TRUKESE-ENGLISH DICTIONARY

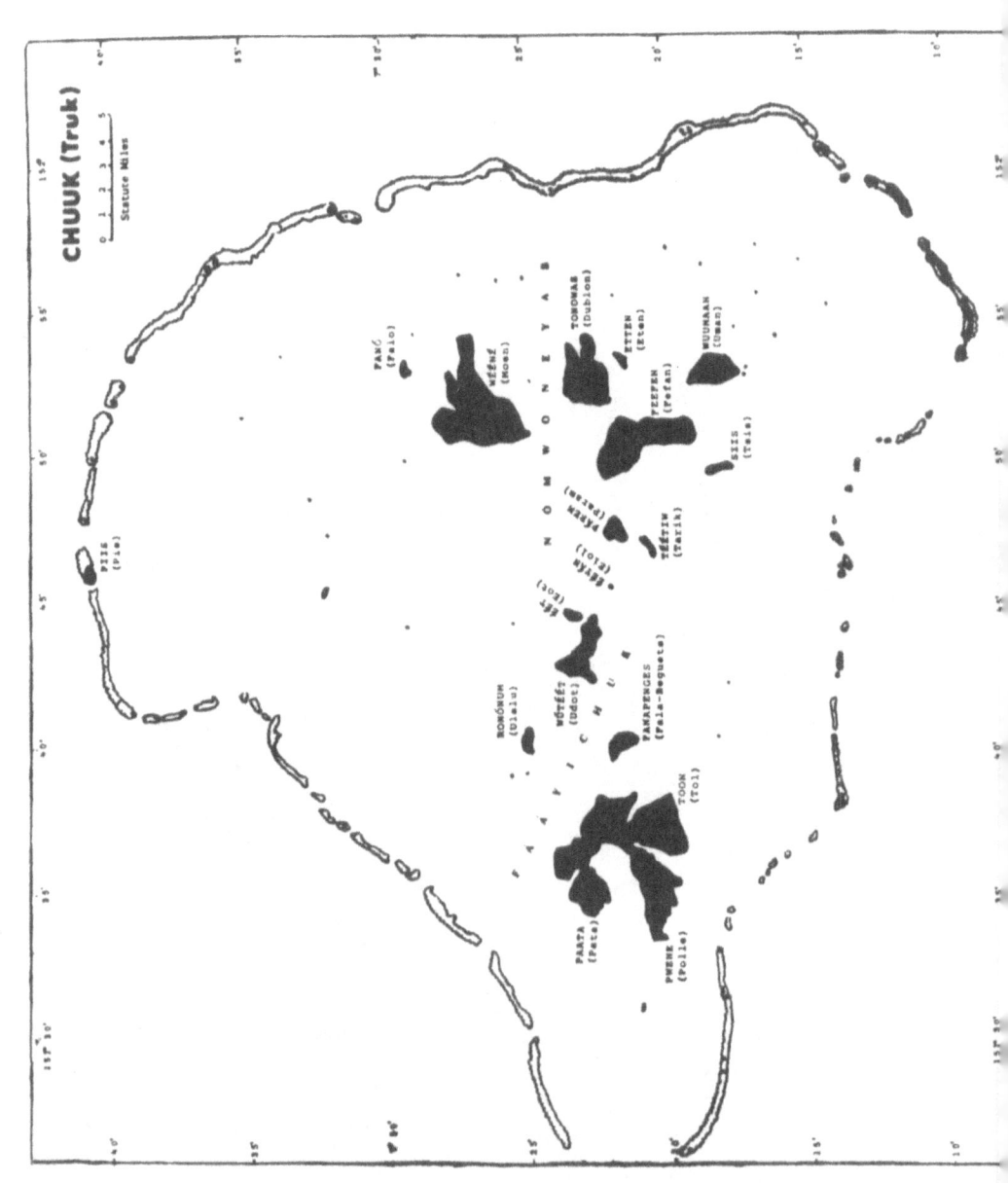

MEMOIRS OF THE
AMERICAN PHILOSOPHICAL SOCIETY
Held at Philadelphia
For Promoting Useful Knowledge
Volume 141

TRUKESE–ENGLISH DICTIONARY

PWPWUKEN TETTENIN FÓÓS: CHUUK-INGENES

Compiled by
WARD H. GOODENOUGH and HIROSHI SUGITA

In Collaboration with:

Boutau K. Efot, Kimeuo Kimiuo, Eiue Rewi,
Net Sangau, Sochiki Stephen

With Contributions by:

Domingo Asor, Sachuo Buliche, Wie Fiti,
Frances Bossy Fritz, Redley Killion, Fritz Muritok,
Chuneo Nimwes, Tony Otto, Ancheres Rechim,
Mineko Robi, Joe Suka, Joshua Suka, Marcellino Umwech

AMERICAN PHILOSOPHICAL SOCIETY
INDEPENDENCE SQUARE • PHILADELPHIA
1980

Copyright © 1980 by The American Philosophical Society

Library of Congress Catalog Card Number 79-54277
International Standard Book Number 0-87169-141-8
US ISSN 0065-9738

*Ngeni aramesen Chuuk meyinisin.
Feyiyééch epwe fitiirenó
feyin feyinnóó chék.*

PREFACE

As originally planned, this volume was to include an English to Trukese index or finder-list and, also, a list of all root forms or morphemes together with the words in which they appear. Considerations of time and quantity of material have led us to reserve this index and root list for a companion volume, which is now in preparation.

Our work builds on the dictionary by Samuel H. Elbert, published in 1947. It began in Romónum, Truk, in 1966, when the Trukese-English half of Elbert's dictionary was systematically worked over by Ward Goodenough in collaboration with Boutau K. Efot and the late Eiue Rewi. At that time, much new material was added. The results were being prepared for publication, when the University of Hawaii's Pacific and Asian Linguistics Institute (now the Social Sciences and Linguistics Institute) undertook a series of dictionaries and reference grammars of the languages of Micronesia for the Department of Education of the Trust Territory of the Pacific Islands. Forces were joined, and the materials were worked over again and expanded further by Hiroshi Sugita in collaboration with Kimeuo Kimiuo, Net Sangau, and Sochiki Stephen. Important contributions were also made by a number of others, as well, whose names are listed on the title page. We regret that the rich and meticulously transcribed vocabulary dealing with psychic states and feelings reported by Lothar Käser (*Der Begriff Seele bei den Insulanern von Truk*, 1977) came to our attention too late to be included in this edition.

Financial support was provided by the National Science Foundation (Grants GS 33132 and SOC72-05306), the Department of Education of the Trust Territory of the Pacific Islands, and by the University of Pennsylvania, for which we are most grateful.

It took many people to process the data. Elizabeth Dickie, Benjamin Fuller, and Barbara Cafetz did much of the collating and coding; Alexis Sears, Diane Willing, and Caroline Stuckert labored long at typing; Cynthia Dalrymple and Niall H. Olsen put everything into the computer; and Niall Olsen handled the follow-up computer work, as well. Ann Peters and Robert Hsu provided initial counsel as to computer format and programming, and Robert Hsu guided the computer operations through their various stages. We are much indebted to all of them.

For their decision to recommend an orthography that represents each of the significantly distinctive sounds of the Trukese language, we thank the participants in the Truk Orthography Conference of August, 1972. We are also most grateful to Truk's Director of Education, Chutomu Nimues, for his cooperation with the dictionary project and to Donald Topping, Director of the University of Hawaii's Social Sciences and Linguistics Institute, for his unflagging support and encouragement.

Above all, we wish to thank the people of Truk for their patience with our inability to get the job done sooner. It is their book, and we happily dedicate it to them with our *kinissow chaapwúúr*.

WARD H. GOODENOUGH
HIROSHI SUGITA

INTRODUCTION

1. THE LANGUAGES OF TRUK.

Three closely related languages are spoken in Truk State, Federated States of Micronesia. They are Trukese, Mortlockese, and Puluwatese. This dictionary represents only the first of them, and that one as it is spoken in the lagoon islands of Truk.

Trukese has by far the largest number of speakers in the Truk state. It is spoken in the Hall Islands as well as in Truk lagoon (see the frontispiece). A dialect chain from west to east and north seems to fall into three major divisions. One covers the Hall Islands, the second the northeastern fringe of the Truk lagoon, consisting of Pis, Falo, northern and eastern Moen, and eastern Dublon, and the third the remainder of Truk lagoon. Since this dictionary deals only with the speech of Truk lagoon, it confines itself largely to the third dialect division. It includes some forms from northern Moen dialects, but none from the Hall Islands, where the old distinction between *n* and *l*, lost in all Truk lagoon dialects, is still preserved, and where the retroflex affricate of lagoon Trukese is pronounced as a retroflex continuant.

In recent years a number of immigrants from the Mortlock Islands have settled in Truk, primarily on Moen Island. Their speech retains some items of Mortlockese lexicon and a number of features of Mortlockese phonology. It is not represented in this dictionary.

With dialect differences of its own, Mortlockese is spoken in all of the islands and atolls south of Truk (Etal, Lukunor, Satawan, Namoluk, Nama, and Losap). It has been considered to be a dialect of Trukese, and there is indeed some degree of mutual intelligibility between the two languages. But its phonology and morphology, as well as some of its lexicon, are different enough to require independent treatment in their own right. For example, recent investigation indicates that there may be twelve contrasting vowels in Mortlockese as compared with the nine vowels of Trukese. In both languages the proliferation of vowels from the five vowels of Proto-Oceanic has come about as a result of similar kinds of change, but the changes followed rather different courses in each case, and the twelve vowels of Mortlockese (if that is indeed their number) do not seem to have resulted from an additional step in the series of changes that produced the nine vowels

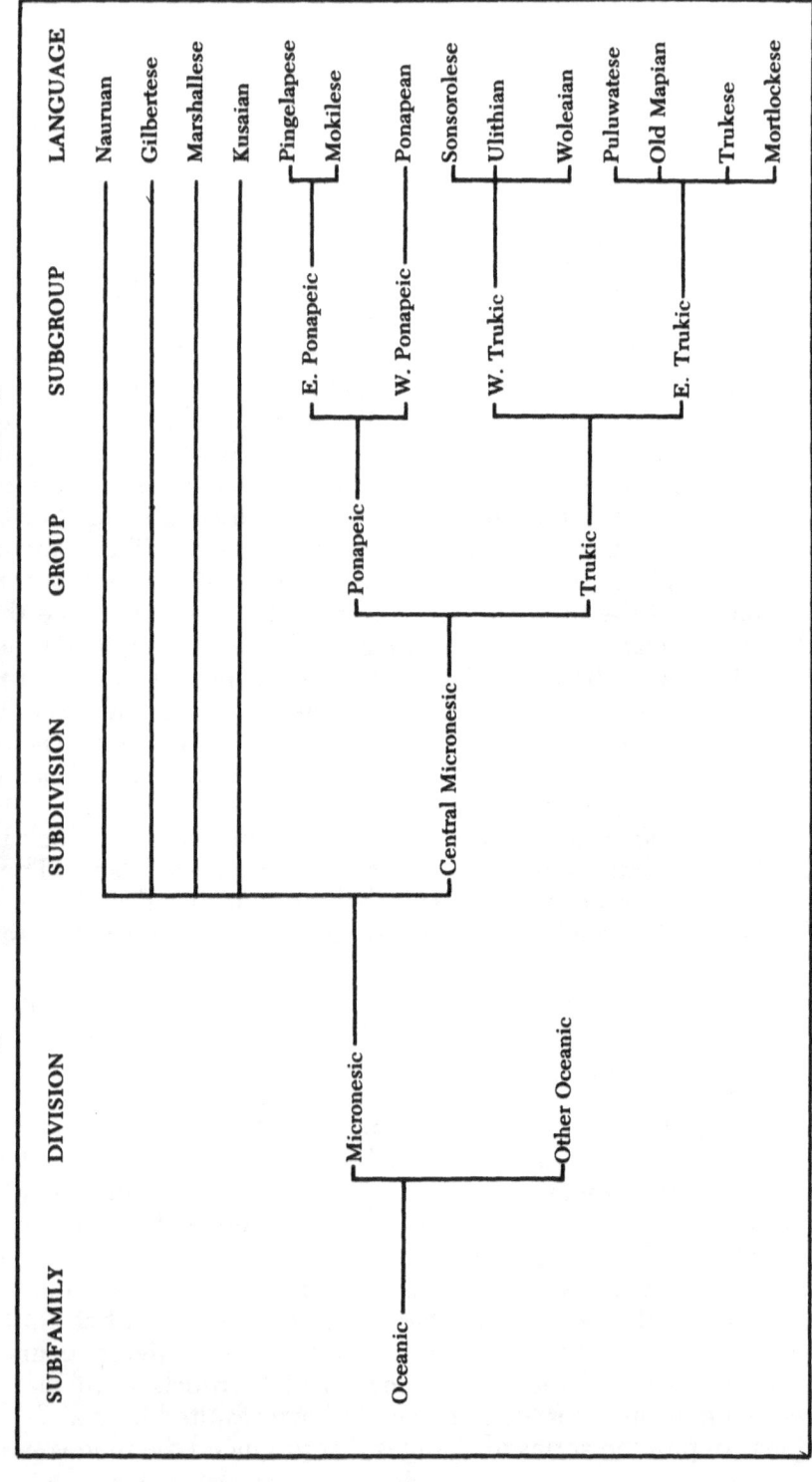

Fig. 1. The Micronesic Division of Oceanic Languages.

of Trukese. There are significant syntactic differences between Mortlockese and Trukese, as well. These considerations make it practical to treat Mortlockese as a distinct language.

Puluwatese is spoken in the atolls west of Truk—Pulusuk, Puluwat, Tamatam, Pulap, and Namonuito—and by the people of Carolinian origin in Tanapag Village in Saipan, Northern Marianas Islands. It, too, subdivides into several dialects. Thus the Trukese words *maas* and *masan* ("eye" and "his eye") are *maah* and *mahan* in Puluwat, *maha* and *mahan* in Ulul (Namonuito), and *mha* and *mhaan* in Pisaras (Nanonuito).

Along with the language formerly spoken on Mapia Atoll (now a part of Indonesia's Irian Jaya), the three languages of the Truk district make up the eastern subgroup of the Trukic group within the Micronesian languages (Fig. 1). The languages of the western group are Woleaian (spoken in several dialects in Satawal, Lamotrek, Elato, Ifaluk, Woleai, Faraulep, and Eauripik, and in Saipan as Saipan Carolinian), Ulithian (spoken in Ulithi, Fais, and Sorol), and Sonsorolese (spoken in several dialects in Tobi, Merir, Sonsorol, and Puloanna).

2. THE ALPHABET.

2.1 Background. The alphabet with which Trukese was written up to 1972 was an adaptation of the English (Roman) alphabet by American Protestant missionaries in the late nineteenth century for translating the Bible and prayerbook into Mortlockese. For some time thereafter local pastors in Truk were heavily recruited from the Mortlock Islands, and Mortlockese or a Mortlockized form of Trukese became the language of liturgy in the Protestant Church throughout the Truk district. The orthography did justice to neither Mortlockese nor Trukese, being very poorly adapted to the meaningful sound distinctions in these languages. Catholic and German Protestant missionaries produced new translations of the Bible and prayerbook in Trukese (still somewhat Mortlockized), adding some vowels with a dieresis but failing as before to represent the language satisfactorily.

By this time the conventions, such as they were, of the first Bible translation had become established for letterwriting and public notices. The alphabet that Trukese children learned to recite went as follows: *a, e, i, o, u, f, s, k, l, m, n, ng, p, r, ch* (also written *tr*), *t*. It reflected the nineteenth-century practice of Protestant missionaries, who listed the vowels and then the consonants in English alphabetical order. The position of *s* and *ch* is consistent with their being equivalent to [h] and a retroflex continuant [ɬ] respectively in Puluwatese. This alphabet and the conventions relating to its use were then brought into the elementary schools and public administration after World War II. The improved orthography in Elbert's *Trukese-English English-Trukese Dictionary* (published in 1947) was ignored.

Dominance of the administration and the educational system by Americans for two decades after the second World War hindered improvement. Americans were happy with a system that did not require them to learn to discriminate the sounds of Trukese they found difficult. Moreover, the system's inadequacies permitted them to dismiss the language as unsuitable for serious literary or expository purposes in the schools. It is ironical, therefore, that the alphabetic reform begun in 1972 in order to do justice to Truk's language should have been perceived by some of Truk's people as an act of American interference with their language. In truth it represented a cooperative effort by Trukese in the administration and Department of Education, in consultation with language specialists, to correct the mishandling of their language by foreigners in the past.

2.2 **Present Alphabet.** The revised alphabet used in this dictionary is based on decisions made at two conferences on orthography, held in Truk in August, 1972, and January, 1975. A workshop in Trukese grammar in July, 1975, found it necessary to modify the representation of one of the sounds of Puluwatese so as to eliminate an unexpected ambiguity in some Puluwatese dialects. The alphabet adopted is aimed at making it possible to represent the sounds of all three languages spoken in the Truk District. It is not, therefore, an alphabet for Trukese alone but for all the eastern Trukic languages. Some of these languages require more alphabetic symbols than do others. It happens that Trukese has the fewest distinct sounds (technically called phonemes): nine vowels, thirteen consonants (of which *l* is needed only in the Hall Islands dialects), and two glides. (We use "glide" in preference to "semivowel," because the Trukese glides are more like consonants than like shortened vowels.) It should be noted that both vowels and consonants may be long as well as short. When long, they are written twice. The sounds, listed in Trukese alphabetical order, are as follows:

    a   a low, central unrounded vowel (like the *a* of English *father*): *fan* "go aground," *faan* "break open (as a boil)."

    á   a low, front, unrounded vowel (like the *a* of English *hat*): *már* "move, be shifted," *máár* "grow (as a plant)."

e	a mid, front, unrounded vowel (like the *e* of English *set*): *wen* "straight," *ween* "well."
é	a mid, contral, unrounded vowel (close to the *u* of English *but*): *té* "crawl," *téé* "uninhabited island."
i	a high, front, unrounded vowel (between the *i* of English *fit* and the *ee* of English *feet*): *it* "emptied," *iit* "name."
o	a mid, back, rounded vowel (like the *o* of English *note*): *rong* "hear," *roong* "magic."
ó	a low, back rounded vowel (like the *aw* of English *law*): *pwór* "curved," *pwóór* "box."
u	a high, back rounded vowel (between the *u* of English *put* and the *oo* of English *boot*): *num* "be bailed," *nuum* "bailer."
ú	a high, central, unrounded vowel (not encountered in standard English): *kú* "be kindled," *kúú* "louse."
f	a voiceless, labiodental spirant (like English *f*): *faat* "shallow water," *ffaat* "be strung (as fish)," *afat* "reveal," *affat* "be made clear," *ááf* "fire."
s	a voiceless, dental spirant (like English *s*): *son* "be deceived," *sson* "damsel fish," *ását* "sword grass," *ássát* "cause to split lengthwise," *maas* "face, eye."
k	a velar, voiceless stop, unaspirated, voiced (unless double) between vowels (like English *k* and *g*) and pronounced with lip rounding if preceded or followed by a back rounded vowel: *kóón* "corn," *kkóón* "lie down," *ika* "if," *ikka* "here they are," *taak* "needle fish."
l	a voiced, dental or alveolar lateral (like the clear *l* of some English speakers). It has merged with *n* in Truk lagoon dialects, but is a distinct sound in the Hall Islands dialects, in Mortlockese, and in Puluwatese. It is not used in this dictionary of lagoon Trukese.
m	a voiced, bilabial, nasal continuant (like English *m*) pronounced without accompanying velar constriction or lip rounding, even when preceded or followed by a back, rounded vowel, and tending (unless double) to be denasalized between vowels, where it approaches a bilabial flap: *mas* "be well joined," *mmas* "opened, bloomed," *amasa* "cause to be joined," *ammasa* "cause to be open," *reem* "for us."
mw	a voiced, bilabial nasal, pronounced with accompanying velar constriction but with lip rounding only when preceded or followed by a back, rounded vowel, and tending

(unless double) to be denasalized between vowels: *mwáán* "man," *mwmwáán* "err," *omwusa* "release him," *omwmwusa* "make him vomit," *reemw* "for you."

n   a voiced, dental or alveolar, nasal continuant (like English *n*), tending (unless double) to be denasalized between vowels, where it sounds more like an alveolar flap: *num* "be bailed," *nnum* "be creased, folded," *anaw* "cordia tree," *annaw* "display platform," *maan* "be adrift."

ng   a voiced, velar, nasal continuant (like the *ng* of English *singer*), tending (unless double) to be partially denasalized between vowels, where it approaches a velar flap: *ngút* "be congested," *ngngút* "be flexible," *nengi* "welsh onion," *nengngin* "girl," *nááng* "sky."

p   a voiceless, bilabial stop, unaspirated (like English *p* and *b*), voiced (unless double) between vowels and pronounced without accompanying velar constriction or lip rounding, even when preceded or followed by a back, rounded vowel: *pan* "be tilted," *ppan* "hillside, steep slope," *apach* "be fastened," *appach* "glue," *sap* "be caught."

pw   a voiceless, bilabial stop, unaspirated, voiced (unless double) between vowels and pronounced with accompanying velar constriction but with lip rounding only when preceded or followed by a back, rounded vowel: *pwó* "be pampered," *pwpwó* "a medicine," *apwang* "channel through mangrove," *apwpwang* "hole cut in a tree trunk for water catchment," *sapw* "not."

r   an alveolar trill, voiced between vowels and tending to be voiceless before or after pause: *rusi* "gather it," *rrus* "be gathered," *kúrúr* "slipping to and fro (as a zipper)," *rúrrúr* "slip, become loose," *iir* "they."

ch   a voiceless, usually retroflex, affricate, voiced (unless double) between vowels. For some speakers it is an alveo-palatal affricate (like English *ch* and *j*), and for some it is an alveolar affricate. It is pronounced more like the English *sh* in Mortlockese: *chú* "extracted," *chchú* "wooden comb," *achawa* "squirrel fish," *achchawa* "make slow," *faach* "pandanus."

t   a voiceless, dental or alveolar stop, unaspirated (like English *t* and *d*), voiced (unless double) between vowels: *taf* "be gathered, picked," *ttaf* "be combed," *metip* "be lonely," *mettip* "spit out," *maat* "brave."

w   a bilabial glide, unrounded except when preceded or followed by a back rounded vowel in Trukese, but always rounded in Mortlockese: *waa* "canoe," *sáwá* "fishing basket," *aaw* "mouth."

y   an alveo-palatal glide, unrounded (not written at the beginning of a word, where it is phonetically absent in some dialects): *éé* (*yéé*) "fishhook," *ááyá* (*yááyá*) "liver," *mááy* or *maay* "breadfruit."

For writing Mortlockese and Puluwatese, the following additional letters are (or may be) necessary:

i̧   a high-mid to low-high, front, unrounded vowel, probably needed for Mortlockese.

u̧   a high-mid to low-high, back, rounded vowel, probably needed for Mortlockese.

u̇   a high-mid to low-high, central, unrounded vowel, probably needed for Mortlockese.

h   a voiceless glottal fricative, needed for Puluwatese.

ṙ   a retroflex continuant similar to American mid-western *r*, needed for Puluwatese and the Hall Islands dialects of Trukese. (The values of *r* and *ṙ* are exactly opposite in Elbert's *Puluwat Dictionary*. The orthography conference of 1972 preferred to keep *r* for the trill in both Trukese and Puluwatese. Its recommendation that *rh* be used for the retroflex had to be abandoned because of the resulting ambiguities in the Pisaras dialect in Namonuito.)

ẇ   a velar glide, unrounded, needed for Mortlockese, where the glides of *naaẇ* "child" and *faaw* "stone" are phonetically distinct, whereas they are phonetically identical in Trukese.

The orthography conference of 1972 determined that all personal names should be rendered as people habitually spell them. Thus we write Boutau and Alexia, instead of Péwútaw and Anessiya. Place names, on the other hand, should be in Trukese. Thus we use Wééné and Feefen in place of Moen and Fefan. It was also determined that entries in this dictionary should appear in Trukese alphabetical order, as listed above.

3. THE FORMAT OF AN ENTRY.

3.1 Kinds of Information Included. Each entry includes several kinds of information. What follows represents the major kinds of information given in the order in which they appear. No one entry includes them all.

1. Headword—the word in the form in which it appears as an entry (see 3.2).
2. The reduplicative type in which the headword appears, if it is a reduplication of a base form, and the number representing its combining form (c.f.) type, given in parentheses (see 4.3 and 4.2).
3. The headword's base form (b.f.), given in small capital letters, or the headword or headwords under which to find its base form and from which this headword is treated as a derivation for reference purpose (see 4.1 and 4.2).
4. The dialect to which the headword is restricted in the form given (see 6.1) and the degree to which the word may be tabu (see 6.2).
5. The source language from which the headword has been borrowed, if it is a loanword, given in parentheses (see 6.3).
6. The name of the author, in brackets, of the work from which the headword has been obtained, when it has not been verified by the compilers (see bibliography).
7. Grammatical or other information pertaining to the headword itself, given in brackets.
8. Variants (var.) in the same or other dialects.
9. The syntactic or grammatical function for which glosses or definitions follow (see Section 5), given in abbreviated form in boldface, together with its inflectional type in the case of nouns and object focused verbs (see 4.4 and 4.5).
10. Glosses and definitions for the syntactic function just given.
11. Special information relating to the gloss or specific syntactic function, given in brackets.
12. Its distributive form or forms (see 4.3).
13. How it is counted and how it is possessed, in the case of nouns, together with any irregularities of inflection.
14. Common phrases, sample sentences, and idiomatic usages.
15. Combinatorial forms into which it enters with directional suffixes (glossed only as necessary) and with various prefixes in the case of numerators.
16. Synonyms and antonyms.
17. The second syntactic or grammatical function for which glosses and definitions are given, followed by the above items 10–15 over again, and so on.

3.2 **Headwords.** A headword usually has for its citation form the form it takes when it occurs by itself without prefixes or suffixes. Some nouns do not ordinarily occur without possessive suffixes; they are usually entered in the combining form (followed by a hyphen) that they exhibit or would appropriately exhibit when they are suffixed by the third person singular possessive pronoun ("his, her, its"): for example, *pwii-* ("sibling of same sex") which appears as *pwiin* with the third singular suffix *-n*.

Object focused verbs are shown in the form in which they are most often encountered, namely with the third person singular objective pronoun attached, a pronoun that also is present when the direct object is given as a separate noun or phrase. This pronoun has the forms: *-y*, *-w*, or "zero" in the absence of directional suffixes, and *-yé-*, *-wé-*, *-wo-*, or *-a-* (*-á-*, *-ó-*) when followed by directional suffixes. Thus the entry *angeey* is from a base *angee-* (consisting of *anga-* plus the verb formative suffix *-e-*) and the third person singular pronoun suffix *-y*.

Suffixes, prefixes, and words that have been recorded only when compounded with other words are entered with a preceding or following hyphen.

4. MORPHOLOGY.

4.1 **The Changing Shapes of Trukese Words.** The elements from which Trukese words are built are of two kinds: nuclei and particles, as we shall call them. Each nucleus and particle is likely to appear in more than one phonemic shape. Thus a nucleus meaning "salt water" appears as *sáát*, *seti-*, and *-set*; a prefixed particle indicating "having the character or quality of" appears as *ma-*, *má-*, *me-*, *mé-*, *mo-*, and *mó-*; and a suffixed particle meaning "condition of being" appears as *-ng*, *-nga-*, *-nge-*, and *-ngo-*. This shifting of shape is probably the most complicated feature of the Trukese language. Actually, there are well-defined patterns in it. Once these patterns are understood, what at first seems very confusing turns out to be highly ordered.

In the distant past, all Trukese words and affixes ended with a vowel. Words, including complex words, usually had a primary stress accent on the vowel of the next to last syllable, and never on the last syllable. The unstressed final vowel became more and more weakly pronounced, being reduced eventually to a whisper and then to nothing. Some other Micronesian languages, such as Gilbertese and Woleaian, show less advanced stages of this same process by which the final vowels of words were lost in Trukese. Before they were lost, however, these vowels affected the pronunciation of the vowels in the immediately preceding syllable in various ways. Lower vowels were raised by following high ones, front vowels were often backed and rounded by following back vowels, and back vowels were often fronted and unrounded by following front vowels. In complex words, an otherwise final vowel that was not now the final vowel in the word was not lost, but its shape also came to be affected by the shape of the vowel that immediately followed it. The result is that Trukese words show at least two and often more than two shapes according to whether or not they stand by themselves or are compounded and, in complex words, according to the shape (present and past) of the other elements with which they are compounded. For a given dialect, the way shapes change is orderly, however, and it is possible to sort words into four major classes (combining form types) according to how they pattern their changes of shape in complex words. Immediately following most entries, therefore, is a number indicating the combining form type of the entry. If the entry is either a simple word or an affix (particle), it is followed in small capital letters by its "base form" (b.f.). From the base form and the indication of combining form type, one can infer for most words just how their shapes change according to what other words and affixes they are compounded with.

For nonnative speakers especially, but for native speakers also, this information is helpful for purposes of constructing new compounds or analyzing compounds not listed in the dictionary into their constituent elements, which may be listed. Trukese is like German and Classical Greek in being highly productive of new compound words to express shades of meaning. Where in English we accomplish this by stringing words together without any change in their shapes, Trukese builds such strings into complex words. The freedom with which this is done is manifested in traditional story telling, even more so in the rhetorical and poetic arts associated with Truk's *itang*. Such word-building will undoubtedly continue to play an important role in rhetoric and in the stylistics of Truk's developing written literature.

4.2 Combining Form Types and Base Forms. In the technical vocabulary of linguistics, each phonemic shape that a nuclear word or particle may have is called a "morph" or "form," and the underlying abstraction of which each morph is a variant representation is called a "morpheme." As the several morphs (*sáát, seti-, -set*) of the nuclear word meaning "salt water" reveal, morphemes in Trukese have different shapes according as they appear as independent words, as the final elements in compound words, or as other than final elements in compound words. Only in the last case does a final vowel appear, this vowel being dropped at the end of a word. Furthermore, a morpheme that has two syllables when it appears as other than a final element in compound words has a different shape in its independent form if it is a noun from the one it has if the independent form is not a noun. If we let C represent any consonant, G any glide, and V any vowel, we can represent schematically how morphemes change their shape, exclusive of changes in the quality of vowels, as shown in Table 1.

In this dictionary, the citation form for each headword is the form it has as an independent word except when it has no independent form. All entries in which a morpheme is represented are referred to one entry as the entry of reference, usually the entry

Table 1. Patterns of the changing syllabic structure of morphemes.

Combining form (non-final)	Combining form (word-final)	Independent form (as verb)	Independent form (as noun)
V-	-Ø	...	...
GV-	-G, -Ø	...	...
CV-	-C	...	...
(G)VV-	-(G)V	(G)V	(G)VV
CVV-	-CV	CV	CVV
(G)VGV-	-(G)VG, -(G)V	(G)VG, (G)V	(G)VVG, (G)VV
CVGV-	-CVG, -CV	CVG, CV	CVVG, CVV
(G)VCV-	-(G)VC	(G)VC	(G)VVC
CVCV-	-CVC	CVC	CVVC
(G)VVCV-	-(G)VVC	(G)VVC	(G)VVC
CVVCV-	-CVVC	CVVC	CVVC
(G)VCVV-	-(G)VCV	(G)VCV	(G)VCV
CVCVV-	-CVCV	CVCV	CVCV
(G)VCVGV-	-(G)VCVG, -(G)VCV	(G)VCVG, (G)VCV	(G)VCVG, (G)VCV
CVCVGV-	-CVCVG, -CVCV	CVCVG, CVCV	CVCVG, CVCV
(G)VCVCV-	-(G)VCVC	(G)VCVC	(G)VCVC
CVCVCV-	-CVCVC	CVCVC	CVCVC
CCV-	-C, -CVC	...	...
CCVV-	-CCV	CCV	CCV
CCVGV-	-CCVG, -CCV	CCVG, CCV	CCVG, CCV
CCVCV-	-CCVC	CCVC	CCVC
(G)VCCV-	-(G)VC, -(G)VVC	(G)VC, (G)VVC	(G)VVC
CVCCV-	-CCVC, -CVVC, -CCVVC	CCVC, CVVC, CCVVC	CCVC, CVVC, CCVVC

Note: C = Consonant, CC = pair of like consonants, G = glide, V = vowel, VV = pair of like vowels, Ø = absence of phonetic expression.

with the independent form. In each entry of reference, the morpheme involved is represented by a "base form," printed in small capital letters immediately after the headword. The key shape most suitable for use as a base form, as Table 1 indicates, is a morpheme's combining form when it is not final in a word, for this form shows the morpheme's underlying pattern of double and single consonants and vowels and retains the final vowel that is otherwise dropped.

A base form's final vowel, technically known as a "stem vowel," may change its phonemic shape as one suffix is replaced by another. Such shifts are in accordance with definite rules involving considerations of harmony with the immediately preceding or immediately following vowels. One can readily grasp these patterns, if one bears in mind the two axes along which Trukese vowels are differentiated, as shown in Table 2.

In the speech of the central lagoon area (Wúéét, Romónum), Trukese morphemes fall into four main classes or combining form types, depending on the shapes of their stem vowels when modifying words (adjectivals) are suffixed to them. Morphemes of type 1 end in a double vowel, which usually remains invariant with a suffixed adjectival. Those of type 2 end in a short high vowel. Those of type 3 never end with a high vowel, but end either with a mid vowel only (type 3a) or with either a mid vowel or a low vowel, depending on the height of the vowel following it (type 3b). There are several patterns for how this works among local dialects. Those of type 4 end in a high, mid, or low vowel, depending on whether the following vowel is correspondingly high, mid, or low. Compare the bases in Table 3 with the suffixed directional adjectivals *-tiw* ("down, west"), *-wu* ("out, north"), *-nong* ("in, south"), *-tá* ("up, east").

The base form used to represent each morpheme in this dictionary is one that accurately reflects its combining form type. Thus *pé* (type 1 in Table 3) has the base form PÉÉ, *peek* the base form PEEKI, *iimw* the base form IMWA, and *sóópw* the base form SÓPWO. That is, the stem vowel in the base form of morphemes

Table 2. Trukese Vowels

	Front unrounded	Central unrounded	Back rounded
High (closed)	i	ú	u
Mid	e	é	o
Low (open)	á	a	ó

xxii

of type 1 is another vowel of the same shape as the one ending the word-final form of the morpheme; the stem vowel in the base form of morphemes of type 2 is a high vowel (*i, ú,* or *u*); in the base form of morphemes of type 3 it is the low vowel *a*; and in the base form of morphemes of type 4 it is the mid vowel *e* or *o*.

The combining form type of the last element in a complex word determines the combining form type of the word. If the final element is a particle, the resulting base has the combining form type that would be had by a simple word whose last two syllables are of same shape. Thus the base of *peekitiw* "western side" is *peekitiwa-* (c.f. type 8), as determined by its final element *-tiw*; and *anga-* plus the verb formative suffix *-e-* produce the complex base *angee-* (c.f. type 1).

4.3 Reduplication or Doubling of Bases. Morphemes may be reduplicated wholly or partially in three ways: doubling the initial consonant (abbreviated as dc. in the dictionary), doubling the base form or its last two syllables (db.), and doubling the first syllable of the base form (ds.).

4.31 Doubling the initial consonant is seen in the following: *ffót* "be planted" (cf. *fótu-ki* "plant it," b.f. FÓTO), *ppos* "be stabbed" (cf. *posu-u-w* "stab him," b.f. POSU), *ttong* "love" (cf. *tonge-e-y* "love him," b.f. TONGA). Comparison with other Pacific languages shows that such doubling of initial consonants reflects an old doubling of the first syllable with subsequent loss of the unstressed first vowel. Doubling the initial consonant occurs with verbs, nouns, and adjectivals. It seems to impart a stative or adjectival meaning to verb bases, especially to object focused verbs, converting them into inactive verbs (often best translated as passives), e.g., *fféér* "be in a state of having been done," *fééri* "do it." The initial double consonant has often been retained in nouns and adjectivals that have been made from such verbs.

The loss of an old **k* (when not preceded by a high vowel) has led to the pairing of initial *kk-* with initial vowel or semivowel in a

Table 3. Combining Form Types

Type 1	Type 2	Type 3a	Type 3b	Type 4
péé-tiw	peeki-tiw	imwe-tiw	pache-tiw	sópwu-tiw
péé-wu	peeki-wu	imwo-wu	pacho-wu	sópwu-wu
péé-nong	peeki-nong	imwo-nong	pacho-nong	sópwo-nong
péé-tá	peeki-tá	imwe-tá	pacha-tá	sópwó-tá
pé "blow"	peek "side"	iimw "house"	pach "attached"	sóópw "district"

number of morphemes, e.g., *kkááp* "transporting" (*cf. áápi* "transport it").

4.32 Doubling the base form, if it consists of two syllables, or doubling the last two syllables, if the base form contains more than two syllables, is illustrated by the following: *waawa* "use a canoe" (cf. *waa* "canoe," b.f. WAA), *núkúnúk* "be convinced" (cf. *núúk* "faith," b.f. NÚKÚ), *mwááneyán* "treat as a brother" (cf. *mwááni-n* "her brother," b.f. MWÁÁNE). In such doublings, the stem vowel appears with the first occurrence of the nucleus but not with the second. Its shape conforms to the patterns already observed for the four combining form types. We should observe in this connection that without other information it is often impossible to distinguish morphemes of combining form types 3 and 4 from their double base forms alone. Those of type 3 have a mid-vowel for stem vowel if the vowel preceding it is a high or mid vowel, and they have a low vowel for the stem vowel if the preceding vowel is a low vowel. The position of the stem vowel from front to back is always the same as that of the preceding vowel in the base, i.g., *manaman* "having supernatural power" (b.f. MANA), *pinepin* "stopper" (b.f. PINA), *pwuropwur* "seethe, bubble, foam" (b.f. PWURA), *wenewen* "straight" (b.f. WENA). Nearly all morphemes of combining form type 4 have a low front or a low back vowel in the syllable before the stem vowel, a fact that results in the stem vowel being a similar low vowel when the base form is doubled, unless the base form begins with a vowel and hence with a *y* glide in compounds. In the latter event the stem vowel is likely to be a mid vowel, especially the mid front vowel *e*. Thus we have *mwárámwár* "garland," (b.f. MWÁRE) and *sórósór* "character" (b.f. SÓRO), but *mwááneyán* "treat as a brother" (b.f. MWÁÁNE) and the competing forms *ónóyón, ónoyón,* and *óneyón* "yellow" (b.f. ÓNO).

4.33 Historically, it seems that with morphemes that have two syllables in their base forms a special development took place if the first and second consonants were identical or were articulated in similar positions. With these morphemes the unstressed stem vowel was dropped when the base form was doubled, and the first of the resulting adjacent consonants assimilated to the second, if they were not already identical, to produce a double consonant, e.g., *nannan* "chatter" (from **nananan,* b.f. NANA), *rarrar* "be trampled down" (from **rararar* b.f. RARA), *tetten* "line, row" (from **teniten,* b.f. TENI), *rúrrúr* "slipping back and forth" (from **núrrúr,* from **núrúnúr,* b.f. NÚRÚ, cf. *nnúr* "slipped"). Doubled base forms such as these presumably provided the model for what is now the widely used doubling of the first syllable with further doubling of the initial consonant, e.g., *fáffátán* "be accustomed to walk" (cf. *fátán* "walk," b.f. FÁTÁNE), *pwúppwúnú* "treat as a spouse" (b.f. PWÚNÚWA), and *ékkéés* "treat as a sibling-in-law" (b.f. ÉÉSA, KÉÉSA). With verbs, doubling the base form and doubling the first syllable of the base form originally had the same meaning, namely pluralizing the action either in the sense of its being repetitive on a given occasion or of its being repeated on different occasions. Thus the semantic effect of doubling is identical in *pwúppwúnú* "treat as a spouse" and *samasam* "treat as a father." There has developed a tendency, however, to associate repetition on a given occasion with doubling the base and repetition on different occasions with doubling the first syllable of the base, so that both forms of doubling are found with some bases, e.g., *fátánátán* "go on walking" and *fáffátán* "be in the habit of walking." In keeping with these developments, moreover, doubling of the first syllable where an old initial *k has been lost, as in *ókkósómwoonu* "be in the habit of paying chiefly respects to" (cf. *ósómwoonu* "pay chiefly respects to"), has been generalized to bases that historically began with a vowel or semivowel as in *wúkkún* "be in the habit of drinking" (c.f. *wún* "drink").

Doubling the first syllable has been extended to forms with double initial consonant, producing new forms with initial *k*, as in *kakkapas* "be wont to make utterance" (cf. *kkapas* "make utterance, be uttered," itself a double initial consonant of the causative prefix *a-* from *ka-*, as found in *apasa* "utter, cause to be said"). Similarly an old base *ngú produced *ngú-ti* "chew and suck" (as sugarcane). The double of the base *ngúngú served as an intransitive verb, from which an old first syllable reduplication gave rise to *ngúngúngú, represented now by *ngngúúng* (*ngúngngú-*) "be chewing and sucking," and this has the newly reduplicated form *ngúngngúúng* "repeatedly be chewing and sucking."

4.4 **Inflection of Nouns.** Inflection involves the suffixing of pronouns. As nouns, Trukese bases often occur with suffixed possessive pronouns, and they almost always occur with a suffixed particle -*n* (or -*ni-*) that links them in relational or possessive construction with a following word (or base in a compound word). Word bases sort into three noun types according to the shape of the stem vowel when this linking or relational particle is suffixed to them: type 1 (T1) when bases end in a double vowel (bases of combining form type 1), type 2 (T2) when the bases end in a single high vowel (bases of combining form types 2 and 4), and type 3 (T3) when the bases end in the mid front vowel *e* (bases of combining forms type 3). Thus, to use our earlier examples in Table 3, we have *péé-n* ("blowing of"), *peeki-n* and *sópwu-n* ("side of" and "district of"), and *imwe-n* ("house of"). The possessive suffixes are as follows.

1st. sg.	-y	(may be dropped after single *i* in some dialects)
2nd. sg.	-mw	(with backing and rounding of the preceding stem vowel of the base, except, in some dialects, when the base ends in a double front vowel)
3rd. sg.	-n	
1st. pl. inc.	-ch	
1st. pl. exc.	-m	(with lengthening of the preceding stem vowel of the base in some dialects if the base does not end in a double vowel)
2nd. pl.	-mi	
3rd. pl.	-r	(with lengthening of the preceding stem vowel of the base if the base does not end in a double vowel)
rel.	-n, -ni-	

Tables 4, 5, and 6 show the noun inflections for each noun type. With type 1 (Table 4) there is a subtype (T1v) showing variation with some forms whose base ends in *aa*, as illustrated by *waa* ("canoe") and *fanaa-* ("adze product"), which contrast with the unvarying pattern of *chcha* ("blood"). This variable subtype shows similar vowel variation when compounding with other forms as well (e.g., *wáá-tawa* "spirit medium") and its combining form type is correspondingly indicated as a variable subtype (1v).

With nouns of type 2 (Table 5), the stem vowel, invariably *i* with the first singular and *u* with the second singular suffixes, is otherwise *i* if the preceding vowel is a front vowel (*siin, pisek, áát*), *ú* if the preceding vowel is a central vowel (*sékúr, fféng, faat*), and *u* if the preceding vowel is a back vowel (*owupw, pwoopw, soór*). The inflection of *naaw* shows a variant pattern in the first singular (found only with some morphemes whose independent form ends in *-aaw*), whereas the inflection of *faaw* is the same as that of *faat*. (This apparently arbitrary difference between *naaw* and *faaw* in the first singular possessive seems to be related to the phonological difference between the two words in Mortlockese, where *naaw* has an unrounded velar glide /ẃ/ but *faaw* has a rounded

Table 4. Noun Inflection: Type 1

	nii "tooth"	peche "foot"	máá "death"	chúú "bone"	téé "islet"	chcha "blood"
1sg.	nii-y	pechee-y	máá-y	chúú-y	téé-y	chchaa-y
2sg.	nii-mw, niyu-mw	pechee-mw, pecheyo-mw	máá-mw, máyó-mw	chuu-mw	too-mw, téyo-mw, téé-mw	chchaa-mw, chchayó-mw
3sg.	nii-n	pechee-n	máá-n	chúú-n	téé-n	chchaa-n
1inc.	nii-ch	pechee-ch	máá-ch	chúú-ch	téé-ch	chchaa-ch
1exc.	nii-m	pechee-m	máá-m	chúú-m	téé-m	chchaa-m
2pl.	nii-mi	pechee-mi	máá-mi	chúú-mi	téé-mi	chchaa-mi
3pl.	nii-r	pechee-r	máá-r	chúú-r	téé-r	chchaa-r
rel.	nii-n	pechee-n	máá-n	chúú-n	téé-n	chchaa-n

	chuuchu "urine"	roo "diaper"	póó "bed"	waa "canoe"	faa- "underside"	fanaa- "adz product"
1sg.	chuuchuu-y	roo-y	póó-y	wáá-y	fáá-y	fánáá-y
2sg.	chuuchuu-mw	roo-mw	póó-mw	wóó-mw	fóó-mw	fónóó-mw
3sg.	chuuchuu-n	roo-n	póó-n	waa-n	faa-n	fanaa-n
1inc.	chuuchuu-ch	roo-ch	póó-ch	waa-ch	faa-ch	fanaa-ch
1exc.	chuuchuu-m	roo-m	póó-m	wáá-m	faa-m	fánáá-m
2pl.	chuuchuu-mi	roo-mi	póó-mi	wáá-mi	faa-mi	fánáá-mi
3pl.	chuuchuu-r	roo-r	póó-r	waa-r	faa-r	fanaa-r
rel.	chuuchuu-n	roo-n	póó-n	wáá-n	fáá-n	fánáá-n

Table 5. Noun inflection: Type 2.

	siin "skin"	pisek "goods"	áat "youth"	sóór "birthmark"	sékúr "back"	naaw "child"	fféng "love"	faat "eyebrow"
1sg.	sini-(y)	piseki-(y)	áti-(y)	sóri-(y)	sékúri-(y)	neyi-(y)	ffengi-(y)	féti-(y)
2sg.	sinu-mw	piseku-mw	átu-mw	sóru-mw	sékuru-mw	nowu-mw	ffengu-mw	fotu-mw
3sg.	sini-n	piseki-n	áti-n	sóru-n	sékúrú-n	néwú-n	ffengú-n	fétú
1inc.	sini-ch	piseki-ch	áti-ch	sóru-ch	sékúrú-ch	néwú-ch	ffengú-ch	fétú-ch
1exc.	sini-im, sini-m	piseki-im, pisekí-m	áti-im, áti-m	sóru-um, sóru-m	sékúrú-um, sékúrú-m	néwú-úm, néwú-m	ffengú-úm, ffengú-m	fétú-úm, fétú-m
2pl.	sini-mi	piseki-mi	áti-mi	sóru-mi	sékúrú-mi	néwú-mi	ffengú-mi	fétú-mi
3pl.	sini-ir	piseki-ir	áti-ir	sóru-ur	sékúrú-ur	néwú-ír	ffengú-úr	fétú-úr
rel.	sini-n	pisekin	áti-n	sóru-n	sékúrú-n	néwú-n	ffengú-n	fétú-n

	owupw "breast"	pwoopw "cause"
1sg.	owupwi-(y)	pwopwi-(y)
2sg.	owupwu-mw	pwopwu-mw
3sg.	owupwu-n	pwopwu-n
1inc.	owupwu-ch	pwopwu-ch
1exc.	owupwu-um, owupwu-m	pwopwu-um, pwopwu-m
2pl.	owupwu-mi	pwopwu-mi
3pl.	owupwu-ur	pwopwu-ur
rel.	owupwu-n	pwopwu-n

Table 6. Noun inflection: Type 3.

	tiip "emotions"	nemenem "authority"	mékúr "head"	ffén "advice"	wuupw "abdomen"	woos "burden"
1sg.	tipe-y	nemeneme-y	mékúre-y	fféne-y	wupwe-y	wose-y
2sg.	tipo-mw	nemenemo-mw	mékúro-mw	fféno-mw	wupwo-mw	woso-mw
3sg.	tipa-n	nemenema-n	mékúra-n	fféna-n	wupwa-n	wosa-n
1inc.	tipa-ch	nemenema-ch	mékúra-ch	fféna-ch	wupwa-ch	wosa-ch
1exc.	tipe-em, tipe-m	nemeneme-em, nemeneme-m	mékúre-em, mékúre-m	fféne-em, fféne-m	wupwe-em, wupwe-m	wose-em, wose-m
2pl.	tipe-mi	nemeneme-mi	mékúre-mi	fféne-mi	wupwe-mi	wose-mi
3pl.	tipe-er	nemeneme-er	mékúre-er	fféne-er	wupwe-er	wose-er
rel.	tipe-n	nemeneme-n	mékúre-n	fféne-n	wupwe-n	wose-n

	faas "nest"	maas "eye"	meen "thing"	sáfey "medicine"	fénú "land"	
1sg.	fase-y	mese-y	mine-y	sáfeye-y	fénúwe-y	
2sg.	faso-mw	moso-mw, meso-mw	mino-mw	sáfeyo-mw	fénuwo-mw	
3sg.	fasa-n	masa-n, mesa-n	mina-n	sáfeya-n	fénúwa-n	
1inc.	fasa-ch	masa-ch, mesa-ch	mina-ch	sáfeya-ch	fénúwa-ch	
1exc.	fase-em, fase-m	mese-em, mese-m	mine-em, mine-m	sáfeye-em, sáfee-m	fénúwe-em, fénúwe-m	
2pl.	fase-mi	mese-mi	mine-mi	sáfee-mi	fénúwe-mi	
3pl.	fase-er	mese-er	mine-er	sáfeye-er	fénúwe-er	
rel.	fase-n	mese-n	mine-n	sáfee-n	fénúwe-n	

labial glide /w/, a distinction that does not occur in lagoon Trukese.)

Nouns of type 3 (Table 6) show the same pattern regardless of the shapes of vowels preceding the stem vowel. In some morphemes in which the vowel before the stem vowel is *a*, however, there is a variable subtype (T3v) characterized by *maas* as inflected in central lagoon and Wuumaan dialects, in which this vowel preceding the stem vowel shifts to *e* and *o* or remains *a* in the same manner as the stem vowel regularly does with nouns of type 3. In other east lagoon and some Toon dialects, however, the vowel before the stem vowel is *e* throughout. Such dissimilation of the next to last vowel of the base (subtype T3d) is also found in *meen* ("thing"), in which the next to last vowel becomes *i* in all its combining forms (combining form subtype 3d).

4.5 Inflection of Verbs. As object focused verbs, bases occur with suffixed objective pronouns. The form of the verb with the third singular pronoun is also the form it takes when the direct object is expressed as a noun or noun phrase rather than as a suffixed pronoun. This form of the verb marks the predicate construction as one that is object focused (see paragraph 5.9). The pronouns are as follows:

1st. sg.		*-yey, -yeyi-*	(after stem vowels *i, e, a, á, ó*)
		-wey, -weyi-	(after stem vowels *é, o, ú, u*)
2nd. sg.		*-k, -ko-*	(with backing and rounding of the preceding stem vowel)
3rd. sg.		*-y, -ye-*	(when preceded by *ii, ee, aa, áá, óó*)
		-w, -wé-	(when preceded by *éé, úú*)
		-w, -wo-	(when preceded by *oo, uu*)
		-Ø, -a-	(when the preceding stem vowel is a short vowel. The naked presence of the stem vowel as the end of a word indicates the presence of a suffix in its "zero" form. The objective pronoun is expressed as *-a-*, in the event there are further suffixes, such as directionals, after it, and then the stem vowel of the verb base always appears as *a*, also, as shown in Table 12 for *wuwe-yi-*.)

1st. pl. inc.	*-kich, -kiche-*	
1st. pl. exc.	*-keem, -kem, -keemi-, -kemi-*	
2nd. pl.	*-kemi, -kemii-*	
3rd. pl.	*-r, -re-*	(with lengthening of the preceding stem vowel except when the base ends in a double vowel)

These pronouns are suffixed directly to the nucleus in the case of causative verbs (when the nucleus has a causative prefix *a-, á-, e-, é-, o-, ó-*, or *ákká-, ekke-, ékké-, okko-, ókkó-*) and sometimes, also, in the absence of a causative prefix, especially with nuclei of combining form type 1. Otherwise, the objective pronouns are suffixed to a verb formative particle that has been suffixed in its turn to the nucleus. Six types of object focused verbs result, three without verb formative suffixes (at least in the third singular) and three with them. In type 1 (see Table 7), the pronouns are suffixed directly to nuclei whose base form ends in a double vowel, e.g., *a-taa-yey* ("destroy me," cf. *ta* "be destroyed"), *nnii-yey* ("kill me"). In type 2 (Table 8), the pronouns are suffixed directly to nuclei whose base forms exhibit a high stem vowel, e.g., *o-wunu-wey* ("poison me," cf. *wun* "be poisoned"). In type 3 (Table 9), the pronouns are suffixed to a verb formative suffix *-á-* (*-ó-* in the second singular) except in the third person singular and plural, when they are suffixed directly to the nucleus, which ends in a stem vowel *a* in the third singular and *e* in the third plural, e.g., *e-chipá-á-yey* ("comfort me," cf. *chip* "be comforted") and *e-chipe-er* ("comfort them"). As the example indicates, the nuclei of verbs of type 3 end in a single low or mid vowel and never in a high vowel. In type 4 (Table 10), the verb formative particles (*-fi-, -si-, -ki-, -mi-, -ni-, -ri-, -ti-, -yi-, -wú-*) are suffixed to bases whose combining form ends in a double vowel, e.g., *féé-ti-yey* ("tie me up" cf. *fééfé* "tied, lashed"). They inflect in the same way as verbs of type 2. In type 5 (Table 11), the same verb formative particles are suffixed to bases ending in single high stem vowels, e.g., *turu-fi-yey* ("seize me," cf. *tur* "be seized"), *fótu-ki-yey* ("plant me," cf. *ffót* "be planted"). Verbs of this type also inflect in the same way as verbs of type 2, except for those with formative particles *-yi-* and *-wú-*. With verbs of this type the formative particle *-yi-* is replaced by *-i-* with fronting of the stem vowel of the nucleus, e.g., *nuki-i-yey* ("haul me on a rope," cf. *nuk,* "be hauled," *nukunuk* "do hauling," base form NUKU). The formative particle *-wú-* is similarly replaced by *-u-* and *-ú-* with nuclei whose base forms end in stem vowels *u* and *ú* respectively, e.g., *posu-u-wey*

Table 7. Object focused verbs of type 1.

	nnii- "smite"	chee- "chase"	afangamáá- "betray"
1sg.	nnii-yey	chee-yey	afangamáá-yey
2sg.	nniyu-k	cheyo-k	afangamáyó-k
3sg.	nnii-y	chee-y	afangamáá-y
1inc.	nnii-kich	chee-kich	afangamáá-kich
1exc.	nnii-keem, -kem	chee-keem, -kem	afangamáá-keem, -kem
2pl.	nnii-kemi	chee-kemi	afangamáá-kemi
3pl.	nnii-r	chee-r	afangamáá-r
	éppúrúú- "imitate"	sááyipéé- "fan"	achchaa- "make bleed"
1sg.	éppúrúú-wey	sááyipéé-wey	achchaa-yey
2sg.	éppúruu-k	sááyipoo-k	achchóó-k
3sg.	éppúrúú-w	sááyipéé-w	achchaa-y
1inc.	éppúrúú-kich	sááyipéé-kich	achchaa-kich
1exc.	éppúrúú-keem, -kem	sááyipéé-keem, -kem	achchaa-keem, -kem
2pl.	éppúrúú-kemi	sááyipéé-kemi	achchaa-kemi
3pl.	éppúrúú-r	sááyipéé-r	achchaa-r
	osuu- "see off"	oyoo- "capture"	ópóó- "put on a bed"
1sg.	osuu-wey	oyoo-wey	ópóó-yey
2sg.	osuu-k	oyoo-k	ópóó-k
3sg.	osuu-w	oyoo-w	ópóó-y
1inc.	osuu-kich	oyoo-kich	ópóó-kich
2inc.	osuu-keem, -kem	oyoo-keem, -kem	ópóó-keem, -kem
2pl.	osuu-kemi	oyoo-kemi	ópóó-kemi
3pl.	osuu-r	oyoo-r	ópóó-r

("stab me," cf. *ppos* "be stabbed," base form POSU) and *núkú-ú-wey* ("believe me," cf. *núúk* "faith," *núkúnúk* "be convinced," base form NUKU). These verbs with formative particles *-i-*, *-u-*, and *-ú-* inflect in the same way as verbs of type 1. In type 6 (Table 12), the verb formative particles are suffixed to bases ending in the single mid vowel *e*, e.g., *pwúnúwe-ni-yey* ("marry me," cf. *pwúpwpwúnú* "be married," base form PWÚNÚWA). These verbs inflect in the same way as verbs of type 2. There is a subtype 6b, by contrast with 6a just illustrated, in which a verb formative particle *-e-* is suffixed to the stem vowel *e* of the nucleus, e.g., *tonge-e-ey* ("feel love for me," cf. *ttong* "love," *ttonge-y* "love for me"). This formative suffix *-e-* replaces *-yi-* widely with nuclei of combining form types 3 and 4, but occasional doublets occur, e.g., *wuwe-yi-yey* and *wuwe-e-yey* ("carry me, convey me," base form

Table 8. Object focused verbs of type 2.

	efichi- "like"	ápweni- "teach judo to"	ámwááni- "treat as a man"
1sg.	efichi-yey	ápweni-yey	ámwááni-yey
2sg.	efichu-k	ápwenu-k	ámwáánu-k
3sg.	efichi	ápweni	ámwááni
1inc.	efichi-kich	ápweni-kich	ámwááni-kich
1exc.	efichi-keem, -kem	ápweni-keem, -kem	ámwááni-keem, -kem
2pl.	efichi-kemi	ápweni-kemi	ámwááni-kemi
3pl.	efichi-ir	ápweni-ir	ámwááni-ir
	ésúkú- "wait for"	éwéwú- "make wealthy"	amaanú- "cast adrift"
1sg.	ésúkú-wey	éwéwú-wey	amaanú-wey
2sg.	ésúku-k	éwéwu-k	amaanu-k
3sg.	ésúkú	éwéwú	amaanú
1inc.	ésúkú-kich	éwéwú-kich	amaanú-kich
1exc.	ésúkú-keem, -kem	éwéwú-keem, -kem	amaanú-keem, -kem
2pl.	ésúkú-kemi	éwéwú-kemi	amaanú-kemi
3pl.	ésúkú-úr	éwéwú-úr	amaanú-úr
	owunu- "poison"	ósómwoonu- "treat as a chief"	ónómwu- "cause to stay"
1sg.	owunu-wey	ósómwoonu-wey	ónómwu-wey
2sg.	owunu-k	ósómwoonu-k	ónómwu-k
3sg.	owunu	ósómwoonu	ónómwu
1inc.	owunu-kich	ósómwoonu-kich	ónómwu-kich
1exc.	owunu-keem, -kem	ósómwoonu-keem, -kem	ónómwu-keem, -kem
2pl.	owunu-kemi	ósómwoonu-kemi	ónómwu-kemi
3pl.	owunu-ur	ósómwoonu-ur	ónómwu-ur

WUWA). The formative suffix -é- similarly replaces -wú-, e.g., féné-é-wey ("give me advice," cf. ffén ("be advised," base form FÉNA). Verbs of this subtype (6b) inflect in the same way as verbs of type 1.

4.6 Inflection Types and Combining Form Types. Noun types and verb types bear an obvious relationship to the four combining form types, as summarized below.

	Noun type	Verb type
combining type 1	1	1, 4
combining type 2	2	2, 5
combining type 3	3	3, 6
combining type 4	2	3, 5 or 6b

Table 9. Object focused verbs of type 3.

	echipa- "comfort"	kúna- "see, find"
1sg.	echipá-á-yey	kúná-á-yey
2sg.	echipó-ó-k	kúnó-ó-k
3sg.	echipa	kúna
1inc.	echipá-á-kich	kúná-á-kich
1exc.	echipá-á-keem, -kem	kúná-á-keem, -kem
2pl.	echipá-á-kemi	kúná-á-kemi
3pl.	echipe-er	kúne-er

4.7 Word Boundaries. In ordinary rapid speech, as distinct from slow or deliberate speech, words undergo modification of initial or final phonemes when there is no pause between words. These modifications of word boundaries (technically known as sandhi) have been described in detail by Dyen (1965: 7–10). They may be summarized according to the following rules.

1. Final /n/ may assimilate to a following initial /s/, /r/, /ch/, /t/: *emés sowurong (emén sowurong)*.
2. Initial /n/ may assimilate to a preceding final /s/, /r/, /ch/, /t/: *meyiwor rowumw (meyiwor nowumw)*.
3. Final /t/ and /ch/ may assimilate to a following initial /s/, /ch/, /t/: *efós suupwa (efóch suupwa)*.
4. A final labial consonant (/f/, /m/, /mw/, /p/, /pw/) may assimilate to any other following initial labial consonant: *óóf fóós (óómw fóós)*.
5. A final velar consonant (/k/, /ng/) may assimilate to another following initial velar consonant: *kkowung ngé (kkowuk ngé)*.
6. Final /w/ disappears before a following initial /w/ or a following initial consonant: *posuu pwáápwá (posuuw pwáápwá)*.

Table 10. Object focused verbs of type 4.

	féé-ti- "tie up"	tee-yi- "sew"
1sg.	féé-ti-yey	tee-yi-yey
2sg.	féé-tu-k	tee-yu-k
3sg.	féé-ti	tee-yi
1inc.	féé-ti-kich	tee-yi-kich
1exc.	féé-ti-keem, -kem	tee-yi-keem, -kem
2pl.	féé-ti-kemi	tee-yi-kemi
3pl.	féé-ti-ir	tee-yi-ir

Table 11. Object focused verbs of type 5.

| | turu-fi- | nuki-i- | núkú-ú- |
	"seize"	"haul"	"believe"
1sg.	turu-fi-yey	nuki-i-yey	núkú-ú-wey
2sg.	turu-fu-k	nuki-yu-k	núku-u-k
3sg.	turu-fi	nuki-i-y	núkú-ú-w
1inc.	turu-fi-kich	nuki-i-kich	núkú-ú-kich
1exc.	turu-fi-keem, -kem	nuki-i-keem, -kem	núkú-ú-keem, -kem
2pl.	turu-fi-kemi	nuki-i-kemi	núkú-ú-kemi
3pl.	turu-fi-ir	nuki-i-r	núkú-ú-r

7. Initial /w/ before /ú/, /u/, /o/ disappears after a final consonant: *wochooch uuch* (*wochooch wuuch*).
8. Final /y/ disappears before a following initial consonant or /w/: *ee mwáán* (*eey mwáán*).
9. Final short vowels assimilate to following initial vowels of same height: *na angeey* (*nó angeey*).
10. Final short /e/ combines with following initial /ó/ to form /aa/: *epwa amónnáátá* (*epwe ómónnáátá*).
11. Except for rule 10 above, a final mid vowel and following initial low vowel or a final low vowel and following initial mid

Table 12. Object focused verbs of type 6.

| | ine-ni- (6a) | ange-e- (6b) | féné-é- (6b) |
	"get as a mother"	"take in hand"	"advise"
1sg.	ine-ni-yey	ange-e-yey	féné-é-wey
2sg.	ine-nu-k	ange-yo-k	féno-o-k
3sg.	ine-ni	ange-e-y	féné-é-w
1inc.	ine-ni-kich	ange-e-kich	féné-é-kich
1exc.	ine-ni-keem, -kem	ange-e-keem, -kem	féné-é-keem, -kem
2pl.	ine-ni-kemi	ange-e-kemi	féné-é-kemi
3pl.	ine-ni-ir	ange-e-r	féné-é-r
	wuwe-yi- (6a)	wuwe-e- (6b)	
	"carry" (with -nó)	"carry" (with -nó)	
1sg.	wuwe-yi-yeyi-nó	wuwe-e-yeyi-nó	
2sg.	wuwe-yu-ko-nó	wuwe-yo-ko-nó	
3sg.	wuwe-ya-a-nó	wuwe-e-ye-nó	
1inc.	wuwe-yi-kichi-nó	wuwe-e-kiche-nó	
1exc.	wuwe-yi-keemi-nó	wuwe-e-keemi-nó	
2pl.	wuwe-yi-kemii-nó	wuwe-e-kemii-nó	
3pl.	wuwe-yi-ire-nó	wuwe-e-re-nó	

vowel combine to form a double low vowel at the same position (front, central or back) as that of the second vowel: *iká ápwa attaw* (*ika epwe attaw*).

None of these assimilations at word boundaries are written in the examples of word usage in this dictionary, nor are they ordinarily written by Trukese, unless there is reason to show colloquial speech in written form. Similar assimilations at morph boundaries within words are written, however, as representing the actual shapes of those words.

Another kind of modification at word boundaries occurs when a phrase ends in a monosyllabic word or when a word is followed by a postposed demonstrative. Then the word preceding the monosyllabic word or demonstrative may be modified as follows.

1. If the preceding word ends in a short vowel, that vowel is doubled: *wúpwee wún* (cf. *wúpwe wún suupwa*), *inaa mwo* (*ina mwo*), *fénúú we* (*fénú we*).

2. If the preceding word ends in a consonant or glide, a short high vowel of the same position as the preceding vowel is added to the final consonant or glide: *eeni chék* (*een chék*), *esapwú nó* (*esapw nó*), *inomwu na* (*inomw na*), *semeyi we* (*semey we*).

Final double vowels resulting from these rules are regularly written in examples of word usage in this dictionary, but the added short vowel after a consonant is not written.

5. SYNTAX.

5.1 Syntactic and Other Grammatical Categories. Each gloss or set of glosses in this dictionary is preceded by an indication of the grammatical function (syntactic category) for which the gloss is given, such as noun (n.) or object-focused verb (vo.). In preparing this dictionary, it was necessary to decide on a classification of grammatical functions before grammatical analysis was completed. For this reason, the classification used is to be understood as tentative and to be superseded in the *Trukese Reference Grammar*, being prepared by Hiroshi Sugita. The several categories used here are described below.

5.2 Nouns. The category NOUN (n.) has several subcategories. "Inflected only" (ni.) are nouns that occur only with possessive and relational suffixes and lack an independent form. "Relational only" (nr.) are nouns that occur only with the relational suffix and also lack an independent form. "Uninflected" (nu.) are nouns that do not appear with possessive suffixes but that may occur only with relational suffixes in addition to occurring in independent form. "Separable" (ns.) are complex nouns whose elements appear as a single word in the independent form but as a two-word phrase when they are inflected (e.g., *féwúnúmas* "eyeball," *féwún mesey* "my eyeball"). Nouns are entered as headwords in this dictionary in their independent form, except for those that are inflected only or are relational only. These latter are shown in their combining form followed by a hyphen (e.g., *ana-* "portion of food to eat," *pwúnúwa-* "spouse").

5.3 **Possessive Constructions.** Uninflected nouns enter into possessive constructions as appositive modifiers or specifiers of inflected nouns that most appropriately signify the nature of the possessive relationship. Thus *waa* "canoe" is inflected, but *chitoosa* "automobile" is not. One can say *waa-n* "his canoe," but must say *waa-n chitoosa* "his automobile (for personal use)" or *aa-n chitoosa* "his automobile (in a dealer's inventory)."

Terms for kin relationships, parts of the body, parts of things generally, and for things of which people are immediate beneficiaries can usually take possessive suffixes. Some of these terms are widely used as so-called "possessive classifiers" in possessive constructions with uninflected nouns. Thus *néwú-n* "his child" is used for small, personal objects carried in one's hand or pocket, e.g., *néwú-n nááyif* "his knife." The most widely used of these classifiers is *aa-n* "his general category of object" or "his thing to which he stands in other than a close, part-whole, or personal relationship." This is the classifier used to make noun phrases out of verb phrases and even whole narrative sentences (see 5.10). After each noun in this dictionary we indicate with what classifiers it is usually found in possessive construction, insofar as we have information.

When the possessor is named, the noun that takes a possessive suffix takes the relational suffix and is followed by the name of the possessor and then by the uninflected noun that serves as appositive modifier. Thus we have *wáá-n Eiue* "Eiue's canoe or vehicle," *wáá-n Eiue chitoosa* "Eiue's automobile," and *néwú-n átánaan nááyif* "yonder fellow's knife."

5.4 **Locative, Temporal and Prepositional Nouns.** Nouns that have a LOCATIVE (loc.) or TEMPORAL (temp.) meaning form a special class. They include all place names, words with a locative prefix *nee-*, words indicating points in time (e.g., *nánew* "yesterday," *ikenááy* "today"), and the important subclass of PREPOSITIONAL NOUNS (prep.), such as *nóó-* ("inside"), *wóó-* ("topside, surface"), *faa-* ("underside"), *núkú-* ("outerside, perimeter").

Prepositional nouns take possessive suffixes and enter into noun constructions with a relational suffix -*n*. They often function semantically like locative prepositions in English but are, strictly speaking, a special class of locative nouns. In the past a locative preposition *i-* ("at") was prefixed to these nouns (as is still the case in Gilbertese), but this preposition has gone out of use. It is preserved only in a few expressions, with demonstratives, and in some place names into which it has become incorporated (e.g., *Inúk*, name of the westernmost and most peripheral district on the westernmost island in Truk).

5.5 Partitive Constructions. Some nouns occur with the third person singular possessive suffix in contexts in which no antecedent possessor has been explicitly expressed. Examples are: *nóón ewe soran aa nó* "on that morning he went away," in which *sora-n* (*soor* "morning") occurs with the suffixed possessive pronoun; *nóón ewe mwúún* "in that period (of time)" in which *mwúú-n* (*mwúú* "era, period") again has the possessive suffix. This partitive construction is frequent in temporal and locative phrases and in other expressions in which reference is made to something that is a part or feature of something else.

Partitive constructions have given rise to new forms derived from them, in which the possessive suffix has been reinterpreted as a part of the base of the noun. Thus we have *mwúún* "government, regime, realm," derived from such expressions as *mwúún Ttooyis* "era of the Germans," which became reinterpreted as a noun and adjective meaning "German period" and then "German government." The phrase *nóón ewe mwúún* can thus mean "during that regime" as well as "in that period."

5.6 Pronouns. PRONOUNS (prn.) may be "personal" (pers.), "interrogative" (interrog.), "demonstrative" (dem.), "subjective" (sub.), "objective" (obj.), or "possessive" (pos.). The last two types have already been dealt with under morphology (see 4.4 and 4.5). Subjective pronouns are discussed under predication (see 5.12), and demonstrative pronouns will be taken up in the next section (see 5.7).

The personal pronouns are best thought of as personal nouns because they occur syntactically in exactly the same places that personal names occur. These pronouns are: *ngaang* (lsg.), *een* (2sg.), *iiy* (3sg.), *kiich* (linc.), *áám* (lexc.), *áámi* (2pl.), and *iir* (3pl.). Like other nouns, those with bases of two syllables exhibit doubling of the first vowel in these, their independent, forms (e.g., *kiich* as compared with its suffixed objective counterpart -*kich*).

The interrogative pronouns are *iyé* ("who?", pl. *ikkiyé*), *ifa* ("how, what manner?", pl. *ikkefa*), *iya* ("where?"), *ineet* ("when?"), *meet* ("what?"), *méwút* or *meyit* ("why, to what end?"), *menniiy* ("which one, what one?", cf. *menne* or *minne* "whatever"). Examples are:

iyé epwe etto? "who will come?"
ineet epwe fis? "when will it be done?"
wúse sineey iyé epwe etto "I do not know who will come."
sise sineey ineet epwe fis "we do not know when it will be done."

5.7 Demonstratives. The several uses of the DEMONSTRATIVES (dem.) are a) as pronouns and adjectives, b) as locatives, c) as dictive verbs, and d) as temporals. Cutting across these different uses are five locational distinctions relative to speaker and hearer each with its temporal counterpart relative to the present: 1) near or with speaker (as against hearer) or at the present time, 2) near or with the hearer (as against the speaker) or that just mentioned or said, 3) near both speaker and hearer or as follows or next in the future, 4) removed from both speaker and hearer, but visible, and 5) out of sight of speaker and hearer or in the past or earlier mentioned. The forms resulting from the intersection of these uses and locational distinctions are shown in Table 13.

As adjectives, demonstratives normally precede the nouns they modify: *eey mwáán* "this man," *enaan wuut* "yonder meeting house," *ekkewe feefin* "those women," *een wiik*, "next week." They regularly come after the noun or noun phrase to which they refer in possessive constructions, however: *nowumw na* "that child of yours by you," *nowumw we* "that child of yours (out of sight or past referred to)." As adjectives, demonstratives are also suffixed to a small group of words as shown in Table 14.

5.8 Numerals and Numerical Nouns. NUMERICAL (num.) constructions are of two types. One consists of numerical nouns. They are uninflected in any way and are used either in serial counting without reference to the kind of thing being counted or, sometimes, when referring to a number as an abstract concept by name. For all other purposes, including doing arithmetic, constructions are used that consist of a numerical prefix and "counting classifier" (cc.). In doing arithmetic and in the vast majority of contexts, the general classifier *-uw* is used. Certain other classifiers are in common use as well, such as *-fóch* ("stick-like object"), *-féw* ("lump or glubular object"), *-mén* ("animate object"), *ché* ("sheet-

Table 13. Demonstratives.

	a) "this/that (these/those)" "this one/that one (etc.)"				b) "here/there"	c) "here/there is (are)" "be this/that way"		d) "now/then/thereupon"
	preposed sg.	pl.	postposed sg.	pl.		sg.	pl.	
1. near speaker	eey	ekkeey, kkeey	eey	kkeey	ikeey, ika, eey, iyeey	iyeey, iye	ikkeey, ikka	iyeey
2. near hearer	ena, na, emwuun, oomw	ekkena, ekkana, kkana, ekkemwuun, ekkoomw	na	kkana	ikena, ikana, ikemwuun, ikkoomw	ina, iyemwuun, iyoomw	ikkena, ikkana, ikkemwuun, ikkoomw	
3. near speaker and hearer	een	ekkaan	een	kkaan	ikaan	iyeen	ikkaan	
4. removed from speaker and hearer	enaan, naan	ekkenaan ekkanaan kkanaan	naan	kkanaan	ikenaan, ikanaan	inaan	ikkenaan, ikkanaan	
5. out of sight or in the past	ewe	ekkewe, kkewe	we	kkewe	ikewe	iwe	ikkewe	iwe

Table 14. Demonstrative Constructions

Location	áte- "male"	niye- "female"	nemin "female"	iimw "house"	chóó "group"	iya "locus"	wono- "male"	wonno "male (pej.)"
sg. 1	áteey	niyeey	nemineey	imweyeey			woneey	wonneey
2	átána	niyena	neminna	imwena	chóóna	iyaana	wonna	wonna
	átemwuun	niyemwuun						
	átoomw	niyoomw	neminnoomw				wonoomw	wonnoomw
3	áteen	niyeen	nemineen	imweyeen			woneen	wonneen
4	átánaan	niyenaan	neminnaan	imwenaan	chóónaan	iyaanaan	wonnaan	wonnaan
5	átewe	niyewe	neminnewe	imweewe	chóówe	iyaawe	wonewe	wonnewe
pl. 1	átekkeey	niyekkeey	nemin kkeey	imwekkeey				
2	átákkana	niyekkana	nemin kkana	imwekkana	chóókkana			
	átekkemwuun	niyekkemwuun						
	átekkoomw	niyekkoomw	nemin kkoomw					
3	átákkaan	niyekkaan	nemin kkaan	imwekkaan				
4	átákkanaan	niyekkanaan	nemin kkanaan	imwekkanaan	chóókkanaan			
5	átekkewe	niyewe	nemin kkewe	imwekkewe	chóókkewe			

like object"), *-óch* ("sort or kind"). Terms for linear measures, for containers when they are used as measures, and for parts of the body when used as representatives of the whole or in reference to things worn on them also serve as classifiers, as do counters for tens, hundreds, thousands, and ten-thousands. The basic words go from one to nine.

Table 15 shows the more common constructions. All the constructions of record are listed for convenient reference under each numerical prefix in the dictionary, and every construction of record is entered as a separate headword.

Numbers above ten are formed by using the constructions for tens, hundreds, thousands, etc., in sequence, from the largest to the lowest level, ending with *mé* ("and") followed by the unit-level construction, thus: *engéréw ttiwepwúkú fiik mé fisuuw* "one thousand nine hundred seventy and seven (1977)."

Numerical constructions consisting of numeral prefixes and suffixed counting classifiers may serve as bases for additional prefixes and suffixes as follows: *ruwuuw* "two (general class)," *o-ruwuuwa-n* "second one (of a series)," *okko-ruwuuw* "two by two, two at a time," *eew nne-ruwuuw* "one half" or *eew nne-ruwuuwa-n* "one half of it"; *rúwe* "twenty," *rúwee-somw* "over twenty." Most of the possible expanded constructions of this kind are not listed as separate entries in this dictionary.

5.9 Verbs. The category VERB (v.) has several subcategories. "Inactive" (vi.) are verbs that describe a condition of the subject and have no object. "Active" (va.) are verbs that describe an action of the subject and that may be followed by an object when the relation between the verb and its object is indefinite (as when the effect of the action on the object is partial rather than complete) or when the object is general rather than specific. "Object focused" (vo.) are transitive verbs indicating that the relation between the verb and its object is definite and the object is specific (not general). "Relational" (vr.) are verbs that are linked to a following object by the relational suffix *-n*, the object being in its turn either a noun phrase or a verb phrase. When the object is a verb or verb phrase, a relational verb functions as an auxilliary verb. The following phrases illustrate the several subcategories.

vi.: *aa semwmwen* "he got sick."
wú sááw "I am embarrassed."
aa wún "he smoked (or drank)."
va.: *wúpwe wún ena suupwa (ekkena suupwa)* "I will have a smoke of that cigarette (those cigarettes)."
wúse wúkkún suupwa "I don't smoke cigarettes."

Table 15. Numerical Constructions.

Number	Numerical noun	Numerical prefix	General class	Tens	Hundreds	Animate objects	Stick objects	Lump objects	Sheet objects	Sorts, kinds
1	eet	e-, i-, ó-	eew	engoon	ipwúkú	emén	efóch	eféw	eché	óóch
2	érúúw, ttérúúw	rúwé-, ruwo-	ruwuuw, ruuwu	rúwe	rúwépwúkú	rúwémén	rúwéfóch, ruwofóch	rúwéféw	rúwaché	ruwóóch
3	één	wúnú-, ini-	wúnúngát	iniik	wúnúpwúkú	wúnúmén	wúnúfóch	wúnúféw	wúnúché	wúnúyóch
4	fáán	fé-, fa-, fáá-	rúwáánú	fáayik	fépwúkú	fémén	feféch, fofóch, ffóch	féféw	faché	fóóch
5	niim	nime-	nimuuw	nime	nimepwúkú	nimmén	nimefóch, niffóch	nimeféw	nimaché	nimóóch
6	woon	wono-	wonuuw	wone	wonopwúkú	wonomén	wonofóch	wonoféw	wonaché	wonoyóch
7	fúús	fúú-, fii-, fisu-	fisuuw	fiik	fúúpwúkú	fúúmén	fúúfóch	fúúféw	fúúché	fúúyóch
8	waan	wanú	wanuuw	wanik	wanúpwúkú	wanúmén	wanúfóch	wanúféw	wanúché	wanúyóch
9	ttiiw	ttiwe-	ttiwuuw	ttiwe	ttiwepwúkú	ttiwemén	ttiwefóch	ttiweféw	ttiwaché	ttiweyóch

vo.: *wúpwe wúnúmi ena suupwa (ekkena suupwa)* "I will smoke that cigarette (those cigarettes)."
wúwa sááwáásini átánaan "I am embarrassed by that fellow."

vr.: *aa pwisin mááritá* "it grew up by itself."
aa mwechen ónnut "he wants to sleep."
aa mwechen kkón "he wants breadfruit pudding."
aa mwechen ataayenó enaan iimw "he wants to destroy that house."

It is possible to construe the apparent object of an active verb as a phrase that functions as an adjectival modifier of an intransitive verb, the object thus being a part of or incorporated into an intransitive verb phrase. Such a view is entirely compatible with the indefinite and nonspecific relation of verb and object in va. construction.

An inactive verb may be transformed into an object focused verb by prefixing the causative particle *a-* (or *á-, e-, é-, o-, ó-* according to the next following vowel) and suffixing the objective pronouns directly to the base: *a-para* "make it red" (*par* "red"), *é-métú-ur* "make them satisfied" (*mét* "satisfied").

Object focused verbs of other than causative type are usually formed by suffixing a verb formative particle to the base, to which the objective pronouns are then suffixed in turn. These particles are *-fi-, -si-, -ki-, -mi-, -ni-, -ri-, -ti-, -yi-* (or *-i-, -e-*), *-ú-* (or *-o-*). Some examples are *turu-fi* "grab it" (*tur* "be grabbed"), *wúnú-mi* "drink it" (*wún* "to drink"), *fenúwe-ni* "acquire it as land" (*fénú* "land"), *éé-yi* "hook it" (*éé* "fish hook"), *pwure-e-y* "moor it with a stake" (*pwuur* "mooring stake"), *núkú-ú-w* "put it in readiness" (*núk* "ready"). Contrast the causative *a-para* "make it red" with *pare-e-y* "apply red to it."

Some object focused verbs are formed simply by suffixing the objective pronouns directly to the base without a verb formative suffix or a causative prefix. Examples: *chee-y* "chase him" (*che* "be in motion"), *ssawa* "make him a present of food" (*ssaw* "present of food to a sick person"). Verbs formed in this way may exist along side those with a verb formative suffix on the same base as with *fana* and *fane-e-y* "adze it" (*fanafan* "adzing").

Replacing the causative prefix *a-* with its dc. equivalent *kka-* (double initial consonant), while at the same time dropping the suffixed objective pronouns, serves sometimes to transform an object focused causative verb into an inactive verb with a passive connotation or into an active verb with incorporated object. Thus from *rap* "heated," we get *a-rapa* "cause it to be heated," and from the latter we get *kka-rap* "be made heated"; and from *é* "learned," we get *á-yéé-w* "make it known, teach it," and from this we get *kká-yé* "learn." Similarly, some object focused verbs with verb formative suffixes may be transformed into inactive verbs by dropping the suffixed pronouns and, usually, but not always doubling the initial consonant: *féé-ri* "make it," *féé-r* or *fféé-r* "be made, make." When this happens, the derived inactive verb acquires as a stem vowel a high vowel that is in the same position as the preceding vowel. Thus, we have *féérú-n* "his making or doing" (*cf. féérí-ya-n* "thing made or to be made by him").

5.10 Nouns Constructed from Verbs. Nouns may be constructed from verbs in several ways. A verb or verb phrase may be preceded by a demonstrative or by a possessive construction with the possessive classifier *aa-* and thus be converted into a verbal noun, indicating not the act but the performing of the act. The semantic effect is often similar to that provided by the suffix *-ing* in English. Thus we have: *meyi ngngaw ewe ninni aramas* "that assaulting people is bad"; *wúwa opwut áán átánaan wúkkún suupwa* "I dislike that fellow's smoking cigarettes."

When verbs are converted into nouns in this way, they appear in independent form in the manner of verbs, so that disyllabic bases do not double the first vowel in the way that disyllabic noun bases ordinarily do in the independent form. Thus we have: *ewe wún piyé* "that drinking beer"; *ese sineey á* "he does not know how to swim (he does not know swimming)."

A verb or verb phrase may also be converted into a noun as the first element in relational construction involving the relational suffix *-n*, as in *pwáán iik* "coming to view (sighting) of fish" (from *pwá* "come to view, be discovered").

5.11 Adjectivals. A noun or verb phrase may consist of a "head," which names the topic, followed by one or more modifying or specifying morphemes, which are here termed adjectivals (adj.): *emén mwáán wátte* "a large man (one-animate man large)"; *aa fátán mwittir* "he walked quickly." Some adjectivals, such as *wátte*, may precede the head, but only if accompanied by the relational (or attributive) suffix *-n*: *emén wátteen mwáán* "a large man (one-animate large-of man)." Similarly in verb phrases, an adjectival may precede the head, now functioning as an inactive verb linked to the head by the preposition *ne*: *aa mwittir ne fátán* "he was quick in walking."

If the base form of the adjectival contains two syllables, it is commonly suffixed to the head to make a compound word. Longer morphemes may also be suffixed.

A widely occurring special class of suffixed adjectivals are the DIRECTIONALS (dir.): *-nó* "away from speaker or referrent," *-to* "toward speaker," *-wow* "toward or farther in the direction of person addressed," *-nong* "in" or "south," *-wu* "out" or "north," *-tá* "up" or "east," and *-tiw* "down" or "west." Thus we have *aa turu-tiw* "he fell down," *sópwu-tiw* "lower or western district." The directionals are special in that they normally come after the suffixed objective pronouns with object focused verbs, as in Table 12 where *-nó* is shown affixed to *wuweyi-* and *wuwee-*. Compare *ange-e-ye-tiw* "take it down" and *ange-tiwe-e-y* "take it from below." In the latter case the suffix modifies only *ange-* ("take in hand") to form a complex verb base that is then object focused with *-e-*, followed by the third singular objective pronoun *-y*.

Another special class of suffixed adjectivals are the INTENSIFIERS (intens.) *-fféw, -kkich, -kkus, -numw, -paas, -pwpwich, -chchar, -chchik, -ttik*. The semantic distinctions among them remain to be analyzed, and they have been glossed indiscriminately as "very, extremely."

A few words have been recorded in which the suffixed adjectival does not appear in the usual combining form of the base (for bases of two syllables) but has the shape of the independent nominal form. These words include *imwefaaw* ("stone house," i.e., house made of stone, cf. *tuuféw* "stone digging," i.e., a method of fishing among stones), *nnúffaaw* ("stone mortar," i.e., mortar made of stone), *pwpwúnúchuuk* ("mountain soil," i.e., a coarse soil found on mountain slopes, cf. *wiichuk* "mountain top"), and *soosoomaay* ("beachrock," lit. "fishtrap holder," used as siding for fishtraps). In each case the construction is a noun and consists of a noun with a modifier derived from another noun and retaining something of its nominal meaning.

5.12 **Predication.** Sentences are basically of three types: "equative," "descriptive," and "narrative."

Equative sentences are constructed of two nouns or noun phrases. Introducing a sentence with the negative STATIVE MARKER (st.m.) *sapw* (*esapw* in some eastern dialects) negates the equation.

iiy semey "my father is he (he my father)."
sapw iiy semey "my father is not he (not he my father)."
semey iiy "he is my father (my father he)."
sapw semey iiy "he is not my father (not my father he)."
samach sómwoon átewe "that fellow is our chief."
sapw samach sómwoon átewe "that fellow is not our chief."

átewe samach sómwoon "our chief is that fellow."
sapw átewe samach sómwoon "our chief is not that fellow."

Descriptive sentences consist of a noun phrase as subject and a word or phrase that describes the state or condition (which may include performing an act) of the subject, the descriptive phrase being introduced by the positive stative marker *meyi*. A descriptive sentence is negated by resort to a narrative sentence using a third person subjective pronoun and the negative aspect marker *-se*.

meyi wátte áttewe "that fellow is big (is big that fellow)."
ese wátte átewe "that fellow is not big (he is not big that fellow)."
meyi wokkowochooch aramas ekkewe waasééna "those strangers are cannibals (are [who] eat people those strangers)."
rese wokkowochooch aramas ekkewe waasééna "those strangers are not cannibals."

Descriptive sentences may serve as relative clauses embedded in both equative and narrative sentences.

emén meyi wátte átewe or *átewe emén meyi wátte* "that fellow is someone [who] is big."
emén meyi wátte epwe etto neesor or *neesor epwe etto emén meyi wátte* "someone [who] is big will come tomorrow."

Narrative sentences are introduced by SUBJECTIVE PRONOMINAL PREFIXES (sub.) with or without aspect markers suffixed directly to them. Although the subjective pronouns are written as separate words in the absence of aspect markers, they are better understood as prefixed to the verb or to an intervening adverbial (see 5.13). The subjective pronouns and aspect markers are shown in their combinations in Table 16.

By ASPECT MARKERS (asp.) we have reference to a set of forms that, when present, are always suffixed directly to the subjective pronouns to form the opening word of a narrative predicate construction. The aspect markers have the following semantic effect: 1) action or state has become realized or is in process of realization as of the present or historical present (*-a*, negative *-se*); 2) action or state will be or is supposed to be realized after the present or historical present (*-pwe*, negative *-sapw*); 3) action or state is intended to be or is about to be realized (*-pwene, -ne*, negative *-sene, -te*); 4) action or state will be or is intended to be

Table 16. Subjective Pronouns and Aspect Markers.

Subjective Prefixes	Aspect Markers						
	-a	-se	-pwe	-sapw	-pwene, -ne	-te	-pwaapw
wú- (1sg)	wúwa	wúse	wúpwe	wúsapw	wúpwene	wúte	wúpwaapw
ke- (2sg)	kaa	kese	kepwe, kopwe	kesapw	kepwene, kopwene, kene	kete	kepwaapw, kopwaapw
e- (3sg)	aa	ese	epwe	esapw	epwene	ete	epwaapw
si- (1inc)	siya	sise	sipwe	sisapw	sipwene	site	sipwaapw
éwú- (1exc)	éwúwa	éwúse	éwúpwe	éwúsapw	éwúpwene	éwúte	éwúpwaapw
éwú-, wo- (2pl)	éwúwa, wowa	éwúse, wose	éwúpwe, wopwe	éwúsapw, wosapw	éwúpwene, wopwene, éwúne, wone	éwúte, wote	éwúpwaapw, wopwaapw
re- (3pl)	raa	rese	repwe	resapw	repwene	rete	repwaapw

realized at a later time (*-pwaapw*). Compare the following descriptive and narrative sentences:

meyi semmwen átewe "that fellow is sick (describing his condition or state with no event implied)."

aa semmwen átewe "that fellow has become sick (as a realized event, a change of condition implied)."

5.13 Adverbials and Qualifiers. There is a small set of words that, when used as ADVERBIALS (adv.), come immediately before the verb and immediately after *meyi* in a descriptive clause or immediately before the verb and immediately after the subjective pronoun and aspect marker in a narrative clause. They have the effect of modifying not the verb but the entire predication. Thus we have *mwmwar* ("probably, likely, tentatively") in the sentence *aa mwmwar sineey mwmwey* "he probably knows it better than I do."

Other adverbials are *ekis* ("barely, a little"), *ii* (softening the force of the statement), *kamwo* ("first"), *kan* ("in the habit of; happen to"), *koon* ("most, very, extremely; too"), *mén* or *mmén* ("indeed, very, extremely"), *mwo* ("first, for now, for the time"), *pwan* ("also, again, more; either"), *chék* ("only, merely, just"), *sóór* ("make an effort, have a go at"), *sóór* ("barely, a little").

Some words that function as adverbials also function as QUALIFIERS (qlf.). These consist of a small residual group of words that can be used fairly freely to qualify what is being said. In addition to *ii, kamwo, mwo, chék* above, they are *máá* ("indeed"), *mwaa* ("indeed, so, really"), *mwo* ("even"), *sapw* ("truly, believe me"). The precise conditions governing their occurrence remain to be analyzed.

The dictionary entries in which adverbials and qualifiers appear as headwords provide examples of their use.

5.14 Mood Markers. The words called MOOD MARKERS (md.m.) come at the beginning of a sentence or clause, before the subject or predicate, and indicate the speaker's attitude or feeling about the statement. Thus, with *itá* (indicating a wish or hope with some doubt), we have as an example: *itá wúpwe áni ewe kkón ngé wúse toongeni* "I wanted to (hopefully I would) eat the breadfruit, but I was not able to."

Other mood markers are *anno* and *sanne* (indicating that what follows is contrary to reality or fact), *eni* and *meni* ("perhaps"), *mwmwar* ("would like to, intend to"), *mwoo* (indicating affirmation in an oath), *are* and *ika* ("if," indicating provisionality or uncertainty as to future), *ómwo* ("would that," indicating unattainable wish, often used with *itá*). Examples of their use are given under the entries in which they appear as headwords.

6. OTHER INFORMATION.

6.1 **Dialects.** Local dialect variation in Trukese remains to be studied. Truk's people tend to make a simple division between the eastern and western halves of the lagoon, *Nómwoneyas* (N) and *Fááyichuk* (F) respectively. These designations occur frequently in this dictionary. Actually, dialect variation is more complicated than this grossly stereotypic division suggests.

The bulk of the material for this dictionary was obtained from Romónum people and reflects the pronunciation patterns that characterize the central lagoon islands of Wútéét, Romónum, and Éét. It is in terms of these patterns that we have described the combining form and inflection types under morphology (see 4 above). These patterns largely prevail in northern Toon (Tol) and Paata (Pata) in the western part of the lagoon; but the speech of southern Toon is, in some respects, more like the eastern lagoon dialects, showing, for example, a greater preference for stem-vowel *-e* regardless of adjacent vowels in words of combining form type 3.

Because of the complexity of differences in local usage, dialect designations even below the N and F levels should be regarded as approximate, at best. Many variations that are regional, moreover, are simply listed as variants with no geographical location given.

6.2 **Tabu Words.** Traditionally, there were three levels or degrees of restriction or tabu on the use of words. These levels are marked Tb1, Tb2, and Tb3 respectively (a word being marked as simply Tb. in the absence of information about specific level).

Tb1 words include the names for private parts (genital and anal) of both sexes and for functions of the sexual organs. They may not ordinarily be mentioned in sexually mixed company or by young persons in the presence of elders. Even among persons of the same sex and age, people who are in the kinship categories of sibling of the same sex, of parent and child, and of sibling-in-law of the same sex may not use these words in talk together. These words also provide the vocabulary of deadly public insult.

Tb2 words include the names of parts of the body closely associated with the genital and anal areas and a number of words whose meanings are innocent in themselves but that resemble in pronunciation words of the Tb1 level. Unlike Tb1 words, Tb2 words may be used among kinsmen of the same sex who are related by marriage, and a man may use them in joking with a woman when not in the presence of relatives of opposite sex or older siblings of the same sex of either.

Tb3 words are difficult to characterize, except that in some way they are suggestive of words of the first and second levels. They also include the less polite words for anal functions. For all words of this level and for some of the second level, as well, there are other words of identical meaning that are acceptable in any social context. The only restrictions on Tb3 words are between or in the presence of father and daughter, mother and son, and brother and sister. Restrictions on the use of words of level three have largely disappeared in modern Trukese usage. (For further information, see Goodenough 1975.)

6.3 **Loanwords.** Trukese has many loanwords from English and Japanese and a few from German and Spanish. Most of these loans are identified as such in this dictionary. If the loan is from other than English, the source word in the language from which the loan comes is usually indicated. If it comes from English, the source word is not otherwise indicated if it also appears in the English gloss, but it is indicated if the derivation is in any way obscure. Loanwords from other Micronesian and Austronesian languages, especially if they are not recent borrowings, are difficult to identify and will remain so until the Micronesian languages have been intensively studied comparatively with the methods of historical linguistics. We have been able to identify only a few such borrowings, but it is probable that there are a great many more.

BIBLIOGRAPHY

BOLLIG, P. LAURENTIUS. 1927. "Die Bewohner der Truk-Inseln. Religion, Leben und kurze Grammatik eines Mikronesiervolkes." (*Anthropos Ethnologische Bibliothek*, 3, no. 1.) Münster i.W.: Aschendorffsche Verlagsbuchhandlung. [Contains texts of songs, riddles, and proverbs, as well as the first published description of Trukese grammar.]

DYEN, ISIDORE. 1949. "On the History of the Trukese Vowels." *Language* 25: pp. 420–436. [Shows how the nine vowel phonemes of Trukese can be systematically derived from the vowels and diphthongs of Proto-Austronesian, as they had then been reconstructed from comparison of other Austronesian languages.]

_____. 1965. *A Sketch of Trukese Grammar.* (American Oriental Series, Essay 4.) New Haven: American Oriental Society. [The best published account of Trukese grammar, based on the Romónum dialect.]

ELBERT, S. H. 1947. *Trukese-English and English-Trukese Dictionary.* Pearl Harbor: United States Naval Military Government. [The first published dictionary of the Trukese language.]

GOODENOUGH, WARD H. 1963. "The Long or Double Consonants of Trukese." *The Proceedings of the Ninth Pacific Science Congress, 1957.* 3 (Anthropology and Social Sciences): pp. 77–80. [Shows how the double consonants can be understood as the result of a loss of intervening vowels without loss of syllable length.]

_____. 1966. "Notes on Truk's Place Names." *Micronesica* 2: pp. 95–129. [The fullest published list of place names in Truk in a phonemic orthography with maps.]

———. 1975. "A Similarity in Cultural and Linguistic Change." In M. Dale Kinkade, Kenneth L. Hale and Oswald Werner, editors, *Linguistics and Anthropology, In Honor of C. F. Voegelin*. (Lisse: The Peter de Ridder Press, pp. 263–273). [Deals specifically with usage relating to tabu words in Trukese.]

KÄSER, LOTHAR. 1977. "Der Begriff Seele bei den Insulanern Truk" (Doctoral Dissertation, Albert-Ludwigs-Universität Freiburg i. Br.), published by the author. [Contains excellent vocabulary materials on psychic states and feelings and on ritual pertaining to the spirits of the dead.]

KIMIUO, KIMEUO, VINCENT R. LINARES, TONY OTTO, and HIROSHI SUGITA. 1976. *Pwpwuken Itechikin Fóósun Chuuk (A Short Trukese Spelling Dictionary)*. Social Sciences and Linguistics Institute, University of Hawaii: Bilingual Education Teacher Training Project for Micronesia (mimeographed).

KRÄMER, AUGUSTIN. 1932. *Truk*. (Ergebnisse der Südsee-Expedition 1908–1910, series 2B, vol. 5, edited by G. Thilenius.) Hamburg: Friedrichsen, De Gruyter [Contains some text materials.]

LIST OF ABBREVIATIONS

(References in parentheses refer to numbered sections in the Introduction)

1sg.	first person singular
2sg.	second person singular
3sg.	third person singular
1exc.	first person plural exclusive
1inc.	first person plural inclusive
2pl.	second person plural
3pl.	third person plural
adj.	adjectival (see 5.11)
adv.	adverbial (see 5.13)
ant.	antonym
asp.	aspective; aspect marker (see 5.12)
b.f.	base form (see 4.2)
c.	causative (see 5.9)
cc.	counting classifier (see 5.8)
cf.	compare
c.f.	combining form (see 4.2)
Cham.	Chamorro
conj.	conjunction
const.	construction
cpd.	compound word
cpds.	compound words
ct.m.	courtesy marker
db	doubled base or its equivalent (see 4.3)
dc	doubled first consonant of base or its equivalent (see 4.3)
dem.	demonstrative (see 5.7)
dim.	diminutive
dir.	directional (see 5.11)
dis.	distributive form (see 4.3)
ds	doubled first syllable of base or its equivalent (see 4.3)
Eng.	English
exc.	exclusive (first plural)
excl.	exclamation
E.Wn.	Efengin Wééné (northern Moen Island)
Éét	Éét (Eot Island)
F.	Fááyichuk (West Truk Lagoon)
Ffn.	Feefen (Fefan Island)
Fi.	Fijian
fig.	figurative; figuratively
Gb.	Gilbertese
Ger.	German
inc.	inclusive (first plural)
ind. obj.	indirect object

intens.	intensifier (see 5.11)
interj.	interjection
interrog.	interrogative; interrogative marker
Itang	itang usage
Jap.	Japanese
Lat.	Latin
loc.	locative (see 5.4)
m.	marker
Mck.	Mortlockese; Mortlock Islands
md.m.	mood marker (see 5.14)
mod.	modern usage
N.	Nómwoneyas (East Truk Lagoon)
n.	noun (see 5.2)
n.form.	noun formative
ni.	noun, inflected only (without independent form, see 5.2)
n.phr.	noun phrase
nr.	noun, relational construction only (no independent form, see 5.2)
ns.	noun, separable in possessive constructions (see 5.2)
nu.	noun, uninflected (may be in relational construction, see 5.2)
num.	numerical; numerative (see 5.8)
N.Wt.	Nómwun Wiitéé (Namonuito Atoll)
obj.	objective (serving as object of a verb) (see 4.5)
Obs.	obsolete
PAN	Proto-Austronesian
P.Eng.	Pidgin English
pers.	personal
phr.	phrase
pl.	plural
Plt.	Pwolowót (Puluwat Atoll), Puluwatese
Pn.	Pwene (Polle Island)
p.n.form.	personal name formative
Pon.	Ponapean
pos.	possessive (see 5.3)
pred. phr.	predicate phrase
pref.	prefix
prep.	preposition; prepositional (see 5.4)
prn.	pronoun (see 4.4, 4.5, 5.6)
prns.	pronouns (see 4.4, 4.5, 5.6)
Ps.W.	Piis-Wééné (Pis or Pis-Moen Island)
Pt.	Paata (Pata Island)
ptv.	partitive (see 5.5)
refl.	reflexive
rel.	relational (see 5.2, 5.3, 5.9)
Rmn.	Romónum (Ulalu Island)
r.t.	reduplicative type (see 4.3)
sg.	singular
Sp.	Spanish
st.	stative (see 5.12)

st.m.	stative marker (see 5.12)
sub.	subjective (serving as subject of a verb) (see 5.12)
suf.	suffix
syn.	synonym
T	inflectional type (with nos. 1, 1v, etc.)
Tb.	tabu (see 6.2)
Tb1.	tabu, first degree (most extensively applied, see 6.2)
Tb2.	tabu, second degree (see 6.2)
Tb3.	tabu, third degree (least extensively applied, see 6.2)
temp.	temporal (see 5.4)
Tn.	Toon (Tol Island)
To.	Tongan
Tws.	Tonowas (Dublon Island)
unsp.	unspecified as to type; unspecifiable
u.m.	unknown meaning or function
v.	verb (see 4.5, 5.9)
va.	verb, active and subject focused; when transitive it is indefinite or unspecific as to its object (see 5.9)
v.form.	verb formative (see 4.5)
vi.	verb, inactive and intransitive; it is descriptive of the condition (which may be active) of the subject (see 5.9)
vo.	verb, active and object focused (transitive); it is definite and specific as to its object (see 5.9)
vo.phr.	verb phrase, object focused
v.phr.	verb phrase
vr.	verb, relational (see 5.9)
Wmn.	Wuumaan (Uman Island)
Wn.	Wééné (Moen Island)
Wny.	Woney (Onei District)
Wol.	Woleaian
Wtt.	Wútéét (Udot Island)

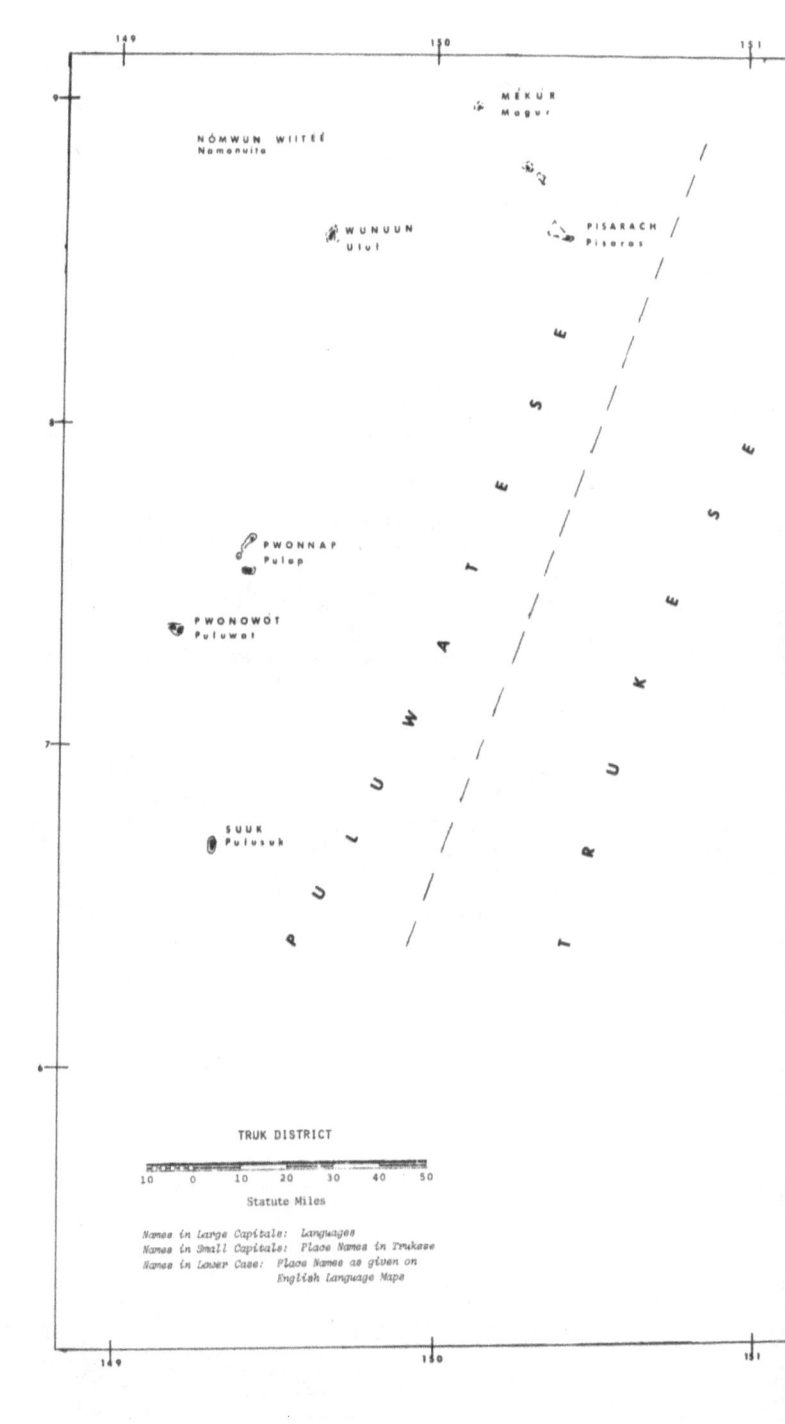

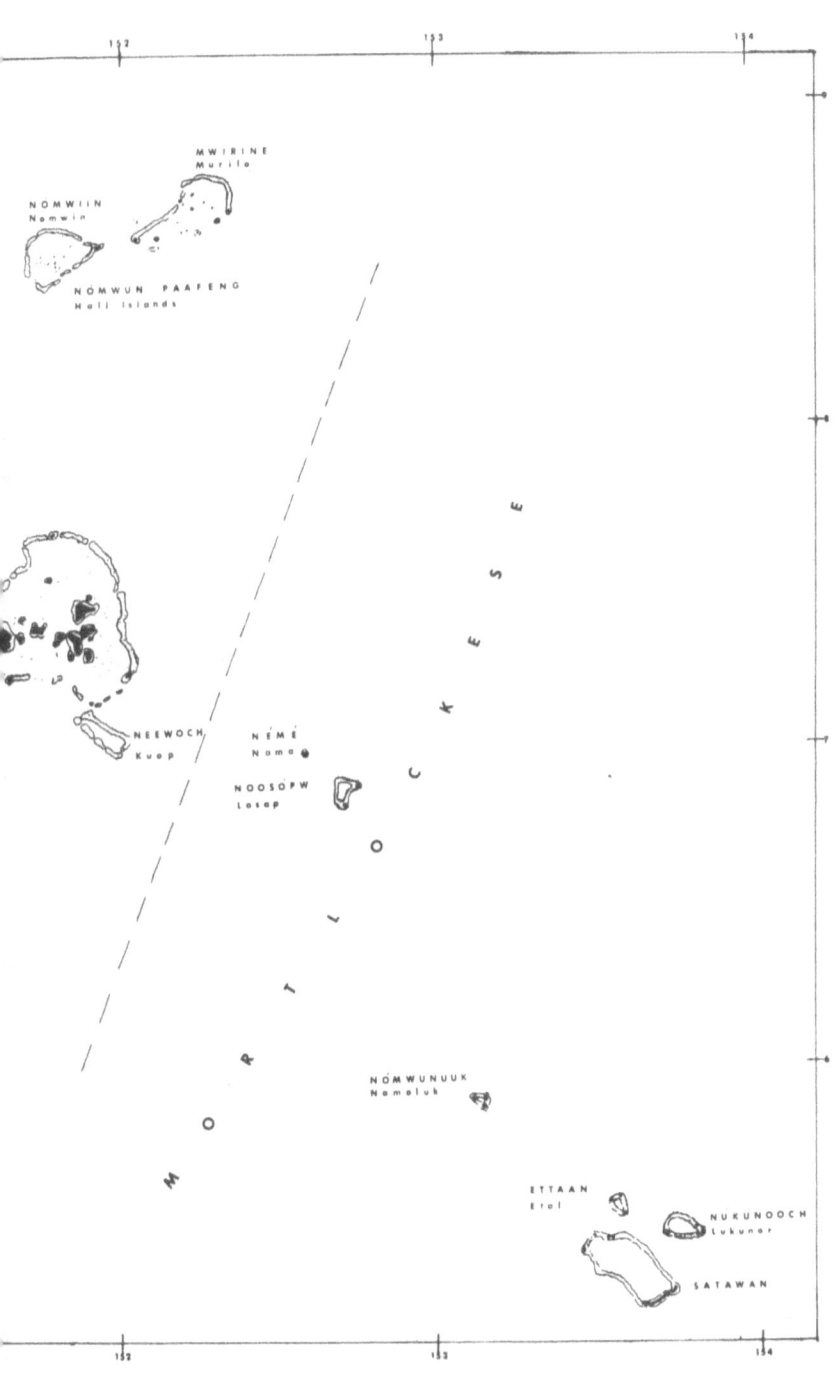

TRUKESE–ENGLISH DICTIONARY

A

a-₁ See *e-₁*. [Used only when followed immediately by the vowel *a*.] Var. *á-₁, e-₁, ó-₁*. pref. (sub.) 3sg. sub. prn.: he, she, it. [Although a prefix, it is written separately except when followed by an aspect marker. Other than with aspect markers, it occurs only in colloquial speech in place of *e-₁*. Sub. prns. are used only at the beginning of narrative constructions and mark them as such.] *aa* he, she, it plus reality aspect marker. *aapw* no (*a-apw* it be not).

a-₂ (3b: *a-, á-, e-, é-, o-, ó-, -ka-, -ká-, -ke-, -ké-, -ko-, -kó-*) A₁, KA₁. [From old **ka-*, the *k* having been lost except when preceded by a prefix ending in *i, u, ú*.] pref. (c.) 1. imparts a causative meaning to the base; causing, making, having the effect of. Dis. *akka-, ákká-, ekke-, ékké-, okko-, ókkó-* (ds). *asséér* be caused to slide, *asséérú* cause to slide, *nikasséér* game of sliding down a slope on coconut fronds (*sséér* be sliding, as one thing against another); *áweesí* cause to be finished, finish (*wees* be finished); *eteni* put in rank order, enumerate (*ten* be in line); *émwéwúna* cause to swing back and forth, *nikémwmwéwún* children's swing (*mwéwúnéwún* swing back and forth); *okkufu* cause to lose, defeat (*kkuf* be defeated); *óónnuta* put to sleep (*ónnut* be asleep); *ópwoow* cause to swell, inflate, *nikópwoopwo* balloon (*pwo* be swollen). Cf. *fa-2*. 2. (In ptv. const.) marks ordinal numbers; (in dis. form) marks numbers at a time. *ááchéén* or *ááyechéén, érúwachéén, éwúnúchéén, afachéén, enimachéén* first, second, third, fourth, fifth leaf or sheet (*eché, rúwaché, wúnúché, faché, nimaché* one, two, three, four, five leaves or sheets). *ákkáyeew, okkoruwuuw, ékkéwúnúngát* one, two, three at a time (*eew, ruwuuw, wúnúngát* one, two, three general kinds of things).

a-₃ (3) A₇. pref. (loc.) at. See *aan₁, ana, anaan*.

a-₄ (3b: *a-, á-, e-, o-, -ka-*) A₈, KA₂. [In cpds. only.] unsp. pertaining to eating. See *ana-, áni, eni₃*.

-a-₁ (1v together with the vowel to which it is suffixed) A₂. Var. *-wa-₁, -ya-₁*. suf. (n.form.; T1v) object or product of an action. [Suffixed to bases of object focused verbs ending in *a* to indicate the thing that is involved in the action. It is used only with suffixed pos. prns. to indicate the actor involved.] *fana-a-* thing adzed or to be adzed by someone (*fana* cut with an adze), *fáná-á-y* thing adzed or to be adzed by me. Cf. *-a-₂*.

-a-₂ (1v together with the vowel to which it is suffixed) A₃. [The noun-formative counterpart of the verb formative suffixes *-e-, -yi-*; also derived from **-ka-*, the *k* having been lost except when preceded by *i, u, ú*, which is the noun-formative counterpart of the verb formative suffix *-ki-*.] suf. (n.form.; T1v) object or product of an action. [Suffixed to the bases of inactive verbs to which the corresponding active-verb formatives may be suffixed. Reference to the actor is indicated by suffixed pos. prns.] *wocha-a-* thing for someone to eat raw, corresponding to *woche-e-y* (from **wocha-yi-*) eat it raw, *wochá-á-y* thing for me to eat raw; *fóta-a-* (from **fóto-ka-*) thing planted or to be planted, corresponding to *fótu-ki* (from *fóto-ki*) plant it, *fótá-á-y* thing planted by me. Cf. *-a-₁*.

-a-₃ (1, 1v together with the vowel to which it is suffixed) A₄. [Suffixed to object focused verbs with bases ending in a single vowel. It is dropped, being the final vowel of the word, in the absence of a further suffix. The final vowel of the verb base becomes *a*, if it was not already *a*, when directional suffixes are added to this suffix.] Var. *-y₂, -w*. suf. (obj.) 3sg. obj. prn.: him, her, it; marker of specific object to follow. *ómonna-a-tá* or *ómonná-ó-tá* prepare it up, *ómonna* prepare it; *fita-a-to* accompany him hither, *fita-a-nó* or *fitó-ó-nó* accompany him away, *fiti* accompany him.

-a-₄ (1v together with the vowel to which it is suffixed) A₅. suf. (v.form.) converts bases of nouns, adjectives, and inactive verbs ending in *a* (c.f. type 3) into object focussed verbs of type 3. [It is absorbed by the final vowel of the preceding base with 3rd sg. and 3rd pl. objective prns.] *kúná-á-yey* see me; *kúnó-ó-k* see you (sg.); *kúna* see him, her, it; *kúná-á-kich* see us (inc.); *kúná-á-keem* see us (exc.); *kúná-á-kemi* see you (pl.); *kúne-er* see them (b.f. KÚNA see *kúnékún*).

-a-₅ A₆. [As the final vowel of a word, it is regularly dropped, its presence being indicated by the retention of the final vowel of the preceding base.] suf. (dem.) here (by me). Syn. *eey*₁. See *ika*₂, *ikka*.

-a₁ (*-wa*, *-ya*) A₉. suf. (asp.) reality aspect marker, indicating realized, past, or effected action. [Suffixed to subjective prns. at the beginning of narrative constructions.] *wúwa* (1sg. with *wú-*); *kaa* (2sg. with *ke-*); *aa* (3sg. with *e-*); *siya*, *saa* (1inc. with *si-*); *éwúwa*, *owa*, *wowa* (1exc. and 2pl. with *éwú-*, *o-*, *wo-*); *raa* (3pl. with *re-*).

-a₂ (1) AA₂. [In cpds. only.] unsp. place, location. See *iya*, *meya*.

aa- (1v) AA₁. ni. (T1v) 1. thing, object (general class, in indefinite or otherwise unspecified relationship to possessor or referent). [Used widely in possessive and relational constructions, the word specifying the object possessed following this one. In rel. const. the possessor or referent comes between this word and the word or phrase specifying the nature of the object possessed. Verbs, verb phrases, and entire sentences may be converted into noun phrases when put in apposition to this word.] *aan* his t.; *áán* t. of. *áán iyé eey raweses* whose are these trousers ("thing of whom these trousers")?; *ááy raweses* my trousers; *áán átewe raweses* that fellow's trousers. *ese núkúúw aach we siya feyinnó Merika* He does not believe that we went to America ("he does not believe the our we went to America"). 2. food portion (deferential usage).

aa₁ (1) AA₅. nu. (T1) name of the low, central, unrounded vowel written *a*; name of the letter thus written.

aa₂ See *a-*₁, *-a*₁. prn. const. 3sg. sub. prn. plus reality aspect marker: he, she, it (past, factual). *aa nó* he has gone; *átewe aa kkapas* that fellow spoke.

aaf (3b) AFFA. n. (T3) intestine, gut. *eyaf a.* one piece of i. *affan* his i.; *affen* i. of.

aas₁ (3b) ASA₁. Var. *-ya*₁. n. (T3) upper part, top, summit, eastern side, above (vertically). *asan* above him, its upper side. *asen ásápwán* windward side; *asen chuuk* mountain top; *asen mékúrey* top of my head. *peekin asan* its upper or eastern side (of Truk and neighboring atolls).

aas₂ (3: *aasse-*) N. Var. *aasaas*. nu. (c.; T2) a tree (*Terminalia catappa*). *aassen iyaan na?* where is that t. from?

aas₃ (Eng.) nu. donkey, ass.

aasaas (db; 3) ASA₂. n. (c.; dis.) a tree (*Terminalia catappa*). [Wood used for paddles; bark used as medicine for infants.] Syn. *aas*₂.

Aakos N. of *Óókos*.

aam (3) AAMA. n. (T3) edge or rim of anything that is concave and can contain things; brim; gunwale. *aaman* its e. *aamen sepi* bowl's rim; *aamen waa* boat's gunwale. *aamen foo-* labia majora (Tb1).

aamenifo (1) See *aam, foo*. Tb1. ns. (T1) labia majora. *aamen foon* her l.

aamw (3) AMWA. n. (T3) wooden spacer joining outrigger boom and outrigger float on canoe. *efóch a.* one spacer. *amwan* its (canoe's) spacer; *aan a.* his spacer.

aan₁ See *a-*₃, *een*₃. F. dem. (loc.) here, at hand (near both speaker and person addressed). *ewe nengngin e móót a. nánew* the girl was sitting here yesterday. Syn. *ikaan*.

aan₂ (3b) ANA. n. (T3) 1. road, street, path, way, route, course (at sea); approach (to a job or problem), method, way (of doing); line of reckoning (in genealogies). *anan* his r. *anen aramas* footpath, sidewalk; *anen feyiyengngaw* way of corruption, road to ruin or misfortune; *anen feyiyééch* way to fortune or blessings; *anen mmak* drawn line, line of type or writing; *anen manaw* way of salvation; *anen neewén* forest or bush road; *anen*

sáay route or way of travel, means of transportation. 2. Milky Way. [Short for *anenimey*.]

aan₃ 3sg. pos. of *aa-*.

Aant Var. *Áánt.* nu. (loc.) Aant Atoll (Eastern Caroline Islands).

aang (3) ANGA₁. n. (T3) span between thumb and forefinger (unit of measure). *eyang* one s.; *fiteyang* how many s.

aangún See *aa-* (?), *ngúnúngún.* nu. (c.) nose flute ("softener"). [Used in former times by young men to serenade young women.] Syn. *nikaangún*.

aap (3b) APA. n. (T3) diaper; cloth a baby sleeps on. *eché a.* one d. *apan* his d.

aapa- (3b) See *ap₁*. [In cpds. only.] vi. (c.) be unfair.

aapa See *ap₁*. [Used with *ngeni epeek*.] vo. (c.; T3) move (something) to one side. *kepwe aapaangeni epeek naan pwóór* you will move that box to one side; *kepwe aapeer ngeni epeek* you will move them to one side. Cf. *aapéngeni*.

aapaangeni See *aapa*.

aapaap (db; 3b) See *ap₁*. vi. (c., dis.) be unfair, show favoritism, discriminate (against others).

aapangngaw (3b) See *aapa-, ngngaw.* vi. (c.) be unfair, selfish, partial. Cf. *inetingngaw, kkefiningngaw*.

aapééch (2: *aapééchchú-*) See *aapa-, ééch.* Var. *aapéyéech.* vi. (c.) be fair, impartial. Cf. *inetééch, kkefiniyéech*.

aapéngeni See *ap₁, ngeni.* [With *epeek*.] Var. *aapaangeni.* vo. (c.; T2) move (something) to one side. *kepwe a. epeek naan pwóór* you will m. that box to one side.

aapéyééch Var. of *aapéech*.

aapw See *a-₁, -apw₁*. v. phr. no ("it not"). *a. iiy* no, not that (in contradiction).

aapwaapw (db; 3) APWA₃. nu. (c.; dis.; T3) a seaweed. [Inedible, growing on sea bottom; used as medicine;]

aar 3pl. pos. of *aa-*.

aara (1) AARAA (?). nu. (T1) 21st night of the lunar month.

aarúng (2) See *arúng.* nu. (c.; T2) breadfruit pudding served with coconut cream (*arúng*).

aarúngi (1) See *érú-₁, ngii₁.* vi. (c.) grind one's teeth (in sleep). Syn. *aarúngú, akkarúngngi*.

aarúngú (1) See *érú-₁, -ngú.* vi. (c.) grind one's teeth (in sleep). Syn. *aarúngi, akkarúngngi*.

aach₁ (3b) ACHA. n. (T3) handle, stem (of fruit). *achan* its h. *achen ama* hammer handle; *achen fináyik* flag pole; *achen maay* breadfruit stem; *achen mwirimwirin chitoosa* steering wheel of automobile; *achen mwirimwirin waa* tiller, ship's wheel. Cf. *paach₁, waas₃*.

aach₂ (3) AACHCHA. (Eng.) nu. (T3) hearts (in cards). *eché a.* one h. card. *aan a., néwún a.* his h. *aachchen kkiing* or *kkiingin aach* king of h.

aach₃ 1inc. pos. of *aa-*.

aat (2: *aatú-*) See *ét.* n. (c.; T2) smoke-cure (for sickness); medicinal steaming. Dis. *aatúwét* (db).

aatere Var. of *antere*.

aatú See *ét.* vo. (c.; T2) smoke, steam, cause to be smoked or steamed (for curing). Dis. *akkaatú* (ds).

aatúpwas (3) See *aat, pwas.* nu. (c.; T3) a medicinal dry steaming or smoking.

aatúwét Dis. of *aat*.

aaw₁ (3b) AWA₁. n. (T3) mouth; opening into something; stem end (of fruit); stalk end (of taro). *awan* his m. *awen machchang* bird's bill or beak; *awen máay* stem end of breadfruit; *awen pwuna* stalk end of *Cyrtosperma* taro; *awen taka* eye of ripe coconut.

aaw₂ nu. 1. a tree (*Ficus carolinensis*). [Bark used as medicine against evil spirits; fruits and leaves used as *itang* medicine; roots used to flavor a special breadfruit pudding; triangular piece of bark symbolized female genitalia and used to be used to prevent yaws in infants;] 2. (Itang) son or *éfékúr* of a chief.

aawúún (ds; 3a: *-wúnné-*) See *wún₃*. vi. stretch (the body).

aawúnna See *aawúún.* Var. *éwúnna.* vo. (refl.; T3) stretch oneself. *wúwa aawúnnááyey* I stretched myself.

aawúti See *aa-, wúti.* vo. (T5) wait for.

aaya (db; 1) See *aa-.* F. Var. *ááyá.* va. (dis.) 1. use (of general-class things in indefinite or otherwise unclassified relationship to the user). *a. fóchófóch* use always, use all the time. With adj. suf.: *aayaffóch* u. always, u. all the time. Cf. *ááni.* 2. eat (deferential usage).

aayaamwánniiy See *aaya, mwmwáán.* vo. (dis.; T5) use without permission.

aayaffóch See *aaya.*

aayamwmwáán (2: *aayaamwánni-*) See *aaya, mwmwáán.* va. use without permission.

aayiti N. of *ááyiti₁.*

af (3b) AFA. vi. arrive. *aa pwani af, aa pwanú af* he also arrived. Syn. *war.*

-af (3) See *aaf.* suf. (cc.; T3) piece of intestine. [Used with num. prefixes.] *eyaf, rúwéyaf, wúnúyaf, féyaf, nimeyaf, woneyaf, fúúyaf, wanúyaf, ttiweyaf, engoon, affan,* one,...ten pieces of i.; *fiteyaf* how many pieces of i. With c. pref. and ptv. const.: *ááyaffan, érúyéyaffan* first, second piece of i. (etc.). With dis. c. pref.: *ákkááyaf, ékkérúwéyaf* be one piece of i. at a time, two pieces of i. at a time (etc.). With pref. *áná-*: *ánááyaf, ánárúwéyaf* sole or only piece of i., sole or only two pieces of i. (etc.).

afaamach (3) AFAAMACHA. nu. (T3) 1. a flowering vine (*Operculum turpethum*). [Flower is used in medicine against *chénúkken* spirits.] 2. white morning glory (*Ipomoea alba*).

afaamwa See *faamw.* vo. (c.; T3) deliver (a baby). *chóón a.* midwife. Syn. *énéwúnéwú.*

afaay See *fa.* vo. (c.; T1) embolden, make brave (of fighting fish; fig. of people).

afak (3) AFAKA. n. (T3) unscented coconut oil. *afakan* his c. o.

afanafan₁ (db; 3) AFANA₁. nu. (T3) formal talk before an audience, lecture, sermon, speech. [Perhaps a causative construction with *fana-₂*.] vi. be making a speech, giving a sermon or lecture.

afanafan₂ (db; 3) AFANA₂. nu. (T3) 1. rattle bean plant (*Crotolaria mucronata*). [Perhaps a causative construction with *fana-₂*.] 2. coffee senna plant (*Cassia occidentalia*).

afanafana See *afanafan₁.* vo. (T3) deliver or give (a talk, sermon, lecture); declaim.

afanaw (3) AFANAWA. nu. (T3) small, unidentified fish (found in piles of sand on the fringing reef, said to be white in color).

afanna See *faan.* vo. (c.; T3) cause to hatch (of eggs), cause to break open (of a boil).

afangamá (1) See *fang, má.* nu. (c.; T1) treachery, betraying ("making death handed over"). *chóón a.* traitor. vi. (c.) be a traitor.

afangamááy See *afangamá.* vo. (c.; T1) betray (someone).

afar (3v: *afara-, éféré-*) AFARA. n. (T3) shoulder (of human, animal, bottle). *afaran* his s. *naan ruume meyi wor afaran* yonder bottle that has shoulders.

afaramwaaw (3) See *afar, mwaaw.* nu. (T3) humble or deferential shoulders.

afat (3) See *faat₂.* vi. (c.) talk about a thing, tell about something, make an explanation. Dis. *akkafat* (ds). *ewe áát ese a. pwe e kúna ekkewe chóón sooná* the boy did not tell that he saw the thieves. Cf. *pwáári.*

Aferika (Eng.) nu. (loc.) Africa. *chóón A.* person of African descent, Negro.

afeyiti See *af, -iti.* vo. (T2) arrive at.

aféé- (1) AFÉÉ₁. ni. (T1) back thigh. *afééy, afoomw, aféén* my, your, his b. t.

aféefee (db; 1) AFÉÉ₂. nu. (T1) male flower and dry pod of breadfruit. [Commonly in the phrase *aféeféén mááy .*]

afékúr N. of *éfékúr.*

afongofong (db; 3) See *fongo-.* va. (c.) sniff.

afongofonga (db) See *fongo-.* vo. (c.; T3) sniff (something).

afor N. of *afór.*

afóósa See *fóós.* vo. (c.; T3) make (someone) talk.

afóna N. of *ófóna.*

afór N. Var. *ófór, afor.* nu. 1. a tree (*Glochidion*). [Its wood is used for rafters.] 2. a shrub (*Securinga flexuesa*). [It is used for firewood.]

affa See *aaf.* vo. (T3) draw, disembowel.

affassa See *ffaas.* vo. (c.; T3) cause to slip.

affanap (3b) See *aaf, nap.* n. (T3) colon, large intestine. *affanapan* his c.

affangara Var. of *affangera.*

affanger (dc; 3) See *fangera-.* vi. (c.) mill around (of a crowd), move to and fro aimlessly within a crowd (of people, fish, etc.). Dis. *akkaffanger* (ds). *ese toongeni kepwe pwerenó neepeekin ewe aan pwún chitoosa meyi chék a.*

fátán it is not possible for you to cross that street because of automobiles that just travel to and fro.

affangera See *fangera-*. Var. *affangara*. vo. (c.; T3) make lie crisscross. *a. ewúti* fold my fingers across one another; *a. peyiy* fold my arms across each other. Cf. *affanger*.

affangerafesenniiy See *fangera-, feseen*. vo. (c.; T5) make lie crisscross.

affat (3) See *ffat* vi. (c.) be made clear, clarified.

affata See *ffat*. vo. (c.; T3) make clear (of water, glass, thoughts, etc.), disclose (of thoughts, words, secrets).

affataffengenniiy See *ffat, ffengeen*. vo. (c.; T5) clarify (something) together.

afféér (dc; 2) See *féér*. nu. (c.; T2) settlement, settling of a dispute. vi. (c.) be settled (of a dispute). *epwe a. neefineer* it will be settled between them.

afféérúúw See *afféér*. vo. (c.; T5) settle (a dispute).

affééw See *ffééw*. vi. (c.) be cold (to the touch, of things); be chilling. *Tiisamper eew ekkewe maramen a.* December is one of the c. months.

affééwú See *ffééw*. vo. (c.; T2) chill, make cold.

afférúúrú (db; 1) See *aaf, rúúrú*₁. n. (T1) small intestine ("curly intestine"). *afférúúrúún* his s. i.

afféw (2) AFFÉWÚ. n. (T2) unifying or joining two things so as to make one (but not of groups of people); mortising (wood); splicing (rope); translating, interpreting (to make common understanding). *afféwún* u. of it; *afféwúúr* joining of them. *chóón a.* interpreter. va. unify, join; translate. Dis. *akkafféw* (ds). vi. be unified, joined, translated.

afféwú See *afféw*. vo. (T2) unify, join; translate. *John aa a. ewe sáán meyi mwmwu* John tied the severed rope. *kepwe a. ááy fóós ngeni kkeey chóón Merika* you will translate my words to these Americans.

afféwúni See *afféw, -ni-*. vo. (T5) unify, join; translate, interpret. *wúpwe a. aar fóós* I shall translate their words. *sipwe afféwúniir* we shall interpret for them. ("we shall join them together").

afkaas (Eng. *half-caste*; or P.Eng. *afkas, apkas*) nu. half-caste, child of ethnically mixed parentage.

asaf (3) ASAFA. nu. (T3) frigate bird. *asafen Chuuk* Trukese f. b. Syn. *mannap*.

asassach (db; 3) See *sach*. F. Var. *achachchach*. vi. (c., dis.) be crowded together (as people in sleeping).

asakka See *assak*. Var. *assaka*. vo. (c.; T3) cut, extract (copra from the coconut shell).

asam (3b, 2c) ASAMA. n. (T3) doorway, door opening, entrance, gateway (as distinct from door). *asaman* its doorway. *éppúngun a.* door (as distinct from doorway). *asamen iimw* house doorway; *asamen maay* entrance of stone fish trap. With dir. suf.: *asamatá* be with doorway to east or upper side; *asaménong* be with d. to south or inner side; *asamútiw* be with d. to west or lower side; *asamúwu* be with d. to north or outer side.

asamatá See *asam*.
asaménong See *asam*.
asamútiw See *asam*.
asamúwu See *asam*.

asamwmwócho (1) See *asam, mwócho*. nu. (T1) window ("thieving door").

asanóng (2) ASANÓNGU. nu. (T2) projecting nub at either end of the hull of a paddle canoe just below the lacings of the end pieces. *asanóngun waa* canoe's p. n.

asangera See *sanger*. vo. (c.; T3) cause to overlap, cause not to match up. With dir. suf.: *asangeraanong* cause (one piece) to overlap inside (the end of another piece).

asangeraanong See *asangera*.

asap (3) See *sap*₁. nu. (c.; T3) clothes hanger.

asapa See *sap*₁. vo. (c.; T3) cause to be stuck, caught, or trapped.

asapwináátiw See *asapwini*.

asapwini See *sapwin*. vo. (c.; T2) let down, let or cause to hang down. With dir. suf.: *asapwináátiw* cause to hang down.

asaram (3) See *saram*. vi. (c.) give or make light, provide illumination.

asarama See *saram*. vo. (c.; T3) illuminate, light up.

asacha See *sach*. F. Var. *achacha*. vo. (c.; T3) wedge in place, pack tightly. *asacheer* crowd them together.

asachopwa See *sachopw*. vo. (c.; T3) break (something) into many pieces.

Asawa (1) ASAWA. Tn. Var. *Achaw*. nu. (loc.) a clan name. *fiin A.*, *fin A.* A. woman; *mwáán A.* A. man. *chóón A.* people of A.

asengúr (2) ASENGÚRÚ. Var. *assúngúr*. nu. a sea cucumber (edible). *emwú a.* one t. *wochááy a.* my T. (to eat).

aseyiro (1) See *aas₁*, *ro₂*. nu. (T1) a house height (such that a person's head just clears under the cross beam without his having to stoop).

aséésé (db; 1) See *sé*. nu. (c.; T1) rest, vacation. vi. (c.) be resting, rest (from work), take a vacation. With intens. suf.: *aséésékkis* take many rests, be inconstant in work.

aséésékkis See *aséésé*.

asééw See *sé*. vo. (c.; T1) cause to rest, make quit work, give a vacation to, lay off (from work).

asiri apatopi (Jap. *hashiri habatobi*) Abbr. *apa*. n. phr. running long jump.

asiri takatopi (Jap. *hashiri takatobi*) n. phr. running high jump.

asoosichiiy N. of *ósoosichiiy* and var. of *asoochikiiy* (see *soosich*).

asoonapa N. of *ósoonapa*.

asoochisiiy Var. of *asoochikiiy* (see *soochis*).

asoochikiiy See *soochik*, *-i-₂*. vo. (c.; T5) save, conserve. *kepwe a. ena mwéngé pwe ete sochchik s.* that food so that it will not be wasted. Syn. *achoochisiiy*, *ósoosichiiy*. Ant. *asochchika*, *ósoonapa*.

asochchika See *sochchik*. N. vo. (c.; T3) waste; discard what was needed. Syn. *ósoonapa*. Ant. *asoochikiiy*, *asoochisiiy*, *ósoosichiiy*.

asómwonnu See *sómwoon*. N. Var. *ósómwoonu*. vo. (c.; T2) treat (someone) with the deference owed a chief, make a chief of.

asór N. of *ósór*.

assak (3) See *sakka-*, *ssaka-*. va. (c.) cut copra, engage in cutting copra.

assaka Var. of *asakka*.

assapana See *ssapan*. vo. (c.; T3) make bloom. *ewe irá aa a. péén* the tree has made its flowers bloom. With dir. suf.: *assapanóónó* make bloom forth.

assapanóónó See *assapana*.

assaraw (3) ASSARAWA. vi. speak ironically or sarcastically; ask for something of which one already has much and others know it; speak as though things were other than they are (in play or with forceful intent). Dis. *akkassarow* (ds). *aa a. ngeni* he spoke ironically to him.

asseya (1) ASSEYAA. nu. (T1) a sea cucumber (edible, found on outer reef). *emwú a.* one t. *wochááy a.* my t. (to eat).

asséék (2) ASSÉÉKÚ. nu. (T2) pudding of fermented breadfruit served with coconut cream. *eew a.* one p. *asséékún épwét* p. of fermented breadfruit.

asséér (2) See *sséér*. vi. (c.) be made to slide against something; be struck (of a match).

asséérúúw See *asséér*, *-ú-*. vo. (c.; T5) cause to slide against something; strike (a match).

assow N. of *ossow*.

assowu N. of *ossowu*.

assúngúr Var. of *asengúr*.

assúraatiw See *assúrú*.

assúrú See *ssúr₁*. N. Var. *éssúrú*. vo. (c.; T2) pour, cause to flow, shed, cause to drip. With dir. suf.: *assúraatiw* cause to flow, drip, pour down.

akakkómw (ds of ds; 3) See *akkómw*. N. vi. (c., dis.) lead the way.

akamw (3) See *-kamw*. Tb. vi., adj. (c.) (be) huge, enormous. *akamwen neminnaan* the huge size of that woman. Cf. *nikkúng*, *ttapwir*, *wátte*.

akarara See *karar*. vo. (c.; T3) cause to make a scraping or rattling noise.

aké Var. of *angké*.

akéttú See *kkéét*. vo. (c.; T2) scratch (an itch). *wúpwe a. núkúnúppomw* I will s. your back.

akka- Dis. of *a-₂*. Routine unambiguous ds forms of this type are not listed as separate entries but may be found under the unreduplicated words beginning with *a-*.

Akkaatopw See *topw*. nu. (pers.) name of the local god of Mt. Winepwéét on Toon (Tol) Island.

akkaay See *kka*. vo. (c.; T1) give something to drink to ("cause thirst to").

akkafachaamas (ds; 3) See *fa-₂, chaa-, maas*. nu. (c.; T3) causing embarrassment or blushing (as when speaking without looking to see who is present); faux pas. *fóósun a.* vocabulary that cannot be freely used in the presence of everyone, containing three levels of restriction: 1. words that cannot be used in any company where sexes are mixed or ages are highly disparate, or in the presence of siblings of the same sex, parent and child of the same sex, or siblings-in-law of the same sex; 2. words that may not be used in the presence of siblings-in-law of same sex or in company where sexes are mixed, except under restricted conditions; 3. words that may not be used in the presence of siblings of opposite sex or parent and and child of opposite sex (observance to tabus relating to this level now largely ignored).

akkapén N. var. of *ékképén.*

akkapénú N. var. of *ékképénú.*

akkar (3) See *kkar.* nu. (c.; T3) sun ("scorcher"). *aa pwan ttin a.* the sun has come out again.

akkara See *kkar.* vo. (c.; T3) cause to be burned; scorch, burn.

akkarúngngi (ds; 1) See *érú-$_1$, ngii$_1$.* nu. (dis.; T1) grinding of the teeth (in sleep only). Syn. *aarúngi, aarúngú.*

akkachawar Dis. of *achawar.*

akkaw (3) AKKAWA. nu. (T3) hat. *imwan a.* his h. *imweyimw a.* wear a h. *imweni a.* acquire a h.

akkawanuuw See *wanuuw.*

akkómw N. var. of *ókkoomw.*

ama (1) AMA$_1$. (Eng. *hammer*). nu. (T1), va. hammer. *efóch a.* one h. *aan a.* his h.

amaam (db; 1) AMA$_2$. vi. (dis.) know something but not admit it. Cf. *niyamaam.*

amaama (db; 1) See *ma.* vi. (c., dis.; T3) do what is embarrassing; cause embarrassment.

amaani See *ama, -ni.* vo. (T4) hammer. *ewe mwáán epwe wiisen a. ewe chúúfén* the man will have the job of hammering the nail.

amaanóónó See *amaanú.*

amaanú See *maan$_3$.* vo. (c.; T2) cast adrift; set to drifting. With dir. suf.: *amaanóónó* set to drifting away.

amaanúúnú See *maanúún.* vo. (c.; T2) thicken, make thicker (of flat objects).

amaat$_1$ (3) See *maata-.* vi. (c.) be ground and polished by rubbing on a stone.

amaat$_2$ (3) See *maataat.* nu. (c.; T3) grater of starchy vegetables made of punctured sheet metal. *eché a.* one g. *amaaten Chuuk* Trukese g. Syn. *feeyiir.*

amaata See *amaat$_2$.* vo. (c.; T3) grate; cause to be grated.

amaay See *ma.* vo. (c.; T1) make ashamed; shame.

amas (3) AMASA. vi., adj. (be) not fully cooked, raw.

amasa See *mas.* vo. (c.; T3) fit together, connect (as in making something out of several pieces or joining things in construction).

amasapwin (2?) See *amas, pwin$_2$.* vi. cook today but leave till tomorrow for pounding into pudding (of *Cyrtosperma* taro only).

amakupw nu. a kind of surgeon fish.

amanaw (3) See *manaw.* nu. (c.; T3) 1. animation; giving life, causing to be alive; sparing (in war). *chóón a.* rescuer, life saver, the Savior. 2. prisoner of war, slave. *néwúni a.* enslave, maltreat, abuse; *aa néwúniyey a.* he enslaved me. vi. be life giving; be given life, be animated. *amanaw sefáán* come back to life. *amanaw-sefáánniiy, amanaw-sefáánniiy* bring (someone) back to life.

amanawa See *amanaw.* vo. (c.; T3) cause to live, give life to, animate; start (an engine); wind (a clock); provide for. *neeniyen a.* starter (of an engine).

amanna See *mman.* vo. (c.; T3) Id. *a. ráán* look at the dawn to determine what the weather will be.

amara (1) AMARAA. nu. (T1) sail. *eché a.* one s. *amaraan waa* boat's sail. Cf. *siipw, steesen, ménsen.*

amaras (3) See *maras.* F. Var. *ámárás.* nu. (c.; T3) 1. gall bladder. 2. medicine made of bark of various plants that have been pounded or grated and mixed with scented coconut oil. [Used to prevent or cure attacks, especially on children, of such spirits as *énúúsowusow* and *chénúkken* .]

amarasa See *amaras.* F. Var. *ámárása.* vo. (T3) give *amaras* medicine to.

améémé (db; 1) See *mé$_2$.* va., vo. (c.; T1) sell. *améméewey, amémook, amémé*

amémúménú (instead of expected *améémééw), amééméékich, amééméékeem, amééméékemi, amééméeér sell me, you, him, us (inc.), us (exc.), you (pl.), them. With dir. suf.: amééméénó sell off, sell away; améémééto sell hither.
aménúménú Var. of eménúménú.
ami (1) AMI. (Jap. *ami*) nu. (T1) wire screening against insects. *eché a.* one screen. *aan a.* his screen.
amóneset nu. a tree (*Messerschmidia argentea*). Cf. *ómón*.
amónna N. of *ómónna*.
amónnaatá N. of *ómónnáátá*.
ammaan (dc; 2) See *maan₃*. nu. (c.; T2) flotsam. See *ápiipi*.
ammasa See *mmas₁*. vo. (c.; T3) cause to be open (as of a louver, clam, sack).
ammasaaw (3b) See *mmas₁*, *aaw₁*. vi. (c.) open the mouth ("cause the mouth to open").
ammanga See *mmang*. vo. (c.; T3) make slow or late, delay, retard.
ammach (3) See *mmach*. nu. (c.; T3) dish made from *meyichéén* or *neeyátin* varieties of breadfruit. [To make it, pick the breadfruit, remove the skin, store until soft, remove the core, shred into a bowl, then pound the young husk of a *ngngúpé* coconut and get the sweet juice of it into the bowl, bundle the mixture in leaves, bake, serve with or without coconut cream added.]
ammacha See *mmach*. vo. (c.; T3) cause to be ripe, ripen.
ammat (3) See *mmat*. n. (c.; T3) 1. sponge. *eew a.* one s. *aan a.* his s. *ammaten Chuuk* Trukese s. Syn. *sopwusopw*. 2. lung. *eew a.* one l. *ammatan* his l. vi. (c.) be soaked up (as water in a sponge).
ammata See *ammat*. vo. (T3) to soak up, sponge up.
ammésék (dc; 2) See *mésék*. vi. (c.) be terrible, awful.
ammésékú See *ammésék*. vo. (c.; T2) scare, frighten, terrify.
ammét (dc; 2) See *mét*. F. vi. (c.) be delicious, satisfying, taste good. Syn. *anné₁*.
ammóót N. of *ómmóót*.
ammón₁ N. of *ómmón₁*.
Ammón₂ N. of *Ómmón₂*.
ampay (2) AMPAYI. [A back formation from *ampayiya*.] nu. (T1) umpiring (in baseball). *iiy e wiisen a.* he has the job of u. *chóón a.* umpire.
ampayiya (1) AMPAYIYAA. (Jap. *ampaiy*, Eng.) nu. (T1) umpire (in baseball). *emén a.* one u. *iiy emán ekkewe a.;* he is one of the umpires. Syn. *chóón ampay*.
amper (2) AMPERI. nu. umbrella. *imwan a.* his u. *amperin sapaan* Japanese u..
amwaar (3b) See *mwaar*. nu. (c.; T3) pleasure.
amwaaraar (db; 3b) See *amwaar*. vi., adj. (c., dis.) be pleasure giving, entertaining, amusing, interesting, delightful, charming, wonderful, praiseworthy; curious; odd. *ááni a.* take pleasure in ("take as pleasure giving").
amwaat (3) See *mwa-, -at₃*. n. (c.; T3) dry coconut frond used on the floor of the house. *amwaatan* its frond. Cf. *paan núú*.
amwaata See *amwaat*. vo. (c.; T3) spread with coconut fronds. *a. nóón eey iimw* spread the inside of this house with fronds. Syn. *eeneni*.
amwaataat (db; 3) See *mwaataat*. vi. (c., dis.) be noisy (in walking or moving about).
amwaataata See *mwaataat*. vo. (c.; T3) cause to rustle (of dry leaves).
amwaateni See *amwaat*, *-ni-*. vo. (c.; T6a) spread coconut fronds in. *a. imwey* spread fronds in my house.
amwas (3b) See *mwas*. Tb2. vi. (c.) dislike. Syn. *opwut*.
amwakena See *mwakeneken*. vo. (c.; T3) incise designs in. Dis. *amwakenekena* (db).
amwakenekena Dis. of *amwakena*.
amwara See *amwaramwar*. Var. *ámwára*. vo. (c.; T3) fool around with (something dangerous).
amwaramwar (db; 3) MWARA₄ N. vi. (c.) fool around (with something dangerous). *kete a. fáán nowumwu na saar pwe site feyiyengngaw* do not f. around with your knife so we won't get hurt.
amwachin (2) AMWACHINI. N. Var. *emwechin*. nu. (T2) general term for man's or woman's loinclothing. *eché a.* one loincovering. *aan a.* his loincovering.

amwachchú (1?) AMWACHCHÚÚ (?). nu. (T1?) edible species of shellfish. *wochááy a.* my s. (to eat).

amwata (1) See *mwata*. vi. cause to climb or ascend speedily. *sáfeen amwataan óós* medicine for making the thatch go up quickly.

amwatang (3) AMWATANGA. nu. (T3) coconut crab (found inland from the beach). *eew a.* one c. c. *néwún a.* his c. c.; *anan a.* his c. c. to eat. Syn. *ménúté, eef.*

amwe (1) AMWEE. Var. *kamwe*. nu. (T1) tridachna clam and shell. *péén a.* tridachna shell.

amwéémwé (db; 1) See *mwé*. vi. (c., dis.) pick for preserving (of breadfruit only). *wúwa a. mááy* I picked breadfruit for preserving.

amwééngún (2) See *mwé, ngúún*. nu. (c.; T2) soul alighting. [Name given to a medicine prepared by spirit mediums for use in seances to bring the souls of men into people's presence for scrutiny.] *sáfeen a.* soul-alighting medicine.

amwéngééni See *mwéngé, -ni-*. vo. (c.; T4) give food to, feed. Dis. *akkamwéngééni* (ds). Syn. *amwéngééw*.

amwéngééw See *mwéngé*. vo. (c.; T1) feed, give food to. Syn. *amwéngééni*.

amwéwúchú N. of *emwéwúchú*.

amwit N. nu. a fish (*Gerres baconensis*). Syn. *chopan*.

amwo N. of *ómwo*.

amwoota See *mwoot₁*. N. Var. *ómwoota*. vo. (c.; T3) make artful in fighting.

amwora N. of *ómwora*.

amwocha See *mwoch*. N., Tn. Var. *ómwmwocha, ómwocha*. vo. (c.; T3) shorten.

amwóru (1) AMWÓRUU. N. Var. *ómwóru, omworu*. vi. be a deception, be a lie, be false, be untrue. *meyi chék a.* it is just a d.

amwóruungeni See *amwóru, ngeni*. Var. *ómwóruungeni, omworuungeni*. vo. (T2) deceive, lie to.

amwuuffengenniiy See *mwuuffengen, -i-₂*. N. vo. (c.; T5) call to meeting, assemble.

amwúch (2) AMWÚCHÚ. N. Var. *émwúch, mwúúch₁*. nu. (T2) firewood. *emwúch a.* one piece of f. *amwúchún Wééné* f. of Wééné (Moen) I.

amwmwéngé (dc; 1) See *mwéngé*. nu. (c.; T1) feeding.

amwmwoot N. of *ómwmwoot*.

amwmwoota N. of *ómwmwoota*.

ana-₁ (3v: *ana-, ene-, ono-, -kan*) See *a-₄, -na-*. ni. (T3v). food to eat; food portion (of cooked starchy food). *eney, onomw, anan* my, your (sg.), his f. Id. *enen chukó* ironweed (*Veronica cinera*). Cf. *chaariya-* (see *chaari*).

ana-₂ (3b) See *aan₂*. [In cpds. only.] vi. be a path or road; lead, go, head (of a path or road). With dir. suf.: *anátá* be a p. east or up; *anonong* be a p. south or in; *anoto* be a p. hither; *ananó, anónó* be a p. away; *anútiw* be a p. west or down; *anewu, anúwu* be a p. north or out.

ana See *a-₃, na*. [Only in const. with *iya*.] dem. (loc.) *ana iya* in that place, at that time (previously named or just referred to).

anaan See *a-₃, naan*. F. dem. (loc.) there, in that place, yonder (within sight of speaker and hearer).

anaanong (3) See *naa-, -nong*. nu. (c.; T3) spear throwing stick, spear thrower. *efóch a.* one s.

anamaaseni See *nam, seni₂*. N. vo. (c.; T2) make forget.

anamaangeni See *nam, ngeni*. N. vo. (c.; T2) remind.

anamanamangngaweey See *namanamangngaw, -e-₂*. vo. (c.; T6b) make appear badly, or look bad; put in a bad light, cause to come out badly. *a. aach angaang* make our work look bad. Cf. *anapanapangngaweey*.

anamwota See *namwot*. N., Tn. Var. *ónómwota*. vo. (c.; T3) make use of.

anana See *nan*. vo. (c.; T3) make (someone or something) the subject of chatter or gossip, spread (something) as gossip. *a. aan féfféér* make his actions the subject of gossip.

ananap (3b) See *aan₂, nap*. nu. (T3) main road, main path (regardless of actual size).

ananó See *ana-₂*.

anang (3) ANANGA. nu. (T3) broken, white branching coral, as found on the strand; coral gravel. *anangen Chuuk* coral gravel of Truk. Syn. *anget, angnget*. Cf. *áán, ápwpwer*.

anangattama See *nangattam*. vo. (c.; T3) make long, make tall, elongate.

anangngaw (3b) See *aan₂, ngngaw.* nu. (T3) bad road, difficult way.

anap (3) ANAPA, ANAPPA. n. (T3) stay of heavy rope from masthead to outrigger yoke on sailing canoe. (F.) *anapen waa, (N.) anappen waa* canoe's s.

anapa See *nap.* vo. (c.; T3) make large, numerous, great; elevate (in status). With dir. suf.: *anapaanó, anapóónó* increase, enlarge, aggrandize further.

anapaanó See *anapa.*

anapanap (3) See *napanap₁* nu. (c.; T3) representation.

anapanapa See *napanap₁.* vo. (c.; T3) plan; decide on the ultimate shape of.

anapanapangngaweey See *napanap₁, ngngaw, -e-₂.* vo. (c.; T6b) make look bad; cause to turn out badly; formulate badly. Cf. *anamanamangngaweey.*

Anapenges (2) See *aan₂, penges.* nu. a school or system of fighting. [Other schools are *Fáánápuuch, Fáán Chéénúkká.*] Cf. *anepenges, anépenges.*

anapóónó See *anapa.*

anaw₁ (3) ANAWA₁. nu. (T3) a grass (*Cassytha filifornis*, common on atolls). *anawen Chuuk* Trukese g.

anaw₂ (3: *-kanaw*) ANAWA₂, KANAWA. nu. (T3) a tree (*Cordia subcordata*). *anawen Chuuk* Trukese t. Syn. *anné₃, ánnikat.*

anátá See *ana-₂.*

anenimey (2) See *aan₂, mááy₂.* nu. (T2) Milky Way. ["path of breadfruit," because on this heavenly path the breadfruit comes from its southern homeland when summoned by the *sowuyótoomey*.]

anepenges (2) See *aan₂, penges.* Var. *anépenges.* nu. (T2) crossroad, path intersection.

anewu See *ana-₂.*

aneyééch (2: *-yéchchú-*) See *aan₂, éech.* Var. *anééch.* nu. (T2) good road, easy path.

aneyiti See *ana-₂, -iti.* vo. (T2) be a path or road to, lead to. *epwe a. Chorong* it will lead to Chorong.

anééné N. of *énééné.*

anéénééw N. of *énéénééw.*

anééch Var. of *aneyééch.*

anénnéew See *nénné.* vo. (c.; T1) cause to be alike, cause to be the same size.

anénnéffengen (2: *-ffengenni-*) See *nénné, ffengeen.* vi. (c.) be alike, same.

anénnéffengenniiy See *anénnéffengeen.* vo. (T5) compare.

anépenges Var. of *anepenges.*

anikitor (Eng.) Var. *anúkitor.* nu. alligator.

aniyon N. of *éniyon.*

anomwa N. of *ónomwa.*

anomwonomw N. of *ónomwonomw.*

anomwonomwa N. of *ónomwonomwa.*

anonong See *ana-.*

anota See *nóót.* Var. *ónota, ónóta.* vo. (c.; T3) bring to a head (of a boil).

anoto See *ana-₂.*

anóót N. of *ónóót.*

anómwu N. of *ónómwu.*

anónó See *ana-₂.*

anónnóón N. of *ónónnóón.*

anú E.Wn. of *énú.*

anúúkiin N. of *énúúki (see anú, -kiin).*

anúút N. vi. be sooty, covered with soot. Syn. *araarúút.*

anúkitor Var. of *anikitor.*

anútiw See *ana-.*

anúwu See *ana-.*

anfapet (Eng.) nu. alphabet.

annaafa See *nnaaf.* vo. (c.; T3) cause to be sufficient, cause to be enough.

annanga See *nnang.* vo. (c.; T3) make a crack, cleft, or slight opening in; make ajar, open at one side, prop up a little on one side. With dir. suf.: *annangaatá* (N.), *annangáátá* (F.) raise or open up a little (of something on one side of a crack or join).

annangaatá See *annanga.*

annaw (3) ANNAWA. nu. (T3) a platform of boards on which to set out food or on which (in former times) to lay out a corpse in the house (instead of burying it). *annawan* its (the corpse's) p.

anné₁ (1) ANNÉÉ₁. N. Var. *nné.* vi., adj. (be) delicious, tasty, savory. Dis. *akkanné* (ds). *meyi akkanné ewe sókkun mwéngé* that kind of food is usually delicious.

anné₂ (1) See *nné₂.* nu. (c.; T1) breadfruit at the stage of being ready for picking or for use in making *épwét* or *maar.* vi. be at this stage.

anné₃ (1) ANNÉÉ₂. nu. (T1) a tree (*Cordia subcordata*). [Its wood is used to make paddles and canoe floats; its fruit is eaten; its flowers are used as a medicine to cure stomach disorders and to clear the minds of students, dancers, fighters, athletes, and carpenters so that they will perform better.] Syn. *anaw₂, ánnikat.*

anniiré (1) ANNIIRÉÉ. Var. *ónniirá.* nu. (T1) a tree. [As described, it seems to be the Pacific Almond, according to legend introduced into Truk from Yap.]

annif N. of *ánnif.*

annim N. (Mck. *allim*). Var. *ánnim* (the more common form). vi., adj. (be) good. [Ordinarily used only in greetings, its use otherwise being considered an affectation.] *raan a. [ng. cay; raan a. o g.* day, sir; *raan a. ne g.* day miss (or ma'am); *neesor a. g.* morning; *neepwoong a. g.* night.

anno md.m indicates that what follows is contrary to reality or fact; when not. *pwata ke ataay a. pisekumw?* Why do you destroy it when [it is] not your property? *wúwa tinaanó pwú a. ke wúreniyey* I sent it off because you did not tell me [not to]. Syn. *sanne, wonne.*

annut N. of *ónnut.*

annuta N. of *ónnuta.*

antaare (1) ANTAAREE. (Lat. *altare*) nu. (T1) altar.

antasiro (1) ANATASIROO. (Jap. *andaasuroo,* from Eng. *under* and *throw*) nu. (T1) underhand throw.

antere (1) ANTEREE. (Ger.) Var. *atere.* nu. (T1) queue, line of people (as at a pay window). *antereen aramas* line of people. *toonong nóón a.* enter a line. vi. queue up, form a line.

antiyos (2) ANTIYOSU. (Sp. *anteojos*) nu. (T2) fishing goggles. *eew peeya a.* one pair of g. *néwún a.* or *mesan a.* his g. *antiyosun Chuuk* Trukese g. vi. do any kind of fishing with goggles.

-ang (3) See *aang.* suf. (cc.) span between thumb and forefinger; entire limb (of the body). [Used with num. prefixes.] *eyang, rúwéyang, wúnúyang, féyang, nimeyang, woneyang, fúúyang, wanúyang, ttiweyang, engoon angan* one,...ten s. With c. pref. and ptv. const.: *ááyangan, érúwéyangan* first s., second s. (etc.). With dis. c. pref.: *ákkayang, ékkérúwéyang* be one s. at a time, two s. at a time (etc.). With pref. *áná-: ánááyang, ánárúwéyang* sole or only s., sole or only two s. (etc.).

anga- (3b) ANGA₂. [In cpds. only.] vi. handle; put hand to; take in hand; perform.

angaang (db; 3b) See *anga-.* n. (dis.; T3) work, handling of things, performance, way of doing things. *angaangan* his w., the way he works; *aan a.* his w. to do, his performance. *a. chééw* common custom. *angaangen koot* devine service, God's work (for us to do); *angaangen marariya* sanitation work, insect spraying; *angaangen namanam* divine service, Christian work; *angaangen nóómw* old way of doing things; *angaangen pisek* working of material goods, how to make things, handicraft. vi. (dis.) be working, engage in work, perform.

angaanga See *angaang.* vo. (T3) put (someone) to work.

angaangaffat (3b) See *angaang, -ffat.* vi. work without pay or to no purpose. Syn. *angaangen nuus, angaang mwáán.*

angaangakkáy (2) See *angaang, kkáy.* vi. work quickly; be quick (in work).

angaangangngaw (3b) See *angaang, ngngaw.* vi. perform badly; be clumsy (in work).

angaangefich (2) See *angaang, -fich.* vi. work well, perform well.

angas (3) See *anga-, -s₁.* vi., adj. (be) adept, naturally able in all kinds of work, widely skilled. *emén meyi a.* one who is naturally able (one cannot say *aa a.,* for this would imply that previously he had not been naturally able, a contradiction in terms).

angasa See *ngaas.* vo. (c.; T3) annoint with *gaas.* Dis. *akkangasa* (ds).

angakkáy See *anga-, kkáy.* vi. handle quickly; work quickly. Ant. *angammang.*

angamaaw See *anga-, maaw.* vi. snatch; take or handle roughly. Ant. *angamwmwaaw.*

angamay (3) See *anga-, maay₁.* F. Var. *angamáy.* vi. catch fish by means of a stone fish trap (*maay*).

angamáy N. of *angamay* (see *anga-, máay*)

angammang See *anga-, mmang.* vi. work slowly; take or handle slowly. Ant. *angakkáy.*

angamwas (3) See *anga-, mwas.* Tbl. vi. handle a thing very badly or clumsily

angamwáán (so as to break); be clumsy. Syn. *angangngaw, angatáp, angepwise, angetteneng, angékkéch, angépwutak.* Ant. *angééch, angeyééch, angeris, angéwútek.*

angamwáán (2: *angamwááni-, angamwáni-*) See *anga-, mwmwáán.* va., vi. take without permission.

angamwáánniiy See *angamwmwáán, -i-₂.* N. Var. *angamwánniiy.* vo. (T5) take without permission.

angamwánniiy F. of *angamwáánniiy.*

angamwmwaaw See *anga-, mwmwaaw.* vi. take or handle gently. Ant. *angamaaw.*

angannap (3) See *anga-, nnap.* vi. do a kind of fishing. [It is done by men only, on the reef, in the day time, with spear and goggles; types of fish taken include *áár, fiticu, gúúwén, ikeféw, maramwen, meyicéécé, mmatow, poro, pweeyas, sewi, sonu, wusap.*]

angangngaw (3b) See *anga-, ngngaw.* Tb3. vi. handle a thing badly or clumsily (so as to break); be clumsy. Syn. *angepwise, angatáp, angamwas, angetteneng, angékkéch, angépwutak.* Ant. *angééch, angeyééch, angeris, angéwútek.* nr. (T3) clumsiness.

angara See *ngar.* vo. (c.; T3) sweeten.

angaraap (3) ANGARAAPA, ANGARAPPA. nu. (T3) bonito fish. *angaraapen Chuuk, angarappen Chuuk* the b. of Truk.

angata (1) See *anga-, ta.* vi. work too hard, work to the point of collapse, be overworking. *angataan átánaan* that fellow's overworking.

angatáp (4) See *anga-, táp.* vi. handle a thing badly or clumsily; be clumsy. Syn. *angangngaw, angamwas, angepwise, angetteneng, angeékkéch, angépwutak.* Ant. *angééch, angeyééch, angeris, angéwútek.*

angatiw Var. of *angetiw.*

angatiweey Var. of *angétiweey.*

angátá (1) See *anga-, -tá.* Var. *angetá.* va., vi. 1. hand up, have in hand reaching up. 2. tell a lie.

angátááy See *angátá.* vo. (T1) take in hand reaching up, take from above.

angeey See *anga-, -e-₂.* vo. (T6b) take (in hand), take hold of. *a. neetipan* capture his heart or emotions. Id. *a. aan achawar* get compensation for adultery from him ("take his loincloth"). With dir. suf.: *angeeyenong,*

angeeyenó, angeeyetá, angeeyetiw, angeeyeto, angeeyewu.

angeeyenong See *angeey.*

angeeyenó See *angeey.*

angeeyetá See *angeey.*

angeeyetiw See *angeey.*

angeeyeto See *angeey.*

angeeyewu See *angeey.*

angengeni See *anga-, ngeni.* Var. *angéngeni.* vo. (T2) handle, take hold of.

angepweteete (1) See *anga-, pweteete.* Var. *angépweteete.* va. take in hand gently, handling gently.

angepwise (1) See *anga-, pwise.* Tb3. vi. handle a thing very badly or clumsily; be very clumsy. Syn. *angangngaw, angamwas, angatáp, angetteneng, angékkéch, angépwutak.* Ant. *angééch, angeyééch, angeris, angéwútek.*

angeris (2) See *anga-, ris₂.* Tb2. vi. handle a thing well; be clever, handy. Syn. *angééch, angeyééch, angéwútek.* Ant. *angangngaw, angamwas, angatáp, angepwise, angetteneng, angékkéch, angépwutak.*

anget (2) ANGETI. N. Var. *angnget.* nu. (T2) broken, dead, white branching coral as found on the strand; coral gravel. Syn. *anang.* Cf. *áán, ápwpwer.*

angetá Var. of *angátá.*

angetiw (3) See *anga-, -tiw.* Var. *angatiw, angétiw.* va. hand down, have in hand reaching down. *a. reey* hand down to me.

angetiweey See *angetiw, -e-₂.* Var. *angatiweey, angútiweey, angétiweey.* vo. (T6b) take in hand reaching down, take from below.

angetteneng (2) See *anga-, tteneng.* Tb1. vi. handle a thing very badly or clumsily; be very clumsy. Syn. *angangngaw, angamwas, angatáp, angepwise, angékkéch, angépwutak.* Ant. *angééch, angeyééch, angeris, angéwútek.*

angeyééch Var. of *angééch.*

angééch (2: *angééchchú-*) See *anga-, ééch.* Var. *angéyééch, angeyééch.* vi. be clever, handy. Syn. *angeris, angéwútek.* Ant. *angangngaw, angamwas, angatáp, angapwise, angetteneng, angékkéch, angépwutak.*

angékkéch See *anga-, kkéch.* Tb1. vi. handle a thing very badly or clumsily; be very clumsy. Syn. *angangngaw,* *angamwas, angatáp, angepwise, angetteneng, angékkéch, angépwutak.* Ant. *angéech, angeyéech, angeris, angéwútek.*

angéngeni Var. of *angengeni.*

angépweteete Var. of *angepweteete.*

angépwutak (3) See *anga-, pwutak.* vi. handle a thing badly or clumsily; be clumsy. Syn. *angangngaw, angamwas, angatáp, angepwise, angetteneng, angékkéch.* Ant. *angéech, angeyéech, angeris, angéwútek.*

angétiw Var. of *angetiw.*

angétiweey Var. of *angetiweey.*

angétúúrú vi. be unmarried, single (either not yet married or widowed). [More polite form than *nipich.*]

angéwumwuné (1) See *anga-, wumwuné.* nu. (T1) fishing for *wumwuné* with a net. vi. fish for *wumwuné.*

angéwútek (2) See *anga-, wútek.* vi. handle a thing well; be clever, handy. Syn. *angéech, angeyéech, angeris.* Ant. *angangngaw, angamwas, angatáp, angepwise, angetteneng, angékkéch, angépwutak.*

angéyéech Var. of *angéech.*

angin (2) ANGINI. nu. sweetheart, lover. *emén a.* one s. *néwún a.* his s. Syn. *kamwmwet.*

angon N. of *óngon.*

angonong (3) See *anga-, -nong.* va., vi. hand in, have in hand reaching in.

angoto (1) See *anga-, -to.* va., vi. hand hither, have in hand reaching hither.

angotoow Var. in 3sg. of *angotooy.*

angotooy See *angoto.* Var. *angotoow* (3sg. only). vo. (T1) take in hand reaching hither, take from here. *angotoowey* take me from here.

angowow See *anga-, -wow.* va., vi. hand toward you, have in hand reaching in your direction.

angowu (1) See *anga-, -wu.* va., vi. hand outward, have in hand reaching to the outside.

angónó (1) See *anga-, -nó.* va., vi. hand away, hand off, have in hand reaching away.

angónóóy See *angónó.* vo. (T1) take in hand reaching away, take from away or yonder.

angútiweey Var. of *angetiweey.*

angúwuuy See *anga-, -wu.* vo. (T1) take in hand reaching outside, take from outside. Cf. *angowu.*

angkachi (1) ANGKACHII. (Jap. *hankachi*) Var. *angkisif.* nu. handkerchief.

angké (1) ANGKÉÉ. (Eng. *anchor*) Var. *aké.* nu. (T1) anchor.

angkisif (Eng.) Var. *angkachi.* nu. handkerchief.

angngana See *ngngan.* Tb1. vo. (T3) beat.

angngawa See *ngngaw.* vo. (T3) make bad, harm, injure, spoil, ruin.

Angngawur nu. (loc.) Angaur Island, Palau Islands.

angnget Rmn. of *anget.*

ap₁ (3) APA₁. [Used with *ngeni epeek.*] vi. be to the side. Dis. *apaap* (db). *ap ngeni epeek* move to one side. Cf. *apéngeni.*

ap₂ (3b) APA₂. vi. be dyed black (of fabrics and fibers by soaking in *ópóchón*).

apa₁ See *ap₂.* vo. (T3) dye black.

apa₂ Abbr. of *asiri apatopi.*

apaap₁ (db; 3) APA₃. N. Var. *apeyap.* vi. be dented. Syn. *ppoch.* Cf. *apeyapúkkis.*

apaap₂ (db; 3) APA₄. nu. (T3) variety of banana. [Its fibers are used for thread in weaving.]

apaap₃ (db; 3) APA₅. va. give a welcoming speech (to), welcome. *a. énú* a type of *féérúwér.*

apaap₄ Dis. of *ap₁.*

apaapa (db; 1) See *paa.* vi. (c.) put out bait, engage in baiting.

apaapaay See *apaapa.* vo. (c.; T1) to bait (as a hook).

apaayetá See *paa₂, -tá.* vo. (c.; T1) flatter. *apaayeyitá, apóókótá* f. me, you.

apasa₁ See *pasa-.* vo. (c.; T3) speak, utter, say. *kepwe a. eey kkapas* you will utter this utterance. With ind. obj.: *apasaangeni* s. to.

apasa₂ See *pas.* vo. (c.; T3) set adrift. With dir. suf.: *apasaanó* cause to drift away; *apasaawu* cause to drift out.

apasaanó See *apasa₂.*

apasaangeni See *apasa₁.*

apasaawu See *apasa₂.*

apakawúch (Eng. *overcoat*) Var. *apokawuch.* nu. raincoat. *wúfey apakawúch* my r. Syn. *sekitin fáán ráán.*

apar₁ (3) See *par.* nu. (c.; T3) 1. red soil from which a red pigment is obtained. *aparen Chuuk* red pigment of Truk. 2. red paint or pigment obtained from this soil. 3. marking in red to guide adzing of canoe hull. *aparen waa* red marking of the canoe.

apar₂ (3) See *para-₂*. N. Var. *áper.* vi. (c.) aim, make an alignment (as with posts, plants, etc.). With ind. obj.: *aparangeni* take aim at.

apara₁ See *par.* vo. (c.; T3) redden, paint red.

apara₂ See *para-₂*. N. Var. *ápera.* vo. (c.; T3) aim at, line (something) up, align.

aparasa See *paras₂*. vo. (c.; T3) cause to fly in all directions, scatter.

aparangngaw (3b) See *apar₂, ngngaw.* N. Var. *áperengngaw.* nu. (T3) poor aim, poor marksmanship.

apareni See *apar₂, -ni-*. N. vo. (T6a) notice, be aware of, realize. *wúsaa mwo fen pwan a.* I am not taking any notice of it. *wúse mwa a. pwe átánaan aa song* I did not realize that he was angry.

aparééch (2: *-echch-u-*) See *apar₂, ééch.* N. Var. *áperééch.* nu. (T2) good aim, good marksmanship.

apach (3b) See *pach.* vi. be fastened; be stuck, pasted, or glued together. *a. sefáán* be put back together, reassembled, fastened together again. *a.-sefááníiy* put (something) back together, reassemble, fasten together again.

apacha See *pach.* vo. (c.; T3) attach, paste, join, connect, glue, add (in arithmetic). With dir. suf.: *apachaanong* include, add (something) in.

apachaaffengenniiy See *apacha, ffengeen, -i-₂*. vo. (c.; T5) stick together; add together; fasten together.

apachaanong See *apacha.*

apachaangeni See *apacha, ngeni.* vo. (c.; T2) attach, stick, fasten, connect (something) to (something).

apachanga See *pachang₂.* vo. (c.; T3) cause to be smeared, besmear.

apachapach (db; 3) See *pach.* nu. (c.; T3) a kind of love magic.

apachachcha See *pachchaach.* vo. (T3) crush, flatten. Syn. *achaapaapa.*

apachón (4) See *ap₂, chón.* Var. *ópóchón.* nu. (T2, T3) 1. type of mud in which fabrics are soaked to dye them black. 2. black dye obtained from mixing mud or earth of same name with the juice of *choyiro* leaves or *taaras* root.

apachchaach (3) See *pachchaach.* vi. (c.) be crushed, flattened.

apachchawa See *pachchaw.* N. vo. (c.; T3) cause to hurry, make speed up, accelerate. *a. eey angaang* speed up this job. *a. eey waa* make this vehicle accelerate.

apat (3) See *pat.* nu. (c.; T3) coolant.

apata See *pat.* vo. (c.; T3) cool, cause to cool; refresh (oneself). Dis. *apatapata* (db). *wúwa apatapatááyey* I cooled myself off, I refreshed myself.

apatapata Dis. of *apata.*

apaya See *pay.* F. Var. *ápáya.* vo. (c.; T3) cause to lean, tilt. Cf. *kkopay.*

apeewun (2) Var. *ápeeyun.* nu. (T2) wall. *apeewunun sóópw* protector of a district or lineage. Cf. *ápe.*

apeni See *aap, -ni-*. vo. (T6b) put a diaper on. Dis. *akkapeni* (ds).

apeyap Var. of *apaap₁.*

apeyapúkkis (db; 2) See *apaap₁, kkis.* N. vi. (dis.) have many small dents, be pocked. Syn. *pochopochokkis.*

apééw₁ See *pé₂.* vo. (c.; T1) wait for (the wind to blow). Dis. *akkapééw* (ds).

apééw₂ See *kapé.* vo. (c.; T1) measure.

apééw₃ See *pé₃.* vo. (c.; T1) make empty.

apéngeni See *ap₁, ngeni.* [Used only with *epeek*.] vo. (T2) *a. epeek* step, move, go to one side; go along the side. *ewe aan aa a. epeek ewe fénú* the road goes along the side of the island. *wúwa a. epeek ewe aan reen átewe* I stepped to one side of the path on account of that fellow. *wúwa a. epeek ewe cheepen* I stepped to one side around the table (cf. *wúwa aapangeni epeek ewe cheepen* I moved the table to one side.

apéchékkúna See *péchékkún.* vo. (c.; T3) strengthen, make strong, make well.

apokawuch Var. of *apakawúch*

apúra (1) APÚRAA. (Jap.) nu. (T1) grease.

apúraani See *apúra, -ni-*. vo. (T4) grease. *a. na waa* grease that auto.

appan (3) APPANA. nu. (T3) neonate or newly born animal, newly hatched bird. *emén a.* one n. *appanen maan* n. of an animal.

appach (3) See *ppach.* nu. (c.; T3) paste, glue. *appachen penik* sticky, whitish threads exuded by the *penik* trepang.

appacha (dc) See *ppach.* vo. (c.; T3) make (something) stick, attach.

appiyo (1) APPIYOO. (Jap. *happyoo*) nu. (T1) announcement, broadcast (by radio). *eché a.* one a. *aan a.* his a.

appiyooni See *appiyo, -ni-*. vo. (T4) announce, broadcast (by radio). *a. eey pworaawus* broadcast this news.

appúng (2) APPÚNGÚ. nu. (T2) fresh water. *appúngún nóón ewe neeni* f. w. of that place. Syn. *kkónik, kkónuk, ónuki, pweke*.

apw (3) APWPWA. vi. be forced open.

-apw₁ [Occurs only in the predicate phrase *aapw*.] vi. be not. *aapw (*e-apw)* no ("it not"); *aapw iiy* not it.

-apw₂ (3) APWA₁. [In cpds. only.] unsp. (u.m.) See *nisiyapw, ssiyapw*.

apwa- (3) APWA₂. ni. (T3) root (of a tooth). *apwan* its r.; *apwen nii* tooth's r. Syn. *wocha-*₁.

apwaapw (db; 3) See *apwa-*. Var. *apwapw*. n. (T3) gums, gum area (of mouth). *apwaapwan* his g.; *apwaapwen nii* gum area or root area of the teeth.

apwaapwa (1) See *pwaapwa*. nu. (c.; T1) celebration, party. vi. (c.) rejoice, have a good time, celebrate.

apwaapwaay See *apwaapwa*. vo. (c.; T1) honor with a party, fete, cheer up, make happy.

apwas (3) APWASA. vi. shout or cry out "wehuhu!" as an exclamation over having nearly fallen down or narrowly escaped an accident, as when carrying a burden down a steep slope. Dis. *akkapwas* (ds). nu. (T3) shout or cry of "wehuhu!". *aan a.* his s.

apwasa See *pwas*. Var. *appwasa*. vo. (c.; T3) dry, cause to be dry.

apwanga See *pwaang*. vo. (c.; T3) make a hole in, puncture.

apwangapwang (db; 3) See *pwanga-*₁. nu. (c.; T3) weakness. vi., adj. (be) weak, without strength, feeble, brittle.

apwapw (3) APWAPWA. Var. *apwaapw*. nu. (c.; T3) teeth arch; gums. Only in the expression *apwapwen nii* gums. Cf. *pwpwa-*.

apwaraay See *pwara*. Tb3. vo. (c.; T1) make brave, encourage.

apwech (3) See *pwech*. nu. (c.; T3) a plant (*Clerodendrum inerme*). [Its white flowers are worn on the ear as a signal in courtship.] *apwechen Chuuk Trukese a.*.

apwéw (2) APWÉWÚ. nu. (T2) species of pompano fish. *apwéwún Chuuk Trukese a..* Cf. *pwéwúr*.

apwichi See *pwich*₁. N. Var. *ápwichi, epwichi*. vo. (c.; T2) broil, roast, heat on a fire.

apworaawusa N. of *ópwóróówusa*.

apwpwa See *apw*. vo. (T3) force (something) open.

apwpwacha See *pwpwach*. vo. (c.; T3) slacken, loosen.

apwpwacho (1) APWPWACHOO. nu. (T1) a species of crab

apwpwich (2?) vi. make breadfruit pudding with coconut cream, make *aarúg*.

apwpwóra N. of *ópwóra*.

ar (3) ARA₁. vi., adj. (be) sweet (to the taste). Dis. *araar* (db). Syn. *ngar*.

araar₁ Dis. of *ar*.

araar₂ (db; 3) ARA₂. nu. (T3) white tern (with some black on the head). *araaren Chuuk Trukese* t.

araarúút F. vi. be covered with soot. Syn. *anúút*.

araf (3) nu. (T3) a kind of fish.

arakak (3) ARAKAKA. n. (T3) 1. ringworm and similar skin diseases. *eféw a.* one r. *arakakan* his r. *arakaken Chuuk Trukese* r. 2. candle bush (*Cassia alata*). [The pounded leaves are used as medicine for ringworm and prickly heat.] vi. have ringworm. *raa a.* they have r.

arama See *ram*. vo. (c.; T3) color a saffron or mustard color (as with turmeric).

aramas (3) ARAMASA. Var. *aramás, árámás*. n. (T3) person, human being; (with suf. pos. prn.) lineage mate, friend; commoner (as against one of chiefly rank); (collectively with reference to a place) people. *emén a.* one p. *aramasan* his lineage mate or friend. *a. tekiya* p. of high rank. *aramasen iya?* p. of what place?; *aramasen Chuuk Trukese* person or people. *aramasen emén* stranger, unknown person; *aramasen núkiisenné* outsider, nonmember of the local polity ("person of the periphery"); *aramasen nóómw* people of old. *aramasen iyé naan?* whose person is that? (of what lineage or family?); *aramasen áán Puruuta (eterekes)* person of Puruuta's (lineage).

aramaki (1) ARAMAKII. (Jap. *haramaki*) nu. (T1) belly-band (to keep the stomach warm). *eché a.* one b. *aan a.* his b.

aramakiini See *aramaki, -ni-*. vo. (T4) wear or put a belly-band on. *a. nuukomw* put a b. on your stomach.

aramás (2) ARAMÁSI. Wn. Var. *aramas, árámás.* n. (T2) person, human being. [For details see *aramas*.] *aramásin Chuuk* Trukese p.

aranga See *rang.* vo. (c.; T3) cause to stiffen in defense, cause to parry, trick into a defensive move by a feint, put on the defensive.

arangaffengenniiy See *rang₁, ffengen, -i-₂.* vo. (c.; T5) cause to throng together.

arap (3b) ARAPA. vi., adj. (be) near, close. Dis. *akkarap* (ds). With dir. suf.: *arapéto* be near here, come near hither.

arapa See *rap.* vo. (c.; T3) broil. Dis. *akkarapa* (ds).

arapakkan (3) See *arap, kkan.* vi. be very near, very close. *a. ngeni* be next to, be along side of.

arapéto See *arap.*

arara₁ See *rar₁.* vo. (c.; T3) heat, make hot.

arara₂ See *rar₂.* vo. (c.; T3) knock down (of grass), pass through (of grass). *emén aa a. ikeey* someone has passed through here (leaving a trail of knocked down grass).

araw₁ (3) ARAWA₁. vi. be fixed, be fast (of blue dye).

araw₂ (3b) ARAWA₂. nu. (T3) color ranging from blue to green. vi., adj. (be) blue to green. Dis. *arawaraw* (db).

arawa See *araw₁.* vo. (T3) fix, make fast (of black dye).

arawépwech (3) See *araw₂, pwech.* nu. (T3) light shade of blue or green. vi. be a light shade of b. or g.

arawóchón (4) See *araw₂, chón.* nu. (T2) dark shade of the color blue to green. vi. be a dark shade of b. or g.

ará (1) ARÁÁ. N. Var. *árá, érá, wúrá.* va. say, utter.

are (1?) AREE (?). N. md.m., conj. if, when (future, uncertain). Syn. *ika.*

areni See *ará, -ni-*. N. Var. *áreni, éreni, wúreni.* vo. (T5) say to, tell (someone).

aretimetik Var. of *aritimetik.*

aretmetik Var. of *aritimetik.*

aréé- (1) ARÉÉ. N. [In cpds. only.] Var. *éréé.* unsp. scraped, sanded, made smooth (by scraping or sanding).

arééti See *aréé-, -ti-*. N. Var. *érééti.* vo. (T4) scrape, sand, smooth by scraping (as with a piece of glass) or sanding.

aréew See *ré₂.* vo. (c.; T1) 1. heat (leaves). 2. (N.) broil (fowl and birds only). Syn. *arapa.*

aritimetik (3) ARITIMETIKA. (Eng.) Var. *aretimetik, aretmetik.* nu. (T3) arithmetic. *aritimetiken Merika* American a.

aro- N. c.f. of *óór.*

arofú See *aro-, fúú.* nu. 27th night of the lunar month.

arosset N. of *órosset.*

aroma (1) AROMAA. N. Var. *óroma.* nu. (T1) 1. a shrub (*Abutilon*). [Fiber used on fish hooks.] 2. nylon fishing line. Syn. *tengús.*

arong (3) ARONGA. N. Var. *órong.* nu. (T3) species of pompano fish. *arongen Chuuk* Trukese p. *péwún a.* sideburns.

aronga N. of *óronga.*

aropwén N. of *óropwén.*

aropwúkú See *aro-, pwúkú* (?). nu. 13th night of the lunar month.

arocha N. of *órocha.*

arúng (2) ARÚNGÚ. nu. (T2) coconut cream (squeezed from grated coconut meat). *arúngún iik* c. c. for fish. Cf. *aarúng.*

achaap (3) See *chaap.* vi., va. (c.) catch, engage in catching (of armored crabs only). *a. kúsún* c. armored crabs.

achaapaapa See *chaapaap.* N. Var. *apachachcha.* vo. (c.; T3) crush, flatten.

achaacha (db; 1) See *chaa-₂.* Tb2. vi. (c.) be big, large, extensive. *achaachaan eey meen* the big size of this thing.

achammach (3) See *aach₁, mmach.* nu. (T3) breadfruit that has formed but is still very small.

achapar (3b) See *aach₁, par.* nu. (T3) a variety of breadfruit ("red stem").

achappa See *chaap.* vo. (c.; T3) cause to be face down; turn face down. Dis. *akkachappa* (ds). With dir. suf.: *achappóónó* turn (something) face down away.

achappóónó See *achappa.*

achar (3) See *char.* nu. (c.; T3) 1. a form of sorcery. 2. an illness resulting from the sorcery of this name.

achara See *char*. vo. (c.; T3) make glow (of coals).
achacha See *chach*. N. Var. *asacha*. vo. (c.; T3) wedge in place, pack tightly, cram.
achachchach (ds; 3) See *chach*. N. Var. *asassach*. vi. (c.) be crowded together (of people in sleeping).
achaw$_1$ (3) ACHAWA$_1$, KACHAWA$_1$. [Derived from *Achaw*$_2$?] nu. (T3) basalt, basaltic rock.
Achaw$_2$ (3: *-kachaw*) ACHAWA$_2$, KACHAWA$_2$. nu. (loc.) Kusaie Island. With pref. *sowu-*: Sowukachaw Lord of Kusaie (legendary ruler of Kusaie).
Achaw$_3$ [Derived from *Achaw*$_2$.] Var. *Asawa*. nu. (loc.) a clan name. *fiin A.*, *fin A. A.* woman; *mwáán A. A.* man. *chóón A.* people of A.
achawa (1) ACHAWAA. nu. (T1) species of squirrel fish.
achawar$_1$ (3) ACHAWARA. [The ds-form *akkachawar* is more commonly used.] n. (T3) loincloth (traditional type, worn by men and woven from banana fibers). *achawaran* his l.
achawar$_2$ (3) [Derived from *achawar*$_1$.] nu. (T3) compensation for a marital offense; indemnity. *achawaren ésúúsú* c. for running off with another man's wife or for adultery; *achawaren kkapas* c. for proposing adultery to another man's wife; *achawaren nisoowu* c. for adultery; *achawaren pwúnúwenóónó* c. for taking another man's wife away in marriage; *achawaren fóór* war indemnity, price of peace; *achawaren ápwichin fénú* payment to an *itang* to keep the enemy from returning; *achawaren eyines* payment to allies in war in recognition of their help. *angeey aan a.* demand or get compensation from him ("seize his loincloth"); *ááni a. seni* pay c. to ("acquire the loincloth from"); *ááni a. ngeni* pay c. to.
achawareni See *achawar*$_1$, *-ni-*. vo. (T6a) acquire a loincloth.
aché (1) ACHÉÉ. Itang. nu. (T1) one who knows *itang* lore but who is not in the direct line of transmission of such lore. [An *aché* is not a member of the *eterekes* or *eyinang* that founded the local school of *itang* or introduced it, nor is he a direct descendent of a male member of that *eterekes* or *eyinang*. He may be a brother-in-law of an *itang* or someone who has paid an *itang* in order to be taught his lore. He is not entitled to use *itang* talk in public meetings if a *chóóyiro* is present, but he may pass on his knowledge to his children and lineage mates and be the introducer of *itang* lore into another locality where it is unknown and be the founder of a line of transmission there.] Syn. *achéémaaraw*.
achéémaaraw (3) See *aché*, *maaraw*. nu. (T3) one who is an *aché* type of *itang*. Syn. *aché*.
achéémmónga See *chéémmóng*. vo. (c.; T3) widen, make wide (of flat objects). Syn. *achéénapa*.
achéénapa See *chéénap*. vo. (c.; T3) widen, make wide (of flat objects). With dir. suf.: *achéénapaanó* widen out. Syn. *achéémmónga*.
achéépéépa See *chéépéép*. vo. (c.; T3) flatten, make broad.
achééwúúw achééwúngeni See *chééw*, *ngeni*. vo. (c.; T2) tell widely to, broadcast to.
achékken (2) See *aach*$_1$, *kken*. F. nu. (T2) a seaweed or seagrass (*Enhalus acoroides*, "sharp stem"). [Used to make fine nets and as medicine for women going out on the water.] Syn. *ónóót*.
achéchchénú (ds) See *chchén*$_1$. vo. (c.; T2) wet (something), make wet.
achi (1) ACHII. (Jap. *hachi*.) nu. (T1) bee. *emén a.* one b. *chénún a.* honey. Syn. *chunen, pwunech*.
achoocho N. of *óchoocho*.
achoochoongeni N. of *óchoochoongeni*.
achomwoch (3) See *aach*$_1$, *mwoch*. nu. (T3) a variety of breadfruit ("short stem").
achopwu N. of *óchopwu*.
achoronga See *chorong*. Var. *achchoronga*. vo. (c.; T3) disturb with noise; (refl.) be noisy; make a disturbance. *kaa chék achorongóókonó pwún kese mwochen rongorong meet ekkeey siya árá* you are just making a disturbance because you do not wish to hear what we are saying.
achómmónga See *chómmóng*. N. Var. *achóómmonga, óchómmónga*. vo. (c.; T3) increase, cause to be many, make numerous. With dir. suf.: *achómmóngaanó* increase on out.

achómmóngaanó See *achómmónga*.
achuki (1) ACHUKII. (Jap. *azuki*) nu. (T1) 1. red bean paste. 2. jelly; jelly doughnut.
achchaay See *chcha*. vo. (c.; T1) cause to bleed, make bloody, shed the blood of. Dis. *akkachchaay* (ds).
achchawa See *chchaw*. N. vo. (c.; T3) make slow or late, delay. Syn. *ammanga*.
achchék$_1$ (2) ACHCHÉKÚ$_1$. n. (T2) skirt (wrap-around), kilt, lavalava (traditional type, worn by women and woven from hibiscus or banana fibers). *eché a.* one s. *achchékún, aan a.* her s. vi. be in a skirt, wearing a skirt; be naked above the waist. Dis. *akkachchék* (ds).
achchék$_2$ (2) ACHCHÉKÚ$_2$. vi., va. be carried (on someone's back); carry (on one's back).
achchékú See *achchék$_2$*. vo. (T2) carry (a child) on one's back. Dis. *akkachchékú* (ds).
achchékúni See *achchék$_1$, -ni-*. vo. (T5) acquire an *achchék* skirt.
achchorong (3) See *chorong*. N. Var. *óchchorong*. nu. (c.; T3) a tree (*Hernandia ovigera*). Syn. *ékúrang*.
achchoronga Var. of *achoronga*.
-at$_1$ (3) ATA$_1$. [In cpds. only.] unsp. (u.m.) See *maat*.
-at$_2$ (3) ATA$_2$. [In cpds. only.] unsp. (u.m.) See *amaat$_1$, amaat$_2$, amaata, kamaat, kkamaat, maata-, maataat*.
-at$_3$ (3) ATA$_3$. [In cpds. only. Perhaps related to -*at$_2$*.] unsp. rustling noise (?). See *amwaat, mwaataat*.
ata- (3) ATA$_4$. [In cpds. only.] unsp. hurry, quick. See *atapwan, mwaat*.
ataataakkisiiy (db) See *ta, kkis, -i-$_2$*. N. Var. *ataatakkisiiy*. vo. (c., dis., intens.; T5) destroy into little pieces, break up into little pieces.
ataatakkisiiy F. of *ataataakkisiiy*.
ataay See *ta*. vo. (c.; T1) destroy, take apart, disassemble, take to pieces, break apart, ruin. *atóók* or *atayók* destroy you (sg.). With dir. suf.: *ataayenó* break apart, take apart; *ataayetiw* disassemble downward (of a structure of a building); *ataayewu* destroy or disassemble in an outward direction.
ataayenó See *ataay*.
ataayetiw See *ataay*.

ataayewu See *ataay*.
atafatafa (db) See *tafa-$_2$*. vo. (c.; T3) unsnarl, disentangle, trace out (of a line).
ataka See *tak*. vo. (c.; T3) finish, complete. Syn. *áweesi*.
atake (1) ATAKEE. (Jap. *hatake*) nu. (T1) garden, plantation, farm. Syn. *máán, tánnipi*. vi. make a garden, do gardening. Syn. *tánnipi, wotoot$_3$*.
atakirikir (db; 2) See *takir*. vi. (c., dis.) be comical, amusing, funny, laughter causing.
atakunu N. of *otokunu*.
atama$_1$ See *tam*. vo. (c.; T3) send off, exile, depose. With dir. suf.: *atamaanong* send in, bring in, install; *atamaawu* send out, chase out, exile, depose, throw out, expunge (of words).
atama$_2$ See *taam*. vo. (c.; T3) turn (a canoe) about so that the outrigger is on the opposite side in relation to the direction of travel.
atamaanong See *atama$_1$*.
atamaawu See *atama$_1$*.
atap (3) ATAPA. vi. wade.
atappa Var. of *attapa*.
Atapwasé nu. (pers.) a traditional storm god. [One of five children of the weather (*néwún ráán*), who live in the gale, sink boats in heavy seas, and blow down trees.]
atapwan (3) See *ata-, -pwan*. Tb3. n. (T3) haste, hurry. *atapwanan, aan a.* his h. vi. be in haste, in a hurry. Syn. *atawaat, pachchaw*. Cf. *kkay, kkáy, mwittir*.
atapwana See *atapwan*. vo. (T3) hurry (someone in what he is doing).
atapwanapwan (db; 3) See *atapwan*. vi., adj. (dis.) (be) temporary. *énnúk a.* t. regulation.
atawaat (3) See *tawaat*. n. (c.; T3) haste, hurry. vi. be in haste, in a hurry. Syn. *atapwan, pachchaw*. Cf. *kkay, kkáy, mwittir*.
atawatta See *tawaat*. vo. (c.; T3) cause (someone) to hurry. Syn. *atapwana*.
atawe (3) See *tawe*. [Used only in n. phrases.] nu. accomplishing. *pisekin a.* tool (e.g., shovel, knife, hammer, etc.); *mwooniyen a.* mutual fund.
ataweey See *atawe*. vo. (c.; T1) finish, complete, do until finished. *a. aach angaang* f. our work. *sipwe a. émétúch pwún sipwe sááy neesor* we shall f.

(preparing) our food for we shall sail tomorrow.
atek Var. of *átek*.
atekini Var. of *átekini*.
atéémén (2) See *té₂, maan*. nu. (c.; T2) devination for who committed a crime ("make-animal-crawl"). [The practitioner fishes with a pole and magic bait in the bush, calling the names of those he suspects. When he calls the guilty party's name a lizard bites the bait. Whatever the practitioner does to the lizard (e.g., breaks a leg) will also befall the guilty person named. If, for example, he throws the lizard far away, the guilty person will leave the island.]
atéépaani See *té₂, paani₂*. vo. (c.; T4) search carefully for.
atééw See *té₂*. vo. (c.; T1) cause or help (someone) to creep, crawl, or climb. With dir. suf.: *atééwétiw* let or cause to climb down.
atééwétiw See *atééw*.
ato (1) ATOO. N., Tn. Var. *óto*. nu. (T1) 1. stem of mangrove fruit. 2. (Itang) younger brother of a chief.
atoon (3) ATOONA. N. Var. *ótoon*. nu. variety of coconut. [Its husk is sweet and is chewed like pandanus.] Syn. *ngngúpé*.
atoononga See *toonong*. N. Var. *ótoononga*. vo. (c.; T3) admit, allow to enter. *atoonongááyey nnón angaang* admit me to work, give me a job.
atoow N. of *ótoow*.
atomwa N. of *ótomwa*.
atu- N. var. of *ótu-*.
atúfi N. of *étúfi*.
atún vi. sleep, be asleep. Syn. *méwúr, ónnut*.
attafa See *ttaf*. Var. *atafatafa, tafa*. vo. (c.; T3) cause to be unsnarled, unravel, follow out (as a line). With dir. suf.: *attafóónó* follow on out, unsnarl on out.
attafóónó See *attafa*.
attama See *ttam*. vo. (c.; T3) make long, make tall. *a. enisan* let his beard grow. With dir. suf.: *attamóónó* make longer, make taller.
attamóónó See *attama*.
attap (3) ATTAPA. nu. (T3) touch, feeling (with the hand).
attapa See *attap*. Var. *atappa*. vo. (T3) touch, feel (with the hand).

attaw (3) ATTAWA. [Perhaps a c. constr. with dc. of *taaw*.] nu. (T3) fishing. *attawen sómwoon* f. in which the entire catch is given to the chief. *a. mwáán* f. done by men; *a. feefin* f. done by women. vi. fish; be, do, or engage in fishing. *a. mwmwáán* f. in a restricted place, f. without permission, trespass in fishing. (N.) *a.-mwáánniiy*, (F.) *a.-mwánniiy* f. without permission in (a place). (N.) *a.-mwáánniiyenó*, (F.) *a.-mwánniiyenó* f. on without permission in (a place).
attawa See *attaw*. vo. (T3) fish, catch (fish). *ekkewe mwáán raa nó a. ooch ááy ikenen améémé* those men went to catch some fish for me to sell.
attof N. of *óttif*.
attofa N. of *óttifa*.
attona Var. of *ótona*.
attonafetáneey N. and Tn. of *óttonofátáneey*.
attu (1) ATTUU. (Sp., *gato*) Var. *áttu, kattu, káttu*. nu. (T1) cat, housecat.
attuf Var. of *óttif*.
attufa Var. of *óttifa*.
awa- (3) AWA₂, KAWA. [In cpds. only.] unsp. beat, strike. See *awata, kkaw, kkawet, wumwukaw*.
awa (1) AWAA. (Eng.) nu. (T1) hour.
awaaséénaangngaw (3b) See *waasééna, ngngaw*. vi. (c.) be inhospitable to visitors.
awaaséénaangngaweey See *awaaséénaangngaw, -e-₂*. vo. (c.; T6b) be inhospitable to (someone).
awaaséénaay See *waasééna*. vo. (c.; T1) entertain, be hospitable to (a visitor).
awaaséénaayééch (2) See *waasééna, ééch*. vi. (c.) be properly hospitable to visitors.
awaaséénaayéchchúúw See *awaaséénaayééch, -ú-*. vo. (c.; T1) be properly hospitable to (a visitor).
awaawaay (db) See *waawa*. vo. (c.; T1) let (someone) use a canoe or vehicle.
awassát (2) See *aaw₁, ssát*. Var. *awessát*. nu. (T2) talkative person. vi. (be) talkative. Syn. *awakkamw, awaparas*. Cf. *awanap*.
awakkamw (3) See *aaw₁, kkamw*. n. (T3) 1. big mouth; person with a big mouth. *awakkamwan* his b. m. 2. talkative person. *emén a.* one t. p. Syn. *awassát*. 3. person who speaks with a loud voice. vi. 1. have a big mouth. 2. talk

awamach

too much, (be) talkative. Syn. *awassát, awaparas.* Cf. *awanap.* 3. talk in a loud voice.

awamach (3) See *aaw₁, macha-* (?). F. Var. *niyawamach.* nu. (T3) species of reef fish.

awanap (3a) See *aaw₁, nap.* vi. be a braggart, be a "big-mouth". Cf. *awakkamw, awaparas, awassát.*

awaniikan See *waniik.*

awanuuwan See *wanuuw.*

awanger Var. of *awenger.*

awaparas (3) See *aaw₁, paras.* n. (T3) talkative person. vi. talk too much, (be) talkative. Syn. *awakkamw, awassát.* Cf. *awanap.*

awapach (3) See *aaw₁, pach.* nu. (T3) deformation of the mouth due to yaws scars ("stuck-mouth"). vi. mispronounce words because of a speech defect or deformation.

awara See *war.* vo. (c.; T3) cause to arrive.

awarawar (db; 3) See *war.* nu. (c.; T3) cause of an arrival. *awarawaren átewe semwmwenin saman* the cause of his arrival is his father's illness. va. be causing to arrive. *aa a. énú* he made spirits come (of a spirit medium).

awata See *awa-, -ta-₂.* vo. (T3) strike, beat, smite, slay. Syn. *mwérúúw, nengeey.* Cf. *namwúti, nniiy, siyeri, wecheey.*

awatá (1) See *aaw₁, -tá.* vi., adj. (be) mouth-up. *aa chi a. faachchamw* he gave voice m.-u. to heaven.

awaw₁ (3a) AWAWA. nu. (T3) veins (ridges) of a leaf, midrib of a coconut frond. *awawen nóón chéén irá* the veins of a leaf. *awawen núú* midrib of a coconut frond. vi. suffer discomfort due to ridges under a sleeping mat; be ridgy under a mat.

awaw₂ (3) See *waw.* N. nu. (T3) a loud popping noise from a particular stroke in mashing breadfruit pudding. *awawen kkón* the popping noise of breadfruit pudding. vi. make a loud popping noise in mashing breadfruit. Syn. *sáánong, eyipwenong, sáákak.*

awaweyinú (1) See *awaw₁, núú.* Var. *awawen núú.* nu. (T1) midrib of coconut frond.

Awayi nu. (loc.) Hawaii.

awásá (1) See *aaw₁, sá.* nu. (T1) species of half-beak fish (upper jaw extended into a beak, lower jaw short). Syn. *fénéwúng.*

awessát Var. of *awassát.*

awenimwi See *aaw₁, -mwi.* Tbl. n. (T3) cervix. *awenimwiin* her c.

awenger (2) See *aaw₁, ngeri-.* Var. *awanger, awúnger.* nu. (T2) species of squirrel fish ("nibble-mouth").

awepeek (2) See *aaw₁, peek₂.* nu. (T2) species of half beak or garfish (lower jaw extended into long beak, upper jaw short; "side-mouth").

awéétúwét (2) See *aaw₁, éét.* vi. be talkative ("smoky mouth").

awémwéch (2) See *aaw₁, mwéch.* vi. be dumb, be unable to speak, be speechless ("fast-mouth").

awémwéchúmwéch (db; 2) See *awémwéch.* vi. stutter, stammer.

awéchén (2) See *aaw₁, chaan.* vi. mispronounce words because of a speech defect or deformation ("wet-mouth").

awiti- (2) See *witi-.* Var. *awúti-.* ni. (c.; T2) thing prepared in advance (for a person). *awitin* t. for him.

awiti See *witi-.* Var. *awúti.* vo. (c.; T2) wait for (someone).

awosukosuka N. of *ówosukasuka.*

awopwo (1) See *aaw₁, pwo.* nu. (T1) a species of fish.

awochopw (2) See *aaw₁, chopw.* nu. (T2) species of pompano fish. *awochopwun Wééné* p. of Wééné (Moen).

awut (3) AWUTTA. (Eng.) vi. be out (in baseball). Ant. *seyif.*

awutta See *awut.* vo. (c.; T3) make (someone) out (in baseball).

awúnúch (2) AWÚNÚCHÚ. nu. (T2) species of snapper fish. *awúnúchún Chuuk* s. of Truk.

awúnger Var. of *awenger.*

awúti- Var. of *awiti-.*

awúti Var. of *awiti.*

ayaangeni (db) See *aa-, ngeni.* vo. (c.; T2) give a general class of thing to ("cause use or possession to"). Dis. *akkayaangeni* (ds).

ayaay (db) See *aa-.* vo. (c.; T1) give a general class of thing to, cause to use or possess. *ayaayey, ayóók* cause me, cause you (sg.) to use. *kepwe a. aan na raweses* you will help him put on his trousers. *kepwe a. óómw na raweses* you will let him wear those (by you) trousers of yours. *kepwe a. Eimun* *reemw* you will give Eimun from yours ("you will cause Eimun to have or use by your agency"). *kepwe a. Eimun reemw óómw kkana raweses* you will give Eimun from among those trousers of yours. *wúpwe a. Eiue reey* I will give Eiue from mine.

ayeewin See *eew$_1$*.

ayis$_1$ F. Var. *eyis*. nu. a tree (*Parinarium glaberrimum*). [The stone of its fruit is used to obtain a fragrant juice for making a perfume known as *néén ómón*.] Syn. *ómón*.

ayis$_2$ (Eng.) nu. ice. *aan a.* his i.

ayispwóks (Eng.) nu. icebox. *aan a.* his i. Syn. *reyichooko*.

ayikiyú (1) AYIKIYÚÚ. (Jap. *haikyuu*) nu. (T1) ration (of food). *óóch a.* one r. *aan a.* his r. va. 1. distribute. 2. purchase or buy (a large quantity). *sipwe nó a. aach pisek me nnón T.T.C.* we will go and purchase some things at Truk Trading Company.

ayin Var. of *eyin$_1$*.

Ayiningnapanap nu. (loc.) Ailinglapalap Island and Atoll (Marshall Islands).

ayinoko (1) AYINOKOO. (Jap. *ainoko*) nu. (T1) half caste, mixed-blood. *ayinokoon Sapaan* one whose father was a Japanese; *ayinokoon Merika* one whose father was an American.

ayipiskas (3) (Eng.) nu. (T3) hibiscus. Syn. *sinifé, sáápwow*.

ayit (3b) See *iit*. vi. (c.) show, give instruction, make demonstration (with *ngeni*). Dis. *akkayit* (ds). Cf. *kkayit*.

Á

á-₁ See *e*-₁. [In this form only when followed immediately by the vowel *á*.] unsp. he, she, it. [Although a prefix, it is written separately. It occurs only in colloquial speech in place of *e*-₁.]

á-₂ See *a*-₂. [Usually in this form when the next following vowel is *á* or *e*.] pref. (c.) imparts causative meaning to the base. Dis. *ákká-* (ds). *áweesi* cause to be finished, finish (*wees* be finished).

á (1) ÁÁ₁. vi. swim, be swimming. Dis. *ákká* (ds). *áán átánaani á* that fellow's swimming; *ese sinee á* he does not know how to swim. With dir. suf.: *áánó* swim away, off; *ááto* swim hither.

-á (1) ÁÁ₆. [In cpds. only.] unsp. (u.m.) See *nissiyá*.

áá-₁ (1) ÁÁ₂. Var. *eyi*-₁. unsp. stick; stick shaped.

áá-₂ (1) ÁÁ₃. [In cpds. only.] unsp. talk, talking. See *ááni*₂, *áániini*.

áá₁ (1) ÁÁ₇. nu. (T1) name of the low, front, unrounded vowel written *á*; name of the letter thus written.

áá₂ (1) ÁÁ₄. interrog. 1. interjection indicating a question (comes at the end of the query). *kenee nó áá?* are you going to go? (the standard goodbye to someone who is leaving). *kene nónnómw áá?* are you going to stay? (the standard goodbye to someone who is remaining behind). 2. eh? (will you say it again?).

ááf (2: *efi-*, *-ef*) EFI₁ (°AFI). F. n. (T2) fire. *efin* his f. *efin nóón naan iimw* the f. in that house. Syn. *ákkey*, *ekkey*, *ettin*.

áás (2) ÁSSI. nu. (T2) flying. *ássin machchang* the bird's f. vi. fly, be in flight. Dis. *áásáás* (db); *ákkáás* (ds). *aa á. ewe sepeniin* the plane was in flight. With dir. suf.: *ássinong*, *ássinó*, *ássitá*, *ássitiw*, *ássito*, *ássiwow*, *ássiwu*.

áásáás Dis. of *áás*.

ááseneetá (1) See *á*, *seneetá*. vi. swim on one's back, swim face up. Syn. *wúrúúrúpwich*.

áásippu (1) See *ási-*, *puu-*₁. Var. *áásipwu*, *ássipu*. vi. (c.) wave (as a flag), be waving; be shaken out (in the wind). Dis. *ákkáásippu* (ds).

áásippuuw See *áásippu*. vo. (c.; T1) shake out, make wave.

áásipwu (1) See *ási-*, *pwu-*₁. Var. *áásippu*, *ássipu*. vi. (c.) wave (as a flag), be waving; be shaken out (in the wind). Dis. *ákkáásipwu* (ds). *ewe fináyik aa ákkáásipwu reen puupuun ewe ásápwán* the flag was waving from the blowing of the wind.

áássaanong See *áássi*.

áássaato See *áássi*.

áássaawow See *áássi*.

áássáátá See *áássi*.

áássáátiw See *áássi*.

áássi See *áás*. vo. (c.; T2) make or cause to fly. With dir. suf.: *áássaanong*, *áássaato*, *áássaawow*, *áássaawu*, *áássáátá*, *áássáátiw*, *áássóónó*.

áássóónó See *áássi*.

áák (2: *eki-*, *-ek*) EKI₁ (°AKI). n. (T2) thought, idea. Dis. *ekiyek* (db, the more commonly used form). *ekin* his t.

áákita- See *ekit*.

áákún See *áá-*₁, *kún*₂ (?). nu. a shrub (*Callicarpa candicans*).

áám₁ prn. (pers.) we, us (exc.). *áám chék* only we; it is up to us.

áám₂ 1exc. pos. of *aa-*.

áámi₁ (1) ÁÁMII. prn. (pers.) you (pl.). *áámii chék* only you; it is up to you.

áámi₂ 2pl. pos. of *aa-*.

áámúnúmún (db; 2) See *á*, *mmún*. Var. *ámmún*. vi. swim the crawl.

áámwa₁ See *emw*. vo. (c.; T3) inspect, investigate, look into, go see. *repwe á. fénúwach* they will inspect our island.

áámwa₂ See *ámwa-*. vo. (c.; T3) pay a sympathetic visit to (someone who is sick). Syn. *emweri*.

áámwáámw (db; 3) See *emw*. vi. (c., dis.) watch, make ongoing or repeated inspections, repeatedly have a look. Dis. *ákkáámwáámw* (ds) customarily make ongoing inspections.

áán₁ (3) ÁNNA. vi. tack back and forth into the wind.

áán₂ (4) ÁNE₁. nu. (T2) a kind of coral (live, white and branching). *ánin wúsúús* c. for making breadfruit pounders. *neeyin á.* among the c. Cf. *anang, angnget, apwpwer.*

áán₃ Rel. of *aa-.*

áán₄ (2) See *áá-₂, -ni-.* [Only in const. with *ngeni;* presumably a back formation from *ááni₂.*] va. *á. ngeni* tell to, sing to. *kete á. ngeniyey áán Wumwowumw michiiyetá Taak* don't tell me [the kind of talk in] Wumwowumw's deceiving Taak.

ááney (2) ÁÁNEYI. nu. (T2) a kind of rooster.

ááni₁ See *aa-, -ni-.* vo. (T4) acquire, take possession of (a general-class thing). *á. achawar ngeni, á. achawar seni* pay compensation for marital offense to (someone). *á. amwaaraar* take delight in, take pleasure in. *á. eew* acquire or take only (whatever named), *wúpwe á. eew mááy* I will have only breadfruit (and nothing else).

ááni₂ See *áá-₂, -ni-.* vo. (T4) tell, sing (a story or song). *á. kkapas* speak, utter speech. *wúpwe á. eché kkéén* I shall sing a song.

áániimaaw (2, 3) See *áá-₂, nii₁, maaw.* vi. argue vigorously. *á. ngeni* a. vigorously against (someone).

áániini (db; 1) See *áá-₂, nii₁.* vi. (dis.) argue violently.

áániiniingeni See *áániini, ngeni.* vo. (dis.; T2) argue violently against, tirade against (someone).

áániicho (1) See *áá-₂, nii₁, choo₂.* vi. argue persistently. *áániichoffengen* a. p. together. *áániichoongeni* a. p. against (someone).

áániichoongeni See *áániicho.*

áániichoffengen See *áániicho.*

áánipé (1) See *eni-₂, pé₂* or *pé₁.* vi. (c.) fan ("make blowing wind"); beckon with downward wave of hand. Dis. *ákkáánipé* (ds). Syn. *áánit, sááyipé.*

áánipééw See *áánipé* vo. (T1) fan (someone); beckon to. Dis. *ákkánipééw* (ds). Syn. *áánita, áánitééw, sááyipééw.*

áánit (3) See *enit.* vi. (c.) fan with a fan. Dis. *ákkáánit* (ds).

áánita See *áánit.* Var. *áánitééw.* vo. (c.; T3) fan (someone) with a fan. Syn. *áánipééw, sááyipééw.*

áánitééw See *áánit, -é-.* [Presumably based on a wrong analogy with *áánipééw* and *sááyipééw.*] Var. *áánita.*

vo. (c.; T6b) fan (someone) with a fan. Syn. *áánipééw, sááyipééw.*

áánó See *á.*

áánna See *een₅.* Var. *ánna₂.* vo. (c.; T3) shoot at, strike at, hurl at (with gun, spear, club). *átewe aa á. neminnewe ngeni eféw faaw* the fellow threw a stone at her ("the fellow threw at the woman with a stone"). Cf. *enna.*

áánneen (db; 3) See *een₅.* N. Var. *ánneen.* nu. (c.; dis.) hurling, throwing, shooting (at things). *neeniyen á.* target ("place for hurling at"). va. shoot at, strike at, hurl at. vi. go shooting at targets.

áánnifich núú n. phr. a grass (*Fleurya ruderalis*).

Áánt Var. of *Aant.*

áángéréwú- See *engeréw.*

áángoona- See *engoon.*

ááp₁ (2) See *ep.* va. (c.) carry (things).

Ááp₂ (2) See *ep.* nu. (T2) 1. a star (probably Spica). 2. a sidereal month, marked by the star of this name and corresponding roughly to November, reported to be so named because people are repeatedly carrying fermented breadfruit from the fermenting pits to their homes at this time (*raa ááp épwét seni neeyin pétéwén* they repeatedly haul fermented breadfruit from the bush).

áápaato See *áápi.*

áápenges (2) See *áá-₁, penges.* Var. *ápenges.* nu. (T2) purlin.

áápengesi See *áápenges.* vo. (T2) put a purlin on.

áápereyingiing See *á, pereyingiing.* F. vi. swim on one's side. Syn. *áátiwiiniin.* Cf. *ááp, kkááp.*

ááp See *ep.* vo. (c.; T2) carry in more than one trip. With dir. suf.: *ááp aato* c. hither in more than one trip; *ááp oónó* c. away in more than one trip.

ááp imar (3b) See *ep, maar.* nu. (c.; T3) basket that is hung in pairs to either end of a shoulder-carrying pole and used by men to haul breadfruit, copra, etc. Syn. *áápimey.*

áápimey (2) See *ep, mááy₂.* nu. (c.; T2) basket hung in pairs at either end of a shoulder-carrying pole and used by men to haul breadfruit, copra, etc. ("breadfruit carrier"). Syn. *áápimar.*

áápiyep (db; 2) See *ep*. vi. (c., dis.) carry repeatedly in many trips.

áápóónó See *áápi*.

ááppásew See *áá-₁, ppásew*. nu. a giant fern (*Acrostichum aureum*).

áápwo (1) See *áá-₁, pwo*. nu. (T1) a tree (*Mischocarpus guillauminii, Cynometra yokotai*).

áár₁ nu. a fish (*Pseudoscarus*).

áár₂ (3) ÁÁRA. Var. *kkáár*. vi. be scooped up with a handnet.

áára₁ See *áár₂*. vo. (T3) scoop up with a handnet. *raa ááreer* they scooped them up.

áára₂ See *ár₁*. vo. (c.; T3) surround; consume entirely (of food). Dis. *ááráára* (db). With dir. suf.: *áárόόnό* consume entirely away (of food).

ááráára Dis. of *áára₂*.

áárer vi. engage in a kind of fishing (done by women at night with hand nets, with or without a moon).

ááriyer (db; 2) See *eri-₂*. ni. (c.; dis.; T2) stripes, lines. *meyi wor ááriyerin* it has stripes or lines. vi., adj. (be) striped, lined.

áárόόnό See *áára₂*.

áách N. nu. milkfish.

áácha See *ách*. vo. (c.; T3) cause (sail) to be shifted (in bringing a canoe about).

ááchipw (3) See *áá-₁, chipwa-*. nu. (T3) tongs for picking up things.

ááchipwa See *ááchipw*. vo. (T2) pick (something) up with tongs.

áát (4: *-át, -kát*) ÁTE, KÁTE. nu. boy. *emén á*. one b. *néwún á*. his b., his son (not yet adult). Ant. *nengngin*. Cf. *áta-*. ni. (T2) (with pref. *nee-*) boyhood. *neeyátin* in his boyhood.

áátipw (3) ÁÁTIPWA. N. nu. (T3) any variety of olive shell (family Olividae). [Used as counters in the game of bingo.] Syn. *pwetek*.

áátiwiiniin (2) See *á, tiwiiniin*. N. vi. swim on one's side. Syn. *áápereyingiing*.

ááto See *á*.

ááwén nu. type of sailing canoe with crescent shaped end pieces; the ceremonial model canoe with a frigate bird perched on it that hangs in the *fanangenimey*. *efóch á*. one c. of this type. *waan á*. his c. of this type.

ááy 1sg. pos. of *aa-*.

ááyá₁ (db; 1) ÁÁ₅. n. (T1) liver *ááyáán* his l. *ááyáán piik* pig's liver.

ááyá₂ (db; 1) See *aa-*. N. Var. *aaya*. vi. (dis.) use a general-class thing.

ááyepó (1) ÁÁYEPÓÓ. nu. (T1) a kind of reef fish.

ááyechéén Tn. of *ááchéén* (see *eché*).

ááyiti₁ See *áá-₂, -iti*. vo. (T2) explain to, point out to, teach, show (someone). Dis. *ákkááyiti* (ds). Syn. *ááyitingeni*.

ááyiti₂ See *á, -iti*. vo. (T2) swim to.

ááyitingeni See *áá-₂, -iti, ngeni*. Var. *áyitingeni*. vo. (T2) explain to, point out to, show (someone). Syn. *ááyiti*.

áfáániyen (db; 2) See *fa-₂, eniyen*. vi. (c., dis.) speak in a way intended to conceal one's meaning from someone present (by using *itang* talk or by using a foreign language). *raa á. neefiineer* they are using *itang* talk among themselves (to test one another's knowledge).

áfáániyeni See *áfáániyen*. vo. (c., dis.; T2) talk or speak about (a person in his presence) in such a way that he does not know what is being said; criticise (someone) indirectly by proverb, parable, or use of *itang* talk.

áfáániyeniyeffengenniir See *áfáániyeni, ffengeen*. [In 3pl. only.] vo. (c., dis., refl.; T2) in the expression *raa á*. they are using *itang* talk to one another (to test one another's knowledge).

áfáánnaanó See *áfááni₁*.

áfááni₁ See *fá-, eni-₃, -ni-*. N. Var. *áfánni*. vo. (c.; T2) form a circle, make (it) a circle (as when fishing or dancing). With dir. suf.: *áfáánnaanó* make (it) off into circle.

áfááni₂ ÁFÁÁNNI. N. Var. *áfánni, áfánniiy*. vo. (T2) pay close attention to, beware of, be careful of, care for, look after, attend to. Dis. *ákkáfááni* (ds). *ke te pwan á*. you (sg.) are welcome (in response to *kinissow* thank you; "don't be further concerned about it").

áfááyika- See *fááyik*.

áfááyichimw (3) See *faa-₁, chiimw*. vi. (c.) wear a garland, handkerchief, or towel on the head.

áfááyichimwa See *faa-₁, chiimw*. vo. (c.; T3) put a garland, handkerchief, or towel on (someone).

áfán (4) ÁFÁNE. nu. (T2) turmeric plant. [Formerly used to make an orange-red cosmetic.]
áfánni F. of áfáánni₁ and áfáánni₂.
áfánniiy Var. of áfáánni₂.
áfánnóónó F. of áfáánnaanó; see áfáánni.
áfára See fár. vo. (c.; T3) confer upon.
áfáchcha See fáchcha-. vo. (c.; T3) spread, spread out (as a mat). Dis. ákkáfáchcha (ds).
áfátána See fátán. Var. áfetána. vo. (c.; T3) drive, make go (of automobile, motorboat).
áfetána N. of áfátána.
áfeyiyengngawa See feyiyengngaw. Var. efeyiyengngawa vo. (c.; T3) cause to go wrong, bring misfortune to, injure.
áfitti See ffiit. N. Var. efitti, fittiiy. vo. (c.; T2) wind (something) up (as a fishline on a stick), cause to be wound up. Dis. ákkáfitti (ds). áfitti óómwu na óó wind up that (by you) fishline of yours.
áffánááng nu. (temp.) 25th (Elbert: twenty-fourth) night of the lunar month.
áffánáng nu. (temp.) 23rd (Elbert: twenty-second) night of the lunar month.
ásá (1) ÁSÁÁ, KÁSÁÁ. nu. (T1) side of canoe without the outrigger, the lee side of a sailing canoe. vi. sail before the wind (of an outrigger sailing canoe).
ásááp (2) ÁSÁPPI. nu. (T2) shuttle (of the loom). efóch á. one s. aan á his s. ásáppin túúr loom's s.
ásááwa See sááw. N. vo. (c.; T3) cause to be ashamed, awkward, or shy; embarrass, shame. Syn. ámáfena, ekini₂.
ásááwe (1) See ásá, we (?). vi. turn in the direction of the outrigger side, go toward the outrigger side.
ásáfááni Var. of ásefááni.
ásápa See sáp. vo. (c.; T3) turn (something). With dir. suf.: ásápáátá turn (something) face up or to the east; take the upper part of.
ásápáátá See ásápa.
ásápásáp (4) See sápe-. nu. (c.; T2) means of prevention. ásápásápin ppéwút a potion to ward off sorcery.
ásápwán See ási-. nu. wind, air. mesen á. wind direction; seni iya mesen eey á. from where is the direction of this wind; pwopwun á. wind direction; asen á. windward; fáán á. leeward.
ását N. of áset.
ásátta See sáát₃. Var. ásetta. vo. (c.; T3) split, break longitudinally.
ásáya (1) ÁSÁYAA. Var. áseya. nu. (T1) species of sea cucumber.
áseeng (3) See seeng. n. (c.; T3) sleeping place in a house. áseengan his s. p. nu. (c.; T3) in á. me nóón and á. me núkún holds or throws in hand-to-hand fighting for disarming an opponent slashing with a bushknife.
áseengesi- (2) ÁSEENGESI. [Used with fáán in pos. const.] ni. (T2) sake, purpose. Dis. ákkáseengesi- (ds). fáán áseengesin for his s. fáán áseengesin manawach for the s. of our lives, for our livelihood; fáán áseengesin aach sipwe sááy for the s. of our impending journey. Syn. iit.
ásefááni See sefáán. F. Var. ásáfááni. vo. (c.; T4) give back, cause to return, pass on. Syn. eniwin-sefáániiy, eniwinisefáániiy, eniwini.
áseneenóóy See seneenó. vo. (c.; T1) take the upper garments from, strip.
áset (2) ÁSETI. Var. ását. nu. (T2) swordgrass (Miscanthus floridulus). [Used in binding thatch.] ásetin Chuuk Trukese s.
ási- (4) ÁSE. [In cpds. only.] unsp. (u.m.) wind (?), blow (?); wave in the wind (?). Cf. áás.
-ási- (2) ÁSI, ESI₄. [Recorded only with the v.form. suf. -ni-.] Var. -esi-. suf. an old passive suffix that is no longer productive as such (cf. Gilbertese -aki). See -ásini, rukáásini, sááwáásini, sikáásini.
ásii- (1) ÁSII. N. [In cpds. only.] unsp. (u.m.) in strips.
ásiiy See ásii-. N. vo. (T1) strip (something) into strips (as with bark, coconut stem). Syn. ettika.
ásineengeni See sine, ngeni. vo. (c.; T2) make known to.
-ásini See -ási-, -ni-. Var. -esini. suf. (vo.; T5) on account of, in response to (something); by, at. [Indicates that the behavior of the subject described by the initial element in the verb construction is a consequence or in response to the verb's object.] wúwa sááwáásini áán átewe féfféér I was

ásipwu embarrassed by (at) his actions. See *kkéyeesini, sikáásini, mwmwusáásini*.
ásipwu Var. of *ásupwu*.
ásupwu See *ási, pwu-₁*. Var. *ásipwu*. vo. (T2) shake out (as with a cloth or towel). Dis. *ákkásupwu* (ds). Syn. *áásippuuw, ópuuw, wichiki*.
ássáát F. of *ássát*.
ássááw (dc; 3) See *sááw*. vi. (c.) be embarrassing, cause embarrassment. *kete á.!*; behave yourself!
ássááy See *ssá*. vo. (c.; T1) cause to run, put to flight.
ássát (3) See *ssát* N. Var. *ássáát*. va. (c.) cause a longitudinal splitting (as with a coconut leaf down the midrib center preparatory to plaiting).
ássefa See *ssef*. vo. (c.; T3) twist up, cause to be bent up.
ássi See *áás* vo. (T2) make fly.
ássiiti See *áás, -iti*. vo. (T2) fly to, fly at. *aa á. Romónum* it flew to Romónum. *wúwa á. átánaan pwe wúwa éfénú* I flew at that fellow and punched him.
ássinong See *áás*.
ássinó See *áás*.
ássipu (1) See *áás, puu-₁*. Var. *áásippu, áásipwu*. vi. wave (as a flag), be shaken out (in the wind).
ássitá See *áás*.
ássitiw See *áás*.
ássito See *áás*.
ássiwow See *áás*.
ássiwu See *áás*.
ákekkey (ds; 2) See *kkey*. vi. (c., dis.) be funny, amusing, comical.
ákká- Dis. of *á-₂*. *Routine, unambiguous ds forms of this type are not listed as separate entries but may be found under the unreduplicated words beginning with á-*.
ákkáámén See *emén*.
ákkáángoon See *engoon*.
ákkáfááyik See *fááyik*.
ákkásápwán (ds) See *ásápwán*. vi. (dis.) be windy, airy.
ákkámángngaw Dis. of *ámángngaw*.
ákkáp (2) ÁKKÁPI. N. Var. *ákkápi*. n. (T2) criticism, fault-finding. *ákkápin* c. of him. *kesapw sowun á.* don't be a fault-finder.
ákkápár (ds; 2) See *ápár*. va. (dis.) use a land plot. *wúpwe á. naan ápár* I shall use yonder land plot.

ákkápáya Dis. of *ápáya*.
ákkápi (1) ÁKKÁPII. F. Var. *ákkáp*. n. (T1) criticism; disparagement; saying something to or about a person to the effect that he is ugly or deformed. *ákkápiin* c. of him.
ákkápiiy See *ákkápi*. vo. (T1) criticize; say something derogatory or disparaging about. Dis. *ákákkápiiy* (ds).
ákkách₁ Dis. of *ách*.
ákkách₂ (ds; 3) See *ácha-*. Rmn. va. (dis.) throw repeatedly. vi. (dis.) be thrown. With dir. suf.: *ákkáchánó* be t. away.
ákkáchánó See *ákkách₂*.
ákkáchcheng (ds; 3) See *chcheng*. vi. (c., dis.) be stained with turmeric.
ákkáya See *kkáy*. vo. (c.; T3) cause to hurry, accelerate.
ákkáyeew See *eew*.
ákkeen (3) ÁKKEENA. Var. *ánneek*. nu. (T3) punting pole. *aan á.* his p. p. *ákkeenen naan waa* punting pole of that canoe. vi. punt.
ákkeena See *ánneeka*. vo. (T3) punt.
ákkey (2) ÁKKEYI. F. Var. *ekkey*. nu. (T2) fire. *aan á.* his f. *ákkeyin Chuuk* Trukese fire. Syn. *ááf*.
ákkeyissuk See *ákkey, ssuk*. vi. make fire by striking flint and steel. See *efissuk*.
ámáámááy (db) See *má*. vo. (c., dis.; T1) curse at, swear at. *ámáámááyey* c. at me; *ámáámáyók* c. at you (sg.). Cf. *ámááy*.
ámáángngawa See *máángngaw*. N. Var. *ámángngawa*. vo. (c.; T3) annoy or provoke (someone) to anger by teasing or playing a practical joke.
ámááre (1) ÁMÁÁREE. nu. (T1) any of several species of fern with alternating leaves (*Nephrolepis, Dryopteris*). [The species *Nephrolepis bisserata* is used in *itang* medicine.]
ámáári See *máár*. vo. (c.; T2) make grow (of plants).
ámáát nu. caulking compound of Trukese manufacture.
ámááy See *má*. vo. (c.; T1) stay with or attend (a dying person); curse *ámááyey* s. w. me; *ámáyók* s. w. you (sg.). Cf. *ámáámááy*.
ámááyirú (1) See *mááyirú*. vi. (c.) give an alarm.
ámááyirúúw See *ámááyirú*. vo. (c.; T1) give an alarm to, scare, frighten;

astonish, surprise. Dis. *ákkámááyirúúw* (ds).
ámáfena See *máfen.* vo. (c.; T3) embarrass, shame. Syn. *ásááwa, ekini₂.*
ámánámána See *mánámán.* vo. (c.; T3) clear (land) of grass and vegetation, prepare (ground) for cultivation. (N.) *á. échchúúw,* (F.) *ámánámánéchchúúw* clear well, clean up well. Id. *á. échchúúw fóós* speak words clearly, carefully, or distinctly.
ámánámánéchchúúw See *ámánámána.*
ámángngaw (3b) See *máá₃, ngngaw.* vi. (c.) be provoking, provocative, teasing. Dis. *ákkámángngaw* (ds). nu. (T2) scorn, derision, provoking a feeling of impotent rage.
ámángngawa F. of *ámáángngawa.*
ámára See *már.* Var. *ámera.* vo. (c.; T3) move or push (something) away, cause to be moved.
ámárás (3) ÁMÁRÁSA. N. Var. *amaras.* nu. 1. gall bladder. 2. medicine made of bark of various plants that have been pounded or grated and mixed with scented coconut oil, used to prevent or cure attacks, especially on children, of such spirits as *énúúsowusow* and *chénúkken.*
ámárása See *ámárás.* N. Var. *amarasa.* vo. (T3) medicate with *ámárás.*
ámeet (3) [Possibly from *á-₂, ma-, it.*] nu. (c.; T3) small forked stick used to strip the barbs from pandanus leaves.
ámeeta See *ámeet.* vo. (T3) strip (pandanus leaves) of barbs with an *ámeet.*
ámesepék (2) See *maas₃, pék.* nu. (c.; T2) variety of banana with large fruit.
ámera Var. of *ámára.*
ámecheresi Var. of *emecheresi.*
ámeyis (2) See *meyi-, -si-.* N. Var. *emeyis.* nu. (c.; T2) sennit sling around back of weaver at the loom. *eché á.* one sling. *ámeyisin túúr* loom sling. Syn. *éwéék, eweyit.*
ámitimit (db; 2) See *mit.* vi. (c.) be slippery. Syn. *kúmitimit, mitimit₂.*
ámmáfen (dc; 3) See *máfen.* vi. be awesome, awe-inspiring.
ámmeseyik (dc; 3) See *meseyik.* vi. (c.) cause excitement, celebrate, rejoice.
ámmeseyika See *ámmeseyik.* vo. (c.; T3) cause to be excited, cause to rejoice, make happy.

ámmeyi See *mmey.* Var. *emmeyi.* vo. (c.; T2) make taut, pull tight. Syn. *ámmeyiya, emmeyiya.*
ámmeyiya See *mmey.* Var. *emmeyiya.* vo. (c.; T3) make taut, pull tight. Syn. *ámmeyi, emmeyi.*
ámmún (2) See *á, mmún.* Var. *áámúnúmún.* vi. swim the crawl.
ámwa- (4) ÁMWE. [In cpds. only.] vi. pay a sympathetic visit to (someone who is sick). Dis. *ámwáámw* (db). Cf. *emw.*
ámwáámw Dis. of *ámwa-.*
ámwáánééch (2) See *mwáán₁, ééch.* vi. phr. (c.) behave in the respectful manner due to a middle-aged man. Syn. *ámwánnifich.*
ámwáánéchchúúw See *ámwáánéech.* Var. *ámwánniyéchchúúw.* vo. phr. (c.; T5) treat (someone) with the respect due a middle-aged man. Syn. *ámwánnifichiiy.*
ámwááni See *mwáán₁.* vo. (c.; T2) treat (someone) as a middle-aged man.
ámwááningngaw (3b) See *mwáán₁, ngngaw.* vi. (c.) treat a middle-aged man as if he were of immature years, treat someone in a manner demeaning to his station.
ámwááningngawa See *ámwááningngaw.* Var. *ámwááningngaweey.* vo. (c.; T3) treat (someone) in a manner ill befitting his or her station as a man, woman, human being, etc.
ámwááningngaweey See *ámwááningngaw, -e-₂.* vo. (c.; T6b) treat (someone) in a manner ill befitting his or her station as a man, woman, human being, etc.
ámwáánna See *mwmwáán.* N. Var. *ámwánna.* vo. (c.; T3) cause to be wrong, make incorrect. Syn. *ámwáánni.*
ámwáánni See *mwmwáán.* vo. (c.; T2) cause to be wrong, make incorrect; misrepresent. *á. fóós* misreport. With dir. suf.: *ámwáánnóónó, ámwmwáánóónó* cause to be further incorrect.
ámwáánnóónó See *ámwáánni.*
ámwáneka See *mwánek.* vo. (c.; T3) cause to be lated, excited, happy, joyful; elate, excite.
ámwánna₁ See *mwmwán.* vo. (c.; T3) let ferment, let sour. Dis. *ákkámwánna* (ds).

ámwánna₂ Var. of ámwáánna.
ámwánnifich (2) See mwáán₁, -fich. vi. conduct oneself in the respectful manner due to a middle-aged man (regardless of the actual age of others present). Syn. ámwáánééch, ámwánniyééch.
ámwánnifichiiy See ámwánnifich, -i-₂. vo. (c.; T5) treat (someone) with the respect due a middle-aged man. Syn. ámwáán échchúúw, ámwánniyéchchúúw.
ámwánniyééch (2) See mwáán₁, ééch. Var. ámwáán ééch. vi. (c.) conduct oneself in the respectful manner due to a middle-aged man, comport oneself most politely and deferentially. Syn. ámwánnifich.
ámwánniyéchchúúw See ámwánniyééch. vo. (c.; T1) treat (someone) with the respect due a middle-aged man, be most polite to. Syn. ámwáánéchchúúw, ámwánnifichiiy.
ámwára Var. of amwara.
ámwárámwára (db) See mwáár. Var. amwaramwara. vo. (c.; T3) put a garland, lei, crown, necklace, wreath on (someone); enwreath.
ámwmwáánóónó See ámwáánni.
ámwmwár (dc; 4) See mwáár. nu. (c.; T2) carrying pole (carried on the shoulder with burden a both ends). efóch á. one c. p. aan á. his c. p.
ámwmwára See ámwmwár. Var. amwmwara, ámwmwera. vo. (c.; T3) carry (something) on the shoulders (with or without a carrying pole). Dis. ákkámwmwára (ds). Syn. mwáreey.
ámwmwera Var. of ámwmwára.
ámwmwet (3) See mwmwet. vi. (c.) 1. cause a skipping or bouncing. 2. make an appeal to a higher court (in law).
ámwmweta See ámwmwet. vo. (c.; T3) 1. cause (something) to skip, jump or bounce. 2. appeal (one's case) to a higher court.
áná- ÁNÁ. [In counting const. only.] pref. sole, only. ánááw (the) only one general-class thing; ánáruwuuw (the) only two general-class things; ánáwúnúngát (the) only three general-class things; ánárúwáánú (the) only four general-class things; ánáámén (the) only one animate being; ánááfóch (the) only one cylindrical object; ánáángoon (the) only ten (lit. only one set of ten) ánárúwe (the) only twenty; ánáyipwúkú (the) only one hundred; ánáángéréw (the) only one thousand; ánáákit, ánákkit (the) only one ten-thousand.
ánáámén See emén.
ánááney Dis. of áney₁.
ánááw See eew₁.
ánáyán (db; 4) ÁNE₂. Var. áneyán. vi. wish.
ánáyáneey See ánáyán, -e-₂. vo. (T6b) wish for. wúwa á. emén piik I wished for a pig.
áneefiina See neefiin. vo. (c.; T3) 1. do wrong in front of (someone), offend against the presence of, affront. Syn. efoo,asa. 2. make room or space in (something). kepwe á. pwú epwe wor neeniyen ekkana ekkóóch pwpwuk make r. in it so there will be a place for those books.
ánees (2) ÁNEESI. nu. (T2) species of pompano or runner fish.
áneetipengngawa See neetipengngaw. vo. (c.; T3) cause to feel bitter or wronged; insult (someone).
-ánef (2?) ÁNEFI (?). [In cpds. only.] adj. (u.m.) See meseyánef.
ánemaaseni See nem, seni₂. Var. anamaaseni. vo. (c.; T2) make forget.
ánemaangeni See nem, ngeni. vo. (c.; T2) remind.
ánenga See nengi-. vo. (c.; T2) glance at, look sideways at.
ánengineng (db; 2) See nengi-. va. (c.) glance, peek, look sideways.
ánepwpwo (1) See áán₂, pwpwo. nu. (T1) a type of coral used to make breadfruit pounders.
ánecha See nech. vo. (c.; T3) cause to ring out, make resound; hit. Syn. necheey.
ánechepéw (2) See nech, paaw. vi. (c.) clap the flat of the palms of the hands together. Syn. episipis₁, ónopwonopw. Cf. ónopwonopw.
ánew (3) See new. nu. (T3) chaser, shover. ánewen méngér the planet Venus as the evening star ("chaser or shooer of flying fish"). vi. (c.) cause a fleeing or shooing (of animals only); wave the hand or fan back and forth to shoo flies. Dis. ánewenew (db).
ánewa See new. vo. (c.; T3) shoo, cause to flee, chase, run off (of animals only).
ánewenew Dis. of ánew.

ánewen ménger See *ánew.*
áney₁ (2) ÁNEYI. Var. *ánney.* vi., adj. (be) long, tall. [Preferred word in the presence of brother and sister, father and daughter, mother and son.] Dis. *ánááney* (ds?). Syn. *nangattam, ttam.* See also *-nááney.* ni. (T2) length; tallness (of people, trees). *áneyin* its l. *ifa wúkúúkún áneyin enaan iinw* what is the length of that house? *ifa áneyin ewe áát* how tall is that boy?
Áney₂ See *áney₁.* nu. Anet Island in Puluwat Atoll ("long").
áneyán Var. of *ánáyán.*
áni- See *a-₄, -ni-.* [In cpds. only.] Var. *eni-.* vi. eat (of cooked starchy food and other foods classed as *mwéngé*).
áni See *a-₄, -ni-.* Var. *eni.* vo. (T5) eat (of cooked starchy food and other foods classed as *mwéngé*).
ánis (2) See *nis.* nu. (c.; T2) assistance, aid. Dis. *áninnis* (db). vi. be helpful, give assistance, give aid.
ánisi See *ánis.* vo. (c.; T2) help, aid, assist, give assistance to.
ánimwáánniiy See *ánimwmwáán, -i-₂.* N. Var. *ánimwánniiy.* vo. (T5) eat without permission.
ánimwánniiy F. of *ánimwáánniiy.*
ánimwmwáán (2: *ánimwáánni-, ánimwánni-*) See *áni-, mwmwáán.* vi. eat without permission.
áninnis (ds; 2) See *ánis.* n. (c.; T2) assistance, help, aid. *áninnisin* a. to him, help for him.
ániyacha See *niyacha.* N. Var. *eniyacha.* vo. (c.; T3) glean (end-of-season breadfruit).
ániyopwut (3b) See *niya-, -pwut.* Var. *eniyopwut, enniyopwut, niyopwut, ninniyopwut.* vi. (c.) be nauseating; feel nausea.
ánupw (2?) ÁNUPWU (?) (*ÁNIPWU ?). nu. a star.
-ánú (1) ÁNÚÚ. suf. (cc.) unknown meaning (possibly a pair). [Only in *rúwáánú*, four.]
ánúk (2) ÁNÚKÚ (*ÁNIKÚ). nu. (T2) small pass or channel in a fringing reef. *ánúkún Neepwukos* the channel of Neepwukos. Syn. *taaw, saraata.* Cf. *mwóóch.*
ánna₁ See *áán₁.* vo. (T3) tack to; beat into the wind to. *siya á. Wééné* we tacked to Moen Island; *repwe ánnáákich* they will tack to us.

ánna₂ Var. of *áánna.*
ánnáámwa See *nne-₁, emw.* vo. (c.; T3) inspect, go to see.
ánnááni N. var. of *ángngááni.*
ánnáya (1) See *nne-₂, aa-.* Var. *ánneya.* nu. (c.; T1) reading, counting, multiplying. vi., va. (c.) read, count, do multiplication, enumerate. Dis. *ákkánnáya* (ds). Cf. *ánney, áney.*
ánnáyaasoosich See *ánnáya, soosich.* F. Var. *ánnáyaachoochis, ánnáyaasoochik.* vi. be obedient, heedful; serve, cater to the wishes of another.
ánnáyaasoosichiiy See *ánnáyaasoosich, -i-₂.* F. Var. *ánnáyaachoochisiiy.* vo. (T5) obey, heed, serve, cater to the wishes of.
ánnáyaasoonap (3b) See *ánnáya, soonap.* vi. be disobedient, heedless, unresponsive to the wishes of another. Syn. *rongonap.*
ánnáyaasoonapeey See *ánnáyaasoonap.* vo. (T6b) disobey, be heedless of, be unresponsive to.
ánnáyaasoochik (2) See *ánnáya, soochik.* vi. be obedient, heedful; serve, cater to the wishes of another.
ánnáyaasoochikiiy See *ánnáyaasoochik.* vo. (T5) obey, heed, serve, cater to the wishes of.
ánnáyaani See *ánnáya, -ni-.* Var. *ánneyaani, ánneyááni.* vo. (c.; T4) count, read, multiply.
ánnáyaachoochis (2) See *ánnáya, choochis.* N. Var. *ánnáyaasoochik, ánnáyaasoosich.* vi. be obedient, heedful; serve, cater to the wishes of another. Dis. *ákkánnáyaachoochis* (ds). *á. ónoon* heed your word.
ánnáyaachoochisiiy See *ánnáyaachoochis, -i-₂.* N. Var. *ánnáyaasoochikiiy, ánnáya choochisiiy.* vo. (T5) obey, heed, serve, cater to the wishes of.
ánneek (3) ÁNNEEKA. Var. *ákkeen.* nu. (T3) punting pole. *efóch á.* one p. p. *aan á.* his p. p. *ánneeken naan waa* punting pole of that canoe. vi., va. punt.
ánneeka See *ánneek.* Var. *ákkeena.* vo. (T3) punt.
ánneen Var. of *áánneen.*
ánneey (2) ÁNNEEYI. vi. put one's breadfruit in another person's earth oven along with the other person's breadfruit (as when one has not picked

ánneeyi

enough to make an earth oven of one's own).
ánneeyi See *ánneey.* vo. (T4) put (breadfruit) in someone else's earth oven. *wúpwe á. ee máay reemw* I shall cook this my-to-eat breadfruit at your place.
ánnenóóy See *nnenó.* vo. (c.; T1) wake, awaken, cause to wake up.
ánnepwut (3) See *nne-₃, pwuta-*, (or *-pwut).* nu. (c.; T3) a tree *(Pittosporum*, "cause bad taste"). [Its bark juice is used as a medicine and perfume.] Syn. *eyirenges.*
ánneta See *nnet.* vo. (c.; T3) 1. speak (something) truly; determine the truth of. 2. be in line with, be straight in relation to.
ánney (dc; 2) ÁNNEYI. Var. *áney.* vi. be long. [Preferred word in the presence of brother and sister, father and daughter, mother and son.] Syn. *nangattam, ttam.* ni. (T2) length, tallness (of person, tree). *ánneyiy, ánneyumw, ánneyin* my, your, his l.
ánneya Var. of *ánnáya.*
ánneyaani Var. of *ánnáyaani.*
ánneyááni Var. of *ánnáyaani.*
ánnif (3) ÁNNIFA. Var. *annif.* vi. move quietly or stealthily, sneak. Dis. *ákkánnif* (ds).
ánnifa See *ánnif.* vo. (T3) move or remove (something) quietly or stealthily.
ánnikát (4) ÁNNIKÁTE. N. nu. (T2) a tree *(Cordia subcordata). ánnikátin Chuuk* the *Cordia* of Truk. Syn. *anaw₂, anné₃.*
ánnim Var. of *annim* and the most widely used form.
ánnimey (2?) ÁNNIMEYI (?). nu. share of fish caught with a new canoe and given to the canoe-builder for his personal consumption.
ángá (1) ÁNGÁÁ. nu. (T1) Micronesian starling *(Aplonis opacus).* Syn. *mwii.*
ángeta See *nget.* vo. (c.; T3) make burst into flame, cause to blaze up.
ángngááni See *ngaa-, -ni-.* N. Var. *ánnááni* vo. (c.; T4) give (someone) food, feed. Dis. *ákkángngááni* (ds). Syn. *amwéngééni, ánnááni.*
ápár (4) ÁPÁRE. n. (T2) a land holding, land plot, land as property. *ápárin* his l. h.

ápára PÁRE₂. vo. (c.; T3) aim (something).
ápárini See *ápár, -ni-.* vo. (T2) acquire tenure in (a land plot). *wúwa á. naan ápár* I have acquired tenure in yonder land plot.
ápáya See *páy.* N. Var. *apaya, ápeya.* vo. (c.; T3) cause to lean, tilt. Dis. *ákkápáya* (ds).
ápáyas (3) ÁPÁYASA. Var. *ápeyas.* nu. (T3) basket (woman's). [Used to keep weaving materials such as fiber threads.] *eew á.* one b. *aan á.* her b. *ápáyasen Chuuk* Trukese b.
ápe (1) See *pe.* va. (c.) fight, attack.
ápeepe (db; 1) See *pe.* vi. (c., dis.) be cursed; be exhausting, killing (as hard labor). Syn. *óóttek.*
ápeepeey See *ápeepe.* vo. (c., dis.; T1) curse. Syn. *óóttekiiy.*
ápeey See *pe.* vo. (c.; T1) defeat (someone).
ápeeyun Var. of *apeewun.*
ápekkusu See *pekkus, peekkus.* vo. (c.; T2) make (someone) tired, exhaust.
ápenges Var. of *áápenges.*
ápeppeet (ds; 3a) See *ppet₂.* vi., adj. (be) shallow. Syn. *ápetpeet, petepeet.*
áper (3) ÁPERA. Var. *apar.* vi. aim, make an alignment (as with posts, plants, etc). With ind. obj.: *áperengeni* take aim at.
ápera See *áper.* Var. *apara.* vo. (T3) aim at, line (something) up, align.
áperengngaw (3b) See *áper, ngngaw.* Var. *aparangngaw.* nu. (T3) poor aim, poor marksmanship. vi., va. be of poor aim, be badly aimed, badly aligned; do to another what one would not have done to oneself.
áperééch (2: *áperééchchú-*) See *áper, ééch.* Var. *aparééch.* nu. (T2) good aim, good marksmanship. vi. be of good aim, be well aimed, be well aligned.
ápetpeet (db; 4) See *ppet₂.* Wmn. vi. (c.) be shallow (of the sea). *ápetpeetin eey neeni* the shallowness of this place. Syn. *ápeppeet, petepeet.*
ápeya Var. of *ápáya.*
ápeyas Var. of *ápáyas.*
ápi- Var. of *epi-₁.*
ápiinen (2) See *epi-₁, neni-₁.* Var. *epiineng.* nu. (T2) horizon. Syn. *óroppeyinen.*
ápiipi (db; 1) See *pi.* nu. (c.; dis.; T1) driftwood, flotsam. *efóch á.* one piece of d.

ápinúkééch (2) See *ep, núuk*₁, *ééch.* N. Var. *epinúkééch.* nu. (T2) optimism. Dis. *ápinúkúnúkééch* (db). Cf. *ápinúkúnúk.* vi. be optimistic, be of good cheer.

ápinúkúnúk (2) See *ep, núúk*₁. N. Var. *epinúkúnúk.* nu. (T2) optimism. *aan ápinúkúnúk* his o. vi. be optimistic.

ápinúkúngngaw (3b) See *ep, núúk*₁, *ngngaw.* N. Var. *epinúkúngngaw.* nu. (T3) pessimism. vi. be pessimistic, be discouraged. Dis. *ápinúkúnúkúngngaw* (db).

ápuuch nu. a tree (*Cretaeva* sp.). [The fruit is eaten; leaves were formerly used as medicine for yaws; the fragrant fruit is used to make garlands; the bark is mixed with saffron and coconut oil as a medicine for skin disease.]

áppán (4) See *ppán.* nu. (c.; T2) a very light driftwood (formerly used to make pillows). *áppánin neeset* the sea's d. vi. be causing to be light, be making light (in weight). Id. *wútaan á.* a medicine to make a slow baby learn to crawl.

áppána See *ppán.* vo. (c.; T3) lighten, make light (in weight).

áppánéw nu. a medicine and spell to treat stingray spear wounds.

áppep (3) See *ppep.* va. (c.) skip (stones).

áppepa See *ppep.* vo. (c.; T3) skip (a stone), cause to skip or bounce along a surface (as on the sea). With n. form. suf.: *áppepaaya-* skipping done (by someone).

ápwá (1) See *pwá.* nu. (c.; T1) gathering or picking (of breadfruit) to be cooked in an earth oven. *ápwáán mááy* the picking of breadfruit for cooking in an earth oven. vi. pick breadfruit for cooking in an earth oven.

ápwááki See *pwáák.* vo. (c.; T4) wait for the recovery of (a sick person), wait for the repair of; fix, repair, cure. Syn. *áchikara.*

ápwáámeerer See *ápwá, meerer.* vi. (c.) pick breadfruit a day ahead of its cooking.

ápwááni See *ápwá, -ni-.* vo. (T4) pick (breadfruit) for cooking in an earth oven.

ápwen (2) See *pwáán.* nu. (c.; T2) teaching, learning, or performance of *pwáán* (judo, rigging, righting overturned canoes). *ápwenin waa* righting of an overturned canoe.

ápweni See *pwáán.* vo. (c.; T2) teach (someone) the art of *pwáán* (judo, rigging, righting overturned canoes).

ápwenna See *pween*₁. vo. (c.; T3) plant (a breadfruit shoot).

ápwereka (1) ÁPWEREKAA. Var. *pwereka.* nu. (T1) a wild yam, tuber and vine (*Dioscorea bulbifera*). [It produces a poor quality yam, very bitter in taste, that is eaten in famines; the pounded fruit is used in steam treatment of swelling of the scrotum.] *ápwerekaan Chuuk* Trukese y.

ápwerika Var. of *epwerika.*

ápwecha See *pwech.* vo. (c.; T3) whiten, make white.

ápwich (2) See *pwich*₁. N. Var. *epwich.* nu. (c.; T2) heating, making hot.

ápwichi See *pwich*₁. N. Var. *epwichi.* vo. (c.; T2) heat, make hot.

ápwpwer (2) ÁPWPWERI. nu. (T2) branching coral. Syn. *áán.* Cf. *anget, angnget, anang.*

ápwpwur (3) See *áá-*₁, *pwpwur*₂. nu. (T3) a tree (*Glochidion puberulum* or *Callicarpa*). [The leathery bark is used for soap; the wood is used for booms on model canoes.]

ár₁ (3a) ÁRA (*ARE). vi. be surrounded; be consumed (of food); be finished (from fishing). With dir. suf.: *árenó* be entirely consumed away; *aretá me neeset* be finished with fishing; *kene árenong, kete semwmwen* finish and go in lest you be sick.

ár₂ (4) ÁRE. vi. be selected, chosen; elected. *wúwa ár nnón ewe wúttúút* I was elected in the election.

árá N. var. of *ará, erá.*

árááni See *rááṇ*₂. vo. (c.; T4) wait for (day to dawn). *siya á. ewe rááṇ* we waited for the day.

áráápinni See *ráá-, pinni.* N. vo. (c.; T2) twist, wring (anything except coconut cream). Syn. *áráápiti.*

áráápiti See *ráá-, piti.* F. vo. (c.; T2) twist, wring (anything except coconut cream). Syn. *áráápinni.*

árámás Wn. of *aramás.*

áreere (db; 1) ÁREE. vi. be uncertain; suppose; try one's luck, take a chance. *aa á. ika meyi wor ika esoor* he is waiting to see whether there is or there is not. *sipwe chék á. ika meyi manaw ika meyi máánó* we shall just wait and see if he is alive or he is

árenong

dead. *wúwa á. ika meyiwor gé wúse wesewesen sineey* I am waiting to see if there is, but I don't really know. *wúpwe chék á. ika wúpwe páás* I will just try my luck to see if I will pass. Cf. *are*.

árenong See *ár₁*.

árenó See *ár₁*.

árer vi. clear the throat.

áretá See *ár₁*.

áretong See *tong*. vi. smart, sting (as of salt on a wound). Dis. *ákkáretong* (ds).

ách (4) ÁCHE. vi. shift sail from one end of a canoe to the other in coming about; change course. Dis. *ákkách* (ds). With dir. suf.: *áchánó, áchenó* s. s. to head away; *áchátá* s. s. to head up or east; *áchenong* s. s. to head in or south; *ácheto* s. s. to head hither; *áchitiw, áchetiw* s. s. to head down or east, *áchiwu, áchewu* s. s. to head out or north.

ácha- (3) ÁCHA. Rmn. [In cpds. only.] unsp. throw; thrown.

áchánó See *ách*.

áchátá₁ See *ách*.

áchátá₂ (1) See *ácha-, -tá*. Var. *áchetá*. nu. (T1) coughing up (as in choking because of food or water, as distinct from coughing up phlegm). *áchátáán mwéngé* coughing up of food. vi. cough up. *á. reen anan we kkón* cough up because of his breadfruit pudding.

ácheenonga See *cheenong*. vo. (c.; T3) let in, admit to membership (in a clan or lineage only). *sipwe á. átánaan nóón eey eyinang* we shall admit that fellow to membership in this clan. Cf. *cheenongeey*.

ácheey See *ácha-*. F. vo. (T6b) throw. With dir. suf.: *ácheeyenong, ácheeyenó, ácheeyeto*. Syn. *móneey*.

ácheeyenong See *ácheey*.

ácheeyenó See *ácheey*.

ácheeyeto See *ácheey*.

áchefenget nu. kind of branching coral.

ácheféw (2) See *che-, faaw*. nu. (c.; T2) caulking material. [It is prepared from coral lime (*pweech*) extracted from *féwúrupw* coral, from charcoal made from the coconut blossom sheath (*moochen epúnget*), and from breadfruit sap (*appachen mááy*).]

ácheféwúúw See *ácheféw, -ú-*. vo. (T5) caulk.

Trukese-English

áchemay (3) See *che-* (?), *maay*. F. nu. (c.; T3) method of driving fish into stone fish traps.

áchemwir (2) See *che-, mwiri-*. nu. (c.; T2) a magic that makes people unable to function in sports or warfare ("causing condition of being behind").

áchen (2) ÁCHENI. nu. (T2) ornamental board carved in form of two facing frigate birds and placed on top of the end-pieces of a paddle canoe. *áchenin waa* canoe's o.b.

áchenechen (db; 3) See *chene-*. nu. (c.; dis.; T3) a shrub (*Polyscias*).

áchenong See *ách*.

áchenó See *ách*.

áchengicheng (db; 2) See *chengi-*. nu. (c., dis.; T2) love, favor, cherish. *áchengichengiy me reemw* my love of you; *áchengichengumw me reey* your love of me. Syn. *cheni-*. vi., adj. (be) dear (esp. in address), beloved. *á. paapa me maama* d. papa and mama.

áchechcha See *chcheech₂*. Var. *áchchecha*. vo. (c.; T3) make tremble, shake. Dis. *ákkáchechcha* (ds).

áchechchem (ds; 3) See *chchem*. nu. (c.; T3) memorial, reminder. *áchechchemen Eiue* thing in memory of Eiue. *féwún á*. memorial stone.

áchechchemeni (ds) See *áchechchem, -ni-*. vo. (c.; T5) commemorate, make a memorial for. nu. (c.; T3) remembrance, reminder, memorial, souvenir. *áchechcheminiyan* remembrance of him.

áchetá See *ách*.

áchetiw See *ách*.

ácheto See *ách*.

áchewu See *ách*.

áchi (1) ÁCHII. nu. (T1) palm toddy (usually in its fermented state), palm wine; alcoholic beverage, liquor. *wúnúman á*. his toddy to drink; *áchiin Merika* American liquor.

áchiin nu. a kind of banana.

áchiiyar (3) See *áchi, ar*. nu. (T3) palm toddy (sweet, unfermented). Ant. *áchimwmwán*.

áchiiyu (1) ÁCHIIYUU. nu. a tree (*Ixoro carolensi*; red fruit).

áchiféw (2) ÁCHIFÉWÚ. nu. (T2) faith, belief (in elegant speech). vi. be true (in elegant speech as contrasted with *pwúng*). Syn. *áchiyéw*.

áchiféwúwa See *áchiféw*. vo. (T3) believe, accept as true. *wúwa á. aan fóós* I believe his talk.
áchiki See *chiki-₂*. N. Var. *echiki*. vo. (c.; T2) blink (one's eyes) in weariness. Dis. *áchikichiki* (db). *wúwa á. mesey* I am blinking my eyes, I am sleepy.
áchikichik (db; 2) See *chiki-₂*. N. Var. *echikichik*. vi. (c., dis.) be sleepy. *aa á. átánaan* that fellow is s.
áchikichiki Dis. of *áchiki*.
áchikun nu. a kind of shellfish.
áchimwmwán (3: *áchiimwánna-*) See *áchi, mwmwán*. nu. (T3) palm toddy (fermented), palm wine.
áchin nu. variety of banana.
áchingi- (2) ÁCHINGI. [In cpds. only.] unsp. (u.m.) See *áchingipa*.
áchinginipa (1) See *áchingi-, paa₂*. N. nu. (T1) remnant of bait on a hook.
áchichchin (ds; 2) See *chin*. vi. (c., dis.) be a cry baby ("cause eyes to be puffy").
áchitiw See *ách*.
áchiwu See *ách*.
áchiyéw (2) ÁCHIYÉWÚ. vi. be true (in elegant speech as contrasted with *pwúng*). *á. kepwe nó Wééné ikenáy?* is it t. that you will go to Wééné today? Syn. *áchiféw*.
áchcha See *ách*. vo. (T3) to bring (a canoe) about by shifting sail.
áchchema See *chchem*. vo. (c.; T3) remind (someone), cause to remember.
áchchenga See *chcheng*. vo. (c.; T3) stain with turmeric or saffron.
áchchenges See *chcheng, -s₂*. n. (c.) offering of goods to an *énúúsór* spirit.
áchchepéw (2) See *chche-₃, paaw₁*. vi. (c.) shake, wave, or jerk one's hands.
áchcheriwa See *chcheriw*. vo. (c.; T3) cause to shine or gleam; shine, polish.
áchcherúwa Var. of *áchcheriwa*.
áchchecha Var. of *áchechcha*.
áchchewucha See *chchewuuch*. F. vo. (c.; T3) cause to ache, make painful. Dis. *ákkáchchewucha* (ds). Syn. *emeteki*.
áchchén (2) See *áá-₁, chchén₁*. Tb. vi. urinate; piss. Syn. *chuuchu*.
áchchi- (db; 4) See *ách*. nr. (T2) shifting sail in coming about. *meyi weyires áchchin eey waa* this canoe is hard to bring about.

áchchik (3) ÁCHCHIKA. n. (T3) lack (of something). *áchchikan* l. of it. Cf. *echik*.
áchchika See *áchchik*. vo. (T3) feel the lack of, miss. Dis. *ákkáchchika* (ds).
áchchinimá (1) See *chchin, má*. vi. (c.) be about to die, on the brink of death.
áta- (3b) ÁTA (*ATE). [In cpds. only.] pref. man, fellow, male person. Syn. *wono-₁*. Ant. *niya-, niye-*. Cf. *áát, nemin*.
átaangas (3) See *áta-, angas*. Var. *áteyangas*. nu. (T3) person who is industrious and naturally capable of effectively accomplishing all kinds of work.
átákkaan Dis. of *áteen*.
átákkana Dis. of *átána*.
átákkanaan Dis. of *átánaan*.
átámaraan (2) ÁTÁMARAANÚ. (Eng.) nu. (T2) admiral, general. *átámaraanún neyifi* naval admiral; *átámaraanún sowunfiyuuw* army general.
átámwaken (3) See *áta-, mwaken*. nu. (T3) liar.
átámwáán See *áta-, mwáán₁*. N. nu. a male, one of male sex (of animals). Syn. *niyamwáán, niyemwáán*. Ant. *niyefeefin*.
átána See *áta-, na*. nu. (dem.) that fellow or male person (near hearer or just mentioned). Dis. *átákkana* those fellows. Syn. *wonna*.
átánaan See *áta-, naan*. nu. (dem.) that fellow (male) yonder. Dis. *átákkanaan* those fellows. Syn. *wonnaan*.
átánecha See *tánech*. vo. (c.; T3) make inattentive.
átángngaw (3b) See *áta-, ngngaw*. Var. *átengngaw*. nu. (T3) ugly, ill-favored, deformed person (of males). Ant. *áteyééch*. Cf. *niyengngaw*.
átápa See *táp*. vo. (c.; T3) cause to be faded, make dull in gloss or brilliance (of the color of clothes, of the glossiness of greased hair).
átápwara (1) See *áta-, pwara*. Var. *átepwara*. nu. (T1) fierce, brave fellow; champion.
áteen See *áta-, een₃*. nu. (dem.) this fellow or male person (near both speaker and hearer). Dis. *átekkaan* these fellows. Syn. *woneen*.
áteey₁ See *te*. vo. (c.; T1) cause to be learned; teach (something) to (with

áteey₂

ngeni). kepwe á. ngeniyey ewe kkéén teach me that song.
áteey₂ See áta-, eey₁. nu. (dem.) this fellow (male) by me. Dis. átekkeey these fellows. Syn. woneey.
átefén̄g (2) See áta-, fén̄g. nu. (T2) man who is popular with women. vi. be much sought after by women.
átefewúnó Var. of átefowunó.
átefowunó (1) See áta-, fowunó. Var. átefewúnó. nu. (T1) famous man.
átefón (4) See áta-, fón. nu. (T3) pampered fellow. Syn. átepwó.
átek (2) See teki-. Var. atek, etek. vi. (c.) engage in towing, dragging, pulling.
átekini See teki-, -ni-. Var. atekini, etekini. vo. (c.; T5) tow, drag, pull.
átekuus See áta-, kuus₁. F. nu. industrious, able fellow. Syn. átepwáák.
átekkeey Dis. of áteey.
átekkemwuun Dis. of átemwuun.
átekkewe Dis. of átewe.
átekkoomw Dis. of átoomw.
átemeet See áta-, meet₁. nu. (inter.) person of what sex? Syn. niyemeet.
átemésékúta (1) See áta-, mésék, ta. nu. (T1) coward (used with either sex). emén á. one c. Syn. nissimwa.
átemmón̄g (4) See áta-, mmón̄g. nu. (T2) big man; fat man.
átemwoot See áta-, mwoot₁. nu. man skilled in hand-to-hand fighting. vi. be such a man.
átemwuun See áta-, -mwuun. N. nu. (dem.) that fellow, that male person (near person addressed). Dis. átekkemwuun those fellows. Syn. átána, átoomw, wonoomw.
átemwuk (3a) See áta-, mwuk₁. nu. (T3) male dwarf. vi. be a m. d.
átemwmwung (3) See áta-, mwmwung. nu. (T3) man who is much liked by women, a lady's man. vi. be such a man.
áten (2) See ten₂. vi. (c.) form a line, go in single file.
áteni See áten. Var. eteni₂. vo. (c.; T2) cause to form a line, put in single file.
áteniyap (3) See áta-, niyap. nu. (T3) successful fisherman.
átepa See tep₁. vo. (c.; T3) make numerous.
átepwara Var. of átápwara.

Trukese-English

átepwáák (2) See áta-, pwáák. N. nu. (T2) industrious fellow. Syn. átekuus. vi. be industrious; (of a man).
átepwó (1) See áta-, pwó. nu. (T1) pampered fellow (male). Syn. átefón.
áterepep (3) See tere-, -pep. va. (c.) skip (stones); be make to skip or bounce along a surface (as on the sea).
átereppepa See tere-, ppep. vo. (c.; T3) cause to skip (as a stone on the sea).
áteri See ter₁. vo. (c.; T2) strip (as land by a tidal wave or leaves from a tree); lay waste, ruin, devastate.
átechófó (1) See áta-, chófó. nu. (T1) industrious, able fellow.
átewe (1) See áta-, -we. nu. (dem.) that fellow (male) (out of sight or past), the male person of reference (in narrative). Dis. átekkewe those fellows. Syn. wonowe. Cf. ewe áát that boy.
átewoch (3) See áta-, woch. nu. (T3) long lived fellow.
átewocheey aramas See áta-, wocheey. n. phr. cannibal ("eat-people-fellow").
átewochooch aramas (db; 3) See áta-, wochooch. n. phr. (dis.) cannibal ("eat-people-fellow").
áteyangas Var. of átaangas.
áteyééch (2) See áta-, ééch. Var. átééch. nu. (T2) handsome person, one pleasing to behold (of males). Ant. átán̄gngaw. Cf. niyayééch.
átééch N. of áteyééch.
átiisow (2) See áát, sowu-₁. Itang. nu. (T2) title of the magistrate or mayor as used on Wuumaan (Uman) Island.
átiisómw See áát, -sómw. Itang. nu. man or men of a chiefly clan.
átinimwár (4) See áát, mwáár. Itang. nu. (T2, T3) man or men of a commoner clan.
átittin₁ (ds; 3) See ttin₁. N. Var. etittin. nu. (c.; T3) examination, investigation, interrogation.
átittin₂ (ds; 2) See tini-₂. va. (c.) take only a little.
átittina See átittin₁. N. Var. etittina. vo. (c.; T3) provide a light for, provide illumination for, shed light on; examine, investigate, inquire of, interrogate.
átittini See átittin₂. vo. (c.; T2) take only a little of (something). kete á., angeey pwan ekkóóch don't take so few of them, take some more.

átoomw See *áta-, oomw.* F. nu. (dem.) that fellow (male, near hearer). Dis. *átekkoomw* those fellows. Syn. *átemwuun, wonoomw.*

átter (dc; 2) See *ter*$_1$. nu. (c.; T2) sweeping blows of knife or club from side to side (a method of approaching an opponent). vi. to swing a knife, whip, or club from side to side.

átteri See *átter.* vo. (c.; T2) make swinging blows at. *raa á. pétéwén ngeni nááyif* they mow down the vegetation with knives.

áttik (2) See *ttik*$_1$. N. Var. *ettik.* nu. (c.; T2) the act of making something sound. *áttikin kitar* playing a guitar. vi. engage in causing to sound, engage in playing (an instrument), make one squeal (as by poking or tickling one in the ribs); whistle between the teeth.

áttiki See *ttik*$_1$. N. Var. *ettiki.* vo. (c.; T2) play (an instrument), whistle to (between the teeth); make (someone) squeal (as by tickling or poking in the ribs).

áttikipwo (1) See *ttik*$_1$, *-pwo. N.* Var. *ettikipwo.* nu. (c.; T1) tickling, act of tickling. vi. engage in tickling.

áttikipwoow See *áttikipwo.* N. Var. *ettikipwoow.* vo. (c.; T1) tickle (someone).

áttina See *ttin*$_1$. N. Var. *ettina.* vo. (c.; T3) make shine, light (a lamp). With dir. suf.: *áttinaatá* make shine brighter, turn (a lamp) up.

áttinaatá See *áttina.*

áttu Var. of *attu.*

áwááyichón (4) See *waal, chón.* nu. (c.; T2, T3) the projection that, when painted black, forms the upper band of black from end to end on the outer side of the hull of a *meniyuk* sailing canoe.

áwátteey See *wáttwe.* vo. (c.; T1) make big, enlarge. With dir. suf.: *áwátteeyenó* make bigger, enlarge further.

áwátteeyenó See *áwátteey.*

áwees (2) See *wees.* vi. (c.) finish, make an ending. *á. meerer* make an ending a day ahead of time.

áweesi See *wees.* F. Var. *aweesi.* vo. (c.; T2) finish, cause to be done, complete. With dir. suf.: *áweesóónó* (F.), *aweesaanó* (N.) finish off, finish up.

áweesóónó See *áweesi.*

áweewe (db; 1) See *weewe.* F. Var. *aweewe.* nu. (T1) explanation. vi. explain, engage in explaining, make something intelligible. With *ngeni*: *áweeweengeni* explain to (someone).

áweeweengeni See *áweewe.*

áweeweey See *áweewe.* vo. (c.; T1) explain, interpret, make intelligible, give the meaning of. *áweeweer ngonuk e.* them to you.

áweeweffengeen (2) See *áweewe, ffengeen.* vi. (c.) make a comparison. Syn. *anéénéffengen.*

áweeweffengenniiy See *áweewe, ffengeen, -i-*$_2$. vo. (c.; T5) compare.

áwesewesa- (db; 3) See *wesewesa-.* [In ptv. const. only.] ni. (loc.; T3) in a line with (something). *áwesewesan* in a l. with it. *áwesewesen eey tiniw* in a l. with this wall plate.

áwesewesa (db) See *wesewesa-.* vo. (c.; T3) bring into alignment with; make even with; make (something) be in line. With *ngeni*: *áwesewesaangeni* be or bring in line in relation to (something). With dir. suf.: *áwesewesáátá* bring up into alignment with.

áwesewesaangeni See *áwesewesa.*

áwesewesáátá See *áwesewesa.*

áwena See *wen.* vo. (c.; T3) straighten, make straight. Dis. *áwenewena* (db) put in a line; align with.

áwenechchara See *wen, -chchar.* vo. (c.; T3) straighten (something) out; tell the truth about (something).

áwenewena Dis. of *áwena.*

áweyires (2) See *weyires.* nu. (c.; T2) making difficulty.

áweyiresi See *weyires.* vo. (c.; T2) make (something) difficult.

áwiisa See *wiis.* N. Var. *ewiisa.* vo. (c.; T3) assign, apportion a share of (something). *sómwoon epwe á. néwún aramas eey mwéngé* the chief will apportion to his people this food.

áwiiwi (db; 1) See *wii-*$_1$. N. Var. *ewiiwi.* vi. (c.) alternate, exchange, change off, trade, swap. Dis. *ákkáwiiwi* (ds). Syn. *ekkesiiwin.*

áyeewi- (2) See *eew.* Tn. [In ptv. const. only.] ni. (T2) first. Dis. *akkáyewi-* (ds). *áyeewin* first one; the first. *ákkáyeewin* first ones; the first (pl.).

áyééw See *é*. Var. *ayééw*. vo. (c.; T1) teach, cause to be learned. [Used with *ngeni*.] Dis. *ákkáyééw* (ds). *ewe chóón fféér kkéén aa á. ngeni kkewe aramas ewe kkéén* the composer taught the song to the people.

áyi- (2) ÁYI. Wn. (Sópwúúk), Tns. (Kuchuwa). Var. *éwú-, eyi-*₃. pref. (sub.) 1exc. sub. prn.: we (not including person addressed).

áyimwu Tws. of *eyimwu*.

áyinepwoch (P.Eng.) Var. *eyinepwóch*. nu. cooking pot, pan, metal cooking vessel.

áyiti Var. of *eyiti*.

áyitingeni Var. of *ááyitingeni*.

áyiye- (3) ÁYIYA. N. [In cpds. only.] Var. *eyiye-*. unsp. condition, state of being. See *áyiyengngaw, áyiyekunukun*.

áyiyeer vi. reform, change one' conduct for the better, "turn over a new leaf;" stand in church and publicly renounce one's former ways.

áyiyesumw (2) See *áyiye-, sumw*. N. Var. *eyiyesumw*. vi. be droopy, floppy (of things).

áyiyessumw (1) See *áyiye-, sumw*. N. Var. *eyiyessumw*. vi. nod the head with sleepiness.

áyiyekunukun (2) See *áyiye-, kun*. N. Var. *eyiyekunukun*. nu. (T2) flickering. vi. flicker.

áyiyengngaw (3b) See *áyiye-, ngngaw*. N. Var. *eyiyengngaw*. nu. (T3) listlessness. vi. be listless.

E

e-₁ E₁. [The standard form; variant forms only in rapid colloquial or *itang* speech.] Var. *a-₁, á-₁, i-₁, ó-₁.* pref. (sub.) 3sg. sub. prn.: he, she, it. [Although a prefix, it is written separately except when followed by an aspect marker. Sub. prns. are used only at the beginning of narrative constructions and mark them as such.] *epwaapw* (indefinite future), *epwe* (future), *epwene* (uncertain future), *esapw* (future negative), *ese* (negative reality), *ete* (purposeful future negative, negative command). See also *aa*.

e-₂ E₂. Var. *i-₂.* pref. (num.) one; a, an; another. [Used with suffixed forms indicating the class of unit enumerated.] *fitemén? emén* how many persons? one person; *wúwa chuuri emén mwáán* I met a man; *sapw iiy, emén* not he, another person. See *echamw, echchi, echchooch, echef₂, eché, echú, echúk, eef₃, eem₂, eféw, effaat, effit, efich₁, efóch, efutuk, engaf, engát, engéréw, engin, engoon, ekis₂, ekit, ekkamw, ekkap, ekkóóch, ekkumw, ekum, ekumwuch, ekup, emach, emas, emataf, emech, emeech, emeet, emén, emma, emmech, emmék, emwénú, emwmwék, emwmwun, emwmwú, emwmwún, emwu, emwú₁, emwú₂, emwúch, ennú, epa, epachang, epan, epeche, epeek, epé, epék, epéw, epino₂, epinúk, epu, epwang, epwey, epwéét, epwi, epwin, epwopw, epwór, epwpwaaw, epwpwún, epwún, esap, esángá, esáwá, eseeng, esen, esópw₁, esópw₂, essaar, essak, essar, essáát, essát, essupw, etáp, etinewupw, etip₁, etit, ettiit, ettún, etú, etúkúm, etún, ewo, ewoch, ewumw, ewupw, ewut₁, ewut₂, ewúk₁, ewúk₂, ewún, ewút, ewúwéw, eyaf, eyang, eyef, eyem, eyep, eyé, eyék, eyi, eyin₃, eyin₄, eyipw, eyiyey, eyó.*

e-₃ See *a-₂.* [Usually in this form in F. dialects when the next following vowel is *e* or *i* .] pref. (c.) imparts causative meaning to the base. Dis. *ekke-* (ds).

e-₄ E₃. [Possibly derived from *e-₂.*] pref. (form.) occurs only with preposed demonstratives. [In N. dialects in *eey, ena, enaan, emwuun, ewe ekkeey, ekkana, ekkena, ekkanaan, ekkaan, ekkemwun, ekkoomw, ekkewe*; in F. dialects in *eey, ewe* only.]

-e-₁ E₄. [Occurs only with numeral bases of c.f. type 3, to form a new base of c.f. type 1. Like all base-final vowels, it is dropped in the absence of a following suffix.] Var. *-ik.* suf. (cc.) unit of ten. *rúwe* twenty, *erúween* twentieth one; *nime* fifty, *enimeen* fiftieth one; *wone* sixty, *owoneen* sixtieth one; *ttiwe* ninety, *ettiween* ninetieth one. *fite* how many specific objects (more than a few and less than hundreds, but without limitations to units of ten).

-e-₂ E₅. [Occurs only with bases of c.f. types 3 and 4.] suf. (v.form.) makes an object focussed verb of the base. *nume-e-y* bail it *(num).*

ee₁ (1) EE. nu. (T1) name of the mid, front, unrounded vowel written *e*; name of the letter thus written.

ee₂ interj. deferential response of inquiry to someone's call. [Used with *ko* or *o* to a man and with *ne* to a woman.] *ee ko?* What is it, sir?

ee₃ interrog. interj. indicating a question (comes at the end of the querry). Syn. *áá.*

eef₁ (2) EFI₁. nu. (T2), suf. (cc.) bunch of ten (of ripe coconuts only). *eyef* or *eef, rúwéyef, wúnúyef, féyef, nimeyef* or *nimeef, wonoyef, fúúyef, wanúyef, ttiweyef* or *ttiweef, engoon efin* one,...ten b. *efin taka* b. of t. ripe coconuts.

eef₂ (2) EEFI. F. nu. (T2) coconut crab. *eew e.* one c. c. *eefin Chuuk* Trukese c. c. Syn. *amwatang, ménúté.*

eef₃ Var. of *eyef.*

eek (2) EKI₂. nu. (T2) kind of turmeric. [Leaves used in love magic by having a spell and medicine made on them in a woman's name, after which they are made into a garland that is worn for several days until it is dry, whereupon it is burned on a fire, and then the

eekita-

woman is said to be irresistably attracted to the man.] *ekin Chuuk Trukese t.*
eekita- See *ekit.*
eem$_1$ (2) EMI$_1$. nu. (T2), suf. (cc.) earlobe. *eyem, rúwéyem, wúnúyem, féyem, nimeyem, wonoyem, fúúyem, wanúyem, ttiweyem* one,...nine e. *emin sening* lobe of the ear.
eem$_2$ Var. of *eyem.*
Een$_1$ (Eng.) nu. Hell.
een$_2$ prn. (pers.) thou, you (sg.). *een na?* is that you? *een iyé* who are you? *een chék!* suit yourself! just as you like!
een$_3$ [Regularly precedes the noun, but follows *peek.*] prn. (dem.) this (near the speaker and person addressed); this (about to be); the next (in temporal const.). Dis. (N.) *ekkaan* (dc with pref.), (F.) *kkaan* (dc). *een mwáán* this man here; *ekkaan mwáán* these men here. *een wiik* next week (cf. *eey wiik*).
een$_4$ (3a, 2) EENA, EENI. n. (T3) spreading of leaves or grass on a surface (of coconut leaves or grass on a house floor, of grass on stones of the earth oven). *eenan* his spreading material. *eenen iimw* floor-spreading of the house. Cf. *wuwas.*
een$_5$ (3: *-en*) ENNA. vi. be shot (as by a spear, bullet, arrow). Dis. *ekkeen* (ds). *aa e. naan machchang reey* that bird was shot by me.
een$_6$ [Used with *me* or *mé.* May be derived from *een$_3$.*] nu. each (of several). *raa niwitto wóón e. mé fénúwan* they returned hither each on his own land. vi. be each (of several). *raa e. me niwiniiti fénúwan* each of them ("they were each and") returned to his land.
eenen (3a) See *een$_4$, -ni-.* vi. put grass on something (as on the stones of an earth oven before putting the food in to cook).
eeneni See *een$_4$, -ni-.* vo. (T5) spread leaves or grass on, spread (something) with leaves or grass. With dir. suf.: *eenenóónó* spread (something) off with leaves or grass; *kepwe eenenóónó na wuumw pwúyi epwe eeninó pwichikkaran* you shall spread that oven off with leaves (or grass) so that its heat will be spread over.
eenenóónó See *eeneni.*

Trukese-English

eeninó (1) See *een$_4$, -nó.* vi. be spread over with leaves or grass (as a house floor or earth oven).
eeng (2) ENGI. Tb1. nu. (T2) genital odor. Dis. *engiyeng* (db). *engiyengin átánaan!* the genital odor of that fellow! Cf. *tteneng.*
eengéréwú- See *engéréw.*
eengéréwú See *engéréw.*
eengi (2, 3) EENGII, EENGIYA. nu. (T2, T3) a strand tree (*Pemphis acidula*). [Hard wood used for clubs and coconut-husking stakes; flowers used as medicine for stomach disorders and diarrhea; used also in hot massage to give strength to children.] (F.) *eengiin fááyinón* or *eengiin fáániinón,* (N.) *eengiyen fááyinón* or *eengiyen fáániinón* species of sea shrub found at considerable depths.
eengoona- See *engoon.*
eengoona See *engoon.*
eengoonu- See *engoon.*
eengoonu See *engoon.*
eep (2) EPPI. Var. *kááp.* nu. (T2) yam (*Dioscorea alata*). [Used as food.] *eféw e.* one y. (tuber). *eppin Chuuk Trukese* y.
eermaano (1) EERMAANOO. (Sp. *hermano*) nu. (T1) catholic lay brother.
eet$_1$ *ETTA. [From an original *etata*, which became *etta* of which *eet* is the independent form. In serial counting the second syllable of *etta* came to be part of the word for "two" *rúúw*, giving rise to the present *ttérúúw, érúúw.*] nu. the number one. [Used in serial counting or to name the number in the abstract, but not used as a numerical adjective.] *eet, ttérúúw, één, fáán* one, two, three, four. Cf. *e-$_2$.*
eet$_2$ (2) ETI$_1$. n. (T2) chin. *eew e.* one c. *etin* his c.
eet$_3$ (2) ETI$_2$. nu. (T2) unopened sheath or pod of a banana or coconut tree in which the immature fruit first begins to form. *efóch e.* one pod. *etin wuuch* banana pod. vi. form a sheath or pod of immature fruit.
eew$_1$ (2) EEWI. [It precedes the word for the thing being enumerated.] nu. (num.; T2) one general-class of thing; another one, a different one. *e. iimw* one house; *eewú chék* or *eewi chék* only one, just one. *sapw ina, e.* not

that, another one; *e. sóókkun* another kind. *fáán e.* once, one time, some day, some time. *pwan e.* once more, once again. *Tiisamper e. ekkewe maramen afééw* December is one [of] the cold (chilly) months. With c. pref. and ptv. const.: (N.) *ayeewin* or *áyeewin*, (F.) *eewin* first. With dis. c. pref.: *ákkáyeew* be one at a time, one by one, by ones. With pref. *áná-*: *anááw* only one, sole, one and only. With pref. *emwi-*: *emwiyeew* only one (in counting breadfruit only).

eew₂ nu. 28th night of the lunar month.

eewin See *eew*₁.

eewúr nu. 17th night of the lunar month.

eey₁ (2: *-ey*) EEYI. [Regularly precedes the noun except in possessive constructions, when it follows the word with the suf. pos. prn. It is suffixed to *áte-, iimw, nemin, chóó,* and follows *peek*.] prn. (dem.) this (associated with the speaker). Dis. *ekkeey* (N.), *kkeey* (F.) these. *eey meen* this thing; *ááy eey meen* this thing of mine; *neyiy eey áát* this son of mine. Cf. *een, ena, enaan, oomw, ewe*.

eey₂ prn. (loc.) here (by the speaker). [Said to be a little more abrupt than *ikeey*.] *ngaang eey* me here, it's me; *eey iye* (N.) here, this place (F. *ikeey iya*).

eey₃ F. prn. (dem.) who (among several), whoever. *e. i miriit neeyimi* whoever understands among you. Syn. *ekka, engát*.

ef (2) EFI₃. vi. pull on a line; be pulled, drawn (as a curtain). Dis. *efiyef* (db). With dir. suf.: *efitá* be pulled up (as a shirt).

efeefina See *feefin*. vo. (c.; T3) allow or enable (someone) to grow into a woman.

efesira See *fesir*. vo. (c.; T3) educate, socialize, reform, tame, pet.

efen₁ (2) EFENI₁. nu. (T2) black species of surgeon fish. *efenin Chuuk* Trukese s. f.

efen₂ nu. 29th night of the lunar month.

efen₃ (2) EFENI₂. F. Var. *efeng, eféng, éfáng*. nu. (T2) north. With suf. adj.: *efeninap* due north; north wind.

efen₄ (2) EFENI₃. nu. (T2) trade wind season (January through April). *maramen e.* months of the trade-wind season; *meyin e.* breadfruit that ripens in the trade-wind season.

efeninap See *efen*₃.

efeningngaw (3b) See *fen*₃, *ngngaw*. nu. (c.; T3) sacrilege, violation of tabu.

efeng (2) EFENGI. N. Var. *efen*₃, *eféng, éfáng*. nu. (T2) north. Syn. *ennefen*.

efeyinaato See *efeyini*.

efeyini See *feyin*₁. vo. (c.; T2) cause (someone) to go, convey, send. With dir. suf.: *efeyinaato* convey hither.

efeyiyengngaw (3) See *feyiyengngaw*. vi., va. (c.) be dangerous; cause injury or misfortune, endanger.

efeyiyengngawa See *feyiyengngaw*. co. (c.; T3) cause (someone) to be injured or to have misfortune, endanger (someone).

efeyiyéchchúúw See *feyiyéech*, *-ú-*. vo. (c.; T5) bless, give good luck to.

eféng (2) EFÉNGÚ. Wn. Var. *efen*₃, *efeng, éféng*. nu. (T2) north; north side. *eféngún Wééné* n. side of Wééné (Moen).

eféw (2) See *e-*₂, *-féw*. num. one globular object (in counting lumps, stones, fruit, and the like). Dis. *kkááféw* some. *e. faaw* one stone. With c. pref. and ptv. const.: *ááféwún* first g. o. at a time. With pref. *áná-*: *ánááféw* only one or sole g. o., one and only g. o.

efiifi See *fiifi*. vi. (c.) (with *neemasa-*) shock a person with language that is tabu or improper in his presence ("cause sparks in the eye"). *aa e. neemesey* he shocked me.

efiis (3a: *efissa-*) See *fi-, sse-*. nu. (c.; T3) ankle bandage used to facilitate tree-climbing. *efissen téétá* climbing bandage.

efiika- See *fiik*.

efiinúún (2) See *fii-, núún*. nu. (c.; T2) feast given when a house, meeting house, or public building is entirely built and its occupants have moved in. [It is given to insure the good health and life of the occupants and refers to making fast the rope lashings.] *efiinúúnún iimw* feast for a house.

efiinúúna See *efiinúún*. vo. (c.; T3) give a house-building feast for (a house).

efiiy See *ef, -i-*₂. vo. (T5) pull on (a line). Dis. *ekkefiiy* (ds). With dir. suf.: *efiiyenó* p. away on; *efiiyetá* p. up on; *efiiyetiw* pull down on; *efiiyeto* p. hither on; *efiiyewu* p. out on.

efiiyetá See *efiiy*.

efiiyetiw See *efiiy*.
efiiyeto See *efiiy*.
efiiyewu See *efiiy*.
efisáátá See *efisi*.
efisi See *fis*. vo. (c.; T2) cause to occur; make, produce, invent, create. With dir. suf.: *efisáátá* cause to occur; create, produce, establish, invent; bring to fruitation. With n. form. suf. *-ya-*: *efisiya-* (ni.; T3) creation, production, invention.
efisifis (db; 2) See *fis*. nu. (c.; T2) accomplisher, clincher. *efisifisin aach mwechen* a. of our wishes; *efisifisin pwúpwpwúnú* a gift that accomplishes permission to marry; *efisifisin tingor* a gift that induces granting one's request, bribe.
efisiya- See *efisi*.
efisuuwa- See *fisuuw*.
efissuk See *ááf, ssuk*. nu. flint and steel (for making fire), strike a light. *aan e.* his f. and s. vi. strike fire with flint and steel.
efin (3, 2) See *fin₁*. nu. a hold in hand-to-hand fighting. [To disarm a man making a downward slash with a bushknife, one seizes the back of his knife hand with one's right hand and twists clockwise at the same time seizing the knife blade with one's left hand and forcing it up in a clockwise direction.]
efina Var. of *effina*.
efinenong (3) See *fin₁, -nong*. nu. (c.; T3) a kind of body blow with the hands in fighting. Syn. *efinewo*.
efinenúka See *finenúk*. vo. (c.; T3) twist.
efinewo (1) See *fin₁*. nu. (c.; T1) kind of body blow with the hands in fighting. Syn. *efinenong*.
efinong (3) See *ef, nong*. nu. (T3) cramp of the arm that pulls the arm into the body. vi. have a cramp of the arm.
efich₁ (3a) See *e-₂, ficha-*. num. one strip of coconut, pandanus, or palm leaf that has been prepared for plaiting mats.
efich₂ (2) See *-fich*. vi. (c.) be pleased. va. (Rmn.) like, take pleasure in, enjoy. [This is the preferred word in mixed company.] *efich ngaang* l. me. *efich ffengen* l. each other, l. mutually. Syn. *saani*.
efichi See *-fich*. N. vo. (c.; T2) like (something).

efichipich (2) See *-fich, pich₂*. nu. (c.; T2) land given by a lineage to the child of a sick member.
efitachéé- See *fitaché*.
efitá (1) See *ef, -tá*. nu. (T1) cramp of the leg muscle that pulls the leg up. *efitáán féwún* cramp of his calf muscle. vi. be pulled up (as a shirt); have a cramp of the leg muscle.
efiteféwú- See *fiteféw*.
efiteménú- See *fitemén*.
efitikopwuta See *fitikopwut*. vo. (c.; T3) make angry by wakening with a noise at night.
efitiyaar (2) See *fiti, -ya-, érú-₁*. vi., adj. (c.) (be) intermingled (as men and women, Trukese and Americans); mingle.
efitiyaarúúw See *efitiyaar, -ú-*. vo. (c.; T5) cause to mingle together (of people).
efituuwa- See *fituuw*.
efitti N. var. of *áfitti*.
efiyef (db; 2) See *ef*. nu. (dis.; T2) fishing with hook and line, in which bait has been loosely attached to a stone by a line that is jerked loose to chum the water around the hook near the bottom (bait is *nippach, senif chúkúfan*, or *mwooch*). vi. (dis.) 1. engage in pulling on a line. 2. fish with hook and line. Dis. *ekkefiyef* (ds).
efiyona See *fiyon*. vo. (c.; T3) starve (someone), make hungry. Dis. *ekkefiyona* (ds).
efiyuuwu See *fiyuuw*. vo. (c.; T2) make (someone) fight. *efiyuuwuwey, efiyuuwuk, efiyuuwu, efiyuuwukich, efiyuuwukeem, efiyuuwukemi, efiyuur* make me, you, him, us (inc.), us (exc.). you (pl.), them f.
efó (1) EFÓÓ. nu. (T1) barnacle. *efóón neeset* b. in the sea.
efór N. of *óófór*.
efóch (4) See *e-₂, fóchu-*. num. one long or stick-like object (e.g., vehicles, canoes, arms, legs, teeth, posts, trees, timbers, cigarettes, pencils, shovels, sticks, strings of fish, burdens of breadfruit on a carrying stick). Dis. *kkááfóch* some. *e. chúúk* one pair of baskets on a carrying pole. With c. pref. and ptv. const.: *ááfóchun* first l. o. With dis. c. pref.: *ákkááfóch* be one l. o. at a time. With pref. *áná-*: *ánááfóch* sole, only l. o.

efótiisómw See *fóto-₂, -sómw.* Itang. nu. corner post in a meeting house where a chief's brothers sit and that symbolizes them. Cf. *iyuusómw.*

efutuk (3) See *e-₂, futuk.* num. one piece of meat.

effaat (3) See *e-₂, ffaat.* num. one string of fish.

Effeng nu. (loc.) local name for the Sowupwonowót clan formerly on Romónum Island. [Derived from the name of its estate on Romónum.]

effina (dc) See *fin₁.* Var. *efina.* vo. (c.; T3) twist (of an arm or body part only). *e. peyiy* t. my arm.

effich (2) EFFICHI. nu. (T2) small leaf package of *kkón* or *aarúng. effichin máay* small p. of breadfruit.

effichiiy See *effich, -i-₂.* vo. (T5) wrap (breadfruit) into small packages.

effit (3) See *e-₂, fitta-,* (or *-ffit*). num. one leaf package of small fish.

esap (3) See *e-₂, saap.* num. one cheek (especially of fish).

esapw See *e-₁.*

esángá (1) See *e-₂, sángá.* num. one basketful of fish. Syn. *esáwá.*

esáwá (1) See *e-₂, sáwá.* num. one basketful of fish. Syn. *esánga.*

ese See *e-₁.*

eseeng (3) See *e-₂, seeng.* num. one between-joints unit of length (as on a bamboo stick).

ese ii wor pred. phr. there is not. [Gentler than *esoor* or *ese wor.*] Ant. *meyi wor.*

esefich (2) See *ssefich₁, ssefich₂.* nu. (c.; T2) arrow, bow and arrow; spool. *efóch e.* one a. or s. *aan e.* his a. *esefichin tereech* spool of thread. *wókuukun e.* bow.

esefichi See *esefich.* vo. (c.; T2) load (a netting needle).

esemwmwen (2) See *semwmwen.* nu. (c.; T2) nursing, caring for the sick. *chóón e.* a nurse.

esemwmweni See *semwmwen.* vo. (c.; T2) nurse, tend, care for (a sick person).

esen (2) See *e-₂, -sen.* num. one coil or hand of rope (from 30 to 100 fathoms of length according to local custom).

eseni See *sáán.* vo. (c.; T2) pay out (rope). With dir. suf.: *esenóónó* p. o. farther.

esenipa See *senip.* vo. (c.; T3) cause desire to well up in (someone).

esenooch nu. technique for righting an overturned vessel in the water. Syn. *pwáán.*

esenóónó See *eseni.*

eseyich (2) ESEYICHI. nu. (T2) snare (general term). *eew e.* one s. *aan e.* his s. *eseyichin Chuuk* Trukese s. va. catch in a snare, trap.

eseyichiiy See *eseyich, -i-₂.* vo. (T5) snare, catch with a snare, trap.

esi-₁ (2: *-kes*) ESI₁, KESI. [In cpds. only.] unsp. fiber thread. See *esiiy, esineenap₁, enikes, enikesiiy.*

esi-₂ (2) ESI₂. ni. (T2) age; sort, kind. *esin* his a. *ifa esin átánaan* what sort of person is he? how old is that fellow?: *ifa esin naan wuut* how old is that meeting house?

esi-₃ (2) ESI₃. [In cpds. only.] unsp. (u.m.) See *esiyes, maasiyes.*

-esi- Var. of *-ási-.*

esiit (3) ESIITA. vi., adj. (be) critical. *kkapas e.* critical talk, criticism.

esiita See *esiit.* vo. (c.; T3) criticize, be critical of. Dis. *ekkesiita* (ds). *aa esiitááyey reen féfféérún ááy angaang* he criticized me on account of the conduct of my work.

esiiwini See *siiwin.* vo. (c.; T2) cause to be exchanged, make a swap of, trade.

esiiy See *esi-₁, -i-₂.* vo. (T5) remove or strip off (barbed edges of pandanus leaf). With dir. suf.: *esiiyenó.*

esiiyenó See *esiiy.*

esissin (ds; 3: *-sinna-*) See *siin₂.* nu. (c.; T3) 1. sign, symbol, insignia; recognition mark. *esissinney* symbol of me (as my name); *esissinnan* sign or symbol of it. *esissinnen eyiis* question mark; *esissinnen mmak* punctuation mark, diacritic mark; *esissinnen meyinap* insignia of an officer, insignia of one of high rank; *esissinnen tetten* insignia of rank. 2. riddle. vi. (c.) guess.

esissinna See *esissin.* vo. (c.; T3) 1. signify, symbolize. 2. guess (a riddle; dis. of *esinna*).

esineenap₁ (3) See *esi-₁, nee-, nap.* nu. (T3) hibiscus fiber thread that hangs from each stake on which the warp of a loom is wound (used to maintain the relative positions of the warp threads in the winding). *esineenapen túúr* loom's *e.* .

esineenap₂ (3) See *sineenap*. nu. (c.; T3) canoe builder's share of fish caught with a new canoe.

esineey See *sine*. vo. (c.; T1) inform, pass information to; (refl.) educate (oneself).

-esini Var. of *-ásini*.

esinna See *siin₂*. vo. (c.; T3) recognize, guess (a riddle). Dis. *esissinna* (ds). *esinná e*. guess it, guess it (formula opening a riddle).

esinnéw nu. kind of mackerel fish.

esingi See *sing*. Tb3. vo. (c.; T2) cause to fart, cause to break wind.

esiyes (db; 2) See *esi-₃*. N. Var. *ekiyek*. nu. (T2) white or fairy tern.

esoor See *e-₁, -se, wor*. [Contraction of *ese wor*.] pred. phr. there is not; it does not exist. *esooru mwo fáán eew* never, not even once. Cf. *eseyi wor*.

esópw₁ (4) See *e-₂, sópwu-₂*. num. one segment, half, division, section. *engoon me nimuuw e*. fifteen and a half.

esópw₂ (4) See *e-₂, sópwu-₃*. num. one burden of tied-together breadfruit.

essaar (dc; 2) See *e-₂, -ssaar*. Var. *essar*. num. one slice (in counting).

essak (dc; 3) See *e-₂, ssaka-*. num. one piece of copra.

essar Var. of *essaar*.

essáát (2) See *e-₂, -ssáát*. num. one sliver, splinter, longitudinal slice.

essát Var. of *essáát*.

essif vi. (c.?) run, go quickly, be speedy.

essupw (2) See *e-₂, ssupwu-*. num. one tiny drop, one droplet.

ek excl. ouch! Syn. *ik*.

ekerikeri (db) See *keri-*. vo. (c., dis.) scratch. *wúwa ekerikeriyey* I am scratching myself.

ekiiki (db; 1) See *ki₂*. va. (c., dis.) engage in lifting, engage in moving by lifting.

ekiiy See *ki₂*. vo. (c.; T1) lift, move (something) by lifting. [Used when the speaker is not among the lifters.] Dis. *ekkekiiy (ds)*. With dir. suf.: *ekiiyenong* move (something) in; *ekiiyenó* move (something) away, carry away; *ekiiyetá* raise, lift up (of things, prices); *ekiiyetiw* lower, lift down; *ekiiyeto* move (something) hither; *ekiiyewow* move (something) toward you; *ekiiyewu* move (something) out, carry outside. Cf. *keki*.

ekiiyenong See *ekiiy*.

ekiiyenó See *ekiiy*.

ekiiyetá See *ekiiy*.

ekiiyetiw See *ekiiy*.

ekiiyeto See *ekiiy*.

ekiiyewow See *ekiiy*.

ekiiyewu See *ekiiy*.

ekis₁ nu. foreign place, distant land, alien land. *e. meyinisin* everywhere, all lands; *fóósun e., kkapasen e*. foreign language, alien language; *meettóóchun e*. something foreign; *finen e*. foreign woman; *ree-e*. foreign man. *wúpwe feyinnó wóón fénúwen e*. I shall journey to a foreign (or distant) land.

ekis₂ (2) See *e-₂, kisi-*. num. one little thing; a little, a bit. Syn. *engin*. adv. (F.) barely, a little. *aa e. toongeni fátán* he was b. able to walk.

ekisi See *kisi-*. vo. (c.; T2) make small, reduce. Dis. *ekisikisi* (db). With dir. suf.: *ekisóónó* make smaller, reduce.

ekisikisi Dis. of *ekisi*.

ekisóónó See *ekisi*.

ekimwaramwar (3) See *áák, mwaramwar₂*. vi. think with uncertainty, be uncertain, be undecided. Syn. *tipemwaramwar*.

ekimwónómwón See *áák, mwónómwón*. vi. have a secret thought.

ekina₁ EKINA. vo. (T3) examine, inspect. Dis. *ekkekina* (ds). *ewú ná ákina (nó ekina) naan mwúúch ika meyi en ika meyi iromw* you (pl.) go e. that wood as to whether it is dry or damp.

ekina₂ See *kin₁*. F. Var. *ekini₁*. vo. (c.; T3) cause to go away, remove, make depart, shift. With dir. suf.: *ekinaato* remove (something) hither; *ekinóónó* remove (something) away, shift (something) to another place, cause to be moved out of the way.

ekinaato See *ekina₂* and *ekini₁*.

ekinasa See *kinas*. vo. (c.; T3) cut, wound.

ekinamwmweey See *kinamwmwe*. Var. *okunamwmweey*. vo. (c.; T1) make comfortable.

ekini₁ See *kin₁*. N. Var. *ekina₂*. vo. (c.; T2) cause to be moved out of the way, remove; (refl.) move out of the way. *wúwa ekiniyey* I moved out of the way. With dir. suf.: *ekinaato* remove hither; *ekinóónó* move (something) away or off out of the way; (refl.) *ekinukunó!* get out of the way!

ekini₂ (2) See *kin₂*. Tn. vo. (c.; T2) make ashamed, shame. Syn. *ámáfena, ásááwa*.

ekinissow (2) See *kinissow*. vi., adj. (c.) (be) naked (of persons).

ekinóónó See *ekina₂* and *ekini₁*.

ekingngaw (3b) See *áák, ngngaw*. vi. have evil intentions.

ekingngawa See *ekingngaw*. vo. (T3) have evil intentions towards, intend to harm.

ekit (3) See *e-₂, -kit*. num. one unit of ten thousand. With c. pref.: *áákita, eekita* (vo.; T3) make (it) ten thousand. With c. pref. and ptv. const.: *áákitan, eekitan* ten thousandth one. With pref. *áná-*: *ánáákit, ánákkit* sole or only ten thousand. Syn. *eew kkitan*.

ekita See *kit*. vo. (c.; T3) make a strong effort at, presevere at, show determination at. *wúpwe e. meet wúpwe toongeni toori ewe maram reen* I shall make a strong e. at (finding) a way that I can get to the moon.

ekitetit (db; 3) See *kit*. vi. (c., dis.) presevere, be zealous, work hard toward a goal. *e. mwaken ngaang ngé esoor nómwotan* zealous at lying I, but it's to no avail (words of a song).

ekiyáánniiy See *kiyáán, -i-₂*. vo. (c.; T5) cause a boundary to be established on.

ekiyek₁ (db; 2) See *áák*. n. (dis.; T3) thought, thinking; idea; opinion, view; whim, fancy; mind. *ekiyekin, aan e.* his. t. *ekiyekin aramas* human view or opinion, popular opinion; *ekiyekin fenúúfaan* view or opinion of people everywhere, universal point-of-view. *ekiyekin sooná* cunning, crafty, insincere, or dishonest ideas.

ekiyek₂ (db; 2) F. Var. *esiyes*. nu. white or fairy tern.

ekiyekééch (2: *-échchéu-*) See *ekiyek₁, ééch*. n. (T2) good, pure, noble thoughts. *ekiyekéchchún átánaan* the good t. of that fellow.

ekiyekéchchúúw See *ekiyek₁, ééch*. vo. (T5) think (something) through; concentrate one's thought on (something).

ekiyekiiy (db) See *áák, -i-₂*. vo. (dis.; T5) think (something), have (something) in mind. With dir. suf.: *ekiyekiiyetá* get the idea of, think (something) up.

ekiyekiiyetá See *ekiyekiiy*.

ekiyekingngaw (3b) See *ekiyek₁, ngngaw*. vi. worry, be anxious, think ill.

ekiyekiya See *kiyeki*. vo. (c.; T3) spread (a mat). With ind. obj.: *ekiyekiyaangeni* (vo. c.; T2) s. (a mat) for (someone). *ekiyekiyaangeniyey chéén pwereka* spread *pwereka* leaves (as a mat) for me.

ekiyekiyaangeni See *ekiyekiya*.

ekiyééch (2) See *áák, ééch*. vi. have good intentions, be well disposed.

ekiyéchchúúw See *ekiyééch, -ú-*. vo. (T5) have good intentions toward, be well disposed to, think well of.

ekum (2) See *e-₂, kumu-*. num. one mouthful or swallow (of liquid). Cf. *ekkumw*.

ekumwuch (2) See *e-₂, kumwuch*. num. one hoof, paw, foot (of animal); one handful, fistful.

ekup (2) See *e-₂, kupu-*. num. one or a broken piece (of a long, rigid object). *e. kupun sóók* one b. p. of chalk.

ekka N. prn. (dem.) who (among several), whoever. *e. i miriit neeyimi* whoever understands among you. Syn. *eey₃*.

ekkaan Dis. of *een₃*.

ekkamw (3b) See *e-₂, kkamw*. num. one fragment or torn piece (of cloth, paper).

ekkana Dis. of *ena*.

ekkanaan Dis. of *enaan*.

ekkap (3) See *e-₂, kkap*. num. one cupful. Cf. *eew kkap* one cup (object).

ekke- Dis. of *e-₃*. Routine, unambiguous ds forms of this type are not listed as separate entries but may be found under the unreduplicated words beginning with *e-*.

ekkeen Dis. of *een₅*.

ekkeey Dis. of *eey₁*.

ekkefisuuw See *fisuuw*.

ekkesiiwin (ds; 2) See *siiwin*. [Regularly in this form rather than *esiiwin*.] va. (c., dis.) trade, swap, make an exchange.

ekkemwuun Dis. of *emwuun*.

ekkena Dis. of *ena*.

ekkeni See *kken*. vo. (c.; T2) make sharp, sharpen.

ekkenimuuw See *nimuuw*.

ekkettiwuuw See *ttiwuuw*.

ekkey N. var. of *ákkey*.

ekkeyis (ds; 2) See *iis.* vo. (c., dis.) engage in stripping bark strips from the midrib of a coconut frond.

ekkeyissuk See *ekkey, ssuk.* N. vi. make fire by striking flint and steel. Syn. *efissuk.*

ekkinóóy See *kki-, -nó.* vo. (c., refl.; T1) make (oneself) weak from hunger, from a spasm of laughter or crying, or from holding one's breath under water. *wúwa ekkinóóyey* I make myself weak; *kaa ekkinóók* you make yourself weak.

ekkóóch See *óóch.* N. Var. *ókkóóch, kkóóch.* num. some, few, several assorted things. *fáán e.* sometimes, a few times, occasionally (but not frequently).

ekkumw (2, 3) See *e-₂, kkumw₁.* num. one portion of premasticated food. Cf. *ekum.*

em (2) EMI₂. vi., adj. (be) trimmed (of hair only).

emas (3) See *e-₂, -mas.* num. one thing worn on the eyes (e.g., goggles, lens) or attached as point to a piercing weapon (e.g., spear point).

emach (3) See *e-₂, macha-.* num. one fishtail.

emataf (3) See *e-₂, matafa-.* num. one or a small portion, small amount, little bit.

emeech (2) See *e-₂, mechchi-.* F. Var. *emech, emmech.* num. one portion of mashed breadfruit.

emeet (3) See *e-₂, meet₂.* num. one strand (of hair or rope).

emenimen (db; 2) See *meni-.* Var. *emmen.* vi. (c., dis.) smile, be smiling.

emeres (2) EMERESI. vi. be unfolded, spread out.

emeresi See *emeres.* vo. (T2) unfold, unfurl, spread out.

emeriika See *meriik.* vo. (c.; T3) irritate (the throat).

emerimer (db; 2) EMERI. va. see dimly, have a glimpse.

emerimeri See *emerimer.* vo. (T2) see (something) dimly, glimpse.

emeripa See *merip.* F. Var. *emeripi.* vo. (c.; T3) shatter.

emeripi See *merip.* N. Var. *emeripa.* vo. (c.; T2) shatter.

emeriyek (2) EMERIYEKI. nu. (T2) kind of fishing done at night by both men and women with coconut fronds used as seines. *emeriyekin Chuuk* Trukese *e.* vi. do *e.* fishing.

emech N. var. of *emeech, emmech.*

emecheresi See *mecheres.* Var. *ámecheresi.* vo. (c.; T2) make easy.

emechiyor nu. fishing with a float attached to one's line.

emechchi See *mechchi-.* vo. (c.; T2) divide (mashed breadfruit) into portions.

emeteki See *metek.* vo. (c.; T2) give pain to, cause to pain.

emeten nu. 12th night of the lunar month.

emey (2) See *meyi-.* nu. (c.; T2) heavy rope. *esen e.* one r. Syn. *sáán.*

emeyaw (3) EMEYAWA. N. vi. urinate (of little children only). Cf. *áchchén, chuuchu, sir.*

emeyis (2) See *meyi-, -s₂.* Var. *ámeyis.* nu. (c.; T2) loom sling. *emeyisin túúr* s. of a loom.

emén (2) See *e-₂, maan₁.* num. one person or creature (with people, mammals, birds, fish, insects, but not lobsters, crabs, sea cucumbers, or shell fish); one knife, gun, file, scissors. Dis. *kkáámén* some. *e. mwáán* one, a man; *e. nááyif* one knife. *esooru mwe (mwo) e. ikanaan* there is no one there. *e. chék* just one; *e. chék neeyiin* anybody, anyone; *e. me e.* each one. With c. pref. and ptv. const.: *ááménún* first one. With dis. c. pref.: *ákkáámén* be one at a time, by ones, one by one. With pref. *áná-*: *ánáámén* sole, only one; *ánáámén néwún* his only child.

emiis₁ (2) EMIISSI. nu. (T2) painter (for a boat), tether (for an animal) mooring line. *esen e.* one p. *emissin waa* boat's p.; *emissin piik* pig's t.

emiis₂ (2) EMIISI. nu. (T2) contest. *emiisin ssá* running contest, race, track meet; *chóón e.* contestant. vi. be in a contest. *e. ffengeen* compete with one another.

emiisi See *emiis₂.* vo. (T2) judge (a contest). *chóón e.* (n. phr.) judge (in a contest).

emiiy See *em, -i-₂.* vo. (T5) trim (of hair only).

emissini See *emiis₁, -ni-.* vo. (T5) moor, tie up (a boat), tether (an animal).

eminefééw See *minafé.* vo. (c.; T1) renew, refresh.

eminiwi (3: -wiya-) See *miniwi.* nu. (c.; T3) a smoother or sander made from *miniwi*. va. apply *miniwi* as a smoother or sander.

eminiwiya See *eminiwi*. vo. (c.; T3) rub, smooth, sand (lumber) with *miniwi*.

emiriiti See *miriit*. vo. (c.; T2) train. make understand, educate, instruct, correct, reprimand.

emma (1v) See *e-₂, -mma*. num. one mouthful of premasticated food.

emmach (3) EMMACHA. nu. (T3) 16th night of the lunar month.

emmen (dc; 2) See *meni-*. Var. *emenimen*. vi. (c.) smile.

emmech N. var. of *emech, emeech*.

emmeyi Var. of *ámmeyi*.

emmeyiya See *mmey*. Var. *ámmeyi, emmeyi*. vo. (c.; T3) make taut, pull tight.

emmék (2) See *e-₂, mékkú-*. num. one fragment.

emmisi See *mmis*. vo. (c.; T2) polish, make gleam.

emmit (2) See *mmit₁*. vi. (c.) smack (with lips or mouth, as when sucking in the breath or eating).

emmiti₁ See *emmit*. vo. (c.; T2) smack (the lips or mouth), cause to smack, make a smaking noise with. *aa e. awan* he smacked his mouth; *aa e. anan mwéngé* he smacked his food.

emmiti₂ See *mmit₂*. vo. (c.; T2) make slippery, make slick, cause to slide easily.

emw (3b) EMWA. vi., adj. (be) inspected, investigated, looked at. With dir. suf.: *emwewu* emerge into view. Cf. *ámwa-*.

emweses (2) EMWESESI. nu. (T2) a tree (*Glochidion*).

emwekinikini See *mwekinikin*. vo. (c.; T2) tickle.

emweri See *ámwa-, -ri-*. vo. (T5) pay a sympathetic visit to (someone who is sick). Syn. *áámwa*.

emwechin F. of *amwachin*.

emwewu See *emw*.

emweyir (3) See *mweyir*. nu. (c.; T3) song sung while carrying *mwatún* to present to the district chief. vi. sing an *e.* song.

emweyira See *emweyir*. vo. (T3) sing *emweyir* upon (food presented to the chief). *raa e. mwatún* they s. an *emweyir* on the *mwatún*.

emwénú (1) See *e-₂, mwénúú-*. num. one ell (unit of length from elbow to fingertips).

emwi- (2) EMWI. Var. *emwú-* (before a following *ú*). pref. only (used with numerical nouns only in counting breadfruit). *emwiyeew, emwiruwuuw* or *emwiruu, emwiwúnúngát* or *emwúwúnúngát, emwúrúwáánú, emwinimuuw, emwiwonuuw, emwifisuuw, emwiwanuuw, emwittiwuuw, emwiyengoon* only one, two,...ten.

emwiicha See *mwiich*. vo. (c.; T3) call to a meeting, assemble.

emwifisuuw See *emwi-*.

emwikka See *mwiik*. vo. (c.; T3) make peppery.

emwinimuuw See *emwi-*.

emwirimá (1) See *mwir, má*. Var. *emwirinimá*. nu. (T1) dying instructions, deathbed testament.

emwirimwir (db; 2) See *mwir*. nu. (c.; dis.; T2) 1. instructions, orders. 2. legacy. va. leave instruction to, leave a message for.

emwirinimá Var. of *emwirimá*.

emwirinnééw See *mwirinné*. Var. *émwúrinnééw*. vo. (c.; T1) improve, cause to be good. With dir. suf.: *emwirinnééwénó* improve, cause to be better.

emwirinnééwénó See *emwirinnééw*.

emwiringngawa See *mwiringngaw*. vo. (c.; T3) give bad luck to.

emwiruu See *emwi-*.

emwiruwuuw See *emwi-*.

emwittiri See *mwittir*. vo. (c.; T2) hurry, make go fast, speed up. *sipwe e. ee* (*eey*) *waa* we shall speed up this boat.

emwittiwuuw See *emwi-*.

emwiwanuuw See *emwi-*.

emwiwonuuw See *emwi-*.

emwiwúnúngát See *emwi-*.

emwiyaatá See *mwi, -tá*. vo. (c., dir.; T3) cause (someone) to wheeze or pant.

emwiyeew See *emwi-*.

emwiyetá (1) See *mwi, -tá*. va. (c.) cause to wheeze or pant. vi. be a cause of wheezing or panting.

emwu E.Wn. of *emwú₂*.

emwuun See *e-₄, -mwuun*. N. prn. (dem.) that (near person addressed). Dis. *ekkemwuun* (ds) those. Syn. *oomw*. Cf. *ena*.

emwú₁ (1) See *e-₂, mwúú-₁*. num. one segment, torn piece (of rag or string).

emwú₂ (1) See *e-₂, mwúú-₂*. num. one sea cucumber; one piece of feces.

emwúrúwáánú See *emwi-*.

emwúch (2) See *e-₂, mwúchú-*. num. one piece of firewood.

emwúwúnúngát See *emwi-*.

emwmwen₁ (2) See *mwmwen*. vi. (c.) stop, be finished. Syn. *emwmwéw*.

emwmwen₂ (2) See *mwmwa-, -ni-*. vi. lead, go first.

emwmweni₁ See *mwmwa-, -ni-*. vo. (c.; T6a) lead, go before, precede.

emwmweni₂ See *emwmwen₁*. vo. (c.; T2) make stop, put a stop to, make an end of, be finished with, terminate. *wúpwe e. aach angaang* I shall be finished with our work.

emwmweningngaw (3) See *emwmwen₂, ngngaw*. va. (c.) mislead.

emwmwék (2) See *e-₂, mwékkú-*. N. num. one bit or morsel (of mashed food). Syn. *epwey*.

emwmwéw (2) See *mwmwéw* vi. (c.) come to an end, stop, cease, be finished, be terminated, be halted. Syn. *emwmwen, mwmwen*.

emwmwéwú See *emwmwéw*. vo. (c.) stop (something), terminate, bring to an end, halt. *wúpwe e. naan chitoosa* I will stop that automobile.

emwmwir (2) See *mwir*. nu. (T2) 1. message. vi. 1. leave a message.

emwmwiri₁ (dc) See *mwir*. vo. (c.; T2) ask an errand of, give an errand to. Dis. *ekkemwmwiri* (ds).

emwmwiri₂ (dc) See *mwiri-*. vo. (c.; T2) decant the water off of (something).

emwmwun (3) See *e-₂, mwmwuna-*. num. one portion of *mwatún*.

emwmwú N. of *emwú₁*.

emwmwún F. of *emwmwun*.

en vi. be dry and good for burning (of wood and coconut fronds). Cf. *iromw*.

ena See *e-₄, na*. N. [Regularly precedes the noun and is not used in pos. const.] prn. (dem.) that (near person address or the thing just mentioned). [In this form only when it precedes the noun or stands by itself. Otherwise it is replaced by *na*.] Dis. *ekkana, ekkena* (ds) those. *meet ena?* what is that (that was just mentioned or that you have there)? Cf. *emwun, oomw*.

enaan See *e-₄, naan*. N. [Regularly precedes the noun and is not used in pos. const.] prn. (dem.) that yonder (visible but at a distance from both speaker and person addressed). Dis. *ekkanaan* (ds) those yonder. Cf. *naan*.

Enanganap nu. (loc.) Elangelap Island (Puluwat Atoll).

Enato nu. (loc.) Elato Island and Atoll (Central Caroline Islands).

ene- See *ana-₁*.

ene (1) ENEE. nu. (T1) swordgrass (*Miscanthus floridulus*). [It is used as a rod around which to sew ivory nut leaves in making thatch.]

eneen interj. maybe, maybe not! search me! I have no idea! perhaps! Cf. *eni₁*.

eneeniya See *neeni*. vo. (c.; T3) find a place for, give shelter to, provide with shelter.

eneeniyengngawa See *neeni, ngngaw*. vo. (c.; T3) 1. put (something) in a place that is bad or inappropriate for it. 2. take (correction or scolding) in a bad spirit.

eneeniyéchchúúw See *neeni, ééch, -ú-*. vo. (c.; T5) 1. put (something) in a place that is good or appropriate for it. 2. take (correction or scolding) in a good spirit.

eneetipengngawa See *neetipengngaw*. vo. (c.; T3) hurt (someone's) feelings; insult.

enes nu. a vine (*Piper* sp., *Piper betel, Piper fragile*).

enemóót (4) See *ene, móót*. nu. a sitting dance. [Performed by women in association with a female medium in honor of a good spirit, *énúúsór*, using reed sticks from swordgrass, *ene*, as dance wands.]

enenikké (1) See *ana-₁, -kké*. nu. (T1) a sedge (*Fimbristylis polymorpha* or *Fimbristylis cymosa*). [Used for stomach disorders in children.] Syn. *pwuker*.

enen chukó See *ana-₁*.

Enengeyitaw (3) See *anang* (?), *taaw* (?). nu. (loc.; T3) a clan name.

eni-₁ (2) See *a-₄, -ni-*. [In cpds. only.] Var. *áni-*. unsp. eat, eating.

eni-₂ (2) ENI₁. [In cpds. only.] unsp. wind, blow.

eni-₃ (2) ENI₂. [In cpds. only.] unsp. in a circle. Dis. -*eniyen* (db). See *áfáánni*₁, *fáán*₆, *fáániyen*.

eni₁ (1) ENII₁. F. md.m. perhaps, maybe (immediately precedes the predicate construction). *e. sipwe fééri neesor* maybe we shall do it tomorrow. *e. aa máánó nánew* or *e. epwe máánó nánew* perhaps he died yesterday. *ngé e. éwúwa fóókkun wúreni ewe aramas wo epwenee sú* but maybe in fact you told that human that she should flee. Syn. *meni*.

eni₂ (1, 3) ENII₂, ENIYA. nu. (T1, T3) bass fish. *eniyen Chuuk* or *eniin Chuuk Trukese* b.

eni₃ Tn. of *áni*.

eniiser (2, 3a) See *eni*₁, *ser*. vi. be accidental, be by chance. *epwaapw e. ika sipwe chuffengen* it will later on be a. if we should meet. *aa e. ewe iik wóón wókii we* that fish was accidently on my spear.

eniiserengngaw (3b) See *eniiser, ngngaw*. vi. be a mischance, be an unfortunate accident.

eniisereyééch (2: *-yéchchú-*) See *eniiser, ééch*. vi. be of good chance; be a fortunate accident.

eniiseri- (2) See *eniiser*. [In ptv. const. only.] ni. (loc; T2) (by) accident, (by) chance. *eniiserin pwú wúpwe turutiw nánew* or *eniiserin wúwa turutiw nánew* by accident I fell down yesterday.

eniimw See *enimw*.

eniiti See *eni-*₂, *-iti*. vo. (T2) blow upon. Dis. *ekkeniiti* (ds).

enifechefech Var. of *ennifechefech*.

eniffóch (3b) See *eni-*₂, *ffóch*. vi. blow steadily.

enis (3) ENISA. n. (T3) whiskers, beard, mustache. *eyé e.* one w. *enisan* his w.

enisow (2?) ENISOWU (?). vi. marry the brother or sister of one's deceased spouse. *aa e. reen* he has made such a marriage with her. Syn. *ánimóng*.

enikapter (Eng.) nu. helicopter.

enikes (db; 2) See *eni-*₃, *esi-*₁. nu. (T2) winding the warp threads. *efóch e.* one stake on which the warp is wound. *enikesin túúr* w. the warp of the loom.

enikesiiy See *enikes, -i-*₂. vo. (T5) wind the warp on (the loom).

eniken (2) ENIKENI. nu. (T2) variety of breadfruit. *enikenin Chuuk* Trukese *e.*.

enikéchéwúnúúnú See *nikéchéwúnúún*. vo. (c.; T2) anaesthetize, make numb. Syn. *éwúnúúnú*.

eniki See *nik*. vo. (c.; T2) cause to be disliked, as by use of spells or by carrying tales (with *reen*). *wúwa e. Alexia (me) reen Boutau* I have caused Alexia to be disliked by Boutau.

enikinik (db; 2) See *nik*. vi. (c., dis.) be causing dislike, making bad relations between people, sewing discord (by use of spells or slander).

Enikoosich nu. (pers.) traditional spirit of the trunks of breadfruit trees. [Completion feasts for houses, *ósópwun iimw*, were made in his honor.]

enimaaw See *eni-*₂, *maaw*. vi. blow strongly (as a gale).

enimaté (1) ENIMATÉÉ. nu. (T1) 1. a star. 2. a month in the traditional sidereal calendar (named for the star).

enimee- See *nime*.

enimenima See *nimenim*. vo. (c.; T3) clean, make tidy.

Enimuuw See *nimuuw*. nu. (temp.) Friday ("Fifth"). *Ketin, kaa fiti Koowag nóón ewe Enimuuw aa nó?* Ketin, did you ride the Koowag last F.? *Enimuuw epwe war* he will arrive on F.

enimuuwa- See *nimuuw*.

enimuuwa See *nimuuw*.

enimw (3) ENIMWA. [Also recorded as *eniimw*.] nu. (T3) variety of breadfruit. *enimwen Chuuk* Trukese *e.*.

enimwmwuka See *nimwmwuk*. vo. (c.; T3) make big, enlarge. With dir. suf.: *enimwmwukóónó* make larger, enlarge.

enimwmwukóónó See *enimwmwuka*.

Enin nu. (loc.) Elin Island (Nomwin Atoll).

eninap (3) See *eni-*₁, *nap*. nu. (T3) large Samoan or mangrove crab. [It is considered the best tasting and hence a food of chiefs.] Syn. *ánimóng*.

eninó (1) See *eni-*₂, *-nó*. vi. blow away (of wind).

ening (3b) See *ning*. nu. (c.; T3) 3rd night of the lunar month ("glimpsed").

eninga See *ning*. vo. (c.; T3) look for a glimpse of, look for (someone or something) to appear.

eningngaw₁ (3b) See *eni-₁, ngngaw.* n. (T3) stomach upset, nausea. *eningngawan* his s. u. *eningngawen nuukey* upset of my stomach. vi. be upset in the stomach, feel nausea.

eningngaw₂ (3b) See *eni-₂, ngngaw.* nu. (T3) ill or unfavorable wind. vi. blow unfavorably (of the wind).

enipaapa (1) See *eni-₁, paa₁.* nu. (T1) species of garfish (one upper beak only).

enipatapat (3b) See *eni-₂, pat.* vi. blow coolly (of a breeze).

enichippúngú See *nichippúng.* vo. (c.; T2) disappoint, make sorry, make regretful.

enit (3) See *eni-₂, -ta-₂.* vi. be slowed by the wind. *aa e. Roopet reen ewe cheepen* Roopet is s. by the wind on account of that table (he is carrying).

enita- (3) See *enit.* nr. (T3) slowing effect (of wind). *eniten ásápwán* s. e. of the wind.

enita See *enit.* vo. (T3) cause (someone) to be slowed by the wind.

eniti- (2) See *eniti.* ni. (T2) heater, warmer. *enitin iyé?* h. for whom?; *enitin Eyiwe* h. for Eiue. *kepwee nó waato enitin ááf* go bring here a h. of fire.

eniti ENITI. vo. (refl.; T2) heat or warm oneself. *wúpwe enitiyey reen ááf* I shall warm myself by the fire.

enito (1) See *eni-₂, -to.* vi. blow hither (of wind).

eniw (3) ENIWA. nu. (T3) sauce made from the seafood *nikos* (*eniwen nikos*).

eniwa See *niw.* vo. (c.; T3) frighten, scare.

eniweniw (db; 3) See *niw.* vi. (c., dis.) be frightening, terrifying.

eniwini See *niwin.* vo. (c.; T2) send back (persons), return (things), pay back (debts), deny (requests). With dir. suf.: *eniwinóónó.*

eniwinóónó See *eniwini.*

eniwin-sefáániiy See *niwin, sefáán, -i-₂.* vo. phr. (c.; T5) return (something) back again, send back.

eniwokkus See *niwokkus.* vi. (c.) be startling, cause one to start or jump with fright.

eniyacha F. of *ániyacha.*

eniyen₁ (db; 2) See *eni-₂.* nu. (dis.; T2) blowing, breeze. *eniyenin ásápwán* b. of wind, breeze; *eniyenin ngasangas* b. of breath. vi. blow; spread word. *aa e. fátán* he walks about and spreads the word ("he walks and blows").

eniyen₂ vi., va. (c.?) walk quickly, hurry; fetch (someone).

eniyééch₁ (2: *-yéchchú-*) See *eni-₁, ééch.* nu. (T2) good feeling. vi. feel well ("eat well").

eniyééch₂ (2: *-yéchchú-*) See *eni-₂, ééch.* nu. (T2) favorable wind. vi. blow favorably.

eniyéchchúúw See *niyééch, -ú-.* vo. (c.; T5) consider (a woman) pretty, admire the beauty of (a woman), be pleased by the appearance of (a woman) ("make a beautiful woman of").

eniyossuuw See *niyoos, -u-.* vo. (c.; T5) make an image, statue, or picture of (someone).

enna See *eens.* vo. (T3) shoot at, strike at, hurl at (with gun, club, spear). Cf. *áánna.*

ennefen (2) See *eni-₂, efen₃.* nu. north.

ennet (2, 3) See *nnet.* vi., adj. (c.) (be) honest, truthful.

ennifechefech (db; 3) See *nnifech.* Var. *ennifechifech.* vi. (c., dis.) shake one's body from side to side (as in disagreement).

ennifechifech Var. of *ennifechefech.*

ennifechifechi See *nnifech.* vo. (c., dis.; T2) make (one's body) shake from side to side.

ennimet (2) See *nnimet.* vi. (c.) have pride, have high standards for oneself, be a neat performer.

ennimwékút (dc; 2) See *ni-₂, mwékút.* vi. (c.) be set in motion, be started.

ennimwékútú See *ni-₂, mwékút.* vo. (c.; T2) set in motion, start (a machine).

enninga See *nning.* vo. (c.; T3) brighten, beautify, decorate, make pretty, make colorful; expose (the glans of the penis by pulling back the foreskin).

enniwin (dc; 2) See *niwin.* n. (c.; T2) cause of a repetition; a contribution that forces a further contribution by the first contributor in a money-raising party or *tééchap. enniwinin* cause repetition by him. *enniwin sefáán* make a repetition over again. *enniwin-sefáániiy* (vo. phr.) repeat over again, make a repetition of.

enniwini (dc) See *ni-₂, win₁.* vo. (c.; T2) repeat, do over again.

enniyap (3) See *ni-₁, apaap₁.* n. (T3) canine tooth. *enniyapan* his c. t. *enniyapen nii* canine tooth ("the canine of the teeth"). *enniyapen oppong* central prong of the many-pronged fish-spear. Cf. *niyap.*

ennú (1) See *e-₂, nnúú-.* num. one portion or loaf of breadfruit pudding; one amount of breadfruit for mashing into a pudding loaf.

engaf (3) See *e-₂, ngaaf.* num. one fathom (distance from fingertip to fingertip of out-stretched hands). With c. pref. and ptv. const.: *áángafan* first f. With dis. c. pref.: *ákkáángaf* be one f. at a time. With pref. *áná-: ánáángaf* only, sole f.

engát (4) See *e-₂, -ngát.* num. one concave or hollow object; (less common) one general-class of thing.

engéréw (2) See *e-₂, -ngéréw.* num. one thousand. *e. aramas* one t. people. With c. pref.: *áángéréwú, eengéréwú* (vo.; T2) make (it) one t. With c. pref. and ptv. const.: *áángéréwún* one thousandth. With dis. c. pref.: *ákkáángéréw* (vi) be one t. at a time. With suf. adj.: *engéréwúpár* one t. plus, something more than one t.; *engéréwúsomw* more than one t. With pref. *nne-₂: nnáángéréw* thousandth (fraction).

engéréwúsomw See *engéréw.*

engéréwúpár See *engéréw.*

engi (1) See *ngi.* nu. (c.; T1) song of lament (in love or mourning); chant. *eché e.* one s. of l. *aan e.* his s. of l. *engiin nóómw* lament of old. *ááni eey e.* sing this s. of l. va. sing a song of lament; chant.

engiiy See *ngi.* [Recorded with dir. suf.] vo. (c.; T1) begin, give voice to, sound the first note of (a song). With dir. suf.: *engiiyetá* begin (a song). Cf. *echiiy, echiya, ngiiri.*

engin (2) See *e-₂, ngin.* num. a little, a bit; one bit or little piece. Syn. *ekis₂.*

engini See *ngin.* vo. (c.; T2) make small, make smaller, reduce. With dir. suf.: *enginóónó* make smaller, reduce away.

enginóónó See *engini.*

engir (2) ENGIRI. nu. (T2) down feathers. *engirin machchang* bird's d. f.

engiyeng Dis. of *eeng.*

engoon (2, 3) See *e-₂, -ngoon.* num. ten, one unit of ten. [Except with general class objects and animate objects, it is followed by a classifying noun in ptv. const.] *e. angan* t. spans ("t. spans of it"); *e. efin* t. bunches of ripe coconuts; *e. éénan* t. hairs; *e. ffaaten iik* or *e. faaten iik* t. strings of fish; *e. iyeyiyan* t. hands of bananas. *e. me eew* eleven general-class things; *e. me emén* eleven animate things. With c. pref.: *áángoonu, eengoonu* (vo.; T2) make (it) t. With c. pref. and ptv. const.: *áángoonun, áángoonan, eengoonun, eengoonan* tenth one. With dis. c. pref.: *ákkáángoon* (vi.) be t. at a time. With pref. *áná-: ánáángoon* one and only t., sole t. With pref. *nne-₂: nnáángoon* tenth (fraction). With dir. adj.: *engoonupár* t. plus, something more than t.; *engoonusomw* more than t.

engnginó (1) See *ngngi-, -nó.* vi. keep straining, endure.

engngiya See *ngngi.* vo. (c.; T3) make (someone) suffer. Cf. *áweyiresi, eriyáfféwú.*

ep (2) EPI₁. va. make more than one carrying trip. Dis. *áápiyep* (c., db); *ekkep* (ds); *kkááp* (dc). With dir. suf.: *epinong, epinó, epitiw, epito, epiwu.*

epa (1) See *e-₂, -pa.* num. one frond, garland, or stalk with leaves (of palm trees, banana trees, *Cyrtosperma* taro, and also of leis or garlands, necklaces, and bead belts). Cf. *epan.*

epan (3) See *paan₁.* num. one branch with its leaves (of trees other than palms and bananas). Syn. *epachang.* Cf. *epa.*

epachang (3) See *e-₂, pachang₁.* num. one branch with leaves. Syn. *epan.*

epeek (2) See *e-₂, peek₂.* num. one side, page.

epeep₁ (db; 3) EPA₁. nu. (T3) lee platform (of outrigger sailing canoe), platform on opposite side from the outrigger. *epeepen waa* canoe's lee platform. *núkún e.* woodcarving design (used on *epeep* and elsewhere). *papen e.* planks of the lee platform. *pecheen e.* beams supporting the lee platform.

epeep₂ (db; 3) EPA₂. nu. (T3) ornamental cape.

epeey nu. 11th night of the lunar month.

epene (1) See *pene*. nu. (c.; T1) winding thread on a spool or shuttle (in weaving).

epeneey See *epene*. vo. (c.; T1) wind thread on. *ósówpun e. túúr* completion feast on weaving a man's loincloth (done in honor of the goddesses *Nisáreere* and *Nipáánaw*).

epengesi See *penges*. vo. (c.; T2) be perpendicular to, cross (as a T).

epereyingiingi See *pereyingiing*. vo. (c.; T2) cause to be on its side or edge. Syn. *etiwiiniini*.

epeche (1) See *e-$_2$, peche*. num. one lower or hind limb (of humans, birds, and animals only).

epé (1) See *e-$_2$, péé*. num. one empty container.

epék (2) See *e-$_2$, péék*. num. one chip, chopped off piece, cigarette butt.

epénget Var. of *epúnget*.

epéw (2) See *e-$_2$, -péw*. num. one wing or thing worn over the hand or arm (e.g., glove).

epi-$_1$ (2) EPI$_2$, KEPI. Var. *ápi-*. ni. (T2), suf. (cc.) butt end, lower end, bottom, west end, trailing edge, trailing end, end opposite to where stem attaches (of fruit). *eyep, rúwéyep, wúnúyep, féyep, nimeyep, wonoyep, fúúyep, wanúyep, ttiweyep* one,...nine b. e. *epin* its b. e. *epin éwúwé* variety of breadfruit associated with stream banks; *epin fanang* type of earth oven; *epin fénú* west end of an island; *epin kkama* bottom of large iron pot; *epin kkap* bottom of a cup; *epin kúú* back of the head; nape of the neck; *epin kúún nnúf* side of a mortar or pounding block that is toward the worker; *epin nááyif* butt end of a knife, back of a knife blade; *epin nisses* bottom of a wooden bowl; *epin núú* end of coconut opposite the eyes; *epin sepi* bottom of a bowl or pan; *epin taka* end of ripe coconut opposite the eyes; *epin towunómw* back end of mosquito canopy. Cf. *neesópwu-, maas*.

epi-$_2$ (2) EPI$_3$. [Occurs with v. form. *-ti-* and n. form. *-ta-*.] unsp. having to do with annointing.

epiineng (2) See *epi-$_1$, nááng*. Var. *ápiinen*. nu. (T2) horizon. Syn. *óroppeyinen*.

epiipiiy (db) See *pii-*. Var. *eppiiy*. vo. (c.; T1) hold up to view, hold up for inspection.

epiiraw (3) See *pii-, rawaraw*. nu. (c.; T3) variety of breadfruit.

epiita See *piit$_2$*. vo. (c.; T3) cause to lose interest; dissuade. *e. aan ekiyek* dissuade him from his idea.

epiitaa- (1) See *epi-$_1$, taa*. F. Var. *epiitar*. ni. (T1) body cavity (of fish only). *epiitaan* it's b. c. *epiitaan iik* fish's b. c.

epiitar (3) See *epi-$_1$, tara-*. N. Var. *epiitaa-*. n. (T3) body cavity (of fish only). *epiitaran* its b. c. *epiitaren iik* fish's b. c.

epiiy See *ep, -i-$_2$*. vo. (T5) repeatedly carry or transport, haul, lug (of goods only). *wúwá e. pisekiy wóón waa* I hauled my belongings on the boat. With dir. suf.: *epiiyenong, epiiyenó, epiiyetá, epiiyetiw, epiiyeto, epiiyewu*.

epiiya- (3) See *ep, -i-$_2$, -ya-*. ni. (c.; T2) large quantity of things requiring that they be carried in more than one trip; something to be transported in more than one trip. *epiiyan* his things to be carried in more than one trip.

epiiyenong See *epiiy*.

epiiyenó See *epiiy*.

epiiyetá See *epiiy*.

epiiyetiw See *epiiy*.

epiiyeto See *epiiy*.

epiiyewu See *epiiy*.

episipis$_1$ (db; 2) See *pisi-$_1$*. vi. (c.) clap the hands together (as in applause), make a clapping. Syn. *ánechepéw, ónopwonopw*.

episipis$_2$ (db; 2) See *pisi-$_2$*. vi. (c.) make a whispering sound (as to babies to put them to sleep).

episipisi$_1$ See *episipis$_1$*. vo. (c.; T2) applaud.

episipisi$_2$ See *episipis$_2$*. vo. (c.; T2) make a whispering sound to.

epissúk (2) See *pissúk*. vi. (c.) make a squirting, squirt. *e. ngeni* squirt at. *wúwa e. ngonuk nóón neyi nikésúk* I squirted water on you (from) inside my (water) pistol. Cf. *pissúkiiti*.

epissúkú See *pissúk*. vo. (c.; T2) cause (something) to squirt.

epikirupw (2) nu. (T2) fishing spear made of mangrove wood (no longer used). *epikirupwun Chuuk* Trukese *e*.

epina See *piins$_5$*. vo. (c.; T3) inspect; examine the appearance, shape, or size of.

Trukese-English epúúk

epinap (3) EPINAPA. nu. (T3) small, informal feast. *eew e.* one f. *aach e.* our (inc.) f.

epinengngaw (3b) See *piin₃, ngngaw.* vi. (c.) be heedless, ignore ridicule, disregard the words of others, be inattentive, be disobedient, continue doing wrong in spite of other's criticism, continue in one's course as if nothing were wrong in spite of everything ("make a bad appearance"). With dir. suf.: *epinengngawónó* go on being h.

epinengngawónó See *epinengngaw.*

epinééch (2) See *piin₃, ééch.* vi. (c.) dissemble (e.g., deny one is hungry when one really is, act as if nothing were wrong, claim ignorance of something about which one really has knowledge, agree to something that one doesn't really want to do), be formally polite or ceremonious, disguise one's true feeling ("make a good appearance"). *kete e.* don't stand on ceremony, do as you please, make yourself at home. Cf. *epiniyééch.*

epinéchchúúw₁ See *epinééch, -ú-.* vo. (c.; T5) disguise (one's feelings), put a false front on, conceal the faults of.

epinéchchúúw₂ See *pin, ééch, -ú-.* Var. *epiniyéchchúúw.* vo. (c.; T5) observe (a tabu) well.

epini See *pin.* vo. (c.; T2) forbid, prohibit, put under restriction or tabu; bless (of a priest blessing those in church), confirm (in the church).

epinikú (1) See *epi-₁, kúú₁.* nu. (T1) back of the head, nape of the neck. *epin kúúy, epin kuumw, epin kúún* back of my, your (sg.), his h.

epiningngaw (3b) See *pin, ngngaw.* nu. (c.; T3) breach of tabu, violation of a prohibition, sacrilege.

epiningngawa See *epiningngaw.* vo. (c.; T3) break or violate (a tabu or prohibition).

epinipin (db; 2) EPINI. [Apparently a secondary formation from *epin* butt end of, its butt end; see *epi-₁.*] nu. (T2) butt end of arm or leg, elbow, heel. *epinipinin peyi* my elbow; *epinipinin pecheey* my heel.

epiniyaw (3b) See *pin, aaw₁.* vi. (c.) put a restriction on one's mouth, refrain from speaking, refrain from eating.

epiniyééch (2: *-yéchchú-*) See *pin, ééch.* vi. observe a tabu, honor a prohibition. Cf. *epinééch.*

epiniyéchchúúw Var. of *epinéchchúúw.*

epino₁ (1) EPINOO. nu. (T1) fish net (general term). *eew e.* one f. n. *aan e.* his f. n. *epinoon Chuuk* Trukese f. n. Syn. *cheew.*

epino₂ (1) See *e-₂, pino.* num. one small package of breadfruit pudding.

epinong See *ep.*

epinó See *ep.*

epinúk (2) See *e-₂, pinúk.* num. one tied bundle, ream of paper.

epinúkééch F. of *ápinúkééch.*

epinúkúnúk F. of *ápinúkúnúk.*

epinúkúnúkééch (2) See *pi-, núúk₁, ééch.* F. vi. (c.) be optimistic, hopeful.

epinúkúngngaw F. of *ápinúkúngngaw.*

epinget Rmn. of *epúnget.*

epichéw nu. headdress consisting of frigate bird feathers fastened to a stock of mangrove wood, which is in turn fastened to the handle of a wooden comb.

epichi See *pich₂.* vo. (c.; T2) untie, unfetter; forgive, pardon. With dir. suf.: *epichóónó* untie, unfetter; forgive, pardon.

epichóónó See *epichi.*

epit (3) See *epi-₂, -ta-₁.* n. (T3) hair oil, ointment, perfume, pommade. *epitan* his pommade.

epitá See *ep.*

epiti See *epi-₂, -ti-.* vo. (c.; T2) annoint with oil or perfume; grease (a car). Dis. *ekkepiti* (ds).

epitiw See *ep.*

epitiya- (2) See *epiti, -ya-.* ni. (T3) annointing material; annointment. *epitiyan* his annointment.

epitiyo (1) See *epi-₂, -ti-, o₂.* vi. annoint the hair with coconut cream and not wash it out afterwards (formerly tabu because it would result in the death of a kinsman).

epito See *ep.*

epiwu See *ep.*

epu (1) See *e-₂, puu-₂.* num. one stroke in swimming (in measuring distance).

epúúk (2) EPÚÚKKÚ. nu. (T2) crossbeam on the outerposts of the end porch or shed on old style houses and meeting houses. *epúúkkún* its c.

epúnget (2) Var. *epénget, epinget.* nu. (T2) coconut pod or sheath (within which are newly formed coconuts); coconut cloth. *epúngetin núú* p. of the coconut tree.

eppet (2) See *ppet₃.* n. (c.; T2) hindrance, screen, thing in the way. *eppetin* thing in his way. va. (c.) block, screen off, get in the way.

eppeti See *ppet₃.* vo. (c.; T2) block, screen off, get in the way of, put something in the way of, wall off.

eppeyis (3) See *ppeyis.* vi. (c.) strive to endure physical stress (as in holding one's breath for a long time or withstanding pain without flinching).

eppeyisenó See *eppeyis.*

eppiiy (dc) See *pii-.* Var. *epiipiiy.* vo. (c.; T1) hold up to view or inspection.

eppis (2) EPPISI. nu. (T2) a game in which bamboo sticks are bounced on the ground. vi. play the game of this name.

eppiseki (dc) See *pisek.* vo. (c.; T2) give goods to, cause to have goods.

eppisi See *eppis.* vo. (c.; T2) throw (a bamboo stick) so as to make it bounce on the ground (in the game of *eppis*).

eppinas (3) EPPINASA. nu. (T3) patch, mending. vi., adj. (be) patched. va. patch, mend.

eppinasa See *eppinas.* vo. (T3) patch, mend.

eppini See *ppin.* vo. (c.; T2) tangle, make snarled, snarl.

eppich (dc; 2) See *pichi-.* nu. (c.; T2) bow and arrow, rubber sling and dart. *eppichin Chuuk* Trukese b. and a. vi. shoot a b. and a.

eppichi See *eppich.* vo. (c.; T2) flick, snap (as one's eyes or a slingshot), shoot (a bow). With dir. suf.: *eppichóónó* flick away, shoot (an arrow) off.

eppichóónó See *eppichi.*

Epreyin (Eng.) nu. April.

epwaapw See *e-₁.*

epwang (3) See *e-₂, pwaang.* num. one hole, cave, cavity, pit, tunnel, hollow. Syn. *engát.*

epwe See *e-₁.*

epwene See *e-₁.*

epwerika See *pwerik.* Var. *ápwerika.* vo. (c.; T3) scratch. *wúwa epwerikááyey* I scratched myself.

epwey (2) See *e-₂, -pwey.* num. one pinch or morsel (of food). Syn. *emwmwék.*

epwéét (2) See *e-₂, pwéét.* num. one nose.

epwi (1) See *e-₂, pwii-₁.* num. one school, group, crowd, flock, herd, swarm, convoy, etc.

epwisipwis See *pwisipwis.* vo. (c.; T2) beat (the lips) together without making any noise; make (something) barely move. *aa e. awan* h. barely moves his mouth.

epwin (2) See *e-₂, pwiin₃.* num. one night.

epwiri See *-pwir.* vo. (c.; T2) cause to be swift, throw, hurl; (refl.) make haste, hie oneself. *wúwa epwiriyey* I made haste. With dir. suf.: *epwiróónó* hie oneself off.

epwiróónó See *epwiri.*

epwich F. of *ápwich.*

epwichi F. of *ápwichi.*

epwichikkara See *pwich₁, kkar.* vo. (c.; T3) heat, make burning hot.

epwopw (2) See *e-₂, pwoopw.* num. one trunk (of tree), base, foundation, cause, source, beginning, origin, reason.

epwór (4) See *e-₂, pwóór.* num. one box or crate (of something); one coffin.

epwún See *e-₂, pwúún₁.* Var. *epwpwún.* num. one broken-off piece.

epwpwaaw (2) See *e-₂, pwpwaaw.* num. one home-made cigarette.

epwpwis (2) See *pwpwis.* vi. (c.) make another person angry, be anger provoking.

epwpwisi See *pwpwis.* vo. (c.; T2) make (someone) angry, infuriate.

epwpwún N. of *epwún.*

er₁ Var. *kker* (dc). vi., adj. (be) tired (of doing something).

er₂ (2) ERI₁. vi. call out in fear or pain, cry out; bawl, bellow, moo, roar. Syn. *ér₂.*

erá N. var. of *érá.*

ereepi (1) EREEPII. nu. (T1) large *nichchik* shell and shellfish.

erefi See *rááf₁.* vo. (c.; T2) divide with a divider.

ereki See *reek.* vo. (c.; T2) wonder about (something).

ereni N. var. of *éreni.*

eri-₁ (2: *-keri-*) ERI₂, KERI. [In cpds. only.] unsp. scratch, scrape.

eri-₃ (2) ERI₃. [In cpds. only.] unsp. strip, line.

eriiy See *eri-₂, -i-₂.* vo. (T5) make lines or stripes on, make a line on, cause to have lines or stripes. With dir. suf.: *eriiyenó* line (something) off, make a line on (something) in the direction away from the speaker; *eriiyenó faan* underline it; *eriiyeto* make a line on (something) in the direction toward the speaker.
eriiyenó See *eriiy.*
eriiyeto See *eriiy.*
erikeri (db) See *eri-₁.* vo. (dis.; T2) scratch.
eriki See *rik.* vo. (c.; T2) cause to turn or change direction.
erimon nu. species of parrot fish.
eriyááni See *riyá, -ni-.* vo. (c.; T4) make miserable, be cruel to, torture, oppress, torment, persecute.
eriyáffewú See *riyáfféw.* vo. (c.; T2) make miserable, torture, persecute, oppress, torment, be cruel or mean to.
echamw (3) See *e-₂, -chamw.* num. one forehead, brow, or similarly classed object (e.g., visor, stem base of a coconut frond); one fishhead. With c. pref. and ptv. const.: *ááchamwan* first f. With dis. c. pref.: *ákkááchamw* be one f. at a time. With pref. *áná-: ánááchamw* sole or only f.
echáy Itang. nu. child of a chief. Syn. *éfékúren sómwoon.*
echeerewe (1) ECHEEREWEE. nu. (T1) species of sea cucumber (black and up to a yard long). *emwú e.* one t. *echeereween Chuuk* Trukese t.
echef₁ nu. 30th and last night of the lunar month.
echef₂ See *e-₂, -chef.* Tn. num. 1. one tentacle (of octopus or squid). *e. éwútún nippach* one octopus t. Syn. *ewút, eyó.* 2. one piece of firewood. *e. émwúch* one p. of f.; *e. masis* one match.
echeni See *cheni-.* vo. (c.; T2) love, cherish, be fond of, value, prize, favor. Dis. *ekkecheni* (ds). *emén meyi fóókkun e. fénúwan* one who is very fond of his land. Syn. *éwúchcheyaani.*
echepw (2) ECHEPWI. Tn. nu. (T2) breadfruit. *echepwin Chuuk* Trukese b.
eché (1) See *e-₂, -ché.* num. one leaf, sheet, thin flat object; one song *e. toropwe* one sheet of paper; *e. kkéén* one song. With c. pref. and ptv. const.:

ááchéén first l. With dis. c. pref.: *ákkááché* be one l. at a time. With pref. *áná-: ánááché* sole or only l.
echifepwéét (2) See *chif₂, pwéét₂.* vi. wrinkle one's nose as as expression of contempt or dislike. Syn. *pwéét káwáng.*
echik (3) ECHIKA. vi. be hungry. Syn. *fiyon.* Cf. *áchchik.*
echikara See *chikar.* vo. (c.; T3) wait for (the weather) to clear.
echikepin (2) See *echik, pin.* vi. fast, observe tabu against eating ("be tabu-hungry").
echiki See *chiki-₂.* vo. (c.; T2) blink (one's eyes) from weariness. Dis. *echikichiki* (db). *echikichiki masan* be blinking his eyes.
echikichik (db; 2) See *chiki-₂.* vi. (c., dis.) be sleepy, be blinking one's eyes from weariness.
echin va. hunt, search (as for crabs and lobsters). *sipwe e. nipwpwey* we shall hunt crabs. *aa e. ne nennenóór* he looked and looked for them ("he hunted in looking for them").
echinichin (db; 2) See *chin.* F. Var. *echichchin.* vi. (c.) cry all the time; be swollen eyed from crying.
echipa See *chip.* vo. (c.; T3) comfort, console, stop from crying.
echipwa See *chiipw.* vo. (c.; T3) divine for (something) by bending the midrib of a coconut leaf.
echipwanga See *chipwang.* vo. (c.; T3) make tired, make weary. *naan angaang aa echipwangááyey* that work has made me tired.
echipwangaangeni See *echipwanga, ngeni.* vo. (c.; T2) trouble (someone). *kese mwechen kepwe echipwangaangonuk ááy naan pisekin óófis kepwee mwo waato* will you please trouble yourself with my office things and fetch them here.
echichchin (ds; 2) See *chin.* N. Var. *echinichin.* vi. (c., dis.) cry all the time.
echiwechiw (db; 3) See *chiwa-.* va. (c., dis.) sing a lullaby.
echiwechiwa (db) See *chiwa-.* vo. (c., dis.; T3) sing a lullaby to.
echiya See *chi.* vo. (c.; T2) begin (of sound), sound the first note of. With dir. suf.: *echiyáátá* begin (of sound, song).

echiyáátá See *echiya*.

echiyo (1) ECHIYOO. Tb. nu. (T1) gonorrhea, urethritis. [The disease is said to have come to Truk from Kusaie and the Marshall Islands, presumably as a result of intensive contact with whalers.] Syn. *rimpiyo*.

echú (2) See *e-₂, chúú*. num. one bone segment (of meat).

echúk (2) See *e-₂, chúúk*. nu. one coconut leaf basket.

echcheriwa See *chcheriw*. Tb1. vo. (c.; T3) make shiny.

echchi (1) See *e-₂, -chchi*. num. one drop.

echchiiy See *-chchi*. vo. (c.; T1) sprinkle.

echchik (2) See *chiki-₂*. vi. (c.) wink, blink. Cf. *áchikichik*.

echchimwa (dc) See *chimw*. vo. (c.; T3) oblige, obligate, force (someone) to consent.

echchini See *chchin* vo. (c.; T2) speed, hurry (one's speech).

echchipwa See *chchipw*. vo. (c.; T3) warp, bend (by fire).

echchipwéér Var. of *echchipwér*.

echchipwér (2) vi. (c.) be excellent.

echchooch (3) See *e-₂, chchooch*. num. one armful.

etáp (2) See *e-₂, táppi-*. num. one age group, one generation; another age group, another generation. *e. aramas* one (or another) generation of people (usually to refer to a generation that has passed on).

ete See *e-₁*.

etek (2) See *teki-*. Var. *atek, átek*. vi. (c.) engage in dragging, towing, pulling.

etekini See *teki-, -ni-*. Var. *atekini, átekini*. vo. (c.; T5) drag, haul, tow. Dis. *ekketekini* (ds).

etekiyaay See *teki-, -ya₁*. vo. (c.; T1) cause to be high, elevate.

etenek (2) ETENEKI. vi., adj. (be) careful, considerate, have concern for others. *emén meyi e.* one who is c.

etenekiiy See *etenek, -i-₂*. vo. (T5) care for, look after, see to, nurse; be hospitable to, entertain. *e. waasééna* be hospitable to a visitor.

etenecha See *tenech*. vo. (c.; T3) cause to be inattentive.

eteni₁ See *ten₁*. vo. (c.; T2) melt, dissolve; (of colors) cause to run, cause to fade.

eteni₂ See *ten₂*. Var. *áteni*. vo. (c.; T2) put in rank-order, enumerate.

etenimas (3v) ns. (T3v) alveolar region of the mouth. *eten masan* his a. r. *niin e.* upper incisor teeth.

eteniten (db; 2) ETENI. nu. (T2) a vine (*Ipomoes digitata*). [Its flowers are used as a medicine for inflammation of the eyes.]

eterekes (2) ETEREKESI. Var. *eterenges*. nu. (T2) lineage group (matrilineal and estate-holding). [The form *eterekes* is preferred over *eterenges* and is said to be related in meaning to *enikes* on the loom, the idea being the common purpose and interest of the several parts.] *eew e.* one l.; another l. *aan e.* his l. *eterekesin Chuuk* lineages of Truk, Trukese lineage.

eterenges Var. of *eterekes*.

eteriiy See *ter₂, -i-₂*. vo. (c.; T5) terminate, remove, lift (a sex tabu) by appropriate spell. With dir. suf.: *eteriiyenó* remove away (a tabu or prohibition), finish (something) off.

etetten (ds; 2) See *ten₂*. vi. (c., dis.) be put in rank order, be enumerated. *aa e. kkeey mettóóch* these things have been put in r. o. Syn. *kketen*.

etetteni (ds) See *ten₂*. vo. (c., dis.; T5) line up, put in rows, arrange in order, file; list; conjugate (a verb), decline (a noun). With dir. suf.: *etettenóónó* list off, arrange forth.

etettenóónó See *etetteni*.

eti- (2) See *ti-₁*. [In cpds. only.] vi. (c.) move, go. With dir. suf.: *etinong* go in, go south; *etinó* go off, go away; *etiwow* go toward you; *etiwu* go out, go north; *ettá* go up, go east; *ettiw* go down, go west; *etto* come hither.

eti See *ti-₁*. vo. (c.; T2) accompany, attend. *wúpwe e. ewe mwiich* I shall attend the meeting.

etiip (3a: *etippa-*) See *ti-₂, ppa-*. n. (c.; T3) wall, partition (of a house); room (in a house). *etippan* his room.

etifi See *tifi-*. Var. *atúfi, étúfi, itifi*. vo. (c.; T2) scoop; dip up, dip out.

etik₁ (2) ETIKI. nu. (T2) a Lethrinid fish (very good to eat). *etikin Chuuk* Trukese *e*.

etik₂ (2) See *tik*. nu. (c.; T2) fishing method using a spear of mangrove wood (*epikirupw*).

etikaanong See *tik, nong*. vo. (c.; T2) insert, put (something) in between.

etikka See *ettik*₁. N. Var. *ettika*. vo. (c.; T3) peel (a banana only).
etimitim (db; 2) See *timi-*. Var. *ettim*. vi. (c.) make a smacking noise by pouting out the lips. [It has no social significance.]
etimwir (2) See *ti-*₁, *mwiri-*. vi. (c.) weed (a garden), do weeding.
etimwiriiy See *etimwir, -i-*₂. vo. (c.; T5) weed (a garden).
etimwmwa ETIMWMWA. Obs. vo. (T3) look at, see.
etinaanong See *etini*.
etinááta See *etini*.
etineepat (3) ETINEEPATA. nu. (T3) meddling, trouble making. *etineepaten átánaan* that fellow's m. vi. meddle, make trouble, engage in calumniation, stir up persons to quarrel or fight.
etinewupw See *e-*₂, *tinewupw*. num. one yard (unit of length from center of chest to outstretched fingertips).
etini See *tin*₂. vo. (c.; T2) insert, put between. With dir. suf.: *etinaanong, etinááta*.
etiniffengen (2) See *tin*₂, *ffengen*. vi. (c.) overlap, interpenetrate.
etiniffengenniiy See *etiniffengen, -i-*₂. vo. (c.; T5) cause to overlap, fold together (one's hands).
etiniki (1) ETINIKII. nu. (T1) hard, white coral. [It was used to make the *tiketik* adze.]
etinimach (3) See *tini-*₂, *mach*. vi. (c.) run a finger under the nose to sniff something on it (a sign of mutual easiness between lovers in connection with genital odors). Syn. *etinimwas*.
etinimacheey See *etinimach, -e-*₂. vo. (c.; T6b) run a finger under the nose of (someone). Syn. *etinimwaseey*.
etinimwas (3) See *tini-*₂, *mwaas*. Tbl. va. (c.) run a finger under the nose to sniff genital odors on it. [This is a sign of mutual easiness between lovers.] Syn. *etinimach*.
etinimwaseey See *etinimwas, -e-*₂. Tbl. vo. (c.; T6b) cause (someone) to sniff the genital odors on one's finger. Syn. *etinimacheey*.
etiningeni See *tini-*₂, *ngeni*. F. Var. *etinngeni*. vo. (c.; T2) give (to someone) to smell, cause (someone) to perceive the odor of. *wúwa etiningonuk eey iik* I held up this fish for you to smell.
etinong See *eti-*.
etinó See *eti-*.
etinnúk (2) See *ti-*₁, *nnúk*₂. F. nu. (c.; T2) pile of stone and coral built in shallows to attract fish. [When it is destroyed, the fish flee into the surrounding nets and baskets.] Syn. *púnúpun*.
etinngeni Var. of *etiningeni*.
etip₁ (3) See *e-*₂, *tiip*₂. num. one slice, chunk, or cut segment (of breadfruit or taro only).
etip₂ (3) See *tiip*₂. F. va. (c.) pass chunks of breadfruit from the oven to those who are pounding them into breadfruit pudding. Syn. *ngngen*.
etipachchema See *tipachchem*. vo. (c.; T3) educate, make smart, make knowledgable.
etipeyeewi See *tipeyeew*. vo. (c.; T2) cause to agree, cause to be in agreement, cause to be of one mind.
etipitipingngawa See *tipitipingngaw*. vo. (c.; T3) cause (someone) to feel the emotion of acute shame and guilt at being caught in a wrongful act.
etippa See *etiip*. vo. (c.; T3) enclose with a wall (in a house), provide with a partition or screen. *e. átewe* screen that fellow (from view). With dir. suf.: *etippóónó* screen off, wall off; *etippóónó naan iimw* screen off that house.
etipwo (1) ETIPWOO. nu. (T1) variety of *Alocasia* taro.
etirá (1) See *eti, -rá*₁. Tn. n. (T1) son, daughter, child (of someone). *etirúán* his c., c. of. Syn. *naaw*.
etiru (1) ETIRUU. nu. (T1) plaited coconut-leaf matting, made with frond midribs at the outer edges. [Used for sitting and for housewalls.] *eché e.* one c.-l. mat. *kiyan e.* his c.-l. mat. *etiruun iimw* m. of the house.
etit (2) See *e-*₂, *-tit*. num. one string (of breadfruit, usually ten in number). Syn. *ettiit*.
etittin F. of *átittin*.
etittina F. of *átittina*.
etiwa See *tiwa-*₂. vo. (c.; T3) welcome, greet, receive (a visitor), be hospitable to. With dir. suf.: *etiwóónó* see (someone) off; set free, release, let go.
etiwáátiw See *tiwa-*₁ or *tiwa-*₂, *-tiw*. vo. (c.; T3) unload.

etiwiiniini See *tiwiiniin.* vo. (c.; T2) cause to be on its side or edge. Syn. *epereyingiingi.*

etiwokkos (3a) See *eti-, woos₂.* va. (c.) imitate the voice or accent. *aa e. kosokosen fénú* he imitated the accent of the island.

etiwow See *eti-.*

etiwóónó See *etiwa.*

etiwu See *eti-.*

etiya- (3) See *eti, -ya-.* ni. (T3) (In cpds.) companions; (with pos. prn.) spouse, husband, wife. *etiyan* his spouse.

etiyeppach (3b) See *etiya-, pach.* vi. (c.) be crowded together, packed tightly. *wúwa osukosuk pwú raa e. chóón wááy* I am having to work hard because the people in my boat are very crowded.

etiyet (db; 2) ETI₃. nu. (T2) wedge. *etiyetin waa* canoe wedge.

etú (3) See *e-₂, túú.* Tb1. num. one vulva (in counting sexual encounters).

etúkúm (3) See *e-₂, túkúm.* num. one package or packet (in counting).

etún (2) See *e-₂, túnú-.* F. Var. *ettún.* num. one portion of *mwatún* pudding. Syn. *emwmwun.*

Ettaan nu. (loc.) Etal Island and District (Mortlock Islands).

ettá See *eti-.*

Etten nu. (loc.) Eten Island.

etteyira See *tteyir.* vo. (c.; T3) cause to be healed, heal.

etti ETTI. vo. (T2) take (something) out with the hands. *e. ngeni powumwu chék* or *e. ngenii chék powumw* take it with just your hands. Cf. *wútti.*

ettiit (2) See *e-₂, ttiit₁.* nu. (num.; T2) one string of ten breadfruit. Syn. *etit.*

ettik₁ (3) ETTIKA. F. vi. 1. be scraped or peeled (of roast breadfruit peeled with a stick). Syn. *safet.* 2. be peeling (as skin after sunburn). Syn. *sifin.* 3. be stripped into strips (of bark, coconut stem). Syn. *kkási.*

ettik₂ F. of *áttik.*

ettika See *ettik₁.* F. vo. (T3) 1. strip (something) into strips. Syn. *ásiiy.* 2. peel (a banana or vegetable). Syn. *seey.* 3. scrape or peel (roasted breadfruit) with a stick. Syn. *safeti.*

ettiki F. of *áttiki.*

ettikipwo F. of *áttikipwo.*

ettikipwoow F. of *áttikipwoow.*

ettim (dc; 2) See *timi-.* Var. *etimitim.* vi. (c.) make a smacking noise with the lips.

ettina F. of *áttina.*

ettinááta F. of *áttinaatá.*

ettipisi See *ttipis.* vo. (c.; T2) cause to do wrong, lead into crime, seduce; put in the position of having done wrong; make a sinner or criminal of.

ettiw See *eti-.*

ettiwa (3) See *eti-, -tiw.* ni. (c.) coming down or west. *ettiwan* his coming down.

ettiwee- See *ttiwe.*

ettiwuuwa- See *ttiwuuw.*

ettiwuuwa See *ttiwuuw*

etto (1) See *eti-, -to.* vi. (c.) come, come hither. nu. (T1) a kind of incantation used to summon a spirit.

ettún N. of *etún* (See *ttúna-*).

ewe (1) See *e-₄, we.* prn. (dem.) that (in the past or not now in sight); the (already mentioned); the one that. [Regularly comes before the word for the thing denoted, when it is expressed, except in possessive construction, when it is replaced by *we* which immediately follows the word for the thing denoted. It also follows *peek.*] Dis. *ekkewe* (N.), *kkewe* (F.) those. *ewe áát* that boy (cf. *átewe* that fellow, that male person; *neyii we* that child of mine, *neyii we áát* that boy-child of mine). *ewe aa nó* the one who has gone.

ewer See *e-₁, -wer.* v. phr. yes (emphatic), indeed, certainly, verily (may accentuate a positive statement or indicate the contrary to a negative). *esaa mwo su? ewer, aa su* he hasn't gone yet? Yes, indeed, he has gone. Cf. *wúú.*

ewetina See *wetin₂.* vo. (c.; T3) break, shatter.

eweyit (2) See *weyit₂.* Tn. nu. (c.; T2) coconut fiber sling around the back of a weaver at the loom. *eweyitin túúr* loom's s. Syn. *ámeyis, emeyis, éwéék.*

ewiisa F. of *áwiisa.*

ewiich nu. a kind of a breadfruit pudding reserved for *itang. eew e.* one *e. . enen itang e.* the *e.* of an *itang* to eat.

ewiiwi F. of *áwiiwi.*

ewini See *win₁.* vo. (c.; T2) turn, change the position of; cause to be moved or shifted. With dir. suf.: *ewinóónó* transform, alter, cause to be changed.

ewinóónó See *ewini.*

ewiri See *wir-*. vo. (c.; T2) permit, allow. Dis. *ekkewiri* (ds). *aa ewiriyey ááy wúpwe feyinnó Wééné* he permitted me to go to Moen.

ewiriwiri (db) See *wiri-*. vo. (c., dis.; T2) look about for.

ewo (1) See *e-₂, -wo.* num. one clump (of bananas).

ewoch See *e-₂, -woch.* Tn. Var. *ooch.* num. one sort, kind, variety, ration, species (in counting). Syn. *óóch.*

ewumw (2) See *e-₂, wumwu-₂.* num. one branching stalk (of bananas, fruit, pandanus keys, coral).

ewupw (2) See *e-₂, wupwu-₁.* num. one breast.

ewut₁ (2) See *e-₂, wutu-.* num. one core; one chunk of cooked breadfruit.

ewut₂ (3) See *e-₂, owut.* Var. *óówut.* num. one row of thatch (in counting).

ewúk₁ (2) See *e-₂, wúúk₁.* num. one tail, rear end.

ewúk₂ (2: *wúkkú-*) See *e-₂, wúúk₂.* num. one fingernail, toenail, claw.

ewún (3a) See *e-₂, wúún₁.* num. one feather, hair, fish scale.

ewút (2) See *e-₂, -wút.* num. one finger or toe; one tentacle (of octopus); one leg (of insect or centipede). Cf. *echef, eyó.*

ewúwéw (2) See *e-₂, -wúwéw.* num. one amount of fermented breadfruit suitable for kneading.

-ey (2: *-wey, -yey*) EYI₁. suf. (obj.) 1sg. obj. prn.: me. *fitiyey* accompany me (see *fiti*), *fitiyeyinó* accompany me away.

eyaf (3b) See *e-₂, -af.* num. one piece of intestine.

eyang (3) See *e-₂, -ang.* num. one finger span (in counting); one entire limb of the body.

eyáf Var. of *eyef.*

eyef (2) See *e-₂, eef₁.* Var. *eef₃, eyáf.* num. one bunch of ten ripe coconuts. Syn. *eef₃.*

eyem (2) See *e-₂, eem₁.* Var. *eem₂.* num. one earlobe.

eyep (2) See *e-₂, epi-₁.* num. one butt end, lower part, or west end.

eyé (1) See *e-₂, éé-.* num. one hair (in counting).

eyék (2) See *e-₂, ékkú-.* num. one net.

eyi-₁ (2) EYI₂. [In cpds. only.] unsp. stick, pole, tree. Syn. *áá-₁.* See *eyiniwow.*

eyi-₂ (2) EYI₃. [In cpds. only.] unsp. state, condition. Syn. *eyiye-.*

eyi-₃ Var. of *áyi-.*

Eyi-₄ (2) EYI₄. pref. (pers. n.form.) common initial element in traditional personal names, marking the name as a man's, usually when the second element is a monosyllable, e. g., *Eyifár, Eyimén, Eyimwun, Eyinus, Eyitipey, Eyiwe, Eyiwer, Eyiwúr, Eyiya.* Cf. *Ina-, Na-, Neyi-.*

eyi (3) See *e-₂, -i.* Rmn. num. one hand of bananas. Syn. *eyin₃, eyiyey.*

eyiis (2) EYIISI. vi. ask a question, make inquiry. Dis. *ekkeyiis* (ds). *e. paat* ask to distraction; *e. tichchik* make a searching inquiry; *kkapas e.* a question (also *kkapaseeyiis*).

eyiisifföch (3b) See *eyiis, -fföch.* va. ask questions continually. Syn. *eyiisittof.*

eyiisini See *eyiis, -ni-.* vo. (c.; T5) ask, interrogate. Dis. *ekkeyiisini* (ds).

eyiisittof See *eyiis, -ttof.* va. ask questions continually. Syn. *eyiisifföch.*

eyiipwórópwór (db; 3b) See *ii-, pwór.* vi., adj. (be) curved, make a curving course.

eyif (3) EYIFA. nu. (T3) subdivision of a district or chiefly domain; named plot of land; lineage or land-holding corporation within a district; a district, larger division of land, or region when it is being referred to as a subdivision of something even larger. *eyifen iyé Nómwuchchu? eyifen Effeng* whose land is Nómwucchu? lineage land of Effeng. *efifen iya Chorong? eyifen nóón Romónum* land of what place is Chorong? a land in Romónum. *eyifen wóón me eyifen Chuuk* the region of the ruling power and the region of Truk, i.e., America and the islands of Truk (when the larger world of both Truk and the United States is the point of reference).

eyis (3) EYISA. (Eng.) nu. (T3) ace (in cards *eyisen kaas*).

eyisi See *iis.* vo. (c.; T2) strip (bark strips) from the midrib of a coconut frond. Dis. *ekkeyisi* (ds).

eyisiisi (db) See *isiis.* vo. (c.; T2) cause to hiss.

eyimanaato See *eyi-₂, man, -to.* vo. (T3; dir.) make miraculously powerful hither. *kepwe e. pwichin awey mé wóón nááng* make m. p. hither from heaven the heat of my mouth (from the *sooyénú* rite).

eyimweyimwa (db) See *iimw.* vo. (c., dis.; T3) house, build a house for, provide (someone) with housing.

eyimwu (1) See *imwu.* N. Var. *áyimwu, eyimwú.* nu. (c.; T1) subtraction (in arithmetic). vi., adj. (be) separated, removed; divorced (in marriage); subtracted or reduced (in arithmetic). With dir. suf.: *eyimwuunó.*

eyimwuunó See *eyimwu.*

eyimwuuw See *eyimwu.* N. Var. *eyimwúúw.* vo. (c.; T1) separate, remove, subtract.

eyimwú F. of *eyimwu.*

eyimwúúfesenniiy See *eyimwú, -feseen, -i-₂.* F. vo. (c.; T5) separate apart.

eyimwúúnó F. of *eyimwuunó (see eyimwu).*

eyimwúúw F. of *eyimwuuw.*

eyin₁ (2, 3) EYINA, EYINI. (Eng.) Var. *ayin.* nu. (T3, T2) iron (for clothing). *néwún e.* his i. *eyinen wúúf, eyinin wúúf* clothes iron.

eyin₂ (3) See *ina-₂.* vi. (c.) be an ally, be allied. Dis. *eyineyin* (db) be allies. *e. ffengen* be allied together (in war).

eyin₃ (3) See *e-₂, ina-₃.* N. num. one hand of bananas. Syn. *eyi.*

eyin₄ (2) See *e-₂, ini-₂.* num. one shoot.

eyinang (3) See *ina-₂, -ng.* n. (c.; T3) clan. [Clan membership is based on matrilineal descent.] *eew e.* one c., another c. *eyinangan, aan e.* his c. *meet óómw e.?* or *meet eyinangomw?* what is your clan? *Eyinangen Wéneya* a clan name.

Eyinangeyinúk (2) See *eyinang, -i-₁, núkú-₁.* nu. (loc.) a clan name ("clan of the outside").

eyineffengenniiy See *ineffengen, -i-₂.* vo. (c.; T5) join together, set (bones).

eyines (2) See *eyin₂.* nu. (T2) ally (in war). *achawaren e.* payment to allies in war in recognition of their help.

eyineni See *eyin₂, -ni-.* vo. (c.; T6a) take as ally, be allied to.

eyineniyeew (2) See *eyin₂, eew₁.* va. become allies.

eyinepwóch (3) EYINEPWÓCHA. (P.Eng. from Eng. *iron pot*) Var. *áyinepwoch.* nu. (T3) cooking pot, pan, metal cooking vessel. *aan e.* his c. p. *eyinepwóchen Chuuk* Trukese c. p. Cf. *eyin₁, pwóóch.* vi. be cooked in a pot or pan.

eyinepwócha See *eyinepwóch.* vo. (c.; T3) cook (something) in a pot or pan.

eyineyin Dis. of *eyin₂.*

eyini See *ini-₂.* vo. (c.; T2) transplant, plant (a shoot).

eyiniika- See *iniik.*

eyinimwey (2) EYINIMWEYI. nu. (T2) sexual desire, lust; amatory pursuits. Syn. *nisoowu.*

eyinimweyiffengen (2) See *eyinimwey, ffengen.* vi. be in love with one another, have mutual desire.

eyinimweyingeni See *eyinemwey, ngeni.* vo. (T2) have sexual desire for, lust after.

eyinini See *ini-₄, -ni-.* vo. (c.; T5) make an edge on (something).

eyiniwoow See *eyi-₁, wuwoow.* vo. (T6a) carry (something) with a carrying pole.

eyiniwow (3a) See *eyi-₁, wuwo-.* nu. (T3) 1. carrying pole. *eföch e.* one c. p. *aan e.* his c. p. *áán iyé e.* or *áán iye e.?* whose carrying pole? 2. a throw in hand-to-hand fighting. [Against an opponent slashing with a bushknife one grabs his slashing arm at the wrist with both hands, twists under his arm and brings it down hard on one's shoulder, breaking his elbow, and then one bends forward, pulling down and pitching him forward over one's shoulder.] vi. carry with a carrying pole.

eyinga See *ing.* vt. (c., refl.; T3) boast, brag ("make a marvel of oneself"). *wúwa pwisin eyingááyey* I boasted.

eyipw (3) See *e-₂, -ipw.* num. one step, footprint, sole; one item of footwear.

eyipwenong (3) See *ipwenong.* F. vi. (c.) make a loud popping noise in pounding breadfruit pudding. Syn. *awaw₂.*

eyipwétú See *ipwét.* vo. (c.; T2) cook (something) until done.

eyipwúkúú- See *ipwúkú.*

eyipwúkúúw See *ipwúkú, -ú-.* vo. (c.; T1) make it one hundred.

eyira- (3a) EYIRA. [In cpds. only.] unsp. peer out, look out.

eyira See *eyira-.* vo. (T3) peer out at, look out for.

eyirenges See *eyi-₁, reng, -s₂*. nu. a tree (*Pittosporum*). *néén e.* perfume made from bark juice of *e.*. Syn. *ánnapwut*.
eyiriffenginniiy See *ireffengeen, -i-₂*. vo. (c.; T5) cause to be healed.
eyiromwu See *iromw*. vo. (c.; T2) soak, drench.
eyirúk (2) EYIRÚKÚ. nu. (T2) heart of palm. [Classed with *mwéngé*.] *eyirúkún núú* h. of coconut palm; *eyirúkún kiniyaw* h. of Truk palm. Cf. *woopw₁, wuwapw*.
eyirúkúúw See *eyirúk, -ú-*. vo. (T5) cut the heart out of (the palm).
eyit (3) See *iit*. vi. (c.) say a name, speak a name. With *ngeni: eyit ngeni, eyitengeni* give a name to.
eyita₁ See *iit*. vo. (c.; T3) name, say the name of; (with *wóón*) earmark (something) for. *wúpwe eyitóók wóón ewe waa* I will earmark that canoe for you ("I will say your name on that canoe"). With *ngeni: eyitaangeni* give the name of (someone) to (someone).
eyita₂ See *it*. vo. (c.; T3) finish up, use up, get (something) finished.
eyitaangeni See *eyita₁*.
eyitekkáyeey See *it, kkáy, -e-₂*. vo. (c.; T6b) finish quickly. With dir. suf.: *eyitekkáyeeyenó* finish off quickly.
eyitekkáyeeyenó See *eyitekkáyeey*.
eyitenngaw (3b) See *iit, ngngaw*. n. (c.; T3) bad name, bad reputation. *eyitengngawan* his b. n. vi. have a bad name.
eyitengach (3) See *itengach*. vi. (c.) lean on the elbows.
eyitengeni See *eyit*.
eyitengngawa See *eyitengngaw*. vo. (c.; T3) give a bad name to, accuse.
eyitepwá (1) See *iit, pwá*. vi. (c.) boast emptily, show off ("make one's name visible"); be known for empty boastfulness or for making false claims about oneself.
eyitewóón nu. simple spear made of mangrove wood. Syn. *pwonosáp*.
eyiteyita Dis. of *eyita₁*.
eyitéchchú See *eyit, ééch*. N. Var. *eyitéchchúúw*. vo. (c.; T2) 1. speak well of, give a good name or reputation to. 2. (refl.) clear one's name.
eyitéchchúúw See *eyit, ééch, -ú-*. F. Var. *eyitéchchú*. vo. (c.; T5) 1. speak well of, give a good name or reputation to. 2. (refl.) clear one's name.
eyiti See *iti-₂*. Var. *áyiti*. vo. (c.; T2) change the location of; bring, fetch; (with *ngeni*) hand, pass (food at table), give, bring. *epwe e. ngonuk naan meettóóch* he will bring you that thing. With dir. suf.: *eyitiyeto, eyitiyenong, eyitiyenó, eyitiyetá, eyitiyetiw, eyitiyewu*. fetch or bring out.
eyitifesenniiy See *itifeseen, -i-₂*. vo. (c.; T5) cause to lie apart.
eyitiféwúwacheey See *itiféwúwach, -e-₂*. vo. (c.; T6b) cause to lie obliquely.
eyitiffengenniiy See *itiffengen, -i-₂*. vo. (c.; T5) cause to lie side by side, cause to lie next to each other
eyitipengesiiy See *itípenges, -i-₂*. vo. (c.; T5) cause to lie across, cause to lie athwart or at a right angle to.
eyitipwpwóruuw See *iti-₂, pwór, -u-*. vo. (c.; T5) cause to lie crookedly or not straightly. *pwata kaa e. naan pwóór* why did you set that box so that it isn't straight.
eyitiyenong See *eyiti*.
eyitiyenó See *eyiti*.
eyitiyetá See *eyiti*.
eyitiyetiw See *eyiti*.
eyitiyeto See *eyiti*.
eyitiyewu See *eyiti*.
eyittiw (3) See *ittiw*. nu. (c.; T3) line from which to hang things, clothesline.
eyittiwa See *ittiw*. vo. (c.; T3) suspend, cause to hang. *e. wóón* hang it on it.
eyiwen (3a) See *eyi-₂, wen*. nu. (T3) lying down. vi., va. lie down. With dir. suf.: *eyiwenitiw* l. d. while someone is off on a momentary errand; *eyiwennó* go l. d.
eyiwenitiw See *eyiwen*.
eyiwennó See *eyiwen*.
eyiye- (3a) EYIYA. F. [In cpds. only.] Var. *áyiye-*. unsp. state, condition. Syn. *eyi-₂*.
eyiyesumw (2) See *eyiye-, sumw*. N. Var. *áyiyesumw, eyiyessumw*. vi. nod the head (in sleepiness):
eyiyessumw F. of *áyiyesumw, eyiyesumw*.
eyiyekunukun (db; 2) See *eyiye-, kun*. nu. (dis.; T2) flickering (of fire or light). *eyiyekunukunun naan ááf* the flickering of yonder fire; *eyiyekunukunun reen ááf* the

eyiyenáámá

flickering of it (the light) an account of the fire. vi. (dis.) flicker, be flickering.

eyiyenáámá (db; 1) See *eyiye-, má*. nu. (T1) moribund state, dying condition. vi. be near death, moribund.

eyiyengngaw See *eyiye-, ngngaw*. n. (T3) listlessness, listless state. *eyiyengngawan* his l. vi., adj. (be) listless.

eyiyepwos (2) See *eyiye-, pwos*. nu. (T2) late meal (at night), midnight snack. *aan e.* his l. m. vi. have a late meal.

eyiyepwosuuw See *eyiyepwos, -u-*. vo. (T5) give (someone) a late meal.

eyiyey (3) See *e-$_2$, iyeyiya-*. num. one hand of bananas. Syn. *eyi, eyin$_4$*.

eyiyoffengenniiy See *iyoffengen, -i-$_2$*. vo. (c.; T5) cause to assemble together.

eyiyonoon (db; 3) See *eyi-$_2$, wonoon*. vi. droop (of plants in drought, of people from overheat or overwork).

eyiyón (3a) See *eyi-$_2$, -ón*. nu. (T3) drought.

eyó (1) See *e-$_2$, óó$_1$*. num. one tentacle (of octopus or squid). Syn. *echef, ewút*.

É

é- See *a-₂*. [Usually in this form, in F. dialects, when the next following vowel is *é* or *ú*.] pref. (c.) imparts causative meaning to the base. Dis. *ékké-* (ds). *méwúr* sleep, *éméwúrú* put (someone) to sleep; *wúng* be blown (of a trumpet), *éwúngú* blow, cause to be blown.

-é- É. [Occurs only in const. with bases of c.f. type 3.] Var. *-e-₂, -o-*. suf. (v.form.) makes an object focussed verb of the base (vo. type 6b).

é (1) ÉÉ₁. vi. 1. be learned, taught. *aa é reey seni Masayichi* I learned it from Masaichi. 2. learn. *wúwa é* I have learned, I know.

-é (1: *-é, -yé, -ké*) ÉÉ₂, KÉÉ₁. suf. (cc.) thread, hair (in counting). *eyé, rúwayé, wúnúyé, fayé, nimayé* or *nimeyé, wonayé* or *woneyé, fúúyé, wanúyé, ttiwayé* or *ttiweyé* one,...nine h.; but *engoon éénan* ten h. Cf. *één₂*.

éé₁ (1) ÉÉ₃, KÉÉ₂. nu. (T1) fishhook. *efóch éé* one f. *aan éé* his f. Syn. *fisuk*. Cf. *ké*.

éé₂ ÉÉ₄. N. v. phr. (?) yes. Syn. *wúú*.

éé₃ (1) ÉÉ₅. nu. (T1) name of the mid, central, unrounded vowel written *é*; name of the letter thus written.

éés (3) ÉÉSA. [Possibly derived from *éé₁* and *-sa-*.] n. (T3) sibling-in-law of same sex; any male consanguineal relative of wife in wife's generation, husband of any female consanguineal relative of a man in his generation, any female consanguineal relative of husband in husband's generation, wife of any male consanguineal relative of a woman in her generation. *éésan* his s.-in-l.

ééseni See *éés, -ni-*. vo. (T6a) acquire (someone) as a sibling-in-law of the same sex.

ééséés (db; 3) See *éés*. Var. *ékkéés*. vi. (dis.) be siblings-in-law of same sex. va. (dis.) treat (someone) as a sibling-in-law of same sex.

éésor nu. in *rongen é*. a form of sorcery that causes ringworm, and in *sáfeen é*. medicine to cure ringworm so caused.

ééssong (3) ÉÉSSONGA. Var. *ééssóng*. vi. reach out for something that is not within reach, reach out and fall short of one's goal; try and fail.

ééssongeey See *ééssong, -e-₂*. vo. (T6b) reach for and fall short of.

ééssóng Var. of *ééssong*.

éék excl. oops! [Uttered when one has misspoken, slipped, or suddenly remembered something forgotten.] *neesor kepwe feyinnó Wútéét...éék!...Wééné* tomorrow you will go to Udot...oops!...Moen.

éékúm (3) ÉÉKÚMA. nu. (T3) bundle (as of things in a cloth or mat). *eew é*. one b. *éékúmen mettóóch* bundle of things. Cf. *túkúm*.

éékúma See *éékúm*. vo. (T3) bundle, make a bundle of. With dir. suf.: *éékúmóónó* bundle (something) up, bundle away. Cf. *túkúmi*.

éékúmóónó See *éékúma*.

éémé (1) ÉÉMÉÉ. nu. (T1) a tree (*Cynometra bijuga*). [It is used for firewood.]

één₁ (2: *énú-, ini-, wunu-, wúnú-*) ÉNÚ₁, WÚNÚ₃. nu. (T2) the number three. [Used in serial counting or to name the number in the abstract, but not used as a numerical adjective.] Cf. *wúnú-₁*.

één₂ (3) See *-é, -na-*. nu. (T3) fiber thread used in weaving; strand of hair. *eyé* one t.; *engoon éénan* ten t. *éénen wuuch* banana fiber t.; *éénen sinifé* hibiscus fiber t. *éénen mékúr* head hair; *eyé éénen mékúr* one strand of head hair.

éénaw (3) ÉÉNAWA. nu. (T3) platform on the outrigger booms of a canoe between the body of the canoe and the float (made up of three boards). *éénawen waa* canoe's outrigger p.

éénenippéw (2) See *één₂, -ppéw*. nu. form of magic that makes others unable to function in sport or war.

éépwúún (2) See *éé₁, pwúún₁*. nu. (T2) method of fishing with women's hand nets.

éér (2: *-ér, -ar*) ÉÉRÚ, ÉRÚ₁. nu. (T2) south. *é. meesón* a little south of west ("south from level"); *e mén é*. it is a south wind.

éereni₁ ÉÉRENI. N. [Possibly derived from é plus the formative -ra- plus -ni-. Cf. Wol. *yééri* be familiar with.] Var. *éerúni*. vo. (T2) do (something) regularly, be accustomed to, be used to. Dis. *ékkééreni* (ds). *wúse é*. I am not used to it; I don't do that. Cf. *éreni*.

éereni₂ (3) See *éereni₁, -ya-*. N. Var. *éerúni*. nu. (T3) custom, tradition. *éereniyan* or *aan é*. his c. *éereniyen Chuuk* Trukese c.

éerúnap (3) See *éer, nap*. nu. (T3) 1. due south. 2. south wind.

éerúni F. of *éereni₁* and *éereni₂*.

ééch (2) ÉCHCHÚ. Tb3. Var. *kéch*. vi., adj. (be) good, suitable, proper, appropriate, fitting, pleasing. *meyi é*. it is good, it is a good thing; *aa é*. it has become good. Syn. *mwirinné, wútek*. n. (T2) goodness, suitability, pleasing quality, suitable thing. *échchún* thing suitable for him. *meyi échchiy eey angaang* this work is suitable for me, this work is what I am good at (or what I like doing). *échchún eey mettóóch* the goodness of this thing.

éét₁ (2) ÉTÚ₁. nu. (T2) smoke. *étún suupwa* or *étús suupwa* cigarette smoke. *étún ómwun nifóro* sea spray.

Éét₂ [From *éét₁*.] nu. (loc.) Eot Island.

éétiw (3b) ÉÉTIWA. nu. east. *e mén é*. it is an east wind; *é. soonong* a little south of east; *é. soowu* a little north of east.

éétiwááfen (2) See *éétiw, efen₃*. nu. (T2) northeast.

éétiwenewen (3) See *éétiw, wen*. nu. (T3) due east.

éétiwéér (2) See *éétiw, éér*. nu. (T2) southeast.

ééw interj. indeed! really!

Ééyán nu. (loc.) Eiol Island.

ééyi See *éé₁, -yi-₂*. vo. (T4) hook (something) on a fishhook. Dis. *ékkééy* (ds). *wúwa é. ngeni ewe éé* I hooked it with the fishhook. *meyi éech eey éé pwún meyi ékkééy iik fáán chómmóng* this is a good fishhook because it hooks fish often.

ééyin (3) ÉÉYINA. nu. (T3) stripes (usually black, of woven loin skirt). *ééyinen chééyitúr* s. of the loin skirt.

ééyitte (1) See *éé₁, -i-₁, tee-₁*. nu. (T1) awl, bone punch. *eföch é*. one a. *aan é*. his a. *ééyitteen Chuuk* Trukese awl.

éfékúr (3) ÉFÉKÚRA. Var. *afékúr*. nu. (T3) child of male member of a matrilineal lineage or clan, person related through his father (connotes "heir"). *néwún é*. his é. child. *éfékúren Wééné* child of a Wééné (Moen) man.

éfén (2) See *fén₁*. nu. (c.; T2) boxing, striking with the fist. Dis. *ékkéfén* (ds). *chóón é*. boxer; *éfénún Merika* American boxing. Syn. *kkéfén*.

éfénú See *éfén*. vo. (c.; T2) strike (someone) with the fist, smite with the fist.

éfeng Var. of *eféng*.

éféréchchuku (2) See *afar, chuku-₁*. vo. (T2) elbow or shoulder one's way through.

éféw (2) See *faaw*. nu. (c.; T2) making into a ball (as when applying scented plants to a loin cloth to make it smell sweet). *éféwún achawar* making a ball of scented plants and a loin cloth.

éféwú See *faaw*. vo. (c.; T2) apply scented plants to (by rolling into a ball).

éffúrú See *ffúr*. vo. (c.; T2) catch (something that drips) in a container.

ésúúsú (db; 1) See *sú*. va. run off with another's wife, have an affair with another's wife, elope. *achawaren é*. compensation paid for sexual relations with another's wife. *aa máá ii é*., or *aa ésúúsúú má* he has indeed run off with another's wife.

ésúúcha (1) See *sú, chaa*. nu. (c.; T1) kite fishing, done to catch needle fish.

ésúúw See *sú*. vo. (c.; T1) cause to leave, depart, or go away; chase off, run off, clear out; elope with, run off with (another's wife); have an affair with (another's wife). With dir. suf.: *ésúúwénó*.

ésúúwénó See *ésúúw*.

ésúk (2) ÉSÚKÚ₁. nu. (T2) fruit that is almost fully formed but not yet ready to pick. *ésúkún mááy* not fully formed breadfruit.

ésúkaawu See *ésúkú₁*.

ésúkú₁ See *súk₁*. vo. (c.; T2) make protrude, make stick out, make not flush. With dir. suf.: *ésúkaawu* make stick out, cause to protrude.

ésúkú₂ See *súk₂*. vo. (c.; T2) wait for (something) to appear; expect, anticipate. *wúwa wetin é. wááyi we* I

waited and waited for my canoe to appear.
ésúkú₃ ÉSÚKÚ₂. vo. (T2) wonder at, marvel at, be amazed at. Dis. *ésúkúsúkú* (db); *ékkésúkú* (ds).
ésúkúsúk (db; 2) See *ésúkú₃*. nu. (T2) wonder, amazement. *ésúkúsúkún Eiue reen ewe sepeniin* Eiue's amazement at that airplane. vi. be amazed, marvel, wonder.
ésúkúsúkú Dis. of *ésúkú₃*.
éssúkú See *ssúk₂*. vo. (c.; T2) cause to bleed or flow (of blood, sap, etc.).
éssúkúchcha (1) See *ssúk₂, chcha*. nu. (T1) bloodshed.
éssúráátiw F. of *assúraatiw* (see *assúrú*).
éssúrú₁ F. of *assúrú*.
éssúrú₂ See *ssúr₂*. vo. (c.; T2) catch in a container (as with rain).
ékéttú See *kkéét*. F. Var. *akéttú*. vo. (c.; T2) scratch. *wúwa ékéttúwey* I s. myself.
ékúúw See *kú₁*. vo. (c.; T1) light (a fire), cause to glow.
ékúúwef (2) See *kú₁, ááf*. nu. (c.; T2) fire signal (made with a coconut frond torch). [It is meaningful as a signal only when made right after sundown.]
ékúkkúffengenniiy See *kúkkúffengeen, -i-₂*. vo. (c.; T5) bring close together, cause to be close together.
ékúkkúnáátiw See *ékúkkúnú*.
ékúkkúnú See *kúkkún*. vo. (c.; T2) cause to be small, make small. With dir. suf.: *ékúkkúnáátiw* make smaller, make less, lessen, decrease.
ékúna₁ See *kún₁*. vo. (c.; T3) make (someone) successful in his quest, grant a request to. *kese mwechen kepwe ékúnááyey ááy eey tingor* will you please grant to me this my request?
ékúna₂ See *kúna-*. vo. (T3) show. With *ngeni*: *ékúnaangeni* show to.
ékúnaangeni See *ékúna₂*.
ékúnna See *kúun*. vo. (c.; T3) wait for (the sea) to be high tide. *siya é. sáát* we are waiting for the sea to be high tide.
ékúrang₁ (3) See *kúra-₂, -ng*. nu. (c.; T3) rattle, rustle, noise of people speaking. *ékúrangen aramas* the noise of people talking. vi. be noisy, rustle (of trees in wind), rattle. *wúse rongorong pwe chóón imwey ngé ré é*. I didn't hear because of the people of my house and the noise of their talking.
ékúrang₂ (3) See *ékúrang₁*. nu. (c.; T3) a tree (*Hernandia ovigera*). [Its name refers to the noise of its fruit rattling in the wind. The bark is used as a medicine for illness caused by sea spirits; the flowers are used as medicine for stiffness of the joints.] Syn. *achchorong*.
ékúranga See *ékúrang₁*. vo. (c.; T3) cause to be noisy, make (something) rattle.
ékúrúrú See *kúrúr*. vo. (c.; T2) slip or slide (curtain or zipper) apart or together. Syn. *érrúrú*.
ékké- Dis. of *é-*. Routine, unambiguous ds forms of this type are not listed as separate entries but may be found under the unreduplicated words beginning with *é-*.
ékkéés (ds; 3) See *ées*. Var. *éesées*. vi. (dis.) be siblings-in-law of same sex. va. (dis.) treat (someone) as a sibling in law of the same sex.
ékkénúk (ds; 2) See *énúk*. n. (dis.; T2) belt, cummerbund, something tied or fastened around the waist. *ékkénúkún* his b. vi. (dis.) wear something fastened around the waist.
ékképén (ds; 2) PÉNÚ. Var. *akkapén*. nu. (c., dis.; T2) oath, affirmation. va. (c., dis.) swear (by), make affirmation. *wúwa é. semey (wúwé ékképés semey)* I s. by my father.
ékképénú See *ékképén*. Var. *akkapénú*. vo. (c., dis.; T2) swear by. *wúwa é. semey* I swear by my father.
ékkérúwáánú See *rúwáánú*.
ékkérúwe See *rúwe*.
ékkérúwémén See *rúwémén*.
ékkét Dis. of *ét*.
ékkéwú- (ds; 2) See *éwú-₂*. ni. (T2) width, thickness, diameter, circumference, girth. *ékkéwiiy, ékkéwumw, ékkéwún* my, your (sg.), his girth.
ékkú- (2: *-yék*) ÉKKÚ. ni., suf. (cc.) net (in counting). *eyék, rúwéyék, wúnúyék, féyék, nimeyék, wonoyék, fúúyék, wanúyék, ttiweyék, engoon ékkún* one,...ten n.; *fiteyék* how many n. Cf. *wuuk*.
ékkúúngeni See *kkúúw₁, ngeni*. vo. (c.; T2) cause (one) to bite; let bite. *kete ékkúúngeniyey naan konaak* don't let that dog to bite me.

ékkúk (2) See *kkúk* nu. (c.; T2) 1. upper rim of ear. *ékkúkún sening* ear's u. r. 2. clamp, pin. *ékkúkún mékúr* bobby pin; hair pin; *ékkúkún mangaak* clothespin.

ékkúkóónó See *ékkúkú*.

ékkúkú See *kkúk* vo. (c.; T2) pin (as with hairpin or clothespin); close. With dir. suf.: *ékkúkóónó* close (as a door, handcuff).

ékkúm (3b) See *kkúm*. vi. (c.) make oneself rigid, become rigid. With dir. suf.: *ékkúmúnó* brace oneself, become more rigid.

ékkúma See *ékkúm*. vo. (c.; T3) make rigid, cause to be rigid.

ékkúmúnó See *ekkúm*.

ékkúmúnóóngeni See *ékkúm, -nó, ngeni*. vo. (c.; T2) brace oneself against.

ékkúné (1) ÉKKÚNÉÉ. F. Var. *kúné*. nu. (T1) mission, errand, charge. *chóón é*. messenger, errand boy; legate, apostle. vi. be sent on an errand.

ékkúnééw See *ékkúné*. vo. (c.; T1) charge, give a mission to, send (someone) on an errand, give an order to.

émékupw (2) ÉMÉKUPWU. nu. (T2) species of surgeon fish, convict tang. *émékupwun* s. f. of (a given region). Syn. *kiirach*.

émékkú See *mmék*. vo. (c.; T2) shatter, break.

éménúúnúúw See *ménúúnú*. vo. (c.; T1) make tired, fatigue.

éménúkotu See *ménúkot*. vo. (c.; T2) make an offering to (spirits).

éménúménú (db) See *maan*₁. vo. (c.; T2) stay with (someone) so that he will not be lonely; keep (someone) company.

éménúwénú (db; 3) See *ma-, núw*. vi. (c.) be nonchalant, unconcerned.

éméngú See *méng*. Var. *émméngú*. vo. (c.; T2) soften; cure (pandanus leaf by scraping with a shell, as when preparing for mat making); deflate (a tire).

éméréwúna See *méréwún*. vo. (c.; T3) remove scales from, scale (a fish), pluck feathers or hairs from. Syn. *étéréwúna*.

émérúk vi. be dried up (of the four types of taro: *pwuna, kká, óni, woot*).

émét (2) See *mét*. n. (c.; T2) food to eat on a trip or journey. *émétún* his f. for a journey.

émétú See *mét*. vo. (c.; T2) feed to satisfy, cause to be sated (with food or drink); (refl.) eat or drink to satiety. *wúwa émétúwey* have eaten to satiety.

éméw (2) ÉMÉWÚ. Tb. nu. (T2) sexual intercourse with a woman without her knowledge. *éméwún neepinu* s. i. with a woman when her husband is present and asleep and the woman thinks her lover is really her husband.

éméwú See *éméw*. Tb. vo. (T2) have sexual intercourse with (a woman) without waking her.

éméwúr (2) See *méwúr*. vi. (c.) shut one's eyes (as in sleep). *éméwúrún maas* (n. phr.) staring at the ground or closing one's eyes in anger; winking at someone as a sign of affection.

éméwúrú See *méwúr*. vo. (c.; T2) put (someone) to sleep.

émúúmú (db; 1) See *mú*. vi. (c.) be melancholy (of person or song).

émmék (2) See *mmék*. vi. be hatched.

émméréwú See *mméréwu-*. vo. (c.; T2) flatter.

émmérupu (1) See *puu*-₁. vi. (c.) blink.

émméwúr₁ (2) See *méwúr*. vi. (c.) shut one's eyes (as in sleep).

émméwúr₂ (2) See *émméwúr*₁. nu. (T2) small bud. *émméwúrún irá* tree's s. b.

émmún (2) ÉMMÚNÚ. n. (T2) liver. *eché é.* one l. *émmúnún* his l. *makkeey wóón chéén émmúniy* inscribe it in my heart ("inscribe it on the leaves of my liver"). Cf. *mmún*.

émwékút (2) See *mwékút*. nu. (c.; T2) acceleration, making speedier. *oowun é.* acceleration fee, paid to a canoe builder to make alterations on a canoe so that it will go faster. va. (c.) accelerate, go faster. Dis. *émwékútúkút* (db).

émwékútú See *mwékút*. vo. (c.; T2) accelerate, make speedier; cause to move or run (as with a machine), start (an engine). Dis. *émwékútúkútú* (db).

émwénéw (2) ÉMWÉNÉWÚ. va. practice the art of hand-to-hand fighting. nu. (T2) art of hand-to-hand fighting.

émwénéwú See *émwénéw*. vo. (T2) practice (hand-to-hand fighting).

émwér (2) ÉMWÉRÚ. vi. difficult to mash (of breadfruit). Dis. *émwérúmwér* (db). *wúsúúsún é.* its mashing is difficult. Syn. *épwék*.

émwérú (3) See *émwér*. vo. (T2) mash with soft strokes in order to deal with hard breadfruit that has been inadequately cooked.

émwérúmwér Dis. of *émwér*.

émwécháátá See *émwéchú*.

émwéchú See *mwéch*. vo. (c.; T2) grasp, take hold of, retain, hold fast to; (fig.) learn; remember. Dis. *ékkémwéchú* (ds). *é. núkún* memorize, learn by heart. With dir. suf.: *émwécháátá* haul up with one's hands.

émwéchúnnúkúúw See *mwéch, nnúk, -ú-*. vo. (c.; T5) hold very tightly; memorize; obey faithfully.

émwéwúna See *mwéwúnéwún*. vo. (c.; T3) cause to swing back and forth; wag. Dis. *émwéwúnéwúna* (db).

émwéwúnéwúna Dis. of *émwéwúna*.

émwéwúchú See *mwéwúchúúch*. Var. *amwawúchú*. vo. (c.; T2) jiggle. Dis. *émwéwúchúúchú* (db).

émwéwúchchú See *mwéwúch*. vo. (c.; T2) startle.

émwúúmey (2) See *mwú₂, mááy₂*. F. nu. (c.; T2) end of the breadfruit season; last ceremonial making of breadfruit pudding; traditional feast for termination of the breadfruit season. vi. make the feast to celebrate the end of the breadfruit season.

émwúúw See *mwú₂*. F. Var. *omwuu*. vo. (c.; T1) make stop, let stop, wait for (something) to stop. *émwúúw ráán, émwúúw wúút* wait for the rain to stop, let the rain stop. With dir. suf.: *émwúúwetiw* make an end downward of; pick the last of (the breadfruit crop).

émwúúwetiw See *émwúúw*.

émwúrinnééw See *mwúrinné*. Var. *emwirinnééw*. vo. (c.; T1) improve, make good. With dir. suf.: *émwúrinnééwénó* improve, make better.

émwúch (2) ÉMWÚCHÚ. F. Var. *amwúch, mwúúch₁*. nu. (T2) firewood. *emwúch é., echef é.* one piece of f.

émwúchchú See *mwmwúch*. vo. (c.; T2) terminate, bring to an end, do for the last time, put an end to.

émwúchchúnó See *émwmwúch*.

émwmwúch (2: *émwúchchú-*) See *mwmwúch*. nu. (c.; T2) making a termination. With dir. suf.: *émwúchchúnó* termination conclusion, end; *émwúchchúnóón eey pworóówus* the end of this account. vi. be a termination, be a last time. *epwe oow wóón saman pwú epwe emwúchchún aan nnengeni masan* he will take funeral gifts to his father for it will be the last time he will look upon his face. With dir. suf.: *émwúchchúnó* be terminated.

énééné (db; 1) See *néé₂*. Var. *anééné*. va. (c.) fill with liquid.

énéénééw See *néén₂*. Var. *anééééw*. vo. (c.; T1) put liquid contents into, fill with liquid, make flooded.

énéffáán N. of *énúfáán*.

énéwúnéw (db; 2) See *naaw*. vi. (c.) deliver a baby. Dis. *ékkénéwúnéw* (ds). *chóón énéwúnéw* midwife.

énéwúnéwú See *naaw*. vo. (c.; T2) 1. deliver (someone) of a baby, be midwife to. 2. make or allow (someone) to use something.

éniyon (Eng.) Var. *aniyon*. nu. onion. Syn. *tamaningi*.

énú-₁ (2) ÉNÚ₂. [In cpds. only.] Var. *énúwa-*. unsp. color.

énú-₂ (2) ÉNÚ₃. [In cpds. only.] unsp. youth, young man. See *énúffé, énúmwáán, énúwén*.

énú (1) ÉNÚÚ. Var. *anú*. nu. (T1) god, spirit, spirit of the dead, ghost. *énúún aramas* spirit of a dead person that has acquired someone as a medium (otherwise a person's spirit or soul is *ngúnún aramas*); *énúún ápiipi* spirits of driftwood that cause illness (*semwmwenin winikápiipi*) to pregnant woman; *énúún mááy* (or *maay*) spirit of breadfruit; *énúún mwárisi* god of the rainbow (cf. *resiim*). *énúwen ommung* (instead of *énúún ommung*) goddess of love; *énúwen maay* spirit of breadfruit.

énúúfeefin (3) See *énú, feefin*. nu. (T3) female spirit or ghost.

énúúso (1) See *énú, so₂*. nu. (T1) nightmare, bad dream. vi. have a nightmare.

énúúsooso₁ (db; 1) See *énú, so₁* (?). nu. (T1) a rite of sorcery used in war to weaken the enemy. Syn. *sooyénú*. Cf. *énúúso*.

Énúúsooso₂ nu. (pers.) god of war, a spirit causing illness and death unless counteracted by the appropriate spell.

enúúsór See *enú, -sór*. nu. spirit of the dead that can be summoned by a spirit medium, summonable spirit. Syn. *enúúyéech*.

enúúki₁ (1) See *enú, -ki*. F. Var. *anúúkiin, enúúkiin*. nu. (T1) rash on babies caused by a spirit and leading to death if not cured by a spell. *sáfeen é*. medicine to cure the rash. vi. have a rash.

enúúki₂ See *enú, -ki*. nu. (T1) eccentric, unpredictable, or precipitous behavior. *enúúkiin átánaan* the eccentric behavior of that fellow. vi. behave in an eccentric, unpredictable, or precipitous manner.

enúúkiin Var. of *enúúki₁*.

enúúmaamaaw (3) See *enú, maamaaw*. vi. insult a heavenly god or good spirit of the dead; (by extension) be ill as a result of failure to obey one's parents, a chief, a priest, or the rules of conduct. [The cure is to confess one's errors and obtain forgiveness from the spirit or offended person.]

enúúmanaw (3) See *enú, manaw*. nu. (T3) any of the ancestral founders of *itang* (such as Sowuwóóniiras, Sowufa, or Sowukuwopw); Jesus.

enúúmwáán (4) See *enú, mwáán₁*. nu. (T2) male spirit or ghost.

Énúúnap (3) See *enú, nap*. nu. (pers.) chief god in the pre-Christian pantheon; the Christian God. [He lives in the region of the sky named *Faachchamw* and rules over everything.]

enúúnúpwwún (2) See *enú, pwpwún*. nu. (T2) earth spirits whose bite causes illness.

enúúngngaw (3b) See *enú, ngngaw*. nu. (T3) a person's bad soul. Syn. *ngúnúngngaw*. vi. be maleficent; be a person who practices sorcery or who does evil to others. *emén meyi é*. one who is m.

enúúroch (3) See *enú, roch*. nu. (T3) bad soul; evil spirit. Syn. *enúúngngaw, soope*.

enúúyaramas (3) See *enú, aramas*. Var. *enú aramas*. nu. (T3) a god, any class of beings with the characteristics of people (*aramas*) and of invisible spirit-beings (*soope*) simultaneously in that they may be invisible or make themselves visible in human form.

enúúyéech (2: *-yéchchú-*) See *enú, ééch*. nu. (T2) good spirit of the dead (the kind that has a relationship with a spirit medium). Syn. *enúúsór*.

enúfáán See *éen₁, fáán₁*. Var. *enéffáán*. nu. the combined number three-four in serial counting by twos (formed from elements for both three and four).

enúffach (3) See *enú-₁, ffach*. vi., adj. (be) light brown colored (not bright).

enúffé (1) See *enú-₂, -fé*. nu. (T1) young one, youngster (of people or animals). *emén chék é*. one that is just a youngster. vi., adj. (be) young, be a youngster. *iir meyi chiwen é*. they are still youngsters.

enúk (2) See *núkú-₃*. n. (c.; T2) belt, cummerbund; something fastened or worn around the waist. *enúkún* his b. vi. wear something around the waist, be belted.

enúkáát (4) See *enú-₂, áát*. nu. (T2) teenaged boy, youth.

enúkúni See *enúk, -ni-*. vo. (c.; T5) acquire (a belt), acquire (something) as a belt.

enúkúnúk (db; 3) See *núkú-₃*. nu. (c.; T2) tightening, making tight. *sáfeen é*. medicine against *mwusochcha* (vomiting blood) [said to tighten the stomach so as to stop bleeding].

enúkúnúkú (db) See *núkú-₃*. vo. (c., dis.; T2) 1. tighten, make firm; check, prove (an arithmetic problem). 2. prepare (something) against disaster, make safe or secure.

enúkúnúkúngngaw (db; 3b) See *núúk, ngngaw*. vi., adj. (c., dis.) (be) untrustworthy, not to be believed.

enúkúnúkúngngawa (db) See *núkúnúkúngngaw*. vo. (T3) make a mess of; cause to look bad or to be untidy; put in disarray.

enúkúng (2) See *enú-₁, kúng*. vi., adj. (be) brown colored.

enúmwáán (2) See *enú-₂, mwáán₁*. nu. (T2) man in his prime (35 to 45 years old).

enúnnúch (ds; 2) See *nnúch*. va. (c., dis.) make a clicking noise (as with the teeth). *é. nii* click the teeth.

enúpar (3b) See *enú-₁, par*. vi. be red colored.

enúpwech (3) See *enú-₁, pwech*. vi. be white colored.

énúwa- (3) See énú-₁, -wa-. ni. (T3) color (of something). énúwan his c. énúwan meyi pwech his color is white; énúwen foorket purple ("color of forget-me-nots"). Syn. énúwén, énúyén.
énúwaay See núwa. vo. (c.; T1) wait for (the sea or weather) to be calm.
énúwén₁ (db; 2) See énú-₂. n. young man. é. áát very young man, teen aged youth. vi. be a y. m.
Énúwén₂ (db; 2) See één₁. nu. (T2) 1. constellation of the three stars in Orion's belt (Delta, Epsilon, and Zeta Orionis). 2. the name for a month in some calendars.
énúwén₃ (db; 2) See énú-₁. Var. énúwa-, énúyén. n. (T2) color. énúwénún its c.
énúwénúsich See énúwén₁, -sich₂. nu. very young man, teen aged youth ("barely an énúwén").
énúyén (db; 2) See énú-₁. Var. énúwa-, énúwén₃. n. (dis.; T2) color. énúyénún its c. énúyénún fetin green, grass color.
énnáátiw See énnú.
énnéw (dc; 2) See naaw. nu. (T2) midwifery. fin énnéw midwife. vi. do midwifery, be a midwife.
énnú See nnú-. vo. (c.; T2) fold up (a mat or sail); lower (a sail). With dir. suf.: énnaatá f. up. énnaatiw, énnáátiw lower (a sail) down; unfold, spread out (a mat); énnóónó f. up.
énnúk (2) See nnúk₂. nu. (c.; T2) law, edict, order, regulation, command, rule, ordinance. énnúkún Kangkúres law passed by Congress; é. atapwanapwan temporary regulation. emén meyi kkémwéch é. one who clings or holds to the law; chóón é., chóón angeey é. law enforcement officer, administrator of the law. vi., adj. (be) restricted.
énnúkú₁ See énnúk. vo. (c.; T2) enact (a law, rule, ordinance), legislate, issue (an edict, order).
énnúkú₂ See nnúk₂. vo. (c.; T2) tighten (a knot, belt); make steady, firm, tight; restrict.
énnúnó (1) See nnú-, nó. vi. (c.) be folded up (of a mat or sail), be folded away.
énnúrú₁ See nnúr₂. vo. (c.; T2) give shade to, cause to be shaded.
énnúrú₂ N. Var. érúrú, érrúrú. vo. (T2) slip or slide (something) out or together (as with a curtain). With dir. suf.: énnúraanong s. inside; énnúraatá s. up.
énnúch (2) See nnúch. vi. (c.) make something snap or click.
énnúchóónó See énnúchú.
énnúchú See nnúch. vo. (c.; T2) cause to snap or click; click, fasten (a lock). é. wóón ngii bite between the teeth (as to kill a louse). With dir. suf.: énnúchóónó lock (something) up or away.
-éngú- (2) [In cpds. only.] unsp. soft, pliable. See maangúwéng.
éngúnúwa See ngúún, -wa-. vo. (c.; T3) reflect (something, as in a mirror).
éngútú See ngút. vo. (c.; T2) cause to be stopped up, cause to be tightly fitted.
éngngún (dc; 2) See ngúnúngún. nu. (c.) song accompanying a pwérúk dance.
éngngúngú See ngngúúng₂. vo. (c.; T2) cause (someone) to chew and suck (sugarcane or pandanus).
épékúpékúúw (db) See ppék, -ú-. vo. (c., dis.; T5) make even, make the same. Syn. éppékú.
épénúwa See pénú. vo. (c.; T3) be a navigator for, navigate. epwe é. eey waa he will be the n. for this vessel.
épéréén (2) ÉPÉRÉÉNÚ. nu. (T2) coconut leaflet decorations hung from the gunwale of a paddle canoe. épéréénún waa canoe's c. l. d. wáán épéréén lines strung along gunwale of canoe from which to hang c. l. d.
épét₁ (2) ÉPÉTÚ₁. nu. (T2) flower bud. épétún its bud.
épét₂ (1) ÉPÉTÚ₂. nu. (T1) a kind of foul-smelling coral.
épétúmá (1) See épét₂, má. nu. (T1) deadly foul-smelling coral (from a spell).
épúngáátiw See épúngú₃.
épúngépúnga (db) PÚNGA. vo. (c., dis.; T3) admire (a person). Dis. ékképúngépénga (ds).
épúngú₁ Var. of éppúngú.
épúngú₂ See púng₁. vo. (c.; T2) cause to explode, detonate, cause to slam.
épúngú₃ See púng₂. vo. (c.; T2) cause to fall (of rain, mosquito net, etc.). With dir. suf.: épúngáátiw cause to fall down.
épúngúmóng (2) See púng₂, móóng. vi. (c.) wear one's hair long and loosely down the back.

épúngúpúng (db; 2) See *púng*₁. va. (c.) make explode, shoot off, set off, detonate.

épúngúchééwúúw See *púng*₁, *chééw*, *-ú-*. vo. (c.; T5) fire continously (as a machine gun).

éppékú See *ppék*. vo. (c.) make exactly alike, make uniform, make even, make the same. *sipwe é. wúfach* we shall make our clothes exactly alike. Syn. *épékúpékúúw*.

éppénúffengen (2) See *ppénú*, *ffengen*. va. (c.) cause to be in opposition. Syn. *ékképpénú*.

éppénúwa See *ppénú*. vo. (c.; T3) 1. answer, pay (someone) back, reply to (someone). Cf. *ppénúweni*. 2. make a pair of, match. *kopwe é. nowumw na choori ngeni ena meyi araw* You will match your zori with that blue one.

éppéchénú See *ppéchén*. vo. (c.; T2) feed (someone) breadfruit or taro that is dipped into water before it is eaten.

éppún (2) ÉPPÚNÚ. nu. (T2) very soft meat of young drinking coconut (*éppúnún núú*); white of an egg (*éppúnún sókun*).

éppúng₁ (2) ÉPPÚNGÚ. nu. (T2) lower part of the back. *éppúngún* l. p. of his b.

éppúng₂ (2) See *ppúng*. n. (T2) lid, cover. *éppúngún* its l. *éppúngún asam* door; *éppúngún nakkich* rat-trap; *éppúngún pwóór* box lid; *éppúngún ruume* bottle stopper, cork, bottle cap.

éppúngaatiw See *éppúngú*.

éppúngáátiw See *éppúngú*.

éppúngóónó See *éppúngú*.

éppúngú See *ppúng*. Var. *épúngú*₁. vo. (c.; T2) put a lid on, close up, shut. Dis. *ékképpúngú* (ds). With dir. suf.: *éppúngáátiw, éppúngaatiw* put a lid down on; *éppúngóónó* shut away.

éppúrú (1) ÉPPÚRÚÚ. nu. (T1) copying, imitating, mimicking. *aan é.* his c. *chóón é.* copier, copycat; *nemenem wóón é.* copyright. vi. be copied. va. copy, mimic, make an imitation. Dis. *ékképpúrú* (ds).

éppúrúúw See *éppúrú*. vo. (T1) copy, make a copy of, mimic, imitate. Dis. *ékképpurúúw* (ds). *ááy é. óómw angaang* my copying your work. *kepwe éppúrúúwey nóón imwey* you will share my house with me ("you will do as I do in my house").

épwék (2) See *pwék* vi. (c.) be hard to mash (of breadfruit). Syn. *émwér*.

épwékú See *épwék*. vo. (T2) mash (breadfruit) with difficulty.

épwénúwétá See *pwénúwe-, -tá*. vo. (c., dir.) cause to be done or accomplished; bring to pass.

épwét (2) ÉPWÉTÚ. nu. (T2) preserved or fermented breadfruit. *anan é.* his p. b. (to eat), *maraan é.* his p. b. (that he has prepared). Syn. *maar*.

épwéwúkúúkú See *pwéwúkúúk*. vo. (c.; T2) cause to shake or tremble.

épwúnnú See *pwúún*₁. vo. (c.; T2) break, cause to be broken.

épwúng (2) See *pwúng*₁. Var. *kképwúng*. nu. (c.; T2) determination of what is right; legal hearing, trial.

épwúngóónó See *épwúngú*.

épwúngú See *pwúng*₁. vo. (c.; T2) correct, put right; determine the right course for, determine the truth of; arrive at a judicial decision about; (with suf. obj. prn.) advise (someone) of (his) mistakes. *aa épwúngúwey* he corrected me, he advised me of my errors; *sipwe épwúngú pwúngún* we shall determine the truth of it; *repwe épwúngú aar angaang* they will determine the right course for their work. With dir. suf.: *épwúngóónó* determine the right course for (work, action, etc.).

épwúngúpwúng (db) See *pwúngú-*. F. nu. species of flounder. *épwúngúpwúngún Chuuk* Trukese f. Syn. *fichan*.

épwúpwpwúnú (ds; 3) See *pwpwúnú*. nu. (c.; T3) marriage, wedding.

épwúpwpwúnúúw (ds) See *pwpwúnú*. F. Var. *épwúpwpwúnúwa*. vo. (c.; T1) cause to be married, find a spouse for; marry (as by a priest). Cf. *pwúnúweni*.

épwúpwpwúnúwa (ds) See *pwpwúnú*. N. Var. *épwúpwpwúnúúw*. vo. (c.; T3) cause to be married, marry (as by a priest). Cf. *pwúnúweni*.

épwpwékú See *pwpwék*. vo. (c.; T2) awaken, cause to lie awake. Dis. *ékképwpwékú* (ds).

épwpwén (dc; 2) See *pwénú-*₂. n. (c.; T2) cover, lid. *épwpwénún* its c. *épwpwénún omos* operculum of the turban shell (cats eye); *épwpwénun maas* eyelid. vi., adj. (be) covered.

épwpwénú See *épwpwén.* vo. (c.; T2) cover, put a lid on.

épwpwún₁ (2) See *pwpwún₁.* nu. (c.; T2) black paint made from mangrove (*woong*) bark, hibiscus charcoal, and water. *épwpwúnún waa* canoe's b. p.

épwpwún₂ (2) See *pwpwún₁.* nu. (c.; T2) small, black crab frequenting the muddy regions of mangrove swamps. *épwpwúnún Chuuk* Trukese *é.* .

épwpwúnú₁ See *pwpwún₁.* vo. (c.; T2) soil, stain, make dirty (as of clothing).

épwpwúnú₂ See *épwpwún₁.* vo. (c.; T2) paint with *éppwún* paint.

ér₁ (2) See *érú-₂.* vi. be pale, have pallor (of skin). With dir. suf.: *érúnó* become pale; *aa érúnó wóón masan* his face became pale. Syn. *kkiyér.*

ér₂ (2) ÉRÚ₂. [In cpds. only.] Var. *wérú-.* unsp. call out in fear or pain, cry out; bawl, bellow, moo, roar. Dis. érúwér, erúyér (db). Syn. *er₂.* See *érúyér, féérúwér, pwuchéér.*

érá (1) ÉRÁÁ. N. Var. *ará, árá, erá, wúrá.* va. say, utter. Dis. *ékkérá* (ds). *wúwa akkérá (wúwa ékkérá) ii chiyeney* I have been saying (hence supposing) that he is my friend. Cf. *éreni.*

éreni See *érá, -ni-.* N. Var. *areni, áreni, ereni, wúreni.* vo. (T5) say to, talk to, speak to, tell. *érenuku ne* you are talking to yourself, sir (i.e., no one is paying attention to what you say). Cf. *ééreni₁.*

éré (1) ÉRÉÉ. nu. (T1) heron (general name).

éréé- (1) ÉRÉÉ, KÉRÉÉ. F. [In cpds. only.] Var. *aréé-.* unsp. scrape, sanded, make smooth by scraping or sanding.

éréépwech (3) See *éré, pwech.* nu. (T3) kind of heron ("white or light h.").

éréér (3) ÉRÉÉRA. nu. (T3) coconut blossom or spathe from within which a new cluster of nuts will form and from which *áchi* is taken before it opens. *éééren núú* coconut's blossom.

éréchón (4) See *éré, chón.* nu. (T2, T3) kind of heron ("black or dark h.").

éréchcha (1) See *éré, chcha.* nu. (T1) kind of heron ("blood-colored h.").

érééti See *éréé-, -ti-.* F. Var. *aréétí.* vo. (T4) scrape, sand, make smooth by scraping (as with a piece of glass) or by sanding.

érétopw (2) See *éré, topw.* nu. (T2) kind of heron ("dull-colored h.").

érú-₁ (2: *-ér, -ar*) ÉRÚ₃. vi. stirring with a stick, spoon, or other object; leveling off the hot stones in an earth oven preparatory to putting food on them.

érú-₂ (2) ÉRÚ₁. nr. (T2) pallor (of skin). *érún masan* the pallor of his face.

érúú Var. of *érúúw₁.*

érúúkéw See *rúúké.* vo. (c.; T1) surprise, astound, astonish.

érúúrúúw See *rúúrú₁.* vo. (c.; T1) curl (hair), make curly or wavy.

érúúw₁ See *rúwa-.* [Derived from the counting sequence **etta *rúúw*, which is now *eet érúúw* or *eet ttérúúw*.] Var. *érúú.* nu. (num.) the number two. [Used in serial counting or to name the number in the abstract, but not used as a numerical adjective, for which see *rúwa-.*] Syn. *ttérúúw.*

érúúw₂ See *érú-₁, -ú-.* vo. (T5) stir (something) with a stick, spoon, etc.; level (an oven) with a stick (by stirring the hot stones). Dis. *ékkérúúw* (ds), *érúwérúúw* (db). *é. nóón* stir it inside, stir the inside of it. *é. ewe wuumw* level off the earth oven's hot stones.

érúúw₃ See *érú-₃, -ú-.* vo. (T5) call out to (someone) from a distance; disturb (a meeting), call (someone) from a meeting or from his house. *kesapw é. wuut pwúú pinin* you shall not disturb (call to) the meeting house because it is forbidden. *emén aa érúúwey mé nóón imwey* someone called me from inside of my house.

érúúwénú (1) See *érúúw₃, énú.* nu. (T1) a type of *féérúyér* used traditionally when someone was ill or going to war.

érúkú See *rúk.* vo. (c.; T2) make unsteady, cause to tip. Dis. *érúkúrúkú* (db).

érúkúfen (2) See *rúkúfen.* vi. (c.) be tickled; be having a sexual thrill.

érúkúfeni See *érúkúfen.* vo. (c.; T2) tickle; stimulate sexually.

érúkúrúkú Dis. of *érúkú.*

érúnó See *ér₁.*

érúróónó See *érúrú.*

érúrú See *rúrú-.* Var. *érrúrú.* vo. (c.; T2) slip or slide (curtain or zipper) apart or together. *wúwa arúrú (wúwa é.) ááy pwotow* I have zipped my typewriter case. With dir. suf.: *érúróónó* zip (something) shut. Cf. *sukkóónó.*

Érúwáánú (1) See *rúwáánú.* nu. (c.; T1) Thursday ("Fourth").

érúwáánúú- See *rúwáánú*.

érúwee- See *rúwe*.

érúwéménú- See *rúwémén*.

érúwér₁ (db; 2) See *érú*-₁. nu. (T2) stirring stick used to arrange the hot stones in an earth oven; stick used by women to hunt octopus. *efóch é*. one s. s. *aan é*. his s. s. vi., adj. stir with a stick, spoon, or other object; (be) cooked by stone boiling in a wooden vessel (of preserved breadfruit: *maar meyi é., épwét meyi é*.).

érúwér₂ Var. of *érúyér*.

érúyér Dis. of *ér*₂.

érrúrú (dc) See *rúrú*-. Var. *érúrú*. vo. (c.; T2) slip or slide (curtain or zipper) apart or together. Syn. *ékúrúrú*.

échéén (2) ÉCHÉÉNNÚ. vi., adj. (be) smooth (of a surface). Syn. *mwótow*.

échéénnú See *échéén*. vo. (T2) smooth, make smooth with adze or plane or on a whetstone. *kepwe é. eey irá* you will make this beam smooth. Syn. *ómwmwótowu*.

échéchchénú See *chéchchén*. vo. (c., dis.; T2) make wet, moisten, dampen.

échúún (3) ÉCHÚÚNNA. vi. fast, refrain from eating.

échúúnna See *échúún*. vo. (T3) refrain from eating (food).

échúna See *chún*. vo. (c.; T3) cause to tip.

échúngúchúng (db; 2) See *chúngú*-. va. (c., dis.) make a vibration (as from walking heavily).

échúngúchúngú (db) See *chúngú*-. vo. (c., dis.; T2) cause to vibrate, make vibrate; rattle (a door).

échúwa See *chú*. N. vo. (c.; T3) pull up, take out, remove (of something that requires effort, as a spot).

échúwétip (3) See *chú, tiip*₁. nu. (c.; T3) gift to the wife and children of a man who is a *sowurong* in order to persuade them to give permission for the *sowurong* to use his knowledge on someone else's behalf.

échchékún (3) vi. be naked from the waist up, be clad only in loinclothing. Cf. *achchék*. ni. (T3) nakedness *échchékúnan* his n.

échchékúna See *échchékún* vo. (T3) let go-naked. *aa é. ewe áát* he let the boy go n.

échchémaawa See *chchémaaw*. vo. (c.; T3) harden, make hard. With dir. suf.: *échchémaawaanó* harden, make harder.

échchémaawaanó See *échchémaawa*.

échchiiti See *éech, -iti*. Var. *échchúúti, kéchchiiti*. vo. (T5) be good for, be suitable for, suit well. *meyi é. ewe semwmwen eey mwéngé* this food is good for that illness. *ese échchiitikich naan mwéngé* that food is not good for us.

échchúúti Var. of *échchiiti*.

échchúúw See *éech, -ú*-. Var. *kéchchúúw*. vo. (T5) make good, make suitable, improve.

échchúngeni See *éech, ngeni*. Var. *kéchchúngeni*. vo. (T2) 1. be good to, kind to. 2. be suitable for.

échchúngú See *chchúng*. vo. (c.; T2) make vibrate (as from walking heavily).

échchúpwér See *éech, -pwér*. N. vi. be very good, very fine, very suitable.

ét (2) See *éét*₁. vi. smoke; be smoky. Dis. *étúyét, étúwét* (db); *ékkét* (ds) be smoked (as fish).

étéréwúna See *téréwún*. F. vo. (c.; T3) scrape scales or hair from, scale, depilate; pluck feathers from; strip leaves from. Syn. *eméréwúna*.

étiiti See *éét*₁, *-iti*. vo. (T2) smoke, steam (something). Cf. *aatú*.

étú- (2) ÉTÚ₂. unsp. (u.m.) See *étúfi*.

étú See under *pwoong*.

étúúfichi See *túúfich*. F. Var. *ótuufichi*. vo. (c.; T2) render (someone or something) suitable or capable; make convenient, reinterpret (with *ngeni*). Syn. *étúúfichiiy*.

étúúfichiiy See *túúfich, -i-*₂. F. vo. (c.; T5) render (someone or something) suitable or capable; make convenient, reinterpret (with *ngeni*). Syn. *étúúfichi*.

étúútú (db; 1) See *túútú*. nu. (c.; T1) a medicinal bath; any preparation a person bathes himself with.

étúútúúw See *túútú*. vo. (c.; T1) bathe (someone).

étúúw See *tú*. vo. (c.; T1) bow (the head). *aa é. mékúran* he bowed his head.

étúfi See *étu-, -fi-*. F. Var. *atúfi, etifi, itifi*. vo. (T5) dip up, dip out (liquid from a container); scoop.

étúr (2) See *túúr*. nu. (c.; T2) strips of midrib of ivory-nut palm leaf inserted across the warp of a loom at the beginning of weaving in order to keep

the starting ends of the warp from unravelling.
étúwét₁ (db; 2) ÉTÚ₃. nu. (T2) a plant (*Wedelia biflora*). [Its flowers are used to prepare medicine for inflammation of the eyes.]
étúwét₂ Dis. of *ét*.
étúyét Dis. of *ét*.
éttúngú See *ttúng*. vo. (c.; T2) cause to flow.
éwéék (2) ÉWÉKKÚ. F. n. (T2) coconut fiber sling around back of weaver at the loom. *éwékkún* his s. Syn. *ámeyis, emeyis; eweyit*.
éwéén nu. tree (*Ficus tenctoris*). [Its fruit may be eaten in time of famine.]
éwérúúw (3) ÉWA, RÚWA. nu. the combined numbers one-two in serial counting by twos (formed from elements for both one and two). Cf. *eet, érúúw*.
éwéwú See *wéw*. vo. (c.; T2) make wealthy.
éwéwúngngaweey See *wéw, ngngaw, -e-₂*. vo. (c.; T6b) impoverish, make unwealthy.
éwéwúyéchchúúw See *wéw, éech, -ú-*. vo. (c.; T5) make wealthy.
éwú-₁ (2) ÉWÚ₁. [The most widely used form.] pref. (sub.) 1exc. sub. prn.: we (excluding persons addressed, var. *áyi-*); 2pl. sub. prn.: you, (var. *o-₂, owu-, wo-*). [Although a prefix, it is written separately except when followed by an aspect marker. Sub. prns. are used only at the beginning of narrative constructions and mark them as such.] *éwúwa* (reality), *éwúne* (immediate future), *éwúpwe* (future, unreality), *éwúsapw* (future negative), *éwúse* (negative reality), *éwúte* (immediate future negative, negative command).
éwú-₂ (2) ÉWÚ₂. ni. (T2) width, thickness, diameter, circumference. Dis. *ékkéwú-* (ds). *éwiy, éwumw, éwún* my, your (sg.), his w. *ifa awumw (éwumw)* what is your thickness or girth?
éwú-₃ (2) ÉWÚ₃. [In cpds. only.] unsp. stick; long slender object.
éwú-₄ (2) ÉWÚ₄. [In cpds. only.] unsp. current, flow (of water). See *éwúrá, éwút₁, éwúwé₁*.
éwú (1) See *wú₃*. nu. (c.; T1) mast. *éwúún waa* canoe's m. Cf. *maasto*.

éwúúsening (3a) See *wú₃, sening*. va. (c.) cock one's ear, cup one's ear with the hand so as to hear better. Cf. *éwússening*.
éwúúngeni (3a) See *wú₃, ngeni*. v. phr. heed, pay attention to. *é. seningomw ena pwóróówus* heed, listen to that story.
éwúúngngaw (3b) See *wú₃, ngngaw*. vi. (c.) be badly built.
éwúútopw (2) See *wú₂, topw*. vi. (c.) be painted black; be repainted black (of something that has become gray or faded) ("cause end of dullness").
éwúútopwu See *éwúútopw*. vo. (c.; T2) paint or repaint (something) black.
éwúúw₁ See *wú₂*. vo. (c.; T1) make stop, stop, halt.
éwúúw₂ See *wú₃*. vo. (c.; T1) make stand, erect, build, construct (a building).
éwúúwa- (3) See *éwúúw₂, -wa-*. ni. (T3) construction by (someone). *éwúúwan* c. by him. *éwúúwen Rikar* Rikar's c., something built by Rikar.
éwúúyééch (2) See *wú₃, ééch*. vi. (c.) be well built.
éwúfa See *wúúf*. vo. (c.; T3) cause to be clothed, clothe. Dis. *éwúféwúfa* (db) clothe, dress (in clothes for upper part of the body).
éwúfár nu. short handled hoe or mattock used in precolonial times.
éwúféwúfa Dis. of *éwúfa*.
éwúsapw See *éwú-₁*.
éwúse See *éwú-₁*.
éwússes (2) ÉWÚSSESI. nu. (T2) coconut cloth. *éwússesin núú* cloth of the coconut tree.
éwússening (3a) See *éwú-₂, sening*. va. (c.) listen, pay attention, pay heed, obey, give ear. Cf. *éwúúsening*. nu. (c.) listening, attending. *neeniyen é.* radar station, listening post.
éwússeningemmang (3) See *éwússening, mmang*. vi. be heedless, pay no attention.
éwúkáátiw See *éwúkú₂*.
éwúkisikiis (2) See *éwú-₂, kisikiis*. vi. be slim, narrow. Syn. *éwúchikichiik*.
éwúkú₁ See *wúkú-₁*. vo. (c.; T2) decide, determine; measure (quantity or depth).
éwúkú₂ See *wúk*. vo. (c.; T2) put an end to (something before it is finished), interrupt, disrupt. *aa é. aach fóós* he disrupted our talk. With dir. suf.:

éwúkáátiw terminate or postpone (what is going on before it is finished); *siya éwúkáátiw aach fóós* we have terminated our talk for the time being; *sipwe mwo éwúkáátiw* we shall stop it for now. Cf. *wúkúfi*.

éwúkúúk (db; 2) See *wúkú*-$_1$. nu. (c.; T2) extent, quantity. *ewúkúúkún* e. of it. va. (c.) 1. measure, make a measurement. 2. decide, make a decision.

éwúkúkkún (2) See *éwú*-$_2$, *kúkkún*. vi. be narrow, slim.

éwúma See *wúma*-. vo. (c.; T3) shape, give shape to.

éwúmanaw (3) See *éwú*-$_2$, *manaw*. vi., adj. (be) well filled out, healthy, of good size, husky, thriving. Ant. *éwúmáámá*.

éwúmáámá (1) See *éwú*-$_2$, *má*. vi., adj. be weak, emaciated (of animals), slightly wilted (of plants), shriveled, moribund. Ant. *éwúmanaw*.

éwúmmóng See *éwú*-$_2$, *mmóng*. vi., adj. be thick, fat, of large circumference or girth. Syn. *éwúwátte*.

éwún nu. kind of tuna or albacore.

éwúna See *wúné*-. vo. (c.; T3) shoot (a sling).

éwúnaangeni See *éwúna*, *ngeni*. vo. (c.; T2) shoot (a sling) at. *éwúnaangenney* shoot it at me. *wúpwé é. átánaan* I will shoot it at that fellow.

éwúnap (3) ÉWÚNAPA. vi. wrestle. Syn. *simwmwo*.

éwúnaw (3) See *wúnaw*. nu. (c.; T3) food given (or to be given) in welcome to a visitor. va. (c.) bring food to a visitor in welcome.

éwúnawa See *éwúnaw*. vo. (c.; T3) give breakfast to; bring food in welcome to.

éwúnaweey See *éwúnaw*, *-e*-$_2$. vo. (c.; T6b) give breakfast to; bring food in welcome to.

éwúne See *éwú*-$_1$.

éwúnenipwin nu. a shrub (*Jussiaea suffruticosa*). [Its leaves are used as a fixative in making dye.] Syn. *choyiro*.

éwúniyár$_1$ nu. whirlwind, waterspout, tornado. Cf. *ménúmén*.

Éwúniyár$_2$ nu. (pers.) a traditional storm god. [One of five children of the weather (*néwún ráán*), who live in the gale, sink boats in heavy seas, and blow down trees.]

éwúnú Var. of *éwúnnú*.

éwúnúún (db; 4) See *wúné*-. nu. (c.; dis.; T2) braided sling (weapon); braided headband. *éwúnúúnún Chuuk* Trukese sling.

éwúnúúnú See *wúnúún*$_1$. vo. (c.; T2) anesthetize, make numb.

éwúnúngát$_1$ (4) See *wúnúngát*. vi. (c.) have three wives or husbands at one time.

Éwúnúngát$_2$ (2) See *wúnúngát*. nu. (c.; T2) Wednesday ("Third").

éwúnúngáta- See *wúnúngát*.

éwúnúngáti- See *wúnúngát*.

éwúnna See *wún*$_3$. vo. (c.; T3) stretch (the body). Syn. *aawúnna*.

éwúnnú (dc) See *wún*$_1$. Var. *éwúnú*. vo. (c.; T2) give a drink to.

éwúnnúngeni See *wún*$_3$, *ngeni*. vo. (c.; T2) lean against.

éwúng (3) See -*wúng*. n. (c.; T3) chest (of body). *éwúngan* his c. Syn. *neewúng* (preferred), *fáán mwár*.

éwúngéwúng (db; 3) See -*wúng* (?). F. nu. (c.; T3) variety of very poisonous crab. Syn. *nichin*.

éwúngin (2) See *éwú*-$_2$, *ngin*. vi. be small (in width or circumference); be waning (of the moon). Cf. *éwúchik*.

éwúngú See *wúng*. vo. (c.; T2) cause to be blown or sounded (of a trumpet), blow, sound.

éwúpwe See *éwú*-$_1$.

Éwúr$_1$ nu. (loc.) mythical southland and home of breadfruit; (according to Bollig) a region of heaven and source of all things that are good to eat. [Bollig says it is divided into two regions, *Éwúrúnap* and *Éwúrúchik*.]

éwúr$_2$ (3) See *wúúr*$_2$. n. (c.; T3) crutch, cane, support. *efóch é.* one c. *éwúran* his c.

éwúra$_1$ See *wúra*-. vo. (c.; T3) explain, teach (something). Dis. *éwúréwúra* (db).

éwúra$_2$ (1v) See *éwúra*$_1$, *-a*-$_1$. nu. (c.; T1) instruction. *mwa, éwúráán iyé naan áát aa inaan angééchchún ne mwirimwir chitoosa?* my, by whose instructions has yonder fellow become that skilled in driving a car?

éwúraangeni See *éwúra*$_1$, *ngeni*. vo. (c.; T2) explain or teach (something) to (someone).

éwúrá (1) See *éwú-₄, -rá₂*. nu. (T1) stream, river. Syn. *éwúwé₁*. Cf. *chénúpwuupwu*.

éwúráátá See *éwúrú₂*.

éwúráátiw See *éwúrú₂*.

éwúres (2) See *wú-₅, resi-*. va. (c.) lay an egg.

éwúrek (2) See *wú-₅, -rek₁*. vi. (c.) worry, brood, have a nagging thought. Dis. *ékkéwúrek* (ds).

éwúrekiiy See *éwúrek, -i-₂*. vo. (T5) dread (something), worry about (something or someone). *éwúrekiyuk* worry about you. *wúwa é. áán átánaan epwe etto* I dread yonder fellow's coming here.

éwúreni See *éwúr₂, -ni-*. vo. (c.; T6a) acquire (something) as a crutch or cane.

éwúréwúr (db; 3) See *éwúr₂*. va. (c., dis.) use a crutch or cane; use (something) as a c.

éwúréwúra See *éwúra₁*.

éwúrú₁ See *wúrú-₁*. vo. (c.; T2) beware of, watch out for. *é. átánaan pwe ete sooná* beware of yonder fellow lest he steal.

éwúrú₂ See *wúr*. vo. (c.; T2) drag, haul, hoist. With dir. suf.: *éwúráátá* haul up (sail); *éwúráátiw* lower (sail). Syn. *wúri₂*.

éwúchamw (3) See *éwú-₃, chaamw*. nu. (T3) crossbeam of house or building (each end resting on the longitudinal beams or wallplates). *éwúchamwen iimw* house's c. *éwúchamw meenúk* c. lying along outer side of the regular end-crossbeam (installed for constructing an end-shed on old style house or meeting house); *éwúchamw nuuk* interior c.

éwúchik (2) See *éwú-₂, chiki-₁*. vi., adj. (be) slim, slender, narrow, not thick. Dis. *éwúchikichiik, éwúchikichik* (db). nu. (T2) slimness, narrowness. *éwúchikin maram* the s. of the moon (old moon or new moon); *éwúchikin me yéétiw* old moon (fourth quarter), *éwúchikin me notow* new moon (first quarter). Cf. *éwúngin*.

éwúchimw (3b) See *éwú-₃, chiimw*. n. (T3) strand of hair. *éwúchimwan* his s. of h.

éwúchche (1) ÉWÚCHCHEE. Var. *awúchche*. vi., adj. (be) precious, valuable, important, dear; high (in price). Syn. *éwúchcheeya*. nu. (T1) preciousness. *féwún é.* precious stone.

éwúchcheeya (1) See *éwúchche, aa-*. Var. *awúchcheeya, éwúchcheya*. vi. be precious, valuable, important, dear, prized; high in prices. Syn. *éwúchche*. Cf. *ácheng*.

éwúchcheeyaangeni See *éwúchcheeya, ngeni*. vo. (T2) be valuable to (someone).

éwúchcheeyááni See *éwúchcheeya, -ni-*. Var. *éwúchcheyaani*. vo. (T4) cherish, value, prize, appreciate, take good care of, treasure. Syn. *echeni*.

éwúchcheya Var. of *éwúchcheeya*.

éwúchcheyaani Var. of *éwúchcheeyááni*.

éwút₁ (3) See *éwú-₄, -ta-₁*. n. (T3) current (at sea), eddy. [Occurs in ptv. const.] *éwúten neeset* c. in the sea; *meyiwor éwútan* there is a c. vi. have or be a current.

éwút₂ (2) ÉWÚTÚ, KÉWÚTÚ. n. (T2) finger, toe, digit; leg (of insect); tentacle (of octopus or squid, syn. *óó*). *ewút é.* one f.; *engoon éwútún* ten f. *éwútún* his f. *é. sepwáák* fourth f.; *éwútiy é. sepwáák* my fourth f. *éwútún pecheech* our toes; *éwútún péwúch* our fingers. *éwútún kunók* clock's hand; *ewútún oppong* fishspear's prongs. Id. *éwútún pecheen áát* penis ("boy's toe").

éwúta See *wúút₂*. vo. (c.; T3) bring rain to, cause to be rained upon.

éwúte See *éwú-₁*.

éwútúkis (2) See *éwút₂, kisi-*. N. nu. (T2) little finger. *ewút é.* one l. f. *éwútún é.* his l. f. Syn. *éwútúngin*.

éwútúnap (3) See *éwút₂, nap*. n. (T3) thumb. *ewút é.* one t. *éwútúnapan* his t.

éwútúnuuk (3a) See *éwút₂, nuuk₁*. nu. (T3) middle finger. *ewút é.* one m. f. *éwútún é.* his m. f.

éwútúngin (2) See *éwút₂, ngin*. F. nu. (T2) little finger. *ewút é.* one l. f. *éwútún é.* his l. f. Syn. *éwútúkis*.

éwútúros (3a) See *éwút₂, ros*. vi., adj. (be) short fingered; without fingers.

éwútúttiit (1) See *éwút₂, -ttiit*. nu. (T1) index finger. *ewút é.* one i. f. *éwútún é.* his i. f.

éwúwa₁ See *wú₁*. vo. (c.; T3) honor, respect, observe (a law or tabu).

éwúwa₂ [Cf. *éwúwéw* from whose base, *éwú-*, this word is apparently derived.] vo. (T3) knead.

éwúwa₃ See *éwú-*₁.

éwúwátte (1) See *éwú-*₂, *wátte*. n. (T1) fatness, thickness. *éwúwátteen* his f. vi., adj. (be) fat, thick, of large girth. Syn. *éwúmmóng*.

éwúwé₁ (1) See *éwú-*₄, *-wé*. nu. (T1) stream, brook, creek, river. *eew é.* one s. *kkewe é. wóón Wééné* or *éwúwéén wóón Wééné* the streams on Wééné. Syn. *éwúrá*. Cf. *chónúpwuupwu*.

éwúwé₂ (1) ÉWÚWÉÉ. nu. (T1) species of snapper fish.

éwúwééch (2) See *wú*₁, *ééch*. Var. *éwúwéyééch*. va. (c.) respect, honor, observe (laws or tabus).

éwúwééchchúúw See *éwúwééch, -ú-*. vo. (c.; T5) honor well, observe well, comply well with (law or tabu).

éwúwéfar (3v) See *éwú-*₃, *afar*. Var. *éwúwéfár*. nu. (T3v) carrying pole. *efóch é.* one c. p. *aan é.* his c. p. Syn. *ámwmwár*.

éwúwéfara See *éwúwéfar*. vo. (T3) carry (something)on a pole. Dis. *ékkéwúwéfara* (ds).

éwúwéfár Var. of *éwúwéfar*.

éwúwénú (1?) See *éwú-*₃ (?), *énú* (?). nu. (T1?) a traditional social sitting dance.

éwúwéngngaw (3b) See *wú*₁, *ngngaw*. va. (c.) fail to honor, respect, or observe laws or tabus.

éwúwéngngawa See *wú*₁, *ngngaw*. vo. (c.; T3) fail to honor, respect, or observe (laws or tabus).

éwúwéw (db; 3) ÉWÚ₅. va. (dis.) knead; do kneading. Cf. *éwúwa*₂, *-wúwéw*.

éwúwéyééch Var. of *éwúwééch*.

éwúyááyá (1) See *éwú-*₂, *áá-*₁. vi., adj. (be) long and slender.

I

i-₁ See *e-₁*. [Occurs in this form only when the next following vowel is *i, ú,* or *u.*] Var. *a-₁, á-₁, e-₁, ó-₁.* pref. (sub.) 3sg. sub. prn.: he, she, it. [Although a prefix, it is written separately.] *i isóni* he stores it; *i minen* he intends; *i tupw reey* he is duped by me; *i wúrá* he says. *ekka i miriit neeyiimi* whoever understands among you.

i-₂ See *e-₂*. [Occurs in this form only with *-pwúkú.*] pref. (num.) one. See *ipwúkú*.

i-₃ (2) I₁. pref. (loc.) at, in (of place or time). See *ifa₂, ika₂, ikaan, ikana, ikanaan, ikeey, ikemwuun, ikena, ikenaan, ikenááy, ikewe, ikka, ikkaan, ikkana, ikkanaan, ikkeey, ikkefa, ikkemwuun, ikkena, ikkenaan, ikkewe, ikkoomw, ikoomw, ina, inaan, ineet, ineng, inen, inón, inúk, Ipis, itam, iwe, iya, iye, iyeen, iyeey, iyemwuun, iyoomw.*

i-₄ (2) I₂. pref. (u.m.) See *ipar*.

-i-₁ I₃. [Occurs in this form regularly after bases ending in *i* and usually after bases ending in *u* and *ú*, the preceding *u* and *ú* becoming *i* also.] Var. *-wi-, -yi-₁.* suf. (rel.) links its antecedent as an attribute, member, part, property, or possession of what follows; of, for. [It has a more honorific, refined, or polite connotation than *-n* or *-ni-* and is more commonly used in *itang* talk.] *áti-i-sómw* man of chiefly rank (see *áát*, cf. *áti-ni-mwár* man of common rank); *Sópwi-i-ram* a place name (see *sóópw*, cf. *Sópwu-ni-féw*); *Núki-i-sóton* a place name (see *núkú-₁*).

-i-₂ I₄. [Occurs in this form after bases ending in *i, u, ú,* the preceding *u* or *ú* becoming *i* also to form an extended base ending in *ii*.] Var. *-yi-₂, -e-₂.* suf. (v.form.) one of a class of suffixes that joined to a base make the resulting construction an object focussed verb (vo.). *fichi-i-y* snip it (see *fichi-*); *nuki-i-y* tow it (see *nuk*).

-i (3) IYA₁. F. [In cpds. only.] suf. (cc.) hand of bananas. *eyi, rúweyi, wúnúyi, féyi, nimeyi, woneyi, fúúyi, wanúyi, ttiweyi* one,...nine h. of b.; *engoon iyeyiyan* ten h. of b.; *fiteyi* how many h. of b. Syn. *ina-₂.* Cf. *iyeyiya-*.

ii- (1) II₁. nr. (T2) direction, tendency. *iin ásápwán* direction of the wind. vi. tend, head, have a course. [In cpds. only.] With dir. suf.: *iinong* head or tend in; *iinó* head or tend away; *iitá* head or tend up or east; *iitiw* head or tend down or west; *iito* head or tend hither; *iiwu* head or tend out. *raa iinó Wééné* they headed off to Wééné (Moen).

ii₁ (1) II₂. nu. (T1) name of the high, front, unrounded vowel written *i*; name of the letter thus written.

ii₂ avd., qlf. serves to soften the force of a statement. *kepwe ii pwisin tingor* you had better ask yourself (cf. *kepwe pwisin tingor* ask yourself); *kesapw ii eyiis* you had better not ask (cf. *kesapw eyis* you must not ask); *wúsapw pwan ii mwéngé pwún ese nnaaf* I had better not also eat because there isn't enough; *siya kan ii angaang ikeey* we are, if we may, working here; *kete ii wosukosuk* don't worry, don't trouble yourself; *aapw ii* not really; *inaa chék ii* better leave it be (cf. *inaa chék* leave it be); *siya ii nó* we are indeed off (cf. *siyaa nó* we're off, let's go).

iifich (2) See *ii-, -fich.* vi. be right handed. Syn. *iiwen, iiyééch.* Ant. *iiméng, iingngaw.*

iis (2) ISI₁. nu. fiber strip from the stalk of a coconut frond or ivory nut frond, used to sew leaves together on a reed in making thatch or to string fish (see *sáriniipw*). *eché i.* one f. s. *isin núú* coconut f. s.; *isin rúpwúng* ivory nut f. s.

iik (3a: *ika-, ikana-*) IKA₁, IKANA. nu. (T3) fish. *emén i.* one f.; *echchú i., effaat i., efóch i.* one string of f. *wocháán i.* his f. (to eat); *iken* (N.), *ikenen* (F.) f. of. *ikenen Chuuk* Trukese f. *iken wooch* general name for reef f. *iken neeyin áán* (N.), *ikenen neyin áán* (F.) f. found in branching coral.

iiméng (2) See *ii-, méng.* vi. be left handed. Syn. *iingngaw.* Ant. *iifich, iiwen, iiyééch.*

iimw (3a) IMWA. n. (T3) house, building, hut, shelter, shed; (with suf. pos. prns.) any kind of cover over one's head (e.g. hat, umbrella, roof). *eew i.* one h. *imwan* his h. *imwen aséésé* rest house; *imwen assak* copra-drying shed; *imwen chitoosa* car top; *imwen feyinnó* toilet, outhouse; *imwen kképwúng* courthouse; *imwen mwéngé* restaurant; *imwen nipich* h. of prostitution, h. for unmarried people; *imwen nó núkún* menstrual hut (tabu expression, cf. *imwerá*); *imwen ómwu* toilet, outhouse; *imwen pinché* (taboo expression) toilet, outhouse; *imwen póó* h. with a raised floor; *imwen pwise* toilet, outhouse (tabu expression); *imwen sáfey* dispensary, hospital; *imwen semwmwen* hospital; *imwen sene* or *imwes sene* adze handle; *imwen tipis* jail; *imwen waasééna* hotel, inn. With suf. dem.: *imweyeey* this h. (by me), *imwena* that h. (by you), *imweyeen* this h. (by us), *imwenaan* that h. (yonder), *imweewe* that h. (out of sight or past).

iin (3a) INA₁. n. (T3) mother; (with suf. pos. prn.) one's mother, aunt, grandmother, kinswoman of any senior generation, kinswoman of one's father's lineage or clan, any such kinswoman of one's spouse; (less commonly, also with suf. pos. prn.) any woman of a man's lineage. *inan* his m. *emén iney* a senior kinswoman of mine. Cf. *inenap.*

iinong See *ii-.*

iinó See *ii-.*

iingngaw (3) See *ii-, ngngaw.* vi. be left handed. Syn. *iiméng.* Ant. *iifich, iiwen, iiyééch.*

iipw (3) IPWA. n. (T3) instep, sole (of foot); (with suf. pos. prn.) something pertaining to the foot. *eyipw* one i. *ipwan* his i. *rasen i.* footprint. *ipwach suus* our shoes. Cf. *pachapach.*

iir (3) IRA₁. prn. (pers.) they, them. *i. ffengen, i. ffengeen* they together. *i. chóón Merika* they are Americans. *wúwa efich i.* I like them.

iich₁ (2) ICHCHI. nu. a star.

iich₂ (2) ICHI. nu. (T2) bamboo (*Bambusa vulgaris, Schizostachym glaucifolium*). *ichin Chuuk* Trukese b. *pwúkúwen i.* b. joint; *seengin i.* length between b. joints. Syn. *pwaaw₂.*

iit (3a) ITA₁. n. (T3) name. *eew i.* one n. *itan* his n. *fáán itan* in his name, for his sake; *fáán iten* for the sake of.

iitá See *ii-.*

iitiw See *ii-.*

iito See *ii-.*

iiw (3) IWA. nu. (T3) grindstone. *iwen took g.* for a bush knife.

iiwe Polite form of *iwe₂.*

iiwen (3a) See *ii-, wen.* vi. be right handed. Syn. *iifich, iiyééch.* Ant. *iingngaw, iiméng.*

iiwu See *ii-.*

iiy (3a) IYA₂. prn. (pers.) he, she, it; him. *i. emén mwáán wátte* he is a big man. *ifa i. Eiue* where is Eiue; *inaan i.* there he is yonder. *wúwa efich i.* I like him.

iiyééch (2: *-yéchchú-*) See *ii-, ééch.* vi. be right handed. Syn. *iifich, iiwen.* Ant. *ingngaw, iiméng.*

ifa₁ (1) IFAA₁. nu. (T1) weft, woof (in weaving or basketry). *ifaan túúr* w. of a loom; *ifaan wuu* w. of a wicker fish trap.

ifa₂ (1) IFAA₂. nu. (loc.; inter.) where, how, what; location, condition (followed by *iiy* in connection with persons, mammals, birds, fish, or creatures classed as *maan*, provided they are alive; otherwise without *iiy*.). Dis. *ikkefa* (ds). *ifaan* its location, location of (with things only). *i. iiy?* where is he?; *i. iiy Eiue?* where is Eiue?; *i.* or *ifaan ewe mettóóch* where is that thing?; *ikkefa iir?* where are they?; *ikkefa* or *ikkefaan kkewe mettóóch?* where are those things? *wúse sineey ika i.* (polite) or *wúse sineey i.* (curt) I don't know where; *wúse sineey ika ifaan* (polite) or *wúse sineey ifaan* (curt) I don't know where. *i. wusun?* how? in what way? how is he?; *i. wusumw? i. wussumw?* how are you? *i. esin átánaan?* what sort of person is that fellow? how old is that fellow?; *i. esin naan wuut?* how old is yonder meeting house? *i. itomw* what is your name?

ifaan See *ifa₂.*

ifet (2) IFETI. vi. be scooped out (of clam shell or coconut), be removed from inside as by a knife or pin (of the contents of various shells).

ifetiiy See *ifet, -i-₂.* vo. (T5) scoop out, remove with knife or pin. Syn. *ipweyiiy, chúúri.*

Ifénúk nu. (loc.) Ifaluk (Ifalik) Atoll (Western Caroline Islands).

isapwich N. Var. *isipwich.* vi. be speedy, fast (of a person running, of an automobile, of a throw).

ise- (3a) ISA. N. [In cpds. only.] unsp. put away, stored. Syn. *isó-.*

isen- See *iseni-.*

isenaanong See *iseni.*

isenaatá See *iseni.*

isenaatiw See *iseni.*

iseni- (2) See *ise-, -ni-.* N. [In cpds. only.] vi. be stored, deposited, put away. With dir. suf.: *isennong* be s. inside (from *iseni-nong); isettá* be s. up on something (from *iseni-tá); isettiw* be s. down (from *iseni-tiw).*

iseni See *ise-, -ni-.* N. vo. (T6a) put away, store, put for safekeeping. With dir. suf.: *isenaanong, isenaatá, isenaatiw.* Syn. *isóni.*

isennong See *iseni-.*

isettá See *iseni-.*

isettiw See *iseni-.*

isewoch (3) See *ise-, woch.* N. Var. *isówoch.* vi. be thrifty, be a careful storer, be a saver.

iseyis (db; 3a) See *ise-.* vi. (dis.) be deposited, parked, stored, put away. Syn. *isóyis.*

isiis (db; 2) ISI₂. vi. (dis.) hiss, swish.

isipwich F. of *isapwich*

isongasii (Jap. *isongasii, isogasii*) vi. be busy. *siya i. reen ekkewe aramas* we are b. because of those people.

isó- (3b irreg.) ISÓ. F. [In cpds. only.] unsp. put away, stored. Syn. *ise-.*

isón- See *isóni-.*

isónaanong See *isóni-.*

isónáátá See *isóni.*

isónáátiw See *isóni.*

isóni- (2) See *isó-, -ni-.* F. [In cpds. only.] vi. be stored, deposited, put away. With dir. suf.: *isónnong* be s. inside (from *isóni-nong); isóttá* be s. up on something (from *isónitá); isóttiw* be s. down (from *isóni-tiw).* Syn. *iseni-.*

isóni See *isó-, -ni-.* F. vo. (T6a) put away, deposit, park, store, put for safekeeping. Dis. *ikkisóni* (ds). With dir. suf.: *isónaanong, isónáátá, isónáátiw.* Syn. *iseni.*

isónnong See *isóni-.*

isóttá See *isóni-.*

isóttiw See *isóni-.*

isówoch F. of *isewoch* (See *isó-, woch).*

isóyis (db; 3b irreg.) See *isó-.* vi. (dis.) be deposited, parked, stored, put away. Syn. *iseyis.*

ik excl. ouch! Syn. *ek.*

-ik₁ (3) IKA₂. [Occurs in this form with numeral bases of c.f. types 1 and 2.] Var. *-e-*₁. suf. (cc.) unit of ten. *iniik* (from *wúnú-ik*) thirty; *eyiniikan* thirtieth; *fááyik* (from *faa-yik*) forty; *áfááyikan* fortieth; *fiik* (from *fúú-yik*) seventy; *efiikan* seventieth; *waniik* (from *wanú-yik*) eighty; *awaniikan* eightieth.

-ik₂ (3) IKA₃. [In cpds. only.] unsp. (u.m.) See *wáániik.*

ika (1) IKAA. Var. *iká.* conj., md.m. expresses uncertainty: if, whether (at beginning of phrase); maybe, perhaps (at end of phrase); (*ika...ika...*) whether...or..., maybe...maybe... *i. e púng wúút wú sapw angaang* if it rains I shall not work. *wúpwe feyinnó reen tóókoche i.* I shall go to the doctor perhaps. *kete eyiis i. ngaang iyé* do not ask who I am. *wúse sineey i. ifa* I do not know where. *wúse sineey i. epwe máánó* I do not know whether he will die. *wúse sineey i. iyéén epwe fééri* I do not know who will do it. *i. epwe sááy i. esapw sááy* either (maybe) he will travel or (maybe) he will not travel. *wúse sineey i. epwe afanafan i. esapw afanafan or wúse sineey i. epwe afanafan i.* I do not know whether he will make a speech or not. (N.) *ikaa pwé...,* (F.) *ikaa wo...* if it should be that... Syn. *are.*

ika₂ See *i-₃, -ka-₂, -a-₅.* N. dem. (loc.) here (by me), in this (by me) place. Syn. *ikeey.* Cf. *ikka.*

ikaan See *i-₃, -ka-₂, een₃.* Var. *ikan.* dem. (loc.) here, there (near us). Syn. *aan*₁. Cf. *ikkaan.*

ikan N. var. of *ikaan.*

ikana See *i-₃, -ka-₂, na.* F. Var. *ikena.* dem. (loc.) there (by you or where you said), in that (near you or jest mentioned) place. *ikana...me iya* that is where... Cf. *ikkana.*

ikanaan See *i-₃, -ka-₂, naan.* F. Var. *ikenaan.* dem. (loc.) there (yonder), in that place (distant from us but visible). Cf. *ikkanaan.*

iká Wn. of *ika*₁.
ikááng (2) IKÁÁNGI. nu. grown mullet.
ikeey See *i*-₃, *-ka*-₂, *eey*₁. Var. *ikey*. dem. (loc.) here (by me), in this (by me) place. (F.) *i. iya*, (N.) *i. iye* here, this place. (F.) *ikeey...me iya*, (N.) *ikeey...me iye* this (here) is where... Syn. *ika*₂. Cf. *ikkeey*.
ikefénúfén (2) See *iik, fénúfén*. nu. (T2) any fish equipped with sharp, stiff spines or thorny projections. [No such fish may be eaten by a shark conjurer. Such fish include *wumwuné, peniwa, marawen, meyichééché, nuunupis*.] Syn. *ikeninnis*.
ikeféw (2) See *iik, faaw*. nu. (T2) a kind of fish.
ikesááw See *iik, sááw* (?). nu. a freshwater fish.
ikekkar (3b) See *iik, kkar*. nu. (T3) 1. species of bass fish. *ikekkaren Chuuk* Trukese bass. 2. name of a spell (*rongen i.*) and of an associated illness (*semwmwenin i.*) involving sore throat and headache. *sáfeen i.* medicine to counter the effects of the *i.* spell.
ikemwuun See *i*-₃, *-ka*-₂, *-mwuun*. N. dem. (loc.) there (not far from us). Syn. *ikoomw*. Cf. *ikkemwuun*.
iken (2) IKENI. (Eng.) nu. (T2) eagle. *ikenin Merika* American e.
ikena N. var. of *ikana*.
ikenaan N. var. of *ikanaan*.
ikenááy [Derivation uncertain; perhaps from *i*-₃, *kena*- (a possible var. of *ana*-₁), and *eey*₁.] Var. *ikinááy*. dem. (tem.) today.
ikeninnis (2) See *iik, ninnis*. nu. (T2) any fish equipped with sharp, stiff spines or thorny projections. [No such fish may be eaten by a shark conjurer. Such fish include *wumwuné, peniwa, marawen, meyichééché, nuunupis*.] Syn. *ikefénúfén*. Cf. *nnis*.
ikenipwin (2) See *iik, pwiin*₃. nu. (T2) fish that can be caught at night.
ikewe See *i*-₃, *-ka*-₂, *we*. dem. (loc.) there (out of sight), in that place (out of sight, past). Cf. *ikkewe*.
ikey N. var. of *ikeey*.
ikeyiné (1) See *iik, née*₂. nu. (T1) a fish (*Gymnocranius microdon*).
ikéér (2) See *iik, érú*-₁ (?). nu. (T2) a species of moray eel (*Gymnothorax thyrsoideus*). *ikéérún Chuuk* Trukese m. e.

ikéwúngúúng See *iik, wúng* (?). nu. a kind of fish. *ropen i.* fishing method using a sweep (*roop*).
ikinááy Wn. of *ikenááy*.
ikoomw See *i*-₃, *-ka*-, *oomw*. F. dem. (loc.) there (not far from us). Syn. *ikemwuun*. Cf. *ikkoomw*.
ikka (1) See *i*-₃, *kka*-₂, *-a*-₅. N. dem. (loc., dis.) here they are (by me). [It is structurally the dis. of *iye*₁.] Syn. *ikkeey*. Cf. *ika*.
ikkaan Dis. of *iyeen* (cf. *ikaan*).
ikkana F. dis. of *ina* (cf. *ikana*).
ikkanaan F. dis. of *inaan* (cf. *ikanaan*).
ikkang (Jap.) excl. end of game! game's over!
ikkeey Dis. of *iyeey*₂ (syn. *ikka*, cf. *ikeey*).
ikkefa Dis. of *ifa*₂.
ikkefaan See *ifa*₂.
ikkemwuun Dis. of *iyemwuun* (syn. *ikkoomw*, cf. *ikemwuun*).
ikkena N. dis. of *ina* (cf. *ikena*).
ikkenaan N. dis. of *inaan* (cf. *ikenaan*).
ikkewe Dis. of *iwe*₁ (cf. *ikewe*).
ikkoomw Dis. of *iyoomw* (cf. *ikoomw*).
impang (3) IMPANGA. (Jap. *inban*) Var. *impwang*. nu. (T3) rubber stamp. *impangen Merika* American r. s.
impwang Var. of *impang*.
imwaanis nu. a form of sorcery used in war. [After a battle, the enemy dead are decapitated and their heads are placed in a circle on the battlefield. The sorcerer recites spells over the heads calling on the ghosts of the slain to "eat" the survivors among the enemy.]
imweewe See *iimw, ewe*.
imwefaaw (2) See *iimw, faaw*. nu. (T2) stone house, house built of stone or concrete blocks. Cf. *féwúwimw*.
imwesárá (1) See *iimw, sárá*. nu. (T1) Japanese or European type of house with floor raised off the ground, storeyed house.
imwesimeen (2) See *iimw, simeen*. nu. (T2) cement house, house built of cement.
imwekkan (3) See *iimw, kkan*. nu. (T3) neighboring house, nearby house.
imwemangaak (2) See *iimw, mangaak*. nu. (T2) tent. Syn. *imwetaapwoonen*.

imwena See *iimw, na.*
imwenaan See *iimw, naan.*
imwenannan (3b) See *iimw, nannan.* vi. talk a lot, chatter.
imweni See *iimw, -ni-.* vo. (T6a) acquire (a house, shelter, umbrella, hat, or tree from which thatch is made). *imweni rúpwúng* acquire an ivory nut tree (whose leaves are standard thatching material). With dir. suf.: *imwenóóto* acquire and bring hither (an umbrella, hat, etc.). Cf. *imweyimw.*
imwenifen (2) See *iimw, fáán₃.* nu. (T2) church building (Protestant usage). Syn. *imwen fáán.* Cf. *imwenipin.*
imwenikkuk (2) See *iimw, kkuk.* nu. (T2) cook house. Syn. *imwen kkuk.*
imweningún (2) See *iimw, ngúún.* ns. (T2) navel ("house of the soul"). *imwen ngúniy* my n.
imwenipin (2) See *iimw, piin₁.* nu. (T2) church building (in Catholic usage). Cf. *imwenifen.*
imweniwún (2) See *iimw, wún₁.* nu. (T2) bar, saloon ("house of drinking"). *i. piyé* beer hall.
imwenóóto See *imweni.*
imwepi (1) See *iimw, pii-₁.* Itang. nu. (T1) thought of one's spouse.
imwepwut (3) See *iimw, pwuta-.* Obs. nu. (T3) menstrual hut. Syn. *imwen nó núkún, imwerá.*
imwepwpwún (2) See *iimw, pwpwún.* nu. (T2) house with a dirt floor, traditional type of dwelling house.
imwerá (1) See *iimw, -rá₁.* nu. (T1) menstrual hut (used to isolate a girl at menarche. [This is a permissible word (cf. *imwen nó núkún*).] Syn. *imwen nó núkún, imwepwut.*
imwetaapwoonen (2) See *iimw, taapwoonen.* nu. (T2) tent. Syn. *imwemangaak.*
imweyeen See *iimw, een₃.*
imweyeey See *iimw, eey₁.*
imweyiffátán (4) See *iimw, fátán.* vi. reside apart in several separated houses (of the members of a lineage). Syn. *imweyimw fátán.*
imweyimw (db; 3a) See *iimw.* vi. (dis.) use or occupy a house, wear a hat, carry an umbrella, use a shelter of any kind. Cf. *imweni.*
imweyimwen omos (2) See *iimw, omos.* n. phr. kind of reef formation.

imweyiché (1) See *iimw, chééché.* nu. (T1) large lineage dwelling house (housing the women of a lineage with their husbands and children).
imworoch (3) See *iimw, roch.* nu. (T3) eclipse (of sun or moon).
imworocheey See *imworoch, -e-₂.* vo. (T6b) eclipse (the sun or moon). *emén aa i. maram* someone has eclipsed the moon (by sorcery).
Imwó (1) IMWÓÓ. nu. (loc.) a clan name. *fin I.* or *fiin I.* I. woman; *mwáán I.* I. man. *chóón I.* people of I.
imwu (1) See *i-₃, mwu.* N. Var. *imwú.* vi. be separated, be apart. With dir. suf.: *imwuunó* be separated off; secede.
imwuufeseen (2) N. Var. *imwúúfeseen.* vi. be separated, be apart from one another.
imwuuseni See *imwu, seni₂.* N. Var. *imwúúseni.* vo. (T2) be separated from.
imwuunó See *imwu.*
imwú F. of *imwu.*
imwúúfeseen F. of *imwuufeseen.*
imwúúseni F. of *imwuuseni.*
in (3b) INA₂. vi. be docked, brought to land; parked (of a car). *aa in ewe waa* that canoe came to land. With dir. suf.: *inenong, inenó. aa inenong nóón naan iimw* it was parked in yonder building. *aa inenó reen naan woroor* it was docked away by yonder pier.
Ina-₁ (3b: *Ina-, Iná-, Ine-, Iné-, Ino-, Inó-*) INA₃. [Presumably derived from *iin.*] pref. (pers. n.form.) feminine prefix in traditional personal names. Examples: *Inaameti, Inaamén, Inaanin, Inaapwúng, Inaasomur, Inaasor, Inachaw, Inamataw, Inapwe, Inááreyong, Inááyichem, Inátipin, Inechen, Ineettiw, Inefes, Ineffár, Inefiicho, Inekinátip, Inemetek, Inemwiriyóng, Ineperey, Ineppich, Inepwiniiti, Inerikiyóng, Inewin, Ineyiya, Inechuwesap, Inemes, Inenikes, Inééwúk, Inééwúwetip, Inékú, Inésú, Inéwú, Inomataw, Inooma, Inoomwmwan, Inoopaw, Inoossúk, Inoota, Inottungur, Inowuwa, Inóóromó.* Cf. *Na-, Neyi-, Eyi-₃.*
ina-₂ INA₄. [In cpds. only.] Var. *ini-.* vi. be joined. Cf. *in. ni.* (T3) suf. (cc.) (N.) hand of bananas. *eyin, rúweyin, wúnúyin, feyin, nimeyin, woneyin, fúúyin, wanúyin, ttiweyin* one,...nine h. of b. Syn. *-i, -iyey.*

ina-₃ (3) INA₅. [In cpds. only.] unsp. held in the teeth.
ina See *i-₃, na.* dem. (loc.) there it is (by you); as you say; *i. iiy* there he (she) is (of a person). Dis. (F.) *ikkana,* (N.) *ikkena* there they are (of things); *ikkana iir, ikkena iir* there they are (of persons). *ina...* that (the just mentioned) is...; *inaa na...* (F.), *ina ena...* (N.) that is what...; *ina menne...* (F.), *ina minne...* (N.) that is the reason..., therefore...; *ina wusun* that is the way of it, that is how it is, *inaa chék* that's enough, that's all. *inaa mwo* that's enough for now; *inaa mwo pwe...* even though..., granted that... vi. be thus, be that way (with you). *aa inaa chék aar angaang* that was all they did ("it was just that their work"). *pwata ina mmangomw na?* why are you slow? ("why is it that way your being slow there?").
inaan See *i-₃, naan.* dem. (loc.) there it is (far from us but visible); it is yonder; *i. iiy* there he (she) is (of a person). Dis. (F.) *ikkanaan,* (N.) *ikkenaan* there they are (of things); *ikkanaan iir, ikkenaan iir* there they are (of persons). *ikkenaan ekkewe mettóóch wúwa kkapas wussun nánew* those are the things I talked about yesterday. vi. be thus, be that (yonder) way. *mwa, éwúráán iyé naan áát aa i. angéechchún ne mwirimwir chitoosa?* my, by whose instruction has yonder fellow become that skilled in driving a car?
-inaf (3) INAFA. [In cpds. only.] unsp. (u.m.) See *wúnniinaf.*
inaka (1) INAKAA. (Jap.) nu. (T1) rural place. *chóón i.* bumpkin, hick.
inacho Var. of *inócho.*
Iná- See *Ina-₁.*
Inááanifót nu. (loc.) a clan name. *fin I., fiin I.* I. woman; *mwáán I.* I. man. *chóón I.* people of I.
Ine-₁ See *Ina-₁.*
ine-₂ (3) INA₆. [In cpds. only.] unsp. (u.m.) See *inefi, inekékú, inemowuuch.*
ineet See *i-₃, nee-, -t.* dem. (tem., interrog.) when? *i. epwe feyitto?* w. will he come? *wúse sineey i. epwe feyinnó* I don't know w. he will go.
ineey See *ina-₃, -e-₂.* F. Var. *ineyi.* vo. (T6b) hold (something) in one's teeth.
inefeseen (2) See *iin, feseen.* vi. have a different mother, be a mother apart (genealogically). *wúwa chék i. mé Piiyóng* I am just a m. apart from Piiyóng (i.e., Piiyóng's mother and my mother were sisters).
inefi (1) See *ine-₂, fi₂.* N. nu. (T1) lightning. Syn. *fiifi.*
ineffengeen Var. of *ineffengen.*
ineffengen (2) See *in* or *ina-₂, ffengen.* Var. *ineffengeen, iniffengen.* vi. be joined together, be set (as broken bones).
inesooch (2) INESOOCHU. nu. (T2) large hermit crab. Cf. *wumwowumw.*
inekékú (1) See *ine-₂, kú₁.* vi. burn down a large tree.
inekékúúw See *inekékú.* vo. (T1) burn down (a large tree).
Inemárew nu. (loc.) a clan name. *fin I., fiin I.* I. woman; *mwáán I.* I. man. *chóó I.* people of I.
Inemes₁ See *iin, maas₃.* nu. (pers.) traditional goddess of love. [She lives in the sky, is patroness of the *éwúwénú* dance, and is invoked commonly in connection with magic to win or punish a lover.]
inemes₂ See *Inemes₁.* vi. call on Inemes.
inemowuuch (3: -wuchcha-) See *ine-₂, ma-, -wuuch.* F. Var. *inemowuch.* nu. (T3) being a hard taskmaster, slave driving. vi. be a hard taskmaster, be a slave driver, work people hard.
inemowuch N. of *inemowuuch.*
inemowuchcheey See *inemowuuch, -e-₂.* vo. (T6b) drive (people) in work, be a harsh taskmaster to (people) or in (work). *i. ekkewe aramas* d. those people in work; *i. ewe angaang* d. the work.
inen (2) See *i-₃, neni-₁.* nu. (T2) sky, heaven. *wóón i.* in heaven (possibly from *wóó-ni-nen*). Syn. *ineng.*
-inen (2) INENI. [In cpds. only.] unsp. (u.m.) See *nóniinen.*
inenap (3a) See *iin, nap.* n. (T3) mother or grandmother (as distinct from aunts and great aunts). [Indicates the woman in the principal sociological role of mother or grandmother, whether by birth, adoption, or fosterage.] *inenapan* his m.
ineni See *iin, -ni-.* vo. (T6a) acquire (someone) as a mother, have (someone) as mother.
Inenikes See *iin, esi-₁.* nu. (pers.) name of goddess of favorable wind. [Invoked

to produce, lessen, or increase the wind.]

inenong See *in*.

inenó See *in*.

ineng (2) See *i-₃, nááng.* Var. *inen.* nu. (T2) sky, heaven. *wóón i.* in heaven (possibly from **wóó-ni-neng*).

inepwiinéw (2) See *iin, pwii-₂, naaw.* nu. (T2) family unit consisting of a woman, her children, and her daughter's children. *eew i.* one f. Cf. *eterekes, eyinang, faameni, futuk, owunnun.*

inet (2) INETI. nu. (T2) division into parts or shares; division in arithmetic. *inetin kkewe mettóóch* division of these things. vi. be divided, be apportioned; divide into shares. Dis. *ikkinet (ds). i. ffengen* distribute mutually, give to one another, share with one another.

inetiiy See *inet, -i-₂.* vo. (T5) divide, distribute, apportion; divide (in artihmetic). *meet kkana e i.* what are those things he is distributing.

inewuch Var. of *inowuch*.

ineyi See *ina-₃, -yi-₂.* N. Var. *ineey.* vo. (T6a) hold (something) in one's teeth.

ineyisema- (3) See *iin, saam.* ni. (T3) paternal aunt, paternal grandmother; any female relative through one's father who is in a senior generation.

ineyin (db; 3) See *iin.* vi. (dis.) treat or use as a mother or sister.

ineyinééch (2) See *ineyin, ééch.* vi. treat one's mother or sister well (with *ngeni). wúpwe i. ngeni iney we* I will t. my m. well.

ineyinó (1) INEYINÓÓ. N. nu. (T1) species of scorpion fish. Syn. *wúsen.* Cf. *noow, nuunupis.*

Iné- See *Ina-₁*.

ini-₁ (2) See *wúnú-₁.* [In this form only in *iniik.*] pref. (num.) three.

ini-₂ (2) INI₁. ni. (T2), suf. (cc.) shoot, short sucker, runner (as of banana, taro, bamboo). *eyin, rúweyin, wúnúyin, feyin, nimeyin, woneyin, fúúyin, wanúyin, ttiweyin, engoon inin* one,...ten s. *inin* its s. *inin irá* tree s.

ini-₃ (2) INI₂. ni. (T2) fin (dorsal or anal, but not pectoral or ventral). *inin* its f. *inin iik* fish's f. *inin wóón* dorsal fin. *inin faan* anal fin. Cf. *paaw₁, peen₁.*

ini-₄ (2) INI₃. [In cpds. only. Presumably related to *ini-₃.*] Var. *ingi-.* unsp. edge, ridge.

ini-₅ (2) INI₄. [In cpds. only.] Var. *ina-.* unsp. joined, united. See *iniffengen, wocheyin.*

iniik (3) See *ini-₁, -ik₁.* num. thirty. With c. pref.: *eyiniika* (vo., T3) make it t. With c. pref. and ptv. const.: *eyiniikan* (ni., T3) thirtieth one. With dis. c. pref.: *ekkeyiniik* (vi.) be t. at a time. With suf. adj.: *iniikipár* over t., t. plus; *iniikisomw* more than t.

iniikisomw See *iniik*.

iniikipár See *iniik*.

iniin₁ (db; 2) See *ini-₂.* nu. (T2) 1. offspring; scion. *iniinin aramas* o. of humans; *iniinin énú* o. of spirits (in the case of children badly deformed at birth, who in pre-Christian times were judged truly spirit rather than human if their condition failed to respond to medicine, but were allowed to live until they died naturally). *iniinin neepwén* a small plover bird (See *iniinneepwén*). 2. a small plover bird (short for *iniinneepwén*).

iniin₂ (db; 2) See *ini-₄.* ni. (T2) edge, ridge. *iniinin* its e. *iniinin cheepen* table's edge; *iniinin sékúr* each of two fleshy ridges on the human back along the spinal column.

iniinneepwén (2) See *iniin₁, nee-, pwéén.* nu. (T2) a small plover bird ("swamp offspring"). [It is smaller than the *kuning* and frequents swamps.] Syn. *iniin₁, iniinin neepwén.*

inifeefin (3) See *ini-₃, feefin.* nu. (T3) anal fin. Syn. *inin faan.*

iniffengeen Var. of *iniffengen*.

iniffengen (2) See *ini-₅, ffengen.* Var. *iniffengeen.* vi. sit together in talk.

inis₁ (2) INISI. n. (T2) body, hull (of boat); person. *inisin* his b. *wóón inisin* in person; *wúse opwut inisin* I don't dislike him personally.

inis₂ (Eng.) nu. inch. *eew i.* or *i. eew* one i. *fituuw i. eey irá?* how many inches (long is) this timber?

inikasaf (3) See *ini-₂, a-₂, saaf₂.* Var. *inikesaf, inikisaf.* nu. (T3) a new shoot (of banana, sugarcane, taro) coming up around the old plant.

inikesaf Var. of *inikasaf*.

inimwáán See *ini-₃, mwáán₁.* nu. dorsal fin. *i. wóón wúkún* soft d. f. ("dorsal fin on its tail"). Syn. *inin wóón.*

inipar (3b) See *ini*-3, *par*. F. nu. (T3) a kind of fish ("red fin"). *emén i.* one f. Syn. *sara*.

Ino- See *Ina*-1

inowuch (2, 3) INOWUCHU, INOWUCHA. Var. *inewuch*. nu. (T2, T3) a kind of sea cucumber. [It is yellowish in color and called by this name when it is large, but is called *tomwun* when it is small.] *inowuchun Chuuk* or *inowuchen Chuuk* Trukese s. c.

Inó- See *Ina*-1

inó (1) INÓÓ. nu. (T1) shaft (of a spear). *inóón máchew* s. of war spear; *inóón óppong* s. of multipronged fish-spear.

inón See *i*-3, *nónu*-. nu. (loc.) underwater.

inócho (1) INÓCHOO. Var. *inacho*. vi. be swollen eyed, puffy eyed. *aa i. mesen naan ááát* yonder boy's eyes have become swollen.

inúk₁ (2) See *i*-3, *núkú*-1. nu. (T2) outer or ocean side (of an island). *inúkún fénú* island's outer or uninhabited s. (cf. *mósóórun fénú* island's inner or inhabited s.). *sipwe feyinnó i.* we shall go to the outer s; *aa nónnómw i.* it is located at the outer s.

Inúk₂ (2) See *inúk*₁. nu. (loc.; T2) name of the western extremity of Pwene (Polle) Island.

inchin (Eng.) nu. engineer. *emén i.* one e.

intiko (1) INTIKOO. (Eng.) nu. (T1) dye. *intikoon mangaak* d. for cloth.

ing (3a) INGA. vi. be astonished, be amazed, be filled with admiration, marvel.

ingemwaar (3) See *ing*, *mwaar*. nu. (T3) admiration. vi. be filled with admiration, marvel. *wúwa i. reen* I am f. with a. on account of him.

ingemwaareyiti See *ingemwaar*, *-iti*. vo. (T2) admire, marvel at.

Ingenes (Eng.) nu. English. *fóósun I.* E. language.

Ingenen (Eng.) nu. (loc.) England.

ingeyiti See *ing*, *-iti*. vo. (T2) admire, marvel at, be amazed at.

ingi- (2) INGI. [In cpds. only.] Var. *ini*-4. unsp. edge, ridge. See *pereyingiing*.

ingik (2, 3) INGIKI, INGIKA. (Eng.) nu. (T2, T3) ink. *ingikin manneng*, *ingiken manneng* fountain pen i.

ipar (3b) See *i*-4, *par*. nu. (T3) a variety of banana. [It is red-skinned and reserved for *itang*; used by *itang* in the *wochowuuch* divination.]

Ippenges nu. (loc.) a clan name. *fin I.*, *fiin I.* I. woman; *mwáán I.* I. man. *chóón I.* people of I.

Ippeyach nu. (loc.) a clan name. *fin I.*, *fiin I.* I. woman; *mwáán I.* I. man. *chóón I.* people of I.

-ipw (3) See *iipw*. suf. (cc.) step, footprint, sole; item of footwear. *eyipw, rúweyipw, wúnúyipw, féyipw* or *feyipw, nimeyipw, wonoyipw, fúúyipw, wanúyipw, ttiweyipw, engoon ipwan* one,...ten s.

ipweni See *iipw*, *-ni*-. vo. (T2b) acquire (shoes, sandals, or other footwear). Cf. *ipweyipw*.

ipwenong (3) See *iipw*, *-nong*. va. set foot in (with *nóón*). *i. nóón sáát* s. f. in the sea.

ipwenúk (2) See *iipw*, *núkú*-3. vi. sprain an ankle; have a sprained ankle.

ipweyiiy IPWEYI (?). vo. (T5?) remove (something) with a knife or pin (of the contents of the *siim, amwe, ómóót,* and *tto* shells). Syn. *chúúri, ifetiiy.* Cf. *pweeyi.*

ipweyipw (db; 3) See *iipw*. va. (dis.) wear or use (shoes, sandals, or other footwear). Cf. *ipweni*.

ipwét (2) See *i*-3, *-pwét*. F. vi. be finished cooking, done (of cooking food). Syn. *mwoot*₂.

ipwo (1) IPWOO. nu. (T1) longer stick framing the edge of a handnet. *efóch i.* one framing s. *ipwoon cheew* handnet's framing s.

ipwúkú (1) See *i*-2, *-pwúkú*. nu. (num.) one hundred. With c. pref. and ptv. const.: *eyipwúkúún* one hundredth one. With suf. adj.: *ipwúkúúpár* over one h., one h. plus; *ipwúkúúsomw* more than one h.

ipwúkúúsomw See *ipwúkú*.

ipwúkúúpár See *ipwúkú*.

ir₁ (3a) IRA₂. Tbl. vi. be filled (as a hole); be buried (as driftwood by sand); be healed (as a wound). Dis. *ireyir* (db, permissable in mixed company). *ineet epwe ireyir enaan soomá?* when will the body be buried? With dir. suf.: *irenó* (permissable in mixed company).

ir₂ (2) IRI. Tbl. vi. masturbate.

-ir (3a) See *iir*. [In this form only when the final vowel of the preceding base is *i*.] Var. *-er, -r, -ur, -úr*. suf. (obj.) 3pl. obj. prn.: them. *fitiir* accompany them (see *fiti*). With dir. suf.: *-irenong, -irenó, -iretá, -iretiw, -ireto, -irewu. fitiirenó* accompany them off, go away with them. suf. (pos.) 3pl. pos. prn.: their; of or for them. *iniiniir* their offspring (see *iniin*).

Iras (3) IRASA. nu. (loc.; T3) a district at the northwest end of Wééné (Moen) Island.

irá (1) IRÁÁ. nu. (T1) tree, stick, timber, log. *efóch i.* one t. *iráán eey fénú* trees of this island; *iráán nóón iimw* timbers of the house. Cf. *ráá*.

irááfénúfén (2) See *irá, fénúfén*. nu. (T2) a shrub (*Bougainvillea spectabilis*). [Flowers worn on the ear.]

iráápenges (2) See *irá, penges*. nu. (T2) the Cross; modern name of the constellation Crux or Southern Cross (old name *pwuupw*).

iráápengesiiy See *iráápenges, -i-₂*. vo. (T5) crucify. With dir. suf.: *iráápengesiiyenó*.

iráápengesiiyenó See *iráápengesiiy*.

irááchchi Var. of *iráchchi*.

irááttong (3a) See *irá, ttong*. nu. (T3) a shrub (*Bougainvillea* "love tree").

iránnap (3a) See *irá, nap*. nu. (T3) forest.

iráchchi (1) See *irá, chii-*. Var. *irááchchi*. nu. (T1) Christmas tree ("drops tree" from its decorations).

ireey See *ir*₁, *-e-*₂. vo. (T6b) bury, inter, fill up (of a hole).

ireffengeen Var. of *ireffengen*.

ireffengen (2) See *ir*₁, *ffengen*. Var. *ireffengeen*. va. heal, become healed (of a wound).

irenó See *ir*₁.

ireyir Dis. of *ir*₁.

iriiy See *ir*₂, *-i-*₂. Tbl. vo. (refl.; T5) masturbate. Dis. *ikkiriiy* (ds).

iromw (2) IROMWU. vi. be soaked, drenched, wet through. *wúwa fóókkun i. reen eey ráán* I have become thoroughly s. by this rain.

-ichi (1) ICHII. suf. (adj.) firstborn, senior, oldest, first, highest ranking (of siblings and lineage mates). See *finniichi, mwáániichi*.

ichiich (db; 2) nu. (T2) species of pompano fish (light in color and large).

it (3) ITA₂. vi. be all gone, used up, finished, consumed. *aa it* it is all gone; *ineet epwe it?* when will it be finished. Syn. *ros*.

ita- (3a) ITA₃. [In cpds. only.] vi., va. press, weigh down. Dis. *iteyit* (db). With dir. suf.: *itetá* press from above; *itetiw* press down.

ita (1) ITAA. nu. (T1) an operation in plaiting of mats in which all leaflets running to the right are bent downward a quarter turn to the right, each leaflet being placed under each adjacent leaflet to the right so as to hold the plait in place during the next operation. Cf. *ita-*.

itaani See *ita, -ni-*. vo. (T4) do the *ita* operation to (in plaiting). Syn. *itaay*.

itaay See *ita* vo. (T1) do the *ita* operation to (in plaiting). Syn. *itaani*.

itam (3b) See *i-*₃, *taam*. nu. (loc.; T3) outrigger side of a canoe (*itamen waa*). Cf. *ásá*.

Itani (Eng.) nu. (loc.) Italy.

itang (3) ITANGA. nu. (T3) a specialist in rhetoric, political, military, and diplomatic history, lore, and magic; the body of lore and magic known by *itang. emén i.* one *i.. itangen Chuuk* Trukese *i.. ese sineey i.* he doesn't know *i.* lore. *fóósun i.* a special style of poetic discourse, or rhetoric rich in metaphor, obscure allusion, and hidden meaning, and forming a part of *i.* lore.

itangúpwpwún (2) See *itang, pwpwún*. nu. (T2) an *itang* of the highest grade. Cf. *chóóyiro*.

itá (1) ITÁÁ. md.m. introduces a narrative construction (used with *-pwe*) to indicate intent or wish to do something, often with implication of doubt as to its feasibility. *i. wúpwe áni ewe kkón ngé wúse toongeni* I wanted to eat that breadfruit but I was not able to. *i. wúpwe nniiy emén kaattu ngé aa chék eniiser wóón emén konaak* I meant to kill a cat but it [my shot] just accidentally <hit> on a dog. *wúú i.* yes, I intend to! *wusun i....* just as if..., just like... *ómwo i....* if only..., would that... (expressing desire contrary to fact or frustrated intent); *ómwo i. wúpwe néwúni emén piik* if only I could acquire a pig.

Itááchék See *itá, chék*. nu. (pers.) a Sóór man who played a prominant role in the legendary history of Wuumaan

(Uman), helping Woonap in the reconquest of Wuumaan from Feefen (Fefan) overlordship.

itemóng (2) See *ita-, móóng*. nu. (T2) blow with the hands to a person's head in fighting.

itenap (3a) See *iit, nap*. nu. (T3) general name (as for a genus); title, subject, topic (of a book or talk); significance or gist of what has been said. *itenapan* its general n. *itenapen aan afanafan* the subject (or point) of his talk.

itenapeey See *itenap, -e-₂*. vo. (T6b) emphasize; name (the title, subject, topic); give the general name of; indicate the main point of.

itenáátá See *iteni₂*.

itenáátiw See *iteni₂*.

iteni₁ See *iit, -ni-*. vo. (T6a) acquire the name of, have the name of; take the place of. *Herbert aa i. itan* Herbert has taken his place ("his name").

iteni₂ See *ita-, -ni-*. vo. (T6a) press, weigh down on. Dis. *iteyiteni* (db). With dir. suf.: *itenáátá* press (something) from above; *itenáátiw* press (something) down.

itenipwin (2) See *iit* or *ita-, pwiin₃*. nu. (T2) any kind of night time activity (e.g.,dancing, singing, serenading, love making, murdering).

itenipwiniiy See *itenipwin, -i-₂*. vo. (T5) attack or murder (someone) at night.

itenngeni See *iit, -ni-, ngeni*. Pt. [An unusual form, the common word being *eyitengeni*.] vo. (T2) name, give a name to. Cf. *eyita₁*.

itengach (3) See *ita-, -ngach*. vi. lean on elbows with hand under chin.

itengngaw (3b) See *iit, ngngaw*. n. (T3) bad name, bad reputation. *itengngawan* his b. n. *meyi wor itengngawan* he has b. n.

itechik (2) See *iit, chiki-₁*. nu. (T2) spelling. *ifa itechikin na fóós?* what is the spelling of that word? va., vi. spell, do spelling.

itechikiiy See *itechik, -i-₂*. vo. (T5) spell.

itetá See *ita-*.

itetiw See *ita-*.

itewuunó (1) See *iit, -wu, -nó*. n. (T1) reputation, fame, renown. *itewuunóón* his r. vi. be famous.

itewuuyééch (2: *-yéchchú-*) See *iit, -wu, ééch*. nu. (T2) fame. vi., va. be famous, famed.

itewumw (2) See *ita-, wuumw*. nu. (T2) carrying of *mwatún* in large bowls in procession in formal presentation to a chief, (*itewumwun sómwoon*) or head of a land-owning lineage (*itewumwun sowufénú*).

itewungngaw (3b) See *iit, -wu, ngngaw*. n. (T3) bad reputation. *itewungngawan* his b. r. vi. be infamous, have a bad reputation.

iteyééch (2: *-yéchchú-*) See *iit, ééch*. F. Var. *itééch*. nu. (T2) good name, reputation, honor. *iteyéchchún ewe sómwoon aa ta* the good name of the chief is ruined. vi. have a good name.

iteyit₁ (db; 3) See *iit*. va., vi. (dis.) use a name; have one's name. *kepwe i. itey* you shall use my name. *ngaang wúwa i. nóón kkapasen itang* I have my name from *itang* talk.

iteyit₂ (db; 3a) See *ita-*. vi., va. (dis.) press, weigh down.

iteyita- (db; 3b) See *iit*. ni. (dis.; T3) total count, total number, all, each and every one. *iteyitan* all of it. *ifa iteyitan?* how many in all? what is its total count? *fitemén iteyitemi* how many of you in all? *ifa iteyitan óómw fiti sukuun?* how often do you attend school ("what the total-count-of-it your attending school"). *iteyiten ráán* every day; *iteyiten mettóóch* every single thing.

iteyiteni See *iteni₂*

iteyó (1) See *ita-, óó*. nu. (T1) handling a trolling line. *chóón i.* trolling line handler.

itééch N. of *iteyééch*.

iti-₁ (2) ГП₁. vi. point, be toward, face. With dir. suf.: *itinong* p. inwards or southwards; *itinó* p. away; *ititá* p. upwards or eastwards; *ititiw* p. downwards or westwards; *itito* p. hither; *itiwu* p. outwards or northwards.

iti-₂ (2) ГП₂. [In cpds. only.] vi. be situated, be arranged. With dir. suf.: *ittiw* hang down, be suspended; *ittiw wóón* hang down from it.

iti ГП₃. E.Wn. vo. (T2) accompany, go with, attend. Syn. *fiti*.

-iti (2) See *iti-₁*. vo. suf. (T2) toward, until, to, in the direction of, upon. *pwiniiti* become night upon (someone); *wuteyiti* rain upon; *ááyiti* swim to.

itiit₁ (db; 2) See *iti-₁*. n. (T2) direction in which something faces or points, orientation. *itiitin* d. in which he faces. *ifa itiitin?* where does it point? in what d. does it face? *itiitin ewe panen irá* d. in which the tree-branch points.

itiit₂ (db; 2) See *iti-₂*. nu. (dis.; T2) arrangement, order. *itiitin fóós* grammar, syntax, word order.

itiitiyééch (2: *-yéchchú-*) See *itiit₂, ééch*. nu. (T2) proper arrangement. *itiitiyéchchún fóós* grammar, syntax.

itifeseen (2) See *iti-₂, feseen*. vi. lie apart.

itifeyiyach (3) See *iti-₂, feyiyach*. N. Var. *itiféwúwach*. vi. lie obliquely.

itiféwúwach F. of *itifeyiyach* (see *iti-₂, féwúwach*).

itifi N. var. of *étúfi*.

itiffengeen Var. of *itiffengen*.

itiffengen (2) See *iti-₂, ffengen*. vi. lie next to each other.

itini See *iti-₁, -ni-*. vo. (T5) point or face towards.

itinong See *iti-₁*.

itinó See *iti-₁*

itin mataw (3) See *iti-₂*. n. phr. calm of the sea (metaphor for calm and peaceful emotions in *itang* talk).

itipenges (2) See *iti-₂, penges*. vi. lie directly across or perpendicularly, lie athwart.

itipwut (2) See *iti-₂, -pwut*. nu. (T2) rafter braces. *itipwutun nóón iimw* house's r. b.

itipwpwór (2, 3b) See *iti-₂, pwpwór*. vi. lie crookedly or not straightly.

ititá See *iti-₁*.

ititiw See *iti-₁*.

itito See *iti-₁*.

itiwu See *iti-₁*.

itiyééch (2: *-yéchchú-*) See *iti-₂, ééch*. vi. be neatly arranged, be such that everything is in its place.

ito (1) ITOO. (Jap. *ido*) nu. (T1) well. *eew i.* one w. *aan i.* his w.; *itoon* w. of.

ittiw See *iti-₂*.

iwe₁ See *i-₃, we*. dem. (loc.) there it is (out of sight), there it was (past); *i. iiy* there he (she) is (of a person). Dis. *ikkewe* there they are, there they were (of things); *ikkewe iir* there they are (of persons). *iwe nóón imwey* there it is in my house. vi. be thus, be that way (as already indicated). *aa iwe áán ewe feefin we aa pochcheey ne ssá* it was thus with that woman, she stuck diligently to running. Cf. *iyeen*.

iwe₂ See *iwe₁*. [Regularly introduces a statement that expresses the consequence of an action referred to in the immediately prior statement or that picks up the next step in a narrative.] Var. *iiwe*. conj. then, well, so, and so, thereupon. *ika ese mwochen, iwe kesapw sááy* if he does not wish it, then you shall not set off (on your journey). *...chóón Paata raa akkasómwonnu Sowupaata. Iwe raa wukkumwuni, wukkumwusómwoon ngeni iteyiten ráán. Aa inaa chék aar angaang. Iwe, mwirin, Woneniyap aa kan nennengeni áán ewe mwáán we angaang*. The people of Paata rendered chiefly honors to Lord-of-Paata. And so they kept making ovens, kept making chief's ovens for him every day. That was all they did. Then, after a while, Woneniyap was ever watching what that man was doing. *iwe iwe!* go on! yes, yes! tell more! very well, then! *iwee ngé* and also, moreover.

iwi (1, 3) IWII, IWIYA. nu. (T1, T3) rich or fatty taste. *iwiyen* or *iwiin eey mwéngé* the r. taste of this food. vi. be or taste rich or fatty.

iwu (1) IWUU. nu. (T1) filth resulting from coconut grease or oil (*iwuun taka*). vi. be soiled from coconut grease or oil.

iya (1) See *i-₃, -a₂*. Var. *iye*. n. (loc.; T1) location, place, whereabouts; place where, where, what place. *iyaan* its location, location of. *wúse sineey iyaan* I do not know its whereabouts. *wúse sineey iyaan ewe fénú* I do not know the location of that island. *epwe tééta me i. wóón ewe waa* he will board the canoe from where? *eey i.* this place (by speaker); *ikeey i.* in this place; *ana i., ikana i.* in that (by you) place; *ikaan i.* in that (near us) place; *ikanaan i.* in that place yonder; *ewe i.* that (not visible) place. *iya...iya* (F.), *iya...iye* (N.) place...at, where. *i. kepwee nó iya* where are you going? *emén meyinap epwe finiirenó i. repwe angaang i.* an important person will select the places they will work at. *sise sineey i. re nómw i.* we don't know where they are ("we do not know the place they are staying at"). *nóón ewe i. si. mómmóót iya* in that place we

iyaanaan

were sitting at. *iya...me iya* (F.), *iya...me iye* (N.) place... from? *wúse sineey i. epwe feyitto me i.* I do not know where he will be coming from ("I do not know the place he will be coming from").

iyaanaan See *iya, naan.* nu. (loc.; dem.) that place yonder. Id. *iyeey me i.* from here to who knows where (expression of indefinite distance, lit. "this place here and that place there").

iyaach (Eng.) nu. yard (unit of measure). *eew i.* or *i. eew* one y. Syn. *tinewupw.*

iyas (3) IYASA. nu. (T3) picking pole (for breadfruit). *efóch i.* one p. p. for breadfruit. *aan i.* his p. p. *iyasen mááy* p. p. for breadfruit.

iyasay (2) IYASAYI. (Jap. *yasai*) nu. (T2) vegetables. *iyasayin Merika* American v.

iyakiyu (1) IYAKIYUU. (Jap. *yakyuu*) Var. *iyakiyú.* nu. (T1) baseball (game of), baseball game. *eew i.* one b. game. vi. play baseball.

iyakiyuffengen (2) See *iyakiyu, ffengen* vi. play baseball together. *i. ngeni na kkúmi* play b. together with ("against") that team.

iyakiyú Var. of *iyakiyu.*

Iyap₁ nu. (loc.) Yap Islands (Western Caroline Islands).

iyap₂ (3) IYAPA. nu. (T3) a variety of banana (named for Yap Island). *iyapen Chuuk* Trukese *iyap.*

iyá (1) IYÁÁ. N. [Commonly used in ptv. const.] Var. *kiyá.* n. (T1) boundary, limit. *iyáán* its b.; b. of.

iyáánniiy See *iyá.* N. [Presumably formed by treating the ptv. const. *iyáán* as a base with v. form. suf. *-i-*₂.] Var. *kiyáánniiy.* vo. (T5) establish a boundary on (something).

iye₁ See *i-*₃, *-e.* dem. (loc.) (emphatic) here, here it is! Dis. *ikka.* Syn. *iyeey.*

iye₂ In *iya...iye* (see *iya*).

Iyeesuus (Lat.) Var. *Iyeyisuus.* nu. (pers.) Jesus. *I. Kristuus* Jesus Christ. Syn. *Siises.*

iyeen See *i-*₃, *een*₃. Var. *iyen.* dem. (loc.) here it is (by us); *i. iiy* here he (she) is (of a person). Dis. *ikkaan* here they are (of things); *ikkaan iir* here they are (of persons). vi. (dem.) do or be thus (as follows). *ke pwe i.* you will do thus. Cf. *iwe*₁.

iyeey₁ See *iya, eey*₁. nu. (loc.; temp.; dem.) this place (by speaker), here; now. *iyeeyi chék* right now. *i. neesossor* this morning, this very morning. Id. *i. me iyaanaan* from here to who knows where (expression of indefinite distance, lit. "this place here and that place there"). Cf. *ikeey.*

iyeey₂ See *i-*₃, *eey*₁. Var. *iyey.* dem. (loc.) here it is (by speaker); *i. iiy* here he (she) is (of a person). Dis. *ikkeey* here they are (of things); *ikkeey iir* here they are (of persons).

iyemwuun See *i-*₃, *emwuun.* N. dem. (loc.) there it is (near you). Dis. *ikkemwun* there they are (near you). Syn. *iyoomw.*

iyen N. var. of *iyeen.*

iyepwórópwór (2, 3b) See *pwór.* vi. be pliable, easily bent.

iyer (2) IYERI. (Eng.) n. (T2) year; age. *eew i.* one y. *iyerin* his age. *fituuw iyerin* how old is he ("how many his years"). *i. sééfé* new year. *nnón eey (ewe, een) i.* this (last, next) y. Cf. *efen*₄, *ráás.*

iyerini See *iyer, -ni-.* vo. (T5) have an age of, reach an age of. *aa i. engoon* he is ten years old. *aa i. iyerin áteey* he is this fellow'a age.

iyering (3) IYERINGNGA. (Eng.) nu. (T3) ear ring. *eew i.* one e. r. *néwún i.* his e. *iyeringngen Sapan* Japanese e. r.

iyeriyer (db; 2) See *iyer.* vi. (dis.) last for many years, be year in and year out. *aa i. ne semwmwen* he has been sick for years ("he has been for many years in sickness").

iyey N. var. of *iyeey*₂.

Iyeyisuus Var. of *Iyeesuus.*

iyeyiya- (db; 3: *-iyey*) See *-i-.* ni. (dis.; T3), suf. (cc.) hand of bananas. *eyiyey, rúweyiyey, wúnúyiyey, feyiyey, nimeyiyey, woneyiyey, fúúyiyey, wanúyiyey, ttiweyiyey, engoon iyeyiyan* one,...ten h. of b.; *fiteyiyey* or *fiteyi iyeyiyan* how many h. of b. *iyeyiyen wuuch* h. of b. Syn. *ina-*₂. Cf. *féwún wuuch, wumwun wuuch.*

iyé (1) IYÉÉ. prn. (interrog.) who, what person. *een iyé* who are you? *kete eyiis ika ngaang iyé* don't ask who I am; *iyé epwe ánisiyey?* or *iyéén epwe ánisiyey?* who will help me? *wúse sineey ika iyéén epwe fééri* I don't know who will do it; *iyé kkaan?* who are they (by you)?

iyéén See *iyé*.

iyo- (3 irreg.) IYO. [In cpds. only.] vi. be assembled, assemble.

iyoomw See *i-₃, oomw*. F. dem. (loc.) there it is (near you). Dis. *ikkoomw* there they are (near you). Syn. *iyemwuun*.

Iyoowa (Lat.) nu. (pers.) Jehovah. Syn. *Siyoowa*.

iyoffengeen (2) See *iyo-, ffengen*. Var. *iyoffengeen*. vi. be assembled together, assemble together.

iyoni See *iyo-, -ni-*. vo. (T6a) assemble, collect, bring together. *sipwe i. aramas* we shall a. the people.

iyoyi (db; 3 irreg.) See *iyo-*. vi. be assembled; assemble. *raa i. nóón ewe mwiich* they assembled in the meeting. *i. ffengen* assemble together. nu. (T3) assemblage, pile. *iyoyiyen pii* pile of trash. Cf. *mwiich*.

iyóótek (3) IYÓÓTEKA. nu. (T3) prayer. *eew i.* one prayer. *aan i.* his prayer. vi. pray. *i. ngeni Koot* pray to God. Cf. *óttek*.

iyóótekeppék (2) See *iyóótek, ppék*. vi. pray in concert, pray together.

iyuusómw See *i-₃, wú₃, -sómw*. Itang. nu. the corner post in a meeting house that a chief sits at or that symbolizes a chief. Cf. *efótiisómw*.

Iyuurop (Eng.) nu. (loc.) Europe.

O

o-$_1$ See e-$_1$. [In this form only when immediately followed by the vowel o.] pref. (sub.) he, she, it. [Although a prefix, it is written separately. It occurs only in colloquial speech in place of e-$_1$.]

o-$_2$ Wn. and Tns. contraction of the 2pl. sub. prn. owu- or éwú-$_1$.

o-$_3$ See a-$_2$. [Usually in this form when the next following vowel is o or u.] pref. (c.) imparts causative meaning to the base. Dis. okko- (ds).

-o- O. [Occurs only in const. with bases of c.f. type 3.] Var. -e-$_2$, -é-. suf. (v.form) makes an object focussed verb of the preceding base (v.o. type 6b).

o$_1$ (1) OO$_1$. ct.m. sir. meet o? what, sir?; ifa o? where, sir?; e nnet o! that's right, sir!; ningéchchún naan feefin o! The beauty of that woman, sir!; Boutau o! Boutau sir!

o$_2$ (1) OO$_2$. vi. be caught, captured (as a fleeing person, chicken, etc.). Dis. okko (db). aa o reey he was c. by me; epwee o reemw it will be c. by you; ese o it was not c.

oo$_1$ (1) OO$_3$. nu. (T1) omen. [oo as distinct from pwee (knot divination) are manifested in the sound of thunder, the appearance of the moon, the appearance of a house's or canoe's construction, the appearance of a medicine prepared by a sowurong, or the appearance of a knot diviner's teaching diagrams (as distinct from knot divination itself).] See oosuni.

oo$_2$ OO$_4$. Var. woo$_4$. conj. and. aa kkechiw oo apasa... he wept and said...

oo$_3$ (1) OO$_5$ nu. (T1) name of the mid, back, rounded vowel written o; name of the letter thus written.

oos (3) OOSA. F. Var. woos$_3$. nu. (T3) 1. any of a class of male spirits inhabiting the deep sea (commonly also referred to as oosen mataw). [Resembling a bright torch that sinks below the sea, these spirits cause sickness and death among infants. They leave orange-yellow excrement (páán o.) by people's houses, thus manifesting their presence.] 2. sickness caused by spirits of this name. 3. medicine (sáfeen o.) and spells (rongen o.) to cure the sickness caused by spirits of this name.

oosuni See oo$_1$, -si-, -ni-. [Presumably the base oosu- derives from a vi. *oos, from a vo. *oosi meaning "portend."] Var. woosuni. vo. (T5) interpret or read (an omen), foretell from or the future of. o. nóón paaw palmistry; chóón o. (or sowuyoosuni) nóón paaw palmist. Cf. oo, pwee$_1$.

oomrang (3) OOMRANGA. (Jap. hoomuran) nu. (T3) home run (in baseball). eew o. one h. r. wecheyiyan o. his (hit by him) h. r.

oomw F. [Normally precedes the noun, but it is suffixed to áte, wono-, wonno-, nemin.] prn. (dem.) that (near person addressed). Dis. kkoomw those. Syn. emwuun. Cf. ena.

oonngaw (3b) See oo$_1$, ngngaw. nu. (T3) false omen. Ant. ooyééch.

oopw (2, 3) OPWPWA, OPWPWU. F. Var. woopw. nu. (T2, T3) species of pompano (up to 5 ft. long). opwpwen, opwpwun p. of (a given kind) opwpwun mataw a species of p.

oopwin nu. a tiny fish (fighting fish). [Used by boys in contests to see whose fish will be dominant in pools made of banana leaves.]

ooch Var. of ewoch.

ootay (2) OOTAYI. (Jap. hootai) nu. (T2) bandage. eféw o. one roll of b.; eché o. one piece of b. aan o. his b.

oow (2) OOWU. nu. (T2) payment (of goods); fee; burial gift, funeral gift (to the dead). oowun sáfey p. for medical treatment; oowun rawa p. for massage treatment; oowun pwee p. for knot divination; owun fanafan p. for building a canoe; oowun iimw p. for building a house. oowun émwékút acceleration fee (paid to a canoe builder to make alterations on a canoe so that it will go faster). oowun ewe meyimá burial gift for the dead person. vi. (with wóón) bring burial gifts to ("make gifts upon").

oowuni See oow, -ni-. vo. (T5) pay a fee to; make a burial gift to. sipwene o. ewe meyimá (ewe sowuwimw, etc.) we are going to make payment to the dead person (the master housebuilder, etc.).

ooyééch (2) See oo_1, *ééch*. nu. (T2) true omen. Ant. *oongngaw*.

osiriko Var. of *osirúko*.

osiroy (2) OSIROYI. (Jap. *oshiroi*) nu. (T2) baby powder. *aan o*. his b. p.

osiroyini See *osiroy, -ni-*. vo. (T5) apply baby powder to.

osirúko (1) OSIRÚKOO. (Jap. *oshiruko*) Var. *osiriko*. nu. (T1) a soup-like drink with dumplings in hot water. *anan o*. his *o.*.

osu (1) See *su*. nu. (c.; T1) 1. seeing off. 2. rites to send away the spirits that have caused an illness and make them content not to return. *osuun chénúkken* r. to see off the sea spirits.

osuunó (1) See *su, -nó*. nu. (c.; T1) seeing off (on a journey). *kkópwongen o*. farewell greeting, godspeed.

osuuw See *su*. vo. (c.; T1) see off (on a journey). With dir. suf.: *osuuwonó*. *sipwe osuuwonó átewe wóón waan we* we shall see that fellow off in his boat.

osuuwonó See *osuuw*.

osukosuk Var. of *wosukosuk*.

osukuun (3) See *sukuun*. F. Var. *ósukuun*. nu. (c.; T3) teaching, instruction. *aan o*. his t. *wúse nniyen meneey áán átánaan we o*. I did not understand that fellow's t. very well.

osukuuna See *sukuun*. F. Var. *ósukuuna*. vo. (c.; T3) teach, instruct (people). va. (c.) study, practice (subjects and things).

osumwu See *sumw*. N. vo. (c.; T2) pick (a bunch of bananas). Syn. *weyiti*.

osunu See *sun*. vo. (c.; T2) beat, defeat (in a race). Cf. *okkufu*.

ossow (dc; 2) See *sowu-*$_2$. F. Var. *assow*. vi. (c.) be reserved or saved for use at an appropriate time.

ossowu See *sowu-*$_2$. F. Var. *assowu*. vo. (c.; T2) reserve or save (something) for an occasion, put aside for future use.

ossuuku See *ssuuk*. vo. (c.; T2) cause to be open.

ossupwu See *ssupw*. vo. (c.; T3) cause to drip; catch (drops).

-ok (3) OKA. [In cpds. only.] unsp. (u.m.) See *siyok, nisiyok*.

okoyikoy (db; 2) See *koyi*-$_1$. nu. (c.; T2) a small whistle; referee's whistle. *eew o*. one w. *neyi o*. my w.; *okoyikoyin* w. of (a given type). Syn. *koroniita*.

okuusa See *kuus*$_2$. vo. (c.; T3) cover with a cloth.

okusóónó See *okusu*.

okusu See *kus*. vo. (c.; T2) cause to escape, let get away. With dir. suf.: *okusóónó*.

okukkunowu See *kunow*. vo. (c., dis.; T2) cause (someone) to visit (with the subject of the verb). *aa okukkunowuwey* he caused me to v. (with him); *ngaang wúwa o*. I caused him to v. (with me).

okunamwmweey See *kunamwmwe*. Var. *ekinamwmweey*. vo. (c.; T1) make (someone) comfortable.

okunnu See *kkun*. vo. (c.; T2) make turn around, make revolve, make go around.

okuchchaanong See *okuchchu*.

okuchchu See *kkuch*. vo. (c.; T2) grant admission to, admit ("cause to be fitted in"). With dir. suf.: *okuchchaanong* grant admission into; *okuchchuweyinong nóón angaang* admit me to work; *okuchchaanong itey nóón angaang* enroll me in (admit my name to) work.

okuwara See *kuwar*. vo. (c.; T3) make muddy (of water).

okko- Dis. of *o*-$_3$ (var. of *akka-*).

okko Dis. of o_2.

okkopwu See *kkopw*. vo. (c.; T2) make dull.

okkoruwuuw See *ruwuuw*.

okkowone See *wone*.

okkowonuuw See *wonuuw*.

okkowun (2) See *wun*. vi. (c., dis.) use extreme insults (of the kind used only to provoke a fight). [Much more severe than *ámáámááy* or *óttekiiy*.] nu. (c.; dis.; T2) extreme insults. *okkowunun móówun* i. used in battle.

okkowuna See *okkowun*. vo. (c.; T3) insult in the extreme.

okkuf See *kkuf*. vi. (c.) compare or compete to see which is poorer or less; see what loses by comparison. *o. ffengen (okkuffengen)* bring together to compare.

okkufu See *kkuf*. vo. (c.; T2) defeat in a fight, war, game (but not a race). Cf. *osunu*.

okkuffengen See *okkuf*.

okkusu See *kkus.* vo. (c.; T2) make spurt, spit out. With dir. suf.: *okkusóónó* make s. out (as blood).

okkun (2) See *kkun.* nu. (c.; T2) large ball of sennit rope. *okunnun sáán* b. of rope.

omos (2) OMOSU. nu. (T2) turban shell (*Turbo petholatus* L.). *omosun* t. s. of (a given region). *épwpwénún o.* cat's eye (operculum of the t. s., syn. *wuwáán wooch*); *imweyimwen o.* a kind of reef formation.

omorokunnu See *mara-, kkun.* vo. (c.; T2) cause to revolve, make spin.

omoruk (3) See *ma-, ruk.* nu. (c.; T3) quick withering of plants after first sprouting up.

omwopwu See *mwopw.* vo. (c.; T2) cause to suffocate, asphyxiate (as by fumes, drowning, etc.).

omwotowutowu See *mwotowutow.* vo. (c.; T2) make smooth, smooth.

omwusa See *mwus.* vo. (c.; T3) untie, release; forgive, absolve from. With dir. suf.: *omwusóónó* (the more common form).

omwusomwus (db; 3) See *mwus.* vi. apologize, confess (to a priest), seek forgiveness. *o. ngeni* (vo. phr.) apologize or confess to, seek forgiveness from.

omwusóónó See *omwusa.*

omwura (3) See *mwuromwur.* vi. (c.) add water (by sprinkling) to breadfruit pudding so as to make it pound well and give it an even (unlumpy) consistency.

omwurenipwin (2) See *mwuromwur, pwiin*₃. nu. (c.; T2) dew ("water-adding of night"). Cf. *omwura.*

omwmwopwura See *mwmwopwur.* vo. (c.; T3) load (a boat) to the point of near swamping.

omwmwung (3) See *mwmwung.* nu. (c.; T3) spell for attracting someone's affection; love magic. [Such a spell may be made on cigarettes, garlands, perfume, ornaments, jewelry, etc.] Dis. *okkomwmwung* (ds). *aan o.* his s. Syn. *pwénúpwén.* vi. (c.) make a love spell.

omwmwunga See *omwmwung.* vo. (c.; T3) make love magic on or on behalf of ("cause to be loved"). *kepwe omwmwungááyey* you shall make l. m. on me (to make me irresistable).

-on (2) ONU (*ONE?). [In place names only.] unsp. (u.m.) Example: *Pisiniyon* name of a reef between Romónum and Féwúúp, Toon.

Oniyon (db; 2) See *-on.* nu. (loc.) in *mwóóchun O.* Aleon Pass.

onomw See *ana-*₁.

onusu See *nus.* vo. (c.; T2) remove from one place to another; remove from its socket or holder, pluck out, chisel out. Cf. *onnusu.*

onussóónó Var. of *ónussaanó.*

onussu Var. of *ónussu.*

onumwu See *nuumw.* vo. (c.; T2) smear.

onupa See *nup.* Var. *ónupa.* vo. (c.; T3) 1. make capsize, tip over, turn over. With dir. suf.: *onupáátá* turn right side up; *onupáátiw* tip or turn down. 2. make flash on and off (of a light). *o. kinaas* rock or flash a mirror. With dir. suf.: *onupaanong* flash (it) in or southwards (as towards Wútéét from Romónum).

onupaanong See *onupa.*

onupáátá See *onupa.*

onupáátiw See *onupa.*

onuponup (db; 3) See *nup.* nu. (c.; T3) a form of sorcery in which a medicine is placed in food and a spell is said over it (also known as *rongen o.*). [It causes spitting, coughing, or vomiting blood.] *sáfeen o.* medicine to counteract the effects of *o.* sorcery.

onupwu See *nupw.* vo. (T2) ripen; wait for (something) to become ripe.

onnusu (dc) See *nus.* vo. (c.; T2) cause to jump or hop. Cf. *onusu.*

onnut Var. of *ónnut.*

opereyitor (Eng.) nu. telephone operator. *emén o.* one t. o.

opi (1) OPII. (Jap. *obi*) nu. (T1) sash worn around the waist (especially at an athletic meet). *eché o.* one s. *aan o.* his s.

opoop (db; 4) OPO. Var. *wopoop.* vi. be depressed, dented (of a surface); have a depression.

opos (2) See *posu-.* nu. (c.; T2) men's hairpin with bead string attached. *néwún o.* his h.; *oposun* h. of (a given kind).

opow (2) OPOWU. vi. prepare breadfruit by broiling, peeling, and gently pounding to make it soft. Dis. *okkopow* (ds).

opowin (2) See *wop, wiin*₁. nu. (T2) method of hunting turtles. vi. hunt turtles by the *o.* method.

opowu See *opow.* vo. (T2) prepare (breadfruit) by broiling, peeling, and gently pounding to make it soft.

opu (1) OPUU. nu. (T1) 1. starch flour that is the residue washed from turmeric in processing turmeric dye or from manioc to be used for food. *anan o.* his s. f. *opuun teyuk* turmeric s. Syn. *toow*₁. 2. yolk (of an egg). *opuun sókun, opuun chukó* egg y., chicken y.

oppos (2) See *ppos.* nu. (c.; T2) innoculation, injection. vi. (c.) 1. be stuck, pierced (by spear, knife, etc.), shot (by medicinal needle); have an innoculation. 2. do innoculations.

opposu See *ppos.* vo. (c.; T2) 1. spear, stab; innoculate. Syn. *posuuw.* 2. tamp down.

opwooyiset (2) See *pwo, sáát*₁. nu. (c.; T2) a form of sorcery that cripples the limbs of children.

opwuupwuuw Dis. of *opwuuw*₂.

opwuuw₁ See *pwu*₁. vi. (c.; T1) cause to flow. With dir. suf.: *opwuuwonó* drain off.

opwuuw₂ See *pwu*₂. vo. (c.; T1) blow, sound (of trumpet). Dis. *opwuupwuuw* (db).

opwuuwonó See *opwuuw*₁.

opwunaasa See *pwunaas.* vo. (c.; T3) make (someone) drunk.

opwupwpwun Dis. of *opwpwun*.

opwuroppi (3) See *pwur*₁, *ppi*₂. nu. (T3) a hold in hand-to-hand fighting that locks the arms of an opponent and plunges his face and eyes into the sand.

opwurók Var. of *ópwurók.*

opwucha See *pwuch.* vo. (c.; T3) drive (someone) crazy.

opwut See *pwuta-*. F. Var. *opwuta, ópwuta.* va. (c.) dislike. *wúwa o. een* I don't like you; *raa o. ffengen* they d. each other. With dir. suf.: *opwutónó* have no use for.

opwuta See *pwuta-*. N. Var. *ópwuta.* vo. (c.; T3) dislike. With dir. suf.: *opwutaanó* have no use for.

opwutaanó See *opwuta.*

opwutónó See *opwut.*

opwpwoyi See *pwpwoy.* vo. (c.; T2) scald.

opwpwuffengen (dc; 2) See *pwu-*₂. *ffengen.* vi. (c.) collide, bump into one another.

opwpwusón nu. a grass (*Hedyotis biflora*).

opwpwun (3) See *pwpwun*₁. n. (c.; T3) causing to be lit, illumination. Dis. *opwupwpwun* (db). *opwupwpwunan* his i. *aa wor opwpwunen ewe sómwoon ewe fúú seni nááng* the star from heaven became a light for the chief; *opwpwupwunen ewe wuumw* illumination of the food presentation.

opwpwuna See *pwpwun*₁. vo. (c.; T3) cause to be lit up; cause to blaze, flame, flash; illuminate; provide light for. *wúpwe o. aach angaang* I shall provide light for our work.

opwpwun mataw See *oopw.*

opwpwura See *pwpwur*₂. vo. (c.; T3) boil, cause to boil.

opwpwuri See *pwu-*₂, *-ri-*. vo. (T2) collide with, bump, stub against. Syn. *ópwpwura.*

oris (2) ORISI. (Eng.) nu. (T2) horse. *emén o.* one h. *néwún o.* his h. *orisin neeset, orisin sáát* sea horse. Syn. *óós*₁.

oroken (Eng.) nu. organ (musical instrument). *pwuupwuun o.* o. pedal.

oruuwuwa- Var. of *oruwuuwa-* (see *ruwuuw*).

oruka See *ruk.* vo. (c.; T3) lead astray, make lose track, make confused, cause to go wrong, divert; cause to be lost. Dis. *orukoruk* (db). *wúwa resin o. ttongomw* I have tried and tried to cause love of you to get lost (I have tried and tried to forget you).

orukoruk (db; 3) See *ruk.* va. (c.) lead astray, make lose track, make confused, make get lost.

orupa See *rup*₂. vo. (c.; T3) cause to fight.

oruwa See *ru*₂. vo. (c.; T3) cause to be out of place.

oruwuuw₁ (3) See *ruwuuw.* vi. (c.) have two wives or husbands at the same time, be a bigamist.

Oruwuuw₂ (3) See *ruwuuw.* F. Var. *Óruuwu.* nu. (c., temp.; T3) Tuesday ("second").

oruwuuwa- See *ruwuuw.*

ochooch Var. of *wochooch.*

ochopw (2) OCHOPWU. nu. (T2) a head garland worn by both sexes in the dance. *mwárin o.* his h. g.; *ochopwun* h. g. of (a given kind).

ochopwu F. of *óchopwu.*

ochoropwpwuna See *choropwpwun.* vo. (c.; T3) cause to flash.

ochow (2) See *chowu-₁.* vi. (c.; T2) have a separate dining arrangement including separate preparation of food, be tabu from eating with others (of *itang* and *pénú*). *iir raa o. faansowun meyinisin* they have a separate mess at all times.

ochuunna See *chuun.* vo. (c.; T3) make blind, blind.

ochuuw See *chu.* vo. (c.; T1) cause (someone) to meet (with *me*). *o. me átánaan* cause him to meet with that fellow.

ochuffengenni See *chuffengeen.* vo. (c.; T2) cause to meet together; put together, join together.

ochuffengenniiy See *chuffengen, -i-₂.* Var. *ochuffengenni.* vo. (c.; T5) cause to meet together, put together, join together.

ochukuchuk (db; 2) See *chuku-₂.* vi. (c.) cluck at, call to (chicks by a chicken). Syn. *óchokochok.*

ochukuchuku See *ochukuchuk.* vo. (T2) cluck at, call to (chicks by a chicken). Syn. *óchokochoka.*

ochchuwa See *chchuwa-.* vo. (c.; T3) look sideways at, look at (someone) from the corner of one's eyes (as in a covert signal).

otokunu See *tokun.* Var. *atakunu.* vo. (c.; T2) cause to revolve; make spin. Dis. *okkotokunu* (ds). Syn. *omorokunnu.*

otomwuna See *tomwun₁.* vo. (c.; T3) peel; let rot. With dir. suf.: *otomwunóónó* peel off; let go soft or rotten.

otomwunóónó See *otomwuna.*

otopay (2) OTOPAYI. (Jap. *ootobai*) nu. (T2) motorcycle. *efóch o.* one m. *waan o.* his m.

otopwu See *topw.* vo. (c.; T2) make dull (not bright), tarnish; obscure (as by clouds). *kuchu aa o. akkar* clouds have obscured the sun.

otuka See *tuk₁.* vo. (c.; T3) make numerous.

otungngaf (3) See *tuu-₃, ngaaf.* nu. (T3) a long stride.

otupwu₁ See *tupw₂.* vo. (c.; T2) fool, deceive, trick, dupe.

otupwu₂ See *tupw₃.* vo. (c.; T2) get (something) smeared. *wúwa o. wúfey nóón pwise* I got my clothes s. in excrement.

oturaatiw See *oturu₂.*

oturaawu See *oturu₂.*

oturénnú (1) See *tura-, nnú.* vi. (c.) be a tease, make sport of someone (as by refusing to take seriously what is being said in earnest). n. (c.; T1) teasing, making sport (of people). *oturénnúún t.* of him. *aan oturénnúúy* his t. of me.

oturénnúúw See *oturénnú.* vo. (c.; T1) tease, make sport of.

oturóónó See *oturu₂.*

oturu₁ See *tur₁.* vo. (c.; T2) cause to be arrested; accuse of a crime. *wúwa o. átánaan reen pwonis* I have caused that fellow to be arrested by the police.

oturu₂ vo. (c.; T2) let or cause to fall; drop With dir. suf.: *oturaatiw* let fall down, cast down; *oturaawu* let fall out, cast out; *oturóónó* cast off or away, throw away. Cf. *kkotur.*

oturunóónó (1) See *tur₂, -nó.* va. (c., dis.) abandon, discontinue; let drop (over time).

ottumwu₁ See *ttumw₁.* vo. (c.; T2) cause to stagger or stumble.

ottumwu₂ See *ttumw₂.* vo. (c.; T2) suck (on); sip from or at. *aa o. ewe kkap* he sipped at the cup; *aa o. owupwun inan* he sucked (on) his mother's breasts.

ottumwu₃ See *ttumw₃.* vo. (c.; T2) cause (someone) to be inadequately supplied or short.

ottur nu. a sea crab.

owa See *o-₂, -a₁.* Var. *éwúwa, owuwa, wowa.* prn. const. 2pl. sub. prn. plus reality aspect marker: you (pl., past or factual). *o. nónnómw ikeey iye* y. remained here.

owosuwos (db; 2) See *wos₃.* nu. (c.; T3) a magic that makes others unable to function in sport or war.

owoneen See *wone.*

owonuuwan See *wonuuw.*

owu- (2) OWU. Wn., Tns. Var. *éwú-₁, o-₂, wo-.* pref. (sub.) 2pl. sub. prn.: you. [Although a prefix, it is written separately except when followed by an aspect marker.] *owuwa* (reality); *owune* (immediate future); *owupwaapw* (indefinite future); *owupwe* (future, unreality); *owusapw* (future negative); *owuse* (negative reality); *owute* (immediate future negative, negative command).

owusapw See *owu-*.

owuse See *owu-*.

owusuus (db; 2) See *wusu-₂*. N. nu. (c.; T2) a tree (*Excoecaria agallocha*). [Poisonous sap, whence its name; fruit used as medicine for eye trouble.] Syn. *rowusuus, wiisuusu, wusuus₂*.

owuka See *wuk*. vo. (c.; T3) do (something) in the early morning. Syn. *wukeey₁*.

owumw (2) See *wuumw*. vi. (c.) take gifts of food to a new mother. [They are brought by her husband's as well as by her own kin.]

owumwes See *wumwes*. vo. (c.; T2) bother to distraction, confuse ("drive crazy").

owumwuumw (db; 2) See *wumwu-₁*. vi. (c., dis.) show one's envy in one's face; be sullen faced. *o. ngeni* (vo. phr.) be sullen towards.

owun (2, 3) See *wun*. N. vi. (c.) be poisonous (of food and drink only). *naan mwéngé meyi o.* that food is p. Syn. *menin*. Cf. *pwich*. nu. (T2) poison. *owunun nóón naan mwéngé* the p. in that food.

owuna See *wun*. vo. (c.; T3) give poison to. Cf. *owunu*.

owune See *owu-*.

owunu See *wun*. vo. (c.; T2) poison; be poisonous for. *ewe iik aa owunuk* that fish has poisoned you (preferable to say *kaa wun reen ewe iik* you are poisoned by that fish). Cf. *owuna*.

owunusa See *wunus*. vo. (c.; T3) cause to be entire, make a whole thing of.

owunnun nu. a nuclear family. [Consisting of a woman, her children (by however many husbands), and her current husband.] *eew o.* one n. f. *aan o.* his n. f. Cf. *eterekes, eyinang, faameni, futuk, inepwiinéw*.

Owung nu. (loc.) a clan name.

owungowunga See *wungowung*. vo. (c.; T3) make high; elevate. With dir. suf.: *owungowungáátá*.

owungowungáátá See *owungowunga*.

owupw (2) See *wupwu-₁, wupw*. n. (c.; T2) breast. *ewupw o.* one b. *owupwun* her b. *owupwun pwpwo, owupwun wúsúús* small decorative knobs or nipples on top of a breadfruit pounder.

owupwaapw See *owu-*.

owupwaatiw See *owupwu*.

owupwáátiw See *owupwu*.

owupwe See *owu-*.

owupwu See *wupw*. vo. (c.; T2) beget, bear (children). With dir. suf.: *owupwaatiw* (N.), *owupwáátiw* (F.) bear, give birth to.

owupwuupw (2) See *wupw*. vi. (c., dis.) produce many offspring, have great increase (of children). Cf. *Nikowupwuupw*.

owupwuta See *wupwut*. vo. (c.; T3) put young coconut leaves on (someone); dress or bedeck (someone) with young coconut leaves.

owura See *wur₁*. vo. (c.; T3) fill, make full. Dis. *okkowura* (ds). With dir. suf.: *owuraawu* fill to overflowing; *owuráátá* fill up.

owuraawu See *owura*.

owuráátá See *owura*.

owurinnaw (3) OWURINNAWA. vi. (c.) tease in a friendly way, joke. *kete kkapasen o.* don't joke. *o. ngeni* (vo. phr.) tease, joke with, josh. Cf. *wur₂*.

owuru See *wur₂*. vo. (c.; T2) amuse (a child); take (someone) for a walk or excursion; visit (someone). Dis. *owuruuru* (db).

owuruur (db; 2) See *wuru-₃*. vi. (c.), va. inspect, examine (visually). nu. (c.; T2) act of inspecting, examining (visually). *kinassen o.* mirror.

owuruuru₁ Dis. of *owuru*.

owuruuru₂ (db) See *wuru-₃*. vo. (c.; T2) inspect, examine (visually).

owurumééw See *wurumé*. vo. (c.; T1) push around, jostle, treat roughly; man handle.

Owurupik nu. (loc.) Eauripik Island and Atoll (Central Caroline Islands).

owuchuuch (db; 2) OWUCHU. nu. (T2) hibiscus bark pompom decorating the end-pieces of a canoe. [The word is not used for similar decorations on a sling.] *owuchuuchun waa* canoe's *o.*. Cf. *wuchuuch*.

owut (3) OWUTA. n. (T3), suf. (cc.) ascending row of thatch. [Used in stating the size of buildings.] *óówut* or *ewut, rúwóówut* or *ruwóówut, wúnúyowut, fóówut, nimóówut, wonóówut, fúúyowut, wanúyowut, ttiwóówut, engoon owutan* one,...ten r. of t.

owuta

owuta (1) OWUTAA. nu. (T1) a species of tuna (skipjack).

owute See *owu-*.

owuwa See *owu-*.

owuwá (1) OWUWÁÁ. vi. whistle (of humans). Dis. *okkowuwá* (ds).

owuwáári See *owuwá*, *-ri-*. vo. (T4) whistle to. Dis. *okkowuwáári* (ds).

owuwoow (db; 3) See *wuwa-₁*. [Apparently from *owuwowu.] nu. (c.; T3) things to be conveyed; shipment, load. Cf. *owuwowuwa-*, *owuwowuwaaya-*. va. (c.) give to be conveyed or shipped; consign for shipping.

owuwomóng (2) See *wuwa-₁*, *móóng*. vi. (c.) carry on one's head.

owuwomónga See *owuwomóng*. N. vo. (c.; T3) carry (something) on one's head. Syn. *owuwomóngeey*.

owuwomóngeey See *owuwomóng*, *-e-₂*. F. vo. (c.; T6b) carry (something) on one's head. With n. form. suf. *-ya-*: *owuwomóngeeya-* (ni.; T3) head burden.

owuwomóngeeya- See *owuwomóngeey*.

owuwochchowu See *wuwochchow*. vo. (c.; T2) load heavily.

owuwowuwa- (db; 3) See *wuwa-₁*. n. (c.; T3) thing (for someone) to convey, load. *owuwowuwan* thing for him to convey, his load to carry. ni. (c.; T3) sign, portent, indication ("conveyance"). *owuwowuwen aan epwene máánó* s. that he is going to die.

owuwowuwa (db) See *wuwa-₁*. vo. (c., dis.; T3) 1. cause to be conveyed; ship, send; mail, post (of letters). With dir. suf.: *owuwowuwóónó* send off, mail off. *wúwa o. neyi toropwe ngeni chiyeney* I have mailed off my letter to my friend. With n. form. suf. *-ya-*: *owuwowuwaaya-* (N.), *owuwowuyááya-* (F.) (ni.; T3) thing given (by someone) to be conveyed, shipment sent (by someone). 2. cause (someone) to be a carrier. *wúpwe o. átánaan pwe epwe wuweey pisekiy* I shall make that fellow a carrier so that he will carry my things.

owuwowuwaaya- See *owuwowa*.

owuwowuwááya- See *owuwowuwa*.

owuwowuwóónó See *owuwowuwa*.

Ó

ó-₁ See *e-*₁. [Used only in rapid or colloquial speech and only when followed by the vowel *ó*.] Var. *á-*₁, *a-*₁, *e-*₁. pref. (sub.) 3sg. sub. prn.: he, she, it. [Although a prefix, it is written separately.] *ó nó Toon* he is off to Toon (Tol) Island.

ó-₂ See *a-*₂. [Usually in this form when the next following vowel is *ó*.] pref. (c.) imparts causative meaning to the base. Dis. *ókkó-* (ds).

ó-₃ See *e-*₂. [In this form only when immediately followed by *ó*.] pref. (num.) one; a, an; another. [Used with suffixed forms indicating the class of unit enumerated.] See *óóch, óówut*.

óó- (1) ÓÓ₁. [In cpds. only.] unsp. relating to cursing. See *óóri*.

óó₁ (1) ÓÓ₂. nu. (T1) fishline. *efóch óó, esen óó* one f. *aan óó* his f. n. (T1), suf. (cc.) tentacle (of octopus or squid). *eyó, rúwéyó, wúnúyó, féyó, nimeyó, wonoyó, fúúyó, wanúyó, ttiweyó, engoon óón* one,...ten t. *eyó óón nippach* one octopus t. Syn. *éwút*₂.

óó₂ (1) ÓÓ₃. nu. (T1) name of the low, back, rounded vowel written *ó*; name of the letter thus written.

óófes (2) ÓÓFESI. (Eng.) nu. (T2) office (place).

óófi See *óó*₁, *-fi-*. vo. (T4) hook (on a hook and line, in fishing).

óófór (4) ÓÓFÓRO. Var. *efór*. nu. (T2) a tree. *óófórun* t. of (a given location). Cf. *ófór*.

óós₁ (2) ÓÓSU. (Eng.) nu. (T2) horse. *emén ó.* one h. *newún ó.* his h. *óósun* h. of (a given kind). Syn. *oris*.

óós₂ (4) ÓSO. nu. (T2) a prepared sheet of thatch; thatch shingle; any sheet of roofing material of any kind; roof. [It is traditionally made of ivory palm leaves stitched to a reed one fathom long.] *emén ó.* one sheet or shingle of traditional t.; *eché ó.* a sheet of metal roofing. *ósun iimw* house's t.

óósooso (db; 1) See *óó*₁, *so*₂. nu. (T1) fishing in which the line is cast out into the water.

Óókos (Eng.) Var. *Aakos*. nu. (temp.) August.

óókkách Var. of *ókkách*.

óón₁ (4) See *ón*₂. nu. (c.; T3) wiping clean. *pééyinin ó.* coconut husk for cleaning; *tóropween ó.* toilet paper.

óón₂ (4) ÓNO₅. nu. (T2) food (especially for an occasion). *aan ó.* his f. *ónun waa* f. for the canoe (given to the canoe builder while he works on the canoe); *ónun iimw* f. for the house (given to the housebuilders); *ónun taka* f. for the copra (given to one's copra cutters). Cf. *ónu-*.

óón₃ E.Wn. of *één*₁.

óónet (2) See *óno-, -ti-*. vi. (c.) be opened out or unfolded (as coconut leaves in connection with mat weaving). Cf. *kkóónet*.

óóneti See *óno-, -ti-*. vo. (T2) spread (something) out flat (as a mat), unfold, open out. Dis. *ókkóóneti* (ds). *ó. kkanaan kiyeki* spread out those mats; *siya ókkóóneti eey kiyeki nóón imwach* we customarily spread this mat in our house. Syn. *ónoti*. Cf. *kkóónet*.

óónu (1) ÓÓNUU. n. (T1) slapping the hollow of the elbow crooked against the chest with cupped hand so as to make a loud popping sound (as in dancing or by men after bathing). [When done repeatedly it is a challenge to war.] *óónuun* his s.

Óónuk nu. (pers.) name of an evil spirit that preys on pregnant women.

óónnuta See *ónnut*. vo. (c.; T3) put to sleep.

óópa See *wop*. Var. *woopa*. vo. (c.; T3) hide, conceal. Dis. *ókkóópa* (ds). With dir. suf.: *óópóónó*.

óópoop (db; 4) See *opoop* (?). nu. (c.; T2, T3) weaving sword. [A lath used to spread the warp threads in weaving and to beat the weft threads into place.] *óópoopun* or *óópoopen túúr* loom's w. s.

óópóónó See *óópa*.

óópwunes nu. a fishing method. [The fish are surrounded and frightened into holes in the reef whence they are speared.]

óór (4) ÓRO. n. (T2) 1. outer surface of skin. *órun* his o. s. 2. the side of óóri

something. *órun waa* side of canoe; *órun pwóór* sides of a box. 3. immediate surroundings, environs, vicinity. *órun iimw* environs of a house.

óóri See *óó-*, *-ri-*. vo. (T4) curse. Syn. *ápeepeey*, *óóttekiiy*, *óttekiiy*.

óóror (3: *-kóóror*) See *wor*, *-ra-* (?). nu. (c.; T3) 1. deliberation or decision as to what is correct, good, or true. 2. (Obs.) thing; something that is. Syn. *mettóóch*. vi. (c.) plan, think something through, think about how things should be.

óórora See *óóror*. vo. (c.; T3) plan; deliberate or decide upon (as to the truth or solution of a matter); diagnose. *tóókoche epwe ó. meet sóókkun semwmwen aa wúri átánaan* the doctor will decide what kind of sickness has taken that fellow.

óóroréech (2) See *óóror*, *éech*. vi. plan or decide well, be of good counsel.

Óórorofich See *óóror*, *-fich*. nu. (pers.) a traditional god who lives in the sky. [Brother of *Semenkóóror* and *Semewútéwút* he presides over good relations among peoples.]

óórorongngaw (3b) See *óóror*, *ngngaw*. vi. plan or decide badly.

óórór (3) See *óór*, *-ra-*. vi. (c.) frequent or hang around a place; keep coming back to a place because of some desire one has in relation to it.

óóróra See *óórór*. vo. (c.; T3) frequent; hang around, keep coming around to. *pwata aa ó. neminnewe?* why does he hang around that girl?

óóch (4) See *e-₂*, *-óch*. num. one sort, kind, variety, species, ration; another sort, etc.; an indefinite amount, some (as with water, fire, sand); anything. Dis. *ekkóóch* (N.), *ókkóóch* (F.), *kkóóch* (F.) several kinds or indefinite amounts, a miscellany or assortment. *ó. paa* some bait, a piece of bait; *ó. pwóróówus* another kind of talk (i.e. a disguised talk). *ó. sóókkun* a different kind, different; *ó. sóókkun aramas* another sort of person, one who is different. *aa fis ó.? ese fis ó.* did anything happen? nothing happened. *fáán ekkóóch* (N.), *fáán ókkóóch* (F.), a few times, infrequently. Syn. *ewoch*, *ooch*.

óót₁ (4, 3) ÓTTO, ÓTTA. nu. (T2, T3) inner bud or spongy core of sprouting coconut. *eew ó.*, *eféw ó.* one i. b. *óttun*, *óttan* its i. b. *óttun taka*, *ótten taka* ripe coconut's i. b.; *pwúkún ó.* coconut's sprout. vi. form an inner bud.

óót₂ nu. a kind of hanging basket.

óóta See *óto-*, *woot₂*. vo. (c.; T3) arrange, put in order, make ready. Dis. *ókkóóta* (ds). Cf. *kkóót*.

óótóót (db; 3) See *óto-*, *woot₂*. nu. (c.; T3) arrangement; program, procedure; agenda. *ifa wusun óótóóten eey mwiich* what is the agenda of this meeting? vi. (c.) be arranged, in order, ready.

óóttek (2) See *óó-*, *-ttek*. Var. *óttek*. vi. (c.) be cursed. Syn. *ápeepe*. Cf. *iyóótek*.

óóttekiiy See *óóttek*, *-i-₂*. Var. *óttekiiy*. vo. (c.; T5) curse. Syn. *ápeepeey*, *óóri*.

óówut Var. of *ewut₂*.

óóyepa (1) See *óó₁*, *epa*. nu. (T1) a long single strand of black beads in a necklace.

óóyó (db; 1) See *óó₁*. nu. (T1) strap or rope handle, carrier made of rope or line. *óóyóón péér* carrier for coconut water bottle; *óóyóón pwekit* bucket handle. vi. be strung (as a line between two trees).

ófósoosoow See *fósooso*. vo. (c.; T1) make uneven (in height or length).

ófóna See *fón*. vo. (c.; T3) pamper, coddle, cherish, spoil (children). Cf. *fóóneni*, *ffóónuni*.

ófónónó (1) See *ó-₂*, *fónónó*. Var. *kófónónó*. vi. (c.) be keeping silent.

ófór F. of *afór*.

ófóta₁ See *fóto-₁*. N. vo. (c.; T3) look at. Dis. *ókkófóta* (ds). Cf. *kkófót*.

ófóta₂ See *fóto-₂*. vo. (c.; T3) plant, cause to be stuck firm (in something).

ósoosichiiy See *soosich*, *-i-₂*. vo. (c.; T5) save, conserve. Syn. *asoochikiiy*, *asoochisiiy*. Ant. *asochchika*, *ósoonapa*.

ósoomá (1) See *soomá*. nu. (c.; T1) offering of tobacco, food or fish to a spirit. *ó. ngeni* (or *wóón*) *soomá o.* to spirits. *pwukopwuken ó.* overhand knot used in tying an offering with a young coconut leaf.

ósoomáángeni See *ósoomá*, *ngeni*. vo. (T2) make an offering to.

ósoonapa See *soonap*. Var. *asoonapa*. vo. (c.; T3) discard (something) needed, make a waste of; regard as or consider to be wasted; feel for (someone) who has suffered a loss of something he needed. *wú fen ó.* I actually got rid of what I need; *wúwa ó. neminnaan reen niyéchchún ngé ese sineey angaang* I regard her as wasted because she is beautiful but does not know how to work. Syn. *asochchika.*

óso̱onga See *soong.* vo. (c.; T3) make angry.

óso̱ochisiiy F. of *asoochisiiy.*

óso̱ochikiiy F. of *asoochikiiy.*

óso̱ow$_1$ See *so̱₂.* vo. (c.; T1) cause to alight; land (a plane).

óso̱ow$_2$ See *so̱₃.* vo. (c.; T1) make precipitate out (as the starch from the washing of grated arrowroot or grated manioc root).

óso̱kini (1) See *óós₂, kini.* nu. (T1) thatch made of plaited coconut frond matting. Syn. *ósopáásini.*

óso̱koopw Short for *ósokoopwure.*

óso̱koopwure (1) See *óós₂, koopwure.* Var. *ósokoopw.* nu. (T1) sheet metal roofing. *eché ó.* one sheet of r. Syn. *ósomáchá.*

óso̱kúwé (1) See *óós₂, kúwé.* nu. (T1) nipa palm thatching.

óso̱máchá (1) See *óós₂, máchá.* nu. (T1) sheet metal roofing. *eché ó.* one sheet of r. Syn. *ósokoopwure.*

óso̱na See *son.* vo. (c.; T3) deceive, trick, fool. Cf. *ókkóson.*

óso̱páásini (1) See *óós₂, paa₁, sini.* nu. (T1) thatch made of coconut frond matting.

óso̱rúpwúng (2) See *óós₂, rúpwúng.* nu. (T2) ivory palm thatching.

óso̱wu See *sowu-₁.* vo. (c.; T2) lead, guide (in an activity). *aa ó. ewe angaang* he led the work.

óso̱yetiru (1) See *óós₂, etiru.* nu. (T1) thatching of plaited coconut matting.

óso̱ów (2) ÓSÓÓWU. vi. give a catch of fish to a neighboring district (by a district) or lineage (by a lineage) as an expression of gratitude for past cordial relations. [Done on occasions when the receiving group is preparing a ceremonial feast.]

óso̱ówu See *ósóów.* vo. (T2) make a formal gift of fish to (a lineage or district by a lineage or district). *si pwe ó. Winisi* we shall *ó.* Winisi district. Syn. *ósóówuni.*

óso̱ówuni See *ósóów, -ni-.* vo. (T5) make a formal gift of fish to (a lineage or district by a lineage or district). *si pwe ó. Winisi* we shall *ó.* Winisi district. Syn. *ósóówu.*

óso̱kuun F. of *ósókun.*

óso̱kun (2) See *sokun₂.* N. Var. *ósókuun.* vi. (c.) lay an egg.

óso̱mwoonééch (2) See *sómwoon, ééch.* nu. (c.; T2) appropriate deference. *angaangen ó.* proper deferential behavior.

óso̱mwoonu See *sómwoon.* Var. *asómwonnu, ósómwonnu.* vo. (c.; T2) treat (someone) with the deference owed a chief or ruler; make a chief of.

óso̱mwonnu Var. of *asómwonnu, ósómwoonu.*

óso̱na See *són.* vo. (c.; T3) level (ground), prepare as a site.

óso̱nóng$_1$ (2) ÓSÓNÓNGU. nu. (T2) cutwater (downward projecting, triangular point at the base of each end of a canoe). *ósónóngun waa* canoe's c.

óso̱nóng$_2$ (3) ÓSÓNÓNGA. nu. (T3) <Elbert> a species of squirrel fish (very red). *ósónóngen* s. f. of (a given region).

óso̱ng nu. necklace composed entirely of red shell beads.

óso̱pw (2) See *sópw.* nu. (c.; T2) completion feast (in house building, canoe building, and other activities). [Involves the lineage for whom the house or canoe is built. In the case of completion of the frame of a house, it is done to insure the good health and life of its future occupants. Failure to do it will result in their sickness and death because of the spells used in connection with its construction to insure that it will be a proper building.] *ósópwun iimw* c. f. of a house (in honor of Enikoosich); *ósópwun mááy* c. f. of the cycle of breadfruit ritual (in honor of Sowuyéwúr); *ósópwun nuunu* c. f. of the ritual model canoe of a breadfruit summoner or fish summoner (in honor of Sineenap); *ósópwun sepi* c. f. of a ceremonial wooden bowl (in honor of Sineenap); *ósópwun tukuyá* c. f. of the men's stick dance (in honor of the *énúúsór* for whom the dance was performed); *ósópwun waa* c. f. of a canoe (in honor of Sineenap); *ósópwun wáátawa* c. f. of a spirit medium (following a possession and in honor of the possessing spirit); *ósópwun wuut* c.

ósópwa

f. of a meeting house or boat house (in honor of Enikoosich). Cf. *sópweyéech, sópwóngngaw.*

ósópwa See *sópw.* vo. (c.; T3) finish, complete. Syn. *ósópwuuw.*

ósópwiisek (2) See *sópw, -sek.* vi. (c.) be (doing something) against one's will; be under duress. *iiy ese mwechen ngé aa chek ó. ne féérí* he didn't want to but was just doing it against his will. Cf. *wosenimwú.*

ósópwuuw See *sópw, -u-.* vo. (c.; T5) finish, complete. Syn. *ósópwa.*

ósópwuni See *ósópw, -ni-.* vo. (c.; T5) make a completion feast for (a building or canoe).

ósór (4) See *-sór.* Var. *asór.* nu. (c.; T2, T3) offering (as in church). *ósórun mwooni, ósóren mwooni* o. of money. vi. (c.) make an offering. [Said to be a loanword from Mck. but perhaps only in Christian usage. Originally something presented to a spirit of the dead, *énúúsór*, to summon or call him.]

ósóra See *-sór.* vo. (c.; T3) call, cause to be summoned. Syn. *ósóreey.*

ósóreey See *-sór, -e-₂.* vo. (c.; T6b) call, cause to be summoned. Syn. *ósóra.*

ósukuun N. of *osukuun.*

ósukuuna N. of *osukuuna.*

ósuni See *óós₂, -ni-.* Var. *óssuni.* vo. (c.; T5) thatch, apply thatch to, put a roof on.

óssaanú (1) See *sse-₁, énú.* [Presumably from an original *ka-sso-yanú.] nu. (c.; T2) preparatory ritual for a seance ("spirit-calling"). [It consists of hanging up the valuables that are an offering to the spirit, gathering and preparing the medicine, and laying out the place in which the medicine is to be put.]

óssooná (1) See *sooná.* vi. (c.) make accusation of stealing, claim that something has been stolen. Id. *ó. ngeni* shirk or be uncooperative in relation to.

óssoonááy See *sooná.* vo. (c.; T1) accuse (someone) of stealing.

óssuni Var. of *ósuni.*

Óschééniya (Eng.) nu. (loc.) Australia.

ókoka See *kok.* vo. (c.; T3) submerge (something) partially, swamp.

ókukkumosu See *kukkumos.* vo. (c.; T2) make round.

ókkách (3) See *óó, -ácha-.* Var. *óókkách.* vi. fish with hook and line ("be casting line"). Cf. *kkáách.*

ókkoomw (3) See *mwmwa-.* F. Var. *akkómw.* vi. (c., dis.) go before, precede, go ahead, be first. *kepwe ó. mwmwey* you shall go ahead in front of me. Ant. *kuukuumwir.* Cf. *kamwo.*

ókkoomwa See *ókkoomw.* vo. (c., dis.; T3) let or have (someone) go first or ahead. *Eiue aa ókkoomwááyey* Eiue had me go ahead.

ókkoomweyiti See *ókkoomw, -iti.* vo. (T2) arrive ahead or first at (a place). *Eiue aa ó. Romónum* Eiue arrived first at Romónum.

ókkopaya See *kkopay.* vo. (c.; T3) cause to be aslant, oblique, not straight, not true.

ókkot (3) ÓKKOTA. n. (T3) food that one contributes to a common meal. *ókkotan* his f. that he has contributed. vi. (c.) contribute food to a common meal where it is put together with the food contributed by others.

ókkota See *kkot.* vo. (c.; T3) wait for low tide.

ókkó- Dis. of *ó-₂* (var. of *akka-*).

ókkóóna See *kkóón.* Var. *ókkóónna.* vo. (c.; T3) make lie down, put to bed. With dir. suf.: *ókkóónnóónó.*

ókkóónna Var. of *ókkóóna.*

ókkóónnóónó See *ókkóóna.*

ókkóóch Dis. of *óóch.*

ókkóson (ds; 3) See *son.* vi. (c., dis.) tease or criticize someone by telling the opposite of the truth. Cf. *ósona.*

ókkóru (ds; 1) See *óruu-.* n. (c.; T1) 1. hibiscus fiber cloth woven on the traditional broadloom. 2. women's traditional skirt. *ókkóruan* her s. vi. (dis.) 1. use a cloth woven on the broadloom. 2. wear a traditional skirt. Cf. *óruuni.*

ókkótupw (2) See *kkótupw.* vi. (c.) wear a dress; (Rmn.) wear any upper garment (shirt, dress, jacket, coat, etc.).

Óktooper (Eng.) nu. (temp.) October.

ómonna See *moon.* vo. (c.; T3) supply with firewood, gather firewood for (an oven). With dir. suf.: *ómonnaato.* Cf. *ómónna.*

ómonnaato See *ómonna.*

ómonnomeerer See *moon, meerer.* vi. (c.) gather firewood a day ahead of time.

ómó (1) ÓMÓÓ. nu. (T1) booby bird. [Found on atolls, not in Truk itself.] emén ó. one b. b. ómóón b. b. of (a given region).

ómóómó (db; 1) See mó. nu. (c.; T1) a kind of sorcery ("obliterator"). [In it a plant called niyóór or wumwukaw is used a) to destroy the murderous thoughts of an enemy and render him no longer dangerous; b) to be put in or near the house of an enemy and to render the enemy's lineage unable to bear girls and thus die out; c) to be put into the mwatún of a food presentation (as from éfekúr to parent lineage) so that the receivers who eat it will die of illness and its women will have no female children.]

ómóóta See móót. vo. (c.; T3) place, set. With dir. suf.: ómóótáátiw put down (cf. ómóóttiwa).

ómóótáátiw See ómóóta.

ómóóttiwa See móóttiw. vo. (c.; T3) make sit down, seat.

ómóóy See mó. vo. (c.; T1) get rid of, erase, obliterate, wipe out, finish off. With dir. suf.: ómóóyenó.

ómósóna See ma-, són. vo. (T3) be suspicious of, watch suspiciously or guardedly. Cf. mósónósón.

ómón (4?) ÓMÓNO (?). nu. (T2?) a tree (Parinarium glaberrimum). Syn. ayis. Cf. amóneset.

ómóna See món. vo. (c.; T3) make waterproof.

ómónna See ómmón₁. Var. amónna. vo. (T3) prepare. With dir. suf.: ómónnáátá. Cf. ómonna.

ómónnááta See ómónna.

ómór (4) See mór. vi. (c.) go fishing in shallow flats at low tide.

ómóra See mór. vo. (c.; T3) cause to evaporate; erase. Dis. ókkómóra (ds).

ómórupurup (db; 2) See ma-, rup₁. vi. (c., dis.) flicker, blink, flash.

ómmóót (2) ÓMMÓÓTU, KÓMMÓÓTU. Var. ammóót, nikómmóót. nu. trochus (shell and shellfish). eféw ó. one t. s. ómmóótun t. s. of (a given region).

ómmósow (dc; 3) See mósow. nu. (c.; T3) parts. vi. (c.) be divided into parts. ena kkapas "miriitiiy" aa ó. fáán fituuw the expression "understand" is divided into a number of parts (things to be understood).

ómmón₁ (3) See mmon. Var. ammón. nu. (c.; T3) preparation. ómónnen p. of (something). vi. (c.) be prepared, made ready.

Ómmón₂ See ómmón₁. Var. Ammón. nu. (temp.) Saturday. [So called because the Protestant tabu against any work on Sunday required preparation of food on Saturday.] Syn. Ráánin Ómmón.

ómwo (1) ÓMWOO. [Perhaps derived from a-₂ and mwo₂.] Var. amwo. md.m. indicates a wish contrary to fact or (with itá pwe) to expectation; would that...; if only... ó. wúwa mwéngé mááy would that I were eating breadfruit; ó. ke pe would that you were dead; ó. itá! I would it should be so (but I don't expect it to be)!; ó. itá wúpwe néwúni emén piik if only I could acquire a pig! Cf. itá.

ómwoota F. of amwoota.

ómwoow See mwo₃. vo. (c.; T1) sink, drown. With dir. suf.: ómwoowonó, ómwoowotiw.

ómwoowonó See ómwoow.

ómwoowotiw See ómwoow.

ómwonna See mwmwoon. vo. (c.; T3) make acid, make sour (as with lime juice), let get sour.

ómwora- (2) See mwor₁. nr. (c.; T3) in the phrase ómworen mékúr gift of first fruits (as cooked food). [Presented to the sowutánnipi (actual maker or or planter of a garden) by the person on whose behalf it was planted or who now possesses the harvest rights to the garden.]

ómwora See mworomwor₁. Var. amwora. vo. (c.; T3) strew (of small grains or seeds, as in sowing seeds); granulate, make into small grains; adz into fine chips.

ómwoch (3) ÓMWOCHA. nu. (T3) necklace of three strings with red, white, and black beads. [Elbert gives the meaning on Puluwat as a kind of red shell used in ornaments, imported from Truk and the Mortlock Islands and sent as tribute via Satawal to Yap.]

ómwocha F. of amwocha.

ómwóón (4) See mwóón. n. (c.; T2) bait (in fishing). ómwónnun his b. ómwónnun or ómwóónun óó fishline's b. (idiomatically used with óó, fishline, rather than with éé, hook).

ómwóna See *mwón₁*. vo. (c.; T3) hide, cover, conceal. Dis. *ómwónómwóna, ómwónomwóna* (db) make (something) secret.

ómwónomwóna See *ómwóna*.

ómwónómwóna See *ómwóna*.

ómwónna See *ómwóón*. vo. (c.; T3) bait, put bait on. *wúpwe ó. óómw óó* I shall b. your fishline.

ómwóru (1) ÓMWÓRUU. [Possibly derived from *a-₂, mwa-, ru* with an analogical change in c.f. type.] nu. (T1) deception, lie, trick. vi. deceive, play a trick. Dis. *ókkómwóru* (ds).

ómwóruungeni See *ómwóru, ngeni*. vo. (T2) deceive.

ómwóruuw See *ómwóru*. vo. (T1) deceive.

ómwu (1) ÓMWUU. [Possibly derived from *a-₂, mwu₂*.] n. (T1) feces, excrement; defecation. [It is a permissable word in mixed company.] *emwu ó., emwú ó.* one piece of f. *ómwuun* his f. Syn. *páá, pwíse*. vi. defecate.

ómwuchcha (1) See *ómwu, chcha*. nu. (T1) dysentery. vi. have dysentery.

ómwmwoot (db; 3) See *mwoot₂*. Var. *amwmwoot*. vi., va. (c.) be cooked; cook.

ómwmwoota See *ómwmwoot*. Var. *amwmwoota*. vo. (c.; T3) cook.

ómwmwocha F. of *amwocha*.

ómwmwóón (dc; 4) See *mwóón*. F. va. (c.) make (food) enticing ("cause to be hungered for"). *pwata kaa ó. onomw mwéngé ngé wúwa mwóón?* why have made your food enticing so I am hungry?

ómwmwón (4: *ómwónnu-*) See *mwóón*. N. nu. (c.; T2) desire, thing craved.

ómwmwócho (dc; 1) See *mwócho*. vi. (c.) shirk, malinger, fail to do one's part or share. Dis. *ókkómwmwócho* (ds).

ómwmwóchoow (dc) See *mwócho*. vo. (c.; T1) accuse or suspect of theft.

ón₁ (4) ÓNO₁. vi., adj. (be) yellow. Dis. (N.) *óneyón,* (F.) *ónoyón-* (db). Cf. *-ón*.

ón₂ (4) ÓNNO. vi. be wiped clean, erased. Cf. *ónna*.

-ón (4) ÓNO₂. [In cpds. only.] nu. (T2) sun. Syn. *akkar*. Cf. *ón₁*.

óna- (3) ÓNA, KÓNA. unsp. twisting (of cordage). See *kkón, óna*.

óna See *óna-*. vo. (T3) roll or twist (of fibers in making cordage). Dis. *ókkóna* (ds).

ónááya- (3) See *óna, -ya-*. ni. (T3) what is rolled or twisted (by someone in making cordage), strand of cordage. *efóch ó.* one s. of c. *ónááyan* s. of c. made by him.

óneyas (3) See *óón₂, aas₁* (?). Var. *ónóyas*. nu. (T3) a variety of breadfruit (with seed, self-propagating). [It is eaten raw as well as cooked.]

óneyón Dis. of *ón₁*.

óni (3) ÓNIYA. F. nu. (T3) taro (*Colocasia esculenta*). [Corms eaten, fruit worn in hair and ears.] *eféw ó.* one corm of t. *óniyen* t. of (a given kind). Syn. *sawa, woot₁*.

óno- (4) ÓNO₃, KÓNO₁. [In cpds. only.] unsp. horizontally at rest.

ónoo- (1) See *noo-*. ni. (c.; T1) what someone said, word, utterance ("causing to be"). *ónoon* his word; word of. *ewe fóós paapa ónoon áát me nengngin* the word papa is said by boys and girls. *ónoon iyé?* who said so?; *ónoon Sowukuwopw* the word of Sowukuwopw.

ónoongngaw (3b) See *ónoo-, ngngaw*. vi. be bad-tempered (of man or beast). Cf. *órochongngaw*.

ónokkenitá (1) See *-ón, kken, tá*. vi. be noon.

ónomwa See *nomw*. Var. *anomwa*. vo. (c.; T3) make gurgle by shaking (of a coconut or bottle). Dis. *ónomwonomwa* (db).

ónomwonomw (db; 3) See *nomw*. Var. of *anomwonomw*. va. (c., dis.) make gurgle by shaking.

ónomwonomwa Dis. of *ónomwa*.

ónongngaw (3b) See *ónu-, ngngaw*. vi. be difficult to mash (of breadfruit).

ónopwa See *nopw*. vo. (c.; T3) clap (hands). Dis. *ónopwonopwa* (db).

ónopwonopw (db; 3) See *nopw*. vi. (c., dis.) clap the cupped palms of one's hands together. Syn. *ánechepéw, episipis₁*.

ónopwonopwa Dis. of *ónopwa*.

ónota Var. of *anota, ónóta*.

ónotáátiw See *ónoti*.

ónoti See *óno-, -ti-*. vo. (T2) spread (something) out so that it lies flat (as a mat). Dis. *ókkónoti* (ds). With dir. suf.: *ónotáátiw* spread (it) down. Syn. *óóneti*. Cf. *kkóónet, óónet*.

ónoyééch (2) See *ónu-, ééch*. vi. be easy to mash (of breadfruit).

ónoyón Dis. of *ón₁*.

ónóót N. Var. *anóót*. nu. a seaweed or seagrass (*Enhalus acoroides*). [It is used in net making and as medicine for women going on the water.] Syn. *achékken*.

ónómwota See *nómwot*. vo. (c.; T3) make use of.

ónómwotéchchúúw See *nómwot, éech, -ú-*. vo. (c.; T5) cause to be well used or employed; make efficient use of.

ónómwotongngawa See *nómwot, ngngaw*. vo. (c.; T3) use poorly; make inefficient use of.

ónómwóónó See *ónómwu*.

ónómwu See *nómw*. Var. *anómwu, ónnómwu*. vo. (c.; T2) cause to remain. With dir. suf.: *ónómwóónó* save away.

ónón (4) See *nónu-*. vi. (c.) be deep (underwater), far down (from a height). Syn. *nónnóón, ónónnóón* (the preferred forms). Cf. *fááyinón, inón*.

ónóna See *nónu-*. vo. (c.; T3) deepen. Syn. *ónónnóóna*.

ónóniinen (2) See *nóniinen*. vi. (c.) be anxiety-provoking, fearsome.

ónónnóón (4) See *nónu-, nóó-*. F. [Apparently a back formation from *ónón nóón*, deep inside of it.] Var. *anónnóón, nónnnóón*. vi. be deep (underwater), far down (from a height). Syn. *ónón*. nu. (T2) depth; draft (of a boat). *ónónnóónun eey neeni* depth of this place; *ónónnóónun féén waa* draft of a ship.

ónónnóóna See *nónnóón*. vo. (c.; T3) deepen. Syn. *ónóna*.

ónóta See *nóót*. Var. *anota, ónota*. vo. (c.; T3) bring to a head (of a boil).

ónóyas Var. of *óneyas*.

ónu- (4) ÓNO₄, KÓNO₂. nr. (T2) ease of mashing (of breadfruit). *meyi ééch ónun eey mááy* this breadfruit is good for easy mashing. Cf. *kkón₂*.

ónuuw See *nu*. vo. (c.; T1) skip, miss (as a line of print); cause to miss, parry (as a blow). *wúwa ó. wókun* I parried his club. *kepwe ó. rúwáánú kunók kesapw mwéngé* you will go four hours without eating. With dir. suf.: *ónuuwonó* let get away, let go off (of model canoes only).

ónuuwonó See *ónuuw*.

ónussaanó See *ónussu*.

ónussu See *nuus₂*. Var. *onussu*. vo. (c.; T2) waste (as money, time, food). With dir. suf.: *ónussaanó* or *onussóónó*.

ónuki (1) ÓNUKII. nu. (T1) fresh water. *ónukiin nóón ewe neeni* f. w. of that place. Syn. *appúng, kkónik, kkónuk, pweke*.

Ónumas (3) nu. (loc.; temp.) 1. a star or constellation. [It is probably to be equated with Crater.] 2. a sidereal month in the traditional calendar.

ónupa Var. of *onupa*.

ónna See *ón₂*. vo. (T3) wipe away, erase.

ónnoow (2) See *nnoow*. vi. (c.) be disgusting, repelling, repugnant. nu. (T2) disgusting thing.

ónnomw (2) ÓNNOMWU. nu. (T2) men's loincloth. *eché ó.* one l. *aan ó.* his l. *ónnomwun* l. of (a given type).

ónnómwu Var. of *ónómwu*.

ónnut (2, 3) See *óno-, nu-, -ti-* or *-ta-₂*. Var. *annut*. vi. sleep ("lie crumpled"?). Dis. *ókkónnut* (ds). With intens. suf.: *ónnutuffóch, ókkónnutuffóch* s. all the time. With dir. suf.: *ónnutonó* go to s.

ónnuta See *ónnut*. vo. (T3) put (someone) to sleep.

ónnutonó See *ónnut*.

ónnutuffóch See *ónnut*.

óngin (2) ÓNGINI. nu. (T2) a plant (*Cucurma* sp.). [Leaves used to wrap fish for broiling over a fire.] Cf. *áfán*.

óngon (3) See *ngon*. Var. *angon*. vi. (c.) 1. be attractive in appearance or conduct (with *meyi*). *emén meyi ó.* one who is a. 2. attract attention (with *aa*); show off. *aa ó.* he attracts attention, behaves so as to attract attention.

óngona See *ngon*. vo. (c.; T3) show (someone) off, display.

óngonongon (db; 3) See *ngon*. nu. (c.; T3) vanity. vi. be vain.

óngóóngóóy (db) See *ngóóngó*. vo. (c.; T1) give cause to (someone) for ridicule.

ópóóy See *póó*. vo. (c.; T1) put on a platform or rack (as copra).

ópóssa See *póós*. vo. (c.; T3) make steady or firm. With dir. suf.: *ópóssáátá* lay in successive layers on top of each other (as lumber or clothes).

ópóssáátá See *ópóssa*.

ópór (4?) ÓPÓRO (?). nu. (T2?) shrub with tiny white flowers (*Desmodium*

unbellatum). [Its small beans are crushed to make a laxative.]
ópóchón Var. of *apachón*.
ópuuw See *puu*-₁. N. vo. (c.; T1) shake out (as a cloth). Syn. *ásupwu*.
óppong (2) ÓPPONGU. nu. (T2) multipronged fish spear. *aan ó*. his s.; *óppongun* s. of (a given type).
ópwoow See *pwo*. vo. (c.; T1) cause to swell; blow up (as a balloon).
ópwooyisam (3) See *pwoo, saam*. vi. (c.) be impatient or rude to one's father.
ópwonna See *pwoo-, nne*-₁ (?). vo. (c.; T3) smell, sniff.
ópwóóy See *pwó*. vi. (c.; T1) pamper; treat with great solicitude, ply with food or attention; relieve of all work; venerate.
ópwónów (2) ÓPWÓNÓWU. vi. cook (breadfruit) in a cooking pot. Cf. *pwónów*.
ópwónówuuw See *ópwónów, '-u-*. vo. (T5) cook (breadfruit) in a cooking pot. Cf. *pwóchchuni*.
ópwóra See *pwór*. Var. *apwpwóra*. vo. (c.; T3) cause to be curved, bent.
ópwóróówus (3) See *pwóróówus*. vi. (c.) make an explanatory talk. Cf. *ótuttun*.
ópwóróówusa See *pwóróówus*. Var. *apworaawusa*. vo. (c.; T3) 1. interrogate, pump, ask news of. 2. tell news of, tell about, give an account of; explain, delineate (verbally). Cf. *ótuttuna*.
ópwórutiwa See *pwór, -tiw*. vo. (c.; T3) cause to be curved, bent, or bowed down.
ópwuropwur (db; 3) See *pwuur*₂. vi. (c., dis.) (of swine) root, turn up soil with the snout.
ópwurók nu. fire plow; making fire by the fire-plow method. vi. make fire by the fire-plow method. Syn. *wútúút*.
ópwuta Var. of *opwuta*.
ópwpwona See *pwpwon*. vo. (c.; T3) swear in (as a witness), cause to be sworn.
ópwpwóro (1) See *pwpwór, ro*₂. [Apparently a contraction of *ópwpwóroro*.] vi. (c.) crouch forward in passing by another as a mark of deference. Dis. *ókkópwpwóro* (dc). *kepwe ó. mé wóóy* you will c. from being above me (i.e., you will crouch before me). With dir. suf.: *ópwpwórooto, ópwpwóroonó*, *ópwpwórootiw, ópwpwóroonong, ópwpwórootá, ópwpwóroowu*.

ópwpwóroongeni See *ópwpwóro, ngeni*. vo. (T2) crouch to (someone) as a sign of deference; show deference to.

ópwpwura See *pwur*₁. vo. (c.; T3) collide with, bump into, stub against. Syn. *opwpwuri*.

óro- See *óór*.

óro (1) See *ro*₁. va. (c.) catch crabs or lobsters on moonlit nights when they are congregating to lay. *si pwe ó. wúúr* we shall hunt for lobsters.

óroottungur See *óro-, óttungur*. vi. be of a patient disposition.

óroow See *ro*₂. vo. (c.; T1) cause to bend. With dir. suf.: *óroowotiw, óroowotá, óroowowu*.

óroffóón (3a) See *óór, ffóón*. vi. be homesick; pine. Syn. *óropwpwos*.

óros (3a) See *ros*. vi. (c.) be exterminated, annihilated.

órosa See *ros*. vo. (c.; T3) finish up, use up, cause to be used up; annihilate.

órosommateeyenó See *ros, mmat, -e*-₂, *-nó*. vo. (c., dir.; T6b) exterminate utterly. [From a chant in the *sooyénú* rite.]

órosset (2) See *óór, sáát*₁. F. Var. *arosset*. nu. (T2) shore, coast, seaside; area between vegetation and water on the rim of an island; boundary between sea and land. *órossetin fénú* island's s.

órossúngngeni See *óór, -ssúng, ngeni*. vo. (T2) bump against.

órokopwánni See *rokopwáán*. vo. (c.; T2) cause to circulate.

óroma F. of *aroma*.

óromwoy₁ (2) nu. (loc.; temp.; T2) 1. a star (probably Arcturus). 2. a month in the traditional sidereal calendar.

óromwoy₂ (2) See *óór, mwoy*. vi. be in the early stage of gnat disease (of breadfruit).

órong F. of *arong*.

óronga See *rong*. Var. *aronga*. vo. (c.; T3) cause to listen, make pay attention.

órongeniféw (2) See *órong, faaw*. nu. (T2) species of large pompano (fish).

órongéchchúúw See *rong, ééch, -ú-*. vo. (c.; T5) bring good news to, cause to hear good news.

Órongotá nu. (loc.) a clan name.

órongngaw (3b) See *óór, ngngaw*. vi., adj. have (having) ugly skin.

óropat (3b) See óór, pat. vi. be cool-skinned; fecund or fertile (of humans). Dis. óropatapat (db).
óropatapat Dis. of óropat.
óroppa- (3a) See óór, ppa-. ni. (loc.; T3) edge (of path), bank (of stream), rim (of heaven). óroppan its e. óroppen aan (at) the road's e.; óroppen kkónik (at) the water's e. Syn. wúnúppa-.
óroppeyinen See óroppa-, neni-$_1$. nu. (loc.; T2) horizon; rim of heaven. Syn. ápiinen, epiineng.
óroppi (3) See óór, ppi$_2$. nu. (loc.; T3) (at) the edge of or (in) the vicinity of the beach; (by) the sand.
óroppoch (3) See óór, ppoch. vi. be dented in the side(s).
óropwén (2) See óór, pwéén$_1$. F. Var. aropwén. nu. <Elbert> strand vine (pinkish flowers). óropwénún s. v. of (a given region).
óropwich (2) See óór, pwich$_1$. vi., adj. 1. have (having) hot skin. 2. (be) infertile (of humans).
óropwichikkar (3b) See óropwich, kkar. vi., adj. 1. have (having) hot skin. 2. (be) infertile (of humans).
óropwpwos (2) See óór, pwos. vi. be homesick; pine. Syn. óroffóón.
óroch$_1$ (3) See roch. nu. (c.; T3) cardinal fish. [It is a tabu of knot diviners, who don't eat it.] órochen c. f. of (a given region).
óroch$_2$ (3a) See roch. vi. (c.) 1. wait for dark. 2. fight under cover of darkness.
órocha See roch. Var. arocha. vo. (c.; T3) 1. darken. With dir. suf.: órochóónó. 2. fight or kill at night, attack under cover of darkness.
órochongngaw (3b) See rocho-, ngngaw. vi. (c.) be mean, harsh, cranky, bad-tempered, savage, quick-to-attack (of dog or man). Cf. ónoongngaw.
órochoyééch (2) See rocho-, ééch. vi. (c.) be gentle, easy-going, kind.
órochóónó See órocha.
óroyééch (2) See óór, ééch. vi., adj. have (having) nice skin.
órósón (4) See óór, sóón$_4$. vi. be invalided in one's house as a result of a wound from a stingray-tipped spear.
órókófáániyeni See rókófáániyen. vo. (c.; T2) make a circle around, go around, encircle.
óruu- (1) ÓRUU. ni. (T1) woman's skirt or waist mat or other fabric woven on a traditional broadloom. óruun her s. Cf. ókkóru.
óruuni See óruu-, -ni-. vo. (T4) acquire a woman's skirt, mosquito-netting, or other fabric woven on the traditional broadloom. Cf. achawareni, ótupwuni, wúfeni.
Óruuwu N. of Oruwuuw$_2$.
órunupwoch (3) See óór, pwooch. nu. (T3) turtle-shell-edge (a unit of measure from the finger tips to the middle of the forearm, i.e., to the edge of the turtle-shell bracelet). eew ó. one t.-s.-e.
-óch (4: -óchchu-) ÓCHCHO. Var. woch. suf. (cc.) sort (in counting rations, kinds, varieties, species). óóch, ruwóóch, wúnúyóch, fóóch, nimóóch, wonoyóch, fúúyóch, wanúyóch, ttiwóóch, engoon one,...ten s. With c. pref. and ptv. const.: óóchchun, oruwóchchun first, second one or kind; ese pwanú wor oruwóchchun it is unique (there is not a second one or kind).
óchoomanaw (3b) See cho, manaw. nu. (c.; T3) rape.
óchoomanawa See óchoomanaw. vo. (c.; T3) rape (someone).
óchoochisiiy See choochis, -i-$_2$. vo. (c.; T5) save.
óchoocho$_1$ (db; 1) See cho. nu. (c.; T1) a form of magic that makes others unable to function in sport or war.
óchoocho$_2$ (db; 1) See cho. Var. achoocho. vi. (c.) strive, try hard. óchoochoongeni (vo., T2) strive towards.
óchoochoongeni See óchoocho$_2$.
óchokochok (db; 3) See choka-. vi. (c.) cluck at, call to (chicks by a chicken). Syn. ochukuchuk.
óchokochoka See óchokochok. vo. (c.; T3) cluck at, call to (chicks by a chicken). Syn. ochukuchuku.
óchopwu See chopw. Var. achopwu, ochopwu. vo. (c.; T2) 1. cause to resound; beat or hammer upon, strike (of resounding things). Dis. óchopwuchopwu (db). 2. cut, chop, or split in two (of hollow things). aa ó. taka he c. a ripe coconut in two.
óchopwuchopwu Dis. of óchopwu.
óchómmónga F. of achómmónga.
óchóna See chón. vo. (c.; T3) blacken, darken (of color).

óchukuchuk (db; 2) See *chuku-*₁. vi. (c., dis.) elbow one's way through a crowd. [Evidence of arrogance *mwáaneson*.] Cf. *éféréchchuku*.

óchchorong F. of *achchorong*.

óchchowu See *chchow*. vo. (c.; T2) make heavy, burdensome. *wúwa ó. aan angaang* I have made his work b. Cf. *ochow*.

óteey See *óto-, -e-*₂. Var. *woteey*. vo. (T6b) clear (land), weed (a garden); husk (a coconut).

ótik (2) ÓTIKI. nu. (T2) a vine (*Cassytha filiformis*). [It can be used as food or medicine.]

ótikipwin See *ótik, -pwin*. Var. *ótukupwin*. nu. <Elbert> a vine (*Piper*). Syn. *wénnúmey*.

óto- (4) ÓTO. [In cpds. only.] Var. *woot*₂. cleared, weeded; husked (of a coconut).

óto F. of *ato*.

ótoomey (2) See *too-, máay*₂. nu. (c.; T2) breadfruit summoning (a ritual specialty).

ótoon F. of *atoon*.

ótoononga See *toonong*. vo. (c.; T3) grant entrance to; convey in.

ótoor (3a) See *too-, -ri-*. [Only with *ngeni*.] vi. (c.) cause to be delivered or conveyed. *ó. ngeni átewe áay toropwe* deliver my letter to him. Cf. *toori*.

ótooto (db; 1) See *too-*. va. (c.) convey; grant admission to; represnt.

ótootongngaw (db; 3b) See *too-, ngngaw*. Var. *ótootoongngaw*. vi. (c., dis.) be unprepared. nu. (c.; dis.) turmoil, confusion.

ótoow See *too-*. Var. *atoow, otoow*. vo. (c.; T1) cause to be present, cause to come; bring, convey, deliver; admit, grant admission to; represent (as in a legislature). *kepwe ó. ááy fóós ngeni átewe* or *kepwe ó. ngeni átewe ááy fóós* you shall deliver my message to that fellow.

ótoowaawa See *toowaaw*. vo. (c.; T3) cause to be distant, put at a distance.

ótoowik (3a) See *too-, iik*. nu. (c.; T3) fish summoning (a ritual specialty).

ótoowuuw See *too-, -wu*. vo. (c.; T1) convey out, grant exit to; dismiss, send away; fire (an employee).

ótomwa See *tomw*. Var. *atomwa*. vo. (c.; T3) cause to disintegrate or to come apart; untie, loosen (a rope).

ótona See *ton*. Var. *attona*. vo. (c.; T3) make visible; look at.

ótongotong (db; 4) See *tong*. nu. (c.; T3) midrib of any palm leaf. *ótongotongen núú* coconut palm leaf's m.; *ótongotongen rúpwúng* ivory palm leaf's m.

ótopwutopw (db; 2) See *topw*. nu. (c.; T2) a magic that makes others unable to function in sport or war.

ótow Tb1. vi. swell internally (of the vaginal membranes when stimulated sexually).

ótó (1) ÓTÓÓ. nu. (T1) thing.

ótóót (db; 3) See *óta-*. Var. *wotoot*. vi. (dis.), va. clear (land), weed (gardens); husk (coconuts). nu. (T3) cleared field, garden.

ótóra See *tór*. vo. (c.; T3) disarrange, mix up, put in disorder, disorganize; break, defile (a tabu).

ótórómmóng (2) See *tór, mmóng*. vi. (c.) make lots of disarray, mess things up; be a "bull in a china shop".

ótu- (2) ÓTU. F. Var. *atu-*. nr. (T2) time (of or for something). *ótun attaw* time for fishing. *ifa ótun óómw nónnómw Chuuk* what was the time of your staying in Truk? (when were you in Truk?); *ina ótun siya kkémwéch ewe miriit* that is the time when we have taken hold of understanding.

ótuufichi N. of *étúúfichi*.

ótuutu (db; 1) See *tuu-*₂. va. shower leis, money, or perfume on someone in appreciation. *raa ó. wóón Neyisiyop néé* they s. perfume on Neyisiyop.

ótukupwin Var. of *ótikipwin*.

ótumwutumw (db; 2) TUMWU. vi. (c., dis.) pout, look sullen. Syn. *owumwuumw*.

ótunungngir (2) See *ótu-, ngngir*. nu. (T2) time of biting (when fish bite).

ótupwu- (2) ÓTUPWU. [Possibly derived from *tupw*₂?] unsp. pertaining to a woman's dress or upper garment.

ótupwuni See *ótupwu-, -ni-*. Rmn. vo. (T5) acquire a dress or upper garment. Syn. *wúfeni*. Cf. *kkótupw*.

óturaanó N. of *oturóónó*.

óturokáppeey See *turokáppe*. vo. (c.; T1) tease, make sport of.

ótuttun (ds; 3a) See *tuno-*. vi. (c.) make a speech, give a lecture, give an informative or explanatory talk. See *ópwóróówus*.

óttuttuna (ds) See *tuno-*. vo. (c.; T3) explain, delineate in talk. Cf. *ópwóróówusa*.

óttek Var. of *óóttek*.

óttekiiy Var. of *óóttekiiy*.

óttif (3a) ÓTTIFA. Var. *attof, attuf, óttof*. n. (T3) saliva, spittle. *óttifan* his s. vi., va. spit, spit at.

óttifa See *óttif*. Var. *attofa, attufa*. vo. (T3) spit at.

óttifengngaw (3b) See *óttif, ngngaw*. vi. spit badly (where one should not).

óttifeyiti See *óttif, -iti*. Var. *óttofeyiti*. vo. (T2) spit on.

óttof N. of *óttif*.

óttofeyiti N. of *óttifeyiti*.

óttomwa See *ttomw*. vo. (c.; T3) cause to fall and burst.

ótton (2) ÓTTONU. [Presumably a back formation from an old *ótto-n*, it's core (see *óót*).] nu. (T2) core of a breadfruit. *óttonun mááy* breadfruit's c.

óttona (dc) See *ton*. vo. (c.; T3) look at. Cf. *kkóton₁*.

óttonofátáneey (dc) See *ton, fátán, -e-₂*. F. Var. *attonafetáneey*. vo. (c.; T6b) make a search for, walk about looking for.

óttonúk (2) See *óót, núkú-₃*. vi. (c.) having a full grown spongy sprout core (of a coconut).

óttong (3a) See *ttong*. vi. (c.) be pitiable, evoking sympathy (of a person). *meyi ó. ewe meyi wumwes* that crazy person is pitiable.

óttonga- (3) See *ttong*. F. ni. (c.; T3) 1. friend, loved one, dear one, relative or other person of whom one is fond or for whom one has positive feeling. *óttongan* his f. Syn. *óttongeeya-*. 2. remembrance, keepsake (of someone one has loved). *óttongen ewe meyimá* r. of the dead person.

óttongeeya- N. of *óttonga-* (see *ttong, -e-₂, -ya-₁*).

óttungur vi. be patient, not easily put out.

ówosu See *wos₃*. vo. (c.; T2) give trouble to, cause to be in want or in a bad way. Syn. *ówosupwpwanga*.

ówosukosuka See *wosukosuk*. Var. *awosukosuka*. vo. (c.; T3) interfere with (another's work), cause (someone) to be beset or burdened with work, be a trouble to, be a nuisance to.

ówosupwpwanga See *wosupwpwang*. vo. (c.; T3) give trouble to, cause to be in want or in a bad way. [Formerly a tabu word.] Syn. *ówosu*.

ówona See *won*. vo. (c.; T3) put to sleep; kill.

ówopoopa See *wopoop*. vo. (c.; T3) dent.

ówota See *wot*. vo. (c.; T3) cause to go aground, run on a reef.

ówut (Eng.) vi. be out (in baseball).

óyin (2) ÓYINNA. (Eng.) nu. oil. *óyinnen torakkú* truck o.

óyoow See *o₂*. vo. (c.; T1) catch, capture. Dis. *ókkóyoow*. (ds)

U, Ú

-u- See -wu-. [Occurs in this form after bases ending in *u*.] Var. *-ú-, -wu-, -wú-*. suf. (v.form.) one of a class of suffixes that joined to a base make the resulting construction an object focussed verb (vo.). *posu-u-w* stab it.

-u N. of *-uw*.

-ur (3a) See *iir*. [In this form only when the preceding base ends in *u*.] Var. *-er, -ir, -r, -úr*. suf. (obj.) 3pl. obj. prn.: them. *ósómwoonuur* treat them as chiefs (see *ósomwoonu*). suf. (pos.) 3pl. pos. prn.: their; of or for them. *sópwuur* their district (see *sóópw*).

-uw (3) WUWA₁. F. [In cpds. only.] Var. *-u*. suf. (cc.) nonspecific or general class of object. *ruwuuw, nimuuw, wonuuw, fisuuw* or *fusuuw, wanuuw, ttiwuuw* two, five, six, seven, eight, nine n. o.; *fituuw* how many n. o. *oruwuuwan, enimuuwan, owonuuwan, efisuuwan, awanuuwan, ettiwuuwan* second, fifth, sixth, seventh, eighth, ninth one. Cf. *eew₁, -ánú, -ngát*.

-ú- See -wú-. [Occurs in this form after bases ending in *ú*.] Var. *-u-, -wu-, -wú-*. suf. (v.form.) one of a class of suffixes that joined to a base make the resulting construction an object focussed verb (vo.). *núkú-ú-w* believe it.

-úr (3a) See *iir*. [In this form only when the preceding base ends in *ú*.] Var. *-er, -ir, -r, -ur*. suf. (obj.) 3pl. obj. prn.: them. *émésékúúr* frighten them (see *émésékú*). suf. (pos.) 3pl. pos. prn.: their; of or for them. *sékúrúúr* their backs (see *sékúr*).

-úw [In cpds. only.] unsp. a poisonous tree. See *wuwáánúúw*. Cf. *wúúp*.

F

f- See *fé-₁*. [Occurs in this form only when the following base begins with *f*.] Var. *fa-₁, fé-, fo-*. **pref.** (num.) four. See *fféw₂, ffóch*.

fa-₁ See *fé-₁*. [Occurs in this form only when the first vowel of the following base is *é*.] Var. *f-, fé-, fo-*. **pref.** (num.) four. See *faché, fapé, fayé*.

fa-₂ (3b: *fa-, fá-, fe-, fé-, fo-, fó-*) FA₁. [Fossil form.] **pref.** (c.) activating, doing, making. See *fachaacha, fátán, fóós*. Cf. *fee-₁*.

-fa- (3) FA₄. **suf.** (n.form.; T3) noun formative, suffixed to bases that take v.form. suf. *-fi-*.

fa (1) FAA₁. **vi.** be bold, brave (of fighting fish and figuratively of people). Pvb. *fa neené* be brave only in one's own yard ("be brave in the pool").

-fa (1) FAA₅. [In cpds. only.] **unsp.** old place name associated with Feefen (Fefan) Island. See *meyifa, Sowufa*. Cf. *fóó-*.

faa-₁ (1v) FAA₂. **ni.** (loc.; T1) underside, under. *faan u.* him; *fáán* under, in, with, during; times (with numbers). *peekin faan* lower or western side (of Truk and surrounding atolls); *fáán akkar* in the sun; *fáán ásápwán* in the lee, leeward; *fáán áseengesin* on behalf of, for the sake of; *fáán chómmóng* frequently, often, many times; *fáán éés* backward sloping portion of prow and stern of *meniyuk* sailing canoe; *fáán eew* once, some day, sometime (*wúse feyinnó mwo Feefen fáán eew* I have never once been to Fefan Island); *fáán ekkóóch* rarely, seldom, a few times, sometimes; *fáán Fapeweri* during February; *fáán iten* for the sake of, in the name of; *fáán maas* before one's eyes, in one's presence (*kepwe suunó mé fáán mesey* get out of my sight); *fáán nááng* under or lower heaven; *fáán nemeniyan* under his jurisdiction or rule; *fáán nnúr* in the shade; *fáán ókkóóch* rarely, seldom, a few times; *fáán paaw* armpit; *fáán pachapachey* sole of my foot; *fáán peche* on foot (*sipwe fátán chék fáán pecheech* we shall just walk on our feet); *fáán pwaapwa* with joy; *fáán pwasuk* a variety of breadfruit; *fáán ruwuuw* two times, twice (*ruwuuw fáán ruwuuw aa weewe mé rúwáánú* two times two equals four); *fáán tengki* with, under, or by electric light or flashlight; *fáán waasi* a hold in fighting; *fáán wóók* with stick or cane.

faa-₂ (1) FAA₃. [In cpds. only.] Var. *fáá-₂*. **unsp.** apply the sole of the foot.

faafa (db; 1) FAA₄. **nu.** (T1) coughing. *áán átánaan f.* yonder fellow's c. **vi.** cough. Syn. *moor₂*.

faas (3) FASA₁. **n.** (T3) nest (of animal or bird). *eew f.* one n. *fasan* its n. *fasen chukó* chicken's n. Cf. *fas*.

faassowu- Var. of *faansowu-*.

faak (3) FAAKKA. **n.** (T3) thin film of light perspiration. *faakkan* his p. **vi.** have a thin film of p. *aa f. inisiy* my body has a film of p. Cf. *moonoon*.

faameni Var. of *faamini*.

faamini (Eng.) Var. *faameni*. **nu.** family, lineage. *eew f.* one f. *aan f.* his f.

faamw (3) FAAMWMWA. **nu.** (T3) giving birth, parturition, delivery (of child). *aan f.* her giving b. *emén f.* a new mother. **va.** give birth, bear a child.

faamwónómwónu- Dis. of *faamwónu-*.

faamwónu- (4) See *faa-₁, mwón*. [In ptv. const. only.] **ni.** (T2) figurative, hidden, or allegorical meaning. Dis. *faamwónómwónu-* (db). *faamwónun* its hidden m.

faan (3) FANNA. **vi.** break open (of boil). *aa f. machey* my boil has broken open.

faansowu- (2) See *faa-₁, sowu-₃*. [In ptv. const. only.] Var. *faassowu-, fassowu-*. **ni.** (temp.; T2) time, tense (of verb), season, turn; (with rel. suf.) at the time of, during, while. *aan faansowun* his turn. *faansowun akkar* dry season; *faansowun epwe etto* the future, in the future; *faansowun ffééw* time of cold, winter; *faansowun iyeey* the present, at the present time; *faansowun meyinisin* always, at all times; *faansowun nóómw* the past, in the past; *faansowun wúút* rainy season; *iteyiten faansowun* every time; *nóón ewe faansowun* at that time (in the past); *nóón na faansowun* at that particular time, at the time just indicated; *nóón eey faansowun* at this time. Cf. *nupwen, ótu-*.

faapach (3b) See *faa-₁, pach.* nu. (T3) the shorter of the two sticks that frame the edges of the hand fishing net. *efóch f.* one net-framing stick. *faapachen cheew* the net's shorter stick.

faar₁ (3) FARA₁. nu. (T3) dance wand or other staff from which is hung garlands and other offerings to the spirits and gods. [It was customarily placed across a spirit canoe that had been suspended from the house rafters.] *faren énú* staff for a spirit.

faar₂ (3) FARA₂. n. (T3) core of a breadfruit. *eféw f., efóch f.* one c. *faran* its c. *faren mááy* breadfruit's c.

faares (2) See *faa-₂, resi-*. vi. rub one's feet back and forth against the ground or floor in anger or distress; paw the ground.

faariker (db; 2) See *fa-₂, eri-₁*. va. scratch lightly on the leg of the person next to oneself to indicate that he is to follow one's lead, that he is to back one's move (a fight is imminent), or to show affection to a sweetheart.

faach (3a) FACHA. nu. (T3) pandanus tree or fruit (*Pandanus tectorius*). *eféw f.* one p. key; *ewumw f.* one cluster of p. keys; *efóch f.* one p. tree. *aan f.* his p.; *ngútan f.* his chew of p. *fachen Chuuk* Trukese p.; *fachen kiyeki* any variety of p. used for making mats. *féwún f.* p. fruit; *méngún f.* p. leaf.

Faachchamw (3) See *faa-₁, chaamw.* [From *Faa-ni-chamw.*] Var. *Fááchchamw.* nu. (loc.; T3) the true sky or heaven (now largely replaced by *nááng*). [It is the region above the stars and the abode of the traditional gods.] *aa chi awatá F.* he gave voice mouth-up to heaven. Syn. *nenichamw.*

faat₁ (2) FÉTÚ. Var. *féét.* n. (T3) eyebrow. *fétiy, fotumw, fétún* my, your (sg.), his e.:

faat₂ (3) FATA. nu. (T3) area of clear, shallow water where the bottom is visible from the surface; lagoon between shore and fringing reef. *faten eey fénú* the lagoon area around this island. Cf. *ffat.*

faata- (3) FAATA. [In ptv. const. only.] Var. *ffaata-*. nr. (T3) string of fish (*faaten iik*). *effaat* one s. of fish.

faateni See *faata-, -ni-.* vo. (T6a) string (fish) on a string.

faati See *faa-₂, -ti-*. Var. *fááti.* vo. (T4) kick with the sole of the foot. Dis. *faffaati* (ds).

faaw (2: *feyi-, féwú-, fowu-, -fey, -féw*) FÉWÚ₁. nu. (T2) stone, rock, coral. *eféw f.* one s. *aan f.* his s. *féwún áchechchem* memorial stone; *féwún kkamaat* stone used to grind and polish stone and shell; *féwún neeset* coral (general term); *féwún peyiyas* gravestone; *féwún seyim* grindstone; *féwún wóón* stone or shell bead from Japan. ni. (T2) lump, chunk, ball, globule; nut, seed, fruit, burr; tuber. *féwiy, fowumw, féwún* my, your (sg.), his l. *féwún ngasangas* heart; *féwún maas* eyeball; *féwún móót, féwún neeniyen móót* buttock (polite term); *féwún nikésúk* bullet, shell; *féwún niwit* buttock (tabu word); *féwún paaw* bicep muscle; *féwún peche* calf muscle; *féwún rúpwúng* ivory nut; *féwún siffich* gizzard; *féwún wuuch* banana fruit. adj. made of stone. *imwefaaw* stone house; *nnúféfaaw* stone mortarboard. Cf. *-féw.*

faawúwe (1) FAAWÚWEE. vi. turn in the direction of the outrigger side, go toward the *itam* side (of canoe).

faayine (1) See *faa-₁.* N. Var. *fááyine.* nu. (T1) variety of breadfruit.

faayiton (3) See *faa-₁, toon.* N. Var. *fááyiton.* nu. (T3) variety of breadfruit.

faayiyór See *faa-₁, óór.* N. Var. *fááyiyór.* nu. (T3) variety of breadfruit.

faffaati Dis. of *faati.*

faffana Dis. of *fana₁.*

faffaneey Dis. of *faneey.*

fas (3) See *faas.* vi. nest (of bird).

fasafas (db; 3) FASA₂. vi. (dis.) be speckled with white (of breadfruit skin only and a sign that the breadfruit is especially tasty).

fasang (3) FASANGA. [Recorded only with *nee-*.] n. (T3) torso, trunk.

fasar (3) FASARA. nu. (T3) sprout, shoot (from the side of a tree). *efóch f.* one s. *fasaran* its s. vi. sprout, be in sprout. *aa f.* it has sprouted.

faseeni See *fasey, -ni-*. vo. (T4) peel, skin, free (something) of its outer covering.

fasey (3) FASEYA. vi. be peeled, skinned, be freed of outer covering (of bananas, breadfruit, bark, fish, etc.).

Trukese-English   fanépéw

fassowu- Var. of *faansowu-*.
fasto (1) FASTOO. (Jap. *faasuto*, from Eng. *first*) nu. (T1) first base (in baseball). *aan f.* its f. b.
fakafak (db; 3) FAKA. nu. (T3) itchy swelling on the body, hives. *sáfeen f.* medicinal oil prepared from copra to apply to the itchy area.
fakun N. var. of *fókun.*
fakkun N. var. of *fókkun.*
fan (3b) FANA₁. vi. go aground (of ship or canoe). *aa fan efóch waa* a canoe has gone aground. With dir. suf.: *fanátá* go aground; come on something unexpectingly; *wúwa fanátá wóón ewe iimw* I came unexpectedly on the house.
fana-₁ (3v) See *fan.* [In cpds. only.] nu. (T3v) shoal or low island. In the place names *Fanaanú, Fanapenges, Fanó, Fánáápi, Fánáásich, Fánáyik, Fánemwoch, Fénawaw, Fénéchu, Fénénuuk, Fénékkúk, Fénémwú, Fenenááney, Feneppi, Fenessich, Fónónó.*
fana-₂ (3b) FANA₂. [In cpds. only.] vi. attend visually, peer, look, stare. Dis. *fanafana-* (db.). With dir. suf.: *fananó, fanafananó, fónónó, fónófónónó* peer or stare off, keep silent; *fanatá* peer up (but not with head tipped back); *fanetiw* p. down; *fanénong, fanonong* p. in; *fanoto, fanóto* p. hither; *fanowu, fanúwu* p. out. Syn. *roo-₂*.
fana₁ See *fanafan.* vo. (T3) adze, cut or shape with an adze. Dis. *faffana* (ds). Syn. *faneey.*
fana₂ (1) FANAA. nu. (T1) small needle fish (*taak*). *emén f.* one n. f. *fanaan* n. f. of (a given region).
fanaa- (1v) See *fanafan, -a-₂.* ni. (T3) adzed thing. *fanaan* thing adzed by him. *fánáán iyé* thing adzed by whom. Syn. *fanaaya-, faneeya, fánááya-*.
fanaan (3) FANAANA. nu. (T3) variety of *Cyrtosperma* taro, considered very good eating. *eféw f.* one C. corm; *efóch f.* one C. plant. *fanaanen Chuuk* Trukese C.
Fanaanú See *fana-₁, énú.* nu. (loc.) Fananu Island (Nomwin Atoll, Hall Islands).
fanafan₁ (db; 3) FANA₃. nu. (dis.; T3) adzing, adze work. *aan f.* his a. *fanafanen waa* adzing of a canoe. vi. (dis.) be adzed; use an adze. *raa f.*

they are adzing. *meyi f. reen Eiue* it was adzed on behalf of Eiue. va. (dis.) adze. *raa f. waa* they adzed canoes.
fanafan₂ (db; 3) FANA₄. nu. (T3) a hold in hand-to-hand fighting by which an opponent's hand is twisted; a blow in which an opponent's upper arm is hit hard with the edge of the flat hand.
fanafananó See *fana-₂*.
fanafanangngaw (db; 3b) See *fana-₂, ngngaw.* vi. (dis.) grieve, brood, be disappointed, be lonely.
fananó See *fana-₂*.
fanang (3) FANANGA. nu. (T3) ash, dust; fireplace, hearth; site of an earth oven; cookhouse; place where men of a locally land-holding lineage assemble to prepare food for ceremonial or festive occasions; a locally land-holding lineage (with its clients or affiliated persons) forming a constituent socio-political division of a *sóópw. fanangen kkuuk* kitchen; *fanangen koon* coal ash; *fanangen mwúúch* wood ash; *fanangen pwpwún* dust. *sómwoonun f.* lineage chief, head of a *fanang* (cf. *chóón neefanang* person in charge of work in a *fanang*). Id. *f. seneeng* naked, unclothed, bare (of a person).
fanangenimey (2) See *fanang, mááy₂.* nu. (T2) hearth site of a breadfruit summoner (*sowuyótoomey*). [It is where the *ááwén* model canoe is suspended from the rafters.]
fanangngat (3) See *fana-₂, ngaat.* vi. sit quietly and not take part in an activity.
Fanapenges See *fana-₁, penges.* nu. (loc.) Fala-Beguets Island.
fanatá See *fana-₂*.
fanawa (1) See *fanafan₁, waa₁.* nu. canoe making, canoe building, canoe adzing.
fanayipw (3) See *fanafan₁, iipw.* nu. (T3) notch cut in a tree trunk to facilitate climbing.
fanátá See *fan.*
faneey See *fanafan, -e-₂.* vo. (T6b) adze, shape or cut with an adze. With n. form. suf.: *faneeya-* (ni.; T3) thing adzed by (someone). Syn. *fana₁*.
fanémménú (1) See *fana-₂, mménú.* vi. brood silently.
fanénong See *fana-₂*.
fanépéw (2) See *fana-₂, paaw.* nu. (T2) form of magic that makes its victims unable to function in sport or war.

111

fanonong See *fana-₂*.
fanoto See *fana-₂*.
fanowu See *fana-₂*.
Fanó (1) FANÓÓ. nu. (loc.; T1) Falo Island.
fanóto See *fana-₂*.
fanúwu See *fana-₂*.
fannó Var. of *fáánnó*.
fang (3b) FANGA. vi. be handed over; give up. *aa f. ewe mwesiin? ese f. reey* has the engine been h. over? it hasn't been h. over by me. With dir. suf.: *fanganó* hand or give away (with *ngeni*); *fangatá* give up (as a bad job), give in, acknowledge defeat; confess; *fangóto* hand or give hither.
fangana- (3v) See *fang, -na-₁* ni. (T3v) gift or present (given as distinct from received), prestation, thing handed over. *fangeney, fangonomw, fanganan, fanganach, fangeneem, fangenemi, fangeneer* my, your (sg.), his, our (inc.), our (exc.), your (pl.), their g. (to someone).
fanganó (1) See *fang, -nó*. vi. be handed or given away. va. hand or give away (with *ngeni*).
fangangeni See *fang, ngeni*. vo. (T2) hand over to, give to. *fangangeniyey, fangangenney* h. over to me; *fangongonuk* h. over to you (sg.).
fangangngaw (3b) See *fang, ngngaw*. nu. (T3) stinginess, niggardliness. *emén chóón f.* a stingy person. vi. give little, be stingy, be niggardly.
fangatá (1) See *fang, -tá*. vi. give up (as a bad job), give in, acknowledge defeat; confess.
fangera- (3) FANGERA. [In cpds. only.] unsp. crisscross.
fangeyééch Var. of *fangééch*.
fangééch (2) See *fang, ééch*. Var. *fangeyééch*. nu. (T2) generosity. *fangééchchún átánaan* that fellow's g. vi., adj. give generously, (be) generous. *emén chóón f.* a generous person.
fangóto (1) See *fang, -to*. vi. be handed or given hither. va. hand or give hither.
Fapeweri (Eng.) nu. February. *fáán F.* during F.
fapé (1) See *fa-₁, péé-₁*. num. four empty containers. With c. pref. and ptv. const.: *afapéén* fourth e. c. With dis. c. pref.: *akkafapé* be four e. c. at a time. With pref. *áná-*: *ánáfapé* sole or only four e. c.

fara- (3b) FARA₃. [In cpds. only.] Var. *fóro-*. unsp. strangling, hanging (by the neck). See *farapach*.
faraf (3) FARAFA. nu. (T3) windward triangular platform covering the outrigger booms adjacent to the body of a *meniyuk* sailing canoe. *farafen waa* canoe's *f.*. Id. *mesen f.* (n.phr.) method of hand-to-hand fighting on canoes ("edge of the outrigger platform").
farapach (3b) See *fara-, pach*. F.; Tb3 Var. *fóropach*. va., vi. embrace, engage in petting; be embraced.
farayin (Eng.) Var. *fúrayin*. va. fry. vi., adj. (be) fried.
farayipáán (Eng.) Var. *fúrayipan* nu. frying pan. *eew f.* one f. p. *aan f.* his f. p.
faréseyin (2) See *faar₂*. nu. (T2) spongy core of the ripe coconut when it is fully formed but still quite soft. *eféw f.* one c. *faréseyinin taka* coconut's c. Cf. *óót, choofar*.
fachaacha (db; 1) See *fa-₂, chaa-*. Tb1. Var. *fachachcha*. vi., adj. (be) reddish colored (of women's genitals).
fachachcha Var. (ds) of *fachaacha*.
fachessis (2?) See *faach, ssis*. nu. (T2) wild, inedible variety of pandanus (*Pandanus tectoris*). [Its leaves are used to make plaited mats.] Syn. *facheniwén, fachenúwén*.
fachekiyeki (3) See *faach, kiyeki*. nu. (T3) variety of pandanus whose leaves are used in making plaited mats.
facheniwén (2) See *faach, wénú-*. Var. *fachenúwén*. nu. (T2) wild, inedible variety of pandanus (*Pandanus tectoris*). [Its leaves are used to make plaited mats.] Syn. *fachessis*.
fachenúwén Var. of *facheniwén*.
fachengeringer (2) See *faach, ngeringer*. nu. (T2) variety of pandanus. [Its fruit is eaten by gnawing and sucking out the sweet juice.]
facheyirá (1) See *faach, irá*. nu. (T1) variety of pandanus with edible but not very good fruit. [Its leaves are used to make plaited mats.]
faché (1) See *fa-₁, -ché*. num. four thin flat objects of any kind (e.g., sheets leaves, planks); four songs. With c. pref. and ptv. const.: *afachéén* fourth one. With dis. c. pref.: *akkafaché* four

at a time. With pref. *áná-*: *anáfaché* the sole or only four.

fachéméng (2) See *faach, méng*. nu. (T2) a variety of inedible pandanus. [Its leaves are used to make mats.]

fachémwurek See *faach, mwurek*. nu. a short pandanus tree. [It is a symbol of humility and deference in *itang* talk.]

Fayeer nu. (pers.) an evil spirit that preys on pregnant women.

fayé (1) See *fa-*₁, *-é*. Var. *feyé*. num. four hairs. With c. pref. and ptv. const.: *afayéén* fourth hair. With dis. c. pref.: *akkafayé* (be) four h. at a time.

Fayiyeweyirek nu. (loc.) Gaferut Island (Central Caroline Islands). [This name is misapplied to what is called West Fayu on maps.] Syn. *Féyiyew*.

fayiyonin (3) FAYIYONINNA. (Eng.) nu. (T2) violin. *eew f.* one v. *néwún f.* his v.; fayiyoninnen v. of (a given make). Syn. *payiyorin*.

fá- Var. of *fa-*₂.

fáá-₁ FAA₆. pref. (num.) four. See *fáán, fááyik*. Cf. *fé, rúwáánú*.

fáá-₂ (1) FÁÁ. [In cpds. only.] Var. *faa-*₂. unsp. apply the sole of the foot.

fááf (2) FÁÁFI. nu. (T2) evening meal, dinner, main meal of the day. *eew f.* one e. m. vi. take the evening meal, dine.

fááfá (db; 1) See *fáá-*₂. nu. (T1) foot brace in the form of a stationary block or board underneath the warp beam of the loom. *fááfáán túúr* loom's f. b.

-fáák [In cpds. only.] unsp. (u.m.) See *rééfáák*.

fáán₁ See *fáá-*₁. [Corruption of an original *faa* from the effect of the following *niim* in serial counting, but cf. Wol. *fangi*.] nu. (num.) the number four. [Used in serial counting or to name the number in the abstract, but not used as a numerical adjective.]

fáán₂ (4) FÁNE₁. nu. (T2) building, dwelling house, meeting house. *fánin Koot* church (building).

fáán₃ (2) FENI₁. nu. (T2) Christian worship, divine service (general term). *fenin neekkunuyón* evening worship, evening prayer; *fenin neesossor* morning worship, morning prayer; *fenin wóón peyiyas* burial service. *fiti f.* go to worship, attend church. vi. engage in worship. *siya f.* we engaged in worship. Syn. *fen*₂. Cf. *namanam, miisa, rosariyo*.

fáán₄ (4) FÁNE₂. nu. (T2) mark (as made by a pencil or pen). *fánin piin* pencil or pen mark. Cf. *mmak*.

fáán₅ Rel. form of *faa-*₁.

fáán₆ (2) See *fá-, eni-*₃. vi. circle, go in a circle (as in a dance or fish in a pond). Cf. *fáániyen*.

fáánaap (3) FÁÁNAAPA. vi. clap under the breast with the hand (done by men in dancing).

Fáánaaw See *faa-*₁, *aaw*₂. nu. (loc.) a clan name ("under the *Ficus* tree"). *fiin F., fin F.* F. woman; *mwáán F.* F. man. *chóón F.* people of F.

Fáánápuuch See *faa-*₁, *ápuuch*. nu. a school or system of fighting ("under the *Cretaeva* tree"). [It is named for its founder, who, according to legend, was defeated by Wonoto. Other schools are *Anapenges, Fáánchéénúkká*.]

Fáánéwú (1) See *faa-*₁, *éwú*. nu. (T1) a school of navigation. [Other schools are *Fáánuuch* and *Weriyeng*.]

fáániinón See *faa-*₁, *inón*. Var. *fááyinón*. nu. (loc.) under water.

fáániipw (3) See *faa-*₁, *iipw*. Var. *fáánipw*. ns. (loc.; T3) in the lee, downwind side. *fáán ipwen ásápwán* in the lee of the wind ("under the foot of the wind"); *fáán ipwen ewe fénú* downwind side of the island.

fáánimas (3) See *faa-*₁, *maas*. ns. (T3v) in front (of someone), before one's eyes. *fáán mesey* in front of me, before my eyes. *papen f.* loom beam that is immediately in front of the weaver, cloth beam.

Fáánimey (2) See *faa-*₁, *mááy*. nu. (loc.) a clan name. *fin F., fiin F.* F. woman; *mwáán F.* F. man. *chóón F.* people of F:

fáánimwmwár (2) See *faa-*₁, *mwáár*. ns. (T2) lower part of the chest. *fáán mwárin, fáán mwárimwárin* lower part of his c.

fáánipéwúúw See *faa-*₁, *paaw*, *-ú-*. vo. (T5) hold (something) under the arm.

fáánipw Var. of *fáániipw*.

fáániyen (db; 2) See *fá-, eni-*₃. nu. (T2) circle, ring. vi. talk around a subject (rather than directly). Cf. *fáán*₆.

Fáánuuch See *faa-*₁, *wuuch*. nu. a school of navigation; name of the school's founder. [It is followed by the atolls to the west of Truk and by the western islands within Truk. Other schools are *Fáánéwú* and *Weriyeng*. The *Weriyeng* school is followed by the eastern islands within Truk and by the Mortlock Islands. According to legend, *Fáánuuch* and *Weriyeng* engaged in a debate or contest, and the followers of each claim the victory for their side to the present day.]

fáánú nu. in *péérún f.* an oblong pendant made of coconut shell. See *péér*.

fáánnó (1) Var. *fannó*. nu. (T1) in *papen f.* loom beam that is away from the weaver.

Fáánchéénúkká (1) See *faa-₁, chéé, kká*. nu. (T1) a school or system of fighting ("under the *Alocasia* leaf"). [Other schools are *Anapenges, Fáánápuuch*.]

fááriyap (3) nu. (T3) mountain apple tree (*Eugenia*). [Its wood is used for outrigger booms, bowls; its fruit is edible; it is very rare in Truk.] *fááriyapen Chuuk* Trukese m. a.

Fááchchamw Var. of *Faachchamw*.

fáát (2) FETI. nu. (T2) groove that goes longitudinally along the bottom of the paddle canoe. *fetin waa* canoe's g. Syn. *péén wuuch*.

-fáát [In cpds. only.] unsp. (u.m.) See *nechefáát*.

fááti See *fáá-₂, -ti-*. Var. *faati*. vo. (T4) kick with the sole of the foot. Dis. *fáffááti* (ds).

fááyik (3) See *fáá-₁, -ik₁*. num. forty. With c. pref. and ptv. const.: *áfááyikan* fortieth one. With dis. c. pref.: *ákkáfááyik* be forty at a time. With pref. *nne-₂*: *nnefááyik* fortieth (fraction). With suf. *-somw*: *fááyikisomw* be more than forty.

fááyikisomw See *fááyik*.

fááyine F. of *faayine*.

fááyineng See *faa-₁, nááng*. Tb. nu. (T2) lower heaven. Syn. *fáán nááng*. Cf. *Nenichang*.

fááyinón See *faa-₁, inón*. Var. *fáániinón*. nu. (loc.) under water.

fááyiro (1) See *faa-₁, ro₂*. nu. (T1) a house height (such that the head must be slightly bowed to pass under the crossbeam) ("below bowing"). vi. be bowing; be respectful. [Said in greeting by a nonkinsman to a chief or *itang* in pre-colonial times, accompanied by a bow of the head.] With dir. suf.: *fááyirootá* be respectful up (to one of higher rank); *fááyirootiw* be respectful down (to one of lower rank).

fááyirootá See *fááyiro*.

fááyirootiw See *fááyiro*.

Fááyichuk (2) See *faa-₁, Chuuk₂*. nu. (loc.; T2) name of the western group of islands in the Truk lagoon ("lower Truk").

fááyiton F. of *faayiton*.

fááyiyór F. of *faayiyór*.

fáffá Dis. of *ffá*.

fáffááti Dis. of *fááti*.

fáffátán Dis. of *fátán*.

fán₁ Var. of *fen₁*.

fán₂ (4) See *fáán₄*. vi. be distinct, easily seen (as something written or marked); be marked.

fáná- See *fana-₁*.

Fánáápi See *fana-₁, ppi₂*. nu. (loc.) overall name for the atolls around Truk (used by the people of Truk proper). F. *Ennefen* Hall Islands (syn. *Nómwun Paafeng, Nómwun Soomá, Nóórowanú*); F. *Éér* atolls south of Truk (Upper and Lower Mortlock Islands); F. *Notow* Western Islands (Pulusuk, Puluwat, Pulap, Namonuito; syn. *Nómwun Pattiw*).

fánángngaw (3b) See *fán₂, ngngaw*. vi. be difficult to distinguish, blurred.

fánáy (2) FÁNÁYI. nu. courting stick (carried by young men in precolonial times). *efóch f.* one c. s. *wókun f.* his c. s.

fáneyééch (2) See *fán₂, ééch*. vi. be easily distinguished.

fár (4) FÁRE. vi. be conferred (of chiefship, with *wóón*). [The allusion seems to be to the act of placing the cord symbolic of chiefship around the new chief's neck, the original meaning possibly being "encircled."] *aa f. ewe sómwoon wóón Boutau* the chiefship was c. upon Boutau. With dir. suf.: *fárátá* be c. up (of the chiefship).

fárátá See *fár*.

fáráyap (3v) See *fár, ap₂*. nu. (T3v) manta, devilfish. *emén f.* one m. *fáráyepen Chuuk* Trukese m.

fárisi See *fár, -si-*. vo. (T5) put (something) over the shoulders (as a wreath or necklace).

fáriyap (3) See *fár, ap₁*. nu. (T3) 1. band of red shell beads worn over the left

shoulder and under the right arm as a decoration in dancing. 2. a plant.
fáchcha- (3) FÁCHCHA. unsp. spread out (as a mat). See *áfáchcha*.
fátán (4) See *fa-₂, táni-*. Var. *fetán*. n. (T2) walking; movement; course; progress; evolution, history. *fátánin* his progress. *fátánin aramas* history of mankind; *fátánin wuruwoon fénú* history of the lore of the land. Id. *fátánin órupiyá* a trick throw in fighting. vi. walk; move, go, proceed. Dis. *fáffátán* (ds), *fátánetán* (db). *fátán, fátán, fátán* go on and on (common phrase in stories to indicate the passage of time); *f. ffengeen* w. toward one another; *f. maaw* w. strongly and heavily, tramp; *f. mwéémwé* limp, w. haltingly; *f. neepwin* w. about or prowl at night (in search of women); *f. nikoyikoy* limp, w. haltingly; *f. paat* be constantly on the go, gad about (also *feyin paat*); *f. rúkúrúk* limp, totter, tip from side to side or be unsteady in walking (as a cripple); *f. sékúr* w. backwards (also *nimárámár*); feyin f. come and go, go back and forth. With intens. suf.: *fátánekkis* w. constantly. Ant. *téété*.
fátánetán Dis. of *fátán*.
fátáneyiti Var. of *fátániiti*.
fátániiti See *fátán, -iti*. Var. *fátáneyiti*. vo. (T2) walk to, go to.
fátánnap (3) See *fátán, nap*. nu. (T3) festive meal; holy communion; a collective bringing of food as gift to a visitor to one's community. vi. make a festive meal; make a collective bringing of food to a visitor.
fátánnapeey See *fátán, nap, -e-₂*. vo. (T6b) make a collective bringing of food as a gift to (someone).
fáyiyór Var. of *fááyiyór*.
fe-₁ (3) FA₂. pref. mutually. [An old pref. no longer productive.] See *feseen, ffengeen, ffengen*.
fe-₂ N. var. of *fé-₁* occurring when immediately followed by *y* or when the following vowel is *i, e, á*. See *fechchi, feffit, fefich, fengát, fengin, fekit, fepino, fepinúk, fepwi, fepwin, fesángá, fesáwá, feseeng, fesen, fetinewupw, fitip, feyaf, feyang, feyef, feyem, feyep, feyé, feyin₂, feyin₃, feyipw, feyiyey, feyó*.
fe (1) FEE₁. Tbl. vi. engage in sexual intercourse, fuck. Cf. *fee-₁, fee-₂*.

fee-₁ (1) FEE₂. [Var. of *fa-₂*.] Var. *fáyi-, feyi-*. pref. (c.) doing, making. See *feet, feettik*. Cf. *fa-₂*.
fee-₂ (1) FEE₃. [In cpds. only.] Var. *féé-*. unsp. pertaining to a sexually productive woman. See *feefin, féépwún*. Cf. *fe*.
Feefen nu. (loc.) Fefan Island.
feefin (3) See *fee-₂, fina-₁*. nu. woman; womanhood; middle-aged woman (about 40 years old). *emén f.* one w. Ant. *mwáán*. Cf. *feefina-, féépwún, mesefeefin*. suf. (adj.) female; left (hand or side). Ant. *mwáán*.
feefina- (3) See *feefin*. ni. (T3) sister (of a man), a blood relative of same generation as and opposite sex to a man. *feefinan* his s. Ant. *mwááni-*.
feefineni See *feefina-, -ni-*. vo. (T6a) acquire (a woman) as a sister (of a man).
feet (3) See *fee-₁, -t*. vi. be what for (with *meyi*); do what. *meyi f. eey mááy?* what is this breadfruit for?; *ke f.?* what are you doing?
feettik (2) See *fee-₁, ttik₁*. Var. *feyittik*. va. pinch with the fingers ("make squeal").
feey See *fe*. Tbl. vo. (T1) have sexual intercourse with, fuck.
feeyiir (3) FEEYIIRA. va. engage in grating on a grater (of taro, banana, arrowroot, and manioc, but not of ripe coconut). Cf. *pweyiker*.
feeyiira- (3) See *feeyiir*. nr. (T3) act of grating. *feeyiiren pwuna* the grating of *Cyrtosperma* taro.
feeyiira See *feeyiir*. vo. (T3) grate (banana, taro, arrowroot, or manioc).
Feeyis₁ nu. (loc.) Fais Island (Western Caroline Islands).
feeyis₂ See *Feeyis₁*. nu. type of dry-land taro (*woten F*.) said to be from Fais Island.
-feeyisin unsp. (u.m.) See *wunufeeyisin*.
fefich N. of *féfich*.
feffen Dis. of *ffen₂*.
feffeyin Dis. of *feyin*.
feffeyinnó Dis. of *feyinnó*.
feffeyittik Dis. of *feyittik*.
feffeyiyéech Dis. of *feyiyéech*.
feffit N. of *féffit*.
fesángá N. of *fésángá*.
fesáwá N. of *fésáwá*.

feseen

feseen (2: -*seenni*-, -*senni*-) See *fe*-₁, *seni*₂ (?). adj. away from each other, apart, separate, different. *feyin f.* travel away from each other; *imwúúfeseen* be separated, apart; *mwúúfeseen* be broken apart, torn apart; *sóókkofeseen* be of different kind. Ant. *ffengen, fengeen.*
-feseenniiy See -*feseen,* -*i*-₂. Var. -*fesenniiy.* vo. suf. (adj.; T5) apart, separate, different. *afangerafeseenniiy, afangerafesenniy* cause (something) to lie criss-cross. Ant. -*ffengenniiy.*
feseeng N. of *féseeng.*
fesen N. of *fésen.*
-**fesenniiy** Var. of -*feseenniiy.*
Fesinimw nu. (loc.) a clan name. *fin F., fiin F.* woman of F.; *mwáán F.* man of F. *chóón F.* people of F.
fesir (3) FESIRA. N. nu. (T3) honest, trustworthy; socialized; tame, housebroken (of animals). Syn. *mwótuk.*
fekit N. of *fékit.*
fen₁ (3) See *fa*-₂, -*n*₂. Var. *fán*₁. vr. or adv. be really, indeed, already; certainly, for sure (with future). *ke saamwo fééri? wúwa f. fééri* you haven't done it yet? I have already done it to completion. *wusun chék f. ááyiwe mwesiin eey* just as if this were really my engine.
fen₂ (2) See *fáán*₃. vi. 1. engage in worship. 2. be tabu, prohibited, sacred. Syn. *pin.*
fene-₁ See *fana-*₁.
fene-₂ (3) FENA. vi. peck. Dis. *feffen* (ds).
feneey See *fene-*₂, -*e-*₂. vo. (T6b) peck.
fenes (2) FENESI. Obs. (Eng. *flask*) Var. *fenesikko.* nu. (T2) bottle, flask. Cf. *ruume.*
fenengeni See *fen*₂, *ngeni.* vo. (T2) worship *siya f. Koot* we worshiped God.
feni- (2) FENI₂. vi. anal discharge (?); bad smell (?).
fenisikko (1) FENESIKKOO. Obs. (Eng. *flask*) Var. *fenes.* nu. (T1) bottle, flask. Cf. *ruume.*
fenitong See *feni-, tong.* vi. break wind, fart. [Preferred when siblings of opposite sex or parent and child of opposite sex are both within hearing.] Syn. *sing, sin, pwpwir.*
-**feng** (2) FENGI. [In cpds. only.] unsp. duration, age. See *neefeng.*

fengát N. of *féngát.*
fengin N. of *féngin.*
fepino N. of *fépino.*
fepinúk N. of *fépinúk.*
fepwi N. of *fépwi.*
fepwin N. of *fépwin.*
-**fech** (3, 2) FECHA, FECHI. [In cpds. only.] unsp. turn to the side (of one's body or a canoe). Dis. *fechefech, fechifech* (db).
fechchi N. of *féchchi.*
fet (2) See *fáát.* vi. make a longitudinal groove along the bottom of a paddle canoe.
fetán Var. of *fátán.*
fete- (3) FETA. Var. *fété-, pété-.* unsp. (u.m.) See *fetepwpwún.*
feteey See *fa-*₂, -*t,* -*e-*₂. vo. (T6b) do what with? *wúpwe f. eey pisek?* what shall I do with this stuff? Id. *sipwe f.* what will we do with it [anyhow]? (implying acceptance of a bad situation or shrugging something off). Cf. *feet.*
fetepwpwún (2) See *fete-, pwpwún.* Var. *fétépwpwún, pétépwpwún.* vi. be soiled, dirty.
fetiiy See *fáát,* -*i-*₂. vo. (T5) scoop out (the soft meat of a drinking coconut). Cf. *assaka.*
fetin (2) FETINI. nu. (T2) general term for a class of plants including grasses, sedges, and ferns. *efóch f.* one blade of grass, one fern, etc. *fetinin Nómwochchek* a plant (*Cuphea hyssopifolia* or *Blechum brownei*). *fetinin wumwuné* a grass (*Paspolum conjugatum, Centotheca latifolia*, used as medicine for diarrhea in children); *fetinin wuumw* a grass (*Ischaemun* sp.); *f. pwérúk* a grass. vi., adj. (be) grassy. *aa f. ikeey* it has become grassy here.
fetinewupw N. of *fétinewupw.*
fetinniyap (3) See *fetin, niyap.* nu. (T3) a grass (*Ischaemum muticum, Manisuris*). [Used to line earth ovens.]
fetip N. of *fétip.*
fettik Var. of *feyittik.*
fettikiiy Var. of *feyittikiiy.*
feyaf N. of *féyaf.*
feyang N. of *féyang.*
feyef N. of *féyef.*
feyem N. of *féyem.*
feyep N. of *féyep.*

Trukese-English

feyé N. of *fayé*.
feyi- (2) FEYI. [Derived from *fa-₂*.] Var. *fee-*. pref. (c.) doing, making.
feyiimw (3a) See *faaw, iimw*. Var. *féwúwimw*. nu. (T3) cave ("shelter-rock").
feyisiyuu nu. a fish (*Epibulus insidiator*).
feyisseni₁ (3?) See *feyin₁, seni₂, -ya-* (?). nu. (T3?) diarrhea, discharge of any kind. vi. have diarrhea.
feyisseni₂ See *feyin₁, seni₂*. vo. (T2) leave, depart from, go or travel from.
feyisset E.Wn. of *feyittá*. See *feyin₁*.
feyin₁ (2) FEYINI. nu. (T2) course, route. *feyinin aach sááy* route of our journey. With dir. suf.: *feyitto* arrival (*feyittooy, feyittoomw* my, your a.). vi. travel; go, walk (curt usage). *f. feseen* t. away from one another; *f. ffengeen* t. toward one another; *f. paat* be on the go constantly, gad about; *f. fátán* come and go, go back and forth; *f. feyinnó* continuing on; *f. feyinnóó chék* continuing on forever. With dir. suf.: *feyiniwu, feyinúwu* t. or go outside; *feyinnong* t. or go inside or south; *feyinnó* t. or go away; *feyittá* t. or go up or east; progress, ascend, make progress; *feyittiw* t. or go down or westward; descend; *feyitto* t. or come hither.
feyin₂ (3) See *fe-₂, ina-₂*. N. num. four hands of bananas. Syn. *feyiyey, féyi*.
feyin₃ (2) See *fe-₂, ini-₂*. num. four shoots.
feyiniiti See *feyin₁, -iti*. vo. (T2) travel or go to.
feyiniffatoto (1) See *feyin₁, -ffat, -to*. vi. come without any visible purpose.
feyiniffatónó (1) See *feyin₁, -ffat, -nó*. vi. go without any visible purpose.
feyinisi (1) FEYINISII. nu. (T1) goatfish.
feyinikkáy (2, 3) See *feyin₁, kkáy*. vi. come or go quickly.
feyiniwi See *faaw, -wi*. Var. *féwúniwi*. nu. grease and fat in belly of turtle.
feyiniwu See *feyin₁*.
feyinná E.Wn. of *feyinnó*. See *feyin₁*.
feyinnong See *feyin₁*.
feyinnó See *feyin₁*.
feyipw N. of *féyipw*.
feyicho (1) See *feyi-, cho*. va. beg pardon (with *wóón*). *f. wóómw!* [I] beg your pardon!; excuse me! Syn. *féwúwico₂, tirow, fááyiro*.

feyiyééch

feyiti See *fa-₂, -iti*. vo. (T2) arrive at, reach.
feyittá See *feyin₁*.
feyittás E.Wn. of *feyittá*. See *feyin₁*.
feyitte E.Wn. of *feyitto*. See *feyin₁*.
feyittes E.Wn. of *feyittá*. See *feyin₁*.
feyittik (2) See *feyi-, ttik₁*. Var. *fettik*. va. pinch with the fingers ("make squeal"). Dis. *feffeyittik* (ds).
feyittikiiy See *feyittik, -i-₂*. Var. *fettikiiy*. vo. (T5) pinch.
feyittiw See *feyin₁*.
feyitto See *feyin₁*.
feyiya- (3) FEYIYA. [In cpds. only.] vi. fare, proceed, happen, go. See *feyiyengngaw, feyiyééch*.
feyiyangngaw Tn. of *feyiyengngaw*.
feyiyach (3) FEYIYACHA. N. Var. *féwúwach*. adj. obliquely.
feyiyán (2) FEYIYÁNI. (Eng.) nu. (T2) file. *emén f.* one f. *feyiyánin Merika* American f.
feyiyemwmwen (2) See *feyiya-, mwmwen*. nu. (T2) parting gift of food, given to a visitor on his departure after the visit. *feyiyemwmwenin* p. g. to him. *feyiyemwmwenin neeyaw* last meal given to a visitor before his departure in the absence of food for him to take with him ("parting-gift-of-food-for in-the-mouth").
feyiyengngaw (3b) See *feyiya-, ngngaw*. Tb3. Var. *feyiyangngaw*. nu. (T3) bad luck, misfortune. vi. fare ill or badly, have bad luck, have an accident, go wrong; suffer injury, be wounded; be wronged, injured, upset. *kese f.?* are you all right? ("you haven't fared badly?" "you haven't been hurt?"). Syn. *feyiyepwutak*.
feyiyepwutak (3) See *feyiya-, pwutak*. [The preferred form in the presence of father and daughter, mother and son, and brother and sister.] vi. fare ill or badly, have bad luck, have an accident, go wrong; suffer injury, be wounded; be wronged, injured, upset. Syn. *feyiyengngaw*.
feyiyey (3) See *fe-₂, iyeyiya-*. num. four hands of bananas. Syn. *feyi, feyin₂*.
feyiyééch (2: *-yéchchú-*) See *feyiya-, ééch*. Tb3. n. (T2) good luck, blessings, good fortune, welfare, prosperity. *feyiyéchchún* his g. l. *feyiyéchchún fenúúfaan* worldly goods or blessings; *feyiyéchchún ngúún* spiritual goods or

blessings; *feyiyéchchuún inis* bodily goods or blessings, health. vi. be blessed, have good luck, prosper, be fortunate. Dis. *feffeyiyééch* (ds). Syn. *feyiyéwútek*.

feyiyéchchúni See *feyiyééch, -ni-*. vo. (T5) acquire as good luck or as a blessing. *feyiyéchchúni feyiyéchchún* acquire his blessings (fortune).

feyiyéwútek See *feyiya-, wútek*. [The preferred form in the presence of father and daughter, mother and son, and brother and sister.] vi. be blessed, have good luck, prosper, be fortunate. Syn. *feyiyééch*.

fé-₁ (3b: *f-, fa-, fe-, fé-, fo-*) FA₃. [Most usually in this form.] pref. (num.) four. Syn. *fáá-*₁, *fáán*₁, *rúwáánú*. See *féchamw, féchef, féchchi, féchchooch, féchú, féchúk, féféw, féffaat, féffit, féfich, féfóch, féfutuk, féngaf, féngát, féngéréw, féngin, fékis, fékit, fékkamw, fékkap, fékkumw, fékum, fékumwuch, fékup, fémach, fémas, fémataf, fémech, fémeech, fémeet, fémén, fémma, fémmeék, fémwénú, fémwmwék, fémwmwun, fémwmwú, fémwmwún, fémwu, fémwú*₁, *fémwú*₂, *fémwúch, fénnú, fépa, fépachang, fépan, fépeche, fépeek, fépék, fépéw, fépino, fépinúk, fépu, fépwang, fépwey, fépwéét, fépwi, fépwin, fépwopw, fépwór, fépwpwaaw, fépwpwún, fépwúkú, fépwún, fésap, fésángá, fésáwá, féseeng, fésen, fésópw*₁, *fésópw*₂, *féssaar, féssak, féssáát, féssupw, fétinewupw, fétip, fétit, féttiit, féttún, fétú, fétúkúm, fétún, féwumw, féwupw, féwúk*₁, *féwúk*₂, *féwún, féwút, féwúwéw, féyaf, féyang, féyef, féyem, féyep, féyék, féyi, féyipw, féyó*.

fé-₂ Var. of *fa-*₂.

fé (1) FÉÉ₁. Var. *-ffé*. adj. new.

-fé (1) FÉÉ₂. suf. (adj.) hibiscus. [Found only in *sinifé*, the present name for hibiscus, but originally meaning "hibiscus bark".]

féé-₁ (1) FÉÉ₄. [In cpds. only.] vi. tied, lashed.

féé-₂ (1) FÉÉ₅. [Presumably derived from *fa-*₂. Cf. *fee-*.] unsp. doing, activating. See *fééri*.

féé (1) FÉÉ₃. nu. (T1) hull cavity of canoe or boat (*féén waa*). Id. *neefééféén sékúriy* at the groove of my back.

fééfé (db; 1) See *féé-*₁. nu. (dis.; T1) lashing, tying. *fééféén ewe iimw* the l. of that house; *fééféén nikeppich* bow string. vi. be lashed, tied.

féépwún (2) See *fee-*₂, *pwún*₁. nu. (T2) young woman (between puberty and middle age). *emén f.* one y. w. *f. nengngin* a very young woman, teen-aged young woman. With adj. suf.: *féépwúnúsich* girl who has just become a young woman, who is just past puberty.

féépwúnúsich See *féépwún*.

féér (2, 3a) FÉÉRÚ. [Presumably a back formation from *fééri*.] n. (T2) deed, action. Dis. *féfféér* (ds) deeds, doings; practice. *féérún, féfféérún, aan féfféér* his d. *féfféérún nóómw* practice of olden times. *aan féfféér meyi ééch* his good deeds. Cf. *fféér*. vi. do, act. Dis. *féfféér* (ds). *meet kaa f.* what did you do? *f.-fichiiy* (vo. phr.) do (something) very carefully or well. *f. sefáán* (vi. phr.), *f.-sefánniiy* (vo. phr.) do again, redo, repeat.

féérááta See *fééri*.

fééreya (1) See *féé-*₂, *-ra-, -ya*₂. vi. be difficult or hard to do.

fééri See *féé-*₂, *-ri-*. vo. (T4) do, make, build, construct. *f. menimenich* fix our faces [in a pleasing expression], make ourselves look attractive. With dir. suf.: *fééráátá*. With n. form. suf.: *féériya-* thing made, product, handiwork. *féériyen iyé eey chitoosa?* who made this automobile ("product of whom this automobile?").

féériya- See *fééri*.

féérúwér (db; 2) See *fa-*₂, *ér*₂. Var. *féérúyér*. nu. (c.; dis.; T2) spell, incantation. *féérúwérún pachaaw* shark spell. vi. recite a spell.

féérúwérúúw See *féérúwér, ú-*. Var. *féérúyérúúw*. vo. (T5) recite a spell upon.

féérúyér Var. of *féérúwér*.

féérúyérú See *féérúyér*. vo. (dis.; T2) recite a spell upon.

féérúyérúúw Var. of *féérúwérúúw*.

féét Var. of *faat*₁.

féétek (2) See *féé-*₁, *-tek*. vi., adj. (be) tied, bound, fettered (as a prisoner).

féétekini See *féétek, -ni-*. vo. (T5) tie up, bind, fetter.

fééti See *féé-*₁, *-ti-*. vo. (T5) tie, lash together. With dir. suf.: *féétóónó* tie (something) off; suppress, curb (an impulse).

fééttóónó See *fééti.*

fééwo (1) See *féé-₁, woo₁.* nu. (T1) tying on the rafters to a house. *sáfeen f.* medicine prepared by a master builder (*sowuyímw*) and drunk by him and his workers preparatory to putting the rafters on a house.

féféw (2) See *fé-₁, -féw.* Var. *fféw.* num. four lumps or globular shaped objects (e.g., stones, balls). *f. faaw* four stones.

féfich (3a) See *fé-₁, ficha-.* Var. *fefich.* num. four strips of coconut, pandanus, or palm leaf prepared for plaiting mats.

féfóch (2) See *fé-₁, fóchu-.* Var. *ffóch.* num. four long and roundish or sticklike objects (e.g. trees, vehicles, shovels, canoes, arms, legs).

féfutuk (3) See *fé-₁, futuk.* num. four pieces of meat (animal or fish).

féffaat (3) See *fé-₁, ffaata-.* num. four strings of fish.

fééfféér Dis. of *féér* and *ffééŕ.*

fééféérééch (2) See *féér, éech.* n. (T2) good deeds, good performance. *féfféérechchún* his g. d. vi. do good; be good to do.

fééféérúngngaw (3b) See *féér, ngngaw.* n. (T3) bad deed. *féféérúngngawan* his bad deed. vi. do bad things; be bad to do.

féfféew Dis. of *fféew.*

féffén (ds; 2) See *fén₁.* nu. (dis.; T2) bruises. *aan f.* his bruises. va. (dis.) bruise.

féffénú (ds; 3) See *fénú.* va. (dis.) use land. *wúwa chék f. eey fénú ngé wúse wesewesen fénúweni* I am just using this land but I have not really acquired title to it. Cf. *fénúweni.*

féffit (3) See *fé-₁, -ffit.* Var. *feffit.* num. four leaf packages of small fish.

fésap (3) See *fé-₁, saap.* num. four cheeks (especially of fish).

fésángá (1) See *fé-₁, sángá.* Var. *fesángá.* num. four basketfuls of fish. Syn. *fésáwá.*

fésáwá (1) See *fé-₁, sáwá.* Var. *fesáwá.* num. four basketfuls of fish. Syn. *fésángá.*

féseeng (3) See *fé-₁, seeng.* Var. *feseeng.* num. four lengths between joints or nodes.

fésen (2) See *fé-₁, -sen.* Var. *fesen.* num. four coils or hanks of rope. [Each coil is 30 to 100 fathoms long according to local custom.]

fésópw₁ (4) See *fé-₁, sópwu-₂.* Var. *fosópw.* num. four sections, divisions, segments.

fésópw₂ (4) See *fé-₁, sópwu-₃.* num. four burdens of tied together breadfruit.

féssaar (2) See *fé-₁, -ssaar.* Var. *féssar.* num. four slices.

féssak (3) See *fé-₁, ssaka-.* num. four pieces of copra.

féssar N. of *féssaar.*

féssáát (3) See *fé-₁, -ssáát.* Var. *féssát.* num. four slivers, longitudinal slices, splinters.

féssát N. of *féssáát.*

féssupw (2) See *fé-₁, ssupwu-.* num. four tiny drops.

fékis (2) See *fé-₁, kisi-.* num. four little things or bits.

fékit (3) See *fé-₁, -kit.* Var. *fekit.* num. forty thousand ("four ten thousands"). Syn. *fááyik ngéréw.*

fékum (2) See *fé-₁, kumu-.* num. four mouthfuls or swallows of liquid.

fékumwuch (2) See *fé-₁, kumwuch.* num. four fistfuls, handfuls (of something); four hooves, paws, feet (of animals).

fékkamw (3b) See *fé-₁, kkamw.* num. four fragments or pieces (of cloth, paper).

fékkap (3) See *fé-₁, kkap.* num. four cupfuls.

fékkumw (2, 3) See *fé-₁, kkumw₁.* num. four portions of premasticated food.

fémas (3) See *fé-₁, -mas.* num. four things worn on the eye (e.g., lenses of goggles) or attached to a piercing weapon (e.g., spear points).

fémach (3) See *fé-₁, macha-.* num. four fishtails.

fémataf (3) See *fé-₁, matafa-.* num. four small portions, small amounts, little bits.

fémeech (2) See *fé-₁, -meech.* F. Var. *fémmech, fémech.* num. four portions of mashed breadfruit.

fémeet See *fé-₁, meet₂.* num. four strands (of hair, fiber).

fémech Var. of *fémmech, fémeech.*

fémén (2) See *fé-₁, maan₁.* num. four persons or creatures (used with people, mammals, birds, fish, insects, but not with lobsters, crabs, sea cucumbers, or

fémma

shell fish); four knives, guns, files, scissors.

fémma (1) See *fé-*₁, *-mma*. num. four mouthfuls of premasticated food.

fémmech (2) See *fé-*₁, *-mmech*. N. Var. *fémeech*, *fémech*. num. four portions of mashed breadfruit.

fémmék (2) See *fé-*₁, *mékkú-*. num. four fragments.

fémwénú (1) See *fé-*₁, *mwénúú-*. num. four ells (lengths from elbow to fingertips).

fémwu E.Wn. of *fémwú*₂.

fémwú₁ (1) See *fé-*₁, *mwúú-*₁. num. four torn fragments (of rag or string).

fémwú₂ (1) See *fé-*₁, *mwúú-*₂. num. four sea cucumbers; four pieces of feces.

fémwúch (2) See *fé-*₁, *-mwúch*. num. four pieces of firewood.

fémwmwék See *fé-*₁, *mwékkú-*. N. num. four bits or morsels (of mashed food). Syn. *fépwey*.

fémwmwun (3) See *fé-*₁, *mwmwuna-*. N. Var. *fémwmwún*. num. four portions of *mwatún*. Syn. *fétún*.

fémwmwú N. of *fémwú*₁.

fémwmwún F. of *fémwmwun*.

fén₁ (2) FÉNÚ₁. vi. be bruised; bleed (euphemism for *chcha*). va. bruise. Dis. *féffén* (ds).

fén₂ (2) FÉNÚ₂. nu. (T2) any instrument used to strike a thorn or sharp object and cause it to puncture (as in lancing a boil). Cf. *ffén*₁. vi. be pricked (as by a thorn, needle, nail, tattooing instrument).

féna- (3) FÉNA. [In cpds. only.] unsp. advise, correct, admonish, counsel.

féné- See *fana-*₁.

fénééw See *féna-*, *-é-*. vo. (T6b) advise, correct, exhort, counsel, reprimand, admonish. *fonook* advise you.

fénéwúng nu. species of half-beak fish (upper jaw extended into a beak, lower jaw short). Syn. *awásá*.

fénú- (2) See *fén*₁. ni. (T2) blood (euphemism for *chcha*). *fénún* his b.

fénú (1, 3a) FÉNÚÚ, FÉNÚWA. nu. inhabited island; land, country. *eew f.* one i. Cf. *téé*. ni. (T3) land, country, homeland; landholding. *fénúwan* his l. *fénúwen éfékúr* land received from a father or mother (whose personal property it already was) or land given by a lineage (*eterekes*) to the children of one of its men by unanimous consent of the lineage's members, such land being referred to by the owner as *fénúwey me reen semey (iney)* my land from my father (mother). *fénúwen kkamé* purchased land; *fénúwen naaw* land given by a man to his children or by a lineage to the children of one of its male members and not subject to subsequent demanded return; *fénúwen naaw seni eterekes* land given by a lineage to the children of one of its men; *fénúwen naaw seni kkamé* land that a man has purchased and passed to his children.

fénúúfaan (1) See *fénú*, *faa-*₁. [Occurs only in ptv. construction, as shown, with 3sg. pos. suf. *-n*.] nu. (loc.) world, earth (as contrasted with heaven). Ant. *nááng*.

fénúúpéén See *fénú*, *péé-*₁. [In ptv. const. with 3sg. pos. suf. as shown here.] nu. (loc.) uninhabited island or land, empty land, desert. Cf. *fénú*, *téé*.

fénúúw See *fén*₂, *-ú-*. vo. (T5) prick, tattoo.

fénúfén (db; 2) See *fén*₂. nu. (dis.; T2) any instrument used to strike a thorn or other sharp object and cause it to puncture. vi., adj. (be) thorny.

fénúweni See *fénú*, *-ni-*. vo. (T6a) acquire title to (a landholding). Cf. *féffénú*.

fénúwepi (1) See *fénú*, *pii-*₁. Itang. nu. (T1) thought of one's land.

fénúwékkamé (1) See *fénú*, *kkamé*. nu. (T1) purchased land. *fénúwan f.* his p. l. Syn. *fénúwen kkamé*.

Fénúwénong (3) See *fénú*, *-nong*. [Bollig] nu. (loc.; T3) a place in the traditional heaven ("Inner Land").

Fénúwowu (1) See *fénú*, *-wu*. [Bollig] nu. (loc.; T1) a place in the traditional heaven ("Outer Land").

fénnú (1) See *fé-*₁, *nnúú-*. num. four portions or loaves of breadfruit pudding; four pudding-loaves' worth of breadfruit to be mashed.

féng (2) FÉNGÚ₁. ni. (T2) love (of someone), affection (for someone). *féngún* l. of or for him. vi. be loved, be the object of affection.

féngaf (3) See *fé-*₁, *ngaaf*. num. four fathoms.

féngát (2) See *fé-*₁, *-ngát*. Var. *fengát*. num. four concave or hollow objects; (less common) four nonspecific or general-class things. Cf. *fépwang*, *rúwáánú*.

féngéréw (2) See *fé-*₁, *-ngéréw*. num. four thousand. Syn. *rúwáánú ngéréw*.

féngin (2) See *fé-*₁, *ngini-*. Var. *fengin*. num. four bits or pieces.

féngúféng (db; 2) FÉNGÚ₂. vi. rouse someone from sleep, wake someone up.

féngúni See *féngúféng, -ni-*. vo. (T5) rouse (someone), wake (someone) up. *fongunuk* rouse you.

fépa (1) See *fé-*₁, *-pa*. num. four fronds, garlands, stalks with leaves (of palm trees, banana plants, *Cyrtosperma* taro, and also of leis and garlands, necklaces, bead belts).

fépan (3) See *fé-*₁, *paan*₁. num. four branches with leaves (of trees other than palms or bananas). Syn. *fépachang*.

fépachang (3) See *fé-*₁, *pachang*₁. num. four branches (with their leaves). Syn. *fépan*.

fépeek (2) See *fé-*₁, *peek*₂. num. four sides, pages.

fépeche (1) See *fé-*₁, *peche*. num. four lower or hind limbs (of humans, birds, and animals only).

fépék (2) See *fé-*₁, *péék*. num. four chips, chopped off pieces, cigarette butts.

fépéw (2) See *fé-*₁, *-péw*. num. four wings or things worn on hands or arms (e.g. gloves).

fépino (1) See *fé-*₁, *pino*. Var. *fepino*. num. four small packages of breadfruit pudding.

fépinúk (2) See *fé-*₁, *pinúk*. Var. *fepinúk*. num. four tied bundles; four reams (of paper).

fépu (1) See *fé-*₁, *puu-*₂. num. four strokes distant or deep (in swimming).

fépwang (3) See *fé-*₁, *pwaang*. num. four holes, caves, cavities, pits, tunnels, hollows. Cf. *féngát*.

fépwey (2) See *fé-*₁, *-pwey*. num. four pinches or morsels (of food). Syn. *fémwmwék*.

fépwéét (2) See *fé-*₁, *pwéét*. num. four noses.

fépwi (1) See *fé-*₁, *pwii-*₁. Var. *fepwi*. num. four groups, groves, flocks, schools, herds, swarms, convoys, etc.

fépwin (2) See *fé-*₁, *pwiin*₃. Var. *fepwin*. num. four nights.

fépwopw (2) See *fé-*₁, *pwoopw*. Var. *fopwopw*. num. four tree-trunks, bases, causes, origins, reasons, foundations, sources, beginnings.

fépwór (4) See *fé-*₁, *pwóór*. num. four boxes or crates (of something).

fépwúkú (1) See *fé-*₁, *-pwúkú*. num. four hundred.

fépwún (2) See *fé-*₁, *pwúún*₁. Var. *fépwpwún*. num. four broken-off pieces.

fépwpwaaw (2) See *fé-*₁, *pwpwaaw*. num. four home-made cigarettes.

fépwpwún N. of *fépwún*.

féchamw (3) See *fé-*₁, *-chamw*. num. four foreheads, brows, or similarly classed objects (e. g., visors, stem-bases of coconut fronds); four fishheads.

féchef See *fé-*₁, *-chef*. num. four tentacles (of octopus or squid); four pieces of firewood. Syn. *féwút, féyó*.

Féchéwúnap nu. (loc.) Faraulep Island and Atoll (Central Caroline Islands).

féchú (1) See *fé-*₁, *chúú*. num. four bone segments of meat.

féchúk (2) See *fé-*₁, *chúúk*. num. four coconut leaf baskets.

féchchi (1) See *fé-*₁, *-chchi*. Var. *fechchi*. num. four drops.

féchchooch See *fé-*₁, *chooch*. num. four armfuls or bunches.

fété- (3) FÉTA. Var. *fete-, pété-*. unsp. (u.m.) See *fétépwpwún*.

fétépwpwún (2) See *fété-, pwpwún*. Var. *fetepwpwún, pétépwpwún*. vi. be soiled, dirty.

fétinewupw (2) See *fé-*₁, *tinewupw*. Var. *fetinewupw*. num. four yards (lengths from center of chest to outstretched fingertips).

fétip (3) See *fé-*₁, *tiip*₂. Var. *fetip*. num. four slices, chunks, or cut segments (of breadfruit and taro only).

fétit (2) See *fé-*₁, *-tit*. num. four strings (of breadfruit, usually ten to a string). Syn. *féttiit*.

fétú (3) See *fé-*₁, *túú*. Tb1. num. four vulvas (in counting sexual encounters).

fétúkúm (3) See *fé-*₁, *túkúm*. num. four packages or packets.

fétún₁ (3) FÉTÚNA. nu. (T3) paddle (for canoe). *efóch f.* one p. *aan f.* his p. *fétúnen waa* canoe's paddle. Syn. *tuutu*₂. va. paddle.

fétún₂ (2) See *fé-₁, túnú-*. F. Var. *féttún*. num. four portions of *mwatún* pudding. Syn. *fémwmwún*.

féttiit (2) See *fé-₁, ttiit₂*. num. four strings of ten breadfruit.

féttún N. of *fétún*.

-féw (2) See *faaw*. suf. (cc.) lump, chunk, globule, spherical object. [Used with numerical prefixes in counting stones, rocks, pieces of coral, nuts, seeds, fruits, burrs, tubers, etc.] *eféw, rúwéféw, wúnúféw, féféw* or *fféw, nimeféw, wonoféw, fúúféw, wanúféw, ttiweféw, engoon féwún* one,...ten l.; *fiteféw* how many l. *eféw faaw* one stone; *eféw wuuch* one banana. With c. pref. and ptv. const.: *ááféwún, érúwéféwún* first l.; second l. (etc.). With dis. c. pref.: *ákkááféw, ékkérúwéféw* be one l. at a time, two l. at a time (etc.). With pref. *áná-: ánááféw, ánárúwéféw* sole or only l., sole or only two l. (etc.).

féwumw (2) See *fé-₁, wumwu-₂*. Var. *fowumw*. num. four branching stalks (of bananas, fruit, clusters of pandanus keys, coral).

féwupw (2) See *fé-₁, wupwu-₁*. num. four breasts.

féwú-₁ (2) FÉWÚ₂. [In cpds. only.] unsp. plaiting (of mats and baskets).

féwú-₂ (2: *féwú-, fowu-*) FÉWÚ₃. adj. talked about. *féwún weyiyerek* place good for or reputed for trolling. See *féwúni*.

féwúúw See *faaw, -ú-*. vo. (T5) put stones on (an earth oven).

féwúféw₁ (db; 2) See *féwú-₁*. nu. (dis.; T2) plaiting. va., vi. plait; be plaited.

féwúféw₂ (db; 2) See *faaw*. vi. (dis.), adj. 1. (be) stony. 2. (be) solid, compacted.

féwúféwiirokumw (db; 3) See *féwú-₁, rokumw*. nu. (T3) simple coconut leaf basket.

féwúsan (3) See *faaw, -san*. nu. (T3) stone used to weight a burial bundle prepared for sea burial.

féwússuk (2) See *faaw, ssuk*. nu. (T2) flint (for striking fire). Syn. *féwúkkékú*.

féwúk₁ (2) See *fé-₁, wúúk₁*. num. four tails (in counting fish).

féwúk₂ (2) See *fé-₁, wúúk₂*. num. four fingernails, toenails, claws.

Féwúkasé (1) See *faaw, ka-₂, sé*. [Bollig] nu. (loc.; T1) a place in the layer of heaven called *Nenisu* ("sunset glow rock" or "repose rock"). [Associated with it is *Táániyón*. Bollig quotes a saying: *wú tupw me Táániyón, wú mwé Féwúkasé; wú tupw me Féwúkasé, wú mwé Táániyón* I disappear from T., I alight at F.; I disappear from F., I alight at T.]

féwúkéré (1) See *faaw, éréé-*. F. Var. *péwúkéré*. n. (T1) shoulder socket. *féwúkéréén* his s. s. *núkún f.* shoulderblade.

féwúkúkkún (2) See *faaw, kúkkún*. nu. (T2) coins, small change. vi., adj. be small (of globular objects).

féwúkkékú (1) See *faaw, kkékú*. nu. (T1) flint (for striking fire). Syn. *féwússuk*.

féwúmanaw (3) See *faaw, manaw*. nu. (T3) a kind of coral. [It is hard, sharp, and round, grows fast, and is used for lime.]

féwúmwo (1) See *faaw, -mwo*. Var. *fowumwo*. nu. (T1) small pebbles; pebbly soil. Dis. *féwúmwoomwo, fowumwoomwo*.

féwúmwoomwo (1) See *féwúmwo*. Var. *fowumwoomwo*. vi., adj. (dis.) (be) pebbly.

féwúmwoch (3) See *faaw, mwoch*. nu. (T3) variety of banana ("short fruit"). Syn. *wuchuféwúmwoch, wuchun Saamawa*.

féwúmwuunó (1) See *faaw, mwuu-, nó*. nu. (T1) cliff. nu. (loc.) name of a cliff and mountain on Paata.

féwún (3a) See *fé-₁, wúún₁*. num. four feathers, scales, hairs.

féwúni See *féwú-₂, -ni-*. vi. (T5) call or speak the name of; talk about (someone) in a positive or envious way. Syn. *paani*.

féwúniwi (1) See *faaw, -wi*. Var. *feyiniwi*. nu. (T1) grease and fat in the belly of a turtle.

féwúnó Var. of *fowunó*.

féwúnón (4) See *faaw, nónu-*. nu. (T2) an illness caused by sorcery and characterized by swelling of the abdomen. [It is treated by *sáfeen faaw*.]

féwúnúkkáách See *féwú-₂, kkáách*. nu. good place for hook-and-line fishing. vi. be such a place.

féwúnúmas (3d, 3v) See *faaw, maas*. ns. (T3v) eyeball. *féwúnúmasan, féwún masan* his e.

féwúnúppi See *faaw, ppi₂*. nu. (num.) hundred thousand ("ball of sand"). Syn. *engoon kkitan, ipwúkú ngéréw*.

féwúnúch (2) See *faaw, núch*. nu. (T2) loose or tippy rocks or stones that make a clatter under one's feet. [According to Bollig, the road to Neetiiti in the lowest layer of heaven is made up of such stones, whose clatter announces the arrival of new souls of the dead.]

féwúpar (3b) See *faaw, par*. nu. (T3) red shell beads; necklace or garland of same.

féwúparapar (db; 3b) See *faaw, par*. nu. (T3) a soft red stone. [Euphemism for *féwúpwarapwar*.]

féwúpotopot (db; 3) See *faaw, potopot*. nu. (T3) a kind of stone (found on land).

féwúpwarapwar (db; 3b) See *faaw, pwaar*. Tbl. nu. (T3) a soft red stone. Cf. *féwúparapar*.

féwúpwech (3) See *faaw, pwech*. nu. (T3) white shell discs used as beads.

féwúpwós (4) See *faaw, -pwós*. nu. (T2) a large slab of stone. [Such a stone was used traditionally in building a *tinemey* type of house. The housebuilder lies down in the center of the house, and the stone is placed on his chest. It is then buried beneath the floor of the center of the house.]

féwúrupw Var. of *fowurupw*.

féwúrúpwúng (2) See *faaw, rúpwúng*. nu. (T3) kidney (?). *féwúrúpwúngún maan* animal's k.

féwúchón₁ (4) See *faaw, chón*. nu. (T2, T3) basalt. Syn. *achaw*.

féwúchón₂ (4) See *faaw, chón*. nu. (T2, T3) black beads made from mangrove wood or coconut shell.

féwúchchi (1) See *faaw, chii-*₁. nu. (T1) not yet fully formed turtle egg (*féwúchchiin pwáápwá*)

féwút (2) See *fé-*₁, *-wút*. num. four fingers, toes, tentacles, insect legs. Cf. *féchef, féyó*.

féwútún (3) See *faaw, túna-*. Tbl. n. (T3) clitoris. *féwútúnan* her c. Syn. *michikken*.

féwúwa- (3) See *féwú-*₁, *-wa-*. ni. (T3) thing plaited (by someone). *féwúwan* t. p. by him.

féwúwaramas (3) See *faaw, aramas*. nu. (T3) an isolated, large, upright stone ("human stone"), monolith.

féwúwach F. of *feyiyach*.

féwúwenewen (db; 3) See *féwú-*₁, *wenewen*₁. nu. (T3) straight weave in plaiting. vi. be woven straight.

féwúweney (2) FÉWÚWENEYI. nu. (T2) wooden bowl (small to medium-sized, flat-bottomed). *eew f.* one b. *sepiyan f.* his b. *féwúweneyin Chuuk* Trukese b. Cf. *namwmweechún*.

féwúwééw See *féwú-*₁, *-wééw*. nu. twill weave in plaiting.

féwúwéw (2) See *fé-*₁, *-wúwéw*. num. four amounts of fermented breadfruit suitable for kneading.

féwúwimw (3a) See *faaw, iimw*. Var. *feyiimw*. nu. (T3) cave ("shelter rock").

féwúwinuk (2) See *féwú-*₂, *nuk*. nu. (T2) place good for trolling (inside the Truk lagoon).

féwúwirá (1) See *faaw, irá*. nu. (T1) fruit (of a tree).

féwúwicho₁ (1) See *faaw, choo*₂. n. (T1) bicep or calf muscle. *féwúwichoon* his b. or c. m.

féwúwicho₂ (1) See *féwú-*₂ (?), *cho*. vi. beg pardon (with *wóón*). *aa f. wóón átánaan* he begged yonder fellow's pardon; *f. wóómw!* [I] beg your pardon! excuse me! Syn. *feyicho, tirow*.

féwúyeféw (2) See *faaw, eféw*. nu. (T2) mussel-shell pendant.

féwúyen (3) See *féwú-*₂, *een*₅. vi. be a good marksman. *emén meyi f.* one who is a good m.

féyaf (3b) See *fé-*₁, *-af*. Var. *feyaf*. num. four pieces of intestine.

féyang (3) See *fé-*₁, *-ang*. Var. *feyang*. num. four finger spans; four entire limbs (of the body).

féyef (2) See *fé-*₁, *eef*₁. Var. *feyef*. num. four bunches of ten ripe coconuts each.

féyem (2) See *fé-*₁, *eem*. Var. *feyem*. num. four earlobes.

féyep (2) See *fé-*₁, *epi-*₁. Var. *feyep*. num. four butt ends, lower ends, west ends.

féyék (2) See *fé-*₁, *ékkú-*. num. four nets.

féyi (3) See *fé-*₁, *-i*. num. four hands (of bananas). Syn. *feyin*₂, *feyiyey*.

féyipw (3) See *fé-*₁, *-ipw*. Var. *feyipw*. num. four steps; footprints, soles, pieces of footwear.

Féyiyew nu. (loc.) Gaferut Island (Central Caroline Islands). [This name is misapplied to what is called West Fayu on maps.] Syn. *Fayiyeweyirek*. Cf. *Kaferut*.

féyó (1) See *fé-$_1$, óó$_1$*. Var. *feyó*. num. four tentacles (of octopus or squid). Syn. *féchef, féwút*.

fi- (2) FI$_1$. Var. *fii-, ffi-*. unsp. attached, clinging.

-fi- FI$_2$. suf. (v.form.) makes an object focussed verb (vo.) of the base.

fi$_1$ (3) FIYA. vi., va. be squeezed, be pressed (of a button); squeeze. Dis. *fiyefi* (db). *fi kúsún* catch armored crabs (referring to method of killing them by squeezing between thumb and forefinger). *ewe feefin aa fi kúsún* the woman caught armored crabs.

fi$_2$ (1) FII$_1$. vi. flash, throw a spark (of lightning, electricity). Dis. *fiifi* (db). Cf. *ménúng, paach$_2$*.

fii- Var. of *fi-*.

fii (1) FII$_2$. nu. (T1) name of the consonant (unvoiced, labiodental spirant) written *f*; name of the letter thus written.

fiifi (db; 1) See *fi$_2$*. nu. (dis.; T1) flashing, sparkling, lightning; radiance. Cf. *inefi*. vi. (dis.) be flashing (as a light flashing on and off or as lightning).

fiisi$_1$ See *fi$_2$, -si-*. vo. (T4) transfer fire to, light (something) from a fire, set fire to (something) by holding (it) in a fire. Syn. *kkeni*. Cf. *ékúúw*.

Fiisi$_2$ (1) FIISII. (Eng.) nu. (loc.) Fiji.

fiisika (1) FIISIKAA. nu. (T1) fish spear. *efóch f.* one f. s. *wókun f.* his f. s. *fiisikaan Chuuk* Trukese f. s.

fiissópw N. of *fissópw*.

fiisnayin (Eng.) nu. fishline. *efóch f.* one f. *aan f.* his f. Syn. *óó*.

fiik (3) See *fúú-, -ik$_1$*. nu. (num.; T3) seventy. With c. pref. and ptv. const.: *efiikan* seventieth one. With suf. *-pár* or *-somw*: *fiikipár, fiikisomw* seventy plus, more than seventy. With pref. *nne-$_2$*: *nnefiik* seventieth (fraction).

fiikisomw See *fiik*.

fiikipár See *fiik*.

fiikkar (3) See *fi$_2$, kkar*. vi. be stubborn (in relation to an idea or opinion).

fiimwár (4) See *fii-, mwáár*. nu. flower garlands offered to gods and spirits of the newly dead by hanging them on a *faar* (staff or rod for this purpose).

fiimwáreey See *fiimwár, -e-$_2$*. vo. (T6b) offer garlands to.

fiin (3) FINA$_1$. F. [Uninflected in locative construction.] Var. *fin$_2$*. nu. (T3) woman, female person. *finen ekis* foreign w. *fiin iya na?* or *fiin iyan na?* w. of where that one with you? *fiin ikeey iya* or *fiin eey iya* w. of this place. *fiin Chuuk* w. of Truk, Trukese w.; *fiin ekis* foreign w.; *fiin Merika* American w.; *fiin Pwereka* w. of the Pwereka clan.

fiinó (1) See *fi, -nó*. vi. flash.

fiingngaw Var. of *finengngaw*.

fiipa (2) FIIPAA. nu. (T1) sickness associated with eating fermented breadfruit (symptoms being chills, fever and headache; also associated with tuberculosis).

fiir (2) FIRI. Tb1. n. (T2) labia minora. *firin* her l. m.

fiirowurow (2) See *fi$_2$ (?), -rowurow*. nu. (T2) a traditional rite in which the clothes and immediate personal effects of a dead person are burned on the fourth day after burial. [The deceased's good soul ascends to heaven in the smoke of the fire.]

fiffiit Dis. of *ffiit*.

fiffini Dis. of *fini*.

fiffich Dis. of *ffich*.

fiffiyon Dis. of *fiyon*.

fis (2) FISI. vi. happen, occur, take place, come to fruition, be brought to completion, be made, be accomplished. With dir. suf.: *fisitá*. Syn. *pwénútá*.

fisikéét (2: *-kéttú-*) See *fis, kéét*. vi. scratch a lot, keep scratching oneself. *aa men fóókkun f. átánaan* that fellow surely keeps scratching himself. *pwata ina fisikéttumw na?* why do you keep scratching yourself?

fisikkor (3) See *fis, kkor*. Tb1. vi. have an abundance of pubic hair.

fisingan Var. of *fisingngan*.

fisingngan (3b) See *fis, ngana-*. Tb1. vi. be tired from sexual intercourse (as after orgasm).

fisitá See *fis*.

fisu- (2) FISU. Var. *fusu-* pref. (num.) seven. [In this form used only with the cc. *-uw*.] Syn. *fúú-*. Cf. *fúús*.

fisuuw (3) See *fisu-, -uw*. Var. *fusuuw*. num. seven general class or non-specific things. With c. pref. and ptv.

const.: *efisuuwan* seventh one. With dis. c. pref.: *ekkefisuuw* be seven at a time. With pref. *nne-₂*: *nnefisuuw* seventh (fraction).

fisuk (Eng.) nu. fishhook. Syn. *éé*.

fissómwoon (2) See *fini-₁, sómwoon*. vi. choose a chief, hold an election.

fissópw (2) See *fini-₂, sópwu-₁*. Var. *fiissópw*. nu. (T2) wrapping of coconut cloth and rope on the end-piece of a canoe. Cf. *ffisópw*.

fin₁ (3a, 2) FINA₃, FINI₃. vi., adj. be twisted (of a part of the body only). Cf. *fittek, pinni, piti*.

fin₂ (3) See *fiin*. N. nu. woman [Used in locative construction.] *fin Chuuk* w. of Truk, Trukese w.; *fin Merika* American w.; *fin Pwereka* w. of the Pwereka clan. *fin iya na?* or *fin iyan na?* w. of where that one? *fin ikeey iya* or *fin eey iya* w. of this place. Cf. *mwáán, re*.

fina- (3) FINA₂. unsp. blow (of wind or breath). See *finefin*.

fináátá See *fini*.

fináng (2) FINÁNGNGI. nu. (T2) species of surgeon fish. *finángngin Chuuk* Trukese s. f.

fináyik (3) FINÁYIKA. (Eng.) nu. (T3) 1. flag. *fináyiken Merika* American f. 2. major administrative division of Truk from time of German rule until 1956 (since then replaced by island municipalities). *sómwoonun f.* flag chief (appointed head of major administrative division). Cf. *kúmi*.

finefin (db; 3) See *fina-*. nu. (dis.; T3) blowing. *finefinen ásápwan* b. of the wind. va. blow. With dir. suf.: *finefinenong, finefinenó, finefinetá, finefinetiw, finefineto, finefinewow, finefinewu*.

finefinenong See *finefin*.
finefinenó See *finefin*.
finefinetá See *finefin*.
finefinetiw See *finefin*.
finefineto See *finefin*.
finefinewow See *finefin*.
finefinewu See *finefin*.

finenipich (2) See *fiin, nipich*. nu. (T2) spinster, unmarried woman (including one formerly married), nun.

finenúk (2) See *fin₁, núkú-₃*. vi. be twisted (of arm).

finengngaw (3) See *fin₁, nngaw*. Var. *fiingngaw*. nu. (T3) sprain; strain of genital area; wrong cut or unsatisfactory planing of wood. *finengngawen pecheey* s. of my leg. vi. be sprained; strained; cut wrong. *aa f. pecheey* my leg has been s.

fineyiti See *fina-, -iti*. vo. (T2) blow upon, blow towards, blow at (of wind or breath). *ásápwán aa fineyitiyey* the wind blew upon me; *ngasangasey aa fineyituk* my breath has been blown upon you.

fini-₁ (2) FINI₁ unsp. choosing, selecting; electing, appointing.

fini-₂ (2) FINI₂. unsp. wrapping, bandaging. Cf. *fi-*.

fini See *fini-₁*. vo. (T2) choose, select, elect, appoint. Dis. *fiffini* (ds). With dir. suf.: *fináátá* elect, appoint. With n. form. suf.: *finiya-* (ni., T3) choice, thing chosen (by someone).

finifin (db; 2) See *fini-₂*. nu. (T2) wrapping, bandage. *finifinin sópwún waa* w. of a canoe's end-piece. vi. be wrapped, bandaged.

finikumwuch (2) See *fin₁, kumwuch*. nu. (T2) a hold or throw in hand-to-hand fighting. [One grasps an opponent's right wrist with one's left hand and the back of his right hand with one's right hand; then one twists his wrist clockwise and bends back his hand at the same time.]

finikúúween (2) See *fin₁, kúúween*. nu. kind of hold or throw in hand-to-hand fighting ("lizard twist"). [To make an unarmed opponent helpless, one seizes his left wrist with one's left hand, bringing his left arm down across his body, at the same time grabbing his right hand with one's right hand and bringing it across his left arm. One then runs one's right arm under his upper left arm and over his upper right arm, grabbing his left wrist in one's right hand. Then one bends him forward and grabs his other wrist from behind between his legs.]

Finipiin (Eng.) nu. (loc.) Philippines.

finipiineey See *Finipiin, -e-₂*. vo. (T6b) block (in cutting hair).

finiti See *fini-₂, -ti-*. vo. (T5) bandage; wrap cloth or matting around (end-piece of a canoe).

finiya- See *fini*.

finniichi See *fiin, -ichi*. [Presumably from *fine-ni-ichi*.] nu. first daughter; oldest of a group of sisters; oldest of a group of siblings of both sexes. Cf. *mwááníichi.*

fintosi Var. of *funtosi.*

fires (2) FIRESI. Var. *fúres.* nu. (T2) braid. *eew f.* one b. *aan f.* his b. *firesin mékúrey* b. of my head; *firesin pwotow* b. (handle) of my carrying case; *firesin éwéék* b. of a loom's backstrap. va. braid. Cf. *fi-.*

firesini See *fires, -ni-.* vo. (T5) braid. With n. form. suf.: *firesiniya-* (ni., T3) thing braided (by someone). Syn. *ffiresi.*

firesiniya- See *firesini.*

firosiki (1) FIROSIKII. (Jap. *furoshiki, huroshiki*) nu. (T1) cloth wrapper; parcel in a c. w. *eché f.* one c. w.; *eew f.* one parcel in a c. w. *aan f.* his c. w. Cf. *túkúm.*

-fich (2) FICHI₁. suf. (adj.) well, thoroughly; right handed. *angaangefich* work well; *ámwánnifich* conduct oneself in the respectful manner due to a middle-aged man (*mwáán*); *iifich* be right-handed.

ficha- (3a) FICHA. [As ni. in ptv. const. only.] ni. (T3), suf. (cc.) strip of coconut, pandanus, or other palm leaf prepared for plaiting mats. *efich, rúwéfich, wúnúfich, féfich, nimefich, wonofich, fúúfich, wanúfich, ttiwefich, engoon fichan* one,...ten s. of palm leaf; *fitefich* how many s. of palm leaf. *fichen núú* s. of coconut leaf; *fichen faach* s. of pandanus leaf; *fichen ténaaw* leaf s. for a mat.

fichan (3) FICHANA. N. [Presumably derived from *ficha-*.] nu. (T3) species of flounder. *emén f.* one f. *fichanen Chuuk* Trukese flounder. Syn. *épwúngúpwúng, ficheyitowunómw.*

fichekúkkún (2) See *ficha-, kúkkún.* F. vi. be of fine or narrow weave. Syn. *fichekkiis.*

fichekkiis (2) See *ficha-, -kkiis.* N. vi. be of fine or narrow weave. Syn. *fichekúkkún.*

fichemwoch (3) See *ficha-, mwoch.* vi. be woven of short strips.

fichenipwe (1) See *ficha-, pwee.* nu. (T1) young coconut leaf strips suitable for making knots (*pwee*) in divining.

fichennap (3a) See *ficha-, nap.* vi. be of wide weave. nu. (T3) third grade of pandanus mat (plaited from original, undoubled, inch-wide leaves). Syn. *nifichennap.*

ficheyitowunómw See *ficha-, towunómw.* N. nu. species of flounder ("leaf-strip of mosquito canopy"). Syn. *fichan, épwúngúpwúng.*

fichi- (2) FICHI₂. [In cpds. only.] unsp. snip (of scissors), snap (of a bowstring, of a camera or photograph).

fichiiy₁ See *fichi-, -i-₂.* vo. (T5) snip, cut (with scissors); snap (a camera or picture); photograph, take a picture of. *wúpwe f. sasingumw* I will snap your picture.

fichiiy₂ See *-fich, -i-₂.* vo. (adj.; T5) well, thoroughly. *féér fichiiy* do (something) well; *sineefichiiy* know (something) well.

fichipaat See *fichi-, paat₂.* vi. be always or continually snipping (with scissors) or snapping (with camera).

fichichééw (2) See *fichi-, chééw.* vi. be always snipping (with scissors) or snapping (with camera).

fichitoneey See *fichi-, toon₁, -e-₂.* vo. (T6b) snip or pinch the top or growing end off (a young tree). Cf. *pekútoneey, wuwapwpweey.*

fita- (3b: *fita-, fite-, fité-, fito-, fitó-*) FITA. [Possibly a cpd. of *fi-,* and *-t.*] Var. *fitu-.* pref. (num.) how many. [Used with suffixed counting classifiers.] See *fitaawut, fitaché, fitapé, fitayé, fite, fitechamw, fitechef, fitechchi, fitechchooch, fitechú, fitechúk, fitefew, fiteffaat, fiteffit, fitefich, fitefóch, fitefutuk, fitengaf, fitengát, fitengéréw, fitengin, fitekis, fitekkamw, fitekkap, fitekkumw, fitekum, fitekumwuch, fitekup, fitemach, fitemas, fitemataf, fitemech, fitemeech, fitemeet, fitemén, fitemma, fitemmech, fitemmék, fitemwénú, fitemwmwék, fitemwmwun, fitemwmwú, fitemwmwún, fitemwu, fitemwú₁, fitemwú₂, fitemwúch, fitennú, fitepa, fitepachang, fitepan, fitepeche, fitepeek, fitepék, fitepéw, fitepino, fitepinúk, fitepu, fitepwang, fitepwey, fitepwéét, fitepwi, fitepwin, fitepwopw, fitepwór, fitepwpwaaw, fitepwpwún, fitepwúkú, fitepwún, fitesap, fitesángá, fitesáwá, fiteseeng, fitesen, fitesópw₁, fitesópw₂, fitessaar, fitessak, firessar, fitessáát, fitessát, fitessupw, fitetinewupw, fitetip, fitetit, fitettiit, fitettún, fitetú, fitetúkúm, fitetún, fitewo, fitewoch, fitewumw, fitewupw, fitewúk₁, fitewúk₂, fitewún,* *fitewúwéw, fiteyaf, fiteyang, fiteyef, fiteyem, fiteyep, fiteyék, fiteyi, fiteyin₁, fiteyin₂, fiteyipw, fiteyiyey, fiteyó, fitéwút, fitowut, fitóówut.*

fitaanong See *fiti*.

fitaanó See *fiti*.

fitaato See *fiti*.

fitaawu See *fiti*.

fitaawut Var. of *fitóówut*.

fitapé (1) See *fita-, péé-₁*. num. how many empty containers?:

fitaché (1) See *fita-, -ché*. num. how many thin, flat objects (e.g., sheets, leaves, planks); how many songs? With c. pref. and ptv. const.: *efitachéén* what one (in a numbered series). With dis. c. pref.: *ekkefitaché* be how many at a time.

fitaw₁ (3) FITAWA. nu. (T3) a vine (*Merremia peltata*). [It is used for stringing breadfruit, and its large leaves are used to cover cooking pots in cooking breadfruit.] *fitawen Chuuk* Trukese *f.*. Cf. *fi-*.

Fitaw₂ [Presumably from *fitaw₁*.] nu. (loc.) a clan name. *fin F., fiin F.* F. woman; *mwáán F.* F. man. *chóón F.* people of F.

fitayé (1) See *fita-, -é*. num. how many threads or hairs?

fitá (1) FITÁÁ. nu. (T1) species of rudder fish.

fitáátá See *fiti*.

fitáátiw See *fiti*.

fite- See *fita-*.

fite (1) See *fita-, -e-₁*. num. how many nonspecific or general class of things (especially if the expected number is more than a few but less than hundreds). *f. párin* how many left over (when a large remainder is anticipated, cf. *fituuw párin*); *f. somwan* or *soomwan* how many more, how much more. Cf. *fituuw, fitengát*.

fiteféw (2) See *fita-, -féw*. num. how many lumps or globular objects (e.g., stones, balls, bananas).

fitefich (3a) See *fita-, ficha-*. num. how many strips of coconut, pandanus, or other palm leaf prepared for plaiting mats.

fitefóch (2) See *fita-, fóchu-*. num. how many long and roundish or sticklike objects (e.g., trees, vehicles, shovels, canoes, arms, legs, teeth, cigarettes).

fiteffaat (3) See *fita-, ffaata-*. num. how many strings of fish.

fiteffit (3) See *fita-, fitta-*. num. how many leaf packages of small fish.

fitesap (3) See *fita-, saap*. num. how many cheeks (especially of fish).

fitesángá (1) See *fita-, sángá*. num. how many basketfuls of fish. Syn. *fitesáwá*.

fitesáwá (1) See *fita-, sáwá*. num. how many basketfuls of fish. Syn. *fitesángá*.

fiteseeng (3) See *fita-, seeng*. num. how many lengths between joints or nodes.

fitesen (2) See *fita-, -sen*. num. how many coils or hanks of rope. [Each coil is 30 to 100 fathoms in length according to local custom.]

fitesópw₁ (2) See *fita-, sópwu-₂*. num. how many sections, divisions.

fitesópw₂ (4) See *fita-, sópwu-₃*. num. how many burdens of tied together breadfruit.

fitessaar (2) See *fita-, -ssaar*. Var. *fitessar*. num. how many slices.

fitessak (3) See *fita-, ssaka-*. num. how many pieces of copra.

fitessar Var. of *fitessaar*.

fitessáát (3) See *fita-, -ssáát*. Var. *fitessát*. num. how many slivers, longitudinal slices, splinters.

fitessát Var. of *fitessáát*.

fitessupw (2) See *fita-, ssupw-*. num. how many tiny drops.

fitekis (2) See *fita-, kisi-*. num. how many little things or bits.

fitekum (2) See *fita-, kumu-*. num. how many mouthfuls or swallows of liquid.

fitekumwuch (2) See *fita-, kumwuch*. num. how many fistfuls, handfuls (of something); how many hooves, paws, feet (of animals).

fitekkamw (3b) See *fita-, kkamw*. num. how many torn fragments or pieces (of cloth, paper).

fitekkap (3) See *fita-, kkap*. num. how many cupfuls.

fitekkumw (2, 3) See *fita-, kkumw₁*. num. how many portions of premasticated food.

fitemas (3) See *fita-, -mas*. num. how many things worn on the eyes (e.g., lenses of goggles) or attached to piercing weapons (e.g., spear points).

fitemach (3) See *fita-, macha-*. num. how many fishtails.

fitemataf (3) See *fita-*, *matafa-*. num. how many small portions, small amounts, little bits.

fitemeech (2) See *fita-*, *-meech*. F. Var. *fitemech*, *fitemmech*. num. how many portions of mashed breadfruit.

fitemeet (3) See *fita-*, *meet$_2$*. num. how many strands (of hair, fiber).

fitemech N. of *fitemeech*.

fitemén (2) See *fita-*, *maan$_1$*. num. how many persons or creatures (used with people, mammals, birds, fish, insects, but not with lobsters, crabs, sea cucumbers, or shell fish); how many knives, guns, files, scissors.

fitemma (1) See *fita-*, *-mma*. num. how many mouthfuls of premasticated food.

fitemmech N. of *fitemeech* (see *fita-*, *-mmech*).

fitemmék See *fita-*, *mékkú-*. num. how many shattered fragments.

fitemwénú (1) See *fita-*, *mwénúú-*. num. how many ells (lengths from elbow to fingertips).

fitemwu N. of *fitemwú$_2$*.

fitemwú$_1$ (1) See *fita-*, *mwúú-$_1$*. num. how many torn fragments (of rag or string).

fitemwú$_2$ (1) See *fita-*, *mwúú-$_1$*. num. how many sea cucumbers; how many pieces of feces.

fitemwúch (2) See *fita-*, *-mwúch*. num. how many pieces of firewood.

fitemwmék See *fita-*, *mwékkú-*. N. num. how many bits or morsels (of mashed food). Syn. *fitepwey*.

fitemwmun (3) See *fita-*, *mwmwuna-*. N. num. how many portions of *mwatún*. Syn. *fitetún*.

fitemwmwú N. of *fitemwú$_1$*.

fitemwmún F. of *fitemwmun*.

fitennú (1) See *fita-*, *nnúú-*. num. how many portions or loaves of breadfruit pudding; how many puddings' worth of breadfruit to be mashed.

fitengaf (3) See *fita-*, *ngaaf*. num. how many fathoms.

fitengát (2, 3) See *fita-*, *-ngát*. num. how many concave or hollow objects; (less common) how many nonspecific or general class of objects, how many holes. Cf. *fituuw*, *fite*, *fitepwang*.

fitengéréw (2) See *fita-*, *-ngéréw*. num. how many thousand.

fitengin (2) See *fita-*, *ngini-*. num. how many bits or pieces.

fitepa (1) See *fita-*, *-pa*. num. how many fronds, garlands, stalks with leaves (of palm trees, banana plants, *Cyrtosperma* taro, and also of leis and garlands, necklaces, bead belts).

fitepan (3) See *fita-*, *paan$_1$*. num. how many branches with leaves (of trees other than palms or bananas). Syn. *fitepachang*.

fitepachang (3) See *fita-*, *pachang$_1$*. num. how many branches (with their leaves). Syn. *fitepan*.

fitepeek (2) See *fita-*, *peek$_2$*. num. how many sides or pages.

fitepeche (1) See *fita-*, *peche*. num. how many lower or hind limbs (of humans, birds, and animals only).

fitepék (2) See *fita-*, *péék*. num. how many chips, cigarette butts.

fitepéw (2) See *fita-*, *-péw*. num. how many wings or things worn over hands and arms (e.g., gloves).

fitepino (1) See *fita-*, *pino*. num. how many small packages of breadfruit pudding.

fitepinúk (2) See *fita-*, *pinúk*. num. how many tied bundles, reams (of paper).

fitepu (1) See *fita-*, *puu-$_2$*. num. how many strokes distant or deep (in swimming).

fitepwang (3) See *fita-*, *pwaang*. num. how many holes, caves, cavities, pits, tunnels, hollows. Cf. *fitengát*.

fitepwey (2) See *fita-*, *-pwey*. num. how many pinches or morsels (of food). Syn. *fitemwmék*.

fitepwéét (2) See *fita-*, *pwéét*. num. how many noses.

fitepwi (1) See *fita-*, *pwii-$_1$*. num. how many groups, groves, flocks, herds, schools, swarms, convoys, etc.

fitepwin (2) See *fita-*, *pwiin$_3$*. num. how many nights.

fitepwopw (2) See *fita-*, *pwoopw*. num. how many tree trunks, bases, causes, origins, reasons, foundations, sources, beginnings.

fitepwór (4) See *fita-*, *pwóór*. num. how many boxes or crates (of something).

fitepwúkú See *fita-*, *-pwúkú*. num. how many hundred.

fitepwún (2) See *fita-*, *pwúún$_1$*. Var. *fitepwpwún*. num. how many broken-off pieces.

fitepwpwaaw (2) See *fita-, pwpwaaw.* num. how many home-made cigarettes.
fitepwpwún N. of *fitepwún.*
fitechamw (3) See *fita-, -chamw.* num. how many foreheads, brows, or similarly classed objects (e.g., visors, stem bases of coconut fronds); how many fishheads.
fitechef See *fita-, -chef.* num. how many tentacles (of octopus or squid); how many pieces of firewood. Syn. *fitéwút, fiteyó.*
fitechú (1) See *fita-, chúú.* num. how many bone segments (of meat).
fitechúk (2) See *fita-, chúúk.* num. four coconut leaf baskets.
fitechchi (1) See *fita-, -chchi.* num. how many drops.
fitechchooch (3) See *fita-, chchooch.* num. how many armfuls.
fitetinewupw See *fita-, tinewupw.* num. how many yards (lengths from the middle of one's chest to outstretched fingertips).
fitetip (3) See *fita-, tiip$_2$.* num. how many slices, chunks, or cut segments (of breadfruit and taro only).
fitetit (2) See *fita-, -tit.* num. how many strings (of breadfruit, usually ten to a string). Syn. *fitettiit.*
fitetú (3) See *fita-, túú.* Tb1. num. how many vulvas (in counting sexual encounters).
fitetúkúm (3) See *fita-, túkúm.* num. how many packages or packets.
fitetún (2) See *fita-, túnú-.* F. Var. *fitettún.* num. how many portions of *mwatún* pudding. Syn. *fitemwún.*
fitettiit (2) See *fita-, ttiit$_2$.* num. how many strings of ten breadfruit.
fitettún N. of *fitetún.* (See *ttúna-*).
fitewo (1) See *fita-, -wo.* num. how many clumps (of bananas).
fitewoch See *fita-, -woch.* Tn. num. how many kinds, sorts, rations, varieties, species. Syn. *fitóóch.*
fitewumw (2) See *fita-, wumwu-$_2$.* num. how many branching stalks (of bananas, fruit, clusters of pandanus, coral).
fitewupw (2) See *fita-, wupwu-$_1$.* num. how many breasts.
fitewut Var. of *fitowut.*
fitewúk$_1$ (2) See *fita-, wúúk$_1$.* num. how many tails (in counting fish).
fitewúk$_2$ (2) See *fita-, wúúk$_2$.* num. how many fingernails, toenails, claws.
fitewún (3a) See *fita-, wúún$_1$.* num. how many feathers, scales, hairs.
fitewúwéw (2) See *fita-, -wúwéw.* num. how many amounts of fermented breadfruit suitable for kneading.
fiteyaf (3b) See *fita-, -af.* num. how many pieces of intestine.
fiteyang (3) See *fita-, -ang.* num. how many finger spans; how many entire limbs (of the body).
fiteyef (2) See *fita-, eef$_1$.* num. how many bunches of ten ripe coconuts each.
fiteyem (2) See *fita-, eem.* num. how many earlobes.
fiteyep (2) See *fita-, epi-.* num. how many butt ends, lower ends, west ends.
fiteyék (2) See *fita-, ékkú-.* num. how many nets.
fiteyi (3) See *fita-, -i.* F. num. how many hands (of bananas). Syn. *fiteyin$_1$, fiteyiyey.*
fiteyin$_1$ (3) See *fita-, ina-$_2$.* N. num. how many hands of bananas. Syn. *fiteyi, fiteyiyey.*
fiteyin$_2$ (2) See *fita-, ini-$_2$.* num. how many shoots.
fiteyipw (3) See *fita-, -ipw.* num. how many footprints, soles, pieces of footwear.
fiteyiyey (3) See *fita-, iyeyiya-.* num. how many hands of bananas. Syn. *fiteyi, fiteyin$_1$.*
fiteyó (1) See *fita-, óó$_1$.* num. how many tentacles (of octopus or squid). Syn. *fitechef, fitéwút.*
fitéwút (2) See *fita-, -wút.* num. how many fingers or toes; tentacles, insect legs. Cf. *fiteyó, fitechef.*
fiti-$_1$ (2) See *fi-, ti-$_1$.* unsp. cling, adhere, attach.
fiti-$_2$ (2) See *fi-, ti-$_1$.* unsp. snarl, tangle, entwining.
fiti See *fiti-$_1$.* vo. (T2) accompany, go with, attend (school, a meeting), go in (a vehicle), take part in, be a member of, participate in; be the fault of, be attributable to, adhere to (of blame). *aa fituk* he accompanied you; it's your own fault (i.e. it goes with you). *epwe f. sepeniin* he will go by airplane. *f. fáán* go to church, attend church. With dir. suf.: *fitaanong, fitaanó* or

fitóónó, fitaato, fitaawu, fitaatá or *fitáátá, fitaatiw* or *fitáátiw*. Syn. *iti*.

fitikooko (1) See *fiti-₂, kooko*. nu. (T1) confusion, disorder. vi. be confused, entangled, mixed up, in disorder (political and social as well as material). Syn. *fitikuuku*.

fitikopwut (3b) See *fiti-₂, opwut*. vi. be awakened by a noise at night.

fitikuuku (1) See *fiti-₂, kuukuu-*. nu. (T1) confusion, disorder. vi. be in confusion, entangled, mixed up. Syn. *fitikooko*.

fitipach (3b) See *fiti-₁, pach*. vi. cling, stay with another constantly; be one who clings. *emén meyi f.* one who constantly clings (of a child).

fitipacheey See *fitipach, -e-₂*. vo. (T6b) cling to.

fitichu nu. kind of reef fish.

fitiyénú (1) See *fiti-₁* (or *fiti-₂*), *énú*. vi. be possessed by an evil spirit (with the result being some form of madness or seizure).

fitowut (2) See *fita-, wutu-*. Var. *fitewut*. num. how many cores (especially of breadfruit).

fitóónó See *fiti*.

fitóówut (3) See *fita-, owut*. Var. *fitaawut*. num. how many rows of thatch; what size of building.

fitu- Var. of *fita-*, found only in *fituuw*.

fituuw (3) See *fitu-, -uw*. num. how many nonspecific or general-class things (especially if the expected number is small). *f. párin* how much is left over (when the expected remainder is small; cf. *fite párin*); *f. somwan* or *soomwan* how much more. With c. pref. and ptv. const.: *efituuwan* what one (of a numbered series). Syn. *fitengát*. Cf. *fite*.

fitun (2) FITUNU. F. nu. (T2) ginger, white ginger (*Zingiber serumbet*). [It is used in food and medicines.] *fitunun Chuuk* Trukese g. Syn. *tunun, sinser*.

fitta- (3: *-ffit*) FITTA. ni. (T3), suf. (cc.) leaf package of small fish. *effit, rúwéffit, wúnúffit, féffit, nimeffit, wonoffit, fúúffit, wanúffit, ttiweffit, engoon fittan* one,...ten l. p.; *fiteffit* how many l. p. Syn. *túkúm*.

fittek (2) See *fin₁, -tek*. vi. be twisted, writhe.

fittiiy See *ffiit, -i-₂*. vo. (T5) wind upon, twine about; wind (something) up (as a fishline on a stick), cause to be wound up or twined about. Syn. *áfitti, efitti*.

fittinikoch vi. turn the hands back and forth in dancing. Cf. *fin₁*.

fiyeey See *fi₁, -e-₂*. vo. (T6b) squeeze between the fingers, press with the fingers, strangle. *f. nowumw tengki* press (the button on) your flashlight.

fiyefi Dis. of *fi₁*.

fiyefiya- (db; 3) See *fi₁*. [In ptv. const. only.] ni. (T3) thing to be pressed or squeezed. *fiyefiyan* its (the flashlight's) button. *fiyefiyen tengki* flashlight button, light switch.

fiyefiyeey See *fi₁, -e-₂*. vo. (dis.; T6b) massage by squeezing (as a calf muscle). *etto f. pecheey eey* come m. my leg here. Cf. *rawááni*.

fiyekúsún (2) See *fi₁, kúsún*. nu. (T2) armored crab catching ("crab squeezing," crabs being squeezed between thumb and fingers to kill them when they are caught).

fiyemas (3) See *fi₁, maas₃*. nu. (T3) thumbing an opponent's eye in fighting.

fiyepwerik (3) See *fi₁, pwerik*. nu. (T3) species of surgeon fish (*Zebrasoma vileferum* <Kuiyama>). [Said to be very scratchy or bitter (*pwerik*) to the taste.]

fiyon (3) FIYONA. nu. (T3) hunger. *aan f.* his h. vi. be hungry. Dis. *fiffiyon* (ds). *wúwa f.* I am h.

fiyuus nu. sickness with the symptoms of advanced tuberculosis of the bones, accompanied by physical collapse, rot, and stench.

fiyuuw (2) FIYUUWU. nu. (T2), vi. fight. *sowun f.* soldier.

fo- See *fé-₁*. [Occurs in this form only when first vowel of following base is *o, ó, u*.] pref. (num.) four. See *fofóch, fopwopw, fosópw, fowoch, fowo, fowumw, fowut₂*.

foo (1) FOO. Tbl. n. (T1) labia majora. *foon* or *aamen foon* her l. m.

foones nu. elevated sitting board extending from the lee platform across the body of a sailing canoe (one on each side of the mast).

foorket (Eng.) nu. forget-me-not. *énúwen foorket* purple.

fofóch Var. of *féfóch*.

fosópw Var. of *fésópw*.

Trukese-English fóós

fokunun (2) nu. (T2) kind of fish.
fonuupwa (1) FONUUPWAA. nu. (T1) an alcholic drink made from the sap of the unopened coconut blossom. [It differs from *áchimmwán* in that a large container is kept under the blossom for a longer period so that fresh sap mixes with the already fermenting sap in the container, and the result is a sweet drink that is intoxicating rather than a sour one.]
fongo- (3a) FONGA. [Presumably derived from c. pref. *fa-$_2$* and an old *ngo.] vi. sniff, blow through the nose. With dir. suf.: *fongotá* sniff up through the nose; *fongotiw* blow down through the nose.
fongopwéét (2) See *fongo-, pwéét.* vi. blow the nose.
fongoti See *fongo-, -ti-.* vi. (T5) blow (one's nose). *kepwe f. pwootumw* b. your nose.
fopwopw Var. of *fépwopw.*
fochchuk Var. of *fóchchuk.*
fochchukuuw Var. of *fóchchukuuw.*
fotu- Var. of *fóto-$_2$.*
fotuki Rmn. of *fótuki.*
fowo (1) See *fo-, -wo.* num. four clumps (of bananas).
fowoch See *fo-, -woch.* Tn. num. four sorts, kinds, varieties, species, rations. Syn. *fóóch.*
fowumw Var. of *féwumw.*
fowumwo Var. of *féwúmwo.*
fowumwoomwo Dis. of *fowumwo* (see *féwúmwo* and *féwúmwoomwo*).
fowunó (1) See *féwú-$_2$, -nó.* Var. *féwúnó.* nu. (T1) be much talked about (in a positive or envious way), be famous. *iiy meyi f.* he is famous.
fowurupw (2) See *faaw, rupwu-.* Var. *féwúrupw.* nu. (T2) mushroom coral. *fowurupwun neeset* m. c. in the sea.
fowucho (1) See *faaw, choo$_2$.* nu. (T1) very hard stone. *eféw f.* one h. s.
fowut$_1$ (3) FOWUTA. n. (T3) adornment, ornament, decoration, best clothing, costume. [It may be used to refer to deeds as things subsequently adorning the performer.] *fowutan* his a. *ningééchchún fowuten átánaan!* how handsomely yonder fellow is dressed! vi. be ornamented, decorated with ornaments, bedecked, dressed up. Dis. *fowutowut* (db). *neminnaan aa kon nniyen fowutowut* that woman is o. too much.

fowut$_2$ (2) See *fo-, wutu-.* num. four cores (especially of breadfruit), four chunks of cooked breadfruit.
fowuteey See *fowut, -e-$_2$.* vo. (T6b) decorate (someone) with ornaments, adorn, dress (someone) up. *wúpwe fowuteeyey* I shall dress myself up; *wúpwe fowuteyok* I shall adorn you.
fowutong See *faaw, tong.* nu. sharp coral (painful to touch).
fó-$_1$ See *fé-$_1$.* [Occurs in this form only when first vowel of following base is *o, ó.*] Var. *f-, fa-, fé-, fo-.* pref. (num.) four. See *fóóch, fówo, fóówut.*
fó-$_2$ Var. of *fa-$_2$* (see *fóchchuk, fóós, fóssó*).
fóó- (1) FÓÓ. unsp. (u.m.) element in place names. *Fóó-nu-pi* Ponape; *Fóó-són* a district on Toon (Tol) Island, so named because the ground is level (*sónósónééch*). Cf. *-fa.*
fóós (4) FÓÓSO. [Perhaps derived from *fó-$_2$* and *woos$_2$.*] n. (T2) spoken word; language; vocabulary. *aan f.* his words (what he says). *f. énnúkún roong* the special injunctions surrounding every item of magical knowledge (*roong*), such as food tabus and other restrictions upon the conduct of a practitioner and his clients; *f. meyi mááyirú, fóósun mááyirú* exclamation of alarm; *f. mwónómwón* secret talk, encoded talk, talk whose meaning is disguised, parable; *f. nangattam* sentence; *f. niyoos* depiction in words, verbal sketch; *f. péchékkún* hard language, rough or coarse talk, talk that does not mince words. *fóósun Chuuk* Trukese language; *fóósun akkafachaamas* vocabulary that cannot be freely used in the presence of everyone, shocking talk; (for details see *akkafachaamas*); *fóósun kkééneemóówun* or *fóósun kékkééneemóówun* any word of the first order of prohibited usage (tabu level 1), chiefly the vocabulary relating to male and female genitalia ("words for calling in combat"); *fóósun nenneyiruk* exclamation of surprise; *fóósun nukunuk waa* the technical vocabulary of navigation. va. speak. *f. ámááyirú* exclaim with alarm; *f. mwaramwar* speak with uncertainty; *f. mwónómwón* speak in secret, in parables; *f. niyoos* depict something in words; *f. paat* talk all the time. With

fóóseey   Trukese-English

dir. suf.: *fóósónó wóón* speak ahead of (someone), take precedence in speaking over (someone), stand and speak in the presence of ("speak off above one"); use *itang* language during the lifetime of an older brother; make a speech in the presence of one's chief.

fóóseey See *fóós, -e-$_2$*. vo. (T6b) talk about. *raa fóóseyok* they talked about you.

fóósechchin Var. of *fóósuchchin.*

fóósón (4) See *fóó-, sóón$_4$*. nu. (loc.; T2) region of slightly higher, fairly level ground back from the shore (traditionally preferred for settlement and cultivation).

fóósónó See *fóós.*

fóósumw nu. netting technique by which sling stone carriers are made.

fóósuchchin (2) See *fóós, chchin.* Var. *fóósechchin.* vi. be hurried in speech, talk rapidly. *kete f.* don't talk fast.

fóók (2) FÓÓKKU. (Eng.) nu. (T2) fork. *fóókkun Merika* American f. *re mwémwmwéngé ngeni f.* they eat with forks.

fóókkeey See *fóók, -e-$_2$*. vo. (T6b) eat (something) with a fork, apply a fork to.

fóókkii Var. of *fóókkun* (used before monosyllables).

fóókkun Var. of *fókkun.*

Fóónupi nu. (loc.) Ponape Island, Eastern Caroline Islands. Syn. *Pwonape.*

fóór (2) FÓÓRU. nu. (T2) variety of banana. [Its fiber is used in loom weaving.] *efóch f.* one b. tree. Id. *achawaren f.* war indemnity or price of peace (paid by the losers to the victors in settlement of a war).

fóóróchón (3) See *fóór, chón.* nu. (T3) variety of banana (not the same as *fóór*).

fóóch See *fó-$_1$, -óch.* num. four sorts, kinds, varieties, species, rations. Syn. *fowoch.*

fóówut (3) See *fó-$_1$, owut.* num. four rows of thatch.

fósooso (1) FÓSOOSOO. [Possibly from *fó-$_2$* and *soo-$_1$*.] vi. be uneven or unequal in height or length (of long or tall things), be irregular in arrangement (as books on a shelf).

fóssó (1) See *fó-$_2$, ssó.* nu. (T1) step or rung (of a ladder).

fókun F. Var. *fakun.* nu. variety of breadfruit.

fókkun FÓKKU. Var. *fakkun, fóókkun, fókkii, fóókkii.* vr. indeed, very, absolutely (intensifies positive or negative aspect of an utterance). *f. éech* be very fine, very nice, fine indeed. *ese f. wor* (or *ese fókkii wor*) there is absolutely none. *f. meyi wor* there really is; is there really?

fón (3) FÓNA. vi. be pampered, coddled, cherished, spoiled (of children). Syn. *pwó.* Cf. *ffóón$_2$.*

fónófónónó See *fana-$_2$.*

fónónó See *fana-$_2$.*

fónnuni See *ffóón$_2$, -ni-.* vo. (T5) raise, tend, herd (an animal). Cf. *afóna.*

fóro- (4) FÓRO. Var. *fara-.* unsp. strangling, hanging (by the neck).

fóropach (3b) See *fóro-, pach.* N., Tb3. Var. *farapach.* vi. embrace, engage in petting; be embraced (as with husband and wife in sleep).

fórusi See *fóro-, -si-.* vo. (T5) strangle, hang (someone) by the neck; embrace. *aa pwisin f.* he hanged himself.

fócha- (4) FÓCHO$_1$. [In dc and db forms only.] unsp. always, continuously, all the time, constantly; for good.

fócho- (4) FÓCHO$_2$. unsp. facial set, mien.

fóchofóch (db; 3b) See *fócho-.* vi. be sullen faced.

fóchongngaw (3b) See *fócho-, ngngaw.* vi. be cranky, scolding, cross.

fóchoyéech (2) See *fócho-, éech.* vi. be of cheerful disposition, be pleasant faced.

fóchófóch (db; 3b) See *fócha-.* adj. (dis.) constantly, all the time, always, continuously. *aaya f.* use c.

fóchu- (4) FÓCHO$_3$. [As ni. in ptv. const. only.] ni. (T2), suf. (cc.) cylindrical, sticklike, or long and rounded object (e. g., canoe, vehicle, arm, leg, tooth, post, tree, timber, cigarette, pencil, shovel, string of fish, piece of rope, burden of breadfruit on a carrying pole). *efóch, rúwéfóch* or *rúwofóch, wúnúfóch, ffóch* or *féfóch* or *fofóch, nimefóch* or *niffóch, wonofóch, fúúfóch, wanúfóch, ttiwefóch, engoon fóchun* one,...ten c. objects; *fitefóch* how many c. objects? *efóch waa* one canoe; *efóch suupwa* one cigarette. With c. pref. and ptv. const.: *ááfóchun* or *áyefóchun, érúwéfóchun* first c. object, second c. object (etc.). With dis.

c. pref.: *ákkááfóch* or *ákkáyefóch, ékkérúwéfóch* one c. object at a time, two at a time (etc.). With pref. *áná-*: *ánááfóch* or *ánáyefóch, ánárúwéfóch* sole or only c. object, sole or only c. objects (etc.).

fóchchuk (2) See *fó-₂, chuku-₁*. Var. *fochchuk*. va. elbow one's way, engage in hitting or pushing aside with the elbows. nu. (T2) distance from the outstretched fingertips of right hand and arm across the chest to the elbow of the left arm when the fingertips of the left hand are touching the middle of the chest (a unit of measure). *eew f.* one unit of d.

fóchchukuuw See *fóchchuk, -u-*. Var. *fochchukuuw*. vo. (T5) elbow (someone).

fótaa- (1v) See *fóto-₂ -a-₂*. [From an earlier **fótoka-*.] Var. *fotaa-*. ni. (T1v) plant, thing planted or to be planted. *fótaan* thing planted by him. *fótáán átánaan* thing planted by that fellow.

fóto-₁ (4) FÓTO₁. unsp. pertaining to scrutiny and hence betrothal.

fóto-₂ (4) FÓTO₂. Var. *fotu-*. unsp. planting.

fótoneeyimw (3) See *fóto-₁ nee-, iimw*. Wmn. nu. (T3) marriage by a man with his paternal cross-cousin or with a woman of his father's *eterekes*.

fótopwasuk (2) See *fóto-₂ pwasuk*. Var. *fótopwósuk*. vi. kneel. Syn. *fótopwúkú, fótupwúkú*.

fótopwósuk Var. of *fótopwasuk*.

fótopwúkú Var. of *fótupwúkú*.

fótónap (3) See *fóto-₂, nap*. nu. (T3) feast. Syn. *mwéngéénap*.

fótukáátiw See *fótuki*.

fótuki See *fóto-₂, -ki-*. vo. (T5) plant (something). With dir. suf.: *fótukáátiw*. With n. form. suf.: *fótukiya-* (cf. *fótaa-*) thing planted (by someone). *fótukiyomw efóch cheepen* your responsibility is one table (of food for the party)("the thing to be planted by you is one table").

fótukiya- See *fótuki*.

fótupwúkú (3) See *fóto-₂, pwúkú*. Var. *fótopwúkú*. vi. kneel. Syn. *fótopwasuk, fótopwósuk*.

fówo (1) See *fó-₁, -wo₁*. num. four clumps (of bananas).

fuu- See *fúú-*.

fuuto (1) FUUTOO. (Jap. *fuutoo*) Var. *fúúto*. nu. (T1) envelope (for mailing). *eché f.* one e. *aan f.* his e.

fuuwut (2) See *fúú-, wutu-*. num. seven cores (especially of breadfruit), seven chunks of cooked breadfruit.

fusu- Var. of *fisu-*.

fusuuw Var. of *fisuuw*.

funtosi (1) FUNTOSII. (Jap. *fundoshi, hundoshi*) Var. *fintoosi, fúntoosi*. nu. (T1) string-fastened loincloth (of Japanese type). *eché f.* one l. *aan f.* his l.

furay (2) FURAYI. (Jap. *furai*, from Eng.) nu. (T2) fly ball (in baseball). *eew f.* one f. b.

furayini See *furay, -ni-*. vo. (T5) hit (a fly ball, in baseball). *f. na pwoor* h. the ball (as a fly).

furayipaang (3) FURAYIPAANGA. (Jap. *furaipan, huraipan*, from Eng.) Var. *farayipáán*. nu. (T3) frying pan, skillet. *eew f.* one f. *aan f.* his f.

furiyo (1) FURIYOO. (Jap. *furyoo*) nu. (T1) bad person.

futong (3) FUTONGA. (Jap. *futon*) Var. *ftong*. nu. (T3) mattress. *eew f.* one m. *futongen Merika* American m.

futuk (3) FUTUKA. n. (T3) 1. meat, flesh, muscle (of humans, animals, fish). *efutuk* one piece of m.; *óóch f.* one indefinite amount (some) of m. *wochaan f.* his meat (to eat); *aan f.* his meat (for eating but not his portion). *futuken inisiy* flesh of my body; *futuken iik* fish meat; *futuken kkowu* beef; *futuken piik* pork. 2. matrilineage (matrilineal lineage), a group of people descended matrilineally from a single ancestress with the active tradition of a common ancestral source; (with suf. pos. prn.) lineage or kindred mate, fellow member of one's matrilineage or of one's personal consanguineal kindred (whether matrilineally related or otherwise). *futukan* his lineage; his lineage or kindred mate. suf. (cc.) piece of meat. *efutuk, rúwéfutuk, wúnúfutuk, féfutuk, nimefutuk, wonofutuk, fúúfutuk, wanúfutuk, ttiwefutuk* one,...nine p. of m.

futukopar (3b) See *futuk, par*. nu. (T3) red flesh exposed by a cut. vi. have r. f. exposed by a cut.

futukopwa (1) See *futuk, pwa*. nu. (T1) proud flesh (i.e., what remains after pus has been removed from a wound or infected area); spoiled meat, contaminated meat.

futukotuk (db; 3) See *futuk*. vi. (dis.) be fleshy, meaty.

fúú- (1: *fii-, fuu-, fúú-*) FÚÚ₂. pref. (num.) seven. Syn. *fisu-, fusu-*. See *fiik, fuuwut, fúffat, fúnnú* or *fúúnnú, fúpwpwaaw, fúúchamw, fúúchef, fúúchchi, fúúchchooch, fúúché, fúúchú, fúúchúk, fúúféw, fúúffit, fúúfich, fúúfóch, fúúfutuk, fúúngaf, fúúngát, fúúngéréw, fúúngin, fúúkis, fúúkit, fúúkkamw, fúúkkap, fúúkkumw, fúúkum, fúúkumwuch, fúúkup, fúúmach, fúúmas, fúúmataf, fúúmech, fúúmeech, fúúmeet, fúúmén, fúúmma, fúúmmech, fúúmmék, fúúmwénú, fúúmwmwék, fúúmwmwun, fúúmwmwú, fúúmwmwún, fúúmwu, fúúmwú₁, fúúmwú₂, fúúmwúch, fúúpa, fúúpachang, fúúpan, fúúpeche, fúúpeek, fúúpé, fúúpék, fúúpéw, fúúpino, fúúpinúk, fúúpu, fúúpwang, fúúpwey, fúúpwéét, fúúpwi, fúúpwin, fúúpwopw, fúúpwór, fúúpwpwún, fúúpwúkú, fúúpwún, fúúsap, fúúsángá, fúúsáwá, fúúseeng, fúúsen, fúúsópw₁, fúúsópw₂, fúússaar, fúússak, fúússar, fúússáát, fúússát, fúússupw, fúútinewupw, fúútip, fúútit, fúúttiit, fúúttún, fúútú, fúútúkúm, fúútún, fúúwéw, fúúwo, fúúwoch, fúúwumw, fúúwupw, fúúwúk₁, fúúwúk₂, fúúwún, fúúwút, fúúyaf, fúúyang, fúúyef, fúúyem, fúúyep, fúúyé, fúúyék, fúúyi, fúúyin₁, fúúyin₂, fúúyipw, fúúyiyey, fúúyowut, fúúyó, fúúyóch.* Cf. *fúús.*

fúú (1, 3) FÚÚ₁, FÚÚWA. nu. (T1, T3) star. *fúúwen nááng, fúún nááng* s. of heaven. *aa áás eféw f.* there was a shooting star ("a star has flown").

fúúféw (2) See *fúú-, -féw.* num. seven lumps or globular shaped objects (e.g., stones, balls, bananas, seeds).

fúúfich (3a) See *fúú-, ficha-.* num. seven strips of coconut, pandanus, or other palm leaf prepared for plaiting mats.

fúúfóch (2) See *fúú-, fóchu-.* num. seven cylindrical, sticklike, or long rounded objects (e. g., cigarettes, sticks, trees, vehicles, canoes, teeth, arms, legs).

fúúfutuk (3) See *fúú-, futuk.* num. seven pieces of meat.

fúúffit (3) See *fúú-, fitta-.* num. seven leaf packages of small fish.

fúús (2, 3) FÚSA, FÚSÚ. nu. (num.) the number seven. [Used in serial counting or to name the number in the abstract, but not used as a numerical adjective.] Cf. *fisu-, fusu-, fúsewaan, fúú-.*

fúúsap (3) See *fúú-, saap.* num. seven cheeks (especially of fish).

fúúsángá (1) See *fúú-, sángá.* num. seven basketfuls of fish. Syn. *fúúsáwá.*

fúúsáwá (1) See *fúú-, sáwá.* num. seven basketfuls of fish. Syn. *fúúsángá.*

fúúseeng (3) See *fúú-, seeng.* num. seven lengths between joints or nodes.

fúúsemwékút (2) See *fúú, se, mwékút.* nu. (T2) North Star (Polaris) ("star-not-moving").

fúúsen (2) See *fúú-, -sen.* num. seven coils or hanks of rope. [Each coil is 30 to 100 fathoms long according to local custom.]

fúúsópw₁ (2) See *fúú-, sópwu-₂.* num. seven sections or divisions.

fúúsópw₂ (4) See *fúú-, sópwu-₃.* num. seven burdens of tied together breadfruit.

fúússaar (2) See *fúú-, -ssaar.* Var. *fúússar.* num. seven slices.

fúússak (3) See *fúú-, ssaka-.* num. seven pieces of copra.

fúússar N. of *fúússaar.*

fúússáát (2) See *fúú-, -ssáát.* Var. *fúússát.* num. seven slivers, longitudinal slices, splinters.

fúússát N. of *fúússáát.*

fúússupw (2) See *fúú-, ssupwu-.* num. seven tiny drops.

fúúkis (2) See *fúú-, kisi-.* num. seven little things or bits.

fúúkit (3) See *fúú-, kita-.* num. seventy thousand, seven units of ten thousand.

fúúkum (2) See *fúú-, kumu-.* num. seven mouthfuls or swallows of liquid.

fúúkumwuch (2) See *fúú-, kumwuch.* num. seven fistfuls, handfuls (of something); seven hooves, paws, feet (of animals).

fúúkkamw (3b) See *fúú-, kkamw.* num. seven torn fragments or pieces (of cloth or paper).

fúúkkap (3) See *fúú-, kkap.* num. seven cupfuls.

fúúkkumw (2, 3) See *fúú-, kkumw₁.* num. seven portions of premasticated food.

fúúmas (3) See *fúú-*, *-mas*. num. seven things worn on the eyes (e.g., lenses of goggles) or attached to piercing weapons (e.g., spear points).

fúúmach (3) See *fúú-*, *macha-*. num. seven fishtails.

fúúmataf (3) See *fúú-*, *matafa-*. num. seven small portions, small amounts, little bits.

fúúmeech (2) See *fúú-*, *-meech*. F. Var. *fúúmmech*. num. seven portions of mashed breadfruit.

fúúmeet (3) See *fúú-*, *meet$_2$*. num. seven strands (of hair, rope).

fúúmech N. var. of *fúúmeech*.

fúúmén (2) See *fúú-*, *maan$_1$*. num. seven persons or creatures (with people, mammals, birds, lizards, insects; but not with lobsters, crabs, sea cucumbers, or shellfish); seven knives, guns, files, scissors.

fúúmma (1) See *fúú-*, *-mma*. num. seven mouthfuls of premasticated food.

fúúmmech N. of *fúúmeech* (see *fúú-*, *-mmech*).

fúúmmék (2) See *fúú-*, *mékkú-*. num. seven shattered fragments.

fúúmwénú (1) See *fúú-*, *mwénúú-*. num. seven ells (lengths from elbow to fingertips).

fúúmwu N. of *fúúmwú$_2$*.

fúúmwú$_1$ (1) See *fúú-*, *mwúú-$_1$*. num. seven torn fragments of rag or string.

fúúmwú$_2$ (1) See *fúú-*, *mwúú-$_2$*. num. seven sea cucumbers; seven pieces of feces.

fúúmwúch (2) See *fúú-*, *-mwúch*. num. seven pieces of firewood.

fúúmwmwék See *fúú-*, *mwékkú-*. N. num. seven bits or morsels (of mashed food). Syn. *fúúpwey*.

fúúmwmwun (3) See *fúú-*, *mwmwuna-*. N. Var. *fúúmwmwún*. num. seven portions of *mwatún* pudding. Syn. *fúútún*.

fúúmwmwú N. of *fúúmwú$_1$*.

fúúmwmwún F. of *fúúmwmwun*.

fúúnnú Var. of *fúnnú*.

fúúngaf (3) See *fúú-*, *ngaaf*. num. seven fathoms.

fúúngát (2) See *fúú-*, *-ngát*. num. seven concave or hollow objects; (less common) seven nonspecific or general-class things.

fúúngéréw (2) See *fúú-*, *-ngéréw*. num. seven thousand.

fúúngin (2) See *fúú-*, *ngini-*. num. seven bits or pieces.

fúúpa (1) See *fúú-*, *-pa*. num. seven fronds, garlands, stalks with leaves (of palm fronds, banana leaves, Cyrtosperma taro stalks, leis, garlands, necklaces, bead belts).

fúúpan (3) See *fúú-*, *paan$_1$*. num. seven branches with leaves (of trees other than palms and bananas). Syn. *fúúpachang*.

fúúpachang (3) See *fúú-*, *pachang$_1$*. num. seven branches with leaves. Syn. *fúúpan*.

fúúpeek (2) See *fúú-*, *peek$_2$*. num. seven sides, pages.

fúúpeche (1) See *fúú-*, *peche*. num. seven lower or hind limbs (of humans, birds, and animals only).

fúúpé (1) See *fúú-*, *péé-$_1$*. num. seven empty containers.

fúúpék (2) See *fúú-*, *péék$_2$*. num. seven chips, cigarette butts.

fúúpéw (2) See *fúú-*, *-péw*. num. seven wings or things worn over hand or arm (e.g., gloves).

fúúpino (1) See *fúú-*, *pino*. num. seven small packages of breadfruit pudding.

fúúpinúk (2) See *fúú-*, *pinúk*. num. seven tied bundles, reams (of paper).

fúúpu (1) See *fúú-*, *puu-$_2$*. num. seven strokes in swimming (in measuring distance).

fúúpwang (3) See *fúú-*, *pwaang*. num. seven holes, caves, cavities, pits, tunnels, hollows. Cf. *fúúngát*.

fúúpwey (2) See *fúú-*, *-pwey*. num. seven pinches or morsels (of food). Syn. *fúúmwmwék*.

fúúpwéét (2) See *fúú-*, *pwéét*. num. seven noses.

fúúpwi (1) See *fúú-*, *pwii-$_1$*. num. seven groups, groves, flocks, schools, herds, swarms, convoys, etc.

fúúpwin (2) See *fúú-*, *pwiin$_3$*. num. seven nights.

fúúpwopw (2) See *fúú-*, *pwoopw*. num. seven tree trunks, bases, foundations, causes, sources, beginnings, origins, reasons.

fúúpwór (4) See *fúú-*, *pwóór*. num. seven boxes or crates (of something).

fúúpwúkú (1) See *fúú-*, *-pwúkú*. num. seven hundred.

fúúpwún (2) See *fúú-, pwúún₁*. Var. *fúúpwpwún*. num. seven broken off pieces.

fúúpwpwún N. of *fúúpwún*.

fúúráán (2) See *fúú, ráán₂*. nu. (T2) Venus as the morning star.

fúúchamw (3) See *fúú-, -chamw*. num. seven foreheads, brows, or similarly classed objects (e.g., visors, stem bases of coconut fronds); seven fishheads.

fúúchef See *fúú-, -chef*. num. seven tentacles (of octopus or squid); seven pieces of firewood. Syn. *fúúwút, fúúyó*.

fúúché (1) See *fúú-, -ché*. num. seven thin, flat objects (e.g., leaves, sheets of paper, planks); seven songs.

fúúchú (1) See *fúú-, chúú*. num. seven bone segments (of meat).

fúúchúk (2) See *fúú-, chúúk*. num. seven coconut leaf baskets.

fúúchchi See *fúú-, -chchi*. num. seven drops (as of rain).

fúúchchooch (3) See *fúú-, chchooch*. num. seven armfuls.

fúútinewupw (2) See *fúú-, tinewupw*. num. seven yards (lengths from center of chest to outstretched fingertips).

fúútip (3) See *fúú-, tiip₂*. num. seven slices, chunks or cut segments (of breadfruit or taro).

fúútit (2) See *fúú-, -tit*. num. seven strings (of breadfruit, usually ten to a string). Syn. *fúúttiit*.

fúútú (3) See *fúú-, túú*. Tbl. num. seven vulvas (in counting sexual encounters).

fúútúkúm (2, 3) See *fúú-, túkúm*. num. seven packages or packets.

fúútún (2) See *fúú-, túnú-*. F. Var. *fúúttún*. num. seven portions of *mwatún* pudding.

fúúttiit (2) See *fúú-, ttiit₂*. num. seven strings of ten breadfruit.

fúúttún N. of *fúútún* (see *ttúna-*).

fúúwéw (2) See *fúú-, -wúwéw*. num. seven amounts of fermented breadfruit suitable for kneading.

fúúwo (1) See *fúú-, -wo₁*. num. seven clumps (of bananas).

fúúwoch Tn. of *fúúyóch* (see *fúú-, -woch*).

fúúwumw (2) See *fúú-, wumwu-₂*. num. seven branching stalks (of bananas, fruit, clusters of pandanus, coral).

fúúwupw (2) See *fúú-, wupwu-₁*. num. seven breasts.

fúúwúk₁ (2) See *fúú-, wúúk₁*. num. seven tails, rear ends.

fúúwúk₂ (2) See *fúú-, wúúk₂*. num. seven fingernails, toenails, claws.

fúúwún (3a) See *fúú-, wúún₁*. num. seven feathers, hairs, fishscales.

fúúwút (2) See *fúú-, -wút*. num. seven fingers or toes, tentacles, insect legs. Cf. *fúúchef, fúúyó*.

fúúyaf (3b) See *fúú-, -af*. num. seven pieces of intestine.

fúúyang (3) See *fúú-, -ang*. num. seven finger spans; seven entire limbs (of the body).

fúúyef (2) See *fúú-, eef₁*. num. seven bunches of ten ripe coconuts each.

fúúyem (2) See *fúú-, eem*. num. seven earlobes.

fúúyep (2) See *fúú-, epi-*. num. seven butt ends, lower ends, west ends.

fúúyé (1) See *fúú-, -é*. num. seven hairs, threads. Cf. *fúúmeet*.

fúúyék (2) See *fúú-, ékkú-*. num. seven nets.

fúúyi (3) See *fúú-, -i*. Rmn. num. seven hands of bananas. Syn. *fúúyin₁, fúúyiyey*.

fúúyin₁ (3) See *fúú-, ina-₂*. N. num. seven hands of bananas. Syn. *fúúyi, fúúyiyey*.

fúúyin₂ (2) See *fúú-, ini-₂*. num. seven shoots.

fúúyipw (3) See *fúú-, -ipw*. num. seven steps, footprints, soles; seven items of footwear.

fúúyiyey (3) See *fúú-, iyeyiya-*. num. seven hands of bananas. Syn. *fúúyi, fúúyin₁*.

fúúyowut (3) See *fúú-, owut*. num. seven rows of thatch.

fúúyó (1) See *fúú-, óó₁*. num. seven tentacles (of octopus or squid). Syn. *fúúchef, fúúwút*.

fúúyóch See *fúú-, -óch*. Var. *fúúwoch*. num. seven sorts, kinds, rations, varieties, species.

fúffaat (3) See *fúú-, ffaata-*. num. seven strings of fish.

fúsawaan Var. of *fúséwaan*.

fúséwaan See *fúús, waan*. Var. *fúsawaan, fúsúwaan*. nu. (num.) the combined number seven-eight in serial counting by twos (formed from elements for both seven and eight).

fúsúwaan Var. of *fúséwaan*.
fúkúro (1) FÚKÚROO. (Jap. *fukuroo, hukuroo*) nu. (T1) owl; (fig.) person who sits up late at night, night-owl. *emén f.* one o. *néwún f.* his (pet) o.
fúnnú (1) See *fúú-, nnúú-*. Var. *fúúnnú*. num. seven portions or loaves of breadfruit pudding; seven puddings' worth of breadfruit to be mashed.
fúntoosi Var. of *funtosi*.
fúpwpwaaw (2) See *fúú-, pwpwaaw*. num. seven home-made cigarettes.
fúrayin Var. of *farayin*.
fúres Var. of *fires*.
ffa Var. of *ffá*.
ffaas (3) See *ffa, aas₁*. vi. slip, lose one's footing; be slippery. Dis. *faffaas* (db). *ewe aan meyi f.* the path that is slippery; *ewe aan aa f.* the path has become slippery. *wúwa f. mé wóón ewe aan* I slipped on that path. Syn. *mit*. Cf. *ttumw*.
ffaat (dc; 3) See *faata-*. vi. be strung (of fish only).
ffaata- (dc; 3) See *faata-*. ni. (T3), suf. (cc.) string of fish. *effaat, rúwéffaat, wúnúffaat, féffaat, nimeffaat, wonoffaat, fúúffaat, wanúffaat, ttiweffaat, engoon ffaaten iik* one,...ten s. of f.; *fiteffaat* how many s. of f.?
ffas (3) FFASA₁. [In cpds. only.] vi. be in want, in need, deprived (in a harsh sense). *ke pwayi f.* you are yet in need (expression of harsh refusal of a request). Cf. *ffaas, -ffas*.
-ffas (3) FFASA₂. unsp. object of laughter, sport, mischief. See *turunuffas*. Cf. Wol. *ffasa*.
ffach (3) FFACHA. vi., adj. (be) light brown.
ffat (dc; 3) See *faat₂*. vi., adj. (be) clear, transparent (of water, glass, meaning, etc.). *aa f. eey kkónik* this fresh water has become clear. *ese f. aan fóós* his words are not clear.
-ffat (3) FFATA. suf. (adj.) just, that's all, without apparent reason, without apparent purpose; (with numerals) exactly, precisely, just. *angaangaffat* work without pay, work that's all, work for no purpose; *feyiniffatoto* come here for no visible reason; *feyiniffatónó* go away without apparent purpose; *téffatonong* enter without invitation; *téffatoto* come without invitation.

eewúffatú chék only just one; *engoonuffat* exactly ten; *nimménúffat* just five (living creatures).
ffá (dc; 1) See *fáá-₂*. Var. *ffa*. vi. kick with the sole of the foot. Dis. *fáffá* (ds). Cf. *fááti, faati*.
ffes (2) FFESI. nu. (T2) pool of money for some common purpose. *mwooniyeniffes, mwooniyen f.* money in a p. va. pool (money). *siya f.* we have pooled (our money).
ffesini See *ffes, -ni-*. vo. (T5) pool (money). *siya f. néwúch we mwooni* we have pooled our money.
ffen₁ (dc; 2) See *feni-*. vi. have diarrhea; be diarrhetic.
ffen₂ (dc; 3) See *fene-₂*. vi. peck (as a chicken). Dis. *feffen* (ds).
ffenichcha (1) See *ffen₁, chcha₁*. vi. have dysentery.
ffengeen (2: -ngenni-) FFENGENNI. [Possibly derived from *fe-₁* and *ngeni*.] Var. *ffengen*. adj. toward one another, together. *angaang f.* work together; *efich f.* like each other; *feyin f.* travel toward one another; *opwut f.* dislike each other. *epwe ina wusumi f.* that will be your way toward one another.
-ffengenniiy See *ffengeen*. vo. suf. (adj.; T5) together, toward one another.
ffey (2, 3) FFEYI, FFEYIYA. N. nu. (T2) stingray; ray fish. *emén f.* one s. *ffeyin Chuuk* Trukese ray. Syn. *sikách*.
ffeyiyenap (3a) See *ffey, nap*. nu. (T3) species of stingray.
ffeyiyennifaro (1) See *ffey, nifóro*. nu. (T1) species of stingray.
ffeyiyepwúk (2?) See *ffey*. nu. (T2?) species of stingray.
-ffé (dc; 1) See *fé*. suf. new. See *énúffé, niyeniffé*.
fféér (dc; 2) See *féér*. nu. (T2) making, manufacture, production. Dis. *féfféér* (ds). *fféérún* or *féfféérún chitoosa* m. of automobiles. vi. be made, done, built. *aa f.* it has been done.
ffééw (2) FFÉÉWÚ. nu. (T2) cold, being cold. Dis. *féfféew* (ds) chills. *aan féfféew* his chills. *faassowun f.* winter, time of cold. vi. feel cold, be cold, feel chilly. Dis. *féfféew* (ds) have chills. *aa f. reen eey ráán* he is cold because of this rain.

ffén₁

ffén₁ (dc; 2) See *fén₂.* nu. (T2) thorn (as on orange and lime trees). [It is used in tattooing.] *ffénún* its thorns.

ffén₂ (dc; 3) See *féna-.* n. (T3) advice, correction, scolding. *ffénan* a. to him; *aan f.* his advising, his advice (to someone). *fféney me reen átánaan* advice to me from yonder fellow.

ffénéngeni See *ffén₂, ngeni.* vo. (T2) instruct, correct, admonish. Syn. *fénééw.*

fféw₁ (dc; 2v: *fféwú-, ffowu-*) See *faaw.* vi. form tubers or globules; get calloused, become hard or solid. With dir. suf.: *fféwúnó* or *ffowunó.*

fféw₂ Var. of *féféw.*

-fféw (2) FFÉWÚ. [In cpds. only.] adj. (intens.?) very (?). See *riyáfféw.*

ffi nu. eff (the letter). *meseni f.* the letter eff. *meyi péchékkún ewe meseni f.* the letter eff is hard (as distinct from soft).

ffiif (ds; 2: *fiffi-*) See *fi-.* vi. (dis.) be tangled.

ffiit (2: *fiitti-, fitti-*) See *fi-, ti-₁.* nu. (dis.; T2) snarl, tangle, entwining. *fiittin* (N.), *fittin* (F.) s. of. *fiittin (fittin) ááy eey óó* the s. of this my fishline. vi. be snarled, tangled; be wound around. Dis. *fiffiit* (ds). Cf. *fin₁.*

ffisópw (dc; 2) See *fi-, sópwu-₁.* vi. wrap ends of a canoe with coconut cloth and wind them with rope. Cf. *fiissópw, fissópw.*

ffin (dc; 2) See *fini-₁.* vi. be chosen, selected, appointed, elected. *aa f. sememi sómwoon?* has your chief been c.?

ffires (dc; 2) See *fires.* nu. (T2) braiding. vi. be braided.

ffiresi (dc) See *fires.* vo. (T2) braid. Syn. *firesini.*

ffich (dc; 2) nu. (T2) scissors; camera trigger. *emén* or *efóch f.* one s. *néwún f.* his s. vi. be cut, snipped (as by scissors); be snapped, taken (of a photograph). Dis. *fiffich* (ds).

-ffit See *fitta-.*

ffiyamw (dc; 3) See *fi-, aamw.* vi. (of outrigger stanchions) be lashed to the outrigger boom of a canoe.

ffiyamweey See *ffiyamw, -e-₂.* vo. (T6b) lash the outrigger stanchions to (a canoe).

ffiyó (1) FFIYÓÓ. vi. have a pain in the testicles from being hit suddenly.

ffowunó See *fféw₁.*

ffóón₁ (dc; 3a) See *fa-₂, won.* nu. (T3) longing, homesickness.

ffóón₂ (dc; 4) FÓNNO. va. raise (animals). *wúpwe f. piik* I will raise pigs. *chóón f. siipw* shepherd. Cf. *fónnuni.*

ffóóneyiti See *ffóón₁, -iti.* vo. (T2) miss, long for, be homesick for, pine for.

ffór (dc; 4) See *fóro-.* vi. 1. be strangled, hanged (by the neck). 2. (of man and woman) be in embrace.

ffóch (2) See *f-, fóchu-.* Var. *féfóch.* num. four cylindrical or stick shaped objects (legs, trees, canoes, teeth, cigarettes, etc.).

-ffóch (dc; 4) See *fócha-.* suf. (adj., dis.) constantly, all the time, always, continuously; for good. *aayafföch* use constantly; *fátáneffóch* walk constantly; *mwéngéffóch* eat all the time; *ókkónnutuffóch, ónnutuffóch* sleep all the time; *weesiffóch* quit and not return, be finished for good, be forever absent (as from work), be fired. Syn. *fóchófóch.*

ffót (dc; 4) See *fóto-₂.* vi. be planted, be stuck (into something). va. plant, stick. Id. *f. cheepen* give a big party ("plant tables"); *esapw pwan wor f. cheepen* there will be no big party.

ffuch (2) FFUCHU. (Eng.) nu. foot (unit of measure). *eew f.* one f.

ffúr (2) FFÚRÚ. vi. be caught in a container (of dripping water, etc.).

Fraans (Eng.) Var. *Franis.* nu. (loc.) France.

Franis Var. of *Fraans.*

ftepwoor Var. of *ftopwoor.*

ftong Var. of *futong.*

ftopwoor (Jap. *futtobooru,* from Eng.) Var. *ftepwoor.* nu. any ball game that uses a big ball of the size of a volleyball.

S

-s₁ (3) SA₁. [Perhaps related to sa-₂.] suf. (u.m.) See *angas, pwunaas*.

-s₂ (2) SI₅. suf. (u.m.) See *áchchenges, emeyis, eyirenges*.

sa-₁ See *se-₁*.

sa-₂ (3b: *sa-, sá-, se-, sé-, so-, só-*) SA₂. pref. of its own accord, spontaneously. [No longer productive.]

-sa- (3) SA₃. suf. (n.form.) noun formative, suffixed to some bases that take verb formative suffix *-yi-*.

sa See *si-₁, -a₁*. N. [Contraction of *siya*.] prn. const. 1pl. inc. prn. plus reality aspect marker: we (past, factual). *sa efich* we liked it. *saa nó* or *sóó nó* we are off, let's go (same as *siyaa nó*).

saa (1) SAA. Tb3. n. (T1 irreg.) abdomen, belly. *saay, sóómw, saan, saach, saam, saami, saar* my, your (sg.), his, our (inc.), our (exc.), your (pl.), their b. Cf. *nuuk, taa, wuupw₂*.

saaf (3) SAFA. n. (T3) 1. lichenification (infected cracks) on soles of feet or palms of hands or between fingers. *safan* his l. 2. (F.) vitiligo (smooth white spots from loss of pigment) on hands or feet. *safan* his v. Syn. *sinnot*.

Saafa (Eng.) nu. (loc.) Java.

saasa (db; 1) See *saa*. va. like, be fond of.

saasaf (3) SAASAFA. (Eng.) nu. (T3) soursop (*Annona muricata*). *eféw s.* one s. fruit; *efóch s.* one s. tree. *saasafen s.* of (a given region).

saam (3v, 3d) SAMA, SEMA. n. (T3v, T3d) (without pos. suf.) one who is a father, fathers; (with pos. suf.) father, grandfather, uncle, any male relative of higher generation in one's own or one's spouse's father's lineage. [Used also in pos. const. for unrelated men who are in a position of authority in relation to oneself, e.g., *semey sense* my teacher, *semey sómwoon* my chief.] *semey, somomw* or *semomw, saman* or *seman, samach*, or *semach, semeem, sememi, semeer* my, your (sg.), his, our (inc.), our (exc.), your (pl.), their f.

Saamawa₁ nu. (loc.) Samoa. *wuchun S.* a variety of banana.

saamawa₂ (1) See *Saamawa*. nu. (T1) a variety of banana. Syn. *wuchun Saamawa*.

-saa mwo See *-se*.

saamwú (1) See *saa, mwú₁* or *mwú₃*. F. vi. be angry.

saan (2) SAANÚ. n. (T2) sickness attributed to working too soon after childbirth (of women). *saanún* her s.

saani See *saa, -ni-*. Tb3. vo. (T4) like, enjoy (have a positive feeling for something because of what one gets from it). Syn. *nuukeni*. Cf. *efich, tongeey*.

saap₁ (3) SAPA₁. n. (T3), suf. (cc.) cheek, side (of the face), area forward of the gills (on a fish). *esap, rúwésap, wúnúsap, fésap, nimesap, wonosap, fúúsap, wanúsap, ttiwesap, engoon sapan* one,...ten fish c.; *eew s.* one c. (of person). *sapan* his c. *sapen eey iik* this fish's c.; *esap sapen iik* one fish c. Cf. *pa-₁*.

saap₂ (3) SAAPA. nu. (T3) knife.

saar (2) SAARÚ. Var. *ssaar*. nu. (T2) small knife, table knife, pocket knife, hunting knife. *emén s. néwún s.* his k. *saarún assak* copra k. *s. kkóóp* pocket k. ("hidden k.").

saaras (3) SAARASA. N. Var. *taaras*. nu. (T3) a shrub (*Sonneratia caseolaris*). [Bark used in dye making, wood as firewood.] *saarasen s.* of (a given region).

saarúúw See *saar, -ú-*. vo. (T5) apply a small knife to, whittle.

saatiin (Eng.) nu. sardine. vi. be witless, lose one's head (especially from alcoholic drink).

saato (1) SAATOO. (Jap. *saado*) nu. (T1) third base (baseball).

saayimw (3a) See *sa-₂, a-₂, iimw*. nu. (T3) conical hat of pandanus leaf. *eew s.* one h. *imwan s.* his h. *saayimwen Chuuk* Trukese h. *waan s.* base of a h.

saf (3b) See *saaf₁*. vi. 1. be in a condition of lichenification (have infected cracks of the skin on hands or feet). Dis. *safasaf* (db), *sassaf* (dc). 2. (F.) have vitiligo (white patches of skin on hands or feet).

safasaf Dis. of *saf*.
safet (2) See *saf*, *-ti-*. N. vi. be scraped or peeled (of roasted breadfruit peeled with a stick). Syn. *ettik₁*.
safeti See *saf*, *-ti-*. N. vo. (T2) peel or take the skin from a roasted breadfruit, using a stick. Syn. *ettika*.
sasimi (1) SASIMII. (Jap. *sashimi*) Var. *sasúmi*. nu. (T1) sliced raw fish, sashimi. *eew s.* one s. *wochaan s.* his s.
sasimiini See *sasimi*, *-ni-*. vo. (T4) make sashimi of.
sasing (2) SASINGI. (Jap. *shashin*) n. (T2) camera; photograph, picture. *eew s.* one c.; *eché s.* one p. *sasingin* p. of him; *néwún s.* his c. *wúpwe fichiiy sasingumw* I will take your picture. Cf. *pikisé*. vi. take a picture.
sasingiiy See *sasing*, *-i-₂*. vo. (T5) take a picture of.
sasúmi Var. of *sasimi*.
sassaf Dis. of *saf*.
sakanto Var. of *sekanto*.
sakatachi (1) SAKATACHII. (Jap. *sakadachi*) vi. stand on one's head.
sakaw (3) SAKAWA. (Pon.) nu. (T3) liquor, alcoholic beverage. *wúnúman s.* his l. to drink. *sakawen Chuuk* Trukese l. vi. be under the influence of liquor, be drunk.
sake (1) SAKEE. (Jap. *sake*) nu. (T1) Japanese rice wine, sake. *wúnúman s.* his r. w.
sako (1) SAKOO. (Jap. *shako*) nu. (T1) garage.
sakupwoo (1) SAKUPWOO. (Jap. *shaku, boo*) nu. (T1) long measuring stick (for measuring distances or length). *efóch s.* one m. s. *néwún s.* his m. s.
sakú (1) SAKÚÚ. (Jap. *shaku*) nu. (T1) ladle, dipper. *efóch s.* one l. *aan s.* his l.
sakúúni See *sakú*, *-ni-*. vo. (T4) dip something with a ladle.
sakúra (1) SAKÚRAA. (Jap.) nu. (T1) a shrub (*Stachyterpheta indica, Stachyterpheta cayennensis, Stachyterpheta urticaefolia*). [Introduced from Japan.]
sakka- Var. of *ssaka-*.
sakkak (3) See *sa-₂, -kkak*. vi. split, crack, check (as of wood when dried too quickly or skin on the soles of the feet). *s. feseen* s. apart.
sakramento (1) SAKRAMENTOO. (Sp.) nu. (T1) sacrament.

samasam (db; 3v) See *saam*. va. treat as a father.
samasamangngaw (3b) See *samasam, ngngaw*. vi. treat as a father badly.
samasamééch (2) See *samasam, ééch*. vi. treat as a father well.
samminne (1) See *sapw₁, minne*. vi. would not be that or for. *s. ke pwe mééni eey mettóóch* [it] would not be for you to buy this thing. *e s. re esiffengeen* it would not be that they are the same age.
samwaaw (3) SAMWAAWA. N. (Pon.) nu. (T3) sickness, illness. *óóch s., eew s.* one illness. *aan s.* his i. vi. be sick, ill. Syn. *semwmwen*.
samwaawútter (2) See *samwaaw, ter₁*. nu. (T2) epidemic. Syn. *semwmwenitter*.
samwo (1) SAMWOO. (Jap. *shamo*) nu. (T1) a kind of fighting rooster.
samwoon Var. of *sómwoon*.
samwmwochi (1) SAMWMWOCHII. (Jap. *shamoji*) nu. (T1) large wooden spoon (for scooping rice or soup). *efóch s.* one s. *aan s.* his s.
san (3v) SANA₁. vi. set bones by massage.
-san (3) SANA₂. unsp. (u.m.) See *féwúsan*.
Sanet nu. (loc.) a clan name.
Saneweri Var. of *Sanéwei*.
Sanéweri (Eng.) Var. *Saneweri, Sanéwéri*. nu. (temp.) January.
Sanéwéri Var. of *Sanéweri*.
sannap N. of *sennap*.
sanne md.m., conj. indicates that what follows is contrary to reality or fact; when not. *pwata ke ataay s. pisekumw?* why do you destroy it when [it is] not your property? *wúwa tinaanó pwú s. ke wúreniyey* I sent it off because you did not tell me not to. Syn. *anno, wonne*.
santang Short form of *santangtopi*.
santangtopi (1) SANTANGTOPII. (Jap. *sandantobi*) nu. hop, step, and jump (track event). vi. do the hop, step, and jump.
sanger (3) SANGERA. vi. fail to match (of two things); protrude, be uneven. *meyi s. feseen* fail to be even with one another at the ends, overlap at the ends (as of two pieces of wood). *pwata aa s. óómw we pwpwon ngeniyey?* why did your pledge to me fail to match [your deeds]?
sap₁ (3b) SAPA₂. vi. be caught, stuck, snagged, trapped, hung up. With dir.

suf.: *sapanó. aa sapanó naan áát wóón naan mangko* that boy has got stuck in that mango tree.

sap₂ (3) SAPA₃. vi. (?) be with open palm (of the hand).

sap₃ (3a) See *sa-₂, pa-₁*. N. [With dir. suf. or in place names only.] Var. *sáp.* vi. face (in a given direction); change direction. With dir. suf.: *sapenong* f. in or south; *sapenó* f. away; *sapetá* f. up or east; *sapetiw* f. down or west; *sapeto* f. hither, f. this way; *sapewow* f. towards you (hearer); *sapewu* f. outwards or north. *e sapeto (sápeto) mé notow* it is the second quarter of the moon ("it faces hither from the west"). Cf. *saap₁*.

sapa See *sap₂*. vo. (T3) hold (something) on the open palm of the hand. Dis. *sassapa* (ds).

Sapaan (Eng.) nu. (loc.) Japan. *chóón S.* a Japanese; *fóósun S.* the Japanese language. *fin-S., fis-S., fiin S.* Japanese woman; *re-S.* Japanese man. *meyi mesen re-S. átánaan* that fellow looks Japanese.

sapanó See *sap₁*.
sapenong See *sap₃*.
sapenó See *sap₃*.
sapetá See *sap₃*.
sapetiw See *sap₃*.
sapeto See *sap₃*.
sapewow See *sap₃*.
sapewu See *sap₃*.

sapw₁ (3?) See *sa-₁, -pwe.* st.m. be not. [Introduces a negative equative sentence.] *s. ngaang!* not I! (i.e., not I the one who...). *s. iiy neyiy chóón angaang* he is not my employee. suf. (asp.) negative future or future intentional aspect marker: will not, shall not, would not; do not, don't (negative future imperative). [Suffixed to sub. prns.: *wúsapw* (1sg.), *kesapw* (2sg.), *esapw* (3sg.), *sisapw* (1pl. inc.), *éwúsapw* (1pl. exc., 2pl.), *áyisapw* (1pl. exc.), *osapw* or *wosapw* (2pl.), *resapw* (3pl.).] *esapw máánó* he will not die. *kesapw etto neesor* do not (you will not) come tomorrow. Cf. *samminne*.

sapw₂ qlf. truly; believe me. *iwe s. raa toori imwen ewe soomáá we, iwe raa toonong* then they truly did arrive at the ogre's house, and then they entered; *s. ngaang wúse fóókkun mwechen feyinnó ngé wúwa feyinnó pwún wúwa sááw reemw* believe me, I didn't really want to go, but I went because I was embarrassed on your account.

sapwin (2) See *sa-₂, pwin₁.* vi. be hanging down. With dir. suf.: *supwinitiw*.

sapwo- Itang of *sópwu-*.

Sapwon nu. (pers.) a sea god. [Invoked for good fishing.]

sara (1) SARAA. N. nu. (T1) yellow-lined squirrel fish (*Holocentrus ensifer* Jordan and Evermann). Syn. *inipar*.

saraata (1) SARAATAA. nu. (T1) small pass or channel in a fringing reef. Syn. *ánúk, taaw*.

saram (3b) See *sa-₂, ram.* nu. (T3) light. *saramen akkar* sunlight. Ant. *kkiroch*. vi., adj. (be) bright, full of light, lit up, illuminated. Dis. *saramaram* (db).

saramaram Dis. of *saram*.

saramata Var. of *sarúmata*.

sarapwar (3) SARAPWARA. nu. (T3) reaching into the womb of a woman in labor to turn the infant in the case of a breach birth. vi. turn an infant in the womb. Cf. *pwaar*.

saraw (3) SARAWA. nu. (T3) barracuda. *sarawen* b. of (a given region).

sarawaraw (db; 3) See *se-₁, raaw₂.* vi. be rowdy, disrespectful, immodest.

sarimata Var. of *sarúmata*.

sarof Var. of *sórof*.

sarú (1) SARÚÚ. (Jap. *saru*) nu. (T1) monkey. *emén s.* one m. *néwún s.* his (pet) m. Syn. *mwook, mwongki, mwóngki*.

sarúmata (1) SARÚMATAA. (Jap. *sarumata*) Var. *saramata, sarimata.* nu. (T1) undershorts. *eché s.* one pair of u. *aan s.* his u. Cf. *panchu*.

sach (3) See *sa-₂, cha-.* vi., adj. (be) wedged, fastened with wedges, crowded; dense, thick, pressed together.

sachawer nu. 1. a plant (*Urena lobata*). 2. a plant (*Triumfetta indica*). Cf. *chchawer, wer*.

sachopw (2) See *sa-₂, chopw.* vi. be broken into many pieces.

sachúmayimwo (1) SACHÚMAYIMWOO. (Jap.) nu. (T1) Japanese sweet potato.

Satawan nu. (loc.) 1. Satawan Island and District (Mortlock Islands). 2. Satawal Island (Central Caroline Islands).

sawa- (3) SAWA. [In cpds. only.] unsp. look after, watch over (?).

sawa (1) SAWAA. nu. (T1) taro (*Colocasia esculenta*). *sawaan Chuuk* Trukese t. Syn. *óni, woot₁*.

sawaan N. of *sewáán*.

saweey See *sawa-, -e-₂*. vo. (T6b) make the rounds of. Cf. *ssaw*.

sawit (2) SAWITI. Var. *sóót*. vi. begin to form breadfruit. nu. (loc.; T2) in *sawitin mááy* time of the early forming of breadfruit.

Sayini (Eng.) nu. (loc.) China.

sá (1) SÁÁ₁. vi. be removed; be emptied (of an earth oven); come loose (of an outrigger float). Cf. *ssá*.

sáá- (1) SÁÁ₂. [In cpds. only.] unsp. noisy. See *sáákak, sáánong*.

sáás (2) See *sá, -si-*. va. stub (as one's toe or foot). *wúwa s. ngeni pecheey ewe faaw* I stubbed my foot against the stone ("I stubbed with my foot the stone"). Cf. *sáási*.

sáásá (db; 1) See *sáá-*. nu. (T1) a small bat. [Its squeaking is associated with ghosts.] *emén s.* one b.

sáási See *sá, -si-*. vo. (T4) remove (as of clothes), take away (from a place), swing out (of arms), remove or peel off (of skin), swing (of a fish pole); chase away into exile (of persons).

sáák (2) SÁKKI. (Eng.) nu. (T2) jack (in cards). *sákkin chayimen* j. of diamonds.

sáákak (3) See *sáá-, kak*. vi. pop loudly (of cooked breadfruit when pounded with a special stroke in mashing it into pudding). Syn. *awaw₂, eyipwenong, sáánong*.

sáán (2) SENI₁. nu. (T2) rope, coil of rope, heavy duty sennit. *esen s.* one coil of rope; *emwú s.* one fragment or piece of r. *aan s.* his r. *senin Chuuk* Trukese r. Cf. *ten₂*.

sáánif (2) SÁÁNIFI. (Eng.) nu. (T1) shelf. *sáánifĭn s.* in (a structure).

sáánong (3) See *sáá-, -nong*. F. vi. pop loudly (of cooked breadfruit when pounded with a special stroke in mashing it into pudding). Syn. *awaw₂, eyipwenong, sáákak*.

sáánó (1) SÁÁNÓÓ. (Eng.) nu. (T1) sailor.

sáápwow (2) SÁÁPWOWU. nu. (T2) hibiscus tree (*Hibiscus tiliaceus*); hibiscus bark. *sáápwowun Chuuk* Trukese h. t. Syn. *sinifé*.

sááchúk (2) See *sá, -chúk*. Tb1. vi. (of a woman) remove all one's clothes and taunt and jeer another woman with one's nakedness, daring her to do the same and see who is the better endowed with attractive private parts. [Done as a form of fighting among women.]

sáát₁ (2) SETI₁. nu. (T2) salt water, sea, salted water. *setin s. w.* of (a given region).

sáát₂ (2) See *sáát₁*. Rmn. Var. *sset*. nu. (T2) illness caused by sea spirits called *chénúkken*. *aan s.* his illness. *aa wúri s. átewe* illness has stricken that fellow. *rongen s.* medicine and spells to cure the *s.* illness.

sáát₃ (4) SÁTTE. nu. (T2) sliver, broken off piece; slice (of bread). *essáát* (F.), *essát* (N.) one s. *sáttin irá* s. of wood; *sáttin kinaas* s. of glass.

sááw (3b) SÁÁWA. N. vi. be ashamed, embarrassed, bashful, shy. *wú s. reen átánaan* I am embarrassed or awkward in that fellow's presence, I am ashamed on account of that fellow. *s. mmang* be shameless, hard to embarrass, without shame. Syn. *ma, máfen*.

sááwáásini (db) See *sááw, -ásini*. vo. (T5) be ashamed or embarrassed by or at (something).

sááweyiti See *sááw, -iti*. vo. (T2) be embarrassed in the presence of.

sááy (2) SEYI₁. nu. transportation; journey, travel. nr. (T2) ship, vessel, vehicle, automobile (in reference to a country, region, or function, but not in reference to a person as owner or user, cf. *waa₁, waawa, wááni*). *seyin iya?* ship from where?; *seyin kkááp* cargo or merchant s.; *seyin kkááp aramas* passenger s.; *seyin neyifĭ* naval vessel, navy s.; *seyin paasiisé* passenger s.; *seyin Sapaan* Japanese s.; *seyin wuwoow sepeniin* aircraft carrier. vi. depart, set out, sail, take off (in connection with transportation); journey, travel. *ineet sipwe s.?* when shall we d.? With dir. suf.: *seyinong, seyinó, seyitá, seyitiw, seyito, seyiwu*. *kepwe seyinó iya?* where are you going to travel to?

sááyipé (1) See *sá, pé₂*. nu. (T1), vi. fan.

sááyipééw See *sááyipé*. vo. (T1) fan.

sáfáán Var. of *sefáán*.

sáfeeni See *sáfey, -ni-*. vo. (T6a) give medicine to, medicate; apply a liquid chemical to; develop (a film).

sáfey (3) SÁFEYA. n. (T3) medicine; any preparation administered to a person to relieve him of symptoms of illness or prevent him from harm (it may be worn as well as be taken internally); any chemical preparation intended to change the form of something or to protect it from pests or other injury. *aan s.* his m. that he knows how to prepare; *sáfeyan* m. for him to take; *wúnúman s.* his m. to drink; *sáfeen* medicine of. *sáfeen amwataan óós, sáfeen kket* m. prepared by the *sowuyimw* and drunk by him and workers preparatory to putting on thatch (it makes the thatch ascend speedily); *sáfeen asaram* m. used to cure the sickness *neeroch*, to help students, performers, etc., to perform well, and to make a spirit medium receptive to his familiar spirit; *sáfeen chimwinúúr* m. prepared by the *sowuyimw* and drunk by him and workers on erecting the cornerposts and wallplates of a house or *wuut*; *sáfeen énúkúnúk* m. against vomiting blood; *sáfeen énúúsór* m. to become a spirit medium; *sáfeen faaw* m. to cure *féwúnón*; *sáfeen fééwo* m. prepared by the *sowuyimw* and drunk by him and workers preparatory to putting the rafters on a house; *sáfeen kinas* m. for treating cuts; *sáfeen máán* m. to counteract blindness from overexposure to bright sunlight; *sáfeen máápwut* m. against madness caused by *máápwut* sorcery; *sáfeen neeroch* m. for *neeroch* sickness; *sáfeen Nimwoyi* m. for sickness caused by Nimwoyi, a *chénúkken* local to Wútéét (Udot); *sáfeen nippach* squid m. (known to *itang* and used to prevent or cure the distorted mouth and swollen neck said to result from sharing a meal of squid with an *itang*); *sáfeen niyang* m. against colic in infants; *sáfeen ngerengereyinó, safeen nóó* m. to cure laryngitis (*ngerengeriyinó,*) caused by the wave spirit (*soopeen nóó*); *sáfeen Núkúnaayo* m. to cure sickness caused by a local *chénúkken* spirit inhabiting Núkúnaayo reef, Romónum Island; *sáfeen onuponup* m. against spitting, coughing, or vomiting blood caused by sorcery; *sáfeen pwéét* m. prepared by the *sowuyimw* and drunk by him and the workers on erecting the king-posts (*pwéét*) and ridgepole of a house or *wuut*; *sáfeen sópwiinos* m. associated with housebuilding ("m. of the mat end"); *sáfeen tétténún óó* m. to cleanse a fishline (after it has been touched by a man who had sexual relations the previous night); *sáfeen winikápiipi* m. to cure *semwmwenin winikápiipi*.

sáse- (3) SÁSA. [In cpds. only.] vi. overflow. With dir. suf.: *sásenong, sásewu*.

sásenong See *sáse-*.

sásewu See *sáse-*.

sássá Dis. of *ssá*.

sássár₁ Dis. of *sár₁*.

sássár₂ (db; 2) See *ssár₁*. nu. (dis.; T2) tier, storey or floor of house, step of a stair, shelf of a cupboard. *fituuw sássárin naan kkapet* how many shelves in that cupboard. *sássárin nááng* tiers or levels of heaven, according to Bollig consisting of *nenichang, nenisú, nenikkun* or *neninap, faachchamw* or *nenichamw* (?) and *nenimwúch* (?).

sássi- (2) SÁSSI. nr. (T2) rising, eastern position (of a star). Syn. *tona-*. Ant. *tupwu-*.

sámmey (2) See *ssá, mmey*. vi. move vigorously (in walking or running).

sámmééng (2) See *sá, mééng*. vi. cut pandanus leaf.

sámmééngúúw See *sámmééng, -ú-*. vo. (T5) cut (pandanus leaves).

sáná- (4) SÁNE. [In cpds. only.] unsp. (u.m.) (?) prominent, standing out (cf. Gb. *tane* clear, distinct). See *sánápwapw*.

sánápwapw (3) See *sáná-, pwpwa-*. Var. *sánepwapw*. nu. (T3) Moorish idol fish (*Zandus canescens* L.). Syn. *nikeriker*.

Sánemwón (Eng.) nu. (loc.) Solomon Islands.

sánepwapw Var. of *sánápwapw*.

sánikú Var. of *sánúkú*.

sánúkú (1) See *sáná-, kúú₁*. Var. *sánikú*. nu. tiny species of pompano (white ulua or jack; *Carangoides ajax* Snyder). Cf. *kú₂*.

sángá (1) SÁNGÁÁ. nu. (T1) fishing basket (fairly fine weave); (Wtt.) basket of *kuumar* type. *eew s.* one b. Syn. *sáwá*. suf. (cc.) basketful of fish. *esángá, rúwésángá, wúnúsángá, fésangá, nimesánga, wonosángá, fúúsángá, wanúsangá, ttiwesangá, engoon sángáán* one,...ten b.

sángáápé (1) See *sángá, pé₃*. Wtt. vi. be with empty basket.

sáp (3a) See *sa-₂, pa-₁*. F. Var. *sap₃*. vi. face, present a side (in a given direction); change direction. With dir. suf.: *sápenong* f. in or south; *sápenó* f. away; *sápetá* f. up or east; *sápeto* f. this way; *sápetiw* f. down or west; *sápewow* f. towards you, f. in your direction; *sápewu* f. outwards or north. *e sápeto mé notow* it is the second quarter of the moon ("it faces hither from the west").

sápe- (4) SÁPE. [In cpds. only.] unsp. prevented, countered, warded off (?). See *ásápásáp*.

Sápesis See *sáp, -sis*. [Kraemer] nu. (loc.) district of Feefen (Fefan) Island ("Upper or Eastern side").

sápenong See *sáp*.

sápenó₁ See *sáp*.

Sápenó₂ See *sáp, -nó*. nu. (loc.) a clan name.

sápengeni See *sáp, ngeni*. vo. (T2) face toward.

sápetá See *sáp*.

sápetiw See *sáp*.

sápeto See *sáp*.

sápewow See *sáp*.

sápewu See *sáp*.

sápúk Tn. nu. sugarcane (*Saccharum officinarum*). Syn. *woow*.

sápwpwach (3) See *sá, pwpwach*. vi. amble, saunter, walk slowly and relaxedly.

sár₁ (4) SÁRE₁. vi., adj. (be) moving, not staying in one place; moved (of a house, disassembled and set up on a new site). Dis. *sássár* (db). Cf. *sen*.

sár₂ (4) SÁRE₂. vi. be over, ended, finished.

sárá (1) See *ssár₁*. vi., adj. (be) tiered, storied, have wooden floor raised off the ground; have shelves (of a cupboard). *meyi s. naan kkapet* that cupboard has shelves.

sárem (3) SÁREMA. n. (T3) bedcover, top sheet, coverlet. *eché s.* one b. *sáreman* his b. Syn. *chchenikam, kuus₂*.

sárepwéét (2) See *sár₂* (?), *pwéét*. nu. (T2) a blow to the nose in fighting.

sári- (4) See *sár₂*. ni. (T2) being finished. *sárin* his being f. *sárich we me angaang nánew siya een mé nó nóón imwan* after we had finished our work yesterday we went each to his own house. *Sárin Fáán* Monday ("worship's being f.").

sárifáátá See *sárifi*.

sárifi See *ssár₁, -fi-*. vo. (T5) open (of a box), lift the lid of, raise (a curtain, mosquito net). With dir. suf.: *sárifáátá*.

sárisi See *sár₁, -si-*. vo. (T5) move from its place, remove (of houses only), disassemble and move (of a house).

sáriniipw (3) See *ssár₂* (?), *iipw* (?). nu. (T3) fiber band from the midrib of the coconut frond on which fish are strung. *sáriniipwen iik* f. b. for fish.

Sárin Fáán See *sári-*.

sáchúng (2) See *sa-₂, chúngú-*. n. (T2) backaches and headaches attributed to excessively hard work (treated by massage). *sáchúngún* his aches. vi. suffer from backaches and headaches; sprain one's back.

sátu nu. a move in fighting that involves catching one's opponent's leg and pulling him off balance.

sáwá (1) SÁWÁÁ. nu. (T1) fishing basket (fairly fine weave). [Made only by women.] *eew s.* one f. b. Syn. *sángá*. suf. (cc.) basketful (of fish). *esáwá, rúwésáwá, wúnúsáwá, fésáwá, nimesáwá, wonosáwá, fúúsáwá, wanúsáwá, ttiwesáwá, engoon sáwáán* one,...ten b.

se-₁ (3b) SA₄. Var. *sa-₁*. pref. (neg.) not. *semiriit* small child ("not understand", cf. *miriit*).

se-₂ See *sa-₂*.

-se (3b) See *se-₁*. [This is its usual form.] Var. *-sa*. suf. (asp.) not; negative reality aspect marker (present or past action); negative of stative marker *meyi*. *ese fééri* he has not done it, he is not doing it; *ese ééch* it is not good. *esoor* (*ese wor*) there is (exists) not; *ese ii wor* there is not (polite or gentle). *esaa mwo, esee mwo* it not now, not yet, not already.

see (1) SEE₁. Tb1. n. (T1) penis. *seen* his p.

seemwas (3) See *see, mwas*. Tb1. vi. having a smelly penis.

-see mwo See *-se*.

seeng (3) SEENGA. n. (T3), suf. (cc.) length between two joints (as on an arm, leg, bamboo, sugarcane, etc.). *eseeng, rúwéseeng, wúnúseeng, féseeng, nimeseeng, wonoseeng, fúúseeng, wanúseeng, ttiweseeng, engoon* *seengan* one,...ten l. *seengen iich* a piece of bamboo between two of its joints or nodes; *seengen paaw* segment between arm joints, e.g. upper arm or lower arm; *seengen peche* upper leg or lower leg.

seepech (3) See *see, pech.* Tbl. nu. (T3) erect penis.

seerupw (2) See *see, ruupw.* Tbl. nu. (T2) syphilitic sore on the penis.

seeta (1) SEETAA. (Eng.) nu. (T1) sweater.

Seetan₁ (Eng.) nu. (pers.) Satan. *kkéénún S.* love song.

seetan₂ (3) SEETANA. nu. (T3) sand burr (*Cenchrus chinatus*).

seetipap (3) See *see, tipap.* Tbl. vi. having a dirty penis.

seewachep (2) See *see, wachep.* Tbl. nu. (T2) big penis. vi. have a big penis. Cf. *chep.*

seey SEE₂. N. vo. (T1) peel (a banana or the skin of vegetables). Syn. *ettika.*

seeya (1) SEEYAA. (Eng.) nu. (T1) chair. *eew s., efóch s.* one c. *aan s.* his c.

sefáán (2) SEFÁÁNI, SEFÁNNI. Var. *sáfáán.* adj. again, once more, over again, anew. *féér s.* do again; *féér-sefáániiy, féér-sefánniiy* (vo., T5) do (something) again. Cf. *fáán*₆.

sefáániiy See *sefáán.*

sefánniiy See *sefáán.*

seféw (2) See *sa-*₂ (?), *faaw.* nu. (T2) breadfruit that has been gathered at the edge of the fermenting pit preparatory to storing for fermentation.

sefich (2) See *se-*₁, *fichi-.* nu. (T2) black ant ("not snip," i.e. not sting). *emén s.* one b. a. *sefichin Chuuk* Trukese b. a. Cf. *niffich.*

sessees Dis. of *ssees.*

sessen₁ (ds; 2) See *sáán.* vi. be roped.

sessen₂ Dis. of *sen.*

sesseni Dis. of *sseni.*

sessepi (ds; 3) See *sepi.* va. use a bowl, dish, or platter. Cf. *sepiyeni.*

sesseppi- (ds; 2) See *seppi-.* [With dir. suf. only.] Var. *peppesse-.* vi. in the opening formula for a story: *sesseppinó, sesseppito*... going forth and coming hither...(i.e., once upon a time...).

sesseppinó See *sesseppi-.*

sesseppito See *sesseppi-.*

sesset (ds; 2) See *sáát*₁. vi. be cooked in a mixture of water, salt water and coconut cream (of fish and other *seni*). Cf. *setiiy.* adj. briny. See *peche.*

-sek (2) SEKI. [In cpds. only.] unsp. pandanus mat (?). Cf. Plt. *háki.*

sekanto (1) SEKANTOO. (Jap. *sekando*) Var. *sakanto.* nu. (T1) second base (in baseball).

seken (Eng.) nu. second (unit of time).

seker (2) SEKERI. (Ger.?) nu. (T2) secretary. *néwún s.* his s. *sekerin eey mwiich* s. of this meeting. Syn. *seketeri.*

seketeri (Eng.) nu. secretary. Syn. *seker.*

sekiita (1) SEKIITAA. (Jap. *sekiita*) nu. (T1) sluice board. *eché s.* one s. b. *aan s.* his s. b.

sekit (2) SEKITI. (Eng.) nu. (T2) jacket, coat. *wúfan s., aan s.* his j. *sekitin fáán ráán* raincoat (syn. *apakawúch, kaappa*).

seme- See *saam.*

semenap (3a) See *saam, nap.* n. (T3) biological father or grandfather (not used for stepfather or adoptive father), genitor. *semenapan* his b. f.

semeni See *saam, -ni-.* vo. (T6a) acquire (someone) as a father (e.g., when one's mother remarries, or one is adopted).

Semenkóóror See *saam, óóror.* nu. (pers.) traditional god of deciding what is good and right. [He lives in the sky and is brother to *Óórorofich* and *Semewútéwút.*]

Semewútéwút See *saam, wúút*₂. nu. (pers.) traditional god of rain. [Brother of *Semenkóóror* and *Óórorofich*, he lives in the sky and is appealed to by weather conjurors (*sowunó*).]

semiriit (2) See *se-*₁, *miriit.* N. nu. (T2) child (to about 8 years of age; "not understanding"). *s. áát* boy; *s. nengngin* girl. Syn. *ménúkón, monukón, nooyiroch, nooyiis, setipeen, tipate.*

Semtemper (Eng.) Var. *Sémtooper, Septemper.* nu. (temp.) September.

semwmwen (2) See *se-*₁, *mwmwen.* nu. (T2) sickness, illness ("not up to what should be"). *aan s.* his s. *chóón s.* patient, sick person; *imwen s.* hospital (syn. *piyowing, piyoying*). *semwmwenin chukó* a kind of s. (syn. *máán chukó*); *semwmwenin feefin, semwmwenin maram* menstruation;

semwmwenin nisoowu veneral disease; *semwmwenin Núkúnaayo* s. caused by a local *chénúkken* spirit inhabiting Núkúnaayo reef, Romónum Island, manifested in one case by a rotting infection of the foot and leg; *semwmwenin rayis* beriberi ("rice s."); *semwmwenin Seniwis* gonorrhea ("Jaluit s.," syn. *rímpiyo*); *semwmwenin suke* diabetes ("sugar s."); *semwmwenin winikápiipi* s. caused by *énúún ápiipi* (driftwood spirits), manifested by excessive swelling of a pregnent woman's abdomen in the early stages of pregnancy and by accompanying swellings of arms, legs, and face. vi., adj. be sick, ill. Syn. *samwaaw*.

semwmwenichchow (2) See *semwmwen, chchow*. vi. be very or gravely sick.

semwmwenitter (2) See *semwmwen, ter₁*. nu. (T2) epidemic. Syn. *samwaawútter*.

semwmwúch (2) See *se-₁, mwmwúch*. vi., adj. (be) everlasting, without end.

sen (2) SENI₂. vi., adj. (be) ephemeral, intermittent, having the quality of coming and going. [F.: of coconuts only; N.: of coconuts and rainsqualls.] Dis. *sessen* (db). With dir. suf.: *seninó* disappear (intermittent away); *senito* appear (intermittent hither).

-sen (2) See *sáán*. suf. (cc.) coil or hank of rope (from 30 to 100 fathoms of length, according to local custom). *esen, rúwésen, wúnúsen, fésen, nimesen, wonosen, fúúsen, wanúsen, ttiwesen, engoon sáán* one,...ten coils.

senááni (Mck.) vo. (T4) protect, succor, save, redeem. Syn. *túmwúnúúw*.

sene (1) SENEE₁. nu. (T1) adze. *eché s.* one a. *aan s.* his a. *seneen Chuuk* Trukese a.

-sene See *-se, -ne*. suf. (asp.) not about to, not going to; negative immediate or intentional future aspect marker expressing a little uncertainty. [Suffixed to subjective pronouns.] *kesene feyinnó* you are not about to depart.

senee-₁ (1) See *se-₁, ne₁* (?). [In cpds. only.] unsp. naked, a cause of embarrassment. See *seneeng*.

senee-₂ (1) SENEE₂. [In cpds. only.] vi. face (in a given direction). With dir. suf.: *seneenó* f. away; *seneetá* f. up; *seneeto* f. this way, f. hither.

seneekuun (2) See *sene, kkun*. nu. (T2) spout adze, canoe adze (hafted on a swivel).

seneeni See *sene, -ni-*. vo. (T4) chop with an adze.

seneenó₁ (1) See *senee-₁, -nó*. vi. be naked from the waist up, half-naked; be naked.

seneenó₂ See *senee-₂*.

seneeng (3) See *senee-₁, -ng*. vi., adj. (be) bare, exposed, uncovered. *fanang s.* naked, unclothed ("bare ashes, uncovered hearth").

seneepw (3) See *senee-₁* (?), *pwpwa-*. nu. (T3) species of surgeon fish. *seneepwen Chuuk* Trukese s. f.

seneetá See *senee-₂*.

seneeto₁ (1) See *senee-₁, -to*. vi. come hither half naked, come without putting on a shirt.

seneeto₂ See *senee-₂*.

seneti₁ See *sáán, -ti-*. vo. (T5) untie, loosen (a rope).

seneti₂ See *san, -ti-*. vo. (T6a) set the bone of (by massage), massage (someone who has suffered a fall from a height). *aa s. ewe aramas* he s. the person's bones.

seneyich (2, 3) SENEYICHI, SENEYICHA. (Eng.) nu. (T2, T3) slate. *eché s.* one s. *seneyichin* or *seneyichen Merika* American s.

seni- (2) SENI₃. [In cpds. only.] unsp. parting, going from, leaving. See *senichcha*.

seni₁ (3) SENIYA. n. (T3) side dish (preferably of fish or meat), food eaten as accompaniment to the main starch dish. *seniyan* his s. d.

seni₂ See *seni-*. vo. (T2) from; than. *seniyey, sonuk* from me, you (sg.). *seni iya mesen eey ásápwán* from where is the wind coming? *eey pwóór meyi nap s. naan* this box is bigger than that one. *pwan s.* likewise with, the same with; *kkewe waasééna meyi nónnómw Romónum raa opwut átánaan pwú meyi ngngaw aan féfféér; pwan s. chóón Romónum, raa pwan opwut iiy* the foreigners who live on Romónum dislike that fellow because his conduct is bad; likewise with the people of Romónum, they also dislike him.

seni₃ See *sáán*. N. vo. (T2) coil, wind up (rope). Syn. *seniiy*.

seniisópw (2) See *sáán, sópwu-*₁. nu. (T2) fore and back stay of *meniyuk* sailing canoe ("end rope").

seniiy See *sáán, -i-*₂. F. vo. (T5) coil, wind up (rope). Syn. *seni*₃.

senif (3) SENIFA. nu. (T3) herring. *senifen Chuuk* Trukese h.

senifané (1) See *senif, nêé*₂ (?). nu. (T1) species of herring.

senis (Eng.) nu. cent or cents, penny or pennies (in counting); an amount of coins, small change, or money. *s. eew* one c.; *s. fítuuw* how much money, how many c. Cf. *ssen*.

senisen (db; 2) SENI₄. n. (T2) tinea (not as heavy and horny as *arakak*). *senisenin* his t.

senikásá (1) See *seni-* (?), *ásá*. N. nu. (T1) board connecting the outrigger boom ends on the side of a canoe away from its outrigger (on the lee side of a sailing canoe). *senikásáán waa* canoe's *s.*. Syn. *tinikásá*.

seninó See *sen*.

sening (3a) SENINGA. n. (T3) ear. *seningan* his e. *emin s.* earlobe; *s. wunowun* extended earlobes (from the traditional practice of cutting and stretching the lobes). *seningen anú* or *énú* (N.), *seningen soomá* or *soope* (F.) any of a large number of fungi ("ghost's or spirit's ear") such as *Auricularia, Ganoderma tropicum, Polyporus grammocephalus, Poria, Psilocybe, Pycnoporus sanguineas, Schizophyllum radiatum, Tyromyces*. *seningen nisses* vertical projection at each end of a wooden bowl; *seningen taam* holes in outrigger float for lashing. Pvb. *seningen nippach meyi mwirinné, seningen pókó meyi ngngaw* squid ears are good, shark ears are bad (a saying meaning that squid have only one ear and can hear only one thing, but sharks have many ears and hear many different and conflicting things that give them much trouble and concern; also, having one ear, a squid is obedient, but having several, a shark is not obedient).

seningening (db; 3) See *sening*. vi. (dis.) hear only what one wants to hear, be inattentive to what people have to say.

seningengngaw (3b) See *sening, ngngaw*. vi. be disobedient.

seningepúng (2) See *sening, púng*₁. vi. be deaf. Syn. *seningepwpwas*.

seningepwpwas (3) See *sening, pwpwas*. vi. be deaf. Syn. *seningepúng*.

seningewú (1) See *sening, wú*₃. vi., adj. (be) attentive ("cocked eared").

seningeyééch (2) See *sening, ééch*. vi. be obedient.

senip (3a) SENIPA. nu. (T3) welling up of desire. With dir. suf.: *senipetá*.

senipetá See *senip*.

senichcha (1) See *seni-, chcha*. Tb2. nu. (T1) dysentery.

senito See *sen*₁.

Seniwis nu. (loc.) Jaluit Atoll (Marshall Islands). *peney S.* poker (card game); *semwmwenin S.* gonorrhea (syn. *rimpiyo*).

seniyeni See *seni*₁, *-ni-*. vo. (T6a) put as a side dish or as an accompanying food to. *sipwe s. kkón* we shall have some fish as s. d. to breadfruit pudding.

sense (1) SENSEE. (Jap. *sensei*) Var. *sensey*. nu. (T1) teacher. *emén s.* one t. *newún* or *saman s.* his t.

senseeni See *sense, -ni-*. vo. (T4) be a teacher of (a class). *epwe s. naan mwiich* he will be the t. of that class.

sensey Var. of *sense*.

sensiyu (1) SENSIYUU. (Jap.) nu. (T1) athletic team.

sennap (3) SENNAPA. F. Var. *sannap*. nu. (T3) canoe builder. Cf. *sineenap*.

senné (1) See *sáán, nénné*. nu. (T1) (traditionally) an area for a meeting marked off in an *wuut* by rope lines on which were hung young coconut leaves (*wupwut*) and on which an *itang* had placed a spell so that no one not a qualified member of the meeting could enter without being ill from the spell; (in modern usage) an area within which people are assembled in actual meeting.

senniya (1) SENNIYAA. (Sp. *sandia*) nu. (T1) watermelon. *eew s., eféw s.* one w. *senniyaan* w. of (a given region).

senta (1) SENTAA. (Jap. *sentaa*) nu. (T1) center field (in baseball).

sengeseng (db; 3) SENGA. n. (dis.; T3) gait, manner of walking. *sengesengan* his g. *átánaan wusun sengesengen feefin* that fellow walks in the manner of women.

sengir (2) See *sa-*₂, *ngiri-*. nu. (T2) yellowtail tuna fish. *sengirin* f. of (a given region).

sengko   Trukese-English

sengko See *katorisengko*.
sep (3a) SEPA. vi. be cut off, lopped of (of coconut fronds and pandanus leaves).
sepesaato See *sepesi*.
sepesep (db; 3a) See *sep*. nu. (T3) cutting or lopping off (of pandanus leaves and coconut fronds). va. cut or lop off.
sepesi See *sep*, *-si-*. vo. (T6a) cut or lop off (coconut fronds or pandanus leaves). With dir. suf.: *sepesaato* cut and bring hither.
sepeniin (2) SEPENIINI. (Ger. *Zeppelin*) nu. (T2) airplane, aircraft. *efóch s.* one a. *waan s.* his a. *sepeniinin Merika* American a. *neeniyen s.* airfield; *s. rúwáánú taapen* four- engined a.; *seyin wuwoow s.* aircraft carrier.
sepi (3) SEPIYA. n. (T3) 1. bowl, dish, platter, plate (general term for food receptacle). *eew s.* one b. *sepiyan* his b. *sepiyen Chuuk* Trukese b.; *sepiyen wóón* European b. 2. a constellation of stars in Delphinus.
sepiyeni See *sepi*, *-ni-*. vo. (T6a) acquire a bowl, dish, or platter. Cf. *sessepi*.
sepiyepach (3b) See *sepi*, *pach*. nu. (T3) double bowl (made of wood). [Made of two bowls joined by a handle.]
seppi- (2) SEPPI. [With dir. suf. only.] vi. (u.m.) See *seppito*, *sesseppi-*.
seppito (1) See *seppi-*, *-to*. vi. (u.m.) word used by a spirit medium when calling an *énúúsór* to come and possess him. nu. (T2) a type of *féérúwér* used by a spirit medium to call an *énúúsór*. Syn. *kkééyénú*.
Septemper (Eng.) Var. *Semtemper*, *Sémtooper*. nu. (temp.) September.
sepwá (1) See *se-*₁, *pwá*. vi. be invisible.
ser (3a) SERA. vi. be met accidentally.
seram (3) SERAMA. N. n. (T3) bed cover, sheet. *seraman* his b. c. Syn. *chchenikam*.
seres vi., adj. sail, be sailing; go on a sailing vessel. *waa s.* sailing vessel (ship or outrigger canoe). vi. reef a sail, shorten sail (on an outrigger canoe with lateen rig). Cf. *riif*.
sereni See *ser*, *-ni-*. vo. (T6a) meet accidentally, chance upon.
serengngaw (3b) See *ser*, *ngngaw*. vi. be unluckily or unhappily encountered; suffer mishap, have an unhappy fate, be unlucky.

serepenit (2) SEREPENITI. (Eng.) nu. (T2) snake, serpent. *emén s.* one s. *serepenitin Merika* American s.
Serepwén (3) SEREPWÉNA. nu. (T3) a star or constellation (probably in Corvus); a month in the traditional sidereal calendar. *Serepwénen efeng* a star (same as *Serepwén*).
sereyééch (2) See *ser*, *ééch*. vi. happily or luckily meet by accident; be lucky, have a happy fate.
seri (1) SERII. (Jap. *seri*) nu. (T1) water cress. *efóch s.* one piece of w. c. *anan s.* his w. c. (to eat).
-set E.Wn. of *-tá*.
seti- (2) SETI₂. [In cpds. only.] unsp. (?) child. See *setipeen*, *setipwitur*.
setiiy See *sáát*₁, *-i-*₂. vo. (T5) cook (fish or other *seni*) in mixture of water, salt water, and coconut cream. Cf. *sesset*.
setikken (2) See *sáát*₁, *kken*. vi. taste salty, taste of sea water.
setipeen See *seti-*, *-peen*. N. nu. small child. Syn. *ménúkón*, *monukón*, *nooyiroch*, *nooyis*, *semiriit*, *tipate*.
setipwitur (2) See *seti-*, *pwitur*. Var. *setipwútúr*. nu. (T2) youngest child of a woman ("skirt child"). *néwún s.* her y. c.; *pwiin s.* his y. sibling (by the same mother). *setipwiturun aach faameni* the y. c. of our family.
setipwiturungngaw (3b) See *setipwitur*, *ngngaw*. Var. *setipwitúrúngngaw*. nu. (T3) the very youngest sibling or child.
setipwitúrúngngaw Var. of *setipwiturungngaw*.
setipwur (3) See *sáát*₁, *pwur*₂. n. (T3) elephantiasis. *setipwuran* his e.
setipwútúr Var. of *setipwitur*.
Setonen nu. (loc.) a clan name.
sewáán F. Var. *sawaan*. nu. a variety of breadfruit.
seweyinón (2) See *sawa-*, *inón*. nu. (T2) species of goatfish. *seweyinónun* g. of (a given region).
sewi₁ (1, 3) SEWII₁, SEWIYA. nu. (T1) any of a number of genera of bass (Elbert: *Plectropomus* fish). *sewiin Chuuk* Trukese b.
sewi₂ (1) SEWII₂. nu. (T1) 1. triton shell <*Tritonia (Charonia) tritonis* L.>; any large triton, helmet or frog shell. *sewiin fáánung* lamp triton. Cf. *nikepikken*. 2. trumpet made from triton shell. *néwún s.* his shell trumpet.

sewiiya (1) See se-₁, wii₁, aa-. nu. (num.; T1) no remainder over four (or over a multiple of four) in knot divination.

sewiiyaw (3) See sewi₁, aaw₁. F. nu. (T3) a species of bass (huge, up to six feet long, probably the jawfish). Syn. seyiyaw.

sewiyechcha (1) See sewi₁, chcha. nu. (T1) Japanese bass.

sey (2) See sááy. Itang. vi. voyage, travel.

seyi- (2) SEYI₂. [In cpds. only.] Var. séé-₂, sii-. unsp. protrude (?); be out of place (?).

seyif (Jap. seifu) vi. be safe (in baseball).

seyifeseen (2) See seyi-, -feseen. vi. be of different length, be uneven.

seyiseni See seyi-, seni₂. vo. (T2) protrude from.

seyikaan (Eng.) vi. shake hands. s. ngeni (vo. phr., T2) s. h. with (someone).

seyikaanong See seyiki.

seyikaato See seyiki.

seyikaawu See seyiki.

seyikáátá See seyiki.

seyikáátiw See seyiki.

seyiki See seyi-, -ki-. N. Var. sééki, siiki. vo. (T2) cause to move, shove, push. With dir. suf.: seyikaanong cause to move in; seyikaato cause to move hither; seyikaawu cause to move out; seyikáátá cause to move up, elevate, raise up (as to high office); seyikáátiw cause to move down, lower; seyikóónó cause to move away. Cf. sseyik.

seyikóónó See seyiki.

seyim (2) SEYIMI. nu. (T2) whetstone, sharpener. seyimin piin pencil sharpener. vi. do sharpening. féwún s. whetstone, grindstone.

seyimi See seyim. vo. (T2) sharpen, whet. Cf. sseyim.

seyin (2) SEYINI. (Eng.) nu. (T2) chain. efóch s. one c. seyinin Merika American c.

seyinó See sááy.

Seyipen nu. (loc.) 1. Saipan. [Said by some itang to be derived from Seyineepwin, because it was discovered at night in a legendary Trukese voyage of exploration.] 2. a variety of banana. wuchun S. banana of S.

seyitiw (3) See seyi-, -tiw. nu. (dir.; T3) a spirit that causes a sickness; the sickness so called. [A term of approbrium when used in address.]

seyiyaw (3) See seyi-, aaw₁. N. nu. (T3) a species of bass (huge, up to six feet long, probably the jawfish). Syn. sewiiyaw.

sé (1) SÉÉ₁. vi. be quieted (of fear, emotion, pain, wind), be calmed, at rest; subside, be subsided (of a wind, pain); set (of sun).

séé-₁ (1) SÉÉ₂. [In cpds. only.] unsp. year (?), season (?). See sééfé. Cf. sowu-₃.

séé-₂ (1) SÉÉ₃. [In cpds. only.] Var. seyi-, sii-. unsp. be out of place (?). See sééki, sséék.

séé (1) See sé. nu. (T1) sunset glow, rosy clouds in west just after sunset.

sééfé (1) See séé-₁, fé. vi., adj. (be) new. nóón eey iyer s. in this n. year. Syn. minafé.

séésé (db; 1) SÉÉ₄. vi. (dis.) 1. engage in a kind of fishing. [It is done by either sex in the shallows in the daytime with hand nets.] 2. catch a wide variety of fish in the daytime.

sééséew Var. of séew₂.

séék (2) SÉKKÚ, SÉÉKÚ. nu. (T2) coconut shell (cut in half and copra removed, often used as a dish); large rings of coconut shell suspended from ears in precolonial times. séékún (sékkún) mékúr skull cap (top of skull); séékun (sékkún) pwasuk knee cap; séékún (sékkún) taka coconut half shell.

séékaanong See sééki.

sééki See séé-₂, -ki-. F. Var. seyiki, siiki. vo. (T2) cause to move or slide; push, shove. With dir. suf.: séékaanong slide (something) in, insert. Cf. sséék.

Séémén (Eng.) nu. (loc.) Germany, German. fin-S. G. woman; re-S. G. man. Syn. Tooyis.

séech (2) SÉCHCHÚ. (Eng.) nu. (T2) shirt. eché s. one s. wúfan s. his s. séchchún Merika American s.

Sééta (1) SÉÉTAA. nu. (T1) 1. a star (probably Alpha Equulei). 2. fourth month in the traditional sidereal calendar.

sééw₁ (2) SÉÉWÚ. [Perhaps from sa-₂, éwú-₂?] nu. (T2) green coconut (best stage for drinking). eew s. one g. c. séewún g. c. of.

sééw₂ Var. séésééw. nu. porcupine fish. Nómwun S. bay between Woney (Onei) and Paata (Pata).

séewúmaaw (3) See sééw₁, maaw. nu. (T3) stage just past séew stage of

séewúr

ripening coconut (beginning to turn brown).

séewúr (2) SÉEWÚRÚ. nu. (T2) plumeria or frangipani (*Plumeria sp.*). *séewúrún Chuuk* Trukese p.; *séewúrún wóón* foreign p. (*Plumeria acutifolia, Plumeria rubra*).

séewúriinen (2) See *séewúr, inen*. nu. (T2) name of plumeria or frangipani attributed to spirits and used by spirit mediums when possessed by a spirit ("plumeria of heaven"). [Elbert: Cerbera tree, fruit used in leis.]

séewútaap (3) See *séew₁, taap*. nu. (T3) fifth stage of coconut growth, just before *séew* stage. [First soft slimy meat appears, milk not yet very sweet.]

séfén (2) SÉFÉNÚ. (Eng.) nu. (T2) shovel. *efóch s.* one s. *aan s.* his s. *séfénún Merika* American s.

sékúr (2) SÉKÚRÚ. n. (T2) back (of people, animals). *sékúrún* his b. *metek s.* backache, arthritis or rheumatism of the back.

sékúrúpi (1) See *sékúr, pi*. nu. (T1) a Lethrinid fish. *sékúrúpiin Chuuk* Trukese l. f. Cf. *metiin*.

sékúrúpwpwór (4) See *sékúr, pwpwór*. nu. (T2) hunchback.

Sémtooper Obs. (Eng.) Var. *Semtemper, Septemper*. nu. (temp.) September.

sétút (2) SÉTÚTÚ. nu. (T2) species of small marine crab. *eew s.* one m. c. *sétútún Chuuk* Trukese m. c.

si-₁ (2) SI₂. [The standard form; it may be shortened to *s-*, as in *saa nó*.] pref. (sub.) 1pl. inc. sub. prn.: we. [Although a prefix, it is written separately except when followed by an aspect marker. Sub. prns. are used only at the beginning of narrative constructions and mark them as such.] *sipwaapw* (indefinite future), *sipwe* (future), *sipwene* (uncertain future), *sisapw* (future negative), *sise* (negative reality), *site* (purposeful future negative, negative command), *siya* (reality).

si-₂ (2) SI₃. pref. be such as is...(with verbs); the condition of being such as is...(with nouns). See *nisimwúút, sichón₁, sichón₂, siin₂, sine, sineey*. Cf. *ki-*.

-si- (2) SI₄. suf. (v.form.) makes an object focussed verb of the base.

si (2) SI₁. excl. hey! [Harsh, impolite, rude, expressing comtempt for person to whom used.]

-si (1) SII₁. suf. (u.m.) See *mwárisi*.

sii- (1) SII₂. [In cpds. only.] Var. *seyi-, séé-₂*. unsp. be out of place (?); move (?). See *siiki, ssiik*.

sii (1) SII₃. nu. (T1) name of the consonant (unvoiced, dental spirant) written *s*; name of the letter thus written.

Siis₁ See *-sis*. nu. (loc.) Tsis Island.

siis₂ (2) SISSI. nu. (T2) shed-like projection at either end of native house or meeting house. *sissin iimw* house's p.

Siises (Eng.) nu. (pers.) Jesus. *S. Krayis* Jesus Christ. Syn. *Iyeesus*.

siikaanong See *siiki*.

siikaato See *siiki*.

siikááta See *siiki*.

siikáátiw See *siiki*.

siike (2) SIIKEE. (Ger. *Ziege*) nu. (T2) goat. *emén s.* one g. *siikeen Chuuk* Trukese g.

siiki See *sii-, -ki-*. N. Var. *seyiki, sééki*. vo. (T2) slide; cause to move. With dir. suf.: *siikaanong* slide in, insert; *siikaato* slide hither; *siikááta* slide up, raise, elevate (to office); *siikáátiw* lower, cause to move down. Cf. *kii, ssiik*.

siim (3) SIIMA, SIMMA. nu. (T3) medium sized tridachna shell (smooth upper surface). *eew s.* one t. s. *siimen (simmen) Chuuk* Trukese t. s. *féwún nóón s.* pearl in the t. s.

siimsón N. of *tiimsón*.

siin₁ (2) SINI₁. nu. (T2) skin, bark. *sinin* his s. Syn. *kiin*.

siin₂ (3: *sinna-*) See *si-₂, -nna-*. vi. be known (as fact, as something seen). Dis. *sissiin* (ds). *aa s. reey* it is known by me (of something seen, or of an idea, answer to riddle). Cf. *sine, sineey*.

siing (2) See *sing*. Tbl. n. (T2) fart. *eew s.* one f. *singin* his f.

siipw₁ (3) SIPWPWA₁. (Eng.) nu. (T3) ship. *efóch s.* one s. *sipwpwen neeman* railroad train, automobile, truck, etc. (obsolete).

siipw₂ (2, 3) SIPWPWA₂. (Eng.) nu. (T3) jib. *sipwpwen pwoot* boat's j.

siipw₃ (3) SIPWPWA₃. (Eng.) nu. (T3) sheep. *emén s.* one s. *sipwpwen Merika* American s. *chóón ffóón s.* shepherd.

siipw₄ (3) SIPWPWA₄. nu. (T3) spider lily (*Crinum asiaticum*). [Stem used in

medicine for *chúúnúket*; flowers worn as a signal in courtship.] *efóch s.* one s. l. *sipwpwen Chuuk Trukese s.* l.
siir (2) SIRI. Tbl. n. (T2) urine. *sirin* his u.
siiwin (2) See *sii-*, *win₁*. n. (T2) exchange, swap, trade, replacement. *siiwinin* his replacement (the one who takes his place). vi. exchange, swap, trade, replace, make a change, be changed. *angeey siiwinin* take revenge for it; *siiwinin kkapas* translation of talk.
siiwini Var. of *siwini*.
siiwiniiti See *siiwin*, *-iti*. Var. *siwiniiti*. vo. (T2) change into (something), be transformed into.
siiwiniiy See *siiwin*, *-i-₂*. Var. *siwiniiy*. vo. (T5) replace, take the place of, make a swap or trade for, change (money); translate (speech). Syn. *siiwini*, *siwini*.
sifin (3) SIFINA. N. n. (T3) peeling (of sunburned skin). *sifinan* his p. vi. be peeling. Syn. *ettik*. Cf. *karakar*.
-sis [Appears only in place names.] suf. (dir.) <Kraemer> up, east.
sisen (2) SISENI. (Eng.) nu. (T2) chisel. *efóch s.* one c. *néwún s.* his c.; *sisenin* c. of.
sisech (2) SISECHI. (Eng.) nu. (T2) scissors. *efóch s.* one pair of s. *néwún s.* his s.; *sisechin* s. of.
sissiin Dis. of *siin₂*.
sik (3b) SIKA₁. vi. be one who flaunts himself, be vain, be lascivious, loose (of a person); be indiscriminate and lustful in one's sexual appetite, constantly dressing so as to attract the attention of the opposite sex (said of both men and women), flirtatious. ni. (T3) lasciviousness, wantoness. *sikan* his l.
sika (3) SIKA₂. (Eng.) nu. (T3) cigar. *efóch s.* one c. *wúnúman s.* his c.
sikaato Var. of *súkaato*.
sikapwoot (Eng. *checkerboard*) nu. checkers. vi. play checkers.
sikáásini See *sik*, *-ásini*. vo. (T5) be vain about, inordinately proud of, flaunt.
sikách (4) SIKÁCHE. F. nu. (T2) stingray; ray fish. *sikáchin Chuuk* Trukese s. *máchewen s.* s. spine. Syn. *ffey*.
sikepwpwach (3) See *sik*, *pwpwach*. vi. be lascivious, wanton, flirtatious, loose or promiscuous sexually.
sikerong (3) See *sik*, *roong*. vi. brag about or flaunt one's special knowledge.

sikiyaki (1) SIKIYAKII. (Jap. *sukiyaki*) nu. (T1) sukiyaki. *eew s.* one s. *anan s.* his s.
sikowuru nu. (temp.) 2nd night of the lunar month.
simeen (2) SIMEENI. (Eng.) nu. (T2) cement; filling (dental). *simeenin Merika* American c. adj. made of cement.
simiis (2) SIMIISI. (Eng. *chemise*) nu. (T2) petticoat. *aan s.*, *wúfan s.* her p. *simiisin Merika* American p.
simiiten nu. a variety of *Cyrtosperma*. [Said to have been introduced from the Marshall Islands.]
simpúng (2) SIMPÚNGÚ. (Jap. *shimbun*) nu. (T2) newspaper. *eché s.* one n. *néwún s.* his n.
simwmweta (1) nu. (T1) false poinciana (*Asclepias curassavica*).
simwmwo (1) SIMWMWOO. (Jap.) vi. wrestle. Syn. *ewúnap*.
simwmwos (Jap.) nu. muslin cloth.
sin (2) SINI₂. Tbl. Var. *sing*. vi. break wind, fart. Syn. *pwpwir*.
sináyik (3) SINÁYIKA. (Eng. *slack*) vi., va. be slacked off (of rope); slacken.
sináyikeey See *sináyik*, *-e-₂*. vo. (T6b) slacken, let out (rope).
sine (1) See *si-₂*, *-na-*, *-e-₂*. [Cf. Gb. *kinai*.] va. know how, be skilled (in). *ááy sina (sine) aretimetik* my being skilled in arithmetic. nu. (T1) knowledge (as ability to do), skill. *aan s.* his k. Cf. *siin₂*, *sineey*.
sineefichiiy See *sine*, *-fich*, *-i-₂*. vo. (T5) know well.
sineeffengennii- See *sine*; *ffengeen*, *-i-₂*. [In plural only.] vo. (refl.) recognize one another. *sise sineeffengenniikich* we don't r. one another.
sineenap (3) See *sine*, *nap*. n. (T3) 1. great skill or training, expertise. *sineenapan* his g. s. 2. one who is highly skilled, an expert; expert adzman, one who knows how to make canoes, wooden bowls, and paddles. Cf. *sennap*. 3. traditional god of wood working (numbered among the sky gods). vi. be highly skilled, expert, knowledgeable. *meyi s. ne fóós átánaan* that fellow is h. s. in the use of words.
sineey₁ See *si-₂*, *-na-*, *-e-₂*. vo. (T6b) know (persons, ideas, intentions, etc.);

recognize. *ááy sineyok* my knowledge of you. Cf. *sine*.

sineey₂ (3) See *sineey₁, -ya-*. n. (T3) knowledge (based on verbal explanation, as distinct from demonstration and doing); knowledge of persons, ideas, intentions, etc. (as distinct from knowing how to do something). *aan s., sineeyan* his k. *meet sineeyomw reen ewe féfféér* what do you know about that affair. Cf. *sine*.

sines (2) SINESI. nu. (T2) plain fighting spear made from coconut wood. *wókun s.* his s. *sinesin Chuuk* Trukese s.

sinéw (2) SINÉWÚ. N. Var. *tinéw*. nu. (T2) wall plate beam (in a house). *sinéwún iimw* houses w. p. b.

sini (1) SINII. [In cpds. only.] Var. *kini*. adj. made of plaited coconut frond matting.

sinifer (2) SINIFERI. (Eng.) nu. (T2) silver. *siniferin Merika* American s.

sinifé (1) See *siin₁, -fé*. nu. (T1) hibiscus (*Hibiscus tiliaceus*); hibiscus bark. [Fruit used as medicine against sea spirits; bark used for cordage and threads in weaving; flowers used as medicine for inflammation of the eyes; wood used to make breadfruit pickers.] *sinifèén Chuuk* Trukese h. Syn. *ayipiskas, sáápwow*.

sinifèénúwén (2) See *sinifé, wénú-*. nu. (T2) person of low degree ("wild hibiscus"); commoner.

sinik (2) SINIKI. (Eng.) nu. (T2) silk. *sinikin Sapaan* Japanese s.

sinini See *ssin, -ni-*. F. Var. *sinni*. vo. (T2) dig up.

sinipwa (1) See *sin, pwa*. Tb1. vi. be flatulent; be offensive because of flatulency.

sinipwut (3) See *siin₁, pwuta-*. N. nu. (T3) species of parrot fish. *sinipwuten Chuuk* Trukese p. f. Syn. *kinipwut*.

sino (1) SINOO. (Eng.) nu. (T1) snow. *sinoon Merika* American s.

sinser (2) SINSERI. (Eng.) nu. (T2) white ginger (*Hedichium cylindrica*). *sinserin Chuuk* Trukese w. g. Syn. *fitun, tunun*.

sinneni See *siin₂, -ni-*. vo. (T6a) recognize (someone).

sinni N. of *sinini*.

sinnot (2, 3) See *siin₁, woot₁*. N. n. (T2, 3) vitiligo (white spots on hands and feet, believed caused by handling taro tubers). *sinnotun, sinnotan* his v. Syn. *saaf*.

sing (2) SINGI. Tb1. Var. *sin*. vi. break wind, fart. [To do this in public is shameful through most of Truk.] Syn. *pwpwir*.

singenes (2) SINGENESI. (Eng. *singlet*). nu. (T2) general term for undershirt, sleeved or sleeveless. *eché s.* one u. *wúfan s.* his u. *singenesin Merika* American u. Cf. *nipéwúttún, ranning*.

sipa (1) SIPAA. (Jap. *shiba*) nu. (T1) a grass (good for preventing erosion); turf, lawn. *aan s.* his g. *sipaan Sapaan* Japanese g.

sipeet (Eng.) Var. *sipeyit*. nu. spades (in cards).

sipeyit Var. of *sipeet*.

sipiringngú (2) SIPIRINGNGÚÚ. (Jap. *supuringu*) nu. (T2) T-shirt. *eché s.* one T. *wúfan s.* his T.

sipor (2) SIPORU. nu. (T2) a small reef fish. *siporun Chuuk* Trukese r. f.

sipuun (3) SIPUUNA. (Jap. *supuun*) nu. (T3) spoon. *efóch s.* one s. *aan s.* his s.; *sipuunen* s. of. Syn. *sipwuun*.

sipw vi. be a superb performer, do a good job; be polished, having a sheen. *meyi s. áteey nóón (wóón) eey angaang* this fellow does an excellent job in this work. *meyi s. eey fétún* this paddle is polished (i.e., is properly finished off).

sipwuun (2) SIPWUNNU. (Eng.) nu. (T2) spoon. *efóch s.* one s. *aan s.* his s.; *sipwunnun* s. of. Syn. *sipuun*.

sipwpwumw (2) SIPWPWUMWU. (Eng. *jib-boom*) nu. (T2) bowsprit. *sipwpwumwun waa* boat's b. Cf. *siipw, pwuumw*.

sir (2) See *siir*. Tb1. vi. urinate.

sirayik (Jap. *sutoraiku*) nu. strike (in baseball). *eew s.* one s.

sirip (3) SIRIPA. nu. (T3) partridge-like dove. [It runs on the ground, has a white head and brownish-red neck, and is delicious eating.] *siripen Chuuk* Trukese d.

sirippa (1) SIRIPPAA. (Jap. *surippa*) nu. (T1) slippers. *eew s.* one pair of s.; *eyipw s.* one slipper. *ipwan s., néwún s.* his s.

siro (1) SIROO. (Eng.) nu. (T1) zero.

sirkumsayis (2) SIRKUMSAYISI. (Eng.) vi. be circumsized.

sirkumsayisiiy See *sirkumsayis, -i-₂*. vo. (T5) circumsize.

-sich (2) SICHI. F. Var. *-chis, chiki-*₁. suf. (adj.) a little bit; incipient, just at the beginning. See *énúwénúsich, móósich, neefááfisich.*

sichiring (2) SICHIRINGI. (Jap. *shichirin*) nu. (T2) small portable stove, hibachi. *eew s.* one s. *aan s.* his s.

sichón₁ (4) See *si-*₂, *chón.* nu. (T2?) plant (*Microlepis speluncae*). [It is used as an *itang* medicine.]

sichón₂ (4) See *si-*₂, *chón.* nu. (T3) species of black worm about six inches long. *sichónen Chuuk* Trukese w. Syn. *niyén.*

sitaam (3) SITAAMA, SITAMMA. (Eng.) nu. (T3) stamp, postage stamp. *sitaamen fénú* deed or title paper to land.

sitakin (2) SITAKINI. (Eng.) nu. (T2) stocking, sock. *efóch, eew s.* one s. *néwún s.* his s. *eew peya s.* a pair of s. *sitakinin Sapaan* Japanese s.

sitammeey See *sitaam, -e-*₂. vo. (T6b) stamp, put a stamp on; register (land).

sitiima (1) SITIIMAA. (Eng. *steamer*) nu. (T1) passenger ship. [It may be any size.] Cf. *timma.*

sitoof (3) SITOOFA. (Eng.) Var. *stoof.* nu. (T3) stove. *eew s.* one s. *aan s.* his s. *sitoofen Merika* American s.

sitoowa (1) SITOOWAA. (Eng.) nu. (T1) store, shop. *chóón s.* storekeeper, shopkeeper, store clerk.

Siwiiten (Eng.) nu. (loc.) Sweden.

Siwiiternán (Eng.) nu. (loc.) Switzerland.

siwini- Var. in cpds. of *siiwin.*

siwini See *siwini-*. Var. *siiwini.* vo. (T2) substitute for, take the place of. *John aa s. George* John substituted for George. Syn. *siiwiniiy, siwiniiy.*

siwiniiti Var. of *siiwiniiti.*

siwiniiy Var. of *siiwiniiy.*

siwinifátáneey See *siwini-, fátán, -e-*₂. vo. (T6b) change the location of.

siya See *si, -a*₁. Var. *sa, só.* prn. const. 1pl. inc. prn. plus reality aspect marker: we (past, factual). *siyaa nó* (N.), *siyóó nó* (F.) we are off (often used in coordinating group effort, as in lifting heavy objects).

Siyemwaw nu. (pers.) name of an evil spirit that preys on pregnant women.

siyeri vo. (T2 or T5) hit, strike (people or things). Syn. *namwúti.* Cf. *awata, mwérúúw, nengeey, nniiy, wecheey.*

siyéé- (1) SIYÉÉ. [In cpds. only.] unsp. call (for help). With dir. suf.: *siyéétá* c. up (to heaven). Cf. *chi.*

siyéétá See *siyéé-*.

Siyoowa (Eng.) nu. (pers.) Jehovah. Syn. *Iyoowa.*

siyok (3) See *si-*₂, *-ok.* vi. peep (of a chick). Syn. *ssiyapw.*

siyokarafi (Eng.) nu. geography.

siyóyinen (2) SIYÓYINENI. nu. (T2) a plant (*Malvastrum coromandelianum, Sida acuta, Sida rhombifolia*). [Its bark, leaves, and flowers are used in medicine.] *siyóyinenin Chuuk* Trukese p.

so₁ (1) SOO₁. vi. be kindled, be lit (of oven, fire, etc.).

so₂ (1) SOO₂. vi. be alighted, landed, come to rest (of flying objects only); alight, come to rest, land. *aa s. ewe machchang* the bird has alighted. With dir. suf.: *soonó, sootiw, sooto. aa sootiw ewe sepeniin* the plane has landed.

so₃ (1) SOO₃. vi. precipitate out (as the starch from the water in which arrowroot or manioc root gratings have been washed). With dir. suf.: *sootiw.*

soo-₁ (1) SOO₄. vi., adj. (be) on the side (of something, e.g. on the near or western side). Dis. *soosoo-* (db). With dir. suf.: *soonó, soosoonó* on the far side, the other side, beyond; *sootá* on the eastern side, to the east, on the upper side, above; *sootiw* on the western side, to the west, on the lower side, below; *sooto, soosooto* on this side, on the near side. *kkapasen sootá* eastern dialect (in Truk). *soosoonóón naan waa* the far side of yonder canoe.

soo-₂ (1) SOO₅. Var. *choo-*₁. unsp. waste, loss, being without what is needed. See *soochik, soochis, soosich, soonap, sochchik.*

soo-₃ (1) SOO₆. unsp. be immersed, under water. See *sooni, sooso*₃.

soo-₄ (1) SOO₇. [In cpds. only.] unsp. person (?). See *soomá, soope, sooná, soopach, sootupw.* Cf. *sowu-*₁.

soo (1) See *so*₃. nu. (T1) precipitate; starch flour precipitated from the washing of any of several roots. *soon áfán* turmeric flour; *soon mwékúmwék* arrowroot flour; *soon tapiyooka* sweet manioc flour.

soof (2) SOFFU. nu. (T2) scrub rag. *aan s.* his s. r. vi. scrub with a wet rag, be scrubbed (of things only). Dis. *sossoof* (ds). *soffun cheepen* scrubbing the table.

soosich (2) See *soo-₂, -sich.* F. vi. be saved, put away, kept (so as not to be wasted); obedient. Syn. *soochik, choochis.*

sooso₁ (1) SOO₈. nu. (T1) 1. (basic meaning) holder, fastener. 2. outrigger fastener in the form of a rope used to lash the outrigger float to the outrigger booms and stanchions (*soosoon taam, soosoon waa*). 3. thatch holder of coconut fronds laid over thatch to keep it from being ripped up in the wind (*soosoon masawu*).

sooso₂ (db; 1) See *soo-₃.* va. soak, immerse, lay a fish trap; drown an opponent in sea fighting by holding him down under water from above on a canoe. Cf. *sooni₂.*

soosoomaay (ds; 3) See *soo-₁, maay₁.* nu. (T3) beach rock. [Used to polish coconut shell flasks.] Syn. *piru.*

soosooni See *sooso₁, -ni-.* vo. (T4) apply the outrigger fastening rope to (the float or the canoe).

soosoonó See *soo-₁.*

soosoongeni (db) See *soo-₁, ngeni.* vo. (T2) be near, be on the side toward.

soosooto See *soo-₁.*

sooko (1) SOOKOO. (Jap. *sooko*) nu. (T1) warehouse. *eew s.* one w. *aan s.* his w.

soomá (1) See *soo-₄, má.* n. (T1) a corpse; spirit, ghost, general term for any invisible being with human emotions. *soomáán* his c. *soomáán iimw* spirit of housebuilding named *Sowurawan.* Cf. *soope, sootupw.*

soomechemech (db; 3) See *soo-₁, meche-.* vi. be precariously situated.

soon (3) SOONA. F. Var. *sson.* nu. (T3) damsel fish. *soonen Chuuk* Trukese d. f.

soonap (3a) See *soo-₂, nap.* n. (T3) waste, discard, failure to realize an opportunity. *soonapan* w. for him, his loss of an opportunity or something he needed. *soonapen átánaan* the waste of that fellow (in reference to someone of handsome appearance but bad character, i.e. the handsome appearance was thrown away on him when someone else who was deserving could have used it). Id. *soonapey!* if only I had known! vi. be wasted; be discarded or lost when needed. Syn. *sochchik.* Ant. *soochis, soochik, soosich.*

sooná (1) See *soo-₄, -ná.* vi., adj. be thievish, tricky; steal. *chóón s.* thief; *peney s.* cheating at cards; *tipachchem s.* knowledgeable to the extent that one can steal with impunity if one wishes to.

soonááni See *sooná, -ni-.* vo. (T4) steal; acquire by stealing. Cf. *soonááy.*

soonáátá See *sooni₁.*

soonáátiw See *sooni₁, sooni₂.*

soonááy See *sooná.* vo. (T1) steal. Cf. *soonááni.*

soonefen (2) See *soo, efen₄.* nu. (T2) coral rock (standing up on reef). *soonefenin wunooch* c. r. of the reef surface.

soon ekiyek See *so₂, ekiyek₂.* n. phr. a hold or throw in hand-to-hand fighting ("fairy tern's alighting"). [Against an opponent striking with a club, one parries the blow with one's left hand and pulls his head down with one's right hand. Then one reaches around behind him with one's left hand and grabs his left arm from between his legs.]

sooni₁ See *so₁, -ni-.* vo. (T4) lay, kindle (of fire, oven, etc.). With dir. suf.: *soonáátá* kindle (a fire or oven); *soonáátiw* put down or lay (a fire).

sooni₂ See *soo-₃, -ni-.* vo. (T4) soak, immerse (in water); lay, set down (a fish trap under water). With dir. suf.: *soonáátiw* soak, immerse; push someone down under water to drown him. Cf. *sooso₂.*

soonó See *so₂, soo-₁.*

soong (3a) SOONGA. vi. be angry, cross. *s. ngeni* be a. at; *s. reen* be a. because of. Cf. *ningeringer.*

soongeyiti See *soong, -iti.* vo. (T2) be angry at. Syn. *soong ngeni.*

soongokkáy (2, 3) See *soong, kkáy.* vi. be impatient, quickly angered.

soopach (3) See *soo-₄, pach.* vi., adj. (be) together (of people), sleep together.

soope (1) See *soo-₄, pe.* nu. (T1) spirit, ghost; general term for any invisible being with human-like emotions, old-time god, soul of dead person, evil spirit (e.g. *chénúkken*). [Cannot be used to refer to a corpse.] *soopeen nóó*

wave spirit (causes sickness resulting in wheezy breathing with loss c" voice and sore throat). Cf. *soomá.*
soopw (2) SOOPWU, SOPWPWU. (Eng.) nu. (T2) soap. *eféw s.* one piece of s. *aan s.* his piece of s. *soopwun* or *sopwpwun Merika* American s. vi. be washed (of clothes); do laundry.
soor (3a) SORA₁. n. (T3) morning. [Usually in ptv. const.] Dis. *sossor* (ds). *soran* its m.; *soren* m. of. *nóón eey soran, nóón eey sossoran* this m.; *nóón ewe soran aa nó* on that past m. *soren efituuw?* what morning?; *soren ewe Ewúnúngát* last Wednesday morning. Cf. *neesor.*
soochis Var. of *soochik* (see *soo-₂, -chis*).
soochik (2) See *soo-₂, chiki-₁.* N. Var. *choochis, soochis, soosich.* vi. be saved, put away, kept (so as not to be wasted). Cf. *sochchik.*
soochu (1) SOOCHUU. (Jap. *soochuu*) nu. (T1) strong alcoholic drink made from coconuts; brandy. *wúnúman s.* his d.
soota (1) SOOTAA. (Eng.) nu. (T1) soda.
sootam (3) SOOTAMA. F. Var. *chóótam.* nu. (T3) stage of growth of a coconut (not yet full sized).
sootá See *soo-₁.*
sootiw₁ See *so₂, so₃, soo-₁.*
sootiw₂ (3) See *so₂, -tiw.* nu. (T3) a hold or throw in hand-to-hand fighting. [Against an opponent thrusting with club or knife, one grabs his thrusting (right) arm at the wrist and, stepping low behind him, pulls his arm down, grabs it from behind between his legs with one's left hand, pulling back and up and at the same pushing forward on his backside with the right hand.]
sooto₁ (1) SOOTOO. (Jap. *shooto*) nu. (T1) shortstop (in baseball).
sooto₂ See *so₂, soo-₁.*
sootupw (2) See *soo-₄, tupw₁.* nu. (T2) corpse, dead body (people only). *emén s.* one c. *sootupwun átewe* that fellow's c. Cf. *soomá.*
soow (2) SOOWU. nu. (T2) midrib of coconut palm leaf (as used in brooms). *efóch s.* one m. *soowun núú* coconut's m.
sooyenú (1) See *soo-₄, énú.* nu. (T1) a form of sorcery used in war. [A corpse or wooden image of a person is propped up or buried with head above ground, with mouth open and facing

the locality of the intended victims, who are devoured by the *énú penemóówun*. Resulting illnesses are *chúúnúket* and *achar.*] Syn. *énúúsooso.*
sooyu (1) SOOYUU. (Jap. *shooyu*) Var. *soyiyú.* nu. (T1) soy, soy sauce. *sooyuun Sapaan* Japanese s. s.
soffuuw See *soof, -u-.* vo. (T5) scrub with a wet rag.
sossich F. of *chochchis.*
sossor See *soor.*
sossora- (ds; 3) See *soro-.* nr. (T3) turning. *sossoren fóós* changing the import of words, falsifying a message to its opposite.
soker (2) SOKERI. (Eng.) nu. (T2) joker (in cards). *sokerin kaas* j. in cards.
sokopen vi. tumble, roll over and over.
sokun Var. of *sókun.*
somwa- (3) SOMWA₁. ni. (T3) amount or number more or over. [In ptv. const. only.] *fituuw (fite, fiteféw) somwan* how many more than it; *nimuuw somwan* five more than it. suf. (adj.) more than. [Used with tens, hundreds, and thousands, but not with one through nine.] *engoonusomw, rúweesomw, iniikisomw, fááyikisomw, nimeesomw, fiikisomw, waniikisomw, ttiweesomw, ipwúkúúsomw* more than ten, twenty,...one hundred. *engéréwúsomw* more than one thousand.
somwori See *ssomw, -ri-.* vo. (T6a) snatch up in one's mouth, snap up, gobble.
son (3) SONA. vi., adj. (be) deceived, tricked, fooled. Syn. *tupw₂.*
sonu nu. <Elbert> a species of damsel fish.
sonpeepa (1) SONPEEPAA. (Eng.) nu. (T1) sandpaper.
songosong (db; 3) SONGA. nu. (T3) a variety of breadfruit. Syn. *neesén.*
sopor (2) SOPORU. nu. (T2) dolphin (fish). *soporun Chuuk* Trukese d.
sopwon (2) SOPWONU. adj. (u.m.) See *móngosopwon.*
sopwusopw (db; 2) SOPWU. Rmn. nu. (T2) sponge (thing and animal).
sopwpwuni See *soopw, -ni-.* vo. (T5) wash (clothes), launder.
sor (3a) See *soor.* vi. be morning. *aa s.* it was morning. With dir. suf.: *soronó* dawn, become morning.

soreey See *soro-, -e-₂*. vo. (T6b) turn, change the direction of, change the import of (words). With dir. suf.: *soreeyenong, soreeyenó, soreeyetá, soreeyetiw, soreeyeto, soreeyewow, soreeyewu*.

soren (2) SORENI. nu. (T2) a small mackerel fish (baby *pétú*). *sorenin Chuuk* Trukese m.

soro- (3a) SORA₂. vi. be turned. With dir. suf.: *soronong, soronó, sorotá, sorotiw, soroto, sorowow, sorowu. eey iimw meyi sorotá asaman Tunnuuk* this house has its door turned east from Tunnuuk.

sorofeseen (2) See *soro-, -feseen*. vi. be turned in opposite directions, be head to foot.

soronong See *soro-*.

soronó See *sor, soro-*.

soropwang (3) SOROPWANGA. (Jap. *soroban*) nu. (T3) abacus. *soropwangen Sapaan* Japanese a.

sorotá₁ See *soro-*.

sorotá₂ (1) See *soro-, -tá*. nu. (T1) day after tomorrow. [Short for *sorotáán neesor*.]

sorotiw See *soro-*.

soroto See *soro-*.

sorowow See *soro-*.

sorowu See *soro-*.

soroyeew See *soro-, eew₁*. vi. be turned or facing the same way.

socha- (3) SOCHA. nr. (T3) in the phrase *sochen mááy* tabu marker of breadfruit. [It consists of a rod with a young coconut leaf tied to it, which is planted beside a breadfruit tree to mark it as ritually tabu.]

sochungiyo (1) SOCHUNGIYOO. (Jap.) nu. (T1) graduation (from school). *mwiichen s. g.* exercise.

sochchik (2) See *soo-₂, -chchik*. N. vi. be wasted (of something discarded or lost that is needed). Syn. *soonap*. Cf. *soochik*.

sowu-₁ (2) SOWU₁. pref. (with nouns) leader of, proprietor of, practitioner of, expert in, one who goes first regarding; (with verbs) frequently engaging in, skilled in, experienced in. *sowufénú* proprietor of land; *sowukkéén* leader in song. *sowufééri* experienced in doing (something). Cf. *soo-₄, ssow*. nr. (T2) leader of, proprietor of. [Permitted, but rarely used.] *sowun ákkáp* fault-finder; *sowun fiyuuw* military person, soldier; *sowun fiyuuwun neeman* army person, soldier; *sowun fiyuuwun neeset* naval person, sailor; *sowun fiyuuwun neeset pwan neeman* marine; *sowun kképwúng* judge; *sowun koowa* deacon (Protestant) (loanword from Pon.); *sowun peták* or *sowun páták* minister, pastor, religious leader (loanword from Pon.).

sowu-₂ (2) SOWU₂. unsp. greeting, honoring. See *kinissow, sowun, sowuni*.

sowu-₃ (2) SOWU₃. [In cpds. only.] unsp. time, season. See *faansowu-, ossow, ossowu*. Cf. *séé-₁*.

Sowufa nu. (pers. and loc.) 1. legendary first chief of Feefen (Fefan) Island. 2. a clan name.

sowufanafan (3) See *sowu-₁, fanafan₁*. nu. (T3) master canoe builder.

Sowufanachik nu. (loc.) a clan name.

Sowufáár nu. (loc.) a clan name.

sowufééri See *sowu-₁, fééri*. vo. (T4) be experienced in doing (something).

sowufén (2) See *sowu-₁, fén₁*. nu. (T2) specialist in treating wounds from knives or sling-stones.

sowufénú (1, 3a) See *sowu-₁, fénú*. nu. (T3) proprietor of the land; land recorder, master of land lore. [May be used of a district chief or a *sowuppwún* (proprietor of soil).]

Sowuféwúúp nu. (pers.) legendary first chief of Féwúúp, Toon (Tol) Island. [He had the soubriquet Mwéchiineesápúk.]

sowufiiwu N. of *sowufiyuuw*.

sowufiyuuw (2) See *sowu-₁, fiyuuw*. Var. *sowufiiwu*. nu. (T2) soldier, military person. *sowufiyuuwun Merika* American s. Syn. *sowun fiyuuw*.

sowufóós (2) See *sowu-₁, fóós*. nu. (T2) orator, master of rhetoric; prophet. vi., adj. (be) talkative.

Sowufóónupi nu. (pers.) legendary chief and founding spirit of Ponape.

sowusan (3v) See *sowu-₁, san*. nu. (T3v) one who knows *san*; masseur, bone-setter.

Sowusatawan nu. (loc.) a clan name.

sowusáfey (3) See *sowu-₁, sáfey*. nu. (T3) one who knows how to prepare medicines. Cf. *sowurong*.

Sowusát nu. (loc.) a clan name.

sowuset (2) See *sowu*-₁, *sáát*₁. nu. (T2) master fisherman.
Sowuk Var. of *Suuk*.
Sowukachaw See *sowu*-₁, *Achaw*₃. nu. (pers.) Lord of Achaw, legendary King of Kusaie.
sowukásissin (3) See *sowu*-₁, *esissin*. nu. (T2) master of signs and portents, soothsayer.
sowukoowa (1) See *sowu*-₁, *koowa*. (Pon.) nu. (T1) deacon (in Protestant Church). Syn. *sowun koowa, sewiin koowa*.
sowukunow (2) See *sowu*-₁, *kunow*. vi. be experienced in loafing.
Sowukuwopw nu. (pers.) name of legendary first chief of Wuumaan (Uman) Island.
Sowukútú nu. (loc.) the chiefly lineage of Kútú, Satawan Atoll.
sowukkes (2) See *sowu*-₁, *kkes*. nu. (T2) enthusiast.
sowukkéén (2) See *sowu*-₁, *kkéén*. nu. (T2) songmaster, leader in song.
sowukképwúng (2) See *sowu*-₁, *kképwúng*. nu. (T2) judge. Syn. *sowun kképwúng*.
sowumáchew (3) See *sowu*-₁, *máchew*₂. nu. (T3) sting-ray conjurer. [He treated those wounded by spears tipped with sting-ray spines.]
Sowumey See *sowu*-₁, *mááy*₂. nu. (pers.) 1. traditional founder and patron saint of breadfruit ritual. [Mythical leader of a group of emigrants from *Éwúr* to *Suuk*, he planted an outrigger float made of breadfruit wood and performed rites that caused the float to take root, sprout, and become a breadfruit tree. The rites he performed have been repeated ever since by *sowuyótoomey* to help ensure good breadfruit harvests.] 2. breadfruit ritual specialist. Syn. *sowuyotoomey*.
sowumwar (3) nu. (T3) in *sáfeen s.* a medicinal steaming used for postpartum illness in women.
Sowumwaror See *sowu*-₁, *mwaror*. Var. *Sowumwóror*. nu. (pers.) a traditional god. [An inhabitant of *Éwúr*, he is patron of dancing (*pwérúk*) that is done for entertainment alone.]
Sowumwerikes nu. (pers.) name of an evil spirit that preys on pregnant women. [It causes insanity in mothers of small infants so that they eat their babies. New mothers are, therefore, attended in their houses, because if left alone they may fall victim to *S.*]
Sowumwir nu. (loc.) a clan name.
Sowumwóóch nu. (loc.) a clan name. Syn. *Mwóóch*₂.
Sowumwóror F. of *Sowumwaror*.
Sowumwmwáár nu. (pers.) legendary first chief of *Wútéét (Udot) Island*.
sowun See *sowu*-₂, -*ni-*. va. in *s. ngeni* greet with (something). *kepwe wuweey néwún átewe kunók ke pwe s. ngeni* take his watch and greet him with it; *wúwa s. ngeni átánaan pecheey* I greeted that fellow with my foot (i.e., I tripped him). Cf. *sowuni*.
sowunakik See *sowu*-₁, *nakik*. nu. thief.
sowuneerongun See *sowu*-₁, *neerongun*. nu. specialist in *neerongun* magic. [He treated those wounded by war-clubs.]
sowuneng (2) See *sowu*-₁, *nááng*. nu. (T2) Christian, one who has been baptized.
sowuné (1) See *sowu*-₁, *néé*₁. nu. (T1) dance specialist.
sowuni See *sowu*-₂, -*ni-*. vo. (T5) greet (a visitor on his arrival). *sise sineey menne epwe sowunikich nóón eey iyer sééfé* we do not know what will greet us (happen to us) in this new year. Cf. *sowun ngeni*.
sowunisoowu (1) See *sowu*-₁, *nisoowu*. nu. (T1) fornicator.
sowunó (1) See *sowu*-₁, *nóó*. nu. (T1) weather conjurer.
Sowunóón₁ See *sowu*-₁, *nónu-*. nu. (pers.) god living under the earth and below the ocean floor, in charge of things below. Cf. *nónnóón*.
sowunóón₂ (4) See *sowu*-₁, *nónu-*. nu. (T2) professional diver. Cf. *nónnóón*.
Sowunuuk nu. (loc.) a clan name.
sowupa (1) SOWUPAA. adj. (u.m.) See *cháásowupa*.
Sowupaata nu. (pers.) legendary first chief of Paata. [He had the soubriquet of Wumwusómwoon and is equated with Sómwooniyóng.]
sowupachaaw (3) See *sowu*-₁, *pachaaw*. nu. (T2) shark conjurer. [He treats those wounded by knuckle-dusters or shark-bite and those who are ill from *rongen pachaaw* sorcery.] Syn. *sowupókó*.
sowupeták See *sowu*-₁, *peták*. (Pon.) nu. pastor, religious teacher (in the

Protestant Church). Syn. *sowun páták, sowun peták.*

Sowupeyinó See *sowu-₁, pa-₁, nóó.* nu. (pers.) traditional god of mild waves and gentle seas. [According to Bollig he lives in *Éwúr.*]

Sowupinay nu. (loc.) a clan name.

sowupókó (1) See *sowu-₁, pókó.* nu. (T1) shark conjurer. [He treats those wounded by knuckle-dusters or shark-bite and those who are ill from *rongen pachaaw* sorcery.] Syn. *sowupachaaw.*

Sowupúng (2) See *sowu-₁, púng₁* or *púng₂.* [Bollig] nu. (pers.) a traditional god. [An inhabitant of *Éwúr*, he is associated with breadfruit.]

sowuppeyinen (2) See *sowu-₁, ppeyinen.* nu. (T2) expert in spells and medicine relating to the illness in infants caused by *Ppeyinen*, god of the horizon.

sowuppéwút (2) See *sowu-₁, ppéwút.* nu. (T2) expert in sorcery; sorcerer. Syn. *sowuyénúúngngaw.*

sowupwe (1) See *sowu-₁, pwee₁.* nu. (T1) knot diviner (one who is versed in the *pweewunus* form of divination).

sowupwen (2) See *sowu-₁, pwáán.* nu. (T2) master of Trukese judo.

Sowupwech nu. (pers.) a traditional god of cooking, earth ovens, and preserving breadfruit.

sowupwénúpwén (2) See *sowu-₁, pwénúpwén₂.* nu. (T2) master of love magic.

sowupwérúk (2) See *sowu-₁, pwérúk.* nu. (T2) dance leader.

Sowupwonowót nu. (loc.) a clan name. [It used to be known locally as *Effeng* on Romónum.]

Sowupwonnap nu. (pers.) name of the legendary chief of Pulap (*Pwonnap*) and of its chiefly lineage.

Sowupwór nu. (pers.) a god. [He is the navigator or captain of the sailing canoe of the wind goddess *Inenikes.*]

sowupwúng (2) See *sowu-₁, pwúúng.* nu. (T2) legislator. nu. (pers.) chief spirit of the traditional spirits of *itang*.

sowupwpwen (2) See *sowu-₁, pwpwen.* nu. (T2) slanderer.

sowupwpwó (1) See *sowu-₁, pwpwó.* nu. (T1) one who knows *pwpwó*.

sowupwpwún (2) See *sowu-₁, pwpwún₁.* nu. (T2) proprietor of the soil; land owner. [He is usually the head of the lineage that is said to control (*nemeni*) the soil as distinct from the party actually occupying the land and using it. The latter makes gifts of *mmwen ppwún* (first fruits of the soil) to the *sowuppwún*.] Cf. *sowufénú.*

sowuraw (3b) See *sowu-₁, raaw₂.* nu. (T3) adviser or planner in diplomacy and war. [Traditionally such advisors were necessarily *itang*.]

sowurawa (1) See *sowu-₁, rawa.* nu. (T1) masseur, master of massage.

Sowurawan nu. (pers.) spirit of house and *wuut* building. [Invoked in spells, he helps the *sowuwimw* or *sowuwut* (housebuilder) to make the construction right, but he requires the *ósópw* feast in order to bring well-being to the building's future occupants.]

sowureyirey (2) See *sowu-₁, reyirey.* nu. (T2) surgeon.

sowurong (3a) See *sowu-₁, roong.* nu. (T3) one who knows all or a great many *roong* or bodies of special knowledge; one who knows the *roong* required in a given situation. [Often used for one who knows the *roong* associated with the causes and cures of illnesses, i.e., as a synonym of *sowusáfey*.] *sowurongen ikekkar* a specialist in the *rongen ikekkar*; *sowurongen oos* specialist in the spells and medicines relating to ailments caused by the sea spirits called *oos* or *wosen mataw*; *sowurongen sáát* specialist in the spells and medicines relating to the spirits called *chénúkken*, especially to the ailments caused by them. Cf. *sowusáfey.*

sowuchipw (3) See *sowu-₁, chiipw.* nu. (T3) diviner (by the *chiipw* method of divination).

sowutakkich (2) See *sowu-₁, takkich.* nu. (T2) master of the *takkich* method of fishing.

sowutánnipi See *sowu-₁, tánnipi.* nu. master gardener, farmer.

sowutónap (3) nu. (T3) 1. a chiefly title (?). 2. a model canoe race (?).

sowuwa (1v) See *sowu-₁, waa₁.* nu. (T1v) canoe owner, owner or manager of a canoe house.

Sowuwafar nu. (loc.) a clan name.

sowuwachar (3) See *sowu-₁, achar.* nu. (T3) specialist in the magic and

medicine to cure sickness caused by *achar* sorcery.
Sowuwefeng nu. (loc.) a clan name.
Sowuwen nu. (loc.) a clan name. Cf. *Sowuwén*.
Sowuwene nu. (loc.) a clan name.
Sowuweney nu. (loc.) a clan name. Cf. *Sowuyáney*.
Sowuwén nu. (loc.) a clan name. Cf. *Sowuwen*.
Sowuwépwún nu. (loc.) a clan name.
sowuwimw Var. of *sowuyímw*.
Sowuwiyap Var. of *Sowuyap*.
sowuwo (1) See *sowu-*$_1$, *oo*$_1$. Var. *sowuyo*. nu. (T1) one who knows how to interpret omens.
sowuwomwmwung Var. of *sowuyomwmwung*.
Sowuwoneyopw nu. (pers.) name of the chiefly lineage in Woneyopw, Mortlock Islands.
Sowuwóóniiras nu. (pers.) traditional title of the high chief of Wééné (Moen) Island and highest ranking chief in the *Máchewen Sópwunupi* league; the legendary first high chief of Wééné and the patron spirit of the school of *itang* lore associated with the Sópwunupi clan and league.
sowuyamwééngún (2) See *sowu-*$_1$, *amwééngún*. nu. (T2) master of *amwééngún*, usually a spirit medium.
sowuyangaang (3b) See *sowu-*$_1$, *angaang*. nu. (T3) leader in work.
Sowuyap Var. *Sowuwiyap*. nu. (pers.) lord of Yap (legendary high chief of Yap Island in the Western Carolines).
sowuyatéémén (2) See *sowu-*$_1$, *atéémén*. nu. (T2) one who knows and practices divinations to detect criminals (*atéémén*).
sowuyattaw (3) See *sowu-*$_1$, *attaw*. nu. (T3) leader in fishing.
sowuyawarawar (3) See *sowu-*$_1$, *awarawar*. nu. spirit caller, spirit medium (as one who causes a spirit to be present).
sowuyákekkey (2) See *sowu-*$_1$, *a-*$_2$, *kkey*. nu. a clown.
Sowuyáney nu. (loc.) a clan name. [*Áney* is the name of an islet in Puluwat Atoll.] Cf. *Sowuweney*.
sowuyek (2) See *sowu-*$_1$, *áák*. nu. (T2) scientist, philosopher, master thinker. Dis. *sowuyekiyek* (db).

sowuyekiyek Dis. of *sowuyek*.
Sowuyéér nu. (loc.) a clan name.
sowuyénúúngngaw (3) See *sowu-*$_1$, *énúúngngaw*. nu. (T3) sorcerer. Syn. *sowuppéwút*.
sowuyénnúk (2) See *sowu-*$_1$, *énnúk*. nu. (T2) legislator; attorney, lawyer.
Sowuyéwúr See *sowu-*$_1$, *Éwúr*. nu. (pers.) traditional god of breadfruit and good harvests. [Chief of the mythical land of *Éwúr*, home of breadfruit, he is appealed to by breadfruit summoners (*sowuyótoomey*) and fish summoners (*sowuyótoowik*).]
sowuyéwúwénú (1) See *sowu-*$_1$, *éwúwénú*. nu. (T1) specialist in the *éwúwénú* dance.
sowuyimw (3a) See *sowu-*$_1$, *iimw*. Var. *sowuwimw*. nu. (T3) master builder (of houses).
sowuyimwaanis See *sowu-*$_1$, *imwaanis*. nu. specialist in a form of sorcery used in war.
sowuyimworoch (3) See *sowu-*$_1$, *imworoch*. nu. (T3) eclipse specialist. [He was called upon to undo the sorcery causing an eclipse and restore the sun or moon.]
sowuyo Var. of *sowuwo*.
sowuyoosuni See *sowu-*$_1$, *oosuni*. vo. (T5) be skilled in interpreting (an omen).
sowuyomwmwung (3) See *sowu-*$_1$, *omwmwung*. Var. *sowuwomwmwung*. nu. (T3) specialist in love magic.
sowuyósór (4) See *sowu-*$_1$, *ósór*. nu. (T2, T3) traditional priest ("leader in offerings").
sowuyótoomey (2) See *sowu-*$_1$, *ótoomey*. nu. (T2) breadfruit summoner. [He performs the ritual intended to induce the spirit of breadfruit to come each year from its southern homeland to Truk and insure a good breadfruit harvest.]
sowuyótoowik (3a) See *sowu-*$_1$, *ótoowik*. nu. (T3) fish summoner. [He knows and performs the rites to insure a plentiful supply of fish.]
soyiyú (1) SOYIYÚÚ. (Jap. *shooyu*) Var. *sooyu*. nu. (T1) soy sauce, shoyu. *wúnúman s.* his s.
só Var. of *siya*.
sóók (2) SÓÓKU. (Eng.) nu. (T2) chalk. *efóch s.* one piece of c. *néwún s.* his piece of c. *sóókun Merika* American c.

sóókkofeseen (2) See *sóókku-, -feseen*. Var. *sókkofeseen, sókkofesen*. vi. be different, of different kind. nu. (T2) difference.

sóókkoseni See *sóókku-, seni₂*. vo. (T2) be different from.

sóókkopaat (3) See *sóókku-, paat₂*. vi. be of many kinds.

sóókkowumwes (2) See *sóókku-, wumwes*. vi. be a bit crazy, eccentric.

sóókkoyeew (2) See *sóókku-, eew₁*. vi. be of the same kind, one kind, similar.

sóókkónó (1) See *sóókku-, -nó*. Var. *sókkónó*. vi. be different. *meyi s. napanapen átánaan* that fellow is of different appearance.

sóókku- (4) SÓÓKKO. Var. *sókku-*. ni. (T2) kind, sort, nature, manner, way, race, breed, variety. *sóókkun* or *sókkun* his k. of (something). *oóch sóókkun* different, a different kind; *meet sóókkun suupwa eey* what kind of cigarette is this? *iiy wusun chék sóókkiy* he is the same kind as I am. Id. *sóókkun mé sóókkun* and so forth, etcetera.

sóón₁ (2) SÓÓNU. nu. (T2) 1. a tree (*Barringtonia racemosa, Barringtonia asiatica*). *sóónun Chuuk* Trukese Barringtonia. Syn. *kuun*. 2. croton. [Not native to Truk, named because of resemblance to Barringtonia.]

sóón₂ (4) SÓÓNO₁. vi. be in bloom, be open (of flowers). With dir. suf.: *sóónónó* bloom.

sóón₃ (4) SÓÓNO₂. (Eng.) nu. (T2) salt. *sóónun Merika* American s.

sóón₄ (4) SÓNO. nu. (T2) 1. (obsolete) the earth (as distinct from heaven). 2. level place, prepared site. *sónun atake* garden site; *sónun iimw* house site.

sóóneey See *sóón₃, -e-₂*. vo. (T6b) salt (food).

sóóneni See *sóón₃, -ni-*. vo. (T6a) salt (food); apply salt to.

sóónónó See *sóón₂*.

sóópach nu. (temp.) 22nd night of the lunar month.

sóópw₁ Var. of *sópw*.

sóópw₂ (2) SÓÓPWU. nu. (T2) heron. *emén s.* one h. *sóópwun Chuuk* Trukese h. Syn. *kawakaw*.

sóópw₃ (4) See *sópwu-₂*. n. (T2) district (major political division of an island or atoll); village. *sópwun* his home d. *sópwun fénú* island's d. With dir. suf.: *sópwonong* inner d.; *sópwótá* eastern or upper d.; *sópwutiw* western or lower d.; *sópwuwu* outer d.

Sóópwu nu. (loc.) a clan name.

sóór₁ (4) SÓRO₃. n. (T2) birthmark. *sórun* his b.

sóór₂ adv. (in exhortation) make an effort to, have a go at. *ke pwe s. ppiiy ika si pwee nó neesor* will you make an effort to determine whether we shall go tomorrow; *ke pwe s. sóttuni fátán* make an effort to try to walk. Cf. *mwmwan, sótun*.

sóór₃ N. adv. barely, a little. *aa s. toongeni fátán* he was barely able to walk. Syn. *ekis₂*.

Sóór₄ nu. (loc.) a clan name.

sóót₁ (2) SÓÓTU. Var. *sawit*. vi. begin to form breadfruit. nu. (loc.; T2) in *sóótun mááy* time when breadfruit is at its early stage of growth.

sóót₂ (Eng.) vi., adj. (be) short of money.

sóssót (ds; 4) See *sót*. n. (T2) trial, temptation, testing, examination. *sóssótun* testing, temptation or examination of him. vi. be attempted, tried, tested, tempted.

sókósók (db; 4) SÓKO₁. n. (T2) character, personality, nature. *sókósókun* his c. Cf. *sókun₁, sóókku-*.

sókósókééch (db; 2) See *sókósók, ééch*. vi., adj. (be) kind, of good character.

sókósókóngngaw (db; 3b) See *sókósók, ngngaw*. vi., adj. (be) of bad character.

sókuun (2: -*kunnu-*) See *sa-₂, kkun*. F. Var. *sokun, sókun₂*. nu. (T2) egg (of chicken, bird or turtle). *sókunnun chukó* chicken egg; *sókunnun pwunech* comb honey. vi. lay eggs.

sókun₁ (4) SÓKO₂. [Occurs, as shown, only with rel. suf. -*n₂*.] vr. be originally, to begin with, formerly. *meyi s. wátte ngé aa ta reen ewe áát, ina pwata aa kúkkúnúnó iyeey* it was big to begin with but it was broken by the boy, that's why it is smaller now; *meyi s. wur eey sepi ngé Oliver aa áni esópw, ina pwata aa esópw chék* this bowl was full originally but Oliver ate half, that's why it has become only a half [full]. Cf. *sókósók*.

sókun₂ (2) See *sa-₂, kkun*. N. Var. *sokun, sókuun*. nu. (T2) egg (of chicken, bird, or turtle). *eféw s.* one e. *néwún s.* its egg (that it laid); *wochaan s.* his e. (to eat). *néwún chukó s.* chicken's e.; *sókunun chukó* chicken e. vi. lay eggs.

sókkofeseen Var. of *sóókkofeseen*.

sókkofesen Var. of *sóókkofeseen*.

sókkónó Var. of *sóókkónó*.

sókku- Var. of *sóókku-*.

-sómw [Apparently a secondary derivation from *sómwoon* chief.] Itang. [In cpds. only.] unsp. chiefly rank. Ant. *-mwár* (see *mwáár*). See *átiisómw*.

sómwoon (2) SÓMWOONU. Var. *samwoon*. nu. (T2) chief, ruler; one who rules over something. *saman s.* his c. (old usage); *néwún s., aan s.* his c. (modern usage). *sómwoonun fanang* c. of a land-owning lineage; *sómwoonun fénú* district c. (old usage), island c. or magistrate (modern usage); *sómwoonun fináyik* flag c. (an administrative title under German and Japanese rule); *sómwoonun kkapas* executive c. of a district (not entitled to food tribute); *sómwoonun Merika* president of the United States; *sómwoonun mwéngé* hereditary and symbolic c. of a district (entitled to food tribute); *sómwoonun sóópw* district c.

Sómwooniyóng nu. (pers.) legendary ancestor of the people of Paata. [He had the soubriquet Wumwusómwoon and is equated with Sowupaata.]

són (4) See *són₄*. vi. be level.

sónééch (2) See *són, ééch.* vi. be level, even, flat (of ground or surface). Dis. *sónósónééch* (db).

sónopwúkúpwúk (db; 2) See *són, pwúúk.* vi. be uneven, bumpy, rough (of ground).

sónowut (2) SÓNOWUTU. nu. (T2) small species of porgy fish. *sónowutun Chuuk* Trukese p. f.

sónósónééch Dis. of *sónééch*.

sónósónóngngaw Dis. of *sónóngngaw*.

sónóngngaw (3b) See *són, ngngaw.* vi. be uneven, rough, bumpy (of ground or surface). Dis. *sónósónóngngaw* (db).

-sóngósóng (db; 4) SÓNGO. [In cpds. only.] adj. roasted or charred (in flavor). See *nnesóngósóng*.

sóppach (3b) See *sópwu-₁, pach.* adj. (of a canoe) having low ends that are of one piece with the body of the hull. *waa s.* low-ended canoe. Cf. *sópwósá.* nu. (T3) a breadfruit summoner's model canoe, used by him in ritual model canoe races.

sópw (4) SÓPWO₁. Var. *sóópw.* vi. be at an end, terminated, finished, completed (of a job, story, activity). Id. *mwúúch mee sópw, tere me iyeey* finished and ended, complete as of now (formula for ending a *túttúnnap* type of story). With dir. suf.: *sópwónó* be finished off.

sópweey₁ See *sópw, -e-₂.* vo. (T6b) complete, fill out, bring to completion, add to (to make sufficient). With dir. suf.: *sópweeyenó* complete; *kepwe s. óómw sukun* you shall c. your schooling.

sópweey₂ See *sópwósópw₁, -e-₂.* vo. (T6b) continue.

sópweyééch (2) See *sópw, ééch.* vi. be completed well (said of a house or *wuut* whose residents live in it in health and without more than the usual amount of death). Ant. *sópwóngngaw.* Cf. *ósópw*.

sópwiinos (3) See *sópwu-₁, noos.* nu. (T3) mat end. *safeen s.* a medicine associated with housebuilding.

sópwonong See *sóópw₃*.

sópwonopwon (db; 3a) See *sa-₂, pwon₂.* vi., adj. (be) variegated; (be) camouflaged in coloring.

Sópworeenong nu. (loc.) a clan name.

sópwósá (1) See *sópwu-₁, sá.* adj. (of a canoe) having ends that are high and pointed and of separate pieces from the body of the hull. *waa s.* high-ended canoe. Cf. *sóppach*.

sópwósópw₁ (db; 4) SÓPWO₂. vi. be continuing, continue.

sópwósópw₂ (db; 4) See *sópwu-₂.* nu. (T2) a kind of turmeric cosmetic prepared in a single half coconut-shell mold. Cf. *péér₁*.

sópwónó See *sópw*.

sópwónóó- (1) See *sópw, -nó.* [In ptv. const. only.] ni. (T1) end, termination, last (of something). *sópwónóón* its e.; finally, last of all.

sópwóngngaw (3b) See *sópw, ngngaw.* vi. be completed badly (said of a house or *wuut* whose residents suffer more than the usual amount of sickness and death). Ant. *sópweyééch.* Cf. *ósópw*.

sópwótá See *sóópw₃*.

sópwu-₁ (4) See *sópw.* [In ptv. const. only.] ni. (T2) end (of something). *sópwun nisses* flat projection at top of each end of a wooden bowl; *sópwun waa* end piece of a canoe. Cf. *neesópw.*

sópwu-₂ (4) SÓPWO₃. Var. *sapwo-*. ni. (T2), suf. (cc.) division, section; half. *esópw, rúwésópw, wúnúsópw, fésópw, nimesópw, wonosópw, fúúsópw, wanúsópw, ttiwesópw, engoon sópwun* one,...ten sections. *kkunók engoon esópw* half past ten, ten-thirty o'clock. *sópwun irá* section of tree trunk, log; *sópwun nóón pwpwuk* chapter of a book. Cf. *sóópw*₃.

sópwu-₃ (4) SÓPWO₄. ni. (T2), suf. (cc.) burden of a varying number of breadfruit that have been tied together. *esópw, rúwésópw, wúnúsópw, fésópw, nimesópw, wonosópw, fúúsópw, wanúsópw, ttiwesópw, engoon sópwun* one,...ten b. of breadfruit.

Sópwun nu. (loc.) a clan name.

Sópwunupi nu. (loc.) 1. a clan name. [Said to be the highest ranking chiefly clan in Truk.] 2. name of a major political league of pre-colonial Truk. 3. a school of *itang* lore. [Its patron spirit is Sowuwóóniiras and it is associated with Wééné (Moen) Island.]

sópwutiw See *sóópw*₃.

sópwuwu See *sóópw*₃.

sópwpwún (2) See *sópw, pwpwún*₁. nu. (T2) the residue of copra from which coconut oil has been extracted. *sópwpwúnún taka* copra r.

-sór (4) SÓRO₁. [In cpds. only.] adj. called, besought. See *ósór, énúúsór*. Cf. Fi. *taro* ask, Gb. *taromauri* engage in worship.

sóro- (4) SÓRO₂. [In cpds. only.] unsp. appearance, conduct, self-manifestation; character. See *sórósór.*

sórof (3) See *sóro-, -fa-*. Var. *sarof*. n. (T3) gait, style of walking. *sórofan* his g. *ifa wusun sórofen átánaan?* what sort of g. does he have?

sórofééch (2) See *sórof, ééch*. nu. (T2) good gait, seemly or gracely walk.

sórofommang (3) See *sórof, mmang*. vi. be indifferent to the fate others.

sórofongngaw (3b) See *sórof, ngngaw*. nu. (T3) bad gait; unseemly or ungainly walk.

sórosooná (1) See *sóro-, sooná*. vi. be thievish, rascally.

sórongngat (3) See *sóro-, -ngngat*. vi. be unresponsive, impassive, taciturn. Syn. *sóropwpwang.*

sóropwpwang (3) See *sóro-, -pwpwang*. Tb3. vi. be unresponsive, impassive. Syn. *sórongngat.*

sóropwpwech (3) See *sóro-, pwech*. vi. be pallid, pale, having a pallor.

sórósór (db; 4) See *sóro-*. n. (T2) manner, character (of one's actions), bearing, appearance. *sórósórun* his m.

sórósórééch (2) See *sórósór, ééch*. vi. be of good character, have a good manner or appearance. nu. good character or manner.

sórósórongngaw (3b) See *sórósór, ngngaw*. vi. be of bad character, have a poor appearance or manner. nu. bad or ugly character or manner, unkempt or dirty appearance.

sóchóówun (3) See *sa-₂, chóó, wun*. n. (T3) unpopularity. *sóchóówunan mé reen aramas* his u. with the people. vi. be unpopular, disliked.

sót (4) SÓTO. va. try, attempt. *kepwe s. muusik* you should try harmonicas. See *sótun, sótuni, sóssót, ssót.*

sóton (3) See *sa-₂, ton*. nu. (T3) beach rock ("appears of its own accord" in reference to the way slabs of beach rock form in sandy areas).

sótun (2) See *sót, -ni-*. vi. (in exhortation) have a try, make an effort, have a go, come on. *sótun wúpwe kkóton* come on, I want to have a look. Cf. *mwmwan, sóór*₂.

sótuni See *sót, -ni-*. vo. (T5) try, attempt, test, examine, tempt, taste.

sóttik (2) SÓTTIKI. nu. (T2) species of goatfish. *sóttikin Chuuk* Trukese g.

su (1) SUU₁. vi. set off (on a journey), depart, leave, set sail, get under way.

suu- (1) SUU₂. [In cpds. only.] unsp. open. See *ossuuku, ssuuk, suuki.*

suuf (2) SUFU. nu. (T2) burrow or burial place in sand (of crabs and turtles). *sufun amwatang* crab's b.; *sufun wiin* turtle's b.

suufén (2) vi. be respectful, deferential; be hesitant, timid, bashful, self-effacing (in relation to someone in authority). [There is embarrassment (*sááw*) associated with *suufén*.] *siya s. ngeni sómwoon* we are r. toward chiefs.

suuféniiti See *suufén, -iti*. vo. (T2) respect, defer to.

suus₁ (2) SUSSU. (Eng.) nu. (T2) shoe, shoes. *eyipw s.* one s.; *eew s.* one pair of s. *ipweni s.* acquire s.; *ipweyipw s.* wear s. *sussun Merika* American s.

Suus₂ (Eng.) nu. Jewery, Jewish ethnicity. *chóón S.* Jewish person, Jewish people; *fin-S.* or *fiin S.* Jewish woman; *namanamen S.* Jewish religion, Judaism; *re-S.* Jewish man.

-suusu Metathesized var. of *wusuus₂* (see *wiisuusu₂*).

suuskiloos (3) SUUSKILOOSA. (P.Eng.) nu. (T3) suit of clothes. *aan s.* his s. *suuskiloosen Merika* American s.

Suuk Var. *Sowuk.* nu. (loc.) Pulusuk Island. Syn. *Pwúnúsuk.*

suuki See *suu-, -ki-.* vo. (T4) open. With dir. suf.: *suukóónó* open (something) up. Cf. *érúrú.*

suukóónó See *suuki.*

suun₁ (2) SUNU₂. Tb1. n. (T2) testicles and scrotum together. *sunun* his t. and s. *féwún s.* testicle. Syn. *wuun₁.*

Suun₂ (Eng.) nu. (temp.) June (month). *S. nóón eey iyer* J. of this year.

Suunaaye (Eng.) nu. (temp.) July (month).

suupini (1) SUUPINII. (Eng.) nu. (T1) jubilee; celebration on completion of twenty-five years' service as a Protestant pastor.

suupw₁ (2) SUPWU₂. nu. (T2) dripping (as of rain), fluid discharge from eyes or skin. *supwun rááń* rain's d.; *supwun inisiy* my body's fluid discharge; *supwun mesey* water of my eyes.

suupw₂ (3) SUPWPWA. (Eng.) nu. (T3) soup. *wúnúman s.* his s. *supwpwen Merika* American s. va. make a soup of something.

suupwa (1) SUUPWAA. nu. (T1) tobacco, tobacco plant (*Nicotiana tabacum*); cigarette. *efóch s.* one cigarette; *etúkúm s.* one pack of cigarettes; *eew s.* one carton of cigarettes. *wúnúman s.* his t. or cigarette (to smoke), his smoke. *s. Chuuk* locally cultivated t. vi. smoke tobacco.

suf (2) See *suuf.* vi., adj. (be) buried in sand (as a crab or turtle).

sussuuk Dis. of *ssuuk.*

sussuk Dis. of *ssuk.*

sussukuun Dis. of *sukuun.*

suspen (Eng.) nu. one who has a suspended jail sentence and is on probation for the term of the sentence. [He may not play bingo, travel out of the community, play cards, or attend feasts or sports. He must do the work of his livelihood. Someone must be responsible for him and report on his behavior. If he misbehaves then he must serve the jail sentence.] vi. give a suspended sentence.

suke (1) SUKEE. (Eng.) nu. (T1) sugar. *wúnúman s.* his s. (to eat). *sukeen Merika* American s.

sukeeni See *suke, -ni-.* vo. (T4) put sugar on, sugar.

sukuun (3) SUKUUNA, SUKUNNA. (Eng.) nu. (T3) school. *aan s* his s. *chóón s.* pupil, student. *sukunnen* or *sukuunen mwúú* or *mwúún* government s.; *sukuunen namanam* church school, religious school, parochial school. vi. study, practice; be studied, practiced. Dis. *sussukuun* (ds). *sussukuun wóón* be studying about (a subject).

sukuuna (1) SUKUUNAA. (Eng.) nu. (T1) schooner (sailing ship). *efóch s.* one s. *waan s.* his s.

sukuuw See *ssuk, -u-.* vo. (T5) beat, knock, strike, pound. *wúwa s. eey cheepen* I struck this table.

sukuni See *ssuk, -ni-.* vo. (T5) bump against, jostle.

sukuru (1) SUKURUU. (Eng.) nu. (T1) screw. *efóch s.* one s. *sukuruun Sapaan* Japanese s.

sumw (2) SUMWU. vi. droop, bend down (of the top or tip of something, as a tree or tree branch that has broken). Dis. *sumwusumw* (db). With dir. suf.: *sumwunó* droop off (of persons in sleep or death).

sumwusumw Dis. of *sumw.*

sumwunó See *sumw.*

sun (2) SUNU₁. F. vi. lag behind, trail (as in a race), lose, be defeated (in racing only). Syn. *mwú₃.* Ant. *kakkay, kákkáy, mwittir.* Cf. *kkuf.*

sunummach (3) See *suun₁, mmach.* n. (T3) elephantiasis of the scrotum. *sunummachan e.* of his s. Syn. *sunupwo.*

sunupwo (1) See *suun₁, pwo.* n. (T1) elephantiasis of scrotum, swelling of s. *sunupwoon e.* of his s. Syn. *sunummach.*

suppék (2) See *su, ppék.* vi. leave or depart together or in company.

supw (2) SUPWU₁. vi. be snatched, grabbed; be caught (as a ball).

supwusupw (db; 2) See *supw*. n. (dis.; T2) catching, dexterity in catching. *supwusupwun* his c. *ifa wusun supwusupwumw* how is your c.? (how good are you at c.?).
supwunóóy See *supw*, *-nó*. vo. (T1) catch (something) from yonder.
Supwunumén nu. (pers.) god of knot divination (*pwee*).
supwungngaw (3b) See *supw*, *ngngaw*. vi. be clumsy in catching.
supwuri See *supw*, *-ri-*. vo. (T5) snatch, grab; catch.
supwutááy See *supw*, *-tá*. vo. (T1) grab or catch from above.
supwutiweey See *supw*, *-tiw*, *-e-*$_2$. vo. (T1) grab or catch from below.
supwuyééch (2) See *supw*, *ééch*. vi. be dexterous in catching.
suri (1) SURII. nu. (T1) species of parrot fish. *suriin Chuuk* Trukese p. f.
suru (1) SURUU. nu. (T1) small unidentified fish. *suruun Chuuk* Trukese f.
suwosu (db; 3) SUWA. nu. (T3) dish of grated *Cyrtosperma* taro (*pwuna*). [It is stone boiled in coconut cream.]
sú (1) SÚÚ$_1$. vi. run away, flee; go away, leave, depart, clear out, scram, vamoose; fly (of birds, insects, but not people). With dir. suf.: *súúnong*, *súúnó*, *súútá*, *súútiw*, *súúwu*. *súúnó faa-* carry off, abscond with.
súú (1) SÚÚ$_2$. (Jap.) nu. (T1) vinegar. *súún Merika* American v.
súúsú (db; 1) See *sú*. vi. fly (of birds, insects, but not of people). Cf. *áás*.
súúnong See *sú*.
súúnó See *sú*.
súúri See *sú*, *-ri-*. vo. (T4) go off to, fly to. *aa s. chúúnúket átánaan* the *chúúnúket* sickness has flown to that fellow. Cf. *súúyiti*.
súútá See *sú*.
súútiw See *sú*.
súúwu See *sú*.
súúyiti See *sú*, *-iti*. vo. (T2) go off to, fly to (of birds). Cf. *súúri*.
súk$_1$ (2) SÚKÚ$_1$. vi. project, stick out, be not flush.
súk$_2$ (2) SÚKÚ$_2$. vi. appear, come into view. Cf. *ssúk*$_2$.
súkaato (1) SÚKAATOO. (Jap. *sukaato*, from Eng.) Var. *sikaato*. nu. (T1) skirt. *eché s.* one s. *aan s.* her s.

súkiyaki Var. of *sikiyaki*.
súkúseni See *súk*$_1$, *seni*$_2$. vo. (T2) project from or beyond.
súmi (1) SÚMII. (Jap.) nu. (T1) charcoal. *eféw s.* one p. of c. *súmiin Sapaan* Japanese c.
súngú- (2) SÚNGÚ. [In cpds. only.] unsp. bump, collide. See *nisúngúr*, *-ssúng*, *súngúri*.
súngúri See *súngú-*, *-ri-*. vo. (T5) bump into, collide with.
súrúsúr Dis. of *ssúr*.
ssaar Var. of *saar*.
-ssaar (dc; 2) See *saar*. suf. (cc.) slice. *essaar*, *rúwéssaar*, *wúnússaar*, *féssaar*, *nimessaar*, *wonossaar*, *fúússaar*, *wanússaar*, *ttiwessaar*, *engoon ssaarún* one,...ten slices.
ssaka- (3) SSAKA, SAKKA. Var. *sakka-*. ni. (T3), suf. (cc.) slice or piece of copra or meat of the ripe coconut. *essak*, *rúwéssak*, *wúnússak*, *féssak*, *nimessak*, *wonossak*, *fúússak*, *wanússak*, *ttiwessak*, *engoon ssakan* or *sakkan* one,...ten piece of c.
ssapan (ds; 3b) See *sa-*$_2$, *paan*$_1$. vi. be in bloom. With dir. suf.: *ssapananó*.
ssapananó See *ssapan*.
ssaw (dc; 3) See *sawa-*. n. (T3) present of food to a sick person. *ssawan* the p. for him as a sick person; *aan s.* his p. for a sick person. vi. 1. make a present of food to a sick person. 2. (Wmn.) pay court to a woman at night. Cf. *tééfán*.
ssawa See *ssaw*. vo. (T3) make a present of food to (someone who is ill).
ssá (1) SSÁÁ. vi. run. Dis. *sássá* (ds). Cf. *sá*.
ssáák Rmn. nu. canoe race. Syn. *káár*, *kitir*$_2$. Cf. *ssá*.
ssáát (dc; 4) See *sáát*$_3$. F. Var. *ssát*. vi. be split, splintered, broken longitudinally.
-ssáát (dc; 4) See *sáát*$_3$. F. Var. *-ssát*. suf. (cc.) sliver, broken off piece, slice (of bread). *essáát*, *rúwéssáát*, *wúnússáát*, *féssáát*, *nimessáát*, *wonossáát*, *fúússáát*, *wanússáát*, *ttiwessáát*, *engoon sáttin* one,...ten s. *essáát sáttin irá* one s. of wood.
ssár$_1$ (dc; 4) SÁRE$_3$. vi. be capable of being elevated or lifted up. Cf. *sárifi*, *sássár*$_2$.
ssár$_2$ (3) SSÁRA. n. (T3) fetter, bonds, rope binding hands or legs; snare. *ssáran* his bonds. vi. be snared, trapped in a snare.

ssára See *ssár₂*. vo. (T3) bind the legs or hands of, fetter; snare. Syn. *ssáreey*.

ssáreey See *ssár₂*, *-e-₂*. vo. (T6b) bind the legs or hands of, fetter; snare, trap in a snare.

ssát N. of *ssáát*.

-ssát N. of *-ssáát*.

sse-₁ (3a) SSE₁. [In cpds. only. Presumably from an older **sso-*, cf. Fi. *toso*.] vi. move, spread; (with dir. suf.) stray, go astray or off course. With dir. suf.: *ssenong* stray to the south or inwards; *ssenó* s. off, misspeak; *ssetá* s. eastwards or upwards; *ssetiw* s. westwards or down; *sseto* s. hither; *ssewu* s. to the north or outwards, s. beyond one's destination.

sse-₂ (3a) SSE₂. [In cpds. only.] unsp. built or stacked one on top of another.

ssees (ds; 3a: *sesse-(?)*) See *sse-₂*. F. Var. *sses*. vi. be built up or laid one on top of another (as papers, books, stones in a wall, etc.). Dis. *sessees* (ds).

ssef (3) SSEFA. vi. be bent up, twisted up (as a twig in a fire).

ssefich₁ (2) See *sse-₂*, *-fich*. vi. be loaded (of a netting needle).

ssefich₂ (2) See *sse-₁*, *fichi-*. vi. bounce, rebound, snap away, hop, shoot out of one's hands (as a piece of soap); be shot (as an arrow). With dir. suf.: *ssefichinó*.

ssefichiiti See *ssefich₂*, *-iti*. vo. (T2) snap or rebound to.

ssefichifich (db; 2) See *ssefich₂*. vi. (dis.) be wriggling, thrashing about (as a fish in one's hands).

ssefichinó See *ssefich₂*.

sses N. of *ssees*.

ssemay (3) See *sse-₂*, *maay₁*. F. Var. *ssemáy*. vi. build a stone fish trap.

ssemáy N. of *ssemay*.

ssen Obs. (Jap. *sen*) nu. sen (one hundreth of a yen), cent. Cf. *senis*.

sseni See *sse-₂*, *-ni-*. vo. (T6a) build up, stack up (as with stones in a wall, strakes on a canoe, paper in a stack). Dis. *sesseni* (ds). *aa s. ewe woroor* he built the stone wall; *repwe s. eey waa* they will b. up the sides of this canoe.

-ssening (dc; 3) See *sening*. adj. moldy. See *pwossening*.

ssenong See *sse-₁*.

ssenó See *sse-₁*.

sset (dc; 2) See *sáát₁*. vi. be sick or ill because of the sea spirits known as *chénukken*. *aa s. áteey* this fellow has become s. nr. (T2) illness, being ill because of *chénúkken*. *ssetin* his i. Syn. *sáát₂*.

ssetá See *sse-₁*.

ssetiw See *sse-₁*.

sseto See *sse-₁*.

ssewu See *sse-₁*.

sseyas (3) See *sse-₁*, *aas₁*. vi. stray out of course to the eastward (in sailing).

sseyik (dc; 2) See *seyi-*, *-ki-*. N. Var. *sséék*, *ssiik*. vi. be moved, pushed, shoved. With dir. suf.: *sseyikitá* be pushed up, elevated. Cf. *seyiki*.

sseyikitá See *sseyik*.

sseyim (dc; 2) See *seyim*. vi. be sharpened (of knife, axe); do sharpening. Cf. *seyimi*.

sséék (dc; 2) See *séé-₂*, *-ki-*. F. Var. *sseyik*, *ssiik*. vi. be moved, slid, pushed, shoved. With dir. suf.: *sséékúnong* moved or slid in, inserted; *sséékúnó* moved away; *sséékútá* moved up or east, raised; *sséékútiw* moved down or west, lowered; *sséékúto* moved hither; *sséékúwu* moved out. Cf. *sééki*.

sséékúnong See *sséék*.

sséékúnó See *sséék*.

sséékútá See *sséék*.

sséékútiw See *sséék*.

sséékúto See *sséék*.

sséékúwu See *sséék*.

sséér (2) See *séé-₂*, *-ri-*. vi. slide (against something). With dir. suf.: *sséérúnó*, *sséérúnong*, *sséérútá*, *sséérútiw*, *sséérútó*, *sséérúwu*. Cf. *ssiik₁*, *sséék₁*.

sséérúnong See *sséér*.

sséérúnó See *sséér*.

sséérútá See *sséér*.

sséérútiw See *sséér*.

sséérúto See *sséér*.

sséérúwu See *sséér*.

ssi- (2) SSI. [In cpds. only.] unsp. bite. See *ssiiy*, *ssis*. Cf. *kkú-*.

ssiik (dc; 2) See *sii-*, *-ki-*. Var. *sseyik*, *sséék*. vi. be slid, moved, pushed, shoved. With dir. suf.: *ssiikinong* be s. in, inserted; *ssiikitá* be s. up, raised, elevated (to office); *ssiikitiw* be s. down, lowered. Cf. *siiki*.

ssiikinong See *ssiik*.

ssiikitá See *ssiik*.

ssiikitiw See *ssiik*.

ssiiy See *ssi-*, *-i-₂*. vo. (T5) bite off or in two.

ssis (ds; 2: *sissi-*) See *ssi-*. vi. be bitten off or in two.

ssin (dc; 2) SINI₃. va. dig up (of potatoes or other root crops). Cf. *sinini, sinni.*

ssiyapw (dc; 3) See *si-₂, -apw₂*. vi. peep (of chick). Syn. *siyok.*

ssomw (dc; 3) SOMWA₂. vi., adj. (be) omniverous, fond of all kinds of food, not particular about food. Cf. *somwori.*

sson (3) SSONA. N. Var. *sson₁*. nu. (T3) damsel fish. *ssonen Chuuk* Trukese d. f.

ssopw (2) SSOPWU. nu. (T2) wooden chest. [Traditionally made of breadfruit wood and used to store turmeric and other valuables.] *eew s.* one c. *aan s.* his c. *ssopwun Chuuk* Trukese c.

ssor (dc; 3a) See *soro-*. vi., adj. (be) turned, changed in direction; changed in import or meaning (of words); falsified.

ssow See *sowu-₁*. nu. name of the prefix *sowu-₁*.

ssó (1) SSÓÓ. nu. (T1) thwart of a canoe. *emén ssó* one t. Cf. *fóssó.*

ssóónufót (4) See *ssó, -n₂, fóto-₂*. nu. (T2) thwart at extreme end of a sailing canoe and into which the upper yard is stepped ("planting thwart").

ssót (dc; 4) See *sót*. vi. be attempted, tried, tested, tempted. Dis. *sóssót* (db).

ssuuk (dc; 2) See *suuki*. vi., adj. (be) open, opened. Dis. *sussuuk* (ds). va. open.

ssuk (dc; 2) SUKU. vi., adj. knock, beat, rap, strike, pound; (be) struck. Dis. *sussuk* (ds). *wúwa s. wóón eey cheepen* I beat (knocked) on this table.

ssupw (dc; 2) See *suupw₁*. vi. drip, drip down (as rain from eaves), run (with sweat); water (of eyes), give forth fluid from the body. *aa s. chénún mesey* my tears dripped down.

ssupwiiti See *ssupw, -iti*. vo. (T2) spatter, sprinkle, drip onto.

ssupwu- (dc; 2) See *suupw₁*. ni. (T2), suf. (cc.) droplet, tiny drop (as of sweat, tears, water dripping from trees). *essupw, rúwéssupw, wúnússupw, féssupw, nimessupw, wonossupw, fúússupw, wanússupw, ttiwessupw, engoon ssupwun* one,...ten d.

ssúk₁ (2) SSÚKÚ₁. n. (T2) hiccough. *ssúkún* his h. vi. hiccough.

ssúk₂ (2) SSÚKÚ₂. vi. bleed, flow (of blood, sap of trees). *aa s. chchaan* his blood flowed. Cf. *fén₁, súk₂*.

-ssúng (dc; 2) See *súngú-*. [In cpds. only.] unsp. bump, collide. See *órossúng*. Cf. *ssuk.*

ssúr₁ (2) SSÚRÚ₁. nu. (T2) drop (large). Cf. *ssupw*. vi. flow, drip, be dripping, be adrip, be flowing. Dis. *súrúsúr* (db) be dripping, dropping, shedding, pouring.

ssúr₂ (2) SSÚRÚ₂. vi. be caught in a container (of dripping rain, etc.).

ssúriiti See *ssúr₁, -iti*. vo. (T2) spatter, pour on.

ssúrúyaw (3b) See *ssúr₁, aaw₁*. vi. slobber, be slobber-mouthed.

spaak (2) SPAAKÚ. (Eng.) nu. spark.

Speyin (Eng.) nu. (loc.) Spain.

spiiker (Eng.) nu. speaker (in a legislature).

steesen (2) STEESENI. (Eng.) nu. (T2) staysail. *steesenin waa* ship's s.

stoof Var. of *sitoof.*

stoop (Eng.) vi. stop (cease activity).

K

-k₁ (3a: -ko-) KO₁. [Suffixed to base of transitive form of verb with modification of preceeding vowel to a back rounded vowel of same vowel height: *i, ú* to *u; e, é* to *o; á, a* to *ó.*] suf. (obj.) 2sg. obj. prn.: thee, you. *fitu-k* accompany thee, *fitu-ko-nó* accompany thee away (*fiti*); *épwúngu-k* advise or correct thee (*épwúngú*); *ottumwu-k* cause thee to stagger (*ottumwu*); *fichiyu-k* give thee a haircut (*fichii-y*); *éppúruu-k* imitate thee (*éppúrúú-w*); *osuu-k* see thee off (*osuu-w*); *cheyo-k* chase thee (*chee-y*); *sááyipoo-k* fan thee (*sááyipéé-w*); *oyoo-k* capture thee (*oyoo-w*); *afangamáyó-k* betray thee (*afangamáá-y*); *achchóó-k* make thee bleed (*achchaa-y*); *ópóó-k* put thee on a bed (*ópóó-y*); and with doubling of the final vowel of the base *awatóó-k* smite thee (*awata*).

-k₂ (3) KA₃. suf. (u.m.) See *mwiyak, pwutak*.

ka-₁ See *ke-*.

ka-₂ Var. of *a-₂* (causative prefix).

-ka- (3b: -*ka-, -ke-, -ko*) KA₄. [Occurs only with locative prefix *i-*₃ and suffixed demonstratives.] unsp. place, locus. See *ika₂, ikaan, ikana, ikanaan, ikeey, ikemwuun, ikena, ikewe, ikoomw*.

kaa- (1) KAA. [In cpds. only.] unsp. thirst; low tide.

kaa See *ke-*.

kaaf₁ (Eng.) nu. gaff (on sailing ship). *efóch k.* one g.

kaaf₂ (Eng.) nu. calf. *emén k.* one c. *néwún k.* his c.

kaas (3) KASSA, KAASA. (Eng.) nu. (T3) playing card or cards. *eché k.* one c. *neyiy k.* my c. *kassen* or *kaasen Merika* American c. Cf. *kaat₂*.

kaak Var. *káák, kkek₂*. excl. exclamation at a bad odor.

kaaka (db; 1) See *kaa-*. vi. (dis.) be thirsty; be at low tide.

kaamété (1) KAAMÉTÉÉ. (Eng.) Var. *kaamwété, kaapété.* nu. (T1) carpenter; carpentry. Syn. *tayikú*.

kaamwété Var. of *kaamété*.

kaamwmwet Var. of *kamwmwet*.

Kaangires Var. of *Kangkúres*.

kaapété Var. of *kaamété*.

kaache (1) KAACHEE. (Jap. *gaaze*) nu. (T1) gauze.

kaat₁ (Eng.) nu. cot.

kaat₂ (Eng.) nu. card. Cf. *kaas*.

Kaatenik (Eng.) nu. member of the Roman Catholic Church. *emén K.* one m. of C. C. vi. be a Catholic.

kaato (1) KAATOO. (Jap. *kaado*) nu. (T1) medical chart.

Kaferut (Eng.) nu. (loc.) Gaferut Island (Central Caroline Islands). [The name derives from a Carolinian name for a mythical phantom island, the real island now designated by this name on maps being properly called *Féyiyew*.]

kafiye (1) KAFIYEE. (Jap. *kafee*, from Fr.) nu. (T1) teahouse, café, small restaurant. *eew k.* one t. *aan k.* his t.

kasakas (db; 3) KASA. vi. (dis.) talk aloud.

kasi (1) KASII. (Jap. *kaji*) nu. (T1) tiller, helm, steering wheel. *efóch k.* one t. *kasiin waa* boat's t. vi. steer; drive a car. Syn. *mwirimwir*.

kasiini See *kasi, -ni-*. vo. (T4) steer (a boat), drive (a car).

kasoring (Jap. from Eng.) nu. gasoline. Syn. *kasúning, káás, kásenin*.

kasúning Obs. (Eng.) nu. gasoline. Syn. *kasoring, káás, kásenin*.

kassooro (1) KASSOOROO. (Jap. *kassooro*) nu. (T1) airport.

kak (3) KAKA. Var. *kkak.* vi. ring (as a bell, as metal on stone); caw (as a bird). Dis. *kakkak* (ds). *aa k. ewe peen* the bell rang.

-kak (3) KAKA. [In cpds. only.] unsp. muddy; muck. See *pwakak*.

kakiros (2) KAKIROSU. (Eng.) nu. (T2) brown cockroach. *emén k.* one c. *kakirosun Merika* American c.

kakkak Dis. of *kak*.

kakkapas Dis. of *kkapas*.

kakkaré Dis. of *kkaré*.

kakkay Var. of *kákkáy*.

kakkayé Dis. of *kkayé*.

kaktay (2) KAKTAYI. (Jap. *gakutai)* nu. (T2) musical band, orchestra. *eew mwiichen k.* one band group.

-kam (3) KAMA. [In cpds. only.] unsp. (u.m.) See *chchenikam.*

kamaat (3) See *ka-₂, maata-.* nu. (c.; T3) a kind of coral [It is used as an abrasive to make wood smooth.]

kametip (2, 3) KAMETIPI, KAMETIPA. (Pon.) nu. (T2, T3) informal feast, picnic. *kametipen* or *kametipin Chuuk* Trukese picnic. vi. hold an informal feast, have a picnic.

kampes (2) KAMPESI. (Eng.) nu. (T2) compass. *eew k.* one c. *kampesin Merika* American c.

-kamw (3) KAMWA₁. Tb. [In cpds. only.] unsp. huge, enormous. See *akamw, céékamw.*

kamwa- (3b) KAMWA₂. [In cpds. only.] unsp. piece, shred, or fragment of cloth, paper, etc.

kamwakamw (db; 3b) See *kamwa-.* vi. (dis.) be in rags, tatters; or shreds (of cloth, paper, etc.).

kamwe (1) KAMWEE. Var. *amwe.* nu. (T1) tridachna clam.

kamweey See *kamwa-, -e-₂.* vo. (T6b) tear, shred (cloth, paper, etc.).

kamwo (1) See *ka-₂, mwo₁.* N. adv., qlf. first (before doing something else). *kepwe k. fééri imwey eey, kepwaapw feyinnó mwirin* you will f. fix my house here, you will then go away afterwards. *witi k.* wait f. Cf. *ókkoomw.*

kamwmwet Var. *kaamwmwet.* nu. sweetheart, lover. *emén k.* one s. *newún k.* his s. *néwúni emén k.* acquire a s. Syn. *angin.* vi. be sweethearts, lovers. *raa k. ffengen* they are s. together.

kan (2?) KANI(?). Var. *kayi.* adv. be wont to, be in the habit of; be one's lot to; happen to. [Used frequently as a softening word to make a statement less abrupt and more gentle in polite discourse.] *aa k. wees* it happens to be finished; *kese k. mwochen* if you please, will you please ("don't you happen to want to"); *wúse k. miriitiiy minne wúpwe wúrá* I don't happen to know what I shall say.

kanapwuus Var. of *kanapwus.*

kanapwuusseey Var. of *kanapwuseey.*

kanapwus (3) KANAPWUSA. (P.Eng.) Var. *kanapwuus.* nu. (T3) jail, prison, calaboose. *eew k.* one j. *aan k.* his j. *chóón k.* prisoner.

kanapwuseey See *kanapwus, -e-₂.* Var. *kanapwuusseey.* vo. (T6b) imprison, arrest.

-kanaw See *anaw₂.*

kanuf (3) KANUFA. nu. (T3) large, multicolored lizard. [Introduced by the Japanese to kill rats.] *emén k.* one l. *kanufen Sapaan* Japanese l.

kansino (1) KANSINOO. (probably from Spanish *concilio* council) vi. confess to a priest, make confession.

kansoku (1) KANSOKUU. (Jap. *kansoku* observe) nu. (T1) radar station, long-distance observation station.

kanchi (1) KANCHII. (Jap. *kanji* executive officer.) nu. (T1) captain (of a team, as in baseball). *emén k.* one c. *néwún k.* his c.; *kanchiin* c. of. Cf. *meyinap.*

kanten (Eng.) nu. candle. *efóch k.* one c. *néwún k.* his c.

kantokú (1) KANTOKÚÚ. (Jap. *kantoku)* nu. (T1) boss, manager; watchman. *emén k.* one b. *néwún k.* his b.

kangkootang (3) KANGKOOTANGA. (Jap. *kankoodan.)* nu. (T3) tourist party, tour group. *kangkootangen Sapaan* Japanese t. p. vi. tour or do sight-seeing in a group. *siya nó k. Sapaan* we are off to do sight-seeing in Japan. Cf. *tuuris.*

Kangkúres (2) KANGKÚRESI. (Eng.) Var. *Kaangires.* nu. (T2) congress, legislature. *Kangkúresin Chuuk* The Truk Congress.

kangngit (2) KANGNGITI. nu. (T2) mango tree and fruit *(Mangifera indica). eféw k.* one m. fruit; *efóch k.* one m. tree. Syn. *mangko, manako.*

kangngof (2) KANGNGOFU. (Jap. *kangofu.)* nu. (T2) nurse. *emén k.* one n. *néwún k.* his n.; *kangngofun* n. of.

kapé (1) See *ka-₂, pé₃.* va. (c.) measure (especially of length and width, as with a ruler). Cf. *apééw₂.*

kapi (1) KAPII. (Eng.) nu. (T1), vi. copy.

kapiini See *kapi, -ni-.* vo. (T1) copy (something).

Kapingamarang (Pon.?) nu. (loc.; T3) Kapingamarangi Atoll.

kapú₁ (1) KAPÚÚ₁. (Jap. *kabu)* nu. (T1) stock company (in which shares are bought); Truk Trading Company

(spelled *Kapú*). *kapúún Chuuk* Trukese stock company. vi. form a pool (as with money).
kapú₂ (1) KAPÚÚ₂. (Jap. *kaabu* from Eng.) nu. (T1), vi. curve (in baseball pitching). *k. kichcho* incurve (Jap., *gichcho* left-handed). *k. kkotur* drop.
kappa (1) KAPPAA. (Jap. *kappa*, from Port. *capa*) nu. (T1) raincoat. *eché k.* one r. *aan k., wúfan k.* his r. *kappaan Merika* American r.
kaptin (Eng.) Var. *kepitin*. nu. captain (of a ship). *emén k.* one c. *néwún k.* his c.
kara- (3b) KARA. [In cpds. only.] unsp. scorched.
karasin (3; *karasinna-*) KARASINNA. (Eng.) nu. (T3) kerosene. *karasinnen Merika* American kerosene.
karakar (db; 3b) See *kara-*. vi. (dis.) 1. be scorched, sunburned. With dir. suf.: *karakarónó* be s. to ruination, burned (in cooking). 2. dried up. *meyi wor karakaren kkón wóón eey cheepen* there is some dried-up breadfruit pudding on this table.
karakarónó See *karakar*.
Karanayin (Eng.) nu. (loc.) Caroline Islands. *nómwun K.* Caroline Archipelago.
karar (3) KARARA. nu. (T3) 1. scraping, scratching or rattling noise (as by a stick along the side of a leaf-thatched house). 2. diarrhea. *meyi wúriyey k.* I have d. vi. rattle, make a scraping or rattling noise; have diarrhea. Dis. *kararrar* (ds).
kararrar Dis. of *karar*.
karereyón [Elbert] nu. bush with conspicuous bright yellow flowers (*Hibiscus moschatus*). [Unknown to Romónum speakers.]
karis nu. close-order drill. vi. do close-order drill.
Kachaw See *Achaw*.
Kachering (Jap.) nu. (loc.) Kwajalein Atoll (Marshall Islands). Syn. *Kuwachenen*.
kachito (1) KACHITOO. (Jap. *katsudoo*.) nu. (T1) motion picture, moving picture, cinema. *eew k.* one m. p. *kachitoon Merika* American m. p.
kachúpisi (1) KACHÚPISII. (Jap. *katsubushi*, from *katsuobushi*.) nu. (T1) dried bonito. *efóch k.* one d. b. *aan k.* his d. b. (to sell); *anan k.* his d. b. (to eat).
katek (2) KATEKI. (Pon.) vi., adj. (be) kind. [Only in *niyenkatek*, nun.]

katorisengko (1) KATORISENGKOO. (Jap. *katorisenkoo*) Var. *sengko*. nu. (T1) mosquito coil (a repellent).
kattu (1) KATTUU. (Sp. *gato*) Var. *attu, áttu, káttu*. nu. (T1) cat. *emén k.* one c. *kattuun Merika* American c. Syn. *kichi*.
kawakaw (db; 3) KAWA. nu. (T3) heron (general name). *emén k.* one h. *kawakawen Chuuk* Trukese h. Syn. *sóópw₂*.
kayakú (1) KAYAKÚÚ. (Jap. *kayaku*) nu. (T1) gunpowder. *néwún k.* his g.
kayi Var. of *kan*.
Kayingan nu. (loc.) Kayangel Atoll (Palau Islands).
kayirú (1) KAYIRÚÚ. (Jap. *kaeru*) nu. (T1) frog. *emén k.* one f.
kayicho (1) KAYICHOO. (Jap. *kaijo* cancellation of warning) nu. (T1) peace, truce, armistice (from the original meaning "call off an alert").
kayiya (1) KAYIYAA. (Jap. *gaiya*) nu. (T1) outfield (in baseball).
ká- See *ke-*.
-ká- See *a-₂*.
kááféw See *eféw*.
kááś (Eng.) nu. gasoline, gas. Syn. *kasoring, kasúning, kásenin*.
káák Var. of *kaak*.
kááká (db; 1) KÁÁ. Tbl. n. (T1) female genitalia. *káákáán* her g.
kááp (2) KÁPPI, KÁÁPPI. nu. (T1) yam. *eféw k.* one y. *káppin* (*káppin*) *Chuuk* Trukese yam. Syn. *eep*.
káár N. nu. canoe race. Syn. *kitir, sáák₂*.
kásenin (Eng.) nu. gasoline. Syn. *kasoring, kasúning, kááś*.
kákkáy (ds; 2) See *kkáy* Var. *kakkay*. vi. (dis.) 1. be speedy, hurry. Syn. *mwittir*. Ant. *mmang*. 2. win (in a race). Ant. *sun, mwú*.
káneng (2) KÁNENGI. vi., adj. cross-eyed, cock-eyed, strabismic. *meyi k. mesen enaan mwáán* that man's eyes are strabismic. See *mesekáneng*.
károt (2, 3) KÁROTU, KAROTA. (Eng.) nu. (T2, T3) carrot. *károtun, károten* c. of (a given kind). Syn. *ninching*.
káttu Var. of *kattu*.
ke- (3b) KE. [The standard form in deliberate speech; also used in rapid colloquial speech when the next vowel is *e* or *i*.] Var. *ka-* (only when immediately followed by *a*), *ká-* (only

in rapid speech when the next vowel is *á*), *ké-* (only in rapid speech when the next vowel is *é* or *ú* or when followed by a consonant plus the vowel *a*), *ko-* (in rapid speech when the next vowel is *o* or *u* and occasionally in combinations like *kopwe, kosapw, kose,* and *kote*), *kó-* (only in rapid speech when the next vowel is *ó*). <These rules are not strictly followed in some dialects.> pref. (sub.) 2sg. sub. prn.: thou, you (sg.). [Although a prefix, it is written separately except when followed by an aspect marker. Sub. prns. are used only at the beginning of narrative constructions and mark them as such.] *kaa* (reality aspect), *kene* or *kepwene* (uncertain future), *kepwaapw* (indefinite future), *kepwe* or *kopwe* (future), *kesapw* (future negative), *kese* (negative reality), *kete* (purposeful future negative, negative command). *kete ássááw* don't misbehave. *meet ena ke eyiis?* what is that you ask? *meet ena ká áni?* what is that you are eating? *pwata ká táyiri átánaan?* why do you make sport of that fellow? *meet ena ké féér?* what is that you are doing? *meet ena ké mwareey?* what is that you have across your shoulders? *meet ena ké wúrá?* what is that you are saying? *kó nó iya?* where are you going?

-keem (2) KEEMI. F. Var. *-kem.* suf. (obj.) 1exc. obj. prn.; us. *wuweyikeem* carry or convey us (see *wuweyi*), *wuweyikeeminó* carry or convey us away.

keen (2) KEENI, KEENNI. nu. (T2) pen, enclosure. *keenin piik* pig pen.

keenniiy See *keen, -i-*₂. vo. (T5) pen, put (something) in an enclosure.

keeri (1) KEERII. (Jap. obs. *keiri*) nu. (T2) policeman; police. *emén k.* one p. *néwún k.* his p. *ekkewe k.* those police.

keech adj. in *pwéét k.* wrinkle the nose (as a signal to someone).

kesapw See *ke-*.

kese See *ke-*.

-kek [In cpds. only.] unsp. (u.m.) See *tikek*.

kekkechiw Dis. of *kkechiw*.

kekkey Dis. of *kkey*.

kekkeyisini Dis. of *kkeyisini*.

-kem N. of *-keem*.

-kemi (1) KEMII. suf. (obj.) 2pl. obj. prn.: you. *wuweyikemi* carry you (see *wuweyi*), *wuweyikemiinó* carry you away.

-ken (2) KENI. [In cpds. only.] adj. sharp, keen. See *kken, ménúken*.

kena- (3) KENA. unsp. (u.m.) See *amwakena, mwakeneken*.

kene See *ke-*.

kengkang (3) KENGKANGA. (Jap. *genkan*) nu. (T3) hall, vestibule, room at the main entrance to a house. *eew k.* one h.

kepina (1) KEPINAA. (Pon. *kepina*, from Eng. *governor*) nu. (T1) colonial governor, district administrator (of Truk District). *emén k.* one g. *saman k., néwún k.* his g.

kepitin Obs. (Eng.) nu. ship's captain. Syn. *kaptin*.

kepwaapw See *ke-*.

kepwe See *ke-*.

kereeta (1) KEREETAA. (Cham. *kareta*, from Sp. *carreta*) nu. (T1) cart, wagon. *efóch k.* one c. *waan k.* his c. *kereetaan Merika* American c.

kereker (db; 3) KERA. nu. (T3) small, narrow boat (without outrigger and for paddling) of Okinawan type. *efóch k.* one b. *waan k.* his b.

keri- (2) KERI. [In cpds. only.] Var. *eri-*₁. unsp. scratch, scrape.

ket See *ka-*₂, *te-*. [Only in *chúúnúket*.] vi. (c.) be made to dissolve (?).

keta (1) KETAA. (Jap. *geta*) nu. (T1) clogs (of Japanese type), wooden zori. *eew k., eyipw k.* one c. *néwún k., ipwan k.* his c.

kete See *ke-*.

Ketemaang nu. (loc.) a clan name.

ké- See *ke-*.

ké (1) KÉÉ₃. vi. be permanently distorted or twisted (as by disease). Cf. *éé*₁.

kéék excl. exclamation of appreciation of a good odor. Ant. *kaak, káák, kkek*₂. Cf. *kék*.

kék excl. exclamation at an odor. Cf. *kaak, káák, kéék, kkek*₂.

kékké Dis. of *kké*.

kékkéén Dis. of *kkéén*.

kékkééneemóówun Dis. of *kkééneemóówun*.

kékkééri Dis. of *kkééri*.

kéro (1) KÉROO. [Elbert] nu. (T1) species of scorpion fish. [Unknown to Romónum speakers.]

kéch (2) KÉCHCHÚ. Ps.W. Var. ééch. vi., adj. (be) good, suitable, proper, appropriate. Cf. kkéch. nr. (T2) goodness. kéchchún eey mettóóch the g. of this thing.

kéchúúw Ps.W. of échchúúw (See kéch, -ú-).

kéchchiiti Ps.W. of échchiiti (See kéch, -iti).

kéchchúngeni Ps.W. of échchúngeni (See kéch, ngeni).

ki- (2) KI_1. pref. (u.m.) See kimaanééné, kippach, kipwaanééné, kipwpwey, kipwpwén. Cf. ku-, si-$_2$.

-ki- (2) KI_2. suf. (v.form.) makes an object focussed verb (vo.) of the base.

ki_1 (1) KII_1. vi. assemble. With dir. suf.: kiinó, kiito.

ki_2 (1) KII_2. vi. 1. be lifted, be moved by lifting. ese ki eey faaw reey I cannot lift this rock. With dir. suf.: kiinong, kiinó, kiitá, kiitiw, kiito, kiiwu. Cf. $siiki_1$, $ssik_1$. 2. be accomplished, realized, carried out. aa ki aach we ekiyek our thought has been realized. nr. (T1) act of lifting. meyi weyires kiin eey waa the l. of this canoe is difficult.

-ki (1) [In cpds. only; possibly derived by wrong analogy from -kiin.] Var. -kiin. unsp. skin; skin rash. See énúúki. Cf. kii-.

kii- (1) KII_3. [In cpds. only.] unsp. pertaining to shellfish or other marine life. See kiikap, kiinen, kiinún, kiirach, kiiroch, kissaf. Cf. -ki.

kii (1) KII_4. nu. (T1) name of the consonant (velar stop) written k; name of the letter thus written.

kiifaanong See kiifi.
kiifaanó See kiifi.
kiifaato See kiifi.
kiifaawu See kiifi.
kiifáátá See kiifi.
kiifáátiw See kiifi.

kiifi KIIFI. vo. (T4) spit (something) from the mouth. aa k. ngonuk he s. it toward or at you. With dir. suf.: kifaanong, kifaanó or kifóónó, kifaato, kifaawu, kifáátá, kifáátiw. Cf. kiteey, kusufi.

kiifóónó See kiifi.

$kiis_1$ (3b) KISA. n. (T3) gift that does not obligate the recipient (the recipient is not kinissow by virtue of the gift). [Normally made only to relatives by marriage.] kisan his gift (to someone).

$kiis_2$ (3) KIISA. [Presumably a back formation from $kiis_1$.] va. give a gift of $kiis_1$ type (with ngeni). Dis. kikkiis (ds).

-kiis (2) See kisi-. adj. little, small, tiny.

kiisenóónó See $kiis_2$, -ni-, -nó. vo. (T5) give away as a $kiis_1$ type of gift.

kiikap (3) See kii-, ap_2 or $apaap_1$ (?). nu. (T3) a bivalve (edible). Cf. kiipap.

kiikiiwu Dis. of $kiiwu_2$.

kiimweyimw (db; 3b) See ki_2, iimw. nu. (T3) house on lee platform of sailing canoe (kiimweyimwen waaseres). eew k. one h. Id. kiimweyimwen maram halo around the moon.

$kiin_1$ (2) $KINI_1$. (Mck.) nu. (T2) rash, skin irritation; skin (in some compounds). eew k. one r. kinin Kuchuwa prickly heat (from Kuchuwa, Tonowas Island, where the mission schoolboys are said to have gotten prickly heat from wearing clothes); kinin nuuk pox ("stomach rash"); kinin poro dark, itchy rash (said to be caused by a spell); kinin woró pox with swollen spots over the body (said to result from the spell named woró). aa wúri enaan mwáán ewe k. that man got the rash.

$kiin_2$ (3, 2) $KINA_1$, $KINI_2$. nu. (T3) woman's belt or necklace of shell beads. eché k. one b. énúkún k. her b.; mwárin k. her n. kinen Chuuk Trukese b. núkúni eché k., énúkúni eché k. acquire a b.; núkúnúk k. wear a b. kinin pattiw b. of a Puluwat type; kinin tiwáán b. with féwúpar and féwúpwech in the middle; kinin wóón b. with féwúpar and féwún wóón (decorative beads of shell or stone from Japan).

$kiin_3$ Var. of kin_1.

kiinen (2) See kii-, $neni-_1$ (?). nu. (T2) a crab (small, black, with two red front claws, found in mangrove swamps). eew k. one c. kiinenin Chuuk Trukese c.

kiinenong Var. of kinenong.
kiinenó Var. of kinenó.
kiineto Var. of kineto.
kiinewu Var. of kinewu.
kiinong See ki_2.
kiinó See ki_1, ki_2.

kiinún See *kii-, nnú-*. nu. any cone shell (family Conidae); white ear discs cut from cone shells.

kiipap (3) See *kii-*. nu. (T3) a bivalve (edible). Cf. *kiikap*.

kiipw (3) KIPWPWA. nu. (T3) a plant. *kipwpwen* p. of (a given region). Syn. *ttong*.

kiirach (3) See *kii-, -rach*. nu. (T3) species of surgeon fish, convict tang. *kiirachen Chuuk* Trukese s. f.

kiiroch (3a) See *kii-, roch*. nu. (T3) sea snail (*Nerita polita* L.).

kiich$_1$ (3a) KICHA. prn. (pers.) 1inc. prn.: we, us.

kiich$_2$ (2) KICHI. nu. (T2) wont, character.

kiit (3: *kita-*) KITA$_3$. nu. (T3) waste, leftovers, scraps. *kiten kofi* coffee grounds; *kiten mwéngé feces; kiten taka* copra flakes from which coconut cream has been squeezed.

kiitá See *ki*$_2$.

kiitiw See *ki*$_2$.

kiito See *ki*$_1$, *ki*$_2$.

kiiwu$_1$ See *ki*$_2$.

kiiwu$_2$ (1) See *ki*$_2$, *-wu*. vi. overflow, spill out, swarm out. Dis. *kiikiiwu* (db)

kiiwúfer (2) KIIWÚFERI. (Ger. *Koffer*) Var. *kúúwiifer, kiwiifer*. nu. (T2) suitcase.

kisáásew See *kiis*$_1$. vi. be generous with *kiis*$_1$ gifts, be generous to one's wife's kin. *emén meyi k. átánaan* one who is g. with *kiis* that fellow.

kiseengey (2) KISEENGEYI. nu. (T2) variety of breadfruit. *kiseengeyin Chuuk* Trukese b.

kisenngeni See *kiis*$_1$, *-ni-, ngeni*. Var. *kiis ngeni, kisengeni*. vo. (T2) give a *kiis*$_1$ type of gift to (someone).

kisengeni See *kiis*$_1$, *ngeni*. Var. *kiis ngeni, kisenngeni*. vo. (T2) give a *kiis*$_1$ type of gift to (someone).

kisi- (2) KISI. ni. (T2), suf. (cc.) bit, little thing; assistant (to). *ekis, rúwékis, wúnúkis, fékis, nimekis, wonokis, fúúkis, wanúkis, ttiwekis, engoon kisin* one,...ten bits; *fitekis* how many bits. *kisin fináyik* assistant flag chief (under Japanese rule). Syn. *ngin*.

kisiiti See *kisi-, -iti*. vo. (T2) be too small for. Syn. *kúkkún ngeni*.

kisikiis (db; 2) See *kisi-, -kkiis*. N. vi. (dis.) be little, tiny, small. With dir. suf.: *kisikiisinó* get smaller, become reduced. Syn. *kúkkún, nginingiin*.

kisikiisinó See *kisikiis*.

kisinom [Elbert] nu. a tree (*Randia carolinensis*). [Unknown to Romónum speakers.]

kisinó (1) See *kisi-, -nó*. vi. decrease, get smaller. Dis. *kisikiisinó* (db).

kissaf (3b) See *kii-* or *kin*$_2$, *saaf*. nu. (T3) any of a wide variety of small gastropods, including moon shells (Natacidae), most miter shells (Mitridae), augur shells (Terebridae), ear shells (Ellobiidae).

kikanchú (1) KIKANCHÚÚ. (Jap. *kikanjuu*) nu. (T1) machine gun. *efóch k.* one m. g. *néwún k.* his m. g.

kikkiis Dis. of *kiis*$_2$.

kikkik Dis. of *kkik*$_1$, *kkik*$_2$.

Kimaanééné See *ki-*$_1$, *ma-, a-*$_2$, *nééné*. nu. (pers.) one of two benevolent guardian spirits of the spring Winikachaw in Mecchitiw, Wééné (Moen) Island.

kimenes (Eng.) nu. gimlet, brace. *efóch k.* one g. *aan k.* his g. *mesen k.* brace's bit.

kimichi (1) KIMICHII. (Kor. *kimchi*) nu. (T1) kimchee. *eew k.* one jar of k. *wochaan k.* his k. (to eat).

kimpa (1) KIMPAA. (Jap. *kinba*) vi., adj. (be) gold-capped, have gold crown (of a tooth).

kin$_1$ (3a) KINA$_2$. N. Var. *kiin*$_3$. vi. be removed, move (oneself), leave, go away; (excl.) scram. With dir. suf.: *kinenong, kinenó, kineto, kinewu. kinewu mé wóón eey aan* move off of this road. Syn. *sú*. Cf. *kineenó, kineeto*.

kin$_2$ (2) See *kiin*$_1$. vi. be ashamed (without implications of awe). *wúwaa k.* I am a. Cf. *ma, máfen, sááw*.

kin$_3$ (2) KINI$_3$. vi., adj. (be) cut, separated, segmented, picked (of fruit). *aa k. mé éétiw* it (the moon) is in the third quarter; *aa k. mé notow* it (the moon) is in the first quarter.

kinaas (3) KINASSA. (Eng.) nu. glass; mirror. *aan k.* his g.; *masan k.* or *mesan k.* his eye-glasses, spectacles; *néwún k.* his mirror. *kinassen owuruur, kinassen woori* mirror.

kinas (3) KINASA. n. (T3) cut, cut wound. *kinasan* his c. *sáfeen k.* medicine for treating cuts. vi. be cut, wounded.

kinamwmwe Var. of *kunamwmwe*.

kinap (3) KINAPA. nu. (T3) card game (like draw poker, but played with a limit of

four players and using only the honor cards: ace, king, queen, jack, ten).
kinapis (Eng.) nu. clubs (in playing cards).
kineenó (1) See *kin₁, -nó.* [Imperative only.] vi. go on farther, keep going; (excl.) go away, scram.
kineeto (1) See *kin₁, -to.* [Imperative only.] vi. come more this way, keep coming.
kineseni See *kin₁, seni₂.* vo. (T2) go away from.
kinenong See *kin₁.*
kinenó See *kin₁.*
kineto See *kin₁.*
kinewu See *kin₁.*
kiney nu. (temp.) 20th night of the lunar month.
kini (3, 1) KINIYA, KINII. Var. *sini* (in cpds. only). nu. (T3) a kind of mat (made of coconut leaves with midribs down the middle of the mat). *eché k.* one mat. *kiyan k.* his m. *kiniyen, kiniin* m. of (a given place). *siya féwúféw k.* we plaited *k.* mats. Cf. *etiru.* adj. made of plaited coconut frond matting. [In cpds. only.]
kiniiy See *kin₃, -i-₂.* vo. (T5) cut, separate, segment, pick; divide. With n. form. suf.: *kiniiya-* (ni.; T3) thing picked (by someone); *kiniiyan* thing picked by him.
kiniiya- See *kiniiy.*
Kinissimas Var. of *Kiriisimas.*
kinissow (2) See *kin₂, sowu-₂.* nu. (T2) social condition in which thanks or apologies are due another. vi. be in a condition of owing thanks or apologies. *kinissow!* thanks! *k. chaapwúúr!* thank you very much!
kinissowiiti See *kinissow, -iti.* vo. (T2) be in awe of, be diffident toward. *wúse toongeni kkapas ngeni ewe samwoon pwe wú k.* I couldn't speak to the chief because I was in a. of him.
kinissowungeni See *kinissow, ngeni.* vo. (T2) express thanks or apologies to.
kinikin (db; 2) See *kin₃.* nu. (dis.; T2) partition, division, section. *eew k.* one partition or division. va., vi. (dis.) engage in cutting, separating, segmenting, picking.
kinimw (3) KINIMWA. nu. (T3) small, armored crab (found in sea). *eew k.* one c. *kinimwen neeset* c. of the sea.

kiningngaw (3b) See *kiin₁, ngngaw.* nu. (T3) any slight skin disease. vi. have a rash.
Kinipech (Eng.) nu. (loc.) Gilbert Islands. *Nómwun K.* Gilbert Islands chain.
kinipwut (3) See *kiin₁, pwuta-.* F. nu. (T3) species of parrot fish. *kinipwuten Chuuk* Trukese p. f. *rongen k.* a form of sorcery causing blindness; *sáfeen k.* medicine against blindness caused by *k.* sorcery. Syn. *sinipwut.*
kiniyaw (3) KINIYAWA. nu. (T3) species of palm, native to Truk. *kiniyawen Chuuk* Trukese p.
kiniyoch (3) KINIYOCHA. nu. (T3) repairing, fixing something up; thing that fixes up.
kiniyocheey See *kiniyoch, -e-₂.* vo. (T6b) repair, mend, fix up; maintain.
kinospiin (Eng.) nu. clothespin.
kinomw (2) KINOMWU. F. nu. (T2) lizard. *emén k.* one l. *kinomwun Chuuk* Trukese l. Syn. *kúúween.*
kinsipakútang (3) KINSIPAKÚTANGA. (Jap. *genshi bakudan*) Var. *kinsúpakútang.* nu. (T3) atom-bomb. *eféw k.* one a. b. *newún k.* his a. b.; *kinsipakútangen* a. b. of.
kinnu (1) KINNUU. Var. *kunnu.* nu. (T1) a small shellfish. *eew k.* one s. *kinnuun Chuuk* Trukese *k.*
kippach (3b) See *ki-₁, pach.* n. (T3) friend. *kippachan* his f.
Kipwaanééné See *ki-₁, pwe₁, a-₂, nééné.* nu. (pers.) a spirit who is guardian of the spring Winikachaw in Mechchitiw, Wééné (Moen) Island.
kipwin (2) KIPWINI. nu. (T2) seed. *kipwinin mááy, kipwinin ónóyas* breadfruit s., *kipwinin kurukur* orange s. *kipwinin pecheey* my ankle knuckle (protruding on both sides of the ankle).
Kipwinittúún nu. (pers.) a traditional storm god. [One of five children of the weather (*newún rááń*), who live in the gale, sink boats in heavy seas, and blow down trees.]
kipwpwaaw (3) KIPWPWAAWA. nu. (T3) pawpaw or papaya tree or fruit (*Carica papaya*). *efóch k.* one p. tree, *eféw k.* one p. fruit. *kipwpwaawen Chuuk* Trukese p.
kipwpwey (2) KIPWPWEYI. nu. (T2) pinching. *chóón k.* a pincher. va. pinch.

kipwpweyi See *kipwpwey.* vo. (T2) pinch. *kipwpweyuk* p. you.

kipwpwén (2) See *ki-₁, pwénú-₂.* N. nu. (T2) lid, cover (in the expression *kippwénún maas* eyelid) Syn. *épwpwén.*

kiriis (2) KIRIISI. (Eng.) nu. (T2) pommade, hair grease. *epitan k.* his p. *kiriisin Chuuk* Trukese p.

Kiriisimas (3) KIRIISIMASA. (Eng.) Var. *Kiriismas, Kirisimas, Kinissimas.* nu. (temp.) Christmas.

Kiriismas Var. of *Kiriisimas.*

kiriiy Tb2. [Presumably formed from a base *kiri* plus v.form. suf. *-i-₂.* The base may be related to *ir₂.*] vo. (T5) roll (trouser legs, shirt sleeves, etc.). [Used only in unmixed company because of similarity to the tabu word *iriiy.*] With dir. suf.: *kiriiyetá* roll up.

kiriiyetá See *kiriiy.*

Kirisimas Var. of *Kiriisimas.*

kirikir (db; 2) KIRI. n. (T2) conduct, social behavior. *kirikirin* his c.

kirikiréech (2: *-échchú-*) See *kirikir, éech.* nu. (T2) kindness, good conduct. *kirikiréchchún átánaan* that fellow's k. vi. be kind, act or behave well.

kirikiringngaw (3b) See *kirikir, ngngaw.* nu. (T3) unkindness, ingratitude, bad conduct. vi. be unkind, ungrateful, inhospitable, untrustworthy, act or behave badly.

Kirinis (Eng.) nu. (loc.) Greenwich Islands (Kapingamarangi).

-kich (3a) See *kiich₁.* suf. (obj.) 1exc. obj. prn.: us. *wuweyikich* carry us (see *wuweyi*), *wuweyikichenó* carry us away.

kichi (Eng. *kitty*) nu. cat. *emén k.* one c. *néwún k.* his c. Syn. *attu, áttu, kattu, káttu.*

kichini See *kiich₂, -ni-.* vo. (T5) frequent, spend most of one's time in; hang about (a person). *Ichiro aa k. Siro ne tingoreey mwooni* Ichiro is hanging about Siro to tease him for some money.

kichiniwén (2) See *kiich₂, wénú-.* Var. *kichinúwén.* nu. (T3) bush dweller, person of low degree, commoner, outcaste. vi., adj. (be) uncivilized, untutored, wild.

kichinúwén Var. of *kichiniwén.*

kichingngaw (3b) See *kiich₂, ngngaw.* nu. (T3) stinginess. vi. 1. be stingy, ungenerous; hold out on another. *wúwa opwut átánaan pwú aa mén k. ngenney* I dislike yonder fellow because he has been very s. toward me. 2. be of low carrying capacity.

kichiyéech (2: *-yéchchú-*) See *kiich₂, éech.* nu. diligence, generosity, industriousness. vi., adj. (be) diligent, generous, industrious, energetic.

kichuyán Var. of *kuchuyen.*

kichúúchú Var. of *kichchúúchú.*

kichcho (1) KICHCHOO. (Jap. *gitcho*) nu. (T1) left-handed person. *emén k.* one l. h. p.

kichchúúchú (1) See *kiin₁* or *kiti-, chúú.* Var. *kichúúchú.* vi., adj. be thin, skinny. With dir. suf.: *kichchúúchúúnó.* Syn. *chúúchú.* Ant. *kitinnupw.*

kichchúúchúúnó See *kichchúúchú.*

kit (3) KITA₁. vi. be strong, firm, steady. Dis. *kitekit* (db).

-kit (3) KITA₂. suf. (cc.) ten thousand. [Replaced by *kkit* in the schools.] *ekit, rúwékit, wúnúkit, fékit, nimekit, wonokit, fúúkit, wanúkit, ttiwekit, engoon kkitan* one,...ten t. t. With c. pref. and ptv. const.: *áákitan, érúwékitan* first t. t., second t. t. (etc.). With pref. *áná-: ánáákit, ánákkit* sole or only t. t. Cf. *kkit.*

kitar (3) KITARA. (Eng.) nu. (T3) guitar. *eew k.* one g. *néwún k.* his g. *kitaren Merika* American g. vi. play a g.

kiteey See *kiit, -e-₂.* vo. (T6b) spit out (food). With dir. suf.: *kiteeyenó, kiteeyetiw, kiteeyewu.* Cf. *kiifi.*

kiteeyenó See *kiteey.*

kiteeyetiw See *kiteey.*

kiteeyewu See *kiteey.*

kitekit Dis. of *kit.*

kiti- (2) KITI. [In cpds. only.] unsp. (u.m.) [Possibly a variant of *kii-,* or a cpd. of *ki-₁* and *ti-.*] See *kitinnupw, kitipéppé, kitipwén, kitipwoopwo, kichchúúchú.*

kitinnupw (2) See *kiti-, nupw.* n. (T2) obesity, condition of being fat. *kitinnupwun* his o. vi. be fat, obese. Ant. *kichchúúchú.*

kitipéppé (1) See *kiti-, pé₁* (?). vi. squirm, thrash about, writhe, wriggle violently (as a newly caught fish).

kitipwén (2) See *kiti-, pwénú-₂* (?). nu. (T2) a kind of shellfish (small and edible). *eféw k.* one s. *kitipwénún Chuuk* Trukese s. Syn. *nittumw.*

kitipwoopwo (1) See *kiti-, pwo.* vi. have multiple swellings.

kitir₁ (2) KITIRI₁. N. **nu.** (T2) fruit or flower of any plant (including that of the coconut). *kitirin irá* f. of the tree. vi. bear fruit or flowers.

kitir₂ (2) KITIRI₂. nu. (T2) contest, match, competition, race. *kitirin waa* canoe race. vi. be in a contest, contend, compete, vie, be in a race.

kitir₃ (2) [Short form of *kitirinippi*.] nu. (T2) kind of clam (bivalve, radial lines, pubescent, small, found in sand). *eféw k.* one c. *kitirin Chuuk* Trukese c.

kitiriféw See *kitir₁, faaw.* Var. *kitirifféw.* vi. be lumpy, not uniformly soft (of breadfruit and other such things that are mashed).

kitirifféw Var. of *kitiriféw.*

kitirinippi (3) See *kitir₁, ppi₂.* nu. (T3) kind of clam (bivalve, radial lines, pubescent, small, found in sand). Syn. *kitir₃.*

kitirup (3) See *kiti-, rup₂.* nu. (T3) wrestling or tussling in play (when lying down). vi. wrestle. *k. ngeni* w. with.

kituun (2) KITUUNU. nu. (T2) offering of a drinking coconut to a spirit or to the spirit of a dead person on his grave. *kituunun ewe meyimá* o. for the dead one.

kiwiifer Var. of *kúúwiifer.*

kiwiin (Eng.) nu. queen (in cards).

kiya- (3) KIYA. ni. (T3) plaited mat, sleeping mat. *kiyan* his m. *toonong nóón kiyan* went in to her sleeping m. Id. *fitaché kiyomw?* how many are your m.? (how many times have you been instructed in *itang?* how much *itang* do you know?)

kiyach (3) KIYACHCHA. (Jap. *kyacchi, kyacchaa,* from Eng.) nu. (T3) catcher (in baseball). *emén k.* one c. *néwún k.* his c.; *kiyachchen* c. of. vi. play or be catcher. *een kepwe k.* you shall be c.

kiyá₁ (1) KIYÁÁ₁. Var. *iyá.* n. (T1) boundary, limit. *kiyáán* its b., b. of. *ekkewe mwáán raa féérí ewe k. neefiinen fénúweer kkewe* those men established the boundary between their lands. Syn. *kiyáán.*

kiyá₂ (1) KIYÁÁ₂. N. nu. (T1) nipa palm. [Its leaves are used for thatch and to prepare hot massages.] *efóch k.* one n. p. tree; *eché k.* one n. p. leaf. Syn. *kiyé, kúwé.*

kiyááfeseen (2: *-fesenni-*) See *kiyá₁, -feseen.* vi. split, divide (of a lineage).

kiyááfesenniiy See *kiyá₁, -fesenniiy.* vo. (T5) split, divide (as land).

kiyáán (2) See *kiyá₁.* F. [Presumably formed by treating the ptv. const. *kiyáán* as the independent form of a new base KIYÁÁNNI.] n. (T2) limit, boundary. *kiyáánnin* its b., b. of.

kiyáánniiy See *kiyáán, -i-₂.* F. Var. *iyáánniiy.* vo. (T5) establish a boundary on.

kiyeki (db; 3) See *kiya-.* nu. (T3) sleeping mat (made of plaited pandanus leaf). *eché k.* one m. *kiyan k.* his m. Syn. *ténaaw.*

Kiyer nu. (pers.) a traditional god (said to live in *Ewúr* and be benevolent).

kiyé Var. of *kúwé.*

kiyopw (2) KIYOPWU. nu. (T2) variety of spider lily with large red stems. *kiyopwun Chuuk* Trukese s. l.

kiyó (1) KIYÓÓ. nu. (T1) outrigger boom on a canoe. *efóch k.* one o. b. *kiyóón waa* canoe's o. b. Syn. *siyá.*

ko-₁ Var. of *ke-,* commonly with *-pwe* in *kopwe.*

ko-₂ Var. of *o-₃.*

ko-₃ (4) KO₂. [In cpds. only.] unsp. pertaining to lines, knots, or their appearance. Cf. *kko-₂, kokko-.*

ko (1) KOO₁. Var. *o₁.* ct.m. sir (polite form in addressing a man or calling him by name). *ee ko!* what is it, sir! (polite way to answer to a man of higher rank when he calls one's name); *áámi ko* you sirs; *een ko* you sir. *kepwe kan ko mwúút ngeniyey eey ááy tingor* you will please, sir, grant to me this my request.

koos (3) KOSA. n. (T3) speech accent, speech intonation. Dis. *kosokos* (db). *kosan* his s. a. *kosen Merika* American a.; *kosen Wééné* Wééné (Moen) a. Cf. *woos.*

kooskake (1) KOOSKAKEE. (Jap. *koshikake*) nu. (T1) chair. *eew k., efóch k.* one c. *aan k.* his c.

kookang₁ (3) KOOKANGA₁. (Jap. *kookan*) vi., va. exchange. *sipwe k. aach rawúses* let us e. our trousers.

kookang₂ (3) KOOKANGA₂. (Jap. *kookan,* from *kookandai* switchboard) nu. (T3) switchboard; operator! (used only to

kookoo-

draw a telephone operator's attention). *eew k.* one s. *aan k.* his s. *chóón k.* operator. Cf. *opereyitor.*

kookoo- (db; 1) KOO₂. unsp. (u.m.) See *fitikooko.* Cf. *kuukuu-.*

kookuupwokang (3) KOOKUUPWOKANGA. (Jap. *kookuubokan*) nu. (T3) airplane carrier. *efóch k.* one a. c. *waan k.* his a. c.

koomw (3) KOOMWMWA. (Eng.) n. (T3) comb. *efóch k.* one c. *aan k.* his c. *koomwmwen feefin* women's c.

koomwmweengeni See *koomwmweey, ngeni.* vo. (T2) comb (something). *wúwa k. mékúrey* I have combed my hair ("my head").

koomwmweey See *koomw, -e-₂.* vo. (T6b) comb (someone). *wúwa koomwmweeyey* I have combed my hair ("combed myself"). Cf. *koomwmweengeni.*

koon₁ Var. *kon, kkon(?).* adv. most, very, extremely (in a positive sense); too (in a negative sense). *e k. nap seni éwúchcheyaan iyeey* it was very much greater than the value of it now. *aa k. mwittir* he was swiftest (of winner of a race); *aa k. ning* it is most (very) beautiful; *aa k. ééch* it is best, it is very good. *aa k. ngar eey kofi* this coffee is too sweet.

koon₂ (2) KOONU₁. (Eng.) nu. (T2) gold. *néwún k.* his g. *koonun Merika* American g.

koon₃ (2) KOONU₂. (Eng.) nu. (T2) coal. *eew k.* one piece of c. *aan k.* his c.

-koongi [In cpds. only.] unsp. (u.m.) See *túrúkoongi.* Cf. *woongi.*

koopwure (1) KOOPWUREE. (Sp. *cobre*) nu. (T1) tin, corrugated iron. *eché k.* one sheet of t. *aan k.* his t.

Kooreya (1) (Eng.) nu. (loc.; T1) Korea. Syn. *Chooseng.*

koori (1) KOORII. (Jap. *koori*) nu. (T1) ice; mixture of water and ice. *eféw k.* one lump of i. *wúnúman* his i. (to suck).

Kooroor nu. (loc.) Koror Island (Palau Islands).

Koot (3) KOOTA. (Eng.) nu. (pers.; T3) God. *emén K.* one G. *néwún K.* his G. *Kooten nááng* heavenly God.

koowa (1) KOOWAA. (Pon.) nu. (T1) in *sowun k., sewiin k.* deacon (in Protestant Church).

kooyeng (3) KOOYENGA. (Jap. *kooen* park) nu. (T3) playground. *eew k.* one p. *aan k.* his p.

Kofénú nu. (loc.) a clan name.

kofi (1) KOFII. (Eng.) nu. (T1) coffee. *wúnúman k.* his drink of c. *kofiin Merika* American c.; *kiten k.* c. grounds; *kona k.* instant (powdered) c.

kosi (1) KOSII. nu. (T1) a throw (in fighting or wrestling).

kosiini See *kosi, -ni-.* vo. (T4) throw (someone) in fighting or wrestling.

kosimaki (1) KOSIMAKII. (Jap.) nu. (T1) woman's wrap-around undergarment. [Made of cotton cloth, it was worn during period of Japanese rule.] *eché k.* one u. *aan k., wúfan k.* her u.

kosokos See *koos.*

kok (3a) KOKA. vi., adj. (be) partly submerged or sunk. With dir. suf.: *kokonó* be swamped (of a boat), sink; *kokotiw* be swamped (of a boat), sink (of a person).

kokonó See *kok.*

kokotiw See *kok.*

kokko- (ds; 4) See *kko-₂.* [In cpds. only.] unsp. appear, look. Cf. *ko-₃.*

kokkongngaw (3b) See *kokko-, ngngaw.* vi. appear badly, look badly.

kokkoyééch (2: *-yéchú-*) See *kokko-, ééch.* vo. appear well; look well.

kompeni (3) KOMPENIYA. (Eng.) nu. (T3) company. *kompeniyen Chuuk* Trukese c. vi. (with *ngeni*) associate (with).

komwaapw Var. of *kómwópw.*

komwu F. of *kómwu.*

komwusin (2) KOMWUSINI. (Eng.) nu. commission, profit.

komwuniyo (1) KOMWUNIYOO. (Lat.) nu. (T1) holy communion (R.C.).

kon Var. of *koon₁.*

kona (1) KONAA. (Jap. *kona*) nu. powder. *k. kofi* instant (powdered) coffee; *k. soopw* soap p.

konaak (3) KONAAKA. nu. (T3) dog. *emén k.* one d. *néwún k.* his d.; *masan k.* his seeing-eye dog. *konaaken Chuuk* Trukese d.

koneeta (1) KONEETAA. nu. (T1) be-still tree (*Thevetia peruviana*).

Konowaay nu. (pers.) traditional god of *tuttunnap* (stories and fables). [He lives in the sky and is a brother of *Naanúken.*]

Konusukis nu. (pers.) Little Claus (of the fairy tale).
Konusunap nu. (pers.) Big Claus (of the fairy tale).
kontrák (2) KONTRÁKKI. (Eng.) nu. (T2) contract. *kontrákkin meet?* c. for what?
kongkúri (1) KONGKÚRII. (Jap. *konkuri* from *kongkuriito* from Eng.) nu. (T1) concrete. *aan k.* his c.; *kongkúriin* c. of.
kopwe See *ke-*.
kopwur (3) KOPWURA. n. (T3) stomach. *kopwuran* his s.
koro (1) KOROO. (Jap. *goro*) nu. (T1) grounder (in baseball). *eew k.* one g.
-koch [In cpds. only.] unsp. (u.m.) See *morenikoch*.
kocha (1) KOCHAA. (Jap. *goza*) nu. (T1) straw mat (Japanese type). *eché k.* one m. *kiyan k.* his m.
kochokoch (db; 3) KOCHA. nu. (dis.; T3) short hairs on top of forehead (especially of women). *emeet k.* one s. h. *néwún k., aan k.* his s. h.
kochchuuni N. (loan source unknown) vo. (T4) cook (something) in coconut oil.
kota- (3) KOTA. [In cpds. only.] unsp. dried, parched, low tide.
kotokot (db; 3) See *kota-*. vi. (dis.) be low tide ("be dry"). With dir. suf.: *kotokototá* become l. t.; *meyi k. eey sáát* the sea here has become l. t.
kotokototá See *kotokot*.
kowuruur (db; 2) See *wur₂*. Itang. vi. (c., dis.) cause visitings.
koyi-₁ (2) KOYI₁. [In cpds. only.] unsp. piping sound, whistle. See *koyikoy, okoyikoy*.
koyi-₂ (2) KOYI₂. [In cpds. only.] unsp. hop on one leg. See *nikkoy, nikoyikoy*.
koyikoy (db; 2) See *koyi-₁*. nu. (T2) a bird (pipes at dawn and dusk).
koyiyasi (1) KOYIYASII. (Jap. *koyashi*) nu. (T1) fertilizer.
kó-₁ Var. of *ke-*.
kó-₂ Var. of *ó-₂*.
kóókó (db; 1) KÓÓ. nu. baby. *emén k.* one b. *néwún k.* his b. Cf. *nikkó*.
kóón (2) KÓÓNU. (Eng.) nu. (T2) corn, maize. *eféw k.* one kernel of c.; *efóch k.* one ear of c. *anan k.* his c. (to eat). *kóónun Merika* American c. Syn. *meyiis*.
kóópeni (3) KÓÓPENIYA. Obs. (P.Eng.) Var. *kompeni*. nu. (T3) mercantile company. *kóópeniyen Chuuk* Trukese c.
kófónónó Var. of *ófónónó*.
kófót (3) See *fóto-₁*. vi. (c.) have a look, watch, observe. Syn. *kkaton, kkóton, kkanges*. Cf. *kkófót*.
kómwópw (Eng. *come up?*) Var. *komwaapw*. nu., vi. ante (in poker).
kómwu (1) KÓMWUU. (Cham. *kamuti*, from Nahuatl) Var. *kkómwu, komwu*. nu. (T1) sweet potato. *eféw k.* one s. p. *kómwuun Chuuk* Trukese s. p. Syn. *kómwuti*.
kómwuti (1) KÓMWUTII. (Cham. *kamuti*, from Nahuatl) Var. *kkómwuuti*. nu. (T1) sweet potato.
-kópo (1) [In cpds. only.] nu. (u.m.; T1) See *meseyikópo*.
kóto- (4) KÓTO. unsp. (u.m.) See *nikótókót₁, nikótókót₂*.
ku- (2) KU. pref. (u.m.) See *kupach*. Cf. *ki-₁*.
ku (1) KUU₁. vi. be more than enough; be fed up.
kuus₁ F. vi., adj. (be) able, skilled, industrious. Syn. *pwáák*.
kuus₂ (3) KUUSA. n. (T3) coverlet or cover of woven material; sheet, blanket. *eché k.* one c. *kuusan* his c. Syn. *chchenikam, sárem*.
kuukuu- (db; 1) KUU₂. unsp. going, proceeding (?). Syn. *kookoo-*. See *fitikuuku, kuukuumwir*.
kuukuumwir (2) See *kuukuu-, mwiri-₁*. vi. go behind, follow.
kuukuumwiriiy See *kuukuumwir, -i-₂*. vo. (T5) go behind, follow (someone).
kuum See *ku, -mi-*. [Presumably a back formation from *kuumi₁*.] vi. shut, closed. *k. ffengenniiy* close (something) together.
kuumar (3) KUUMARA. nu. (T3) type of basket. *eew k.* one b. *aan k.* his b. Cf. *sángá, sewá*.
kuumi₁ See *ku, -mi-*. vo. (T4) close (something) up, shut.
kuumi₂ See *kumu-*. [Derivation obscure.] vo. (T4) hold (something) in the mouth without swallowing. Syn. *kumuuw*.
kuun (3) KUUNA, KUUNNA. nu. (T3) a tree (*Barringtonia asiatica, Barringtonia racemosa*). [Fruits are used as fish poison and to cauterize wounds.]

kuunen Chuuk, kuunnen Chuuk Trukese Barringtonia. Syn. *sóón₁, wuwáánúúw₁*.

-kuun See *kkun*.

kuunón (4) See *kuukuu-, nónu-*. vi. be seriously ill. With dir. suf.: *kuunónónó* take a serious turn for the worse; *aa kuunónónó átánaan reen aan semwmwen* that fellow has taken a serious turn for the worse with his sickness.

kuunónónó See *kuunón*.

kuunun nu. scar.

kuup (3: *kuppa-*) See *ku-, ppa-*. nu. (T3) bulkhead of paddle canoe (lashed to outrigger boom where it crosses body of canoe). *kuppen waa* canoe's b.

kuupw (3) KUPWPWA. nu. (T3) pod that forms at tip of breadfruit branch and that opens to reveal the male flower. *kupwpwen mááy* male flower-pod of breadfruit. Cf. *kuwapw*.

kuuch (3) KUUCHA. (Eng.) nu. goat. *emén k.* one g. *néwún k.* his g. Syn. *siike*.

kus (2) KUSU. vi. spurt out, be squirted out, flow (of blood); escape, get away; (coarse talk) appear, emerge, come to view. *aa kus chcha* blood flowed. With dir. suf.: *kusunó,* emerge going away; *kusuto* emerge or appear hither; *kusutiw* emerge downwards, pour or fall down (of liquids from a faucet or hose). Cf. *kkus*.

Kusaye nu. (loc.) Kusaie Island (Eastern Caroline Islands). [This is the ordinary name in use today; cf. old *itang* name of *Achaw* or *Kachaw*.]

kusiiti See *kus, -iti.* vo. (T2) squirt upon, spurt upon.

kusufi See *kus, -fi-*. vo. (T5) spit (something) out; spit on (someone). *k. ewe kkónik* s. out the water; *k. ewe aramas* s. on that person. Cf. *kiifi*.

kusukus₁ (db; 2) See *kus.* nu. (dis.; T2) chewing and spitting of medicine on a patient. vi. to chew and spit medicine on someone.

kusukus₂ (db; 2) See *kus.* nu. (dis.; T2) lisp, speech distortion; (of a person) chronic liar. vi. be lisped; lie chronically.

kusunó See *kus*.

kusutiw See *kus*.

kusuto See *kus*.

kukkuus (ds; 3) See *kuus₂*. va. (dis.) use a blanket or coverlet, cover oneself with a coverlet. *ewe mwáán aa k. ewe chchenikam* the man has covered himself with a sheet.

kukkumos (ds; 3) See *kumosa-*. nu. (T3) circularity, roundness. *kukkumosen maram* fullness of the moon. vi. be round, circular, globular. *meyi k. eey cheepen* this table is round. Syn. *kumosumos*.

kukkun (ds; 2) See *kkun*. nu. (T2) direction of facing. *kukkunun fénú* direction in which the island faces ("the turn of the land"). vi. (dis.) revolve, rotate, turn, roll repeatedly.

kukkunow Dis. of *kunow*.

kumosa- (3, 2) KUMOSA, KUMOSU. [In cpds. only.] unsp. round, circular, globular. See *kukkumos, kumosumos*.

kumosu- See *kumosa-*.

kumosumos (db; 2) See *kumosa-*. Var. *kukkumos*. vi. (dis.) be round, circular, globular.

kumu- (2) KUMU. [In cpds. only.] unsp. holding or swishing fluid in the mouth without swallowing. Cf. *kkumw₁*. suf. (cc.) mouthful or swallow of liquid. *ekum, rúwékum, wúnúkum, fékum, nimekum, wonokum, fúúkum, wanúkum, ttiwekum* one,...nine m. of l.; *fitekum* how many m. of l.

kumuuw See *kumu-, -u-*. vo. (T5) hold or swish (a fluid) in the mouth without swallowing, rinse out the mouth with (a fluid). *siya k. ewe kkónik* we held the water in our mouth without swallowing it. Syn. *kuumi₂*.

kumukum (db; 2) See *kumu-*. vi. (dis.) hold a fluid or swish it in the mouth without swallowing it.

kumwuch (2) KUMWUCHU. n. (T2) fist; hoof, foot, paw (of animal). *efóch k.* one f. *kumwuchun* his f. suf. (cc.) fistful, handful; hoof, foot, paw (of animal). *ekumwuch, rúwékumwuch, wúnúkumwuch, fékumwuch, nimekumwuch, wonokumwuch, fúúkumwuch, wanúkumwuch, ttiwekumwuch* one,...nine f., etc. (*wúnukumuch rayis* three fistfuls of rice; *wúnúkumuch kumwuchun piik* three pig's feet).

kun (2) KUNU. vi. be extinguished, go out (of fire, stove, lamp). Dis. *kunukun* (db). With dir. suf.: *kununó*.

kunamwmwe (1) KUNAMWMWEE. Var. *kinamwmwe, kunamwmwey.* n. (T1) comfort, tranquility, peace.

Trukese-English   kurupw₁

kunamwmween his c. vi., adj. (be) comfortable, quiet, tranquil, at peace. *méwúr k.* sleep comfortably, sleep well. Syn. *kúréwúren.*

kunamwmwey Var. of *kunamwmwe.*

kuniing₁ (3) KUNIINGA. nu. (T3) false ridgepole. [It lies on top of the rafters directly over the ridgepole and parallel to it.] *kuniingen iimw* house's f. r.

kuniing₂ Var. of *kuning.*

kuning (3) KUNINGNGA, KUNINGA. Var. *kuniing.* nu. (T3) plover (bird). *emén k.* one p.

kuningeey Var. of *kuningngeey.*

kuningngeey See *kuning, -e-₂*. vo. (refl.; T6b) brag, boast. *kaa kuningngeyok* you b.

kunow (2) KUNOWU. nu. (T2) recreation, excursion, ride, sail, walk, sport, visit. Dis. *kukkunow* (ds). *aan k.* his r. Syn. *wur₃.* vi. engage in recreation, play, take a walk, go for a ride, visit about. Dis. *kukkunow* (ds). *siya kukkunowu chék* we are just visiting about or taking a walk. With intens. suf.: *kukkunowukkis* visit about constantly.

kunowukkis See *kunow.*

kunowungngaw (3a) See *kunow, -ngngaw.* Tn. vi. take a walk without any particular purpose.

kunuuw See *kun, -u-.* vo. (T5) extinguish (a fire, stove, lamp).

kunukun (db; 2) See *kun.* nu. (dis.; T2) extinguishing. *neeniyen k.* ashtray. *seyin k.* firetruck, fire engine, fireboat. vi. (dis.) being extinguished.

kunun (3) KUNUNA. n. (T3) sore, abcess. *eew k.* one s. *kununan* his s.

kununó See *kun.*

kunnu Var. of *kinnu.*

kunnuun vi. move freely inside, rattle around inside. *meyi k. pecheey me nnón neyiy kkeey suus pwún raa koon wátte* my feet move freely in these shoes of mine because they are too big. *aa k. nóón* it rattled around inside of it.

kunnuuw See *kkun, -u-.* vo. (T5) turn (something).

kup (2) KUPU. vi. be broken, or cut short or off (of long, rigid objects). Dis. *kupukup* (db) be in a broken condition, be jointed, fold up (as legs on a card table).

kupach (3b) See *ku-, pach.* vi. stay fixed in one place. *ewe nengngin aa mmen k. nnón imwan we* the always stays home and never goe out.

kupen (2) KUPENI. nu. (T2) sling stone. [It is ground to be pointed at both ends.] *kupenin éwúnúún* sling's s.

kupet (2) KUPETI. vi. be scattered, dispersed, spread out. *k. feseen* be scattered or spread apart.

kupeti See *kupet.* vo. (T2) disperse, spread out. *siya k. taka wóón póó* we have spread out copra on racks. With dir. suf.: *kupetóónó. kepwe wún sáfey pwún epwe k. semwmwenin nóón nuukomw* you will drink some medicine for it will disperse the illness in your belly.

kupetóónó See *kupeti.*

kupiiy See *kup, -i-₂*. vo. (T5) break or cut (something) short or off (of long objects); fold (something) up (as the legs of a card table).

kupu- (2) See *kup.* ni. (T2) broken piece. *ekup, rúwékup, wúnúkup, fékup, nimekup, wonokup, fúúkup, wanúkup, ttiwekup, engoon kupun* one,...ten b. p. *ekup kupun sóók* one b. p. of chalk; *eey kupun* this b. p. (of it).

kupukup Dis. of *kup.*

kupwpwosón nu. succulent weed (*Portulaca*). [It is eaten in periods of famine.]

kuroop (2) KUROPPU. (Jap. *guroobu*, from Eng. *glove*) Var. *kuroopw.* nu. (T2) baseball glove. *epéw k.* one b. g. *péwún k.* his b. g. *kuroppun iyakiyu* g. for baseball.

kuroopw Var. of *kuroop.*

kuru- (2) KURU₁. [In cpds. only.] pref. (intens.?) See *kuruffat, kuruppep.*

kuruffat (3) See *kuru-, ffat.* vi. be very clear, transparent.

kurukur (db; 2) KURU₂. nu. (T2) orange (tree, fruit, or wood) *eféw k.* one o. *wochaan k.* his o. (to eat). *kurukurun Chuuk* Trukese o. (a variety); *kurukurun Ttooyis* German o. (a variety).

kuruppep See *kuru-, ppep.* vi. (dis.) bounce along (as a boat on the waves, a flying fish, or land seaplane).

kurupw₁ (2) KURUPWPWU₁. nu. (T2) node or joint (of arm, leg, tree, bamboo). *eew k.* one n. *kurupwpwun paaw* wrist; *kurupwpwun peche* ankle; *kurupwpwun irá* node of a tree.

kurupw₂ (2) KURUPWU₁, KURUPWPWU₂. nu. (T2) tiny coconut in first stage of growth (up to about three inches in diameter). *eew k., eféw k.* one c. *kurupwpwun núú* coconut tree's tiny nut.

kurupwusset (2) See *kurupw₂, sáát₁*. nu. (T2) first sour water in a young coconut.

kurupwurupw₁ (db; 2) See *kurupw₁*. vi. (dis.) be full of nodes.

kurupwurupw₂ (db; 2) KURUPWU₂. vi. be soft and chewable (of bones of young animals). *meyi k. eey chúún piik* this pig's bone is s. and c.

kurutong (Jap.) nu. croton.

kuchu (1) KUCHUU. nu. (T1) cloud. *eew k.* one c. *kuchuun nááng* clouds of heaven.

kuchuupwech (3) See *kuchu, pwech*. nu. (T3) white cloud.

kuchuuchón (4) See *kuchu, chón*. nu. (T2) dark cloud.

kuchuuchu (db; 1) See *kuchu*. vi. (dis.) be cloudy.

Kuchuwa nu. (loc.) easternmost district of Tonowas (Dublon) Island, seat of the Protestant Church. *kinin K.* prickly heat.

kuchuyen (2) KUCHUYENI. (Eng.) nu. (T2) accordion. *kuchuyenin Sapaan* Japanese a. vi. play the accordion.

kuchchungngaw (3b) See *kkuch, ngngaw*. vi. fit badly. *meyi k. ewe pwóór nnón ewe asam* the box is too big to go through this doorway.

kuchchuyééch (2: *-yéchchú-*) See *kkuch, ééch*. vi. fit well.

Kuwaamw nu. (loc.) Guam. [Said by some *itang* to be derived from *kúúwamw* because the *aamw* of a legendary canoe on a voyage of exploration hit (*kkúúw*) the land.]

kuwapw (3) KUWAPWPWA. Var. *wuwapw*. nu. (T3) leaf bud at the growing tip of a tree or plant before the leaves have opened. *kuwapwpwen irá* tree's l. b. Syn. *machang*. Cf. *kuupw*.

kuwar (3) See *ku-, warawar*. nu. (T3) muddiness, roiled state (of water). *kuwaren eey kkónik* m. of this water. vi. be muddy or roiled (of fresh and salt water only). Ant. *ffat*.

Kuwachenen nu. (loc.) Kwajalein Atoll (Marshall Islands). Syn. *Kachering*.

kuwoku (db; 3) KUWA. n. (T3) groove in the buttocks at the base of the spine. *kuwokuwan* his g. *chúún k.* bone at the end of the spinal column, tailbone, coccyx; hipbone, innominate bone.

Kuwopw nu. (loc.) ancient name of Wuuman (Uman) Island. [It was erroneously given by cartographers to Kuop Atoll, just south of Truk, whose correct name is *Neewoch*.]

kuwó (1) KUWÓÓ. nu. (T1) a kind of fish.

kú₁ (1) KÚÚ₁. vi. catch fire, be lit (of a fire); glow (of a single coal or piece of wood). Cf. *kun*.

kú₂ (1) KÚÚ₂. vi. form a dense school (of fish). *raa kú ekkewe iik* the fish formed a dense s.

kúú-₁ See *kú₂*. nr. (T1) school (of fish). *kúún iik* s. of fish.

kúú-₂ (1) KÚÚ₃. [In cpds. only.] unsp. break, tear, disarrange. See *kkúút₂, kúúti*.

kúú-₃ (1) KÚÚ₄. [In cpds. only.] unsp. (u.m.) bump, hit, strike.

kúú₁ (1) KÚÚ₅. n. (T1) back or nape of head and neck. *kúún* back of his h. *epin kúúy* the extremity of the back of my h. (see *epinikú*).

kúú₂ (1, 3) KÚÚ₆, KÚÚWA₁, KÚWA. n. (T1, T3) louse, flea. *emén k.* one l. *kúúwan* his l.; *kúúwen* l. of (someone). *kúún konaak* dog flea; *kúún káttu* cat flea. *kúún meef, kúwen meef* maggot.

kúú₃ Var. of *kúúw*.

kúús (3) KÚÚSA. nu. (T3) octopus. *kúúsen Chuuk* Trukese o. Syn. *nippach*.

Kúúseyinen See *kúús, neni-₁*. nu. (pers.) evil spirit invoked in cursing. *K. een! K. youl; wochóómw K!* your food K.! (the idea being that once in your stomach, K. will eat you); *ómwo K. epwe wocheyok!* may K. eat you!

kúúkú (db; 1) KÚÚ₇. nu. (T1) 1. dialect. *kúúkúún fóós* d. of speech. 2. verse (of a song); word or expression of a special speech. *wúse sineey kúúkúún ewe kkéén* I do not know the verse of the song. *kúúkúún fóósun itang* words and expressions of *itang*.

kúúmech See *kúú-₃, meche-*. N. vi. have a good memory, be quick to learn, be smart. Syn. *chuumech*.

kúún (3) KÚNNA, KÚNA₃. Var. *kkún*. n. (T3) high tide. *kúnnan* its h. t. *kúnnen sáát* h. t. of the sea water. vi. be at high tide. *aa k. ewe sáát* the sea water has come to h. t. With dir. suf.: *kúnnénong, kúnnoto* come in (of the tide).

kúúnúféw (2) See *kúú₂, faaw.* nu. (T2) 1. species of small bass (fish). 2. a form of sorcery such that if a person eats the fish of this name in company with a person who knows the sorcery, he can be made ill by the spell put on it. 3. a medicine to cure the illness resulting from the sorcery of this name.

kúúnúmmas (3) See *kúú₂, mmas₃.* nu. (T3) crab louse. *emén k.* one c. l. *kúúwan k.* his c. l. Syn. *nikúwenimmas.*

kúúnger (?Jap. *kuuger* from Ger. *Kugel*) nu. small cucumber. Cf. *kúúri₂.*

kúúpé (1) KÚÚPÉÉ. nu. (T1) variety of banana (green when ripe).

kúúri₁ See *kú₁, -ri-.* vo. (T4) burn, scorch, consume with fire. *ewe ááf aa k. ewe irá* the fire burned the tree.

kúúri₂ (1) KÚÚRII. (Jap. *kyuuri*) nu. (T1) cucumber. *eféw k., eföch k.* one c. *wochaan k.* his c. (to eat). Cf. *kúúnger.*

kúúti See *kúú-₂, -ti-.* vo. (T4) break up, tear apart, disarrange. *wúwa k. ewe iyoyiyen pii* I have broken up the pile of trash.

kúúw (3) KÚÚWA₂. Var. *kúú.* nu. (T3) 1. porpoise. [It is classed with fish as *iik* rather than with mammals as *maan.*] 2. a star (probably Beta Andromedae, cf. *ngiinikú*). 3. the traditional sixth sidereal month, according to most sources, but given by Elbert as the fifth month.

kúúween (2) KÚÚWEENI. Var. *kúween, kúweni-.* nu. (T2) species of lizard (long, brown). *emén k.* one l. *k̊úúweenin Chuuk* Trukese l. Syn. *kinomw.*

kúúwiifer Var. of *kiiwúfer.*

kúúyiti See *kú₁, -iti.* vo. (T2) 1. glow until. 2. (of fire) spread to. *ewe ekkey aa k. ewe iyoyiyen pii* the fire spread to the pile of garbage.

kúsúúwonó Var. of *kkúsúúwonó.*

kúsún (2) KÚSÚNÚ. nu. (T2) species of armored crab (light yellowish with blueish tips on claws, edible). *eew k.* one c. *kúsúnún Chuuk* Trukese c.; *fi k.* catch crabs.

kúkkú- (ds; 2) KKÚ₁. [In cpds. only.] unsp. side.

kúkkúúw Dis. of *kkúúw.*

kúkkúffengeen (2) See *kúkkú-, ffengeen.* vi. be close together.

kúkkúk (db; 2) See *kkú-.* vi. (dis.) bite, be wont to bite. *ese k. naan konaak* that dog does not b.

kúkkún (ds; 2) See *-kkún.* vi., adj. (be) small, little. *néwún we k.* his little one, his child; (Rmn.) his sweetheart. *emén k. nengngin, emén kúkkúnún nengngin* one small girl. Syn. *kisikiis, mwékkún, nginingiin.* Ant. *nimwmwuk, wátte.* Cf. *kkú-.*

kúkkúna Dis. of *kúna.*

kúkkúnong (3) See *kúkkú-, -nong.* n. (T3) inner side, inside; inland. *kúkkúnongan* inside of him. Ant. *kúkkúwu.*

kúkkúnó (1) See *kúkkú-, -nó.* n. (T1) the side yonder or away. *kúkkúnóón* off from him, the far side of him.

kúkkúnúngngaw (3b) See *kúkkún, ngngaw.* vi. be smallest, very small.

kúkkúngeni See *kúkkú-, ngeni.* vo. (T2) be close to, be beside. Syn. *kkanengeni.*

kúkkútá See *kúkkú-, -tá.* n. (T1) upper or eastern side. *kúkkútáán* his u. or e. s. vi. (Tn.) be high or lofty. Syn. *tekiya.*

kúkkútiw (3) See *kúkkú-, -tiw.* nu. (T2) lower or western side. *kúkkútiwan* his l. or w. s.

kúkkúto (1) See *kúkkú-, -to.* n. (T1) this side. *kúkkútoon* this s. of him.

kúkkúwow See *kúkkú-, -wow.* nu. your side, the side by person addressed. Cf. *peekiwow.* vi. be beside you.

kúkkúwu (1) See *kúkkú-, -wu.* n. (T2) outer side, seaward side. *kúkkúwuun* his o. s. *kúkkúwuun fénú* outer or seaward s. of the island. Ant. *kúkkúnong.*

kúmékúm Dis. of *kkúm.*

kúmi (3) KÚMIYA. (Jap. *kumi*) nu. (T3) an administrative district established by Japan and comprising one or more traditional districts (*sóópw*) within an island (*fénú*). [Such districts were maintained only on Tonowas (Dublon) Island under American administration.] *kúmiyen fénú* d. of the island. Cf. *kkúmi.*

kúmitimit (db; 2) See *mit.* vi. (dis.) be slippery, slick. Syn. *ámitimit, mitimit₂.*

kúmwachen N. nu. a green lizard. *emén k.* one l. Syn. *nipwáárech, nipwóóroch.*

kún₁ (3) See *kúna-.* vi. be successful in one's petition or begging of a favor, succeed in one's quest; be allowed, permitted (of a person, not of his request). *wúwa k. ááy wúpwe nó* I am permitted to leave. *ke k. óómw na tingor?* is your request granted? Cf. *kúna-.*

kún₂ (3) vi., adj. (be) hard (of cooked breadfruit). *aa k. eey kama* (the breadfruit in) this pot has been cooked hard. Cf. *kkúm.*

kúna- (3) KÚNA. [In cpds. only.] unsp. be seen, found, come upon.

kúna See *kúna-.* vo. (T3) see, behold; find, succeed in one's search for; come upon; catch (a sickness), experience (an injury); (refl.) see, have a vision. Dis. *kúkkúna* (ds). *aa k. ewe semwmwen* he caught the illness; *aa k. feyiyengngaw* he experienced an injury; *siya toongeni kúnáákich* we are able to see. Syn. *weri, wúri₁.* Cf. *kún₁.*

kúneyiti See *kúún, -iti.* vo. (T2) overtake with high tide. *sáát aa kúneyitiyey* the sea has overtaken me with high tide.

kúné (1) KÚNÉÉ. N. Var. *ékkúné.* vi. be sent (of a person on a mission, used only in combination with *chóón*). *chóón k.* messenger, helper, servant.

kúnékún (db; 3) See *kúna-.* va. (dis.) see (things generally). *siya toongeni k. mettóóch* we are able to s. things. *kaa k. aramas? wúwa kúna emén chék* did you s. any people? I saw only one person.

kúnnénong See *kúún.*

kúnnoto See *kúún.*

kúng (2) KÚNGÚ. vi., adj. (be) brown. Dis. *kúngúkúng* (db).

kúngúkúng Dis. of *kúng.*

kúra-₁ (3) KÚRA₁. Tbl. unsp. exposed (of the prepuce), drawn back (of the foreskin).

kúra-₂ Var. of *wúra-.*

kúreey See *kúra-₁, -e-₂.* Tbl. vo. (T6b) pull back (the foreskin), circumcize.

kúréwúren (db; 2) See *kúra-₂* or *wúra-, -ni-.* Tb3. vi. be comfortable. Syn. *kunamwmwe.*

kúrú- (2) KÚRÚ. [In cpds. only.] unsp. (u.m.) See *kúrúwén.*

kúrúr (2) KÚRÚRÚ. nu. (T2) 1. a slipping or sliding apart or together (as a zipper or curtains). Cf. *rúrú-.* 2. a move (in fighting) in which a person ducks under an opponent's arm and throws him.

kúrúwén (2) See *kúrú-, wénú-.* Tn. nu. (T2) a common shrub (*Macaranga carolinensis*). Syn. *ttupw₂, tuupw, tupwpwunuwén.*

kúchún (2) KÚCHÚNÚ. nu. (T2) a kind of turmeric. [Traditionally used to make a cosmetic by grating the root or corm of the plant, washing out the starch, and then packing the starchy flour into the shell of a very young coconut. The resulting lipstick-like product is *teyuk.*] *kúchúnún Chuuk* Trukese t. Syn. *áfán.*

-kút (2) KÚTÚ. unsp. move (not be at rest). Dis. *-kútúkút* (db). See *mwékút.*

Kútú nu. (loc.) Kutu Island and District (Satawan Atoll).

kútta See *kkúút₁.* vo. (T3) look for, search for. With dir. suf.: *kúttaato* look for (it) hither.

kúttaato See *kútta.*

kúween Var. of *kúúween.*

kúwen (2) KÚWENI. nu. (T2) variety of *Cyrtosperma* taro (*pwuna*). *kúwenin Chuuk* Trukese t.

kúwenen (2) KÚWENENI. nu. (T2) variety of banana. [It was reserved for chiefs and *itang* in former times.] *kúwenenin Chuuk* Trukese b.

kúweni- Var. of *kúúween* in cpds.

kúwenifat (3) See *kúweni-, faat₂.* nu. (T3) bonefish ("lizard of the shallow flats").

kúwennité (1) See *kúweni-, té₂.* nu. (T1) a house height (*chimwennúúren iimw*) such that one must crawl on hands and knees to pass under the crossbeam ("lizard's crawl"). vi. crawl on one's belly (a sign of extreme deference).

kúwé (1) KÚWÉÉ. F. Var. *kiyé.* nu. (T1) nipa palm. [Its leaves are used for thatch and to prepare hot massages.] *efóch k.* one n. p. tree; *eché k.* one n. p. leaf. *kúwéén Chuuk* Trukese n. p. Syn. *kiyá₂.*

kka-₁ Dc. of *a-₂.* See *kkanges, kkamaat, kkamas, kkamé, kkapach, kkapas, kkapwas, kkapwich, kkarap, kkaré₁,* *kkaré₂, kkasupw, kkatamonong, kkatamowu, kkawet, kkayé, kkayít.*

kka-₂ (3b: *kka-, kká-, kke-, kkó-, kko-*) KKA₁. [Occurs only in dem. and num. constructions.] pref. (dis.) plural marker. See *ekkaan, ekkana, ekkanaan, ekkeey, ekkewe, ekkóóch, kkaan, kkana, kkanaan, kkáámén, kkááfóch, kkeey, kkewe.*

kka (dc; 1) See *kaa-*. vi. be thirsty; be at low tide.

kkaan F. dis. of *een*₃.

kkasupw (dc; 2) See *ási-, pwu-*₁. vi. be shaken out (as a cloth).

kkak (dc; 3) See *kak*. nu. (T3) ring, ringing sound (of a bell, of metal on stone). *aan k.* its ring. *kkaken peen* sound of a bell; *kkaken took* ring of a bushknife (striking a stone). vi. make a sudden sharp noise (as metal on metal); cackle, caw; break (of a voice singing too high). Dis. *kakkak* (ds).

-kkak (3) KAKKA (?). [In cpds. only.] unsp. be split, cracked, checked (of wood or skin). See *sakkak.*

kkaki (Eng.) nu. khaki trousers. *eew k.* one pair of k. t. *aan k.* his k. t.

kkama (1) KKAMAA. (Jap. *kama.*) nu. (T1) large, iron cooking pot. *eew k.* one c. p. *aan k.* his c. p.

kkamaani See *kkama, -ni-*. vo. (T4) prepare (food) in a *kkama.*

kkamaat (dc; 3) See *amaat*₁. nu. (c.; T3) grinding and polishing. *féwún k.* stone for g. and p. shell and stone artifacts. *féwún kkamaaten ngiingi* stone for g. and p. a shell breadfruit peeler. va. grind and polish.

kkamas (dc; 3) See *mas*. vi. (c.) be joined (as in a mortise or as planks edge to edge on a canoe). Cf. *afféew.*

kkamé (dc; 1) See *mé*₂. vi. (c.) buy.

kkamééseni See *kkamé, seni*₂. vo. (c.; T2) buy from.

kkamééngeni See *kkamé, ngeni*. vo. (c.; T2) sell to, attend to (customer).

kkamw (dc; 3b) See *kamwa-*. n. (T3) suf. (cc.) fragment, torn piece, shred (of paper, cloth). *ekkamw, rúwékkamw, wúnúkkamw, fékkamw, nimekkamw, wonokkamw, fúúkkamw, wanúkkamw, ttiwekkamw, engoon kkamwan* one,...ten fragments, rags, shreds, etc. *eché kkamwen mangaak* a torn piece of cloth, a rag, a tatter. vi., adj. (be) torn, ripped, shredded (of cloth, paper, etc.). *epwe k. óómw rawúses* your trousers will be t.

kkan (3) KKANA. vi. be near, close. *k. ngeni* be close to; have sexual relations with. *k. ffengeen* be close together.

kkana F. dis. of *na*.

kkanaan F. dis. of *naan*.

kkanapanó (dc; 1) See *nap, -nó*. vi. (c.) be enlarged, magnified, increased. Cf. *anapa.*

kkanéngeni See *kkan, ngeni*. F. vo. (T2) be close to; be related genealogically or by marriage to; have sexual relations with. Syn. *kúkkúngeni.*

kkanges (dc) va. (c.) have a look, watch, observe. Syn. *kkaton, kkóton, kófót.*

kkap (3) KKAPA. (Eng.) nu. (T3) cup. *eew k.* one c. (cf. *ekkap* one cupful). *ruwuuw kkapen Merika* two American c. suf. (cc.) cupful. *ekkap, rúwékkap, wúnúkkap, fékkap, nimekkap, wonokkap, fúúkkap, wanúkkap, ttiwekkap* one, ...nine c.

kkapa (1) KKAPAA. (Eng.) nu. (T1) penny. *eew k.* one p. *néwún k.* his p.

kkapas (dc; 3) See *pasa-*. Var. *kkapás*. nu. (c.; T3) talk, speech, utterance, language. *eew k.* one utterance; a saying. *aan k.* his talk. *k. chééw* talk that is not attended to (that drones on); *k. esiit* criticism; *k. mwúúmwú* halting speech; *k. paat* talking all the time; *k. pweteete* courteous or polite speech; *k. rikirik* misleading talk. *kkapasen Chuuk* language of Truk; *kkapasen fénú* legend of the land, dialect of the island; *kkapasen sootá* eastern dialects of Truk; *kkapasen wurumwmwot* teasing, joshing, joking, playful talk. vi. (c.) speak, say, talk. Dis. *kakkapas* (ds) converse.

kkapaseeyiis (2) See *kkapas, eyiis*. nu. (T2) question.

kkapaséppék (2) See *kkapas, ppék*. vi. converse, talk freely together.

kkapach (dc; 3) See *pach*. nu. (c.) addition. vi. be added, attached; add. *ruwuuw k. ruwuuw weewen rúwáánú* two plus two equals four.

kkapás (2) Wn. Var. *kkapas*. nu. (c.; T2) talk, speech, utterance, language. *kkapásin Chuuk* language of Truk.

kkapet (2) KKAPETI. (Eng.) nu. (T2) cupboard. *eew k.* one c. *aan k.* his c. *kkapetin mwéngé* cupboard for food.

kkapékinaas (3) See *kkap, kinaas.* (Eng.) nu. (T3) drinking glass. *eew k.* one d. g.

kkapwas (dc; 3) See *pwas.* nu. (c.; T3) drying. vi. (c.) be dried, dried out.

kkapwich (dc; 2) See *pwich₁.* Var. *kkepwich.* vi. (c.) be broiled, roasted, or heated on an open fire (of fish, breadfruit, water, etc.).

kkapwichi See *kkapwich.* vo. (c.; T2) roast, broil. *siya k. naan mááy* we roasted yonder breadfruit.

kkapwong Var. of *kkópwong.*

kkar (dc; 3b) See *kara-.* vi. be burned, scorched, sunburned. *aa k. ewe iimw* the house has been b.

kkarap (dc; 3) See *rap.* vi. (c.) be heated (of tobacco, coconut, pandanus, or other leaves).

kkaré₁ N. of *kkéré.*

kkaré₂ (dc; 1) See *ré₂.* N. vi. (c.) be broiled (of chickens, birds); be burned out, cauterized (as in treating ringworm by heating the midrib of a coconut leaf and applying the hot tip to the infected area). va. light (a cigarette).

kkata (dc; 1) See *ta.* vi., va. (c.) broken, destroyed, disintegrated; break, destroy. Cf. *ataay.*

kkatamonong (dc; 3) See *tam, -nong.* va. (c.) send in, bring in, install. *ekkewe mwáán raa k. ekkewe pisek nnón ewe iimw* those men brought the things into the house.

kkatamowu (dc; 1) See *tam, -wu.* va. (c.) remove, exile, depose, send out. vi. (c.) be removed, exiled, deposed.

kkaton Var. of *kkóton₁* and *kkóton₂.*

kkatur N. of *kkotur.*

kkaw (dc; 3) See *awa-.* nu. (T3) 1. octopus stick (used by women to catch octopus). *efóch k.* one o. s. *aan k.* her o. s. 2. method of octopus fishing (in which women knock with a stick against a hole in the reef where there is an octopus thereby causing it to come out so that it can be picked up by hand). *kkawen Chuuk* Trukese o. s. or method of o. fishing. va. catch (octopus) using an octopus stick.

kkawa See *kkaw.* vo. (T3) catch (an octopus) using an octopus stick.

kkawet (dc; 2) See *awa-, -ti-.* vi. be beaten. *ewe mwáán aa k. reen ewe pwonis* the man was b. by the policeman.

kkayé (dc; 1) See *é.* Var. *kkáyé.* nu. (c.; T1) learning, studying. va. study, learn. Syn. *kkayit, pengkiyo.*

kkayingún (2) KKAYINGÚNÚ. Obs. (Jap. *kaigun*) nu. (T2) 1. navy. 2. sailor. *emén k.* one s. Syn. *neyifi.*

kkayit (dc; 3b) See *ayit.* Var. *kkáyit₂.* nu. (c.; T3) thing shown, demonstration, instruction. Cf. *kkáyit₁.* va. learn, study. Syn. *kkayé, pengkiyo.*

kká- Dc. of *á-₂.* See *kkáách, kkáámw, kkááp, kkáár₁, kkású, kkáte, kkáter.*

kká (1) KKÁÁ. nu. (T1) elephant-ear dryland taro (*Alocasia macrorhiza*). [An itch, *pwerik*, is caused by handling it.] *kkáán Chuuk* Trukese t. Syn. *pwerik.*

kkááfóch Dis. of *efóch.*

kkáámén Dis. of *emén.*

kkáámw (dc; 3b) See *emw.* nu. (c.; T3) inspection, investigation. *chóón k.* inspector.

kkááp (dc; 2) See *ep.* nu. (c.; T2) repeated carrying, hauling. va. (c.) carry repeatedly, haul. *seyin k. pisek* cargo ship or cargo-carrying vehicle.

kkáár₁ (dc; 2) See *eri-₂.* nu. (c.; T2) running race. *kkáárin waafétún* r. of paddling canoes. vi. race, run a race; draw a line.

kkáár₂ (dc; 3) See *áár₂.* vi. be scooped up with a handnet.

kkáách (dc; 3) See *ácha-* (?). vi. (c.) fish with hook and line; angle. Cf. *póón.*

kkáfis Var. of *kkefis.*

kkáfinitá Var. of *kkefinitá.*

kkási (dc; 1) See *ásii-.* N. vi. be stripped into strips (as bark, coconut stems). Syn. *ettik.*

kkású (dc; 1) See *sú.* vi. (c.) be chased away, sent away, exiled. Cf. *kkésú.*

kkáki Var. of *kkeki.*

kkánáán F. vr. for the first time; only just now. Syn. *pwáráán.* Cf. *kkáráán, kkeráán, kkéráán.*

kkánis (dc; 2) See *ánis.* nu. (T2) aiding, assistance, helping. vi. aid, assist, help. *wúpwe nó k. nnón naan angaang* I will go and help with that work.

-kkáp (dc; 4) KÁPE. [In cpds. only.] unsp. (u.m.) See *nikkáp.*

kkáper (dc; 3) See *para-₂.* vi., va. (c.) be aimed; aim. Cf. *apara₂, ápera.*

kkáráán Var. *kkeráán, kkéráán.* vr. begin to, start to; (with aspect marker *-a*) just now. *aa k. feyitto* he has just now arrived. Syn. *kkánáán, pwáráán.*

kkáte (dc; 1) See *te.* va. (c.) learn, practice (of a song or dance).

kkáter (dc; 2) See *ter₁.* va. (c.) strip, devastate; clear land of vegetation. *ewe mwáán aa k. irá* the man cleared the land of trees.

kkátinaas Var. of *ketinaas.*

kkáwáng adj. in *pwéét k.* wrinkle or turn up one's nose as an expression of contempt or dislike (syn. *echifepwéét*).

kkáy (2, 3) KKÁYI, KKÁYA. vi., adj. (be) fast, quick; hurry, go quickly. Dis. *kákkáy* (ds). With dir. suf.: *kkáyito, kkáyeto* hurry hither; *kkáyinó, kkáyenó* hurry away. *ewe feefin aa mwochen néwún we epwe kkáyenó nnón ewe sukuun* the woman wanted her child to go to school quickly.

kkáyé Var. of *kkayé.*

kkáyit₁ (dc; 2) See *iti-₁.* nu. (c.; T2) fetching, handing. *kkáyitin sómwoon* a gesture in which the right hand is extended palm-up to give or receive something while the left hand grasps the rear part of the right forearm ("fetching or handing of chiefs"). Cf. *áyiti, kkayit.*

kkáyit₂ Var. of *kkayit.*

kkáyito See *kkáy.*

kke-₁ (3) KKA₂. [In cpds. only.] unsp. burn, be afire. See *kkeek.*

kke-₂ Var. of *kka-₁.* See *kkechiw, kkefinitá, kkefis, kketen, kkeyang.*

kkeek (ds; 3: *kekke-*) See *kke-₁.* Var. *kkek₁.* nu. burning off of vegetation preparatory to cultivation. vi. burn off vegetation; be aflame, burn; burn someone with a cigarette (as among lovers). *ewe mwáán aa k. nnón fénúwan we* the man burned off his field. Cf. *niképwét.*

kkeey F. dis. of *eey.*

kkefis (2) See *fis.* Var. *kkáfis.* nu. (c.; T2) product, creation. *kkefisin nóón menniiy iyer?* a p. of what year? vi. be made, created, established. With dir. suf.: *kkefisitá* be pretended (as in playing a game), be made up (in the sense of telling a lie, giving a false report, or singing a pretended song); *aa kkefisitá ewe pworaawus* the story was made up (was false).

kkefisitá See *kkefis.*

kkefinitá (1) See *fini-₁.* Var. *kkáfinitá.* vi. (c.) be chosen, elected. *Siipen aa k. me reen ekkewe aramas pwe iiy sómwoon* Siipen has been elected by the people to be chief.

kkes (2) KKESI. n. (T2) enthusiasm. *kkesin* his e. vi. be enthusiastic, be enthused.

kkesip (dc) vi. (c.) be closed.

kkek₁ Var. of *kkeek.*

kkek₂ Var. of *kaak.*

kkeki (dc; 1) See *ki₂.* Var. *kkáki.* vi., va. (c.) move something by lifting it; lift (something, when the speaker is among the lifters). Cf. *ekiiy.*

kkemwuun N. dis. of *-mwuun.*

kken (dc; 2) See *-ken.* vi., adj. 1. (be) sharp. 2. salty (as sea water).

kkenaato See *kkeni.*

kkeni See *kke-₁, -ni-.* vo. (T5) set fire to, kindle, ignite, light (a lamp, cigarette). *sipwe k. piich eey* let us burn our trash here. With dir. suf.: *kkenaato* light (something) hither; *kkenóónó* burn (something) away. *ika kese tongeey nanen awey ngonuk, kepwe chék kkenóónó* if you don't like the talk from my mouth toward you, you may just burn it away (a courtship saying).

kkenóónó See *kkeni.*

-kkep (2) KKEPI. [In cpds. only.] nu. (u.m.) See *nikkep.*

kkepich (dc; 2) See *pich₂.* vi. (c.) be untied, released, pardoned. Cf. *epichi.*

kkepit (dc; 2) See *epiti.* vi., va. be annointed, perfumed; annoint, perfume.

kkepwich Var. of *kkapwich.*

kker Var. (dc) of *er₁.*

kkeráán Var. of *kkáráán.*

kkechiw (dc; 3) See *chiwa-.* vi. (c.) cry, weep. Dis. *kekkechiw* (ds).

kket (2) KKETI. va. tie thatch to the rafters of a house, do thatching. *sipwe k. iimw ikenááy* let us thatch houses today.

kketen (dc; 2) See *ten₂.* vi. (c.) be put in rank order. *aa k. kkeey mettóóch* these things have been put in r. o. *esaa mwo k. aach kkewe angaang* our work assignments have not yet been worked out. Syn. *etetten.*

185

kketi See *kket*. vo. (T2) thatch, tie thatch to. *sipwene k. eey iimw* we are going to t. this house.

kketinaas (3) KKETINAASA. (Eng.) Var. *kkátinaas*. nu. (T3) sword, cutlass. *efóch k., emén k.* one s. *néwún k.* his s. *kketinaasen Merika* American s.

kkewe F. dis. of *ewe*.

kkey (2) KKEYI. vi. laugh (polite word, cf. *takir*). Dis. *kekkey* (ds).

kkeyang (dc; 3) See *aang*. n. (c.; T3) fork, crotch (as on a tree or fish tail). *kkeyangan* its f. *kkeyangen irá* crotch or f. of a tree; *kkeyangen wúkún iik* f. of a fish's tail.

kkeyisini See *kkey, -si-, -ni-*. vo. (T5) laugh at, mock. Syn. *takiriiy*.

kkeyik (2, 3) KKEYIKI. (Eng.) nu. (T2) cake. *eew k.* one c. *anan k.* his c. *kkeyikin* or *kkeyiken Merika* American c.

kkeyinepaan Var. *kkeyinapaan*. nu. leprosy, especially in its more advanced stages. vi. be in an advanced stage of leprosy.

kké- Dc. of *é-*. See *kkékú, kkémwéch, kképúng₁, kképúng₂, kképwúng, kkéré, kkéréét, kkésú, kkéwú, kkéwúk*.

kké (1v: *kkéé-, kkoo-*) KKÉÉ₁. vi. call, cry, shout. Dis. *kékké* (ds). With dir. suf.: *kkéénó* or *kkoonó, kkéétá, kkéétiw, kkééto* or *kkooto, kkééwu* or *kkoowu*. Cf. *kkéén*.

-kké (1) KKÉÉ₂. unsp. See *enenikké, winikké*.

kkéé- (1) See *kké*. ni. (T1) shout, cry, call. *kkééy, kkéémw, kkéén* my, your, his s.

kkéén (2) KKÉÉNÚ. [Possibly a dc form derived from the same original base as *ááni₃*.] nu. (T2) song. *eché k.* one s. *kkéénún Chuuk* Trukese s.; *kkéénún fénú* s. of the land (as sung by an *itang*); *kkéénún núkún* secular s.; *kkéénún tattapw* round, roundelay. *ááni eché k.* sing a s. *chéén k.* sheet of song music, musical score. vi. sing. Dis. *kékkéén* (ds). *k. nikatattapw* sing a round. Cf. *kké*.

kkééneemóówun (2) See *kké, nee-, móówun*. Var. *kkéénnemóówun*. nu. (T2) war taunt, insult hurled at any enemy (involves use of tabu 1 words with reference to a person's mother). Dis. *kékkééneemóówun* (ds) insulting language. *fóósun kkééneemóówun* any word of the first order of prohibited usage (tabu 1), chiefly the vocabulary relating to male and female genitalia.

vi. make an insult, hurl a war taunt. Dis. *kékkééneemóówun* (ds).

kkéénó See *kké*.

kkéénúúw See *kkéén, -ú-*. vo. (T5) sing (a song); sing about (someone). *aa k. eché kkéén* he sang a song.

kkéénnemóówun Var. of *kkééneemóówun*.

kkééngeni See *kké, ngeni*. vo. (T2) call or shout to (someone).

kkééraanong See *kkééri*.

kkééraato See *kkééri*.

kkééraawu See *kkééri*.

kkééráátá See *kkééri*.

kkééráátiw See *kkééri*.

kkééri See *kké, -ri-*. vo. (T4) call to, call out to, shout to (someone). Dis. *kékkééri* (ds). *kkééruk*, or *kkooruk* call to you (sg.). With dir. suf.: *kkééraanong, kkééraato, kkééraawu, kkééráátá, kkééráátiw, kkééróónó*.

kkééróónó See *kkééri*.

kkéét (2) KÉTTÚ, KÉÉTTÚ. vi. itch; scratch an itch. Syn. *pwerik*.

kkéétá See *kké*.

kkéétiw See *kké*.

kkééto See *kké*.

kkéétukkachang (3) See *kké, tuu-₂, chang*. vi. call from a distance to someone who is in his house (tabu behavior, especially in precolonial times).

kkééwu See *kké*.

kkééyénú (2) See *kké, énú*. nu. (T1) a type of *féérúwér* used by a spirit medium to call an *énúúsór* to possess him. Syn. *seppito*.

kkééyiti See *kké, -iti*. vo. (T2) call out to (a place), call so the sound reaches (a person or place).

kkésú (dc; 1) See *sú*. Var. *kassú*. vi. (c.) elope; run off together. *ewe mwáán me ewe feefin raa k. neepwinewe* the man and the woman ran off together last night. Cf. *kkású*.

kkékú (dc; 1) See *kú₁*. va. (c.) be causing to catch fire. *ewe feefin aa k. ekkey* the woman is building a fire.

kkémwéch (dc; 2) See *mwéch*. vi. (c.) be held, clutched (in the hand). *meyi k. nóón péwún* it is h. in his hand. va. (c.) hold, clutch; heed, obey. *wúwa k. átánaan* I held yonder fellow. *neeniyen k.* handle; *chóón k. fináyik* chief of a *fináyik* (political division established under German rule, now

terminated) ("person who holds the flag").
kképúng₁ (dc; 2) See *púngú-*. vi. (c.) be shut, closed, covered (with a lid).
kképúng₂ (dc; 2) See *púng₁*. vi. (c.) explode, detonate, be set off.
kképwúng (dc; 2) See *pwúng₁*. nu. (c.) determination of what is right; legal hearing or trial. *imwen k.* courthouse. Syn. *épwúng*.
kkéráán Var. of *kkáráán*.
kkéré (dc; 1) See *éréé-*. F. Var. *kkaré*. vi. be scraped (as pandanus and banana leaves or other fibers preparatory to plaiting and weaving, as a face in shaving). va. scrape.
kkérééi (dc) See *éréé-*, *-ti-*. va., vi. sand or scrape smooth; be sanded or scraped smooth. *ekkewe feefin raa k. chéén faach* the women scraped pandanus leaves smooth.
kkéch Tb1. vi. stink, smell bad. *meyi k.* it stinks. Cf. *kéch*.
kkéwú₁ (dc; 1) See *wú₃*. va. (c.) make upright, make stand, erect, build. With dir. suf.: *kkéwúútá* erect, make stand up (as a house, flagpole); *kkéwúútiw* plant upright (as the corner posts of a house).
kkéwú₂ (dc; 1) See *wú₂*. vi. stop, pause. With dir. suf.: *kéwúúnó* stop altogether, cease, halt.
kkéwúúnó See *kkéwú₂*.
kkéwúútá See *kkéwú*.
kkéwúútiw See *kkéwú*.
kkéwúk (dc; 2) See *wúkú-₁*. nu. (c.; T2) measuring instrument, measure. va., vi. measure; be measured.
kkéyeesini See *kké*, *-ásini*. vo. (T5) call out (news, announcements).
kki- (2) KKI. pref. (u.m.) See *kkinó*, *kkipwin*, *kkiroch*, *kkiyér*.
kkiis (Eng.) vi. kiss (by rubbing noses or touching with nose); embrace affectionately. *k. ngeni* kiss (someone).
-kkiis (dc; 2) See *kisi-*. suf. (adj.) small.
kkiin (3) KINNA, KIINNA. (Eng.) nu. (T3) keel. *eföch k.* one k. *kinnen (kiinnen) waa* boat's keel.
kkiing (3) KKIINGA, KIINGNGA. (Eng.) nu. (T3) king, monarch; king in cards. *emén k.* one k. (person); *eché k.* one k. (card). *ewe kkiingen (kiingngen) nóón Merika* the k. in America.
kkiiy (3) KKIIYA. (Eng.) nu. (T3) key. *kkiiyen nóók k.* for a lock.

kkiiyeey See *kkiiy*, *-e-₂*. vo. (T6b) unlock. With dir. suf.: *kkiiyeeyenó* lock (something) up.
kkiiyeeyenó See *kkiiyeey*.
kkis adj., suf. (intens.) constantly, repeatedly. *aséésékkis* be taking many rests, be repeatedly resting; *ataatakkis* destroy to bits, break to pieces; *fátánekkis* walk constantly; *kunowukkis* visit about constantly; *mwéngékkis* eat constantly. Cf. *-kkich*, *-chchik*.
kkik₁ vi. squeal (as a mouse). Dis. *kikkik* (ds).
kkik₂ (2) KIKKI. vi. move, change location. Dis. *kikkik* (ds). Cf. *ki₂*.
kkino (1) KKINOO. (from Ger. *Kilogramm*) nu. (T1) scale. *eew k.* one s. *aan k.* his s. *kkinoon Merika* American s. ni. (T1) weight. *kkinoon* his w. *fituuw kkinoon ewe piik* what is the w. of the pig? va., vi. weigh; be weighed. *sipwe k. piik* we are going to w. pigs.
kkinooni See *kkino*, *-ni-*. vo. (T4) weigh (something) on a scale.
kkinó (1) See *kki-*, *-nó*. vi. be weak (from hunger, from a spasm of laughing or crying, or from holding one's breath under water).
kkipwin (2) See *kki-*, *-pwin*. vi. be bitter.
kkiroch (3) See *kki-*, *roch*. nu. (T3) darkness. *kkirochen eey pwinin!* how dark it is tonight! ("the d. of this night"). Ant. *saram*. vi. be dark. *meyi k. nnón eey ruumw* it is d. in this room.
-kkich (2) KKICHI (?). Var. *-chchik*. adj. (intens.) very, absolutely. *chónokkich* very black; *mwakenekkich* lie outrageously, big falsehood; *parakkich* very red; *patekkich* very cold; *rochokkich* very dark, pitch dark; *soonáákkich* big or frequent stealing. Cf. *-kkis*.
kkit (dc; 3) See *-kit*. nu. (num.; T3) ten thousand. *eew k., ruwuuw k.,...engoon kkitan* one, two,...ten units of t. t. With pref. *áná-*: *ánákkit* sole or only unit of t. t. Syn. *engoon ngéréw*.
kkiyér (2) See *kki-*, *érú-₂*. vi., adj. (be) pale, have pallor. Syn. *ér₁*. nr. (T2) pallor, paleness. *kkiyérún masan* the p. of his face.
kko-₁ Dc. of *o-₃*. See *kkotur*, *kkowumw*.

kko-₂ (4) KKO. pref. pertaining to condition, state, or appearance (?). Dis. *kokko-* (ds). See *kkopay*. Cf. *ko-₃*.

kkoomw Dis. of *oomw*.

kkoonó See *kké*.

kkooto See *kké*.

kkoowu See *kké*.

kkoma (1) KKOMAA. (Eng.) nu. (T1) comma.

kkon Var. (?) of *kon*.

kkonu₁ Var. of *kkónu*.

kkonu₂ (dc; 1) See *nu*. vi. (c.) be passed by; escape attack. Cf. *ónuuw*.

kkopay (dc; 3) See *kko-₂, pay*. Var. *kkopáy*. vi., adj. (be) aslant, oblique; not straight, not true; leaning to one side. *meyi k. péwún ewe mwáán* his arm is not straight. *fátánekkopay* walk obliquely. Ant. *wenechchar*.

kkopáy N. of *kkopay*.

kkopw (2) KKOPWU. vi., adj. (be) dull, not sharp. *meyi k. eey nááyif* this knife is d.

kkor (3) KKORA. Tbl. n. (T3) underarm hair, pubic hair. *emeet k.* one h. *kkoran* his h.

kkochu (dc; 1) See *chu*. vi. (c.) be joined, connected. Cf. *ochuuw*.

kkot (dc; 3) See *kota-*. nu. (T3) low tide, low water. *pwata ina kkoten eey sáát?* why is this seawater (tide) so low? vi. be low tide; be thirsty, be dried out (as a dead tree).

kkoteyiti See *kkot, -iti.* vo. (T2) bring low tide to. *aa kkoteyitikich* we have been overtaken by l. t.

kkotu (dc; 1) vi., va. (c.) be soaked; soak. Cf. *tú*.

kkotupw Var. of *kkótupw*.

kkotur (dc; 2) See *tur₂*. F. Var. *kkótur, kkatur*. va. (c.) drop. *raa k. pakútang mé wóón sepeniin* they dropped bombs from airplanes. Cf. *oturu₂*. vi., adj. (c.) (be) dropped, discontinued, abandoned. *kapú k.* drop (in baseball pitching). With dir. suf.: *kkoturunó* (F.), *kkóturunó, kkaturunó* (N.) be abandoned.

kkoturunó See *kkotur*.

kkowu (1) KKOWUU. nu. (T1) cow; beef; corned beef. *emén k.* one cow; *eew k.* one tin of corned beef. *kkowuun Merika* American c. *k. manaw* live cow (as distinct from beef).

kkowuk (2) KKOWUKU. nu. (T2) axe. *eché k., efóch k., emén k.* one a. *aan k., néwún k.* his a. *kkowukun Merika* American a. vi. chop with an axe.

kkowumw (dc; 2) See *wumwu-₁*. vi. be spiteful, malicious (*ngeni* towards); bear a grudge. *ewe feefin aa k. ngeni átenaan* the woman is spiteful towards that man. nu. (c.; T2) envy, spite, malice, dislike (of people). *aan k.* his feeling of e.

kkó- Dis. of *ó-₂*.

-kkó (dc; 1) See *kóókó*. suf. (dim.) diminutive (for infants). *nikkó* baby girl; *wukkó* baby boy.

kkóón (dc; 4) See *óno-*. nu. (c.; T2) lying, reclining. *áán átánaan k.* that fellow's l. *kkóónun rééfa* former practice in which a man gave his wife to a senior kinsman for a night preparatory to asking for something of great value from him the next day. vi. lie, recline. Dis. *kókkóón* (ds). With dir. suf.: *kkóónnó* go lie down, go into a reclining position; *kkóónutiw* wait for someone while he is on a momentary errand. Syn. *eyiwen*.

kkóónet (dc; 2) See *óónet*. va., vi. spread out or be spread out (of a mat). *wúpwe k. tanaaw* I will spread a mat. Cf. * óóneti*.

kkóónutiw See *kkóón*.

kkóónnó See *kkóón*.

kkóóp (dc; 3) See *wop*. F. Var. *woop*. va., vi. (c.) hide or be hidden, conceal or be concealed. *ewe áát aa k. peen* the boy hid pens.

kkóóch Dis. of *óóch*.

kkóót (dc; 3) See *wota-*. n. (c.; T3) arrangement, putting in order. *kkóótan* a. of it. *kkóóten eey pisek* arrangement of these goods. vi. (c.) be arranged, be put in order. *aa wees kkewe pwpwuk ne k.* the books are finished being a. va. arrange (things). *kepwe k. pwpwuk* you will a. books.

kkófót (4) See *fóto-₁*. vi. (be) betrothed, engaged to marry. *Fritz me Maria raa k.* Fritz and Maria are b. ni. (T3, T2) betrothed, affianced, fiancé, fiancéé. *kkófótan, kkófótun* his b.

kkófóteni See *kkófót, -ni*. Var. *kkófótuni*. vo. (T6a) betrothe, become engaged to.

kkófótuni Var. (T5) of *kkófóteni*.

kkómwu Var. of *kómwu*.

kkómwuuti Var. of *kómwuuti*.

kkón₁ (dc; 3) See *óna-*. va., vi. roll or be rolled on the thigh (of threads in the making of cordage), twist or be twisted together. *sipwe k. núún* we are going to make ropes.

kkón₂ (dc; 4) See *ónu-*. nu. (T2) pounded breadfruit pudding (without anything added). *anan k.* his b. p. to eat; *túkúmiyan k. b. p.* packaged by him. Cf. *mwatún, chééwúch*.

kkóneey₁ See *kkón₁, -e-₂*. vo. (T6b) roll (fibers) together.

kkóneey₂ See *kkón₂; -e-₂*. N. vo. (T6b) make into breadfruit pudding. *kepwe k. eey maay* you will make this breadfruit into b. p.

kkóniineewoch (3) See *kkón₂, neewoch*. nu. (T3) breadfruit pudding presented to a canoe builder by the canoe owner when the builder is ready to set the outrigger booms into the notches (*neewoch*) in the side of the canoe. [The builder smears the notches with some of the pudding.]

kkónik (2) KKÓNIKI. Var. *kkónuk*. nu. (T2) fresh water. *kkónikin eey neeni* f. w. of this place. Syn. *appúng, ónuki, pweke*. Cf. *chaan*.

kkónofich See *kkón₁, -fich*. vi., va. be twisted on the right thigh with the right hand; have a right-hand twist; twist with a right-hand twist.

kkónoséék (2) See *kkón₂, séék*. vi. take special care in the making of breadfruit pudding for a chief; prepare *chééwúch*.

kkónommééng See *kkón₁, -mmééng*. vi., va. be twisted on the left thigh with the left hand; have a left-hand twist; twist with a left-hand twist.

kkónómá (1) See *kkón₂, má*. nu. (T1) stale breadfruit pudding.

kkónu (dc; 1) See *nu*. Var. *kkonu₁*. vi. (c.) have missed a menstrual period; be pregnant, have conceived a child.

kkónuk N. of *kkónik*.

kkópwong (dc; 3) See *pwoong*. Var. *kkapwong*. nu. (c.; T3) greeting, salutation. *aan k.* his g. (to someone). *kkópwongen osuunó* farewell, godspeed. vi. make greeting, make salutation. *k. ngeni* greet, salute (someone).

kkóton₁ (dc; 3a) See *ton*. Var. *kkaton*. va. (c.) have a look, watch, observe. Syn. *kófót*. Cf. *óttona*.

kkóton₂ (2) KKÓTONU. (Eng.) Var. *kkaton*. nu. (T2) 1. cotton; cotton plant (*Gossypium barbadense*). *kkótonun Merika* American c. 2. kapok; kapok tree (*Ceiba pentandra*). [Recently introduced. Its floss is used to stuff pillows.]

kkótupw (dc; 2) See *ótupwu-*. Var. *kkotupw*. nu. (T2) dress (woman's), frock. *eché k.* one d. *wúfan k.* her d.

kkótur₁ (dc; 2) See *tur₁*. nu. (c.) a method of fishing.

kkótur₂ N. of *kkotur*.

kkóturunó N. of *kkoturunó*.

kkuum vi., adj. (be) closed (as the neck of a bag or a flower bud); (be) uncircumcised (but see *nikichuur*). *k. ffengenniiy* close (something).

kkuf (2) KKUFU. vi. be overcome (in a fight, war, or game); be defeated, lose. [Not used in connection with a footrace.] *wúwa k. reen* I was defeated by him, I lost to him. Syn. *miis*. Ant. *win*. Cf. *sun, mwú₃*.

kkus (dc; 2) See *kus*. Tb1. vi. spurt, be discharged, be spit, be squirted (of liquid spurting suddenly and quickly); be ejaculated (of sperm). With dir. suf.: *kkusutiw* s. down (Tb, cf. *kusutiw*).

-kkus adj. (intens.) very, extremely. *maakkus* be very ashamed (*ma* be ashamed).

kkusiiti See *kkus, -iti*. Tb. vo. (T2) be squirted or ejaculated upon; (refl.) have an emission. Cf. *kusiiti*.

kkusutiw See *kkus*.

kkuk (2) KKUKU. (Eng.) va., vi. cook; be cooked. Cf. *mwoot*.

kkukuuw See *kkuk, -u-*. vo. (T5) cook (something). Syn. *amwoota*.

kkumi (1) KKUMII. (Ger. *Gummi*) nu. (T1) rubber, rubber-like plastic; rubber hose. *eché k.* one sheet of r.; *efóch k.* one length of hose. *aan k.* his r. *kkumiin Merika* American r.

kkumw₁ (2, 3) KKUMWU₁, KKUMWA. n. (T3), suf. (cc.) portion of premasticated food. *ekkumw, rúwokkumw, wúnúkkumw, fékkumw, nimekkumw, wonokkumw, fúúkkumw, wanúkkumw, ttiwekkumw, engoon kkumwan* one,...ten portions of premasticated food. (in certain dialects) *kkumwey, kkumwomw* or *kkumwumw, kkumwan* my, your (sg.), his portion of p. f.; *anan k.* his portion of p. f. vi. be fed premasticated food.

kkumw₂　　　　　　　　　　　　　　　　　　　　　　　　　**Trukese-English**

ewe semeriit aa k. reey the baby was f. p. f. by me. Cf. *kumu-*.

kkumw₂ (2) KKUMWU₂. nu. (T2) type of lashing to produce a diamond-shaped or lozenge-shaped pattern.

kkumwuuw₁ See *kkumw₁, -u-*. vo. (T5) feed (someone) premasticated food. *wúwa k. ewe ménúkón* I have fed the child p. f.

kkumwuuw₂ See *kkumw₂, -u-*. vo. (T5) lash (something) in a diamond or lozenge pattern.

kkun (2: *kunnu-, -kuun*) KUNNU. n. (T2) turning, rotation. *kunnun* its t. vi. revolve, be turned; roll, turn around; go on the opposite tack (through the wind, as in a European sailboat, cf. *ách*). Cf. *otokun*.

kkunók (Eng.) nu. clock, watch. *eew k.* one c. or w. *néwún k.* his c. or w. nu. (temp.) hour (on the clock); something o'clock, a time. *k. fítuuw iyeey?* what is the hour now? what time or o'clock is it now? *k. engoon esópw* half past ten, ten-thirty o'clock. *k. eew minich engoon* ten minutes after one o'clock. *engoon minich mwmwen k. ruwuuw* ten minutes before two o'clock.

kkuch (2) KUCHCHU. vi. fit. *meyi k. pecheey nnón ekkeey suus* these shoes fit my feet. Syn. *tá*.

kkú- (dc; 2) KKÚ₂. [In cpds. only.] unsp. bite; bitten. See *kkúk, -kkún, kúúw, mwékkú-*. Cf. *ssi-*.

kkú (2: *kkú-, -wúk*) KKÚ₃. Tn. [An analogical back formation from a ni. *kkú-*.] Var. *wúúk₂*. n. (T2) fingernail, toenail, claw. *ewúk* one f. *kkún* his f.

kkúúngeni (dc) See *kúú-₃, ngeni*. vo. (T2) bump, hit, strike against (something).

kkúút₁ (3) KÚTTA. Var. *kkút*. nu. (T3) search. *aan k.* his s. vi., va. search, engage in search; search for. *re k. wiin* they are searching for turtles. Syn. *rúúr*.

kkúút₂ (dc; 2) See *kúú-₂, -ti-*. [Presumably a back formation from *kúúti*.] vi. be broken up, torn apart, disarranged.

kkúútaka (dc; 1) See *kúú-₃, taka*. nu. (T1) being struck by a falling coconut. *máán k.* death from being s. by a f. c.

kkúúw₁ See *kkú-, -ú-*. vo. (T5) bite. Dis. *kúkkúúw* (ds). *kkuuk* bite you. *naan konaak e kan kúkkúúwey* that dog keeps biting me. With dir. suf.: *kkúúwonó* bite (something) off.

kkúúw₂ (dc) See *kúú-₃*. vo. (T1) bump, hit, strike. *aa kkúúwey kitirin ewe núú* the coconut hit me.

kkúúwonó See *kkúúw₁*.

kkúsú (1) See *kkú-, sú*. nu. (T1) sorcery, black magic. *kkúsúún Chuuk* Trukese s. Syn. *ppéwút, rongongngaw₂*. Ant. *rongééch₂*.

kkúsúúnó (1) See *kkúsú, -nó*. vi., adj. be lost, be mislaid. [More gentle than *péwútúnó*.]

kkúsúúngeni See *kkúsú, ngeni*. vo. (T2) make black magic against.

kkúsúúwonó See *kkúsú, -nó*. vo. (T1) lose, mislay. [More gentle than *péwútóónó*.]

kkúk (ds; 2: *kúkkú-*) See *kkú-*. vi. bite (of fish or insects). *aa mmen k. nikken ikeey* mosquitos bite here (i.e., this is a bad place for mosquitos).

kkúm (3) KKÚMA. n. (T3) rigidity. *kkúman* his r. vi., adj. (be) rigid, tense, stiff, unflinching, tough, indestructable, durable (of persons or things). Dis. *kúmékúm* (db). *aa mmen k. futuken ewe iik* the meat of the fish is very tough.

kkúmi (1) KKÚMII. (Jap. *kumi*) nu. (T1) team (athletic). *eew k.* one t. *aan k.* his t. Cf. *kúmi*.

kkún Var. of *kúún*.

-kkún (2) KKÚNÚ. [Apparently a back formation from *kkú-* plus *-n₂*.] unsp. small, little. See *kúkkún, mwókkún*.

-kkúng unsp. big, large. See *nikkúng*.

kkúr (dc; 3) See *kúra-₁*. Tb1. vi. be drawn back (of foreskin), be exposed (of prepuce), be circumcized.

kkúch (2) KKÚCHÚ. nu. (T2) species of squirrel fish. *kkúchún Chuuk* Trukese s. f.

kkút Var. of *kkúút*.

Krayis (Eng.) Var. *Kérayis*. nu. (pers.) Christ. Syn. *Kristuus*.

Kristuus (Lat. *Christus*) Var. *Kiristuus*. nu. (pers.) Christ. Syn. *Krayis*.

M

-m (2) MI₁ (from *MMI). [In this form with all noun bases in N. dialects but only after bases ending in double vowels in F. dialects; with other bases in F. dialects, the final vowel of the base is doubled with this suffix.] suf. (pos.) 1exc. pos. prn.: of us (excluding person or persons addressed); belonging to, on behalf of, for, or pertaining to us. *chchaa-m* our blood, *pwéétú-úm* (F.) or *pwéétú-m* (N.) our nose, *fénúwe-em* (F.) or *fénúwe-m* (N.) our land.

ma- (3b: *ma-, má-, me-, mé-, mo-, mó-*) MA₁. pref. (adj.) indicates that what is described is an appearance or a condition of being. Cf. *che-, mwa-, -ng*.

-ma- (3) MA₂. suf. (n.form.; T3) object or product of an action. [Suffixed to bases of inactive verbs, to which the corresponding active-verb formative *-mi-* may be suffixed.]

ma (1) MAA₁. N. vi. be ashamed. *aanú ma* his being a. *wúwaa ma reen átenaan* I am ashamed of him. Syn. *máfen, sááw, kin*.

maa (1) MAA₂. Var. *máá₃*. n. (T1) behavior, manner, habit. See *maayicha*. Cf. *ma*.

Maas₁ (3) MAASA₁. (Eng.) nu. (loc.; T3) March (the month).

maas₂ (3) MAASA₂. (Eng.) nu. (T3) march, marching; a dance with a marching step in imitation of close-order drill. *maasen Chuuk* Trukese m.

maas₃ (3d, 3v: *masa, mesa, mesá-, mese-, mesó-, -mas, -mes*) MASA₁, MESA₁. n. (T3d, T3v) eye, face (of living creature and fig. of some things); (with pos. suf.) anything worn on the eyes or face. *eféw m.* one e.; *eféw féwún m.* one eyeball; *emas mesen kinaas* one lens (of spectacles). *masan, mesan* his e.; *mesen* e. of. *féwún m.* eyeball. *mesen cheew* mesh or hole in a net; *mesen taka* coconut eye. *meyi mesen re-Sapaan* look Japanese ("be face of Japanese person"). *mwoo mesen semey* even my father's eyes (an oath implying that one's father will go blind if one has lied). Id. *masan chék* it makes no difference; its all the same to me ("his eye only"). nr. (loc.; T3d, T3v) leading, piercing, working, cutting end or edge (of something); beginning (of day); direction (of wind); front (of a building); means (of money); point (of pencil, needle, etc.). *emas mesen sines* one spear point. *mesen awan* his lips ("edge of his mouth"); *mesen ásápwáán* direction of the wind; *mesen kimenes* point of a gimlet, bit (of brace and bit); *mesen nááyif* knife blade; *mesen owupw* nipple (of breast or baby's bottle); *mesen piin* pin point, pencil point. *raa toowu mesen ewe wuut* they came out in front of the meeting house. *siya angeey mesen maak* we got it with (by means of) dollars. Id. *mesen faraf* (n. phr.) method of hand-to-hand fighting ("edge of the outrigger platform").

Maasan (Eng.) nu. (loc.) Marshall Islands. *fénúwen M.* M. I.

Maasané (1) MAASANÉÉ. nu. (loc.) a clan name. *fin M.* or *fiin M.* M. woman; *mwáán M.* M. man. *chóón M.* people of M.

maasiyes (db; 2) See *ma-, esi-₃*. nu. (T2) treeless place, field, open area without shade.

maasuuwa (1) MAASUUWAA. vi. be exhausted (of soil). Syn. *móówuuwa*.

maaskkú (1) MAASKKÚÚ. (Jap. *masuku*, from Eng.) Var. *maskú*. nu. (T1) catcher's mask (baseball). *eew m.* one c. m. *masan m., mesan m.,* his c. m.; *maaskkúún* c. m. of.

maasta (1) MAASTAA. (P.Eng.) Var. *masta*. nu. (T1) headman, master. *emén m.* one h. *néwún m.* his h. *maastaan eyinang* clan h.; *maastaan iimw* household h.

maasto (1) MAASTOO. (Jap. from Eng.) nu. (T1) mast. *maastoon pwoot* ship's m. Syn. *éwú*.

maak (3) MAAKKA. (Ger. *Mark*) nu. (T3) money; (obs.) mark. *eew m.* one monetary unit, one dollar; *fituuw m.* how much m. *néwún m.* his m. *maakken Merika* American m. Syn. *mwooni*.

maake (1) MAAKEE. nu. (T1) boat pulley, capstan.

maakkus See *ma, -kkus*. nu. great shame. *aan m.* his g. s. vi. be very ashamed.

maama (1) MAAMAA. [Used for own mother (by birth or adoption) in address and reference by children, but not by adults.] nu. (T1) mother. *inan m.* his m. Cf. *iin.*

maamaaw (db; 3) See *maa, maaw*. nu. (T3) hard place; shallow area studded with sharp coral projecting from sand so that walking is not possible (also *wóón m.*). *maamaawen ene, maamaawen iich* joint (hard place) of a bamboo. vi., adj. (be) hard, tough, strong, healthy; (with *wóón*) prevail over, defeat. *aa m. wóón* he defeated him.

maan$_1$ (2: *ménú-, mén-, man-, monu-, -mén*) MÉNÚ$_1$ nu. (T2) living creature of land or air (other than human). *emén m.* one c. *m. feffetán* walking animal (e.g., dog, cat, etc.); *m. mwócho* wild or untamed animal; *m. mwóchoonó* animal gone wild; *m. ákkáás, m. súúsú* bird (general term, syn. of *machchang*); *m. téété* creeping or crawling creature (esp. of crabs and lizards). Cf. *aramas, iik*. nr. (T2), suf. (cc.) living creature of land, sea, or air (as cc. including people, mammals, birds, fish, lizards, and knives, but not lobsters, crabs, sea cucumbers, or shellfish). *emén, rúwémén, wúnúmén, fémén, nimmén, wonomén, fúúmén, wanúmén, ttiwemén, engoon* one,...ten c. *ménún chunen* bee; *ménún neeman* land animal; *ménún neepaayinú* coconut-leaf miner (inhabiting the opening leaf); *ménún neeset* sea creature (including fish, shellfish, sea cucumber); *ménún rayis* rice weevil; *ménún semwmwen* bacterium, disease germ.

maan$_2$ (2) MAANÚ. vi. 1. be becalmed, adrift; drift. Dis. *mammaan* (ds). With dir. suf.: *maanúnó* drift off, float away; *maanúto* drift or float hither. 2. soar (without flapping wings), glide. 3. do a dance movement with outstretched arms.

Maan$_3$ nu. (loc.) a star or constellation (to be equated probably with Sirius or Procyon); a month in the traditional sidereal calendar.

maaniiti See *maan*$_2$, *-iti*. vo. (T2) drift to, float to.

maanúún (db; 2) See *ma-, wúnú-*$_2$. vi. be thick (of flat objects). *aa mmen m. chenikamwomw na panangkeet* your blanket is very t.

maanúúniiti See *maanúún, -iti*. vo. (T2) be too thick for.

maanúnó See *maan*$_2$.

maanúto See *maan*$_2$.

maangúwéng (db; 2) See *ma-, -éngú-*. vi. be soft, pliable. Syn. *méngúméng*.

maap (3) MAPPA, MAAPPA. (Eng.) nu. (T3) map. *mappen* or *maappen fénú* island m.

maar (3) MARA. nu. (T3) preserved (fermented) breadfruit. [For possessives see *maraa-*.] *maren meyimeet?* p. b. of what variety of b.? Syn. *épwét*. vi. pick and preserve breadfruit.

maaraw (3b) See *ma-, araw*$_2$. vi. be at a green stage, be green (of fruit such as bananas, mangoes, etc.). Syn. *ménguch*. nu. (T3) species of parrot fish.

maach (3v) MACHA$_1$. n. (T3) tail (of fish). *emach m.* one t. *machan* its t. *mechen iik* fish's t. Cf. *wúúk*$_1$.

maat (3) See *ma-, -at*$_1$. vi., adj. (be) brave. Syn. *pwara*. Ant. *nisiin, nissimwa, nissiyá*.

maata- (3) See *ma-, -at*$_2$. [In cpds. only.] unsp. rough of surface.

maataat (db; 3) See *maata-*. vi., adj. (be) rough to the touch (but not to the eye).

maaw (3) MAAWA. vi., adj. (be) hard, firm; ready to pick but not yet fully ripe; (of bananas, papayas, oranges, mangoes, etc., but not of breadfruit); strong, powerful. *fátán m.* walk strongly and heavily, tramp; walk restlessly in the presence of an important person. Cf. *nné*$_2$.

maay$_1$ (3) MAYA. F. Var. *mááy*$_1$. nu. (T3) stone fish trap (built on reef flat). *eew m.* one f. t. *mayen iik* f. t. for fish. vi. drive fish into a f. t.

maay$_2$ N. of *mááy*$_2$

maayicha Var. of *mááyicha*.

mas (3) MASA$_2$. vi. well joined, fitted together. *meyi m. wóón pecheemw ekkena suus?* do those shoes fit your feet?

-mas (3) See *maas*$_3$. suf. (cc.) something worn on the eyes (e.g., lens of goggles glasses; something attached to the piercing or working end, tip (e.g. metal spear point); mesh (of net). *emas,* *rúwémas, wúnúmas, fémas, nimemas, wonomas, fúúmas, wanúmas, ttiwemas* one,...nine lenses or points.

masamas (db; 3) See *maas₃*. nu. (T3) species of porgy fish (with big eyes).

masaché (1) See *maas₃, chéé*. nu. (T1) leaves of trees or *kká* placed directly on food in an *wuumw*.

masachééni See *masaché, -ni-*. vo. (T4) apply leaves as a cover to. *m. eey wuumw* cover the food in this *wuumw* with leaves.

masawu (1) See *maas₃, -wu*. nu. (T1) edge of thatch at each end of a house. [It is often held down by overlaid coconut fronds, *sooso*.]

mases (2) MASESI. (Eng.) Var. *masis*. nu. (T1) matches. *efóch m.* one m.; *eew m.* one box of m. *masesin Sapaan* Japanese m.

masééé (db; 1) See *ma-, sé*. vi. be eased, allayed, mitigated, alleviated, (of pain, fear, distress, anger, wind).

masiing (Jap.) nu. machine or motor oil.

masis Var. of *mases*.

masow Var. of *mósow*.

maskú (1) MASKÚÚ. (Jap. *masuku*, Eng. *mask*) Var. *maaskkú*. nu. (T1) catcher's mask (in baseball). *eew m.* one c. m. *masan m., mesan m.* his c. m.; *maskúún* c. m. of.

masta Var. of *maasta*.

makú (1) MAKÚÚ. (Jap. *maku*) nu. curtain.

makúwawúri (1) MAKÚWAWÚRII. (Jap. *makuwauri*) nu. (T1) melon (*Cucumis melo*). *eféw m.* one m. *wochaan m.* his m. (to eat). *makúwawúriin Sapaan* Japanese m.

makkeey See *mmak, -e-₂*. vo. (T6b) write, inscribe. Dis. *mammakkeey* (ds). *m. wóón chéén émmúniy* inscribe it in my heart ("inscribe it on the leaves of my kidney").

makkekkáy (2, 3) See *mmak, kkáy*. nu. quick writing. vi. write quickly.

makkengeni Var. of *makkéngeni*.

makkeppék Var. of *makképpék*.

makketichchik (2) See *mmak, tichchik*. N. Var. *makkétichchik*. vi. be written very thoroughly with great detail.

makkeya- (3) See *mmak, -a-₁*. ni. (T3) written work, written product, thing written (by someone). *makkeyan* his w. w.

makkeyééch (2: *-yéchchú-*) See *mmak, ééch*. nu. (T2) good writing.

makkéngeni See *mmak, ngeni*. Var. *makkengeni*. vo. (T2) write with (something). *m. piin* w. with a pencil.

makképpék (2) See *mmak, -ppék*. vi. write at the same time.

makkétichchik F. of *makketichchik*.

mame (1) MAMEE. (Jap. *mame*) nu. (T1) bean. *eféw m.* one b.; *efóch m.* one bean-pod (with beans), one b. plant. *wochaan m., anan m.* his b. (to eat); *aan m.* his b. (to sell); *fótaan* or *fátaan m.* his b. (to plant).

mammaan Dis. of *maan₃*.

mammasa Dis. of *mmasa*.

mammakkeey Dis. of *makkeey*.

mammanaw Dis. of *manaw*.

mammang Dis. of *mmang*.

mammach Dis. of *mmach*.

man (3) MANA. vi. have divine, magical, or supernatural power (a quality of being, not a form of knowledge); be miraculous, magically powerful. Dis. *manaman* (db). *aa m. ewe sáfey* the medicine has become powerful.

manako Var. of *mangko*.

manaman (db; 3) See *man*. nu. (dis.; T3) divine, magical, or supernatural power (as distinct from knowledge). vi. (dis.) have divine, magical, or supernatural power (as an ongoing condition); be miraculous, magically powerful.

manaw (3b) See *ma-, -naw*. n. (T3) 1. life, health; (figuratively) salvation; erection (of penis). *manawan* his 1. *m. semwmwúch, m. ese mwmwúch* 1. everlasting, eternal 1., 1. without end. With dir. suf.: *manawetá* (n.; T1) revival, resurrection. 2. character. *meyi ngngaw manawan* his c. is bad. *raa sineey manawan* they know his c. (what sort of person he is). vi., adj. (be) alive, healthy, recovered (from illness); saved (spiritually); erect (of penis). Dis. *mammanaw* (ds). *m. sefáán* be alive again, rise from the dead, revive, be resurrected. With dir. suf.: *manawanó* (N.), *manawónó* (F.) give birth, bear young; *manawetá* come back to life, revive; *manawetiw* come down safely; *manawenong* come in safely.

manawenong See *manaw*.

manawetá See *manaw*.

manawetiw See *manaw*.

manaweyiti See *manaw, -iti*. Var. *manawiiti*. vo. (T2) live until; reach safely. *wúse sineey ika wúpwe m. nnón*

manawééch   **Trukese-English**

een iyer I don't know if I will live until next year. *aa feyiyééch pwe aa m. ewe fénú* he was lucky because he reached the island safely.

manawééch (2) See *manaw, ééch.* nu. (T2) good character, health. *manawééchchún fénú* (n.phr.) public welfare, public interest. vi. be healthy; be of good character. *manawééchchún fénú* (vi.phr.) be of the public welfare, be in the public interest.

manawiiti Var. of *manaweyiti*.

manawónó See *manaw*.

manayita (1) MANAYITAA. (Jap. *manaita*) nu. (T1) chopping board. *eché m.* one c. b. *aan m.* his c. b. *manayitaan Chuuk* Trukese c. b.

manúté Var. and N. of *ménúté*.

manna- (3: *-man*) MANNA₁. [In cpds. only.] unsp. clearing, cleared ground. See *mannaan, neeman*.

mannaan (ds; 3) See *manna-*. nu. (T3) grassland (treeless, open).

mannap (3) See *maan₁, nap*. Itang. nu. (T3) frigate bird or man-of-war bird. Syn. *asaf*.

manneew (2) See *maan₁, eew₁*. nu. (T2) small outrigger canoe of *meniiyuk* type (for one or two men only).

manneng (2) MANNENGI. (Jap. *mannenhitsu*) nu. (T2) fountain pen. *efóch m.* one f. p. *néwún m.* his f. p. *mannengin Merika* American f. p.

manneyiti See *mman, -iti.* vo. (T2) overtake by dawn; dawn upon. *ráán aa m. átánaan* day has dawned upon that fellow.

manchú (1) MANCHÚÚ. (Jap. *manjuu*) nu. (T1) 1. a kind of dumpling stuffed with red bean jam. *eféw m.* one d. *anan m.* his d. (to eat). *manchúún Sapaan* Japanese d. 2. soft sweetstuff.

mangaak (2) MANGAAKÚ. Var. *mangaaku*. nu. (T2) cloth. *eché m.* one sheet of c.; *ekkamw m.* one torn fragment of c. *mangaakún Sapaan* Japanese c.

mangaaku Var. of *mangaak*.

mangane (1) MANGANEE. (Jap. *mengane*) Var. *mengane*. nu. (T1) spectacles, glasses. *eew m.* one pair of s. *néwún m., masan m., mesan m.* his s. *manganeen fáán akkar* sunglasses; *manganeen nennengngaw* corrective glasses; *manganeen chuun* glasses for the blind.

mangko (1) MANGKOO. (Eng.) Var. *manako*. nu. (T1) mango (*Mangifera indica*). *eféw m.* one m. fruit; *efóch m.* one m. tree. *aan m.* his m. tree; *woochaan m.* his m. fruit (to eat). *mangkoon Chuuk* Trukese m. Syn. *kangngit*.

mangnga (1) MANGNGAA. (Jap. *manga*) nu. (T1) farce, comedy, cartoon. vi. play a farce.

mara- (3v: *márá-, mere-, méré-, moro-*) See *ma-, ra-*. [In cpds. only.] pref. (adj., intens.) indicates that what is described in appearance or condition of being is in an extreme state.

maraa- (1v) See *maar, -a-₁*. ni. (T1v) preserved breadfruit. *mirááy, móróómw, maraan, maraach, márááḿ, márááḿi, maraar* my, your (sg.), his our (inc.), our (exc.), your (pl.), their p. b.; *márááń* p. b. of.

maras (3) See *ma-, -ras*. F. Var. *márás*. vi., adj. (be) bitter, acid. nu. (T3) a tree.

maram (3) See *ma-, ram*. nu. (T3) 1. moon. *aa wunus m.* the m. is full; *aa kin m. mé notow* the m. is in the first quarter; *aa kin m. mé éétiw* the m. is in the third quarter; *aa mmék m. mé éétiw* there is no m. ("the m. has disintegrated in the east"). 2. month (lunar or calendar); sidereal division of the year. *eew m.* one m. *m. Suun* m. of June. *maramen efen* months of *efen* season (Jan.-Apr.). *nóón ewe m.* in the past m., last m.; *nóón een m.* during next m. vi. be moonlight, be moonlit; (with numbers) be -- month(s) old. *neyiy eey aa m. eew* my child has become one month old.

marameni See *maram, -ni-*. vo. (T6a) be -- month(s) old ("acquire-months --"); spend -- month(s). *m. eew* be one m. old. *wúpwe nó m. eew wóón naan téé* I am going off to spend one month on that island.

marameyiti See *maram, -iti*. vo. (T2) shine moonlight upon.

maramwen F. nu. a yellow reef fish. Syn. *mwaramwar₁*.

marariya (1) MARARIYAA. (Eng. *malaria*) nu. (T1) insect spraying; sanitation. *chóón m.* sanitation worker; *angaangen m.* sanitation work, insect spraying.

marétip (3) See *maar, tiip₂*. nu. (T3) a method of preserving breadfruit.

Mariiya (Lat.) nu. (pers.) Mary (mother of Jesus, in Catholic usage). Cf. *Meeri*.

mach (3) MACHA₂. vi., adj. (be) very ripe, rotten; stink.

macha- (3) See *maach*. suf. (cc.) tail (of fish, in counting fish). *emach, rúwémach, wúnúmach, fémach, nimemach, wonomach, fúúmach, wanúmach, engoon machan* one,...ten t. Syn. *wúúk*₁.

machamach (db; 3) See *maach*. nu. (T3) species of small fish. *emén m.* one m..

machang (3) MACHANGA. nu. (T3) leaf bud at tip of the growing point of a tree or plant (at the plant's apex only). *machangen irá* tree's growing point. Syn. *kuwapw, wuwapw.* Cf. *machchang*.

machchang (3) See *maan*₁, *chang*. nu. (T3) 1. bird. Syn. *maan súúsú, maan ákkááś.* 2. (N.) shellfish.

machchach (3) MACHACHCHA (P). vi., adj. (be) muddy, having mud puddles. Syn. *pwakak, pwakakkaak*.

machchéénap (3b) See *maan*₁, *chéénap*. nu. (T3) cockroach (black and bad smelling).

matafa- (3) MATAFA. ni. (T3), suf. (cc.) scrap; (in counting) small portion or amount, little bit. *emataf, rúwémataf, wúnúmataf, fémataf, nimemataf, wonomataf, fúúmataf, wanúmataf, ttiwemataf* one,...nine bits; *fitemataf* how many bits. *emataf rayis* a little bit of rice.

mataw (3) See *ma-, taaw*. nu. (T3) a deep, the deep sea, sea. *eew m.* one d. *matawen Chuuk* a d. of Truk. *Matawen Pasifik* the Pacific Ocean.

matto (1) MATTOO. nu. (T1) pumice stone. [According to Bollig, it was traditionally associated with *Éwúr* and a talisman that ensures a plentiful harvest.] *eféw m.* one p. s. *néwún m., aan m.* his p. s.

maw (3) MAWA. vi. steam. nr. (T3) steam. *mawen wuumw* earth oven's s. With dir. suf.: *mawatá*.

mawatá See *maw*.

maweyisor (3a) See *maw, sora-*. nu. (T3) dark clouds in the east at dawn that threaten rain in the day but in fact quickly dissipate ("steam of morning").

Maying (Pon.) nu. (pers.) Lord (used only of the Christian God). *M. Siises* Lord Jesus.

má (1) See *mááᵢ*. vi. die, lose consciousness, lose sensation, become paralysed; (fig.) be overcome with fatigue, hunger, or other physiological want; be extinguished (of a light), stop (of an engine). *aa m.* he died; *aanú wee m.* his dying. With dir. suf.: *máánó* die (cease to live); *máátiw* die off (as a family's membership).

máá- (1) MÁÁ₃. [In cpds. only.] unsp. (u.m.) See *Mááchik, Máánap*.

máá₁ (1) MÁÁ₁. n. (T1) death; loss of consciousness; collapse; paralysis; disease, illness, sickness, pestilence. *máán* his d. (cf. *aanú wee má* his dying). *máán feyiyengngaw* d. by accident; *máán kkúútaka* d. from being hit by a falling coconut; *máán chukó, máámáán chukó* a kind of sickness (also called *semwmwenin chukó*); *máán épwét* sickness with symptoms of fever and general disability, including aching limbs, said to result from eating fermented breadfruit (also called *chúnen épwét*); *máán fénú* wrong conduct that is widely engaged in ("disease of the land"); *máán kawakaw, máán éré* sickness resulting from disregarding a *sochen mááy* tabu sign (Kraemer: falling sickness); *máán neetip* death from severe constipation said to result from excessive sexual activity, the antidote for it being *rongen neetip*. With dir. suf.: *máánó* death (permanent); *aan m.* his d.; *ifa wusun máánóón átewe?* how did he die?

máá₂ (1) MÁÁ₂. [Underscores or emphasizes the immediately preceding word. It may be shortened to *má* with lengthening of the final vowel of the preceding word.] adv., qlf. indeed. *iyé aa fééri? ngaang m.!* Who did it? I did! *aa máá iiy ésúúsú* or *aa ésúsúú má* he i. has run off with another's wife or he has run off i. with another's wife. Id. *m. ngaang* by golly!

máá₃ (1) MÁÁ₄. [In cpds. only.] Var. *maa*. n. (T1) behavior, manner, habit. *máán mwéngé* stinginess with food, failure to invite a passing relative to share one's food when one is eating (preferred in mixed company to *mááyicha*).

máásen (2) See *máá*₁, *seni-*. nu. orphan ("death parted"). *emén m.* one˚ o.

máákkáy (2, 3) See *má, kkáy.* vi. die young, die quickly.

máám (2) MÁÁMI. nu. large species of wrasse fish (up to six feet long). *emén m.* one w. f. Cf. *merer.*

máámá₁ (db; 1) See *máá*₃. n. (dis.; T1) negligence, heedlessness. *máámáán* his n. *mwa meyi feet máámáámw, áteen* say, to what end is your negligence, fellow?; *mwa pwata ina máámáámw* oh, why such carelessness on your part? vi. (dis.) be negligent, heedless, careless, inconsiderate.

máámá₂ (db; 1) See *má.* vi., adj. listless, feeble, weak. *meyi m. ne angaang* be l. at work; *angaang m.* work listlessly.

máán₁ (2) MÁNNI. n. (T2) swidden field, land cleared of trees and grass for cultivation. *mánnin* his f. Cf. *mánámán, manna-.*

máán₂ nu. affliction of the eyes from overexposure to bright sun, resulting in partial blindness. *sáfeen m.* medicine against blindness from overexposure to bright sun (syn. *sáfeen kinipwut, sáfeen mósóroch*).

Máánap₁ (3a) See *máá-, nap.* nu. (loc.; T3) the star Altair; the third month in the traditional sidereal calendar. [Altair's rising marks what was taken as due east in the traditional sidereal compass.] *Máánapen efeng* constellation consisting of the Little Dipper (without the handle). *tonen* or *sássin M.* rising of A., A. in the east (due east); *tupwun M.* setting of A., A. in the west (due west).

máánap₂ (3a) See *máá*₁, *nap.* nu. (T3) pestilence, plague. Dis. *máánapanap* (db).

máánapanap Dis. of *máánap*₂.

máánééné (1) See *má, nééné*₂. nu. (T1) seasickness. vi. be seasick.

máániffór (4) See *máá*₁, *ffór.* vi. be strangled, hanged. nu. (T2) death by hanging, strangling.

máánikát (4) See *máá*₃, *áát.* vi., adj. (be) childish (in behavior).

máánó See *má, máá*₁.

máánóóroch (3a) See *máánó, roch.* nu. (T3) murder at night. vi. be murdered at night.

máángngaw (3b) See *máá*₃, *ngngaw.* Var. *mángngaw.* vi. be fooled, teased (as by a practical joke); be irritated, provoked.

máángngaweyiti See *máángngaw, -iti.* Var. *mángngaweyiti.* vo. (T2) be annoyed at, angry at, irritated at, provoked at. Syn. *ningeriiti.*

mááppúng Var. of *máppúng.*

máápwut (3) See *máá*₁, *pwuta-.* nu. (T3) a form of sorcery (also known as *rongen m.*) that causes madness. *sáfeen m.* medicine to counter the effects of *m.* sorcery.

máápwpwas (3) See *máá*₁, *pwpwas.* nu. (T3) emaciation; death by thirst. vi. be emaciated, wasted (of the body); die of thirst.

máár (2) MÁÁRI. vi. grow (of plants). With dir. suf.: *mááritá* grow up, shoot up; *máárito* grow again after being damaged.

mááráár (db; 4) MÁÁRE. Var. *mááreyár.* n. (T2) kinsman, relative of any distance. *mááráárin* his k. vi. be kin, related.

mááreyár Var. of *mááráár.*

máárééch (2) See *máár, ééch.* vi. grow well (of plants).

máárikkáy (2, 3) See *máár, kkáy.* vi. grow quickly (of plants).

mááringngaw (3b) See *máár, ngngaw.* vi. grow badly (of plants).

mááritá See *máár.*

máárito See *máár.*

máách (2) MÁÁCHI. nu. (T2) shell from which ear discs are made; discs made of shell. *mááchin Chuuk* Trukese ear discs.

Mááchik₁ (1) See *máá-, chiki-*₁. nu. (loc.; T2) a star; a sidereal month in the traditional calendar.

máátiw See *má.*

máátter (2) See *máá*₁, *ter*₁. nu. (T2) epidemic.

mááwún (2) See *máá*₁, *wún* (?). nu. (T2) an illness. *rongen m.* spell to cure the *m.* illness.

mááy₁ N. of *maay*₁.

mááy₂ (2) MEYI₃. Var. *maay*₂, *meey*₂. nu. (T2) breadfruit, breadfruit tree (*Artocarpus altilis*). *efóch m.* one b. t.; *eew m.* one b. fruit. *aan m.* his b. tree; *anan m.* his b. to eat. *meyin woró, meyin wóón wúnúmar* or *meyin wúnúmar, meyin neefin, meyin efen* the four minor seasons (the first two in *ráás* and the third and fourth in *efen*), b. of each of these seasons;

meyin ráás the *ráás* season, b. of that season.
mááyineng (2) See *máá*₁, *nááng*. nu. (T2) famine. *mááyinengin nóón ewe faansowun* famine of that time.
mááyirú (1) See *máá*₃, *rú*₁. nu. (T1) alarm. vi. be alarmed, be astonished, surprised, scared, frightened.
mááyicha (1) See *máá*₃, *chaa*. Var. *maayicha*. Tb2. vi. be stingy, niggardly, selfish; refuse to share; be stingy with food, not inviting passing relatives to share one's food. n. (T1) stinginess, niggardliness, selfishness (especially with food). Syn. *máán mwéngé*.
mááyichaangeni See *mááyicha*, *ngeni*. vo. (T2) be stingy to (someone, especially with food).
máfen (3) MÁFENA. F. nu. (T3) embarassment, shame. *aan m.* his e. vi. be embarrassed, ashamed. Syn. *ma, sááw*.
mánámán (db; 4) MÁNE. nu. (T2) place of habitation, populated area, inhabited area. vi. be cleared of grass and vegetation, be a field (for cultivation). Cf. *máán*₁.
mánefenef (db; 3) MÁNEFA. vi. shimmer, be shimmering (of the vapors from a gasoline tank or the reflection of the sun on water or on sand). nu. (T3) shimmer; shimmering. *mánefenefen sáát* s. of the sea.
mángngaw Var. of *máángngaw*.
mángngaweyiti Var. of *máángngaweyiti*.
mángngawiiti See *mángngawiiti*.
máppúng (2) See *má, púng*₂. Var. *mááppúng*. vi. 1. be exhausted, weary, tired; "be in a bad way", "be feeling it", "be hurting" (from fatigue, hunger, lack of cigarettes, etc.). Syn. *pekkus, peengngaw*. 2. (fig. with *reen*) burn with love for; *wúwa m. reen naan nenggin* I am burning with love for that girl.
már (4) MÁRE. vi. move, shift; be moved, removed, shifted; have gotten out of the way, have made space for. With dir. suf.: *máránó, máreto*.
márá (1) MÁRÁÁ. nu. (T1) yard or cleared ground around a house or meeting house; houseyard. *eew m.* one y.
márás N. of *maras*.
máránó See *már*.

máráchcháán (2) See *mara-, chche-*₃, *eni-*₂ (?). nu. (T2) gleaming, glaring, sparkling. *pwata ina máráchcháánin ósun ena iimw?* why is the roof of that house glaring like that? vi., va. gleam, glare, sparkle (as the sea with phosphorescence or glass in the sun).
máreseni See *már, seni*. vo. (T2) move from (a place).
márech (2) MÁRECHCHI. nu. (T2) variety of banana. *márechchin Chuuk* Trukese b.
máreto See *már*.
márewerew (db; 3) MÁREWA. nu. (T3) barely discernible movement (as of a canoe at night). vi. be barely discernible from its movement.
márisi See *már, -si-*. vo. (T2) move; (refl.) move (onself) out of the way. *márisuk m.* yourself, m. over (said when trying to get someone to move enough to permit one to pass through a crowd).
máchá (1) See *máche-, -ya-*. Var. *mechá*. nu. (T1) 1. sharp, pointed, long projection; beak (of a fish), horn, spine (of a fish); metal nail. *efóch m.* one nail. *mácháán chúúfén* metal nail. 2. large species of unicorn fish. adj., nu. (T1) metal.
máche- (4) MÁCHE. [In cpds. only.] unsp. long, pointed projection; spike, spine.
máchemeyaas (3b) See *máche-, me*₁, *aas*₁. nu. (T3) sidereal compass position (having reference to the position in the east of the star that forms the spine of the constellation *pwuupw*); a star (?).
máchew₁ (3b) MÁCHEWA. nu. plant (*Monerma repens, Lepturus repens*) used in love medicine; a variety of large, swamp taro (*Cyrtosperma*).
máchew₂ (3) See *máche-, -wa-*. n. (T3) 1. stingray tailbone; spear; throwing spear with stingray spines attached. *efóch m.* one s. t. or spear. *máchewan* its s. t. *máchewen sikách* stingray's s. t. Syn. *ninget*. 2. school of *itang*. *M. Sópwunupi* school of *itang* associated with Wééné (Moen) Island; *M. Wunaap* school of *itang* associated with Wuumaan (Uman) Island.
Mácheweyichchún See *máchew*₂, *chchún*. nu. school of *itang* lore. [Its patron spirit is Soon of the Imwó clan, and it is associated with Tonowas (Dublon) and Feefen (Fefan) Islands.]
mátár (4) MÁTÁRE. Var. *metár*. nu. (T2) fringe of hair or thread. *mátárin mesey* my eyelash (see *mátárinimas*); *mátárin*

chééyitúr warp-thread f. on a piece of cloth; *mátárin kiyeki* f. on a mat. Cf. *meet₂*.

mátárinimas See *mátár, maas₃*. ns. (T3v) eyelash. *mátárin masan* his e.

máyirú Var. of *mááyirú*.

me- See *ma-*.

me See *mé₁*.

mee- (1) MEE. [Historically derived from *mé₁* (*ma) and *i-₃*] unsp. coming from; place (other than where speaker is). See *meenúk, meesón, meey₁*.

meefáátá See *meefi₁*.

meefi₁ MEEFI. vo. (T4) sense, be aware of, perceive, feel, taste; realize, appreciate. *wúwa m. péchékkún* I feel well. *wúwa meefuk kepwe toongeni fééri* I feel that you will be able to do it. *wúwa m. óómw fóós* or *wúwa meefuk óómw fóós* I sensed or heard your words (as in my sleep). *wúse meefiyey reen ewe tókter* I didn't feel anything at the doctor's. *kaa mwmwan meefuk?* do you feel better? *wúwa m. nómwotan* I appreciated the need of it.

meefi₂ (3) See *meefi₁, -a-₁*. nu. (T3) values, sentiments; sensation, feeling. *meefiyan, aan m.* his v. *meet meefiyomw reen ááy eey mwochen?* what do you think of this wish of mine?

meesón (4) See *mee-, són*. adj. a little off of west ("coming from level"). *éér m.* a little south of west.

meem (2) MEMI. nu. (T2) midrib of a leaf, inner cord of a sea cucumber. *memin wupwut* midrib of the coconut or pandanus leaf; *memin penik* white longitudinal cord inside a *penik* sea cucumber (sometimes edible, sometimes not).

meen (3d) MINA. n. (T3d) thing; man (not woman); relative, friend; polite term of address to a man whom one is not *pin me wóón* (used by men and women); used as a substitute for one's own name in narration where one's name is called by another. *miney, minomw, minan* t. for me, you (sg.), him. *minen nóómw* old t.

meenúk (2) See *mee-, núkú-₁*. nu. (T2) outer barrier reef of Truk.

meenne Var. of *menne*.

meerer nu. (temp.) a day ahead of time. *sipwe áwees m.* we shall finish a d. ahead of t.

Meeri (Eng.) nu. (pers.) Mary. Cf. *Mariiya*.

meech (2) MECHCHI₂. nu. (T2) species of surgeon fish. *mechchin Chuuk* Trukese s. f.

-meech (2) See *mechchi-*. F. Var. *-mmech, -mech*. suf. (cc.) portion of mashed breadfruit. *emeech, rúwémeech, wúnúmeech, fémeech, nimemeech, wonomeech, fúúmeech, wanúmeech, ttiwemeech* one,...nine portions of m. b.

meet₁ See *mee-, -t*. Var. *meeta*. prn. (interrog.) what? [The use of *meet* or *mwaa meet* in answer to someone's call is impolite; the polite response is *ee*.] *m. ena?* what is that?; *m. kepwe fééri?* what will you do? *wúse sineey m. wúpwe fééri* I don't know what I shall do.

meet₂ (3) MEETA. nu. (T3), suf. (cc.) strand (of hair or rope). *emeet, rúwémeet, wúnúmeet, fémeet, nimemeet, wonomeet, fúúmeet, wanúmeet, ttiwemeet* one,...nine s. *meeten mékúr* s. of hair; *meeten sáán* s. of rope; *meeten tereech* s. of thread. Cf. *mátár*.

meeta N. of *meet₁*.

meetekúkkún (2) See *meet₂, kúkkún*. vi., adj. (be) fine-haired; have fine hair. Syn. *meetekkiis*.

meetekkiis (2) See *meet₂, -kkiis*. vi., adj. (be) fine-haired; have fine hair. Syn. *meetekúkkún*.

-meew (2) See *ma-, eew₁*. [In cpds. only.] unsp. single, only, solitary. *Pisemeew* "solitary sand islet" (name of an islet in Truk). See *nimeew*.

meey₁ See *mee-*. F. Var. *meya*. adj. (interrog.) coming from where, whence. *ke náá m.? ke nóó m.?* where are you coming from? where have you been? *mé anayiya aa pwopwutá m. ewe kkéén* that is the place whence the song came. Syn. *me iya*.

meeyar (3) MEEYARA. nu. (T3) coconut fiber bag; net-like carrier for sling stones. *aan m.* his b. *meeyaren Chuuk* Trukese b.

mes (2) MESI. vi., adj. (be) worn out (of household goods and clothes); be fragile with age. *ewe mesin mwárámwár* the w. o. garland. With dir. suf.: *mesinó*.

mesa-₁, mese-1 See *maas*₃.
mesa-₂, mese-2 (3a) MESA₂. [In cpds. only.] unsp. act disruptively. See *mesepaat, mesemesekkis.*
mesaaraw (3) See *maas*₃, *araw*₂. nu. (loc.; T3) fairly deep, blue water beyond a reef (between *neepwech* and *neechón*).
mesaroch Var. of *mósóroch.*
mesááres (2) See *maas*₃, *a-*₂, *ráás*. nu. (temp.; T2) season just before breadfruit harvest (early May).
meseerááni (2) See *maas*₃, *ráán*. nu. (loc.; T2) east, east end. *meseeráánin Romónum* e. end of Romónum Island.
mesefeefin (3) See *maas*₃, *feefin*. nu. (T3) woman aged 25 to about 32.
mesefú See *maas*₃, *fúú*. nu. (temp.) 8th night of the lunar month.
mesekáneng See *maas*₃, *-káneng*. vi. be cross-eyed; cock-eyed. Syn. *meseyánef.*
mesekinaas (3) See *maas*₃, *kinaas*. nu. (T3) spectacles; glasses. *eew m.* one pair of s. *néwún m., mesan m.* his s.
mesekitikitiiy (db) See *mesa-*₂, *kiti-, -i-*₂. vo. (dis.; T5) tease. [Preferred when siblings of opposite sex or parent and child of opposite sex are both within hearing.] Cf. *táyiri.*
mesemaama (db; 1) See *maas*₃, *ma.* vi. be embarrassed. Ant. *mesemaaw.*
mesemaaw (3) See *maas*₃, *maaw*. vi. be unembarrassed, poised, at ease, self-possessed (as when speaking in public). Ant. *mesemaama.*
mesemese- (db; 3) See *maas*₃. ni. (dis.; T3) by one's eyes! [An oath or exclamation.] *mesemesey, kepwenee nó* by my eyes, you should go away. *mesemesey mwaa, kesapw akkafar!* by my eyes, you shouldn't tell anybody about it!
mesemesekkis (db) See *mesa-*₂, *kkis*. vi. (dis.) commonly act disruptively, be a bother to others.
mesemwáán (2) See *maas*₃, *mwáán*₁. nu. (T2) man aged about 28 to 40. vi. be a man aged about 28 to 40.
mesen See *maas*₃.
mesenap (3) See *maas*₃, *nap*. nu. (T3) proximal cross-board (next to gunwhale) of outrigger platform on paddle canoe. *mesenapen waa* canoe's proximal c.-b.
mesenifé (1) See *maas*₃, *féé*. nu. (T1) either of two oblique braces connecting the outrigger beams to the canoe hull. *meseniféén waa* canoe's b. *m. mé mwmwan* forward b.; *m. mé mwirin* aft b. Syn. *mesereewu.*
mesenifén (2) See *maas*₃, *fén*₂. nu. (T2) point of thorn on tattooing instrument.
mesenimw (3) See *maas*₃, *iimw.* [Shortened from **meseniimw.*] nu. (T3) a move in hand-to-hand fighting, designed for use at the door of a house.
meseninnúf (3) See *maas*₃, *nnúf*. nu. (T3) the side of a breadfruit pounding board away from the worker, i.e., its outer side.
mesening (3) See *maas*₃, *ning*. nu. (temp.), vi. 4th night of the lunar month ("first appearing").
mesenipik See *maas*₃, *piik*₂ (?). nu. an insect (leaf-scale eating, minute, white, cushiony, found on breadfruit and coconut leaves).
meseniyaw (3) See *maas*₃, *aaw*₁. ns. (T3) lips, external region of the mouth. *mesen awan* his l. Syn. *mesen aaw.* ni. (T3) flattery, insincere speech. *meseniyawan* his f. ("from the front of his mouth"). vi. be insincere, not from the heart. *kete m. ngenney* don't be i. with me.
mesepaat (3) See *mesa-*₂, *paat*₂. nu. (T3) mischief. Syn. *turunuffas.* vi., adj. be mischievous, do mischief; fool around; play idly with something (as in doodling with a pencil).
mesepach (3b) See *maas*₃, *pach*. vi. be with closed eyes; be slit-eyed (like Orientals). nu. person with closed eyes; slit-eyed person. *emén m.* one p. with c. e.
mesepwech (3) See *maas*₃, *pwech*. vi. be white-faced; have a face with light complexion. nu. (T3) spear armed with ray spines (tip painted white). Syn. *niyawépwech, niyawúwépwech.*
mesepwúkú (3) See *maas*₃, *pwúkú*. vi. walk on one's knees (a sign of deference).
mesepwpwach (3) See *maas*₃, *pwpwach.* nu. (T3) wrinkled face. *mesepwpwachan* his w. f. vi. be wrinkle-faced.
mesereewu (3) See *maas*₃, *-reewu*. nu. (T3) either of two oblique braces connecting the outrigger boom to the canoe hull. *mesereewuwen waa* the canoe's b. Syn. *mesenifé.*

meserech See *maas₃, rech₂*. nu. variety of banana.

mesechééw (2) See *maas₃, chééw*. Itang. [A play on *chééw* "continuous" and *cheew* "net".] nu. (T2) net mesh (instead of the literal "featureless face"). Cf. *mesechcheew, meseyichew, mesen cheew*.

mesechón (4) See *maas₃, chón*. nu. (T2) variety of breadfruit. [It has a very long fruit and deeply incised leaves; found mostly on Toon (Tol) Island.]

mesechuun (3) See *maas₃, chuun*. vi. be blind.

mesechcha (1) See *maas₃, chcha₁*. nu. (T1) species of snapper fish.

mesechcheew (2) See *maas₃, cheew*. nu. (T2) net mesh. Syn. *meseyichew, mesen cheew*. Cf. *mesechééw*.

meseta (1) See *maas₃, ta*. n. (T1) bloodshot eye. *aa wúriyey m.* I have bloodshot eyes. vi. be bloodshot (of eyes).

mesetiw (3a) See *maas₃, -tiw*. nu. (temp.), vi. 9th night of the lunar month.

mesetton (3a) See *maas₃, ton*. vi. be hazy or bleary-eyed (as of a sick person); have a far-away look in the eyes.

mesewen (3a) See *maas₃, wen*. nu. (temp.), vi. 7th night of the lunar month ("straight face"); moon at the half.

meseyaraw (3b) See *maas₃, araw₂*. nu. (T3) blue-green sea just beyond reef and before reaching dark-appearing deep sea, usually with visible bottom. vi. be blue-eyed.

meseyánef See *maas₃, -ánef*. vi. be cross-eyed. Syn. *mesekáneng*.

meseyeew (2) See *maas₃, eew₁*. vi. be uniform, unvaried.

meseyiset (2) See *maas₃, sáát*. nu. (T2) whirlpool.

meseyik (3) See *maas₃, iik*. vi. be pleasantly excited. *wúwa m. reen tepen ewe iik nánew* I got excited at the size of the school of fish yesterday.

meseyikeyiti See *meseyik, -iti*. vo. (T2) be pleasantly excited about (at).

meseyikópo See *maas₃, kópo*. vi. be easily pleased; made happy by little things.

meseyinómw (4) See *maas₃, nóómw₁*. nu. (T2) lagoon area between barrier reef and a reef island ("lagoon edge").

meseyichew (1, 2) See *maas₃, cheew₁*. ns. (T1, T2) mesh or hole in a net. Syn. *mesechcheew, mesen cheew*. Cf. *mesechééw*.

meserú (3) See *maas₃, rúwa-*. nu. (T3) a constellation of two stars ("two eyes").

mesinó See *mes*.

mesóón (3a) See *maas₃, ón*. nu. (temp.), vi. 5th night of the lunar month ("yellow edge").

memmettip Dis. of *mettip*.

meneey MENEE. vo. (T1) understand, sense the thought of, read the mind of; be satisfied with, be pleased with. *wúse nniyen m. áán átánaan we osukuun* I did not understand his teaching very well. *pwata kaa pwan meneer aar repwe fitikich?* why do you keep thinking ("understanding them") that they will accompany us? *kaa m. meet wúwa ngonuk?* are you satisfied with what I have given you?

menennen (2) See *ma-, nne-₁, -ni-*. vi., adj. (be) transparent.

meni- (2) MENI. ni. (T2) smile; pleased facial expression. Dis. *menimeni-* (db). *menin* his s.

meni (1) MENII. N. md.m. maybe, perhaps (immediately precedes the predicate construction). *m. sipwe fééri neesor* maybe we will do it tomorrow. Syn. *eni*.

meniiyuk (3) MENIIYUKA. nu. (T3) sailing canoe with forked prow design. *meniiyuken Chuuk* Trukese s. c.

menimen (db; 2) See *meni-*. n. (dis.; T2) pleased facial expression (especially a smiling one); smile, smiling. *menimenin* his p. f. e. *fééri menimenich* fix our faces in a pleasing expression, make ourselves look attractive. vi. be appreciative, pleased. *aa m. soosich (choochis) ngeni óóm niffang* he is a. of your gift.

menimenééch (db; 2) See *menimen, ééch*. n. (dis.; T2) pleasant facial expression. Ant. *meniningngaw*. vi. have a pleasant facial expression.

menimenimmang See *menimen, mmang*. vi. be unappreciative, disparaging. *aa m. ngeni óómw niffang* he was u. of your gift.

menimeningngaw (db; 3a) See *menimen, ngngaw*. nu. (dis.; T3) unpleasant or displeased facial expression. Ant. *menimenééch*. vi. have an unpleasant facial expression.

menin (2) MENINI. nu. (T2) poison (only of things eaten or drunk). *meninin nóón naan mwéngé* the p. in that food. vi. be poisonous (of food or drink). *meyi m. na mwéngé* that food by you is p. Syn. *owun.*

meningngaw (3) See *meni-, ngngaw.* vi., adj. show an injured or hurt expression in the face (as after being reprimanded); be embarrassed. Syn. *mitingngaw.* Cf. *meniyééch.*

meniyééch (2) See *meni-, ééch.* vi. be cheerful faced; pleasant faced, smiling faced. Cf. *meningngaw.*

menne (1) See *meen, ne₃.* F. Var. *meenne, minne.* prn. whatever, whoever (not in relation to concrete objects); what, who (indefinite). *m. chék áámi mwochen* whatever you want, whoever you want; *m. neeyiir* who among them. Id. *ina m.* that is why, therefore; *meyi chék kúna m. meyi toowaaw seni* is just seeing whatever is far away from him. Id. *ina m.* that is why, therefore. Cf. *meet, menniiy.*

menni Var. of *menniiy.*

menniin (2) MENNIINI. Var. *mennin.* vi. be timid, cautious, respectful, apprehensive, slightly afraid or embarrassed (as in the presence of one's sister or a chief, or as when balanced precariously on a log). *m. ngeni* be respectful towards, wary of. Cf. *nisiin, nnis, nissimwa, nissiyá.*

menniiniiti See *menniin, -iti.* Var. *menniniiti.* vo. (T2) be cautious or careful in relation to; be respectful towards, be wary of. Syn. *menniin ngeni.*

menniinimmang (3) See *menniin, mmang.* Var. *menninimmang.* vi. be bold, incautious, reckless, audacious, without regard for others; be disrespectful.

menniiy See *meen.* Var. *menni.* prn. what one, which one. [In relation to concrete things, but not in relation to actions, ideas, people, etc.] *wúse sineey m. wúpwe aaya* I don't know what one I shall use; *m. neeyiir* what one among them; *meyi wor eey pétéwén wóón m. fénú? m. chék kaa toori.* These plants occur on what island? Just whatever one you come to. Cf. *menne.*

mennin Var. of *menniin.*

menniniiti Var. of *menniiniiti.*

mengane Var. of *mangane.*

menger₁ (2) See *ma-, nger.* vi. be hoarse, speak huskily. Dis. *mengeringer* (db).

menger₂ Var. of *méngér.*

mengeringer Dis. of *menger.*

mengiiy See *ma-, ngi.* N. vo. (T1) admire. Syn. *méngúúw.*

mengiringir (db; 2) See *ma-, ngiringir.* nu. (T2) feeling of guilt. *aan m.* his f. of g. vi. have a feeling of guilt, feel guilty; hurt (of the conscience).

mere- See *mara-.*

merengetenget (db; 3) See *mara-, nget.* vi. (dis.) flame up.

merepwpwun Var. of *moropwpwun.*

merer nu. large species of wrasse fish (about 3 feet long). Cf. *máám.*

merettin (3) See *mara-, ttin*₁. vi. shine brightly, glare. Syn. *merepwpwun.*

meriik (3) MERIIKA. nu. (T3) throat irritation. *meriiken suupwa* t. i. from tobacco. vi. be irritated in the throat. *wúwa m. reen ewe sika* I got sore throat from the cigar.

Merika (Eng.) nu. (loc.) America; United States of America. *M. efeng* North A.; *M. yéér* South A.

merip (3) See *ma-, -rip.* Var. *márip.* vi. be shattered, broken into pieces. Dis. *meriperip* (db).

meriweriw (db; 3) See *ma-, -riw.* vi. glitter (as the surface of the sea in the early morning sun).

Meriyanis (Eng.) nu. (loc.) Mariana Islands. Syn. *Weyichón.*

merong (2) MERONGU. (Jap. *meron,* from Eng.) nu. (T2) melon; cantaloupe. *eféw m.* one m. *wochaan m.* his c.

-mech N. var. of *-meech.*

mechá Var. of *máchá.*

meche- (3) MECHA. [In cpds. only.] unsp. facile. See *mecheres.*

mechen (2) MECHENI. nu. (T2) no-trepassing sign in the form of a stick set up on a reef, shallow area, or land plot; a tabu against trespass. [It may be set up to increase the supply of fish or fruit or to mourn someone recently dead.] *mechenin meyimá* burial marker. *mechenin róóng* sign of prohibition against trespass, made from young coconut leaves (*wupwut*) that may simply girdle a tree or stake or be strung to form an enclosure around the prohibited or restricted area. Cf.

mecheniiy *pwaaw, róóng.* vi. be marked as tabu against trespass.

mecheniiy See *mechen, -i-₂.* vo. (T5) mark with a sign against trespass.

mecheres (2) See *meche-, resi-.* vi. be easy, not difficult.

mecheresiiti See *mecheres, -iti.* vo. (T2) be easy for; go easily to. *aa kan m. ewe neeni* he was able to go to the place easily.

mecheyichey (db; 2) See *ma-, cheyi-.* Tb. vi., adj. be slimy, mucous-like. nu. (T2) vaginal fluid; moist flow on cow's nose.

mechikow (2) MECHIKOWU. nu. sea bird larger than a *kuning* (plover), seen only occasionally (probably the sooty-tern, cf. Wol. *mashigowu*). *emén m.* one *m..*

Mechiro nu. (loc.) Majuro Atoll (Marshall Islands).

mechiyenimey (2) See *ma-, chi, mááy.* nu. (T2) special loincloth worn by *sowuyótoomey* (breadfruit summoner). [It is also worn by men who take part in the model-canoe races in breadfruit ritual.]

mechchi- (2: *-meech, -mmech, -mech*) MECHCHI₁. ni. (T2) portion of mashed breadfruit. [In ptv. const. only.] *engoon mechchin* ten p. of m. b. Cf. *-meech.*

Mechchitiw nu. (loc.) district and village on Wééné (Moen) Island.

metár Var. of *mátár.*

metek (2) METEKI. vi., adj. pain, hurt; (be) painful. Dis. *metekitek* (db). *m. cheeche* spasmodic pain; *m. sékúr* backache, arthritis or rheumatism of the back. Syn. *ngiiyów.*

metekinón (4) See *metek, nónu-.* vi. be sore or painful inside.

metekitek Dis. of *metek.*

metiin nu. a Lethrinid fish. Cf. *sékúrúpi.*

metip (3) See *ma-, tiip₁.* vi., adj. (be) lonely. *wúwua kan m. pwe ese wor chiyeney* I am lonely because I don't have company.

metipeyiti See *metip, -iti.* vo. (T2) miss, long for.

mettip (2) METTIPI. vi. spit out (particles) from the mouth (as of food). Dis. *memmettip* (ds).

mettipiiy See *mettip, -i-₂.* vo. (T5) spit out (particles) from the mouth (as of food).

mettóóch (2) See *meet₁, -óch.* Var. *meettóóch.* nu. (T2) thing. *mettóóchun ekis* something foreign. Id. *esoor m.* there is nothing (to offer you) [The polite thing to say to visitors to whom one is not able or prepared to offer something to eat or drink]. Cf. *óóror₁.*

meya (1) See *mé-, -a₂.* N. Var. *meey₁.* adj. (loc., interrog.) from where, whence, from what place. *ke náá m.?* where are you coming from? where have you been?

meyi- (2) MEYI₁. [In cpds. only.] unsp. pull taut. See *ámeyis, mmey.*

Meyi₁ (Eng.) nu. (temp.) May.

meyi₂ MEYI₂. Var. *mén₁, mmen, mmén₁.* st.m. be, is, are; have the quality or attribute of; who is, that is. [Links a noun or pronoun with a word or construction that specifies a quality, attribute, or condition of what is denoted by the noun or pronoun.] *m. ééch* it is fine (cf. *aa ééch* it has become fine). *ika áámi m. tipeyeew ffengen meyinisen* if you are all of one sentiment together. *m. ét ikeey* it is smoky here; *m. mwochomwoch neenuukan* he is quick tempered. *m. wátte ewe mwáán* or *ewe mwáán m. wátte* the man is big; *ewe mwáán m. wátte aa war* the man who is big has arrived; *m. wátte ewe mwáán aa war* the man who has arrived is big. pref. (st.) one who is, one that is. *emén meyinap aa war* an important person has arrived (cf. *iiy emén meyi nap* he is someone who is important).

meyiis (2) MEYIISI. (Eng.) nu. (T2) maise, corn. *meyiisin Merika* American m. Syn. *kóón.*

meyiiton (3) See *mááy₂, Toon₂.* nu. (T3) variety of breadfruit.

meyifanang (3) See *mááy₂, fanang.* nu. (T3) variety of breadfruit.

meyisópw (4) See *mááy₂, sópw.* nu. (T2) variety of breadfruit.

meyikoch (3) See *mááy₂, kochokoch* (?) or *woch* (?), or *wocha-₂* (?). N. nu. (T3) a variety of breadfruit. *m. chéémón* variety of breadfruit like *meyikoch* in its fruit but different in its leaves, which are unserrated. Syn. *meyiror.*

meyimanaw (3b) See *meyi₂, manaw.* nu. (T3) living being or creature.

meyimá (1) See *meyi₂, má.* nu. (T1) dead body, corpse. Syn. *meyipe.*

meyimeet See *mááy₂, meet.* nu. (interrog.) what kind of breadfruit?

maren meyimeet fermented breadfruit of what k. of b.?; *meyimeet ena?* what k. of b. is that?

meyimwotow (2) See *mááy₂, mwotowutow*. nu. (T2) variety of breadfruit. Syn. *neepwoopwo, wúnniinaf*.

meyinap (3a) See *meyi₂, nap*. nu. (T3) person of importance or consequence, chief, officer, old person, "V.I.P."; manager, boss, supervisor. *emén m*. one important p.

meyiniin (db; 2) MEYINI. nu. (T2) distant sound. *meyiniinin waa* d. s. of a canoe; *meyiniinin kékké* d. s. of a call or shout.

meyiniipis See *mááy₂*. nu. variety of breadfruit ("b. of Ipis").

meyinifa (1) See *mááy₂, -fa*. nu. (T1) variety of breadfruit.

meyinisi- (2) See *mé₁* or *ma-, inis₁*. [In ptv. const. only.] ni. (T2) totality, entirety; all, every one (of something). *kiich meyinisin* all of us. *meyinisin kkewe aramas* all those people. Syn. *mowunusa-*.

meyinimmas (3) See *mááy₂, mmas₂*. nu. (T3) a breadfruit tree that has been selected by a breadfruit summoner as the special tree for ritual purposes in a given year's ritual cycle.

meyipe (1) See *meyi₂, pe*. nu. (T1) corpse, body of a dead person. Syn. *meyimá*.

meyipin (2) See *meyi₂, pin*. nu. (T2) saint. *emén m*. one s.

meyipwech (3) See *mááy₂, pwech*. nu. (T3) variety of breadfruit.

meyipwó (1) See *mááy₂, pwó*. nu. (T1) variety of breadfruit (much favored). Syn. *winikké*.

meyiror See *mááy₂, -ror*. F. nu. variety of breadfruit. Syn. *meyikoch*.

meyichéén (2) See *mááy₂, chéé-₁* (?). Var. *meyichén*. nu. variety of breadfruit. [Considered the best variety, its fruit has smooth skin, a round shape, and is of medium size.] *meyichéénún Pwonape* variety of b. introduced from Ponape.

meyichééché (1) See *meyi₂, chééché*. nu. (T1) kind of fish.

meyichén Var. of *meyichéén*.

meyichóópwut (3) See *mááy₂, chóópwut*. nu. (T3) variety of breadfruit (with long fruit, rough skin).

meyit (3) See *meyi₂, -t*. N. Var. *méwút*. prn. (interrog.) why, what for. *m. ena?* what is that for? *m. ii chék kaa chonomwas pwe sipwe nó Wééné?* why did you lie that we would go to Wééné (Moen)? Syn. *meyittaa, meyitte*.

meyiter (2) See *mááy₂, teri-*. nu. (T2) variety of breadfruit (with quick-ripening fruit).

meyittaa See *meyit*. N. prn. (interrog.) what for. *m. na maay* what is that breadfruit for? Syn. *meyitte, méwút*.

meyitte See *meyit*. N. prn. (interrog.) what for. *m. na maay* what is that breadfruit for? Syn. *meyittaa, méwút*.

meyiyeew (2) See *mááy₂, eew₁*. nu. (T2) the first breadfruit to ripen on a particular plot of land. [It should be presented to the chief.]

meyiyón (4) See *mááy₂, óno-₂*. nu. (T2) variety of breadfruit. [It is easy to mash into pudding.]

mé- See *ma-*.

mé₁ (3) MÉ. F. Var. *me*. conj. and, or; with, in conjunction with. *iiki mé, kkáá mé, kkónu mé, mááyi mé* fish and taro and pudding and breadfruit. *kiich mé rúwémén* we two (inc.); *áám mé Ruut* Ruth and I. *siya pwiipwi ffengen mé átánaan* we (inc.) are brothers together with that fellow. Cf. *oo₂, woo₄*. prep. from. *mé reen Eiue* from Eiue's; *mé nóón ewe pwóór* from inside the box; *mé wóón ewe waa* from on the canoe; *mé Wééné* from Moen. *aa péétá mé notow* it blows from the west. Id. *me anayiya* at that time. Id. *me reey, ese nifinifin* as for me, it makes no difference.

mé₂ (1) See *méé-₁*. vi. be traded, sold, paid for. *aa m. wóómw we?* is your car paid for? With dir. suf.: *méénó* be sold out.

méé-₁ (1) MÉÉ₁. ni. (T1) return, thing received in exchange; price, cost; pay, fee, salary. *méey, moomw, méén* my, your (sg.), his fee or pay. *wesewesen méén ewe kkama* the true cost of the iron cooking bowl.

méé-₂ (1) MÉÉ₂. unsp. unpleasantly, roughly. See *méméénúmwmwus, wurumé*.

méékisikiis (db; 2) See *méé-₁, kisikiis*. N. vi. be inexpensive, cheap. Syn. *méékúkkún*. Ant. *méémmóng, mééwátte, mééttapwir*.

méékúkkún (2) See *méé-₁, kúkkún.* F. vi. be inexpensive, cheap. Syn. *méékisikiis.* Ant. *méémmóng, méewátte, méettapwir.*

méémé (db; 1) MÉÉ₃. nu. (T1) unidentified edible thing from the sea.

mééméénuumwmwus Var. of *méémeénúmwmwus.*

méémeénúmwmwus (db; 3) See *méé-₂, nú, mwmwus.* Var. *méémeénuumwmwus.* vi. (dis.) retch.

méémmóng (2) See *méé-₁, mmóng.* vi. be expensive. Syn. *méewátte.* Ant. *méékisikis, méékúkkún.* Cf. *méettapwir.*

Méén (3) MÉÉNA₁. [Elbert] nu. (loc.; temp.) star (probably to be identified with Vega); sidereal month in the traditional calendar. [Elbert identifies it with Orion.] Cf. *méena-.*

méena- (3) MÉÉNA₂. [Possibly derived from *ma-* and *wún₃.*] ni. (T3) male flower of the banana. *méenan* its m. f. Cf. *Méén.*

méenaato See *méeni.*

méenérú See *Méén, rúwa-.* nu. (loc.) a star (unidentified).

méeni See *méé-₁, -ni-.* vo. (T4) buy. With dir. suf.: *méenaato* b. hither. With n. form. suf.: *méeniya-* (ni.) purchase, thing purchased by (someone); *fénúwey méeniyey* my land purchased by me.

méenó See *mé₂.*

méeng (2) See *méng.* nu. (T2) pandanus leaf (especially when made soft by scraping with a shell). *méngún faach* cured p. l.

-méeng Var. *-mméeng.* suf. (adj.) left handed. Syn. *kichcho.* Cf. *méng.*

méettapwir (2) See *méé-₁, ttapwir.* vi. be too high in cost or price, very expensive (in relation to expectation). *méettapwirin eey pwpwuk* the very high cost of this book. Cf. *méewátte.*

méew nu. species of snapper fish.

méewátte (1) See *méé-₁, wátte.* vi. be expensive. Syn. *méemmóng.* Ant. *méékisikiis, méékúkkún.* Cf. *méettapwir.*

mésék (2) MÉSÉKÚ. vi. be afraid.

mésékiiti See *mésék, -iti.* vo. (T2) fear, be terrified by.

mésékúta (1) See *mésék, ta.* vi. be cowardly. *emén meyi m.* a coward.

mékú (1) See *ma-, kúúkú* (?). vi. belch. [A sign of satiety in eating, but not marked as either polite or impolite behavior.] nu. (T1) belch, burp. *pwata aa ina óómw na m.?* why did you belch like that?

mékúr₁ (3a) MÉKÚRA. n. (T3) head; (fig.) hair. *eew m.* one h. *mékúran* his h. *mékúren wúsúús* knob forming the top of a breadfruit pounder. Syn. *móóng.*

Mékúr₂ nu. (loc.) Magur Island (Namonuito Atoll).

mékúrechchen (3a) See *mékúr, chchen.* Var. *mékúréchchen.* vi. be light haired, blond, red-haired. Cf. *mékúréyón.*

Mékúrechik nu. (loc.) Magererik Island (Namonuito Atoll, locally known as *Makúre'rik*).

mékúréngngaw (3b) See *mékúr, ngngaw.* vi. be stupid, silly, not smart.

mékúrépaan (3: *-panna-, -paanna-*) See *mékúr, paan₂.* vi. be bald-headed. Cf. *mékúromwor.*

mékúréchchen Var. of *mékúrechchen.*

mékúréchchow (2) See *mékúr, chchow.* vi. be patient, good tempered, self-controlled. Syn. *móngochchow.*

mékúréyón (4) See *mékúr, ón₁.* Var. *mékúróyón.* vi. be yellow-haired, blond. Cf. *mékúrechchen.*

mékúromoy See *mékúr, moy.* vi., adj. (be) gray-haired, white-haired. Cf. *mékúrotopw.*

mékúromwor (3) See *mékúr, mwor₁.* vi. be completely bald-headed. Cf. *mékúrépaan.*

mékúrotopw (2) See *mékúr, topw.* nu. (T2) grey-hairedness. *mékúrotopwun átánaan* the g.-h. of that fellow. vi. be gray-haired. Cf. *mékúromoy.*

mékúróyón Var. of *mékúréyón.*

mékkú- (2: -mmék) MÉKKÚ. ni. (T2), suf. (cc.) 1. fragment. *emmék, rúwémmék, wúnúmmék, fémmék, nimemmék, wonommék, fúúmmék, wanúmmék, ttiwemmék, engoon mékkún* one,...ten f. *mékkún kinaas* broken piece of glass. 2. lacerated wound. *mékkún chamwan* l. w. on his forehead.

mékkúkkáy (3) See *mékkú-, kkáy.* vi., adj. (be) easily shattered, fragile.

mémméngú (ds; 1) See *ménguú-.* vi. (dis.) speak, talk. Syn. *ménguúngú.*

mén₁ Var. of *meyi₂* and *mmén₁.*

mén₂ Var. *mmén₂.* adv. indeed, very, extremely. *wúwa wopwut átánaan pwú aa m. kichingngaw ngenney* I

dislike that fellow because he treated me very badly.
mén₃ (2) MÉNÚ₂. vi. blow, be a wind. *e mén efeninap* it blows from due north. nr. (T2) something blown by the wind. *ménún ákkey* burned fragment of grass or paper as blown by the wind.
-mén See *maan₁*.
ménék (2) MÉNÉKU. Var. *ménéng*. nu. (T2) mangrove swamp. *ménékún* m. s. of.
ménéng (2) MÉNÉNGÚ. Var. *ménék*. nu. (T2) mangrove swamp. *ménéngún* m. s. of.
ménéngúnéng (db; 2) See *ménéng*. vi. (dis.) be soft, spongy.
méniineemas (3) See *maan₁, nee-, maas₃*. vi. make a facial gesture consisting of a slight shake of the head, flutter of the eyelids, and flick of the eyebrows as a warning to a friend to wait and not talk ("insect in the eye"). *m. ffengen* make such gesture to one another.
ménuus (2) See *maan₁, wusu-₂*. nu. (T2) species of tiny ant that stings. *emén m.* one a.; *ewumw m.* one swarm of ants. vi. be aswarm or swarming with tiny stinging ants. *aa m. ena kkeyik* that cake is a. with ants.
ménuwó Var. of *ménúwo*.
ménú nu. scabies. vi. break out in scabies. *wúwa m.* I got scabies.
ménúúnú (db; 1) See *ma-, núú-*. vi. (dis.) be tired, fatigued.
ménúúw See *mén₃* (?), *-ú-*. vo. (T5?) pull with a jerk. *wúpwe m. een paan núú* I will pull off this coconut frond.
ménúken (2) See *mén₃, -ken*. nu. (T2) surprise raid (military).
ménúkeniiy See *ménúken, -i-₂*. vo. (T5) raid against.
ménúkot (2) MÉNÚKOTU. nu. (T2) offering to spirits. [It is made especially to *Énúún Mwáresi*, god of navigation.]
ménúkón Var. of *monukón*.
ménúmanaw (3b) See *maan₁, manaw*. nu. (T3) living creature.
ménúmén (db; 2) See *mén₃*. nu. (dis.; T2) severe storm. Cf. *cheepenikú, puunumén*. vi. blow severely (as a typhoon), be stormy.
ménúméniiti See *ménúmén, -iti*. vo. (T2) storm upon, overtake (of a strom). *aa ménúméniitikich* it storms upon us, we have been caught by a storm.

ménúmwuk (3a) See *maan₁, -mwuk*. nu. (T3) adult person.
ménún See *maan₁*.
ménúng (2) MÉNÚNGÚ. N. nu. (T2) thunder. *ménúngún nááng* sky's t. Syn. *paach₂*.
ménúté (1) See *maan₁, té₃*. F. Var. *manúté*. nu. (T1) coconut crab. *eew m., emén m.* one c. c. Syn. *amwatang, eef₂*.
ménúwo (1) See *maan₁, -wo₂*. Var. *ménuwó*. nu. (T1) 1. kind of sea eagle. 2. a mythical bird, the flapping of whose wings makes a wind that topples trees.
ménsen (2) MÉNSENI. (Eng.) nu. (T2) mainsail. *ménsenin waa* ship's m.
ménnúúki See *ma-, nnú, -ki-*. vo. (T4) forget; leave behind. *wúwa m. ááy wúpwe kkééruk nánew* I forgot to call you yesterday. *wúwa m. ááy kkewe kkiiy nnón ewe iimw* I left my keys in the house.
ménnúkamw (3b) See *maan₁, kamwa-*. N. nu. (T3) centipede. *emén m.* one c. *ménnúkamwen Chuuk* Trukese c. Syn. *ménnúpwin, niménnúké*.
ménnúkowukow (2) nu. (T2) variety of giant swamp taro (*Cyrtosperma*). [Said to have been introduced from the Marshall Islands.] *efóch m.* one t. (plant); *eféw m.* one t. (root). *fótaan m.* his t. (plant, root); *wochaan m.* his t. (to eat).
ménnúpwin (2) See *maan₁, pwin₁*. nu. (T2) centipede. *emén m.* one c. *ménnúpwinin Chuuk* Trukese c. Syn. *ménnúkamw, niménnúké*.
ménnúyepeep (3) See *maan₁* (?), *epeep₁*. nu. (T3) very large paddle canoe (with a lee platform). *efóch m.* one c. *waan m.* his c.
méng (2) MÉNGÚ. vi., adj. (be) soft, supple, pliable, deflated, springy (not stiff, rigid, or brittle). Dis. *méngúméng* (db). *aa m. óómw na táyiya* your tire has become soft. Syn. *maangúwéng*.
méngér (2) MÉNGÉRU. Var. *menger, niméngér*. nu. (T2) flying fish. *méngérún Chuuk* Trukese f. f. *ánewen m.* planet Venus as the evening star ("chaser of flying fish").
méngúú- (1) See *ma-, ngú*. unsp. sound of the human voice.
méngúúngú (db; 1) See *méngúú-*. n. (dis.; T1) 1. sounding of voice, sound of

méngúúw

voices. *méngúúngúún* his s. of v. 2. sobriquet, epithet, nickname. [Based on characteristic action or notable conduct.] *méngúúngúún Sowuféwúúp Mwéchiineesápúk, ménguúngúún Sowupaata Wumwusómwoon* the s. of Sowuféwúúp was Mwéchiineesápúk, the s. of Sowupaata was Wumwusómwoon. vi. (dis.) speak, talk. Syn. *mémméngú.* Cf. *mwénguúngú.*

ménguúw See *mengúú-*. F. vo. (T1) admire. *wú m. átenaan reen aan napanap* I a. him for his good behavior. Syn. *mengiiy.*

menguméng Dis. of *méng.*

ménguónan (3) See *méeng, nan.* n. (T3) tongue. *mengúnanan* his t. Syn. *chéennaaw, chéennékan.*

Méngúnufach See *méeng, faach.* nu. (loc.) a clan name ("pandanus leaf"). *fin M.* M. woman; *mwáán M.* M. man. *chóón M.* people of M.

ménguch (3) MÉNGÚCHA. nu. (T3) green or unripe fruit. *menguchan* its g. f. *ménguchen kangngit* green mango. vi. be green, unripe, not yet ready to be picked (of fruit). Syn. *maaraw.*

méré- See *mara-*.

mérékúukú (db; 1) See *mara-, kú₁.* nu. (T1) spark. *mérékúúkúún tengki* electric s. vi. be sparky, throw sparks (of a fire, electricity); bright (with a lot of light). *aa mmen m. ttinen nowumw na tengki* your flashlight is very sparky.

mérewún (3) See *méré-, wúún₁.* nu. (T3) body or animal hair (as a whole), fur, scales (of fish), feathers. *mérewúnan* his h. Syn. *térewún.* vi. be hairy (of body), furry, scaley, feathered. Dis. *mérewúnewún* (db).

mérewúnewún Dis. of *mérewún.*

mérúúp nu. variety of breadfruit.

mét (2) MÉTU. vi. be satisfied, sated (with food or drink).

méwúnáng (4) MÉWÚNÁNGE. nu. (T2) insect that destroys wood (probably a termite). *méwúnángin* i. of.

méwúr (2) MÉWÚRÚ. vi. sleep. *m. kunamwmwe* s. well. With dir. suf.: *méwúrúnó* go to s., fall asleep. Syn. *atún, ónnut, onnut.*

méwúriiráán (2) See *méwúr, -i-₁* or *i-₃, ráán₂.* vi. nap, sleep in the daytime.

méwúrupwut (3?) See *méwúr, pwuta-* (?). nu. (T3?) species of parrot fish.

Trukese-English

méwúrúkkin See *méwúr, kin₃.* N. nu. restless sleep, broken sleep. vi. sleep restlessly, sleep poorly due to being bothered by spirits or worries. Syn. *wonokkin.*

méwúrúnó See *méwúr.*

méwút (3) See *meyi₂, -t.* F. Var. *meyit.* prn. (interrog.) why, what for. *m. eey ruume* what is this bottle for? *m. ena?* what's that for?; *m. na mááy* what is that breadfruit for? *ngé m.* never mind; *ngé m. ii* never mind that (polite). Syn. *meyittaa, meyitte.*

-mi- (2) MI₂. suf. (v.form.) makes an object focussed verb of the base.

-mi (1) MII₁. suf. (pos.) 2pl. pos. prn.: of you (pl.); belonging to, on behalf of, for, or pertaining to you. *chcha-mi* your blood, *pwéétú-mi* your nose, *fénúwe-mi* your land.

mii (1) MII₂. nu. (T1) name of the consonant (voiced, bilabial, nasal continuant) written *m*; name of the letter thus written.

miis (2) MIISI. N., Tn. vi. lose, be beaten (in a contest). Syn. *kkuf.*

miisa (1) MIISAA. (Lat.) nu. (T1) mass (Catholic).

miiya (1) MIIYAA. nu. (T1), vi. baa, bleat (of sheep or goat). Syn. *mmáá.*

misi- (2) MISI. [In cpds. only.] unsp. gleam, shine.

misimis (db; 2) See *misi-.* vi. (dis.) be gleaming, shining. Syn. *mmis.*

misin (Eng.) nu. mission (Christian). *chóón m.* missionary.

misineri (Eng.) nu. missionary. Syn. *chóón misin.*

misiwi (1) MISIWII. nu. (T1) spring (of water). *misiwiin Romónum* s. of Romónum. Syn. *miror.*

miso (1) MISOO. (Jap. *miso*) nu. (T1) bean paste. *anan m.* his b. p. (to eat).

mina- See *meen.*

mina See *meen.* vo. (T3) do something to; fix, take care of, attend to; disturb, mess with, fool with; spoil, harm. *kesapw m. átenaan* don't harm that fellow.

minaangeni See *mina, ngeni.* vo. (T2) do something to; mess with, fool with.

minafé (1) See *meen, -fé.* vi., adj. (be) new. Syn. *seéfé.*

mine- See *meen.*

minen See *meen* (?), *-ni-.* vr. intend, mean to.

206

minik (2) MINIKI. (Eng.) nu. milk. *óóch m.* some (one indefinite amount of) m.

minich (Eng.) nu. (temp.) minute. *eew m.* one m.; *fituuw m.* how many m. *kkunók rúwáánú m. engooñ* ten m. after four o'clock; *engoon m. mwmwen kunók rúwáánú* ten m. before four o'clock.

miniwi (3) MINIWIYA. nu. (T3) a kind of seaweed (low, spreading). [Seawater is said to spring from it; it is used as sandpaper.]

miniyon (Eng.) nu. (num.) million. *eew m.* one m.; *fituuw m.* how many m.

minne N. of *menne*.

miriit (2) MIRIITI. nu. (T2) understanding, sophistication, knowledge, wisdom. *aan m.* his u.; *miriitin* u. of (something). vi. understand, be knowledgeable, be wise. *esaamwo m.* he does not yet u.; *meyi m.* he is knowledgeable.

miriitiiy See *miriit, -i-₂.* vo. (T5) understand, know. *kesaamwo m. óómw kopwe suufén ngeni inomw me somwomw* you don't yet u. that you should respect your mother and father.

miror (3) MIRORA. nu. (T3) spring (of water). *eew m.* one s. *miroren eey fénú* s. of this island. Syn. *misiwi*.

mich (2) MICHI. vi. be deceived, duped, fooled, gulled, tricked. *wúwaa m. reen átánaan* I was d. by that fellow. Syn. *tupw₂.* Cf. *michimich*.

michiiy See *mich, -i-₂.* vo. (T5) deceive, trick, fool, gull, dupe, con.

michikken (2) MICHIKKENI. Tb1. nu. (T2) clitoris. *efóch m.* one. c. *michikkenin feefin* woman's c.

michimich (db; 2) See *mich.* vi. (dis.) be a deceiver; be deceiving, tricking, duping, gulling, conning. va. deceive, trick, fool, gull, dupe, con, sweettalk.

michiyapwúra (1) MICHIYAPWÚRAA. (Jap. *mizuabura*) nu. (T1) hair oil. *eew m.* one container of h. o. *epitan m.* his h. o.; *michiyapwúraan* h. o. of.

micho (1) MICHOO. (Jap. *mizo*) nu. (T1) ditch.

mit (2) MITI₁. vi. slip, slide; be slick, slippery. With dir. suf.: *mititiw.* Syn. *ffaas*.

miti- (2) MITI₂. [In cpds. only.] unsp. smack with lips or mouth. See *emmit, emmiti₁, mitimit₁, mitinné, mitiri, mmit₁*.

mitimit₁ (db; 2) See *miti-.* vi., va. (dis.) make smacking noises with lips or mouth (as in eating or kissing); smack.

mitimit₂ (db; 2) See *mit.* vi. (dis.) be slippery, slick. Syn. *kúmitimit*.

mitinné (1) See *miti-, nné₁.* vi. eat food with a smacking and sucking of lips in appreciation of its goodness. *aa fen m. awen átemwuun ne mwéngé* that fellow surely does smack and suck with relish in eating.

mitingngaw (3) See *mit, ngngaw.* vi., adj. (be) humilated, embarassed. Cf. *meningngaw*.

mitiri See *miti-, -ri-.* Var. *mmitiri.* vo. (T4) smack upon; kiss or suck noisily. *wúwa m. peyiy* I sucked noisily on my hand.

mititiw See *mit*.

mitto (1) MITTOO. (Jap. *mitto*) nu. (T1) catcher's mitt (baseball). *eew m.* one c. m. *péwún m.* his c. m.

mo- See *ma-*.

moon (3) MONNA. vi. be supplied with firewood (of an earth oven).

moonoon (db; 4) MOONO. nu. (T2, T3) sweat, perspiration. *moonoonen inisiy, moonoonun inisiy* s. of my body. vi. perspire, sweat. Cf. *faak*.

moong (3) MONGA. nu. (T3) mucous, nasal discharge. Dis. *mongomong* (db). *mongan* his m. *mongomongen ekinissow* semen; vaginal fluid.

moor₁ (3) MORA. n. (T3) thread of coconut husk fiber, banana fiber, or hibiscus bark. *emeet moren sinifé* one strand of hibiscus thread. *moren taka* coconut t.; *moren wuuch* banana t.

moor₂ nu. head cold, chest cold, the common cold. vi. have a cold; cough. Cf. *faafa*.

mooch (3) MOOCHA. nu. (T3) hot coals; charcoal. *óóch m.* one batch of c. *moochen ááf* c. of the fire; *moochen epúnget* coconut sheath charcoal (used in making caulking).

moot (3) MOOTA. vi. be finished cooking. Syn. *ipwét*.

mosomw See *maas₁*.

momwu- (2) MOMWU. nu. (u.m.; T2) See *momwuchis, momwusich*.

momwusich F. of *momwuchis*.

momwuchis See *momwu-, -chis*. N. Var. *momwusich*. nu. (T2) mackerel.

monukón (4) See *maan₁, óno-*. F. Var. *ménúkón*. baby, infant, little child (not yet capable of walking, "lying creature"). Syn. *nooyiroch, nooyis, semiriit.*

monuponup (db; 3) See *ma-, nup.* vi. be flashing, shimmering (of reflected light, of flashing light signals).

monnotá See *mmon.*

monnow nu. a plant (said to be a kind of *fetin*). Cf. *nnow, mónnow.*

mongomong Dis. of *moong.*

mongochcha (1) See *moong, chcha.* nu. (T1) nose bleed. vi. have a nose bleed. Cf. *fongo-.*

morenikoch See *moor$_1$, -koch.* nu. thread of any kind (banana, hibiscus, etc.) used on a loom (general term).

moro- See *mara-.*

morokkun (2) See *mara-, kkun.* vi. spin, rotate, turn round and round. Dis. *morokukkun* (db). *meyi m. fénúúfaan* the earth is rotating. *aa m. taapenin enaan sepeniin* the propeller of that airplane has begun turning.

moropw (2) n. (T2) coverlet, cover, sheet. *wúfan m., moropwun* his c.

moropweey See *moropw, -e-$_2$.* N. Var. *moropwuuw.* vo. (T6b) cover with a coverlet or sheet. With dir. suf.: *moropweeyenó* c. over; (refl.) lie under a cover.

moropweeyenó See *moropweey.*

moropwuuw See *moropw, -u-.* F. Var. *moropweey.* vo. (T5) cover with a coverlet or sheet. With dir. suf.: *moropwuuwonó* c. over; (refl.) lie under a cover.

moropwuuwonó See *moropwuuw.*

moropwunopwun Dis. of *moropwpwun.*

moropwpwun (3b) See *mara-, pwpwun$_1$.* Var. *merepwpwun.* vi. flame up; flash with phosphorescence (as the sea at night); shine brightly, glare. Dis. *moropwunopwun* (db). Syn. *merettin.* nr. (T3) flashing, flaming up, phosphorescence. *moropwpwunen sáát* phosphorescence of the sea. nu. (loc.) <Bollig> a region of heaven.

mororof (3) nu. (T3) a vine (*Luffa cylindrica*). [Leaf is rubbed on ringworm and similar skin conditions to cure them. The plant is also used as a medicine to cure illness resulting from violation of *itang* prerogatives.]

morottuun (3) See *mara-, ttuun.* vi., va. revolve, rotate, spin round and round; roll fibers on the thigh so as to twist them into cordage.

morottuuna See *morottuun.* vo. (T3) spin, rotate, twirl (something); stir.

morowuk (3) See *moor$_1$, wuuk$_1$.* nu. (T3) bag made of sennit.

morowukuuk (db; 3) See *moor$_1$, wuuk$_1$.* nu. (T3) spider web. Syn. *wuken ninnim.*

mowunusa- (3a, 2) See *mé$_1$* or *ma-, wunus.* [In ptv. const. only.] ni. (T3, T2) totality, entirely. *mowunusan, mowunusun* wholly, entirely, totally. Syn. *meyinisi-.*

mowunusu- See *mowunusa-.*

moy (2) MOYI. vi. be gray, white (of hair only). *meyi m. mékúran* he is white-haired ("his head is white").

mó- See *ma-.*

mó (1) MÓÓ$_1$. vi. be gotten rid of, erased, wiped out, finished off; cured. *aa m. ááy we rimpiyo* my gonorrhea has been cured. With dir. suf.: *móónó* gotten rid of, etc.; divorced (of marriage).

móó- (1) MÓÓ$_2$. [In cpds. only.] unsp. (u.m.) See *móósich, móónap.*

móó (1) See *mó.* nu. (T1) remains, scar, site, location (of past activity, structure, etc.). *móón iimw* house site; *móón fanang* cooking site; *móón angaang* work site; *móón fanafan* adzing site. *móón ngééngé* mark of sucking kiss on neck; *móón kinaas* cut scar; *móón ipwen aramas* footprint.

móósich (2) See *móó-, -sich.* F. Var. *móóchis.* nu. (T2) finger from tip to first knuckle, first finger-joint (a unit of measure). *eew m.* one f. Cf. *móónap.*

móón (2) MÓÓNU. nu. (T2) hollow, concavity. vi. be hollow, concave.

móónap (3) See *móó-, nap.* nu. (T3) finger between tip and second knuckle (a unit of measure). *eew m.* one f. Cf. *móóchis, móósich.*

móóniyow vi. depart from a place that is not one's own. [With *wóón* or *nóón*.] *wúwa m. nóón imwen John* I have departed from John's house; *wúwa m. wóón Romónum* I have departed from Romónum. Cf. *mó.*

móónowa (1) MÓÓNOWAA. (Eng.) nu. (T1) warship, man-of-war. *efóch m.* one w. *móónowaan Merika* American w.

móónó See *mó.*

móónupis (4) See *móó, piis₁*. nu. abandoned garden site.

móónnow nu. type of hand-to-hand fighting used in disputes over the picking of breadfruit. [Refers to a plant common under breadfruit trees.]

móóng (4) MÓNGO. [More common in cpds. than as an independent word.] n. (T2) head. *móngun* his head. Syn. *mékúr*.

móóchis (2) See *móó-, -chis*. N. Var. *móósich*. nu. (T2) finger from tip to first knuckle, first finger-joint (a unit of measure). *eew m.* one f. Cf. *móónap*.

móót (4) MÓÓTO. vi. sit, be seated. Dis. *mómmóót* (ds). *m. mwmwáán* s. idle. *mómmóót ffengen* s. together. With dir. suf.: *móóttiw* sit down.

móótiisómw See *móót, -sómw*. Itang. Var. *móótiisómwoon*. vi. sit as if a chief.

móótiisómwoon (2) See *móót, sómwoon*. Itang. Var. *móótiisómw*. vi. sit as if a chief.

móótong (2, 3) MÓÓTONGU, MÓÓTONGA. nu. (T2, T3) removable board across outrigger booms between gunwhales of paddle canoe. *móótongen waa, móótongun waa* canoe's r. b.

móóttiw See *móót*.

-móów [In cpds. only.] adj. reddish brown (?). See *núúmóów*.

móówuuwa (1) MÓÓWUUWAA. vi. be exhausted (of soil). Syn. *maasuuwa*.

móówun (2) See *ma-, o-₃, wun*. nu. (T2) war, battle. *eew m.* one b. *Oruuwen Móówunun Fénúúfaan* World War II. vi. fight a war, do battle.

móówunuuw See *móówun, -u-*. vo. (T5) war against, battle against. *siya m. ewe sóópw* we warred against that district.

mósow (3) MÓSOWA. Var. *masow*. n. (T3) 1. contents, parts. *mósowan* its c. *mósowen nóón fénú meyinisin* all the c. of the land; *mósowen nóón iimw* c. of the house. 2. knowledge, expertise. *mósowan* his k. 3. member, follower, disciple. *mósowen Mácheweyichchún* followers of the *M.* school of *itang*; *mósowen ewe sense* followers (pupils) of that teacher. vi. have contents.

mósóór (4) See *maas₃, óro-*. Var. *mesóór*. nu. (loc.; T2) proximate, inner or inhabited side, lagoon side (of an island). *mósóórun fénú* island's p. s.;

wúwa fátánnó m. I walked to the p. s. Ant. *inúk₁, núkúnap*.

mósónósón (db; 4) See *ma-, són*. vi. be humble, lowly; inoffensive, meek, gentle; of quiet behavior, even tempered. *emén meyi m.* a humble man, a gentleman.

mósónósóneyiti See *mósónósón, -iti*. vo. (T2) be humble to, gentle with.

mósóroch (3) See *maas₃, roch*. Var. *mesaroch*. nu. (T3) wooziness (as when ill). vi. be woozy.

mómmóót Dis. of *móót*.

mómmón (ds; 3) See *móna-*. vi., va. (dis.) be thrown; engage in throwing; throw.

mómmór Dis. of *mór*.

món (4) MÓNO₂. Var. *mwón*. vi., adj. (be) waterproof, not leaky. *aa m. ewe waa* the canoe doesn't leak. Ant. *nnich*.

móna- (4?) MÓNO₁. [In cpds. only.] unsp. throw, cast, hurl.

móneey See *móna-, -e-₂*. vo. (T6b) throw, cast, hurl. *m. ewe pwoor* t. that ball. *kepwe m. enaan machchang ngeni eféw faaw* you will throw a stone at that bird. With dir. suf.: *móneeyenong* t. it inside; *móneeyenó* t. it away; *móneeyeto* t. it here. With n. form. suf.: *móneeya-* (ni.; T3) thing thrown to or by (someone); *móneeyey na pwoor* throw me that ball you have ("thing thrown to me that-by-you ball"); *meyi isipwich móneeyen átánaan* that fellow's throwing is speedy.

móneeya- See *móneey*.

móneeyenong See *móneey*.

móneeyenó See *móneey*.

móneeyeto See *móneey*.

mónnow nu. 1. a tree (*Acalypha trukensis*). [Wood is used for fire by friction, breadfruit picking poles and in house construction; flowers are used as eye medicine.] 2. a tree (*Acalypha wilkesiana*, a Japanese introduction). Cf. *monnow, nnow*.

móngosopwon (2) See *móóng, sopwon*. nu. (T2) fontanel, soft spot (of baby). *mógosopwonun monukón* baby's f.

móngochchow (2) See *móóng, chchow*. vi. be patient, self-controlled. Syn. *mékúréchchow*.

móngópaan (3: *-panna-*) See *móóng, paan₂*. n. (T3) baldness. *móngópannan* his b. vi. be bald. Syn. *mékúrépaan*. Cf. *mékúromwor*.

mór

mór (4) MÓRO. vi. be at low tide; evaporate, boil away. Dis. *mómmór* (ds). With dir. suf.: *mórónó* evaporate entirely, disappear. nr. (T2) evaporation. *mórun kkónik* evaporation of water.

mórónó See *mór*.

mótow nu. a kind of fish. *emén m.* one f. Cf. *mmótow*.

muusik (2) MUUSIKI. (Eng.) nu. (T2) harmonica. *eew m., efóch m.* one h. *néwún m.* his h. *muusikin Merika* American h. vi. play a harmonica. *meyi m.* he is playing a h.; *kepwe sót m.* try the h.; try to play the h.

muun (3) MUNNA, MUUNNA. nu. (T3) caterpillar, insect larva. [Eats the leaves of *kká* taro (*Alocasia*).] *emén m.* one c. *munnen Chuuk* Trukese c.

musuwe (1) MUSUWEE. adj. long ago, ancient.

mú (1) MÚÚ. vi. be full of emotion, feel pity, feel sad. Dis. *múmmú* (ds). *átewe aa mú reen ekkewe kkéén* he was filled with e. by the songs.

múú- (1) See *mú*. nr. (T1) emotion; pity. *múún meet ena?* e. about what that? *múún ááy eey pwpwos* e. of this homesickness of mine.

múúti See *mú, -ti-*. Var. *múyiti*. vo. (T4) love, pity, feel for. [Refined speech.] *múútuk* love you. Cf. *tongeey*.

músúwen nu. (temp.) 6th night of the lunar month.

múmmú Dis. of *mú*.

múnúmún (db; 2) See *mmún*. adj. involving the upper back or shoulders (in *áámúnúmún* swim the crawl).

múyiti Var. of *múúti*.

mma (1v) MMAA. nu. (T1v) premasticated food for infants. *emma* one mouthful of p. f. *anan m.* his p. f. (to eat).

-mma (1) See *mma*. suf. (cc.) mouthful of premasticated food. *emma, rúwémma, wúnúmma, fémma, nimemma, wonomma, fúúmma, wanúmma, ttiwemma, engoon* one,...ten m.

mmaani Var. of *mmááni*.

mmas₁ (3) MMASA₁. Var. *mmás*. vi. have opened, have bloomed (of a flower or a clam). *aa m. ena péén irá* that flower has bloomed. With dir. suf.: *mmasónó* have o. forth.

mmas₂ (dc; 3) See *maas₃*. vi. stand watch. *chóón m.* guard, watchman. *chóón mmasen siipw* shepherd.

mmas₃ (3) MMASA₂. nu. (u.m.) See *kúúnumas, nikúwenimmas*.

mmasa See *mmas₂*. vo. (T3) watch over, guard. Dis. *mammasa* (ds).

mmasónó See *mmas₁*.

mmak (3a) MAKKA. (Eng. *mark*) nu. (T3) writing. *aan m.* his w. (cf. *makkeya-*). *makken perees* printed w., printed-style w.; *makken ráán annim* script or cursive w.; *makken wóón paan núú* long hand printing style of w.; *mmakken wóón pááney* carved w. (as initials or names) on a dried frond; printing form of w. (as distinct from cursive); *makken wóón perees* printed type-script. va., vi. write; be written. *m. wóón naam* signal by blinker lights.

mman (3) MMANA, MANNA₂. nu. (T3) first light of dawn. *aa té mmanen ráán* the dawn of day has crept (forth). *aa piinó ewe m.* the dawn has spread forth. vi. dawn. With dir. suf.: *mmanenó* dawn forth.

mmanenó See *mman*.

mmang (3) MMANGA. vi., adj. (be) slow, late, tardy, dilatory. Dis. *mammang* (ds). With dir. suf.: *mammangoto* come late or slowly. ni. (T3) slowness, lateness, tardiness. *mmangan* his s. With dir. suf.: *mmangoto* (nu.;T1) late arrival; *aan m.* his l. a.; *mmangotoon átánaan* that fellow's l. a.

mmangen See *mmang, -ni-*. vr. be slow in, late in, a long time in; delay in. *kete m. mómmóót pwú ese metek sékúrumw* do not be a long time in sitting so that your back will not hurt.

mmangeni See *mmang, -ni-*. vo. (T6a) be as slow as, as late as, as tardy as. *kepwe chék m. mmangey* you will just be as late as me ("as slow as my slowness").

mmangeyiti See *mmang, -iti*. vo. (T2) be late to (in arriving at). *aa m. aach we mwiich* he was l. to our meeting.

mmangoto See *mmang*.

mmach (dc; 3) See *macha-*. n. (T3) boil (on the skin). *eféw m.* one b. *mmachan* his b. vi., adj. 1. have a boil (on the skin); (be) swollen. 2. be very ripe (of anything). Dis. *mammach* (ds). *aa m. enaan mangko* that mango is v. r.

mmacheyiti See *mmach, -iti*. vo. (T2) get ripe by (a certain date). *enaan wuuch meyi toongeni m. Kirisimas* that stalk of bananas may be ripe by Christmas.

Trukese-English

mmat (3) MMATA. nu. (T3) low tide. vi. be at low tide. Syn. *kkot*. Ant. *kkún*.

mmaw (3) MMAWA. vi., nu. (T3) yawn. *aan m.* his y.

mmáá (1) MMÁÁ. nu. (T1), vi. baa, bleat (of sheep or goat). *mmáán* b. of. Syn. *miiya*.

mmááni See *mma, -ni-*. Var. *mmaani*. vo. (T4) feed with premasticated food. With n. form. suf.: *mmááníya-* (ni.; T3) food premasticated by (someone).

mmááníya- See *mmááni*.

mmás E.Wn. of *mmas*₁.

mmen Var. of *meyi*₂ and *mmén*₂.

mmer vi. be partially clear, murky (of sea water in the area between shallow and deep water. *sipwe attaw ikeey pwe meyi m.* we are going to fish here because it is murky.

-mmech N. of *-meech*.

mmey (dc; 2) See *meyi-*. vi. be stretched taut, pulled tight. *meyi m. ena kkumi* that rubber band is stretched taut. Cf. *wey*.

-mmééng (dc) Var. *-mééng*. suf. (adj.) left handed. See *kkónomméeng*.

mmék (dc; 2) See *mékkú-*. vi. be shattered, broken to pieces; break into pieces, (of glass, globular containers, dishes, etc.). *aa m. ewe kkap* the cup has been broken to pieces. Syn. *rup*₁. Cf. *pwúún*₁, *mwmwú*.

-mmék See *mékkú-*.

mmén₁ Var. of *meyi*₂.

mmén₂ (dc) See *mén*₂. Var. *mmen*. qlf. very, extremely, indeed. *aa mmén ééch ráánich eey nóón eey pwinin* it is v. nice weather we are having tonight ("it is v. nice this our day tonight").

mménú (dc; 1) See *ma-, nnú.* vi. be tired, fatigued. Syn. *ménúúnú*.

mméréwú- (2) unsp. flattered. See *émméréwú*.

mmis (dc; 2) See *misi-*. vi., adj. shine, gleam; be shiny, glossy, gleaming (as of greased hair or certain types of cloth, polished steel, etc.). Dis. *misimis* (db).

mmit₁ (dc; 2) See *miti-*. nu. (T2) smacking, (of lips, or mouth). *mmitin awey* s. of my mouth. vi. smack or make a loud kissing noise; be smacked. Dis. *mitimit* (db). *aa mmit awey* my mouth smacked.

mmit₂ (dc; 2) See *mit*. vi. slip, slide, glide. Dis. *mitimit*₂ (db). With dir. suf.: *mmititiw*.

mmititiw See *mmit*₂.

mmon (3) MONNA. vi. be prepared, ready. *kaa m. reen óómw kepwene ónnut?* are you ready to go to sleep? With dir. suf.: *monnotá.* ni. (T3) preparation. *monnan* its p. Cf. *ómmón*.

mmóng (4) MMÓNGO. vi., adj. (be) big, large, on a large scale, huge. [Preferred when siblings of opposite sex or parent and child of opposite sex are both within hearing.] *mwéngé m.* eat heavily. ni. (T2) bigness, large size. *mmóngun eey mettóóch* the big size of this thing. Syn. *wátte*. Ant. *nginingiin, kisikiis*.

mmótow nu. large species of *Pectropomus* fish. *emén m.* one P. f. Cf. *mótow*.

mmún (2) MÚNNÚ. nu. (T2) upper back, back of the shoulder. *múnniy., munnumw, múnnún* my, your, his u. b.

MW

-mw (2) MWU. [Has the effect of backing and rounding the final vowel of the base to which it is suffixed.] **suf.** (pos.) of you (sg.), of thee; belonging to, on behalf of, for, pertaining to you. *chchaa-mw* or *chchayó-mw* your blood, *pwéétu-mw* or *pwootu-mw* your nose, *fénúwo-mw* your land.

mwa- (3b: *mwa-, mwá-, mwe-, mwé-, mwo-, mwó-*) MWA. **pref.** (adj.) having a variable condition, as with oscillatory movement, variegated surface, etc. Cf. *che-, ma-*.

mwa Tn. of *mwaa₁*.

-mwa (1) MWAA₃. [In cpds. only.] **unsp.** (u.m.) See *nissimwa*.

mwaa₁ (1) MWAA₁. Var. *mwa*. **qlf.** indeed, so, really. [Used after kinship terms in cursing.] *mw.* meet what, indeed? exactly what? What do you know? how about that?; *mw. pwata* why indeed? *emén chééyiro mwaa átánaan* a real *chééyiro* he *áá mw. áá?* or *ee mw. áá?* Isn't that so?

mwaa₂ (1) MWAA₂. Tb1. **n.** (T1) vagina. *mwaan* her v.; v. of. *pwangen mw.* vaginal orifice.

mwaas (3) MWASA. Tb1. **n.** (T3) stench. Dis. *mwasamwas* (db). *mwasan* his s. *mwasen inomw* (Tb1) the s. of your mother (a curse that requires retaliation in fighting); *mwasen iiy ne, mwasen iiy, mwasamwasen iiy* (Tb2) the s. of it (a milder curse).

mwaak (3) MWAKKA. **nu.** (T3) large strand tree (*Pisonia grandis*). [Its soft wood is used for firewood.] *mwakken Chuuk* Trukese *Pisonia*.

mwaar (3) See *mwa-, ar.* **vi.** be astonished (positively), delighted, entertained, filled with admiration, rapt in admiration. *wúwa mw. reer* I am a. by them. **ni.** (T3) astonishment. *pwata ina mwaarumw na* why are you astonished? (why your a.?).

mwaareyiti See *mwaar, -iti.* **vo.** (T2) admire, praise, glorify.

mwaat (3) See *mwa-, ata-.* **vi., adj.** (be) quick, fast.

mwaataat (db; 3) See *mwa-, -at₃.* **n.** (T3) rustling (of leaves and fronds); making a rustling, rubbing, or splashing noise. *mwaataatan* its r. **vi.** (c.) rustle; make a rustling, rubbing, or splashing noise.

mwaaw (3b) See *mwa-, aaw₁.* **vi., adj.** (be) humble, deferential.

mwas (3) See *mwaas.* Tb1. **vi., adj.** stink, smell badly (especially in relation to the odor of unwashed genitals); stinking. [Used with reference to someone's mother, it is a challenge to fight and an insult of the highest order.] Dis. *mwasamwas* (db). Cf. *eeng.*

mwasamwas Dis. of *mwaas, mwas*.

mwasiin Var. of *mwesiin*.

mwaken (3) MWAKENA. **n.** (T3) lie, prevarication. *mwakenan* his l. *mwakenomw!* you're kidding! With intens. suf.: *mwakenekkich* (n.; T2) big l.; *mwakenekkichin* his b. l. With dir. suf.: *mwakenetá* (n.; T1) making up a l.; *mwakenetáán* his m. up a l. **vi.** lie, prevaricate; be false. With intens. suf.: *mwakenekkich* tell a big l. With dir. suf.: *mwakenetá* make up a l.

mwakeneken (db; 3) See *mwa-, kena.* **vi.** 1. be incised, having incised designs. 2. have many colors, be variegated.

mwakenekkich See *mwaken*.

mwakenetá See *mwaken*.

-mwan (3) MWANA. [In cpds. only.] **unsp.** (u.m.) See *neemwan*.

mwanú (1) MWANÚÚ. [In cpds. only.] **unsp.** (u.m.) See *neemwanú*.

mwangerenger (db; 3) See *mwa-, nger* (?). **vi., adj.** (be) tiny and profuse (as fine print or extremely fine weaving).

-mwar (3) MWARA₁. [In cpds. only.] **adj.** uncertain. Dis. *-mwaramwar* (db).

mwara- (3) MWARA₂. N. Var. *mwári-*. **unsp.** something carried on the shoulders (as a burden) or worn around the neck or head (as a garland).

mwaramwar₁ (db; 3) MWARA₃. N. **nu.** (T3) a yellow reef fish. Syn. *mwaramwen*.

mwaramwar₂ (db; 3) See *-mwar.* **vi., adj.** (be) uncertain; uncertainly; vague. *fóós mwaramwar* speak with uncertainty; *núkúuw mwaramwar* believe it with uncertainty. *itá wúpe feyinnó neesor ngé wúwa mw. pwún meyi chóómmóng ááy angaang* I hope to depart tomorrow but I am u. because there is a lot of work for me to do. *ke sapw mw. nóón óómw pwóróówus* do not be vague in your account.

mwaramwar₃ N. of *mwárámwár* (see *mwara-*).

mwarangarang (db; 3b) See *mwa-, rang₂*. vi. be rough, bristly, spiny; stiff and frizzy (of hair); rough to eye as well as touch. Ant. *mwotowutow*. Cf. *maataat*.

mwareey N. of *mwáreey* (see *mwara-*).

mwareton (3) See *mwara-, toon*. nu. (T3) a throw (in fighting) in which one catches a person by the hands and throws him forward from behind one's back over one's shoulder.

Mwariirong nu. (pers.) a traditional storm goddess. [One of five children of the weather (*néwún ráán*), who live in the gale, sink boats in heavy seas, and blow down trees.]

mwaror See *mwa-, -ror*. unsp. (u.m.) See *Sowumwaror*.

mwaché (1) See *mwa-, chéé₁*. vi. be shaded, overshadowed (of growing plants and crops). *pwata iyeey mwachéén eey irá?* why is this tree shaded?

mwata (1) MWATAA. vi., adj. (be) nimble or speedy in climbing.

mwatún (2) See *mwa-, túnú-*. Var. *mwétún*. nu. (T2) a preparation of food consisting of breadfruit, taro, or other starchy base with coconut cream added.

mwatúnúúw See *mwatún, -ú-*. vo. (T5) add coconut cream to. *etto wúpwe mw. onomw na rayis* come here and I will add c. c. to your rice.

mwawúchúúch (db; 2) See *mwa-, wúchúúch₁*. vi. flap, wave, bounce up and down (of wings in flight, tree branches in wind, a boat in a rough sea), jiggle.

mwayisa (1) MWAYISAA. nu. (T1) orientation of mind, attitude, preoccupation (especially in relation to living or dying). *pween mw*. know divination to determine a sick person's attitude.

mwayin (Eng.) nu. mile. *eew mw*. one m.; *fituuw mw*. how many m.

mwáán₁ (4) MWÁÁNE. nu. (T2) adult man (from middle age to when he begins to become feeble with old age). *emén mw*. one a. m. *aan mw*. his older male lineage mate (of a male), his sublineage head; *néwún mw*. his adult son. *mw. nipich* unmarried man. Ant. *feefin*. Cf. *mwááni-, napa-*. vi. be or become an adult man. Cf. *mwááneyán*. adj. male (of animals); right (of a side, as opposed to left). Ant. *feefin*.

Mwáán₂ See *mwáán₁*. nu. (loc.) name of a district on Wééné (Moen) Island, from which the English name of the island is derived. [It is situated on the right hand side of the island as one faces down wind. Mwáánitiw (West Mwáán) is similarly situated on Wútéét (Udot), and the districts named Peniyamwáán (Mwáán side) are on the right side of the smaller islands of Párem (Perem) and Fanapenges (Fala Beguets) as one faces them from the neighboring larger islands with which they are geographically and politically associated. The meaning of the name is now interpreted in the sense of "adult man" rather than "right" ("man side"), because an adult man is said to be capable of all things and to be the most resourceful of persons, and Mwáán is the district of Truk most endowed with all kinds of food resources and, traditionally, a place to which others resort in times of hunger.]

mwááneson (3) See *mwáán₁, son*. Tb3 nu. (T3) putting down; disdain, contempt for others; behavior or action expressive of disdain; making a mockery of people and social customs. [*mwáánewús* is preferred over this word in the presence of brother and sister, father and daughter, and mother and son.] *aan mw*. his p. d. behavior. Syn. *mwáánewús*. Cf. *namanam tekiya, mwááneyas*.

mwáánewús (2) See *mwáán₁, wúsú-*. nu. (T2) putting down; disdain, contempt for others; behavior or action expressive of disdain; making a mockery of people and social customs. [Preferred over *mwááneson* when siblings of opposite sex or parent and child of opposite sex are both within hearing.] *aan mw*. his p. d. behavior. Syn. *mwááneson*. Cf. *mwááneyas, namanam tekiya*.

mwááneyas (3b) See *mwáán₁, aas₁.* nu. (T3) disrespectful behavior, arrogance, behavior that disregards the presence or status of others. Cf. *mwááneson, mwáánewús, namanam tekiya.*

mwááneyán (db; 4) See *mwááni-.* F. vi. be brother and sister. *mw. ffengen* be b. and s. to one another. va. treat (someone) as a brother (by a woman). Syn. *mwongeyang.*

mwááni- (4) See *mwáán₁.* F. ni. (T2) brother, cousin (of a woman); any consanguineal male relative of a woman reckoned in her generation. *mwáánin* her b.

mwáániinúk (2) See *mwáán₁, núkú-₁.* n. (T2) younger brother (of a male), younger lineage mate (of a male). *mwáániinúkún* his younger b.

mwáániichi (1) See *mwáán₁, -ichi.* nu. (T1) eldest brother in a set of siblings; eldest male in a generation in a lineage or sublineage; senior male in a lineage or sublineage.

Mwáánitiw See *Mwáán₂, -tiw.* nu. (loc.) a district on Wútéét (Udot) Island ("West Mwáán").

mwáániyen (db; 2) See *mwa-, eniyen.* nu. (T2) dizziness. *aan mw.* his d. *mwáániyenin mékúrey* d. of my head. vi. be dizzy.

mwáánninó See *mwmwáán.*

mwááng (2) MWÁÁNGI. nu. (T2) sprain, strain, or similar physical injury. *mwááŋgin peyiy* s. of my hand. vi. be sprained, etc; *aa mw. pecheey* my leg has been s.

mwáár (4) MWÁRE. [Rare form.] n. (T2) something carried on or pertaining to the shoulders; garland, lei, necklace; (by extension) crown; collar. *mwárin* his g. *mwárin feeyis* collar bone, clavicle. *mwárin irááfénúfén* crown of thorns. See the more common *mwárámwár.*

mwánek (3) See *mwa-, nek.* vi. be elated, stirred with joy; excited with happy anticipation. With dir. suf.: *mwáneketá. átewe aa mwáneketá reen ewe kkéén* he was e. by the song.

mwánekenek (db; 3) See *mwa-, nek.* vi. wobble, move rapidly back and forth (as a device on an engine).

mwáneketá See *mwánek.*

mwánenep nu. a sea cucumber.

mwánninó See *mwmwáán.*

mwárá (1) MWÁRÁÁ. vi. sponge or cadge food from people frequently. With intens. suf.: *mwáráákkich* (vi.; T2) be a big sponger or cadger of food.

mwáráákkich See *mwárá.*

mwárááyiti See *mwárá, -iti.* vo. (T2) sponge or cadge food from.

mwáráfach Var. of *mwárefach.*

mwárámwár (db; 4) See *mwáár.* Var. *mwaramwar₃.* nu. (T2) garland, lei, necklace; crown, wreath. *mwárin mw.* his g. va. wear (a garland, etc.). Cf. *mwárini.*

mwáreey See *mwári-, -e-₂.* Var. *mwareey.* vo. (T6b) carry on the shoulders, put on or around one's shoulders. Syn. *ámwmwára.*

mwárefach (3a) See *mwáár, faach.* Var. *mwáráfach.* n. (T3) species of surgeon fish (*Acanthurus olivaceus* Bloch and Schneider; orange spot on tang and neck). [Head used in scenting coconut oil in former times.] *mwárefachen Chuuk* Trukese s. f.

mwáresi N. of *mwárisi.*

mwárenong (3) See *mwári-, -nong.* vi. put one's shoulder under (with *faan*).

mwárepwu (3) See *mwáár, pwuwa-.* nu. (T3) condition in which the umbilical cord is twisted around the neck of a human fetus. vi. be twisted around the neck of a fetus (of the umbilical cord).

mwári- (4) See *mwáár.* Var. *mwara-.* ni. (T2) something carried on the shoulders (as a burden) or worn around the neck or head (as a garland, necklace, crown). [Used in possessive and relational constructions.] *mwárin* his shoulder burden, garland, etc.

mwárisi (1) See *mwáár, -si.* F. Var. *mwáresi.* nu. (T1) rainbow. *mwárisiin náang* rainbow in the sky. *énúún mw.* god of the rainbow, god of *pénú. aa wú mw.* a rainbow has appeared ("stood"). Syn. *resiim.*

mwárini See *mwáár, -ni-.* vo. (T5) acquire a garland, lei, necklace, crown. Cf. *mwárámwár.*

mwácheenap (3) See *mwa-, che, -nap.* vi. unthinkingly break something or mess something up because one's attention is directed elsewhere, be inattentive to what one is doing. *mw. ngeni* be inattentive towards.

mwácheeni See *mwa-, che, -ni-*. Tb3 vo. (T4) fool around with, play with. *ke te mwácheenuk* don't play with yourself (i.e., don't play with your genitals); *ke te mw. na naam* don't f. with that lamp.

mwáchey (3) MWÁCHEYA. n. (T3) deformity. *mwácheyan* his d. vi., adj. be deformed, misshapen.

mwe Var. of *mwo₂*.

-mwe (1) MWEE. suf. (u.m.) an element in place names. *Pisamwe* Pisamoe Islet; *Wonomwe* Onamue Islet.

mween (2) MWENI. nu. (T2) mainsheet (of sailing canoe). *mwenin waa* canoe's m. Cf. *wáánimwen*.

mweeriker₁ (db; 2) See *mwa-, -eri₁*. nu. (T2) rough coconut basket for fish, taro, or fermented breadfruit. *eew mw. one b. aan mw.* his b.

Mweeriker₂ (db; 2) See *mweeriker₁*. nu. (T2) the constellation Pleiades; a sidereal month in the traditional calendar.

mweerikeriiy See *mweeriker₁, -i-₂*. vo. (T5) put (something) in a *mweeriker* basket.

mwesi (3) MWESIYA. Var. *mwmwesi*. vi. sneeze.

mwesiin (3) MWESIINNA. (Eng.) Var. *mwasiin*. nu. (T3) machine, engine, motor. *mw. otokun* hand-turned sewing machine; *mw. pwuupwu* pedal-operated sewing machine. *mwesinnen Merika* American m.; *mwesiinnen teete* sewing machine; *mwesiinnen tengki* generator (electric).

mwekinikin (db; 2) See *mwa-, kiin₁*. F. nu. (T2) tickling. *mwekinikinin naan semiriit reen átánaan* the t. of that baby by that fellow. vi. be tickled.

mwen (2?) vi., adj. (be) crippled from birth. Cf. *mwmwék*.

mweneene (db; 1) See *mwa-, nee-* (?). vi. be destitute, very poor, indigent; without property, family or possessions; bereft of everything.

mweniik (3) MWENIIKA. nu. (T3) species of wrasse fish. *mweniiken Chuuk* Trukese w. f.

mwereng (2) MWERENGI. nu. (T2) a kind of coral. [Its branches are short and close together.]

mwechen (2) See *mwa-, cheni-*. Var. *mwochen*. va. desire, want. *kese mw.* if you please, please ("don't you want").

n. (T2) desire. *aan mw., mwechenin* his d.

mwecheniya (1) See *mwechen, aa-*. Var. *mwocheniya*. n. (T1) unreasonable desire; desire for what is not appropriate, covetousness, greed. *mwecheniyaan* his d. vi. have an unreasonable desire; covet. *aa mw. reen* he has an unreasoned impetuous desire for (on account of) it.

mwecheyinap (3a) See *mwechen, nap*. nu. (T3) ambition. vi. be ambitious.

mwet (3a) MWETA. Var. *mwmwet*. vi. 1. jump, spring, leap. Dis. *mwetemwet* (db) bounce up and down, be bouncy. With dir. suf.: *mwetetá, mwetewu*. Syn. *nus*. 2. take first place in competition, win.

mweteey See *mwet, -e-₂*. vo. (refl.; T6b) 1. (with *wóón*) jump or leap over or onto. *wúwa mweteeyey wóón átánaan* I jumped over that fellow. 2. (without *wóón*) be outstanding, first rate. *kaa mweteyok* you are o.

mwetemwet Dist. of *mwet, mwmwet*.

mwetetá See *mwet*.

mwetewu See *mwet*.

mwetikitik (db; 2) See *mwa-, tiki-*. vi. be very tiny.

mweyán (4) MWEYÁNE. nu. (T2?) a *mwatún* made from chunks of breadfruit, banana, or *Cyrtosperma* that have been boiled in a tridacna shell. vi. make *mweyán*. Cf. *áni-*.

mweyáneey See *mweyán, -e-₂*. vo. (T6b) make (breadfruit, banana, or *Cyrtosperma*) into *mweyán*.

mweyir (3?) MWEYIRA (?). nu. (T3?) traditional dance of exhultation. [Done only by women.] Cf. *emweyir*.

mwé (1) MWÉÉ. vi. kneel (on one or two knees); alight (of birds, airplanes, spirits). With dir. suf.: *mwéétiw*.

mwéék (2) MWÉKÚ. nu. (T2) arrowroot (*Tacca leontopetaloides*). [Formerly cultivated, its roots were made into a starch flour, from which a tapioca-like pudding was made.] Dis. *mwékúmwék* (db).

mwéémwé (db; 1) See *mwé*. vi. (dis.) be lame, halt; limp.

mwéén (2) MWÉÉNÚ. nu. (T2) species of squirrel fish (*Myripristis*; red and large-eyed). *mwéénún Chuuk* Trukese s. f.

mwéech (2) See *mwéch*. n. (T2) gift to a sweetheart (to hold his or her affections). Dis. *mwéchúmwéch* (db). *mwéchún ngeniyey* her g. to me.

mwéétiw See *mwé*.

Mwékin nu. (loc.) Mokil Island and Atoll (Eastern Caroline Islands).

mwékúmwék Dis. of *mwéék*.

mwékút (2) See *mwa-, -kút*. vi. move. Dist. *mwékútúkút* (db) be in motion, move about, run (as an engine).

mwékútúkút Dis. of *mwékút*.

mwékkú- (2) See *mwa-, kkú-*. N. [In cpds. only.] ni. (T2), suf. (cc.) bit or morsel (of mashed food). *emwmwék, rúwémwmwék, wúnúmwék, fémwmwék, nimemwmwék, wonomwmwék, fúúmwmwék, wanúmwmwék, ttiwemwmwék, engoon mwékkún* one,...ten b. Syn. *-pwey*.

mwékkún (2) See *mwa-, -kkún*. vi., adj. (be) small, little. Syn. *kúkkún*. Cf. *mwékkú-*.

mwékkúnong See *mwmwék*.

mwékkúnó See *mwmwék*.

mwénúú- (1) MWÉNÚÚ. ni. (T1), suf. (cc.) ell, length from elbow to fingertips. *emwénú, rúwémwénú, wúnúmwénú, fémwénú, nimemwénú, wonomwénú, fúúmwénú, wanúmwénú, ttiwemwénú, engoon mwénúún* one,...ten e.

mwénúnnúr (ds; 2) See *mwa-, nnúr₂*. vi., adj. (be) disguised, in code (of talk or messages). *kkapas mw*. talk that conceals the true meaning from all but its intended hearer, coded message.

mwéngé (1) MWÉNGÉÉ. nu. (T1) food (any cooked starchy food, bread, any leafy vegetable, cooked or uncooked, cooked fish, copra; but *not* uncooked bananas or other fruit, uncooked fish, or cooked or uncooked meat, for which see *wochooch, wocheey, wochaa-*). *anan mw*. his f. (to eat); *aan mw*. his f. (to present or sell to others, or for purposes other than to consume it personally). *mwéngéén neeyónowas* lunch, noon meal. vi. eat. *siya mw*. let us eat.

mwéngéénap (3a) See *mwéngé, nap*. nu. (T3) festive meal, banquet, feast. Syn. *fótónap*.

mwéngéépaat (3) See *mwéngé, paat₂*. vi. eat continually, eat between meals. Syn. *mwéngéfföch*.

mwéngééturunuffas (3) See *mwéngé, turunuffas*. nu. (T3) bad manners in eating. vi. eat in a way that disregards social conventions, be unmannerly in eating; eat mischievously.

mwéngéfföch (3b) See *mwéngé, -fföch*. nu. (T3) eat between meals, eat all the time, eat continually. Syn. *mwéngéépaat*.

mwéngémmóng (2) See *mwéngé, mmóng*. vi. eat heavily.

mwéngúúngú (db; 1) See *mwa-, ngú*. vi. (dis.) make vocal sound; groan, moan Cf. *méngúúngú*.

mwéngúnúngún (2) See *mwa-, ngúnúngún*. nu. (T2) whisper. vi., adj. whisper, speak very softly so that no one will hear; (be) whispering.

mwérúúw MWÉRÚÚ (?). vo. (T1?) strike, slay, kill (a person or living creature). *mwérúúwey, mworuuk* s. me, you (sg.). With dir. suf.: *mwérúúwetiw*. Syn. *awata, nengeey*.

mwérúúwetiw See *mwérúúw*.

mwéch (2) MWÉCHÚ. vi., adj. (be) held, fastened, stuck; (be) staying in one place; (be) restrained. *aa mw*. he is restrained; *meyi mw*. it is stuck. With dir. suf.: *mwéchúnó* be held fast.

mwéchúmwéch Dis. of *mwéech*.

mwéchúmwéchiiti (db) See *mwéch, -iti*. vo. (dis.; T2) stick to, hold fast to, keep to (of one task or responsibility at the expense of other tasks and responsibilities).

mwéchúmwéchútiw (db; 3) See *mwéch, -tiw*. vi. (dis.) stay or remain where one is; fail to progress; be left behind.

mwéchúni See *mwéech, -ni-*. vo. (T5) acquire (something) as a gift to one's sweetheart.

mwéchúnó See *mwéch*.

mwétún Var. of *mwatún*.

-mwéw (2) MWÉWÚ. [In cpds. only.] unsp. (u.m.) See *núkúmwéw*. Cf. *mwmwéw*.

mwéwúkkay nu. (T3) a tree (*Guettarda* sp.). [Wood used for bowls and platters.] Syn. *mwoosor*.

mwéwúnéwún (db; 3a) See *mwa-, wún₃*. Var. *mwmwéwún₂*. vi. swing back and forth, wag (as of a hanging object or a tail); flap. Cf. *nikéwúnéwún, nikémwmwéwún*.

mwéwúch (2) See *mwa-, wúchú-₁*. vi. be startled (as by a sudden noise).

mwéwúchúúch (db; 2) See *mwa-*, *wúchú-*₁. vi. (dis.) jiggle up and down. Cf. *mwawúchúúch*.

mwi (3a) MWIYA. vi., adj. have a cough; (be) breathless, out of breath; (be) asthmatic. *epwene peenó reen aanú mwi* he is going to die from his being asthmatic.

-mwi (1) MWII₁. [In cpds. only.] n. (u.m.; T1) See *awenimwi*.

mwii₁ (1) MWII₂. nu. (T1) starling (small, black bird). *emén mw.* one s. *mwiin Chuuk* Trukese s. Syn. *ángá*.

mwii₂ (1) MWII₃. nu. (T1) name of the consonant (velarized, voiced, bilabial, nasal continuant) written *mw*; name of the digraph thus written.

mwiik (3) MWIKKA, MWIIKA. nu. (T3) pepper plant (*Capsicum frutescens*); hot pepper. [Pounded fruit used as a condiment in food.] *mwikken Chuuk, mwiiken Chuuk* Trukese *mw.*. vi. be peppery, hot. *aa mw. noón awach* it gets p. in our mouths.

mwiir [In this form in idiomatic usage only.] Var. *mwir*. vi. Id. *mw. me sóópw* give word before and after (of one's activity); *si pwe mw. me sóópw ngeni sómwoon* we shall give word b. and a. to the chief.

mwiich (3) MWIICHA. nu. (T3) meeting, gathering of people for any purpose, group, team, class. *mwiichen aramas* gathering of peoples; *mwiichen kkéén* singing group, choir; *mwiichen itewumw* group for carrying *mwatún* to a chief; *mwiichen móówun* army, navy, airforce, military band or group of any kind, war party; *mwiichen sochungiyo* graduation exercise. vi. meet, assemble. Cf. *iyoyi*.

mwiichepin (2) See *mwiich, pin*. Var. *mwiichipin*. nu. (T2) church meeting.

mwiichipin Var. of *mwiichepin*.

mwiiy (3) See *mwi*. n. (T3) cough; asthma; breathlessness, panting. *mwiyan* his c.

mwikkeey See *mwiik, -e-*₂. vo. (T6b) make peppery; put pepper on.

mwin (3) MWINA. vi. go or come in company, go together. Dist. *mwinemwin* (db.) stay together. *wú pwe mw. me emén* I shall go with someone; *si pwe mw.* we shall go together. Cf. *mwiich*.

mwinemwin Dist. of *mwin*.

mwir (2) MWIRI₁. Var. *mwiir*. vi. inform before hand, ask permission. [Used only in the expression *mw. mé wóó-*.] *mw. mé wóóy* ask my p. Cf. *mwiri-*.

mwiri- (2) MWIRI₂. ni. (prep.; T2) after, behind, following, subsequent; aft, stern (of a boat); past (in telling time). Dis. *mwirimwiri-* (db) following; continuation, continual recurrence. *mwirin* after him; thereafter, afterwards, later; *mwirimwirin* junior or younger member, membership, or generation (in a lineage). *tettenin mwirin* the subsequent generation.

mwiriitupw (2) See *mwiri-, tupw*₁. nu. (T2) afterglow in sky immediately following sunset ("after-set"). [A symbol of beauty.] *mwiriitupwun akkar* afterglow of the sun. *wupwutiwen noón eeni mman éfékúren noón een mw.* born in the dawn-glow and sired in the afterglow (a phrase in love-talk describing a woman's beauty). Syn. *séé*.

mwiriiy See *mwiri-, -i-*₂. vo. (T5) 1. resemble, look like, take after. 2. steer. 3. be the hindermost of; be the anchor-man of (a relay team).

mwirifóchófóch (db; 4) See *mwiri-, fócha-*. vi. be last (as of canoes or people in a line). ni. (T2, T3) last one (in a line). [In ptv. const. only.] *mwirifóchófóchan* (N.), *mwirifóchófóchun* (F.) last (of it).

mwirisefáán See *mwiri-, sefáán*. vi. retrace one's course or steps.

mwirisefáániiy See *mwirisefáán, -i-*₂. vo. (T5) return (a ship) to its course.

mwirimwir (db; 2) See *mwiri-*. n. (T2) steering device. *mwirimwirin* its s. d. *mwirimwirin chitosa* automobile's steering wheel; *mwirimwirin paasiken* bicycle's handlebar; *mwirimwirin waa* boat's tiller, ship's wheel, helm. ni. (T2) continuation (of something), continual recurrence (of something); descendents (of someone), subsequent or junior generations (of a lineage). va. (with *wóón*) steer. *wúpwe mw. wóón eey waa* I shall steer on this boat.

mwirin See *mwiri-*.

Mwiriné nu. (loc.) Murilo Atoll and Island (Hall Islands).

mwirinóó- (1) See *mwiri-, -nó*. ni. (loc., temp.; T1) after the end of (something):

mwirinné (1) See *mwiri-, nné₁*. F. Var. *mwurinné, mwúrinné.* vi., adj. (be) good, pretty, fine, nice. *mw. seni* better than; *mw. seni meyinisin* best; *fóókkun mw.* very g.

mwiringngaw (3b) See *mwiri-, ngngaw.* vi. do something before an undertaking that will bring it bad luck.

mwirichchik (2) See *mwiri-, -chchik.* vi. be very last, last of it all. ni. (T2) very last (of something). [In ptv. const. only.] *mwirichchikin* the v. l. of it.

mwichimwich Var. of *mwmwich*.

mwittir (2) MWITTIRI. vi., adj. 1. (be) quick, fast, speedy, early; hurry. With dir. suf.: *mwittirito* hurry here. Syn. *kkay, kkáy.* Ant. *mmang.* Cf. *atapwan, atawat.* 2. win a race. Ant. *sun, mwú.* ni. (T2) quickness, speed. *pwata ina mwittirimi?* why are you (pl.) in a hurry? ("why that quickness of yours?").

mwittirito See *mwittir*.

mwiyak (3) See *mwi, -k₂.* nu. (T3) asthma; bad coughing, coughing sickness. *aan mw.* his c.

mwiyemwi (db; 3a) See *mwi.* n. (T3) asthma, breathlessness, serious coughing, coughing sickness (tuberculosis), dyspepsia, breathing with difficulty. *mwiyemwiyan* his breathlessness. Syn. *mwmwi*.

mwiyengngas (3b) See *mwi, ngas.* n. (T3) panting, hard breathing. *mwiyengngasan* his p. vi. pant, breath hard (as from running).

mwiyepos See *mwi, -pos.* vi. have a chronic cough (as with tuberculosis).

mwo₁ (1) MWOO₁. adv., qlf. for now, for the time being, for a bit, for a little while; instead; at that time. *inaa mwo* that's enough for now, leave be for now. *wúsapw angaang ikeey ngé wúpwe mwoo nó Wééné* I shan't work but I shall for the time being (instead) go to Wééné (Moen). *Kepwe nó iya? Wúpwe nó Wééné. Kaa (Kepwee) mwo méénaato etúkúm wúnúmey suupwa* Where are you going? I am going to Wééné (Moen). Will you at that time buy hither a pack of cigarettes for me? *witiwiti mwo* wait a bit; *wúpwe nóó mwo chuuri pwiiyi we* I am going to see my sister for a bit.

mwo₂ (1) MWOO₂. Var. *mwe (before words beginning with e).* qlf. even. [May be used to soften an utterance or make it more polite or gentle.] *esooru mwo (mwe) emén ikanaan* there is no one (not even one) there. *ikaa mwo* even if; *ikaa mwo wú nó Wééné neesor, wúsapw kkamé onomw rayis* even if I go to Wééné (Moen) tomorrow, I shall not buy your rice. *wúse feyinnó mwo Feefen fáán eew* I have not been to Feefen (Fefan) even once. *Eiue mwo ngé pwan óchoocho* even Eiue worked hard, too. *rese mwochen repwe tekiyaa mwo ngé kkapas* they did not want them to be insolent (haughty) even in talk. *pwanú mwo sómwoon ngé aa feyitto* even the chief came, too.

mwo₃ (1) MWOO₃. F. Var. *mwmwo.* vi., adj. be sunk (of ship), submerged, drowned (of person). Dis. *mwoomwo* (db), *mwomwmwo* (ds) sink by degrees, founder. With dir. suf.: *mwoonó, mwootiw*.

-mwo (1) MWOO₄. unsp. (u.m.) Dis. *-mwoomwo* (db). See *féwúmwo*.

mwoo-₁ (1) MWOO₆. unsp. hunger, craving. See *mwoosset, mwosset*.

mwoo-₂ (1) MWOO₇. [In cpds. only.] unsp. (u.m.) See *mwoochón* Cf. *móó*.

mwoo (1) MWOO₅. md.m. by. [Affirmative exclamation in oaths.] *mw. pwiiy, meyi pwúng!* by my brother, it is true!; *mw. mesen semey!* by the eyes of my father!; *mw. manawomw!* you bet your life!

Mwooses (Eng.) nu. (pers.) Moses.

mwooseng (2) MWOOSENGI. nu. mature stage of coconut (not yet *taka*). [Best stage for grating the meat.] *mwoosengin núú* coconut's m. s.

mwoosor (2) MWOOSORU. nu. (T2) a tree (*Guettarda* sp.); shoots (of this tree) planted on either side of a house in the *osu* ceremony. [Used in making bowls and paddles.] *mwoosorun Chuuk* t. of (a given region). Syn. *mwéwúkkay*.

mwoosset Var. of *mwosset*.

mwook (Eng.) nu. monkey. Syn. *mwóngki, mwongki, sarú*.

mwoomwo Dis. of *mwo₃*.

-mwoomwo Dis. of *-mwo*.

-mwoon (2) MWOONU. [In cpds. only.] unsp. (u.m.) See *winimwoon*.

mwooni (3) MWOONIYA. (Eng.) nu. (T3) money. *neyi mw.* my m. *mwooniyen nóngónóngun mwúún* m. of the government treasury. *nussun mw*.

change ("left-over money"). Cf. *chana, féwúkúkkún, maak*. Cf. also *mwoni*.

mwoonó See *mwo₃*.

mwoor (3) MWORA₁. nu. (T3) strong wind, windy condition; rough condition (of the sea). *mworen iyeey* the w. of now. Ant. *núwa*. Cf. *moor*.

mwooch nu. species of surgeon fish (when grown). [Black, about 7 inches long, found on reefs.] Cf. *ningús*.

mwoochaap (3b) See *mwo₃, chaap*. F. Var. *mwoochap*. vi. sink after having turned over (of a boat), sink face down.

mwoochap N. of *mwoochaap*.

mwoochón (4) See *mwoo-₂, chón*. vi. be bruised.

mwoot₁ (3) MWOOTA₁. vi., adj. (be) artful in fighting.

mwoot₂ (3a) MWOOTA₂. N. vi. cook; be cooked. Syn. *ipwét*.

mwoota (1) MWOOTAA. (Eng.) nu. (T1) motor boat. *efóch mw*. one m. b.

mwootiw See *mwo₃*.

mwootokkay N. of *mwootokkáy*.

mwootokkáy (2, 3) See *mwoot₂, kkáy*. F. Var. *mwootokkay*. vi., adj. (be) cooked quickly.

mwootommang (3) See *mwoot₂, mmang*. vi., adj. (be) cooked slowly.

mwootonong (2, 3) See *mwoot₁, -nong*. nu. (T2, T3) a type of rooster (red and black), said to be found on Mt. Tonaachaw, Wééné (Moen) Island. [It is the bird and emblem of the Sópwunupi clan (*ménún Sópwunupi*), more specifically of its school of *itang*.] *mwootonongun, mwootonongan* r. of (a given region).

mwootongngaw (3b) See *mwoot₂, ngngaw*. vi., adj. (be) cooked badly.

mwooy (2) See *mwoy*. nu. (T2) gnat that is said to destroy breadfruit.

mwosset (2) See *mwoo-₁, sáát*. Var. *mwoosset*. nu. a want or desire for fish or *seni* (side dish, traditionally fish, to go with starch staple). vi. have a desire for fish or *seni*. *siya mwossetin iik* we have a *seni*-desire for fish.

mwokus (2) See *mwa-, kuus*. Var. *mwókos*. vi., adj. (be) quick and wise thinking, able to learn quickly and think profoundly; able to make quick and apt decisions, able to size up a situation quickly and intelligently (commonly used of magicians and fighters).

mwokkáy (2, 3) See *mwo₃, kkáy*. Var. *mwmwokkáy*. vi. sink or submerge quickly.

mwommang (3) See *mwo₃, mmang*. Var. *mwmwommang*. vi. sink or submerge slowly.

mwomwmwo Dis. of *mwo₃*.

mwomwmwongeyang Var. of *mwongeyang*.

mwomwmwor Dis. of *mwor₂*.

mwoni (3) MWONIYA. nu. (T3) burned wood coals. *mwoniyen ááf* c. of fire; *mwoniyen mwúúch* c. of firewood. Cf. *mwooni*.

mwoniyok (2, 3) MWONIYOKU, MWONIYOKA. (Eng.) nu. (T2, T3) sweet manioc, tapioca, cassava (*Manihot esculenta*). [Cultivated as food.] *mwoniyokun* or *mwoniyoken Merika* American m. Syn. *tapiyooka*.

mwongas (3) MWONGASA. nu. (T3) stage of growth of coconut in which it is brown on the outside with some firm meat. Syn. *naawupwut*. vi. be at the *mw*. stage of growth.

mwongeya- (3) MWONGEYA. N. ni. (T3) brother of a woman, any consanguineal male relative of a woman reckoned in her generation. *mwongeyan* her b. Syn. *mwááni-*.

mwongeyang (3) See *mwongeya-, -ng* (?). N. Var. *mwomwmwongeyang* (ds). vi. (dis.) be brother and sister. *mw. ffengen* be b. and s. to one another. va. treat (someone) as a brother (by a woman). Syn. *mwááneyán*.

mwongki Var. of *mwóngki*.

mwopw vi., adj. (be) asphyxiated, suffocated (as from drowning, fumes, fire).

mwor₁ (3) MWORA₂. Var. *mwmwor*. vi. 1. fall of its own accord (as ripe fruit); be fallen. With dir. suf.: *mworotiw, mworomworotiw* (db). 2. be bald, shed, without fur or feathers. *aa mw. mékúran* his head is bald; *aa mw. wúnan* its feathers are shed (i.e., it is bald). Cf. *paan₂*.

mwor₂ See *mwoor*. vi. be windy, be a strong wind; be made rough by the wind (of the sea). Dis. *mworomwor* (db), *mwomwmwor* (ds). With dir. suf.: *mworotá* get rough or windy; *mworonó* get rougher or windier. Ant. *núwa*.

mworeyiti See *mwoor, -iti.* vo. (T2) blow upon (of a wind), be a strong wind upon.

mworoffóch (4) See *mwor₂, -ffóch.* vi. be continuously windy or rough.

mworosoosich See *mwoor, soosich.* F. Var. *mworosoochis.* vi. be an effectively used breeze, wind or rough sea (as with a well-designed sailing vessel or well- planned fishing trip).

mworosoonap (3) See *mwoor, soonap.* vi. be a wasted breeze, wind or rough sea (as with a poorly designed sailing vessel or poorly planned fishing trip).

mworosoochis N. of *mworosoosich.*

mworokúkkún (2) See *mwoor, kúkkún.* nu. a gentle breeze or sea. vi. be a gentle breeze or sea.

mworokkis See *mwoor, kkis.* vi. be continually or recurringly windy or rough (day after day).

mworokkus See *mwoor, -kkus.* vi., adj. (be) very windy or rough.

mworomwor₁ (db; 3) MWORA₃. n. (T3) crumb, grain (as of bread, sand). *mworomworan* c. of it. vi., adj. 1. (be) strewn with crumbs, grains, small seeds, etc. 2. trickle (of grainy things, such as rice, sugar, coffee, but not water). With dir. suf.: *mworomworotiw.*

mworomwor₂ Dis. of *mwor₂.*

mworomworotiw See *mwor₁, mworomwor₁.*

mworonó See *mwor₂.*

mworotá See *mwor₂.*

mworotiw See *mwor₁.*

mworoyééch (2: *-yéchchu-*) See *mwoor, ééch.* nu. (T2) an agreeable breeze, a pleasant breeze. vi. be a pleasant breeze.

mwoch (3) MWOCHA. Var. *mwmwoch.* vi., adj. (be) short, abbreviated; temporary. Dis. *mwochomwoch, mwochomwooch* (db). *meyi mwochomwoch neenuukan* he is short (quick) tempered. *núkúúw mw.* believe it temporarily. Syn. *mwurek.*

mwochen N. of *mwechen.*

mwocheniya N. of *mwecheniya.*

mwochomwooch Dis. of *mwoch.*

mwochomwoch Dis. of *mwoch.*

Mwochunong nu. (loc.) Mortlock Islands. Syn. *Mwóchunók.*

mwotowutow (2) See *mwa-, towu-.* Var. *mwótowutow.* vi., adj. (be) smooth. Ant. *mwarangarang.* ni. (T2) smoothness (of something). *mwotowutowun eey cheepen* the s. of this table.

mwoy (2) MWOYI₁. vi. be diseased (of breadfruit, attributed to gnats). *aa mw. eey mááy* this breadfruit has become d.

mwoyimwoy (db; 2) MWOYI₂. nu. (T2) mountain dove (green and white).

mwóón (4) MWÓNNO. Var. *mwmwón.* vi., va. crave, hunger (for), have an appetite (for). Dis. *mwómwmwóón* (ds). *wúwa mw. pinawa* I hunger (crave) for bread.

mwóóch₁ (4) See *mwa-, wooch.* nu. (T2) a pass through a reef (suitable for large vessels). *mwóóchun nóón Chuuk* the passes in Truk. Cf. *taaw, ánúk.*

Mwóóch₂ See *mwóóch₁.* nu. (loc.) 1. a clan name. Syn. *Sowumwóóch.* 2. Mor or Moch Island and District (Satawan Atoll).

Mwóóchonap (3a) See *mwóóch₁, nap.* Var. *Mwóóchónap.* nu. (loc.) name of Truk's Northwest Pass ("Main Pass" or "Great Pass").

Mwóóchónap Var. of *Mwóóchonap.*

mwóssu- (2) MWÓSSU. [In cpds. only.] unsp. pertaining to spirits. See *mwóssuni.*

mwóssuni See *mwóssu-, -ni-.* vo. (T6a) possess (someone) (of a spirit). *aa mw. soomá* a spirit has possessed him. Syn. *chchúni.*

mwókos Var. of *mwokus.*

mwómwmwóón Dis. of *mwóón.*

mwómwmwóót Dis. of *mwmwóót.*

mwón₁ (4) MWÓNO. vi. be covered, sheltered; secret, hidden, disguised. Dis. *mwónómwón, mwónomwón* (db). *fóós mwónómwón* (n.phr.) a secret, parable; (v.phr.) speak in secret. With dir. suf.: *mwónónó* disappear.

mwón₂ Var. of *món.*

mwónómwón Dis. of *mwón₁.*

mwónónó See *mwón₁.*

mwónneyiti See *mwóón, -iti.* vo. (T2) have a craving, appetite, hunger for (something).

mwóngki (Eng.) Var. *mwongki.* nu. monkey. Syn. *mwook, sarú.*

mwórooro (db; 1) See *mwa-, ro₂.* vi. sway (as a seated dance or a tree); totter (in walking).

mwócho (1) MWÓCHOO. vi., adj. 1. steal, (be) thievish; (be) rascally. *ewe meyi* *mw.* that rascal, thief; *asam mw.* window ("stealing door"). 2. (be) wild, untamed. *maan mw.* wild animal, untamed animal. With dir. suf.: *maan mwóchoonó* animal gone wild. Ant. *fesir, mwótuk.*

mwóchukiiset (2) See *mwa-, chuuk, sáát₁.* nu. (T2) shoreline; area between vegetation and sea on an island shore, whether sandy or rocky. Syn. *mwóchukunuppi.*

mwóchukunuppi (1) See *mwa-, chuuk, ppi₁.* nu. (T1) shoreline; area between vegetation and sea on an island shore, whether sandy or rocky ("piling of flotsam"?). *mwóchukunuppiin fénú* islands *mw.*. Syn. *mwóchukiiset.*

Mwóchunók (Eng.) nu. (loc.) Mortlock Islands. *fénúwen Mw.* island of M. Syn. *Mwochunong.*

mwótow (2) See *mwa-, towu-.* vi., adj. (be) smooth. Dis. *mwótowutow* (db).

mwótowutow Dis. of *mwótow* and var. of *mwotowutow.*

mwótuk F. vi., adj. (be) tame (not wild). Syn. *fesir.* Ant. *mwócho.*

mwóttonong See *mwmwóót.*

mwóttotiw See *mwmwóót.*

mwu₁ (1) N. [Commonly with dir. suf.] vi. be assembled, be in meeting together. With dir. suf.: *mwuuto.* Cf. *chu.*

mwu₂ N. of *mwú₁.*

mwuu- N. of *mwúú-₁, mwúú-₂.*

mwuufeseen N. of *mwúúfeseen.*

mwuuffengeen (2) See *mwu₁, ffengeen.* N. vi. meet together, assemble.

mwuuseni N. of *mwúúseni.*

mwuumwu N. of *mwúúmwú.*

mwuun Var. of *mwúún.*

-mwuun N. suf. (dem.) that (near hearer). Dis. *kkemwuun* (dc). Syn. *oomw.* See *átemwuun, emwuun, ekkemwuun, niyemwuun.*

mwuunón (4) See *mwu₂, nónu-.* nu. (T2) a strain. *mwuunónun sékúriy* s. in my back. vi. have a strained muscle (in arm or back).

mwuunu (1) MWUUNUU. nu. (T1) polisher made of sennit. [For polishing wooden objects.] *aan mw.* his p. *mwuunuun Chuuk* Trukese p.

mwuuch (2) nu. (T2) anchovy, a small fish. *mwuuchun Chuuk* Trukese a.

mwuut Var. of *mwúút₂* and *mwúút₃.*

-mwuut (2) MWUTTU. Var. -*mwúút.* unsp. (u.m.) See *nikamwuut.*

mwuuti N. of *mwúúti.*

mwuuto See *mwu₁.*

mwus (3) MWUSA. vi., adj. (be) untied, released, forgiven, absolved. Cf. *mwmwus.*

mwuk (3a) MWUKA₁. vi. be slow in growing (of persons and plants). With dir. suf.: *mwukonó* have lived a long time; *mwuketiw* be slowed down in growing.

-mwuk (3a) MWUKA₂. [Perhaps related to *mwuk.*] adj. large, huge, big, enormous. See *nimwmwuk, wachemwuk, wachimwuk.*

mwukonó See *mwuk.*

mwumwmwus Dis. of *mwmwus.*

mwurek (Mck.) vi., adj. (be) short. Syn. *mwoch.*

mwuré (1) MWURÉÉ. nu. (T1) pigeon. *mwuréén Chuuk* Trukese p.

mwurinné Var. of *mwírinné.*

mwuromwur (db; 3) MWURA. vi., adj. (be) smooth, without lumps (of breadfruit pudding).

mwuto (1) MWUTOO. nu. (T1) coral head. *eew mw.* one c. h.

mwú₁ (1) MWÚÚ₁. F. Var. *mwu.* vi., adj. (be) severed, broken apart, torn apart (as a string, piece of cloth); adopted (of a child); divorced, separated (of a spouse). Dis. *mwúúmwú* (db). *mw. seni owupw* be weaned; *kkapas mwúúmwú* halting speech.

mwú₂ (1) MWÚÚ₂. vi. come to an end, cease, terminate. *aa mwú rááán* the rain has ended. Syn. *mwmwúch, mwúúch₂.*

mwú₃ vi. lose in a race. Syn. *sun.* Ant. *mwittir, kakkay, kákkáy.* Cf. *kkuf.*

mwúú-₁ (1) See *mwú₁.* Var. *mwuu-.* ni. (T1), suf. (cc.) fragment, broken or cut piece or segment of rag or string. *emwú, rúwémwú, wúnúmwú, fémwú, nimemwú, wonomwú, fúúmwú, wanúmwú, ttiwemwú, engoon mwúún* one,...ten f. *mwúún sáán* f. of rope; *emwú sáán* one f. of rope.

mwúú-₂ (1) MWÚÚ₄. F. [In counting only.] Var. *mwuu-.* ni. (T1), suf. (cc.) sea cucumber, trepang; piece of feces. *emwú, rúwémwú, wúnúmwú, fémwú, nimemwú, wonomwú, fúúmwú, wanúmwú, ttiwemwú, engoon mwúún* one,...ten s. c.

mwúú-₃ (1) See *mwú*₁. [In cpds. only.] unsp. allotted; granted; permitted.

mwúú (1) MWÚÚ₃. n. (T1) 1. lifetime, era, epoch, period, time. *mwúúy, mwuumw, mwúún* my, your (sg.), his l. *nóón eey (ewe) mw.* in this (that) time; *nóón ewe mwúún* in that time (ptv. const.); *mwúún éfékúr, mwúún winipós* time of the children, time of the fathers (in traditional history). *neemwúúr* in their time. Cf. *mwú*₁. 2. government, dynasty, kingdom, rule, realm, state. *mwúún* his g. (of which he is ruler); *aan mw.* his g. (of which he is citizen or subject). *mwúún Sapaan* Japanese times, era, rule, government. Cf. *mwúún.*

mwúúfeseen (2) See *mwú*₁, *feseen*. Var. *mwuufeseen.* vi. be broken apart, torn apart. Cf. *imwúúfeseen.*

mwúúseni See *mwú*₁, *seni*₂. vo. (T2) be torn from, broken apart from; weaned from; divorced from.

mwúúmwú (db; 1) See *mwú*₁. nu. (dis.; T1) adoption (of a child). vi. be adopted. *neyiy mw.* my adopted child.

mwúúmwúúngeni (db) See *mwúú-*₃, *ngeni*. vo. (dis.; T2) be granted to. *aa mw. átewe aan epwene nó sowufiiwu* it was g. to him that he go be a soldier.

mwúúmwúútá (db; 1) See *mwúú-*₃, *-tá*. vi. be permitted (of a request). nu. (T1) permission. *tóropween mw.* license, permit.

mwúún [A back formation from *múú* plus the rel. suf. *-n*.] Var. *mwuun.* nu. government, nation, kingdom, state, rule, realm. *sukunnen mw.* g. school; *chóón mw.* g. worker, g. representative; *mw. Merika* American nation, United States rule (of Truk); *mw. Sapaan* Japanese nation, Japanese rule (of Truk); *mw. Ttoyis* German nation, German rule (of Truk); *eew mw.* another state, nation; *eewú chék mw.* a single realm.

mwúúnúppi (3) See *mwúú-*₁, *ppi*. nu. (T3) sandbar. Syn. *mwúútenippi.*

mwúúr (2) MWÚRÚ. n. (T2) wart; sucker on squid or octopus. *mwúrún* his w.

mwúúch₁ (2) MWÚCHÚ. F. Var. *amwúch, émwúch.* n. (T2) wood (as a material), firewood. *emwúch mw.* one piece of wood; *efóch mw.* one log or stick of wood. *mwúchún* his f.; *mwúchún ááf* firewood.

mwúúch₂ (2) F. Var. *mwmwúch.* vi. be finished, ended, terminated (of work, stories, activities). Id. *mw. mee sópw, tere me iyeey* finished and done, completed as of now (standard ending of a story; in some dialects *tere meyimey* "completed tightly").

mwúút₁ (3) See *mwúú-*₃, *-ta-*₁. n. (T3) allotment, grant, allowance, share (of property). *mwúútan* his a.

mwúút₂ (2) See *mwúú-*₃, *-ti-*. Var. *mwuut.* va. allot; grant; permit, allow (with *ngeni*).

mwúút₃ (2) MWÚÚTTÚ. Var. *mwuut.* vi. be quick, (Tn.) run; (Rmn.) walk or run. Dis. *mwúmwmwúút* (ds). With dir. suf.: *mwúúttúto, mwúúttúnó.* Cf. *mwittir.*

-mwúút (2) MWÚTTÚ. Var. *-mwuut.* unsp. (u.m.) See *nikamwúút, nisimwúút.*

mwúútááta See *mwúúti*₂.

mwúútenippi (3) See *mwú*₁, *-ta-*₁, *ppi*. nu. (T3) sandbar. Syn. *mwúúnúppi.*

mwúúti₁ See *mwú*₁, *-ti-*. F. Var. *mwuuti.* vo. (T4) break apart (as a line, marriage); adopt (as a child). *mw. seni owupw* wean. With dir. suf.: *mwúútóónó* break off, away.

mwúúti₂ See *mwúú-*₃, *-ti-*. [Recorded only with dir. suf.] vo. (T4) allot; grant (land). With dir. suf.: *mwúútááta.*

mwúúto Var. of *mwuuto.*

mwúútóónó See *mwúúti*₁.

mwúúttúnó See *mwúút*₃.

mwúúttúto See *mwúút*₃.

mwúmwmwúút Dis. of *mwúút*₃.

mwúnú (1) MWÚNÚÚ. nu. (T1) a variety of giant dryland taro (*Alocasia*). [It is said to be not very good.] *eché mw.* one t. leaf; *efóch mw.* one t. plant or tuber. *anan mw.* his t. to eat; *fótaan mw.* his t. to plant. *mwúnúún Chuuk* Trukese t.

mwúrinné N. of *mwirinné.*

mwúchú- (2) See *mwúúch*₁. ni. (T2), suf. (cc.) stick or piece of firewood. *emwúch, rúwémwúch, wúnúmwúch, fémwúch, nimemwúch, wonomwúch, fúúmwúch, wanúmwúch, ttiwemwúch, engoon mwúchún* or *engoon fóchun mwúch* one,...ten s. of f.

mwúchúmwúch (db; 2) See *mwúúch*₁. va. use firewood. vi. be supplied with firewood. *aa mw. ena kkama?* has that cooking pot been supplied with f.?

mwúchúni See *mwúúch₁, -ni-*. vo. (T5) get or acquire firewood.

mwúttir N. of *mwittir*.

mwmwa- (3) MWMWA. ni. (loc.; prep.; T3) 1. front; before, in front (of), ahead (of); than (in positive comparison). *mwmwey, mwmwomw, mwmwan* before me, you (sg.), him. *mwmwen wa* boat's bow. *iiy meyi nap mwmwey he* is older than I; *siya mwmwar niyap mwmwen nánew* we have probably caught more than (we did) yesterday. 2. first (of food or crops). *mwmwen mááy* first breadfruit (presented to a chief); *mwmwen mwéngé* first food crop (presented to a chief or landowner); *mwmwen pwpwún* first fruits of the soil (presented to the *sowupwpwún*). Syn. *mwmwee-*. Cf. *nimwamw*.

mwmwaaren (3) MWMWAARA. [Only with rel. suf.] vr. be almost, nearly. *aa mw. feyiyengngaw* he almost had an accident. Cf. *mwmwar*.

mwmwaaw (3) MWMWAAWA. vi., adj. (be) gentle, easy (of actions). *aa mw.* he became g.; *meyi mw.* it is g.

mwmwan (3) MWMWANA. vi. go check, have a look, investigate. Cf. *mwmwa-, sóór₂, sótun*.

mwmwar (dc; 3) See *-mwar*. adv. probably, likely; tentatively. [Expresses the speaker's uncertainty about the truth of a statement or the fulfillment of a request, or the outcome of an action, but his inclination toward certainty.] *aa mw. sineey mwmwey he* p. knows it better than I do; *siya mw. toori* we have p. reached it. Cf. *mwmwaaren*. md.m. would like to, intend to. *mw. wúpwe kkóton* I would like to have a look.

mwmwáán (2) MWÁÁNNI, MWÁNNI. vi., adj. err, make a mistake; (be) wrong, mistaken, incorrect; done improperly, without permission. *aaya mw.* use improperly; *angaang mw.* work badly or incorrectly; *attaw mw.* fish without permission. *mw. feseen* be unmatched, different, opposite irregular; *mw. fesenniiy* (vo.; T5) make different or irregular. With dir. suf.: *mwáánninó* (N), *mwánninó* (F).

mwmwán (db; 4) MWÁNNE. vi., adj. (be) fermented, soured (from fermentation, as of *áchi, núú, kkón*).

mwmwee- (1) MWMWEE. [A contraction of *mwmweeye-*, from *mwmweey, -a-₁*.] nr. (T1) presentation of first fruits to chiefs and owners of soil. *mwmween pwuna* p. of *Cyrtosperma*; *mwmween kká* p. of *Alocasia*; *mwmween épwét* p. of fermented breadfruit; *mwmween woot* p. of taro; *mwmween suupwa* p. of tobacco; *mwmween mááy* p. of breadfruit. Cf. *mwmwa-*.

mwmweemw₁ (ds; 3: *mwemwmwe-*) See *mwmwa-*. vi. (dis.) present first fruits to a chief or landowner.

mwmweemw₂ nu. (T3?) method of fishing. [It is done by men and women together, in the daytime, on the reef. The women use hand nets and *kuumar*; the men use spear and goggles. Many types of fish are caught.] vi. do *mw.* fishing.

mwmweey See *mwmwa-, -e-₂*. vo. (T6b) present as first-fruits. *mw. eey mááy ngeni enaan sómwoon* p. this breadfruit to yonder chief.

mwmwesi (dc; 3) See *mwesi*. vi. sneeze. n. (T3) sneezing. *mwmwesiyan* his s.

mwmwemey (2) See *mwmwa-, mááy₂*. nu. (T2) first breadfruit from a holding, cooked as *wumwun mw.* for presentation to the chief.

mwmwen (2) MWMWENI. vi. be done, finished (as with eating, working, etc.); be up to what should be; stop, come to an end. *e mw.* it is d. (i.e., no further need to bother). *wúwa mw., wúsapw chchiwen fééri* I am d., I won't do it any more. Syn. *emwmwen, emwmwéw, mwmwéw*.

mwmwenááni See *mwmwa-, ná, -ni-*. vo. (T4) guide, lead, go before.

mwmwenó (1) See *mwmwa-, nó₂*. vi. go first. ni. (T1) the one who goes first. [In ptv. const. only.] *mwmwenóón eterenges* senior male of a lineage.

mwmwenuwa (1) See *mwmwa-, wuwa*. nu. (T1) first fruits on any plot and which the chief has exclusive right to eat.

mwmwechikichiki- (db; 2) See *mwmwa-, chiki-₁ (?)*. ni. (prep.; T2) (in) front (of), before, ahead (of). *mwmwechikichikin waa* boat's bow. *epwe mwmwechikichikumw* he will go ahead of you.

mwmwet (dc; 3a) See *mwet*. vi. jump, spring, hop. *mw. wóón* jump over.

mwmwetefátán

Syn. *nus, nnus.* nr. (T3) muscle cramp. *mwmweten féwún peche* c. in the leg.

mwmwetefátán (4) See *mwmwet, fátán.* vi. go hopping along, keep on hopping; keep moving from place to place, keep jumping around.

mwmweteseni See *mwmwet, seni.* vo. (T2) hop away from.

mwmwék (2) MWÉKKÚ. vi. be unable to walk. *aa mw. átenaan* or *aa mwékkúnó átánaan* he is u. to w. With dir. suf.: *mwékkúnong neeyimw* be bedridden. Cf. *mwen.*

-mwmwék See *mwékkú-.*

mwmwérú vi. limp (in walking).

mwmwéw (2) MWMWÉWÚ. vi. come to an end; cease, be finished. Syn. *emwmwen, emwmwéw, mwmwen.*

mwmwéwún$_1$ (3) See *mwmwa-* (?), *wúún*$_5$. n. (T3) aerial root (of mangrove). *efóch mw.* one a. r. *mwmwéwúnan* its a. r. *mwmwéwúnen chiya* mangrove's a. r.

mwmwéwún$_2$ (dc; 3) See *mwa-, wún*$_3$. vi. rock back and forth. Cf. *mwéwúnéwún.*

mwmwi (dc; 3a) See *mwi.* nu. (T3) asthma, panting, gasping, shortness of breath. Syn. *mwiyemwi.*

mwmwich (dc; 2) MWICHI. Var. *mwichimwich.* nu. (T2) species of seaweed. *mwmwichin Chuuk* Trukese s.

mwmwo N. of *mwo*$_3$.

mwmwoon (3, 2) MWONNA, MWOONNA, MWOONNU. vi. be acid, sour (to the taste, as with lime juice). *mwonnan* (F.); *mwoonnan, mwoonnun* (N.) its being a. Cf. *ómwonna.*

mwmwokkáy N. of *mwokkáy.*

mwmwommang N. of *mwommang.*

mwmwopwur (3) See *mwmwa-* (?), *pwur*$_2$. vi. be on the verge of being swamped but not actually swamped (as of an overloaded boat). *aa mw. reen aramas* it is on the verge of being swamped because of [too many] people.

Trukese-English

mwmwor (dc; 3) See *mwor*$_1$. vi. 1. fall of its own accord (as ripe fruit); be fallen. With dir. suf.: *mwmworotiw.* 2. become bald; be balding; be shed (of hair). *mwmworen mékúrey* balding of my head. With dir. suf.: *mwmworonó.*

mwmworonó See *mwmwor.*

mwmworotiw See *mwmwor.*

mwmwoch N. of *mwoch.*

-**mwmwot** (4) MWMWOTO. [In cpds. only.] unsp. (u.m.) See *wurumwmwot.*

mwmwóót (4: *mwótto-*) See *mwa-, tto-.* vi. have a hollow; be cupped. Dis. *mwómwmwóót* (ds). With dir. suf.: *mwóttonong* be dented; have a hollow, groove, concavity; *mwóttotiw* be cupped; have a hollow, concavity.

mwmwón Var. of *mwóón.*

mwmwus (3) MWMWUSA. vi. vomit, throw up. Dis. *mwumwmwus* (ds). nu. (T3) vomiting. Cf. *mwus.*

mwmwusáásini See *mwmwus, -ásini.* vo. (T5) vomit, throw up (something or on account of something).

mwmwuna- (3: -*mwmwun*) MWMWUNA. N. Var. *mwmwúna-.* ni. (T3), suf. (cc.) portion of *mwatún* (in counting). *emwmwún, rúwémwmwun, wúnúmwmwun, fémwmwun, nimemwmwun, wonomwmwun, fúúmwmwun, wanúmwmwun, ttiwemwmwun, engoon mwmwunan* one,...ten p. Syn. *túnú-, ttúna-.*

mwmwung (3) MWMWUNGA. vi. be loved (by someone of opposite sex), be someone's sweetheart. *aa tééfán neepwinewe ngé ese mw.* he went 'house-crawling' last night but he wasn't l.

mwmwú (dc; 1) See *mwú*$_1$. vi., adj. (be) fragile; easily broken, torn, shattered.

mwmwúú- N. of *mwúú-*$_1$.

mwmwúna- F. of *mwmwuna-.*

mwmwúch (2) MWÚCHCHÚ. Var. *mwúúch*$_2$. nu. (T2) end, finish, termination (of work, speech, stories, but not of the end of a thing, such as the end of a table or pencil). *mwúchchún eey tuttunnap* the e. of this story. vi. be finished, ended, terminated. *ese mw.* be without end, eternal. Syn. *mwú*$_2$.

N

-n₁ (3) NA₁. suf. (pos.) 3sg. pos. prn.: of him, her, it. [Used in partitive construction in many expressions where it would not appear in English, as in expressions of time, but not consistently. Thus it is used in: *nóón eey sossoran* this morning; *nóón eey pwinin* this night; *nóón na faansowun* at that particular time; *nóón ewe ráánin* on that day. But it is not used with: *ewe wiik* that week; *ewe maram* that month; *ewe iyeer* that year.]

-n₂ (2: *-ni-*, *-nu-*, *-nú-*) NI₁. [The variant forms *-nu-*, *-nú-* occur in compounds when the following element begins with a labial, *-nú-* if the preceding vowel is a central vowel and *-nu-* if it is a back vowel, as in *Méngú-nú-fach*, *tupwu-nu-pwin*, *turu-nu-ffas*.] suf. (rel.) of, pertaining to.

Na- (3b) NA₂. [Used when following vowel is *a*.] Var. *Ná-*, *Ne-*, *Né-*, *No-*, *Nó-*. pref. (pers. n.form.) feminine prefix in personal names Cf. *Ina-*, *Neyi-*, *Eyi-₃*.

-na-₁ (3) NA₃. suf. (n.form.; T3) object of an action. *fanga-na-* (someone's) gift to someone (*fang* be handed over); *chiye-na-* companion (*chiyechi* be companions). Cf. *-ni-*.

-na-₂ Var. of *-nna-*.

na [In F. dialects it regularly precedes the noun except in possessive constructions, when it follows the word with the suf. pos. prn. It also follows pers. prns. and *peek* and is suffixed to *áta-*, *iimw*, *nemin*, *chóó*. In N. dialects it is replaced by *ena* when preceding the noun but remains *na* otherwise.] prn. (dem.) that (assoc. with person addressed.). Dis. *kkana* (ds). *meet na* what is that (you've got there)? *na meen* that thing; *een na?* is that you? *nowumw na nááyif* that (by you) knife of yours; *chóóna* that group (of yours); *neminna* that woman (by you); *átána* that fellow (by you). Cf. *een₃*, *eey₁*, *ewe*, *oomw*, *naan*.

naa- (1) NAA₁. N. [In cpds. only.] Var. *ná-*, *nó-*. unsp. going, proceeding. See *anaanong*, *chénaa-*.

Naa (1) NAA₂. nu. a star (probably Beta Pegasi); 5th month in traditional sidereal calendar (according to most authorities). [According to Elbert, the 6th month.]

naas (3b) NASA. nu. (T3) hole (in the ground), pit. *eew n.* one h. *nasen épwét* pit of fermented breadfruit; *nasen pakútang* bomb crater.

naakkich (2) See *naa-*, *-kkich*. Var. *nakkich*. nu. (T2) rat, mouse. *emén n.* one r. *éppúngún n.* rat trap.

naam (3) NAMA₁. (Eng.) nu. (T3) lamp. *eew n.* one l. *néwún naam* his l.

naamwáár nu. hawkfish.

naan [In F. dialects it regularly precedes the noun except in possessive constructions, when it follows the word with the suf. pos. prn. It also follows pers. prns. and *peek* and is suffixed to *áta-*, *iimw*, *nemin*, *chóó*. In N. dialects it is replaced by *enaan* when preceding the noun but remains *naan* otherwise.] prn. (dem.) that, that there, that yonder (visible, but distant). Dis. *kkanaan* (ds). *n. meen* that thing; *n. áát* that boy; *átánaan* that fellow; *chóónaan* that group.

Naanúken (Pon. *Nahnken*) nu. (pers.) a traditional god who lives in the sky.

-naar Var. of *-raar*.

naaw (2) NÉWÚ. n. (T2) child; (with pos. suf.) son, daughter, nephew, niece, any kinsman of junior generation; pupil, employee, political subject, domestic animal, anyone over whom one has a position of authority; any small object that is intimately associated with the person (usually specified in apposition). *neyiy*, *nowumw*, *néwún* my, your, his c.

naawupwut (3) See *naa-*, *wupwut*. nu. (T3) brown coconut with some firm meat. [Milk is not as sweet as that of *sééw* stage.] Syn. *mwongas*.

nasanas (db; 3b) See *naas*. va. (dis.) put (something) in a pit. Cf. *naseni*.

nasanómw (2) See *naas*, *nómw*. nu. (T2) large pit or hole (in the ground). Syn. *nasékkochu*.

naseni See *naas, -ni-*. vo. (T6a) put (something) in a pit. Cf. *nasanas*.

nasékúkkún (2) See *naas, kúkkún*. nu. (T2) small pit or hole (in the ground).

nasékkochu (1) See *naas, kko-₁, chu*. nu. (T1) large pit or hole (in the ground). Syn. *nasanómw*.

nasú (1) NASÚÚ. (Jap. *nasu*) nu. (T1) eggplant. *eféw n.* one e. *wochaan n.* his e. (to eat).

naka- Var. of *nanga-*.

naka (1) NAKAA. nu. (T1) person, fellow, guy. [Used in a somewhat disrespectful way, much as English "guy," but for either sex.]

nakafaffaas (3) See *naka-, ffaas*. vi. be wet from continual slipping on a wet and slippery path.

nakatáán (3) See *naka-, táána-*. Var. *nákátáán*. nu. (T3) variety of banana (regarded as very tasty).

nakattam Var. of *nangattam*.

nakik unsp. *chóón n.* thief.

nakkich Var. of *naakkich*.

nam (3b) NAMA₂. N. Var. *nem*. vi. be in mind, be on one's mind. With dir. suf.: *namanó, namónó* be forgotten; *naméto* be remembered.

namanam (db; 3b) See *nam*. n. (dis.; T3) character, quality, morals, deportment. *namanaman* his c. *meyi feet namanamomw* what sort of person are you? n. *tekiya* pride, conceit; rudeness. nu. (dis.; T3) religion, philosophy, doctrine, ideology; Christianity. *aan n.* his r. *chóón n.* a Christian. *namanamen nóómw* the r. of before, the pre-Christian r.; *namanamen Pirostan* Protestantism; *namanamen Kaatenik* Catholicism; *namanamen Suus* Judaism. vi. be of (a specified) character. n. *tekiya* be proud, conceited, presumptuous; presume above one's rightful station; be rude.

namanamangngaw (db; 3b) See *namanam, ngngaw*. nu. (T3) a bad religion. vi., adj. (be) of bad character.

namanamónó (db; 1) See *nam, -nó*. vi. be regretful (with *reen*).

namanó See *nam*.

namayiki (1) NAMAYIKII. (Jap. *namaiki*) vi. be impudent. nu. (T1) impudence.

nameseni See *nam, seni₂*. N. Var. *nemeseni*. vi. (?) be forgotten. Syn. *namanó, namónó*.

namenaanó See *nameni*.

namenaato See *nameni*.

nameni See *nam, -ni-*. N. Var. *nemeni₃*. vo. (T6a) think about, have (something) on one's mind; recall, remember. With dir. suf.: *namenaanó* forget; *namenaato* think of, remember, bring to mind.

namewerewer (3) See *naam, wer*. Var. *naméwerewer*. nu. (T3) flashlight, searchlight.

naméfeefin (3) See *nam, feefin*. Var. *nemefeefin*. vi. have women on one's mind.

naméfénú (1, 3a) See *nam, fénú*. Var. *nemefénú*. vi. have one's land or home on one's mind.

naméto See *nam*.

naméwerewer Var. of *namewerewer*.

Namoro nu. (loc.) a clan name. *fin N.* or *fiin N.* N. woman; *mwáán N.* N. man. *chóón N.* people of N.

namónó See *nam*.

nampa (1) NAMPAA. (Eng.) n. (T1) number. *nampaan* his n. (in row of people, lottery). *nampaan iimw* house number (street address).

namwot N. of *nómwot*.

namwotongngaw N. of *nómwotongngaw*.

namwmweechún nu. large, flat-bottomed wooden bowl. Cf. *féwúweney*.

nan (3b) NANA. vi. chatter. Dis. *nannan* (ds).

nanapaat See *nan, paat₂*. vi. harangue, rant.

nanenipwuch (3) See *nan, pwuch*. vi. talk crazily.

naneyiti See *nan, -iti*. vo. (T2) scold, rant at.

nanéngeni See *nan, ngeni*. vo. (T2) scold.

nanéchééw (2) See *nan, chééw*. vi. chatter a great deal; talk to oneself.

nanéchchow (2) See *nan, chchow*. vi. speak harshly, be insulting (with *ngeni*).

nano- Var. of *nónu-*.

nanowó Var. of *nónówó*.

nannan (db; 3b) See *nan*. nu. (dis.; T3) chattering. *aan n.* his c. vi. (dis.) chatter.

Nantakú (Jap.) nu. (loc.) locale of Truk District's administrative center on Wééné (Moen) I. [Traditional name is *Wunuungenota* or *Wunuunganata*.]

nanten (Eng.) nu. lantern. *eew n.* one l. *néwún n.* his l.

nanga- (3) NANGA. [In cpds. only.] Var. *naka-*. unsp. appearance, shape, configuration.

nangakúchú (1) NANGAKÚCHÚÚ. (Jap. *nagagutsu*) nu. (T1) boot. *ipwan n.*, *néwún n.* his b.

nanganang (db; 3) See *nanga-*. n. (dis.; T3) appearance, shape, configuration. *nanganangan* his a. Syn. *napanap₁*.

nangatattam See *nangattam*.

nangattam (3a) See *nanga-, ttam*. Tb3. Var. *nakattam*. n. (T3) length, height. *nangattaman* its l. vi., adj. (be) long, tall. Dis. *nangatattam* (ds.) Syn. *áney*.

nangattameyiti See *nanga-, ttam, -iti*. Tb3. vo. (T2) be as long or as tall as.

nangkiyú (1) NANGKIYÚÚ. (Jap. *nankyuu*) nu. (T1) liner (in baseball). *eew n.* one l.

nap (3a) NAPA₁. Var. *nnap*. vi., adj. (be) big, large, great; principal, main. Dis. *napanap* (db). *n. seni* more than, larger than, older than.

-nap (3) NAPA₂. [In cpds. only.] adj. badly, illy; contrarily. See *mwácheenap, rongonap*. Cf. *ngngaw, pwutak*.

napa- (3a) See *nap*. N. ni. (T3) older brother (of man); older sister (of woman). *napan* his o.b. Cf. *mwáán₁*.

napanap₁ (db; 3a) See *nap*. n. (dis.; T3) appearance, configuration, shape; plan; conduct, manner; matter, affair. *napanapan* his a. *napanapan me reey* my plan for it (its appearance according to me), the way I see it. *mwaa, meyi feet napanapomw, áteen?* say, what sort of conduct is that, fellow? Syn. *nanganang, wunuun₂*. vi. seem, look, appear (as specified). *n. ffengeen* look alike, be similar (in appearance).

napanap₂ Dis. of *nap*.

napanapangngaw (3) See *napanap₁, ngngaw*. nu. (T3) bad appearance, bad manner of acting.

napanapééch (2) See *napanap₁, ééch*. nu. (T2) good appearance, good manner of acting.

nape (1) NAPEE. (Jap. *nabe*) nu. (T1) cooking pan, pot. *eew n.* one p. *aan n.* his p.

napeyiti See *nap, -iti*. vo. (T2) be old enough to have been living during (a period). *kaa n. faansowun ewe móówun?* were you living at the time of the war?

napéseni Var. of *nap seni* (see *nap*).

napwpwa (1) NAPWPWAA. (Jap. *nappa*) nu. (T1) green vegetables, greens. *efóch n.* one g. v. (stalk or plant). *anan n.* his g. v. (to eat).

naté (1) NATÉÉ. (Eng.) Var. *nnaté*. nu. (T1) ladder, stair.

Natiin (Eng.) nu. Latin.

-naw (3b) NAWA₁. [In cpds. only.] unsp. alive, animate. See *manaw*. Cf. *nnaw*.

nawa- (3v: *newe-*) NAWA₂. unsp. (u.m.) See *neweyinón*.

nawanaw Dis. of *nnaw*.

nayisen (2) NAYISENI. (Eng.) nu. (T2) license. *néwún n.* his l.

nayité (1) NAYITÉÉ. (Eng.) nu. (T1) lighter, small vessel. *efóch n.* one l. *waan n.* his l.

nayiya (1) NAYIYAA. (Jap. *naiya*) nu. (T1) infield (in baseball). *n. furay* infield fly.

nayiyon (Eng.) nu. lion. *emén n.* one l.

Ná- Var. of *Na-* (used when following vowel is *á* without an intervening consonant).

ná (1) NÁÁ₁. E.Wn. [Used in colloquial speech in other dialects when the next following word begins with *á*.] Var. *naa-, náá, nó₂*. vi. go, proceed (away from place of reference). *wúpwenee ná* I am about to go off, I am about to leave. *ewú ná ákina (nó ekina)* you (pl.) go examine it.

-ná₁ E.Wn. of *-nó*.

-ná₂ (1) NÁÁ₂. [In cpds. only.] unsp. thievish, tricky (?). See *sooná*.

náá Var. of *ná*, appearing only in the expression *ke náá meya* (N.) or *ke náá meey?* (Éét, Rmn., Wtt.) where are you coming from?

náán (2?) NENI₁ (?). nu. (T2?) model double canoe that traditionally served as the shrine of an *énúúsór* spirit. Cf. *neni-₁*.

nááná (db; 1) NÁÁ₃. Var. *neene*. n. (T1) bracelet, ring, earring. *efóch n.* one b. *náánáán* his b. Cf. *nikum*. vi. wear as a bracelet or ring.

náánááni See *nááná, -ni-*. vo. (T4) acquire or own as a bracelet, ring, or earring.

-nááney (2) See *áney₁*. adj. long, tall. [Recorded only in the reef name *Fenenááney*. Cf. Plt. *lááláy*.]

nááng (2) NENGI₁. Var. *neni-*₁. nu. (T2) heaven, sky. [According to Bollig, it has several tiers or levels, consisting of *Nenichang, Nenimwékút* or *Nenisú, Nenikkun* or *Neninap, Faacchamw* or *Nenichamw,* and *Nenimmwúch*.] *chóón n.* angel (cf. *sowuneng*); *fáán n.* lower h.

nááyif (3a) NÁÁYIFA. (Eng.) nu. (T3) knife. *emén n.* one k. *néwún n.* his k. *mesen n.* k. blade.

nááyifekken (2) See *nááyif, kken.* nu. (T2) sharp knife.

nááyifekkopw (2) See *nááyif, kkopw.* nu. (T2) dull knife.

nákásááp (2) nu. (T2) species of wrasse fish.

nákásássá (ds; 1) See *naka-, ssá.* Var. *nekesássá.* vi. run very fast. Syn. *nikásássá.*

nákátáán Var. of *nakatáán.*

nánew (2) NÁNEWI. nu. (temp.) yesterday.

náyimis (2) NÁYIMISI. (Eng.) nu. (T2) lime (tree and fruit, *Citrus aurantifolia*). vi. be limed (with lime juice).

náyimisiiy See *náyimis, -i-*₂. vo. (T5) put lime juice on (something).

náyin (2) NÁYINI. (Eng.) nu. (T2) line (as marked on paper); line (as rope). *efóch n.* one l. *náyinin wóón eey toropwe* lines on this paper.

náyiré (1) NÁYIRÉÉ. nu. (T1) noddy tern. Syn. *pwooniik.*

Ne-₁ Var. of *Na-* (used when following vowel is *i* or *e*, with or without intervening consonant, or *á* with intervening consonant).

ne-₂ Var. of *nee-.*

ne₁ (1) NEE₁. interj. expression of admiration. *Nnengeni wááy eey waa. Wúú ne, mé échchún wóómw na* Look at my canoe here. Yes *ne,* for the fineness of your canoe there. ct.m. miss; ma'am; sir. [Polite form in addressing women or calling them by name; may also be used in addressing men.] *ee ne!* polite way to call to a woman of higher rank. *érenuku ne!* You're talking to yourself, sir! Cf. *nee.*

ne₂ NE₁. [Although properly a prefix, it is written separately or with a hyphen.] pref. (loc., temp.) in, at, while, during (with verbs). *ne fátán* in walking. *meyi angangngaw átánaan ne ppek* that fellow does badly at shooting (he is a bad shot).

-ne NE₂. [Used only with a preceding *pwe* (or other aspect marker) except in the second person singular and plural when the *pwe* may be omitted.] suf. (asp.) future particle expressive of a little uncertainity. [Polite in that it softens the force of a statement.] *kene feyinnó* you are going to depart; *kenee nó* goodbye ("you will be going"). *wúpwene feyinnó neesor* I expect or I guess that I shall depart tomorrow (cf. *wúpwe feyinnó neesor* I shall depart tomorrow).

nee- (1) NEE₂. Var. *ne-*₂. pref. (loc., temp.) place, location, time; in, at. [Freely prefixed to nouns, it occurs in many place names.] *neemataw* at sea, on the sea (*mataw* sea); *neepwin* at night, night time (*pwiin* night). Cf. *ne*₃.

nee NEE₃. ct.m. miss, ma'am, sir. [Polite particle attached to person's name when calling from a distance.] *nee o* or *nee ko* polite call to a man; *nee ne* polite call to a woman. Cf. *ne*₁.

neefasang (3) See *fasang.* n. (loc.; T3) torso, trunk (of person); neck (of breadfruit pounder). *neefasangan* his t.

neefanang (3) See *fanang.* nu. (loc.; T3) site of a lineage hearth, at the lineage hearth. *chóón n.* person in charge of work at a l. h. site.

neefat (3) See *faat*₂. nu. (loc.; T3) (in or at the) shallow lagoon (between fringing reef and shore).

neefááf (2) See *fááf.* nu. (temp.; T2) time of the main meal (*fááf*); dinner-time; the period just after nightfall until around 9:00 P.M. during which the main meal is usually taken. *n. maaw* after about 8 P.M., late *n.*; *n. otonó* from 9 to 11 P.M.

neefááfisich F. of *neefááfichis.*

neefááfichis (2) See *neefááf, -chis.* N. Var. *neefááfisich.* nu. (temp.; T2) the beginning of *neefááf,* time immediately after dark.

neefeng (2) See *-feng.* n. (T2) age. *neefengin* his a. *fítuuw neefengumw* how old are you.

neefé (1) See *féé.* nu. (loc.; T1) (in the) hull. *neefeén waa* in the canoe's h.

neefééfé (db; 1) See *féé.* nu. (loc.; T1) the groove of one's back. *neefééféén sékúriy* the g. of my back.

neeféwúchóchchón (4) See *féwúchón*₁. nu. (loc.; T2) very deep, dark water.

neefiina- (3) See *fi-, ina-₂*. ni. (loc.; T3) between. *neefiinan mé néwún* b. him and his child; *neefiinach* b. us. *ifa wusun neefiinen tekiya mé tekisón?* what is the character of (relations between) socially high and low?

neefóós (4) See *fóós*. nu. (temp.; T2) during speech, at speaking.

neesaa- (1) See *saa*. ni. (loc.; T1) emotions, disposition. *neesaan* (in) his e.; e. of. *meyi ééch neesaan* he is of good disposition.

neesemiriiti- (2) See *semiriit*. ni. (temp.; T2) (one's) childhood. *neesemiriitin* (in) his c. Syn. *neenooyiis, neenooyirochu-*.

neeset (2) See *sáát₁*. nu. (loc.; T2) (at) sea, (in the) salt water. *chóón n.* fisherman.

neesékúr (2) See *sékúr*. nu. (loc.; T2) at one's back.

neesén nu. a variety of breadfruit. Syn. *songosong*.

neesossor See *neesor*.

neesossorochis See *neesor*.

neesossorusich See *neesor*.

neesor (3a) See *soor*. nu. (temp.; T3) morning; tomorrow. Dis. *neesossor* (ds) in the morning. *n. ánnim* good morning. *neesoren nánew* yesterday morning; *neesoren n., nesossoren n.* tomorrow morning; *neesorowe* this (past) morning. *sorotáán n.* day after tomorrow; *pwénnóónun n.* day after the day after tomorrow. *neesossorochis* (N.), *neesossorusich* (F.) very early morning (after dawn). Syn. *néwú*.

neesóósó (db; 1) nu. (T1) a variety of breadfruit.

neesómwoon (2) See *sómwoon*. nu. (T2) food contest between the chiefly and commoner clans. [For a stated number of days they vie to see which side can produce more food to give to the other.]

neesópwónóó- (1) See *neesópwu-, -nó*. ni. (loc.; T1) (at the) end, conclusion (of something). *neesópwónóón* at its e.

neesópwu- (4) See *sópwu-₁*. ni. (loc.; T2) end (of an object, as distinct from its side); pointed end (of a pencil). *neesópwun* its e. *neesópwun cheepen* table's e.; *neesópwun iimw* house's e.; *neesópwun waa* canoe's e. Ant. *neepeek*. Cf. *epi-₁*.

neesópwúúkúúkú- (db; 2) See *neesópwu-, wúkúúk₂*. ni. (loc.; T2) very end, very last (of something). [In ptv. const. only.]

neekiyá (1) See *kiyá₁*. Var. *neekiyáán*. n. (loc.; T1) (at the) boundary. *neekiyáán* at its b.

neekiyáán (2) See *kiyáán*. Var. *neekiyá*. n. (loc.; T2) (at the) boundary. *neekiyáánnin* at its b.

neekupukup (db; 2) See *kup*. nu. (loc.; T2) joint (of the body or of something that folds up, as a carpenter's rule). *neekupukupun éwút* finger j.

neekkamas (dc; 3) See *kkamas*. n. (loc.; T3v) place of juncture (as between two boards in a floor). *neekkamasan* its p. of j. *neekkamesen kkewe paap* p. of j. of those boards.

neekkapwin nu. blow to the genital area (in fighting).

neekkeyang (dc; 3) See *kkeyang*. n. (loc.; T3) between the fingers. *neekkeyangan* between his f.

neekkeyina- (3) See *kke-₂, ina-₂*. ni. (loc.; T3) joint, point of juncture. *neekkeyinen chúún* j. of his bones; *neekkeyinen kkaan irá* j. of those timbers; *neekkeyinen pecheey* j. of my leg (knee, ankle).

neekkeyinechú (1) See *neekkeyina-, chúú*. Var. *neekeyinen chúú*. nu. (loc.; T1) joint (of the bones).

neekkot (3) See *kkot*. nu. (loc.; T3) shallows between an island and its fringing reef.

neekkóón (2) See *kkóón*. nu. (loc.; T2) inner side of the bend of a joint. *neekkóónun pecheey* inner or back side of my knee; *neekkóónun peyiy* inner side of my elbow.

neekkunuyón (4) See *kun, -ón*. Var. *nekkuniyón, nekkunuyón*. nu. (temp.; T2) late afternoon (around 4:00 P.M. to dark). *n. ánnim!* good afternoon! *neekkunuyónun neesor* l. a. tomorrow.

neekkunuyónopwin (2) See *neekkunuyón, pwin₂*. nu. (temp.; T2) twilight time. Syn. *neekkunuyónoroch*.

neekkunuyónoroch (3a) See *neekkunuyón, roch*. nu. (temp.; T3) twilight time. Syn. *neekkunuyónopwin*.

neemaasiyes (2) See *maasiyes*. nu. (loc.; T2) place of treelessness.

neemasa- (3v) See *maas₃*. ni. (loc.; T3v) before the face or eyes, presence, front region. *neemesey, neemosomw, neemasan* in front of me, you, him.

neeman (3) See *manna-*. nu. (loc.; T3) inland (especially in relation to settlement area); ashore, pertaining to land. *ménún n.* a land animal.

neemataw (3) See *mataw.* nu. (loc.; T3) the deep sea.

neemán (2) See *máán*₁. nu. (loc.; T2) swidden field, land cleared of trees and grass for cultivation.

neemánánán (db; 4) See *mánámán.* nu. (loc.; T2) place of habitation.

neemese- See *neemasa-*.

neemesopwut (3) See *neemasa-*, *pwuta-*. nu. (T3) person with the natural ability to see the soul of someone who is about to die.

neemóón (2) See *móón.* n. (loc.; T2) hollow, concavity, hollow place; valley; inner l. side; (with suf. pos. prn.) hollow of one's arm. *neemóónun* its h. *n. ngééngé* red mark from a sucking kiss. *neemóónun peyiy* hollow of my arm; *neemóónun chuuk* mountain valley.

neemóton (3) See *ma-, ton.* n. (T3) white stripe of a *chééyitúr. neemótonan* its w. s.

neemwan (3) See *-mwan.* nu. (T3) cut-away section at the end of the handle of an *oppong* spear for its prongs to set against. *neemwanen oppong* spear's cut-away section.

neemwanú (1) NEEMWANÚÚ. n. (T1) inside or hollow of the knee. *neemwanúún, neemwanúún pecheen* inside of his k. Cf. *neekkóón, neemóón.*

Neemwey nu. (loc.) a clan name. *fin N.* or *fiin N.* N. woman; *mwáán N., re-N.* N. man. *chóón N.* people of N.

Neemwóóch nu. (loc.) name of an Wútéét (Udot) Island *eyif* in Tunnuuk district. [Important in Wútéét legend as the home and name of a lineage of powerful sorcerers.]

neemwókkúnú- (2) See *mwókkún.* ni. (temp.; T2) in the youth of.

neemwúú- See *mwúú.* ni. (temp.; T1) in the time (of someone's life). *neemwúún* in his t.

neene (db; 1) NEE₄. F. Var. *nááná.* n. (T1) bracelet, ring, earring. *efóch n.* one b. *neeneen* his b. vi. (dis.) wear as a bracelet or ring.

neeni (3) See *nee-, -ni-, -ya-*₁. n. (T3) place where a thing properly belongs, hence home, container, etc.; the place or location of something. *neeniyan* his home, place where he is. *neeniyen amanawa* starter (of engine or car); *neeniyen angaang* place of work, office; *neeniyen áánnen* target (place for being shot at); *neeniyen éwússening* radar station, listening post; *neeniyen fóós* telephone, microphone, loud speaker, radio station; *neeniyen káás* gasoline container, gas tank; *neeniyen kkémwéch* handle; *neeniyen maak, neeniyen mwooni* purse; *neeniyen móót* buttocks ("sitting place"); *neeniyen ossupwun kkónik* spout; *neeniyen peyiyas* cemetery, place of graves; *neeniyen pii* garbage or trash container, trashcan, garbage can, wastebasket; *neeniyen sepeniin* airfield; *neeniyen wurummót* playground.

neeningafé (1) See *ningafé.* nu. (temp.; T1) time of new shining (of the moon). *neeningaféén maram* time of the new moon. Syn. *neeningetáá-*.

neeningetáá- (1) See *ning, -tá.* [Used only with *maram*.] nr. (temp.; T1) in *neeningetáán maram* time of the new moon. Syn. *neeningafé.*

neeniyach (3) See *niyach.* nu. (temp.; T3) season when there is little breadfruit left. [Period between *ráás* and *effen* in August and September.]

neeniyeni See *neeni, -ni-.* vo. (T6a) acquire or have a place of one's own; inhabit a place. Cf. *nenneeni.*

neeniyenipwu (1) See *neeni, pwu*₃. nu. (T1) foot stool, footrest.

neenooyiis (2) See *nooyiis.* Tn. n. (temp.; T2) time of small childhood. *neenooyiisin* in his early c. Syn. *neenooyirochu-, neesemiriiti-.*

neenooyirochu- (2) See *nooyiroch.* ni. (temp.; T2) time of one's childhood. *neenooyirochun* in his early c. Syn. *neenooyiis, neesemiriiti-.*

neenómw (2) See *nóómw*₁. nu. (loc.; T2) lagoon area; in a lagoon.

neenuuk (3a) See *nuuk*₁. n. (loc.; T3) middle; stomach, belly; seat of emotions or feelings, heart; psyche, personality. *neenuukan* his m. *sipwe ekiyek neenuukach* we shall think in our hearts. *meyi mwochomwoch neenuukan* he is quick-tempered.

neenuukékkan (3) See *neenuuk, kkan.* N. Var. *neenuukokkan.* vi., adj. (be) quick-tempered.

neenuukokkan F. of *neenuukékkan*.
neepat (3b) See *pat*. nu. (T3) variety of breadfruit. [So called because it is *patapat* in taste.]
neepeeki- (2) See *peek₂*. ni. (loc.; T2) long side (as of a table or house), side wall (of house). *neepeekin* its l. s.
neepeniya- (3) See *peniya-*. ni. (loc.; T3) side (of person). *neepeniyan* his s.
neeppi (3) See *ppi₂*. nu. (loc.; T3) beach; on the beach.
neepwekiiki (db; 1) See *pwekiiki*. Var. *neepwokuuku*. nu. (loc.; T1) back corner. *neepwekiikiin neeyimw* b. c. of the inside of a house; *neepwekiikiin awach* b. c. of one's jaw (where teeth leave off).
neepwech (3) See *pwech*. nu. (loc.; T3) relatively shallow area with a sandy bottom next to the outer slope of a fringing reef.
neepwin (2) See *pwiin₃*. nu. (temp.; T2) night time, at night. *neepwineey* tonight; *neepwinewe* last night. Cf. *neepwong*.
neepwineey See *neepwin*.
neepwinewe See *neepwin*.
neepwoopwo (db; 1) nu. (T1) a variety of breadfruit. Syn. *meyimwotow, wúnniinaf*.
neepwokuuku (db; 1) See *pwokuuku*. Var. *neepwekiiki*. nu. (loc.; T1) back corner. *neepwokuukuun neeyimw* b. c. of the inside of a house; *neepwokuukuun awach* b. c. of one's jaw (where the teeth leave off).
neepwona- (3) See *pwon₂*. ni. (loc.; T3) region beyond visibility; depths. *neepwonen neemataw* (in the) depths of the sea.
neepwong (3) See *pwoong*. (Mck. *leepwong*) nu. (temp.; T3) night time, at night. [Used only in the expression *n. annim!* good evening! good night!] Cf. *neepwin*.
neepwopwu- (2) See *pwoopw*. ni. (temp.; loc.; T2) beginning (of something). [In ptv. const. only.] Syn. *neechepi-*.
neepwúkúwa- (3) See *pwúkú*. ni. (loc.; T3) joint (of arm or leg). *neepwúkúwen pecheey* my knee, ankle; *neepwúkúwen peyiy* my wrist, elbow.
neeraán (2) See *raán₂*. nu. (temp.; T2) daytime, in the day.
neerás N. var. of *neeres*.

neeres (2) See *ráás*. Var. *neerás*. nu. (temp.; T2) time of the breadfruit season.
neerongun nu. 1. a kind of magic. 2. sickness caused by the *n*. magic.
neeroch (3a) See *roch*. nu. (temp., loc.; T3) 1. time of darkness, in the dark. 2. a spell causing sickness. 3. sickness caused by the *n*. spell. 4. a blow to the solar plexus (in fighting).
neechepi- See *chááp*. Tb1. ni. (temp.; T2) beginning (of something). [In ptv. const. only.] Syn. *neepwopwu-*.
neechimónnu- (2) Tb2. ni. (loc.; T2) lap, inner region of the thighs. *neechimónnun* his l.
neechón (4) See *chón*. nu. (loc.; T2) deep, black water (where bottom cannot be seen).
neechú (1) See *chúú*. n. (loc.; T1) body interior; (fig.) character, attitude. *neechúún* his b. i. *meyingngaw neechúún átánaan* that fellow's attitude is bad; *e chchow neechúún* he is angry.
neetang (3) See *taang*. n. (loc.; T3) crotch (of a person).
neetip (3) See *tiip₁*. ni. (loc.; T3) place of emotions, (in one's) feelings, heart, soul (as a place in the body). *neetipan* his p. of e. *angeey neetipan* capture or win his heart or emotions. nu. (T3) severe constipation; a serious illness accompanied by stomach and general disorders; the magic and medicine associated with this illness. [It is said to be caused by excessive indulgence in sex. There is a spell to cure it, *rongen n.*] *aan n.* his c.
neetipengngaw (3b) See *neetip, ngngaw*. vi. feel badly; be disappointed, disturbed; be sad, unhappy. Syn. *neetipechchow*.
neetipechchow (2) See *neetip, chchow*. vi. be aggrieved, bitter; feel wronged; (be) sad, heavy-hearted, sorrowful; feel badly, be disappointed, be disturbed. Syn. *neetipengngaw*.
neetipeta (1) See *neetip, ta*. vi. be broken-hearted, grief-striken. nu. (T1) broken heart signal of sweethearts (involving wearing the *Canna* flower). *pwata ke néwúnéw na n.?* why are you wearing that "broken-heart"? Cf. *nini, paachaw*.
neetiwiinum (3) See *-tiw, nuum*. nu. (loc.; T3) bailer's place in a canoe. [The

neeweesi-

bailer sits on the thwart nearest the central platform and facing that platform.]

neeweesi- (2) See *wees.* Var. *neeyáweesi-*. nu. (temp., loc.; T2) the finish (of something). [In ptv. const. only.]

neewén₁ (2) See *wénú-*. nu. (loc.; T2) (in the) forest, bush.

Neewén₂ (2) See *wénú-*. nu. (loc.; T2) a clan name. *fin N.* or *fiin N.* N. woman; *mwáán N., re-N.* N. man. *chóón N.* people of N.

neewo (1) See *-wo*₂. nu. (loc.; T1) 1. origin, source, base; ancestor, senior lineage mate. *aan n.* his lineage ancestor. *neewoon kkewe aramas* or *áán kkewe aramas n.* o. of these people; *neewoon eyinang* clan's o. *neewoon paaw* upper arm close to the shoulder; *neewoon peche* upper thigh, lap; *neewoon irá* tree's base or trunk. 2. talk or accounting of origins.

neewooni See *neewo, -ni-*. vo. (T4) give an account of the origins of.

Neewooreng (3) See *neewo, reng*. nu. (loc.; T3) a clan name. *fin N.* or *fiin N.* N. woman; *mwáán N., re-N.* N. man. *chóón N.* people of N.

neewoch₁ (3) See *wocha-*₃. n. (T3) notch in the side of a canoe into which the outrigger boom is set. *neewochan* its n. *neewochen waa* canoe's n.

Neewoch₂ See *wooch.* nu. (loc.) Kuop Atoll.

neewota (1) nu. (T1) variety of breadfruit.

Neewow nu. (loc.) a clan name. *fin N.* or *fiin N.* N. woman; *mwáán N., re-N.* N. man. *chóón N.* people of N.

Neewuureng nu. (loc.) a clan name.

neewut (2) See *nee-, wutu-*. n. (loc.; T2) core, at the core; inside of the body, interior (of people, animals, fruit, things). *neewutun* c. of him. *neewutun eey kkunók* interior of this watch. Cf. *wutun mááy* breadfruit core (as an excised object).

neewuwapwpweyichuk (2) See *nee-, wuwapw, chuuk*₁. nu. (loc.; T2) summit or tip of a high mountain.

neewú (3) See *nee-, wúú*₂. n. (T3) voice; accent, pronunciation. *esinna neewúwan* recognise his v. *neewuwomw!* a curse in Mck. usage.

neewúnú- (2) See *wúún*₃. ni. (loc.; T2) top (of something). [In ptv. const. only.] *neewúnún chuuk* mountain top.

neewúng (3) See *-wúng.* n. (loc.; T3) chest (of body). *neewúngan* his c. Syn. *éwúng*.

neewúwékken (2) See *neewú, kken*. vi. be shrill voiced.

neey Rmn., Wtt., Éét. Var. *neya, nóóy.* vi. go where? *ke pwe n.?* where are you going?

neeyam (3) See *aam*. nu. (T3) a throw in hand-to-hand fighting on canoes ("at the gunwhale"). [Against an opponent slashing with a club, one crosses one's arms to block the blow and turn it past one's body; then stepping behind him one pushes him overboard or grabs his leg from behind and trips him overboard.]

neeyamwawukowuk See *mwa-, wukowuk*. nu. (temp.; T3) crack of dawn, time of earliest beginning of morning light. Syn. *neeyamwóyimwóy*.

neeyamwóyimwóy See *mwoyimwoy* (?). N. nu. (temp.; T2) crack of dawn, the time of earliest beginning of morning light, just after dawn. Syn. *neeyamwawukowuk*.

neeyanopan Var. of *neeyónopan*.

neeyanowas Var. of *neeyónowas*.

neeyapar (3b) See *par*. nu. (T3) variety of breadfruit, reddish within.

neeyaw₁ (3b) See *aaw*₁. nu. (loc.; T3) inside of the mouth. *feyiyemwmwenin n.* last meal given to a visitor before his departure.

neeyaw₂ (3) NEEYAWA. nu. (T3) band of shell bead decoration on the neckline of locally woven shirt worn by men of high rank; shirt or cape so decorated.

neeyáti- (4) See *áát*. ni. (temp.; T2) boyhood. *neeyátin* (in) his b.

neeyáweesi- (2) See *wees*. Var. *neeweesi-*. ni. (temp., loc.; T2) at the finish (of something). *neeyáweesin* at the f. of it.

neeyefen (2) See *efen*₄. nu. (temp.; T2) trade wind season. [January to April; time of very little breadfruit.]

neeyénú nu. a form of divination. [Performed by *itang* and *sowurong* and involving the recitation of a verbal spell. Recitation without error or faltering is a favorable sign.]

neeyénúfféé- (1) See *énúffé.* ni. (temp.; T1) time of youth. *neeyénúfféén* (in) his y.

neeyi- (2) NEEYI. nr. (loc.; T2) in, among, at, place of. Cf. *nee-, neeyii-.*

neeyii- (1) See *ii-* (?). [Not used with 1sg. or 2sg. pos. prns.] Var. *neyii-.* ni. (loc.; T3) among, the midst of. *neeyiin* midst of it; *neeyiir* among them. Id. *emén chék neeyiin* anybody; *neeyiin ráán chék* any day.

neeyimw (3) See *iimw.* nu. (loc.; T3) inside of a house. *neepwekiikiin neeyimw* back corner of the i. of a h. *inaan iiy n.* there he is in the h.

neeyónokken (2) See *-ón, kken.* nu. (temp.; T2) noon, midday ("sharp sun time"). Syn. *neeyónowas.*

neeyónopan (3) See *-ón, pan.* Var. *neeyanopan, nóónopan.* nu. (temp.; T3) early afternoon (noon to about 3:30 P.M., "tilted sun time"). *neeyónopanen neesor* early afternoon tomorrow.

neeyónowas (3b) See *-ón, aas₁.* Var. *neeyanowas, nóónowas.* nu. (temp.; T3) midday, noon (from about 10:00 a.m. to about 2:00 p.m. "high sun time"). *neeyónowas ánnim* good midday (greeting that may be used at this time). Syn. *neeyónokken.*

nesen (2) (Eng.) nu. (T2) lesson, schoolwork. *aan n.* his l. *kepwe pengkiyooni ewe nesenin aretimetik* you should study the arithmetic l.

nessaar (2) See *nee-, ssaar.* n. (T2) waistband ("knife place"). *nessaarún* his w.

nek (3) NEKA₁. vi. gyrate the hips in dancing.

nekatayimw (Eng.) Var. *nektayimw.* nu. necktie.

nekeey See *nekenek, -e-₂.* vo. (T6b) cut a love scar on; scarify. Dis. *nekenekeey* (db).

nekenek (db; 3) NEKA₂. (Pon.) n. (T3) ornamental scar; love scar (as cut by sweethearts on each other as tokens of bravery and love). [A custom said to be introduced from Ponape. The scars are cut on the upper arm, inner thigh, and chest.] *nekenekan* his s. va. scarify.

nekenekeey Dis. of *nekeey.*

nekkuniyón Var. of *neekkunuyón.*

nekkunuyón Var. of *neekkunuyón.*

nektayimw Var. of *nekatayimw.*

nem (3a) NEMA₁. F. Var. *nam.* vi. be in mind, be on one's mind. With dir. suf.: *nemeto* be remembered; *nemenó* be forgotten.

neman md.m. probably. *n. wú pwe feyinnó neesor* I will p. leave tomorrow. *n. eni* presumably.

Nemáneyé See *Ne-₁, mánámán.* nu. (pers.) traditional goddess of land clearing. [She lives in the sky and presides over clearing, weeding, and general neatness of the land, house yards, and paths.]

neme- (3) NEMA₂. ni. (T3) affair, authority, business. *neman* his a. *nemeyi chék* it is my business, up to me, my affair.

nemefeefin (3) See *nem, feefin.* Var. *naméfeefin.* vi. have women on one's mind.

nemefénú (1, 3a) See *nem, fénú.* Var. *naméfénú.* vi. have one's land on one's mind.

nemeseni See *nem, seni₂.* F. Var. *nameseni.* vi. (?) be forgotten. Syn. *nemenó.*

nemenaanó See *nemeni₁, nemeni₃.*

nemenaato See *nemeni₃.*

nemenem (db; 3) See *neme-.* n. (dis.; T3) control, power, authority, responsibility. *nemeneman* his c. *nemenemen saam me iin* authority of father and mother to make decisions relating to what their children will do. (The way they do this represents *nemeniyeer wóón néwúúr* their government or rule of their children.). *n. wóón éppúrú* copyright. vi. be in authority, be responsible.

nemenema- (db; 3) See *nem.* nu. (dis.; T3) reminder (of someone). *nemeneman r.* of him or her (any one of several types of grasses worn on the ear as a message in courtship).

nemenemenó (db; 1) See *nem, -nó.* F. vi. be regretful (with *reen*). *wúwa n. reen ááy féfféér* I am r. of (because of) my actions.

nemenemengngaw (db; 3b) See *neme-, ngngaw.* nu. (dis.; T3) misrule, bad exercise of power or authority.

nemeni₁ See *neme-, -ni-.* vo. (T6a) exert power or control over, govern, rule, boss, supervise, be responsible for. *pwisin n.* be independently, autonomously, or freely in control of; *wúwa pwisin nemeniyey* I am in autonomous control of myself, I am

nemeni₂

free, independent. *aan n. ewe angaang* his supervising the work. With dir. suf.: *nemenaanó, nemenóónó.*
nemeni₂ (3: *nemeniya-*) See *nemeni₁, -ya-*. n. (T3) government, authority, supervision; (with pos. suf.) sphere of authority, jurisdiction, thing governed. *nemeniyan* his sphere of a. *nemeniyen ewe angaang* a. over the work. *fáán nemeniyey* under my a. *chóón n.* supervisor, official, boss.
nemeni₃ See *nem, -ni-*. F. Var. *nameni.* vo. (T6a) think about, have on one's mind. With dir. suf.: *nemenaato* think of, remember, bring to mind; *nemenaanó, nemenóónó* forget.
nemenó See *nem.*
nemenóónó See *nemeni₁, nemeni₃.*
nemeto See *nem.*
nemin (3d) See *ne-₁, meen.* nu. (dem.) woman; miss, ma'am; polite term of address to a woman that one is not *pin mé wóón. n. kkeey, n. kkaan* these, those women. Ant. *áta-, wono-₁.*
neminna (3) See *nemin, na.* nu. (dem.) that woman by you. Dis. *nemin kkana.*
neminnaan See *nemin, naan.* nu. (dem.) that woman yonder. Dis. *nemin kkanaan.*
neminneen See *nemin, een₃.* nu. (dem.) this woman here by us. Dis. *nemin kkaan.*
neminneey (2) See *nemin, eey₁.* nu. (dem.) this woman here by me. Dis. *nemin kkeey.*
neminnewe (1) See *nemin, -we.* nu. (dem.) that woman (out of sight or past), the female person of reference (in narrative). Dis. *nemin kkewe.*
neminnoomw See *nemin, oomw.* nu. (dem.) this woman here by us. Dis. *nemin kkoomw.*
Nemwmwes nu. (pers.) legendary daughter of Sowuyap (Sowuwiyap). Pvb. *aa seningeni seningen N.* he has acquired the ears of N. (he does not heed the advice of a father or a chief).
neni-₁ (2) NENI₂. Var. *nááng.* ni. (T2) heaven, sky. *nenin énú* regions of heaven where the gods live. Cf. *náán.*
neni-₂ (2) NENI₃. [In cpds. only.] unsp. (u.m.) See *neniinúk.*
neniinúk (2) See *neni-₂, núkú-₁.* nu. ear ornament consisting of a disc attached to a hole made in the upper rim of the ear.

Nenisú (1) See *neni-₁, sú.* [Bollig] nu. (loc.) the second level of heaven (*nááng*). [It is the region of clouds, the "going" or "flying heaven."] Syn. *Nenimwékút.*
Nenikkun (2) See *neni-₁, kkun.* [Bollig] nu. (loc.) the third level of heaven (*nááng*). [It is the region of the stars, the "revolving heaven."] Syn. *Neninap.*
Nenimwékút (2) See *neni-₁, mwékút.* [Bollig] nu. (loc.) the second level of heaven (*nááng*). [It is the region of clouds, the "moving heaven."] Syn. *Nenisú.*
Nenimwmwúch (2) See *neni-₁, mwmwúch.* [Bollig] nu. (loc.) the highest part of heaven (*nááng*).
Neninap (3) See *neni-₁, nap.* [Bollig] nu. (loc.) the third level of heaven (*nááng*). [It is the region of the stars, the "main" or "great heaven."] Syn. *Nenikkun.*
Nenichamw (3) See *neni-₁, chaamw.* [Bollig] nu. (loc.) the fourth level of heaven (*nááng*). [It is the region of the gods, the "brow heaven."] Syn. *Faachchamw.*
Nenichang (3) See *neni-₁, chang.* [Bollig] nu. (loc.) the lowest level of heaven (*nááng*). [It is the region where birds fly, the "flight heaven."]
nenne- Dis. of *nne-₁, nne-₃.*
nenneeni (ds; 3) See *neeni.* va. (dis.) use or stay in a place without owning it. Cf. *neeniyeni.*
nennesset Var. of *nnesesset.*
nennenó Dis. of *nnenó.*
nennengar Dis. of *nnengar.*
nennengeni Dis. of *nnengeni.*
nennengngaw₁ Dis. of *nnengngaw* bad tasting.
nennengngaw₂ (ds; 3) See *nne-₁, ngngaw.* vi. have bad vision.
nennech (ds; 3) See *nech.* nu. (T3) striking, tapping, ringing (of a bell). vi. be striking, tapping, be ringing.
nennetá Dis. of *nnetá.*
nenneyar Dis. of *nneyar.*
nenneyééch₁ Dis. of *nneyééch* good tasting.
nenneyééch₂ (2) See *nne-₁, ééch.* vi., adj. have good vision.
nenneyiruk (3) See *nne-₁, ruk.* nu. (T3) surprise. *fóósun n.* exclamation of s. vi. be surprised, astonished.

nengi- (2, 3) NENGI₃, NENGA. unsp. glance, peek, look sideways. See *ánenga, ánengineng*. Cf. *nne-*₁.
nengi (1) NENGII. (Jap. *negi, neni*) nu. (T1) Welsh onion, leek. *efóch n.* one W. o. *anan n.* his W. o.
nengipwechepwech (3) See *nááng, pwechepwech.* nu. (T3) drought. [Traditionally attributed to the goddess Nipwechepwech.]
nengita (1) See *nááng, ta.* vi. be in famine, starving ("ruined heaven").
nengngin (2) See *ne-*₁, *ngin.* nu. (T2) girl; salesgirl in store. [Formerly coarse word, now standard.] *néwún n.* his g. child; his sweetheart (Rmn.). *n. Achaw* g. of Achaw clan. *féépwún n.* adolescent girl (teen age). Syn. *niyerá.*
nepwpwekit (3) See *nee-, pwpwekit.* nu. (loc.; T3) (in) pocket. *waasen n.* pocket watch.
nepwpwech (3) See *nee-, pwech.* nu. (loc.; T3) sandy shallows close to shore before deep water.
nepwpwo (1) nu. (T1) most advanced grade in the *Sópwunupi* school of *itang.* Cf. *pwpwo*₃.
nech (3) NECHA. vi. be struck sharply, tapped, rapped; be rung (of a bell, chimes, clock, metal object that gives a ringing sound; of a drum). Dis. *nennech* (ds.), *nechenech* (db.).
necheey See *nech, -e-*₂. vo. (T6b) 1. strike or tap sharply; ring, beat (of bell, chimes, drum). 2. shape by pecking (as in making a pestle of hard coral). 3. break (the top off a drinking coconut) with sharp tapping blows.
nechefáát (2) See *nech, -fáát.* nu. (T2) the top that has been cut off of a drinking coconut.
nechenech (db; 3) See *nech.* nu. (dis.; T3) 1. striking sharply, tapping, rapping. 2. shaping by pecking (of a pestle). vi. (dis.) 1. be shaped by pecking. 2. be cut (of drinking coconuts) [It is tabu for an *itang* to drink from a coconut that has been cut.]
nechisneyitér (Eng.) nu. legislator.
nechimóósi (1) NECHIMÓÓSII. (Jap. *nejimawashi*) nu. (T1) screwdriver. *efóch n.* one s. *aan n.* his s.
nechimóósiini See *nechimóósi, -ni-.* vo. (T4) screw (something) with a screwdriver.

nechchón (dc; 4) See *nee-, chón.* nu. (T2) deep place, deep water. Cf. *pwechepwech.*
new (3) NEWA₁. vi. flee, run away (of animals).
newenew (db; 3) NEWA₂. n. (T3) pronunciation, accent. *newenewan* his p.
neweyinón (4) See *nawa-, nónu-.* nu. (T2) cargo board laid in the inside of a canoe to provide a dry platform. *neweyinónun waa* canoe's c. b.
Newuwomá (1) See *ne-*₂, *wuwa-, má.* nu. (loc.) Romónum Island's highest hill (Mt. Wichuk on maps). [*Wiichuk* is the name of the land plot on the hill's summit and not the real name of the hill.]
Newúmá nu. (pers.) name of the legendary founder of a school of judo-like fighting. Cf. *newúwémá.*
newúwémá (1) See *ne-*₂, *wúú*₃, *má.* N. nu. (T1) throat lock in Trukese judo (*pwáán*). Syn. *chiyoromá.*
neya N. Var. *neey, nóóy.* vi. go where. *kepwe n.?* where are you going?
neyang (3) NEYANGA. Var. *nneyang.* nu. (T3) any true conch shell. [Any of the genus *Strombus* or the genus *Lambis*, including spider conchs.]
Neyi- pref. (pers. n.form.) feminine prefix in personal names. Cf. *Ina-, Na-, Eyi-.*
neyii- Var. of *neeyii-.*
neyifi (1) NEYIFII. (Eng.) nu. (T1) 1. navy. 2. sailor. *emén n.* one s. Syn. *kkayingún.* vi. be without underpants ("navy style").
neyis (2) NEYISI. (Eng.) nu. (T2) lace.
Neyinopw See *neyi-, nopw.* nu. (pers.) traditional goddess associated with breadfruit. [She lives in *Éwúr* and catches the breadfruit essence as it responds to the call of the breadfruit summoner (*sowuyótoomey*), holding it tightly in her hands so that it cannot fly away. If the breadfruit is late in forming, the *sowuyótoomey* performs a rite in which he fans with a fan and chants a spell. He repeats this until *Neyinopw* goes to sleep, opens her hands, and releases the breadfruit.]
Neyitinimataw See *ne-*₁, *itin mataw.* nu. (pers.) name of a legendary woman.
neyiy See *naaw.*
Né- Var. of *Na-* (used when the following vowel is *ú* or *é*).

né (1) See *nééₐ*. vi., adj. (be) liquified, melted, become liquified. With dir. suf.: *nééno*.

néé- (1) NÉÉ₃. [In cpds. only.] unsp. scraped, peeled (as skin of breadfruit).

nééɪ (1) NÉÉɪ. nu. (T1) perfume, cosmetic oil. *óóch* n. one indefinite amount or kind of p. *aan* n. his p. that he owns; *epitiyan* n. his p. to use. *néén afak, néén taka* unscented coconut oil; *néén ayis, néén ómón* coconut oil p. scented with the nut of the *ómón* tree (*Parinarium glaberrimum*); *néén eyirenges* p. from *Pittosporum* tree; *néén Fanaanú* p. in which a spell has been made that makes a woman crazy (symptoms include nymphomania); *néén Wóón* imported p.; *néén wúchúúch* unscented coconut oil (obtained by pressing).

nééₐ (1) NÉÉ₃. nu. (T1) pond, pool, flooded place. *néén attaw* a fishing pool; *néén wuu* a pool for fishtraps.

nééné₁ (db; 1) See *néé-*. va. (dis.) scrape, peel (as the skin off breadfruit). nu. (T1) scraping, peeling (the act).

nééné₂ (db; 1) See *nééₐ*. nu. (dis.; T1) liquid contents of something. *néénéén nóón* the l. c. in it; *néénéén owupw* breast milk. vi., adj. (dis.) have liquid contents; (be) flooded, brimming; full of liquids.

nééno See *né*.

néépwpwuk N. of *népwpwuk*.

nèét nu. tree (*Messerschmidia argentea*); fruit used as medicine. Syn. *amóneset*. Cf. *nnét*.

nééti See *néé-, -ti-*. vo. (T4) scrape, peel (as the skin off of breadfruit). [A specially cut cowrie shell is used as peeler.]

nékénék (db; 3) NÉKA. N. vi., adj. (be) selfish.

nékkéféw (2) See *nééɪ, kké-ₐ, féwú-ₐ* (?). nu. (T2) scented pressed coconut oil. Ant. *néén afak, néén taka, néén wúchúúch*. Cf. *népwpwuk*.

Némé nu. (loc.) Nama Island.

nénné (ds; 1) NNÉÉ₁. n. (T1v) size, measure; equal. *nénnéén* his s. *iiy nénnééyi chék* he is just my s., he is just like me (the equal of me). *nénnéé chék mé...* just the same as... *ifa nénnéén imwomw* how big is your house?, what is your house like? *nénnéénú wee chék* just the same as before. vi. be of a size; be the same, be uniform (in size or appearance, of two or more things). *siya nénnéé chék* we are the same s., we are just alike.

nénnééyéch (2) See *nénné, ééch*. vi. be of right size, of good size.

nénnééyiti See *nénné, -iti*. vo. (T2) be of same size as, fit the size of.

nénnéffengen (2) See *nénné, ffengen*. vi. be compared.

népwpwuk (2, 3) See *nééɪ, pwpwuk₁* (?). Var. *néépwpwuk*. nu. (T2, T3) scented coconut oil. *népwpwukun, népwpwuken* c. o. of. Cf. *nékkéféw*.

nétú nu. (temp.) 18th night of the lunar month.

néwú- See *naaw*.

néwú E.Wn., Ps. nu. (temp.) tomorrow. Syn. *neesor*.

néwúmanaw (3b) See *naaw, manaw*. vi. have children that live. Ant. *néwúmá*.

néwúmá (1) See *naaw, má*. vi. have many stillborn children or many children that die in infancy. Ant. *néwúmanaw*.

néwúmwéch (2) See *naaw, mwéch*. nu. (T2) a form of sorcery that makes childbirth difficult.

néwúnaatá See *néwúni*.

néwúnaatiw See *néwúni*.

néwúnap (3a) See *naaw, nap*. [Not used in pos. const.] nu. (T3) stepchild, spouse's child from before one's marriage to one's spouse.

néwúnapeey See *néwúnap, -e-ₐ*. vo. (T6b) be a stepparent to.

néwúnáátá See *néwúni*.

néwúnáátiw See *néwúni*.

néwúnéw (db; 2) See *naaw*. va. (dis.) have children; behave as a parent to; use, borrow, wear (of anything that one possesses as *néwún*).
néwúnéwúffengen (va.) use together, use jointly, share.
néwúnéwúffengenniiy (vo.; T6a); use (something) jointly, share. nu. (T2) being a parent, parenting; *néwúnéwún pwáápwá* parenting of a turtle (proverb said of a father who does not care properly for his children, because male turtles eat their young).

néwúnéwúffengen See *néwúnéw*.

néwúnéwúffengenniiy See *néwúnéw*.

néwúni See *naaw, -ni-*. vo. (T5) have or acquire as a child; be a parent to; acquire as an employee, subject, domestic, animal, or small personal object (anything that one possesses as *néwún*). *n. amanaw* (vo. phr.) maltreat, abuse, enslave. *n. emén kaamwmwet* acquire a sweetheart. With dir. suf.: *néwúnaatá* (N.), *néwúnáátá* (F.) raise, bring up (a child); *néwúnaatiw* (N.), *néwúnáátiw* (F.) bear, give birth to (a child).

néwúnurunó (1) nu. (T1) a species of fish.

néwúngngaw (3b) See *naaw, ngngaw.* vi. be bad to children or employees, be a bad or neglectful parent; have bad children. Ant. *néwúyéech.*

néwúngngaweey See *néwúngngaw, -e-₂.* vo. (T6b) be a bad parent to. Ant. *néwúyéchchúúw.*

néwúwepweteete (1) See *ne-₂, wúú₂, pweteete.* vi., adj. (be) soft of voice.

néwúwiis (2, 3) See *naaw, wiis₁.* nu. (T2, T3) public office; office holder (e.g. chief, treasurer, secretary, policeman, pastor, etc.). *néwúwiisin* or *néwúwiisen nóón fénú* p. o. of the island (municipality). Syn. *wiis₂.*

néwúyéech (2) See *naaw, éech.* vi. be good to children; be a good parent; have good children. Ant. *néwúngngaw.*

néwúyéchchúúw See *néwúyéech, -ú-.* vo. (T5) be a good parent to. Ant. *néwúngngaweey.*

ni-₁ (2) NI₂. pref. (n.form.) 1. thing that, one who (approximately equivalent to English *-er*). [Prefix in name of many animals, birds, fishes, shells, insects, plants, spirit beings, person, followed by an expression of a characteristic or activity.] *Nikowupwuupw* Producer-of-many-offspring (cf. *owupwuupw* produce many offspring). 2. the act, activity, or doing of (something).

ni-₂ (2) NI₃. pref. (intens.) very, truly, much, all the time, habitually. [Often difficult to distinguish from *ni-₁.*] *nisowukásissin* one who truly knows how to read signs and portents (cf. *sowukásissin*); *nikekkechiw* be a crybaby, cry a lot (cf. *kekkechiw*).

-ni- (2) NI₄. suf. (v.form.) 1. in vo. const. with bases that take suffixed pos. prns. in first or second person, it implies the possession or acquisition as owner or proprietor of whatever is denoted by the base. *ááni* acquire as a general type of object (see *aa-*); *fénúweni* acquire as land (see *fénú*); *imweni* acquire as shelter (see *iimw*). 2. in vo. const. with other bases, it implies application to the object of whatever is denoted by the base, and in vi. const. with these bases it implies the application to the subject of whatever is denoted by the base. *chééni* (vo.) wrap in leaves (see *chéé*); *chééchéén* (vi.) be centered (see *chééché*).

nii- (1) NII₂. [In cpds. only.] unsp. pour; be poured.

nii₁ (1) NII₁. Var. *ngii.* n. (T1) tooth. *niin* his t. *mesen n. t. edge; enniyapen n.* canine tooth; *apwaapwen n.* gums. *niin etenimas* upper incisor tooth; *niin mesen pwukos* lower incisor tooth; *niin ngáách* molar or premolar tooth; *niin núú* canine tooth; *niin nánit* tattooing needle (made from frigate bird bone and having three or four prongs).

nii₂ (1) NII₃. nu. (T1) name of the consonant (voiced, dental, nasal continuant) written *n*; name of the letter thus written.

niim (3b) NIMA₁. Var. *nniim.* nu. (num.) the number five. [Used in serial counting or to name the number in the abstract, but not used as a numerical adjective.] Cf. *nima-, nimu-.*

niinaanong See *niini₁.*

niináátiw See *niini₁.*

niini₁ See *nii-, -ni-.* vo. (T4) pour. With dir. suf.: *niinaanong, niináátiw, niinóónó.*

niini₂ (db; 1) See *nii-.* vi. (dis.) pour. With dir. suf.: *niiniitiw.*

niiniitiw See *niini₂.*

niinó (1) See *nii-, -nó.* vi. be poured off.

niinóónó See *niini₁.*

niipw (3) NIPWA₁. n. (T3) pit for soaking coconut husks preparatory to making rope from their fibers. [It is made in a fringing reef or mangrove swamp.] *nipwan* his p.

niit (2) NIITI. nu. (T2) squid, cuttlefish. *niitin* s. of (a kind or region). Syn. *nimárámár.*

nifanakkén nu. a species of fish (small, beaked, black on top and light underneath).

nifanan. (3) F. Var. *nifanang.* nu. (T3) a species of sea cucumber. [Considered inedible in Truk, it was used to force octopuses out of their holes.]

nifanang (3) See *ni-₁, fanang* N. Var. *nifanan.* nu. (T3) a species of sea cucumber.

nifaro

nifaro N. of *nifóro*.
nifach (3a) See *ni-₁, faach*. nu. (T3) 1. a vine (*Freycinetia* sp.). [Resembling a poor pandanus, it is usable for mat plaiting.] 2. a species of pandanus (*Pandanus comensii micronesicus*).
nifááánipwpwún (2) See *ni-₁, faa-₁, pwpwún₁*. nu. (T2) action that caused another's downfall without one's own actions in the matter being known ("underground affair"). [Example is to steal from a man in such a way as to cast suspicion on a formerly trusted employee so that the employee will be accused of the theft, the object being the employee's downfall not the possession of the stolen goods.]
nifeefeechón (db; 4) See *ni-₁, fe, chón*. Tb1. nu. (T2) dragonfly. Syn. *wusekiichén*.
nifech₁ nu. limpet.
nifech₂ Var. of *nnifech*.
nifecheyiti Var. of *nnifecheyiti*.
nifechéech Var. of *nniféchéech*.
niféééféeyiyas (ds; 3) nu. (T3) species of Moorish idol fish. Cf. *nikasakas, nikásseres*.
niféfféew (ds; 2) See *ni-₂, féfféew*. vi., adj. (be) very sensitive to cold; have chills.
nifén (2) nu. (T2) a sea cucumber (edible, small, found in *achékken* coral).
nifétúfét (db; 2) See *ni-₂, faat₁*. nu. (T2) serrated war-club ("many-browed-thing").
niféwúféw (db; 2) See *ni-₁, féwúféw₂* (?). nu. (T2) 1. trunk fish. 2. damsel fish. Syn. *wononum*.
niféwúmesepwpwun (3b) See *ni-₁, féwúnúmas, pwpwun₁*. N. nu. (T3) a species of bird (tiny, bright green in color, with white around the eyes; "blaze-eyes-thing"). Syn. *nichché, nichchéénófor*.
Niféwúnmesechchawerchchawer (db; 3) See *ni-₁, féwúnúmas, chchawer*. nu. (pers.; T3) name of an ogre in a story ("Pupily-eyeballs-thing").
nifinifin (db; 2) See *ni-₂, fini-₁*. vi., adj. (be) a matter of choice; (be) a choosy person, fastidious, particular, fussy. *ese n.* it is not a m. of c., it makes no difference; *meyi n.* it is a m. of c., it makes a difference; *emén meyi n.* a choosy, fussy, fastidious person; *wúse n.* I am not choosy, it makes no

difference to me; *aa n. anan mwéngé* his food makes a difference (to him) (i.e., he is choosy about his food).
nifinifintowunómw (ds; 2) See *ni-₁, finifin, towunómw*. nu. (T2) giant skate, manta. Syn. *ninumunum*.
nifich (2) See *ni-₂, -fich*. vi. be skillful.
nifichennap (3) See *ni-₁, fichennap*. nu. (T3) third grade of pandanus mat (plaited from original, undoubled, inch-wide leaflets). Syn. *fichennap*.
nifichifichimas (3) See *ni-₁, fichi-, maas₃*. nu. (T3) grasshopper. *nifichifichimasen* g. of (a type or region).
nifóro (1) Var. *nifaro*. nu. (T1) a bird (living in burrows by day, a great fisher). *étún ómwun n.* sea spray.
niffang (dc; 3b) See *ni-₁, fang*. nu. (T3) gift, present. [The recipient is obligated to the giver; cf. *kiis₁.*] *eew n.* one g. *aan n.* his g. *ááy n. ngonuk* my g. to you. vi. give a gift.
niffátán See *ni-₁, fátán*. nu. a cerithid or horn shell.
niffich (dc; 2) See *ni-₁, ffich*. nu. (T2) species of large, black, stinging ant.
niffóch Var. of *nimefóch*.
nis (2) NISI. vi. be without resources of any kind, be utterly destitute.
nisaangas (3) See *ni-₁, se-₁, angas*. vi. be naturally awkward or inept in all kinds of work. Ant. *angas*.
nisáásáánipwin (db; 1) See *ni-₁, sáá-, pwiin₃*. nu. (T2) a species of land bird (small, black; "night-noisy-one").
nisááw N. of *niseew*.
nisássááw (ds; 3b) See *ni-₂, sááw*. vi. be very shy, bashful, easily embarrassed.
nisáráfach (3) nu. (T3) <Elbert> a species of snapper fish (black spot near tail and black eye).
Nisáreere nu. (pers.) traditional goddess of loom weaving. [A sister of *Énúúnap*, she lives in the sky and is invoked, along with her sister *Nipáánaw*, by women for good products from the loom.]
niseew (2) F. Var. *nisááw*. nu. (T2) Portuguese man-of-war (jellyfish). *eew n.* one P. m. *niseewin* P. m. of (a given region). Cf. *nimóótong*.
Nisem nu. a school of *itang* lore (also said to be a grade within the *Sópwunupi* school). [Its patron spirit is Sowumwáár of the Keteman clan, and

it is associated with Mwáánitiw District, Wútéét (Udot) Island.]

nisemwáániyón (4) nu. (T2) a species of eel (black and white stripes).

nisenisenkámey (ds; 2) See *ni-₁, sáán, emey* N. nu. (T2) species of sea cucumber; (long and inedible, elastic and stretches up to 20 feet in length). Syn. *nimwúúmwúúkemey.*

niseningening (db; 3b) See *ni-₁, sening.* nu. (T3) 1. whitish eel. 2. <Elbert> vulgar name for the clitoris.

nisiin vi. be fearful, timid. Syn. *nissimwa, nissiyá.*

nisimwúút (2: *-mwúttú-*) See *ni-₁, si-₂, -mwúút.* n. (T2) tail (of a land animal, not of a bird). *nisimwúttún* its t.

nisiyapw (3) See *ni-₁, ssiyapw.* nu. (T3) chick, little chicken. *nisiyapwen* c. of (a given region or kind). Syn. *nisiyok, niyók.*

nisiyok (3) See *ni-₁, siyok.* nu. (T3) chick, little chicken. *nisiyoken* c. of (a given region or kind). Syn. *nisiyapw, niyók.*

nisoong (3a) See *ni-₁, soong.* nu. (T3) variety of large moth.

nisoowu (1) See *ni-₁* or *ni-₂, soo-₁ , -wu.* nu. (T1) the desire, the thought, or the act of sexual intercourse (whether legitimate or illegitimate). [Not a tabu word.] Syn. *eyinimwey.* vi. have the desire for, the thought of, or engage in the act of sexual intercourse. *kete n.* don't indulge in sex thoughts.

nisossong (ds; 3a) See *ni-₂, soong.* vi., adj. (be) easily angered, touchy, crabbed, hot tempered, cranky, choleric.

nisowukásissin (3: *-sissinna-*) See *ni-₂, sowukásissin.* nu. (T3) one who is truly master of reading signs and portents.

nisónop nu. a type of woman's wrap-around skirt (*chééyitúr*).

nisópwpwunen Kachaw n. phr. a small eel. [Romónum people do not eat it, but Wééné people are said to do so.]

nisúngúr (2) See *ni-₁, súngú-, -ri-.* nu. (T2) a variety of chicken. [It is claimed to have originated in Wútéét (Udot) Island and is an emblem of the Sópwunupi clan in Fááyichuk and of its *itang* school.]

nissefich (2) See *ni-₁, ssefich₂.* nu. (T2) an insect caused disease affecting *Colocasia* and *Alocasia* taros.

nisses (2) See *ni-₁, ssees* (?). nu. (T2) small wooden bowl (kind of *sepi*). *eew n.* one b. *sepiyan n.* his b.; *nissesin* b. of (a given make). *sópwun n.* flat projection at top of each end of the b.; *seningen n.* nose-like vertical projection at each end of the b.; *epin nisses* bottom of the b.

nissimwa (1) See *ni-₁* or *ni-₂, si-₂, -mwa.* vi. be cowardly, fearful, timid. Syn. *nisiin, nissiyá.* Ant. *maat, pwara.*

nissiyá (1) See *ni-₁* or *ni-₂, si-₂, -á.* vi. be cowardly, fearful, timid. Syn. *nisiin, nissimwa.* Ant. *maat, pwara.*

nisso (dc; 1) See *ni-₁, so₂.* nu. (T1) small girl's jumping game.

nissomw (3) See *ni-₁, ssomw.* nu. (T3) a species of damsel fish. *nissomwen* d. f. of (a given region).

nik (2) NIKI. vi. be discarded; be rejected, disliked. With dir. suf.: *nikinó* be alienated. *aa nikinó mé neetipey* she has become alienated from my heart.

nika- (3b: *nika-, niké-, niko-, nikó-*) cpd. pref. (c.) 1. thing that causes... See *ni-₁, a-₂.* 2. habitually or often causing... See *ni-₂, a-₂.*

nika (1) See *ni-₁, kaa-* (?). nu. (T1) a species of sea cucumber. [It is wrapped in breadfruit leaf and stored in a *kuumar* basket for two days until it smells high and is then eaten raw. Its rough outer skin is rubbed off on a stone before it is stored.]

nikaanen (2) See *ni-₁, aa-* (?), *neni-₁.* nu. (T2) 1. a toy propellor on a stick (made of coconut leaves). *efóch n.* one t. p. *aan n.* his t. p.; *nikaanenin* t. p. of. 2. <Elbert> a drill, drilling tool.

nikaanipwpwún Var. of *nikaanúpwpwún.*

nikaanúpwpwún (2) See *nika-, áni, pwpwún.* N. Var. *nikaanipwpwún.* nu. (T2) a species of earthworm. Syn. *nikénúúnúpwpwún.*

nikaangún (2) See *ni-₁, aa-* (?), *ngúnúngún.* nu. (T1) reed nose flute. *efóch n.* one r. n. f. *néwún n.* his r. n. f. *nikaangúnún Chuuk* Trukese r. n. f. Syn. *aangún.*

nikasafasaf (db; 3b) See *nika-, saf.* nu. (T3) tall swamp grass (*Cyperus javanicus, Sclenia margarifera*). [It is used as fishing medicine.]

nikasakas (db; 3) See *ni-₁, kasakas.* nu. (T3) a species of Moorish idol fish. Cf. *nifééfééyiyas, nikásseres.*

nikasésséér Dis. of *nikasséér*.
nikassaka (1) nu. (T1) men's head garland. *mwarin n.* his h. g.
nikasséér (2) See *nika-, sséér*. nu. (T2) the game of sliding down a slope on coconut fronds. vi. slide down a slope on coconut fronds. Dis. *nikaséssér* (ds) do surfing, skate.
nikasso Dis. of *nikóssó*.
nikamwaawúch (2) vi. swing on a branch. Cf. *mwawúchúúch*.
nikamwachché (1) See *nika-, mwa-, chééché*. vi. put one's arm around another person's shoulders or waist (as in walking together).
nikamwatté (1) See *nika-, mwa-, té$_2$*. vi. try to climb on someone's back. With dir. suf.: *nikamwattéétá. pwata kaa nikamwattéétá wóóy?* why did you try to climb up on my back?
nikamwuut Var. of *nikamwúút*.
nikamwúút (2: -*mwúttú*-) See *nika-, -mwúút*. Var. *nikamwuut*. n. (T2) tail (of a land animal, not of a bird). *nikamwúttún* its t. Syn. *nisimwúút*.
nikach (3) nu. (T3) a species of sea cucumber.
nikatapar (3) See *ni-$_1$, par*. nu. (T3) a species of sea cucumber (inedible, black on top and red underneath).
nikatattapw (ds; 3b) See *nika-, ttapw*. vi. (dis.) be strung out in a line, one after another. *kkéén n.* round, roundelay; sing a round.
nikatuttumw (ds; 2) See *nika-, ttumw$_1$*. vi. be stumbling.
nikattik (2) See *nika-, ttik$_1$*. N. Var. *nikettik*. nu. (T2) any musical instrument, whistle.
nikattow N. of *nikóttow*.
nikááp (2) See *nika-, ep* or *epi-$_1$*. nu. (T2) land bird (brown, long tail, timid and afraid of other birds).
nikáátápar Var. of *niteyikepar*.
nikásássá (ds; 1) See *nika-, ssá*. vi. run very fast. Syn. *nákásássá, nekesássá*.
nikásseres See *nika-, seres*. nu. species of Moorish idol fish. Cf. *nifééfééyiyas, nikasakas*.
nikáppich Var. of *nikeppich*.
nikekkechiw (ds; 3) See *ni-$_2$, kkechiw*. vi. be a crybaby, cry very much.
nikepikken (2) See *ni-$_1$, epi-$_1$, kken*. nu. (T2) triton trumpet shell (a kind of sewi).

nikeppis (2) See *nika-, ppis* (?). nu. (T2) light throwing spear.
nikeppich (2) See *nika-, ppich*. Var. *nikáppich, nikoppich*. nu. (T2) 1. bow and arrow; rubber sling and dart; fishing done with iron dart and rubber sling (by both men and women wearing goggles). 2. snare involving a noose attached to a sprung pole or sapling, released with a trigger. vi. fish with dart and sling.
nikeppichiiy See *nikeppich, -yi-$_2$*. vo. (T5) shoot with bow and arrow.
nikepwerik (3) See *nika-, pwerik*. nu. (T3) rozelle plant ("itchy thing" from its scratchy leaves).
nikeriker (db; 2) See *ni-$_1$, keri-*. nu. (T2) general name for butterfly fish. Syn. *sánápwapw*.
nikechin (2) See *nika-, chin*. nu. (T2) small pimple. *eféw n.* one s. p.
nikettik F. of *nikattik*.
nikewiiwi Var. of *nikkewiiwi*.
nikeyitepar Var. of *niteyikepar*.
niké (1) See *ni-$_1$, éé$_1$*. nu. (T1) the pickly chaff-flower (*Achyranthes aspera*).
nikééké (db; 1) See *ni-$_1$, éé$_1$*. nu. (T1) person who can't be separated from the company of his or her spouse ("hooked one").
nikéfénúnnúr (2) See *nika-, fa-$_2$, nnúr$_1$*. nu. (T2) bow knot, slip knot.
nikéfénúnnúrúúw See *nikéfénúnnúr, -ú-*. vo. (T5) tie with a bow knot or slip knot.
nikésúk$_1$ (2) See *nika-, ssúk$_2$* (?). nu. (T2) a vine (*Flagellaria indica*).
nikésúk$_2$ (2) See *nika-, ssúk$_1$* or *ssúk$_2$*. nu. (T2) gun, firearm of any kind (i.e. pistol, rifle, shotgun). *eföch n.* one g. *néwún n.* his g.; *nikésúkún* g. of (a certain manufacture). Syn. *ppek*.
nikémméwúr (dc; 2) See *nika-, méwúr*. nu. (T2) 1. a plant (*Phyllanthus neruru*). [It is used to make a medicine used in breadfruit summoning ritual.] 2. a plant (*Kyllinga pumila* or *Cyperus brevifolius*).
nikémwméwún (dc; 3a) See *nika-, mwméwún$_2$*. nu. (T3) children's swing. Syn. *nikéwúnéwún*. vi. swing on a swing. Cf. *mwéwúnéwún*.
nikénúúnúpwpwún (2) See *nika-, núúnú$_1$, pwpwún*. F. nu. (T2) an

earthworm; an intestinal worm. Syn. *nikaanúpwpwún.*
nikénúnnúkúúw See *nika-, nnúk₂, -ú-*. vo. (T5) tie up tight.
niképpúrú (1) See *ni-₁, éppúrú.* nu. (T1) plagiarism, cheating by copying (as on school examinations). vi. cheat by copying, plagiarize.
niképwét (2) See *nika-, -pwét.* nu. (T2) 1. burn scar. [Such scars were once common as a result of cauterizing ringworm; more recently they are made on the arms of young men and women lovers as tokens of affection.] *niképwétún* his b. s. 2. coconut-leaf midrib used in making burn-scars. vi. to make burn scars.
niképwétúúw See *niképwét, -ú-*. vo. (T5) make a burn-scar on.
nikéchéwúnúún (2) See *nika-, che-, wúnúún₁.* vi. be numb.
nikétúttúr (2) See *nika-, túr.* nu. (T2) ankle band. Syn. *riiriin peche.*
nikéw nu. lizard fish.
nikéwúnéwún (db; 3a) See *nika-, wún₃.* Var. *nikéwúnúún.* nu. (T3) 1. swing. *nikéwúnéwúnen, nikéwúnúúnen* s. of. Syn. *nikémwmwéwún.* 2. method of felling a tree by swinging a sharp stone against its trunk in order to chop it down.
nikéwúnúún Var. of *nikéwúnéwún.*
nikéwúngúúng (db; 2) See *nika-, wúng.* nu. (T2) bull-roarer (noise-maker made of coconut leaf on a string, said to cause a wind). *kete n. pwú ete ásápwáán* don't use the b. lest it be windy.
nikéwútúros (3a) See *ni-₁, éwútúros.* nu. (T3) person with short fingers.
nikiinóng Var. of *núkiinong.*
nikiitú vi. stay or engage in something for a long time; concentrate on something for a long time.
nikinik (db; 2) NIKI. vi. stand watch, guard. *aa n. nóón imwey* he s. g. in my house.
nikinikiiy See *nikinik, -i-₂.* vo. (T5) watch over, guard.
nikinikin (db; 2) See *ni-₁, kiin₁.* nu. (T2) shape, appearance. *nikinikin* its s. Syn. *napanap, wúméwúm.*
nikiniko (1) See *nik, ko* (?). vi. forget, be neglectful.

nikirááffit (2) See *ni-₂, irá* (?), *ffiit.* vi. twirl.
nikichuur₁ nu. 1. papal miter shell (*Mitra papalis* L.). 2. partridge tun shell (*Tonna perdix* L.). 3. small sea shell (like an ear shell, but with some flattening on two sides and with pronounced teeth on both sides of the aperture). Syn. *pachar.*
nikichuur₂ Tb. vi. be uncircumcized. Cf. *kkuumw.*
nikit (3) See *nik, -ta-₁.* nu. (T3) what is left over, left behind, left out; leavings, remains. *nikitan* what is left of it.
nikitaanó See *nikiti.*
nikiti See *nik, -ti-*. vo. (T5) leave (something) over or behind. With dir. suf.: *nikitaanó* (N.), *nikitóónó* (F.).
nikitirúúng Rmn. nu. small bird with bright green body and red tail. Syn. *niwúkúpar, túrin wén, wúkúpar.*
nikitóónó See *nikiti.*
nikoffiif (2: *-fiffi-*) See *ni-₂, ko-₃, ffiif.* vi. be confused, tangled (of line only). Syn. *nikopinipin.*
nikof núnnúr See *ni-₁, ko-₃, fi-, nnúr₁.* N. n. phr. slip knot. Syn. *nikorurrur.*
nikos nu. a seafood.
nikosi nu. dancing motion involving swaying body wnd hands.
nikomotiif (Eng.) nu. locomotive.
nikopinipin (db; 2) See *ni-₂, ko-₃, pini-.* adj. tangled, snarled (as a fish line). Syn. *nikoffiif.*
nikoppich Tn. of *nikeppich.*
nikorurrur (2) See *ni-₁, ko-₃, -rurrur.* nu. (T2) slip knot. Syn. *nikof núnnúr.*
nikochopwuchopw (db; 2) See *nika-, chopw.* nu. (T2) a plant (*Dendrobium* sp., *Robiquetia lutea*).
nikochchuwa (1) vi. a facial gesture consisting of dropping the eyelids and at the same time looking aside after catching the eye of a person of opposite sex. [It expresses interest and shyness at the same time.]
nikotuupwén (2) See *nika-, tuu-₂, pwénú-₂.* nu. (T2) veil worn on the heads of women during mass.
nikotupwutupw (db; 2) See *nika-, tupw₂.* nu. (T2) pitfall, trap (real or figurative).
nikowusuus (2) See *nika-, wusuus.* nu. (T2) frog triton or frog shell (family Bursidae).

nikowun₁ (2) See *nika-, wun.* vi. feel nausea from eating too much fat or grease. Syn. *wunun kiriis.*

nikowun₂ nu. an offering of coconuts placed on a grave immediately after burial and made to the good soul of the deceased.

nikowunowun (db; 3) See *nika-, wunowun.* nu. (T3) kind of swamp grass (*Cyperus javanica*).

Nikowupwuupw (db; 2) See *ni-₁, owupwuupw.* nu. (pers.) legendary sister's daughter of Sowukachaw ("bearer of many"); Truk's founding ancestress. [Likened to a coconut tree, she is the putative ancestress of the people and clans of Truk.]

nikoyikoy See *nikkoy.*

nikósso (dc; 1) See *nika-, soo-₃.* F. Var. of *nikasso.* nu. (T1) any small cowrie shell (family Cypraeidae), including the money cowrie. [Used as a counter in the game of *chaangke.*] Syn. *nimwárá₂.* Cf. *ngiingi₁.*

nikómmóót (2) See *ni-₁, ómmóót.* N. nu. (T2) trochus, trochus shell. Syn. *ómmóót.*

nikónókóón (db; 4) See *ni-₁, kkóón* (?). nu. (T2) a plant (*Abelmoschus moschatus*).

nikópwoopwo (db; 1) See *nika-, pwo.* nu. (T1) balloon.

nikópwór (4) See *nika-, pwór* (?). nu. (T2) mist on a mountain.

nikóchopwuchopw (db; 2) See *nika-, chopw.* nu. (T2) a species of orchid ("popper"). [So named because the leaves pop when snapped. The leaves are pounded to put in a concoction to reduce swelling of the scrotum.]

nikóto (1) See *nika-, -to.* vi. grab hold of another with one's hand. *wúwa n. wóón átánaan* I grabbed hold of that fellow.

nikótomwotomw (db; 3b) See *nika-, tomw.* vi. be loosely tied.

nikótókót (db; 4) See *ni-₁, kóto-.* nu. 1. a vine (*Cantella asiatica*). [Leaves and root used as medicine for pain in legs; leaves used with fruit of *nopwur* for medicine to reduce swelling from being pierced by a porcupine fish.] 2. tiny black swamp crab with bright red foreclaws.

nikótupwutupw (db; 2) See *ni-₂, tupw.* vi. be deceitful, tricky, sly.

nikóttow (2) See *nika-, towu-.* F. Var. *nikattow.* nu. (T2) species of lizard. [Said to be the same as *nichéwúpach* but used in reference to small ones.]

nikówuche (1) nu. (T1) woman's traditional wrap-around skirt or kilt. [Woven of hibiscus fiber.] *óruun n.* her s. (to wear).

nikóyóóyó (db; 1) See *nika-, óó.* nu. (T1) long line or wire.

nikukkutong N. of *nikúkkútong.*

nikum (3) NIKUMA. nu. wrist band, bracelet. *néwún n.* his b.; *nikumen* b. of. Cf. *kumosa-.*

nikúúch (2) nu. (T2) sea cucumber. *nikúúchún* s. c. of (a given region).

nikúúchéwúch (db; 3) nu. (T3) skink; small lizard with yellow strips.

nikúkkútong See *ni-₁, kkú-, tong.* F. Var. *nikukkutong.* nu. ant.

nikúweniin nu. sea horse. Syn. *orisin neeset, orisin sáát.*

nikúwenimmas (3) See *ni-₁, kúú₂, mmas₃.* nu. (T3) crab louse. Syn. *kúúnúmmas.*

nikkapwi N. of *nikkepwi.*

nikkáp Wn. of *nikkep.*

nikken (2) See *ni-₁, kken.* nu. (T2) mosquito. *emén n.* one m. *nikkenin* m. of (a given region).

nikkep (2) See *ni-₂, -kkep.* Var. *nikkáp.* vi. be big, large (of things and of wind). *meyi n. ásápwán* the wind is strong. Syn. *mmóng, nikkúng, nimwmwuk, wáchemwuk, wáchimwuk, wátte.* Ant. *-kkiis, kúkkún, ngin.*

nikkepwi (3) See *ni-₁, kke-₂, pwii.* F. Var. *nikkapwi.* nu. (T3) traditional upper garment (worn by women poncho-style). *eché n.* one g. *nikkepwiyen* g. of.

nikkewiiwi (db; 2) See *ni-₂, kke-, wii-₁.* Var. *nikewiiwi.* va. alternate, exchange, change off, trade, swap.

nikké (1) See *ni-₁, kké.* nu. (T1) whitish sand crab ("caller," because said to be able to call comrades when buried in the sand). *eew n.* one s. c.

nikkich (2) See *ni-₁, -kkich.* Tb. nu. (T2) Peeping Tom. vi. peep, peek (as a Peeping Tom).

nikkichiiy See *nikkich, -i-₂.* Tb. vo. (T5) watch (someone) as a Peeping Tom, peep or peek at.

nikkoy (dc; 2) See *ni-₂, koyi-₂*. vi. hop on one foot. Dis. *nikoyikoy* (db) limp. Cf. *koyikoy.*

nikkó (1) See *ni-₁, kóókó*. [In reference and address.] nu. (T1) baby girl. Cf. *wukkó.*

nikkóóch (2) See *ni-₁, óóch*. nu. (T2) childrens game. [One player makes several holes in the sand and then, scooping up sand, drops it into the holes, dropping a small stone or shell in one of them so that the sand covers it. The other player is to guess in which hole it has been dropped. If he guesses right he gets the stone and the other player has to guess.]

nikkumwuch (dc; 2) See *ni-₁, kumwuch*. nu. (T2) knuckle-duster (usually studded with shark's teeth).

nikkúng (2) See *ni-₂, -kkúng*. vi., adj. (be) big, large. [Traditionally a preferred word in the presence of brother and sister, father and daughter, and mother and son.] Syn. *mmóng, nikkep, nikkúng, nimwmwuk, wáchimwuk, wátte.* Ant. *-kkiis, kúkkún, ngin.* nr. (T2) bigness, large size. *nikkúngún eey mettóóch!* the b. of this thing!

nima- (3b: *nif-, nim-, nima-, nime-, nimé-, nimo-, nimó-*) See *niim*. pref. (num.) five. See *niffóch, nimaché, nimapé, nimayé, nime, nimechamw, nimechchi, nimechchoch, nimechú, nimechúk, niméféw, nimeffaat, nimeffit, nimefich, nimefóch, nimefutuk, nimengaf, nimengát, nimengéréw, nimengin, nimekis, nimekit, nimekkamw, nimekkap, nimekkumw, nimekum, nimekumwuch, nimekup, nimemach, nimemas, nimemataf, nimemech, nimemeech, nimemeet, nimemma, nimemmech, nimemmék, nimemwénú, nimemwmwék, nimemwmwun, nimemwmwú, nimemwmwún, nimemwu, nimemwú₁, nimemwú₂, nimemwúch, nimennú, nimepa, nimepachang, nimepan, nimepeche, nimepeek, nimepék, nimepéw, nimepino, nimepinúk, nimepu, nimepwang, nimepwey, nimepwéét, nimepwi, nimepwin, nimepwopw, nimepwór, nimepwpwaaw, nimepwpwún, nimepwúkú, nimepwún, nimesángá, nimesáwá, nimeseeng, nimesen, nimesópw, nimessaar, nimessak, nimessar, nimessáát,*

nimessát, nimessupw, nimetinewupw, nimetip, nimetit, nimettiit, nimetú, nimetúkúm, nimetún, nimewo, nimewoch, nimewumw, nimewupw, nimewut, nimewúwéw, nimeyaf, nimeyang, nimeyef, nimeyem, nimeyep, nimeyék, nimeyi, nimeyin₁, nimeyin₂, nimeyipw, nimeyiyey, niméwúk₁, niméwúk₁, niméwún, niméwút, nimmén, nimowo, nimowumw, nimóóch, nimóówut, nimówo. See also *nimuuw.*

nimaataat (db; 3) See *ni-₁, maataat*. nu. (T3) species of unicorn fish.

nimaatong Var. of *nimóótong.*

nimapé (1) See *nima-, péé-₁*. num. five empty containers.

nimaché (1) See *nima-, -ché*. num. five thin flat objects of any kind (e.g. sheets, leaves, planks).

nimayé (1) See *nima-, -é*. num. five hairs.

nimárámár (db; 3b) See *ni-₁, már*. nu. (T3) a kind of squid, cuttlefish. Syn. *niit*. vi. walk backward. Syn. *fátán sekúr.*

nime- (3a) NIMA₂. unsp. clean, neat, pure. See *nimenim, nimengngaw, nimeti, nimééch, ninnim₂, nnim, nnimet.*

nime (1) See *nima-, -e-₁*. num. fifty. With c. pref. and ptv. const.: *enimeen* fiftieth one. With dis. c. pref.: *ekkenime* be fifty at a time, by fifties. With suf. *-somw*: *nimeesomw* be more than fifty.

nimeesomw See *nime.*

nimeew See *ni-₁, -meew*. nu. a kind of jellyfish. [Small, dark, stinging, it has only one dangling streamer; its sting is more severe than that of a portuguese man-of-war.]

niméféw (2) See *nima-, -féw*. num. five lumps or globular shaped object (e.g. stones, balls).

nimefich (3a) See *nima-, ficha-*. num. five strips of coconut, pandanus, or palm leaf prepared for plaiting mats.

nimefóch (4) See *nima-, fóchu-*. Var. *niffóch*. num. five long objects (e. g. vehicles, legs, teeth, timbers, shovels).

nimefutuk (3) See *nima-, futuk*. num. five pieces of meat.

nimeffaat (3) See *nima-, ffaata-*. num. five strings of fish.

nimeffit (3) See *nima-, fitta-*. num. five leaf packages of small fish.

nimesap (3) See *nima-, saap.* num. five cheeks (especially of fish).
nimesááféw (2) See *ni-₁, maas₃, eféw.* nu. one-eyed person. *emén n.* one o.-e. p. vi. be one-eyed. *iiy meyi n.* he is (or he who is) o.-e.
nimesángá (1) See *nima-, sángá.* num. five basketfuls of fish. Syn. *nimesáwá.*
nimesáwá (1) See *nima-, sáwá.* num. five basketfuls of fish. Syn. *nimesángá.*
nimeseeng (3) See *nima-, seeng.* num. five lengths between joints.
nimesemechééw (db; 2) See *ni-₁, maas₃, chééw.* nu. (T2) one who gropes about unable to see ("the-featureless-faced"). vi. grope about.
nimesen (2) See *nima-, -sen.* num. five coils of rope. [Each coil is 30 to 100 fathoms in length according to local custom.]
nimesepwpwun See *ni-₁, maas₃, pwpwun₁.* nu. lantern fish.
nimesopwut (3) See *ni-₁, maas₃, pwuta-.* nu. (T3) person with a natural ability to see and communicate with ghosts. Cf. *wáánaanú, wáátawa.*
nimesópw₁ (2) See *nima-, sópwu-₂.* num. five segments.
nimesópw₂ (4) See *nima-, sópwu-₃.* num. five burdens of tied together breadfruit.
nimessaar (2) See *nima-, -ssaar.* Var. *nimessar.* num. five slices.
nimessak (3) See *nima-, ssaka-.* num. five pieces of copra.
nimessar N. of *nimessaar.*
nimessáát (2, 3) See *nima-, -ssáát.* Var. *nimessát.* num. five slivers, longitudinal slices, splinters.
nimessát N. of *nimessáát.*
nimessupw (2) See *nima-, ssupwu-.* num. five tiny drops.
nimekis (2) See *nima-, kisi-.* num. five little things or bits. Syn. *nimengin.*
nimekit (3) See *nima-, -kit.* num. fifty thousand.
nimekum (2) See *nima-, kumu-.* num. five mouthfuls or swallows of liquid.
nimekumwuch (2) See *nima-, kumwuch.* num. five fistfuls or handfulls (of something); five hooves, paws, feet (of animals).
nimekkamw (3b) See *nima-, kkamw.* num. five fragments or pieces (of cloth, paper).

nimekkap (3) See *nima-, kkap.* num. five cupfuls.
nimekkumw (2, 3) See *nima-, kkumw₁.* num. five portions of premasticated food. Cf. *nimemma.*
nimemas (3) See *nima-, -mas.* num. five things worn on the eyes (e.g., lenses of goggles) or attached to piercing weapons (e.g., spear points).
nimemach (3) See *nima-, macha-.* F. num. five fishtails (in counting fish). Cf. *niméwúk₁.*
nimemataf (3) See *nima-, matafa-.* num. five small portions, small amounts, little bits.
nimemeech (2) See *nima-, -meech.* F. Var. *nimemech, nimemmech.* num. five portions of mashed breadfruit.
nimemeet (3) See *nima-, meet₂.* num. five strands.
nimemech N. var. of *nimemeech.*
nimemma (1) See *nima-, -mma.* num. five mouthfuls of premasticated food. Cf. *nimekkumw.*
nimemmech N. var. of *nimemeech.*
nimemmék (2) See *nima-, mékkú-.* num. five fragments.
nimemwénú (1) See *nima-, mwénúú-.* num. five ells (lengths from elbow to fingertips).
nimemwu E.Wn. of *nimemwú₂.*
nimemwú₁ (1) See *nima-, mwúú-₁.* F. Var. *nimemwmwú.* num. five torn fragments (of rag or string).
nimemwú₂ (1) See *nima-, mwúú-₂.* Var. *nimemwu.* num. five sea cucumbers; five pieces of feces.
nimemwúch (2) See *nima-, -mwúch.* num. five pieces of firewood.
nimemwmwék See *nima-, mwékkú-.* N. num. five bits or morsels (of mashed food). Syn. *nimepwey.*
nimemwmwun (3) See *nima-, mwmwuna-.* N. Var. *nimemwmwún.* num. five portions of *mwatún.* Syn. *nimetún.*
nimemwmwú N. of *nimemwú₁.*
nimemwmwún F. of *nimemwmwun.*
nimenim (db; 3a) See *nime-.* vi. (dis.) be clean, neat, pure. Cf. *nnim.* n. (T3) neatness. *nimeniman* his n. *nimenimen eey neeni!* the neatness of this place!
nimenimengngaw Dis. of *nimengngaw.*

Trukese-English nimetip

nimenimééch Dis. of *nimééch*.

nimennú (1) See *nima-, nnúú-*. num. five loaves of breadfruit pudding or amounts of breadfruit to be mashed into pudding loaves.

nimengaf (3) See *nima-, ngaaf*. num. five fathoms, five times the distance from fingertip to fingertip of outstretched arms.

nimengát (4) See *nima-, -ngát*. num. five concave or hollow objects;(less common) five things of most any kind. Cf. *nimepwang, nimuuw*.

nimenger (3) See *ni-₁, menger*. nu. (T3) edible sea cucumber (found in *áán* coral).

nimengéréw (2) See *nima-, -ngéréw*. num. five thousand.

nimengin (2) See *nima-, ngini-*. num. five little things or bits. Syn. *nimekis*.

nimengngaw (3b) See *nime-, ngngaw*. vi. be dirty, messy, disarrayed. Dis. *nimenimengngaw* (db).

nimepa (1) See *nima-, -pa*. num. five fronds, garlands, stalks with leaves. [Of palm trees, banana trees, *Cyrtosperma*, and also of leis or garlands, necklaces, bead belts.] Cf. *nimepan*.

nimepan (3) See *nima-, paan₁*. num. five branches with leaves (of trees other than palms and bananas). Syn. *nimepachang*. Cf. *nimepa*.

nimepachang (3) See *nima-, pachang*. num. five branches with leaves. Syn. *nimepan*.

nimepeek (2) See *nima-, peek₂*. num. five sides, pages.

nimepeche (1) See *nima-, peche*. num. five lower or hind limbs (of humans, birds, and animals only).

nimepék (2) See *nima-, péék₂*. num. five chips, chopped off pieces, ciagarette butts.

nimepéw (2) See *nima-, -péw*. num. five wings or things worn over hand or arm (e.g., gloves); five armlengths (from finger-tips to shoulder).

nimepino (1) See *nima-, pino*. num. five small packages of breadfruit pudding.

nimepinúk (2) See *nima-, pinúk*. num. five tied bundles, reams of paper.

nimepu (1) See *nima-, puu-₂*. num. five strokes in swimming (in measuring distance).

nimepwang (3) See *nima-, pwaang*. num. five holes, caves, cavities, pits, tunnels, hollows. Cf. *nimengát*.

nimepwey (2) See *nima-, -pwey*. num. five pinches or morsels of breadfruit pudding. Syn. *nimemwmwék*.

nimepwéét (2) See *nima-, pwéét*. num. five noses.

nimepwi (1) See *nima-, pwii-₁*. num. five groups, groves, flocks, schools, herds, swarms, convoys, prides, etc.

nimepwin (2) See *nima-, pwiin₃*. num. five nights.

nimepwopw (2) See *nima-, pwoopw*. num. five tree-trunks, bases, foundations, causes, sources, beginnings, origins, reasons.

nimepwór (4) See *nima-, pwóór*. num. five boxes or crates (of something).

nimepwúkú (1) See *nima-, -pwúkú*. num. five hundred.

nimepwún (2) See *nima-, pwúún₁*. Var. *nimepwpwún*. num. five pieces (broken off).

nimepwpwaaw (2) See *nima-, pwpwaaw*. num. five home-made cigarettes.

nimepwpwún N. of *nimepwún*.

nimechamw (3) See *nima-, -chamw*. num. five foreheads, brows, or similarly classed objects (e.g., visors, stem-bases of coconut fronds); five fishheads.

nimechef See *nima-, -chef*. num. five tentacles (of octopus or squid). Syn. *nimeyó, niméwút*.

nimechú (1) See *nima-, chúú*. num. five bone segments (of meat).

nimechúk (2) See *nima-, chúúk*. num. five coconut-leaf baskets (of something).

nimechchi (1) See *nima-, -chchi*. num. five drops.

nimechchooch (3) See *nima-, chchooch* num. five armfuls.

nimetaawu See *nimeti*.

nimeti See *nime-, -ti-*. vo. (T2) clean, clean up, neaten, make neat, spruce up. With dir. suf.: *nimetaawu* clean out.

nimetinewupw (2) See *nima-, tinewupw*. num. five yards (lengths from center of chest to outstretched fingertips).

nimetip (3) See *nima-, tiip₂* num. five slices, chunks, cut segments (of breadfruit and taro only).

nimetit   Trukese-English

nimetit (2) See *nima-*, *-tit*. num. five strings (of breadfruit, usually ten to a string). Syn. *nimettiit*.

nimetú (3) See *nima-*, *túú*. Tbl. num. five vulvas (in enumerating sexual encounters).

nimetúkúm (3) See *nima-*, *túkúm*. num. five packages of breadfruit pudding.

nimetún (2) See *nima-*, *túnú-*. F. Var. *nimettún*. num. five portions of *mwatún* pudding. Syn. *nimemwmwun*.

nimettiit (2) See *nima-*, *ttiit₂*. num. five strings of ten breadfruit. Syn. *nimetit*.

nimettún N. of *nimetún*.

nimewo (1) See *nima-*, *-wo*₁. Var. *nimowo*, *nimówo*. num. five clumps (of bananas).

nimewoon (3) See *niim*, *woon* nu. (num.) the combined number five-six in serial counting by twos (formed from elements for both five and six).

nimewoch See *nima-*, *-woch*. Tn. num. five sorts, kinds, rations, varieties, species. Syn. *nimóóch*.

nimewumw (2) See *nima-*, *wumwu-*₂. Var. *nimowumw*. num. five stalks of bananas.

nimewupw (2) See *nima-*, *wupwu-*₁. num. five breasts.

nimewut (2) See *nima-*, *wutu-*. num. 1. five cores (especially of breadfruit). 2. five chunks of cooked breadfruit.

nimewúwéw (2) See *nima-*, *-wúwéw*. num. five amounts of fermented breadfruit suitable for kneading.

nimeyaf (3b) See *nima-*, *-af*. num. five pieces of intestine.

nimeyang (3) See *nima-*, *-ang*. num. five finger spans; five entire limbs (of an animal).

nimeyef (2) See *nima-*, *eef*₁. num. five bunches of ripe coconuts.

nimeyem (2) See *nima-*, *eem*. num. five earlobes.

nimeyep (2) See *nima-*, *epi-*₁. num. five butt ends, lower ends, west ends.

nimeyék (2) See *nima-*, *ékkú-*. num. five nets.

nimeyi (3) See *nima-*, *-i*. Rmn. num. five hands (of bananas). Syn. *nimeyin*₁, *nimeyiyey*.

nimeyin₁ (3) See *nima-*, *ina-*₂. N. num. five hands of bananas. Syn. *nimeyi*, *nimeyiyey*.

nimeyin₂ (2) See *nima-*, *ini-*₂. num. five shoots.

nimeyipw (3) See *nima-*, *-ipw*. num. five steps, footprints, soles; five items of footwear; five feet (distance from heel to toe).

nimeyiyey (3) See *nima-*, *iyeyiya-*. num. five hands of bananas. Syn. *nimeyi*, *nimeyin*₁.

nimeyó (1) See *nima-*, *óó*₁. num. five tentacles (of octopus or squid). Syn. *nimechef*, *niméwút*.

nimééch (2) See *nime-*, *ééch*. vi. be pretty, neat, beautiful, clean. Dis. *nimenimééch* (db).

niménnúké (1) See *ni-*₁, *maan*₁, *éé*₁. F. nu. (T1) centipede. Syn. *ménnúkamw*.

ninéngér Var. of *méngér*.

niméwúk₁ (2) See *nima-*, *wúúk*₁. num. five tails (in counting fish). Cf. *nimemach*.

niméwúk₂ (2) See *nima-*, *wúúk*₂. num. five fingernails, toenails, claws.

niméwún (3a) See *nima-*, *wúún*₁. num. five feathers, scales, hairs.

niméwút (2) See *nima-*, *-wút*. num. five fingers or toes; five octopus tentacles, insect legs. Cf. *nimechef*, *nimeyó*.

nimong (3) See *ni-*₁, *moong*. nu. (T3) any of a wide number of small marine gastropods, including the periwinkle and little dove shell.

nimowo Var. of *nimewo*.

nimowumw Var. of *nimewumw*.

nimóóch See *nima-*, *-óch*. num. five sorts, rations, kinds, varieties, species. Syn. *nimewoch*.

nimóótong See *ni-*₁, *maa*, *tong*. Var. *nimaatong*, *nimmóótong*. nu. Portuguese man-of-war (jellyfish). [Said to come from Éwúr, it is a taboo object to be avoided because of its sting and its association with supernatural power.] Cf. *niseew*.

nimóówut (3) See *nima-*, *owut*. num. five rows of thatch.

nimówo Var. of *nimewo*.

nimu- Var. of *nima-* five (see *nimuuw*).

nimuu N. of *nimuuw*.

nimuuw (3) See *nimu-*, *-uw*. F. [From earlier *nimowu*.] Var. *nimuu*, *numuu*. num. five general-class things. With c. pref. and ptv. const.: *enimuuwan* fifth one. With dis. c. pref.: *ekkenimuuw* be five at a time, by fives. Syn. *nimengát*.

nimmang (3) See *ni-*₁, *mmang*. nu. (T3) brown heron. Syn. *nichchaw*, *niwoowo*.

nimmén (2) See *nima-, maan₁*. num. five persons or creatures (of people, mammals, birds, fish, and insects; but not of lobsters, crabs, sea cucumbers, or shellfish); five knives, guns, files, scissors.

nimmóótong Var. of *nimóótong*.

nimwamw (3) See *ni-₁, mwmwa-* (?). nu. (T3) woman's head garland, lei. [Its use as a term of address is insulting.] *mwárin* n. her g.; *nimwamwen* g. of (a particular type).

nimwanúk (2) See *ni-₁, mwa-, núk.* nu. (T2) gad-about. vi. gad about.

nimwaramwarsapwon (3) nu. (T3) zebra eel. *nimwaramwarsapwonen* z. e. of (a given region).

nimwárá₁ (1) See *ni-₁, mwárá.* nu. (T1) sponger or cadger of meals. *emén* m. one s.

nimwárá₂ (1) nu. (T1) any small cowrie, including the money cowrie. [Elbert gives N. *nimmwere*.] Syn. *nikósso, chaangke₂*. Cf. *ngiingi₁*.

nimwékútútiw (3) See *ni-₂, mwékút, -tiw.* vi. move down.

nimwékkútúúw See *ni-₁, mwa-, -kút, -ú-*. Tb. vo. (T5) masturbate. Cf. *mwékút*.

nimwémwmwéngéyásápwán See *ni-₁, mwéngé, ásápwán.* nu. a small bat ("wind-eater").

nimwérúng nu. species of small fish. *chuun* n. net with fine mesh.

nimwiimwi (db; 1) nu. (T1) outrigger sailing canoe of the type with short blunt endpieces. [Common in the Mortlocks.]

Nimwootonong nu. (pers.) name of a god in Ponape.

Nimwoyi nu. (pers.) famous *chénúkken* spirit that lives in a hole by the rocky water's edge at Núkúnúféw, Wútéét (Udot) Island. *sáfeen N.* medicine for sickness caused by N.

Nimwóóchow nu. (pers.) a traditional god. [An inhabitant of *Éwúr*, he is patron of the *pwérúkún wuwáán irá* (dance of tree fruits), performed as a part of traditional increase rites.]

nimwuumwuukámey N. of *nimwúúmwúúkemey*.

nimwuk nu. angel fish.

nimwúúmwúúkemey (db; 2) See *ni-₁, mwúú-₂, emey.* F. Var. *nimwuumwuukámey.* nu. (T2) species of sea cucumber. [It is long, inedible, and elastic, stretching up to 20 feet in length.] *emwú* n. one s. c.

nimwmwereyón (4) See *ni-₁, mwara-, -ón.* nu. (T2) rudder fish.

nimwmwet (3a) See *ni-₁, mwmwet.* nu. (T3) mud skipper fish (*Periophthalmus*). *nimwmweten* m. s. of. Syn. *nusupaat*.

nimwmwuk (dc; 3a) See *ni-₂, -mwuk.* vi., adj. (be) very big, large, huge, enormous. [This is a preferred form in the presence of brother and sister, father and daughter, and mother and son.] With dir. suf.: *nimwmwukonó* get bigger, increase, grow (in size). Syn. *mmóng, nikkep, nikkúng, wáchemwuk, wáchimwuk, wátte*. Ant. *-kkiis, kúkkún, ngin*.

nimwmwukonó See *nimwmwuk*.

nini (1) NINII. (Eng.) nu. lily flower (*Canna*). [Worn on the ear as a sign of a broken heart, *neetipeta*.] Syn. *paachew*.

ninimwmwun (2) nu. (T2) pole of reed or hibiscus, about 5 feet long, to which banana fibers are lashed preparatory to setting up a loom. *ninimwmwunun* p. of.

ninumunum (db; 2) See *ni-₁, numu-.* nu. (T2) manta, giant skate ("folder"). Syn. *nifinifintowunómw*.

ninnen See *ni-₁, nne-₁* (?). nu. a very small fish, (*Gerres baconensis*).

ninni (ds; 1) See *nnii-.* vi. (dis.), va. be assaulted (physically); assault, kill. *kesapw n. aramas* you shall not assault (kill) people. With dir. suf.: *ninniinó* be assaulted, be killed.

ninniinó See *ninni*.

ninnis₁ (2) NINNISI₁. vi. (dis.) watch over a place, stand guard. Cf. *nnis*.

ninnis₂ (2) NINNISI₂. nu. (T2) diagnosis of illness by rubbing the patient's arms. *chóón n.* one who can diagnose by this method.

ninnisiiy₁ See *ninnis₁, -i-₂.* vo. (T5) watch, guard.

ninnisiiy₂ See *ninnis₂, -i-₂.* vo. (T5) diagnose the illness of (someone) by rubbing the patient's arms.

ninnikopwuupwu (ds, db; 1) See *nika-, pwuupwu₁.* nu. (T1) flotsam carried down in a stream or river ("streaming-things").

ninnim₁ (2) nu. (T3) many-colored spider. *emén n.* one s. *ninnimin* s. of. *wuken n.* spider web.

ninnim₂ (ds; 2) See *nime-*. va. clean.

ninnich Dis. of *nnich*.

ninnupwe (1) nu. (T1) species of small fruit bat.

ninching (Jap. *ninjin*) nu. carrot, panax. Syn. *károt*.

ning (3b) NINGA. vi. come into view, appear, become visible. *aa n. maram* the moon has appeared (of a new moon). Cf. *nning.* nr. (T3) appearance, coming to view. *ningen maram* new moon.

ningafé (1) See *ning, -fé₁*. vi. appear anew (of the moon).

ningengngaw Var. of *nningengngaw*.

ningeriiti See *ningeringer, -iti*. vo. (T2) exhibit one's dislike toward. Dis. *ningeringeriiti* (db). Syn. *máángngaweyiti*.

ningeringer (db; 2) See *ni-₂, ngeringer*. vi. exhibit one's dislike in one's face. Cf. *soong*.

ningeringeriiti Dis. of *ningeriiti*.

ninget (2) NINGETI. nu. (T2) spear. *ningetin sikách* sting-ray spine.

ningúúngúúmeech Var. of *ningúúngúúmech*.

ningúúngúúmech (ds; 3) See *ni-₁, ngúúngú₂, meche-* (?). Var. *ningúúngúúmeech*. nu. (T3) creature that lives underground and makes a groaning noise ("facile-groaner").

ningúúchew nu. a kind of toadstool.

ningús (2) See *ni-₂, ngús*. nu. young or little *mwooch* fish (species of surgeon fish).

ningnger (dc; 2) See *ni-₁, ngnger*. nu. (T2) tiny species of louse, young louse.

nipa (1) See *ni-₁, paa₁*. nu. (T1) mat of the finest grade plaited from pandanus. *eché n.* one m. *kiyan n.* his m.; *nipaan* m. of (a particular make).

Nipááñaw nu. (pers.) traditional goddess of loom weaving. [A sister of *Nisáreere*, she lives in the sky and is patroness of *enikesin túúr* (winding the warp and placing it on the loom).]

nipechemmach (3) See *ni-₁, pechemmach*. nu. (T3) man-in-the-moon. Cf. *nipéépéénúmóng₁*.

nipéénéppún (2) See *ni-₁, péé₁, éppún*. nu. (T2) a species of fish (flat, both eyes on same side).

Nipéépé See *ni-₁, pé₃*. nu. (pers.) a traditional goddess. [An inhabitant of *Éwúr*, she causes scarcity of fish and food.]

nipéépéénúmóng₁ (db; 4) See *ni-₂, péé-₁, móóng*. vi. be completely bald. nu. (T2) 1. one with all one's hair cut off, one who is completely bald. 2. man-in-the-moon. Cf. *nipechemmach*.

Nipéépéénúmóng₂ See *nipéépéénúmóng₁*. nu. (pers.) a legendary *itang* and demigod who was the first lord of Fanó (Falo) Island. [He was second to none in his knowledge of spells and was therefore invulnerable.]

nipéppérúnút₁ nu. a blue starfish.

Nipéppérúnút₂ [Elbert: *Nipéppárenút*] nu. (pers.) god of rain (according to Elbert). Cf. *wúút₂*.

nipéwúttún (2) See *ni-₁, paaw₁, ttún*. nu. (T2) sleeveless undershirt. *eché n.* one s. u. *wúfan n.* his s. u.; *nipéwúttúnún* s. u. of (a given make). Syn. *ranning*. Cf. *singenes*.

nipéwúyánney (2) See *ni-₁, paaw₁, ánney*. nu. (T2) crested tern. Cf. *nipuwánney*.

nipéwúyesópw (2) See *ni-₁, paaw₁, esópw*. vi. be half-armed (of someone who has lost part of an arm).

nipich (2) See *ni-₁, pich₂*. nu. unmarried person (not yet married, divorced, or widowed). *emén n.* one u. p. *nipichin* u. p. of (a given place). *fin n., fiin n., finenipich* unmarried woman; *re-n., átenipich, mwáán n.* unmarried man. *n. mwáán esaa wmo pwúpwpwúnú* bachelor; *n. feefin esaa mwo pwúpwpwúnú* spinster, old maid; *n. mwáán meyi máánó pwúnúwan* widower; *n. feefin meyi máánó pwúnúwan* widow. *néwún n.* bastard, child born out of wedlock (no stigma of illegitimacy attaches to such children); *imwen n.* house of prostitution, whorehouse, brothel. Syn. *ángétúúrú*. vi., adj. (be) unmarried.

nipuwánnem (3) Var. *nipuwánney*. nu. (T3) a species of bird (on reef islands). *nipuwánnemen* b. of (a given region).

nipuwánney (2) Var. *nipuwánnem*. nu. (T2) a species of bird (on reef islands). *nipuwánneyin* b. of (a given region). Cf. *nipéwúyánney*.

nippach (dc; 3b) See *ni-₁, pach*. nu. (T3) octopus. *pachen n.* body of the o. at the point where the tentacles emanate. *éwútún n., óón n.* o. tentacle. Cf. *kúús, niit, nimárár.*

nippé (1) See *ni-₁, ppé.* N. nu. (T1) box-shaped ball made of pandanus leaf; game played with this ball. vi. play with an *n.* ball.

nippénú (3?) See *ni-₁, pénú* (?). nu. (T3?) damsel fish.

nippiis (2) NIPPIISI. (Eng.?) n. (T2) urine. *nippiisin* his u. va. urinate.

nippú nu. sand-colored goby fish.

nipw (3) NIPWA₂. vi., adj. (be) hilled up (as around a plant in gardening).

nipwachchaach (3) vi. swim on the back. Syn. *niyááyáánipwin.*

nipwáákééch (2) See *ni-₁, pwáák, ééch.* vi. be skilled, clever, diligent, efficient, able, capable.

nipwáákingngaw (3) See *ni-₂, pwáák, ngngaw.* vi., adj. (be) unskilled, incapable, inept.

nipwáárech N. Var. *nipwóóroch.* nu. a green lizard. Syn. *kúmwachen.*

Nipwe (1) nu. (loc.; T1) alternative name for the *Pwee* clan. [Apparently from the expression *mwáánnipwe* man of *Pwee* (*mwááninipwe).] *fin* N., *fiin* N. N. woman; *mwáán* N., *re-*N. N. man. *chóón* N. people of N.

nipweepwe (db; 1) See *ni-₁, pweepwe₂.* nu. (T1) a serrated war-club.

nipweni₁ nu. a variety of breadfruit.

nipweni₂ See *nipw, -ni-*. vo. (T6a) make a hill in.

nipweni₃ See *niipw, -ni-*. vo. (T6a) acquire (something) as a soaking pit.

nipwenipw (db; 3) See *niipw.* vi. (dis.), va. use a soaking pit.

nipwen kachen n. phr. a cross-lash technique of lashing.

nipwepwpweyiya (1) Var. *nipwepwpweyiyá.* nu. (T1) war-club cut in a pattern of successive diamonds with sharp cleats on the flatter sides. *efóch n.* one w. c. *wókun n.* his w. c. *nipwepwpweyiyaan* w. c. of (a given make).

nipwepwpweyiyá Var. of *nipwepwpweyiya.*

Nipwechepwech See *ni-₁, pwech.* nu. (pers.) traditional goddess of drought and famine. [She lives in *Éwúr.*]

nipwékúpwék (db; 2) See *ni-₁, pwékú-.* nu. (T2) crossmark vi. mark a crossmark.

nipwépwpwérúk (ds; 2) See *ni-₁, pwérúk.* nu. (T2) small brown sea bird ("dancer," so called because it teeters its body and tail).

nipwisipwis₁ (2) See *ni-₁, pwisipwis.* nu. (T2) butterfly ("silent-together-beater"). Syn. *nipwisipwisikkón.*

nipwisipwis₂ (2) vi. be triangular in shape. Cf. Wol. *lipweyisiisi.*

nipwisipwisikkón (3b) See *ni-₁, pwisipwis, kkón₂.* Var. *nipwisipwis.* nu. (T3) butterfly.

nipwich (2) See *ni-₁, pwich₂.* nu. (T2) small mollusc found in seaweed at very low tide (sometimes poisonous to eat). *eféw n.* one m. *nipwichin* m. of.

nipwichach (3) nu. (T3) reed throwing-spear.

nipwo (1) See *ni-₁, pwo.* nu. (T1) puffer fish.

nipwoopwo (db; 1) See *ni-₁, pwoopwo₂.* nu. (T1) 1. a fish (head used in former times to scent pressed coconut oil). 2. <Elbert> a species of surgeon fish (*Hepatus nigrofuscus*).

nipwooton (3a) See *ni-₁, pwo, ton* nu. (T3) a species of goat fish (jet black).

nipwopwpwomw (db; 3) See *ni-₁, pwoomw.* vi. be a mimic. nu. (T3) imitation.

nipwopwpwomweey See *nipwopwpwomw, -e-₂.* vo. (T6b) mimic, ape. Syn. *nipwopwpwomweni.*

nipwopwpwomweni See *nipwopwpwomw, -ni-*. vo. (T6a) mimic, ape. Syn. *nipwopwpwomweey.*

nipwóóroch F. of *nipwáárech.*

nipwúkúpwúk (db; 2) See *nipwúk.* vi. (dis.) be bumpy, uneven, rough.

nipwpwe (1) NIPWPWEE. nu. (T1) twin (of siblings).

nipwpwer nu. tusk (of pig).

nipwpwey (2) See *ni-₁, -pwey.* nu. (T2) land crab ("pincher," found in holes near the sea, but not on the beach itself). *eew n.* one l. c. *nipwpweyin* l. c. of. Syn. *rokumw.*

nipwpwét (2) See *ni-₁, pwpwét* (?). nu. (T2) a species of shellfish and its shell.

nipwpwuch nu. a variety of breadfruit.

nipwpwúk

nipwpwúk (dc; 2) See *ni-₂, pwúk*. nu. (T2) bump, projection; bumps on baby's head (caused by spirits).

niram (3) See *ni-₁, ram*. nu. (pers.) a nickname ("orange-red one").

niréérééféw (ds; 2) See *ni-₁, ré₁, faaw*. nu. (T2) thresher shark. [It is classed as a kind of *pachaaw*.]

nich (2) NICHI₁. [In cpds. only.] Var. *núch*. vi. be disappointed.

nichaase (1) See *ni-₂, cha, see*. Tbl. nu. (T1) fellatio.

nichaatú (1) See *ni-₂, cha, túú*. Tbl. nu. (T1) cunnilingus.

nichéénúkar (3) nu. (T3) a species of edible bivalve shellfish.

nichéénfetin (2) See *ni-₁, chéé, fetin*. nu. (T2) a species of fish.

nichéénkayé (1) nu. (T1) species of surgeon fish.

nichééngeni nu. mackerel when about one inch long.

nichéwúpach (3b) nu. (T3) species of lizard. [Similar to *nikóttow*, but usually of larger adult stage.]

nichi- (2) NICHI₂. [In cpds. only.] unsp. leak. See *nnich*.

nichimwmwú (1) See *nich, mwmwú*. N. vi. feel sunk (as when one has lost all one's money gambling). Syn. *nichippúng*.

nichin (2) See *ni-₁, chin*. N. nu. (T2) species of crab (very poisonous). Syn. *éwúngéwúng*.

nichippúng (2) See *nich, ppúng*. F. vi. feel sunk (as when one has lost all one's money gambling). Syn. *nichimwmwú*. nu. (T2) sunken feeling.

nichopw (2) nu. (T2) second finest grade of pandanus mat.

Nichuuchuumataw (3) See *ni-₁, cheew, mataw*. nu. (pers.) sea goddess who fishes with hand nets ("deep-sea-netter"). [Sailors who are polite and ask her permission to pass so that she can lift her nets come to no harm; those who are arrogant and tear her net by sailing through it are subsequently cursed by her and come to harm.]

nichúkken (2) See *ni-₁, chúú, kken*. nu. (T1) species of porcupine fish ("sharp-bone-thing").

nichchaw (3) See *ni-₁, chchaw*. nu. (T3) brown heron (slow flier). Syn. *nimmang, niwoowo*.

Trukese-English

nichché Short for *nichchéénófor*.

nichchéénófor See *ni-₁, chéé, ófor*. F. nu. a species of bird (tiny, bright green in color, with white around the eyes). Syn. *niféwúmesepwpwun*.

nichchik nu. species of shellfish (with small, vertical veins on shell, different from *kitir₃*).

nichchok (2, 3) See *ni-₁, -chchok*. nu. (T2, T3) a species of land bird (small, with white and orange breast and gray back, probably the bush warbler, *Cettia diphone*). [The bill of this bird is rubbed on the lips of a year-old child to help insure that the child will learn to talk.] *nichchoken, nichchokun* b. of (a given region).

nichchó (1) nu. (T1) a species of shellfish (small, sticks to rocks along coast and to mangrove).

nitáákápar Var. of *niteyikepar*.

nitáátá (db; 1) See *ni-₁, tá*. nu. (T1) a tiny minnow-like fish.

niteyikepar (3) See *ni-₁, teyuk, par*. Var. *nikáátápar, nikeyitepar, nitáákápar*. nu. (T3) 1. variety of breadfruit. 2. ruby-throated honey-eater (small bird with red head and breast, black wings and tail).

nitikitik (db; 2) See *ni-₁, tikitik₁* or *ttik₂*. nu. (T2) a kind of fish.

nitinimwár (4) See *ni-₁, tin₂, mwáár*. nu. (T2) poncho or slip-over garment (with a slit through it to insert one's head) that is ornamented with colored thread rather than with shells ("inserted-collar- ornament-thing").

nitúkútúkúniyos (ds; 2) See *ni-₁, túkútúk, oos₂*. F. Var. *nitúkútúkún woos*. ns. (T2) cocoon. [It is associated with the destruction of taro leaves.]

nitúkútúkún woos N. of *nitúkútúniyos*.

nitter (2) See *ni-₁, tter*. nu. (T2) a land bird (light brown). *nitterin* b. of (a given region).

nittopw ráán See *ni-₁, topw, ráán₂*. n. phr. black spider (said to have no web).

nittumw₁ (3) nu. (T3) a small edible shellfish. *eféw* n. one s. *nittumwen* s. of (a given region).

nittumw₂ (2) See *ni-₂, ttumw₂* (?). nu. (T2) a bivalve used to scrape wood surfaces. *nittumwun* b. of (a given region).

niw (3) NIWA. vi., adj. (be) afraid, scared, frightened. *wúwaa* n. I am scared.

niwanék nu. a species of bird (whitish breast, lives in burrows by day and flies at night, great fisher).
niwees nu. (T2) variety of *Cyrtosperma* taro.
niweffengen (2) See *niw, ffengen.* vi. fear one another.
niweyiti See *niw, -iti.* vo. (T2) fear, be afraid of.
Niweyitipwich nu. a school of *itang* lore. [Its patron spirit is Fánninúk of the Fesinimw clan, and it is associated with districts on Toon Island and Fanapenges, Paata, and Romónum Islands.]
niwékkútiw (Mck.) vi. fall down.
niwin (2) See *ni-$_1$, win$_1$.* n. (T2) return for something, wage, cost or price of something, exchange. *niwinin* return for it, price of it. *niwinin wóók* land acquired in war or by forceful seizure ("return for the club"). With dir. suf.: *niwitto* r. hither; *niwinno* r. yonder. vi. return, come back. *n. sefáán* (vi. phr.) r. back again, go back; *n. sefááníiti* (vo. phr.) r. to, go back to. With dir. suf.: *niwitto* r. hither; *niwinnó* r. yonder; *niwittá* r. up or east; *niwittiw* r. down or west.
niwini See *niwin.* vo. (T2) make return for, pay back for, return.
niwiniiy See *niwin, -i-$_2$.* vo. (T5) make return to, pay (someone) back.
niwinimmang (3) See *niwin, mmang.* nu. (T3) debt, loan, bill. *wúpwe eniwini ngonuk rúwe chana ááy* n. I will return to you my d. of twenty dollars. vi. borrow on credit, be indebted.
niwinimmóng (2) See *niwin, mmóng.* vi. be expensive.
niwiningngaw (3b) See *niwin, ngngaw.* vi. come back or return without having accomplished one's purpose.
niwiniwin (db; 2) See *ni-$_1$, winiwin$_1$.* nu. (T2) small insect (white, stinging, in sand at edge of the sea).
niwiniyééch (2) See *niwin, ééch.* vi. return having accomplished one's purpose.
niwinnó See *niwin.*
niwit (2) NIWITI. Tbl. nu. (T2) anus, anal region, arse; penis (of boy). *niwitin* his a. *féwún* n. buttocks (Tbl).
niwitipin (2) See *niwit, -pin.* Tbl. nu. (T2) paralyzing blow to an opponent's back in hand-to-hand fighting ("plugged anus").
niwitichcha (1) See *niwit, chcha.* Tbl. nu. (T1) piles, hemorrhoids.
niwittá See *niwin.*
niwittiw See *niwin.*
niwittó See *niwin.*
niwo (1) See *ni-$_1$, woo$_1$.* nu. (T1) a reed (*Phragmites karka*). [It is used for rods in making thatch.] Syn. *woowo$_1$.* Cf. *róó.*
niwoowo (db; 1) See *ni-$_1$, wo$_2$.* brown heron (slow flier). Syn. *nichchaw, nimmang.*
niwoowoomén (2) See *ni-$_1$, wo$_2$, mén$_3$.* nu. repeating what another has said ("wind-watching"). vi. repeat what another has said.
niwoowoomenúúw See *niwoowoomén, -ú-.* vo. (T5) repeat after (someone).
niwokkus (dc; 2) See *niw, kus.* Var. *nuwokkus.* vi. be startled, jump with fright; be apprehensive, jumpy.
niwúkúpar (3) See *ni-$_1$, wúúk$_1$, par.* nu. (T3) a bird ("red-tailed-one," with green body and red tail). Syn. *nikitirúúng, túrin wén, wúkúpar.*
niwúkúpwech (2) See *ni-$_1$, wúúk$_1$, pwech.* F. Var. *wúkúpwech.* nu. (T2) a species of trigger fish. *niwúkúpwechin* t. f. of (a given region).
niya- (3b) NIYA. [In cpds. only.] Var. *niye-.* pref. sex, gender, kind, sort (of animals). *niyemeet?* of what sex?; *niyamwáán* of male sex; *niyefeefin* of female sex. nr. (T3), pref. woman, female person.
niyaataf (3) See *niya-, tafa-$_2$.* nu. (c.; T3) plicate miter shell (*Vexillum plicarium* L.).
niyafeefin Var. of *niyefeefin.*
niyamaam (db; 3) See *ni-$_2$, amaam.* vi. (dis.) regret, repent, be sorry.
niyamwáán (2) See *niya-, mwáán$_1$.* F. vi., adj. (be) male (of animals only). Syn. *átámwáán, winiyamwáán.* Ant. *niyefeefin.* nu. (T2) male (of the species). *niyamwáánin chukó* rooster.
Niyanááman nu. (pers.) traditional goddess who provides in time of want. [She lives in the sky and provides food, fire, or fish when invoked in time of want.]
Niyang (3) See *ni-$_1$, anga-.* nu. (pers.; T3) a spirit residing by houses and paths causing cholic in infants ("grabber"). [It

hides by the house and touches or grabs the mother when she comes out to bathe. If she is alone, the N. will follow her and grab her again. Thereafter her baby cries all the time and cannot be comfortable.] *sáfeen N.* medicine against cholic.

niyap (3) NIYAPA. [Presumably derived from *ni-*₁, *apaap*₁; cf. *enniyap*, having reference originally to spearing fish.] n. (T3) a catch (of fish). *niyapan* his c. vi. catch fish, be successful in fishing.

niyapeni See *niyap, -ni-*. vo. (T6a) catch (fish).

niyach (3) See *ni-*₁, *aach*₁. nu. (T3) scanty late crop (of breadfruit only) in August-September. *niyachen mááy* l. c. of breadfruit; *niyachen ráás* l. c. of *ráás* season. vi. become scanty (of breadfruit only).

niyachonnupw (2) See *ni-*₁, *aach*₁, *nupw*. nu. (T2) breadfuuit at the stage of development when stem has become red ("ripe-stem-thing").

Niyaw See *Niyawachcha*.

niyawamach (3) See *ni-*₁, *aaw*₁, *maach*. N. Var. *awamach*. nu. (T3) a reef fish.

niyawapach (3) See *ni-*₁, *aaw*₁, *pach*. nu. (T3) mouth distorted by yaws scars or puckered by wrinkles ("pucker mouth").

Niyawachcha See *ni-*₁, *aaw*₁, *chcha*₁. nu. (pers.) a spirit living in Mechchitiw, Wééné (Moen) and feared because it kills the foetus within a pregnant woman ("bloody-mouthed-one"). [Also called *Niyaw* for short.]

niyawépwech (3) See *ni-*₁, *éwú-*₃ (?), *pwech*. Var. *niyawúwepwech, niyawúwépwech*. nu. (T3) spear armed with spines whose tips are painted white (hence name). [Its spines may be made from stingray spines or from carved mangrove wood.] Syn. *mesepwech*.

niyawúpinik (3) See *ni-*₁, *aaw, pinik*₂. nu. (T3) cormorant.

niyawúwepwech Var. of *niyawépwech*.
niyawúwépwech Var. of *niyawépwech*.

niyayééch (2: *-yéchchú-*) See *niya-, ééch*. nu. (T2) handsome person, one pleasing to behold (of females). Ant. *niyengngaw*. Cf. *áteyééch, niyéech*.

niyááyáánipwin (db; 2) See *ni-*₁, *á, -pwin* (?). vi. (dis.) swim on one's back. Syn. *nipwachchaach*.

niye- Var. of *niya-* and standard form with suffixed demonstratives.

niyeen See *niye-, een*₃. nu. (dem.) this female by you and me. Dis. *niyekkaan*.

niyeey See *niye-, eey*₁. nu. (dem.) this female by me. Dis. *niyekkeey*.

niyefeefin (3) See *niya-, feefin*. Var. *niyafeefin*. vi., adj. (be) female (of animals only). Ant. *átámwáán, niyamwáán*. nu. (T3) female (of the species); *niyefeefinen chukó* hen.

niyeféwúnó Var. of *niyefowunó*.

niyefowunó (1) See *niye-, fowunó*. Var. of *niyeféwúnó*. nu. (T1) famous woman.

niyekak (3) See *niya-, kak*. nu. (T3) a species of bird. [Living in mangroves, it is larger than *kuning* but similar in color, has a long sharp bill, is noisy, and eats gobies and crabs.] *niyekaken* b. of (a given region).

niyekkaan Dis. of *niyeen*.

niyekkana Dis. of *niyena*.

niyekkanaan Dis. of *niyenaan*.

niyekkápe (1) See *niya-, kká-, pe*. nu. (T1) beautiful woman ("knockout"). vi., adj. (be) beautiful, lovely.

niyekkeey Dis. of *niyeey*.

niyekkemwuun Dis. of *niyemwuun*.

niyekkewe Dis. of *niyewe*.

niyekkoomw Dis. of *niyoomw*.

niyemaat (3) See *niya-, maat*. vi. be brave (of a woman).

niyemeet See *niya-, meet*₁. vi. (interrog.) be of what sex (of animals).

niyemésékúta (1) See *niya-, mésékúta*. nu. (T1) coward (of females only). vi. be cowardly (of females).

niyemwaken (3) See *niya-, mwaken*. nu. (T3) liar (of women only). vi. be a liar (of women).

niyemwáán Var. of *niyamwáán*.

niyemwuun See *niye-, -mwuun*. N. nu. (dem.) that female person by you; that female of reference. Dis. *niyekkemwuun*. Syn. *niyena, niyoomw*.

niyemwmwung (3) See *niya-, mwmwung*. nu. (T3) woman popular with or much loved by men.

niyena See *niye-, na*. nu. (dem.) that female person by you; that female of reference. Dis. *niyekkana*. Cf. *niyemwuun, niyoomw*.

niyenaan See *niye-, naan.* nu. (dem.) that female person yonder. Dis. *niyekkanaan.*

niyeniffé (1) See *niya-, fé.* vi., adj. (be) young (of animals).

niyenika (1) See *niya-, kaa-* (?). nu. (T1) blue herring (a small fish).

niyenimwár (4) See *niya-, mwáár.* Itang. nu. (T2) woman of a commoner clan.

niyeniyap (3) See *niya-, niyap.* nu. (T3) good fisherwoman (one who regularly does well at fishing).

niyenkatek (2) See *niya-, katek.* nu. (T2) nun ("kind lady").

Niyenpáánú See *niya-, páá* (?), *núú.* nu. (pers.) local goddess of Mt. Winimwér in Féwúúp, Toon (Tol).

niyengngaw (3b) See *niya-, ngngaw.* nu. (T3) ugly, ill-favored, deformed person (of females). Ant. *niyayéech.* Cf. *átángngaw.*

niyepwó (1) See *niya-, pwó.* nu. (T1) pampered girl child.

niyerá (1) See *niya-, -rá*$_1$. Obs. nu. (T1) girl. [Polite form for *nenggin*, now considered old fashioned.]

niyewe (1) See *niye-, -we.* nu. (dem.; T1) that female person (out of sight or past), the female person of reference (in narrative). Dis. *niyekkewe.*

niyeyisómw See *niya-, -sómw.* Itang. nu. woman of a chiefly clan.

niyeyiroch$_1$ See *Niyeyiroch*$_2$. nu. a kind of love magic. See *ommung, pwénúpwén*$_2$.

Niyeyiroch$_2$ (3) See *niya-, roch.* nu. (pers.) a traditional goddess. [An inhabitant of *Éwúr*, she makes blind a person's thoughts and vision.]

niyéech (2) See *ni-*$_2$, *éech.* vi. be pretty, attractive, (of a girl or woman). *emén n.* a pretty girl or woman. Cf. *niyayéech.*

niyén (2) nu. (T2) species of black worm (about 6 inches long). *niyénún* w. of (a given region). Syn. *sichón.*

niyénúf nu. a species of land worm.

niyéwúmá (3) See *ni-*$_1$, *éwúmáámá.* nu. (T3) file fish.

niyéwúretin nu. tiny mullet (fish).

niyéwút nu. rectangular-shaped leaf package of breadfruit-pudding (very common size). *eew n.* one p. of b. p,.

niyoos (2) NIYOSSU. nu. (T2) statue, doll, picture, representation, image. *niyossun aramas* human image, statue of a man. *fóós n.* (vi. phr.) describe the appearance of something in words, depict in words; (n. phr.) depiction in words, verbal sketch. *niyossun pachaaw* shark image (used in making sorcery).

niyoomw See *niye-, oomw.* F. nu. (dem.) this female person by you. Dis. *niyekkoomw.* Syn. *niyena, niyemwuun.*

niyon nu. millipede (large, purple-staining).

niyowut (3) NIYOWUTA. n. (T3) ear ornament; anything worn in the hole in the ear (e.g. a flower). *eew n.* one e. o. *niyowutan* his e. o. *niyowutey iyering* my earring; *niyowutey koon* my gold earring.

niyóór (4?) NIYÓÓRO (?). nu. (T2, T3) 1. a shrub (*Premna integrifolia*). [It is used for canoe paddles, fire-making sticks, and love magic.] *niyóóren, niyóórun* s. of (a given region). Syn. *wumwukaw.* 2. a spell spoken into *n.* leaves. [It is aimed at preventing a person from doing what he has set out to do.] vi. utter a *n.* spell.

niyóóreey See *niyóór, -e-*$_2$. vo. (T6a) speak a *niyóór* spell against.

niyók nu. small chicken. Syn. *nisiyapw, nisiyok.*

niyóch (3) NIYÓCHA. Tn. nu. (T3) young woman. *niyóchen* y. w. of (a place). Syn. *féépwún.*

No- Var. of *Na-* (used when the following vowel, with or without intervening consonant, is *o* or *u*, e.g., *Nopwot* as a nickname meaning "Miss rough skin," cf. *pwotopwot*).

noo- (1) NOO. [In cpds. only.] unsp. be (at or in a place or time).

noos (3) NOSA. n. (T3) mat (general term), pandanus mat. *eché n.* one m. *kiyan n.* his m.; *nosan* his place of learning *itang* lore. *nosen pénú* m. used by *pénú* in laying out instruction in navigation; *nosen pwee* m. used by *sowupwe* in laying out instruction in knot divination; *nosen itang* mat used by *itang* in instruction. [The mat is spread with red bananas or other items whose arrangements constitute the framework of instruction. The pupils sit around the mat and the *itang* on it, giving his instructions and demonstrations.] *fitaché kiyomw (n.)?* how many are your mats? i.e., how many times have you been instructed in *itang? eew chék noseer, iir mósowen eew* n. only one their mat, they are the contents of the same mat, i.e. they learned their *itang* together from the same source. Syn. *kiyeki.*

Noosópw nu. (loc.) Losop Island and Atoll.

noon (3) NONNA. nu. (T3) hibiscus cord along the edge of a *cheew* fish net connecting the two sticks of the frame; cord along the top of a seine on which floats are strung. *nonnen cheew* fish net's cord.

noot (3) NOTA. nu. (T3) large species of Lethrinid fish. *noten* f. of (a given region).

nooten (2) NOOTENI. (Ger.) nu. (T2) musical notes, tune. *nootenin eey kkéén* the n. of this song.

noow (2: *nuu-*) NUU₁ (*NOWU). Obs. scorpion fish; spotted rockfish. [Old name used in spell chanted by swimmer in deep water to bring the scorpion fish up near the surface to serve as a screen between him and sharks.] Syn. *nuunupis.* Cf. *ineyinó, wúsen, nnoow, noowu.*

noowu nu. anchovy. *chuun n.* a. net. Cf. *noow.*

nooyiis (2) NOOYIISI. Tn. nu. (T2) small child. *neenooyiisin* during his early childhood. Syn. *ménúkón, monukón, nooyiroch, semiriit, tipate.*

nooyiroch (2) NOOYIROCHU. F. nu. (T2) child to about eight years. *nooyirochun* during his early childhood. Syn. *ménúkón, monukón, nooyiis, semiriit, tipate.* Cf. *noo-, roch.*

Nofémper (Eng.) nu. (temp.) November.

noseyirek (2) See *noos, reki-.* Itang. nu. (T2) plaited pandanus mat.

nomi (1) NOMII. (Jap. *nomi*) nu. (T1) chisel. *efóch n.* one c. *néwún n.* his c.

nomiini See *nomi, -ni-.* vo. (T4) apply a chisel to.

nomw (3) NOMWA. vi. gurgle, make a liquid noise (as of a coconut when shaken). Dis. *nomwonomw* (db). ni. (T3) gurgle. *nomwen taka* the g. of a ripe coconut.

nomwonomw Dis. of *nomw.*

nomwu- (2) NOMWU. [In cpds. only.] unsp. stripping skin, bark or leaves by scraping, scratching, or clawing. See *nnomw, nnomwut, nomwuti, nomwuuw.*

nomwuuw See *nomwu-, -u-.* vo. (T5) strip skin, bark, or leaves from (something) by scraping, scratching or clawing. Syn. *nomwuti.* Cf. *nnomw.*

nomwuti See *nomwu-, -ti-.* vo. (T5) strip skin, bark or leaves from (something) by scraping, scratching, or clawing. Syn. *nomwuuw.* Cf. *nnomwut.*

nonno (ds; 1) See *noo-.* vi. (dis.) stay, remain; be (at or in a place or time). Syn. *nónnómw.*

-nong (3) NONGA. adj. (dir.) inward, southward. *toonong* come in; *angonong* hand in. *aa péénong seni ennefen* it blows southward from the north.

nopw (3) NOPWA. vi. be clapped (of cupped palms of hands); clap. Dis. *nopwonopw* (db).

nopwonopw (3) See *nopw* vi. (dis.) be clapping; clap (with cupped hands). nu. (T3) clapping.

nopwonopwa (1) NOPWONOPWAA. (P.Eng. *lavalava*) nu. (T1) women's old-fashioned wrap-around kilt, or skirt, waist-mat (woven of hibiscus fibers). *aan n., óruun n.* her w.-m. Syn. *chééyitúr.*

nopwur (3) NOPWURA. nu. (T3) a tree and its fruit (*Morinda citrifolia*). [The fruit is eaten raw or baked; the leaves and fruit are used as medicine for eye infections and the fruit is used as a cough medicine; the roots are used to make yellow dye.] Cf. *nnopwur.*

nopwut (3) NOPWUTA. Var. *nnopwut.* nu. (T3) eel. *rongen n.* a form of sorcery; *sáfeen n.* medicine to counteract the effects of *rongen n.*.

nopwutochón (4) See *nopwut, chón.* nu. (T2) a kind of eel (black in color).

nopwpwuk (3) NOPWPWUKA. n. (T3) unscented coconut oil. *nopwpwukan* his c. o.

Norweey (Eng.) nu. (loc.) Norway.

notow (3b) NOTOWA. n. (loc.; T3) west. *notowan* w. of it. *e mén n.* it blows from the w.

notowaar (2) See *notow, éér.* nu. (loc.; T2) southwest.

notowanap (3a) See *notow, nap.* nu. (loc.; T3) due west; west wind.

notowááfen (2) See *notow, efen₃.* nu. (loc.; T2) northwest.

nowu-₁ (2) NOWU₁. [In cpds. only.] unsp. twirl (as a rope). See *nnow, nowunow, nowuti.*

nowu-₂ (2) NOWU₂. [In cpds. only.] unsp. stink (?). See *pwoonow.*

nowumwoy (2) NOWUMWOYI. nu. (T2) heddle (of loom). *nowumwoyin túúr* loom's h. Cf. *nowu-₁, mwooy.*

nowunow (db; 2) See *nowu-₁.* nu. (dis.; T2) twirling a rope (as preparatory to throwing).

nowuti See *nowu-₁, -ti-.* vo. (T5) twirl (a rope, sling, lasso).

Nó- Var. of *Na-* (used when following vowel is *ó*).

nó₁ (1) See *nóó.* vi. be wavy, riled, rough (of the sea). Dis. *nóónó* (db, the more usual form).

nó₂ (1) NÓÓ₁. Var. *ná, naa-.* vi. go or be away from speaker, go or be off. Dis. *nóónó* (db) be moving or proceeding away. *siyaa n.* we are off, on our way; *kenee n.* goodbye (to one departing). *n. núkún* (Tb1.; n.phr.) menstruation ("going to the outer side"); *imwen n. núkún* menstrual hut. *ke nóó mey?* (Tn., Pt.) where are you coming from? where have you been? (cf. *náá*).

-nó (1) See *nó₂*. Var. *-ná.* adj. (dir.) away, off.

nóó- (1) NÓÓ₃. [In ptv. const. only.] Var. *nnó-.* ni. (prep.; T1) in, inside; on (of days of the week or month). [Used only of things. Forms with suf. pos. prns. in reference to persons are tabu (level one) where women are concerned and regarded as nonsense where men are concern. Instead one says *nóón awey, nóón ngaang, nóón inisi* in my mouth, inside me, inside my body.] *nóón een rúán* tomorrow; *nóón eew rúán* some other day, some other time; *nóón ekkaan rúán* in the days ahead, someday soon.

nóó (1) NÓÓ₂. nu. (T1) wave, billow. *nóón sáát* waves of the sea.

nóófeefin (3) See *nóó, feefin.* nu. (T3) small waves. [Men are said to wash and pray in them to obtain the love of a woman.] Ant. *nóómwáán.*

nóók (3) NÓKKA. (Eng.) nu. (T3) lock. *eew n.* one l. *aan n.* his l.; *nókken* l. of (a given make). vi. be locked.

nóókis (2) See *nóó, kisi-.* vi. be small (of waves).

nóómmóng (2) See *nóó, mmóng.* vi. be large (of waves). Syn. *nóónap, nóówátte.*

nóómw₁ (4) NÓMWO₂. nu. (T2) an enclosed or relatively enclosed body of water, such as a lagoon, harbor, bay, small sea; an atoll; an archipelago; a region of water associated with an island or group of islands. *Nómwun Chuuk* the atoll of Truk; *Nómwun Wiité* Namonuito atoll (*Nómwon Weyitéé* in the local language); *Nómwun Sééw* name of the bay between Woney and Paata. Cf. *neenómw.*

nóómw₂ nu. (temp.) 1. earlier, first, beforehand. *sipwe fééri n.* we shall do it first. 2. ago, in the past, of old, ancient times. *nóómw nóómw* long ago; *nóómw nóómw nóómw* very long ago, long long long ago. *minen n.* an old thing, something of old; *aramasen n.* people of old; *féfféérún n.* something done long ago or in old times; *éérúniyen n.* former customs.

nóómwáán (2) See *nóó, mwáán₁.* nu. (T2) large waves. [Women are said to wash and pray in these to obtain the love of a man.] Ant. *nóófeefin.*

nóónap (3a) See *nóó, nap.* vi. be large (of waves). Syn. *nóómmóng, nóówátte.*

nóónopan Var. of *neeyónopan.*

nóónowas Var. of *neeyónowas.*

nóónó Dis. of *nó₁*, and *nó₂*.

nóóng₁ (4) NÓNGO₂. nu. (T2) triangular carving at each end of the longitudinal grooving along the keel of a paddle canoe. *nóngun waa* canoe's t. c.

nóóng₂ (4) NÓNGO₃. Var. *nnóng.* nu. (T2) fly (insect). *emén n.* one f. *nóngun f.* of (a given region).

nóópwo (1) See *nóó, pwo.* nu. (T1) ocean swell. Dis. *nóópwoopwo* (db) large swell. vi. have swells (of the sea).

nóópwoopwo See *nóópwo.*

nóópwu (1) See *nóó-, pwu₃.* nu. (T1) socket for mast or yard on sailing canoe.

Nóórowanú See *nee-, óór, énú.* nu. (loc.) Hall Islands. Syn. *Fánáápi Ennefen, Nómwun Paafeng, Nómwun Soomá.*

nóót (4) NÓTO. n. (T2) pus. *nótun* his p.

nóóter (2) See *nóó, ter₁.* nu. (T2) tidal wave.

nóóto (1) See *nóó, -to.* vi. be moving hither (of waves); begin to get wavy.

nóówátte (1) See *nóó, wátte.* vi. be large (of waves). Syn. *nóómmóng, nóónap.*

Nóówuru nu. (loc.) Nauru.

nóóy Tn., Pt. Var. *neey, neya.* vi. go where? *ke pwe n.?* where are you going?

nóku₁ nu. guy (harsh term of address or reference). *ewe n.* that g. *kkanaan n.* you guys.

Nóku₂ See *nóku₁.* nu. (pers.) name of a spirit used in the curse *wochóómw N.!* go eat N.!

nókun (4) NÓKO. [Regularly, as shown, with rel. suf. *-n₂.*] vr. almost, just about. *wúwa n. toori* I almost got to it; *meyi n. wees ika ke fééri* it would be just about finished if you were doing it.

nókkeey See *nóók, -e-₂.* vo. (T6b) lock. With dir. suf.: *nókkeeyenó* l. up, l. away.

nókkeeyenó See *nókkeey.*

nómw (4) NÓMWO₁. Var. *nnómw.* vi. stay, remain, be in (a place), be located, be situated, dwell, be present, be alive. Dis. *nónnómw* (ds). *ese n.* he is not here (there). Syn. *noo-.*

Nómwiisé (1) See *nóómw₁, séé.* nu. (loc.; T1) the body of water bounded by Wonamwe, Pata, Woney, and the outer reef of Truk ("sunset-glow-sea").

Nómwiin nu. (loc.) Nomwin Island and Atoll (Hall Islands).

nómwiiti See *nómw, -iti.* vo. (T2) stay with (someone).

nómwoffengeen (2) See *nómw, ffengeen.* Var. *nómwoffengen.* vi. stay together.

nómwoffengen Var. of *nómwoffengeen.*

nómwokkan (3) See *nómw, kkan.* vi. be near. *n. ngeni* be n. to.

Nómwoneyas (3b) See *nóómw₁, ne-₂, aas₁.* nu. (loc.) East or Upper Truk, comprising the islands and waters of the eastern half of Truk's lagoon. Cf. *Fááyichuk.*

Nómwochchek See *nóómw₁.* nu. (loc.) Lamotrek Atoll (Central Caroline Islands).

nómwot (3a) NÓMWOTA. [Perhaps derived from *nómw, -ta-₁.*] Var. *namwot.* n. (T3) use, utility, need, usefulness. *nómwotan* need of him, his usefulness. *nómwotomw ngeni* your usefulness for (something). vi. be useful, worthwhile. *n. mwmwáán* useless.

nómwotongngaw (3b) See *nómwot, ngngaw.* Var. *namwotongngaw.* vi. be of no use, useless; sit around and do nothing, (be) lazy; be in vain, to no purpose. *aa n. aach sááy* our trip was in vain.

Nómwunuuk See *nóómw₁, nuuk₁.* nu. (loc.) Namoluk Island and Atoll (Mortlock Islands). [Known locally as *Namwoluuk.*]

Nómwun Soomá n. phr. (loc.) Hall Islands. Syn. *Fánáápi Ennefen, Nómwun Paafeng, Nóórowanú.*

Nómwun Nuukeyisen n. phr. (loc.) Ulul Island and its surrounding waters.

Nómwun Paafeng n. phr. (loc.) Hall Islands. Syn. *Fánáápi Ennefen, Nómwun Soomá, Nóórowanú.*

Nómwun Pattiw n. phr. (loc.) atolls immediately to the West of Truk (Pulusuk, Puluwat, Tamatam, Pulap). Syn. *Fánáápi Notow.*

Nómwun Pwonowót n. phr. (loc.) a region consisting of the atolls (and their surrounding waters) of Pulusuk, Puluwat, Tamatam, and Pulap.

Nómwun Wééné n. phr. (loc.) the islands and reefs under the hegemony of Wééné (Moen) Island.

Nómwun Wiité See *nóómw₁, wii-₃, téé₁.* n. phr. (loc.) Namonuito Atoll (excluding Ulul Island). [Known locally as *Nómwon Weyitéé.*]

nóniinen (2) See *nónu-, -inen.* nu. (T2) sorrow, concern, regret, unease, worry. *nóniinenin átánaan* that fellow's concern. vi. be sorry, sad, mournful, regretful, anxious, uneasy, worried (about one's own or another's condition).

nónowó (1) See *nónu-, wóó-* (?). [With *ngeni.*] Var. *nanowó.* vi. feel spiteful, be spitefully envious, feel hate because of one's envy. *n. ngeni* feel s. toward. Cf. *nónnón.*

nónu- (4) NÓNO. [In cpds. only.] Var. *nano-.* unsp. deep; under or below the surface; interior. See *fááyinón, inón, kuunón, metekinón, nóniinen, nónnón, nónnóón, nónówó, ónón, ónóna, ónónnóón.* Cf. *nnó-, nóó-.*

nó núkún N. phr., see *nó₂.*

nónnipéw (2) See *nónu-, paaw₁.* nu. (T2) mid-palm (unit of measure from finger tips to the middle of the palm). *eew n.* one m.-p.

nónnóón (db; 4) See *nónu-*. N. [Apparently an irregular doubling of the base of the type represented by *kisikiis*, in this case with the loss of the stem vowel between like consonants.] Var. *ónónnóón*. vi. be deep (underwater), far down (from a height). Syn. *ónón*. nu. (T2) depth; draft (of a boat).

nónnómw Dis. of *nómw*.

nónnón (ds; 4) See *nónu-*. vi. be envious. Cf. *nónówó*.

nóng (4) NÓNGO$_1$. vi. be propped up. Dis. *nóngónóng* (db).

nóngónóng (4) See *nóng*. vi. (dis.) being propped up. nu. (T2) 1. propping. 2. sleeper, bed, cradle (on which things rest or are propped); (fig.) wealth. *nóngónóngun waa* canoe's cradle. *nóngónóngun mwúún* government's wealth, treasury.

nónguni See *nóng, -ni-*. vo. (T5) prop up.

nóchchú nu. ripe coconut from which two sprouts grow.

Nótókapwin (2) Var. *Nótukupwin*. n. (pers.; T2) spirit on Toon (Tol), whose name is used as a curse. *Nótókapwinumw!* N. to you! or *ómwo kaa wocheey N.* would that you ate N.

Nótukupwin Rmn. and Ps. of *Nótókapwin*.

nu- (2) NU. [In cpds. only.] unsp. bend, fold, crumple. See *nnum, numi*. Cf. *nnú-*.

-nu- See *-n*.

nu (1) NUU$_2$. vi. go beyond, go past, pass by. With dir. suf.: *nuunó* pass by and keep on going; skip, miss (as a line of print); sail away beyond recovery (of a model sailboat).

-nu (1) NUU$_3$. [In cpds. only.] unsp. (u.m.) See *wááyinu*.

nuu- C.f. of *noow*.

nuus$_1$ (2) NUSSU$_1$. n. (T2) remainder, leftovers; remains (of things or people); change (in a purchase); survivor. *nussun* his left-overs (of food); what is left of it; its change (money). *nussun mwéngé* left-over food; *nussun angaang* remaining work; *nussun mwooni* change (of money). Syn. *nuuwek*. Cf. *nu*.

nuus$_2$ (2) NUSSU$_2$. (Eng.) vi. lose (be the poorer); lose (in a contest). Cf. *kkuf, miis, mwú$_3$, sun*.

nuuseni (2) See *nu, seni$_2$*. vi. pass beyond, go past, go beyond, get away.

nuuspeepa (1) NUUSPEEPAA. (Eng.) nu. (T1) newspaper.

nuuk$_1$ (3a) NUUKA. n. (T3) middle, center (of things); abdomen, stomach, belly (of persons). [Seat of emotion, *tiip*.] *nuukan* his a.; *nuuken* m. of, a. of. Cf. *saa, taa, wuupw$_2$*.

Nuuk$_2$ nu. (pers.) a traditional god, also called *Nuukeyinen*.

Nuukan nu. (loc.) a clan name (said to be short for *Nuukanap$_2$*).

nuukanap$_1$ (3a) See *nuuk$_1$, nap*. nu. (loc.; T3) center, exact middle. *nuukanapan* (at) its c.; *nuukanapen* (at) the c. of.

Nuukanap$_2$ (3) See *nuukanap$_1$*. nu. (loc.; T3) a clan name. Syn. *Nuukan*.

nuukeni See *nuuk$_1$, -ni-*. vo. (T6a) like, have positively in mind. Syn. *saani*.

nuukenipwin (2) See *nuuk$_1$, pwiin$_3$*. nu. (temp.; T2) midnight. *n. wotonó* from m. to just before dawn, after m.; *n. wototo* from after dinner to m., before m.

Nuukenfénú See *nuuk$_1$, fénú*. nu. (loc.) a clan name.

Nuukeyisen See *Nómwun Nuukeyisen*.

Nuukeyinen See *nuuk$_1$, neni-$_1$*. nu. (pers.) a traditional god (*énú aramas*) inhabiting the sky world (*Faachchamw*). Syn. *Nuuk$_2$*.

Nuukini (Eng.) nu. (loc.) New Guinea.

nuukochchow (2) See *nuuk$_1$, chchow*. vi. be heavy-hearted, disturbed in one's feelings.

nuukómwoot (3) See *nuuk$_1$, mwoot$_2$*. nu. (T3) skin disease with sores around waist.

nuum (3) NUMA. nu. (T3) bailer. *numen waa* canoe's b.

nuumw (2) NUMWU$_2$. nu. (T2) seaweed, moss; sea algae, scum; coating (on teeth); lubricating fluid from sex organs; smear of food on face. *numwun nii* coating on the teeth, particles of food stuck in teeth.

nuunó See *nu*.

nuunu$_1$ (db; 1) See *noow*. nu. (T1) a type of sea crab.

nuunu$_2$ (db; 1) See *nu*. nu. (T1) model sailing canoe. vi. sail a model canoe.

nuunupis (2) See *noow, piis*. nu. (T2) scorpion fish; spotted rockfish. Syn. *noow*.

nuupw (2) NUUPWU. nu. (T2) type of large wooden bowl. *eew n.* one b. *sepiyan n.* his b.; *nuupwun* b. of (a given make).

nuuwa- (3) NUUWA. [In cpds. only.] unsp. remnant, leaving, left-over. See *nuuwenipa.* Cf. *nuuwek, nuus₁.*

nuuwek (2) NUUWEKI. nu. (T2) what is left, what remains. *nuuwekin mwéngé* left-over food; *nuuwekin angaang* remaining work. Syn. *nuus₁.* Cf. *nu.*

nuuwenipa (1) See *nuuwa-, pa₂.* nu. (T1) remnant of bait on a hook. Cf. *nuus₁, nuuwek.*

nus (2) NUSU. F. Var. *nnus.* vi. 1. jump (from one point to another). Syn. *mwmwet.* 2. be out of its socket or holder.

Nusufer (Eng.) nu. (pers.) Lucifer.

nusumwmwet (3a) See *nus, mwmwet.* vi. bounce, jump, hop.

nusupaat (3) See *nus, paat₁.* nu. (T3) mud skipper fish (*Periophthalmus*).

nuk (2, 3) NUKU, NUKA (*NUKO?). vi. haul on a line; troll for small fish in the Truk lagoon. Dis. *nukunuk* (db). *nukunuk waa* (n. phr.) navigation.

nukamár N. of *nukómár.*

nukeey See *nuk, -e-₂.* vo. (T6b) carry. Cf. *nukiiy.*

nukeyaato See *nukeyi.*

nukeyaawu See *nukeyi.*

nukeyi See *nuk, -yi-₂.* Var. *nukiiy.* vo. (T6a) haul, pull, tow; bring, take along (of persons). With dir. suf.: *nukeyaato, nukeyaawu.*

nukiiy See *nuk, -i-₂.* Var. *nukeyi.* vo. (T5) haul on a line, pull, tow; lead, guide (a blind person holding on to a stick).

nukómár (4) See *nuk, már.* F. Var. *nukamár.* vi. pull on line and back up at the same time.

nukumey (2) See *nuk, mááy₂.* vi. haul a breadfruit log from where it was felled to where it will be adzed into a canoe.

nukunuk Dis. of *nuk.*

num (3) See *nuum.* vi. be bailed (as a boat). Dis. *numonum* (db).

numaanong See *numi.*

numeey See *nuum, -e-₂.* vo. (T6b) bail (a boat).

numi See *nu-, -mi-.* Var. *nnumi.* vo. (T2) bend, fold, crease, crumple. With dir. suf.: *numaanong* fold in. Cf. *nnum.*

numonum Dis. of *num.*

numu- (2) NUMU. [A back formation from *numi.*] unsp. bend, fold.

numuu Wn. of *nimuuw.*

numw₁ (2) NUMWU₁. Tb. vi. be, exist. *ese n.* there is none (syn. *esoor*).

numw₂ (2) See *nuumw.* vi. be smeared, coated.

-numw (2) NUMWU₃. adj. (intens.) very. *chipwangonumw* be very tired.

numwuttar (3) See *numw₂, -ttar.* vi. be spattered with sticky substances (e.g., of paint, glue, food).

nunnus (ds; 2) See *nus.* vi. (dis.) be hopping, jumpy, bouncy (as a ride in a car).

nunnupwuuw Dis. of *nnupwuuw.*

nup (3a) NUPA. vi. rock or roll from side to side; flash on and off (as of a light signal). Dis. *nuponup* (db) be tippy, rocky (of a boat); flashing on and off (of a light). *nupen kinaas* the flash of a mirror. *aa n. kinaas seni Romónum* a mirror has flashed from Romónum. With dir. suf.: *nuponó* capsize, tip over; *nupotá* roll or turn upwards, tip up.

nupenaanong See *nupeni.*

nupenaanó See *nupeni.*

nupenaatá See *nupeni.*

nupenaatiw See *nupeni.*

nupenáátá See *nupeni.*

nupenáátiw See *nupeni.*

nupeni See *nup, -ni-.* vo. (T6a) tilt, tip, tip over, turn over. With dir. suf.: *nupenaanong* tip (it) in (as of water from a container into another one); *nupenaatá, nupenáátá* turn (it) right side up, tip (it) up; *nupenaatiw, nupenáátiw* tip (it) down; *nupenaanó, nupenóónó* turn (it) over.

nupenóónó See *nupeni.*

nupeyiti See *nup, -iti.* vo. (T2) tip toward. *n. epeek* tip it onto its side.

nuponó See *nup.*

nuponup Dis. of *nup.*

nupotá See *nup.*

nupw (2) NUPWU. F. Var. *nnupw.* vi., adj. (be) ripe.

nupwen (3) NUPWA. [Occurs, as shown, only with rel. suf. *-n₂.*] nr. (temp.; T3) when, at the time of, during (past and future). Cf. *faansowu-.*

nupwiiti See *nupw, -iti.* vo. (T2) be ripe by (a date).

nupwuféw (2) See *nupw, faaw.* vi. become ripe with hard spots because of bruising (as bananas).
nuti See *nu-, -ti-.* vo. (T2) tie by a twining process, subject (something) to twining. Cf. *nnut.*
nuwokkus Var. of *niwokkus.*
nú (1) NÚÚ$_1$. vi. regurgitate a bit of food as a result of very heavy eating (a sign of complete satiety). Cf. *núúnú$_1$.*
núú- (1) NÚÚ$_4$. [In cpds. only.] unsp. tired, weary; bored. Cf. *nnúúw.*
núú$_1$ (1) NÚÚ$_2$. nu. (T1) marker (of reef, pass, etc.). *núún ewe faaw* m. of the reef.
núú$_2$ (1) NÚÚ$_3$. nu. (T1) coconut tree; a coconut at the unripe or drinking stage (cf. *taka*). *efóch n.* a coconut tree; *eew n. (éféw* in atoll dialects) a drinking nut. *n. káteete* husked drinking coconuts tied together in a bundle by bits of their husk. *núún péér* variety of coconut especially good for making *pééréchón* coconut shell flasks; *núún sáfey* a coconut tree that has been charmed so as to injure anyone picking from it.
núúfaaw See *nnú-* (?), *faaw* (?). nu. pleated sea snail (*Nerita plicata*).
núúfé (1) See *núú$_2$ -fé$_1$.* nu. (T1) young coconut tree.
núúsessen (2) See *núú$_2$ sessen.* nu. (T2) variety of coconut (sweet and prolific with very small nuts that ripen all at once). [So called because when harvested, the whole cluster of nuts is tied with a rope and lowered to the ground to prevent the nuts from breaking open on impact.]
núúk (2) NÚKÚ$_6$. [Possibly derived from *núkú-$_3$.*] nu. (T2) faith, belief, conviction. *aan n.* his f. Cf. *núkúúw$_3$.*
núúmóów See *núú$_2$, -móów.* nu. a variety of coconut (reddish brown in color).
núúmwin (3) See *núú$_2$ mwin.* nu. (T3) coconuts that are growing together (?).
núún Var. *nnúún.* nu. 1. sennit rope (fine grade). [Made of coconut fiber, it is used in house construction. It is also a symbol of chiefship.] *efóch n.* one piece of r.; *esen n.* one full coil of r. 2. (Itang) sustenance, assistance (by virtue of of the word's resemblance to *núúnú$_1$*, meaning chew or eat, and hence providing a cryptic reference to the chief's exclusive right to eat first fruits, wherefore a necklace of *núún*

rope is placed around the new chief's shoulders when he is being installed in office).
núúnap (3a) See *núú$_2$ nap.* N. nu. (T3) a big coconut. Syn. *númmóng.*
Núúneenap nu. (loc.) a clan name.
núúnú$_1$ (db; 1) See *nú.* va. chew, eat, masticate. [More polite than *áni.*] Cf. *ngúngngúúng.*
núúnú$_2$ (db; 1) NÚÚ$_5$. nu. (T1) large trigger fish (*Odonus niger*). Syn. *ngúúngú$_1$, pwúnúúnú.*
núúnúúw See *núúnú$_1$.* vo. (dis.; T1) chew, eat (in deferential or polite usage). Cf. *áni.*
núúng (2) NÚNGÚ. nu. (T2) ant (small).
núúpen (2) nu. (T2) a mashed breadfruit pudding that has not yet been packaged in leaves.
núúpwiniyách (3) See *núú$_2$, pwin$_1$* (?). nu. (T3) variety of coconut with reddish tinge inside husk.
núúch (3) NÚCHA. n. (T3) ink or black secretion of octopus and squid. *núchan* its i.
núúchimwa- (3) See *núú$_2$ chimw.* nr. (T3) in *núúchimwen sómwoon* coconut trees reserved for a chief's use.
núúchu (1) See *núú$_2$, chu.* nu. (T1) a kind of coconut.
núúwen (3a) See *núú$_2$, wen.* nu. (T3) straight coconut palm. [In *itang* talk a symbol of true chiefship.]
núúwumwuumw (db; 2) See *núú$_2$, wumwu-$_2$.* nu. (T2) any variety of coconut tree that bears many nuts.
núúyaraw (3b) See *núú$_2$, araw$_2$.* nu. (T3) variety of coconut (green colored nuts).
núúyón (4) See *núú$_2$, ón$_1$.* nu. (T2) variety of coconut (yellow colored nuts).
núffé (1) See *núú$_2$, -ffé.* nu. (T1) young coconut tree that has not yet borne fruit.
núk (2) NÚKÚ$_1$. vi. be ready, prepared, set; alerted; assembled. Dis. *núkúnúk* (db). *siya n. reen aach angaang* we are r. for our work. With dir. suf.: *núkúnó, núkútá, núkúto, núkúwu.*
núké (1) NÚKÉÉ. nu. (T1) <Elbert> a species of sea cucumber. *emwú n.* one s. c.
núkiisá (1) nu. (T1) a variety of banana. [Traditionally reserved for *itang*.]
núkiisenné (1) See *núkú-$_1$, senné.* nu. (loc.; T1) outside the area of meeting.

aramasen n. a person who is not a legitimate member of a meeting, an observer of a meeting.

núkiinong (2) See *núkú-₁, -nong* (?). Tb2. n. (T2) back side; back of thigh and buttocks together. *núkiinongun* his b. s.

núkiitang (3) See *núkú-₁, taang.* Tb3. n. (T3) outer surface of one's thigh.

núkú-₁ (2) NÚKÚ₂. ni. (loc.; T2), adj. exterior, outside, outside surface, exterior surface, cover, outer edge, immediate environs; surface of one's skin; secular sphere. *núkún* its outside, surface, cover; surface of his skin. *chóón núkún* heathen, pagan, non-Christian, non-member (of a group); *kkéénún núkún* secular song. *núkún sékúr* surface of one's back; *núkún chiya* on the sea side of the mangroves; *núkún epeep* a woodcarving design used on lee platforms of canoes; *núkún wúwen nippach* back of the neck of an octopus.

núkú-₂ (2) NÚKÚ₃. pref. a little, a bit. See *núkúchéchchén, núkúmwochomwoch, núkúttam, núkúwátte.*

núkú-₃ (2) NÚKÚ₄. [In cpds. only.] unsp. tight, firm, stable. ni. (T2) tightness, firmness. *émwúchú núkún* learn it by heart.

núkú-₄ (2) NÚKÚ₅. [In cpds. only.] unsp. put away, stored, saved. See *núkúúw₄.* Cf. *isóyis.*

núkúúffengenniiy See *núkúúw₁, ffengen, -i-₂.* vo. (T5) tighten (something) up or together; join tightly.

núkúúw₁ See *núkú-₃, -ú-.* vo. (T5) tighten, make firm.

núkúúw₂ See *núúk, -ú-.* vo. (T5) believe, have faith in, trust, depend on. *n. kisikis* b. partially; *n. mwaramwar* b. with uncertainty or doubtfully; *n. mwochomwoch* b. temporarily. *wúse n. ónoon* or *wúse n. aan fóós* I do not b. what he says.

núkúúw₃ See *núk, -ú-.* vo. (T5) put in readiness, prepare; (refl.) get ready. *siya núkúúkich* we have put ourselves in readiness, taken our places.

núkúúw₄ See *núkú-₄, -ú-.* vo. (T5) put away, put in a safe place, save, keep. Dis. *núnnúkúúw* (ds). Cf. *isóni.*

núkúúw₅ (3) See *núúk, -ú-, -wa-.* n. (T3) thing believed, belief, creed, one's faith. *núkúúwan* what he believes, his religious faith. *n. kisikis* little faith; *n. mwochomwoch* temporary belief. Cf. *núkúúw₂.*

núkúmmang (3) See *núk, mmang.* vi. dillydally, be dilatory, slow to be ready or alert, unready, unprepared. Cf. *núkúpwpwach.*

núkúmmach (3) See *núkú-₃, mmach.* vi. be unresponsive to what others say, disobedient, slow to obey, willful, stubborn; lawbreaking, headless of law.

núkúmwaramwar (db; 3) See *núúk, mwaramwar₂.* vi. be of two minds, uncertain, ambivalent.

núkúmwár (4) See *núkú-₁, mwáár.* vi. be veiled; wear clothes over the head and face.

núkúmwetár (4) nu. (T2) string of *séék* discs tied together with hibiscus cord and worn suspended from the large hole in one's earlobe. *néwún n.* his *n..* Cf. *mátár, metár.*

núkúmwéw (2) See *núkú-₁, -mwéw.* n. (T2) clothes. *núkúmwéwún* his c.

núkúmwochomwoch (db; 3) See *núkú-₂, mwoch.* vi., adj. (dis.) (be) a little short, a bit short.

núkúnap (3) See *núkú-₁, nap.* nu. (loc.; T3) ocean side (of island, reef); waters on the ocean side; sea beyond the barrier reef; open sea. *núkúnapen fénú* o. s. of an island; *siya fátánnó n.* we walked to the o. s. Cf. *inúk₁, mósóór.*

núkúni See *núkú-₁, -ni-.* vo. (T5) acquire or own (something as a belt). Cf. *núkúnúk₂.*

Núkúnooch See *núkú-₁, wooch.* nu. (loc.) Lukunor Island and District (Mortlock Islands).

núkúnó See *núk.*

núkúnúú (3) See *núkú-₁, wúú₂.* [From **núkú-ni-wú.*] ns. (T3) back of the neck, nape of the neck. *núkún wúwan* b. of his n. *núkún wúwen nippach* b. of the n. of an octopus.

núkúnúk₁ Dis. of *núk* and *nnúk₂.*

núkúnúk₂ (db; 2) See *núkú-₁.* vi. (dis.) wear around the body (as a belt). *n. kiin* wear a belt. Cf. *núkúni.*

núkúnúk₃ (db; 2) See *núúk.* vi. be convinced. *wúwa n. reen* I have been c. by it.

núkúnúkééch (db; 2) See *núk, ééch.* vi. be well prepared, well set. nu. (T2)

good condition of readiness, preparedness.
núkúnúkú- (db; 2) See *núk*. ni. (T2) readiness, preparedness, alertness. *núkúnúkún* his r.
núkúnúkúmmang (ds; 3) See *núkúnúk₃, mmang.* vi. be slow to believe, distrustful, suspicious, untrusting.
núkúnúkúngngaw (db; 3b) See *núk, ngngaw.* vi. be ill prepared, unready; messy, sloppy, cluttered, slovenly, untidy, in disorder, in disarray.
núkúnúp (3: *-núppa-*) See *núkú-₁, pa-* or *paap.* n. (T3) upper back. *núkúnúppan* his u. b. Cf. *núkúnúpé*.
núkúnúpé (1) See *núkún, péé-₁.* n. (T1) back, outer side of a turtle shell. *núkúnúpééy, -poomw, -péén* my, your, his b. Cf. *núkúnúp.*
núkúnúwéféw (ds; 2) See *núkúnúú, faaw.* [Structurally two words: *núkún wúwéféw.*] nu. (T2) bump on the back of the neck (as on an octopus). vi. be even-tempered, not given to quick anger.
núkúnúwoch (3) See *núkú-₁, wocha-₅.* Tb1. n. (T3) trough or notch immediately back of the head of the penis. *núkúnúwochan* his n..
núkúpéépé (db; 1) See *núkú-₁, pé₃*. vi. fit loosely, be too big.
núkúpwpwach (3) See *núk, pwpwach.* vi. be lackadaisical. Cf. *núkúmmang.*
núkúrár (db; 3) See *núkú-₁, -rár.* vi., adj. (be) squeamish, overly fastidious, inclined to recoil from things that strike one as dirty, slimy, etc. Syn. *núkúcheyang.*
núkúcheyang (3b) See *núkú-₃, che-, anga-.* vi. be squeamish, overly fastidious; inclined to recoil from things that strike one as dirty, slimy, etc. Syn. *núkúrár.*
núkúchén (2) See *núkú-₂, chaan.* nu. (T2) tidal inlet. *núkúchénún fénú* t. i. of the island. Syn. *paat₁*.
núkúchéchchén (db; 2) See *núkú-₂, chchén.* vi. be moist, damp.
núkúchchar (3) See *núkú-₃, chchar.* vi. be very tightly bound together; immovable, stubborn, resistant (of persons and things).
núkútá See *núk.*
núkúto See *núk.*
núkúttam (3a) See *núkú-₂, ttam.* vi. be a bit long.
núkúwátte (1) See *núkú-₂, wátte.* vi. be a bit big.
Núkúwor nu. (loc.) Nukuoro Atoll.
núkúwu See *núk.*
Núkúyep nu. (loc.) Likiep Island and Atoll (Marshall Islands).
nummong (2) See *núú₂, mmong.* nu. (T2) a big coconut. Syn. *núúnap.*
-nún See *nnú-*.
núnnúkúúw Dis. of *núkúúw₄.*
núnnúr Dis. of *nnúr₁.*
núnnúch Dis. of *nnúch.*
núrúnó (1) See *nnúr₁, -nó.* vi. disappear into a hole (as a fish).
núch₁ N. Var. *nich.* vi. be disappointed.
núch₂ (3) See *núúch.* vi. emit ink (of octopus or squid).
núchcha (1) See *núú₂, chcha₁.* nu. (T1) a variety of coconut (red colored nut).
núw (3) NÚWA. vi. be flung out (of arm), slung (of sling stone), swung to and fro (of the body). nr. (T3) act of flinging, slinging, swinging. *núwen inisin* swinging of his body (in dance); *núwen peyiy* flinging out of my arm.
núwa (1) NÚWAA. nu. (T1) calm. Ant. *mwoor.* vi. be calm (of sea or weather). Ant. *mwor₂.* Syn. *choopi, chóórek.*
núwangngaw N. of *núwéngngaw.*
núweti See *núw, -ti-.* vo. (T6a) cast (a fishline); swing out, thrust out (as one's arm). n. *ewúnúún* sling a sling; n. *sáán* throw a rope (e.g. to a boat, or from a boat to a pier); n. *wúwach* swing or fling our head from side to side. With dir. suf.: *núwetóónó*. Cf. *nnúwet.*
núwetóónó See *núweti.*
núwéech (2) See *núw, éech.* Var. *núwéyéech.* nu. (T2) graceful swinging of body in dance.
núwénúw (db; 3) See *núw.* nu. (T3) swinging of the body in dance; swinging of the body in a way calculated to draw attention, sexy handling of one's body (in other than dance). *meyi núwénúwan* he is sexy.
núwéngngaw (3b) See *núw, ngngaw.* Var. *núwangngaw.* nu. (T3) swaying of the body in a way calculated to attract attention; awkward swinging of the body in dance. See *núwénúw.*
núwéyéech Var. of *núwéech.*
-nna- (3) NNA₃. [In cpds. only.] Var. *-na-*. unsp. know. See *siin₂, sine, sineey.*

nnaaf (Eng.) vi. be enough, sufficient; (with *ngeni*) be able. *e se n.* it is not enough; *wú sapw n. ngeni* I won't be up to it (able to do it). Syn. *té.*

nnaar (3) vi. scatter.

nnam (3) vi., va. be trapped; trap.

nnang (3) NNANGA. n. (T3) crack. *nnangan* its c.; *nnangen* c. of. vi. be ajar, have a crack, be not flush, not fit tightly.

nnap Var. of *nap.*

nnape (1) NNAPEE. (Jap. *nabe*) nu. (T1) cooking pot.

nnapeeni See *nnape, -ni-*. vo. (T4) cook (something) in a pot (in hot water). Syn. *pwóchchuni, kochchuuni.*

nnaté Var. of *naté.*

nnaw (dc; 3) NAWA₂. n. (T3) cough. *nnawan* his c. vi. cough. Dis. *nawanaw* (db). Cf. *-naw.*

nnáángéréw (2) See *nne-₂, -ngéréw.* nu. (num.; T2) thousandth (fraction). *eew n.* one t.

nnááng oon (2, 3) See *nne-₂, engoon.* nu. (num.; T2, T3) tenth (fraction). *eew n.* one t.

nnáp (4) NNÁPE. va. thrust.

nne-₁ (3a) NNE. [In cpds. only.] vi. look. Dis. *nenne-* (ds). With dir. suf.: *nneto, nenneto* look hither, look at me; *nnenong, nennenong* look inside; *nnenó, nennenó* look off, look away, wake up, come awake, open one's eyes; *nnetiw, nennetiw* look down; *nnetá, nennetá* look up; *nnewu, nennewu* look outside.

nne-₂ (3a: *nne-, nná-*) NNA₁. pref. (num.) fraction, part. [May be prefixed to any numerical of the general class. Although a prefix, it is usually written as a separate word.] *nneruwuuw* half (*ruwuuw* two); *nnewúnúngát* third (*wúnúngát* three). *ruwuuw nnewúnúngát* two thirds; *ruwuuw wunus wúnúngát nnerúwáánú* two and three fourths; *engoon me nimuuw wunus eew nneruwuuw* (also *engoon me nimuuw esópw*) fifteen and one half; *eew nnewúnúngátiir* one third of them.

nne-₃ (3a) NNA₂. nr. (T3) taste, flavor. Dis. *nenne-* (ds). *nnen* t. of.

nnef va. pass chunks of breadfruit from an oven to those who will pound them into breadfruit pudding. Syn. *etip₂, ₁gngen.*

nnefááyik (3) See *nne-₂, fááyik.* nu. (num.; T3) fortieth (fraction). *eew n.* one f.

nnefiik (3) See *nne-₂, fiik.* nu. (num.; T3) seventieth (fraction). *eew n.* one s.

nnefisuuw (3) See *nne-₂, fisuuw.* nu. (num.; T3) seventh (fraction). *eew n.* one s.

nnesefáán (2: *-fánni-*) See *nne-₂, sefáán.* vi. look back.

nnesesset (db; 2) See *nne-₃, sáát₁.* vi. be salty tasting, brackish. Dis. *nennesset* (ds). Cf. *nnesetirú.*

nnesetirú (1) See *nne-₃, sáát₁, rú₁.* vi. taste salty, brackish. Cf. *nnesesset.*

nnesóngósóng See *nne-₃, -sóngósóng.* vi., adj. having a burned taste or a charred or roasted flavor (as of peanuts).

nnesópwu- (4) See *nne-₂, sópwu-₂.* ni. (T2) half (of something).

nnekit (3) See *nne-₂, -kit.* nu. (num.; T3) ten thousandth (fraction). *eew n.* one t. t.

nnekkáy (2, 3) See *nne-₁, kkáy.* vi. look quickly.

nnekken See *nne-₃, -kken.* vi. taste of salt water, taste salty.

nnemaras (3) See *nne-₃, maras.* nu. (T3) bitter taste. vi. have a bitter taste.

nnemmang (3) See *nne-₁, mmang.* vi. look slowly.

nnemwoon (3: *-mwonna-*) See *nne-₃, mwmwoon.* nu. (T3) sour taste, acid taste. vi. have a sour or acid taste.

nnen (ds; 3: *nenna-*) See *nne-₃.* n. (T3) taste, flavor. *nennan* t. of it.

nneni See *nne-₃, -ni-.* vo. (T6a) taste. Syn. *nneri.*

nnenime (1) See *nne-₂, nime.* nu. (num.; T1) fiftieth (fraction). *eew n.* one f.

nnenimuuw (3) See *nne-₂, nimuuw.* nu. (num.; T3) fifth (fraction). *eew n.* one f.

nnenó See *nne-₁.*

nnenóóy (3) See *nne-₁, -nó.* vo. (T1) look away at.

nneng (dc; 2) NENGI₂. Tb1. vi., adj. (be) smelling bad, have a bad odor (only of women's genitals). Cf. *tteneng.*

nnengar (3b) See *nne-₃, ngar.* vi., adj. (be) sweet. Syn. *nneyar.*

nnengen (2) See *nne-₁, ngeni.* vi. have a look (used as an interjection).

nnengeni See *nne-₁, ngeni.* vo. (T2) look at, regard. Dis. *nennengeni* (ds).

nnengngaw (3b) See *nne-₃, ngngaw*. vi., adj. (be) bad tasting. Dis. *nennengngaw* (ds).

nnepatapat (db; 3) See *nne-₃, pat*. vi. be unsalted, unsweetened, insipid, tasteless.

nneri See *nne-₃, -ri-*. vo. (T6a) taste. Syn. *nneni*.

nnerik (2) See *nne-₁, rik*. nu. (T2) sidelong glance. vi. glance to the side (with *ngeni*). Dis. *nnerikirik* (db). *nnerikirik fátán, nnerikirik feyin* walk or go about looking from side to side (as in apprehension).

nnerikiiy See *nnerik, -i-₂*. vo. (T5) glance at.

nnerikirik Dis. of *nnerik*.

nneruwuuw (3) See *nne-₂, ruwuuw*. nu. (num.; T3) half. *eew n*. one h. Cf. *esópw*.

nnerúwáánú (1) See *nne-₂, rúwáánú*. nu. (num.; T1) fourth (fraction). *eew n*. one f.

nnerúwe (1) See *nne-₂, rúwe*. nu. (num.; T1) twentieth (fraction). *eew n*. one t.

nnet (2, 3) NNETI, NNETA. vi. be true. *e n*: it is t.; *e n. o!* it is t., sir! nr. (T2, T3) truth; verdict (of a trial). *nnetin óómw fóós, nneten óómw fóós* the t. of your words; *nneten kképwúng* a proper or true trial (in court); *ifa nneten ewe kképwúng* what was the verdict of that court?

nnetá See *nne-₁*.

nnetááy See *nne-₁, -tá*. vo. (T1) look up at.

nnetiw See *nne-₁*.

nnetiweey See *nne-₁, -tiw, -e-₂*. vo. (T6b) look down at.

nneto See *nne-₁*.

nnetooy See *nne-₁, -to*. vo. (T1) look hither at. *nnetoowey, nnetook* l. h. at me, you (sg.).

nnettiwe (1) See *nne-₂, ttiwe*. nu. (num.; T1) ninetieth (fraction). *eew n*. one n.

nnettiwuuw (3) See *nne-₂, ttiwuuw*. nu. (num.; T3) ninth (fraction). *eew n*. one n.

nnewaniik (3) See *nne-₂, waniik*. nu. (num.; T3) eightieth (fraction). *eew n*. one e.

nnewanuuw (3) See *nne-₂, wanuuw*. nu. (num.; T3) eighth (fraction). *eew n*. one e.

nnewenewen (db; 3a) See *nne-₁, wen*. vi. look straight ahead. *n. ngeni* l. straight ahead at.

nnewone (1) See *nne-₂, wone*. nu. (num.; T1) sixtieth (fraction). *eew n*. one s.

nnewonuuw (3) See *nne-₂, wonuuw*. nu. (num.; T3) sixth (fraction). *eew n*. one s.

nnewowee- See *nne-₁, -wow, -e-₂*. vo. (T6b) look at person addressed. [Used only with 2sg. and 2pl. objective pronouns.] *nnewoweyok* look at you (sg.); *nnewoweekemi* look at you (pl.).

nnewu See *nne-₁*.

nnewuuw See *nne-₁, -wu*. vo. (T1) look outside at.

nnewúnúngát (2, 3) See *nne-₂, wúnúngát*. n. (num.; T2, T3) third (fraction). *eew n*. one t.; *eew nnewúnúngátin* one t. of it.

nneyang Var. of *neyang*.

nneyapaap (db; 3) See *nne-₃, ap₁* (?). nu. (T3) the taste or feel of milk in one's mouth. [Many dislike this taste, others like it.]

nneyar (3) See *nne-₃, ar*. vi., adj. (be) sweet. Dis. *nenneyar* (ds). Syn. *nnengar*.

nneyééch (2) See *nne-₃, ééch*. vi. be good tasting. Dis. *nenneyééch* (ds).

nneyiniik (3) See *nne-₂, iniik*. n. (num.; T3) thirtieth (fraction). *eew n*. one t.

nneyipwúkú (1) See *nne-₂, -pwúkú*. nu. (num.; T1) hundredth (fraction). *eew n*. one h.

nné₁ (1) NNÉÉ₂. F. Var. *anné₁*. vi., adj. (be) delicious, tasty, savory. Cf. *nénné, nne-₃*.

nné₂ (1) NNÉÉ₃. Var. *anné₂*. vi., adj. (be) firm, ready to pick, but not yet fully ripe (of breadfruit only). Cf. *maaw, nénné*.

nnék (2) NNÉKÚ. vi. plant in a pattern (of taro). *nnékún óni* planting taro in a pattern.

nnékúúw See *nnék, -ú-*. vo. (T5) plant in a pattern (of taro).

nnét (2) NNÉTÚ. nu. (T2) half-flower (*Scaevola frutescens*). [A strand shrub, its berries are used as a medicine for inflamed eyes.] *efóch n*. one h.-f. *nnétún* h.-f. of (a given region). Cf. *nèét*.

nnéw (dc; 2) See *naaw*. vi. have had many children (of man or woman); have been fertile.

nnii- (1) NNII. [In cpds. only.] unsp. strike, smite, beat.

nniim Var. of *niim*.

nniimanaw (3b) See *nnii-, manaw*. vi. commit murder.

nniimanaweey See *nniimanaw, -e-₂*. vo. (T6b) murder, kill.

nniiy See *nnii-*. vo. (T1) strike, beat, smite (a person or animal). With dir. suf.: *nniiyenó* slay, kill; (refl.) commit suicide, kill oneself. *wúpwe pwisin nniiyeyinó* I shall commit suicide.

nniiyenó See *nniiy*.

nnif (2) NNIFI. N. Var. *nnúf.* nu. (T2) flat, wooden mortar (for mashing breadfruit and taro). *eew n.* one m. *aan n.* his m.; *nnifin* m. of (a given make).

nnifech (dc; 3, 2) See *ni-₁* or *ni-₂, -fech-*. Var. *nifech₂*. nu. (T3) turning movement of the body (as in dancing). vi. turn (of body or canoe).

nnifecheyiti See *nnifech, -iti*. vo. (T2) turn one's body towards.

nnifén (2) See *ni-₂, fén₁*. nu. (T2) bruised, injured. va. bruise, injure.

nniféchééch (2) See *nnifech, ééch*. Var. *nifechééch*. vi. turn gracefully (as in dancing); be deft, nimble; (be) quick thinking or acting in an emergency.

nnis nu. a reef fish (similar to *wumwuné*, very timid). Cf. *ikeninnis*.

nnim (dc; 3a) See *nime-*. vi., adj. (be) clean, neat, pure. Dis. *nimenim* (db).

nnimet (dc; 2) See *nime-, -ti-*. vi. (be) neatened, cleaned, spruced up. Cf. *nimeti*.

nning (dc; 3) See *ning*. n. (T3) pleasant hue, glory, beauty. *nningan* his b. vi., adj. (be) of pleasant or bright hue; glorious, beautiful, pretty; exposed (of the end of the penis).

nningengngaw (3b) See *nning, ngngaw*. Var. *ningengngaw*. vi., adj. (be) ugly, unpleasant in appearance; deformed, misshapen.

nningééch (2) See *nning, ééch*. vi., adj. (be) beautiful, pretty.

nnich (dc; 2) See *nichi-*. vi., adj. leak (of house, canoe, container); leaking. Dis. *ninnich* (ds) be leaky. With dir. suf.: *nnichinong, nnichinó, nnichiwu*.

nnichinong See *nnich*.

nnichinó See *nnich*.

nnichiwu See *nnich*.

nniyen (3) NNIYA-. [Regularly, as shown, with rel. suf. -n₂.] vr. be more than expected, too much; (with negative) very, very well, quite, sufficiently. *aa n. wátte* it is bigger than I expected or thought; *ese n. wátte* it is not as big as I expected, it's not very big; *ese n. nééné* it is not quite full. *wúse n. sineey fóósun Chuuk* I don't know the Trukese language very well (as well as you might think); *neminnaan aa kon n. fowutowut* that woman is ornamented too much. Cf. *ni-₂*.

nniyepwut (dc; 3) See *ni-₂, opwut*. vo. (T3) be disgusted with, be nauseated by.

nno- (4) NNO. [In cpds. only.] unsp. inside. See *nnofit*. Cf. *nónu-, nnó-, nóó-*.

nnoow (dc; 2) NNOOWU. va. be disgusted by, be repelled by; abhor. *wúwa n. naan iik pwún meyi pwoono* I am repelled by that fish because it stinks; *aa n. ngaang* he is disgusted by me.

nnoowáásini F. of *nnooweesini*.

nnooweesini See *nnoow, -ásini-*. N. vo. (T5) be disgusted by (something) to the point of future avoidance; be no longer able to stand (something).

nnoowupwétérék See *nnoow, pwétérék*. N. nu. athlete's foot, fungus of the foot. Syn. *nnoowupwpwún*.

nnoowupwpwún (2) See *nnoow, pwpwún-*. F. nu. (T2) athlete's foot, fungus of the foot. Syn. *nnoowupwétérék*.

nnofit (2) See *nno-, fiti-₂*. vi., adj. (be) mixed together, intermingled (as of food ingredients, people of different groups, etc.).

nnofitééch (2) See *nnofit, ééch*. vi., adj. (be) well mixed.

nnofitiiy See *nnofit, -i-₂*. vo. (T5) mix together.

nnofitingngaw (3b) See *nnofit, ngngaw*. vi., adj. (be) badly mixed.

nnofitingngawa See *nnofitingngaw*. vo. (T3) mix badly.

nnokop (2) NNOKOPU. n. (T2) flat leaf package (of broiled preserved breadfruit, or of medicine). *aan n., nnokopun* his p.; *anan n.* his p. to eat. *nnokopun épwét* p. of preserved fermented breadfruit; *nnokipun sáfey* p. of medicine.

nnokopuuw See *nnokop, -u-*. vo. (T5) prepare a flat leaf package of (preserved breadfruit or medicine).

nnokopuni (2) See *nnokop, -ni-*. vo. (T5) prepare a flat leaf package of (preserved breadfruit or medicine). Syn. *nnokapuuw*.

nnomw (dc; 2) See *nomwu-*. vi. be stripped (of skin, bark, or leaves); scraped, scratched, clawed.

nnomwut (dc; 2) See *nomwu-, -ti-*. vi. be scraped (as by a shell); clawed, scratched (as by fingernails so as to lose skin); skinned, stripped (of bark or leaves by scraping). Cf. *nomwuti*.

nnopwur nu. a species of shell fish. Cf. *nopwur*.

nnopwut Var. of *nopwut*.

nnow (dc; 2) See *nowu-*₁. nu. (T2) lasso. vi. be twirled, twirl (as a rope).

nnó- (3 irreg.) NNÓ. [In ptv. const. only.] Var. *nóó-*. ni. (prep.) in, inside. *nnón* in it. Cf. *nónu-, nóó-, nno-*.

nnómw N. of *nómw*.

nnón See *nnó-*.

nnóng (dc; 2) See *nóóng₂*. N. nu. (T2) fly (insect).

nnus N. of *nus*.

nnum (dc; 2) See *nu-, -mi-*. vi. be creased, folded, bent, crumpled. Cf. *numi*. nu. (T2) crease, fold. [Presumably a secondary formation from the verb.] *meyi wor nnumun* it has a crease.

nnumi Var. of *numi*.

nnupw N. of *nupw*.

nnupwuuw See *nu-, pwu-, -u-*. vo. (refl.; T5) jerk, jump with surprise, be startled, twitch. Dis. *nunnupwuuw* (ds). *wúwa nnupwuuwey* I was startled. *meyi nunnupwuuw* it characteristically twitches.

nnut (2) See *nu-, -ti-*. Var. *nnút*. vi. be tied together by a twining process (of reeds or rods, as in making fences or drying racks); tie things together by twining. Cf. *nuti*. nu. (T2) process of tying rod or reeds together by twining. [Presumably a secondary formation from the verb.]

nnú- (2: *-nún*) NNÚ. [In cpds. only.] unsp. folded. See *énnú, énnúnó, nnútiw, nnúún*. Cf. *nu-*.

nnú (dc; 1) See *núú-*. vi. be exasperated, fed up (with *wóó-*₁). *aa n. wóóy* he is fed up with me.

nnúú- (1) NNÚÚ₁. ni. (T1), suf. (cc.) loaf of breadfruit pudding. *ennú, rúwénnú, wúnúnnú, fénnú, nimennú, wononnú,*
fúúnnú or *fúnnú, wanúnnú, ttiwennú, engoon nnúún* one,...ten l.; *fitennú* how many l. *nnúún* l. of it.

nnúún₁ (ds; 2: *núnnú-*) See *nnú-*. vi. be lowered, furled (of a sail); folded up (of a mat).

nnúún₂ Var. of *núún*.

nnúúw NNÚÚ₂. vo. (T1) know (the way, the reefs, etc.); have knowledge of, be familiar with. *wúwa n. ewe aan* I k. the way (road); *ngaang meyi n. kkewe faaw* I am familiar with (have knowledge of) that reef (those rocks). Cf. *núú-*.

nnúf (3a) NNÚFA. F. Var. *nnif*. nu. (T3) flat, wooden mortar (for mashing breadfruit and taro). *eew n.* one m. *aan n.* his m.; *nnúfen* m. of (a given make).

nnúfaachaw (3) See *nnúf, achaw*₁. nu. (T3) stone mortar or pounding board (of basalt or *achaw*). Syn. *nnúféfaaw*.

nnúféfaaw (2) See *nnúf, faaw*. nu. (T2) stone mortar or pounding block. See *nnúfaachaw*.

nnúk₁ (2) NNÚKÚ. nu. (T2) bird's nest fern, (*Asplenium nidus*). *efóch n.* one f. *nnúkún* f. of (a given region).

nnúk₂ (dc; 2) See *núkú-*₃. vi. be tight, firm, stable; tightly bound together (as of the beams of a house). Dis. *núkúnúk* (db).

nnúng (dc) See *núúng*. vi. be infested with ants.

nnúr₁ (dc; 2) NÚRÚ₁. vi. 1. slip, become loose (of a rope). Dis. *núnnúr* (ds). *núnnúrún mááy* a rite in the cycle of breadfruit summoning ritual. Syn. *-rurrur, rúrrúr*. 2. shrink.

nnúr₂ (dc; 2) NÚRÚ₂. n. (T2) shade; (with pos. suf.) shadow. *meyi wor nnúrún* it has a shadow. *kepwe etto fáán nnúrún eey irá* come beneath the s. of this tree; *fáán n.* in the s. vi. be shady, shaded, in the shadow. Dis. *núnnúr* (ds). *meyi n. eey irá* this tree is shady.

nnúch (2) NNÚCHÚ. vi. be snapped (of fingers), clicked (of a lock), ground (of teeth), tick (of a clock); start, begin (doing something). nu. (T2) snapping, clicking, ticking, tapping, grinding. Dis. *núnnúch* (ds). *núnnúchún nii* grinding of teeth.

nnút Var. of *nnut*.

nnútiw (3) See *nnú-, -tiw*. vi. lower sail; be lowered, furled (of sail).

nnúwet (dc; 3) See *núw, -ti-*. vi. be cast (of a fish line); be slung, swung out, flung out (of arm, sling stone). Cf. *núweti*.

NG

-ng (3) NGA. suf. state or condition. See *chipwang, pachang, parang, seneeng, wochang.*

ngaa- (1v) NGAA. [In cpds. only.] unsp. open mouth; be fed, have food. See *ángááni.*

ngaaf (3) NGAFA. n. (T3), suf. (cc.) fathom (distance from fingertip to fingertip of outstretched hands and arms). *engaf, rúwéngaf, wúnúngaf, féngaf, nimengaf, wonongaf, fúúngaf, wanúngaf, ttiwengaf, engoon ngaaf* or *engoon ngafan* one,...ten fathoms; *fitengaf* how many fathoms.

ngaas (3) NGASA. nu. (T3) a kind of perfumed oil. *epitiyan ng.* his p. o. *pwoon ng.* the odor of p. o.

ngaang prn. (pers.) I, me. Emphatic: *nganga, ngaanga. ngaangú chék, ngaang chék* just me, only me.

ngaanga₁ See *ngaang.* Var. *nganga.* prn. (pers.) I, me (emphatic).

Ngaanga₂ (db; 1) Itang. nu. (pers.) in the expression *Ngiingi me Ng.*, the names of either two people or, according to some, of two porpoises in legend.

ngaat (3) NGATA. nu. (T3) hole. [Preferred over *pwaang* in the presence of siblings of opposite sex or parent and child of opposite sex.] *ngaten ómwu* anus (Tb., "faeces hole"). Cf. *-ngát.*

ngas (3b) NGASA. vi. draw or emit breath, breathe. Dis. *ngasangas* (db).

ngasanó (1) See *ngas, -nó.* vi. relax (as after hard work), feel relieved (as after hardship or from pain); (metaphorically) defecate, urinate. *imwen ng.* lavatory.

ngasannap (3a) See *ngas, nap.* n. (T3) deep breathing, sigh. *ngasannapan* his d. b. vi. breathe deeply, sigh.

ngasangas (db; 3b) See *ngas.* n. (dis.; T3) breathing, breath; heart. *ngasangasan* his b. *féwún ng.* heart. vi. (dis.) breathe.

ngasengeni Var. of *ngaséseni.*

ngasepwpwich Var. of *ngasépwpwich.*

ngaséseni See *ngas, seni₂.* Var. *ngasengeni.* vo. (T2) get relief from (sickness, misery, oppression, hardship).

ngasépwpwich See *ngas, -pwpwich.* Var. *ngasepwpwich.* vi. puff, pant.

ngana- (3b) NGANA. Tbl. [In cpds. only.] unsp. sexual orgasm, sexual pleasure.

nganangan (db; 3) See *ngana-.* Tbl. vi., adj. (dis.) (be) having sexual orgasm or sexual pleasure.

nganga See *ngaang.* Var. *ngaanga.* prn. (pers.) I, me (emphatic).

ngar (3b) NGARA. vi., adj. (be) sweet. Dis. *ngarangar* (db). Syn. *ar.*

ngarangar Dis. of *ngar.*

-ngach (2) NGACHA. suf. chin. See *itengach.* Cf. *ngáách.*

ngateni See *ngaat, -ni-.* vo. (T6a) pierce, make a hole in, dig a hole in.

ngá (1) NGÁÁ. vi. make a sudden soft noise (as light waves on a beach, falling rain, the slow breaking of a limb from its weight, tearing of clothes, wheezy breathing).

ngáán (2) NGÁÁNI. nu. (T2) mackerel, Pacific kingfish. *ngáánin Chuuk* m. of Truk.

ngáángá (db; 1) See *ngá.* nu. (T1) sudden soft noise; type of noise children make to frighten people. *ngááángáán chiyorey* wheeze in my throat. vi. make a scary noise.

ngááángáári Dis. of *ngáári.*

ngáári See *ngá, -ri-.* vo. (T4) make a scary noise at (someone); jeer at or mock (someone) by "ááááá...". Dis. *ngááángááári* (db).

ngáách (4) NGÁCHE₁. n. (T2) lower jaw, jaw. *ngáchin* his jaw. *chúún ng.* jawbone. Cf. *-ngach.*

ngááwu (1) See *ngá, -wu.* nu. (T1) miao (of cat). *ngááwuun kattu* cat's m. vi. mew.

-ngách (4) NGÁCHE₂. [In cpds. only.] unsp. (u.m.) See *winingách.*

ngáchángách (db; 4) See *ngáách.* vi., va. use or wear dentures.

Ngáchik Var. of *Ngechik.*

-ngát (4) NGÁTE. ni. (T2, T3), suf. (cc.) concave or hollow object; (less common) thing of most any kind, nonspecific or general class object (regularly used outside of Tn. dialects only for the number three). *engát,*

ngáta-   **Trukese-English**

rúwéngát or *rúwengát, wúnúngát, féngát* or *fengát, nimengát, wonongát, fúúngát, wanúngát, ttiwengát, engoon ngátan* or *engoon ngátin* one,...ten c. or h. objects. *fitengát* how many c. or h. objects? *éwúnúngátan* (N.) or *éwúnúngátin* (F.) the third one. Syn. *-uw, pwaang.* Cf. *ngaat.*

ngáta- See *-ngát.*

ngáti- See *-ngát.*

nge Var. of *ngé.*

-ngen [In cpds. only.] adj. (?) joyful, happy. See *chchengen.*

ngeni NGENI. vo. (T2) give to (someone); (following or suffixed to another verb) toward, to, against, for, with. *ngeniyey* or *ngenney, ngonuk* give me, you, or toward me, you. *wúwa angaang ng. Eiue* I worked for Eiue; *wúwa makkeey ng. eey piin* I wrote it with this pencil; *wúwa ééy ng. ewe éé* I hooked it with the hook. *apasaangeni* tell (something) to (someone); *makkengeni* write with (something).

nger (3) NGERA. vi. be chafed or scratched (as skin); be rough, hoarse, rasping (of voice). *aa ng. péwún reen néwún kkunók* his arm has been c. by his wristwatch. *meyi ng. neewúwan* his throat is hoarse.

ngereey See *nger, -e-₂.* vo. (T6b) saw, cut by chafing.

ngerenger (db; 3) See *nger.* nu. (dis.; T3) saw. *emén ng.* one s. *néwún ng.* his s. *piipiin ng.* sawdust. va. (dis.) saw. vi. (dis.) be sawed.

ngerengereyinó (db; 1) See *nger, nóó.* nu. (T1) sickness whose symptoms are wheezy breathing, loss of voice, and a sore throat, laryngitis. [Said to be caused by the wave spirit *soopeen nóó.*] *sáfeen ng.* medicine for this sickness.

ngeri- (2) NGERI. [In cpds. only.] unsp. nibble, gnaw.

ngeriiy See *ngeri-, -i-₂.* vo. (T5) nibble, gnaw.

ngeringer (db; 2) See *ngeri-.* vi. (dis.) be nibbling, be gnawing.

Ngechik Var. *Ngáchik, Ingechik.* nu. (loc.) Ngatik Atoll.

nget (3) NGETA. vi. be aflame, flaming.

ngé Var. *nge.* conj. but, while, and, whereas. *wúpwe takiriikemi reen ewe eew kinikin ngé ááami osapw takiriiyey?* shall I laugh at you on account of that other half (of the body) but you not laugh at me? *ngaangú chék epwe ruuwu kinikin nóón inisi? ngé áámi? áá?* is it only I who has two divisions in his person? whereas you? eh? *iwee ngé* whereas, and also, moreover; *pwún wiis meyi chék mwochen mwmwetefátán, nóón mwuu; iwee ngé wiis seni pwpwún ese toongeni epwe mwmwet* for an assignment (job) just wants to go hopping (from one person to another), in the government (service); whereas an assignment of soil cannot hop (away from you). *mwo ngé* even; *Eiue mwo ngé pwan óchoocho* even Eiue also exerted himself ("Eiue yet but also exerting"); *rese mwochen epwe tekiyaa mwo ngé kkapás* they did not want him to act above his station even (in) talk. *ngé....ngé* although (albeit)....but (nevertheless); *pwe eey mwéngé wú áni ngé wesetáán eney seni semeyi ngé meyi kkamé* for this food I am eating, although actually my portion from my father, is nonetheless bought. *ngé méwút!* never mind! ("but what for!"); *ngé méwút iiy!* never mind that!

ngéé- (1) NGÉÉ. [In cpds. only.] unsp. suck, kiss in a sucking manner.

ngééngé (db; 1) See *ngéé-.* nu. (dis.; T1) sucking (of infant on breast); sucking kiss (as by lover on the throat). *neemóón ng.* red mark from a sucking kiss. ni. (T1) mark of a kiss. *ngééngéén m.* of a k. on him. vi. be sucked on; be a love mark (from a sucking kiss).

ngééti See *ngéé-, -ti-.* vo. (T4) go all out at, exert oneself in. *aa ng. aanú we angaang* he exerted himself in his work. *raa ng. ne fétún* they went all out in paddling.

ngééwú See *ngéé-, -wú-.* vo. (T4) suck; kiss suckingly (less common than *ngééyi*).

ngééyi See *ngéé-, -yi-₂.* vo. (T4) suck; kiss suckingly. *aa ng. fáán wúwan* he kissed suckingly under her throat. Syn. *ngééwú.*

ngéréw (2) NGÉRÉWÚ. [Back formation from *-ngéréw.*] nu. (T2) thousand. [It has replaced *-ngéréw* in the schools to avoid confusions such as *nimengéréw* (five thousand) with *nime ngéréw* (fifty thousand), which has replaced *nimekit* (five ten-thousands) in the modern arithmetic curriculum.] *eew ng., ruuwu*

ng., wúnúngát ng.,...engoon ng. one, two, three,...ten t.
-ngéréw (2) See *ngéréw.* suf. (cc.) thousand. [Used with numerical prefixes; replaced by *ngéréw* and the general counting classifier in school usage.] *engéréw, rúwéngéréw, wúnúngéréw, féngéréw, nimengéréw, wonongéréw, fúúngéréw, wanúngéréw, ttiwengéréw* one,...nine t.; *fitengéréw* how many t. *engéréw aramas* one t. people. With c. pref. and ptv. const.: *áángéréwún, érúwéngéréwún* one thousandth, two thousandth (etc.). With dis. c. pref.: *ákkaángéréw ékkérúwéngéréw* be one t. at a time, two t. at a time (etc.). With pref. *nne-₂: nnáángéréw* thousandth (fraction).
ngi (1) NGII₁. vi. buzz, hum, sound; sing. Dis. *ngiingi* (db). With dir. suf.: *ngiitá* sing or speak in a high-pitched voice; *ngiitiw* lower the pitch of one's voice.
ngii₁ (1) NGII₂. Wn. and Ps.W. Var. *nii.* n. (T1) tooth. *ngiin* his t.
ngii₂ (1) NGII₄. nu. (T1) name of the consonant (voiced, velar, nasal continuant) written *ng*; name of the digraph thus written.
ngiinikú See *ngii₁, kúúw.* nu. name of a star.
ngiinuuk (3) See *ngi, nuuk₁.* [New word established at the orthography conference of 1972.] vi., adj. (be) mid height (of a vowel; "middle sounding"). [Trukese mid vowels are *e, é, o.*] *wosowá ng.* mid vowel.
ngiingi₁ (db; 1) NGII₃. nu. (T1) 1. any cowrie or bubble shell (families Cypraeidae and Bullidae, especially any of the larger varieties); any shell used to make a breadfruit peeler. *eew ng.* one c. s. *néwún ng.* his c. s. Cf. *nikósso, nimwárá, pwiin₂.* 2. breadfruit peeler.
ngiingi₂ (db; 1) See *ngi.* n. (T1) tune; intonation, accent, voice. *ngiingiin* his accent, voice. vi. Dis. of *ngi.*
Ngiingi₃ (db; 1) Itang. nu. (pers.) in the expression *Ng. me Ngaanga*, the names either of two people or, according to some, of two porpoises in legend.
ngiiráátá See *ngiiri.*
ngiiri See *ngi, -ri-.* vo. (T4) sing, hum (a tune). With dir. suf.: *ngiiráátá* sing (a tune) in a high-pitched voice.

ngiitaw (3) nu. (T3) name of a star.
ngiitá₁ See *ngi.*
ngiitá₂ (1) See *ngi, -tá.* [New word established at the orthography conference of 1972.] vi., adj. (be) high (of a vowel; "high sounding"). [Trukese high vowels are *i, u, ú.*] *wosowá ng.* high vowel.
ngiitiw₁ See *ngi.*
ngiitiw₂ (3) See *ngi, -tiw.* [New word established at the orthography conference of 1972.] vi., adj. (be) low (of vowel; "low sounding"). [Trukese low vowels are *a, á, ó.*] *wosowá ng.* low vowel.
ngiiyów (2) NGIIYÓWU. vi. pain, hurt; be painful. Syn. *metek.* nu. (T2) pain, being painful. *ngiiyówun pecheey* p. in my leg.
ngimmóng (2) See *ngi, mmóng.* vi. sing in a loud voice. With dir. suf.: *ngimmóngótá* raise the singing louder.
ngimmóngótá See *ngimmóng.*
ngin (2: *ngini-, -ngin, -ngiin*) NGINI. F. vi., adj. (be) small, little, tiny. With dir. suf.: *ngininó* become smaller, be reduced. Syn. *kis.*
ngini- (2) See *ngin.* [In ptv. const. only as *ni.*] ni. (T2), suf. (cc.) bit, tiny piece. *engin, rúwéngin* or *rúwengin, wúnúngin, féngin* or *fengin, nimengin, wonongin, fúúngin, wanúngin, ttiwengin, engoon nginin* one,...ten bits.
nginino See *ngin.*
nginingiin (db; 2) See *ngin.* Var. *nginingin.* vi., adj. (be) little, small, tiny. [Preferred over *kisikiis* when siblings of opposite sex or parent and child of opposite sex are both within hearing.] With dir. suf.: *nginingiininó* become smaller, be reduced.
nginingiininó See *nginingiin.*
nginingin Var. of *nginingiin.*
ngiri- (2) NGIRI. [In cpds. only.] unsp. bite, take the bait (of fish).
ngiriiy See *ngiri-, -i-₂.* vo. (T5) bite (the bait), tug (the line) (of fish).
ngiringir (db; 2) See *ngiri-.* vi. (dis.) be biting the bait, be tugging at the line.
-ngoon (2) NGOONU. [Used only with *e-* (one).] suf. (cc.) ten, unit of ten. *engoon* ten. *áángoonun* tenth one. *nnáángoon* tenth (fraction).
ngon (3) NGONA. va. observe with pleasure, behold appreciatively. Dis.

ngonongon (db). *wúwaa ng. ewe wurumwmwot nánew* I watched the play (with appreciation) yesterday.

ngoneyiti See *ngon, -iti*. vo. (T6a) view (something) with pleasure, praise.

ngonongon (db; 3) See *ngon*. nu. (dis.; T3) observing with pleasure, staring appreciatively, ogling. vi. (dis.) be observing with pleasure, stare appreciatively, ogle. *pwata kaa ng.?* why are you staring?

ngonuk See *ngeni*.

ngor vi. sing.

ngot vi. snore.

ngóóngó (db; 1) NGÓÓ. nu. (T1) making faces in ridicule. vi. make faces in ridicule.

ngóóngóóri See *ngóóngó, -ri-*. vo. (T4) make faces in ridicule at (someone).

ngú- (2) NGÚ. [In cpds. only.] unsp. chew and suck (as on sugarcane, coconut husk, pandanus fruit). See *ngngúúng₂, ngúngngúúng, ngúta-, ngúti*.

ngú (1) NGÚÚ₁. vi. moan, groan, grunt. Dis. *ngúúngú* (db).

-ngú (1) NGÚÚ₂. [In cpds. only; a var. of *ñgii*.] unsp. tooth, teeth. See *aarúngú*.

ngúús vi. in *ng. me ng.* give advice or admonish over and over again; a signal or making a signal by wearing a grass with a bushy tuft of seeds behind one's ear to show one's sweetheart that one is paying no attention to people's admonishing against the love affair. Cf. *ngús*.

ngúún (2) NGÚNÚ₂. n. (T2) soul (good or bad of a person); reflection of a person (as a manifestation of the good soul), shadow of a person (as manifestation of the bad soul). *ngúnún* his s. Id. *aa súúnó ngúniy* I was startled ("my soul fled").

ngúúng Var. of *ngngúúng₁*.

ngúúngú₁ (db; 1) NGÚÚ₃. nu. (T1) species of trigger fish (*Odonus niger* <Kuiyama>). Syn. *núúnú₂, pwúnúúnú*.

ngúúngú₂ (db; 1) See *ngú*. nu. (dis.; T1) moaning, groaning, grunting. *ngúúngúún piik* pig's grunting. vi., adj. (dis.) (be) moaning, groaning, grunting.

ngúúngúúres (db; 2) See *ngúúngú₂, resi-*. vi. be groaning or grunting repeatedly.

ngús (2) NGÚSÚ. vi. be agreed upon, coordinated. Cf. *ngúús*.

ngún Var. *ngngún*. vi. hand, be in hand (usually in the imperative). *ng. o!* here it is in my hand for you to take, sir!

Ngúnú nu. (loc.) Ngulu Island and Atoll (Western Caroline Islands).

Ngúnúfen (2) See *ngúún, fen₂*. nu. (T2) The Holy Ghost, Holy Spirit (Protestant usage). Syn. *Ngúnúpin*.

ngúnúngún (db; 2) NGÚNÚ₁. vi. be whispering, talking in a soft voice.

ngúnúngúnúngngaw (3b) See *ngúnúngún, ngngaw*. vi. grumble, mutter, complain.

ngúnúngngaw (3b) See *ngúún, ngngaw*. nu. (T3) bad soul (manifested as a person's shadow, becomes a ghost after death).

Ngúnúpin (2) See *ngúún, pin*. nu. (T2) The Holy Ghost, The Holy Spirit (Catholic usage). Syn. *Ngúnúfen*.

ngúnúyééch (2) See *ngúún, ééch*. nu. (T2) good soul (manifested as a person's reflection, ascends to the sky world after death and may become an *énúúsór*).

ngúngngúúng (ds of ds; 2) See *ngngúúng₂*. nu. (T2) chewing and sucking. va. (dis.) chew and suck. Cf. *núúnú₁*.

ngút (2) NGÚTÚ. vi., adj. (be) congested, stopped up, or stuffed up (of nose, pipe, hose); pinched (as feet in tight shoes); aching (of the head); squeezed or constricted (as an arm by an elastic band); swollen (as an arm). *meyi ng. pwéétiy* my nose is stuffed up.

ngúta- (3) See *ngú-, -ta-₂*. ni. (T3) a chew; thing for chewing and sucking (e. g. sugarcane, coconut husk, pandanus fruit). *ngútan* his c.

ngúti See *ngú-, -ti-*. vo. (T5) chew and suck (sugarcane, coconut husk, pandanus fruit). Cf. *núúnúúw*.

ngútúpwéét (2) See *ngút, pwéét₂*. vi. have a stuffed up nose.

ngútúchchar (3) See *ngút, -chchar*. vi. be firmly stuck inside, be tightly pinched.

ngúwén nu. a kind of fish.

ngngan (dc; 3b) See *ngana-*. Tb1. nu. (T3) orgasm. vi. 1. have orgasm or sexual pleasure. 2. be beaten.

-ngngat (dc; 3) See *ngaat*. adj. emptily. Syn. *-pwpwang*. See *fanangngat, wosungngat*.

ngngaw (3b) NGNGAWA. Tb3. vi., adj. (be) bad, ugly, unfitting, unsuitable, objectionable. *meyi ng.* it is bad; *aa ng.* it has gone bad. Syn. *pwutak.* ni. (T3) badness, ugliness, unsuitability. *ngngawan* his b. *ifa wusun ngngawey?* how am I bad ("what is the manner of my badness")?

ngngaweyiti See *ngngaw, -iti.* vo. (T6a) be bad for, be unfavorable to.

ngngawéngeni See *ngngaw, ngeni.* Var. *ngngawúngeni.* vo. (T2) treat badly, be bad to.

ngngawónó See *ngngaw, -nó.* vi. be gone bad, ruined, damaged, spoiled, broken down, rendered useless.

ngngawúngeni Var. of *ngngawéngeni.*

ngngen N. vi. pass chunks of cooked breadfruit from the oven to those who will mash them into breadfruit pudding. Syn. *etip$_2$*.

ngnger (dc; 2) See *ngeri-.* [With *wóón*.] vi. eat continually, have an insatiable appetite, have a craving to eat, be greedy for food. *meyi ng. wóón ewe wokasi* has a craving for that candy.

ngngi- (2) NGNGI. unsp. strain, make effort. See *engnginó, ngngi.*

ngngi (3) See *ngngi-, -ya-.* vi. be exhausted, be played out, be unable to continue. *ngngiyen átánaan* his being e.

-ngngi (dc; 1) See *ngii$_1$.* Var. *-ngngú.* adj. of the teeth, dental. See *akkarúngngi.*

ngngir (dc; 2) See *ngiri-.* va., vi. bite, take the bait (of fish); be biting; be bitten on. *ótunu ng.* time when fish b. *aa ng. ááy óó* my line has been bitten on; *aa ng. wóón óó* there has been a b. on the line. *eew neeni meyi ng.* a place where fish b.

ngngú- (2) NGNGÚ (*NGÚNGÚ). [In cpds. only.] unsp. throw, flip.

ngngúúng$_1$ (ds; 2: *ngúngngú-*) See *ngngú-.* Var. *ngúúng.* nu. (T2) heddle (on a loom); string used as a heddle, heald string. *efóch ng.* one heald rod. *ngúngngún túúr* loom's h.

ngngúúng$_2$ (ds; 2: *ngúngngú-*) See *ngú-.* vi. (dis.) be chewing and sucking (as sugarcane, coconut husk, pandanus). Syn. *ngúngngúúng.*

ngngún Var. of *ngún.*

ngngúpé (dc; 1) See *ngú-, pé$_3$.* nu. (T1) a type of coconut whose green husk is chewed. Syn. *atoon, ótoon.*

ngngúpwir (2) See *ngngú-, -pwir.* vi. have force, impetus, go fast and far, be thrown fast (of a baseball). *meyi ng. ewe pwoor* the ball has f. *wúse meneey óómw ekiyek ese ng.* I haven't grasped your thought which has no f. (courtship talk).

ngngút vi. (of relatively soft, flexible object like dough) be elastic, strong (not easily broken when stretched).

P

pa-₁ (3b) PA₁. Var. *ppa-*. ni. (loc.; T3) side; edge (of path), bank (of stream), edge or rim (of gully). *pan* its e. *pen ewe aan* (of) edge of the road; *pen ewe kkónik* (at) at the edge of the stream. *e nónnómw pan* it is at the e. of it.

pa-₂ (3a: *-p*) PA₂. [In cpds. only.] Var. *paap, -ppa-*. unsp. board. See *chééchéép, pachchaach*.

-pa (1) See *paa₁*. suf. (cc.) frond, garland, stalk with leaves. [Used with numerical prefixes in counting palm fronds, leis, garlands, banana fronds, *Cyrtosperma*, necklaces, bead belts.] *epa, rúwépa, wúnúpa, fépa, nimepa, wonopa, fúúpa, wanúpa, ttiwepa, engoon paan* one,...ten f. *epa paan núú* one coconut frond.

paa- (1) PAA₃. [In cpds. only.] unsp. condition, state of being. See *pachchaw*. Cf. Wol. *paa-*.

paa₁ (1, 1v) PAA₁. n. (T1) frond, flower garland (something with a series of leaves or petals on it). *epa* one f. *paan* its f.; f. of. *paan kúwé* nipa frond; *paan mwárámwár* garland; *paan núú* coconut frond; *paan pwuna* stalk and leaves of Cyrtosperma; *paan rúpwúng* ivory-nut palm frond; *paan wuuch* leaves of a banana (collectively). Cf. *paan₁*.

paa₂ (1) PAA₂. n. (T1) bait. *óóch p.* some b., one amount of b. *paan* his b.; b. of.

paas₁ (3) PAASA. (Eng.) adj. past (in telling the time). *minich engoon p.* ten minutes past.

paas₂ (3) PASA₃. nu. (T3) boundary marker for land holdings (consisting of small piles of stones).

-paas [In cpds. only.] adj. (intens.) very, much. See *tórópaas*. Cf. *paat₂*.

paasiisé (1) PAASIISÉÉ. (Eng.) nu. (T1) passenger. *paasiiséén waa* canoe's p. *seyin p.* passenger ship.

paasiken (Eng.) nu. bicycle. *efóch p.* one b. *waan p.* his b. *mwirimwirin p.* b. handlebars.

Paasofer (Eng.) nu. Easter (Protestant), Passover. Cf. *Paska*.

paak (3) PAKKA. (Eng.) nu. (T3) barque (type of sailing vessel). *pakken* b. of (a given place).

paaken (2) See *paa₁, -ken*. nu. (T2) variety of tobacco (with hardy leaves).

paan₁ (3) PANA₁. F. n. (T3), suf. (cc.) branch with its leaves (of trees other than palms and bananas). *epan, rúwépan, wúnúpan, fépan, nimepan, wonopan, fúúpan, wanúpan, ttiwepan, engoon panan* one,...ten b. *panen irá* tree's branch; *epan panen mááy* one breadfruit tree b. Syn. *pachang, ráá*. Cf. *paa₁*.

paan₂ (3) PANNA. vi. be bald (of head). Cf. *mwor₁*.

paan₃ (3) PAANA. N. Var. *páán*. nu. (T3) <Elbert> a species of trigger fish.

paanaato See *paani₁*.

Paanaw nu. (loc.) Palau Islands.

paani See *paa₂, -ni-*. vo. (T4) 1. bait (as a hook); put out bait for (as a fish or a spirit); lure. With dir. suf.: *paanaato* bait hither. 2. call; invoke (a name). *p. Eiue* call Eiue; *p. iten Eiue* invoke or speak the name of Eiue.

paap (db; 3a: *papa-, -ppa-, -pap, -p*) PAPA, PPA. Var. *pa-₂*. n. (T3) board, plank; board floor. Dis. *pappa-* (ds). *eché p.* one b. *papen fannó, papen fáánnó* warp beam (on loom); *papen fáánimas* cloth beam (on loom); *papen iimw* house plank or planks (indef. no.); *pappen iimw* house planks (more than one); *papen waa* strake added to the hull of a canoe to elevate its side or patch an imperfection in the base log from which the hull was shaped; *papen wóón faraf* planks on the inner triangular platform on the outrigger booms of a *meniyuk* sailing canoe; *papen wóón kiyó* planks covering outer portion of outrigger booms of *meniyuk* sailing canoe.

paapa₁ (db; 1) See *paa₂*. vi. be baited.

paapa₂ (1) PAAPAA. (Eng.) nu. (T1) papa, father. [Used only by children in address.]

paapa₃ (db; 1) PAA₄. vi. make a welcoming speech in which one apologizes for not having anything to give or for the inadequacy of one's hospitality. *aan p.* his welcome with apology. *chóón p.* official giver of welcome apology in a meeting.

paapaangeni See *paapa₃, ngeni.* vo. (T2) make welcoming apology to.

Paapaapin (2) See *paapa₂, pin.* nu. (T2) Pope.

paar (3b) See *par.* Tb3. nu. (T3) a tree (*Erythrina variegata*). [Its bark is used as medicine for pain in chest stomach; black dye is obtained from the bark.] *paren* t. of (a given region).

paarang (3) PAARANGA. nu. (T3) 1. rust. 2. smallpox, measles. vi. rust, be rusty. With dir. suf.: *paarangónó* rust away.

paarangónó See *paarang.*

paareniyaw N. Var. *pááreyiraw* nu. dried coconut frond that is hanging down from the tree or has fallen to the ground. Cf. *paa₁.*

paaro (1) PAAROO. (Eng.) vi. borrow money. nu. (T1) act of borrowing. *chóón p.* borrower.

paarooni See *paaro, -ni-.* vo. (T4) borrow (money).

paach₁ (3) See *pach.* n. (T3) handle (as of a knife or axe). *pachan* its h. *pachen nippach* body of an octopus at the point where the tentacles emanate. Cf. *aach₁.*

paach₂ (3) nu. (T3) thunder. *wúngúúngún p.* clap or sound of t. *naan iró aa wúngúri p.* the thunder has sounded the tree (the tree was struck by lightning). Syn. *ménúng.* Cf. *fi.*

paache (1) See *paa₁, -che.* nu. (T1) the *Canna* plant. [Flower worn in the ear as a sign of a broken heart, *neetipeta.*] Syn. *nini.*

paachón (4) See *paa₁, chón.* nu. (T2) variety of *Cyrtosperma* (giant swamp taro).

paat₁ (3) PATA, PAATA₁. nu. (T3) tidal inlet, offshore gully in the shallows caused by inflow and/or outflow of water; channel. *paaten eey neeni* i. of this place. *Penipat* placename on Romónum Island ("edge of the inlet"). Syn. *núkúchén.*

paat₂ (3) PAATA₂. adj. very often, continually. *fóós p., kkapas p.* talk all the time. See *fichipaat, mesepaat, wúnnúpaat.* Cf. *chééw, -paas.*

Paata nu. (loc.) 1. Pata Island and Municipality. 2. Pata District, Tonowas (Dublon) Island.

paatere (1) PAATEREE. (Sp. *padre*) nu. (T1) priest (Roman Catholic).

paaw₁ (2) PÉWÚ₁, PEYI. n. (T2) hand and arm together; forelimb (of animal); upper limb; pectoral fin (of fish); wing (of bird or aeroplane). *epéw p.* one a. *peyiy, powumw, péwún* my, your, his a. *fáán p.* armpit; *neewoon p.* upper arm close to shoulder; *seengen p.* segment between arm joints (upper or lower arm). *péwún chukó* chicken wing; small, roofed wing extending obliquely from the corner of a traditional style house; *péwún iik* fish's pectoral fin (cf. *peenen iik*); *péwún máánap me efeng* a star (beta) in Aquila; *péwún máánap me yéér* a star (gamma) in Aquila; *péwún arong* or *órong* sideburns; *péwún wúúf* sleeve of a garment. Ant. *peche, taang.* ni. (T2) something pertaining to or worn over the hand (in possessive construction only). *péwún kuroop* his baseball glove.

paaw₂ (2) PÉWÚ₂, PAAWÚ. nu. (T2) food aboard a ship or canoe. *aan p.* his ship food. *meet paawún aach sááy?* what is the f. for our journeyY? vi. eat aboard a ship or canoe.

paawén (2) See *paa₁, wénú-.* nu. (T2) variety of *Cyrtosperma.* nu. (pers.) patron spirit of the *Wúnnan* school of *itang.*

paayinú (1) See *paa₁, núú₂.* nu. (T1) coconut leaf.

pas (3b) PASA₁. vi. drift. With dir. suf.: *pasónó.* Cf. *pi.*

pasa- (3) PASA₂. [In cpds. only.] unsp. spoken. See *apasa, kkapas.*

paseri See *pas, -ri-.* vo. (T6a) drift to. Syn. *paseyiti.*

paseyiti See *pas, -iti.* vo. (T2) drift to. Syn. *paseri.*

Pasifik (Eng.) nu. (loc.) Pacific. *Matawen P.* Pacific Ocean.

pasónó See *pas.*

Paska (Sp.) nu. Easter (Roman Catholic). Cf. *Paasofer.*

pakayaroo (Jap. *bakayaroo*) excl. (in cursing) Fool!, Stupid!, God damn you!

pake (1) PAKEE. (Jap. *bake*) nu. (T1) feather fish lure. *óóch p.* one l. *néwún p.* his l. Syn. *weyit.*

Pakiin nu. (loc.) Pakin Island (Eastern Caroline Islands).

pakútang (3) PAKÚTANGA. (Jap. *bakudan*) nu. (T3) dynamite, bomb. *eféw p.* one b. *néwún p.* his b. vi., va. use dynamite; catch fish using dynamite.

pakútangeey See *pakútang, -e-₂*. vo. (T6b) dynamite or bomb (something).

pakking (2) PAKKINGI. (Jap. *bakkin*) nu. (T2) fine, penalty. *eew p.* one f. *aan p.* his f. vi. be fined. *wúwa p.* I was fined.

pan (3b, 3v) PANA₂. vi. be tilted, tipped. With dir. suf.: *panénong* tilted inwards; *panónó* tilted off; *panétiw*, *panútiw* tilted down; *panatá* tilted up; *panéwu*, *panúwu* tilted outwards. See *peneyaw*. Cf. *para-₂, pay.*

-pan See *paan*₁.

pana- (3) PANA₃. [In place names only.] unsp. land (?), island (?). See *Panúwu*₁, *Pattiw*. Cf. *fana-*₁.

panaas (3) (Eng.) nu. (T3) flush (in poker or *kinap*).

panangkeet (Eng.) Var. *pinangkeet*. nu. blanket.

panapan Dis. of *ppan.*

panatá See *pan*.

panaw (3) PANAWA. nu. (T3) a tree (*Semicarpus*). [Poisonous to the skin, it is found only on Mt. Winipwéét, Toon (Tol) Island.]

panénong See *pan.*

panétiw See *pan.*

panéwu See *pan.*

panonong (3) See *pan* (?), *-nong*. nu. (T3) removal of infant to a new location in the house following dropping off of the umbilical cord. [Occasion for lifting restrictions on mother of new-born child.]

panónó See *pan.*

panútiw See *pan.*

Panúwu₁ (1) See *pana-, -wu*. nu. (loc.; T1) Pis Island. Syn. *Piis.*

panúwu₂ See *pan.*

pansooko (1) PANSOOKOO. (Jap. *bansookoo*) nu. (T1) adhesive tape. *eché p.* one piece of a. t.; *aan p.* his a. t.

pansookooni See *pansooko, -ni-*. vo. (T4) apply adhesive tape to.

panchú (1) PANCHÚÚ. (Jap. *panchu*, from Eng.) nu. (T1) panties; briefs. *eché p.* one pair of p. *aan p.* her p. Cf. *sarúmata.*

pangkiin (2) PANGKIINI. (Eng.) nu. (T2) pumpkin. *eew p.* one p. *pangkiinin* p. of (a given type).

papatayis (2) PAPATAYISI. (Eng.) nu. (T2) baptism. vi., va. be baptized; baptize.

papatayisi See *papatayis*. vo. (T2) baptize.

Papentuwap nu. (loc.) Babelthuap Island (Palau Islands).

papeyitúr (2) See *paap, túúr*. nu. (T2) loom beam. *papen fáánimas* cloth beam, loom beam immediately in front of the weaver; *papen fannó, papen fáánnó* warp beam, loom beam away from the weaver.

par (3b) PARA₁. Tb3. vi., adj. (be) red. Dis. *parapar* (db). With dir. suf.: *parónó, paranó* become red, blush.

para-₁ (3b) See *par*. Tb2. ni. (T3) vagina (with suffixed pronouns). *paran* her v. Syn. *mwaa*₂.

para-₂ (3v) PARA₂. unsp. (?) aligned, oriented. See *kkáper, pereyinging.*

paras₁ (3) PARASA₁. nu. (T3) gonorrhea. *aan p.* his g. Syn. *rimpiyo.*

paras₂ (3) PARASA₂. nu. (T3) spray, spume; windblown drops of rain or sea spray.

paraseni (2) See *par, seni*₂. vo. (T2) be redder than.

paraseyiset (db; 2) See *paras*₂, *sáát*₁. nu. (T2) sea spray.

paranó See *par*.

parang (3) See *par, -ng*. nu. (T3) flying sparks. *parangen ááf* the flying sparks of the fire. vi. have sparks flying; be sparky. Dis. *parangarang* (db). *meyi parangarang eey ááf* this fire is sparky. Cf. *paarang.*

parangarang Dis. of *parang.*

parapar Dis. of *par.*

parapara- (db; 3b) See *par*. ni. (dis.; T3) hemorrhoids or piles, in the expression *aa turutiw paraparan* he has hemorrhoids (his "reds" have fallen down).

parachón (4) See *par, chón*. vi., adj. (be) dark red.

parattik (2) See *par, -ttik*. vi. (be) bright red, brilliant red. nr. (T2) bright redness. *parattikin wúfen neminnaan* the b. r. of that woman's dress.

pariki (1) PARIKII. (Jap. *bariki*) Var. *parúki*. nu. (T1) horsepower. *parúkin mwesiin* engine's horsepower.

parónó See *par.*

parúki Var. of paríki.
pach (3b) PACHA₁. vi., adj. 1. (be) attached, pasted, joined, added. With dir. suf.: pachatá be a. upwards. 2. (be) sticky.
pachaaw (3, 2) See pach, aaw₁ (?). F. nu. (T3, T2) shark. emén p. one s. pachaawen, pachaawún s. of (a given region). Syn. pókó.
pachang₁ (3) PACHANGA. nu. (T3), suf. (cc.) branch. epachang, rúwépachang, wúnúpachang, fépachang, nimepachang, wonopachang, fúúpachang, wanúpachang, ttiwepachang one,...nine b. pachangen mááy breadfruit branch. Syn. paan₁. Cf. kkeyang.
pachang₂ (3) See pach, -ng. n. (T3) smeared condition. pachangan his s. c. vi. be smeared with sticky substance (such as breadfruit mashings, bread dough, etc.). Dis. pachangachang (db).
pachangachang Dis. of pachang₂.
pachangngaw (3b) See pach, ngngaw. vi. be on poor terms with (with me reen). kiich si p. me reen ewe sómwoon we are on poor terms with the chief (i.e. he does not like us).
pachapach (db; 3b) PACHA₂. n. (T3) foot (of men and animals). efóch p. one f. pachapachan his f. fáán pachapachey sole of my foot. Cf. iipw, peche.
pachar (3) PACHARA. nu. (T3) 1. small sea shell (like an ear shell, but with some flattening on two sides and with pronounced teeth on both sides of the aperture). Syn. nikichuur₁. 2. <Elbert> small convex shell sticking to surface of rocks (too little meat to eat).
pachatá See pach.
pacheri₁ See pach, -ri-. vo. (T6a) cling to (as cloth clings to the body), adhere to. aa p. inisin it clung to his body.
pacheri₂ (3: pacheriya-) See pacheri₁, -ya-. n. (T3) relative, kinsman, clansman. pacheriyan his r.
pacheyiti See pach, -iti. vo. (T2) stick to, fasten on to.
pachingko (1) PACHINGKOO. (Jap. pachigko) nu. (T1) slingshot. eew p. one s. néwún p. his s. vi. use a slingshot.
pachingkooni See pachingko, -ni-. vo. (T4) use a slingshot against (someone).

pachchaach (2) See paa- or pa-₂, -chchaach. F. vi. be crushed. Syn. chaapaap.
pachchaw (2, 3b) See paa-, chchaw. N. nu. (T3) hurry. [This is the preferred word in the presence of brother and sister, father and daughter, and mother and son.] vi. be in a hurry. Syn. atapwan, atawaat.
pachchawammang (3) See pachchaw, mmang. Var. pachchawúmmang. vi. be slow when there is need for haste; dawdle, be unhurried. pwata aa p. átánaan ngé siya atapwan why is that fellow dawdling when we are in a hurry?
pachchawúmmang Var. of pachchawammang.
pat (3b) PATA. vi., adj. (be) cool; fertile. Dis. patapat (db). With dir. suf.: patónó cool off, become cool, turn cold (as a corpse), have less fever; patoto become cool hither. nu. (T3) cooling, process of being or becoming cool. e patoto paten winingách the cooling of pre-dawn is cooling hither.
Patan nu. (loc.) a clan name.
patapat Dis. of pat.
patekkich Var. of patúkkich.
patoto See pat.
patónó See pat.
patúkkich See pat, -kkich. Var. patekkich. vi., adj. (be) very cool, cold, icy.
patta (1) PATTAA. (Jap. batto) nu. (T1) bat (baseball). efóch p. one b.; aan p. his b.
Pattiw (3) See pana-, -tiw. nu. (loc.; T3) Western Islands. Nómwun P. the island chain consisting of Pulusuk, Puluwat, Tamatam, and Pulap.
pay (3a) PAYA. F. Var. páy. vi., adj. lean, slant, tilt; (be) oblique, crooked, not straight, not true. Dis. (F.) payepay, (N.) páyepáy (ds) waver; tilt now this way now that way (as an unsteady pole); reel; swing back and forth; vibrate. Cf. pan, para-₂.
payepay Dis. of pay.
payeyiti See pay, -iti. F. Var. páyeyiti. vo. (T2) lean against, tilt over to.
payiking (2) PAYIKINGI. (Jap. baikin) nu. (T2) germ, bactirium. payikingin his g.; g. of.
payitokú (Jap. baidoku) nu. syphilis. vi. have syphilis.

payiyorin (2) PAYIYORINI. Obs. (Jap. *baiorin*) nu. (T2) violin. *eew p.* one v. *néwún p.* his v. *payiyorinin* v. of (a given make). Syn. *fayiyonin*.

pá (1) PÁÁ. Tb3. vi. defecate. Dis. *páápá* (db) defecate (baby talk). Syn. *ómwu*.

páá (1) See *pá*. Tb3. n. (T1) feces, excrement. *páán* his f. Syn. *ómwu, pwise*.

-páák (Eng.) [In cpds. only.] adj. backwards. See *wochopáák*.

páán F. of *paan₃*.

pááney (2) See *paa₁, áney₁*. Obs. nu. (T2) entire coconut frond ("long frond"). *chamwen p.* part of c. f. from the stem to the first leaf. *makken wóón p.* carved writing (as initials or names) on a frond; printing form of writing (as distinct from cursive).

páápá Dis. of *pá*.

pááreyiraw F. of *paareniyaw*.

pááyiti See *pá, -iti*. vo. (T2) defecate upon.

pánnu nu. variety of banana.

pár (4) PÁRE₁. vi., adj. (be) surplus, extra, left out, left over; be a remainder, be a few more than (what is specified). *engéréwúpár* one thousand plus (be a few more than one thousand). *wúwa p. reemw* I was s. on account of you (you were chosen over me).

-páráák [In cpds. only.] unsp. (u.m.) See *téépáráák*. Cf. *para-₂*.

párápárángngaw (db; 3b) See *pár, ngngaw*. vi., va. be unmatched, be an odd number; match badly with. *maram meyi p. pwinin* the moon matches badly with its nights (i.e., with the days of the month).

párápárééch (db; 2) See *pár, ééch*. vi., va. be well or evenly matched, be an even number; match up well with.

páreseni See *pár, seni₂*. vo. (T2) be surplus in relation to, be left out of (as surplus or extra). *wúwa p. ewe angaang reen átewe* I was left out of that job because of that fellow (who filled it).

Párem nu. (loc.) Param Island.

pári- (4) See *pár*. ni. (T2) remainder, leftover, surplus. [Now obs. in arithmetic.] *párin* its r. *fituuw párin?* what is its r.? (when a small number is anticipated); *ruwuuw párin* its r. is two.

páchcha (1) See *pá, chcha*. vi. have dysentery.

páták Var. of *peták*.

páy N. of *pay*.

páyepáy N. of *payepay*.

páyeyiti N. of *payeyiti*.

pe (1) PEE. vi. lose consciousness, die, be extinguished, stop running (of machine or clock); lose (in war or game), have a hard time; be dead, exhausted. *ómwo kaa pe!* would you were dead! (a curse); *siyaa pe!* we've had it! With dir. suf.: *peenó* die, lose one's life. Syn. *má*. Ant. *manaw*.

peek₁ (2) PEEKI₁. nu. (T2) belt (men's or women's) made of red shell beads (*féwúpar*). [Worn in dancing. According to LeBar, worn only by men.] *eché p.* one b. *énúkin p.* his b.; *peekin* b. of (a given type).

peek₂ (2) PEEKI₂. n. (loc.; T2), suf. (cc.) side, page (of book). Dis. *peppeeki-* (ds). *epeek, rúwépeek, wúnúpeek, fépeek, nimepeek, wonopeek, fúúpeek, wanúpeek, ttiwepeek, engoon peekin* one,...ten s. *p. een, p. naan* that or the other s., the opposite s.; *p. eey* this s. (near speaker); *peekena, p. na* that s. (that is the topic of reference); *p. ewe* that (invisible) s.; *p. oomw* that s. (near addressee). *peekin asan* upper or eastern s. (of Truk or neighboring atolls); *peekin efeng* north s.; *peekin éér* south s.; *peekin éétiw* east s.; *peekin faan* lower or western s. (of Truk or neighboring atolls); *peekin notow* west s. With dir. suf.: *peekinong, peekinó, peppeekinó, peekitá, peekitiw, peekito, peppeekito, peekiwow, peekiwu. e nómw peppeekinóón (peppeekitoon) naan waa* it is on the far side (near side) of that canoe.

peekeen See *peek₂, een₃*. nu. a rank or school of *itang* ("opposite side").

peekinong See *peek₂*.

peekinó See *peek₂*.

peekitá See *peek₂*.

peekitiw See *peek₂*.

peekito See *peek₂*.

peekiwow See *peek₂*.

peekiwu See *peek₂*.

peekkus (2) See *pe, -kkus*. Var. *pekkus*. vi., adj. (be) exhausted, weary, physically very tired (from heavy work). Syn. *mááppúng*.

peen₁ (3) See *pa-₁, ina-₂.* n. (T3) ventral fin (of fish). *peenan* its v. f. *peenen iik* fish's v. f. Cf. *paaw₁, ini-₃.*

peen₂ (2) PENNI. (Eng.) nu. (T2) pen, fountain pen. *efóch p.* one p. *pennin p.* of (a given type).

peen₃ (Eng.) nu. bell. *eew p.* one b.

-peen [In cpds. only.] unsp. (u.m.) See *setipeen.*

peenit (2) PEENITI. (Eng.) nu. belt. *efóch p.* one b. *aan p.* his b. *peenitin waas* wrist-watch band.

peenó See *pe.*

peet (2) PETTI. (Eng.) nu. (T2) bed. *eew p.* one b. *aan p.* his b. *pettin* b. of (a given type).

peey (3) PEYIYA. n. (T3) placenta, afterbirth. *peyiyan* her p.

peeya (1) PEEYAA. (Eng.) nu. (T1) pair. *eew p.* one p. *eew peeyaan suus, eew peeya suus* one p. of shoes. *eew peeyaan kiwiin, eew peeya kiwiin* one p. of queens (in poker).

pese- (3) PESA. [In cpds. only.] unsp. urge, oblige. See *peseey, pesepes.*

peseey See *pese-, -e-₂.* vo. (T6b) urge, exhort, oblige, force. Dis. *peppeseey* (ds).

pesepes (db; 3) See *pese-.* vi. be urged, exhorted, obliged, forced. *meyi p. me reen átánaan* it is u. by that fellow.

pekkiiy See *ppek, -i-₂.* vo. (T5) shoot with a gun or pistol.

pekkus Var. of *peekkus.*

pen See *pa-₁.*

pene (1) PENEE. nu. (T1) crowd, bunch, flock, throng, herd, school. *peneen aramas* c. of people; *peneen iik* school of fish; *peneen iit* bunch of names; *peneen machchang* flock of birds. Syn. *pwii-₁.*

peney (2) PENEYI. (Eng.) nu. (T2) playing cards. *eché p.* a card. *néwún p.* his c. *peney Seniwis* poker; (card game); *peney sooná* cheating at cards. See *kaas.* vi. play cards; gamble at cards. *peneyin mwooni* (n. phr.) gambling at cards for money, (v. phr.) gamble at cards for money.

peneyaw (3b) See *pan, aaw₁.* nu. (T3) <Elbert> a kind of bass. *peneyawen* b. of (a given region).

peneyich (Eng.) nu. dinner plate. *eew p.* one p. *sepiyan p.* his p.

peneyittu (1) See *peney, tuu-₁.* nu. (T1) gambling game with cards. [The deck is cut into a number of piles equalling the number of players. The cards remain face down and the players bet on the piles blind. Piles are then turned up and high card wins.]

peni- (2) PENI. [In cpds. only.] unsp. sea cucumber.

penik (3) See *peni-, -k₂.* nu. (T3) species of sea cucumber. [Edible, found in sand, burrows under sand in daytime and comes to the surface of sand under water at night, exudes whitish threads called *appach*.] *emwú p.* one s. c. *peniken* s. c. of (a given region).

peniké (1) See *peni-, ké.* nu. (T1) <Elbert> a species of sea cucumber (edible, like *penik* but smaller). *emwú p.* one s. c. *penikéén* s. c. of (a given region).

penimaaw (3) See *pa-₁, maaw.* nu. (T3) breadfruit that has grown larger than the *sawit* stage, but the stem has not yet become red.

penipen (db; 2) See *peni-.* nu. (T2) <Elbert> a species of sea cucumber, trepang (rough surface, black, edible). [According to Elbert, eaten by Japanese but not by people of Truk.]

penichón (4) See *peni-, chón.* nu. (T2) <Elbert> a species of black sea cucumber (edible, three inches to one foot in length). *emwú p.* one s. c. *penichónun* s. c. of (a given region).

peniwa (1) See *pa-₁, waa₁.* nu. (T1) a species of fish.

peniya- (3) See *pa-₁, -ni-, -ya-.* ni. (T3) side; helper, assistant. *peniyan* his helper. With dir. suf.: *peniyetiw* lower or western s.; *peniyetá* upper or eastern s.

peniyefeefin (3) See *peniya-, feefin.* nu. (T3) left side. Syn. *peniyemééng.* Ant. *peniyefich, peniyemwáán.*

peniyefich (2) See *peniya-, -fich.* nu. (T2) right side. Syn. *peniyemwáán.* Ant. *peniyefeefin, peniyemééng.*

peniyesis See *peniya-, -sis.* [Kraemer] nu. upper or eastern side on Siis (Tsis) Island (by contrast with *peniyetiw*, lower or western side).

peniyemééng See *peniya-, -mééng.* nu. left side. Syn. *peniyefeefin.* Ant. *peniyefich, peniyemwáán.*

peniyemwáán (2) See *peniya-, mwáán₁.* nu. (T2) right side. Syn. *peniyefich.* Ant. *peniyefeefin, peniyemééng.*

Peniyóór See *peniya-*, *óór*. nu. (loc.) a clan name.

penges (2) PENGESI. vi., adj. (be) athwart, perpendicular, across. *meyi p. seni kkeey fénú* it is perpendicular to these islands. nu. (T2) a cross.

pengkiyo (1) PENGKIYOO. (Jap. *begkyoo*) vi. study. [Used mainly by people who grew up under Japanese rule.] Syn. *kkayé*, *kkayit*.

pengkiyooni See *pengkiyo*, *-ni-*. vo. (T4) study. *ke pwe p. ewe nesenin aretimetik* you should s. the lesson in arithmetic.

pengngaw (3) See *pe*, *ngngaw*. vi. be lovesick. Cf. *máppúng*, *pekkus*.

peppeekinó See *peek₂*.

peppeekito See *peek₂*.

peppeseey Dis. of *peseey*.

peppesse- (ds; 3a) PESSE. [With dir. suf. only.] Var. *sesseppi-*. vi. in the opening formula for a story: *peppessenó*, *peppesseto*... going forth and coming hither... (i.e., once upon a time...).

peppessenó See *peppesse-*.

peppesseto See *peppesse-*.

peppek Dis. of *ppek*.

peppeni Dis. of *ppeni*.

peppep Dis. of *ppep*.

peppeyinit Dis. of *peyinit*.

perees₁ (Eng. *press*) nu. print. *makken p.* printed writing, printing style of writing.

perees₂ (2) PERESSI. [A back formation from *peressin*.] nu. (T2) a variety of banana. Syn. *wuchun Merika*.

Peressin₁ nu. (loc.) Brazil.

peressin₂ See *Peressin₁*. Var. *perees*. nu. a variety of banana. Syn. *wuchun Merika*.

pereyiniin (2) See *para-₂*, *iniin₂*. vi. be square or rectangular in shape. Cf. *pereyingiing*.

pereyingiing (db) See *para-₂*, *ingi-*. F. vi. be on one's side; lean or tip sideways, list; sidle, slip between things by turning one's body sideways. Syn. *tiwiiniin*. Cf. *pereyiniin*.

peri- (2) PERI₁. [In cpds. only.] unsp. shaped, dressed (of wood). See *chiyaaperiper*, *periiy*, *periper*.

periiy See *peri-*, *-i-₂*. vo. (T5) shape, dress (wood only). With n. form. suf. *-ya-*: *periiya-* (ni.; T3) shaping done or to be done by someone. *periiyen iyé?* shaping done by whom?

periiya- See *periiy*.

perikang (3) PERIKANGA. (Jap. *barikan*, from the name of the French manufacturer Bariquand) nu. (T3) hair clipper. *eew p.* one h. c. *néwún p.* his h. c.

perikangeey See *perikang*, *-e-₂*. vo. (T6b) clip with a hair clipper.

periper (db; 2) See *peri-*. vi., va. be shaped, dressed (of wood only); shape or dress wood.

pech (3) PECHA. Tb1. vi. become erect (penis). ni. (T3) erection (of penis). *pechan* his e.

peche (1) PECHEE. n. (T1), suf. (cc.) leg and foot, lower limb (of human, birds); hind leg (of animals). [The preferred word in mixed company.] *epeche*, *rúwépeche*, *wúnúpeche*, *fépeche*, *nimepeche*, *wonopeche*, *fúúpeche*, *wanúpeche*, *ttiwepeche* one,...nine l.; *fitepeche* how many l.; *efóch pecheen aramas* or *epeche pecheen aramas* one human l. *pecheen* his l. *neewoon p.* upper thigh, lap. *pecheen attu* a plant (*Devallia solida* "cat's foot;" its roots are used as medicine against spirits of the hills and mountains); *pecheen epeep* booms supporting the lee platform of a sailing canoe. Syn. *taang*. Ant. *paaw₁*. vi. in *p. sesset* be an immigrant ("have briny legs"), be a returned prisoner-of-war.

pecheemá (1) See *peche*, *má*. vi. (be) paralyzed in the leg or foot; have a withered leg (as from infantile paralysis).

pecheemmach Var. of *pechemmach*.

pecheepwo (1) See *peche*, *pwo*. nu. (T1) elephantiasis of the leg, swollen leg. Cf. *pechemmach*.

pechemmach (3) See *peche*, *mmach*. nu. (T3) boil on or infected swelling of the leg. Cf. *pecheepwo*.

petá (1) See *pa-₁*, *-tá*. n. (loc.; T1) upper or eastern side; (with pos. suf.) upper side of, above, east of. *petáán* on his upper s., above him. *petáán Romónum* upper or eastern s. of Romónum Island. Cf. *peekitá*.

peták (Pon.) Var. *páták*. nu. in *sowun p.* pastor, religious teacher (in the Protestant Church).

pete- (3: *pete-*, *pété-*) PETA. pref. covered with, generally characterized by (?). See *pétépwpwún*, *pétéwén*. Cf. *fete-*.

petepeet Dis. of *ppet₂*.
petewen Var. of *pétéwén*.
peyinit (2) PEYINITI. (Eng.) nu. (T2) paint. vi. paint; be painted. Dis. *peppeyinit* (ds).
peyinitiiy See *peyinit, -i-₂*. vo. (T5) paint.
peyiya- (3) PEYIYA. [In cpds. only.] unsp. grave, tomb; bury. See *peyiyemá*.
peyiyas (3) See *peyiya-, -s₁*. Var. *peyiyás*. nu. (T3) grave. *neeniyen p.* cemetery, place of graves; *féwún p.* gravestone. vi., va. be buried; bury.
peyiyaseni See *peyiyas, -ni-*. vo. (T6a) bury (a corpse).
peyiyás (nu.; T2) Wn. of *peyiyas*.
peyiyásini Wn. of *peyiyaseni*.
peyiyemá (1) See *peyiya-, má*. vi. (of a woman) be one whose husbands die not long after they marry her.
peyiyóóf (Eng.) vi. pay wages, get paid. *ráánin p.* payday. vi. get paid, receive pay.
peyiyór (2) See *paaw₁, óór*. nu. (T2) wound up ball of *núún* cord. *peyiyórun núún* sennit ball. vi. winding sennit on fingers preparatory to making lashings.
pé₁ (1) PÉÉ₁. vi. be parried or warded off with the open hand. *aa pé wókun* his club was p. Cf. *pééni₁*.
pé₂ (1) PÉÉ₂. vi. blow (as wind). Dis. *péépé* (db). *aa pé ásápwán* the wind blew; *e péépé ásápwán* the wind is blowing. With dir. suf.: *aa péétiw seni éétiw* it blows west (down) from the east; *aa péétá seni notow* it blows north (out) from the south; *aa péénong seni ennefen* it blows south (in) from the north. Cf. *pééni₂*.
pé₃ (1) PÉÉ₃. vi., adj. (be) empty, be emptied. *ese toongeni pé reey pwú meyi pinemmóng* it cannot be emptied by me because it is of large capacity.
péé-₁ (1) See *pé₃*. ni. (T1), suf. (cc.) empty container; shell. *epé, rúwapé, wúnúpé, fapé, nimapé, wonapé, fúúpé, wanúpé, ttiwapé, engoon péén* one,...ten e. c.; *fitapé* how many e. c. *péén* his e. c. *péén káás* empty gas container; *péén núú* empty drinking coconut; *péén tinepwu* empty half coconut shell; *péén tirongkang* empty oil drum. *péén amwe* tridachna shell. *péén wuuch, péén wuchchen waa* longitudinal groove along the keel on the bottom of a paddle canoe (syn. *fáát*).
péé-₂ (1) PÉÉ₄. ni. (T1) flower, blossom. *péén* its f.
péésapa See *pé₁, sap₂*. N. Var. *péésapeey*. vo. (T3) slap the face with one's open hand. Dis. *péésapasapa* (db).
péésapasapa Dis. of *péésapa*.
péésapasapeey Dis. of *péésapeey*.
péésapeey See *pé₁, sap₂, -e-₂*. F. Var. *péésapa*. vo. (T6b) slap the face with one's open hand. Dis. *péésapasapeey* (db).
péék (2) PÉKÚ₁. n. (T2), suf. (cc.) chip, chipped off piece. *epék, rúwépék, wúnúpék, nimapék, wonapék, fúúpék, wanúpék, ttiwapék, engoon pékún* one,...ten chips. *pékún* its chip. *pékún suupwa* cigarette butt.
péémwi (1) See *pé₂, mwi*. nu. (T1) form of magic that makes others unable to function in sport or war.
pééni₁ See *pé₁, -ni-*. vo. (T4) parry with the open hand. *wúpwe p. wókun* I will parry his club.
pééni₂ See *pé₂, -ni-*. vo. (T4) blow (something or someone). With dir. suf.: *péénáátiw* blow (it) down.
péénong See *pé₂*.
pééngas (3b) See *péé-₂, ngas*. nu. (T3) a tree (*Fagraea galilai*). [Its flowers are used for garlands.]
pééngút (2) nu. (T2) file fish. *pééngútún* f. f. of (a given region).
péépé₁ Dis. of *pé₂*.
péépé₂ (db; 1) See *péé-₂*. vi. (dis.) be in flower, be in bloom.
péér (3) See *péé-₁, -r₂*. n. (T3) 1. empty whole coconut shell (with meat removed); coconut-shell water bottle or flask; bottle. *eew p.* one c. s. or b. *aan p.* his c. s. of b.; *pééran* its (the coconut's) shell. *pééren néé* perfume b.; *pééren taka* shell of the ripe coconut; *pééren mékúr* skull. 2. concave cap (as of a bottle or knee). *pééran* its c. *pééren pwasuk* knee cap. nu. (T3) type of turmeric cosmetic prepared in a mold made of two coconut half-shells bound together. Cf. *sópwósópw₂*.
péérechón (4) See *péér, chón*. nu. (T2) coconut shell flask.
péérún fáánú n. phr. oblong pendant made of coconut shell. Cf. *péér*.

péechóón (4) See *péé-₁*. nu. (T2) ornate sea snail (*Nerita ornata* Sby.).

péétá See *pé₂*.

péétiw See *pé₂*.

péewu See *pé₂*.

pééyiin (2) See *péé-₁, ini-₂*. nu. (T2) 1. husk and shell of a ripe coconut or copra nut ("sprout container"). *pééyiinin taka* copra nut's husk and shell. 2. dysentery; medicine for dysentery (*sáfeen pééyiin*). [The illness is caused by sorcery perpetrated over the victim's personal husk-soaking pit (*niipw*) on an island's fringing reef or in a mangrove swamp.]

pék (2) See *péék*. vi., adj. (be) chopped, hewn (as with axe or bush knife). Dis. *pékúpék* (db).

pékúúw See *pék, -ú-*. vo. (T5) chop, cut (as with axe or bushknife). Dis. *péppékúúw* (ds). With dir. suf.: *pékúúwoto* c. it hither; *pékúúwetiw* c. it down.

pékúúwetiw See *pékúúw*.

pékúúwoto See *pékúúw*.

pékúnúfan (3) See *péék, fanafan₁*. nu. (T3) the larger piece of wood remaining after something has been chopped from it.

pékúpék (db; 2) See *pék*. va. (dis.) chop (as with axe or bush knife). With dir. suf.: *pékúpékúto* c. and bring hither.

pékúpékéech (ds; 2) See *ppék, ééch*. vi. be even, well matched, uniform, exactly alike.

pékúpékúngngaw (ds; 3b) See *ppék, ngngaw*. vi. be uneven, not uniform, unalike, badly matched.

pékúpékúto See *pékúpék*.

pékútoneey See *pék, toon₁, -e-₂*. vo. (T6b) chop, lop, or cut the top or growing end off (a tree). Cf. *fichitoneey, wuwapwpweey*.

péné (1) PÉNÉÉ. nu. (T1) 1. a tree (*Thespasia populnea*). [It is used in preparing medicine against illness caused by sea spirits; its wood is used to make paddles.] 2. variety of breadfruit.

pének (2) PÉNÉKÚ. vi., adj. (be) muddy, riled (of water).

pénú (3a) PÉNÚWA. nu. (T3) navigator; expert in navigation, seamanship and related arts; navigational arts. *riiriin p.* braided coconut-leaf bracelet and anklet that is a symbol of the navigator's office and worn by him as such.

pénúwéngngaw (3b) See *pénú, ngngaw*. nu. (T3) a poor navigator. vi. navigate badly.

pénúwéyéech (2) See *pénú, ééch*. nu. (T2) a good navigator. vi. navigate well.

péppé Dis. of *ppé*.

péppékúúw Dis. of *pékúúw*.

péré (1) PÉRÉÉ. n. (T1) size. *pééréén* its s.

pérééκúkkún (2) See *péré, kúkkún*. nu. (T2) small size. Syn. *pérééngin, pérékkiis*.

péréémwuk (3a) See *péré, mwuk*. nu. (T3) a dwarf. vi. be dwarfed.

pérééníkkúng (2) See *péré, nikkúng*. nu. (T2) large size. Syn. *pérééwátte, pérémmóng*.

pérééngin (2) See *péré, ngin*. nu. (T2) small size. Syn. *pérééκúkkún, pérékkiis*.

pérééwátte (1) See *péré, wátte*. nu. (T1) large size. Syn. *pérééníkkúng, pérémmóng*.

pérékkiis (2) See *péré, -kkiis*. nu. (T2) small size. Syn. *pérééκúkkún, pérééngin*.

pérémmóng (4) See *péré, mmóng*. nu. (T2) large size. Syn. *pérééníkkúng, pérééwátte*.

péchékkún (3) PÉCHÉKKÚNA. n. (T3) strength; power, force. *péchékkúnan* his s. vi., adj. (be) strong, hard, tough; be well, in good health; prevail or win in a contest or fight; persevere, win through. *fóós p.* hard language, rough language, talk that does not mince words. *p. ngeni* ride herd on, keep after, be forceful towards. Ant. *apwangapwang, kkuf*. Cf. *kún₂*.

pété- See *pete-*.

pétépwúnúpwún Dis. of *pétépwpwún*.

pétépwpwún (2) See *pete-, pwpwún*. Var. *fetepwpwún, fétépwpwún*. vi., adj. (be) soiled, dirty. Dis. *pétépwúnúpwún* (db).

pétéwén (2) See *pete-, wénú-*. Var. *petewen*. nu. (T2) plant (general term), vegetation (uncultivated); tree, bush, shrub, fern, grass. *efóch p.* one p. *pétéwénún mwéngé* food p. *neeyin p.* in the bush; *óóch sóókkun p.* a kind of p. Syn. *rooro*. Cf. *wénúwén*.

pétú (1) PÉTÚÚ. nu. (T1) big-eyed or goggle-eyed scad fish (*Trachurops crumenopthalmus*).

-péw (2) See *paaw*₁. suf. (cc.) wing; forelimb; arm's length (unit of distance from fingertips to shoulder); thing worn over the hand or arm (e.g., glove). *epéw, rúwépéw, wúnúpéw, fépéw, nimepéw, wonopéw, fúúpéw, wanúpéw, ttiwepéw, engoon* or *engoon péwún* one,...ten w. (etc.). *epéw kuroop* one baseball glove; *rúwépéw péwún machchang* two bird wings.

péwúfeefin (3) See *paaw*₁, *feefin*. nu. (T3) left hand and arm. Cf. *péwún feefin*.

péwúkéré (1) See *paaw*₁, *éréé*-. N. Var. *féwúkéré*. n. (T1) shoulder socket. *péwúkéréén* his s. s. *núkún p.* shoulderblade.

péwúmmach (3) See *paaw*₁, *mmach*. vi. have a boil on the arm; have a swelling on the arm.

péwúmwáán (2) See *paaw*₁, *mwáán*₁. nu. (T2) right hand and arm.

péwúpék (2) See *paaw*₁, *pék*. vi. be with amputated arm.

péwúpwo (1) See *paaw*₁, *pwo*. vi. be swollen armed. nu. (T1) elephantiasis of the arm.

péwúpwór (3b) See *paaw*₁, *pwór*. nu. (T3) a hold in hand-to-hand fighting. [The opponent's hand is twisted and thrust back against his chest.]

péwút (2) See *paaw*₁, *-ti-*. [A back formation from *péwuti*.] vi. be abandoned, forsaken; lost; left. *p. seni* be lost from. With dir. suf.: *péwútúnong* left inside; *péwútúnó* put away, divorced (of spouse), let go, thrown away, abandoned; *péwútútá* left up; *péwútútiw* put down, left down, fallen down; *péwútúto* left here; *péwútúwow* left there near you; *péwútúwu* left or put outside. Cf. *ppéwút*.

péwútaanong See *péwúti*.
péwútaato See *péwúti*.
péwútaawow See *péwúti*.
péwútaawu See *péwúti*.

péwútaw (3) See *paaw*₂, *taaw*. nu. (T3) a gift of fish received by a person on the beach when a fishing boat comes in. *péwútawan* his g. of f. *chóón p.* a person waiting on the beach when a fishing boat comes in. vi. give fish to someone waiting on the beach.

péwútaweey See *péwútaw, -e-*₂. vo. (T6b) give a gift of fish to a person on the beach when a fishing boat comes in.

péwútáátá See *péwúti*.
péwútáátiw See *péwúti*.

péwúte (1) See *paaw*₁, *tee-*₂. nu. (T1) fruit bat. *emén p.* one f. b. *péwúteen* f. b. of (a given region).

péwúti See *paaw*₁, *-ti-*. [With dir. suf. only.] vo. (T5) leave, abandon. With dir. suf.: *péwútaanong* leave (it) inside; *péwútaato* bring and leave (it) here; *péwútaawow* leave (it) there (where you are); *péwútaawu* leave (it) outside; *péwútáátá* leave (it) up (on something); *péwútáátiw* leave (it) down, put it down; *péwútóónó* discard, divorce (a spouse), leave, abandon, forsake, desert, have no further use for. *kete péwútikeeminó* do not desert us. Cf. *péwút, ppéwút*.

péwútóónó See *péwúti*.

péwútúmwáánninó (1) See *péwút, mwmwáán, -nó*. vi. (dir.) be discarded or let go without need, wrongly or mistakenly let go of, wrongly forsaken.

péwútúnong See *péwút*.
péwútúnó See *péwút*.
péwútútá See *péwút*.
péwútútiw See *péwút*.
péwútúto See *péwút*.
péwútúwow See *péwút*.
péwútúwu See *péwút*.

pi- (2) PI. pref. (?) held in the hand (?); material goods (?); frame of mind (?). See *epinúkééch, epinúkúngngaw, epinúkúnúk, piit*₂, *piniyech, pino, pinúk* or *ppúnúk, pinúkúúw, piraapa, piraapaani, piireyir, pisek*.

pi (1) PII₁. Var. *ppi*. vi. float, rise. With dir. suf.: *piinó* float away or off (*aa piinó mman* dawn has floated off); *piitá* float up, well up (*aa piitá aach soong seni neenuukach* our anger wells up from our bellies). Cf. *pas*.

pii- (1) PII₂. [In cpds. only.] unsp. appear; appearance. See *epiipiiy, epiipaw, eppiiy, fénúwepi, imwepi, Nowuwopi, ppiifeyin, ppiiy*.

pii₁ (1) PII₃. nu. (T1) trash, rubbish, garbage. Dis. *piipi* (db). *neeniyen p.* garbage or trash container, trash can, garbage can, wastebasket. *piin fanafan* wood chip (from adzing); *piin mwéngé* garbage. *piipiin ngerenger* sawdust.

pii₂ (1) PII₅. nu. (T1) name of the consonant (bilabial stop) written *p*; name of the letter thus written.

piis₁ (4) PISE. nu. (T2) sandy islet (in place names and compounds). [Place names include *Piis₂, Piseech, Pisemeew, Pisarach, Pisin Ménúkómó, Pisar, Pisiniyap, Pisinúún.*] *pisin énú* (according to Bollig) regions of heaven where the gods live. Syn. *piye-*. Cf. *Piik₁, ppi₃*.

Piis₂ (3) PIISA. [Derived from *piis₁*.] nu. (loc.; T3) Pis Island (both in Truk and Losap Atoll). *Piisen Wééné (Chuuk)* P. of Moen Island (Truk); *Piisen Noosópw* P. of Losap Atoll. Cf. *Panúwu, Piik₁*.

Piik₁ (Plt.) [Equivalent of *Piis*, originally meaning "sand island."] nu. (loc.) 1. a clan name. 2. Pikelot Island. [The name from which Pikelot derives properly applies to a former islet in West Fayu that was destroyed by a typhoon.] Cf. *Pikenooch*.

piik₂ (3) PIKKA. (Eng.) nu. (T3) pig. *emén p.* one p. *néwún p.* his p. *pikken nóómw* an old p.

piin₁ (2) PINI₁. nu. (T2) prohibition, restriction on behavior, tabu; commandment. *pinin énúún nóómw* p. relating to the old gods; *pinin feefin* p. relating to women; *pinin Koot* commandment of God; *pinin mwáán* p. relating to men; *pinin mwúún* p. associated with the government; *pinin peyiyas* p. relating to graves; *pinin roong* p. associated with specialized knowledge; *pinin róóng* p. associated with no-trepassing signs; *pinin sáfey* p. relating to medicine.

piin₂ (1) PII₄. [Always, as shown, with rel. suf. -n₂.] vr. be experienced in; formerly, before, in the past. *wúwa p. fééri* I am experienced in doing it; I have done it before. *wúwa p. nónnómw ikeey* I formerly lived here; *wúwa p. wurónuk kesapw wún sakaw* I have told you before not to drink liquor.

piin₃ (3) PINNA₁. (Eng.) nu. (T3) pin. *efóch p.* one p. *pinnen wuuf* safety pin (pin for clothing).

piin₄ (3) PINNA₂. (Eng.) nu. (T3) pencil. *efóch p.* one p. *pinnen p.* of (a given make).

piin₅ (3) PINA₁. nu. (T3) appearance, shape; likeness; size (of men and animals). *pinen núú* size of coconut; *pinen áán iyé eey núú?* whose coconuts does this one resemble in size? *kepwe waato eew pinen ewe núú si wúnúmi nánew* bring a coconut like the one we drank yesterday.

piinaakkich See *ruupw*.

piingk (Eng.) adj. pink.

piingko (1) PIINGKOO. (Eng.) Var. *pingko*. nu. (T1) game of bingo. vi. play bingo.

piipi Dis. of *pii₁*.

piir (2) PIRI. n. (T2) hard lump or growth under the skin. *pirin* his l. *pirin taka* spore of the ripe coconut when beginning to form. Cf. *faréseyin*.

piireyir (db; 3) See *pi-, ir₁*. vi. be anxious, apprehensive, uncertain of the outcome of something about which we have concern.

piiché (1) See *pii₁, chéé.* nu. (T1) leaf trash.

piichcha (1) PIICHCHAA. (Jap. *pichchaa*) nu. (T1) pitcher (in baseball). *emén p.* one p. *néwún p.* his p.; *piichchaan* p. of (a given team).

piit₁ (3) PITTA. (Eng.) vi. beat time, lead a song.

piit₂ (3) See *pi-, it.* vi. be disenchanted, loose one's ardor or interest; be persuaded away from something. Dis. *piiteyit* (db). *wúwa p. reen sukuun* I have lost interest in school. *aa piiteyit ekiyekin ewe feefin neenuuken ewe mwáán* thinking about the woman has lost its ardor in the man's heart.

piitá See *pi*.

piiteyit Dis. of *piit₂*.

Pisarach See *piis₁*. nu. (loc.) Pisaras Island (Namonuito Atoll). [Known locally as *Pihara ŕ*.]

piseey See *piis₁, -e-₂*. vo. (T6b) grow, raise (of garden produce). With n. form. suf.: *piseeya-* (ni.; T3) thing grown or to be grown (by someone), vegetable produce (of someone).

pisek (2) See *pi-, -sek.* n. (T2) movable goods; belongings; parts; supplies; gear, equipment. *pisekin* his m. g. *pisekin angaang* tools; *pisekin iimw* furniture of house; *pisekin inis* body parts; *pisekin mwesiin* engine parts.

pisekisek (db; 2) See *pisek*. vi. (dis.) be rich, wealthy (in material goods). Cf. *wéw*.

pisekini See *pisek, -ni-*. vo. (T5) acquire (movable goods). Cf. *pippisek*.

Pisemeew (2) See *piis*₁, *-meew*. nu. (loc.; T2) Pisemew Islet ("lonely sand").
pisi-₁ (2) PISI₁. [In cpds. only.] unsp. clap, slap (with the hands). See *episipis*₁, *pisipis, pisiri, ppis*.
pisi-₂ (2) PISI₂. unsp. sibilant or spitting sound. See *episipis*₂, *pissúk*.
pisikit (2) PISIKITI. (Eng.) nu. (T2) biscuit, cracker. *eché p.* one b. *pisikitin* b. of (a given kind).
pisimóng (4) See *pisi-*₁, *móóng*. vi. slap or tap the back of the head (a traditional nervous gesture, no longer in fashion).
pisipis (db; 2) See *pisi-*₁. va. (dis.) clap (hands). nu. (dis.; T2) clapping. *pisipisin péwúch* the c. of our hands.
pisiri See *pisi-*₁, *-ri-*. vo. (T5) slap with the hand. Cf. *ppis*.
pissúk (2) See *pisi-*₂, *ssúk*₂. [From *pisissúk.] vi. squirt (as water from mouth or waterpistol).
pissúkiiti See *pissúk*, *-iti*. vo. (T2) squirt upon. *kkónik aa p. átánaan* the water squirted upon him. Cf. *epissúk ngeni*.
pistoor (2) PISTOOR. (Jap. *pisutoru*) nu. (T2) pistol. *eew p.* one p. *néwún p.* his p. *pistoorun Sapaan* Japanese p. Cf. *nikésúk*₂.
Pikené nu. (loc.) West Fayu Island and Atoll (Central Caroline Islands). Cf. *Féyiyeew*.
Pikenooch nu. (loc.) a former islet in West Fayu (Central Caroline Islands) that was destroyed by a typhoon and whose name was misapplied to what is shown as Pikelot Island on maps. Cf. *Piik*₁.
pikisé (1) PIKISÉÉ. (Eng.) n. (T1) photograph, snapshot, picture. *pikiséén* his picture, photograph of him. *fichiiy pikiséémw* take your picture. Cf. *sasing*.
Pikiram Obs. nu. (loc.) Pingelap Island and Atoll (Eastern Caroline Islands). Syn. *Púngúnap*.
pimpong (Jap. *pímpon*) nu. pingpong ball. *eféw p.* one p. b. *néwún p.* his p. b. vi. play pingpong.
pin (2) See *piin*₁. vi., adj. (be) forbidden, prohibited, tabu, restricted as to what can be done; sacred, sanctified. *kiich si p. me wóón átewe* we are tabu from being above him, we are subject to his authority.

-pin (3a) PINA₂. [In cpds. only.] adj. plugged (of a hole). See *pineey, pinenó, pinepin*.
pinakpwoot (Eng.) nu. blackboard. *eew p.* one b.
pinangkeet Var. of *panangkeet*.
pinayin (2) PINAYINI. (Eng.) nu. (T2) plane (tool). *eew p.* one p. *néwún p.* his p. *pinayinin* p. of (a given type).
pinayini See *pinayin*. vo. (T2) plane.
pineey See *-pin*, *-e-*₂. vo. (T6b) plug up (of a hole); contradict (talk).
pinekúkkún (2) See *piin*₅, *kúkkún*. Tb3. vi. be of small size. Syn. *pinengin*.
pinemmóng (2) See *piin*₅, *mmóng*. vi. be of large size. Syn. *pinewátte*.
pinenó (1) See *-pin*, *-nó*. vi. be stopped up, corked, blocked.
pinengin (2) See *piin*₅, *ngin*. vi. be of small size. Syn. *pinekúkkún*.
pinengngaw (3b) See *piin*₅, *ngngaw*. vi. be of improper or inadequate size; of ugly shape.
pinepin (db; 3a) See *-pin*. vi. (dis.) be stopped up, corked, blocked. n. (T3) cork, stopper, plug; door. *pinepinan* its c. *pinepinen iimw* plank door of house that can be closed; *pinepinen péér* coconut-shell bottle stopper.
pinewa (1) PINEWAA. (Eng.) Var. *pinawa, piniwé*. nu. (T1) bread; flour. *p. amas* flour; *p. ipwét* bread; *p. ómwmwoot* bread.
pinewátte (1) See *piin*₅, *wátte*. Tb3. vi. be of large size. Syn. *pinemmóng*.
pini- (2) PINI₂. unsp. snarled, tangled.
piniiy See *pin*, *-i-*₂. vo. (T5) prohibit, forbid.
pinik₁ (3) PINIKA₁. nu. (T3) a small shellfish. *eféw p.* one s. *piniken* s. of (a given region).
pinik₂ (3) PINIKA₂. [In cpds. only; possibly related to *pinik*₁.] adj. scraping (?). [Cf. Pul. *penik* coconut-shell scraper.] See *niyawúpinik*.
pinini See *pin*, *-ni-*. vo. (T5) be under a tabu or restriction with regard to (something); be prohibited from.
Pininiyow nu. (loc.) Peleliu Island (Palau Islands).
piningeni See *pin, ngeni*. vo. (T2) worship. *siya p. Koot* we worshiped God.
pinip (2) PINIPI. nu. (T2) ground lily. *pinipin* g. l. of (a given region).

piniwé Wn. (Mwáán) of *pinewa*.
piniyech (2) PINIYECHI. nu. (T2) leaf bundle of food with the food having been cooked in the bundle on a fire. *piniyechin iik* l. b. of fish.
piniyechiiy See *piniyech*, -*i*-₂. vo. (T5) cook in a leaf bundle.
piniyon (Eng.) nu. billion. *eew p.* one b.
pino (1) PINOO. n. (T1), suf. (cc.) small package of breadfruit pudding. *epino, rúwépino, wúnúpino, fépino, nimepino, wonopino, fúúpino, wanúpino, ttiwepino, engoon pinoon* one,...ten p. of b. p.
pinó (1) See *pi-, nó*₂. n. (T1) age mate, contemporary, person with the same birthday as one's own; generation; persons on a canoe accompanying one's own canoe on a trip. *emón p.* one a. m.; *eew p.* one generation. *pinóón* his a. m.
pinu nu. a type of men's cape, poncho, or cloak. [Woven of banana and hibiscus fibers and decorated with red shell discs around the neck area, it could only be worn by men who had completed military training.]
pinúk (2) See *pi-, núkú*-₃. n. (T2), suf. (cc.) a tied bundle; ream of paper. *epinúk, rúwépinúk, wúnúpinúk, nimepinúk, wonopinúk, fúúpinúk, wanúpinúk, ttiwepinúk, engoon p.* one,...ten t. b. *pinúkún mwúúch* b. of firewood; *pinúkún toropwe* ream of paper. Cf. *ppúnúk.*
pinúkúúw See *pinúk, ú*-. vo. (T5) tie (something) in a bundle.
pinni See *pini-, -ni-.* N. [In cpds. only.] vo. (T2) twist (a limb or muscle, as with a cramp). See *áráápinni.* Cf. *fin*₁*, fittek, piti.*
pinnu (1) PINNUU. (Eng.) nu. pillow.
pinché Var. of *pincho*.
pincho (1) PINCHOO. (Jap. *benjo*) Var. *pinché.* vi. defecate. *imwen p.* outhouse. n. (T1) feces. *eew p.* one pile of f. *pinchoon* his f.
pinchúri (1) PINCHÚRII. (Jap. *bin, tsuri*) nu. (T1) a game. [Each contestant holds, in the manner of a fishing pole, a stick with a string attached. The end of the stick is attached to the middle of a nail. The contestant runs to a narrow-necked bottle, inserts the nail into it, and works it into a horizontal position so it lodges, enabling him to lift the bottle with his pole. In this manner he carries the bottle and runs a certain distance to the goal. He is not allowed to touch either the bottle or the string.]

pingngaw (3b) See *pii*₁*, ngngaw.* nu. (T3) unsightly trash, litter. vi. be littered; make a litter.
pippiiy Dis. of *ppiiy*.
pippisek (ds; 2) See *pisek.* va. (dis.) use (goods, gear, material things). Cf. *pisekini.*
pippin Dis. of *ppin*.
pippinó (ds; 1) See *pinó.* vi. (dis.) go in company (of canoes only); be born on the same day and hence to be of exactly the same age (of persons).
pippit Dis. of *ppit*.
piraas (3) PIRAASSA. (Eng.) nu. brass. *piraassen* b. of (a given region).
piraapa (1) PIRAAPAA. vi. be heaped, stacked.
piraapaani See *piraapa, -ni-.* vo. (T4) stack.
piraapaayéchchúúw See *piraapa, ééch, -ú-.* vo. (T5) stack well.
piresten Var. of *presiten*.
piriis (2) PIRIISI. (Eng.) nu. (T2) bridge. *piriisin ewe éwúwé* the stream's b.
piriik (Eng. *brig*) nu. jail.
piriyoch (3) PIRIYOCHCHA. (Eng.) nu. (T3) period (in punctuation). *piriyochchen mmak* p. of writing.
piroos (3) PIROSSA. (Eng.) nu. (T3) brush. *pirossen* b. of (a given make).
Pirostan (Eng.) Var. *Prostan.* nu. Protestant.
piru (1) PIRUU. nu. (T1) beach rock. *eféw p.* one b. r. *piruun Chuuk* Trukese b. r. Syn. *soosoomaay.*
piruumw (3) PIRUUMWA. (Eng.) nu. (T3) broom.
piruumweey See *piruumw, -e-*₂. vo. (T6b) sweep (with a broom).
pich₁ (2) PICHI₁. vi. form (of fruit), emerge, come out (of stars), come to view. Dis. *pichipich* (db). With dir. suf.: *pichinong, pichiwu.* nu. (T1) forming, emerging. *pichipichin sawit* forming of fruit in its early stage.
pich₂ (2) PICHI₂. vi., adj. (be) untied, unlashed, unfettered; forgiven, pardoned.
pichi- (2) PICHI₃. [In cpds. only.] unsp. vibrate, pulsate; flick, snap. See *pichipich, pichichopw, ppich.*

pichinong See *pich*₁.
pichipich₁ Dis. of *pich*₁.
pichipich₂ (db; 2) See *pichi*-. vi. (dis.) pulse, pulsate, vibrate (as a pulse, watch, violin string). n. (dis.; T2) pulse (of the body); vibration. *pichipichin* his p.
pichichopw (2) See *pichi*-, *chopw*. nu. (T2) bead string hanging from men's hairpin. *pichichopwun opos* hairpin's b. s.
pichiwu See *pich*₁.
piti- (2) PITI. nr. (T2) braiding, twisting (of a given locale, as with rope or leis). *pitin iya* b. of where? (Cf. *pitiyen iyé*).
piti See *piti*-. vo. (T2) braid, twist (hair, rope, leis). With n. form. suf.: *pitiya*- something braided or twisted (by someone); *piteyen iyé?* braided by whom? (cf. *pitin iya*). Cf. *oppit*.
pitik₁ nu. a bivalve, used for scraping wood surfaces.
pitik₂ (3) PITIKA. nu. (T3) matter discharged from the eyes (as with conjunctivitis or at waking in the morning). *pitiken mesey* m. of my eyes.
pitimékúr (3a) See *piti*-, *mékúr*. nu. (T3) hair braided on either side (formerly worn by both sexes). vi. wear the hair braided on either side.
pitimwár (4) See *piti*-, *mwáár*. vi. make a lei.
pitinnúk (2) See *piti*-, *nnúk*₂. vi. wear the hair bound on top of the head or in a knot on the front of the head, held by means of a braided head band (traditionally of men only). nu. (T2) men's braided headband. *aan p.* his h.
pitiya- See *piti*.
pitteey See *piit*₁, *-e-*₂. vo. (T6b) beat the time for.
Piyaanú See *piye*-, *énú*. nu. (loc.) Torres Islet.
piyano (1) PIYANOO. (Eng.) nu. (T1) piano.
piye- (3: -*pi*) PIYA. [In cpds. only, mostly place names.] unsp. sand. *Piyesich* ("Little Sand") name of localities on Wútéét (Udot) and Romónum Islands. See *piyepi, ppi*. Cf. *piis*₁.
piyepi (db; 3) See *piye*-. nu. (T3) low-lying sandy island, flatland (as on an atoll islet or the coastal flats on high islands); beach. *wóón p.* (on) the sandy flat, the sandy flat area before reaching mountain slopes. vi. form a sandy islet or beach.
Piyeyireng (3) See *piye*-, *reng*. [Bollig] nu. (loc.) a place in heaven ("Saffron Sand").
piyé (1) PIYÉÉ. (Eng.) nu. (T1) beer. *imweniwún p.* beer hall, bar.
Piyéénú (1) See *piye*-, *énú*. [Bollig] [Cf. the more usual form in place names *Piyaanú*.] nu. (loc.; T1) a place in heaven ("Spirit Sand").
piyowing Var. of *piyoying*.
piyoying (2) PIYOYINGI. (Jap. *byooin*) Var. *piyowing*. nu. (T2) hospital. *eew p.* one h. *aan p.* his h.
poot (3) POOTA. nu. (T3) sweetfish (both in fresh and salt water). *emén p.* one s. *pooten* s. of (a given region).
pos (2) POSU. vi. land, hit bottom (in a descent). *raa túútiw p. wóón ewe piru* they dived down and land on the beachrock. With dir. suf.: *posutiw.*
-pos suf. (u.m.) See *mwiyepos*.
posu- (2) POSU. [In cpds. only.] unsp. stab, spear. See *posuuw, ppos*.
posuuw See *posu*-, *-u*-. vo. (T5) stab, spear. Syn. *opposu*. Cf. *ppos*.
posto (1) POSTOO. (Jap. *posuto*) Var. *pwoosto*. nu. (T1) post office. *eew p.* one p. *aan p.* his p.
ponnóón (2) PONNÓÓNU. [Formed from an old *poni-nóó-n "night removed" with ptv. const.] nu. (temp.; T2) (day) before yesterday or after tomorrow; some day soon. *ponnóónuwe* day before yesterday; *ponnóónun nánew* day before yesterday; *ponnóónun neesor* day after tomorrow; *ponnóón ponnóón* or *ponnóónun ponnóónuwe* day before the day before yesterday. *sipwe kukkunow p.* we shall visit some day soon. Cf. *pwiin*₃, *pwoong*.
ponga- (3) PONGA. ni. (T3) booming sound, boom (as from a drum or deep voice).
pongeey See *ponga*-, *-e-*₂. vo. (T6b) strike, smite (with open hand); make resound or boom (by striking).
pongkiyo (1) PONGKIYOO. (Jap. *boogekyoo*) nu. (T1) telescope, binocular. *eew p.* one t. *néwún p.* his t.
poro₁ (1) POROO₁. nu. (T1) species of wrasse fish.
poro₂ (1) POROO₂. nu. (T1) name of spell associated with a dark itchy rash (*kinin p.*).

pocho- (3) POCHA. [In cpds. only.] unsp. dented. See *ppoch*.

pochopochokkis (db; 2) See *pocho-*, *kkis*. vi. have many dents, pocked. Syn. *apeyapúkkis*.

pochcheey POCHCHA. vo. (T6b) (refl.) hurry. *kaa pochcheyok* you hurried.

potopot (db; 3) POTA. vi. (dis.) be rough (of surface or skin, as when skin has been scratched).

póó (1) PÓÓ. nu. (T1) platform, sleeping platform, copra drying platform; bed, raised floor rack. *eew p.* one p. *póón his p. ímwen p.* house with raised floor. *póón assak* copra drying rack.

póós (4: *-pós*) PÓSSO. Var. *ppós*. vi., adj. (be) steady, stable, motionless, immobile, stationary; stay in one place without moving; (be) steadfast in one's work or purpose, firm in one's resolve, not responsive to insult or other forms of baiting. With dir. suf.: *póssónó* continue motionless, steady. ni. (T2) steadiness, stability (of something). *póssun s.* of.

póón (3: *-pón, -póón*) PÓNNA. vi. do hook and line fishing; fish with a surface line and chumming; bait one's hook with *éppwún* for the purpose of catching *áár*. Cf. *kkáách, chipón*.

pááni See *póó, -ni-*. vo. (T4) to acquire a platform or rack. Cf. *póópó*.

póópó (db; 1) See *póó*. vi. (dis.) use a platform or rack. Cf. *pááni*.

póów (4) PÓWO. nu. (T2) species of snapper fish. *pówun s.* of (a given region).

pósseyiti See *póós, -iti*. vo. (T2) remain firm, steady, or fixed until.

póssónó See *póós*.

póssu- See *póós*.

pókó (1) PÓKÓÓ. N. nu. (T1) shark (general term): *emén p.* one s. *pókóón s.* of (a given region). Syn. *pachaaw*.

pówun$_1$ (3) PÓWUNA$_1$. (Eng.) Var. *pawun*. n. pound; weight. *fituuw p.?* how many p.? *pówunan* his weight.

pówun$_2$ (3) PÓWUNA$_2$. (P.Eng. from Eng. *found*) nu. (T3) food given to a worker in connection with or in part payment for his work. *aan p.* his f. *pówunen ewe angaang* f. for the work. *ese toonong ááy p. reemw* I haven't gotten my share of food from you (slang for I haven't enjoyed any of your favors, said in jest to a woman).

puu-$_1$ (1) PUU$_1$. [In cpds. only.] unsp. flutter (as eyelids or things in the wind); flap, shake, toss; be blown strongly, blow strongly. See *áásippu, ássipu, ópuuw, puunumén*.

puu-$_2$ (2) PUU$_2$. [In counting only.] ni. (T1), suf. (cc.) stroke in swimming (as a measure of depth of water). *epu, rúwépu, wúnúpu, fépu, nimepu, wonopu, fúúpu, wanúpu, ttiwepu, engoon puun* one,...ten s.; *fítepu* how many s.

puunumén (2) See *puu-*$_1$, *mén*$_3$. nu. (T2) typhoon, hurricane.

puupu (db; 1) See *puu-*$_1$. nu. (T1) strong blowing (of wind). *puupuun ewe ásápwán s.* b. of the wind.

púnúpún (db; 2) PÚNÚ. nu. (T2) 1. kind of fishing done by women using piles of coral. [A large pile is surrounded by women with hand nets and large fish baskets called *tengerik* into which the fish flee as the coral is unpiled. Alternately, women put branching coral in baskets, put the baskets down in the sea, and small fish enter. The women then pick up the baskets with the fish in them.] 2. (N.) pile of coral used to attract fish. vi. do fishing using piles of coral to attract the fish.

púntayicho (1) PÚNTAYICHOO. (Jap. *buntaichoo*) nu. (T1) squad leader (army). *emén p.* one s. l.

púng$_1$ (2) PÚNGÚ$_1$. vi. pop, crack, sound suddenly and sharply; explode, detonate, fire (as a gun); slam (as a door).

púng$_2$ (2) PÚNGÚ$_2$. Var. *pwúng*$_2$. vi. fall (as rain and as in walking on slippery or rough ground). *aa. p. rááán* it has started to rain. With dir. suf.: *púngútiw*.

púngiiti$_1$ See *púng*$_1$, *-iti*. vo. (T2) sound as far as; explode upon.

púngiiti$_2$ See *púng*$_2$, *-iti*. vo. (T2) fall upon (of rain).

púngú- (2) PÚNGÚ$_3$. unsp. cover (with a lid). See *éppúng, éppúngú, épúngú, kképúng, ppúng*.

Púngúnap nu. (loc.) Pingelap Island and Atoll (Eastern Caroline Islands). Syn. *Pikiram*.

púngúpúng (db; 2) See *púng*$_1$. va. make pop (as by slapping the hands on the surface of things, as when women wash clothes).

púngúpúngúri Dis. of *púngúri*.
púngúri See *púng₁, -ri-*. vo. (T5) make (something) pop, crack, or sound explosively, slap (something) resoundingly with the hands (as in doing laundry or beating a drum). Dis. *púngúpúngúri* (db).
púngúchechchech (db; 3) See *púng₁, chcheech₂*. vi. throb (as one's pulse or a pain).
púngúchééw (2) See *púng₁, chééw*. nu. (T2) machine gun. *púngúchééwún Sapaan* Japanese m. g. Syn. *kikanchú*. vi. fire repeatedly (as a machine gun).
púngútiw See *púng₂*.
púngúwonuuw (3) See *púng₁, wonuuw*. nu. (T3) six-shooter, revolver.
púruuk (Ger. *Bruch*) nu. fractions (in arithmetic).
ppa- (dc; 3b: *ppa-, ppe-, ppé-, -p*) See *pa-₁*. ni. (loc.; T3) 1. (at) the side or edge (of), beside. *meyiwor emén ppen ewe asam* there is someone beside the window. 2. aid, help (for something). *ppen manaw* ransom.
-ppa- See *paap*.
ppan (dc; 3) PANA₄. nu. (T3) hillside; steep slope. *eew p.* one h. *ppanen ewe chuuk* side of the hill or mountain. vi., adj. (be) steep. Dis. *panapan* (db) (be) hilly. *meyi p. eey chuuk* this hill or mountain is s. Cf. *pana-, ppa-*.
ppach (dc; 3b) See *pach*. vi., adj. (be) sticky.
ppásew [In cpds. only.] adj. (u.m.) See *ááppásew*.
ppán (4) PPÁNE. vi., adj. (be) light, of little weight. Ant. *chchow*.
ppek (2) PEKKI. vi. shoot (with a gun). Dis. *peppek* (db). *meyi angangngaw átánaan ne p.* that fellow performs badly in shooting. nu. (T2) gun, firearm (general term). *pekkin aramas* gun for shooting people, firearm for war; *pekkin fénú* field gun, cannon; *pekkin maan, pekkin machchang* gun for shooting birds, fowling piece. Syn. *nikésúk*.
ppen vi. (of fruit) be fully formed but not yet ripe.
ppeni See *ppa-, -ni-*. vo. (T6a) help, give assistance to, assist, support (someone), take (someone's) siee. Dis. *peppeni* (ds).
ppep (3: *-pep, -ppep*) PEPPA. vi. skip (as a stone thrown on water); bounce on the surface (as a fish or landing seaplance). Dis. *peppep* (ds) skip or bounce along. Cf. *átereppep, kuruppep*.
ppet₁ (Eng.) nu. a bet. vi. 1. bet (with *wóón*). *wúwa p. wóón senis nime* I bet fifty cents. 2. bid (with *wóón* or *reen*). *wúwa p. ngeni Siro reen ewe kontrák* I bid against Siro for the contract.
ppet₂ (4) PPETE, PEETE (?). F. vi. be shallow (of the sea). Dis. *petepeet* (db). Syn. *ápetpeet*.
ppet₃ (2) See *ppa-, -ti-*. vi. be blocked, screened off, having something in the way of. *wúwa p. reemw* I am blocked by you. Cf. *eppet, eppeti*.
ppeyis (3) PPEYISA. n. (T3) fortitude, ability to endure physical pain, ability to hold one's breath or stay under water for a long time. *ppeyisan* his f. vi. have or show fortitude.
ppeyinen (2) See *ppa-, -nen*. nu. (T2) 1. horizon. Syn. *óroppeyinen*. 2. god of the horizon. [Cause of illness in infants.] *rongen p.* spell to protect against illness in infants; *sáfeen p.* medicine to cure illness in infants; *semwmwenin p.* illness in infants caused by the god of the horizon. See *sowuppeyinen*.
ppé (dc; 1) See *pé₃*. nu. (T1) hollow ball (i.e., football, basketball, soccer ball, traditional square ball of woven pandanus leaves); game played with pandanus-leaf ball. vi. play with a pandanus-leaf ball. Dis. *péppé* (db).
ppék (dc; 2) PÉKÚ₂. adj. 1. in conjunction, at the same time, in unison, together. [Usually suffixed to the word it modifies.] *fátáneppék* walk along side one another; *iyóótekeppék* pray together; *kkapaséppék* talk freely together, converse; *makképpék* write at the same time; *suppék* depart together. Cf. *épékúpékúúw, pékúpékééch, pékúpékúngngaw*. 2. exactly, precisely (with numbers and measures). *engoonuppék* exactly ten; *nénnéppék* exactly even, of equal length or size.
ppénú (3a) PPÉNÚWA. nu. (T3) answer, reply. *aan p.* his a. ni. (T3) opposite number, opposite, opponent, dancing partner, antonym (of word). *ppénúwan* his opponent or dancing partner; its opposite. *ppénúwen ena fóós* antonym

ppénúwefeseen / **Trukese-English**

of that word. vi. reply, answer, respond, counter.

ppénúwefeseen (2) See *ppénú, -feseen*. vi. be odd numbered. [Odd numbers are unlucky in making medicines; and odd numbered nights of the moon are sorcery-making nights.] Cf. *ppénúwéngngaw*.

ppénúweffengen (2) See *ppénú, ffengen*. vi. be even numbered. [Above ten, these numbers are confined to multiples of ten like twenty, thirty, etc. Even numbers are lucky for making medicine, and even numbered nights of the moon are not suitable for making sorcery.] Cf. *ppénúwéyééch*.

ppénúweni See *ppénú, -ni-*. vo. (T5) answer, respond to, reply to, be in opposition to, be a dance partner to. Cf. *éppénúwa*.

ppénúwéngngaw (3b) See *ppénú, ngngaw*. vi. match badly; be an odd number. Cf. *ppénúwefeseen*.

ppénúwéyééch (2) See *ppénú, ééch*. vi. match well, correspond; be an even number. Cf. *ppénúweffengen*.

ppéchén (2) See *ppa-, chaan*. vi. eat breadfruit or taro by dipping it in water before taking it in the mouth.

-ppéw (2) PPÉWÚ. [In cpds. only.] unsp. sorcery (?). Syn. *ppéwút*. See *éénenippéw*.

ppéwút (dc; 2) PPÉWÚTÚ. n. (T2) sorcery, black magic. [Presumably from *péwút*, having reference to leaving the vehicle of the spell in a hidden place in or near the victim's house.] *ppéwútún* s. done on him; *aan p*. his s. (against someone). *ppéwútún nóómw* s. of old times; *ppéwútún soope* s. done to chase away a ghost (the sorcerer does his hair up in knots all over the top of his head and lashes himself to a tree to keep himself from being swept away by the vanishing ghost). *ppéwútiy me reen átewe* s. done on me by that fellow. *chóón p*. sorcerer. Syn. *kkúsú, rongongngaw*. See *sowuppéwút*. va. make sorcery. *p. ngeni* (vo. phr.) make s. against (someone).

ppi$_1$ (dc; 1) See *pi*. vi. (dis.) float. With dir. suf.: *ppiinó, ppiito*.

ppi$_2$ (dc; 3) See *piye-*. nu. (T3) sand, sand spit, beach, sand islet without vegetation. *fáán p*. sandy shallows next to a sandy shore. Cf. *fénú, neeppi, piis, piyepi, téé*.

ppiifeyini (dc) See *pii-, feyin*. vo. (T2) go in search of, look for, search for.

ppiinó See *ppi$_1$*.

ppiito See *ppi$_1$*.

ppiiy (dc) See *pii-*. vo. (T1) examine, inspect, have a look at, see; watch over, look after. Dis. *pippiiy* (ds). *sipwe p*. we shall see; *kepwe p. ika aa feyitto* see if he has come; *p. ke te tupw reen na óyin* look out that you do not get smeared with that oil. With dir. suf.: *piiyeto* find hither. *kese mwechen kepwe ppiiyeto epa mwáriy* please find hither a lei for me.

ppiiyas (3b) See *ppi$_1$, aas$_1$*. vi. float high, ride high (of a boat).

ppis (dc; 2) See *pisi-$_1$*. vi., adj. (be) slapped (with the hand). Cf. *pisiri*. va. slap.

ppin (dc; 2) See *pini-*. vi., adj. (be) snarled, tangled (of fishline, string, thread, rope). Dis. *pippin* (ds). *ppinin* snarling of (something).

ppich (dc; 2) See *pichi-*. vi., adj. (be) snapped, bounced, vibrated; be a stabbing pain. nu. (T2) snap, bounce, vibration.

ppichin (Eng.) nu. pidgin (language).

ppit (dc; 2) See *piti-*. vi. be braided, twisted, twined (of hair, rope, leis). Dis. *pippit* (ds). va. braid, twist, twine.

ppos (dc; 2) See *posu-*. vi., adj. (be) smeared, stabbed. Dis. *poppos* (db). Cf. *posuuw*.

ppoch (3) See *pocho-*. vi., adj. (be) dented (as of a dent in metal).

ppós Var. of *póós*.

ppúnúk (dc; 2) See *pinúk*. vi. be tied up in a bundle, bundled together.

ppúnúkúúw (dc) See *ppúnúk, -ú-*. vo. (T5) tie (something) in a bundle.

ppúng (dc; 2) See *púngú-*. vi., adj. be shut, closed, covered with a lid.

presiten (Eng.) Var. *piresten*. nu. president.

prisman (3) PRISMANA. Obs. (Eng.) nu. (T3) policeman. Cf. *pwonis*.

Prostan (Eng.) Var. *Pirostan*. nu. Protestant.

PW

pwa- (3b: *pwa-, pwá-, pwe-, pwé-, pwo-, pwó-*) PWA. [In cpds. only.] pref. meaning unclear, but seeming to indicate some kind of condition or state. Cf. *che-, -ma-, mwa-, -ng, sa-*.

pwa (1) PWAA$_1$. [In cpds. only.] vi., adj. spoiled, rotten, tainted (of food).

-pwa Var. of *-pwe*.

pwaa- (1) PWAA$_2$. [In cpds. only.] unsp. See *pwaaset*.

pwaaset (2) See *pwaa-, sáát$_1$*. nu. (T2) any shellfish or sea cucumber; (more loosely) any seafood including fish. *pwaasetin Chuuk Trukese s. siya mwosset pwú esoor pw.* we hunger for *seni* because there is no seafood.

-pwaak (3) PWAAKA. suf. (intens.) very, extremely (in a negative sense). See *rochopwaak, tenechepwaak*.

pwaang (3) PWANGA$_1$. Tb3. n. (T3), suf. (cc.) hole, cave, cavity, pit, tunnel, hollow. *epwang, rúwépwang, wúnúpwang, fépwang, nimepwang, wonopwang, fúúpwang, wanúpwang, ttiwepwpwang* one,...nine h. *pwangan* its h. *pwangen mwaa* (Tb1) vaginal orifice; *pwangen sening* large hole stretched in lobe of ear; *pwangen pwéét* nostril. *meyiwor pwangan* it has a h., it is punctured. Syn. *ngaat*.

-pwaapw suf. (asp.) indefinite future; later, by and by, afterwards. [Suffixed to sub. prns. at the beginning of narrative constructions.] *wúpwaapw...mwirin* afterward, I shall... (cf. *wúpwe...* I shall). *sipwaapw pwan chuffengeen* we shall meet again later. *eni eew ráán wúpwaapw sineeyéchchúúw kkapasen Chuuk* maybe someday I shall know how to speak Trukese well. Cf. *-pwe*.

pwaapwa (db; 1) PWAA$_3$. n. (T1) happiness, joy, pleasure, merriment, fun. *aan pw., pwaapwaan* his h. *pwaapwaan mwiich* h. at a social gathering. vi. 1. be happy, merry, glad, delighted. 2. be wearing a flower on the left ear by a man or the right ear by a woman as a symbol of happiness and requited love.

pwaapwaayiti See *pwaapwa, -iti*. vo. (T2) be pleased with.

pwaar (3) PWARA. Tb1. n. (T3) pubic triangle. *pwaran* her p. t.

pwaat F. of *pwata*.

pwaaw$_1$ (2) PWAAWÚ$_1$. nu. (T2) prohibition or taboo on the gathering of food, on fishing, or on trepassing on trees or fishing sites. *pwaawún meyimá* p. on behalf of someone who has died. Syn. *róóng*. Cf. *mechen*.

pwaaw$_2$ (2) PWAAWÚ$_2$. nu. (T3) bamboo (*Bambusa vulgaris*). *pw. Chuuk* or *pwaawún Chuuk* Trukese b. Syn. *iich$_2$*.

pwaaw$_3$ nu. a kind of fish.

pwaawúni See *pwaaw$_1$, -ni-*. vo. (T5) make a tabu or prohibition against trepass on (a place or tree). *sipwe pw. eey neeni* we shall taboo this place.

pwas (3) PWASA. Var. *pwpwas*. vi., adj. (be) dry.

pwasakka (1) See *pwas, kka*. vi. be dry.

pwasuk (2) PWASUKU. Var. *pwásuk*. n. (T2) knee. *pwasukun* his k.

pwakak (3) See *pwa-, -kak*. nu. (T3) mud. vi. be muddy; soft (of sand). Dis. *pwakakkak* (ds).

pwakakkak Dis. of *pwakak*.

pwan Var. *pwayi* (when followed by a monosyllabic word). adv. also, too, again, more, other; either (after a negative). *pw. eew* one more, once more, another thing; *pw. ekis* a little more, some more; *pw. emén* one more person, another person; *pw. ngaang* me too; *pw. seni* likewise with, the same with. *meyi pwanú wor reey* I have more; *meyi pwayi wor* there is more; *ngaang wúse pw. sineey* I don't know it either. *sipwaapw pw. chuffengen* we shall meet together again later. *pwanú mwo...ngé, pwan...mwo ngé* even; *pwanú mwo sómwoon ngé aa feyitto* even the chief has come; *pwan ewe kepinaa mwo ngé aa fiti* even the governor attended; *Eiue mwo ngé pwan óchoocho* even Eiue worked hard, too.

-pwan (3) PWANA$_2$. unsp. (u.m.) See *atapwan*.

pwanang$_1$ (3) PWANANGA$_1$. nu. (T3) <Elbert> ilangilang tree (*Cananga*

pwanang₂

odorata). *pwanangen* t. of (a given region). Syn. *pwuur₁*.

pwanang₃ (3) PWANANGA₂. nu. (T3) roofed porch or shed attached to a house (without walls). *eew pw.* one p. *pwanangen iimw* house's p.

pwanga-₁ (3) PWANGA₂. [In cpds. only.] unsp. weak, feeble (?). See *apwangapwang*.

pwanga-₂ (3) PWANGA₃. [In cpds. only.] unsp. beat, tempo (in music). See *pwangapwang, pwangeey*.

pwangapwang (db; 3) See *pwanga-₂*. vi. beat time to music, conduct a chorus. *chóón pw.* musical conductor.

pwangeey (3) See *pwanga-₂, -e-₂*. vo. (T6b) beat time to, conduct (a musical performance).

pwangeni See *pwaang, -ni-*. vo. (T6a) make a hole or space in. *pw. neefiinen mmak* make a space between letters (on a typewriter).

pwangéwátte (1) See *pwaang, wátte*. Tb3. vi. be big-holed (as of net mesh). *pwangéwatteen eey mesechcheew* the big-holed-ness of this net mesh.

Pwapiyen (2) PWAYIPENI. nu. Bible. *eew Pw.* one B. *néwún Pw.* his B. *Pwayipenin Pirostan* Protestant B.

pwara (1) PWARAA. Tb3. nu. (T1) courage, bravery. vi., adj. (be) brave, bold, strong in war, fierce; dare. Syn. *maat*. Ant. *nissiyá, nisiin, nissimwa*. Cf. *pwaar*.

pwaraawus E.Wn. of *pwóróówus*.

pwaraayiti (2) See *pwara, -iti*. vo. (T2) be brave in the presence of.

pwarapwpwech (3) See *pwaar, pwech*. Tb1. vi. be without pubic hair.

pwachapwach Dis. of *pwpwach*.

pwachen (2) PWACHENI₂. (Eng.) nu. (T2) button. *eféw pw.* one b. *pwachenin Sapaan* Japanese b.

pwachechchen (ds; 4) See *pwa-, chene-*. nu. (T2) tidal pool on reef (at low tide).

pwachú (1) See *pwa-, chúú*. nu. (T1) kind of reef fish. *pwachúún Chuuk* Trukese r. f.

pwata N. Var. *pwaat, woopwat*. interrog. Why?, how come?, how does it happen that...? *pwataa mwo* why instead?, why anyway?, why then?; *pwataa mwo kese ngeni átánaan...* why didn't you give to him instead...?, why didn't you give to him anyway...? *ngé pwataa*

(pwaatú) chék of course!, why not!, surely!, certainly!

pwayip (3) PWAYIPPA. (Eng.) nu. (T3) pipe (for smoking). *efóch pw.* one p. *pwayippen* p. of (a given type).

pwá (1) PWÁÁ₁. vi. come to view, appear; be discovered, found, sighted. *se pwá* be invisible. *pwáán iik* sighting, discovery, or sign of a school of fish (as revealed by a flight of birds birds hovering over and swooping down). With dir. suf.: *pwáánó* emerge into view, unfold into view; *pwáátá* rise to view, raise up (as from one's bed); *pwááto* appear hither, come hither into view.

pwáák (2: *pwááki-*) See *pwa-, áák*. vi. (N.) be able, skilled, (industrious. Syn. *kuus₁, chófó*. (F.) be recovered from illness; be fixed, repaired. Syn. *chikar, kuus₁*.

pwáákini See *pwáák, -ni-*. vo. (T5) cure, repair, fix.

pwáán (2) PWENI, PWÁÁNI. nu. (T2) 1. art of Trukese judo and of disarming a foe. *pwenin Chuuk, pwáánin Chuuk* Trukese judo. 2. art of rigging for carrying huge ceremonial bowls of food or for carrying and erecting logs in house construction or lashing down a house in a storm. 3. art of righting an overturned canoe.

-pwáán Var. of *pween₂* in cpds.

pwáánó See *pwá*.

pwáápwá (db; 1) PWÁÁ₂. nu. (T1) turtle. *eew pw.* one t. *néwún pw.* having children like a turtle (said of a father who does not care properly for his children, because male turtles eat their young). Syn. *wiin₁*.

pwáápwáánó (db; 1) See *pwá, -nó*. vi. be readily visible, in clear view. See *pwáánó*.

pwááráátá See *pwáári*.

pwáári See *pwá, -ri-*. vo. (T4) make visible (with *ngeni*); show, reveal, testify concerning, confess. With dir. suf.: *pwááráátá* describe, reveal; show, confess, declare, testify concerning. Cf. *afat*.

pwáátá See *pwá*.

pwááto See *pwá*.

pwásuk Var. of *pwasuk*.

pwáráán N. vr. be for the first time; be just now (with aspect marker *-a*). Syn. *kkánáán, kkáráán, kkeráán, kkéráán*.

pwáchen (4) See *pwa-, chene-*. nu. (T2) coconut oil (unscented). *pwáchenin taka* oil of the ripe coconut.

pwe₁ PWE₂. N. [It is embedded in the phrase preceding it, which it terminates, being followed by a brief pause.] Var. *pwé₁*. conj. links what follows intentionally with what went before (after verbs indicating thinking or saying); that, as follows, thus. *aa apasaa pwe iiy sómwoon* he said that he was chief. *aa apasaa pwe, "Iwe, sipwene móówun"* he said, "Very well, we are going to do battle". Syn. *wé, wo₂*.

pwe₂ PWE₃. N. [It is embedded in the phrase following it, which it initiates, being preceded by a brief pause.] Var. *pwé₂*. conj. links what follows as the cause or reason for what went before; because, for, as, since; (before a future aspect marker) so that, in order that. *sapw ngaang wúún me aaw me ato, pwe ngaang aramasen núkiisenné* I am not a chief, son of a chief, or brother of a chief, as I am a person from outside. *aa etto pwe epwe mééni wúnúman suupwa* he has come in order to buy cigarettes for himself. Syn. *pwú, pwún₂, pwúnún*.

-pwe PWE₁. [Suffixed to sub. prns. at the beginning of narrative constructions.] Var. *-pwa* (if immediately followed by *a*), *-pwo* (if immediately followed by *o, wo*). suf. (asp.) intentional future aspect marker; will, shall, must, should, ought (often implying a command); (following *pwe₁*) in order that, in order to. *epwe ina?* is that it, is that how it will be?; *epwe wor, epwo wor* there will be. *wúpwe fituk* I shall go with you, let me go with you; *wúpwe fóókkun fituk* I shall indeed go with you, I must go with you. *kepwe waato* bring it here. *aa mwittirinó pwe epwe sowuni kkanaan wasééna* he hurried off in order to greet those visitors over there. See *wúpwe, kepwe, epwe, sipwe, éwúpwe, áyipwe, opwe, owupwe, wopwe, repwe*.

pwee- (1) PWEE₁. [In cpds. only.] unsp. pull up from the sea. See *pweepwe₁, pweewu, pweeyi*.

pwee₁ (1) PWEE₂. nu. (T1) divination done with knots tied in young coconut leaves (since World War II also done with cards). [The most complicated procedure, *pweewunus*, involves casting knots at random into four coconut leaves, counting the number of knots by fours in each leaf so so as to obtain an even number four or a remainder of one, two, or three, and thus providing sixteen permutations for each pair of leaves and 256 permutations for the two sets of sixteen. Every permutation is named and has its meaning in the divination process.] *pween atake* or *pween máárin atake* d. of how a garden will grow; *pween attaw* d. of luck in fishing; *pween fanafan* d. of how a new canoe will perform (consisting of *pween mwittir* for speed and *pween póssun* for stability); *pween manaw* d. of life (to determine whether a sick person is likely to live or die); *pween manaw nóón móówun* d. of survival in war; *pween mwayisa* d. of attitude (to determine whether a sick person's attitude is oriented toward living or dying); *pween ngngúpwir* d. of force (to determine whether a person's affection will go on for ever or will quickly end); *pween rááán* d. of weather.

Pwee₂ nu. (loc.) a clan name. Syn. *Nipwe, Tinik*.

pweefis (2) See *pwee₁, fis*. nu. (T2) a form of knot divination (to determine whether a marriage will be fruitful).

pwees (2) PWEESI, PWESSI. (Eng.) nu. (T2) wallet, billfold, pocketbook, purse. *aan pwees* his wallet. *pweesin Sapaan, pwessin Sapaan* Japanese wallet.

pween₁ (3) PWENNA. n. (T3) shoot of a banana, breadfruit, or *Alocasia* taro. *pwennan* its s. *pwennen wuuch* banana s.; *pwennen mááy* breadfruit s.; *pwennen kká, pwenneni kká* Alocasia s.

pween₂ (2) PWENNI. Var. *-pwáán*. nu. (T2) environs, area around a place. *pwennin Winipwéét* e. of Mt. Winipwéét. vo. (T2) go in a circuit around something, circumnavigate. Dis. *pwepwpween* (ds).

pweeniféng (2) See *pwee₁, féng*. nu. (T2) a form of knot divination (to determine the disposition of the person one loves).

pweeniyas (3b) See *pwee₁, aas₁*. nu. (T3) knot divination done with only one

pweepwe₁ coconut leaf (counting done by fives). Syn. *pweeyeew.*

pweepwe₁ (db; 1) See *pwee-.* va. pull up from the sea. *si pw. wuu* we are pulling up fish traps.

pweepwe₂ (db; 1) PWEE₃. unsp. (u.m.) See *nipweepwe.*

pweech (3) See *pwech.* nu. (T3) powdered lime (made by burning coral limestone *féwúrupw*); white paint of native manufacture. *pwechen* l. of (a given region)q ni. (T3) white hair, gray hair. *pwechan* his w. h.

pweechar (3) PWEECHARA. nu. (T3) snail. *pweecharen neeset* sea s.; *pweecharen neeman* land s.; *pweecharen Chuuk* Trukese land s. (indigenous); *pweecharen wóón* African snail.

pweewu (1) See *pwee-, wuu.* vi. pull up fish traps.

pweewunus See *pwee₁, wunus.* nu. knot divination in its fully elaborated form (involving the use of four coconut leaves and the 256 permutations of two sets of the sixteen permutations of two sets of four).

pweey₁ (2) PWEEYI. F. Var. *pwpwey.* nu. (T2) pearl oyster. [Edible only in part, shell used as a knife in old days.] *eew pw.* (Rmn.), *efóch pw.* (Tn.) one o. *pweeyin Chuuk* Trukese o.

pweey₂ See *pwee₁.* vo. (T1) divine for (something) with knots.

pweeyas (3) nu. (T3) pompano fish. *pweeyasen* p. f. of (a given region).

pweeyeew See *pwee₁, eew₁.* nu. knot divination done with only one coconut leaf (counting done by fives). Syn. *pweeniyas.*

pweeyééch (2) See *pwee₁, ééch.* vi. be a good omen (in knot divination). Ant. *pwengngaw.*

pweeyi See *pwee-, -yi-₂.* vo. (T4) pull up from the sea. *sipwe pw. ewe wuu* we shall p. up the fish trap.

pweeyisár (4) See *pwee₁, sár₂.* nu. (T2) divination of termination (done to determine whether a sickness will end or will continue indefinitely).

pweke (1) PWEKEE. Wn. nu. (T1) water. Syn. *appúng, kkónik, kkónuk, ónuki.*

pwekiiki (db; 2) PWEKII. Var. *pwokuuku.* nu. (T1) corner (as in a house).

pwekit (3) PWEKITA. (Eng.) Var. *pwengit.* nu. (T3) bucket. *eew pw.* one b. *aan pw.* his b. *eew pwekiten kkónik* one b. of water.

pwene₁ (1) PWENEE. nu. (T1) <Elbert> a fish of the bass family (*Plectiropomus*).

Pwene₂ nu. (loc.) Polle Island.

pweniiy See *pwáán, -i-₂.* vo. (T5) use judo against; rig; right (an overturned canoe).

pwenneyisómw (4) See *pween₁, -sómw.* nu. senior line, ranking line (based on matrilineal primogeniture) within a chiefly lineage or clan ("chiefly shoot").

pwenniiy See *pween₂, -yi-₂.* vo. (T5) circumnavigate, go all the way around (as to walk around an island), circle.

pwennifátán (4) See *pween₂, fátán.* vi. proceed all the way around something, circumnavigate. Syn. *pwennifeyin.*

pwennifátáneey See *pwennifátán, -e-₂.* vo. (T6b) travel all the way around (something); circumnavigate.

pwennifeyin (2) See *pween₂, feyin.* vi. travel all the way around (something); circumnavigate. Syn. *pwennifátán.*

pwennifeyiniiy See *pwennifeyin, -i-₂.* vo. (T5) travel all the way around (something); circumnavigate.

pwengit Var. of *pwekit.*

pwengngaw (3) See *pwee₁, ngngaw.* vi. be a bad omen (in knot divination). Ant. *pweeyééch.*

pwepwpween Dis. of *pween₂.*

pwer (3a) PWERA. vi. go, come. *menniiy neeyiin kkaan aan kepwe pw. nóón (wóón)?* which of these roads will you go on? With dir. suf.: *pwerenong, pwerenó, pweretá, pw020retiw, pwereto, pwerewow, pwerewu.*

Pwereka₁ (1) See *pwereka₂.* nu. (loc.) a clan name. *fiin Pw., fin Pw.* Pw. woman; *mwáán Pw., re-Pw.* Pw. man; *chóón Pw.* people of Pw.

pwereka₂ (1) PWEREKAA. [Possibly related to Fijian *mere* (tendon, vine, string) and meaning "famine vine" (cf. *kaa-*).] nu. (T1) a wild yam, vine and tuber (*Dioscorea bulbifera*). [It produces a yam of poor quality that is very bitter, eaten in times of famine. The pounded fruit is used in steam treatment of swelling of the scrotum or epididimitis.] Syn. *ápwereka.*

pwerenong See *pwer.*

pwerenó See *pwer.*

pweretá See *pwer.*
pweretiw See *pwer.*
pwereto See *pwer.*
pwerewow See *pwer.*
pwerewu See *pwer.*
pwereyiti See *pwer, -iti.* vo. (T2) come to, arrive at.
pwerik (3) PWERIKA. [Possibly from *pwa-* and a metathesis of *keri-.*] nu. (T3) 1. itch. 2. dry-land elephant ear taro (*Alocasia macrorrhiza*). [So named because of its irritant nature.] *pweriken* t. of (a given region). vi. itch; scratch an itch; be itchy. Dis. *pwerikerik* (db) have a ticklish irritation (as in the throat, causing a cough). Syn. *kkéét.* Cf. *epwerika, erikeri.*
pwerikerik Dis. of *pwerik.*
pwech (3) PWECHA. vi., adj. (be) white. Dis. *pwechepwech* (db).
pwechepwech (db; 3) See *pwech.* vi., adj. (be) white. nu. (T3) sandy shoal. Cf. *neechón.*
pweteete (db; 1) See *pwa-, teete₃.* vi., adj. (be) gentle, soft, polite. *kkapas pw.* gentle or polite speech; *angaang pw.* take it easy, do gently.
pweteeto (1) PWETEETOO. (Eng.) nu. (T1) potato (sweet and white). *pweteetoon Chuuk* sweet p.; *pweteetoon wóón* white p.
pwetek (2) PWETEKI. nu. 1. any variety of olive shell (of the family Olividae). [Olive shells are used as tokens in the game of bingo.] Syn. *áátip.* 2. blood mouth conch (edible).
pwey (2) PWEYI₁. vi. be mildewed; (N.) be wet, damp (of mats). *pweyin eey kiyeki* the mildewed state of this mat.
-pwey (2) PWEYI₂. F. suf. (cc.) (In counting) pinch or morsel (of mashed food). [Used with num. pref.] *epwey, rúwépwey, wúnúpwey, fépwey, nimepwey, wonopwey, fúúpwey, wanúpwey, ttiwepwey* one,...nine p. Syn. *-mwmwék.*
pweyiker (2) See *pweey₁, keri-.* nu. (T2) coconut grater. *efóch pw.* one c. g. *aan pw.* his c. g. *pweyikerin* c. g. of (a given region). va. grate (coconuts). Cf. *feeyiir.*
pweyikeriiy See *pweyiker, -i-₂.* vo. (T5) grate (a coconut).
pweyinaper (2) PWEYINAPERI. (loan source unknown) nu. (T2) pineapple (*Ananas comosus*). *ewumw pw.* one p. *pweyinaperin Chuuk* Trukese p.
pweyiyónoon (db; 4) See *pweey₁, ón₂.* nu. (T2) a shell (*Atrina*). [It is used to strip banana fibers for making loom threads.]
pwé₁ N. var. of *pwe₁.*
pwé₂ N. var. of *pwe₂.*
pwéék (2) PWÉKÚ₁. nu. (T2) callous (as on hands or feet); bruise (as on banana or breadfruit).
pwéén₁ (2) PWÉNÚ₃. n. (T2) fresh-water swamp; taro-patch. *pwénún* his s. or t. p.
Pwéén₂ nu. (loc.) a clan name. *fiin Pw., fin Pw.* Pw. woman, *mwáán Pw., re-Pw.* Pw. man; *chóón Pw.* people of Pw.
pwéét (2) PWÉÉTÚ. n. (T2), suf. (cc.) 1. nose. *epwéét, rúwépwéét, wúnúpwéét, fépwéét, nimepwéét, wonopwéét, fúúpwéét, wanúpwéét, ttiwepwéét, engoon pwéétún* one,...ten noses. *pwéétiy, pwootumw, pwéétún* my, your, his n. 2. kingpost (of house or meeting house), upright timber between tiebeam and ridgepole. *pwéétún ewe iimw* the house's k. Syn. *wúraté.*
pwéétúút (2) See *pwéét, -wút.* nu. (T2) small species of unicorn fish (*Naso brevirostris* Cuvier and Valenciennes). *pwéétúútún Chuuk* u. f. of Truk.
pwéétúkken (2) See *pwéét, kken.* vi. be sharp-nosed.
pwéétúkkopw (2) See *pwéét, kkopw.* vi. be flat-nosed.
pwék (2) See *pwéék.* vi. be calloused (of hands or feet), bruised (of banana or breadfruit).
pwékú- (2) PWÉKÚ₂. unsp. (u.m.) See *nipwékúpwék.*
pwénú-₁ (2) PWÉNÚ₁. [In cpds. only.] Var. *pwénúwe-.* unsp. finished, accomplished, completed, done. See *épwénúwétá, pwénútá, pwénúúwetá.*
pwénú-₂ (2) PWÉNÚ₂. [In cpds. only.] unsp. cover, lid. See *épwpwén, pwénúpwén, pénúúw.*
pwénúúngeni See *pwénú-₂, -ú-, ngeni.* vo. (T2) cover (something) with (something). *wúpwe pwénúúngeniyey ena tówun* I shall c. myself with that towel; *si pw. mangaak* we c. it with clothing. Cf. *pwénúúw₁.*

pwénúúw₁ See *pwénú-₂, -ú-*. vo. (T5) cover, conceal. *wúpwe pwénúúwey ngeni ena tówun* I shall c. myself with that towel. With dir. suf.: *pwénúúwénó* cover up. Cf. *épwpwén, pwénúúngeni*.

pwénúúw₂ See *pwénúpwén₂, -ú-*. vo. (T5) charm (someone) so that he or she will be loved.

pwénúúwetá See *pwénú-₁, -ú-, -tá.* Var. *pwénúúwétá.* vo. (T5) finish, complete, accomplish. *siya pw. aach angaang* we have finished our work.

pwénúúwénó See *pwénúúw₁*.

pwénúúwétá Var. of *pwénúúwetá*.

pwénúmar (3) See *pwénú-₁, maar.* nu. (T3) one of four traditional annual feasts. [It was made in the *efen* season and involved a substantial presentation of fermented breadfruit to the district chief.]

pwénúni See *pwéén₁, -ni-*. vo. (T5) acquire ownership of a fresh-water swamp or taro patch. Cf. *pwénúpwén₃*.

pwénúpwén₁ (db; 2) See *pwénú-₂*. va., vi. cover with a lid; be covered, be protected by a talisman or magical medicine. nu. (T2) cover, lid, shield. *pwénúpwénún sóópach* side projection near the gunwale from end to end of a sailing canoe, its function being to keep the sea from splashing into the body of the canoe.

pwénúpwén₂ (db; 2) See *pwénú-₁*. nu. (T2) love magic. Syn. *omwmwung*.

pwénúpwén₃ (db; 2) See *pwéén₁*. va. use a fresh-water swamp or taro patch. Cf. *pwénúni*.

pwénútá (1) See *pwénú-₁, -tá*. vi. be accomplished, realized. Syn. *fis*.

pwénútiw (3) See *pwénú-₂, -tiw*. nu. (T3) thatch that caps the ridgepole. *pwénútiwen enaan wuung* t. capping that ridgepole.

pwénúwe- (3) PWÉNÚWA. [In cpds. only.] Var. *pwénú-₁*. unsp. finished, accomplished, done, completed.

pwénúwetá (1) See *pwénúwe-, -tá.* Var. *pwénútá, pwénúwétá*. vi. be finished, accomplished, completed, done.

pwénúwéta Var. of *pwénúwetá*.

-pwér suf. very. *échchúpwér* very good (*ééch* good).

pwerúk (2) See *pwa-, rúk*. nu. (T2) dance, dancing (traditional style). *pwérúkún nóómw* d. of olden times. *pwérúkún fáán maram* a d. performed with an *óppong* in connection with the *sooyénú* rite ("dance under the moon"); *pwérúkún mááy* a sitting d. done by men in the breadfruit summoner's meeting house as part of the cycle of breadfruit ritual; *pwérúkún sowufanafan* a sitting d. in honor of Sineenap, performed at the completion feast of a canoe; *pwérúkún wóók* a d. done with staves in rites in honor of an *enúúsór* spirit, stick dance. vi. dance. Dis. *pwérúkúrúk* (db) be dancing, quiver (of body and arms in dancing, of leaves in the wind). Cf. *pwéwúkúúk*.

pwérúkúnong (3) nu. (T3) species of surgeon fish. *pwérúkúnongen Chuuk* Trukese s. f.

pwérúkúrúk Dis. of *pwérúk*.

pwéchékkún Var. of *péchékkún*.

-pwét (2) PWÉTÚ₁. [In cpds. only.] unsp. indicates something about the condition of food. See *épwét, ipwét*.

pwété (1) PWÉTÉÉ. (Eng.) nu. (T1) butter. *pwétéén Merika* American b.

pwétérék nu. muck; mushy consistency. vi. be mushy, mucky (of breadfruit pudding, swampy ground, etc.).

pwétúpwét Dis. of *opwpwét*.

pwétúr (2) PWÉTÚRÚ. nu. (T2) termite. *pwétúrún Chuuk* Trukese t.

pwéwúkúúk (2) See *pwa-, -wúkúúk*. vi. quiver, tremble, shake, vibrate heavily (as a ship from its engines). Cf. *pwérúk*.

pwéwúr (2) PWÉWÚRÚ. nu. (T2) species of pompano fish. *pwéwúrún Chuuk* p. f. of Truk.

pwi (1) PWII₁. vi. be finished, done, stopped, ceased. *wúwa pw. seni pwúnúwey* I have finished with my wife, I am done with my wife. Syn. *wees*.

pwii-₁ (1) PWII₂. nr. (T1), suf. (cc.) group, company, pair; grove, flock, school, herd, swarm, convoy, pride. *epwi, rúwépwi, wúnúpwi, fépwi, nimepwi, wonopwi, fúúpwi, wanúpwi, ttiwepwi, engoon pwiin* one,...ten g. *pwiin iik* school of fish; *pwiin aramas* group of people; *pwiin irá* grove. Syn. *pene*.

pwii-₂ (1) PWII₃. ni. (T1) sibling of same sex, lineage mate of same sex and generation; relative of same sex whose father is a lineage mate of one's own father; relative by marriage whose spouse is *pwii-* to one's own spouse;

close or initimate friend of same sex. Dis. *pwiipwi* (db). *pwiin* his s. *pwiiy emén chék inach* my s. by the same mother (the highest priority relationship in Truk); *pwiiy winipwúnú* my s. by marriage (spouse of someone who is *pwii-* to my spouse); *pwiiy winisam* my s. by fathers (my s. by the same father or whose father and my father were lineage mates). *pwiimw pwiimw (pwiipw pwiimw) meyi pwúng?* by your s. is it true?; *mwoo pwiiy meyi pwúng* by my s. it is true.

pwii₁ (1) PWII₄. nu. (T1) name of the consonant (velarized, bilabial stop) written *pw*; name of the digraph thus written.

pwii₂ (3) PWIYA. (Mck.) nu. (T1) hole for head and neck in traditional clothing. *pwiyen wúfey* h. of my garment. Syn. *pwaang, ngaat.*

pwiisón (4) See *pwi, sóón₄.* nu. (T2) 1. one or both of the two upright posts to which the warp beam of a loom is lashed. *pwiisónun ewe túúr* post of the loom. 2. frame on which men's headbands are made. 3. a throw in hand-to-hand fighting. [One ducks under a club blow and grabs one's opponent's leg, pitching him forward hard on his face with the momentum of his swing.]

pwiin₁ (2) PWINI₁. n. (T2) swim bladder (of a fish). *pwinin* its s. b.

pwiin₂ (2) PWINI₂. N. nu. (T2) small species of cowrie shell. Cf. *ngiingi.*

pwiin₃ (2) PWINI₃. nu. (T2), suf. (cc.) night. *epwin, rúwépwin, wúnúpwin, fépwin, nimepwin, wonopwin, fúúpwin, wanúpwin, ttiwepwin, engoon pwinin* one,...ten n. *pwinin* its n. *pwinin maram* day (night) of the month (moon), date; *pwinin neesor* tomorrow night. *nóón eey pwinin* tonight, during this present night (cf. *neepwineey*); *nóón ewe pwinin* on that (past) night. Ant. *ráán₂.* Cf. *neepwin, pwin₂.*

pwiini See *pwii-₂, -ni-.* vo. (T4) acquire as a sibling of same sex (as in adoption) or as an intimate friend.

pwiipwi (db; 1) See *pwii-₂.* nu. (dis.; T1) siblings of same sex; relatives who are *pwii-* to one another. *iir pw.* they are s. *pwiipwii chék* lineage mates of same generation and sex; *pw. emén chék ineer* s. by the same mother; *pw.*

winipwúnú s. by marriage (persons whose spouses are *pwii-* to one another); *pw. winisam* s. by fathers (s. by the same father, persons of same sex whose fathers were lineage mates). va. behave or treat someone as a sibling of same sex; be a friend to someone. *wúpwe pw. een* I will treat you as a s. *sipwe pw. ffengeen* we shall treat one another as s.

pwiipwiingngaw (3b) See *pwiipwi, ngngaw.* [Used with *ngeni*.] vi. be a bad sibling of same sex.

pwiipwiiyééch (2: *-yéchchú-*) See *pwiipwi, ééch.* [Used with *ngeni*.] vi. be a good sibling of same sex.

pwiich₁ (3: *pwichcha-*) See *pwii-₁, chche-₂.* nu. (T3) familiar, companion. *pwichchan* his familiar; (jestingly) his close friend. *pwichchen pachaaw* pilot fish; *pwichchen soomá* animal, fish, or bird familiar of a ghost. Syn. *chénaa-*. Cf. *chiyen.*

pwiich₂ (2) See *pwich₁.* n. (T2) warmth, heat. *pwichin* his being warm, his w. Cf. *pwichikkar.*

pwiich₃ (2) See *pwich₂.* nu. (T2) poison. *pwichin eey iik* the p. of this fish.

pwise (1) PWISEE. Tb3. [Not used in pos. const.] nu. (T1) excrement, feces. *imwen pw.* outhouse, toilet. Syn. *ómwu, páá.*

pwisika (1) PWISIKAA. nu. (T1) chicken. *emén pw.* one c. *pwisikaan Chuuk* Trukese c. *sáfeen pw.* medicine used to counteract the effects of sorcery called *rongen chukó* (syn. *sáfeen chukó*). Syn. *chukó, pwuchó.*

pwisin (2) PWISI₁. [Occurs, as shown, only with rel. suf. -n₂.] Var. *pwúsin.* vr. oneself, personally, in person; by itself; naturally, of its own accord. *aa pw. máárítá* it grew up by itself; *aa pw. fisitá ewe semwmwen* the sickness came of its own accord. *aa pw. fórusi* he hanged himself (refl.); *wúpwe pw. nniiyey* I shall kill myself (refl.). *pw. fénúwey* my own land (my land by inheritance rather than by purchase); *pw. neyiy* my very own child; *pw. ngaang* I myself, I in person. Syn. *pwpwúkún.*

pwisipwis (db; 2) PWISI₂. vi. move one's lips without making any noise; barely move.

pwin₁ (2) PWINI₃. vi. be slipped on or off (as clothing into which one inserts

pwin₂

one's body). With dir. suf.: *pwininong* be slipped on; *pwininó* be slipped off; *pwinitiw* be slipped down; *pwiniwu* be slipped out of. Cf. *pwiniti*.

pwin₂ (2) See *pwiin₃*. vi. become night. Ant. *rááng*. Cf. *pwiniiti*.

-pwin (2) PWIN₄. [In cpds. only.] unsp. (u.m.) See *kkipwin*.

pwini See *pwiin₃*. vo. (T2) spend (a night). *sipwe pw. epwin* we shall s. one night.

pwiniiti See *pwin₂*, *-iti*. vo. (T2) become night upon.

pwininong See *pwin₁*.

pwininó See *pwin₁*.

pwinipwin (db; 2) See *pwin₁*. n. (T2) 1. thing taken off and given to someone one meets on the path. 2. a gift of food received in a chance encounter with someone on the road. *pwinipwinin* his gift.

pwinipwiniiy See *pwinipwin*, *-i-₂*. vo. (T5) give a gift of food to (someone) in a chance encounter on the road.

pwinitaanong See *pwiniti*.

pwinitaanó See *pwiniti*.

pwinitaawu See *pwiniti*.

pwinitáátiw See *pwiniti*.

pwiniti See *pwin₁*, *-iti*. vo. (T2) slip (something) on or off (e.g., clothes). With dir. suf.: *pwinitaanong* slip on over one's head (of clothing); *pwinitaanó*, *pwinitóónó* slip off; *pwinitaawu* slip off over one's head (of clothing); *pwinitáátiw* slip down (one's clothing) to undress.

pwinitiw See *pwin₁*.

pwinitóónó See *pwiniti*.

pwiniwochooch (3) See *pwiin₃*, *wochooch*. nu. (T3) odd numbered nights of the moon ("devouring nights"). [Such nights are unlucky and best for making sorcery.]

pwiniwu See *pwin₁*.

pwiniyang (3b) See *pwin₁*, *-ang*. nu. (T3) a hold on another's arms (in fighting).

-pwir (2) PWIRI. [In cpds. only.] unsp. be quick, speedy. See *epwiri*, *ngngúpwir*.

pwich₁ (2) PWICHI₁. vi., adj. (be) hot, warm. Dis. *pwichipwich* (db) be ardent, strong in motivation, very hot. *aa pwichipwich aan sowuneng* he has become an ardent Christian.

pwich₂ (2) PWICHI₂. vi., adj. (be) poisonous; be poisoned. *kepwee pw. reen na mwéngé* you will be p. by that food.

pwichikkar (3b) See *pwich₁*, *kkar*. vi. be burning hot; have a fever. ni. (T3) fever; heat. *pwichikkaran* his f. *aa wúri pwichikkaren ewe roong* the heat of the spell has attacked him. Cf. *pwiich₂*.

pwichipwich Dis. of *pwich₁*.

pwichipwichitá (db; 1) See *pwich₁*, *-tá*. vi. be overheated.

pwichcheyich (db; 3) See *pwiich₁*. vi. (dis.) have a familiar.

pwitur Obs. nu. a type of traditional women's skirt or *chééyitúr*.

pwo (1) PWOO₁. vi., adj. (be) swollen. Dis. *pwoopwo* (db) swollen; pregnant (with child). With dir. suf.: *pwoonó* be inflated, blown up, swollen out. Cf. *pwoo*.

-pwo (1) PWOO₂. [In cpds. only.] adj. (u.m.) See *áttikipwo*, *áttipwoow*, *ettikipwo*, *ettikipwoow*, *takiripwo*.

pwoo- (1) PWOO₃. ni. (T1) odor, smell. Dis. *pwoopwo* (db). *pwoon* his o. *pwoon ngaas* the o. of perfumed oil.

pwoo (1) See *pwo*. nu. (T1) swelling (of any kind). *pwoon* his s.

pwoos₁ (2) PWOSSU₁. (Eng.) nu. (T2) boss, overseer. *pwossun angaang* work b.

pwoos₂ (2) PWOSSU₂. (Eng.) nu. (T2) boss on a pier or boat for making fast a line. *pwossun eey waa* b. of this boat.

pwoosenisen (2) See *pwoo-*, *senisen*. nu. (T2) smell of tinea or ringworm.

pwoosto (1) PWOOSTOO. (Jap. *posuto*) Var. *posto*. nu. (T1) post office. *seyin pw.* mail boat, mail plane.

pwookuungo Var. of *pwookuuwo*.

pwookuuwo (1) PWOOKUUWOO. (Jap. *bookuugoo*) Var. *pwookuungo*. nu. (T1) cave. *eew pw.* one c. *aan pw.* his c.

pwoomaaw (3) See *pwoo-*, *maaw*. vi. smell strong (as body odor).

pwoomach (3) See *pwoo-*, *mach*. vi., adj. stink, smell rotten. *pwoomachen eey iik* the stinking of this fish.

pwoomw (3) PWOMWA₁. n. (T3) motions of a thing; gesture of the body. Dis. *pwopwpwoomw* (ds). *pwomwan* his gesture, its motions. *pwomwen ama* what one does with a hammer, the motions of a hammer (i.e. pounding).

pwoomwas (3) See *pwoo-*, *mwas*. Tbl. vi. have the odor of unwashed genitals, stink. Dis. *pwoomwasamwas* (db).

pwoomwasamwas Dis. of *pwoomwas*.

Trukese-English   **pwomweni**

pwoomwáánennap (3) See *pwoo-, mwáán*$_1$, *nap.* nu. (T3) bad body odor ("old-man-smell").

Pwoonan (Eng.) nu. (loc.) Poland.

pwooniik (3a) See *pwoo-, iik.* nu. (T3) 1. fishy smell. 2. noddy tern. Syn. *nayiré.*

Pwoonopey Var. of *Pwonape.*

pwoonow (2) See *pwoo-, nowu-*$_2$. nu. (T2) very bad smell, stink, stench. *pwoonowun* stench of.

pwoonó See *pwo.*

pwoong (2: *pwongu-, -pwong, -pwung*) PWONGU, PWUNGU. [Occurring mostly in cpds.] nu. (T2) night. *pwongun aara* (v. phr. and n. phr.) time of the first (?) waning (of the moon); *pwongun étú* (v. phr. and n. phr.) be full, time when full (of the moon). Syn. *pwiin*$_3$.

pwoongarangar (db; 3b) See *pwoo-, ngar.* nu. (T3) sweet smell; smell of sweetness (in food).

pwoopw (2) PWOPWU. n. (T2), suf. (cc.) 1. base, basis, trunk (of tree). *epwopw, rúwépwopw, wúnúpwopw, fépwopw, nimepwopw, wonopwopw, fúúwpopw, wanúpwopw, ttiwepwopw, engoon pwopwun* one,...ten b. *pwopwun* its b. 2. source, beginning, origin; reason, cause, final cause or purpose. *pwopwun* his origin, source, ancestor; its cause. *pwopwun ásápwáán* wind direction; *pwopwun ewe fóós* source of what was said; *pwopwun kkónik* spring (of water); *pwopwun mmak* initial letter; *pwopwun aan we mmak* reason for his writing.

pwoopwo$_1$ Dis. of *pwo.*

pwoopwo$_2$ (1) See *pwoo-.* nu. (T1) odor, smell. *pwoon* his o.; o. of.

pwoopwutak (3) See *pwoo-, pwutak.* nu. (T3) bad smell. vi. smell bad. Syn. *pwongngaw.*

pwoor (2) PWOORU. (Jap. *booru*) nu. (T2) ball (in baseball). *eféw pw.* one b. *newún pw.* his b.

pwooch (3) PWOCHA. nu. (T3) scales or armor plating of a turtle's shell or a crocodile's back. *pwochen wiin* turtle's shell. *eché pwochen wiin* one plate of turtle shell.

pwoochú (1) PWOOCHÚÚ. (Jap. *boozu*) nu. (T1) closely clipped hair, crew cut. vi. have closely cropped hair.

pwootakatopi (1) PWOOTAKATOPII. (Jap. *bootakatobi*) vi. do the pole vault.

pwootong (2) See *pwoo-, tong.* nu. (T2) pungent smell.

pwootteneng (2) See *pwoo-, tteneng.* Tb1. Var. *pwotteneng.* vi. have the odor of genitals.

pwoow (2) PWOWU. Var. *pwóów.* nu. (T2) fishing pole. *efóch pw.* one f. p. *pwowun Chuuk* Trukese f. p.

pwoowusuus (2) See *pwoo-, wusuus.* nu. (T2) pungent smell (as of a goat), strong smell (as of old preserved breadfruit).

pwoowútek See *pwoo-, wútek.* vi. smell sweet, smell nice. [Preferred when siblings of opposite sex or parent and child of opposite sex are both within hearing.] Syn. *pwokkus.*

pwooyéech (2) See *pwoo-, ééch.* Tb3. nu. (T2) nice smell. vi., adj. (be) nice smelling, fragrant.

pwos (2) PWOSU. Var. *pwpwos.* vi., adj. be homesick, suffer nostalgia; have longing; be lonely.

pwosiiti See *pwos, -iti.* vo. (T2) be homesick for, miss very much, have longing for, be nostalgic for. *pw. fénú* be homesick; *sipwe pwosiituk* we will miss you.

pwossening (3) See *pwoo-, -ssening.* nu. (T3) moldy smell; earthy smell. vi. smell moldy.

pwokita- (3) PWOKITA. ni. (loc.; T3) because of, due to. *pwokitan* because of him. *pwokiten aan aa mmang* because of his being late. Cf. *pwe*$_2$, *pwú, pwún*$_2$, *pwúnún.*

pwokuuku (1) PWOKUUKUU. Var. *pwekiiki.* nu. (T1) corner (inside, as in a house). *pwokuukuun iimw* c. of (inside) a house.

pwokkéch See *pwoo-, kkéch.* Tb. vi. stink, smell bad.

pwokkus (2) See *pwoo-, -kkus.* Tb3. vi. smell sweet, smell nice (as of perfume). Syn. *pwoowútek.* n. (T2) sweet smell, aroma. *pwokkusun* its s. s.

pwomweey See *pwoomw, -e-*$_2$. vo. (T6b) gesture with, perform the motions with; go through the motions of. *aa pw. ewe angaang* he went through the motions of the work.

pwomweni See *pwoomw, -ni-.* vo. (T6a) demonstrate the motions of, act out, imitate the motions of; practice. *kepwe pw. aar fiyuuw* you shall act out their fight.

pwomwééch (2) See *pwoomw, ééch.* vi. execute the motions of something skillfully, be skillful in performing.

pwomwongngaw (3b) See *pwoomw, ngngaw.* vi. execute the motions of something badly; be unskillful in performing.

pwomwpwomw₁ (db; 2) PWOMWU₁. nu. (T2) passion fruit (*Passiflora foetida*). *pwomwpwomwun Chuuk* Trukese p. f.

pwomwpwomw₂ (db; 2, 3) PWOMWU₂, PWOMWA₂. nu. (T2, T3) diesel-powered fishing boat or small craft. *pwomwpwomwen Chuuk, pwomwpwomwun Chuuk* Trukese f. b.

pwon₁ vi. be enough. Syn. *ku.*

pwon₂ (3a) PWONA. vi. disappear. With dir. suf.: *pwononó.*

Pwonape (Eng.) Var. *Pwoonopey.* nu. (loc.) Ponape Island. Syn. *Fóónupi.*

pwonen (2) PWONENI. (Eng.) nu. (T2) bowline. *eew pw.* one b. *pwonenin sáán* b. of heavy rope.

pwonis (2) PWONISI. (Eng.) nu. (T2) police. *pwonisin Chuuk* Trukese p. *chóón pw.* policeman. Cf. *prisman.*

pwonosáp (4) nu. (T2) simple spear made of mangrove wood. Syn. *eyitewóón.*

Pwonowót nu. (loc.) Puluwat Island and Atoll. [Known locally as *Pwolowat*.]

Pwonnap nu. (loc.) Pulap Island and Atoll. [Known locally as *Pwollap*.]

pwonneng (2?) See *pwoo-, nneng.* Tb1. nu. (T2?) bad smell, stench (of women's genitals only).

pwongusoopach (3) See *pwoong, soopach.* vi. be waning (of the moon). [Nights when husband and wife sleep together.] nu. (T3) time of waning.

pwongunummach (3) See *pwoong, mmach.* vi. be waxing (of the moon). nu. (T3) time of waxing ("nights of eloping"). Syn. *pwongunúúr.*

pwongunúúr (2) See *pwoong, wúr.* vi. be waxing (of the moon). nu. (T3) time of waxing. Syn. *pwongunummach.* Cf. *wúrúúrúnó, wúrúúrúnúpwin.*

pwongngaw (3) See *pwoo-, ngngaw.* Tb3. nu. (T3) bad smell. vi. smell bad. Syn. *pwoopwutak.*

pwopw (2) See *pwoopw.* [Commonly with dir. suf.] vi. be begun, originated. With dir. suf.: *pwopwutá.* Syn. *pwún₁.*

pwopwuuw See *pwoopw, -u-.* vo. (T5) begin, start up, originate. With dir. suf.: *pwopwuuwotá.*

pwopwuuwotá See *pwopwuuw.*

pwopwunnap (3a) See *pwoopw, nap.* nu. (T3) trunk or base of a large tree.

pwopwutá See *pwopw.*

pwopwutááni See *pwopw, -tá, -ni-.* vo. (T4) undertake, start, begin, set out upon, commence.

pwotteneng Var. of *pwootteneng.*

pwow (2) See *pwoow.* vi. fish with a pole and small hook and line, do pole fishing. [Done in fishing for *fokunun, pwowunen, awopwo, peniwa, taak, wéér, inipar, sékúrúpi, néwúnurunó.*]

pwowuuw See *pwow, -u-.* vo. (T5) catch (a fish) with a fishing pole.

pwowunen (2) nu. (T2) a species of fish. *pwowunenin* f. of (a given region).

pwoyin (Eng.) nu. decimal point.

pwó (1) PWÓÓ. vi., adj. (be) pampered. Syn. *fón.* Cf. *chengi-, chen.*

pwóór (4) PWÓRO₁. nu. (T2) box, chest, crate. *eew pw.* one b.; *epwór pwórun* one b. of (something). *aan pw.* his b.; *pwórun* b. of (something as contents). ni. (T2) coffin. *pwórun* his c. (to be buried in). suf. (cc.) box or crate (of something). *epwór, rúwépwór, wúnúpwór, fépwór, nimepwór, wonopwór, fúúpwór, wanúpwór, ttiwepwór, engoon pwórun* one,...ten b. (of something).

pwóóch (2) PWÓCHCHU. (Eng. *pot*) nu. (T2) can, tin can (with its contents). *eew pw.* one c. *pwóchchun iik* c. of fish; *pwóchchun kkowu* c. of corned beef. *péén pw.* empty c. vi. (N.) be cooked in a pan or pot. Syn. *eyinepwóch.*

pwóów (4) PWÓWO. Var. *pwoow.* nu. (T2) fishing pole. *efóch pw.* one f. p. *aan pw.* his f. p. *pwówun Chuuk* Trukese f. p.

pwónów (4) PWÓNÓW. nu. (T2) a species of reef fish (Elbert: tiny, bright blue, with yellow underbody). *pwónówun* f. of (a given region). Cf. *ópwónów.*

pwór (4) PWÓRO₂. vi., adj. made curved, bent (by human action). Dis. *pwórópwór* (db). With dir. suf.: *pwórutiw* be bowed or bent down (as the head). Cf. *pwpwór.* See also *wúrépworopwor.*

pwóreey See *pwór*, *-e-₂*. vo. (T6b) bend, curve. Dis. *pwórópwóreey* (db). With dir. suf.: *pwórópwóreeyetiw* (refl.) b. oneself down.

pwóreyiti See *pwór*, *-iti*. vo. (T2) be bent or curved towards.

pwóróówus (3) PWÓRÓÓWUSA. Var. *pwaraawus*. nu. (T3) communication, news, announcement, information, something worth hearing; saying, proverb. *eew chék pw.* just one announcement; *óóch pw.* another kind of talk (i.e., disguised talk). *aan pw.* what he has to say; *pwóróówusan* news or talk about him; the news he is bringing. *pwóróówusen fénú* information about the land; *pwóróówusen nóómw* legend, history, story of old times, folklore. *pwóróówusen nóón manaw* story of one's life, life history. *pwóróósey seni Wééné* news I am bringing from Wééné. *pw. ffengen* conversation. vi. converse. *pw. ffengen c.* together, exchange information; conversation.

pwórópwór₁ Dis. of *pwór*.

pwórópwór₂ (db; 2) See *pwóór*. vi. be boxed, crated.

pwórópwóreey Dis. of *pwóreey*.

pwórópwóreeyetiw See *pwóreey*.

pwóruni See *pwóór*, *-ni-*. vo. (T5) put in a box or chest, crate.

pwórutiw See *pwór*.

pwóchéwú nu. pendant made of turtle-shell discs. Cf. *pwooch*.

pwóchchuni See *pwóóch*, *-ni-*. N. vo. (T5) cook in a pot or pan. Syn. *eyinepwocha, kochchuuni, nnapeeni*.

pwótow (2) PWÓTOWU. nu. (T2) general term for a basket, satchel, carrying case, suitcase (any container of cloth or basketry designed for carrying things). *eew pw.* one b. *aan pw.* his b. *pw. Chuuk, pwótowun Chuuk* Trukese b.

pwu-₁ (1: *-pw*) PWU₁. [In cpds. only.] unsp. blow, wind. See *ásupwu, kkasupw, pwukos₁, pwuupw*. Cf. *pwu₂*.

pwu-₂ (2) PWU₂. [In cpds. only.] unsp. bump, collide. See *opwpwuffengen, opwpwuri, opwuroppi, ópwpwura, pwur₁, pwuroffengen*.

pwu₁ (1) PWUU₁. vi. flow (of fresh or salt water). Dis. *pwuupwu* (db). With dir. suf.: *pwuunong, pwuunó, pwuutá, pwuuto, pwuutiw, pwuuwu*.

pwu₂ (1) PWUU₂. vi., adj. (be) blown (as a trumpet).

pwu₃ (1) PWUU₃. vi. place one's foot. *wúwa pwu wóón* I put my foot on it. With dir. suf.: *pwuutiw. wúwa pwuutiw wóón pwise* I stepped on some excrement.

-pwu [In cpds. only.] unsp. (u.m.) See *tinepwu*.

pwuu (3) PWUWA. ni. (T3) umbilical cord, navel. *pwuwan* his u. c. *aa ttún pwuwan* his u. c. has dropped off.

pwuus (3) PWUUSA. (Eng.) vi. be pushed.

pwuuseey See *pwuus*, *-e-₂*. vo. (T6b) push. Dis. *pwupwpwuuseey* (ds).

pwuusefáán (2) See *pwu₁, sefáán*. vi. flow again, flow once more (of a stream that had dried up).

pwuuk (3) PWUUKA. nu. (T3) judo. *pwuuken j.* of (a given style). vi. grab hold of someone (in wrestling).

pwuumw (3) PWUUMWA. (Eng.) nu. boom. *pw. neef* boom crutch, boom gallows. Cf. *sipwpwumw*.

pwuun₁ (Eng. *full*) nu. full house (in poker). *eew pw.* one f. h. *neyi pw.* my f. h.

pwuun₂ (3) PWUUNA. nu. (T3) <Elbert> Caproid fish. *pwuunen f.* of (a given region).

pwuunong See *pwu₁*.

pwuunó See *pwu₁*.

pwuupw (db; 2: *pwupwu-, pwú-, -pw*) See *pwu-₁*. nu. (T2) 1. <Elbert> a species of trigger fish. *emén pw.* one t. f. *pwupwun t.* f. of (a given region). Cf. *pwúnúúnú*. 2. (in traditional navigation) the constellation Crux (Southern Cross, under Christian influence popularly known as *iráápenges*). Cf. *táánupw, tupwunupw, wenewenenupw*.

pwuupwu₁ (db; 1) See *pwu₁*. vi. flow (of a stream).

pwuupwu₂ (db; 1) See *pwu₃*. nu. (T1) something to place the foot on; step, tread, treadle, pedal. *mwesinen pw.* sewing machine with treadle; *pwuupwuun mwesin* treadle (on sewing machine); *pwuupwuun oroken* organ pedal; *pwuupwuun paasiken* bicycle pedal.

pwuupwu₃ (db; 1) vi. (dis.) engage in a kind of fishing. [It is done only by women, with hand nets, in sea grass (*achékken*) to catch *peniwa, awanger*, *feyinisi, awopwo, nitikitik, pwowunen, maramwen, pwaaw₃.*]

pwuupwu₄ (db; 1) nu. (T1) variety of banana.

pwuur₁ (3) PWURA₂. nu. (T3) <Elbert> ilangilang tree (*Cananga odorata*). *pwuren* t. o (a given region). Syn. *pwanang₁*.

pwuur₂ (3) PWURA₃. nu. (T3) anchoring or mooring stake carried by a canoe. *pwuren eey waa* this canoe's a. s.

pwuuraatiw See *pwuuri₁, pwuuri₂*.

pwuuráátiw See *pwuuri₁, pwuuri₂*.

pwuuri₁ See *pwu₃, -ri-*. vo. (T4) step on, tread on, run over (of car). With dir. suf.: *pwuuráátiw* (F.), *pwuuraatiw* (N.) tread down on, step down on.

pwuuri₂ See *pwu₁, -ri-*. vo. (T4) carry or wash (something) along (by the flow of a stream). With dir. suf.: *pwuuraatiw* (N.), *pwuuráátiw* (F.) wash down, sweep down (in stream). *aa pwuuriyeyitiw ewe chénúpwuupwu* the stream swept me down.

pwuutá See *pwu₁*.

pwuutiw See *pwu₁, pwu₃*.

pwuuto See *pwu₁*.

pwuuwow See *pwu₁*.

pwuuwu See *pwu₁*.

pwuka- (3a) PWUKA. Var. *pwpwuk*. nr. (T3) knot. *pwuken sinifé* weaver's knot used to tie hibiscus threads together into a continuous warp in weaving; *pwuken wuuch* weaver's knot used to join banana threads into a continuous warp.

pwukeey See *pwuka-, -e-₂*. vo. (T6b) tie (something) in a knot.

pwuker (2) PWUKERI. nu. (T2) 1. a sedge (*Fimbristylis polymorpha* or *Fimbristylis cymosa*). [Used for stomach disorders. Classed as a kind of *fetin* (grass).] *pwukerin Chuuk* Trukese s. Syn. *enenniké*. 2. a plant (*Chrysopogon aciculatus*).

pwukerimwéch (2) See *pwuker, mwéch*. N. nu. (T2) 1. a grass (*Eleusine indica*). [It is used for stomach disorders, especially vomiting blood.] Syn. *tipweek*. 2. a plant (*Paspalum longifolium*).

pwukos₁ (3) See *pwu-₁, koos*. nu. (T3) meaning uncertain, but apparently referring to the making of sound in the mouth ("voice-wind"). *niin mesen pw.* lower incisor teeth.

Pwukos₂ [Apparently related to Wol. *pwugota* meaning "family, family estate, village." See also the place on Wééné named *Neepwukos*.] nu. (loc.) a clan name.

pwukopwuk (db; 3) See *pwuka-*. vi. be knotted, tied in a knot. Cf. *pwpwuk, pwukeey*. nu. (T3) knot. *pwukopwuken ósoomá* an overhand knot in a bight (single bow knot) used in tying an offering (*ósór*) with a young coconut leaf.

pwukkáy (2, 3) See *pwu₁, kkáy*. vi. flow quickly.

pwuna₁ (1) PWUNAA₁. nu. (T1) giant swamp taro (*Cyrtosperma chamissonis*). [Corms are used as food; children's medicine is made from fruit and flower stalk.] *eew pw.* one t. plant, corm, or bed. *pwunaan Chuuk* Trukese t.

pwuna₂ (1) PWUNAA₂. nu. (T1) a species of unicorn fish (*Naso lituratus* Schneider). *emén pw.* one u. f. *pwunaan Chuuk* u. f. of Truk.

pwunaas (3) See *pwu-₂, naa-, -s₁*. vi. be drunk, intoxicated. Syn. *torongki*. Cf. *pwunaasa*.

pwunech nu. honey; (N.) bee. *chénún pw.* liquid honey; *sókunnun pw.* comb honey ("bee eggs"). Cf. *achi, chunen*.

pwunopwun (db; 3b) See *pwpwun₁*. nu. (T3) a tree (*Xylocarpus granatum*). [It has large cannon-ball fruit, tiny white flowers, and grows among the mangrove trees. Its wood ignites quickly, whether freshly cut or seasoned, and hence its name.] *pwunopwunen* t. of (a given region).

pwunu- (2) PWUNU. [In cpds. only.] unsp. affect others. See *pwunungngaw, pwunupwutak, pwunuyééch*. Cf. *pwún₁*.

pwunungngaw (3) See *pwunu-, ngngaw*. Tb3. vi. affect another adversely. Syn. *pwunupwutak*.

pwunupwutak (3) See *pwunu-, pwutak*. vi. affect another adversely; do something that results in injury, misfortune, or loss to another (e.g., send a person on an errand in which he gets hurt or borrow and lose someone's property). Syn. *pwunungngaw*.

pwunuyééch (2: *-yéchchú-*) See *pwunu-, ééch*. vi. affect another favorably; do something from which another benefits.

pwupwuchón (4) See *pwuupw, chón.* nu. (T2) <Elbert> species of trigger fish.

pwupwuyééch (2) See *pwuupw, ééch.* nu. (T2) <Elbert> species of trigger fish.

pwupwpwuuseey Dis. of *pwuuseey.*

pwupwpwuchéér Dis. of *pwuchéér.*

pwur₁ (3) See *pwu-₂, -r₂.* vi. be bumped, stubbed; trip.

pwur₂ (3) PWURA₄. vi., adj. (be) enough; (be) plump, well filled out. *meyi pw. inisin átánaan* that fellow is plump.

pwur₃ (3) PWURA₅. vi. go bad, get spoiled (of *kkón* and *épwét*). *aa pw. eey kkón* this breadfruit pudding has gotten spoiled. *pwata iyeey pwuren eey épwét* why has this fermented breadfruit gone bad?

pwura See *pwuur₂.* vo. (T3) plant (something). With dir. suf.: *pwuraatiw.* Syn. *pwureey.*

pwuraatiw See *pwura.*

pwureey See *pwuur₂, -e-₂.* vo. (T6b) 1. plant (something). Syn. *pwura.* 2. anchor or moor (a boat) with a stake. Syn. *pwureni.*

pwurek (2) PWUREKI. nu. (T2) species of sea cucumber. [Edible, it is found in *achékken* sea grass.] *emwú pw.* one s. c. *pwurekin* s. c. of (a given region).

pwureni See *pwuur₂, -ni-.* vo. (T6a) anchor or moor (a boat) with a stake. Syn. *pwureey.*

pwurey (2) PWUREYI. nu. (T2) a small mullet. *pwureyin* m. of (a given region).

pwuroffengen (2) See *pwur₁, ffengen.* vi. be bumped together, be in collision.

pwuropwur (db; 3a) See *pwpwur₂.* nu. (T3) bubble, foam, suds. vi. (dis.) be boiling, foaming.

pwuch (3) PWUCHA. vi., adj. (be) crazy; beset, driven to distraction. [The preferred word in the presence of brother and sister, father and daughter, and mother and son.] Dis. *pwuchopwuch* (db). Syn. *wumwes.*

pwuchéér (2) See *pwuch, ér₂.* vi. call or cry out *wééw* in distress or for help. Dis. *pwupwpwuchéér* (ds).

pwuchopwuch Dis. of *pwuch.*

pwuchó (1) PWUCHÓÓ. nu. (T1) chicken. *pwuchóón Chuuk* Trukese c. Syn. *chukó.*

-pwut (2) PWUTU. [In cpds. only.] unsp. (u.m.) See *itipwut.*

pwuta- (3) PWUTA. [In cpds. only.] unsp. bad, of negative value. See *chóópwut, kinipwut, opwut, pwutak, sinipwut.*

pwutak (3) See *pwuta-, -k₂.* vi., adj. (be) bad, improper, unsuitable, inappropriate. [Preferred traditionally when siblings of opposite sex or parent and child of opposite sex were both within hearing.] Syn. *ngngaw.*

pwú PWÚ. F. [It is embedded in the phrase following it, which it initiates, being preceded by a brief pause.] Var. *pwún₂, pwúún₃, pwúyi.* conj. links what follows as the cause or reason for what went before; because, for, as, since; (before a future aspect marker) so that, in order that. *wúse fééri pwú wúse mwechen* I did not do it because I did not want to. *aa etto pwú epwe mééni wúnúman suupwa* he has come in order to buy cigarettes for himself. Syn. *pwe₂, pwé₂, pwúnún.*

pwúúk (2) PWÚKÚ. n. (T2) sprout. *pwúkún* its s. Cf. *nipwpwúk, nipwúkúpwúk, pwúk, pwúkú.*

pwúún₁ (2: *pwúnnú-, -pwún*) PWÚNNÚ. F. Var. *pwpwún₂.* vi. break, be broken (of hard or brittle objects). Cf. *mmék, mwmwú.* ni. (T2) fracture (of something). *pwúnnún chúún* f. of his bone. suf. (cc.) fragment, broken piece. *epwún, rúwépwún, wúnúpwún, fépwún, nimepwún, wonopwún, fúúpwún, wanúpwún, ttiwepwún, engoon pwúnnún* one,...ten fragments. *epwpwún sóók* one f. of chalk.

pwúún₂ (2) PWÚNÚ₃. n. (T2) a borrowed thing. *pwúnún* something b. by him.

pwúún₃ Var. of *pwú.*

pwúúng (2) PWÚNGÚ₂. n. (T2) what is agreed on as right, proper, correct, or just; what is agreed on as the right, proper, or appropriate course of action; accord, treaty, agreement. *pwúngún* (with reference to something said) the right of it; (with reference to a person) what is right in his view, what is right for him; *aar pw.* their treaty or agreement. *ina pwúngún* that is the right of it. *pwúngún fénú* what the people of a district or island are in accord about; common goals or objectives for a district or island; what is right or just for the district.

pwúsin Var. of *pwisin*.
pwúk (2) See *pwúúk*. Var. *pwpwúk*. vi. sprout, be sprouted (of a seed).
pwúkú (3: *pwúkúwa-*) See *pwúk*, *-wa-*. n. (T3) node, joint (of body, bamboo, sugarcane); knot (in wood); knee; peninsula. *pwúkúwan* his j., his knee. *pwúkúwen pecheey* my knee or ankle; *pwúkúwen peyiy* my elbow or wrist; *pwúkúwen iich* bamboo node. Syn. *kurupw₁*.
-pwúkú (1) PWÚKÚÚ. suf. (cc.) unit of a hundred. *ipwúkú, rúwépwúkú, wúnúpwúkú, fépwúkú, nimepwúkú, wonopwúkú, fúúpwúkú, wanúpwúkú, ttiwepwúkú* one,...nine h. *eyipwúkúún* one hundredth one.
pwúkúwékú (db; 3) See *pwúkú*. vi. be full of nodes, joints, knots.
pwúkúwépwpwún (2) See *pwúkú, pwpwún*. nu. (T2) house height (*chimwenúúren iimw*) such that one must walk on one's knees to clear under the crossbeam ("dirty knees").
pwún₁ (2) PWÚNÚ₂. vi. be begun, originate. With dir. suf.: *pwúnútá*. Syn. *pwopw*.
pwún₂ F. of *pwú*.
pwúnúúnú (1) See *pwuupw, núúnú₂*. nu. (T1) large trigger fish (*Odonus niger*). Syn. *ngúúngú₁*.
pwúnúúw See *pwún₁, -ú-*. vo. (T5) begin, commence.
pwúnúseni (2) See *pwún₁, seni₂*. vo. (T2) originate from.
Pwúnúsuuk nu. (loc.) Pulusuk Island and Atoll. Syn. *Suuk, Sowuk*.
pwúnún See *pwún₁*. [Occurs, as shown, only with 3rd sg. pos. suf. *-n₁* or the rel. suf. *-n₂*.] ni. (T2) cause, reason. *ina pw.* that is the reason. Syn. *pwoopw*. conj. links what follows as the cause or reason for what went before; because, for, as, since. *wúsapw nó pw. wúse mwechen* I shall not go because I do not want to. Syn. *pwe₁, pwé₁, pwú, pwún₂, pwúyi*.
pwúnúngngaw (3b) See *pwúún₂, ngngaw*. vi. borrow badly, misborrow (as when losing something one has borrowed).
pwúnúpwún Dis. of *pwpwún₁*.
pwúnútá (1) See *pwún₁, -tá*. n. (T1) beginning, source, origin. *pwúnútáán* his origins. vi. be begun, originate.
pwúnúwa- (3) PWÚNÚWA. [Probably from *pwúún₂, -wa-*. Cf. Wol. *pwpwúlúú*.]

ni. (T3) spouse, husband, wife; *pwii-* of one's spouse; spouse of one's *pwii-*. *pwúnúwan* his s.
pwúnúweni See *pwúnúwa-, -ni-*. vo. (T6a) acquire as a spouse, marry. *pwúnúwenuk* or *pwúnúwonuk* marry you (sg.). Cf. *pwúpwpwúnú*.
pwúnúyééch (2: *-yéchchú-*) See *pwúún₂, ééch*. vi. borrow well, be a good borrower.
pwúnnúúw See *pwúún₁, -ú-*. vo. (T5) break. Dis. *pwúpwpwúnnúúw* (ds).
pwúng₁ (2) See *pwúúng*. vi. be correct, right, righteous, just, proper; be the correct thing to do, be the right course. *meyi pw. reemw* you are right. Cf. *pwúngúpwúng*.
pwúng₂ Rmn. of *púng₂*.
pwúngú- (2) PWÚNGÚ₁. [In cpds. only.] unsp. (u.m.) See *épwúngúpwúng*.
pwúngúúw See *pwúúng, -ú-*. vo. (T5) agree to (something) as a proper goal of action.
pwúngúngngaw (3b) See *pwúúng, ngngaw*. nu. (T3) incorrect view of what is right. vi. be incorrect according to the rules.
pwúngúpwúng (db; 2) See *pwúúng*. vi. determine what is right, correct, proper; determine the right course of action; discuss. *pwúngúpwúng ffengen* come to an agreement about the proper thing to do.
pwúngúpwúngúúw See *pwúngúpwúng, -ú-*. vo. (T5) determine the right course of action in regard to (something).
pwúngúch (2) PWÚNGÚCHÚ. nu. (T2) variety of banana. *pwúngúchún* b. of (a given region).
pwúngúyééch (2: *-yéchchú-*) See *pwúúng, ééch*. nu. (T2) a good view of what is right or proper to do. vi. 1. be right or correct according to the rules. 2. be treated justly or properly. *epwe pw. eey fénú* this island will be treated properly.
pwúpwpwún Dis. of *pwpwún₁*.
pwúpwpwúnú (ds; 3) See *pwúnúwa-*. vi. (dis.) be married. va. treat (someone) as a spouse; marry. Cf. *pwúnúweni*.
pwúpwpwúnnúúw Dis. of *pwúnnúúw*.
pwúrúr (2) PWÚRÚRÚ. vi. roar (of a motor). Dis. *pwúrúrrúr* (db). *pwata ina pwúrúrún wóómw na?* why that roaring of your boat?

pwúrúrrúr Dis. of *pwúrúr*.
pwúyi F. of *pwú*.
pwpwa- (dc; 3) PWPWA. ni. (T3) gill arch (of fish). *pwpwan* its g. a. *pwpwen iik* g. a. of a fish. Cf. *apwapw, sánápwapw*.
pwpwaaw (dc; 2) PWPWAAWÚ. ni. (T2), suf. (cc.) cigarette or cigar of traditional home-made type. *epwpwaaw, rúwépwpwaaw, wúnúpwpwaaw, fépwpwaaw, nimepwpwaaw, wonopwpwaaw, fúpwpwaaw, wanúpwpwaaw, ttiwepwpwaaw, engoon pwpwaawún* one,...ten home-made c. vi. roll tobacco leaves in banana leaf to make a traditional cigarette or cigar.
pwpwaawúni See *pwpwaaw, -ni-*. vo. (T5) roll (a cigarette or cigar).
pwpwas (dc; 3) See *pwas*. vi., adj. 1. (be) dry, light (in weight); dried out (as the last stage of a ripe coconut after it has fallen from the tree). 2. (of a coconut) be short, not doubled. Syn. *chchow*.
pwpwamw (3) PWPWAMWA. (Eng.) nu. (T3) pump.
pwpwamweey See *pwpwamw, -e-$_2$*. vo. (T6b) pump. Dis. *pwapwpwamweey* (dc).
-pwpwang (dc; 3) See *pwaang*. Tb3. adj. emptily. Syn. *-ngngat*. See *wosupwpwang*.
pwpwach (dc; 3) PWACHA. vi., adj. (be) loose, slack, wrinkled. Dis. *pwachapwach* (db).
pwpwekit (3) PWPWEKITA. (Eng.) Var. *pwpwengit, pwpwékit*. n. (T3) pocket. *pwpwekitan, pwpwengitan* his p.
pwpwen (1) PWPWENI. nu. (T2) slander.
pwpweni See *pwpwen*. vo. (T5) slander (someone).
pwpwengit Var. of *pwpwekit*.
pwpwey (2) PWPWEYI. N. Var. *pweey*. nu. (T2) pearl oyster. *pwpweyin Chuuk* Trukese o.
pwpwék (2) PWPWÉKÚ. vi. lie awake at night, to visit with a sweetheart at night. *pwata ina pwpwékumw na?* why are you lying awake?
pwpwékiiti See *pwpwék, -iti*. vo. (T2) lie awake until.
pwpwékit Var. of *pwpwekit*.
pwpwékúúw See *pwpwék, -wú-*. vo. (T5) keep watch on (a brother's wife only) at night. *wúwa pw. pwúnúwen pwiiy we* I kept w. on my brother's wife.

pwpwét (dc; 2) PWÉTÚ$_2$. n. (T2) scar (as from a cut, yaws, burn). *pwpwétún* his s. vi., adj. be scarred. Dis. *pwétúpwét* (db).
pwpwétúr (2) PWPWÉTÚRÚ. n. (T2) ugly skin condition. *pwpwétúrún* his ugly s. c. Cf. *pwpwét*.
pwpwis (2) PWPWISI. vi. be angered (by someone's actions).
pwpwin va. dive for fish (of birds over a school). *raa pwpw. iik* they d. for f.
pwpwir (2) PWPWIRI. Tb3. vi. break wind, fart. Dis. *pwipwpwir* (ds). Syn. *sin, sing*.
-pwpwich (2) PWPWICHI. [In cpds. only.] adj. (intens.) a lot, over and over again. See *ngasépwpwich*.
pwpwo$_1$ (1) PWPWOO$_1$. nu. (T1) instruction in traditional navigation (*pénú*); one who knows navigation, navigator. *emén pw.* one navigator.
pwpwo$_2$ (1) PWPWOO$_2$. N. nu. (T1) breadfruit pounder. *efóch pw.* one b. p. Syn. *wúsúús*. Cf. *pwu-$_3$*. vi., va. be pounded; pound (breadfruit pudding).
pwpwooni$_1$ See *pwpwo$_1$, -ni-*. vo. (T4) give instruction in navigation to (someone).
pwpwooni$_2$ See *pwpwo$_2$, -ni-*. N. vo. (T4) pound or mash (breadfruit, taro, etc.). Syn. *wúsi*.
pwpwos Var. of *pwos*.
pwpwosiiti See *pwpwos, -iti*. vo. (T2) be homesick for.
pwpwon (3a) PWPWONA. nu. (T3) promise, agreement; vow, pledge, sworn statement, oath. *aan pw.* his p. *toropween pw.* signed affidavit or declaration. *pwpwonen pwúpwpwúnú* marriage vows. vi. promise, make a contract, take an oath, vow. Dis. *pwopwpwon* (ds).
pwpwonéech Var. of *pwpwonoyéech*.
pwpwonoffengen (2) See *pwpwon, ffengen*. vi. make an agreement, contract, covenant; promise one another; pledge together.
pwpwonomwaken (3) See *pwpwon, mwaken*. vi. make a false promise, break a promise, give false testimony under oath.
pwpwonoyéech (2) See *pwpwon, ééch*. Var. *pwpwonéech*. vi. keep a promise, keep one's word, give true testimony under oath.

pwpwoy

pwpwoy (2) PWPWOYI. vi., adj. (be) scalded. *pwpwoyin sinin átewe* the scalding of that fellow's skin. nu. (T2) blister.

pwpwó (1) PWPWÓÓ. nu. (T1) medicine and spells that strengthen one's own side in dancing contests and weaken one's opponents. [A tabu of the medicine is that one may not eat shortly before dancing or have sexual relations on the preceding night. Violation results in illness.]

pwpwór (dc; 4) See *pwór*. vi., adj. (be) curved, bent (naturally); crooked, dishonest, not straight.

pwpwu (1) PWPWUU. (Yap?) nu. (T1) betel nut palm; betel nut. *efóch pw.* one b. n. palm; *éféw pw.* one b. n. (fruit). *pwpwuun Iyap* b. n. of Yap Island.

pwpwuk$_1$ (dc; 3a) See *pwuka-*. nu. (T2) knot.

pwpwuk$_2$ (3) PWPWUKA. (Eng.) nu. (T3) book. *neeníyen pw.* bookcase. *pwpwuken fóós, pwpwuken tettenin fóós* dictionary.

pwpwukenikát (4) See *pwpwuk$_1$, áát*. nu. (T2) granny knot ("boy's knot").

pwpwukenikáteey See *pwpwukenikát, -e-$_2$*. vo. (T6b) tie (something) in a granny knot.

pwpwukénúk (2) See *pwpwuk$_1$, núkú-$_3$*. nu. (T2) square knot. Syn. *pwpwukonap*. vi. tie a square knot.

pwpwukonap (dc; 3a) See *pwpwuk$_1$, nap*. nu. (T3) square knot. Syn. *pwpwukénúk*.

pwpwukonapeey See *pwpwukonap. -e-$_2$*. vo. (T6b) tie (something) in a square knot.

pwpwun$_1$ (dc; 3b) PWUNA. n. (T3) blaze, flash, flame, flare. *pwpwunan* its b. vi. be lit up, blaze, flash, flame, flare. Cf. *choropwpwun*.

pwpwun$_2$ (3) PWPWUNA. nu. (T3) necklace, beads (of European type). *epa pw.* one n. *pwpwunen Merika* American n.

pwpwunech vi. be difficult to mash (of breadfruit).

pwpwur$_1$ (dc; 3) See *pwuur$_2$*. vi. be planted.

pwpwur$_2$ (dc; 3) PWURA$_1$. vi. be boiling, be in a lather, seethe, foam. Dis. *pwuropwur* (db).

Trukese-English

pwpwúk Var. (dc) of *pwúk*.

pwpwúkún (2) PWPWÚKÚ. [Occurs, as shown, only with rel. suf. -n_2.] vr. oneself, personally, in person; by itself; naturally, of its own accord. *aa pw. nó* he went by himself. *pw. neyíy* my own child; *pw. fénúwey* my natural land (by inheritance rather than by purchase). Syn. *pwisin*.

pwpwún$_1$ (dc; 2) PWÚNÚ$_1$. nu. (T2) soil, earth; dirt, soot. *pw. patapat* fertile soil (Syn *pwpwúnúpat*); *pw. pwichikkar* infertile soil (Syn. *pwpwúnúpwich*). *pwpwúnún piin* lead (in a pencil). vi. be dirty, soiled, sooty. Dis. *pwúnúpwún* (db), *pwúpwpwún* (ds).

pwpwún$_2$ (2: *pwúnnú-, -pwpwún*) See *pwúún$_1$*. N. vi. break, be broken (of hard or brittle objects). Cf. *mmék, mwmwú*. ni. (T2) fracture (of something). *pwúnnún chúún* f. of his bone. suf. (cc.) fragment, broken piece. *epwpwún, rúwépwpwún, wúnúpwpwún, fépwpwún, nimepwpwún, wonopwpwún, fúúpwpwún, wanúpwpwún, ttiwepwpwún, engoon pwúnnún* one,...ten f.; *fitepwpwún* how many f. *epwpwún sóók* one f. of chalk.

pwpwúnú (dc; 3) See *pwúnúwa-*. vi., adj. (be) married. Dis. *pwúpwpwúnú* (ds).

pwpwúnúmwerúche (1) See *pwpwún$_1$, mwerúche*. nu. (T1) pebbly soil, such as is abundant on the plateau of *Romónum*.

pwpwúnúpar (3b) See *pwpwún$_1$, par*. nu. (T3) red soil.

pwpwúnúpat (3b) See *pwpwún$_1$, pat*. nu. (T3) fertile soil. Dis. *pwpwúnúpatapat* (db).

pwpwúnúpatapat Dis. of *pwpwúnúpat*.

pwpwúnúpwich (2) See *pwpwún$_1$, pwich$_1$*. nu. (T2) infertile soil.

pwpwúnúchón (4) See *pwpwún$_1$, chón*. nu. (T2) dark soil of island hillsides. [It is regarded as good for most crops.]

pwpwúnúchuuk (2) See *pwpwún$_1$, chuuk$_1$*. nu. (T2) reddish, very friable soil in upland areas. [It is considered very fertile for gardening.]

R

-r₁ (3a: *-re-*, *-ré-*, *-ro-*) See *iir*. [In this form only when the preceding base ends in a double vowel.] Var. *-er*, *-ir*, *-ur*, *-úr*. suf. (obj.) 3pl. obj. prn.: them. *cheer* chase them (see *cheey*); *amaar* embarrass them (see *amaay*); *nniir* kill them (see *nniiy*); *osuur* see them off (see *osuuw*); *kúúr* bite them (see *kúúw*); *améémér* sell them (see *amééme*); *ámáár* tend them in dying (see *ámááy*). suf. (pos.) 3pl. pos. prn.: their; of or for them. *waar* their canoe (see *waa*); *feyittoor* their arrival (see *feyitto*); *pecheer* their legs (see *peche*); *máár* their death (see *máá*); *chúúr* their bones (see *chúú*); *póór* their platform (see *póó*); *niir* their teeth (see *nii*).

-r₂ (3) RA₁. suf. (u.m.) See *péér*, *pwur*₁.

ra-₁ See *re-*₁. [In this form only when followed immediately by the vowel *a*.] Var. *re-*₁, *ré-*, *ro-*, *ró-*. pref. (sub.) 3pl. sub. prn.: they. [Although a prefix, it is written separately except when followed by an aspect marker. Other then with aspect markers, it occurs only in colloquial speech in place of *re-*₁.] *raa* they (plus reality aspect marker).

ra-₂ (3b) RA₂. pref. male person. See *rangngaw*, *rapaan*, *rapwpwach*. Cf. *áta-*, *fin*, *niya-*, *re-*₂.

ra-₃ (3b: *re-*, *ro-*) RA₃. pref. (intens.) very much. See *chere-*, *mara-*, *rowusuus*.

-ra- (3) RA₄. [Counterpart of verb formative suffix *-ri-*.] suf. (n.form.; T3) object or product of an action. [Reference to the actor is indicated by suffixed pos. prns.]

raaf (3) RAFFA. (Eng.) nu. (T3) raft. *efóch r.* one r. *waan r.* his r.; *raffen r.* of (a given locality).

raas₁ (3) RASA₁. n. (T3) trace, spoor, tracks, remains, or marks of something that passed by or had been in a place. *rasan* mark of him (as when he has been sitting in the sand). *rasen ááf* ashes, remains of fire; *rasen fanafan* remains of a canoe-adzing; *rasen fanang* remains of a fire, remains of a cooking place; *rasen iimw* remains of a house, trace of where a house once stood; *rasen iipw* footprint.

raas₂ N. var. of *rááś*.

raas₃ (3) RASA₂. nu. food (at a feast).

raamen (2) RAAMENI. (Jap. *raamen*) nu. (T2) Chinese-style noodles with soup. [This word seems to have been borrowed into Trukese after the Japanese had left Truk, because in pre-war Japan, the commonly used word for this type of noodle was *shinasoba* ("China-noodle").] *etúkúm r.* one pack of n. *anan r.* his n. (to eat).

Raanúk nu. (loc.) Ralik Archipelago (Marshall Islands).

raapw (3) RAPWA₁. Tbl. n. (T3) trough just back of the head of the penis; trough to either side of the clitoris. *rapwan* his t.

raar (3) RAARA. N. Var. *rááŕ*. nu. (T3) sea urchin. *raaren s. u.* of (a given locality).

-raar Var. *-naar*. unsp. (u.m.) See *takúraar*, *tékúraar*.

Raatek nu. (loc.) Ratak Archipelago (Marshall Islands).

raaw₁ (3) RAWA₁. nu. (T3) whale. *emén r.* one w. *rawen w.* of (a given region).

raaw₂ (3b) RAWA₂. nu. (T3) planning or thinking in relation to social, diplomatic, or military action; plotting, scheming; strategy, tactics.

raaw₃ (3) RAWA₃. nu. (T3) metal cooking pot. Syn. *eyinepwoch*.

-ras (3) RASA₃. [In cpds. only.] unsp. bitter, acid. See *maras*.

rasaras (db; 3) See *-ras*. nu. (T3) a plant (*Sporobulus virginicus*).

raseey See *raas*₁, *-e-*₂. vo. (T6b) clear a site, prepare a site. *sipwe r. neeniyen imwach* we shall c. a site for our house.

ram (3b) RAMA. vi., adj. (be) orange-red, saffron colored, brownish or tannish yellow, mustard color, color of ripe banana. Dis. *ramaram* (db). *niram* a nickname.

ramaram Dis. of *ram*.

ramúne (1) RAMÚNEE. (Jap. *ramune*) nu. (T1) marbles. *eféw r.* one marble. *néwún* his m.

305

ranning (3) RANNINGA. (Jap. *ranningu*, from Eng. *running (shirt)*) Var. *ranningngú*. nu. (T3) sleeveless undershirt. *eché r.* one u. *wúfan r.* his u. *ranningen Sapaan* Japanese u. Syn. *nipéwúttún*. Cf. *singenes*.

ranningngú (1) RANNINGNGÚÚ. (Jap. *ranningu*, from Eng. *running (shirt)*) Var. *ranning*. nu. (T1) sleeveless undershirt. *eché r.* one u. *wúfan r.* his u. Syn. *nipéwúttún*. Cf. *singenes*.

ranchii (1) RANCHII. (Jap. *ranchi*) nu. (T1) a launch. *efóch r.* one l. *waan r.* his .l.

rang₁ (3b) RANGA₁. vi. be crowded, in a throng; go in a crowd. Dis. *rangarang* (db). *r. ffengen* throng together, go in a crowd. With dir. suf.: *rangatá, rangéto* or *rangoto, rangéwu* or *rangúwu, rangéwow* or *rangowow, rangútiw*.

rang₂ (3b) RANGA₂. vi. stiffen in defense, make a defensive move.

rangarang Dis. of *rang₁*.

rangatá See *rang₁*.

rangeyiti See *rang₁, -iti.* vo. (T2) crowd upon.

rangéto See *rang₁*.

rangéwow See *rang₁*.

rangéwu See *rang₁*.

rangoto See *rang₁*.

rangowow See *rang₁*.

rangónó See *rang₁*.

rangútiw See *rang₁*.

rangúwu See *rang₁*.

rap (3) RAPA. vi. be heated. Cf. *ré₂*.

rapaan (3) See *ra-₂, paa-₂, -ni-*. vi. be a wanderer, a bum, one who flits from place to place. *rapaanan* his wandering about. nu. (T3) a wanderer, one who cannot settle down in a place.

rapich (2) RAPICHI. (Eng.) nu. (T2) rabbit. *emén r.* one r. *rapichin Merika* American r.

rapwarapw (db; 3) RAPWA₂. vi., adj. (be) big, large. Syn. *nap, wátte*.

rapwpwa (1) RAPWPWAA. (Jap. *rappa*) nu. (T1) bugle. *eew r.* one b. *newún r.* his b. *rapwpwaan Sapaan* Japanese b. vi. blow a bugle.

rapwpwaani See *rapwpwa*. vo. (T1) drink (something) directly from the bottle ("bugle it").

rar₁ (3) RARA₁. vi., adj. (be) warm. Dis. *rarrar₁* (ds).

rar₂ (3) RARA₂. vi. be knocked down, trampled down (of grass, resulting from someone's having walked through it). Dis. *rarrar* (db).

rareng (3) See *ra-₂* (?), *reng*. Obs. vi., adj. (be) beautiful, pleasing to behold.

rareyiti See *rar₁, -iti.* vo. (T2) carry warmth to.

rarrar Dis. of *rar₁* and *rar₂*.

rarrawa Dis. of *rawa*.

-rach (3) RACHA. unsp. (u.m.) See *kiirach*.

rachiwo (1) RACHIWOO. (Jap. *rajio*) nu. (T1) radio. *eew r.* one r. *newún r.* his r. *rachiwoon Merika* American r.

rataw (3) RATAWA. nu. (T3) a blow to the jaw that breaks it (in hand-to-hand fighting). [Said to be a specialty of the atolls around Truk.]

rawa (1v) RAWAA. nu. (T1) the art of massage. *chóón r.* person treated by massage (cf. *sowurawa*). vi., va. massage. Dis. *rarrawa* (ds).

rawangngaw (3b) See *raaw₂, ngngaw*. nu. (T3) plotting harm to others who trust us, plotting in ways that betray trust; schemes that fail to accomplish their objectives.

rawapwakak (3) See *raaw₂, pwakak*. nu. (T3) concealing one's plan to do another harm by speakly politely to him and luring him into unwariness.

rawaraw (db; 3) RAWA₄. n. (T3) pimple. *rawarawan* his p. vi. (dis.) be pimply, have pimples.

rawááni See *rawa, -ni-*. vo. (T4) massage (someone).

raweey See *raaw₂, -e-₂*. vo. (T6b) work out the tactics of, plan.

raweses (2) RAWESESI. (Eng.) nu. (T2) trousers, pants. *eew r.* one t. *aan r.* his t. *rawesesin nóón* underpants, underdrawers.

rawééch (2) See *raaw₂, ééch*. nu. (T2) planning or scheming about social action that is agreeable to others in its consequences; effective tactics against the enemy.

rayis (2) RAYISI. (Eng.) nu. (T2) rice. *aan r.* his r. (to sell); *anan r.* his r. (to eat). *rayisin Sapaan* Japanese r.

rayisé (1) RAYISÉÉ. (Eng.) Var. *ráyisé*. nu. (T1) razor blade; razor. *pachen r.* razor ("blade holder").

rayiséew See *rayisé*. Var. *ráyiséew*. vo. (T1) shave (someone).

rayito (1) RAYITOO. (Jap. *raito*) nu. (T1) right field (in baseball).

-rá₁ (1) RÁÁ₁. [In cpds. only.] unsp. girl. See *imwerá, niyerá*.

-rá₂ (1) RÁÁ₂. [In cpds. only.] unsp. on land (?). See *éwúrá*.

ráá- (1) RÁÁ₃. [In cpds. only.] unsp. (u.m.) See *áráápinni, áráápiti, ráápiit*.

ráá (1) RÁÁ₄. N. nu. (T1) branch (with leaves). Dis. *ráárá* (db). *ráán irá* tree's b. Syn. *paan₁*.

rááf₁ (2) REFI. n. (T2) partition, divider (in house, oven). *refin* its p., p. of.

rááf₂ nu. a method of hand-to-hand fighting around an earth oven.

rááś (2) RESI₁. Var. *raas, (in cpds.)* *-rek₂.* nu. (T2) breadfruit harvest season (lasting from May through August when the principle crop is harvested); season of westerly winds. *maramen r.* months of *r.*; *meyin r.* breadfruit of *r.*; *niyachen r.* the last of the *r.* harvest. *resin eey iyer* breadfruit season of this year.

Ráák nu. (loc.) a clan name.

ráákkot (3) See *ráá, kkot*. nu. (T3) dried-out dead tree.

ráán₁ (3) RÁÁNI₁. nu. (T2) 1. weather. 2. rain. *ráánin r.* of (a given locality). Syn. *wúút₂*. vi. rain.

ráán₂ (2) RÁÁNI₂. n. (T2) day, daylight. *ráánin* his d. (of birthday). *fituuw r. ikenááy* what d. is it today?; *iteyiten r.* every d.; *nóón een r.* tomorrow; *nóón eew r.* or (Tn.) *r. ewoch* someday, some other d., some other time; *nóón ekkaan ráán* in the days ahead, someday soon; *r. ánnim* good day (greeting from about 10 to 3), say good d., greet; *r. r.* day after day, day in and day out. *nóón ewe ráánin* on that (past) day; *ráánin aséésé* day of rest, holiday; *ráánin apwaapwa, ráánin pwaapwa* day of celebration, holiday. vi. become day, dawn. With dir. suf.: *rááninó*.

Ráánápuuch nu. (pers.) name of the legendary founder of a school of judo-like fighting.

rááneéch (2) See *ráán₁, ééch*. nu. (T2) good weather. vi. be good weather.

ráániiti See *ráán₂, -iti*. vo. (T2) dawn upon, become day upon.

rááníni (2) See *ráán₂, -ni-*. vi. have as a day, spend (a day). *Iyeyisus aa r. rúwe mé nimuuwen Tiisémper nóón wupwutiwan* Jesus had the twenty-fifth of December as his day of birth; *wúpwe r. eey ráán ikenááy ne attaw pwú meyi núwa* I shall spend this day today fishing because it is calm.

Rááninifen (2) See *ráán₂, fen₂*. nu. (T2) Sunday.

rááninipin (2) See *ráán₂, pin*. nu. (T2) holiday, church holiday, day one is not supposed to work by prohibition of religion (e.g. Sunday, Christmas, etc.).

rááninó See *ráán₂*.

rááningngaw (3b) See *ráán₁, ngngaw*. nu. (T3) bad weather. vi. be bad weather.

ráánúk (2) See *ráá, núkú-₁*. nu. (T2) outside branch. *ráánúkún irá* tree's outside b.

ráápiit (2) See *ráá-, piti-*. F. vi. twist (of a limb), cramp (of a muscle). *ráápiitin pecheey* twist or cramp of my leg. Cf. *efitá*.

ráár (2) RÁÁRI. F. Var. *raar*. nu. (T2) sea urchin. *ráárin* s.u. of (a given locality).

ráárá (db; 1) See *ráá*. vi. have many branches. n. (T1) Dis. of *ráá*.

rááché (1) See *ráá, chééché*. nu. (T1) shed stick (on a loom). *efóch r.* one s. s. *rááchéén túúr* loom's s. s.

rááton (3) See *ráá, ton*. nu. (T3) a sea urchin (red, very spiny).

-rár (4) RÁRE. [In cpds. only.] adj. (u.m.) See *núkúrár*.

re-₁ (4) RE₁. [This is the standard form under most conditions.] Var. *ra-₁, ré-, ro-, ró-*. pref. (sub.) 3pl. sub. prn.: they. [Although a prefix, it is written separately except when followed by an aspect marker.] *repwaapw* (indefinite future), *repwe* (future), *repwene* (uncertain future), *resapw* (future negative), *rese* (negative reality), *rete* (purposeful future negative). *re nónnómw neeset* they live in the sea.

re-₂ (3b) RE₂. [It is lengthened to *ree-* under conditions that vary depending on dialect. Some speakers use the long form consistently when the following word has two or less syllables in its terminal combining form. Others use it only when the following word is monosyllabic in its terminal combining form. Yet others use the long form only in the expressions *ree-Chuk, ree-Wóón*.] pref. man of, male person of. [It is conventionally written with a hyphen.] *ree-Chuk* m. of Chuuk (Truk); *ree-Fanó, re-Fanó* m. of Fanó

ree-₁

(Falo) I.; *ree-Pis, re-Piis* m. of Piis (Pis) I.; *ree-Suuk, re-Suuk* m. of Suuk (Pulusuk) I.; *ree-Ton, re-Toon* m. of Toon (Tol) I.; *ree-Wóón* European, national of the ruling colonial power; *ree-Éét, re-Éét* m. of Éét (Eot) I.; *re-Fánáápi* m. of the atolls; *re-Feefen* m. of Feefen (Fefan) I.; *re-Romónum* m. of Romónum I.; *re-Tonowas* m. of Tonowas (Dublon) I.; *re-Pwonowót* m. of Pwonowót (Puluwat) Atoll; *re-Wuumaan* m. of Wuuman (Uman) I.; *re-Wútéét* m. of Wútéét (Udot) I.; *re-Wééné* m. of Wééné (Moen) I.; *re-Fanapenges* m. of Fanapenges (Falabeguets) I. *re-ekis* outsider, foreigner, stranger; *ree-nóómw* man of old; *re-nipich* unmarried man, bachelor; *re-winipós* indigenous person. Cf. *ra-₂*.

ree-₁ See *re-₂*.

ree-₂ (1) REE. ni. (loc.; T1) 1. on account of, on behalf of, because of, by (indicating the beneficiary, source, or agent of an action or event); about (indicating the topic of conversation). *reen meet?* for what reason?; *sipwe kkapas reen* we shall talk about it; *aa kkuf reey* he lost to (on account of) me; *aa fis reen ewe sómwoon* it was done by the chief; *kinissow reemw!* excuse me!, thanks to you! 2. at the home or place of, in the possession of. *e wor pwpwuk reemw?* do you have a book?; *repwe etto reech* they will come to our place; *wúpwe nó reen Eiue* I shall go to Eiue's (house).

reek (2) REKI₁. nu. (T2) thought, thinking. Dis. *rekirek* (db, the common form). *rekin* his t.

reen See *ree-₂*.

reepi (3) REEPIYA. vi. be wise, experienced.

reepiyeey See *reepi, -e-₂*. vo. (T6b) understand, be wise in.

reech (2) RECHI. nu. (T2) a tern (lives in mangroves). *emén r.* one t. *rechin* t. of (a given locality).

reechooko (1) REECHOOKOO. (Jap. *reizooko*) Var. *reyichooko*. nu. (T1) refrigerator, icebox. *eew r.* one r. *aan r.* his r.

-reewu (3) REEWUWA. unsp. (u.m.) See *mesereewu*.

ref (2) See *rááf₁*. vi. be divided by a partition. Dis. *refiref* (db).

refiiy See *ref, -i-₂*. vo. (T5) divide with a divider.

refisú (1) See *ref, sú*. nu. (T1) a hold or throw in hand-to-hand fighting. [One grabs one's opponent's right hand and bends his right arm back up behind him. One then forces him to bend forward and grabs his left hand in one's own left hand from behind between his legs.]

refiref (db; 2) See *ref*. nu. (T2) division by a partition. vi. Dis. of *ref*.

refto (1) REFTOO. (Jap. *refuto*) nu. (T1) left field (baseball).

resi- (2) RESI₂. [In cpds. only.] unsp. repeatedly, again and again. Syn. *-rek₁*. See *ngúúngúúres, resin*.

resiim (3) RESIIMA. nu. (T3) rainbow. *eew r.* one r. *resiimen nááng* rainboow of the sky. Syn. *mwáresi, mwárisi*. nu. (pers.) traditional god of the rainbow. [He lives in the sky and is also god of war and of red ear decorations.] Syn. *Énúún Mwárisi*.

resin (2) See *resi-, -n₂*. vr. over and over again, repeatedly; vainly, in vain; to no avail. *r. púngú mwo ráán ngé wúpwe chék angaang* though it rains and rains, I shall just keep working; *wúwa r. sóttuni ngé wúse toongeni* I tried and tried but I couldn't succeed.

-rek₁ (2) REKI₂. [In cpds. only.] adj. repeatedly. Syn. *resi-*. See *weyiyerek*.

-rek₂ (2) REKI₃. Var. *rááS, raas*. unsp. season of main breadfruit harvest and of westerly winds.

rekiiy See *reek, -i-₂*. vo. (T5) think. Dis. *rekirekiiy* (ds).

rekingngaw (3b) See *reek, ngngaw*. vi. have evil intentions.

rekingngawa See *rekingngaw*. vo. (T3) have evil intentions toward, intend to harm (someone).

rekirek Dis. of *reek*.

rekirekiiy Dis. of *rekiiy*.

rekich (2) REKICHI. nu. (T2) a strand tree (*Calophyllum inophyllum*). [Wood is used to make bowls; crushed leaves are rubbed on the outside of a new canoe hull after painting to fix the paint.] *rekichin* t. of (a given region).

rekiyééch (2) See *reek, ééch*. vi. have good intentions.

rekiyéchchúúw See *rekiyééch, -ú-*. vo. (T5) have good intentions towards, be well disposed to.

rekooto (1) REKOOTOO. (Jap. *rekoodo*) nu. (T1) record, disc. *eché r.* one r. *néwún r.* his r.

remonchúri (Jap. *remon, tsuri*) nu. an obstacle race. [Each contestant is supplied with a piece of string. He runs to a table containing limes and ties the string around a lime in a single loop; then, holding the other end of the loop, he runs to the goal.]

rensú (1) RENSÚÚ. (Jap. *rensyuu*) nu. (T1) practice, exercise. *eew r.* one e. *aan r.* his e. vi. practice, exercise.

rensúúni See *rensú, -ni-*. vo. (T4) help someone to practice.

reng (3) RENGA. adj., vi. (be) yellow, yellow-green, saffron colored (associated with turmeric). Dis. *rengereng* (db). *rengerengen teyuk* yellow-green of turmeric.

rep (3) REPA. vi. be deceived, fooled. Dis. *reperep* (db). *wúwa r. reen átánaan* I was d. by that fellow.

repeey See *rep, -e-₂*. vo. (T6b) deceive, trick, fool.

repwoot (Eng.) nu. report.

rer vi. tremble (with fear).

reri- (2) RERI. ni. (T2) log big enough to burn all night (associated with the needs of old people). *rerin ewe chinnap* the old person's l.

rech₁ vi. make the noise of burning coconut shells. *raa r. kkewe sékkún taka* the coconut shells made *r.* noise.

rech₂ [In cpds. only.] adj. (u.m.) See *chamwerech, meserech*.

reyi- (2) REYI. [In cpds. only.] unsp. cutting, slicing.

reyiiy See *reyi-, -i-₂*. vo. (T5) cut, slice.

reyik (3) REYIKA. (Eng.) nu. (T3) rake.

reyikeey See *reyik, -e-₂*. vo. (T6b) rake.

reyirey (db; 2) See *reyi-*. nu. (T2) cutting, surgery, vaccination, carving. *reyireyin mettóóch* the c. of things. vi. be cut (as with a knife), sliced, medically operated on; carved, vaccinated. va. cut, carve, perform surgery (on).

reyichooko Var. of *reechooko*.

ré- Var. of *re-₁* (only when immediately followed by the vowel *é*).

ré₁ (1: *réé-, roo-*) RÉÉ₁. vi. grope, reach with the hands where one cannot see. Dis. *rééré* (db). *wumwun rééré* (N.) forest overgrowth of leafy branches (F.: *wumwun róóró*). With dir. suf.: *réénong* or *roonong, réénó, rééta,*
réétiw, rééto, réewow, réewu. aa réétiw fáán ewe cheepen he groped down under the table.

ré₂ (1) RÉÉ₂. vi. 1. be heated (of leaves). Cf. *rap.* 2. (N.) be broiled (of chicken or birds). Syn. *kkarap*.

rééfa (1) See *ré₁, faa-₁*. nu. (T1) in *kkóónun rééfa* former practice in which a man allowed a senior kinsman to sleep with his wife for a major favor in return.

rééfáák (2) See *ré₁, -fáák*. vi. pull small weeds by hand.

rééfáákiiy See *rééfáák, -i-₂*. vo. (T5) pull (small weeds) by hand.

rééféw (2) See *ré₁, faaw*. vi. do a kind of fishing at night. [Men and women work together, women with handnets, men with hands only. Men reach into holes with their hands and the fish scoot out into the waiting handnets of the women.]

réénong See *ré₁*.

réénó See *ré₁*.

réépwang (3) See *ré₁, pwaang*. Tbl. vi. fondle a woman's genitals.

rééré Dis. of *ré₁*.

réét (2) See *ré₁* (?), *-ti-*. [Presumably a back formation from *rééti*.] vi. have one's hair in a bun or topknot. [This was the regular style of hair dress by both men and women in pre-colonial times. In sorcery, the hair was done up in many *réét* or small buns.] *meyi r. mékúran* his hair is in a bun.

réétá See *ré₁*.

rééti See *ré₁* (?), *-ti-*. vo. (T2) do (one's hair) up in a knot or knots.

réétiw See *ré₁*.

réétó See *ré₁*.

réewow See *ré₁*.

réewu See *ré₁*.

rééyi See *ré₁, -yi-₂*. vo. (T4) grope for, reach into or under for.

rék (2) RÉKÚ. vi. be scooped out (with hands, spatula, etc.) Dis. *rékúrék* (db). Cf. *tuk₂*.

rékúúw See *rék, -ú-*. vo. (T5) scoop out. *aa r. ewe épwét* he s. out the fermented breadfruit (from the pit).

-ri- (2) RI. suf. (v.form.) makes an object focussed verb of the base. *kkééri* call to (*kké* call, shout).

ri (1) RII₁. vi. be bound, tied up.

rii (1) RII₂. nu. (T1) name of the consonant (alveolar trill) written *r*; name of the letter thus written.

riif (3) RIFFA. (Eng.) vi. reef or shorten sail on western type of sailboat; roll up one's trousers; be rolled up (as trousers or shirt sleeves). Cf. *seres*.

riimey (2) See *ri, mááy₂*. vi. mark a breadfruit tree as reserved or tabu by tying a coconut leaf girdle around its trunk.

riing (3) RINGNGA. (Eng.) nu. (T3) ring. *efóch r.* one r. *néwún r.* his r. *ringngen Merika* American r.

riiri (db; 1) See *ri*. n. (T2) something tied on; band, ribbon; bandage; lashing; bonds; fetters. *riiriin* his b. *riiriin paaw* wrist band, arm band; *riiriin peche* ankle band, leg band; *riiriin pénú* bracelet and anklet of braided coconut leaf worn by a navigator as insignia of his status. va. tie, lash, bind. *riiriin mettóóch* the lashing of things.

riit (2) RIITI. nu. (T2) sterile woman. *emén r.* one s. w. *riitin Romónum* s. w. of Romónum. vi. be barren, sterile (of men and women).

riiy See *ri*. vo. (T1) tie, lash, wind, bind (of thread, rope, etc.). With n. form. suf.: *riiya-* (ni.; T3) tying, lashing, binding (done by someone).

riffeey See *riif, -e-₂*. Tbl. vo. (T6b) take a reef in, roll up.

ris₁ (2) RISI. Tbl. vi. have illicit sexual intercourse by day. Cf. *tééfán*.

ris₂ Tb2. vi., adj. (be) nice, fine, appropriate, good. Syn. *chif₂, ééch*.

risiiy See *ris₁, -i-₂*. Tbl. vo. (T5) have illicit sexual intercourse by day with (someone).

rik (2) RIKI. vi. change direction, turn to one side (as in walking and steering a boat), zig, zag. Dis. *rikirik* (db) zigzag, move from side to side. *rikirik fátán* stagger, reel (as when intoxicated), weave in and out (in driving a car). *kkapas rikirik* misleading talk. With dir. suf.: *rikinong, rikinó, rikitá, rikitiw, rikito, rikiwow, rikiwu*.

rikin (2) RIKINI. (Eng.) nu. (T2) rigging (of boat only). *rikinin waa* canoe's r.

rikinong See *rik*.
rikinó See *rik*.
rikirik Dis. of *rik*.
rikitá See *rik*.

rikitiw See *rik*.
rikito See *rik*.
rikiwow See *rik*.
rikiwu See *rik*.

rikúngún (2) RIKÚNGÚNÚ. Obs. (Jap. *rikugun*) nu. (T2) soldier (army). *emén r.* one s.

rimpiyo (1) RIMPIYOO. (Jap. *rimbyoo*) nu. (T1) gonorrhea or other urethritis (polite word). *aan r.* his g. Syn. *echiyo, paras*. vi. have gonorreha.

-rip (3, 2) RIPA, RIPI. [In cpds. only.] unsp. shatter, break into pieces. Syn. *rup₁*. See *merip, ripiiy*.

ripiiy See *-rip, -i-₂*. vo. (T5) shatter, break into pieces.

rippiyo (1) RIPPIYOO. (Jap. *rippyoo*) nu. (T1) stationary marker on a reef marking a passage.

riching (3) RICHINGA. nu. (T3) a species of flounder. *richingen* f. of (a given region).

-riw (3) RIWA. [In cpds. only.] unsp. glitter. Dis. *-riweriw* (db). See *chcheriw, meriweriw*.

riyaaka (1) RIYAAKAA. (Jap. *riyakaa*, from Eng. *rear car*) nu. (T1) cart, handcart, pullcart. *efóch r.* one c. *waan r.* his c.

riyá (1) RIYÁÁ. vi. be miserable, in torment, in anguish.

riyáfféw (2) See *riyá, -fféw*. nu. (T2) misery, torment, anguish, distress, suffering. vi. be miserable, in torment, in anguish, in distress, oppressed, suffering.

ro- Var. of *re-₁* (occurs only in colloquial speech when followed by the vowels *o, u*).

ro₁ (1) See *roo-₃*. vi. be congregated (of crabs and lobsters or crayfish at time of egg-laying); assemble (Itang). Dis. *rooro* (db) assemble in large numbers (Itang). With dir. suf.: *rooto* assemble hither (Itang).

ro₂ (1) ROO₁. vi. bend the body forward, bow, stoop. With dir. suf.: *rootá* bend the head back, tip the face up; *rootiw* bend down; *rooto* bend hither (said to another when one wants to whisper something to him); *roowu* lean out. Cf. *roo-₂*.

-ro (1) ROO₂. [In cpds. only.] unsp. pertaining to chiefly rank. See *chóóyiro*.

roo-₁ (1) ROO₃. ni. (T1) diaper. *roon* his d.

roo-₂ (1) ROO₄. [With dir. suf. only.] vi. shift one's visual attention, look (in some direction). *rootá* look up; *rooto* look hither; *roowu* look out (as from the house). Syn. *fana-₂*. Cf. *chimw*, *ro₂*.

roo-₃ (1) ROO₅. ni. (T1) egg sack or roe of crab or lobster. *roon* its e. s. Cf. *rúú*.

roos (3) ROOSA, ROSSA. (Eng.) nu. (T3) rose. *roosen* or *rossen Merika* American r.

roosaariyo (1) ROOSAARIYOO. (Sp.) nu. (T1) rosary. vi. say the rosary.

roonaak (3) ROONAAKA. (Eng.) nu. (T3) oarlock, rowlock. *efóch r.* one r. *roonaaken* r. of.

rooni See *roo-₂, -ni-*. vo. (T4) wrap in a diaper, put a diaper on.

roonong Var. of *réénong* (see *ré₁*).

roong (3a) RONGA₂. n. (T3) any endeavor that requires special knowledge and instruction to perform; (with pos. prns.) a specialty that one is competent to perform. [In traditional Trukese endeavors any *roong* included medicine or spells as a part of what had to be known, but one can use the term for modern fields of knowledge as well, e.g. physics.] *rongan* his specialty. *rongey anthropology* my specialty is anthropology. *rongen chukó* medicine and spells for curing the sickness called *máán chukó*; *rongen chúúnúket* medicine and spells relating to *chúúnúket* sickness; *rongen ikekkar* the spells and medicine for curing sore throat and headache caused by *ikekkar* (of uncertain meaning); *rongen mááwún* spell to cure *mááwún*; *rongen neeroch* magic and spells associated with sickness and medicine of the same name; *rongen neetip* spell to treat *neetip* (q.v.); *rongen oos* magic and medicines to pertaining to the ailments caused by the spirits named *oos* or *wosen mataw*; *rongen sáát* spells and medicines that pertain to the class of sea spirits called *chénúkken*. *pwopwun r.* person who knows all the *r.* known by members of his lineage; *panen r.* person who knows only some of his lineage's *r.*.

roop (3) ROPA. nu. (T3) a sweep made of coconut leaves tied together (in fishing); fishing with a sweep. *ropen ikéwúngúúng* sweep for the *ikéwúngúúng* fish (a fishing method).

roor (4) ROORO. nu. (T2) cooking by boiling in a shell vessel (as with breadfruit, *roorun mááy*). vi. cook by boiling in shell vessel.

rooreey See *roor, -e-₂*. vo. (T6b) boil in a shell vessel.

rooro₁ (db; 1) ROO₆. nu. (T1) vegetation, bush; plant. *efóch r.* one plant. *newún r.* his plant. Syn. *pétéwén*.

rooro₂ Dis. of *ro₁*.

Roota nu. (loc.) Rota (Marianas Islands). [Claimed by some *itang* to be derived from *rootá₁* because on a legendary voyage of exploration the people "looked up" and saw the island.]

rootá See *ro₂, roo-₂*.

rootiw See *ro₂*.

rooto See *ro₁, ro₂, roo-₂*.

roowu See *ro₂, roo-₂*.

roffengen (2) See *ro₂, ffengen*. vi. bend heads together (as in intimate conversation).

ros (3a) ROSA. N. vi. be all gone, used up, finished, depleted, consumed (as of food or goods). With dir. suf.: *rosonó*. Syn. *it*.

roseyiti See *ros, -iti*. vo. (T2) be finished or used up by (a given time). *epwe r. Suun* it will be f. by June.

rosonó See *ros*.

rosoto See *ros*.

roko- (3a) ROKA. [In cpds. only.] Var. *rókó-*. unsp. curve, curved.

rokofáániyen (2) See *roko-, fáániyen*. Var. *rókófáániyen*. vi. be circular; be encircled. va. encircle, go around.

rokopwáán (2) See *roko-, -pwáán* or *pween₂*. vi. circulate (as money, water, etc.).

rokumw (3) ROKUMWA. nu. (T3) land crab. *eew r.* one l. c. *rokumwen* l. c. of (a given region). Syn. *nipwpwey*.

Romanum E.Wn. of *Romónum*.

Romónum Var. *Romanum*. nu. (loc.) Ulalu Island.

rong (3a) RONGA₁. va. hear, obey, listen. Dis. *rongorong* (db). *wúwa r. óómw na fóós* I listened to what you said. *rongorong ngeni* listen to, be attentive to.

rongeeya- See *rong, -e-₂, -ya-*. ni. (T3) what was heard (by someone). *rongeeyan* what he heard.

rongééch (2) See *rong, ééch*. vi. hear good news. Ant. *rongongngaw₁, rongopwut, rongopwutak*.

rongosoosich (2) See *rong, soosich.* F. Var. *rongosoochis.* vi., adj. obey; (be) obedient. Syn. *rongochoochis.*

rongosoonap (3) See *rong, soonap.* vi. disobey, fail to do as instructed. Syn. *rongochchaw, rongommang.*

Rongomete nu. (loc.) a clan name.

rongommang (3) See *rong, mmang.* F. vi. fail to obey, be slow to obey, disobey. Syn. *rochochchaw, rongosoonap.*

rongomwéch (2) See *roong, mwéch.* nu. (T2) withholding knowledge of magic or some other specialty from one's heirs. 3. knowledge that is withheld.

rongonap$_1$ (3) See *rong, -nap.* vi. be disobedient, heedless.

Rongonap$_2$ nu. (loc.) Rongelap Island and Atoll (Marshall Islands).

rongongngaw$_1$ (3b) See *rong, ngngaw.* vi. hear bad news. Syn. *rongopwut, rongopwutak.* Ant. *rongééch*$_1$.

rongongngaw$_2$ (3b) See *roong, ngngaw.* nu. (T3) black magic, sorcery. Syn. *kkúsú, ppéwút.*

rongopwut (3) See *rong, pwuta-.* N. Var. *rongopwutak.* vi. hear bad news. Syn. *rongongngaw*$_1$. Ant. *rongééch.*

rongopwutak (3) See *rong, pwutak.* Var. *rongopwut.* vi. hear bad news. Syn. *rongongngaw.* Ant. *rongééch.*

rongorong Dis. of *rong.*

Rongochik nu. (loc.) Rongerik Island and Atoll (Marshall Islands).

rongochoochis (2) See *rong, choochis.* N. vi. obey. Syn. *rongosoosich.*

rongochchaw (3) See *rong, chchaw.* N. vi. fail to obey, be slow to obey, disobey. Syn. *rongommang, rongosoonap.*

Rongowu nu. (loc.) a clan name. Syn. *Rowoow.*

rop (3) See *roop.* vi. fish with a sweep of coconut leaves tied together. Dis. *roporop* (db).

ropeey See *roop, -e-*$_2$. vo. (T4) catch (fish) with a sweep of coconut leaves tied together.

ropey (2) ROPEYI. nu. (T2) small goby fish. [Tabu to knot diviners (*sowupwe*).] *emén r.* one g. *ropeyin Chuuk* Trukese g.

Ropéfénú nu. (loc.) a clan name.

roporop Dis. of *rop.*

-ror [In cpds. only.] unsp. (u.m.) See *meyiror.*

roch (3a) ROCHA$_1$. vi., adj. (be) dark, ignorant. Dis. *rochoroch* (db). *rochen eey pwinin* the darkness of this night. With dir. suf.: *rochonó* get dark.

rocho- (3a) ROCHA$_2$. [In cpds. only.] unsp. having to do with one's behavior or attitude towards others. See *rochongngaw, rochopwaak, rochoyéech.*

rochonó See *roch.*

rochonón (4) See *roch, nónu-.* nu. (T2) 1st night of lunar month ("interior dark"). [The moon is not visible.]

rochongngaw (3b) See *rocho-, ngngaw.* vi. be mean, harsh, cranky, surly, gruff.

rochopwaak (3) See *rocho-, -pwaak.* vi. be savage, unsocialized, without understanding of what is proper conduct, impulsive, governed by impulse.

rochoroch Dis. of *roch.*

rochoyéech (2) See *rocho-, ééch.* vi. be gentle, easy-going, kind.

Rowoow nu. (loc.) a clan name. Syn. *Rongowu.*

rowus (3) ROWUSA. (Eng.) nu. (T3) 1. a shrub (*Hibiscus rosa-sinensis*) with a red flower. [A Japanese introduction. If bright red, the flower is worn on the ear as a symbol of requited love; light and dark red have other meanings.] *rowusen* s. of (a given region). 2. rose.

rowusuus (db; 2) See *ra-*$_3$, *wusu-*$_2$. nu. (T2) a tree (*Excoecoria agallocha*). [Poisonous sap; fruit used as medicine for eye trouble.] Syn. *owusuus, wiisuusu, wusuus*$_2$.

-rowurow (db; 2) ROWU. unsp. (u.m.) See *fiirowurow.*

ró- Var. of *re-*$_1$ (occurring in colloquial speech when the next following vowel is *ó*).

róó- (1) RÓÓ$_1$. [In cpds. only.] unsp. embrace. See *róómi.*

róó (1) RÓÓ$_2$. nu. (T1) rod around which leaves used in thatching are stitched, standard length being one fathom. [These rods are obtained from *woowo* (the grass *Phragmites karka*) or *ását* (also known as *ene*, the sword grass *Miscanthus floridus*).] *róón óós* thatch rod.

róómi See *róó-, -mi-.* vo. (T4) embrace, hug.

róóng (4) RÓNGO. nu. (T2, T3) 1. prohibition against trespass in the name of one who has died (on trees, fishing places, etc.). *róngun* or *róngen ewe neeni* the place's p. against t. Syn. *pwaaw*₁. Cf. *mechen*. 2. altar.

róóró (db; 1) See *róó-*. nu. (T1) embracing. *wumwun r.* (F.) forest overgrowth of leafy branches (N.: *wumwun rééré*).

rókófááníyen Var. of *rokofááníyen*.

róngeey See *róóng*, -e-₂. vo. (T6b) put under a prohibition against trespass, restrict trespass on.

rópwó (1) RÓPWÓÓ. nu. (T1) a variety of breadfruit. *rópwóón Chuuk* Trukese b.

rówun (3) RÓWUNA. (Eng.) vi. make the rounds, walk a beat; go (all the way) around; turn around (as a car or a person). *meyi r. pwanangen eey iimw* the porch of this house goes all the way around.

rówuneey See *rówun*, -e-₂. vo. (T6b) turn (something) around; make the rounds of.

ru- (2) RU. [In cpds. only.] unsp. gather. See *rrus, rusi*.

ru₁ (3a) RUWA₁. vi., adj. rush about, bustle about, hurry to and fro. Dis. *ruworu* (db). With dir. suf.: *ruwonó, ruwoto*.

ru₂ (3) RUWA₂. vi. be out of place, out of joint, dislocated.

ruu N. of *ruwuuw*.

Ruusiya (Eng.) nu. (loc.) Russia.

ruume (1) RUUMEE. nu. (T1) bottle. *eew r.* one b. *ruumeen* b. of (a given kind or source).

ruumw₁ (2) RUMWU. n. (T2) 1. barb. *rumwun* its b. *rumwun máchá* metal spear's b.; *rumwun see* corona of the penis. 2. tenon (in joinery). *rumwun irá* timber's t. *kepwe fééri rumwun na irá pwú epwe afféew* make a t. on that timber so that it will be joined.

ruumw₂ (3) RUMWMWA. (Eng.) n. (T3) room. *rumwmwan* his r. *rumwmwen faan* downstairs; *rumwmwen mwéngé* dining room; *rumwmwen ónnut* bedroom; *rumwmwen waasééna* guest room, parlor; *rumwmwen wóón* upstairs.

ruupw (2) RUPWU₂. nu. (T2) yaws, framboesia. *rupwun* his y. *rupwun Iyap* a pox (not as severe as *paarang*, probably chicken pox); *rupwun naakkich* (N.), *rupwun piinakkich* (F.) yaws on palm of hand or sole of foot; *rupwun pwétúr* progressive rotting away of body beginning at extremities (leprosy).

ruuru (db; 1) RUU. adj. tied. See *tukuruuru*. Cf. *ri*.

ruuw₁ (3) RUUWA. Var. *ruu*. nu. (T3) species of large parrot fish. *emén r., eew r.* one p. f. *ruuwen Chuuk* Trukese p. f.

ruuw₂ Var. of *ruwuuw*.

ruuwu N. of *ruwuuw*.

rus Var. of *rrus*.

rusi See *ru-*, -*si*-. vo. (T2) gather. Cf. *rrus*.

ruk (3a) RUKA. vi. stray from one's course, be astray, take a wrong road, do other than what one intended, lose track, go wrong; be confused. Dis. *rukoruk* (db). *aa rukoruk aan fóós* his speech is mixed up or confused (as of a stutterer). With dir. suf.: *rukonó* go astray, get lost.

rukáásini See *ruk*, -*ásini*. vo. (T2) be surprised at (what has happened).

ruke (1) RUKEE. nu. (T1) morning glory (*Ipomoea gracilis*). [Flowers are used in medicine for conjunctivitis of the eyes; leaves are mixed with palm toddy to make a famine food.] *rukeen Chuuk* Trukese m. g. Syn. *rukuruk*.

rukofeseen (2) See *ruk*, -*feseen*. vi. stray apart, get out of touch, lose track of one another.

rukonó See *ruk*.

rukoruk Dis. of *ruk*.

rukuruk (db; 2) RUKU. nu. (T2) 1. morning glory (*Ipomoea gracilis*). *rukurukun Chuuk* Trukese m. g. Syn. *ruke*. 2. a vine (*Lygodium circinatum*).

rumech (2) RUMECHI. nu. (T2) 1. a small round mollusc. [It sticks to coral and has no shell.] *eféw r.* one m. *rumechin Chuuk* Trukese m. 2. either of two kinds of small fish said to frequent places where molluscs of this name are found. [They are taken, scrubbed to remove the poison exterior and then cooked and eaten.]

rumwmwenikkuk (2) See *ruumw*₂, *kkuk*. nu. (T2) kitchen.

rup₁ (2) RUPU₁. Var. -*rip*. vi., adj. (be) shattered. Dis. *rupurup* (db). Syn. *mmék*, -*rip*.

rup₂ (3) RUPA. vi. fight (of chickens, boys, people). *áám éwúwa r. má átánaan* we fought with that fellow.

rup₃ (2) RUPU₂. Var. *rrup*. vi. be carved in relief (of geometric designs in wood carving).

rupiiy See *rup*₁, *-i-*₂. vo. (T5) shatter. Syn. *ripiiy*.

ruputi See *rup*₃, *-ti-*. vo. (T5) carve geometric designs in relief on (something).

rupwu- (2) RUPWU₁. [In cpds. only.] unsp. (u.m.) See *fowurupw*, *rupwur*, *rupwuri*.

rupwur (2) See *rupwu-*, *-ri-*. vi. be rinsed.

rupwuri See *rupwu-*, *-ri-*. vo. (T5) rinse out, rinse off. *r. awan* r. out his mouth; *r. péwún* r. off his hands.

-rurrur (ds; 2) RURU. [In cpds. only.] vi., adj. slip, become loose (of a rope). Syn. *nnúr*₁, *rúrrúr*.

ruweey See *ru*₁, *-e-*₂. vo. (T6b) hurry towards. With dir. suf.: *ruweeyenó* hurry away with, hurry away to; *ruweeyeto* fetch quickly.

ruweeyenó See *ruweey*.

ruweeyeto See *ruweey*.

ruwo- Var. of *rúwa-*.

ruwoseni See *ru*₂, *seni*₂. vo. (T2) be displaced from.

ruwonó See *ru*₁.

ruwongngaw (3b) See *ru*₁, *ngngaw*. vi. do what one thinks another wants when the other does not in fact want it.

ruworu Dis. of *ru*₁.

ruwocheeche (1) See *ru*₁, *cheeche*. vi. run back and forth.

ruwochchooch (3) See *rúwa-*, *chchooch*. num. two armfuls.

ruwoto See *ru*₁.

ruwowoch See *rúwa-*, *-woch*. Tn. num. two sorts, rations, kinds, varieties, species. Syn. *ruwóóch*.

ruwowumw Var. of *rúwéwumw*.

ruwowupw (2) See *rúwa-*, *wupwu-*₁. num. two breasts.

Ruwó nu. (loc.) Ruo Island (Hall Islands).

ruwóóch (4) See *rúwa-*, *-óch*. num. two sorts, rations, kinds, varieties, species. With c. pref. and ptv. const.: *oruwóchchun* a second kind; *ese pwanú wor oruwóchchun* it is unique (there is not a second one or kind). Syn. *ruwowoch*.

ruwóówut Var. of *rúwóówut*.

ruwu- (2) RUWU. Var. *rúwa-*. pref. (num.) two. See *ruwuuw*.

ruwuuw (3) See *ruwu-*, *-uw*. F. Var. *ruu*, *ruuw*, *ruuwu*. num. two general-class things. With c. pref. and ptv. const.: *oruwuuwan* second. With dis. c. pref.: *okkoruwuuw* be two at a time, by twos.

rú₁ (1) RÚÚ₁. N. [Idiomatic usage only.] unsp. aware. *sipwe rúú chék aa war* we will scarcely know it before he arrives. Syn. *wúrúng*.

rú₂ (3) RÚÚ₂. vi. lay eggs, spawn (of fish). Dis. *rúúrú* (db). Cf. *rúú*.

rúú (3) RÚÚWA, RÚWA₁. n. (T3) roe, fish eggs. *rúúwan* (F.), *rúwan* (N.) its r. Cf. *rú*₂, *roo-*₃.

rúúké (1) See *rú*₁, *éé*₁ *(?)*. vi. be surprised, astounded, astonished. Syn. *máayirú*.

rúúr N. vi. search for scattered objects (as shells). Dis. *rúrrúúr* (ds). Syn. *kkúút*₁.

rúúrú₁ (db; 1) RÚÚ₃. vi. be curly, wavy (of hair).

rúúrú₂ Dis. of *rú*₂.

rúk (2) RÚKÚ. vi. tip, be unsteady; tip with the outrigger going down under water (of outrigger canoes). Dis. *rúkúrúk* (db). *fátán rúkúrúk* limp, tip from side to side or be unsteady in walking (as a cripple). With dir. suf.: *rúkúnó* tip over, capsize. Cf. *chún*.

rúkan (3) RÚKANA. vi. be hard-working, conscientious.

rúkúfen (2) RÚKÚFENI. Tb3. nu. (T2) sensation of being tickled; sensation of sexual stimulation. vi. be ticklish; be tickled.

rúkúnó See *rúk*.

rúngérúng (db; 3) RÚNGA. n. (T3) sputum, mucous coughed up from chest. *rúngérúngan* his s.

rúngúrúng (db; 2) RÚNGÚ. vi. be just beginning to be fully ripe (of breadfruit, mangoes, bananas, which are picked before this stage). *rúngúrúngún máay* almost fully ripe breadfruit.

rúpwúng (2) RÚPWÚNGÚ. nu. (T2) ivory nut palm (*Coelococcus amicarum*). [Thatch materials made from leaves; wood used for rafters.] *imwan r.* his i. n. palm. *rúpwúngún Chuuk* Trukese i. n. *féwún r.* ivory nut; *aa imweni efóch r.* he acquired an i. n. tree.

rúrú- (2) RÚRÚ. vi. be slipped or slid apart or together (as a curtain or zipper). Cf. *kúrúr*.

rúrrúúr Dis. of *rúúr*.
rúrrúr (ds; 2) See *rúrú-*. Rmn. vi. slip, become loose. *rúrrúrún mááy* a rite that is part of the cycle of breadfruit summoning ritual (syn. *núnnúrún mááy*). Syn. *nnúr*, *-rurrur*.
rúwa- (3b: *ruwo-*, *ruwó-*, *rúwa-*, *rúwe-*, *rúwé-*, *rúwo-*, *rúwó-*) RÚWA$_2$. Var. *ruwu-*. pref. (num.) two. See *ruwochchooch*, *ruwowoch*, *ruwowumw*, *ruwowupw*, *ruwóóch*, *ruwóówut*, *rúwaché*, *rúwapé*, *rúwayé*, *rúwáánú*, *rúwe*, *rúweyi*, *rúweyin*$_1$, *rúweyin*$_2$, *rúweyipw*, *rúweyiyey*, *rúwéchamw*, *rúwéchef*, *rúwéchchi*, *rúwéchú*, *rúwéchúk*, *rúwéféw*, *rúwéffaat*, *rúwéffit*, *rúwéfich*, *rúwéfóch*, *rúwéfutuk*, *rúwéngaf*, *rúwéngát*, *rúwéngéréw*, *rúwéngin*, *rúwékis*, *rúwékit*, *rúwékkamw*, *rúwékkap*, *rúwékumwuch*, *rúwékup*, *rúwémach*, *rúwémataf*, *rúwémech*, *rúwémeech*, *rúwémeet*, *rúwémén*, *rúwémma*, *rúwémmech*, *rúwémmék*, *rúwémmwék*, *rúwémwénú*, *rúwémwmwun*, *rúwémwmwú*, *rúwémwmwún*, *rúwémwu*, *rúwémwú*$_1$, *rúwémwú*$_2$, *rúwémwúch*, *rúwénnú*, *rúwépa*, *rúwépachang*, *rúwépan*, *rúwépeche*, *rúwépeek*, *rúwépék*, *rúwépéw*, *rúwépino*, *rúwépinúk*, *rúwépu*, *rúwépwang*, *rúwépwey*, *rúwépwéét*, *rúwépwi*, *rúwépwin*, *rúwépwopw*, *rúwépwór*, *rúwépwpwaaw*, *rúwépwpwún*, *rúwépwúkú*, *rúwépwún*, *rúwésángá*, *rúwésáwá*, *rúwéseeng*, *rúwésen*, *rúwésópw*, *rúwéssaar*, *rúwéssak*, *rúwéssar*, *rúwéssáát*, *rúwéssát*, *rúwéssupw*, *rúwétáp*, *rúwétinewupw*, *rúwétip*, *rúwétit*, *rúwéttiit*, *rúwéttún*, *rúwétú*, *rúwétúkúm*, *rúwétún*, *rúwéwumw*, *rúwéwupw*, *rúwéwúk*$_1$, *rúwéwúk*$_2$, *rúwéwún*, *rúwéwút*, *rúwéwúwéw*, *rúwéyaf*, *rúwéyang*, *rúwéyef*, *rúwéyem*, *rúwéyep*, *rúwéyó*, *rúwofóch*, *rúwokkumw*, *rúwowut*, *rúwóówut*, *rúwówo*.
rúwapé (1) See *rúwa-*, *péé-*$_1$. num. two empty containers.
rúwaché (1) See *rúwa-*, *-ché*. num. two leaves, sheets, flat objects.
rúwayé (1) See *rúwa-*, *-é*. num. two hairs, threads.
rúwáánú (1) See *rúwa-*, *-ánú*. num. four general-class things. *eew nnerúwáánú*, *eew nnerúwáánúún* one-fourth (fraction). With c. pref. and ptv. const.: *érúwáánúún* fourth (in a series), in the fourth place. With dis. c. pref.: *ékkérúwáánú* be four at a time. Cf. *fáá-*$_1$, *fáán*$_1$, *fé-*$_1$.
rúwe (1) See *rúwa-*, *-e-*$_1$. num. twenty. *eew nnerúwe* one twentieth. With c. pref. and ptv. const.: *érúween* twentieth (in a series), in the twentieth place. With dis. c. pref.: *ékkérúwe* be twenty at a time. With suf. *-somw*: *rúweesomw* be more than twenty.
rúweesomw See *rúwe*.
rúweyi (3) See *rúwa-*, *-i*. num. two hands (of bananas). Syn. *rúweyin*$_1$, *rúweyiyey*.
rúweyin$_1$ (3) See *rúwa-*, *ina-*$_2$. num. two hands (of bananas). Syn. *rúweyi*, *rúweyiyey*.
rúweyipw (3) See *rúwa-*, *-ipw*. num. two steps, footprints, soles; two items of footwear.
rúweyiyey (3) See *rúwa-*, *iyeyiya-*. num. two hands of bananas. Syn. *rúweyi*, *rúweyin*$_1$.
rúweyun$_2$ (2) See *rúwa-*, *ini-*$_2$. num. two shoots.
rúwéféw (2) See *rúwa-*, *-féw*. num. two globular shaped objects (e.g. stones, balls).
rúwéfich (3a) See *rúwa-*, *ficha-*. num. two strips of coconut, pandanus, or palm leaf prepared for plaiting mats.
rúwéfóch (2) See *rúwa-*, *fóchu-*. Var. *rúwofóch*. num. two long objects (e.g. vehicles, canoes, arms, teeth, etc.).
rúwéfutuk (3) See *rúwa-*, *futuk*. num. two pieces of meat.
rúwéffaat (3) See *rúwa-*, *ffaata-*. num. two strings of fish.
rúwéffit (3) See *rúwa-*, *fitta-*. num. two leaf packages of small fish.
rúwésap (3) See *rúwa-*, *saap*. num. two cheeks (especially of fish).
rúwésángá (1) See *rúwa-*, *sángá*. num. two basketfuls of fish. Syn. *rúwésáwá*.
rúwésáwá (1) See *rúwa-*, *sáwa*. num. two basketfuls of fish. Syn. *rúwésángá*.
rúwéseeng (3) See *rúwa-*, *seeng*. num. two lengths between joints.
rúwésen (2) See *rúwa-*, *-sen*. num. two coils of rope. [Each coil is 30 to 100 fathoms in length according to local custom.]
rúwésópw (2) See *rúwa-*, *sópwu-*$_2$. num. two segments.

rúwéssaar (2) See *rúwa-, -ssaar.* Var. *rúwéssar.* num. two slices.

rúwéssak (3) See *rúwa-, ssaka-.* num. two pieces of copra.

rúwéssar N. of *rúwéssaar.*

rúwéssáát (2, 3) See *rúwa-, -ssáát.* Var. *rúwéssát.* num. two slivers, longitudinal slices, splinters.

rúwéssát N. of *rúwéssáát.*

rúwéssupw (2) See *rúwa-, ssupwu-.* num. two tiny drops.

rúwékis (2) See *rúwa-, kisi-.* num. two little things or bits. Syn. *rúwéngin.*

rúwékit (3) See *rúwa-, -kit.* num. twenty thousand.

rúwékum (2) See *rúwa-, kumu-.* num. two mouthfuls or swallows of liquid.

rúwékumwuch (2) See *rúwa-, kumwuch.* num. two fistfuls or handfuls (of something); two hooves, paws, feet (of animals).

rúwékkamw (3b) See *rúwa-, kkamw.* num. two fragments or pieces (of cloth, paper).

rúwékkap (3) See *rúwa-, kkap.* num. two cupfuls.

rúwémas (3) See *rúwa-, -mas.* num. two things worn on the eyes (e.g., lenses of goggles) or attached to piercing weapons (e.g., spear points).

rúwémach (3) See *rúwa-, macha-.* num. two fish tails (in counting fish).

rúwémataf (3) See *rúwa-, matafa-.* num. two small portions, small amounts, little bits.

rúwémeech (2) See *rúwa-, -meech.* F. Var. *rúwémech, rúwémmech.* num. two portions of mashed breadfruit.

rúwémeet (3) See *rúwa-, meet$_2$.* num. two strands.

rúwémech N. var. of *rúwémeech.*

rúwémén (2) See *rúwa-, maan$_1$.* num. two person or creatures (people, mammals, birds, fish, insects; but not lobsters, crabs, sea cucumbers, or shell fish); two knives, guns, files, scissors.

rúwémma (1) See *rúwa-, -mma.* num. two mouthfuls of premasticated food.

rúwémmech N. var. of *rúwémeech.*

rúwémmék (2) See *rúwa-, mékkú-.* num. two fragments.

rúwémwénú (1) See *rúwa-, mwénúú-.* num. two ells (lengths from elbow to fingertips).

rúwémwu E.Wn. of *rúwémwú$_2$.*

rúwémwú$_1$ (1) See *rúwa-, mwúú-$_1$.* F. Var. *rúwémwmwú.* num. two torm fragments (of rag or string).

rúwémwú$_2$ (1) See *rúwa-, mwúú-$_2$.* Var. *rúwémwu.* num. two sea cucumbers; two pieces of feces.

rúwémwúch (2) See *rúwa-, mwúch.* num. two pieces of firewood.

rúwémwmwék See *rúwa-, mwékkú-.* N. num. two bits or morsels (of mashed food). Syn. *rúwépwey.*

rúwémwmwun (3) See *rúwa-, mwmwúna-.* N. num. two portions of *mwatún.* Syn. *rúwétún.*

rúwémwmwú N. of *rúwémwú$_1$.*

rúwémwmwún F. of *rúwémwmwun.*

rúwénnú (1) See *rúwa-, nnúú-.* num. two loaves of breafruit pudding or amounts of breafruit to be mashed into pudding loaves.

rúwéngaf (3) See *rúwa-, ngaaf.* num. two fathoms, twice the distance from fingertip to fingertip of outstretched hands.

rúwéngát (4) See *rúwa-, -ngát.* num. two concave or hollow objects; (less common) two things of most any kind. Cf. *rúwépwang.*

rúwéngeréw (2) See *rúwa-, -ngeréw.* num. two thousand.

rúwéngin (2) See *rúwa-, ngini-.* num. two little things or bits. Syn. *rúwékis.*

rúwépa (1) See *rúwa-, -pa.* num. two fronds, garlands, stalks with leaves. [Of palm trees, banana trees, *Cyrtosperma*, and also of leis or garlands, necklaces, bead belts.]

rúwépan (3) See *rúwa-, paan$_1$.* num. two branches with leaves (of trees other than palms and bananas). Syn. *rúwépachang.* Cf. *rúwépa.*

rúwépachang (3) See *rúwa-, pachang.* num. two branches with leaves. Syn. *rúwépan.*

rúwépeek (2) See *rúwa-, peek$_2$.* num. two sides, pages.

rúwépeche (1) See *rúwa-, peche.* num. two lower or hind limbs (of humans, birds, and animals only).

rúwépék (2) See *rúwa-, péék$_2$.* num. two chips, chipped off pieces, cigarette butts.

rúwépéw (2) See *rúwa-, -péw.* num. two wings or things worn over hand or arm (e.g. gloves).

Trukese-English

rúwépino (1) See *rúwa-, pino.* num. two small packages of breadfruit pudding.

rúwépinúk (2) See *rúwa-, pinúk.* num. two tied bundles, reams of paper.

rúwépu (1) See *rúwa-, puu-₂.* num. two strokes in swimming (in measuring distance).

rúwépwang (3) See *rúwa-, pwaang.* num. two holes, caves, cavities, pits, tunnels, hollows. Cf. *rúwéngát.*

rúwépwey (2) See *rúwa-, -pwey.* num. two pinches or morsels of breadfruit pudding. Syn. *rúwémwmwék.*

rúwépwéét (2) See *rúwa-, pwéét₂.* num. two noses.

rúwépwi (1) See *rúwa-, pwii-₁.* num. two groups, groves, flocks, schools, herds, swarms, convoys, prides, etc.

rúwépwin (2) See *rúwa-, pwiin₃.* num. two nights.

rúwépwopw (2) See *rúwa-, pwoopw.* num. two tree trunks, bases, causes, foundations, sources, beginnings, origins, reasons.

rúwépwór (4) See *rúwa-, pwóór.* num. two boxes or crates (of something).

rúwépwúkú (1) See *rúwa-, -pwúkú.* num. two hundred.

rúwépwún (2) See *rúwa-, pwúún₁.* Var. *rúwépwpwún.* num. two pieces (broken off).

rúwépwpwaaw (2) See *rúwa-, pwpwaaw.* num. two home-made cigarettes.

rúwépwpwún N. of *rúwépwún.*

rúwéchamw (3) See *rúwa-, -chamw.* num. two foreheads, brows or similarly classed objects (e.g. visors, stem-bases of coconut fronds); two fishheads.

rúwéchef See *rúwa-, -chef.* num. two tentacles (of octopus or squid); two pieces of firewood. Syn. *rúwéyó, rúwéwút.*

rúwéchú (1) See *rúwa-, chúú.* num. two bone segments (of meat).

rúwéchúk (2) See *rúwa-, chúúk.* num. two coconut-leaf baskets (of something).

rúwéchchi (1) See *rúwa-, chchi-.* num. two drops.

rúwétinewupw (2) See *rúwa-, tinewupw.* num. two yards (lengths from center of chest to outstretched fingertips).

rúwétip (3) See *rúwa-, tiip₂.* num. two slices, chunks, cut segments (of breadfruit and taro only).

rúwowut

rúwétit (2) See *rúwa-, -tit.* num. two strings (of breadfruit, usually ten to a string). Syn. *rúwéttiit.*

rúwétú (1) See *rúwa-, túú.* Tbl. num. two vulvas.

rúwétúkúm (3) See *rúwa-, túkúm.* num. two packages of breadfruit pudding.

rúwétún (2) See *rúwa-, túnú-.* F. Var. *rúwéttún.* num. two portions of mwatún. Syn. *rúwémwmwun.*

rúwéttiit (2) See *rúwa-, ttiit₂.* num. two strings of ten breadfruit. Syn. *rúwétit.*

rúwéttún N. of *rúwétún.*

rúwéwumw (2) See *rúwa-, wumwu-₂.* Var. *ruwowumw.* num. two stalks of bananas.

rúwéwupw (2) See *rúwa-, wupwu-.* Var. *ruwowupw.* num. two breasts.

rúwéwúk₁ (2) See *rúwa-, wúúk₁.* num. two tails (in counting fish). Cf. *rúwémach.*

rúwéwúk₂ (2) See *rúwa-, wúúk₂.* num. two fingernails, toenails, claws.

rúwéwún (3a) See *rúwa-, wúún₁.* num. two feathers, scales, hairs.

rúwéwút (2) See *rúwa-, -wút.* num. two fingers or toes; five octopus tentacles, insect legs. Cf. *rúwéchef, rúwéyó.*

rúwéwúwéw (2) See *rúwa-, -wúwéw.* num. two amounts of fermented breadfruit suitable for kneading.

rúwéyaf (3b) See *rúwa-, -af.* num. two pieces of intestine.

rúwéyang (3) See *rúwa-, -ang.* num. two finger spans; two entire limbs (of an animal).

rúwéyef (2) See *rúwa-, eef₁.* num. two bunches of ripe coconuts.

rúwéyem (2) See *rúwa-, eem.* num. two earlobes.

rúwéyep (2) See *rúwa-, epi-₁.* num. two butt ends, lower ends, west ends.

rúwéyék (2) See *rúwa-, ékkú-.* num. two nets.

rúwéyó (1) See *rúwa-, óó₁.* num. two tentacles (of octopus or squid). Syn. *rúwéchef, rúwéwút.*

rúwofóch Var. of *rúwéfóch.*

rúwokkumw (2, 3) See *rúwa-, kkumw₁.* num. two portions of premasticated food.

rúwowut (2) See *rúwa-, wutu-.* num. 1. two cores (especially of breadfruit). 2. two chunks of cooked breadfruit.

rúwóówut (3) See *rúwa-*, *ówut*. Var. *ruwóówut*. num. two rows of thatch.

rúwówo (1) See *rúwa-*, *-wo$_1$*. num. two clumps (of bananas).

rré (dc; 1) See *ré$_1$*. nu. (T1) groping with the hands (as reaching in a hole). va. grope, grope for. *wúpwe r. nipwpwey* I will g. for crabs (in their holes).

rrus (dc; 2) See *ru-*, *-si-*. Var. *rus*. va., vi. gather; be gathered. Cf. *rusi*.

rrup Var. (dc) of *rup$_3$*.

CH

-ch CHA₁. suf. (pos.) 1inc. pos. prn.: our, of us (including person addressed). *waach* our canoe (*waa*, b.f. WAA), *néwúch* our child (*naaw*, b.f. NÉWÚ), *samach* our father (*saam*, b.f. SAMA), *sinich* our skin (*siin*, b.f. SINI).

cha- (3: -*ch*) CHA₂. [In cpds. only.] unsp. wedged; pressed together.

cha (1) CHAA₁. Tb2. vi. eat; drink; chew; smoke (cigarettes). Dis. *chaacha* (db). Cf. *mwéngé, wochooch, wún, ngngúúng*.

chaa-₁ (1) CHAA₂. [In cpds. only.] unsp. blood.

chaa-₂ (1) CHAA₃. [In cpds. only.] unsp. big, large, extensive. See *achaacha, chéécha*.

chaa (1) See *cha*. Tb2. Var. *chcha₂* n. (T1) food; drink; chew of tobacco. *waato ena ch., sipwe cha* bring that food, we will eat. Cf. *mwéngé*.

chaamw (3) CHAMWA. n. (T3) forehead, brow. *echamw ch.* one f. (see -*chamw*). *chamwan* his f. *chamwen akkaw* visor of a cap [cf. *penin akkaw* brim of a hat]. *chamwen pááney* part of the coconut frond from the stem to the first leaf.

chaan (2) CHÉNÚ. n. (T2) 1. liquid, juice. [Usually in partitive construction with 3rd sg. pos. prn.] *chénún* its l. *chénún maas* tears. *chénún núú* coconut milk. *chénún owupw* breast milk. *chénún owupwun kkowu* cow's milk. *chénún pwunech* liquid honey. 2. fresh water. *chénún chénúttu* well water. Syn. *kkónik, kkónuk, pweke*.

chaap (3b) CHAPPA. F. Var. *chchap*. vi., adj. (be) face down. With dir. suf.: *chappanó, chappónó* turned away face down; *chappetiw* bend over, bow down (as in prayer). *ewe áát aa chappanó pwe aa chepeti ewe faaw* the boy fell face-down because he stumbled on the stone.

chaapaap (3) See *cha-, apaap*₁. N. vi., adj. 1. (be) crushed; flattened. Syn. *pachchaach*. 2. very low. *meyi wor ekkóóch sókkun peet meyi ch.* there are some kinds of beds which are very low. With dir. suf.: *chaapaapanó* fall flat.

chaapwúúr (Mck.) vi., adj. (be) very much (?). [Outside of the Bible, it is used only in the expression *kinissow ch.* "thank you v. m."]

chaari See *cha, -ri-*. Tb2. vo. (T4) eat; drink; chew; smoke (cigarettes). With n. form. suf.: *chaariya-* (ni.; T3) food; something to eat, drink, chew, or smoke. Syn. *áni, wocheey, wúnúmi, ngúti*.

chaacha₁ Dis. of *cha*.

chaacha₂ (db; 1) CHAA₄. Tb1. nu. (dis.) noise made by genitals during sexual intercourse.

chammóng (4) See *cha, mmóng*. Tb2. va. eat or drink heartily. Syn. *mwéngémmóng, wúnúmmóng*.

champang (3) CHAMPANGA. (Jap. *zanpan*) nu. dump, place for disposing refuse; garbage.

-chamw See *chaamw*. suf. (cc.) (in counting) forehead, brow, or similarly classed object (e.g., visor, stem-base of coconut frond); fish head. *echamw, rúwéchamw, wúnúchamw, féchamw, nimechamw, wonochamw, fúúchamw, wanúchamw, ttiwechamw* one,...nine f.; *fitechamw* how many f. *echhamw chhamwen iik* one fishhead. With c. pref. and ptv. const.: *ááchamwan, érúwéchamwan* first f., second f. (etc.). With dis. c. pref.: *ákkááchamw, ékkérúwéchamw* be one f. at a time, two f. at a time (etc.).

chamwan faan See *chaamw, faa-*. n. phr. 26th night of the lunar month ("its brow under it").

chamwekún (3) See *chaamw, kúna-*. vi., adj. (be) bald-headed.

chamwerech See *chaamw, rech₂*. nu. projecting pair of horns that form the prow and stern end-pieces of the *meniyuk* sailing canoe.

chamweyinú (1) See *chaamw, núú*. nu. serrated war-club. *efóch ch.* one w.-c. *aan, néwún* or *wókun ch.* his w.-c.

Chamworo (1) CHAMWOROO. (Cham.) nu. Chamorro (person); (rarely) a person who is a "half-caste" in between a "white" and "dark" skinned person.

chana (1) CHANAA. (Eng. *dollar*). nu. (T1) dollar; money. *eew ch.* one d.; *eché ch.* one d. bill. *néwún ch.* his d. *wúpwe néwúni eféw féwún eew ch.* I want to get a silver d. *wúpwe néwúni óóchh féwúféwún eew ch.* I want one d. in coins. Syn. *maak, mwooni.*

chang (3) CHANGA. vi., adj. fly, (be) flying, (be) in flight. *ewe sepenin aa ch.*. the plane took off (i.e., became flying).

changke₁ (1) CHANGKEE₁. (Jap. *janken*) nu. game of scissors-stone-cloth. vi. play scissors-stone-cloth. excl. *ch. ssi* or *ch. chchi* or *ch. pwpwo* uttered by players in time with throwing their hands.

changke₂ (1) CHANGKEE₂. F. (Jap.?). nu. money cowrie shell. Syn. *nimwárá.*

chappanó See *chaap, chchap.*

chappetiw See *chaap.*

chapwen Tb2. vi., adj. (be) face up; (be) lying on one's back. With dir. suf.: *chapwenetá.* Syn. *seneetá.* Ant. *chaap, chchaap.*

char (3b) CHARA. vi. glow, (be) glowing (of coals). *ewe faaw nnón ewe ekkey aa ch.* the stone in in the fire is glowing. Cf. *kú₁.*

chareyiti See *char, -iti.* vo. (T2) glow until (of coals). *ch. winingách* glow until dawn. Cf. *kúúyiti.*

chach (db; 3) See *cha-.* N. Var. *sach.* vi., adj. (be) wedged, fastened with wedges; crowded, dense, pressed together.

chawang (3) CHAWANGA. (Jap. *chawan*) nu. (T3) rice-bowl. *eew ch.* one r. *aan ch.* his r.

chayimen (Eng. *diamond*) nu. diamond; diamonds (in cards). *eféw ch.* one d. (precious stone); *emén ch.* one d. (card).

chá (1) CHÁÁ. vi., adj. (be) appeased, soothed, calmed (of anger, often by gifts). Dis. *cháácha* (db). With suf. adj.: *chákkáy* be quickly a.; *chámmang* be slowly a. Cf. *chááŕ, chááŕi.*

cháásowupa (1) See *chá, sowupa.* vi., adj. (be) not easily appeased; (be) slowly soothed (of anger).

cháánu (1) CHÁÁNUU. nu. (T1) a variety of *kká* taro (*Alocasia*) with dark leaves.

chááŋeni See *chá, ngeni.* vo. (T2) be appeased (of anger) toward.

chááp (2) CHEPI. Tb1. n. (T2) genitals (general term). *chepin* his g. Cf. *chepitá.*

cháár See *chá, -ri-.* [Presumably a back formation from *chááŕi.*] vi. be appeased, soothed, calmed (of anger). [Used with *sefáán.*] *cháár sefáán* be reconciled, be appeased back again (of anger). *cháár-sefááŋiiy* (vo.phr.) be reconciled with (someone). *aa cháár-sefááŋiikeem me átewe* he has reconciled me and him ("us and him").

chááŕi See *chá, -ri-.* vo. (T4) appease, soothe, calm (someone who is angry). Dis. *cháácháári* (db), *cháchchááŕi* (ds) [The former is preferred]. *Fritz aa resin ne ch. ewe nengngin nge ese fókkun chá* Fritz tried to soothe the girl, but she was not much soothed. Cf. *cháár.*

cháácha (db; 1) See *chá.* vi., adj. (dis.) (be) appeased, soothed, calmed (of anger). va. (dis.) appease, soothe, calm (of anger) *ch. ffengen* soothe one another's feelings.

chááchááŕi Dis. of *chááŕi.*

chákkáy See *chá.*

chámmang See *chá.*

cháchcháák (ds; 2) CHÁÁKI. vi., adj. (be) thin (of flat objects such as leaves, paper, boards).

cháchchááŕi Dis. of *chááŕi.*

che- (3a: *che-, ché-, cho-, chó-, -ch*) CHA₃. Var. *chche-₂.* pref. (adj.) state of being. Cf. *ma-, mwa-, pwa-, sa-.*

che (1) CHEE₁. Var. *chche.* vi. be in motion, move (of only the bowels in this form, but generally in cpds.); flee, run away (in cpds.). *ese che omwu* the bowels have not moved.

-che (1) CHEE₂. [In cpds. only.] unsp. (u.m.) See *paache.*

chee (1) CHEE₃. nu. (T1) a kind of small, sharp coral. *ewumw ch.* one c. (as a whole); *efóch ch.* one c. (stem or branch only).

cheeneeyamw (3) See *che, nee-, aamw.* n. (T3) stringer from outrigger boom to outrigger stanchion on canoe. *esen ch., efóch ch.* one s. *aan ch.* his s. *cheeneeyamwen waa* canoe's s.

cheenong (3) See *che, -nong.* n. (T3) client member, person admitted into or attached to a lineage or clan but who is not a member by birth. *cheenongen eyinang* c. m. of a clan. vi.

be a client member (lit. "move in"). *aa ch. nóón ewe eyinang* he became a c. m. of the clan. Cf. *cheeyenong.*

cheenongeey See *cheenong, -e-₂*. vo. (T6b) join (a clan or lineage only) as a client member. *raa chék ch. áán feefinen semeer we eyinang* they just joined their father's sister's clan. Cf. *ácheenonga.*

cheenó (1) See *che, -nó.* vi. run off, hurry off. Cf. *cheeyenó.*

cheenóóy [Short for *cheenó iya (iye)*.] v. phr. run away to where. *iyaan kkewe féépwún re ch.* where those young women were running away to.

cheengngaw (3) See *che, ngngaw*. Var. *chengngaw*. nu. (T3) accidental mistake, error, misstep. *aan ch.* his m. *omwusóónó reen ááy ch.* pardon my mistake ("pardon it on account of my accidental mistake"). vi. make a mistake, error, mistep. Dis. *cheecheengngaw* (db).

cheepen (2) CHEEPENI. (Eng. *table*) nu. table. *eew ch.* one t. *aan ch.* his t. Id. *ffót ch.* have a big party ("plant tables").

cheepenikú (1) See *che, pa-₁* (?), *kúú-₂* or *kúú-₃*. nu. typhoon, hurricane. Syn. *puunumén.*

cheeraanó See *cheeri.*

cheeraato See *cheeri.*

cheeri See *che, -ri-*. vo. (T4) fetch; go catch; run after and get. With dir. suf.: (N.) *cheeraanó*, (F.) *cheeróónó* f. yonder; *cheeraato* f. hither.

cheeróónó See *cheeri.*

cheeche (db; 1) See *che.* vi. (dis.) be in continuing motion; be moving fast; be running. *ewe áát aa ch. pwe aa chiichi ewe ráán* the boy was running because it was raining.

cheecheengngaw Dis. of *cheengngaw.*

cheew₁ (1, 2) CHUU₃ (*CHEWU), CHEEWI. nu. (T1, T2) fish net (general term). *aan ch., néwún ch.* her n. *chuun n.* for (fishing); *cheewin* n. from (place). *mesen ch.* net's mesh. *chuun kkótur* n. for *kkótur* fishing. *chuun méngér* n. for flying fish; *chuun mweemw* women's n. of largest mesh; *chuun nimwérúng* n. with fine mesh for *nimwérúng* fishing. *chuun nitáátá, chuun niyenika* women's n. with finest mesh; *chuun noowu* anchovy n.; *chuun pétú* mackerel n.; *chuun pwachú* n. for *pwachú* fishing. *chuun senif* herring n.; *chuun wumwuné* net for *wumwuné* fishing. *chuun wiin* turtle n.; also a maneuver in fighting by which an opponent's arms are twisted behind him and broken. *cheewin Chuuk* Trukese fish net.

Cheew₂ [Derived from *cheew₁.*] nu. a star or constellation (probably Corona Borealis); a month in the traditional sidereal calendar (named for the star).

cheewenewen (db; 3) See *che, wen.* vi. move in a straight line. *ewe mwáán aa ch. ngeni imwanú we* the man walked straight to his house. Cf. *chchewenewen.*

cheewu (1) See *che, -wu.* vi. move out; run outside; go outside. *kepwe ch. reen Eiue* you will go outside to where Eiue is. Cf. *cheeyewu.*

cheey See *che.* F. Var. *chchey.* vo. (T1) chase; shoo away; put to rout; pursue; hunt. With dir. suf.: *cheeyenong* c. in; *ewe konaak aa cheeyenong ewe káttu nóón ewe iimw* the dog chased the cat into the house. *cheeyenó* c. away; *cheeyewu* c. out.

cheeyenong See *cheey.*

cheeyenó See *cheey.*

cheeyewu See *cheey.*

cheeyééch (2: -échchú-) See *che, ééch.* vi. be lucky, fortunate.

-chef Tn. suf. (cc.) 1. tentacle (of octopus or squid). *echef, rúwéchef, wúnúchef, féchef, nimechef, wonochef, fúúchef, wanúchef, ttiwechef* one,...nine t. *echef éwútún nippach* one octopus t. Syn. *-wút, óó.* 2. piece of firewood. *echef émwúch* one p. of f.; *echef masis* one match.

chekkáy (2) See *che, kkáy.* vi. hurry. With dir. suf.: *chekkáyito* h. hither.

chekkáyito See *chekkáy.*

cheme- (3a) CHEMA. [In cpds. only.] unsp. remembering, recalling.

chememmang (3) See *cheme-, mmang.* n. (T3) poor memory. vi. be of poor memory.

chen (2) CHENI. Var. *chengi-*. vi. be loved, favored, cherished; pampered. Syn. *áchengicheng, fón, pwó.* ni. (T2) love, favoring, cherishing. *chenin* l. of or for him. *cheniy me reemw* love of me by you; *chenumw me reey* love of you by me. *chenin ewe áát me reen saman we meyi fókkun wátte* the father's love for his son is very great.

chene- (4) CHENE. [In cpds. only.] unsp. light, shiny.

chenechen (db; 3a) See *chene-*. vi., adj. (dis.) (be) glossy, shiny (hence said of someone with a balding head).

chenetaka (1) See *chene-, taka*. nu. (T1) a food prepared from turmeric starch (*opuun teyuk*) and coconut cream, which are mixed and baked.

chenikam Var. of *chchenikam*.

chennaaw Var. of *chéénnaw*.

chennaaweey Var. of *chénnaaweey*.

chennakan Var. of *chénnakan*.

chennakaneey Var. of *chénnakaneey*.

chengi- (2) CHENGI. [In cpds. only.] unsp. loved; cherished. Cf. *chen*.

chep (2) See *chááp*. Tbl. Var. *pech*. vi. become erect (of penis).

chepeti See *chchep$_1$, -ti-*. vo. (T6a) kick. Cf. *chuputi*.

chepitá (1) See *chááp, -tá*. Tbl. (Mck.) nu. (T1) beginning. vi. begin, commence.

chere- (3v: *chere-, choro-*) See *che-, ra-$_3$*. pref. (adj., intens.) state of being very much. See *cheremmis, choropwpwun*. Cf. *mara-*.

cheremmis (2) See *chere-, mmis*. vi. gleam very brightly. *kaa mmen ch. pwúún kaa epituk kiriis* you are very shiny because you put pomade on your hair.

cherepwpwun (3a) See *chere-, pwpwun$_1$*. Var. *choropwpwun*. vi. be flashing (of eyes). Syn. *merepwpwun, mesepwpwun, mesettin*.

cheris (2) CHERISI. nu. a kind of pompano fish. *emén ch.* one p. *wochaan* or *anan* his p. (to eat).

chero (1) CHEROO. (Eng.) nu. (num.; T1) zero. Syn. *woo$_2$*.

chechchem (ds; 3a) See *cheme-*. nu. (dis.; T3) memory; remembering. *aan ch.* his m.; *chechchemen* m. of (something). va. (dis.) remember.

chechchemeni (ds) See *cheme-, -ni-*. vo. (dis.; T6a) remember, recall.

chechchenó Dis. of *chchenó*.

cheyi- (2) CHEYI. Tb. [In cpds. only.] unsp. pertaining to slimy, mucousy body fluids. See *mecheyichey*.

-ché (1) See *chéé*. suf. (cc.) (in counting) leaf; sheet; thin flat object; song. [Used with numerical prefixes.] *eché, rúwaché, wúnúché, faché, nimaché, wonaché fúúché, wanúché, ttiwaché,*

engoon chéén one,...ten l.; *fitaché* how many l. *eché chéé* one leaf; *eché toropwe* one sheet of paper; *eché paap* one board; *eché kkéén* one song. With c. pref. and ptv. const.: *ááchéén, érúwachéén* first l., second l. With dis. c. pref.: *ákkááché, ékkérúwaché* be one l. at a time, two l. at a time. With pref. *áná-*: *ánááché, ánárúwaché* sole or only l.; sole or only two l.

chéé-$_1$ (1) CHÉÉ$_2$. [In ptv. const. only.] ni. (T1) width, breadth (of flat objects only) Dis. *chééchéé-* (db). *ifa chéén* what is its w.; how wide is it? *engoon iyaach chééchéén* its w. is ten yards; it is ten yards wide.

chéé-$_2$ (1) CHÉÉ$_3$. [In cpds. and ptv. const. only.] ni. (T1) payment in settlement of a debt, feud, war. *chéén paaw* gift made to a woman in return for her attending another woman in childbirth ("payment for the hand"); midwife's fee. Cf. *choon wóók*.

chéé (1) CHÉÉ$_1$. n. (T1) leaf, sheet. *eché ch.* one l. *chéén* its l., l. of. *chéén irá* leaf of a tree; *chéén mwéngé* tongue; *chéén núú* coconut leaf (as distinct from frond); *chéén toropwe* sheet of paper. See also *-ché*.

chééfénú (3) See *chéé-$_2$, fénú*. nu. (T3) peace-making (in warfare). *chééfénúwen* p.-m. of. vi. make peace.

chéékamw (3) See *chéé-$_1$, kamwa-*. vi., adj. (be) wide, broad (of flat objects). Syn. *chéécha, chéémmóng, chéénap, chéérapw, chééwátte*. Ant. *chéékis, chéékúkkún*.

chéékis (2) See *chéé-$_1$, kisi-*. vi., adj. (be) narrow (of flat objects). Syn. *chéékúkkún*. Ant. *chéécha, chéékamw, chéémmóng, chéénap, chéérapw, chééwátte*.

chéékúkkún (2) See *chéé-$_1$, kúkkún*. vi., adj. (be) narrow (of flat objects). Syn. *chéékis*. Ant. *chhéémmónng, chhéénap, chhééwátte, chhéékamw, chhééchha, chhéérapw*. nr. (T2) 2. narrowness (of flat objects).

Chééma nu. (loc.) a clan name. *fiin Ch., fin Ch.* C. woman; *mwáán Ch.* C. man. *chóón Ch.* people of C.

chéémmóng (4) See *chéé-$_1$, mmóng*. vi., adj. (be) wide, broad (of flat objects). Syn. *chééwátte, chéékamw, chéécha, chéénap, chéérapw*. Ant. *chéékis, chéékúkkún*.

chéémwón (4) See *chéé, mwón.* nu. variety of breadfruit with unserrated leaves ("waterproof leaf").

chéénap (3b) See *chéé-₁, nap.* vi., adj. (be) wide, broad (of flat objects). Syn. *chééwátte, chéékamw, chéécha, chéérapw, chéémmóng.* Ant. *chéékis, chéékúkkún.* nr. (T3) wideness, broadness (of flat objects).

chééni See *chéé, -ni-.* vo. (T4) wrap in leaves.

chéénúfach (3) See *chéé, faach.* nu. (T3) groove at the bottom of a canoe ("pandanus leaf").

chéépéép See *chéé-₁, pa-.* Var. *chééchéép* (of which this is presumably a corruption), *chépéép.* vi., adj. (be) broad. *meyi fókkun ch. neeyéwúngen ewe mwáán* the man has a very broad chest. Cf. *chaapaap.*

chéépwech See *chéé, pwech.* [Elbert] nu. a tree (*Heritiera*). [Its wood is used for bowls.] *efóch ch.* one ch. . Syn. *seefin.*

chéérapw (3) See *chéé-₁, rapwarapw.* vi., adj. (be) wide, broad (of flat objects). Syn. *chéécha, chéémmóng, chéékamw, chéénap, chééwátte.* Ant. *chéékis, chéékúkkún.*

chéécha (1) See *chéé-₁, chaa-₂.* Tb2. Var. *ché-.* vi., adj. (be) wide, broad (of flat objects). Syn. *chéékamw, chéémmóng, chéénap, chéérapw, chééwátte.* Ant. *chéékis, chéékúkkún.*

chééché (db; 1) CHÉÉ₄. n. (T1) center; middle. *chééchéén anaw* middle board on the outrigger platform of a paddle canoe. *Neechééché* an *eyif* of Romónum Island ("Center Place"). Syn. *nuuk.*

chééchéé- Dis. of *chéé-₁.*

chééchéén See *chééché, -ni-.* vi., adj. (be) true, reliable ("be centered"). *meyi ch. áán áténaan fóós* what that fellow says is true.

chééchéép (3) See *chéé-₁, pa-.* Var. *chéépéép.* vi., adj. (be) flat and broad.

chééchón See *chéé, chón.* nu. (T2) a vine (*Canavalia maritima, Canavalia microcarpa*). [Its leaves are used as medicine.] Syn. *wénúka.*

Chééchchiya See *chéé* or *chééché, chiya.* nu. (loc.) a clan name ("mangrove leaf" or "mangrove center"). *fiin Ch., fin Ch.* C. woman; *mwáán Ch.* C. man. *chóón Ch.* people of C.

chééw (2) CHÉÉWÚ. vi., adj. (be) continuous, uninterrupted, featureless, unbroken; (be) widespread, common (of knowledge). *ch. ffengen* go together as a unit. Cf. *paat₂.*

chééwátte (1) See *chéé-₁, wátte.* vi., adj. (be) wide, broad (of flat objects). Syn. *chéécha, chéékamw, chéémmóng, chéénap, chéérapw.* Ant. *chéékis, chéékúkkún.*

chééwiiti See *chééw, -iti.* vo. (T2) spread to. *ewe máátter aa ch. chóómmóng aramas* the flu s. to a lot of people.

chééwúfátán See *chééw, fátán.* vi. be well known; widespread; widely circulated; everywhere used; of common knowledge. *óómw angaangééch aa ch. wóón Chuuk* Your ability is widely known in Truk.

chééwúch (2) See *chéé, wúchú-2.* nu. (T2) a food made of breadfruit pudding and coconut cream with various herbs, according to different recipes, to flavor the cream.

chééyitúr (2) See *chéé, túúr.* nu. (T2) woman's traditional wrap-around skirt or kilt, woven from hibiscus and banana fibers. *eché ch.* one skirt. *aan ch.* her. *achawar ch.* loin cloth. Syn. *nopwonopwa.*

chéféné (1) See *che-.* vi., adj. (be) in a bad way; unfortunate. *wúwa ch. pwúún aa it ewe pisek* I was unfortunate because the thing had been sold out.

chék (2) CHÉKÚ. adv., qlf. only, merely, just. *kepwe ch. ekiyekiiy meet kepwe fééri* you will just think about what you will do. *ngaangú ch.* only me, just me. *iyeeyi ch.* right now, just now. *ngé eew ch. kepwe ch. wúreniyey* but only tell me just one thing ("but one thing only you will just tell me"). Id. *een ch.* it's up to you; suit yourself; just as you like; *iiri ch.* it's up to them.

chénaa- (1) See *che-, naa-.* Obs. ni. (T1) companion; familiar; pal; buddy. *emén ch.* one c. *chénaan* his c.; c. of. *chénaan pachaaw* dogfish shark. Syn. *pwiich₁.* Cf. *chiyena-.*

chénú- C.f. of *chaan.*

chénúkken (2) See *chaan, kken.* nu. (T2) class or member of a class of dangerous sea spirits. [Usually but not always female, they inhabit the shallow waters and have to be placated when people fish in their vicinity. Children should not swim every day or play around too much in the water or they will make the spirits angry and will get sick. There are many such spirits, each associated with a particular place. The names of of those in the waters of Romónum Island are *Inemeter, Inossow, Inowunong, Inowuwu, Neyinopw, Neyitippi, Nemenis, Néwúrúrúppi, Nimwetekéw, Nipúnúpúnúya, Nipwichchan, Nisékúrúpach, Nóópwór, Nuukenekaraw*.]

chénúpwich (2) See *chaan, pwich₁*. n. (T2) hot water. *chénúpwichin* his h. w. (to use, not to drink).

chénúpwichiiy See *chénúpwich*. vo. (T2) heat, boil (water). *kese mwochen kepwe ch. ekis chénúpwichiy?* will you please heat some water for me?

chénúpwuupwu (1) See *chaan, pwu₁*. nu. (T1) flowing water; stream, river; waterfall. *eew ch.* one stream. Cf. *éwúrá, éwúwé₁*.

chénúchcha (1) See *chaan, chcha*. nu. (T1) a sea worm. [Edible, it is found in branching coral.]

chénúttu (1) See *chaan, ttu₁*. nu. (T1) well ("dug water"). *chénún ch.* w. water.

chénnaaw (3) See *chéé, ne-, aaw*. [From *chéé-ni-ne-yaw*.] Var. *chennaaw*. n. (T3) tongue. *eché ch.* one t. *chénnaawan* his t. Syn. *chéén mwéngé, chénnakan*.

chénnaaweey See *chénnaaw, -e-₂*. Var. *chennaaweey*. vo. (T6b) lick, taste; put one's tongue to. *ewe káttu aa ch. péwún we* the cat licked his paw. Syn. *chénnakaneey*.

chénnakan (3) See *chéé, ne-, ana-*. [From *chéé-ni-ne-kan*.] Var. *chennakan*. n. (T3) tongue. *chénnakanan* his t. Syn. *chéén mwéngé, chénnaaw*.

chénnakaneey See *chénnakan, -e-₂*. Var. *chennakaneey*. vo. (T6b) lick, taste; put the tongue to. Syn. *chénnaaweey*.

chépéép Var. of *chéépéép*.

chéchchén Dis. of *chchén*.

chéwátte Var. of *chééwátte*.

Chéwúkkúk Tn. nu. (loc.) clan name. [Local name for the *Sowuwefeg* clan on Toon (Tol) Island.]

chi- (2) CHI. pref. (u.m.) See *chifféw, chipóón*

chi (3a, 1) CHIYA₁, CHII₄. vi. be uttered; vocalized; begun (of a song). *aa chi awatá Faachchamw* he gave voice mouth-up to heaven. With dir. suf.: *chiyetá* be begun as a vocal sound (in speaking, singing, weeping); *aa chiyetá ewe kkéén* the song began.

chii-₁ (1) CHII₁. [In cpds. or ptv. const. only.] unsp. drip, drop, sprinkle.

chii-₂ (1) CHII₂. [In cpds. only.] unsp. See *chiinnap*.

chii (1) CHII₅. nu. (T1) name of the consonant (retroflex affricate) written *ch*; name of the digraph thus written.

chiimw (3a) CHIMWA. n. (T3) head. [Limited in use as compared with the more common *mékúr*.] *eew ch.* one h. *chimwan* his h.

chiimwéémwé (db; 1) See *chii-₁, mwé*. nu. (T1) sprinkling (of rain). vi. be sprinkling (of rain).

chiineyin (3?) CHIINEYINA (?). nu. (T3?) 1. a species of wrasse fish. 2. a sorcery done with the fish of this name. 3. a sickness caused by the sorcery of this name. 4. a medicine to cure the sickness of this name.

chiinnap (dc; 3) See *chii-₂, nap*. N. Var. *chinnap*. nu. (T3) elder, oldster, old person. *emén ch.* one e. *ch. mwáán* old man ("male e."); *ch. feefin* old woman ("female e."). vi. be old, aged (of people).

chiip (Eng.) nu. jeep.

chiipw (3) See *chipwa-*. nu. (T3) a kind of divination, done by bending the midrib of a coconut leaf many times.

chiichi₁ (db; 1) See *chii-₁*. nu. (T1) dripping, sprinkling. *chiichiin ráán* dripping of the rain. vi. be dripping, sprinkling.

chiichi₂ (db; 1) CHII₃. nu. (dis.; T1) a fern (*Phymotodes*). [It is used for leis and love magic. According to some it is the same as *wénnúmey* (*Polypodium scolopendris*), and according to others it is distinct.] *epwopw ch.* one f.

chiiyew (2) CHIIYEWI. nu. (T2) large leaf package of breadfruit pudding (as much as 3 ft. wide). *eew ch.* or *etúkúm ch.* one l. p. *anan ch.* his l. p.

chif₁ (2) CHIFI. Tbl. va. prod the female genitals with the penis in sexual foreplay. Dis. *chifichif* (db).

chif₂ (3a) CHIFA. Tb3. vi., adj. (be) nice, agreeable. *iiy emén meyi ch.* he is a n. person.

chifengngaw (3b) See *chif₂, ngngaw.* Tb3. nu. (T3) disagreeableness, ugliness. vi., adj. (be) disagreeable, ugly, not nice. *ewe nengngin meyi ch. fáán ekkewe fowut* the girl is ugly with those body decorations.

chiféech (2: *chiféchchú-*) See *chif₂, ééch.* Tb3. nu. (T2) agreeableness. vi., adj. (be) agreeable, very nice.

chifichif Dis. of *chif₁.*

chifiti See *chif₁, -ti-*. Tbl. vo. (T5) prod with the penis.

chifféw (2) See *chi-, faaw.* vi. cook fermented breadfruit in earth oven.

chifféwúúw See *chifféw, -ú-*. vo. (T5) cook in an earth oven for fermented breadfruit.

-chis (2) CHISI. N. Var. *-sich.* suf. (adj.) just beginning, incipient; little. Syn. *chiki-₁.*

chika (1) CHIKAA. vi. choke. [Used only with reference to fish bones.] *aa ch. reen chúún iik* he choked on a fish bone.

chikanta (1) CHIKANTAA. (Jap. *tsukanda*) excl. caught! [Said when a person has caught an opponent in the game of *chintori.*]

chikar (3b) CHIKARA. nu. (T3) (N.) cure; antidote. *chikaren nopwur* a charm or amulet made for babies to wear around their necks at sea to make them invisible to *Resiim*, the rainbow spirit. vi. 1. clear (of weather); subside (of wind). 2. (N.) recover (from illness); be fixed, repaired (of things). *ewe mwáán aa ch. seni aan we semwmwen* the man was cured of his sickness. *ewe waa aa ch.* the canoe was repaired. Syn. *pwáák.*

chiki-₁ (2) CHIKI₁. [In cpds. only.] adj. small, little. Dis. *chikichiiki-, chikichiki-* (db). Syn. *-chis.*

chiki-₂ (2) CHIKI₂. [In cpds. only.] unsp. blink the eyes (in weariness). Dis. *chikichiki-* (db).

chikichiiki- Dis. of *chiki-₁.*

chikongki (1) CHIKONGKII. (Jap. *chikuonki*) nu. (T1) phonograph; record player. *eew ch.* one p. *néwún ch.* his p.

chimék (2) CHIMÉKÚ. nu. (T2) an inedible variety of wet taro.

chimw (3a) See *chiimw.* vi., adj. (be) nodded, nod (once only, up or down). Dis. *chimwechimw* (db). With dir. suf.: *chimwetá* tip the head back; look up in the air; *chimwenong* stick one's head (into something). *ewe konaak aa chimwenong nnón ewe sepi* the dog stuck his head into the bowl.

chimwenong See *chimw.*

chimwenúúr (3a) See *chiimw, wúúr₂.* [From *chimwe-ni-wúr.*] nu. (T3) head-clearance height (of the crossbeam of a house; "head-nod of the corner post"). *meet chimwenúúren naan iimw?* what is the head-clearance height of that house?

chimwechimw (db; 3a) See *chimw.* vi. (dis.) be nodding (in drowsiness); pitch, bob, dip up and down (as a boat).

chimwetá See *chimw.*

chin (2) CHINI₂. F. vi., adj. have a sty. nr. (T2) sty. *chinin maas* s. of the eyes. Syn. *inacho.*

chinnap F. of *chiinnap.*

chintori (1) CHINTORII. (Jap. *jintori*) nu. (T1) children's game in which two teams compete to occupy each other's territory or camp. *eew ch.* one game.

chip (3) CHIPA. vi., adj. (be) comforted, consoled. *aa ch. pwe aa mwéngé wokasi* he was consoled because he ate candies. With dir. suf.: *chipenó.*

chipenó See *chip.*

chipóón Var. of *chipón.*

chipón (3) See *chi-, póón.* Var. *chipóón.* nu., vi. chum (in fishing).

chipóneey See *chipón, -e-₂.* vo. (T6b) chum for (fish).

chippú (1?) CHIPPÚÚ (?). (Jap. *chippu*) nu. (T1?) tip, foul tip (in baseball).

chipwa- (3) CHIPWA. unsp. bending, bowing, warping. See *chiipw, chipwang, chipwechipw, chipweyi.*

chipwang (3b) See *chipwa-, -ng.* vi. be tired, weary (from work); lazy; (with rel. suf.) be tired of. *wúwa chipwangen kúttóók* I have become tired of looking for you. Syn. *wúwet.*

chipwangeyiti See *chipwang, -iti.* vo. (T2) be tired from, weary because of. *wúwa ch. naan angaang* I feel lazy about doing that work.

chipwangonumw (2) See *chipwang, numw₁.* nu. (T2) fatigue, exhaustion (from work). *chipwangonumwun naan* *aramas* that person's fatigue. vi. be exhausted, very tired, very weary.

chipwechipw (db; 3) See *chipwa-*. n. (dis.; T3) curve, arch, bow; zigzag line (with pointed or rounded corners). *meyi wor chipwechipwan* it has a curve. *chipwechipwen fétumw meyi ákkámángngaw* your arched eyebrow is irresistibly provoking (in love talk). vi., adj. (be) curved, bent, arched, bowed (of mountain, cape, pole, stick of wood, eyebrow, etc.).

chipweyi See *chiipw, -yi-$_2$*. vo. (T6a) divine by *chiipw* method. *kepwe ch. mwo neyiy we áát* you will divine (the illness of) my son. Syn. *echipwa*. Cf. *echchipwa*.

chitoosa (1) CHITOOSAA. (Jap. *jidoosha*) nu. (T1) automobile (passenger car only). *efóch ch.* one a. *waan ch.* his a.; *chitoosaan Sapaan* Japanese a.

chiwa- (3a) CHIWA. [In cpds. only.] unsp. crying, weeping.

chiya- (3a) CHIYA$_3$. unsp. accompany; companion. See *chiyena-, chiyeneni, chiyechi*.

chiya$_1$ (1) CHIYAA$_1$. nu. (T1) mangrove tree (*Rhizophora*). *efóch ch.* one m. tree; one stick of m. wood. *aan ch.* his m. tree; *imwan ch.* his wood (as building material); *chiyaan Chuuk* Trukese m. *chiyaan iimw* or *chiyaaniimw* (*chiyaa-ni-imw) species of m. used for house rafters (*R. apiculata*). *chiyaan wuumw* or *chiyaanuumw* (*chiyaa-ni-wumw) species of m. used for firewood (*R. mucronata*). With adj. suf.: *chiyaanap* a large m. tree (not a variety or species) by contrast with *chiya kúkkún*. Cf. *woong*.

chiya$_2$ (1) CHIYAA$_2$. (Eng. *deer*) nu. (T1) deer. *emén ch.* one d. *néwún ch.* his pet d.; *wochaan ch.* his d. (as food); *chiyaan Merika* American d.

chiyaanap See *chiya$_1$*.

chiyaaperiper (2) See *chiya$_1$, peri-*. nu. plain or smooth-sided warclub ("cut-into-shape mangrove"). *emén ch.* or *efóch ch.* one w.

chiyena- (3) See *chiya-, -na-$_1$*. Var. *chchiyena-*. ni. (T3) companion, colleague, fellow-traveler, friend; what goes together with something else (as component parts of something). *emén chiyenan kkewe* one of his friends. *chiyenan* his c. *Keneeto mé chiyenan kkanaan* Keneeto and those companions of his. Id. *chiyenen ménúkón* afterbirth ("infant's c."). Syn. *chiyechi*. Cf. *chénaa-, pwiich*.

chiyeneni See *chiyena-, -ni-*. vo. (T6a) acquire as a companion or friend.

chiyechi (db; 3a) See *chiya-*. n. (dis.; T3) companion, friend, acquaintance (i.e. one with whom one talks). [Said to be less good usage than *chiyena-*.] *emén ch.* one c. *chiyechiyan* his c. Syn. *chiyena-*. Cf. *chénaa-, pwiich*. vi. (d.) be companions, friends. *raa ch. ffengeen* they became c.

chiyetá See *chi*.

chiyor (3a) CHIYORA. [Possibly a cpd. with *chi*.] n. (T3) throat. *chiyoran* his t.

chiyoromá (1) See *chiyor, má*. F. nu. (T1) a hold in hand-to-hand fighting. [Against an opponent slashing with a knife, one grabs his right (slashing) arm with one's left hand, pushing his arm to one's right. At the same time one puts one's right arm under one's own left arm and over the opponent's right arm and pushes one's right wrist or forearm against his throat, pulling back his right arm with one's left hand to provide leverage for pressure against his Adam's apple.] Syn. *newúwémá*.

chiyoromááni See *chiyoromá, -ni-*. vo. (T6a) apply the *chiyoromá* hold to (someone).

cho (1) See *choo$_2$*. vi., adj. (be) strong.

choo-$_1$ (1) CHOO$_3$. N. Var. *soo-$_2$*. vi., adj. (be) wasted, lost. See *choochis*.

choo-$_2$ (1) CHOO$_4$. n. (u.m.) See *choochón*.

choo$_1$ (1) CHOO$_1$. N. nu. (T1) very ripe coconut; copra. *eew ch., eféw ch., engát ch.* one c. *aan ch.* his c. (to dispose of); *anan ch.* his c. (to eat). Syn. *taka*.

choo$_2$ (1) CHOO$_2$. n. (T1) strength. *choon* his s. *choon wóók* land acquired as spoils of war ("strength of the club", cf. *chéé-$_2$*).

choof (3) CHOFA. Tb1. n. (T3) penis. *efóch ch.* one p. *chofan* his p.

choofar (3) See *choo$_1$, faar*. nu. (T3) spongy interior mass of the sprouting coconut. Syn. *óót*. Cf. *fareseyin*.

choosa (1) CHOOSAA. (Jap. *choosa*) nu. (T1) investigation. *choosaan ewe féfféér* i. of that undertaking. vi. conduct an investigation, investigate.

choosaani See *choosa, -ni-*. vo. (T4) investigate. *ewe pwonis aa nó ch.* meet

pwopwun áán ewe mwáán we máánó the policeman went to investigate the cause of the man's death.
Chooseng Obs. (Jap. *Choosen*) nu. (loc.) Korea. Syn. *Kooreya*.
chookkar (3) See *choo*₁, *kkar*. nu. (T3) a medicine made by mixing coconut cream obtained from grilled copra together with coconut milk and herbs. *aan ch.* m. made by him; *wúnúman ch.* m. he takes. va. make *chookkar* medicine. *wúpwe ch. wúnúmen átánaan meyi semwmwen* I shall make *ch.* medicine for that man who is sick.
chookkareey See *chookkar, -e-*₂. vo. (T6b) make and give *chookkar* medicine to (someone).
choomw (3) CHOMWA. nu. (T3) bank (at edge of sea or beach). *fáán ch.* shallows next to a rocky shore where waves break.
chooneesening (3a) See *choo*₁, *nee-, sening*. Var. *choon neesening*. nu. (T3) stage of growth of a coconut just before the fully ripe stage when there is still a little milk inside ("copra in the ear" from the sound when someone shakes it).
choopi nu. calm (of weather, sea), vi. be calm. *aa mmen ch. ikenááy* we have a very calm weather today. Syn. *chóórek, núwa*.
Choor nu. (pers.) a traditional storm god. [One of five children of the weather (*néwún ráán*), who live in the gale, sink boats in heavy seas, and blow down trees.]
choorar (3) See *choo*₁, *rar*₁ n. (T3) massage done with a bundle of herbs, copra, and a hot stone rolled up in a cloth ("warm copra"). *chooraran* m. of or for him.
choori (1) CHOORII. (Jap. *zoori*) nu. (T1) zori type of footwear. *ipwan ch.* or *néwún ch.* his z. (to wear); *aan ch.* his z. (to dispose of); *chooriin Sapaan* Japanese z.
choorikú (1) CHOORIKÚÚ. (Jap. *jooriku*) nu. (T1) invasion, landing in force. vi. make a landing in force.
choorikúúni See *choorikú, -ni-*. vo. (T5) invade, make a landing in force on.
chooriwú (1) CHOORIWÚÚ. (Jap. *jooryuu*) Var. *chooriyú*. va., vi. distill; do distilling.

chooriwúúni See *chooriwú, -ni-*. Var. *chooriyúúni*. vo. (T5) distill (something, as to make alcohol).
chooriyú Var. of *chooriwú*.
chooriyúúni Var. of *chooriwúúni*.
choochis (2) See *choo-*₁, *-chis*. N. Var. *soochik, soochis, soosich*. vi., adj. (be) saved, put away, kept, preserved ("little lost").
choocho₁ (db; 1) CHOO₅. nu. (T1) splinter. *choochoon mwúúch* s. of wood.
choocho₂ (db; 1) CHOO₆. [Elbert] nu. (T1) flying fish.
choochón (4) See *choo-*₂, *chón*. nu. (T2?) vine with purple flowers (*Canavalia microcarpa*); a vine (*Vigna marina*). Syn. *wénúka*.
choffana (1) CHOFFANAA. vi. be lying; telling a lie; prevaricating. With intens. suf.: *choffanakkich* be telling a big lie. Syn. *mwaken, mwakenekkich, chonongngén, chonomwas, chonope, womworú*. Cf. *chon*.
choka- (3) CHOKA. [In cpds. only.] unsp. call, chirp, cluck (of a bird or chicken). See *nichchok, óchokochok*.
chomwochomw (db; 3) See *choomw*. nu. (T3) bank (at edge of the sea or edge of the beach). *wóón chomwochomwen Nómwuchchu* on the b. of Nómwuchchu.
chon (3a) CHONA. Tb3. vi. gossip about members of the opposite sex. Dis. *chochchon* (ds). Cf. *pwóróówus*.
chona- (3a) See *chon*. Tb3. ni. (T3) gossip (about someone). *chonan* g. about him. *chonen iyé* g. about whom?
chona See *chon*. Tb3. vo. (T3) gossip about (someone of the other sex).
chonaa- (1v) See *chon, -a-*₂. Tb3. ni. (T1v) gossip concerning someone of the other sex (by someone); thing gossiped (by someone). *chonaan* thing gossiped by him; *chonáán iyé* thing gossiped by whom?
choneey See *chon, -e-*₂. F. vo. (refl.; T6b) take oneself off, go away (in anger). *wúwa choneeyey* I took myself off; *kaa choneyok* you took yourself off. *ewe mwáán aa choneeyenó núkún enaan iimw* the man ran away to the side of yonder house. With dir. suf.: *wúwa choneeyeyinó* (1sg.), *kaa choneyokonó* (2sg.), *aa choneeyenó* (3sg.).
choneeyenó See *choneey*.

chonomwas (3b) See *chon, mwas.* Tb2. vi. tell a lie (about someone), speak slander. nu. (T3) 1. false information; lie. *eew ch.* one lie. 2. liar. *emén ch.* one l.

chopan (3) CHOPANA. nu. (T3) a fish (*Gerres baconensis*). Syn. *amwit.*

chopw (2) CHOPWU. vi. make a sudden, sharp sound; crack, pop, knock, detonate, explode, crackle (of fire), thunder. *aa ch. ewe fúúseng* the balloon exploded. nr. (T2) a sharp sudden sound; crack, knock, bang, pop, clap (of thunder). Id. *chopwun ama* insincere love talk ("hammer's bang").

chopwunap (3b) See *chopw, nap.* nu. (T3) thunder; boom; loud detonation; sudden loud sound vi. thunder; boom; make a sudden loud sound.

chopwunó (1) See *chopw, -nó.* vi. have diarrhea.

chopwuchopw (db; 2) See *chopw.* nu. (T2) a kind of fish.

choro- See *chere-*.

chorong (3) See *che-, rong.* Var. *chchorong.* vi. be bothered by noise. *siya ch. reen núchúnúchún enaan tayip* we are bothered by the noise of that typewriter. Syn. *chororong.*

choropwpwun (3a) See *chere-, pwpwun₁.* Var. *cherepwpwun.* vi. flash; blaze (as eyes). Syn. *merepwpwun, mesepwpwun, mesettin.*

chororong (3) See *chere-, rong.* Rmn. vi. be bothered by noise. Syn. *chorong.*

chorochor₁ (db; 3) CHORA₁. nu. (T3) a black worm (Elbert: termite; fruit worm, as in mangoes and breadfruit). *emén ch.* one w.

chorochor₂ (3) CHORA₂. vi., adj. (dis.) be spoiled, (of a ripe coconut that has not matured properly).

chochchis CHOCHCHISI (?). N. Var. *sossich.* nu. a vine with red berries.

chochchon Dis. of *chon.*

chowu-₁ (2) CHOWU₁. [In cpds. only.] unsp. heavy, pressing.

chowu-₂ (2) CHOWU₂. [In fish names only.] unsp. (u.m.) See *chowupwáák, chowupwo.*

chowuni See *chowu-₁, -ni-.* vo. (T5) be heavy for; feel anger toward.

chowupwááс N. of *chowupwáák.*

chowupwáák (2) See *chowu-₂, pwáák.* Var. *chowupwáás.* nu. a fish, (family Maurolicidae).

chowupwo (1) See *chowu-₂, pwo.* nu. (T1) balloon fish.

chowuchow (db; 2) See *chowu-₁.* nu. (T2) pressing pole used to extract coconut cream and other things on a *wúchúúch* press. *chowuchowun wúchúúch* p.p. of a press. vi. (dis.) be burdened, weighed down, depressed, heavy in mood.

choyiro (1) CHOYIROO. nu. (T1) a shrub (*Jussiaea suffruticosa*). Syn. *éwúnenipwin.*

chóó- (1) CHÓÓ₂. [In cpds. only.] unsp. strain, filter.

chóó (1) CHÓÓ₁. nu. (T1) 1. group (of people); company, fellowship, team; corporation; descent group, lineage. *eew ch.* one g. *aan ch.* his g. With suf. dem.: *chóóna, chóónaan, chóówe. chóónaan áán Keneeto* those companions of Keneeto, Keneeto's crowd; *chóóna meyi énúúngngaw* that group (you mentioned) does sorcery. 2. (with rel. suf.) member (of a group); participant (in an activity); person (of a kind, occupation, etc.). *chóón afaamwa* midwife; *chóón afangamá* traitor; *chóón afanafan* preacher, lecturer; *chóón Áferika* person of African descent, Negro; *chóón afféw* interpreter; *chóón angaang* worker, laborer; *chóón amanaw* life-saver, rescuer, the Savior; *chóón ampay* umpire; *chóón améémé* seller, salesman; *chóón attaw* fisherman; *chóón Chuuk* Trukese person; *chóón emiis* contestant; *chóón emiisi* judge of a contest, referee, umpire; *chóón esemwmwen* nurse; *chóón éfén, chóón ékkéfén* boxer; *chóón ékkúné* errand boy, legate, apostle; *chóón épwúngú aramas* judge (of disputes); *chóón fféér kkéén* song composer; *chóón ffóón chukó* chicken tender; *chóón ffóón piik* pigkeeper, swineherd; *chóón ffóón siipw* shepherd; *chóón iimw* (or *chóóniimw*) household member; *chóón imwa-* (with suf. pos. prn.) wife; *chóón inaka* bumpkin, hick; *chóón kkáámw* inspector; *chóón kkánis* helper, giver of aid or assistance; *chóón kkémwéch fináyik* government appointed chief during periods of German and Japanese administration ("person who holds the flag"); *chóón kkuk* cook, chef; *chóón marariya* sanitation worker; *chóón mmak* writer, clerk; *chóón mmas* watchman, guard; *chóón mwárá* beggar (of food only); *chóón* *mwuumwu, chóón mwúúmwú* adopter (of a child), adopting parent; *chóón mwúún* government worker, government representative, government spokesman; *chóón nakik* thief; *chóón nááng* angel; *chóón neefanang* person in charge of work in a *fanang*; *chóón neeset* fisherman; *chóón núkún* nonmember (esp. of Church); *chóón oosuni nóón paaw* palmist; *chóón paapa* welcoming speaker at a meeting, whose role is to apologize for the inadequacy of the hospitality; *chóón paaro* borrower; *chóón ppéwút* sorcerer; *chóón péwútaw* person waiting on the beach when a fishing boat comes in; *chóón pwangapwang* conductor (in music); *chóón pwááráátá* witness (in court); *chóón rawa* person treated by massage, patient or client (of masseur); *chóón semwmwen* sick person, medical patient; *chóón sitoowa* storekeeper, shopkeeper, store clerk; *chóón sooná* thief; *chóón sukuun* pupil, student; *chóón Suus* Jew, Jewish people; *chóón tánnipi* gardener, farmer; *chóón táwán* wanderer, vagabond, traveler; *chóón teete* tailor, seamstress; *chóón tengki* electrician; *chóónu san* one who knows *san*; *chóón winipós* person of the place, local person, native, resident; *chóón wóók* fighter, bully ("person of the club or spear"); *chóón wúttúút nii* dentist, dental surgeon ("tooth puller").

chóókis (2) See *chóó, kisi-*. vi. be sparsely populated, of few members. Syn. *chóókúkkún*.

chóókúkkún (2) See *chóó, kúkkún*. vi. be sparsely populated, of few members. Syn. *chóókis*.

chóómmóng Var. of *chómmóng*.

-chóón [In cpds. only.] unsp. (u.m.) See *pééchóón*.

chóóna See *chóó*.

chóónaan See *chóó*.

chóóni See *chóó, -ni-*. vo. (T4) join, become a member of (a group, meeting, etc.).

chóópwut (3) See *chóó, pwuta-*. Tn. nu. (T3) woman. *chóópwuten eey fénú* w. of this island.

chóórek (2) CHÓÓREKI. nu. (T2) calm (of weather, sea). vi. be calm. Syn. *choopi, núwa*.

chóóri See *chóó-, -ri-,* vo. (T4) strain out the starch from.

chóóch (3) See *chóó, cha-*. vi. be packed, jampacked, full, crowded (of people). Dis. *chóóchóóch* (db).

chóóchó (db; 1) See *chóó*. vi. (dis.) be heavily populated, of wide membership. nr. (T1) large population. *meyi wor chóóchóón aramas wóón naan fénú* there is a large p. on that island.

chóóchóó- (db; 1) See *chóó-*. nr. (dis.; T1) strainer and its frame. [Used to wash starch from grated roots.] *chóóchóón áfán* s. of woven hibiscus stretched on a frame and used in making turmeric dye. *chóóchóón mwéék* s. for extracting starch from arrowroot.

chóóchóóch Dis. of *chóóch*.

chóótam (3) CHÓÓTAMA. N. Var. *sootam*. nu. stage of growth of a coconut (not yet full sized).

chóówe See *chóó*.

chóóyisá (1) See *chóó, sá*. nu. (T1) refugee from war; exile; expatriate. [In former times it was a term of opprobrium, indicating that a person didn't really belong where he was residing and was cowardly as well, having been run off his own land.] Syn. *chóóyitur*.

chóóyinum (3a) See *chóó, nuum*. nu. (T3) bailer's thwart. [It is situated immediately fore or aft of where the outrigger booms cross the body of a sailing canoe.]

chóóyiro (1) See *chóó, -ro*. nu. (T1) one who knows *itang* lore and who is in direct line of hereditary entitlement to such lore (i.e., a member of the clan or *eterekes* that founded the local school of *itang* or a direct descendant of such a member through males, i.e. one of the founding clan's *éfékúr*.) [The *mwáániichi* among a set of *chóóyiro* in the same generation of the same *eterekes* is the only one among them entitled to speak as an *itang* in public meeting. In the absence of the *mwáániichi*, the next younger *chóóyiro* may speak in his place. Women may be *chóóyiro* but may not speak in public. A *sómwoonun mwéngé* may not speak if he has an older *eterekes* brother who is *sómwoonun kkapas*.]

chóóyitur (2) See *chóó, tur₂*. nu. (T2) refugee; exile. Syn. *chóóyisá*.

chófó (1) CHÓFÓÓ. F. vi., adj. (be) able; diligent; skilled; industrious. *Fritz aa fókkun ch. ne angaang* Fritz is very diligent at work. Syn. *kichiyééch*.

chókkeey See *chóó, kkeey*. nu. (dem.) these people.

chómmóng (4) See *chóó, mmóng*. Var. *chóómmóng*. vi., adj. (be) many, much, numerous. nr. (T2) muchness, numerousness (of something).

chón (4) CHÓNO. vi., adj. (be) dark (of color); black. [A little less gentle than *chóchchón*.] With intens. adj.: (vi., adj.) *chónekkich, chónokkich, chónukkich* very d., very b.; (nr.) extreme darkness, blackness. *chónekkichin inisumw* the blackness of your skin. Ant. *pwech*.

chóneey See *chón, -e-₂*. vo. (T6b) darken; blacken.

chónekkich See *chón*.

chónokkich See *chón*.

chónukkich See *chón*.

chóchchón (ds; 4) See *chón*. vi., adj. (dis.) (be) dark (of color), black. [A little more gentle than *chón*.] nr. (T2) dark or black part (of something). *chóchchónun maas* iris of the eye. Ant. *pwechepwech*.

chu (1) CHUU₁. vi. meet, come together. Dis. *chuchchu* (ds).

chuu- C.f. of *cheew*.

chuuk₁ (2) CHUKU₃. nu. (T2) mound, pile, heap; hill, mountain. *eew ch.* one m. *chukun Wééné* mountain of Wééné (Moen) Island.

Chuuk₂ [Derived from *chuuk₁*.] nu. (loc.) Truk. *aramasen Ch.* people of T.; *chóón Ch.* Trukese person; *fiin Ch.* Trukese woman; *fóósun Ch., kkapasen Ch.* Trukese language; *ree-Chuk, re Chuuk* Trukese man.

chuukis (2) See *cheew₁, kisi-*. nu. (T2) fishnet of fine mesh. *eew ch.* one f. *aan c.* or *néwún ch.* his f.

chuumaaw (3) See *cheew₁, maaw*. nu. (T3) fishnet with coarse mesh and heavy cord. *eew ch.* one f. *aan ch.* or *néwún ch.* his f.

chuumar (3) See *cheew₁, maar*. nu. (T3) fermented breadfruit (when eaten by a spirit medium because the possessing spirit wishes it). Cf. *épwét*.

chuumech (3) See *chu, meche-*. F. vi., adj. (be) of good memory, quick to learn, smart. Syn. *kúúmech*.

chuuméwúr (2) See *chu, méwúr*. Itang. nu. (T2) social harmony.

chuumwong (2, 3) CHUUMWONGU, CHUUMWONGA. (Jap. *chuumon*) nu. (T2) purchase order. *aan ch.* his p. o.; *chuumwongun pisek* p. o. for goods. vi., va. make a purchase order; order. *ch. ngeni* place an order with, send an order to.

chuumwongeey See *chuumwong, -e-₂*. vo. (T6b) make a purchase order for.

chuun (3) CHUUNNA. nu. (T3) blindness. *aan ch.* his b. vi., adj. (be) blind. *aa ch. mesey* my eyes have become blind.

chuuni See *cheew₁, -ni-*. vo. (T4) net (fish); catch with a net.

chuunnap (dc; 3b) See *cheew₁, nap*. nu. fishnet with large mesh. *eew ch.* one f. *aan ch.* or *néwún ch.* his f.

chuupwutak (3) See *chu, pwutak*. nu. (T3) practical joke; practical joking. [More gentle usage than *chúngngaw*.] vi. be a practical joker.

chuuri See *chu, -ri-*. vo. (T4) meet, encounter, join.

chuuchu (db; 1) CHUU₂. n. (T1) urine, piss. [Preferred word in mixed company.] *ch. nóót* pyuria, pussy urine. *féwún ch., neeniyen ch.* kidney. Syn. *siir*. vi. urinate, piss. Syn. *áchchén, emeyaw, sir*.

chuffengeen Var. of *chuffengen*.

chuffengen (2: -ngenni-) See *chu, ffengen*. Var. *chuffengeen*. vi. meet together.

chukó (1) CHUKÓÓ. nu. (T1) chicken. *emén ch.* one c. *néwún ch.* his c.; *wochaan ch.* his c. (to eat); *chukóón Chuuk* Trukese c. *péwún ch.* chicken wing; section of roof on traditional house that extends from a corner. *máán ch.* or *semwmwenin ch.* a kind of sickness; *rongen ch.* medicine and spells to cure this sickness. Syn. *pwisika, pwuchó*.

chuku-₁ (2) CHUKU₁. [In cpds. only.] unsp. elbowing.

chuku-₂ (2) CHUKU₂. [In cpds. only.] unsp. call, chirp (as a bird). See *ochukuchuk, ochukuchuku*.

Chukuchap (3) See *chuuk₁, chaap* (?). nu. (loc.) name of highest mountain on Feefen (Fefan) Island.

chunen (2) CHUNENI. F. nu. (T2) 1. bee. *emén ch.* one b. *chunenin Chuuk* Trukese b. *minen ch.* honey 2. honey. [This meaning given by some speakers is disputed by others.] *ménún ch.* bee. *wúnúmi ch.* eat h. Syn. *achi.* Cf. *pwunech.*

chuputi See *chchup, -ti-.* vo. (T5) scratch (as a chicken). *aa ch. pwpwún* it scratched the soil. Cf. *chepeti.*

chupwosta (1) CHUPWOSTAA. (Jap. *zubonshita*) nu. (T1) long underpants. *eché ch.* one pair of u. *aan ch.* his u.

chuchchu Dis. of *chu.*

chuchchup Dis. of *chchup.*

chuwopwong See *chú* (?), *pwoong.* nu. 10th night of the lunar month.

chú (3) CHÚWA. vi. be extracted, pulled up, pulled out; come up, come out (of plants, nails, etc., in response to human effort to *wiiy* or *wútti*); move (in response to effort). *aa wiiy naan pétéwén ngé ese chú* he pulled on that plant but it didn't come up.

chúú-₁ (1) CHÚÚ₂. [In cpds. only.] vi. (u.m.) [Possibly a variant of *chu.*] See *chúngngaw, chúngngaweey, chúúngngaw, chúúngngawa.*

chúú-₂ (1) CHÚÚ₃. [In cpds. only; possibly derived from *chúú.*] n. wooden comb.

chúú-₃ (1) CHÚÚ₄. [In cpds. only; possibly derived from *chúú.*] unsp. needlework; pricking with pin or needle.

chúú (1) CHÚÚ₁. n. (T1) bone. *efoch ch.* one b. *chúún* his b. *chúún epinikú* occipital bone; *chúún éwúren maas* bone under the eye; *chúún éwúsap* zygoma, cheekbone; *chúún kuwoku* coccyx, bone at the end of the spinal column. suf. (cc.) bone segment (in a cut of meat). *echú, rúwéchú, wúnúchú, féchú, nimechú, wonochú, fúúchú, wanúchú, ttiwechú, engoon chúún* one,...ten b. s.

chúúfén (2) See *chúú-₃, fén₂.* nu. (T2) nail; nailing (in carpentry). *efóch* one n. *mácháán ch.* metal nail. vi. be nailed.

chúúfénúúw See *chúúfén, -ú-.* vo. (T5) nail, fasten with a nail.

chúúféw (2) See *chúú, faaw.* nu. (T2) a species of wrasse fish.

chúúk (2) CHÚKÚ. nu. (T2) basket made of coconut leaves. [It is made for temporary use by both men and woman.] *echúk ch., eew ch.* one b.; *efóch ch.* one pair of baskets on a carrying pole. *aan ch.* his b. *chúkún kkón* b. of breadfruit pudding; a way of storing breadfruit pudding when leaves are in short supply (done with two puddings to a basket separated by a leaf, the harder pudding underneath and the softer on top). *waasen chúúk* carrying pole with b. at each end. suf. (cc.) *echúk, rúwéchúk, wúnúchúk, féchúk, nimechúk, wonochúk, fúúchúk, wanúchúk, ttiwechúk, engoon chúkún* one,...ten b.

chúúmaaw (3) See *chúú, maaw.* vi., adj. (be) hardened physically, inured, tough.

chúún (3b) CHÚNNA. n. (T3) post, stake (as supporting a mosquito net); fence post, paling, picket. *efóch ch.* one p. *chúnnan* his p. *chúnnen ttiit* fence post. vi. be blocked or concealed from view by trees, posts, or stakes. With dir. suf.: *chúnnónó* be blocked off from view by trees, posts, or stakes; be fenced off.

chúúnap (3b) See *chúú, nap.* n. (T3) backbone *chúúnapan* his b.

chúúnúket See *chúú, ket.* nu. sickness caused by *énúúsooso* or *sooyénú* sorcery. [It adversely affects the fertility of women and men.] *aa súúri ch. átánaan* the ch. sickness has taken ("gone to") that fellow. *rongen ch.* medicine and spells to cure the ch. sickness.

chúúngngaw Var. of *chúngngaw.*

chúúngngawa Var. (vo., T3) of *chúngngaweey.*

chúúpach (3b) See *chúú-₂, pach.* nu. (T3) ornamental comb made of a single piece of wood.

chúúpwún See *chúú, pwúún₁.* vi. be broken boned; have a broken bone.

chúúraanó See *chúúri.*

chúúrááá (1) See *chúú, rááá.* n. (T1) ribs, rib bones. *chúúrááán* his r.

chúúri See *chúú-₃, -ri-.* vo. (T4) 1. apply a pointed object to; remove or extract with a pointed object (e.g., nails). 2. embroider. With dir. suf.: *chúúraanó* forget (polite usage).

chúúchú (db; 1) See *chúú.* vi. (dis.) be bony; skinny. Syn. *kichchúúchú.* Ant. *kitinnupw.*

chúúchúúfeefin (db; 3a) See *chúú, feefin*. nu. (T3) boom (on a sailing canoe). *efóch ch*. one b.

chúúchúúmwáán (4) See *chúú, mwáán₁*. nu. (T2) yard (of sailing canoe). *efóch ch*. one y.

chúkúfan (3) CHÚKÚFANA. nu. (T3) angel fish. [Its head was formerly used to perfume coconut oil.] *emén ch*. one a. f.

chúkúseeyipen See *chúúk, Seeyipen*. nu. Saipan basket (round, flat bottomed).

chúkúseneetá (1) See *chúúk, seneetá*. nu. (T1) open basket.

chúkúni See *chúúk, -ni-*. vo. (T5) apply a basket to (something); put in a basket.

chúkúnúkan (3) See *chúúk, ana-*. [From *chúkú-ni-kan*.] n. (T3) stomach ("food basket"). *chúkúnúkanan* his s.

chúkúchúk (db; 2) See *chúúk*. vi. (dis.) be put in baskets; be basketed. *aa wees mé ch. na kkón? Ewer, aa ch.*. Is that breadfruit finished with being basketed? Yes, indeed, it has been basketed.

chúkkamas (3) See *chúú-₂, kkamas*. nu. (T3) ornamental comb made with transverse wooden pins. *aan ch.* his c.

chún (3a) CHÚNA₁. vi. tip or heel over with outrigger up (of canoe). With dir. suf.: *chúnénó* tip over, capsize. Cf. *rúk*.

chúna CHÚNA₂. vo. (T3) carry with the hands. *wúwa ch. naan pwóór* I carried that box with my hands.

chúnénó See *chún*.

chúnneey See *chúún, -e-₂*. vo. (T6b) fence (something) in with stakes; block (something) from view with trees or stakes. *sipwe ch. ewe imwen piik* we shall fence in the pig house.

chúnnónó See *chúún*.

chúngú- (2) CHÚNGÚ. [In cpds. only.] vi., adj. (be) jarred; shake, vibrate. Cf. *wúchú-₁*.

chúngngaw (3b) See *chúú-₁, ngngaw*. Tb3. Var. *chúúngngaw*. nu. (T3) practical joke, injuring another without provocation only for the pleasure of seeing someone discomfitted, sadistic or mean practical joke. Syn. *chuupwutak*

chúngngaweey See *chúngngaw, -e-₂*. Tb3. Var. *chúúngngawa*. vo. (T6b) play a practical joke on.

chúri (1) CHÚRII. (Jap. *zurui*) vi. cheat. *emén meyi ch.* a cheat, cheater.

chúrikkótó (1) See *chúri*. (Jap. *zurui koto*) nu. (T1) exposed cheat or cheater. *emén ch.* one e. *c. ch. ch. nipanipanipa!* (children's jeer at a cheater).

chúchchú Dis. of *chchú₂*.

chúwéféereya (1) See *chú, féereya*. vi. be difficult to extract or pull out (of a nail, or something someone wants from another).

chcha (dc; 1) See *chaa-₁*. Tb2. n. (T1) blood. *chchaan* his b.; b. of. vi., adj. (be) bloody; bleed; menstruate. *aa ch. pwe emén e pékúúw* he is bleeding because someone cut him. Cf. *achchaay*.

-chchaach (ds; 2: *chachcha-*) See *chach*. [In cpds. only.] adj. dense, crowded. See *pachchaach*.

chchangngaw (3b) See *chcha, ngngaw*. nu. (T3) sickness resulting from being cursed in retaliation for a transgression ("bad blood").

chchap N. of *chaap*.

chchar (3) CHCHARA₁. nu. starfish.

-chchar (3) CHCHARA₂. [In cpds. only.] adj. (intens.) very, extremely. *wenechchar* very straight, very honest.

chchaw (dc; 3) CHAWA. N. vi., adj. (be) slow; late. Syn. *mmang*.

chchawer (3) CHCHAWERA. nu. (T3) pupil (of the eye). *chchaweren maas* p. of the eye. Cf. *wer*.

chche-₁ (dc; 3) CHA₄. [In cpds. and with rel. suf. only.] nr. (T3) covering (of a surface). *eché chche-* one c. *aan chche-* his c. *chchen cheepen* table cover, table cloth. *chchen fáán óós* ceiling ("cover of underside of thatch"). *chchen futong* matress cover. *chchen péwúch* gloves. *chchen pwpwuk* book jacket.

chche-₂ (dc; 3a) See *che-*. [In cpds. only.] Var. *chché-*. pref. (adj.) state of being. *chchemaaw, chchémaaw* be hard (of substance).

chche-₃ (3a) CHCHA (*CHECHE). [In cpds. only.] unsp. shake, quake.

chche Var. of *che*.

chcheech₁ Var. of *chchech*.

chcheech₂ (ds; 3: *chechche-*) See chche-₃ nu. (T3) quake; tremor. *chechchen fénú* earthquake. vi. shake; shiver; quake; tremble. *wúwa ch. pwúún wúwa ffééw* I am shaking because I am cold.

chcheey See *chche-₁, -e-₂.* vo. (T6b) cover, put a covering on. *ch. enaan cheepen ngeni enaan meyi pwech* cover that table with that white one (i.e., table cloth). Syn. *chcheni.*

chchek (2) CHCHEKI. (Eng. *duck*) nu. (T2) duck. *emén ch.* one d. *néwún ch.* his d.; *chchekin Merika* American d.

chchem (dc; 3a) See *cheme-.* vi. remember; recall; have in mind. *kaa pwan ch.?* are you absorbed in reminiscence?

chchemaamaaw Dis. of *chchemaaw.*

chchemaaw (3) See *chche-₂, maaw.* Var. *chchémaaw.* vi., adj. (be) hard (of substance, as distinct from soft), rigid. Dis. *chchemaamaaw* (db). *ewe meyi má aa ch.* the dead body has become r.

chchemeni (dc) See *cheme-, -ni-.* vo. (T5) remember; recall; have in mind. Dis. *chechchemeni* (ds). *ngaang meyi ch. meet siya apasa nánew* I am remembering what we said yesterday.

chchen₁ nu. a strand tree.

chchen₂ (dc; 3a) See *chene-.* vi., adj. (be) light (in color), blond, reddish. *mékúren fín Merika meyi ch.* the hair of American women is l. in color. Cf. *chcheng.*

chcheni See *chche-₁, -ni-.* vo. (T6a) cover, put a covering on. *kepwe ch. ngeniyey naan cheepen* you will cover that table for me. Syn. *chcheey.*

chcheniipw (dc; 3) See *chche-₁, iipw.* ns. (T3) compensation in goods or land for trespass in a house, in the vicinity of a grave, on land or fishing sites marked with a *mechen* or *róóng* ("cover of footprint"). *chchen ipwan* c. paid by him.

chchenikam (dc; 3) See *chche-₁, -kam.* Var. *chenikam.* n. (T3) bedcover, top sheet, coverlet. *eché ch.* one b. *chchenikaman* his b. Syn. *kuus₂, sárem.*

chchenó (1) See *chche-₂, -nó.* vi. be immobile; stay put. Dis. *chechchenó* (ds). *aa chechchenóó chék* he just stays put.

chcheng (dc; 3) CHENGA. vi., adj. (be) stained with turmeric. Cf. *chchen₂.*

chchengen See *chche-₂, -ngen.* vi. be joyful, ecstatic. *aa ch. reey* he is joyful because of me. Syn. *pwaapwa.*

chchep₁ (dc; 3) CHEPA. nu. (T3) kicking (with feet). *meyi sineey ch.* knows how to kick; is a kicker. vi., adj. (be) kicked. va. kick. *siya nó ch. pwoor* let's go and kick balls. Cf. *chchup.*

chchep₂ nu. species of pompano fish (up to 18 inches long).

chcheriw (dc; 3) See *chche-₂, riw.* Tbl (Rmn. only). vi. be shiny, glossy. Dis. *chcheriweriw* (db). *niimw na kimpa meyi chcheriweriw* your gold-capped tooth is shiny.

chcheriweriw Dis. of *chcheriw.*

chchech (ds; 3: *chechche-*) See *chche-₁.* Var. *chcheech₁.* nu. (T3) cover (of a surface). *eché chechchen pinnu* a pillow case. *aan chechchen pinnu* his pillow case. *chechchen cheepen* table cover, table cloth. vi. be covered (of a surface). *ewe cheepen aa ch.* the table is c.

chchetá (1) See *chche-₃, -táp* vi. begin to shake or quake.

chchewenewen (dc, db; 3) See *chche-₂, wen.* vi. (dis.) be standing at attention, be standing straight and still. Cf. *cheewenewen.*

chchewuuch (dc; 3: *-wuchcha-*) See *chche-₂, -wuuch.* n. (T3) pain, ache, hurt. *eew ch.* one p. *chchewuuchchan* his p. Syn. *metek, ngiyóów.* vi. be painful, ache, hurt. *wúwa ch. pwúún wúwa angaang wátte* I ache because I worked hard.

chchey N. of *cheey.*

chcheyiroch (dc; 3a) See *che, í-₃, roch.* va. go in search of a woman at night; keep a night-time assignation. *kesapw ch. nengngin pwe kepwe ch. feefín* don't go after little girls but go after grown-up women. Syn. *tééfán.*

chcheyirocheey See *chcheyiroch, -e-₂.* vo. (T6b) search for (a woman) at night.

chchékún (dc) See *chche-₂, kún₂.* vi., adj. (be) stiff, rigid, hard (of a substance). *ewe iik aa ch. me fáán ewe akkar* the fish became hard in the sun.

chchémaamaaw Dis. of *chchémaaw.*

chchémaaw (dc; 3) See *chche-₂, maaw.* Var. *chchemaaw.* vi. be hard (of substance). Dis. *chchémaamaaw (db)* [The more common form]. With dir.

chchén₁   **Trukese-English**

suf.: *chchémaawúnó* become harder, harden.

chchén₁ (dc; 2) See *chaan*. vi., adj. (be) wet. Dis. *chéchchén* (ds).

chchén₂ nu. land that has been made productive. *fénúwan ch.* his l. *áán ewe sóópw ch.* the productive l. of the village.

-chchi (dc; 1) See *chii-*₁. suf. (cc.) (in counting) drop. [Used with numerical prefixes.] *echchi, rúwéchchi, wúnúchchi, féchchi, nimechchi, wonochchi, fúúchchi, wanúchchi, ttiwechchi* one,...nine d.; *fitechchi* how many d. With c. pref. and ptv. const.: *ááchchiin, érúwéchchiin* first d., second d. (etc.). With dis. c. pref.: *ákkááchchi, ékkérúwéchchi* be one d. at a time, two d. at a time (etc.).

chchif Var. of *chif*₁.

-chchik (2) CHCHIKI. Var. *-kkich*. adj. (intens.) very, absolutely. See *mwirichchik*.

chchin (dc; 2) CHINI₁. vi., adj. (be) hurried, speedy, fast (ordinarily in reference to speech). *aa mmen ch. aan kkapas* his speech is very fast. *aa mmen ch. pecheen ne fátán* he walked with a quick movement of his legs.

Chchiniyón (Eng.) nu. (loc.) Tinian Island. [The name has been equated in meaning by some *itang* with *neekkunuyón* because it is alleged to have been sighted by a Trukese voyage of exploration in the "afternoon."]

chchipw (dc; 3) See *chipwa-*. vi., adj. (be) warped, bent (by fire).

chchiwen (dc; 2) CHIWA. [Usually, as shown, with rel. suf. *-n₂*. Also may occur with rel. suf. *-yi-* when followed by a monosyllabic word.] vr. still, yet; (with neg.) again, longer. *meyi ch. manaw* be still alive. *meyi ch. nómw* it still remains. *ese ch. chómmóng* it is no longer plentiful. *ese chchiweni wor* or *ese chchiweyi wor* there is no more, there no longer is. *neesor wúsapw ch. feyitto* I shall not come again tomorrow.

chchiweyi See *chchiwen*.

chchiyena- Var. of *chiyena-*.

chchooch (ds; 3) CHOCHCHA, CHCHOCHA. n. (T3), suf. (cc.) bunch, armful, fullness (of a bunch). *echchooch, ruwochchooch, wunuchchooch, féchchooch, nimechchooch, wonochchooch, fúúchchooch, wanúchchooch, ttiwechchooch, engoon chochchan* or *chchochan* one,...ten b.; *fitechchooch* how many b. *chchochen ekkanaan núú* the fullness (of the bunch) of those coconuts.

chchorong Var. of *chorong*.

chchotá (1) CHCHOTÁÁ. nu. (T1) finely-plaited, satchel-shaped basket (a kind of *pwótow*); (mod.) women's handbag, shopping bag. *eew ch.* one b. *aan ch.* his b.; *chchotáán Chuuk* Trukese b.

chchow (dc; 2) See *chowu-*₁. n. (T2) weight, heaviness; ill-will, hostility, anger. *chchowun* his w.; *aan ch.* his ill-will. vi., adj. 1. (be) heavy, weighty, burdensome, serious; be angry (of one's heart or mood). *ngaang wúwa ch. reemw pwún ke núkúmmach* I am angry at you because you are naughty. Ant. *ppán*. 2. (of a consonant) be long, double, geminate. Ant. *pwpwas*.

chchuk (2) CHCHUKU. nu. (T2) thorny oyster (edible). *eféw ch.* one o. *chchukun* o. of.

chchup (dc; 2) CHUPU. va. scratch (as a chicken), be scratching. Dis. *chuchchup* (ds). Cf. *chchep*₁.

chchuwa- (3) CHCHUWA. [In cpds. only.] unsp. (u.m.) See *ochchuwa, nikochchuwa*.

chchú- (2) CHCHÚ. [In cpds. only.] unsp. concerning the soul or spirit. See *chchúni, chchúnó*.

chchú₁ (dc; 1) See *chúú-*₂. nu. (T1) wooden comb. [Worn in the hair in precolonial times, its manufacture was a specialty of Pwonowót (Puluwat) Atoll.] *efóch ch.* one c. *aan ch.* his c. Id. *chchúún pwénútiw* small wooden thatch pin that pierces thatch at the ridgepeak and goes between the ridgepole and the false ridgepole so as to pin the thatch in place.

chchú₂ (dc; 1) See *chúú-*₃. nu. (T1) embroidery; embroidering. *aan ch.* her e. va. embroider, do embroidering. Dis. *chúchchú* (ds).

Chchún nu. (loc.) 1. a district of Tonowas (Dublon) Island. 2. name associated with a school of *itang* now based on Feefen (Fefan) Island. See *Mácheweyichchún*.

chchúni See *chchú-, -ni, -a-*₃. N. vo. (T6a) possess, take possession of (of a spirit). *aa ch. soomá* a ghost has possessed him. Syn. *mwóssuni*.

chchúnó (1) See *chchú-, -nó*. n. (T1) shade, shadow (representing a person's *ngúnúngngaw* or bad soul). *chchúnóón* his s., s. of.

chchúng (dc; 2) See *chúngú-*. vi. be shaken, jarred; vibrate, shake (as from being walked on). *aa ch. papen eey waa pwúún aa fan* the bottom ("board") of this canoe shook because it went aground.

T

-t (3) TA₁. suf. (interrog.) indicates a query or question. See *feet, feteey, fita-, meet₁, pwaat, pwata.*

-ta-₁ (3) TA₂. [Counterpart of the verb formative suffix *-ti-*.] suf. (n.form.; T3) object or product of an action. [Suffixed to the bases of inactive verbs to which the corresponding verb formative *-ti-* may be suffixed. Reference to the actor is indicated by suffixed pos. prns.]

-ta-₂ (3) TA₃. Var. *-ti-.* suf. (v.form.) makes a verb of the base.

ta (1) TAA₁. vi. be destroyed, in pieces, in ruins, ruined, disintegrated, disassembled; come or fall apart.

taa (1) TAA₂. F. n. (T1) intestine. *eyaf taan* a piece of its i. *taan* his i., i. of. Cf. *saa.*

taafen (2) TAAFENI. (Ger. *Tafel*) nu. (T2) slate (tablet). *eew t.* one s. *aan t.* his s. *taafenin Merika* American s.

taak (3, 2) TAAKA, TAKÚ, TÉKÚ. [The combining form *taaka-* is apparently a recent formation. Cf. *takúraar, tékúraar*.] nu. (T3) needle fish (twin beaked). *taaken Chuuk* Trukese n. f.

taam (3b) TAMA₁. n. (T3) outrigger float. *efóch tamen waa* one o. f. *aan t.* his o. f.; *taman* its (the canoe's) o. f.

Taanna nu. (loc.) a clan name.

taang (3) TANGA. Tb3. n. (T3) leg and foot together. *tangan* his l. Syn. *peche.* Ant. *paaw₁.*

taap (3) TAPPA. nu. (T3) green coconut with water not yet sweet and no gelatinous meat to speak of yet. *tappen núú* green nut of the coconut.

taapen (2) TAAPENI. (Eng. *turbine*) nu. (T2) propeller (on plane, ship, outboard motor). *eew t.* one p. *taapenin mwesiin* p. of a motor.

taapwoonen (2) TAAPWOONENI. (Eng.) nu. (T2) tarpaulin. *eché t.* one t. *imwan t.* his t. *taapwoonenin Merika* American t.

taaras (3) TAARASA. F. Var. *saaras.* a shrub (*Sonneratia caseolaris*). [Bark is used in dye making; wood is used for firewood.] *taarasen Chuuk* Trukese s.

taaw (3v) TAWA. n. (T3v) small or narrow channel through a reef. *tawan* its c. *tewen Wééné* pass of Moen; *tewen iya ewe taaw* where is that pass?; *Tewee-Romónum* name of two passes on the outer reef that bound the portion of outer reef belonging to Romónum. Syn. *ánúk, saraata.*

taf (3) TAFA₁. vi. be gathered, picked (of green leaves of banana, breadfruit, tobacco, etc.).

tafa-₁ (3v) TAFA₂. n. (interrog.; T3v) what relationship? what part? what place? what use? what nature? *tafan?* what relationship to him? *tefey átánaan?* what relationship is he to me?; *tofomw e metek?* what part of you hurts?; *tefen Wééné?* what part of Wééné?

tafa-₂ (3) TAFA₃. [In cpds. only.] unsp. combed, preened; unraveled, untangled, unsnarled.

tafa See *tafa-₂.* vo. (T3) comb, preen; disentangle, unsnarl (of hair, fishline, etc.). Syn. *attafa.*

tafataf₁ (db; 3) See *taf.* nu. (T3) gathering, picking, plucking (of leaves). *tafatafen chéén irá* g. of tree leaves. va. (dis.) gather.

tafataf₂ (db; 3) See *tafa-₂.* va. (dis.) comb. nu. (T3) combing, preening.

tafeni See *taf, -ni-.* vo. (T6a) gather, pick.

tak (3) TAKA. Wn., obs. vi. be finished. Syn. *pwi, tawe, wees.*

taka (1) TAKAA. [A loanword from an unidentified but related language. Cf. Tongan *mataka* and Gb. *takataka*.] nu. (T1) copra, copra nut; very ripe coconut; dried coconut meat. *awen t.* or *mesen t.* eye of a ripe coconut. Cf. *assak.*

takeyiti See *tak, -iti.* vo. (T2) finish at (a given time). Syn. *taweeyiti, weesiiti.*

takises Var. of *takisis.*

takisis (2) TAKISISI. (Eng.) Var. *takises.* nu. (T2) tax, taxes. *eew t.* one t. *takisisin Chuuk* Trukese t.

takir (2) TAKIRI. Tb3. vi. laugh. Dis. *takirikir* (db) be laughing, jovial; *tattakir* (ds) l. repeatedly. Syn. *kekkey.*

takiriiy See *takir, -i-₂.* Tb3. vo. (T5) laugh at. Syn. *kkeyisini.*

takirikir Dis. of *takir*.
takiripwo (1) See *takir, -pwo*. vi. be convulsed with laughter.
tako (1) TAKOO. (Jap. *tako*) nu. (T1) kite. *eew t.* one k. *néwún t.* his k.
takúnaar N. var. of *tékúnaar*.
takúraar Var. of *tékúraar*.
takúwang (3) TAKÚWANGA. (Jap. *takuwan*) nu. (T3) pickled radish. *efóch t.* one p. r. *woochan t.* his p. r.
takkich (2) See *taak, -kkich* (?). nu. (T2) method of torch fishing in which fish are speared from a moving canoe using an *óppong* fishing spear. [It is done to catch needle fish (*taak*).]
tam (3b) TAMA$_2$. vi. be deposed, chased out, run off, sent away, exiled.
tama- (3) TAMA$_3$. [In cpds. only.] unsp. ability to perform, skill.
tama (1) TAMAA. (Jap. *tama*) nu. (T1) electric light bulb. *néwún t.* his e. l. b. *tamaan Sapaan* Japanese e. l. b.
tamaak (3) TAMAAKA. (Ger. *Tabak*) nu. (T3) tobacco. *wúnúman t.* his t. (to smoke); *tamaaken Chuuk* Trukese t. Syn. *suupwa*.
tamaato (1) TAMAATOO. (Eng.) nu. (T1) tomato. *eféw t., efóch t.* one t. *aan t.* his t. plant; *wochaan t.* his t. (to eat); *tamaatoon Merika* American t.
tamaningi (1) TAMANINGII. (Jap.) nu. (T1) onion. Syn. *éniyon*.
tamangngaw (3b) See *tama-, ngngaw*. nu. (T3) inability to perform, having one's hands full, having one's style cramped, being out of action. Dis. *tamatamangngaw* (db). *wúwa t. reen pwiiy we pwún átewe aa wúreni ónooy we reen* my style is cramped on account of my brother because he told what I said about him (someone already referred to earlier). vi. be unable to perform, have one's hand full. Dis. *tamatamangngaw* (db).
tamachiki (1) TAMACHIKII. (Jap. *tamatsuki*) Var. *tamachki*. nu. (T1) game of marbles that uses five small holes in the ground. vi. play the *t.* game.
tamatam$_1$ (db; 3b) See *taam*. n. (T3) orientation, direction fronting the long inner side (of an island) or the outrigger side (of a canoe). *tamataman* his o.
tamatam$_2$ (db; 3) See *tama-*. n. (T3) ability to perform; skill. *tamataman* his skill.

Tamatam$_3$ See *tamatam$_1$*. nu. (loc.) Tamatam Island (Pulap Atoll).
tamatamangngaw Dis. of *tamangngaw*.
tamatamééch (2) See *tamatam$_2$, ééch*. nu. (T2) ability to perform well. vi. be able to perform well, skillful, master of a situation.
tameni See *taam, -ni-*. vo. (T6a) have or get as outrigger. *ewe waa aa t. ewe irá* the canoe got the log for its o.
tamepichinó (1) See *taam, pich$_2$, -nó*. vi. be without a companion in a strange place ("outrigger float off unlashed").
tamééch (2) See *tama-, ééch*. vi. be right handed. Ant. *tammééng*.
taménotow (3b) See *taam, notow*. vi. be with outrigger to the west; be oriented toward the west. Cf. *tamatam$_1$*.
taméyefeng (2) See *taam, efeng*. vi. be with outrigger to the north; be oriented toward the north. Cf. *tamatam$_1$*.
taméyéér (2) See *taam, éér*. vi. be with outrigger to the south; be oriented toward the south. Cf. *tamatam$_1$*.
taméyéétiw (3b) See *taam, éétiw*. vi. be with outrigger to the east; be oriented toward the east. Cf. *tamatam$_1$*.
tammééng See *tama-, mmééng*. vi. be left-handed. Ant. *tamééch*.
tanaaw Var. of *ténaaw*.
tangngo (1) TANGNGOO. (Jap. *dango*) nu. (T1) dumplings cooked in hot sugared water. Syn. *osiriko*.
tapi (1) TAPII. (Jap. *tabi*) nu. (T1) tabi (rubber-soled sock-like footwear worn by workmen such as construction workers). *eew t.* pair of t.; *eyipw t.* one t. *néwún t., ipwan t.* his t.
tapiyooka (1) TAPIYOOKAA. (Eng.) Var. *tapiyoka*. nu. (T1) tapioca, manioc, cassava (*Manihot esculenta*). Syn. *mwoniyok*.
tapiyookaapwech (3) See *tapiyooka, pwech*. nu. (T3) white tapioca (has white root).
tapiyookaayón (4) See *tapiyooka, ón$_1$*. nu. (T2) yellow tapioca (has yellow root).
tapwa- (3b, 3v) TAPWA. [In cpds. only.] unsp. next after, following; chasing, pursuing. See *tapweey, tapwato, tapwpwaanú, tepwaanú, tepwekinaas, tepwpwaanú, ttapw, ttapwoto*.
tapwato (1) See *tapwa-, -to*. vi. follow, be next after; go or come after.

tapweey See *tapwa-, -e-₂*. vo. (T6b) follow after; chase, pursue.

tapwpwaanú (1) See *tapwa- (?), énú*. N. (Mck.) Var. *tepwaanú, tepwpwaanú*. nu. (T1) mask-like spirit head carved of wood and set up on gable end of Mortlockese canoe house or meeting house; model or replica of same.

tara- (3) TARA. [In cpds. only.] unsp. passage, intestine, gut. [An element in place names, e.g., *Epiitar, Taranap*.] Syn. *taa*. See *epiitar*.

Tarawa nu. (loc.) a clan name (from Gilbert Island atoll of Tarawa?).

taray (2) TARAYI. (Jap. *tarai*) nu. (T2) washtub, basin. *eew t*. one w. *aan t.* his w. *tarayin Sapaan* Japanese w.

taropwe Var. of *toropwe*.

tattam Dis. of *ttam*.

tattapw (ds; 3b) See *tapwa-*. nu. (T3) being in succession, being one after another. *kkéénún t*. round, roundelay.

tattapwoto See *ttapw*.

-tawa (1) TAWAA. [In cpds. only.] unsp. (u.m.) See *wáátawa*.

tawaat (3) TAWATTA. vi. be in a hurry. *een meyi t.?* or *ke t.?* are you in a hurry?

tawasi (1) TAWASII. (Jap. *tawashi*) nu. (T1) scrubbing brush with a handle. *eféw, eew t*. one s. b. *aan t.* his s. b.

tawasiiri See *tawasi, -ri-*. vo. (T4) scrub (something) with a *tawasi*.

tawanap (3a) See *taaw, nap*. nu. (T3) 1. big or main pass or channel in a reef. [It is a common place name.] 2. (Itang) seat of the emotions (syn. *neetip*).

tawe (1) TAWEE. vi. 1. be finished, done. *meyi t. aach angaang* our work is f. Syn. *pwi, tak, wees*. 2. (N.) be convenient. *ika meyi t. kepwe fitiyey* if it is c., you will accompany me. Syn. *túúfich*.

taweeyiti See *tawe, -iti*. vo. (T2) be finished by (a time). Syn. *takeyiti, weesiiti*.

tayifuun Var. of *táyifuun*.

tayikú (1) TAYIKÚÚ. (Jap. *daiku*) nu. (T1) carpenter. *emén t*. one c. *néwún t*. his c. Syn. *kaamété*.

tayikúúni See *tayikú, -ni-*. vo. (T4) do carpentry on, repair (by means of carpentry). *t. na iimw* repair that house.

Tayiwang₁ nu. (loc.) Taiwan.

tayiwang₂ See *Tayiwang₁*. Var. *táyiwang*. nu. (T3) variety of banana.

tayiyo (1) TAYIYOO. (Jap. *taihoo*) nu. (T1) cannon. *efóch t*. one c. *néwún t*. his c.

tá (1) TÁÁ₁. vi. 1. fit. Syn. *kkuch*. 2. come close, skirt.

-tá (1) See *táá-*. Var. *-tás, -tes, -set*. adj. (dir.) up, upward; east, eastward. *aa péétá seni notow* it blows eastward from the west.

táá- (1) TÁÁ₂. nr. (T1) rising, ascent (of something). *táán maram* r. of the moon.

táán (2) TÁÁNI. nu. (T2) species of small mangrove crab. *táánin Chuuk* Trukese m. c.

táána- (3) TÁÁNA. [In cpds. only.] unsp. (u.m.) See *nakatáán, táánáán*.

táánáán (db; 3) See *táána-*. nu. (T3) a variety of banana. *táánáánen Chuuk* Trukese b.

Táániyón (4) See *táá-, -ón*. [Bollig] nu. (loc.; T2) a place in the layer of heaven called *Nenisu ("sunrise")*. [Associated with it is the place called *Féwúkasé*. Bollig quotes a saying: *wú tupw me Táániyón, wú mwé Féwúkasé; wú tupw me Féwúkasé, wú mwé Táániyón* I disappear from T., I alight at F.; I disappear from F., I alight at T.]

táánupw (2) See *táá-, pwuupw*. nu. (loc.) (in traditional navigation) a point of the sidereal compass in the southeastern sky ("rising of Crux").

tááng (2) TENGI. Tb1. n. (T2) penis. *tengin* his p.

ttáángngaw (3b) See *tá, ngngaw*. vi. fit badly.

táári See *tá, -ri-*. vo. (T4) skirt, skim, sail close along the shore of, fly low along.

tááringeey See *ttááring, -e-₂*. vo. (T6b) tear (clothing). Dis. *táttááringeey* (ds).

tááyééch (2) See *tá, ééch*. vi. fit well.

-tás E.Wn. and Ps.W. of *-tá*.

táne (1) TÁNEE. nu. (T1) cat's cradle, string figure. vi. make a cat's cradle.

tánech (3a) TÁNECHA. N. Var. *tenech*. vi. be inattentive to work, nonchalant.

tánechepwaak (3) See *tánech, -pwaak*. N. vi. be very inattentive to work, careless, indifferent, disinterested.

táni- (4) TÁNE. [In cpds. only.] unsp. (u.m.) See *fátán, tánnipi*.

tánnipi (3?) See *táni-, piye-*. nu. (T3?) garden (plot and crops together), plantation, farm. *chóón t*. gardener, farmer. vi. make a garden or plantation.

táp (4) TÁPE. vi. be faded, dulled (in gloss or brilliance). [Said of the color of clothes or of the glossiness of greased hair that has lost its gloss after washing the grease out.] Dis. *tápátáp* (db).

tápátáp Dis. of *táp*.

táppi-₁ (2) TÁPPI. ni. (T2) age-mate, person of nearly identical age. *táppin* his age-mate. Cf. *pinó*.

táppi-₂ (2) See *táppi-₁*. nr. (T2), suf. (cc.) people who have died or passed on. *etáp aramas* one set of people who have passed on, one generation of dead. *kkewe táppin aramas* those people who have passed on.

táttááringeey Dis. of *tááringeey*.

táwán (3) TÁWÁNA. n. (T3) vagabondage, wandering, traveling about. *táwánan* his wandering. *chóón t.* wanderer, traveler, vagabond. *pwata ina táwánomw* why are you such a wanderer? (said to imply that there is something wrong with you that you cannot settle down in one place).

táy (4) TÁYE. Tb3. vi. fool around, play about. *ketee táy* don't f. a. Syn. *wurumwmwot*.

táyifuun (Eng.) Var. *tayifuun*. nu. typhoon. Syn. *ménúmén, puunumén*.

táyinikkich (2) See *táy, -kkich*. Tb3. vi. play about wildly, fool around, horse about.

táyiri See *táy, -ri-*. Tb3. vo. (T5) tease, make sport of. Syn. *wurumwmwoteey, wurumwmwotiiti*. Cf. *mesekitikitiiy*.

táyiwang F. of *tayiwang₂*.

táyiya (1) TÁYIYAA. (Jap. from Eng.) nu. (T1) tire. *eew t.* one t. *aan t.* his t. *táyiyaan Merika* American t.

táyiyaani See *táyiya, -ni-*. vo. (T4) put a tire on (something).

te- (3) TA₄. [In cpds. only.] unsp. dissolved, melted. See *eteni, ket, ten₁, teniiti*.

te (1) TEE₁. vi. be learned, known (after practicing, as a song or dance). *meyi te ewe kkéén* the song is known.

-te₁ TE. suf. (asp.) don't (negative imperative); lest (purposeful future negative, when in a phrase introduced by *pwú, pwún*). *kete feyinnó* don't depart. *repwene feyinnó pwún ewe Énúún Mwaresi ete wocheer* they will leave lest the Rainbow God devour

them (they will leave so that the Rainbow God will not devour them).

-te₂ E.Wn. and Ps.W. of *-to*.

tee-₁ (1) TEE₂. [In cpds. only.] unsp. sew. See *teete₁, teeyi*.

tee-₂ (1) TEE₃. [In cpds. only.] unsp. covering. See *teewunus, teeyaw*. Cf. Gb. *rai*.

tees (Eng.) nu. test, examination.

teek (2) TEKKI. (Eng.) nu. (T2) deck (of a ship). *tekkin waa* ship's d.

Teena nu. (loc.) a clan name.

teep (Jap.) Var. *teyip*. nu. tape recorder. Syn. *teeprekooto*.

teeprekooto (1) (Jap.) nu. tape recorder. Syn. *teep, teyip*.

teechééw (2) See *tee-₁* or *tee-₂, chééw*. vi. be an unbroken succession, be continuous. *pwata aa t. chék rán mwirinné?* why has there just been a continuous succession of nice days? *aa t. chék ewe akkar* the sun just shone without interruption (as in a drought).

teete₁ (db; 1) See *tee-₁*. nu. (T1) sewing. *chóón t.* tailor, seamstress. vi. sew.

teete₂ (db; 1) TEE₄. nu. (T1) small leaf package of breadfruit pudding, grated taro, or banana. *eew t.* one p. *teeteen kkón* p. of breadfruit pudding.

teete₃ (db; 1) TEE₅. [In cpds. only.] unsp. (u.m.) gentle (?). See *pweteete*.

teewunus (3a) See *tee-₂, wunus*. nu. (T3) mother-hubbard dress formerly worn by mission women.

teeyaw (3) See *tee-₂, aaw₁*. nu. (T3) slip-over ornamental upper garment of bright colors and shells worn by men and women in such dances as the *maas*.

teeyi See *tee-₁, -yi-₂*. vo. (T4) sew. *teeyiyey, teeyuk* s. me, you.

tefetef (db; 3) See *tafa-₁*. vi. (dis.) be what relationship?

tefiiy See *tefitef, -i-₂*. vo. (T5) tear, rip; run away.

tefitef (db; 2) TEFI. va. tear, rip.

teffengen (2) See *tee-₁, ffengen*. vi. be sewed together.

-tes E.Wn. and Ps.W. var. of *-tá* (see also *-set, -tás*).

tessiri (1) TESSIRII. (Jap. *tesuri*) nu. (T1) bench attached to an outer wall of a house. *eew t.* one b. *aan t.* his b.

-tek (2) TEKI₁. suf. (v.form.) imparts a passive meaning. [No longer productive.] See *féétek, fittek*.

teki- (2) TEKI₂. [In cpds. only.] unsp. pertaining to position or change in position. See *etekini, tekisón, tekiya.*

tekisón (4) See *teki-, són.* vi. be low, humble, of low rank, of low height. With dir. suf.: *tekisónutiw* become or get lower.

tekisónutiw See *tekisón.*

tekiya (1) See *teki-, -ya*₁. n. (T1) height, greatness, high rank; high point. *tekiyaan* his h. *tekiyaan chuuk* mountain's summit. vi., adj. (be) high, lofty, exalted, of high rank. *aramas t.* person of high rank; *namanam t.* arrogant (lofty) behavior, insolence, disrespectful behavior, pushing above one's station, putting on airs. With dir. suf.: *tekiyaatá* become or get higher.

tekiyaatá See *tekiya.*

tempúra (1) TEMPÚRAA. (Jap. *tempura*) nu. (T1) doughnut. *eféw t.* one d. *anan t.* his d. vi. make doughnuts.

tempwo (1) TEMPWOO. (Jap. *dempoo*) nu. (T1) telegram, radiogram, cablegram. *eché t.* one t. *néwún t.* t. for him.

ten₁ (2) See *te-, -ni-.* vi., adj. dissolve, melt; be faded, run (of colors). *meyi t. wúfey* my clothing is faded (or has run). With dir. suf.: *teninó.*

ten₂ (2) TENI. vi. be in a line, in a row; be arranged in lines or rows. With dir. suf.: *teninó* be extending off in a line or row, be standing or marching in line. nr. (T2) line, row, linear arrangement (of something). *tenin íimw* town, village, encampment, settlement; *tenin néwúnéw* line of descent, lineage; *tenin pwiipwi* generation. *eew tenin néwúnéw me wóón semeer* a line of descent through fathers; *eew tenin néwúnéw me wóón ineer* a line of descent through mothers; *tenin néwúnéw wátte* senior line of descent; *tenin néwúnéw kúkkún* junior line of descent; *tenin pwiipwi wátte* senior generation; *tenin pwiipwi kúkkún* junior generation. Cf. *sáán.*

tenech Var. of *tánech.*

tenechepwaak Var. of *tánechepwaak.*

teniiti₁ See *ten*₁*, -iti.* vo. (T2) melt onto; run onto (of color). *kanten aa t. enaan ténaaw* the candle has run down to the mat.

teniiti₂ See *ten*₂*, -iti.* vo. (T2) form a line to or as far as.

teninó See *ten*₁ and *ten*₂.

tenúngi (1) TENÚNGII. (Jap. *tenugui*) nu. (T1) a towel (of Japanese style). *eché t.* one t. *aan t.* his t.

tenre (1) TENREE. (Jap.) nu. (T1) female go-between (in love affairs). Syn. *towupe.*

tenchi (1) TENCHII. (Jap.) nu. (T1) battery (as in a flashlight). *eféw t.* one b. *néwún t.* his b. *tenchiin neyiy tengki* my flashlight b.

tengerik (3) TENGERIKA. F. nu. (T3) a large *kuumar* or women's fishing basket used in the kind of fishing called *púnúpún. eew t.* one b. *aan t.* her b. *tengeriken púnúpún* b. for *púnúpún* fishing.

tengús (Jap.) nu. nylon fishing line. Syn. *aroma, óroma.*

tengki (1) TENGKII. (Jap. *denki*) nu. (T1) electric light; electricity; flashlight. *eew t.* one flashlight. *néwún t.* his flashlight. *chóón t.* electrician; *mwesiinen t.* generator (electric); *fáán t.* with, under, by electric light or flashlight; *fiyefiyen t.* flashlight button.

tengkiini See *tengki, -ni-.* vo. (T4) give light to.

tengngú (1) TENGNGÚÚ. nu. (T1) tiny gnat. [It is said to have been introduced into Truk just before World War II.] *tengngúún Chuuk* Trukese g.

tep₁ (3) TEPA₁. vi., adj. be many, numerous. Dis. *tepetep* (db) be very numerous. nr. (T3) multitude, numerousness. *tepetepen kkey iik* the m. of these fish.

tep₂ (3) TEPA₂. [Used with plural subject only.] vi. compete, fight, contend (with one another).

tepeey See *tep*₂*, -e-*₂*.* vo. (T6b) hit, strike (people or things). Syn. *namwúti, nengeey, siyeri.*

tepetep Dis. of *tep*₁.

tepúkúro (1) TEPÚKÚROO. (Jap. *tebukuro*) nu. (T1) glove (other than in baseball). *epéw t.* one g. *péwún t.* his g. (to wear).

teppang (3) TEPPANGA. (Jap. *teppan*) nu. (T3) large sheet of iron used as a trough for mixing cement or concrete. *eew t.* one sheet of i. *aan t.* his sheet of i.

tepwaanú Var. of *tapwpwaanú.*

tepwekinaas (3: *-kinassa-*) See *tapwa-, kinaas.* nu. (T3) binoculars.

tepwpwaanú F. of *tapwpwaanú*.
ter₁ (2) TERI₁. vi., adj. (be) devastated, ruined, stripped. With dir. suf.: *terinó*. *aa terinó ewe fénú reen ewe nóóter* the land was devastated by the tidal wave. *aa terinó chéén ewe irá* the leaves of the tree have been stripped away.
ter₂ (2) TERI₂. vi. be finished, completed. *aa t. chék ika mááno aa kisenngeni inisiy pwpwún* it would just be finished if death gave my body to the soil. Id. *mwúúch mee sópw, tere me iyeey* finished and ended, complete as of now (formula for ending a *túttúnnap* story). With dir. suf.: *terinó* be finished off. ni. (T2) end (of something). [In ptv. const. only.] *ika wú máánó epwaapw ina terin* if I die it will afterwards be the end.
tere- (3a) TERE. N. Var. *téré-*. pref. (intens.) very, extremely. *tereféwúféw* very stony.
tereech (2) TERECHCHI. (Eng.) nu. (T2) thread. *efóch t.* a string of t.; *emwú t.* a broken piece of t. *aan t.* his t. *terechchin Sapaan* Japanese t.
tereféwúféw (2) See *tere-*, *féwúféw*₂. Var. *téréféwúféw*. vi. be very stony.
terennif nu. surprise raid in war (especially at night). Syn. *menúken*.
terepep (2) See *tere-*, *ppep*. nu. (T2) species of surgeon fish. *terepepin Chuuk* Trukese s. f.
teri- (2) TERI₃. [In cpds. only.] unsp. speed; speedy.
terinó See *ter*₂.
teritam (3) See *teri-*, *taam*. vi. (in courtship talk) be unenthusiastic, drag one's feet. [The outrigger is seen as a drag on the speed of the canoe; hence the expression as a figure of speech for lack of enthusiasm for something for which others are enthused.]
teriwi (1) See *teri-*, *wi*. vi. grow quickly (of people or plants).
terúútang (3) TERÚÚTANGA. (Jap. *teryuudan*) nu. (T3) hand grenade. *eféw t.* one h. g. *néwún t.* his h. g.
tetten₁ (ds; 2) See *ten*₂. nu. (T2) rank, row, line, list, grade; generation, descent line. *ese nómw nóón tettenin* he is not in his r. *tettenin mwirin* generation following. *pwpwuken tettenin fóós* dictionary.
tetten₂ nu. a kind of yellow-tail pompano.

tettenéech (ds; 2) See *ten*₂, *éech*. vi. be well-arranged, neat, in good order, tidy; be regular (as a verb).
tetteningngaw (ds; 3b) See *ten*₂, *ngngaw*. vi. be in disorder, disordered, disorderly, badly arranged; be irregular (as a verb).
tewe- See *taaw*.
teyik Var. of *teyuk*.
teyikeey See *teyuk*, *-e-*₂. vo. (T6b) annoint with turmeric.
teyinemeet (2) TEYINEMEETI. (Eng.) nu. (T2) dynamite.
teyinemeetiiy See *teyinemeet*, *-i-*₂. vo. (T5) dynamite (something).
teyip Var. of *teep*.
teyuk (3) TEYUKA (*TEYIKO). Var. *teyik*. n. (T3) turmeric; cosmetic stick made of turmeric mixed with coconut oil and perfume. [Orange-yellow in color it was used traditionally as a body paint and was also applied to clothing.] *teyukan* his t.
té₁ (1) TÉÉ₁. vi. be enough. Syn. *nnaaf*.
té₂ (1) TÉÉ₂. vi. 1. walk on the hands; (N.) creep or crawl on all fours. Dis. *téété* (db). With dir. suf.: *téétá* crawl or creep up, clamber up, climb up, ascend, rise (of the sun); *téétiw* crawl or creep down, climb down, descend. 2. (short for *téétá*) rise (of the sun). 3. be invaded, infested.
téé- (1) See *té*₂. ni. (T1) walking on the hands; (N.) creeping or crawling on all fours. *téén* his w. on the h.
téé₁ (1: *-té*, *-téé*) TÉÉ₃ (*TÉÉÉ). n. (T1) an uninhabited or not regularly inhabited low island that has vegetation on it. *téén* his u. i. *téén Chuuk* u. i. of Truk. Cf. *fénú*, *ppi*.
Téé₂ nu. (loc.) Ta Island and District (Mortlock Islands).
tééfán (4) See *té*₂, *fáán*₂. vi. go in search of a woman at night, have illicit sexual intercourse ("house-crawl"). Syn. *chcheyiroch*, *ssaw*₂. nu. (T2) going in search of a woman at night.
tééfáneey See *tééfán*, *-e-*₂. vo. (T6b) have illicit sexual intercourse with (someone) at night.
tééfátán (4) See *té*₂, *fátán*. vi. crawl about (with much coming and going, as of ants).
téési N. of *tééki*₁.
tééki₁ See *té*₂, *-ki-*. Var. *téési*. vo. (T4) invade, infest; (F.) crawl upon. *aa*

téékuk ewe kinin kuchuwa prickly heat has infested you (you have gotten prickly heat).

tééki₂ (1) TÉÉKII. (Eng.) nu. (T1) turkey. *téékiin Merika* American t.

téémey (2) See *té₂, mááy₂*. vi. climb a breadfruit tree.

téémwánninong (3) See *té₂, mwmwáán, -nong*. vi. enter without legitimate purpose. Syn. *téffatonong*.

téémwánnito (1) See *té₂, mwmwáán, -to*. vi. come visit without legitimate reason. Syn. *téffatoto*.

téén (2) TÉÉNÚ. nu. (T2) torch. [Traditionally made of a rolled dried coconut frond.] *efóch t.* one t. *aan t.* his t. *téénún Fanapenges* torches of Fanapenges Island. vi. go torch fishing. *siyaa nó t.* we are off t. f.

téénú (1) See *té₂, núú*. vi. gather drinking coconuts ("do coconut climbing").

téépáráák See *té₂, -páráák*. F. vi. creep or crawl on all fours. Syn. *ténnaw*.

tééppi (3) See *té₂, ppi₂*. nu. (T3) a sea cucumber. [Edible, said to be like *chénúchcha*, but found in the sand.]

téér nu. a sea cucumber. [Edible, known on Wééné (Moen) but not on Romónum.]

téérú Var. of *ttérúúw*.

tééchap (3) See *té₂, chaap*. vi. crawl face down; make a blind opening bet (in poker); engage in money-matching at a money-raising party. [Money-matching parties were invented by the late Petrus Mailo as a means of raising capital for investment purposes. The name refers to "crawling" toward progress.] nu. (T3) party for raising money by money-matching. ni. (T3) matching (someone's) money at a money-raising party. *tééchapan* m. his money.

téétá See *té₂*.

téété (db; 1) See *té₂*. nu. (T1) track of an animal. *téétéén* its trace or track. vi., adj. crawl; (be) crawling, creeping on all fours, walking on the hands; be able to crawl. *t. fátán* c. about. *maan t.* creeping or crawling creature. va. climb or crawl to get something.

téétiw₁ See *té₂*.

Téétiw₂ (3a) See *téé₁, -tiw*. nu. (loc.) Tarik Island.

tééwoch (3) See *té₂, wooch*. nu. (T3) method of fishing. [Men drive fish into women's nets, the men starting from shore and the women waiting with nets on the fringing reef.] Syn. *mwmweemw*.

téffat (3) See *té₂, -ffat*. vi. crawl to no purpose, crawl aimlessly. Id. *téffatonong* enter without invitation or legitimate reason (syn. *téémwánninong*); *téffatoto* come visit without invitation or legitimate reason (syn. *téémwánnito*). With dir. suf.: *téffatátá, téffatetiw, téffátónó*.

téffatátá See *téffat*.

téffatetiw See *téffat*.

téffatonong See *téffat*.

téffatoto See *téffat*.

téffátónó See *téffat*.

tékúnaar See *taak, -naar*. Var. *takúnaar, takúraar, tékúraar*. nu. swordfish, marlin.

tékúraar See *taak, -raar*. Var. *takúnaar, takúraar, tékúnaar*. nu. swordfish, marlin.

témmey (2) See *té₂, mmey*. vi., adj. (be) fast, efficient (as in work).

tén (2) TÉNÚ. vi. be scrubbed, scoured, washed (of hands and dishes, but not clothes); dusted, shined up; erased, rubbed.

ténaaw (3) TÉNAAWA. F. Var. *tanaaw*. nu. (T3) mat. *eché t.* one m. *kiyan t.* his m. *ténaawen Chuuk* Trukese m. Syn. *kiyeki*.

tenóóno See *ténú*.

ténú See *tén*. vo. (T2) wash, scrub, scour; erase, rub; dust, shine (of shoes); wipe. Dis. *tétténú* (ds). With dir. suf.: *ténóónó* wipe off, wash off. *ténóónó chéchchénún kkeey sepi* dry ("wipe off the wetness of") these dishes.

ténúpwpwaseey See *tén, pwas, -e-₂*. vo. (T6b) dry (with a towel), rub dry.

ténnaw (3) See *té₂, -naw* (?). F. vi. creep, crawl on all fours. Syn. *tééparáák*.

téngúrútiw (3a) nu. (T3) kind of body blow with the hands (in fighting).

tépwpwach (3) See *té₂, pwpwach*. vi., adj. 1. (be) diffident, uninterested, lackadaisical, unenthusiastic. 2. (be) slow (in gait, action or speech).

téré- F. of *tere-*.

téréféfféw Dis. of *téréfféw*.

téréféwúféw Dis. of *téréfféw* and var. of *teref éwúféw*.

téréfféw (2) See *téré-, faaw.* vi. be very stony; be rough (of a path). Dis. *téréféfféw* (ds), *téréféwúféw* (db).
téréparapar (3b) See *téré-, parapar.* vi., adj. (be) very red.
térépwichikkar (3b) See *téré-, pwichikkar.* vi., adj. (be) very hot.
téréwún (3a) See *téré-, wúún₁.* n. (T3) scales (of fish), feathers (of bird), skin, hair (of animals and people). *téréwúnan* its s. Syn. *méréwún.*
térúú Var. of *ttérúúw.*
tétten (ds; 2) See *tén.* nu. (T2) washing, scrubbing, scouring; erasing, rubbing. *téttenún mmak* eraser.
téttenú Dis. of *ténú.*
ti-₁ (2) TI₁. [In cpds. only.] unsp. motion, moving, going. See *eti-, fiti-₁.*
ti-₂ (2) TI₂. [In cpds. only.] unsp. fence, wall, enclosure. Cf. *etiip, etippa, ttiit₁, ttiiy.*
ti-₃ (2) TI₃. [In cpds. only.] unsp. penetrate, pierce. See *tik, tikek, tiki₁, ttik₃.*
ti-₄ (2) TI₄. [In cpds. only.] unsp. jab, poke. See *tiki-, tiki₂, -ttiit₂, ttik₂.*
-ti- (2) TI₅. suf. (v.form.) makes a verb of the base. *fééti* tie, lash (*fééfé* tying, lashing).
ti (1) TII₁. vi., adj. be crowded, pushed together; (in cpds.) be persistent, pushy.
tii (1) TII₂. nu. (T1) name of the consonant (dental stop) written *t*; name of the letter thus written.
tiis (Eng.) nu. diesel fuel.
Tiisamper (Eng.) Var. *Tiisémper.* nu. (temp.) December.
Tiisémper Var. of *Tiisamper.*
tiimaaw (3) See *ti, maaw.* vi. deny repeatedly, protest strongly.
tiimsón (4) TIIMSÓNO. (Eng.) Var. *siimsón.* nu. (T2) demijohn. *eew t.* one d. *aan t.* his d. *tiimsónun Merika* American d.
tiin₁ (3) TIINA, TINNA₁. nu. (T3) a shrub (*Cordyline terminalis*). [Unopened leaves are used to treat stomach disorders; bark is used to relieve constipation.] *tiinen Chuuk, tinnen Chuuk* Trukese s.
tiin₂ (3) TINNA₂. (Eng.) Var. *ttiin₂.* nu. (T3) tin, can, metal container. *tinnen piskit* t. of biscuits.
tiinaanó See *tiini.*

tiinaato See *tiini.*
tiini See *ti, -ni-.* vo. (T4) shove, push; send. With dir. suf.: *tiinaato* send hither; *tiinaanó, tiinóónó* send off.
tiinóónó See *tiini.*
tiip₁ (3a) TIPA₁. n. (T3) emotion, feelings, sentiment (located in the abdominal region, *neenuuk*); attitude; mind; spirit. *tipan his e. tipen áát* youthful or boyish spirit; *tipen mwáán* mature spirit, attitude of a mature man. Cf. *neetip.*
tiip₂ (3) TIPA₂. n. (T3), suf. (cc.) slice, chunk, cut segment (of breadfruit and taro only); chip (of wood from adzing). Dis. *tipetip* (db). *etip, rúwétip, wúnútip, fétip, nimetip, wonotip, fúútip, wanútip, ttiwetip, engoon tipan* one,...ten s. *tipen mááy* sliced chunk of breadfruit; *tipen pwuna* sliced chunk of taro. *tipetipen waa* wood chips from making a canoe.
tiipw (3: *tipwa-*) See *tipw.* nu. (T3) auxiliary rods used in complicated weaving; outermost flat lath used to spread thread on the loom. *tipwen túúr* a. r. of a loom. Syn. *wááyitipw.*
tiiti (db; 1) See *ti.* vi., adj. shove, push; shoving, pushing; summoning, inviting. va. summon, send for. *aa t. ngaang* she has sent for me. With dir. suf.: *tiitiinó* transmit, send (as a message); *tiitiito* send hither for. *wúwa tiitiinó fóós ngeni* I sent him a message; *aa tiitiito néwún mwooni reey* she has sent hither for her money that is in my keeping.
tiitiinó See *tiiti.*
tiitiito See *tiiti.*
tiito (1) See *ti, -to.* vi. be sent hither. *aa t. me Merika neyi toropwe* my letter was sent hither from America.
tifi- (2) TIFI. Var. *túfi-.* unsp. scooping. See *etifi.*
tik (2) See *ti-₃, -ki-.* vi. be sticking through, be piercing. *meyi t. nóón* it is s. through it. With dir. suf.: *tikenong.* Cf. *tiki, ttik₃.*
tikek See *ti-₃, -kek.* nu. needle. Cf. *tik.*
tikenong See *tik.*
tiketik (db; 3) TIKA. nu. (T3) straight-edge adze. *eché t.* one a. *aan t.* his a.
tiki- (2) See *ti-₄, -ki-.* [In cpds. only.] unsp. jab, poke; speck, dot.
tiki₁ See *ti-₃, -ki-.* vo. (T5) stitch or sew (thatch). *siya t. rúpwúng* we stitched

tiki₂   **Trukese-English**

ivory nut thatch. With n. form suf.: *tikiya-* (ni.; T3) stitching or sewing (done or to be done by someone); *tikiyan* s. done by him.

tiki₂ See *ti-₄, -ki-*. vo. (T5) 1. poke, touch with the forefinger, tap (as the keys of a typewriter). 2. put a dot on, spot, make a diacritical mark on, put a period on. Cf. *ttik₂*.

tikifúúfú (1) See *tiki-, fúú*. vi. having polkadots ("starry-spotted").

tikisoomá (1) See *tik, soomá*. vi. incur the liability of death (among the relatives of a housebuilder or houseowner) as a result of faulty house construction. [This liability results from the supernatural power used in housebuilding magic.]

tikimaan (2) See *ttik₁, maan₂* (?). nu. (T2) buzzing in the ear, ringing in the ear. [Said to be caused by someone's talking about the person affected.] *tikimaanún nóón seningey* b. in my ear.

tikit₁ (2) TIKITI₁, TIKITTI₁. (Eng.) nu. (T2) ticket. *tikitin* or *tikittin kachito* cinema t.

tikit₂ (2) TIKITI₂, TIKITTI₂. nu. (T2) freshwater eel. *tikitin* or *tikittin Chuuk* Trukese e.

tikitik₁ (db; 2) TIKI₁. nu. (T2) small pile of sand on a fringing reef. [A small fish called *afanaw* is said to live in the hole in such a pile of sand.] *eew t.* one p. of s. *tikitikin* p. of s. of (a given area). *wóón t.* a beach's area of rough sand that is covered at high tide.

tikitik₂ Dis. of *ttik₂*.

tikitik₃ (db; 2) See *ttik₁*. nu. (T2) song, chirping, peeping (of birds). [Used instead of *ttik₁* when sound is faint or indistinct.] *meet eey aa ttik? tikitikin machchang ika meet?* what is this that peeped? the peeping of a bird or what?

tikiya- See *tiki₁*.

tikot (3) TIKOTA. n. (T3) room (in house). *tikotan* his r. *tikoten iimw* house's r.

tikka (1) TIKKAA. nu. (T1) unscented coconut oil. *tikkaan taka* o. of a coconut.

timi- (2) TIMI. [In cpds. only.] unsp. smacking noise made with the lips.

timma (1) TIMMAA. (Jap.) nu. small rowboat, skiff. *efóch t.* one r. *waan t.* his r. *t. kkumi* rubber boat. Cf. *sitiima*.

tin₁ (2) TINI₁. vi. proceed in relation to trees, boulders, houses, or other things that stand up around one. *aa t. neyin kkewe aramas* he proceeded among those people. With dir. suf.: *tininong* or *tinnong, tininó, tiniwu. aa tininong neyin kkewe pétéwén* he went in among the bushes; *aa tiniwu me neyin pétéwén* he emerged from among the bushes.

tin₂ (2) TINI₂. vi. be inserted, put in between. *meyi t. eey piin wóón eey óós* this pencil is inserted up in this thatch; *meyi t. wóón seningey* it is inserted in my ear. With dir. suf.: *tininong*.

tin₃ (3) TINA. vi. be chopped lengthwise; be separated, split. *meyi t. eey ira* this tree is c. lengthwise.

tinemey (2) See *tin₃, mááy ₂*. nu. (T2) house whose frame is built entirely of adzed breadfruit timbers (cornerposts, tiebeams, wallplates, kingposts, ridgepole, and rafters).

tineni See *tin₃, -ni-*. vo. (T6a) chop lengthwise.

tinepwu See *tin₃, -pwu*. vi., adj. (be) cut in half (of a coconut). *péén t.* empty half of a ripe coconut shell.

tinetin (db; 3) See *tin₃*. va. chop lengthwise; separate, split.

tinewupw (2) See *tin₃, wupwu-₁*. n. (T2), suf. (cc.) cloth yard (length from center of chest to outstretched fingertips, one half a *ngaaf* fathom). *etinewupw, ráwétinewupw, wúnútinewupw, fétinewupw, nimetinewupw, wonotinewupw, fúútinewupw, wanútinewupw, ttiwetinewupw* one,...nine y.

tinéw (2) TINÉWÚ. F. Var. *sinéw*. nu. (T2) wall plate (longitudinal beam of a house). *tinéwún ewe iimw* the house's w.

tini-₁ (2) TINI₃. [In cpds. only.] unsp. (u.m.) See *átittin₂*.

tini-₂ (2) TINI₄. [In cpds. only.] unsp. smell, perceive odor. See *etiningeni, etinimach, etinimwas, tini, ttin₂*.

tini See *tini-₂*. vo. (T2) smell, sniff, perceive the odor of. *siya t. pwoon kkanaan iik* we smelled the odor of those fish. Cf. *ttin₂*.

tinifi See *tin₁, -fi-*. vo. (T5) go among.

Tinik nu. (loc.) a local name for the *Pwee* or *Nipwe* clan on Toon (Tol) Island.

344

tinikásá (1) See *tin₂, ásá*. F. nu. (T1) board connecting the outrigger boom ends on the side opposite to the outrigger (on the lee side of a sailing canoe). *tinikásáán waa* canoe's *t.*. Syn. *senikásá*.
tinikken (2) See *tin₁, kken*. vi. be industrious, hard-working ("go among things sharply").
tinikkopw (2) See *tin₁, kkopw*. vi. be lazy, unindustrious ("go among things dully").
tininong See *tin₁, tin₂*.
tininó See *tin₁*.
tinipwu (1) nu. (T1) a species of rudder fish. *tinipwuun Chuuk* Trukese r. f.
tiniwu See *tin₁*.
tiniyókkoomw (3) See *tin₁, ókkoomw*. va. pass, go past, proceed ahead (in connection with walking, driving, etc., but not racing). *aa t. senney* he passed me.
tinoopen (2) TINOOPENI. (Eng.) nu. (T2) can opener, tin opener. *eew t.* one c. o. *aan t.* his c. o. *tinoopenin Merika* American c. o. Syn. *woopen*.
tinneey See *ttiin₁, -e-₂*. vo. (T6b) shuffle (playing cards).
tinnong Var. of *tininong*.
tingar (3) TINGARA. nu. (T3) a fish (*Gnathodentex aurolineatus* Kuiyama).
tingor (3) TINGORA. Var. *tingór, tungór*. nu. (T3) plea, request. *ááy t. ngonuk, ááy t. reemw* my request of you, my plea to you; *kinissow, meyi wor ekis ááy t.* please, I have a small request (a common way of asking a favor). vi. make a plea, request. *t. péchékkún* persist in asking, plead hard; *t. maaw* request shamelessly or with effrontery, or without regard to social considerations.
tingoreey See *tingor, -yi-₂*. vo. (T6b) ask (someone for something). *wúwa t. ewe sómwoon eew neyiy pwpwuk* I asked the chief for a book for me.
tipap (3) TIPAPA. Tbl. nu. (T3) smegma.
tiparoch (3a) See *tiip₁, roch*. Var. *tipóroch*. vi. be ignorant, stupid, unable to learn easily. Ant. *tipachchem*.
tipachchem (3a) See *tiip₁, chchem*. n. (T3) intelligence. *tipachcheman* his i. vi. be intelligent, smart, quick to learn. *t. sooná* so knowledgeable that one can steal with impunity. Ant. *tiparoch*.

tipate (1) See *tiip₁, tee-₂*. Var. *tipáte*. nu. (T1) small child ("covered mind"). Syn. *ménúkón, monukón, nooyiis, nooyiroch, semiriit*.
tipeféereya (1) See *tiip₁, féereya*. vi. be particular, fussy, never satisfied with what has been done. Cf. *mwecheniya*.
tipesé (1) See *tiip₁, sé*. vi. be eased or quieted in one's mind, be relieved (in one's feelings), have one's mind at rest.
tipekúkkún (2) See *tiip₁, kúkkún*. vi. be unselfish, unselfseeking, of modest desire or ambition.
tipekkowumw (2) See *tiip₁, kkowumw*. nu. (T2) envy, spite, malice; misanthropy, dislike of people. *aan t.* his e. vi. feel envious; be disagreeable, quarrelsome.
tipemecheres (2) See *tiip₁, mecheres*. nu. (T2) cooperation. vi. be cooperative, good-natured, agreeable, easy-going.
tipemmóng (2) See *tiip₁, mmóng*. vi. be greedy, selfish, avaricious. Syn. *tipenap₁*.
tipemwaramwar (3) See *tiip₁, mwaramwar₂*. vi. feel uncertain.
tipemwócho (1) See *tiip₁, mwócho*. nu. (T1) thievish or rascally character.
tipenap₁ (3) See *tiip₁, -nap*. N. vi. be selfish, greedy. Syn. *tipemmóng*.
tipenap₂ (3) See *tiip₂, -nap*. vi. be crudely made, be poorly shaped.
tipeni See *tiip₁, -ni-*. vo. (T6a) want, desire, like; be in favor of.
tipennap (3a) See *tiip₂, nap*. vi. slice into big pieces.
tipengeni See *tiip₁, ngeni*. vo. (T2) agree with, share feelings of. Cf. *tipingeni*.
tipengngaw (3b) See *tiip₁, ngngaw*. vi. feel badly (emotionally), have a bad attitude, be antipathetic, be badly disposed; disagree.
tipeppós (3b) See *tiip₁, ppós*. nu. (T3) steadfastness (of persons). vi., adj. (be) steadfast, undeflectable.
tipepwich (2) See *tiip₁, pwich₁*. nu. (T2) ardor, strong desire. vi. have strong desire.
tiperi See *tiip₂, -ri-*. vo. (T6a) slice or cut into chunks.
tiperúwérú (1) See *tiip₁, rúwa-*. vi. be undecided, uncertain, unsure of how one feels or of what one wants, hesitant ("two-minded"). Syn. *tipemwaramwar*. adj. indecisive.

tipetip

tipetip Dis. of *tiip*₂.
tipewen (3a) See *tiip*₁, *wen*. vi., adj. (be) honest, straight-forward, trustworthy.
tipeweyires (2) See *tiip*₁, *weyires*. vi., adj. (be) difficult to get along with, disagreeable.
tipeyeew (2) See *tiip*₁, *eew*₁. vi. be of one mind, of one sentiment, agree; be harmonious, harmoniously shaped. *tipeyeew ffengen* agree together, come to a common sentiment, arrive at one mind.
tipeyééch (2) See *tiip*₁, *ééch*. nu. (T2) pleasant or favorable emotion or attitude; good disposition. vi., adj. (be) well-disposed.
tipi- (2) TIPI. [In cpds. only.] unsp. wrongdoing.
tipingeni See *tipi-*, *ngeni*. vo. (T2) accuse (someone) of wrongdoing, blame.
tipir (2) TIPIRI. nu. (T2) mosquito fish (?). *tipirin Chuuk* Trukese m. f.
tipitip (db; 2) See *tipi-*. vi. (with *ngeni*) make accusation of wrongdoing. *aa t. mwmwáán ngeniyey* he made false accusation against me.
tipitipingngaw (3b) See *tipitip*, *ngngaw*. n. (T3) the emotion of acute shame and guilt at being caught in a wrongful act. *tipitipingngawan* his shame. vi. feel acute shame and guilt at being caught in a wrongful act, hang one's head in shame (when accused of something), act guilty. [Expressed behaviorally by looking at the ground, saying nothing, and scratching the back of one's ear.]
tipóroch Var. of *tiparoch*.
tipw (3) TIPWA. vi., adj. (be) prized, pried, lifted with a lever.
tipweek (2) TIPWEEKI. F. nu. (T2) grass (*Eleusine indica*). [It is used to relieve stomach disorders.] *tipweekin Chuuk* Trukese g. Syn. *pwukerimwéch*.
tipweey See *tipw*, *-e-*₂. vo. (T6b) prize up, lift with a lever; use the *tiipw* on (the loom).
tipwetipw (db; 3) See *tiipw*. vi. use the *tiipw*. *t. wóón ewe túúr* use the *tiipw* on the loom.
tirapw (3) TIRAPWPWA. (Eng. *trap*) nu. (T3) drum (musical instrument). *tirapwpwen Merika* American d. *siya wópwuni ewe t. pwú epwe ttik* we beat the drum so it would sound.

Trukese-English

tiriis (2) TIRISSI. nu. (T2) echo. *tirissin neewuwan* e. of his voice.
tiriffééw (2) See *ttir*, *fféew*. nu. (T2) goosepimples. vi. have goosepimples.
tiriniyon (Eng.) nu. trillion. *eew t.* one t.
tirongkang (3) TIRONGKANGA. (Jap. *doramukan*, from Eng. *drum, can*) Var. *tirungkang*. nu. (T3) drum (container). *eew t.* one d. *aan t.* his d. *tirongkangen Merika* American d.
tirow [With *wóó-*₁.] vi. beg pardon. *t. wóómw* I beg your p., excuse me. Syn. *feyicho*, *féwúwicho*.
tirungkang Var. of *tirongkang*.
tichchik (2) See *ti*, *-chchik*. vi., adj. (be) inquisitive, always wanting to know, always asking about things; pry; pester with questions. *emén meyi t.* busybody, one who pries. *eyiis t.* inquire searchingly.
tichchiki- (2) See *tichchik*. ni. (T2) details (of something).
-tit (2: *titti-*) See *tti-*₂. suf. (cc.) string (of breadfruit, ordinarily ten to a string). *etit, rúwetit, wúnútit, fétit, nimetit, wonotit, fúútit, wanútit, ttiwetit, engoon tittin one,...ten s.* Syn. *-iyef*, *ttiit*₂.
tittiiy See *ttiit*₁, *-i-*₂. vo. (T5) fence, enclose.
tiw (3a) TIWA₂. vi. remain in a place; change one's location. With dir. suf.: *tiwenong* disembark onto land from the sea; *tiwenó* disembark, go ashore, transfer from one vehicle to another, fail to reembark, depart, escape, get away, die (euphemism); *tiwetá* embark, go aboard, climb aboard; *tiweto* embark or disembark hither; *tiwetiw* disembark, go ashore, fail to embark, drop out (of a passenger list), step down; *tiwewu* embark aboard.
-tiw (3a) TIWA₁. adj. (dir.) down; west, westward. *aa péétiw seni éétiw* it blows westward from the east.
tiweey See *-tiw*, *-e-*₂. vo. (T6b) cut down, fell.
tiwenong See *tiw*.
tiwenó See *tiw*.
tiweri See *-tiw*, *-ri-*. vo. (T6a) blow down, strike down (as a tree by wind or lightning).
tiwetá See *tiw*.
tiwetiw₁ (db; 3a) See *-tiw*. nu. (T3) felling, cutting down.

tiwetiw₂ See *tiw*.
tiweto See *tiw*.
tiwewu See *tiw*.
tiwiiniin (2) See *ti-₁, wi, ini-₄*. N. vi., adj. (be) on one's side ("go on edge"); sidle, slip between something by turning one's body sideways. Syn. *pereyingiing*.
tiyor (3) TIYORA. nu. (T3) small coop for penning a fighting cock preparatory to his fighting. *tiyoren chukó* chicken's c.
to (1) See *too-*. vi. be reachable, attainable; be reached, attained.
-to (1) See *too-*. Var. *-te*. adj. (dir.) towards speaker or point of reference, hither, this way. Ant. *-nó*.
too- (1) TOO. [In cpds. only.] unsp. arrive; proceed. With dir. suf.: *toonong* come or go in, enter (with *nóón*); *toonong nóón kiyan* go to his sleeping place or mat (idiom: lit. "enter in his mat"); *tootá* reach the top, arrive up; *tootiw* reach the bottom, arrive down; *toowu* go out, come out, emerge, arrive outside, quit, be fired, be dismissed.
took (3) TOKKA. nu. bush knife. *néwún t.* his b. k. *tokken Sapaan* Japanese b. k.
Tooming (Jap. *toomin*) nu. name by which the Japanese called the people of Truk. [Known primarily to older people, it is felt to have a comtemptuous sense.]
toon₁ (3) TONA₂. nu. (T3) peak, high point, pinnacle; extension of a mast. *tonan* its p. *tonen Chuuk* the highest point of Truk; *tonen éwú* masthead, mast extension; *tonen chukó* chicken's or cock's comb; *tonen pókó, tonen pachaaw* dorsal fin of a shark. Cf. *ton*.
Toon₂ (3) See *toon₁*. nu. (loc.) Tol Island. [It has Truk's highest mountain whose summit is *tonen Chuuk*.]
toonong See *too-*.
toongeni (2) See *too-, ngeni*. vo. (T2) be able to do, can, achieve against. *ese t. angaang* he is unable to work; *ngaang meyi t. fóósun Chuuk* I am able to speak Trukese. nu. (T2) ability, capability. *aan t.* his a.
toori See *too-, -ri-*. vo. (T4) reach, arrive at, come to (a place); achieve (a goal).
tootay (2) TOOTAYI. (Jap. *toodai*) nu. (T2) lighthouse. *eew t.* one l. *aan t.* its l.; *tootayin* l. of.
tootá See *too-*.
tootiw See *too-*.

tooto (db; 1) See *too-*. vi. be uninhibited, ready to do wrong. *átánaan meyi fóókkun t. nóón aan ekiyek* that fellow is very u. in his thinking.
toow₁ (2, 3) TOWU₁, TOOWA₁. N. nu. (T2, T3) turmeric flour or starch; face powder. [Derived from grated and washed turmeric, which is yellow in color, is edible, is used to make *teyuk*, and is also used as a body grease without coconut oil.] *anan t.* his t. f. (to eat); *towun, toowen* t. f. of. Syn. *opu*.
toow₂ (3) TOOWA₂ (from *TOO-AWA). vi. be far, distant. Dis. *toowaaw* (db, the common form).
toowaaw (db; 3) See *toow₂*. nu. (T3) far distance. *toowaawen ewe fénú* f. d. of the island. vi. be far, distant.
toowaay See *toow₁, -a-₄*. vo. (T1) massage with *toow*. *toowaayey, toowayók, toowaay, toowaakich, toowaakeem, toowaakemi, toowaar* m. me, you (sg.), him, us (inc.), us (exc.), you (pl.), them with *t*. (instead of *toowááyey*, etc., as with T3 verbs).
Toowis Var. *Ttooyis*. nu. (loc.) Germany. *re-T*. a German man; *fin T.* or *fiin T.* a German woman; *fóósun T.* German language; *mwúún T.* German rule (of Truk); *kurukurun T.* German orange (a variety).
Toowow nu. (loc.) a clan name.
toowu See *too-*.
toku (1) TOKUU. nu. (T1) yellow-fin tuna, albacore (general name). *tokuun Chuuk* Trukese t.
tokun (2) TOKUNU. vi. revolve, spin, be spun. Cf. *kkun*.
tomw (3b) TOMWA. vi. 1. become untied (of rope). 2. be squashed, burst, disintegrated (of fruit only). *aa ttomw eew mááy, ina pwata meyi t.* a breadfruit fell and burst, that's why it is squashed.
tomwun₁ (3a) TOMWUNA₁. vi. be peeled (of fruit); be decayed, soft, rotten (of fish and seafood). *tomwunen eey iik* the decay of this fish. With dir. suf.: *tomwunonó* be peeled off, gone soft or rotten. Cf. *tomw*.
tomwun₂ (2, 3) TOMWUNU, TOMWUNA₂. nu. (T2, T3) yellowish species of sea cucumber. [Called by this name when small, but called *inowuch* when large.] *tomwunun* or *tomwunen Chuuk* Trukese s. c.

tomwunonó See *tomwun*₁.
ton (3a) TONA₁. vi., adj. (be) visible, discernible, viewed; prominent. *meyi t. ika ese t.* is it v. or is it not v. With dir. suf.: *tononó* fade from being visible; *tonoto* become visible, become more visible.
tona- (3) See *ton*. [In cpds. only.] unsp. under scrutiny. nr. (T3) rising, eastern position (of a star). *tonen Máánap* r. of Altair (due east, on the navigator's sidereal compass). Syn. *sássi-*. Ant. *tupwu-*.
Tonaachaw (3) See *toon*₁, *achaw*₁. nu. (loc.) northernmost mountain on Wééné (Moen) Island ("Basalt Peak"). [Said to be the first place of human settlement, probably because of association with *Achaw*, Kusaie Island, from which Truk's people traditionally derive themselves.]
tonoseni See *ton, seni*₂. vo. (T2) be visible from.
tonosómwoon (2) See *toon*₁, *sómwoon*. Itang. vi. be above a chief.
Tonomwáán (4) See *toon*₁, *mwáán*₁. nu. (loc.) highest mountain on Tonowas (Dublon) Island.
tononó See *ton*.
tonoto See *ton*.
tonoton (3) See *ton*. nu. (T3) type of love magic. vi. make a type of love magic.
tonotoneey See *tonoton, -e-*₂. vo. (T6b) make *tonoton* love magic for. *tonotoneey átánaan reen ewe feefin* make magic for that fellow concerning that woman.
Tonowas (3b) See *toon*₁, *aas*₁. nu. (loc.) Dublon Island ("eastern pinnacle").
tonoya (1) TONOYAA. nu. (T1) throw net. *eew t.* one t. n. *tonoyaan Chuuk* Trukese t. n.
tong (4?) TONGO (?). vi. smart, sting.
tongeey See *ttong, -e-*₂. vo. (T6b) love, pity, have sympathy for. *aan tongeyok* his loving you.
toping (2) TOPINGI. (Jap. *dobin*) nu. (T2) teapot, kettle. *eew t.* one t. *aan t.* his t.; *topingin* t. of.
topw (2) TOPWU. vi., adj. (be) not bright, dull, tarnished, ungreased, opaque, dry (of ungreased hair); (be) gray, gray-brown, gloomy; (be) cloudy, obscured (as by clouds); (be) faint, difficult to see. Dis. *topwutopw* (db). *meyi*
topwutopw akkar ikenáy the sun is obscured today.
topwutopw Dis. of *topw*.
tor (3) TORA. vi. snore, grunt (of pig), purr (of cat).
tora- (3) See *tor*. ni. (T3) snore, heavy breathing in one's sleep, grunt (of pig), purr (of cat). *toran* his s.
torakkú (1) TORAKKÚÚ. (Jap. *torakku*, from Eng.) nu. (T1) truck. *efóch t.* one t. *waan t.* his t. *torakkúún Sapaan* Japanese t.
torikko (1) TORIKKOO. (Jap. *torikko*) nu. (T1) a kind of *tamachiki* game with marbles. vi. play a kind of *tamachiki*.
toro (1) TOROO. (Jap. *torokko*, from Eng. *truck*) nu. (T1) barbell. *efóch t.* one b. *aan t.* his b.
torongki (1) TORONGKII. (Eng.) vi. be drunk, intoxicated. Syn. *pwunaas*.
toropiito (1) TOROPIITOO. (Eng. *torpedo*) nu. (T1) submarine.
toropwe (1) TOROPWEE. Var. *taropwe*. nu. (T1) paper; letter, card; pass, document. *toropween kékké* summons (written); *toropween mwúúmwúútá* permit, license; *toropween pwpwon* signed affidavit or declaration; *toropween tingor* invitation (written).
torotor (db; 3) See *tor*. n. (T3) snoring, grunting, purring. *torotoran* his s. *torotoren kattu* cat's purring.
towu- (2) TOWU₂. [In cpds. only.] unsp. (u.m.) See *mwotowutow, nikóttow*.
towunómw (4) TOWUNÓMWO. n. (T2) mosquito net, sleeping canopy. *towunómwun* his m. n.
towupe (1) TOWUPEE. nu. (T1) female go-between (in love affairs). Syn. *tenre*.
tóó- (1) TÓÓ₁. [In cpds. only.] unsp. rub gently, pat, caress. See *tóóf, tóófeey, tóófi*.
tóóf (3) See *tóó-, -fi-*. [Apparently a back formation from *tóófi*.] vi. give an alcohol rub.
tóófeey See *tóóf, -e-*₂. vo. (T6b) give an alcohol rub to.
tóófi See *tóó-, -fi-*. vo. (T4) rub gently, pat, caress. Dis. *tóttóófi* (ds).
tóók (4) TÓKKO. vi. stop off, make an intermediate stop (on a journey). With dir. suf.: *tókkónó, tókkoto. tókkónó Fanapenges* s. o. at Fanapenges; *tókkoto wóón eey fénú* s. o. here on this island.

tóókoche Var. of *tókoche*.
tóótó (db; 1) TÓÓ₂. nu. (T1) netting needle.
tóówun (2) TÓÓWUNU. (Eng.) Var. *tawun*. nu. (T2) towel. *eché t.* one t. *aan t.* his t. *tóówunun Merika* American t.
tókoche (1) TÓKOCHEE. (Eng.) Var. *tóókoche*. nu. (T1) doctor (medical), physician. *tókocheen sáfey* doctor of medicine. Syn. *tókter*.
tókkónó See *tóók*.
tókter (2) TÓKTERI. (Eng.) doctor (medical), physician. Syn. *tókoche*.
tór (4) TÓRO. vi. be disarranged, disarrayed, mussed, messed up, in a mess, untidy; (of a tabu) be broken, defiled.
tórófátán (4) See *tór, fátán*. vi. have strayed, be out of place.
tórópaas (3b) See *tór, -paas*. Var. *taropaas*. vi. be in confusion, in great disorder, scattered about.
tórótóréech (2) See *tór, ééch*. vi. be orderly, well arranged, neat, well combed.
tórótóróngngaw (db; 3b) See *tór, ngngaw*. vi. be in disorder, mussed up, unkempt, untidy, neglected, clumsy, inept, inappropriate. *fóós t.* clumsy, ungrammatical, inelegant, incorrect or incomplete speech; *meyi t. ááy kkapas* my speech is inelegant. nu. (T3) unsuitability, clumsiness. *tórótóróngngawen eey mwéngé* unsuitability of this food.
tóttóófi Dis. of *tóófi*.
tuu-₁ (1) TUU₁. [In cpds. only.] unsp. dig, excavate. See *ttu₁, ttuuw₁, tuutu*.
tuu-₂ (1) TUU₂. [In cpds. only.] unsp. throw, hurl; stab, pierce. See *kéétukkachang, ttu₂, ttuuw₂*.
tuu-₃ (1) TUU₃. N. [In cpds. only.] Var. *túú-*. unsp. (?) perform, undertake. See *tuufich*.
tuuféw (2) See *tuu-₁, faaw*. vi. do a kind of fishing at night. [It is done by four or five women together with one or two men. The men use a stick of wood, the women use nets. The men dig up stones with the stick, the fish rush out, and women catch them up in their handnets.] Cf. *tuuyán*.
tuufi N. var. of *túúfi*.
tuufich N. of *túúfich* (see *tuu-₃, -fich*).

tuuk (3) TUKA₃. nu. (T3) bag, sack, gunny sack. *eew t.* one b. *aan t.* his b. *tuken rayis* b. of rice. Cf. *túkúm*.
Tuumw nu. (loc.) a clan name.
tuumwu (1) TUUMWUU. vi. dye, do dying (any color).
tuumwuuni See *tuumwu, -ni-*. vo. (T1) dye. *siya t. eey mangaak* we dyed this cloth.
tuuna- (3) TUUNA. [In cpds. only.] unsp. rotating, spinning. See *ttun, ttuun, tuuna*.
tuuna See *tuuna-*. vo. (T3) twirl, rotate, spin (between the palms of the hands). Cf. *ttuun*.
tuungeni See *tuu-₁, ngeni*. vo. (T2) remind (someone) of something bad; speak to, have a word with.
tuupw (2, 3) TUPWPWU, TUPWPWA. F. Var. *ttupw*. nu. (T3) a shrub (*Macaranga carolinensis*). [Big, almost round leaves are used to cover boiling breadfruit.] *tupwpwun* or *tupwpwen Chuuk* Trukese s. Syn. *kúrúwén, tupwpwunuwén*.
tuutá (1) See *tuu-₁, -tá*. vi. be dug up, resurrected, come back to life or memory. Cf. *tuuwotá*.
tuutu (db; 1) See *tuu-₁*. vi. (dis.), va. dig. nu. (T1) 1. digging; ditch, air raid shelter, foxhole (military). 2. (Rmn.) paddle. Syn. *fétún*.
tuutunnap N. var. of *tuttunnap*.
tuuwotá See *tuu-₁, -tá*. vo. (T1) dig up, resurrect (of bad things). Cf. *tuutá*.
tuuyán (4) See *ttu₁, áán₂*. nu. (T2) a kind of fishing done by men and women together in the daytime. [The women surround *áán* coral with nets while the mend dig in the *áán* with sticks and chase out the fish.] Cf. *tuuféw*.
tuk₁ (3a) TUKA₁. vi. be many, numerous, plentiful. *meyi t. kkeey iik* these fish are numerous; *oo mé tuken eey iik!* oh what a lot of fish!
tuk₂ (3a) TUKA₂. va., vi. scoop, shovel (from a larger quantity of material); be scooped out. Dis. *tukotuk* (db). *siya t. ppi* we scoop up sand. Cf. *rék*.
tukeey See *tuk₂, -e-₂*. vo. (T6b) scoop with one's fingers (as of food in eating with the fingers); scoop up, shovel out.
tukeni See *tuuk, -ni-*. vo. (T6a) bag, put in a bag.
tukoppi (3) See *tuk₂, ppi₂*. vi. scoop sand.

tukotuk (db; 3) See *tuk₂*. nu. (T3) scooping, shovelling; scoop. *tukotuken ppi* scooping up of sand; *mwesiinen tukotuken pwpwún* steam shovel, power shovel, power dredge; *tukotuken pwpwún* scoop (on a power shovel). va. (dis.) scoop, shovel. *mwesiinen t. pwpwún* steam shovel, power shovel, power dredge.

tuku- (2) TUKU. [In cpds. only.] unsp. tap, beat; daub. See *tukuuw, tukuyá.* Cf. *ssuk*.

tukuungeni See *tukuuw, ngeni.* vo. (T2) daub (something) on (someone). *aa tukuungeniyey ewe sáfey* he daubed the medicine on me.

tukuuw See *tuku-, -u-.* vo. (T5) daub. *aa t. ewe sáfey ngeniyey* he daubed the medicine on me. Cf. *tukuungeni*.

tukuyá (1) See *tuku-, áá-₁.* nu. (T1) dance with hardwood staves. [Traditionally performed in honor of an *énúúsór* spirit.] *eew t.* one d. *tukuyáán Chuuk* Trukese d. vi. dance a *t*.

Tumwur nu. 1. a star (Antares). 2. name of a traditional sidereal month. [Coming in December, it was the first month of the year.]

tumwuri See *ttumw₂, -ri-.* vo. (T5) sip, suck. *aa t. ewe kkap* he sipped from the cup; *aa t. owupwun inan* he sucked his mother's breast.

tuni (3, 1) TUNIYA, TUNII. nu. (T1) variety of breadfruit. *tuniyen* or *tuniin Chuuk* Trukese b.

tuno- (3a) TUNA. unsp. express or make known in speech.

tunofóós (4) See *tuno-, fóós.* vi. be garrulous in a nasty way, gossip rudely.

tunomichimich (2) See *tuno-, michimich.* vi. speak flatteringly or guilefully (for selfish ends).

tunomúúmú (1) See *tuno-, mú.* vi. pine, be nostalgic (in talk).

tunomúúmúúyiti See *tunomúúmú, -iti.* vo. (T2) pine for, talk with nostalgia of.

tunommóng (4) See *tuno-, mmóng.* vi. exaggerate, talk big.

tunomwúúmwú (1) See *tuno-, mwú₃.* F. Var. *tunumwuumu.* vi. grumble.

tunomwúúmwúúyiti See *tunomwúúmwú, -iti.* F. Var. *tunumwuumwuuyiti.* vo. (T2) grumble about (someone). [Used in relation to persons only.]

tunopwaasik (3) See *tuno-, pwa, sik.* vi. boast outrageously (especially of sexual prowess).

tunumwuumwu N. of *tunomwúúmwú*.

tunumwuumwuuyiti N. of *tunomwúúmúúyiti*.

tunun (2) TUNUNU. N. nu. (T2) ginger (*Zingiber zerumbet*, Elbert: *Hedichium cylindrica*). *tununun Chuuk* g. of Truk. Syn. *fitun, sinser*.

tungurungur (db; 2) TUNGURU. vi. rant, rave (in anger).

tupw₁ (2) TUPWU₁. vi. 1. go, proceed. With dir. suf.: *tupwunong neeman* go inland; *tupwutiw* go down or west, descend, set (of the sun); *tupwuwu neeset* go out in the sea. 2. set (of sun, moon, sunset glow). *aa t. akkar* the sun has s.

tupw₂ (2) TUPWU₂. vi. be fooled, deceived, tricked, duped, trapped. *wúwa t. reen* I was fooled by him. Syn. *son*.

tupw₃ (2) TUPWU₃. [Used with *nóón*.] vi. get smeared. *wúwaa t. nóón pwiise* I got s. in excrement.

tupwiiti See *tupw₂, -iti.* vo. (T2) be fooled by, tricked by. *kete t. átánaan pwú meyi mwaken* don't be fooled by him because he is lying.

tupwu- (2) See *tupw₁.* nr. (T2) setting, western position (of a heavenly body). *tupwun Máánap* s. of Altair (due west on the navigator's sidereal compass).

tupwu (3) TUPWUWA. n. (T3) brain. *tupwuwan* his b.

tupwuniyón (4) See *tupwu-, -ón.* nu. (T2) 1. sunset. 2. (Itang) the western region of *Faachchamw* (heaven). [According to Bollig, it is the abode of the uncles of Énúúnap.]

tupwunong See *tupw₁*.

tupwunupw (2) See *tupwu-, pwuupw.* nu. (loc.) (in traditional navigation) extreme southwestern position on the sidereal compass ("setting of Crux").

tupwunupwin (2) See *tupw₁, pwiin₃.* Itang. nu. (T2) going about at night. Ant. *tupwuyiráán*.

tupwurasé nu. a mythical bird. [Larger than any other bird, it can lift up people and driftwood logs; it causes typhoons in anger at being seen by people.]

tupwutiw See *tupw₁*.

tupwuwu See *tupw₁*.

tupwuyiráán (2) See *tupw₁, ráán₂*. Itang. nu. (T2) going about by day. Ant. *tupwunupwin*.

tupwpwén (2) See *tupw₁, pwénú-₁*. n. (T2) persistency, perseverance, steadfastness, constancy. *tupwpwénún* his p. vi. persist, persevere, be steadfast (with *nóón*). *pwata aa t. nóón angaangangngaw?* why does he p. in doing bad things?

tupwpwunuwén (2) See *tuupw, wénú-*. nu. 1. a shrub (*Macaranga carolinensis*). [Big leaves are used to cover boiling breadfruit.] Syn. *ttupw₂, tuupw, kúrúwén*. 2. a shrub (*Pipturus repandus*).

tur₁ (2) TURU₁. [Used with *wóón*.] vi. be grabbed, taken, seized, captured. *aa t. wóón ewe óó* it was taken on the fishline; *wúwa t. wóómw* I have been seized by you.

tur₂ (2) TURU₂. Var. *ttur*. vi. fall, be fallen; plunge, dive (into the sea). With dir. suf.: *turunó*, (E.Wn.) *turuná* fall away, plunge off (into the sea); *turutiw* fall down, fall from grace or from public office; *turuu, turuwu* fall out.

tura- (3a) TURA. [In cpds. only.] unsp. (u.m.) See *oturénnú, turokáppe*.

turokáppe (1) See *tura-, pe*. vi. be teased, made sport of.

turu- (2) TURU₃. [In cpds. only.] unsp. enter (?). See *turupwén*.

turuu See *tur₂*.

turufi See *tur₁, -fi-*. vo. (T5) catch hold of, seize, snatch, grab hold of, capture, arrest (of police).

turuffengeen Var. of *turuffengen*.

turuffengen (2) See *tur₁, ffengen*. Var. *turuffengeen*. vi. embrace one another.

turukkémwéch (2) See *tur₁, kkémwéch*. vi. have one's hands full and be unable to hold something else.

turuná See *tur₂*.

turunó See *tur₂*.

turunóóy See *tur₁, -nó*. vo. (T1) grab from yonder.

turunuffas (3) See *tur₁, ffas*. nu. (T3) mischief. vi., adj. (be) mischievous; make sport of others; make a show or pretense of something but not really take it seriously (as when someone professes a religion but does not really believe it), play at something rather than do it seriously, make a mockery of something.

turunuffaseey See *turunuffas, -e-₂*. vo. (T6b) make sport of (someone) in an inhuman way, treat as if not a human being, insult or demean in the extreme; mock, taunt.

turupwén (2) See *turu-, pwéén₁*. vi. cultivate wet taro.

turupwpwas Var. of *túrúpwpwas*.

turupwpwaseey See *turupwpwas, -e-₂*. vo. (T6b) pick, apply a pickaxe to. Syn. *túrúpwpwaseengeni*.

turutiw See *tur₂*.

tuttu (ds; 1) See *ttu₃*. va. (dis.) sew thatch. nu. (dis.; T1) sewing thatch.

tuttunnap (dc; 3a) See *tuno-, nap*. Var. *tuutunnap*. nu. (T3) story, tale, legend, fable. [It is for entertainment and does not purport to be true.] *eew t.* one s. *aan t.* his s. (to tell); *tuttunnapan* s. about him. *tuttunnapen nóómw* s. from or about old times; *ááni eew t.* tell a s. Cf. *wuruwo*.

tuttunnapa See *tuttunnap*. N. Var. *tuttunnapeey*. vo. (T3) tell, relate (a story).

tuttunnapeey See *tuttunnap, -e-₂*. F. Var. *tuttunnapa*. vo. (T6b) tell, relate (a story).

tú (1) TÚÚ₁. vi. (be) bowed (of the head); (in cpds.) dive, duck the head under water. With dir. suf.: *túúnó* dive away; *túútá* tip the head back, face upwards, come to the surface (from under water), surface; *túútiw* dive, bow the head and body low (as to Japanese officials).

túú- (1) TÚÚ₂. F. [In cpds. only.] Var. *tuu-*. unsp. (?) perform, undertake. See *túúfich*.

túú (3) TÚWA. Tb1. n. (T3), suf. (cc.) vulva, cunt. *etú, rúwétú, wúnútú, fétú, nimetú, wonotú, fúútú, wanútú, ttiwetú, engoon túwan* one,...ten v. (in counting sexual encounters); *fitetú* how many v.

túúfaato See *túúfi*.

túúfi See *tú, -fi-*. Var. *tuufi*. vo. (T4) dive for. With dir. suf.: *túúfaato* d. for and bring hither.

túúfich (2) See *túú-, -fich*. F. Var. *tuufich*. n. (T2) capability, ability, convenience; suitability. *túúfichin* his c. vi., adj. be capable, convenient, able; suitable. *ese t. ngeniyey* it is not convenient for me; *wúse t.* I am not

túúnó

able, it is not convenient for me; *ika meyi t.* if it is convenient.
túúnó See *tú.*
túúr (2) TÚRÚ. nu. (T2) loom; weave (of a fabric). *eché t.* one l. *aan t.* his l. *túrún Chuuk* Trukese l. *meyi feet túrún wúfomw na?* what sort of weave is your clothing?
túútá See *tú.*
túútiw See *tú.*
túútú (db; 1) See *tú.* vi. (dis.) bathe, take a shower.
túkiyefiiy Var. of *túkúwefiiy.*
túkú- (2) TÚKÚ. [In cpds. only.] unsp. package.
túkúm (3) See *túkú-, -ma-.* n. (T3), suf. (cc.) package, packet. *etúkúm, rúwétúkúm, wúnútúkúm, fétúkúm, nimetúkúm, wonotúkúm, fúútúkúm, wanútúkúm, ttiwetúkúm, engoon túkúman* one,...ten p. *túkúman* p. of it. *túkúmen kkón* p. of breadfruit pudding. Cf. *éékúm, túkúmiya-, túkútúk.*
túkúméwúún (3) See *túkúm, wún₃* (?). nu. (T3) a charm that has been wrapped up and tied in a small bundle. [It may be worn around the neck or attached to an object.]
túkúmi See *túkú-, -mi-.* vo. (T6a) package, wrap up (in a package), make into a bundle; conceal or keep hidden (of thoughts or feelings).
túkúmiya- (3) See *túkúmi, -a-₁.* ni. (T3) package, packet (belonging to someone). *túkúmiyan kkón* his p. of breadfruit pudding. Cf. *túkúm, túkútúk.*
túkúruuru (1) See *túkú-, ruuru.* nu. (T1) tied bundle of breadfruit pudding. [Distinct from a flat package wrapped in leaves but not tied.]
túkútúk (db; 2) See *túkú-.* nu. (T2) package, packet, bundle, parcel. *túkútúkún toropwe* envelope; *túkútúkún kkón* p. of breadfruit pudding. Cf. *túkúm, túkúmiya-.* vi., va. be wrapped, packaged, bundled; wrap, package.
túkúwef (2) See *túkú-, ááf.* Var. *túkúyef.* nu. (T2) leaf package of food for broiling. vi. broil in a leaf package.
túkúwefiiy See *túkúwef, -i-₂.* Var. *túkúyefiiy, túkiyefiiy.* vo. (T5) broil (something) in a leaf package.

Trukese-English

túkúyefiiy Var. of *túkúwefiiy.*
túkúyéf Var. of *túkúwef.*
túkken (2) See *tú, kken.* vi. bathe in the sea, play or go swimming in the sea.
túmwúnééch Var. of *túmwúnúyéech.*
túmwúnéchchúúw See *túmwúnééch, -ú-.* vo. (T5) care well for.
túmwúnú- (2) TÚMWÚNÚ. [In cpds. only.] unsp. care for, safeguard, protect. See *ttúmwún, túmwúnééch, túmwúnú, túmwúnúngngaw, túmwúnúúw, túmwúnúyéech.*
túmwúnú See *túmwúnú-.* N. Var. *túmwúnúúw.* vo. (T2) look after, tend, take care of, protect, safeguard; spare.
túmwúnúúw See *túmwúnú-, -ú-.* F. Var. *túmwúnú.* vo. (T5) look after, tend, take care of, protect, safeguard, defend; spare; (refl.) be careful, look out for oneself. *túmwúnúúwey* spare me. *t. emén seni* protect someone from (someone). Syn. *senááni.*
túmwúnúngngaw (3b) See *túmwúnú-, ngngaw.* vi. be careless, not careful, inattentive.
túmwúnúyéech (2: *-yéchchú-*) See *túmwúnú-, éech.* Var. *túmwúnééch.* vi. be careful, protective, alert, attentive.
túna- (3) TÚNA. F. [In cpds. only.] Var. *túnna-.* unsp. (u.m.) See *féwútún, túnaaw, túnnaaw.*
túna- (3b) See *túna-, aaw₁.* F. Var. *túnnaaw.* nu. (T3) lips. *túnaawan* his l.
túnú- (2) TÚNÚ. F. unsp. detach from larger whole, segment. With dir. suf.: *túnútiw* become detached or break off (downward). ni. (T2), suf. (cc.) portion of *mwmwatún* (in counting). *etún rúwétún, wúnútún, fétún, nimetún, wonotún, fúútún, wanútún, ttiwetún, engoon túnún* one,...ten p. Syn. *ttúna-.*
túnúúw See *túnú-, -ú-.* vo. (T5) detach, pick (of fruit), amputate, decapitate. *wúpwe t. kkeey mááy* I shall pick these breadfruit; *wúpwe t. wuwomw* I will cut off your head.
túnútiw See *túnú-.*
túnna- Var. of *túna-.*
túnnaaw N. of *túnaaw.*
túr (2) See *túúr.* vi. weave on a loom; be woven.
túrin wén (?) n. phr. small bird with bright green body and red tail. Syn. *niwúkúpar, nikitirúúng, wúkúpar.*

Trukese-English   ttérúúw

túriyepeek (2) See *peek₂*. nu. (T2) blow to a person's side in hand-to-hand fighting.

túrúféwúúp nu. raised section of gunwhale in the middle of a paddle canoe.

túrúkoongi (1) See *túúr, -koongi*. nu. (T1) a type of *chééyitúr*.

túrúni See *túúr, -ni-*. vo. (T5) weave.

túrúpwpwas (3) TÚRÚPWPWASA. (Jap. *tsuruhashi*, dial. *tsuruppasi*) Var. *turupwpwas*. nu. (T3) pick, pickaxe. *efóch t.* one p. *aan t.* his p. *túrúpwpwasen Chuuk* Trukese p.

túrúpwpwaseengeni See *túrúpwpwas, -e-₂, ngeni*. vo. (T2) pick, apply a pickaxe to. Syn. *turupwpwaseey*.

túttúún Dis. of *ttúún*.

túttúnúkkis (ds) See *ttún, kkis*. vi. be much fallen out, full of gaps (of teeth).

túwesir (2) See *túú, siir*. Tb1. vi. given to urinating in orgasm.

túwéfachaacha (1) See *túú, fachaacha*. Tb1. vi. having reddish colored genitals (of a woman).

túwéffir (2) See *túú, fiir*. Tb1. vi. be endowed with labia minora.

túwékkor (3) See *túú, kkor*. Tb1. vi. be plentifully endowed with pubic hair (of a woman).

túwémwas (3) See *túú, mwas*. Tb1. vi. have smelly genitals (of a woman).

túwóótow See *túú, ótow*. Tb1. vi. have genitals whose membranes swell markedly when stimulated sexually (of a woman).

tta (1) TTAA. nu. (T1) mesh gauge (for netting). *efóch tta* one m. g. vi., va. make a fish net, do net weaving.

ttaayi See *tta, -yi-₂*. vo. (T4) weave (a net). With n. form suf.: *ttaayiya-* (ni.; T3) netting or net weaving done or to be done (by someone).

ttaayiya- See *ttaayi*.

ttaf (dc; 3) See *tafa-₂*. vi. be combed, preened, disentangled (of hair); be unsnarled (of a line), unraveled. Cf. *ttáf*.

ttam (3a) TTAMA. Tb3. n. (T3) length, tallness. Dis. *tattam* (ds). *ttaman* his l. vi., adj. (be) long, tall (of slender object). With dir. suf.: *ttamónó, ttamanó* lengthen, get taller. Syn. *áney*.

ttamanó See *ttam*.

ttamónó See *ttam*.

ttan (3) TTANA. nu. (T3) dream. *eew t.* one d. *aan t.* his d. vi. dream.

ttana See *ttan*. vo. (T3) dream of, dream about.

ttanasapanó (1) See *ttana, sapanó*. vi. in *t. wóón* dream about (someone).

ttapw (dc; 3b) See *tapwa-*. vi. be next, afterwards; follow. *wúpwe t. mwirumw* I shall be n. after you. *e t. ngé ruwuuw (wúnúngát)* it is second (third). With dir. suf.: *ttapwanó* go next; *ttapwoto* come next, come afterwards. va. chase, pursue, follow. *átánaan aa t. chukó* that fellow chased chickens.

ttapwanó See *ttapw*.

ttapwir (2) TTAPWIRI. vi., adj. (be) very big, huge, enormous. See *mééttapwir*.

ttapwoto See *ttapw*.

-ttar (3) TTARA. [In cpds. only.] adj. laden. See *numwuttar*.

ttá- Var. of *tte-* (?).

ttááring (dc; 3) TÁÁRINGA. vi., va. be torn (as of clothes); tear. Cf. *tááringeey*.

ttáf (4) TTÁFE. nu. (T2) ornamental wooden comb with feather ornament (worn in pre-colonial times in the hair by men and women); feather ornament on a comb. *aan t.* his c. *ttáfin Chuuk* Trukese c. Cf. *ttaf*.

ttárupwurupw (db; 2) See *ttá-, ruupw*. vi. be rough and unattractive (of the skin). *meyi t. wóón mesen átánaan* that fellow's face is r. and u.

tte- Var. *ttá-* (?), *tto-₂*. pref. (intens.) very. See *ttárupwurupw, tteneng, tteyir, ttopwur*.

-ttek (2) TTEKI. [In cpds. only.] unsp. (u.m.) See *óóttek, óóttekiiy*.

tteneng (2) See *tte-, nneng*. Tb1. nu. (T2) genital odor (of women only). *ttenengin* her g. o. Cf. *eeng, -sseneng*.

tter (2) TTERI. va. go about in search of, look for, gather, collect. *wúpwe t. sáfey* I shall go in s. of medicine; *epwe t. attaw* he will go in s. of fishing companions; *epwe t. chóón sááy* he will go in s. of sailing companions.

tteri See *tter*. vo. (T2) go in search of. *aa t. ewe attaw* he went in s. of [people to go on] the fishing trip.

tteyir (3a) See *tte-, ir*₁. vi. be healed (of a wound).

ttérúúw See *rúwa-*. [Derived from the counting sequence **etta *rúúw*, which is now *eet érúúw* or *eet ttérúúw*.] Var.

tti-₁   **Trukese-English**

téérú, térúú. nu. (num.) the number two. [Used in serial counting or to name the number in the abstract, but not as a numerical adjective, for which see *rúwa-*.] Syn. *erúúw*₁.

tti-₁ (dc; 2) See *ti-₂*. [In cpds. only.] unsp. fence, enclosure, wall. See *ttiit*₁, *ttiiy*₁.

tti-₂ (2: *-tit*) TTI. [In cpds. only.] unsp. string on a line (of breadfruit). See *-tit*, *ttiit*₂, *ttiiy*₂.

ttii (1) TTII. (Eng.) nu. (T1) tea. *eew t.* one tin of t.; *eew kkapen t.* one cup of t.; *óóch t.* some t. *wúnúman t.* his drink of t. *ttiin Sapaan* Japanese t.

ttiin₁ (3) TINNA₃. (Eng. *deal*) vi. shuffle (playing cards).

ttiin₂ Var. of *tiin*₂.

ttiit₁ (ds; 2: *titti-*) See *tti-*₁. Var. *ttit.* n. (T2) fence, wall, hedge; pen, enclosure. *tittin* f. that fences him; *aan t.* his f. (that he owns). vi. be fenced, enclosed.

ttiit₂ (ds; *titti-*) See *tti-*₂. vi. be strung on a line (of breadfruit). ni. (T2), suf. (cc.) 1. string (of breadfruit, ordinarily ten to a string). *ettiit, rúwéttiit, wúnúttiit, féttiit, nimettiit, wonottiit, fúúttiit, wanúttiit, ttiwettiit, engoon tittin* one,...ten s. *tittin máay* s. of breadfruit. Syn. *-iyef, -tit.* 2. amulet (in the form of a small bundle of medicine on a string). *tittin aramas* a. to be worn by a person; *tittin iimw* a. to be hung in a house to protect its occupants.

-ttiit (ds; 1) See *ti-*₄. adj. poking, jabbing. See *ewútúttiit.*

ttiiw (3b) See *ttiwa-*. nu. (num.) the number nine. [Used in serial counting or to name the number in the abstract, but not as a numerical adjective, for which see *ttiwa-*.]

ttiiy₁ See *tti-*₁, *-i-*₂. vo. (T5) fence, enclose.

ttiiy₂ See *tti-*₂, *-i-*₂. vo. (T5) string (breadfruit) together.

ttik₁ (dc; 2) TIKI₂. nu. (T2) sound, whistle, song (of birds), chirp, buzz, peep, squeal, squeak, trill, strum, ring. Dis. *tikitik* (db, used when sound is faint or indistinct). *ttikin owuwá* sound of whistling (human); *ttikin machchang* song, chirp, peep of birds; *ttikin piik* squeal of a pig. vi. whistle, chirp, peep, buzz. *meet eey aa t.?* what is this that sounded?

ttik₂ (dc; 2) See *ti-*₄, *-ki-*. nu. (T2) dot (as made by pen or by finger poked in sand), period (in writing), spot, diacritical mark (as dieresis). *eew t.* one dot. Cf. *tiki-*. vi,. va. be jabbed (as with a finger); be dotted; jab, poke. Dis. *tikitik* (db). *meyi t. esissinnan* its diacritical marks are dotted. With dir. suf.: *ttikinong* (as vi.) penetrate, go inside; (as va.) jab, poke.

ttik₃ (dc; 2) See *ti-*₃, *-ki-*. vi., va. be sewn or stitched (of thatch only); sew or stitch (thatch). [Leaves of the ivory nut palm are wrapped in overlapping series around a reed one fathom long and stitched in place with a length of fiber from a coconut frond to make a shingle or piece of thatch.] *siya t. óós* we stitched thatch.

-ttik (2) TTIKI. adj. (intens.) bright, brilliant (of colors). *parattik* bright red.

ttikinong See *ttik*₂.

ttin₁ (3) TTINA. nu. (T3) shine, ray, brightness, beam. *ttinen akkar* the sun's rays, shining of the sun. vi. be bright, shining (of sun, moon). *meyi t. akkar* the sun if shining.

ttin₂ (dc; 2) See *tini-*₂. vi. smell, perceive odor.

ttineey See *ttin*₁, *-e-*₂. F. Var. *ttineyi.* vo. (T6b) shine on.

ttinesich (2) See *ttin*₁, *-sich*₁. nu. (T2) faint shine; dim rays. *ttinesichin maram* f. s. of the moon.

ttinemmóng (4) See *ttin*₁, *mmóng.* vi. be bright (of light).

ttineyi See *ttin*₁, *-yi-*₂. N. Var. *tineey.* vo. (T6a) shine on.

ttineyiti See *ttin*₁, *-iti.* vo. (T2) shine upon.

ttipen TTIPA. [Occurs as shown with rel. suf. *-n*₂.] vr. pretend, simulate. *siya t. wúrá wo kiich pwiipwi* we p. in talk that we are brothers; *wúwa ttipen angaang pwú wúsapw rong aan fóós* I p. to work so that I shall not (as if I did not) hear what he says.

ttipis (dc; 2) See *tipi-, -si-*. n. (T2) error, mistake, fault; sin, wrongdoing. *ttipisin* his error; *aan ttipis* his error. *pwisin ttipisiy* my own fault. *imwen t.* jail; *t. wátte* felony; *t. kúkkún* venial or pardonable sin (Catholic usage). *ómwusóónó ááy t.* forgive me my sin or mistake; I beg your pardon; excuse me. vi. err, make a mistake, sin, transgress, do wrong; be a wrong, be sinfull, be a transgression.

ttipisinap (3a) See *ttipis, nap.* nu. (T3) mortal sin. [Catholic usage.]

ttipwúk (2) See *ttú-* (?), *pwúk.* nu. (T2) nubile girl, girl at puberty. [Possibly meaning "sprouting breast."]

ttir (dc; 2) TIRI. n. (T2) hives, small bumps on the skin (such as are produced by mosquito bites). *ttirin* his bumps. Cf. *tiriffééw.* vi. 1. have hives. *meyi t. inisin* his skin has small bumps.

ttit Var. of *ttiit₁*.

ttiwa- (3b) TTIWA. Var. *ttiwu-.* pref. (num.) nine. See *ttiwaché, ttiwapé, ttiwapék, ttiwayé, ttiwe, ttiwechamw, ttiwechchi, ttiwechchooch, ttiwechef, ttiwechú, ttiwechúk, ttiweféw, ttiweffaat, ttiweffit, ttiwefich, ttiwefóch, ttiwefutuk, ttiwengaf, ttiwengát, ttiwengéréw, ttiwengin, ttiwengoon, ttiwekis, ttiwekit, ttiwekkamw, ttiwekkap, ttiwekkumw, ttiwekum, ttiwekumwuch, ttiwekup, ttiwemach, ttiwemas, ttiwemataf, ttiwemech, ttiwemeech, ttiwemeet, ttiwemén, ttiwemma, ttiwemmék, ttiwemwénú, ttiwemwmék, ttiwemwmwun, ttiwemwmwú, ttiwemwmwún, ttiwemwú₁, ttiwemwú₂, ttiwemwúch, ttiwennú, ttiwepa, ttiwepachang, ttiwepan, ttiwepeche, ttiwepeek, ttiwepéw, ttiwepino, ttiwepinúk, ttiwepu, ttiwepwang, ttiwepwey, ttiwepwéét, ttiwepwi, ttiwepwopw, ttiwepwór, ttiwepwpwaaw, ttiwepwpwún, ttiwepwúkú, ttiwepwún, ttiwesap, ttiwesángá, ttiwesáwá, ttiweseeng, ttiwesen, ttiwesópw₁, ttiwesópw₂, ttiwessaar, ttiwessak, ttiwessar, ttiwessáát, ttiwessát, ttiwessupw, ttiwetinewupw, ttiwetip, ttiwetit, ttiwettiit, ttiwettún, ttiwetú, ttiwetúkúm, ttiwetún, ttiwewoch, ttiwewumw, ttiwewupw, ttiweyaf, ttiweyang, ttiweyef, ttiweyem, ttiweyep, ttiweyék, ttiweyi, ttiweyin₁, ttiweyin₂, ttiweyipw, ttiweyiyey, ttiweyó, ttiwéwúk₁, ttiwéwúk₂, ttiwéwún, ttiwéwút, ttiwowut, ttiwowumw, ttiwóóch, ttiwóówut, ttiwówo.*

ttiwapé (1) See *ttiwa-, péé-₁.* num. nine empty containers.

ttiwapék (2) See *ttiwa-, péék₂.* num. nine chips, chipped off pieces, cigarette butts.

ttiwaché (1) See *ttiwa-, -ché.* num. nine thin flat objects of any kind (e.g., sheets, leaves, planks); nine songs.

ttiwayé (1) See *ttiwa-, -é.* num. nine hairs.

ttiwe (1) See *ttiwa-, -e-₁.* num. ninety. With c. pref. and ptv. const.: *ettiween* ninetieth one, ninetieth place. With dis. c. pref.: *ekkettiwe* be ninety at a time. With pref. *nne-₂: eew nnettiwe* one ninetieth. With suf. *-somw: ttiweesomw* be more than ninety.

ttiweesomw See *ttiwe.*

ttiweféw (2) See *ttiwa-, -féw.* num. nine lumps or globular shaped objects (e.g., stones, balls).

ttiwefich (3a) See *ttiwa-, ficha-.* num. nine strips of coconut, pandanus, or palm leaf prepared for plaiting mats.

ttiwefóch (2) See *ttiwa-, fóchu-.* num. nine long objects (e.g. vehicles, cigarettes, pencils, teeth, timbers, shovels, arms, legs, etc.).

ttiwefutuk (3) See *ttiwa-, futuk.* num. nine pieces of meat.

ttiweffaat (3) See *ttiwa-, ffata-.* num. nine strings of fish.

ttiweffit (3) See *ttiwa-, fitta-.* num. nine leaf packages of small fish.

ttiwesap (3) See *ttiwa-, saap.* num. nine cheeks (especially of fish).

ttiwesángá (1) See *ttiwa-, sángá.* num. nine basketfuls of fish. Syn. *ttiwesáwá.*

ttiwesáwá (1) See *ttiwa-, sáwá.* num. nine basketfuls of fish. Syn. *ttiwesángá.*

ttiweseeng (3) See *ttiwa-, seeng.* num. nine lengths between joints.

ttiwesen (2) See *ttiwa-, -sen.* num. nine coils of rope. [Each coil 30 to 100 fathoms in length according to local custom.]

ttiwesópw₁ (4) See *ttiwa-, sópwu-₂.* num. nine segments.

ttiwesópw₂ (4) See *ttiwa-, sópwu-₃.* num. nine burdens of tied together breadfruit.

ttiwessaar (2) See *ttiwa-, -ssaar.* num. nine slices.

ttiwessak (3) See *ttiwa-, ssaka-.* num. nine pieces of copra.

ttiwessar N. of *ttiwessaar.*

ttiwessáát (4) See *ttiwa-, -ssáát.* num. nine slivers, longitudinal slices, splinters.

ttiwessát N. of *ttiwessáát.*

ttiwessupw (2) See *ttiwa-, ssupwu-*. num. nine tiny drops.

ttiwekis (2) See *ttiwa-, kisi-*. num. nine little things or bits. Syn. *ttiwengin*.

ttiwekit (3) See *ttiwa-, -kit*. num. ninety thousand.

ttiwekum (2) See *ttiwa-, kumu-*. num. nine mouthfuls or swallows of liquid.

ttiwekumwuch (2) See *ttiwa-, kumwuch*. num. nine fistfulls or handfulls (of something); nine hooves, paws, feet (of animals).

ttiwekkamw (3b) See *ttiwa-, kkamw*. num. nine fragments or pieces (of cloth, paper).

ttiwekkap (3) See *ttiwa-, kkap*. num. nine cupfuls.

ttiwekkumw (2, 3) See *ttiwa-, kkum$_1$*. num. nine portions of premasticated food.

ttiwemas (3) See *ttiwa-, -mas*. num. nine things worn on the eyes (e.g., lenses of goggles) or attached to piercing weapons (e.g., spear points).

ttiwemach (3) See *ttiwa-, macha-*. num. nine fishtails (in counting fish). Cf. *ttiwéwúk$_1$*.

ttiwemataf (3) See *ttiwa-, matafa-*. num. nine small portions, small amounts, little bits.

ttiwemeech (2) See *ttiwa-, -meech*. F. Var. *ttiwemech, ttiwemmech*. num. nine portions of mashed breadfruit.

ttiwemeet (3) See *ttiwa-, meet$_2$*. num. nine strands.

ttiwemech N. var. of *ttiwemeech*.

ttiwemén (2) See *ttiwa-, maan$_1$*. num. nine persons or creatures (people, mammals, birds, fish, lizards, and insects; but not lobsters, crabs, sea cucumbers, or shellfish); nine knives, guns, files, scissors.

ttiwemma (1) See *ttiwa-, -mma*. num. nine mouthfuls of premasticated food.

ttiwemmech N. var. of *ttiwemeech*.

ttiwemmék (2) See *ttiwa-, mékkú-*. num. nine fragments.

ttiwemwénú (1) See *ttiwa-, mwénúú-*. num. nine ells (lengths from elbows to fingertips).

ttiwemwu E.Wn. of *ttiwemwú$_2$*.

ttiwemwú$_1$ (1) See *ttiwa-, mwúú-$_1$*. num. nine torn fragments (of rag or string).

ttiwemwú$_2$ (1) See *ttiwa-, mwúú-$_2$*. Var. *ttiwemwu*. num. nine sea cucumbers.

ttiwemwúch (2) See *ttiwa-, -mwúch*. num. nine pieces of firewood.

ttiwemwmék See *ttiwa-, mwékkú-*. N. num. nine bits or morsels (of mashed food). Syn. *ttiwepwey*.

ttiwemwmwun (3) See *ttiwa-, mwmwuna-*. Var. *ttiwemwmwún*. num. nine portions of *mwatún*. Syn. *ttiwetún*.

ttiwemwmwú N. of *ttiwemwú$_1$*.

ttiwemwmwún F. of *ttiwemwmwun*.

ttiwennú (1) See *ttiwa-, nnúú-*. num. nine loaves of breadfruit pudding or amounts of breadfruit to be mashed into pudding loaves.

ttiwengaf (3) See *ttiwa-, ngaaf*. num. nine fathoms (lengths from fingertip to fingertip of outstretched hands).

ttiwengát (4) See *ttiwa-, -ngát*. num. nine concave or hollow objects; (less common) nine things of most any sort. Cf. *ttiwepwang, ttiwuuw*.

ttiwengéréw (2) See *ttiwa-, -ngéréw*. num. nine thousand.

ttiwengin (2) See *ttiwa-, ngini-*. num. nine little things or bits. Syn. *ttiwekis*.

ttiwengoon (2) See *ttiwa-, -ngoon*. Rmn. nu. (num.) the combined number nine-ten in serial counting by twos (formed from elements for both nine and ten). Syn. *engoon*.

ttiwepa (1) See *ttiwa-, -pa*. num. nine fronds, garlands, stalks with leaves. [Of palm trees, banana trees, *Cyrtosperma*, and also of leis or garlands, necklaces, bead belts.] Cf. *ttiwepan*.

ttiwepan (3) See *ttiwa-, paan$_1$*. num. nine branches with leaves (of trees other than palms and bananas). Syn. *ttiwepachang*. Cf. *ttiwepa*.

ttiwepachang (3) See *ttiwa-, pachang$_1$*. num. nine branches with leaves. Syn. *ttiwepan*.

ttiwepeek (2) See *ttiwa-, peek$_2$*. num. nine sides, pages.

ttiwepeche (1) See *ttiwa-, peche*. num. nine lower or hind limbs (of humans, birds, and animals only).

ttiwepéw (2) See *ttiwa-, -péw*. num. nine things worn over the hand or arm (e.g., gloves).

ttiwepino (1) See *ttiwa-, pino*. num. nine small packages of breadfruit pudding.

ttiwepinúk (2) See *ttiwa-, pinúk*. num. nine tied bundles, reams of paper.

ttiwepu (1) See *ttiwa-, puu-₂*. num. nine strokes in swimming (in measuring distance).

ttiwepwang (3) See *ttiwa-, pwaang*. num. nine holes, caves, cavities, pits, tunnels, hollows. Cf. *ttiwengát*.

ttiwepwey (2) See *ttiwa-, -pwey*. num. nine pinches or morsels of mashed food. Syn. *ttiwemwmwék*.

ttiwepwéét (2) See *ttiwa-, pwéét*. num. nine noses.

ttiwepwi (1) See *ttiwa-, pwii-₁*. num. nine groups, groves, flocks, schools, herds, swarms, convoys, prides, etc.

ttiwepwin (2) See *ttiwa-, pwiin₃*. num. nine nights.

ttiwepwopw (2) See *ttiwa-, pwoopw*. num. nine tree trunks, bases, foundations, causes, sources, beginnings, origins, reasons.

ttiwepwór (4) See *ttiwa-, pwóór*. num. nine boxes or crates (of something).

ttiwepwúkú (1) See *ttiwa-, -pwúkú*. num. nine hundred.

ttiwepwún (2) See *ttiwa-, pwúún₁*. Var. *ttiwepwpwún*. num. nine pieces (broken off).

ttiwepwpwaaw (2) See *ttiwa-, pwpwaaw*. num. nine home-made cigarettes.

ttiwepwpwún N. of *ttiwepwún*.

ttiwechamw (3) See *ttiwa-, -chamw*. num. nine foreheads, brows or similarly classed objects (e.g. visors, stem-bases of coconut fronds); nine fishheads.

ttiwechef See *ttiwa-, -chef*. num. nine tentacles (of octopus or squid); nine pieces of firewood. Syn. *ttiweyó, ttiwéwút*.

ttiwechú (1) See *ttiwa-, chúú*. num. nine bone segments (of meat).

ttiwechúk (2) See *ttiwa-, chúúk*. num. nine coconut-leaf baskets (of something).

ttiwechchi (1) See *ttiwa-, -chchi*. num. nine drops.

ttiwechchooch (3) See *ttiwa-, chooch*. num. nine bundles of ten small packages of breadfruit pudding.

ttiwetinewupw (2) See *ttiwa-, tinewupw*. num. nine yards (lengths from center of chest to outstretched fingertips).

ttiwetip (3) See *ttiwa-, tiip₂*. num. nine slices, chunks, cut segments (of breadfruit, taro only).

ttiwetit (2) See *ttiwa-, -tit*. num. nine strings (of breadfruit, usually ten to a string). Syn. *ttiwettiit*.

ttiwetú (3) See *ttiwa-, túú*. Tbl. num. nine vulvas (in counting sexual encounters).

ttiwetúkúm (3) See *ttiwa-, túkúm*. num. nine packages (of something).

ttiwetún (2) See *ttiwa-, túnú-*. Var. *ttiwettún*. num. nine portions of *mwatún*. Syn. *ttiwemwmwun*.

ttiwettiit (2) See *ttiwa-, ttiit₂*. num. nine strings of ten breadfruit. Syn. *ttiwetit*.

ttiwettún N. of *ttiwetún*.

ttiwewoch (2) See *ttiwa-, -woch*. Tn. num. nine sorts, rations, kinds, varieties, species. Syn. *ttiwóóch*.

ttiwewumw (2) See *ttiwa-, wumwu-₂*. Var. *ttiwowumw*. num. nine branching stalks (of bananas, fruit, pandanus keys, coral).

ttiwewupw (2) See *ttiwa-, wupwu-₁*. num. nine breasts.

ttiwewúwéw (2) See *ttiwa-, -wúwéw*. num. nine amounts of fermented breadfruit suitable for kneading.

ttiweyaf (3) See *ttiwa-, -af*. num. nine pieces of intestine.

ttiweyang (3) See *ttiwa-, -ang*. num. nine finger spans; nine entire limbs (of an animal).

ttiweyef (2) See *ttiwa-, eef₁*. num. nine bunches of ripe coconuts.

ttiweyem (2) See *ttiwa-, eem*. num. nine earlobes.

ttiweyep (2) See *ttiwa-, epi-₁*. num. nine butt ends, lower ends, west ends.

ttiweyék (2) See *ttiwa-, ékkú-*. num. nine nets.

ttiweyi (3) See *ttiwa-, -i*. Rmn. num. nine hands (of bananas). Syn. *ttiweyin₁, ttiweyiyey*.

ttiweyin₁ (3) See *ttiwa-, ina-₂*. N. num. nine hands of bananas. Syn. *ttiweyi, ttiweyiyey*.

ttiweyin₂ (2) See *ttiwa-, ini-₂*. num. nine shoots.

ttiweyipw (3) See *ttiwa-, ipw*. num. nine steps, footprints, soles; nine items of footwear.

ttiweyiyey (3) See *ttiwa-, iyeyiya-*. num. nine hands of bananas. Syn. *ttiweyi, ttiweyin₁*.

ttiweyó (1) See *ttiwa-, óó₁*. num. nine tentacles (of octopus or squid). Syn. *ttiwechef, ttiwéwút*.

ttiwéwúk₁

ttiwéwúk₁ (2) See *ttiwa-, wúúk₁*. num. nine tails (in counting birds). Cf. *ttiwemach*.

ttiwéwúk₂ (2) See *ttiwa-, wúúk₂*. num. nine fingernails, toenails, claws.

ttiwéwún (3a) See *ttiwa-, wúún₁*. num. nine feathers, scales, hairs.

ttiwéwút (2) See *ttiwa-, -wút*. num. nine fingers or toes; nine octopus tentacles, insect legs. Cf. *ttiwechef, ttiweyó*.

ttiwowumw Var. of *ttiwewumw*.

ttiwowut (2) See *ttiwa-, wutu-*. num. 1. nine cores (especially of breadfruit). 2. nine chunks of cooked breadfruit.

ttiwóóch (2) See *ttiwa-, -óch*. num. nine sorts, rations, kinds, varieties, species. Syn. *ttiwewoch*.

ttiwóówut (3) See *ttiwa-, owut*. num. nine rows of thatch.

ttiwówo (1) See *ttiwa-, -wo₁*. num. nine clumps (of bananas).

ttiwu- Var. of *ttiwa-* nine (see *ttiwuuw*).

ttiwuu N. of *ttiwuuw*.

ttiwuuw (3) See *ttiwu-, -uw*. F. Var. *ttiwuu*. num. nine general-class things. With c. pref. and ptv. const.: *ettiwuuwan* ninth one. With dis. c. pref.: *ekkettiwuuw* be nine at a time. With pref. *nne-₂*: *eew nnettiwuuw* one ninth part. Syn. *ttiwengát*.

tto-₁ (4) TTO. [In cpds. only.] unsp. hollowed, dented. See *mwmwóót*.

tto-₂ Var. of *tte-*.

tto (1) TTOO. nu. (T1) variety of small tridachna clam. [It is used as food.] *eew t.* one t. c. *ttoon Chuuk* Trukese t. c. Cf. *siim*.

Ttooyis Var. of *Toowis*.

-ttof adj. continually. See *eyiisittof*.

ttomw (dc; 3b) See *tomw*. vi. fall and burst open (as a ripe breadfruit). *aa t. eew mááy, ina pwata meyi tomw* a breadfruit fell and burst, that's why it is squashed.

tton (Eng.) nu. ton. *eew t.* one t.

ttona (1v) TTONAA. nu. (T1v) mixture.

ttonááni See *ttona, -ni-*. vo. (T4) mix.

ttong (dc; 3a) TONGA. nu. (T3) 1. love, affection, sympathy, pity (positive feeling towards others in the sense of wanting to do things for them). *aan t.* his l. for someone; *ttongan* l. for him. *t. núkúchchar* unflinching or firm l.; *ááy t. ngonuk* my l. toward you. 2. a plant. Syn. *kiipw*.

Trukese-English

ttongommang (3) See *ttong, mmang*. vi. be slow to feel sympathy or pity or love; be pitiless, hard-hearted.

ttongomwmwáán (2) See *ttong, mwmwáán*. nu. (T2) unrequited love.

ttopwur (3) See *tto-₂, pwur₃*. vi. be mouldy; have ringworm of the skin. Cf. *arakak*.

ttu₁ (dc; 1) See *tuu-₁*. va., vi., adj. dig; (be) dug. Dis. *tuutu* (db). *sipwe t. pwpwún* we shall d. earth. With dir. suf.: *ttuuto*. Cf. *ttuuw₁*.

ttu₂ (dc; 1) See *tuu-₂*. vi. be thrown, hurled, stabbed, jabbed (of spears only). Cf. *ttuuw₂*.

ttu₃ (dc; 2) See *tuu-₂*. N. vi. be sewn, stitched (of thatch). Cf. *ttuuw₃*.

ttuu (1) See *ttu₂*. nu. (T1) throwing, hurling (of spears). *ttuun ewe máchew* t. of the spear.

ttuumáchew (3) See *ttu₂, máchew*. vi. hurl spears, do spear-throwing.

ttuumwéch (2) See *ttu₂, mwéch*. vi. stab with a spear without letting go of the shaft.

ttuun (dc; 3) See *tuuna-*. Var. *ttun*. vi. be rotated, twirled, spun (between the palms of the hands). Cf. *tuuna*.

ttuuraw (3) See *ttu₂, raaw₁*. vi. hunt whales. Cf. *ttú-*.

ttuuto See *ttu₁*.

ttuuw₁ See *ttu₁*. vo. (T1) dig. *raa t. ewe pwpwún* they dug the earth. With n. form. suf.: *ttuuwa-* (ni.; T3) something dug or to be dug (by someone).

ttuuw₂ See *ttu₂*. vo. (T1) throw, hurl, stab, jab (a spear). *aa t. ewe máchew* he hurled the spear; *t. ngeni* hurl, stab (it) at (him).

ttuuw₃ See *ttu₃*. N. vo. (T1) sew, stitch (thatch). With n. form. suf.: *ttuuwa-* (ni.; T3) something sewn or to be sewn (by someone).

ttuuwa- See *ttuuw₁, ttuuw₃*.

ttuffengen (2) See *ttu₁, ffengeen*. vi. dig towards one another.

ttumw₁ (2) TTUMWU₁. vi. stumble, stagger. *wúwa t. reen chchowun wosey we irá* I staggered from the weight of my load of wood. With dir. suf.: *ttumwunó* stumble and fall down.

ttumw₂ (2) TTUMWU₂. va. sip, suck, drink with a sucking noise. *wúwa t. nóón ewe kkap* I sipped in the cup; *aa t. owupwun inan* he sucked at his mother's breast. Cf. *ttú-*.

ttumw₃ (2) TTUMWU₃. vi., adj. (be) inadequately supplied, short. *wúwa t. reen mwéngé* I am short of food.

ttumwiiti See *ttumw₁, -iti*. vo. (T2) stagger as far as, stumble to.

ttun Var. of *ttuun*.

ttupw₁ (2) TTUPWU. vi. (be) collected, gathered together, assembled (of things).

ttupw₂ (2: *tupwpwa-*) See *tuupw*. N. nu. (T3) a shrub (*Macaranga carolinensis*). [Big, nearly round leaves are used to cover boiling breadfruit.] *tupwpwen Chuuk* Trukese s. Syn. *kúrúwén, tupwpwunuwén*.

ttupwuffengen (2) See *ttupw₁, ffengen*. vi. be collected together; collect together.

ttupwuffengenniiy See *ttupwuffengen, -i-₂*. vo. (T5) collect, gather (something) together.

ttupwuni See *ttupw₁, -ni-*. vo. (T5) contribute.

ttur (dc; 2) See *tur₂*. vi. be fallen. With dir. suf.: *tturunó, tturutiw, tturuu (tturu-wu)*.

tturuu See *ttur*.

tturumménú (dc; 1) See *tur₂, mménú*. vi. be lackadaisical.

tturunó See *ttur*.

tturutiw See *ttur*.

ttú- (2) TTÚ. ni. (T2) breast, teat. *ttiy, ttumw, ttún* my, your (sg.), her b. Cf. *ttúút*.

ttúún (3) TTÚÚNA. vi. be broiled (as taro, bananas, crabs, fish, pork); do broiling. Dis. *túttúún* (ds).

ttúúna See *ttúún*. vo. (T3) broil.

ttúút (ds; 2: *túttú-*) See *ttú-*. va. suck (of a nursing child or animal). *aa t. owupwun inan* he sucked his mother's breast.

ttúmwún (dc; 2) See *túmwúnú-*. vi. be cared for, looked after, safeguarded, protected.

ttún (dc; 2) See *túnú-*. vi. become detached from a main part, hence to fall out, come loose (of teeth, of ripe fruit); be broken out, gapped (as of teeth); be decapitated, amputated. *aa t. eey wuuch* this banana has fallen loose (from its stalk); *aa t. peyiy reen ewe nááyif* my hand was amputated by that knife; *epwe t. wúwey* my head ("neck") will be cut off.

ttúna- (3) TTÚNA. N. [In counting only.] ni. (T3), suf. (cc.) portion of *mwatún* pudding. *ettún, rúwéttún, wúnúttun, féttún, nimettún, wonottún, fúúttún, wanúttún, ttiwettún, engoon ttúnan* one,...ten p. of p. Syn. *túnú-*.

ttúng (2) TTÚNGÚ. vi. flow (of sap, sweat).

W

-w (3a: *-wé-, -wo-*) WA₁. [In this form only when the preceding base ends in *éé, oo, uu, úú*, except when they are directional suffixes. It is dropped after *uu* in N. dialects and after the single vowels *u, ú* in both N. and F. dialects.] Var. *-a-₃, -y₂*. suf. (obj.) 3sg. obj. prn.: *him, her, it. atééw* cause him to creep, *atééwétiw* cause him to climb down (cf. *té*); *óyoow* capture him (cf. *o₂*); *osuuw* or *osuuwonó* see him off (cf. *su*); *ésúúw* or *ésúúwénó* chase him away (cf. *sú*); *éssúrú* catch it in a container (cf. *ssúr₂*); *efiyuuwu* make him fight (cf. *fiyuuw*).

wa- (3) WA₂. [Var. of *wuwa-₁*; used only with 3sg. object and dir. suf.] vo. (T3) carry, bring, take, convey. With dir. suf.: *waato, waawow, waawu, wáátá, wáátiw, wóónó.*

-wa- (3) See *-a-₁*. [Used only with suf. pos. prn.] Var. *-a-₁, -ya-₁*. suf. (n.form.; T3) object or product of an action. [Suffixed to verb bases ending in *-é, -o, -u, -ú* to indicate the thing that is involved in the action in relation to the actor.] *-wan* o. or p. of his action. *ttuuwa-* thatch sewn or to be sewn by someone (see *ttuuw₃*).

waa-₁ (1v) WAA₃. ni. (T1v) tie, tie-rod, stringer, transverse connector; stick. *wáán t. of. wáán anap* outrigger yoke on *meniyuk* sailing canoe; *wáán épéréén* line from which to hang coconut-leaflet decorations along the gunwhale of a paddle canoe; *wáán kesich* transverse bar across the body at each end of a *meniyuk* sailing canoe to which the fore and back stays are attached; *wáán paaw* wrist; *wáán wútúút* grooved stick of the fireplow.

waa-₂ (1) WAA₄. ni. (T1) frame. *waan f. of. waan saayimw* base of *saayimw* hat; *waan wuu* warp elements in weaving a wicker fish trap or lobster pot.

waa-₃ (1) WAA₅. unsp. foot, leg (?). See *waasaas.*

waa₁ (1v) WAA₁. n. (T1v) boat, ship, canoe, vessel, conveyance, automobile, airplane, vehicle; (in const.) medium (of a spirit). *efóch w.* one b. *waan his b.; wáán b. of. w. chitosa* automobile; *w. fétún* paddle canoe; *w. seres* sailboat, sailing ship, sailing canoe; *w. sóppach* canoe with low ends that are of one piece with the full; *w. sópwósá* canoe with high end pieces. *wáán Resimw* title of especially successful warriors who officiated in traditional precombat ceremonies. Cf. *sááy.*

waa₂ (1) WAA₂. n. (T1) vein, artery, blood vessel, tendon, nerve, sinew. *waan his v. waan chcha* blood vessel; *waan inisiy* the veins of my body; *waan meefi* nerve; *waan nii* tooth nerve.

waas₁ (3) WASSA. (Eng.) nu. (T3) watch (clock). *eew w.* one w. *aan w.* his w. *wassen Merika* American w.; *wassen nepwpwekit* pocket watch; *wassen wáán paaw* wrist watch. *peenitin w.* wrist-watch band.

waas₂ (3) (Eng.) vi. stand watch.

waas₃ (3) WAASA. nu. (T3) handle (as of axe or basket), shaft (of speak), pole (for flag). *waasen chúúk* carrying pole for attach baskets; *waasen feeyir* improvised stool to which a *feeyir* grater is attached; *waasen fináyik* flag pole; *waasen kkowuk* axe handle; *waasen máchew, waasen óppong* spear shaft; *waasen pweyiker* stool to which coconut grater is attached. Cf. *waa-₁, aach₁.*

waasaas (db; 3) See *waa-₃, aas₁.* adj. (dis.) quickly, briskly (in walking, "with feet high"). *fátán w.* walk q.

waasan (3) See *waa-₂, -san.* nu. (T3) warp threads (of a loom), warp. *waasanen túúr* loom's w. t.

waaseni See *waas₃, -ni-*. vo. (T6a) provide with a handle.

waasééna (1) See *waa₁, séé-₂, naa-*. nu. (T1) visitor, traveler, person from elsewhere. *imwen w.* inn, hotel.

waamerip (3) See *waa₂, merip.* nu. (T3) miscarriage. *waameripen ewe feefin* the woman's m.

waamwú (1) See *waa₂, mwú₁.* nu. (T1) ruptured sinew, bad strain.

waan (2: *wani-, wanu-, wanú-*) WANÚ₁. nu. (num.) the number eight. [Used in serial counting or to name the number

in the abstract, but not used as a numerical adjective.] Cf. *wanú-*₁.
waapich (2) See *waa*₂, *pich*₁. nu. (T2) phlebitis, varicose veins.
waapichipich (2) See *waa*₂, *pichipich*₂. nu. (T2) artery.
waar (3) WAARA. nu. (T3) root. *waaran* its r. *waaren irá* tree's r.
waato See *wa-*.
waawa (db; 1) See *waa*₁. va. (dis.) use as a vehicle; ride. Cf. *wááni*.
waawow See *wa-*.
waawu See *wa-*.
waawupw (3) See *waa-*₂ (?), *wuupw*₂. nu. (T3) neck tunic of brightly colored cloth formerly decorated with red coral. [Used as a dance costume.] *eché w.* one t. *aan w.* his t. *waawupwen Chuuk* Trukese t. *wúpwe mwárámwár eey w.* I will wear this t.
waay nu. name of the palatal, unrounded glide written *y*; name of the letter thus written.
wanawan (db; 3) WANA. nu. (T3) pepper vine (of the kind used in betel chewing). [Betel chewing is not customary in Truk.]
waneyis nu. a straight in poker in *kinap*.
waniik (3) See *wanú-*₁, *ik*₁. num. eighty. With c. pref. and ptv. const.: *awaniikan* eightieth one. With dis. c. pref.: *akkawaniik* be eighty at a time. With pref. *nne-*₂: *eew nnewaniikan* one eightieth part. With suf. *-somw*: *waniikisomw* more than eighty.
waniikisomw See *waniik*.
wanu- Var. of *wanú-*₁ when next vowel is *o* or *u*.
wanuuw (3) See *wanú-*₁, *-uw*. F. Var. *wanúúw*. num. eight nonspecific or general class objects. With c. pref. and ptv. const.: *awanuuwan* eighth one. With dis. c. pref.: *akkawanuuw* be eight at a time. With pref. *nne-*₂: *eew nnewanuuwan* one eighth part. Syn. *wanúngát*.
wanumwmwur Var. of *wanúmwmwur*.
wanuwumw Var. of *wanúwumw*.
wanuwut (2) See *wanú-*₁, *wutu-*. num. 1. eight cores (especially of breadfruit). 2. eight chunks of cooked breadfruit.
wanú-₁ (2) See *waan*. Var. *wanu-*. pref. (num.) eight. See *waniik, wanuuw, wanuwumw, wanuwut, wanúchamw, wanúchchi, wanúchchooch, wanúchef,*
*wanúchú, wanúchúk, wanúféw, wanúffaat, wanúffit, wanúfich, wanúfóch, wanúfutuk, wanúngaf, wanúngát, wanúngéréw, wanúngin, wanúkis, wanúkit, wanúkkamw, wanúkkap, wanúkkumw, wanúkum, wanúkumwuch, wanúkup, wanúmach, wanúmas, wanúmataf, wanúmech, wanúmeech, wanúmeet, wanúmén, wanúmma, wanúmmech, wanúmmék, wanúmwénú, wanúmwmwun, wanúmwmwú, wanúmwmwún, wanúmwu, wanúmwú*₁*, wanúmwú*₂*, wanúmwúch, wanúnnú, wanúpa, wanúpachang, wanúpan, wanúpeche, wanúpech, wanúpé, wanúpék, wanúpéw, wanúpino, wanúpinúk, wanúpu, wanúpwang, wanúpwey, wanúpwéét, wanúpwi, wanúpwin, wanúpwopw, wanúpwór, wanúpwpwaaw, wanúpwpwún, wanúpwúkú, wanúpwún, wanúsap, wanúsángá, wanúsáwá, wanúseeng, wanúsen, wanúsópw, wanússát, wanússupw, wanútinewupw, wanútip, wanútit, wanúttiit, wanúttún, wanútú, wanútúkúm, wanútún, wanúwo, wanúwoch, wanúwumw, wanúwupw, wanúwúk*₁*, wanúwúk*₂*, wanúwún, wanúwút, wanúwúwéw, wanúyaf, wanúyang, wanúyef, wanúyem, wanúyep, wanúyé, wanúyék, wanúyi, wanúyin*₁*, wanúyin*₂*, wanúyipw, wanúyiyey, wanúyowut, wanúyó, wanúyóch.*
wanú-₂ (2) WANÚ₂. [In cpds. only.] unsp. (u.m.) See *wanúmwmwur*.
wanúúw N. of *wanuuw*.
wanúféw (2) See *wanú-*₁, *-féw*. num. eight lumps or globular shaped objects (e.g., stones, balls).
wanúfich (3a) See *wanú-*₁, *ficha-*. num. eight strips of coconut, pandanus or palm leaf prepared for plaiting.
wanúfóch (4) See *wanú-*₁, *fóchu-*. num. eight long objects (e.g., vehicles, legs, teeth, timbers, shovels).
wanúfutuk (3) See *wanú-*₁, *futuk*. num. eight pieces of meat.
wanúffaat (3) See *wanú-*₁, *ffaata-*. num. eight strings of fish.
wanúffit (3) See *wanú-*₁, *fitta-*. num. eight leaf-packages of small fish.
wanúsap (3) See *wanú-*₁, *saap*. num. eight cheeks (especially of fish).
wanúsángá (1) See *wanú-*₁, *sángá*. num. eight basketfuls of fish. Syn. *wanúsáwá*.

wanúsáwá (1) See *wanú*-₁, *sáwá*. num. eight basketfuls of fish. Syn. *wanúsángá*.

wanúseeng (3) See *wanú*-₁, *seeng*. num. eight lengths between joints.

wanúsen (2) See *wanú*-₁, -*sen*. num. eight coils of rope. [Each coil is 30 to 100 fathoms long according to local custom.]

wanúsópw₁ (4) See *wanú*-₁, *sópwu*-₂. num. eight segments.

wanúsópw₂ (4) See *wanú*-₁, *sópwu*-₃. num. eight burdens of tied together breadfruit.

wanússaar (2) See *wanú*-₁, -*ssaar*. Var. *wanússar*. num. eight slices.

wanússak (3) See *wanú*-₁, *ssaka*-. num. eight pieces of copra.

wanússar N. of *wanússaar*.

wanússáát (2, 3) See *wanú*-₁, -*ssáát*. Var. *wanússát*. num. eight slivers, longitudinal slices, splinters.

wanússát N. of *wanússáát*.

wanússupw (2) See *wanú*-₁, *ssupwu*-. num. eight tiny drops.

wanúkis (2) See *wanú*-₁, *kisi*-. num. eight little things or bits. Syn. *wanúngin*.

wanúkit (3) See *wanú*-₁, -*kit*. num. eighty thousand.

wanúkum (2) See *wanú*-₁, *kumu*-. num. eight mouthfuls or swallows of liquid.

wanúkumwuch (2) See *wanú*-₁, *kumwuch*. num. eight fistfulls or handfuls (of something); eight hooves, paws, feet (of animals).

wanúkkamw (3b) See *wanú*-₁, *kkamw*. num. eight fragments or piece (of cloth, paper).

wanúkkap (3) See *wanú*-₁, *kkap*. num. eight cupfuls.

wanúkkumw (2, 3) See *wanú*-₁, *kkumw*₁. num. eight portions of premasticated food.

wanúmas (3) See *wanú*-₁, -*mas*. num. eight things worn on the eyes (e.g., lenses of goggles) or attached to piercing weapons (e.g., spear points).

wanúmach (3) See *wanú*-₁, *macha*-. F. num. eight fishtails (in counting fish). Cf. *wanúwúk*₁.

wanúmataf (3) See *wanú*-₁, *matafa*-. num. eight small portions, small amounts, little bits.

wanúmeech (2) See *wanú*-₁, -*meech*. F. Var. *wanúmech*, *wanúmmech*. num. eight portions of mashed breadfruit.

wanúmeet (3) See *wanú*-₁, *meet*₂. num. eight strands (of hair, fiber).

wanúmech N. var. of *wanúmeech*.

wanúmén (2) See *wanú*-₁, *maan*₁. num. eight persons or creatures (of people, mammals, birds, fish, insects, but not of lobsters, crabs, sea cucumbers, or shell fish); eight knives, guns, files, scissors.

wanúmma (1) See *wanú*-₁, -*mma*. num. eight mouthfuls of premasticated food.

wanúmmech N. var. of *wanúmeech*.

wanúmmék (2) See *wanú*-₁, *mékkú*-. num. eight fragments.

wanúmwénú (1) See *wanú*-₁, *mwénúú*-. num. eight ells (lengths from elbow to fingertips).

wanúmwu E.Wn. of *wanúmwú*₂.

wanúmwú₁ (1) See *wanú*-₁, *mwúú*-₁. F. Var. *wanúmwmwú*. num. eight torn fragments (of rag or string).

wanúmwú₂ (1) See *wanú*-₁, *mwúú*-₂. Var. *wanúmwu*. num. eight sea cucumbers; eight pieces of feces.

wanúmwúch (2) See *wanú*-₁, *mwúchú*-. num. eight pieces of firewood.

wanúmwmwék See *wanú*-₁, *mwékkú*-. N. num. eight bits or morsels (of mashed food). Syn. *wanúpwey*.

wanúmwmwun (3) See *wanú*-₁, *mwmwuna*-. N. Var. *wanúmwmwún*. num. eight portions of *mwatún*.

wanúmwmwur (3) See *wanú*-₂ *mwuromwur*. Var. *wanumwmwur*. nu. (T3) a variety of breadfruit.

wanúmwmwú N. of *wanúmwú*₁.

wanúmwmwún F. of *wanúmwmwun*.

wanúnnú (1) See *wanú*-₁, *nnúú*-. num. eight loaves of breadfruit pudding or amounts of breadfruit to be mashed into pudding loaves.

wanúngaf (3) See *wanú*-₁, *ngaaf*. num. eight fathoms (lengths from fingertip to fingertip of outstretched arms).

wanúngát (4) See *wanú*-₁, -*ngát*. num. eight concave or hollow objects; (less common) eight things of almost any kind. Cf. *wanúpwang*, *wanuuw*.

wanúngéréw (2) See *wanú*-₁, -*ngéréw*. num. eight thousand.

wanúngin (2) See *wanú*-₁, *ngini*-. num. eight little things or bits. Syn. *wanúkis*.

wanúpa (1) See *wanú*-₁, -*pa*. num. eight fronds, garlands, stalks with leaves. [Of palm trees, banana plants, *Cyrtosperma*, and also of leis or

garlands, necklaces, bead belts.] Cf. *wanúpan.*
wanúpan (3) See *wanú-*₁, *paan*₁. num. eight branches with leaves (of trees other than palms or bananas). Syn. *wanúpachang.* Cf. *wanúpa.*
wanúpachang (3) See *wanú-*₁, *pachang*₁. num. eight branches with leaves. Syn. *wanúpan.*
wanúpeek (2) See *wanú-*₁, *peek*₂. num. eight sides, pages.
wanúpeche (1) See *wanú-*₁, *peche.* num. eight lower or hind limbs (of humans, birds, and animals only).
wanúpé (1) See *wanú-*₁, *péé-*₁. num. eight empty containers.
wanúpék (2) See *wanú-*₁, *péék*₂. num. eight chips, chopped off pieces, cigarette butts.
wanúpéw (2) See *wanú-*₁, *-péw.* num. eight wings or things worn over hand or arm (e.g., gloves).
wanúpino (1) See *wanú-*₁, *pino.* num. eight small packages of breadfruit pudding.
wanúpinúk (2) See *wanú-*₁, *pinúk.* num. eight tied bundles, reams (of paper).
wanúpu (1) See *wanú-*₁, *puu-*₂. num. eight strokes in swimming (in measuring distance).
wanúpwang (3) See *wanú-*₁, *pwaang.* num. eight holes, caves, cavities, pits, tunnels, hollows. Cf. *wanúngát.*
wanúpwey (2) See *wanú-*₁, *-pwey.* num. eight pinches or morsels of mashed food. Syn. *wanúmwmwék.*
wanúpwéét (2) See *wanú-*₁, *pwéét.* num. eight noses.
wanúpwi (1) See *wanú-*₁, *pwii-*₁. num. eight groups, groves, flocks, schools, herds, swarms, convoys, prides, etc.
wanúpwin (2) See *wanú-*₁, *pwiin*₃. num. eight nights.
wanúpwopw (2) See *wanú-*₁, *pwoopw.* num. eight tree-trunks, bases, foundations, causes, sources, beginnings, origins, reasons.
wanúpwór (4) See *wanú-*₁, *pwóór.* num. eight boxes or crates (of something).
wanúpwúkú (1) See *wanú-*₁, *-pwúkú.* num. eight hundred.
wanúpwún (2) See *wanú-*₁, *pwúún*₁. Var. *wanúpwpwún.* num. eight pieces (broken off).
wanúpwpwaaw (2) See *wanú-*₁, *pwpwaaw.* num. eight home-made cigarettes.
wanúpwpwún N. of *wanúpwún.*
wanúchamw (3) See *wanú-*₁, *-chamw.* num. eight foreheads, brows, or similarly classed objects (e.g., visors, stem-bases of coconut fronds); eight fishheads.
wanúchef See *wanú-*₁, *-chef.* num. eight tentacles (of octopus or squid); eight pieces of firewood. Syn. *wanúyó, wanúwút.*
wanúché (1) See *wanú-*₁, *-ché.* num. eight thin flat objects of any kind (e.g., sheets, leaves, planks); eight songs.
wanúchú (1) See *wanú-*₁, *chúú.* num. eight bone segments (of meat).
wanúchúk (2) See *wanú-*₁, *chúúk.* num. eight coconut-leaf baskets (of something).
wanúchchi (1) See *wanú-*₁, *-chchi.* num. eight drops.
wanúchchooch (3) See *wanú-*₁, *chchooch.* num. eight armfuls.
wanútinewupw (2) See *wanú-*₁, *tinewupw.* num. eight yards (lengths from center of chest to outstretched fingertips).
wanútip (3) See *wanú-*₁, *tiip*₂. num. eight slices, chunks, cut segments (of breadfruit and taro only).
wanútit (2) See *wanú-*₁, *-tit.* num. eight strings (of breadfruit, usually ten to a string). Syn. *wanúttiit.*
wanútú (3) See *wanú-*₁, *túú.* Tbl. num. eight vulvas (in counting sexual encounters).
wanútúkúm (3) See *wanú-*₁, *túkúm.* num. eight packages (of something).
wanútún (2) See *wanú-*₁, *túnú-.* F. Var. *wanúttún.* num. eight portions of *mwatún* pudding. Syn. *wanúmwmwun.*
wanúttiit (2) See *wanú-*₁, *ttiit*₂. num. eight strings of ten breadfruit each. Syn. *wanútit.*
wanúttún N. of *wanútún.*
wanúwo (1) See *wanú-*₁, *-wo*₁. num. eight clumps (of bananas).
wanúwoch See *wanú-*₁, *-woch.* Tn. num. eight sorts, kinds, rations, varieties, species. Syn. *wanúyóch.*
wanúwumw (2) See *wanú-*₁, *wumwu-*₂. Var. *wanuwumw.* num.

wanúwupw   Trukese-English

eight branching stalks (of bananas, fruit, clusters of pandanus keys, coral).
wanúwupw (2) See *wanú-₁, wupwu-*. num. eight breasts.
wanúwúk₁ (2) See *wanú-₁, wúúk₁*. num. eight tails (in counting fish). Cf. *wanúmach*.
wanúwúk₂ (2) See *wanú-₁, wúúk₂*. num. eight fingernails, toenails, claws.
wanúwún (3a) See *wanú-₁, wúún₁*. num. eight feathers, scales, hairs.
wanúwút (2) See *wanú-₁, -wút*. num. eight fingers or toes; eight octopus tentacles, insect legs. Cf. *wanúchef, wanúyó*.
wanúwúwéw (2) See *wanú-₁, -wúwéw*. num. eight amounts of fermented breadfruit suitable for kneading.
wanúyaf (3b) See *wanú-₁, -af*. num. eight pieces of intestine.
wanúyang (3) See *wanú-₁, -ang*. num. eight finger spans, five entire limbs (of an animal).
wanúyef (2) See *wanú-₁, eef₁*. num. eight bunches of ripe coconuts.
wanúyem (2) See *wanú-₁, eem*. num. eight ear lobes.
wanúyep (2) See *wanú-₁, epi-₁*. num. eight butt ends, lower ends, west ends.
wanúyé (1) See *wanú-₁, -é*. num. eight hairs.
wanúyék (2) See *wanú-₁, ékkú-*. num. eight nets.
wanúyi (3) See *wanú-₁, -i*. Rmn. num. eight hands of bananas. Syn. *wanúyin₁, wanúyiyey*.
wanúyin₁ (3) See *wanú-₁, ina-₂*. N. num. eight hands of bananas. Syn. *wanúyi, wanúyiyey*.
wanúyin₂ (2) See *wanú-₁, ini-₂*. num. eight shoots.
wanúyipw (3) See *wanú-₁, -ipw*. num. eight steps, footprints, soles; eight items of footwear.
wanúyiyey (3) See *wanú-₁, iyeyiya-*. num. eight hands of bananas. Syn. *wanúyi, wanúyin₁*.
wanúyowut (3) See *wanú-₁, owut*. num. eight rows of thatch.
wanúyó (1) See *wanú-₁, óó₁*. num. eight tentacles (of octopus or squid). Cf. *wanúchef, wanúwút*.
wanúyóch See *wanú-₁, -óch*. num. eight sorts, rations, kinds, varieties, species. Syn. *wanúwoch*.

war (3) WARA₁. vi. arrive.
wara- (3) See *war*. ni. (T3) arrival. *waran his a. warey neesor sipwe...* on my arrival tomorrow we shall...
warawar (db; 3) WARA₂. nu. (T3) ditch. *ewe warawaren nóón Epin Fénú* the d. in Epin Fénú. Cf. *kuwar*.
warawareey See *warawar, -e-₂*. vo. (T6b) dig a ditch in. *wúpwe w. ikeey* I shall dig a ditch in this place.
waresé (1) nu. (T1) a kind of fish.
wareyiti See *war, -iti*. vo. (T2) arrive at.
warúng (2) WARÚNGÚ. Var. *wérúng*. nu. sweet basil (*Ocimum basilicum*). [Flowers are worn as a signal in courtship and are also used in various medicines.]
wachep adj. big, large. See *seewachep*. Cf. *wáche-*.
waw (3) WAWA. vi. resound (of gunfire or the popping of breadfruit pounders in soft pudding). *meyi w. nóón seningey* it r. in my ears. *wawen eey wúsúús nóón seningey* resounding of this pounder in my ears.
way (3) WAYA. F. Var. *woy*. excl. oh; oops. [Indicates suddenly remembering something one had forgotten.]
wayiséech (2) WAYISÉCHCHÚ. (Eng. *white shirt*) nu. (T2) long-sleeved shirt. Cf. *séech*.
wayin₁ (2) WAYINI. (Eng.) nu. (T2) wine. *wayinin Merika* American w.
wayin₂ (3) WAYINNA. (Eng.) vi., va. wind a watch.
wayinneey See *wayin₂, -e-₂*. vo. (T6b) wind (a watch).
wá (1) WÁÁ. vi. be open, be opened; be cleared, opened up (of land). Dis. *wááwá* (db) be roomy, spacious.
wáási See *wá, -si-*. vo. (T4) open, make room for, clear a way for, give way to; comb out with one's hand (of one's hair); (excl.) gangway! *éwúpwe wáásiyey* make room for me.
wáákúkkún (2) See *wá, kúkkún*. vi. be open to a small degree.
wáánaanú (1) See *waa₁, énú*. nu. spirit medium in his role as vehicle of a spirit (after the spirit has descended upon him). Syn. *wáátawa*. Cf. *sowuyawarawar*.
wááni See *waa₁, -ni-*. vo. (T4) acquire a vehicle. Cf. *waawa*.
wáániik (3) See *waa-₁, -ik₂*. nu. (T3) core of the banana trunk that serves as a

Trukese-English

base against which to strip banana fibers for loom threads. *wááníiken wuuch* c. of a banana trunk.

wáánimwen (2) See *waa*-₁, *mween*. nu. (T2) stringer connecting the outrigger booms at a point centrally located over the hull of a sailing canoe and serving as a block around which to run the mainsheet.

wáánipwu (1) See *waa*-₁, *pwu*₁ (?). nu. (T1) longitudinal stringer under and across outrigger booms of paddle canoe. *wáánipwuun waa* canoe's l. s.

wáátawa (1) See *waa*₁, *-tawa*. nu. (T1) spirit medium in his role as vehicle of the spirit. Syn. *wáánaanú*. Cf. *sowuyawarawar*.

wáátá See *wa-*.

wáátiw See *wa-*.

wááwá Dis. of *wá*.

wááyiso (1) See *waa*-₁, *sooso*₁. nu. (T1) distal board across the outrigger booms next to the outrigger stanchions. *wááyisoon waa* canoe's d. b.

wááyinu (1) See *waa*-₁, *-nu*. nu. (T1) cross-tie or stringer underneath the outrigger booms near the body of sailing canoe. [It forms part of the cantilever arrangement of the lee-platform beams and the outrigger booms.]

wááyiché (1) See *waa*-₂, *chééché* (?). nu. (T1) second heddle (used in weaving complicated patterns). *wááyichéén túúr* loom;s s. h.

wááyitipw (3) See *waa*-₁, *tiipw*. nu. (T3) pair of auxiliary rods used in weaving complicated patterns. *wááyitipwen túúr* loom's a. r.

wámmóng (2) See *wá*, *mmóng*. vi. be roomy, spacious.

wáche- (3, 4) [In cpds. only.] unsp. (u.m.) See *wáchemwuk*, *wáchimwuk*, *wáchikún*.

wáchemwuk (3a) See *wáche-*, *-mwuk*. N. Var. *wáchimwuk*. vi. be large, big, huge.

wáchikún (2) See *wáche-*, *kún*₂. vi. be cold.

wáchimwuk F. of *wáchemwuk*.

wátte (1) WÁTTEE. Tb3. [Commonly used with rel. suf. *-n* when it precedes the noun it modifies.] vi., adj. (be) big, large, huge (in bulk size), strong (of wind), of greater proportions. *íimw w.* big house; *emén wátteen iik* a big fish. With dir. suf.: *wátteenó* increase, grow, get larger; get bigger. Syn. *mmóng, nimwmwuk*. Ant. *kúkkún*.

wátteenó See *watte*.

we- (3a) WE. [In cpds. only.] Var. *wú-*₄. unsp. see. See *weri, weriwer*.

we [The equivalent of *ewe* when following rather than preceding the noun it modifies, it is used in possessive constructions, when it follows the word with the suf. pos. prn. It also follows pers. prns., pers. names, and is suffixed to *áta-, íimw, nemin, neesor, neepwin, ponnóón*.] prn. (dem.), suf. (dem.) that (past or not now in sight); the (already mentioned). *Purutaa we* that fellow Puruta; *néwún we monukón* that baby child of his; *ááy we angaang* that work of mine ("that general-thing-of-mine work"); *áán ewe mwáán we angaang* the work of that man (*ewe* modifies *mwáán*, and *we* modifies the preceding possessive construction as a whole). *átewe* that fellow. Cf. *ewe*.

wee- (1) WEE₁. [In cpds. only.] unsp. untied, unfastened. See *weeyi*.

wees (2) WEESI. n. (T2) finishing, being finished. *weesin* his being finished. *kepwe witiwit weesiy ne angaang* wait for my being finished at work. vi. be finished, done, over. *esaa mwo w. ááy angaang* my work isn't f. yet; *meet sóókkun angaang epwe w. reey* what kind of work is there that I am capable of doing? With intens. suf.: *weesifföch* he completely finished, be fired (from a job). With dir. suf.: *weesinó* finished off. Syn. *pwi, tak, tawe*.

weesen (2) WEESENI. (Eng.) nu. (T2) whistle (steam), auto horn, siren. *weesenin angaang* work w.

weesiiti See *wees*, *-iti*. vo. (T2) be finished at (a given time).

weesifföch See *wees*.

weesinó See *wees*.

weeku (1) WEEKUU. nu. (T1) ironwood tree (*Casuarina equisetifolia*). *weekuun Chuuk* Trukese *w.*.

ween (2) WEENI. (Eng.) nu. (T2) well (for water). *weenin Romónum* Romónum's w.

weengú (1) WEENGÚÚ. nu. (T1) a tree (*Callophyllum*). [Used for bowls, clubs, canes; fragrant fruit used in leis.] *weengúún Chuuk* Trukese *w.*.

weet (3) WETA. Tb1. n. (T3) semen, sperm. *wetan* his s.

weewe (db; 1) WEE₂. vi. 1. be alike, same, equal. *weewee chék* be just the same; *weewee chék mé...* be just the same as... 2. (with *reen*) be informed, understand. *wúwa w. reen óómw áweewe pwú meyi weeweeyééch* I understand your explanantion because it is intelligible. With dir. suf.: *weeweenó* understand henceforth. n. (T1) 1. likeness, equal. *ruwuuw kkapach ruwuuw, weeween rúwáánú* two times two equals four ("its equal is four"). 2. meaning, significance, explanation, moral. *weeween* its m.

weeweefeseen (2) See *weewe, -feseen*. vi. be different, unlike, dissimilar (in meaning, size, or shape).

weeweenó See *weewe*.

weeweengngaw (3b) See *weewe, ngngaw*. vi. be unintelligible, unclear in meaning.

weeweeyééch (2) See *weewe, ééch*. vi. be intelligible, informative, clear in meaning.

weey nu. a shrub (*Lumnitzera littorea*). [Fruit is used as a medicine against blood in the stool.]

weeya (1) WEEYAA. (Eng.) nu. (T1) wire. *efóch w.* one w. *aan w.* his w. *weeyaan Merika* American w.

weeyi See *wee-, -yi-₂*. vo. (T4) undo, untie, unfasten. With dir. suf.: *weeyóónó. weeyóónó mékúran* undo her hair.

wesa- (3) WESA. ni. (T3) truth, reality (of something). Dis. *wesewesa-* (db). *wesan, wesewesan* its t. *iwe, ina wesan* very well, that is the t. of it.

wesen (3) See *wesa-*. Var. *wessen*. vr. truly, really. Dis. *wesewesen* (db). *aa wesewesen peenó reen* it truly died on account of it. adj. (preposed) true, real, actual. *wesewesen saman* his true father.

wesetáán See *wesa-, -tá*. adj. (preposed) actual, real, true. *w. íteer* their a. names.

wesewesa- (db; 3) See *wesa-*. [In ptv. const. only.] Var. *wessa-*. ni. (T3) reality, actuality (of something); (in rel. const. with nouns) real, actual, true, exact; (in rel. const. with verbs) really, truly, actually, exactly. *wesewesan* the r. of it, in r. *eey piin meyi nónnómw wesewesen nuukanapen eey cheepen* this pencil is located at the exact center of this table.

wesewesen Dis. of *wesen*.

wessa- (3) WESSA. [In ptv. const. only.] Var. *wesewese-*. ni. (T3) reality, actuality (of something); (in rel. const. with verbs) really, truly, actually, exactly; (in re. const. with nouns) real, actual, exact, true. *wessan* the r. of it, in r. adj. (preposed) true, real, actual. *wessen saman* his true father. vr. truly, really. *aa wessen fééri* he really did it.

wen (3a) WENA. vi., adj. (be) straight, well aligned; (be) honest, sincere; due (in directions). Dis. *wenewen* (db). ni. (T2) straightness; honesty, sincerity; due (of directions). *wenan, wenewenan* his honesty.

wenechchar (3) See *wen, -chchar*. vi., adj. (be) straight, true, correct, honest; straight (of hair). ni. (T3) correction. *wenechcharan* its c.

wenewen₁ Dis. of *wen*.

wenewen₂ (db; 3) See *wen*. nu. (T3) a star (near Aquila).

wenewenenupw (2) See *wen, pwuupw*. nu. (loc.) (in traditional navigation) due south on the sidereal compass ("exactness or meridian point of Crux").

Weney nu. (pers.) patron spirit of knot divination (*pwee*).

Weneya Obs. nu. (loc.) Woleai Atoll. [This is the old form of the name.] Syn. *Woneyaye*.

Weneyopw Var. *Woneyopw*. nu. (loc.) Oneop Island, Mortlock Islands.

weni- Var. of *wénú-* (see *petewen*).

wer (3) WERA. vi. flash (of a light, flashlight).

-wer [Only in the pred. phr. *ewer*. Possibly from a vi. form of *weri*,] vi. be certainly. *ewer (*e-wer)* yes indeed ("it be certainly").

wereey See *wer, -e-₂*. vo. (T6b) flash (a light) on.

weri See *we-, -ri-*. Var. *wúri*₁. vo. (T5) see, behold. Syn. *kúna*.

weriwer (db; 2) WERI. [Presumably a back formation from *weri*.] nu. (T2) seeing, beholding.

Weriyeng See *weriwer, eni*₂. nu. (pers.) name of the founder of a school of navigation (*pénú*); the school of navigation so named for its founder. [This school has as its patron saint Pecheenuuk of the Sowupwonowót clan, but it is said to be followed mainly in eastern Truk and the Mortlock Islands. Other schools are *Fáánéwú* and *Fáánuuch*. The *Fáánuuch* school is followed by the atolls to the west of Truk and by the western islands within Truk. According to legend, *Weriyeng* and *Fáánuuch* engaged in a debate or contest, and the followers of each claim the victory for their side to the present day.]

wech (3) WECHA. Tb2. vi., va. be struck, hit, beaten; beat (as with a stick); flick the clitoris with the penis, have sexual relations. Dis. *wechewech* (db). *aa wecha!*, (Tn.) *aa weche!* (slang) he's kidding; he's full of baloney, he's lying. Cf. *wópw*.

wecheey See *wech*, *-e-$_2$*. Tb2. vo. (T6b) strike, hit, beat; (reflexive) masturbate. Cf. *awata*, *mwérúúw*, *namwúti*, *nengeey*, *nniiy*, *pongeey*, *siyeri*, *wópwuni*.

wecheffengennii- (2) See *wech*, *ffengen*, *-i-$_2$*. vo. (refl.) hit each other. [With pl. suf. prns. only.] *siya wecheffengenniikich* we h. each other; *raa wecheffengenniir* they h. one another.

wechengeni See *wech*, *ngeni*. vo. (T2) hit, strike, beat with (something). *wúpwe wecheey eey áát*, *w. na wóók* I am going to beat this fellow, beat him with that stick.

wechewech (db; 3) See *wech*. Tb2. nu. (T3) hitting, striking, beating; masturbation. vi. (dis.) be hitting, striking, beating; be masturbating.

wetiken (2) WETIKENI. nu. (T2) coconut grater and stool. *efóch w.* one g. *aan w. his g. wetikenin Chuuk* Trukese g. Syn. *pweyiker*. vi. engage in grating (of coconut only).

wetikeniiy See *wetiken*, *-i-$_2$*. vo. (T5) grate (coconut).

wetin$_1$ (2) WETI. [Occurs, as shown, only with rel. suf. *-n$_2$*.] vr. again and again, persistently (with the implication of failure); to the point of giving up; in vain. *wúwa fóókkun w. kútta ngé iyeey wúwa kúna* I have been looking and looking for it, but now I have found it. *wúwa w. wituk ngé kese feyitto* I waited and waited for you but you did not come. *wúwa w. ésúkú wááyiwe* I waited in vain for my canoe to appear. *se wetini mwo*

hardly, barely, scarcely. *wúse wetini mwo kútta ngé wúwa kúna* I hardly looked for it and I found it. Cf. *wúwet*.

wetin$_2$ (3) WETINA. vi. be broken, shattered. *aa w. ewe ruume* the bottle was b. Syn. *mmék*.

wey (2) WEYI$_1$. vi. be pulled in tight, taut; jerk, be convulsed, shudder, twitch. *aa w. inisin* his body shuddered. Cf. *mmey*.

-wey See *-ey*.

weyi- (2) WEYI$_2$. [In cpds. only.] unsp. perform, do. See *weyingngaw*, *weyineey*, *weyires*.

weyineey See *weyi-*. vo. (T6b) do in a hurry; hurry (reflexive). *kepwe weyineyok* hurry up; *kepwe w. óómw fééri pisekiy* hurry your handling of my goods.

weyingngaw (3b) See *weyi-*, *ngngaw*. nu. (T3) incest. vi. commit incest.

weyipw (3) WEYIPWA. nu. (T3) room (in house). *eew w.* one r. *weyipwen iimw*, *weyipwen nóón iimw* r. in (of) a house; *weyipwen méwúr* sleeping r.

weyires (2) See *weyi-*, *resi-*. vi., adj. (be) difficult, hard; (with *wóón*) jealous (about), possessive (of). *meyi w. aach eey angaang* this work of ours is d. *aa w. wóón pwúnúwan* he is jealous about his wife (he doesn't want her to talk to anybody else); *aa w. wóón pisekin* he is possessive of his goods (he doesn't want others to use them). nu. (T2) hardship; difficulty.

weyich (2) WEYICHI. nu. (T2) a weed with a small purple flower. [Symbol of unrequited love.] *weyichin Chuuk* Trukese w.

Weyichón nu. (loc.) Marianas or Ladrones Islands. Syn. *Meriyanis*.

weyit$_1$ (2) WEYITI. nu. (T2) feather fish lure used in trolling. *óóch w.* one l. *néwún w.* his l. *weyitin Chuuk* Trukese l. Syn. *pake*.

weyit$_2$ (2) See *wey*, *-ti-*. vi. be taut, pulled tight. *w. ffengen* (n.phr.) start, being startled; *aan w. f.* his start. *w.-ffengenniiy* (vo.phr.) startle, astound, dismay, astonish, take aback; (refl.) be startled, astonished, astounded, dismayed, taken aback; *kaa w.-ffengenniyuk* you were startled.

weyiti See *wey*, *-ti-*. vo. (T5) 1. shock (a person); pull back (an object) toward oneself, pull in tight; lash together, bind together; (refl.) be shocked, jump,

weyiwey

be startled. *ewe fiifi aa weyitikich* the electricity shocked us. *wúwa w. eey toropwe* I pulled this paper back towards me. *wúwaweyitiyey* I jumped back startled. 2. (F.) pick (a bunch of bananas). Syn. *osumwu*.

weyiwey (db; 2) See *wey*. nu. (T2) lashings. *weyiweyin eey waa* the l. on this canoe.

weyiya- (3) WEYIYA. [In cpds. only.] unsp. voyage, sail (?). See *weyiyerek*. Cf. Wol. *wayiya*.

weyiyerek (2) See *weyiya-, -rek*. nu. trolling in the open sea for large fish. Cf. *nuk*. vi. troll for large fish. Cf. *nuk*.

wé Var. of *wo₂*.

-wé (1) WÉÉ. [In cpds. only.] unsp. water (?). See *éwúwé*.

Wééné nu. (loc.) Moen Island.

wéér (2) WÉÉRÚ. nu. (T2) a species of bass (fish). *wéérún Chuuk* Trukese b.

wééw excl. help!, alas!

-wééw [In cpds. only.] unsp. (u.m.) See *féwúwééw*.

Wéneya Var. of *Weneya* (see *Eyinangen Wéneya*).

wénú- (2) WÉNÚ. Var. *weni-*. unsp. bush, vegetation generally.

wénúka (1) See *wénú-*. nu. (T1) a vine (*Canavalia maritima, Canavalia microcarpa, Vigna marina*). Syn. *chééchón*.

wénúnnap Var. of *wénnap*.

wénúngngaw (3b) See *wénú-, ngngaw*. nu. (T3) useless plant, weed.

wénúngngút See *wénú-, ngngút*. nu. a plant.

wénúpwokkus (2) See *wénú-, pwokkus*. Tb3. nu. fragrant grass or herb.

wénúwén (db; 2) See *wénú-*. nu. (T2) vegetation, bush (uncultivated). *neyiin w.* in the bush. Cf. *pétéwén*. vi. be overgrown (with vegetation).

wénnap (3a) See *wénú-, nap*. Var. *wénúnnap*. nu. (T3) forest, jungle.

wénnúmey (2) See *wénú-, mááy₂*. [From *wénú-ni-mey*.] nu. (T2) 1. <Elbert> a vine (*Piper*). Syn. *ótikipwin*. 2. a fern (*Polypodium* or *Phymatodes scolopendria*). [Used to prepare medicine for chest ailments; classed as a *fetin*.]

wérú- (2) WÉRÚ. [In cpds. only.] unsp. call out in fear or pain, bawl. See *wérúni, wérúwér*. Cf. *ér₂*.

Trukese-English

wérúni See *wérú-, -ni-*. vo. call concerned or alarmed attention to (something); inform with alarm about.

wérúng (2) WÉRÚNGÚ. Var. *warúng*. nu. (T2) mint or sweet basil (*Ocimum basilicum*). [Used for love magic and food flavoring.] *wérúngún Chuuk* Trukese m.

wérúwér (db; 2) See *wérú-*. F. Var. *érúyér*. vi. (dis.) call out in fear or pain; bawl, bellow, moo, roar.

wéw (2) WÉWÚ. vi., adj. (be) rich, wealthy.

wéwú- (2) See *wéw*. ni. (T2) wealth. *wéwiy, wéwumw, wéwún* my, your (sg.), his w.

wéwúngngaw (3b) See *wéw, ngngaw*. n. (T3) poverty. *wéwúngngawan* his p. vi., adj. (be) very poor, destitute.

wéwúyéech (2) See *wéw, ééch*. nu. (T2) wealth. *wéwúyéchchún* his w. vi., adj. (be) wealthy, rich.

wi- (2) WI. [In cpds. only.] Var. *wú-*. unsp. situation, locus, manner (?). See *wini-, witi*.

-wi- (2) See *-i-₁*. [Occurs in this form only occasionally after bases ending in *u, ú*.] Var. *-i-₁, -yi-₁*. suf. (rel.) links its antecedent as an attribute, member, part, property or possession of what follows; of, for. [It has a more honorific, refined, or polite connotation than *-n, -ni-* and is more commonly used in *itang* talk.] *féwú-wi-cho* bicep or calf muscle ("lump of strength").

wi (1) WII₁. vi. pulled up, extracted (of something planted). va. extract, pull up; weed (a garden).

-wi (1) WII₂. [In cpds. only.] unsp. fat in a turtle. See *feyiniwi, féwúniwi*. Cf. *wiin₁*.

wii-₁ (1) WII₃. [In cpds. only.] unsp. replaced, succeeded, exchanged.

wii-₂ (1) WII₄. [In cpds. only.] unsp. arrange, plan. See *wiiwa, wiiwi₁, wiiye-*.

wii-₃ (1) WII₅. [In some cases it can be interpreted as from *wi-, -i-₁*.] pref. (loc.) (at) the top (of), surface (of); at, on. Cf. *wini-*.

wii (1) WII₆. nu. (T1) name of the bilabial glide written *w*; name of the letter thus written.

wiis (3) WIISA. n. (T3) allotment, assignment, share, part, portion, lot; task, responsibility, duty, office. *eew w.*

one a. *wiisan* his a. *wiisen mwáán* men's responsibility (as opposed to women's, as in marriage). *ngúún wiisomw een* take this your portion of food (preferable in polite usage to *onomw,* see *ana-*). *een me wiisan nóón angaang* each his task in work. *wiisen* (also *wiisin*) *nóón fénú* island's public offices (see also *néwúwiis*). vi. take or have responsibility, assume a task.

wiisen See *wiis, -n₂.* vr. perform the office of, serve as, play the role of, have the function of, do the job of, have the duty of. *aa w. sómwoon* he serves as chief. *ewe feefin aa w. mwáán* the woman performed as a man. *aa w. fétúneer* he took the job of paddling them. *aa w. éwúúw eey iimw* he has the job of erecting this house.

wiiseni See *wiis, -ni-.* vo. (T6a) allot to, give a task to, assign to.

wiisenúúr nu. hold or throw in hand-to-hand fighting. [One grasps an opponent's right wrist with one's left hand and the back of his right hand with one's right hand; then one twists his wrist clockwise and bends back his hand at the same time.]

wiisiipw Var. of *wiisipw.*

wiisipw See *wii-₃, sipw.* Itang. nu. (loc.) (on) open and generous hand.

Wiisuusu₁ See *wiisuusu₂.* nu. (loc.) a clan name.

wiisuusu₂ (db; 1) See *wii-₃, -suusu.* nu. (T1) a tree (*Excoecaria agallocha*). [Poisonous sap; fruit used as medicine for eye trouble.] Syn. *owusuus, rowusuus, wusuus.*

wiiski (1) WIISKII. (Eng.) nu. (T1) whiskey. *wiiskiin Merika* American w.

wiik (3) WIKKA₁. (Eng.) nu. (T3) week. *wikken maram* w. of the month; *nóón ewe w.* last w., in the past w.

wiimóówun (2) See *wii-₂, móówun.* nu. (T2) strategy and tactics in war, battle plan. [Could be drawn up traditionally only by an *itang.*]

wiin₁ (2: *wini-, wuni-*) WINI₁. nu. (T2) sea turtle. *eew w.* one t. *wini Chuuk* Trukese t.; *pwochen w.* t. shell. Syn. *woong.* Cf. *-wi.*

wiin₂ (3) WINNA₁. (Eng.) nu. (T3) wheel (of vehicle). *winnen chitoosa* automobile w. Cf. *aach₁.*

wiin₃ (3) WINNA₂. (Eng.) vi. win. ni. (T3) winnings, prize. *winnan* his w.

wiina₁ (1) WIINAA. n. (T1) hip; iliac crest. *wiinaan* his h. *chúún w.* h. bone.

Wiina₂ [Said by *itang* to be derived from *wiina₁.*] nu. (loc.) a clan name.

wiinam (3) WIINAMA. nu. (T3) species of goat fish. *wiinamen Chuuk* Trukese g. f.

wiineni Var. of *winneni.*

wiinis (2) WIINISI. (Eng.) nu. (T2) winch and boom, derrick.

wiinisiiy See *wiinis, -i-₂.* vo. (T5) apply a winch or derrick to.

wiiras (3) See *wii-₃, raas₁.* nu. (T3) in *wiirasen móówun* the field of battle ("the site of war"). [Traditionally a clearing that served as a local interdistrict field of honor to which disputing groups went to fight.]

wiiché nu. a vine (*Ryssoptens abutilifolia*). Cf. *chéé.*

wiichuk (2) See *wii-₃, chuuk₁.* nu. (loc.; T2) region in the immediate vicinity of a mountain top.

wiitekiya (1) See *wii-₃, tekiya.* vi., adj. (be) aloft, a high place, high above. *wiitekiyaan* high above him. *wiitekiyaan ewe éwú* high up on the mast. *ke sapw téétá w.* don't climb up on high.

Wiitéé See *wii-₃, téé₁.* nu. (loc.) a clan name.

Wiitipwen nu. (loc.) name of the highest mountain on Wééné (Moen) Island.

Wiitonnap See *wii-₃, toon, nap.* nu. (loc.) name of the highest mountain of Wútéét (Udot) Island.

wiiwa See *wii-₂, waa₁.* nu. travel plan, course, of a canoe. [Can only be made by an *itang*, and is designed to minimize exposure of the wrong side of the canoe to sorcery from hostile islands and to allow its occupants to greet properly the spirits of reefs and rocks en route.]

wiiwi₁ (db; 1) See *wii-₂.* nu. (T1) 1. strategy and tactics, plan of action (in war or other undertakings). 2. technique for arranging banana fibers into a long line preparatory to setting up a loom.

wiiwi₂ (db; 1) See *wi.* va., vi. (dis.) pull up by the roots (of something planted). nu. (T1) pulling up.

wiiy₁ See *wii-₁.* vo. (T1) take the place of, succeed.

wiiy₂ See *wi*. vo. (T1) pull up (plants).
wiiye- (3) See *wii-₂, -ya-*. ni. (T3) plan, tactic, strategy. *wiiyan* his p. *wiiyen iyé ewe éwúwa fééri nóón ewe móówun* whose p. did you execute in that battle?
wikka- (3) WIKKA₂. (Eng.) unsp. wick. See *wikkeey*.
wikkeey See *wikka-, -e-₂*. vo. (T6b) manipulate the wick of. With dir. suf.: *wikkeeyetá* turn up (a wick); *wikkeeyetiw* turn down (a wick).
wikkeeyetá See *wikkeey*.
wikkeeyetiw See *wikkeey*.
wikkiik (db; 3) See *wiik*. vi. be for a number of weeks. Syn. *wiwiik*.
win₁ (2) WINI₂. vi., adj. be changed (of position), altered, shifted, moved, turned. Dis. *winiwin, winiwiniwin* (db). *ásápwán aa winiwin toori notow* the wind shifted around to the west; *átéwe aa mwechen améémé pisekin, iwe aa winiwiniwin aan ekiyek toori ese chchiwen mwechen áméémé* he want to sell his goods, then his thoughts kept changing until he no longer wanted to sell. With dir. suf.: *wininó* be transformed, altered, changed, shifted, moved, converted (in religion).
win₂ (2) See *win₁*. vi. undulate the body in dancing (while standing) with arms and hands stretched out to one's sides. *aa w. ewe feefin wóón pwérúk* the woman undulated above the dance (the rest of the dancers were seated and she stood to *win wóón*). Syn. *maan₂*.
wini-₁ See *wi-, -n*. Var. *wuno-, wunu-₂, wúnú-₄*. pref. (loc., temp.) on, at. Cf. *wii-₃*.
wini-₂ (2) WINI₃. [In cpds. only.] unsp. breadfruit. See *winifitun, winikké, winipwuna, winiwin₂*.
winiiti- (2) See *wini-₁, iti-₂*. ni. (loc.; T2) location, side. *winiitin néwún feefin* his grown daughter's place or room (referring to the traditional taboo against a man's entering his daughter's room). With dir. suf.: *winiititáán* (at) the upper or east side of (something); *winiititiwen* (at) the lower or west side of (something).
winiiti See *win₁, -iti*. vo. (T2) change into, become.
winiititáá- See *winiiti-*.
winiititiwa- See *winiiti-*.
winifey (2) See *wini-₁, faaw*. Var. *winiféw₂*. nu. (loc.; T2) stony place ("on the stones").
winifénú (3) See *wini-₁, fénú*. nu. (loc.; T3) on land, on shore, ashore. [Used when at sea.] *winifénúwen Romónum* ashore on Romónum Island.
winiféw₁ (2) See *wini-₁, faaw*. nu. (T2) species of sea cucumber. [Edible, it is found in sand on the outer or barrier reef.]
winiféw₂ (2) See *wini-₁, faaw*. Var. *winifey*. nu. (loc.; T2) stony place ("on the stones").
winifitun (2) See *wini-₂, fitun*. nu. (T2) variety of breadfruit. *winifitunun Chuuk* Trukese b.
winisi See *win₁, -si-*. vo. (T5) turn, (refl.) change one's position; displace, remove, transplant. Cf. *winiki*.
winik (2) See *win₁, -ki-*. vi. turn over, roll over. Cf. *winiki*.
Winikachaw (3) See *wini-₁, achaw₁*. nu. (loc.; T3) name of a spring in Mechchitiw, Wééné (Moen) Island. [Important in *itang* lore.]
Winikápiipi (1) See *wini-₁, ápiipi*. nu. (pers.) an evil spirit that preys on pregnant women.
winikéés (2) See *wini-₁, éés*. nu. (T2) those married into a lineage or clan. *winikéésún Achaw* those married to Achaw people.
winiki See *win₁, -ki-*. vo. (T5) turn (it) over. Cf. *winik, winisi*.
winikiyá (2) See *wini-₁, kiyá₁*. nu. (T2) boundaries. *winikiyáán eyif* b. of land plots.
winikké (1) See *wini-₂, -kké*. nu. (T1) variety of breadfruit (much favored). Syn. *meyipwó*.
Winimaraaw nu. (loc.) Olimarao Island and Atoll (West Central Carolines).
winimwoon (2) See *wiin₁, -mwoon*. Var. *wunimwoon*. nu. a species of sea turtle. [It has a dark unattractive shell whose scales are flush with one another, making a smooth surface.] *winimwoonun* t. of (a region). Cf. *winichchen*.
winimwúún (1) See *wini-₁, mwúú*. nr. (temp.; T1) at the time of, when, during.

winimwmweeráán (2) See *wini*-₁, *mwmwa*-, *-i*-₁, *ráán*₂. F. Var. *wúnúmwmweeáán*. nu. (T2) daybreak, early day before dawn. *winimwmweeráánin nánew* d. yesterday.
winin áát See *win*₁, *áát*. v. phr. (be) boyish (of a girl).
wininengngin (2) See *win*₁, *nengngin*. vi., adj. (be) girlish (of a boy).
wininó See *win*₁.
winingách (4) See *wini*-₁, *-ngách*. Var. *wúningách*. nu. (temp.; T2) period just before daybreak or dawn (when cocks begin to crow). *winingáchin nánew* just before d. yesterday. vi. be at daybreak.
winipós (3b: *-póssa-*) See *wini*-₁, *póós*. vi. belonging to a place (of people). *chóón w.* people of the place; *mwúún w.* time of the original people of the place (as oppposed to their *éfékúr*). re-*winipós* indigenous person, aborigine, person whose family has been long established in a locality (as opposed to a newcomer). Ant. *waasééna*.
Winipwéét nu. (loc.) Truk's highest mountain, located on Toon (Tol) Island.
winipwuna (1) See *wini*-₂, *pwuna*₁ (?). nu. (T1) a variety of breadfruit.
winichchen (3a) See *wiin*₁, *chchen*₂. nu. (T3) 1. a species of sea turtle. [It has a shell of light or reddish hue, whose scales at the back are slightly separated.] Cf. *winimwoon*. 2. turtle shell of the turtle of this name.
winiwin₁ Dis. of *win*₁.
winiwin₂ (db; 2) See *wini*-₂. nu. variety of breadfruit.
winiwiniwin Dis. of *win*₁.
winiyamwáán (2) See *wi*-, *niya*-, *mwáán*₁. nu. (T2) a male, one of male sex (of animals). Syn. *niyamwáán*, *átámwáán*. Ant. *niyefeefin*.
winiyór (4) See *wini*-₁, *óór*. n. (T2) neighborhood, vicinity, environs; (with *aramas*) neighbor. *aramasen winiyórun* his neighbor.
winneni See *wiin*₃, *-ni*-. Var. *wiineni*. vo. (T6a) win (something).
wippin (3) See *wi*-, *-pin*. vi., adj. contradict, object; (be) contentious. *w. ngeni* contradict, object to, dispute.
wippineey See *wippin*, *-e*-₂. vo. (T6b) contradict, object to, dispute.

wir (2) WIRI₁. vi. be permitted, granted, allowed. *wúwa w.* I have permission; *meyi w.* it is permitted.
wiri- (2) WIRI₂. [In cpds. only. Presumably a back formation from *wúri*₁.] Var. *wúrú*-₁. unsp. see, aware. See *ewiriwir*.
wichi- Var. of *wúchú*-₁.
wichiiy See *wichiwich*₁, *-i*-₂. vo. (T5) whip, lash; beat (as a drum), strike (a bell).
wichik Var. of *wúchúk*.
wichiki Var. of *wúchúki*.
wichiwich₁ (db; 2) WICHI. n. (T2) whip, lash; whipping, lashing. *efóch w.;* one w. *wichiwichin* the whipping of him.
wichiwich₂ Var. of *wúchúúch*₁.
witi- (2) WITI. [In cpds. only. Presumably a back formation from *witi*.] vi. wait, be waiting.
witi See *wi*-, *-ti*-. Var. *wúti*. vo. (T5) wait for.
witiwit₁ (db; 2) See *witi*-. Var. *wútiwit*. vi. wait, be waiting.
witiwit₂ nu. a species of mountain dove. [It has a beautiful green and white color.]
witiwitinó (db; 1) See *witiwit*, *-nó*. Var. *wútiwitinó*. vi. be postponed, delayed.
witiwitóónó (db) See *witi*-, *-nó*. vo. (T1) postpone.
wiwiik (ds; 3) See *wiik*. vi. be for a number of weeks. Syn. *wikkiik*.
wo- Wn. and Tns. contraction of the 2pl. sub. prn. *owu*- or *éwú*-₁.
wo₁ (1) WOO₁. vi. (be) looked at, examined, scrutinized.
wo₂ WO. F. [It is embedded in the phrase preceding it, which it terminates, being followed by a brief pause.] Var. *wé.* conj. links what follows intentionally with what went before (after verbs indicating thinking or speaking); that, as follows, thus. *aa apasaa wo iiy sómwoon* he said that he was chief. *aa apasaa wo, "Iwe, sipwene móówon"* he said, "Very well, we are going to do battle". Syn. *pwe*₁, *pwé*₁.
-wo₁ (1) WOO₂. suf. (cc.) clump (of bananas). *ewo, rúwówo, wúnúwo, fówo, nimówo* or *nimowo, wonowo, fúúwo, wanúwo, ttiwówo* one,...nine c.
-wo₂ (1) WOO₃. [In cpds. only.] unsp. origin. See *neewo, wuruwo*.
woo₁ (1) WOO₄. n. (T1) vertical rafter. *efóch w.* one r. *woon* its (a house's) r.

woo₂

woo₂ (1) WOO₅. (Eng.) nu. (num.) zero. Syn. *chero*.

woo₃ (1) WOO₆. excl. Oh! [Indicates pleasure with rising then slightly falling pitch, indicates pity with falling then slightly rising pitch.]

woo₄ WOO₇. Var. *oo₂*. conj. and. Cf. *mé₁*.

woos₁ (3) WOSA₁. n. (T3) load, burden, thing carried. *wosan* his l. *wosen iyé* who brought it, who carried it; *wosen chitoosa* things carried on a car; *wosen waa* things carried on a canoe (cf. *woseniwa*).

woos₂ (3a) WOSA₂. n. (T3) voice, tone of voice, accent. *wosan* his v. *wosen kkechiw* the sound of weeping. Cf. *koos*, *kosokos*.

woos₃ (3) WOSA₃. N. Var. *oos*. nu. (T3) 1. any of a class of male spirits associated with the sea (commonly also referred to as *wosen mataw*). [They cause sickness and death among infants.] 2. sickness caused by spirits of this name. 3. medicine to cure sickness of this name.

woos₄ (2) WOOSU. nu. (T2) small moth. *emén w.* one m. *woosun Chuuk* Trukese m.

woomay nu. species of goatfish.

woomeeyas (3) See *wo₁*, *mee-*, *aas₁*. vi. be inattentive, let one's attention wander.

woomey (2) See *woo₁*, *mááy₂*. nu. (T2) house with breadfruit timbers for rafters.

woompees (Jap.) nu. homebase (in baseball).

woomw (3) WOMWA. n. (T3) facial appearance. *womwan* his f. a.

woon₁ (3) WONA₄. nu. (num.) the number six. [Used in serial counting or to name the number in the abstract, but not used as a numerical adjective.] Cf. *wono-*, *wonu-*.

woon₂ (3) WONA₅. n. (T3) comb (of chicken). *wonan* its c. *wonen chukó* chicken's c.

Woonap nu. (pers.) legendary hero of Wuumaan (Uman) Island. [He is said to have reconquered Wuumaan from control by Feefen Island and to have established the hegemony of the Fesinimw clan there.]

woonumas (3) See *woo₁*, *maas₃*. n. (T3) end rafter (of a house). *woonumasen iimw* house's e. r. Cf. *wóón maas*.

woong₁ (3) WONGA. nu. (T3) 1. a variety of mangrove (*Bruguiera conjugata*). [It has red bract flowers and a tall thick trunk.] *wongen Chuuk* Trukese m. 2. sap of the mangrove of this name when expressed from its bark and used to make canoe paint.

woong₂ E.Wn. nu. turtle. Syn. *wiin₁*.

woongi₁ nu. edible seashell.

woongi₂ nu. a variety of breadfruit (prolific but with small fruit).

woop (3) See *wop*. N. [From the c. *ówop*.] Var. *kkóóp*. vi. (c.) be hidden, concealed. va. hunt (turtles). *sipwe w. wiin* we shall h. for turtles.

woopa See *wop*. N. [From the c. *owopa*.] Var. *óópa*. vo. (T3) hide, conceal.

woopen (2) WOOPENI. (Eng.) nu. (T2) can opener. Syn. *tinoopen*.

woopéw (2) See *-wo₂* (?), *paaw*. nu. (T2) length from elbow to fingertips of opposite hand (one and a half yards). *rúwéngat woopéw* two fathoms and one *w.* (used only in this way to express a remainder of fathoms).

woopw₁ (3) WOPWPWA₁. N. Var. *wuwapw*. nu. (T3) growing end (of a palm or banana). *wopwpwen núú* g. e. of a coconut tree. Cf. *eyirúk*.

woopw₂ (3) WOPWPWA₂. N. Var. *oopw*. nu. (T3) a species of pampano. *wopwpwen Chuuk* Trukese p.

woopwat Ffn. var. of *pwata*.

woor₁ (3) WORA₁. n. (T3) fish gills. *woran* its g.

woor₂ (3) WORA₂. nu. (T3) coconut-husk fiber. *woren pééyiin* f. of a ripe coconut.

woori See *wo₁*, *-ri-*. vo. (T4) examine, scrutinize, inspect, look at. Cf. *wóóri*.

wooch (3) WOCHA₇. nu. (T3) reef. *wochen fénú* fringing reef around an island; *wochen meenúk*, *wochen núkúnap* outer barrier reef; *wochen órofénú* reef in the vicinity of an island (not fringing); *wochen neenómw* lagoon reef; *fáán w.* inner side of a reef; *mesen w.* outer side or face of a reef; *wóón w.* surface of a reef. *wochen nii* alveolar bone, gums; *wochen niin wóón* upper alveolar bone; *wochen niin faan* lower alveolar bone.

woochiya (1) See *woo₁*, *chiya₁*. nu. (T1) house with mangrove timbers for rafters.

woot₁ (3a) WOTA₁. N. nu. (T3) taro (*Colocasia esculenta*; general name for swamp and dry-land types). *eféw w.* one corm of t. *néwún w.* his t. (that he has cultivated); *fótaan w.* his t. (that he has planted); *anan w.* his t. (to eat). *woten Iyap* a variety of t.; *woten Sapaan* Japanese t. (*Kanthosoma*). Syn. *óni, sawa.*

woot₂ (3) WOTA₂. nu. (T3) coconut husking stick, digging-stick used in cultivation. [It is made of *Pemphis acidula* wood, if possible.] *eféch w.* one h. s. *aan w.* his h. s. *woten Chuuk* Trukese h. s. Cf. *óto-*.

woot₃ (3) WOTA₃. nu. (T3) funnel-shaped entrance to wicker fish trap or lobster pot. *woten wuu* fish trap's e.

wootay (2) WOOTAYI. (Jap.) Var. *wootáy, wotáy.* nu. (T2) bandage. *eché w.* one b. *aan w.* his b.

wootayini See *wootay, -ni-.* Var. *wootáyini.* vo. (T5) bandage.

wootáy Var. of *wootay.*

wootáyini Var. of *wootayini.*

woow (2) WOWU. nu. (T2) sugarcane (*Saccharum officinarum*). *eföch w.* one stick of s. *ngútan w.* his s. (to chew). *wowun Chuuk* Trukese s. Syn. *sápúk.*

woowo₁ (db; 1) See *woo₁.* nu. (T1) a reed (*Phragmites karka*). [It is used as a thatching rod.] *woowoon Chuuk* Trukese r. Syn. *niwo.* See *róó.*

woowo₂ (db; 1) See *wo₁.* vi. (dis.) engage in a kind of fishing. [It is done only by women, who break up *áán* with their hand, whereupon the fish flee into the nets with which they have surrounded the *áán*.]

woowoonó (db; 2) See *wo₁, -nó.* vi. (dis.) be facing away, looking off.

wofa (1) WOFAA. nu. (T1) variety of breadfruit.

woffan (3) WOFFANA. nu. (T3) heartburn. *aan w.* his h. vi. have heartburn. *wúwa w. reen ewe mwéngé* I had h. from the food.

wos₁ (3) WOSA₅. va., vi. collect or gather firewood. *siya w. mwúúch* we collected wood for f.; *iir meyi w.* they are collecting f.

wos₂ (3) WOSA₄. vi. be cut in half, cut in two. Dis. *wosoos* (db).

wos₃ (2) WOSU. vi. be in trouble, without, in want, in a bad way; be confused.

woseey₁ See *wos₁, -e-₂.* vo. (T6b) collect or gather (wood) for firewood.

woseey₂ See *wos₂, -e-₂.* vo. (T6b) cut in half. Cf. *wocheey₁, woteey.*

wosenimwú (1) See *woos₁* or *woos₂, mwúú-₃.* nu. (T1) grudging or forced acquiescence. *kaa chék fanganó nóón w.* you just gave it away grudgingly. *kaa fééri reen w. chék* you did it only because you were forced to. Cf. *ósópwiisek.*

woseniwa (1) See *woos₁, waa₁.* nu. (T1) a gift to the owner of a canoe or boat in return for its use by another ("boat's burden").

wosen mataw See *woos₃.*

wosiroyi (1) WOSIROYII. (Jap.) nu. (T1) face powder. *wosiroyiin Sapaan* Japanese f. p.

wosománámán (4) See *woos₂, mánámán.* nu. (T2) clear, forceful speech in a meeting. vi. speak clearly and forcefully.

wosommóng (2) See *woos₂, mmóng.* nu. (T2) loud voice. vi. be loud voiced.

wosomwar (3) See *woos₂, -mwar.* [New word established at the orthography conference of 1972.] nu. (T3) semivowel ("indeterminate voice").

wosonáng nu. (temp.) 24th night of the lunar month.

wosonong (3) See *woos₃, -nong.* [New word established at the orthography conference of 1972.] vi., adj. (be) back (fo a vowel; "inner voiced"). [Trukese vowels are *o, ó, u*.]

wosonuuk (3) See *woos₂, nuuk₁.* [New word established at the orthography conference of 1972.] vi., adj. (be) central (of a vowel; "centrally voiced"). [Trukese central vowels are *a, é, ú*.]

wosongngú (1) See *woos₂, ngú.* nu. (T1) sound of moaning, groaning.

wosopin (3) See *woos₂, -pin.* [New word established at the orthography conference of 1972.] nu. (T3) consonant ("obstructed voice").

wosopwich (2) See *woos₃, pwich₁.* nu. (T2) 1. fever caused by the spirit *wosen mataw*. 2. medicine used to treat the fever of this name.

wosopwo (1) See *woos₃, pwo.* nu. (T1) 1. swellings on the skin caused by the spirit *wosen mataw*. 2. medicine used to treat condition of this name.

wosowá (1) See *woos₂, wá*. [New word established at the orthography conference of 1972.] nu. (T1) vowel ("open voice").

wosowey (2) See *woos₃, wey*. nu. (T2) 1. convulsions caused by the spirit *wosen mataw*. 2. medicine and magic to cure the convulsions of this name.

wosowu (1) See *woos₂, -wu*. [New word established at the orthography conference of 1972.] vi., adj. (be) front (of a vowel; "outer voiced"). [Trukese front vowels are *á, e, i*.]

wosukosuk (db; 3) See *woos₃, -k₂*. Var. *osukosuk*. vi. be busy, beset, occupied, burdened with work, in a difficult position. *wosukosuken nóniinen* beset with worry, burdened with concern.

wosungngat (3) See *wos₃, -ngngat*. [Permissible in mixed company.] vi. be in trouble, without, in want, in a bad way. Syn. *wosupwpwang*.

wosupwpwang (3) See *wos₃, -pwpwang*. Tb3. vi. be in trouble, without, in want, in a bad way. Syn. *wosungngat*.

wokasi (1) WOKASII. (Jap. *okashi*) nu. (T1) 1. candy (especially hard candy); sweet crackers. *eféw w*. one c. *anan w*. his c. *w. taka* Trukese c. made from copra. Cf. *manchú*. 2. a variety of banana.

Wokinawa nu. (loc.) Okinawa.

wokkoop Dis. of *woop*.

wokkon Dis. of *won*.

wokkoronó See *wor*.

wokkocheey Dis. of *wocheey₁*.

womwáánis (3) See *woomw, enis*. nu. (T3) beard (facial). *womwáánisan* his b. vi. be bearded (heavily).

womwééch (2) See *woomw, ééch*. vi. be handsome of face.

womwoménúúnú (1) See *woomw, ménúúnú*. vi. be tired-faced, weary-faced.

womwongngaw (3b) See *woomw, ngngaw*. vi. be ugly faced.

won (3a) WONA₁. F. vi. sleep (Rmn.: of fish only, Tn.: of people). Dis. *wonoon* (db), *wokkon* (ds). *meyi w. iik?* do fish s.?; *wúpwe w*. I shall s.; *wonoonen átecy* the sleeping of this fellow. With dir. suf.: *wononó* go off to s.; (Tn.) be quiet, silent. Cf. *óno-, wúnú-₃*.

Wona nu. (loc.) a star.

wonapé (1) See *wono-₂, -é*. num. six hairs.

wonaché (1) See *wono-₂, -ché*. num. six thin flat objects of any kind (e.g., sheets, leaves, planks); six songs.

wone (1) See *wono-₂, -e-₁*. num. sixty. With c. pref. and ptv. const.: *owoneen* sixtieth one. With dis. c. pref.: *okkowone* be s. at a time. With pref. *nne-₂: eew nnewone* one sixtieth. With suf. *-somw: woneesomw* be more than s.

woneesomw See *wone*.

woneen See *wono-₁, een₃*. nu. (dem.) this fellow (male) by you and me. [This is the polite form, cf. *wonneen*.] Dis. *wonokkaan* these fellows. Syn. *áteen*.

woneey See *wono-₁, eey₁*. nu. (dem.) this fellow (male) by me. [This is the polite form, cf. *wonneey*.] Dis. *wonokkeey* these fellows. Syn. *áteey₂*.

wones vi. be too close together (of things planted).

wonen vi. continue on, keep on, go on. With dir. suf.: *woneenó* continue, keep on.

Woneniyap nu. (pers.) name of the local god or tutelary spirit of Woney, Ton (Tol) Island. [He figures in legend as an adversary of Sowupaata.]

wonennó See *wonen*.

Woney nu. (loc.) northernmost peninsula of the Toon (Tol) complex of islands and a municipality of Truk. [The name is said to be derived from Woneyiyap, a variant of Woneniyap, name of Woney's tutelary god.]

woneyaf (3) See *wono-₂, -af*. num. six pieces of intestine.

woneyang (3) See *wono-₂, -ang*. num. six finger spans; six entire limbs (of an animal).

Woneyaye (Eng.) nu. (loc.) Woleai Atoll. Syn. *Weneya*.

woneyi (3) See *wono-₂, -i*. Rmn. num. six hands (of bananas). Syn. *woneyin₁, woneyiyey*.

woneyin₁ (3) See *wono-₂, ina-₂*. num. six hands (of bananas). Syn. *woneyi, woneyiyey*.

woneyin₂ (2) See *wono-₂, ini-₂*. num. six shoots.

woneyiyey (3) See *wono-₂, iyeyiya-*. num. six hands of bananas. Syn. *woneyi, woneyin₁*.

Woneyopw Var. *Weneyopw*. nu. (loc.) Oneop Island (Mortlock Islands). [This is the form by which it is locally known.]

wonéwúk₁ (2) See *wono-₂, wúúk₁*. num. six tails (in counting fish). Syn. *wonomach*.

wonéwúk₂ (2) See *wono-₂, wúúk₂*. num. six fingernails, toenails, claws.

wonéwút (2) See *wono-₂, -wút*. num. six fingers or toes; six octopus tentacles, insect legs. Syn. *wonochef, wonoyó*.

wonéwúwéw (2) See *wono-₂, -wúwéw*. num. six amounts of fermented breadfruit suitable for kneading.

woniyancher (Eng.) nu. oleander. [Leaves and wood are deadly poisonous.]

wono-₁ (3a) WONA₂. [Used only in cpds. with suf. dem.] nu. fellow (of males only). [This is the polite form; cf. *wonno-*.] Syn. *áta-*. See *woneey, wonna, woneen, wonoomw, wonnaan, wonowe*.

wono-₂ (3) See *woon₁*. Var. *wonu-*. pref. (num.) six. See *wonaché, wonapé, wonayé, wone, woneyaf, woneyang, woneyi, woneyin₁, woneyin₂, woneyiyey, wonéwúk₁, wonéwúk₂, wonéwút, wonochamw, wonochchi, wonochchooch, wonochú, wonochúk, wonoféw, wonoffaat, wonoffit, wonofóch, wonofutuk, wonongaf, wonongát, wonongéréw, wonongin, wonokis, wonokit, wonokkamw, wonokkap, wonokkumw, wonokun, wonokumwuch, wonokup, wonomach, wonomas, wonomataf, wonomech, wonomeech, wonomeet, wonomén, wonomma, wonommech, wonommék, wonomwénú, wonomwmwun, wonomwmwú, wonomwmwún, wonomwu, wonomwú₁, wonomwú₂, wonomwúch, wononnú, wonopa, wonopachang, wonopan, wonopeche, wonopeek, wonopék, wonopéw, wonopino, wonopinúk, wonopu, wonopwang, wonopwey, wonopwéét, wonopwi, wonopwin, wonopwopw, wonopwór, wonopwpwaaw, wonopwúkú, wonopwún, wonosap, wonosángá, wonosáwá, wonoseeng, wonosen, wonosópw₁, wonosópw₂, wonossaar, wonossak, wonossar, wonossáát, wonossát, wonossupw, wonotinewupw, wonotip, wonotit, wonottiit, wonottún, wonotú, wonotúkúm, wonotún, wonowo, wonowoch, wonowumw, wonowupw, wonowut₁, wonowún, wonowúwéw,*

wonoyaf, wonoyef, wonoyem, wonoyep, wonoyék, wonoyipw, wonoyó, wonoyóch, wonóówut.

wonoomw See *wono-₁, oomw*. nu. (dem.) that fellow (male, near hearer). [This is the polite form, cf. *wonnoomw*.] Dis. *wonokkoomw* those fellows. Syn. *átemwuun, átoomw*.

wonoon₁ Dis. of *won*.

wonoon₂ (db; 3) WONA₃. nu. likeness. *wonooneyisaraw* l. of a barracuda.

Wonofáát See *wono-₁, fááti*. nu. (pers.) traditional god of magical spells (*roong*). [He lives in the sky, is associated with lightning, is the trickster hero of many stories, and has been equated by Christians with Satan. Once in anger he kicked with his foot and created the string of reef islands in the southeastern part of Truk, whence his name "Kick-fellow."]

wonoféw (2) See *wono-₂, -féw*. num. six lumps of globular shaped objects (e.g., stones, balls).

wonofich (3a) See *wono-₂, ficha-*. num. six strips of coconut, pandanus or other palm leaf prepared for plaiting mats.

wonofóch (4) See *wono-₂, fóchu-*. num. six long objects (e.g., vehicles, legs, teeth, timbers, shovels).

wonofutuk (3) See *wono-₂, futuk*. num. six pieces of meat.

wonoffaat (3) See *wono-₂, ffaata-*. num. six strings of fish.

wonoffit (3) See *wono-₂, fitta-*. num. six leaf packages of small fish.

wonosap (3) See *wono-₂, saap*. num. six cheeks (especially of fish).

wonosángá (1) See *wono-₂, sángá*. num. six basketsfuls of fish. Syn. *wonosáwá*.

wonosáwá (1) See *wono-₂, sáwá*. num. six basketfulls of fish. Syn. *wonosángá*.

wonoseeng (3) See *wono-₂, seeng*. num. six lengths between joints.

wonosen (2) See *wono-₂, -sen*. num. six coils of rope. [Each coil is 30 to 100 fathoms in length according to local custom.]

wonosópw₁ (4) See *wono-₂, sópwu-₂*. num. six segments.

wonosópw₂ (4) See *wono-₂, sópwu-₃*. num. six burdens of tied-together breadfruit.

wonossaar (2) See *wono-₂, -ssaar*. Var. *wonossar*. num. six slices.

wonossak (3) See *wono-₂, ssaka-*. num. six pieces of copra.

wonossar

wonossar N. of *wonossaar*.
wonossáát (2, 3) See *wono-₂, -ssáát*. Var. *wonossát*. num. six slivers, longitudinal slices, splinters.
wonossát N. of *wonossáát*.
wonossupw (2) See *wono-₂, ssupwu-*. num. six tiny drops.
wonokis (2) See *wono-₂, kisi-*. num. six little things or bits. Syn. *wonongin*.
wonokit (3) See *wono-₂, -kit*. num. sixty thousand.
wonokum (2) See *wono-₂, kumu-*. num. six mouthfuls or swallows of liquid.
wonokumwuch (2) See *wono-₂, kumwuch*. num. six fistfulls or handfulls (of something); six hooves, paws, feet (of animals).
wonokkaan Dis. of *woneen*.
wonokkamw (3b) See *wono-₂, kkamw*. num. six fragments of pieces (of cloth, paper).
wonokkana Dis. of *wonna*.
wonokkanaan Dis. of *wonnaan*.
wonokkap (3) See *wono-₂, kkap*. num. six cupfuls.
wonokkeey Dis. of *woneey*.
wonokkewe Dis. of *wonowe*.
wonokkin (2) See *won, kin₃*. F. Var. *méwúrúkkin*. nu. (T2) restless sleep. vi. sleep restlessly (due to being bothered by spirits or worries).
wonokkoomw Dis. of *wonoomw*.
wonokkumw (2, 3) See *wono-₂, kkumw₁*. num. six portions of premasticated food.
wonomas (3) See *wono-₂, -mas*. num. six things worn on the eyes (e.g., lenses of goggles) or attached to piercing weapons (e.g., spear points).
wonomach (3) See *wono-₂, macha-*. F. num. six fishtails (in counting fish). Cf. *wonéwúk₁*.
wonomataf (3) See *wono-₂, matafa-*. num. six small portions, small amounts, little bits.
wonomeech (2) See *wono-₂, -meech*. Var. *wonomech, wonommech*. num. six portions of mashed breadfruit.
wonomeet (3) See *wono-₂, meet₂*. num. six strands.
wonomech N. var. of *wonomeech*.
wonomén (2) See *wono-₂, maan₁*. num. six persons or creatures (of people, mammals, birds, fish, and insects; but not of lobsters, crabs, sea cucumbers,

Trukese-English

or shellfish); six knives, guns, files, scissors.
wonomma (1) See *wono-₂, -mma*. num. six mouthfuls of premasticated food.
wonommech N. var. of *wonomeech*.
wonommék (2) See *wono-₂, mékkú-*. num. six fragments.
wonomwaw nu. (temp.) 15th night of the lunar month.
wonomwénú (1) See *wono-₂, mwénúú-*. num. six ells (lengths from elbow to fingertip).
wonomwu E.Wn. of *wonomwú₂*.
wonomwú₁ (1) See *wono-₂, mwúú-₁*. F. Var. *wonomwmwú*. num. six torn fragments (of rag or string).
wonomwú₂ (1) See *wono-₂, mwúú-₂*. Var. *wonomwu*. num. six sea cucumbers; six pieces of feces.
wonomwúch (2) See *wono-₂, mwúchú-*. num. six pieces of firewood.
wonomwmék See *wono-₂, mwékkú-*. N. num. six bits or morsels (of mashed food). Syn. *wonopwey*.
wonomwmwun (3) See *wono-₂, mwmwuna-*. num. six portions of *mwatún*. Syn. *wonotún*.
wonomwmwú N. of *wonomwú₁*.
wonomwmwún F. of *wonomwmwun*.
wononó See *won*.
wononum nu. damsel fish. Syn. *niféwúféw*.
wononnú (1) See *wono-₂, nnúú-*. num. six loaves of breadfruit pudding or amounts of breadfruit to be mashed into pudding loaves.
wonongaf (3) See *wono-₂, ngaaf*. num. six fathoms (six times the distance from fingertip to fingertip of outstretched hands).
wonongát (4) See *wono-₂, -ngát*. num. six concave or hollow objects; (less common) six things of almost any kind. Cf. *wonopwang, wonuuw*.
wonongéréw (2) See *wono-₂, -ngéréw*. num. six thousand.
wonongin (2) See *wono-₂, ngini-*. num. six little things or bits. Syn. *wonokis*.
wonongngaw (3b) See *won, ngngaw*. vi. sleep restlessly.
wonopa (1) See *wono-₂, -pa*. num. six fronds, garland, stalks with leaves. [Of palm trees, banana trees, *Cyrtosperma*, and also of leis or garlands, necklaces, and bead belts.] Cf. *wonopan*.

wonopan (3) See *wono-₂, paan₁*. num. six branches with leaves (of trees other than palms or bananas). Syn. *wonopachang.* Cf. *wonopa.*

wonopachang (3) See *wono-₂, pachang₁*. num. six branches with leaves. Syn. *wonopan.*

wonopeek (2) See *wono-₂, peek₂*. num. six sides, pages.

wonopeche (1) See *wono-₂, peche*. num. six lower or hind limbs (of humans, birds, and animals only).

wonopék (2) See *wono-₂, péék₂*. num. six chips, chopped off pieces, cigarette butts.

wonopéw (2) See *wono-₂, -péw*. num. six wings or things worn over hand or arm (e.g., gloves).

wonopiiy See *won, pii-₁*. vo. (T1) sit on (eggs or small chicks, of hens).

wonopino (1) See *wono-₂, pino*. num. six small packages of breadfruit pudding.

wonopinúk (2) See *wono-₂, pinúk*. num. six tied bundles, reams of paper.

wonopu (1) See *wono-₂, puu-₂*. num. six strokes in swimming (in measuring distance).

wonopwang (3) See *wono-₂, pwaang*. num. six holes, caves, cavities, pits, tunnels, hollows. Cf. *wonongát.*

wonopwey (2) See *wono-₂, -pwey*. num. six pinches or morsels (of mashed food). Syn. *wonomwmwék.*

wonopwéét (2) See *wono-₂, pwéét*. num. six noses.

wonopwi (1) See *wono-₂, pwii-₁*. num. six groups, groves, flocks, schools, herds, swarms, convoys, prides, etc.

wonopwin (2) See *wono-₂, pwiin₃*. num. six nights.

wonopwopw (2) See *wono-₂, pwoopw*. num. six tree-trunks, bases, foundations, causes, sources, beginnings, origins, reasons.

wonopwór (4) See *wono-₂, pwóór*. num. six boxes or crates (of something).

wonopwu nu. (temp.) 14th night of the lunar month.

wonopwúkú (1) See *wono-₂, -pwúkú*. num. six hundred.

wonopwún (2) See *wono-₂, pwúún₁*. Var. *wonopwpwún*. num. six pieces (broken off).

wonopwpwaaw (2) See *wono-₂, pwpwaaw*. num. six home-made cigarettes.

wonopwpwún N. of *wonopwún.*

wonochamw (3) See *wono-₂, -chamw*. num. six foreheads, brows, or similarly classed objects (e.g., visors, stem-bases of coconut fronds); six fishheads.

wonochef See *wono-₂, -chef*. num. six tentacles (of octopus or squid); six pieces of firewood. Syn. *wonowút, wonoyó.*

wonochú (1) See *wono-₂, chúú*. num. six bone segments (of meat).

wonochúk (2) See *wono-₂, chúúk*. num. six coconut-leaf baskets (of something).

wonochchi (1) See *wono-₂, -chchi*. num. six drops.

wonochchipw (3) See *won, chchipw*. n. (T3) squirming sleep. *wonochchipwan* his s. s. vi. squirm in one's sleep.

wonochchooch (3) See *wono-₂, chchooch*. num. six armfuls.

wonotinewupw (2) See *wono-₂, tinewupw*. num. six yards (lengths from center of chest to outstretched fingertips).

wonotip (3) See *wono-₂, tiip₂*. num. six slices, chunks, cut segments (of breadfruit and taro only).

wonotit (2) See *wono-₂, -tit*. num. six strings (of breadfruit, usually ten to a string). Syn. *wonottiit.*

Wonoto nu. (pers.) 1. name of the legendary founder of a school of judo-like fighting. [He is said to have defeated his rivals *Fáánápuuch* and *Newúmá*.] 2. the system of fighting founded by the man of this name.

wonotú (3) See *wono-₂, túú*. Tbl. num. six vulvas.

wonotúkúm (3) See *wono-₂, túkúm*. num. six packages (of something).

wonotún (2) See *wono-₂, túnú-*. F. Var. *wonottún*. num. six portions of *mwatún* pudding. Syn. *wonomwmwun.*

wonottiit (2) See *wono-₂, ttiit₂*. num. six strings of ten breadfruit each. Syn. *wonotit.*

wonottún N. of *wonotún.*

wonowe See *wono-₁, -we*. nu. (dem.) that fellow (male) (out of sight or past), the male person of reference (in narrative). [This is the polite form, cf. *wonnowe*.] Dis. *wonokkewe* those fellows. Syn. *átewe.*

wonowo (1) See *wono-₂, -wo₁*. num. six clumps (of bananas).

wonowoch See *wono-₂, -woch*. Tn. num. six sorts, kinds, rations, varieties, species,. Syn. *wonoyóch*.

Wonowu nu. (loc.) Ono Island (Namonuito Atoll).

wonowumw (2) See *wono-₂, wumwu-₂*. num. six branching stalks (of bananas, fruit, cluster of pandanus keys, coral).

wonowupw (2) See *wono-₂, wupwu-*. num. six breasts.

wonowut₁ (2) See *wono-₂, wutu-*. num. 1. six cores (especially of breadfruit). 2. six chunks of cooked breadfruit.

wonowut₂ (3) See *won, wuut₁*. vi. sleep in the men's house; be under sexual taboo. Cf. *wonoyimw*.

wonowún (3) See *wono-₂, wúún₁*. num. six feathers, scales, hairs.

wonowúwéw (2) See *wono-₂, -wúwéw*. num. six amounts of fermented breadfruit suitable for kneading.

wonoyaf Var. of *woneyaf*.

wonoyef See *wono-₂, eef₁*. num. six bunches of ripe coconuts.

wonoyem See *wono-₂, eem*. num. six earlobes.

wonoyep (2) See *wono-₂, epi-₁*. num. six butt ends, lower ends, west ends.

wonoyééch (2) See *won, ééch*. nu. quiet sleep. *wonoyéchchún átánaan* the q. s. of that fellow yonder. vi. sleep quietly and well.

wonoyék (2) See *wono-₂, ékkú-*. num. six nets.

wonoyimw (3a) See *won, iimw*. vi. sleep in the house. Cf. *wonowut₂*.

wonoyipw (3) See *wono-₂, -ipw*. num. six steps, footprints, soles; six items of footwear.

wonoyó (1) See *wono-₂, óó₁*. num. six tentacles (of octopus or squid). Syn. *wonéwút, wonochef*.

wonoyóch (4) See *wono-₂, -óch*. num. six sorts, rations, kinds, varieties, species. Syn. *wonowoch*.

wonóówut (3) See *wono-₂, owut*. num. six rows of thatch.

wonu- (2) See *woon₁*. Var. *wono-*. pref. (num.) six. See *wonuuw*.

wonuu Var. of *wonuuw*.

wonuuw (3) See *wonu-, -uw*. F. Var. *wonuu*. num. six nonspecific or general-class objects. With c. pref. and ptv. const.: *owonuuwan* sixth one. With dis. c. pref.: *okkowonuuw* be six at a time. With pref. *nne-₂*: *eew nnewonuuwan* one sixth part. Syn. *wonongát*.

wonna See *wono-₁, wonno-, na*. nu. (dem.) that fellow (male) near hearer or just mentioned. Dis. *wonokkana* (polite), *wonnokkana* (not polite) those fellows. *kete mina w.* don't fool around with that f. Syn. *átána*.

wonnaan See *wono-₁, wonno-, naan*. nu. (dem.) that fellow (male) yonder. Dis. *wonokkanaan* (polite), *wonnokkanaan* (not polite) those fellows. Syn. *átánaan*.

wonne md.m., conj. indicates that what follows is contrary to reality or fact; when not. *pwata ke ataay w. pisekumw?* why do you destroy it when [it is] not your property? Syn. *anne, sanne*.

wonneen See *wonno-, een₃*. nu. (dem.) this fellow (male) by you and me. [This is the impolite form, cf. *woneen*.] Dis. *wonnokkaan* those fellows.

wonneey See *wonno-, eey₁*. nu. (dem.) this fellow (male) by me. [This is the impolite form, cf. *woneey*.] Dis. *wonnokkeey* these fellows.

wonno- (3a) WONNA. [Used only with suf. dem.] pref. fellow (of males only). [This is the harsh, impolite form.] See *wonna, wonnaan, wonneen, wonneey, wonnoomw, wonnowe*.

wonnoomw See *wonno-, oomw*. nu. (dem.) that fellow (male, near hearer). [This is the impolite form, cf. *wonoomw*.] Dis. *wonnokkoomw* those fellows.

wonnokkaan Dis. of *wonneen*.

wonnokkana Dis. of *wonna*.

wonnokkanaan Dis. of *wonnaan*.

wonnokkeey Dis. of *wonneey*.

wonnokkewe Dis. of *wonnowe*.

wonnokkoomw Dis. of *wonnoomw*.

wonnowe See *wonno-, -we*. nu. (dem.) that fellow (male, out of sight or past), the male person of reference (in narrative). [This is the impolite form, cf. *wonowe*.] Dis. *wonnokkewe* those fellows.

wop (3) WOPA. vi. hide; be hidden, concealed.

woperi See *wop, -ri-*. vo. (T6a) be hidden from; spy on, wait in ambush for.

woper-fátáneey See *wop, -ri-, fátán, -e-₂*. vo. phr. (T6b) walk about in concealment from.

wopoop (db; 4) WOPO. Var. *opoop*. vi. depressed, dented (of a surface); have a depression.

wopotáyim (3) WOPOTÁYIMA. (Eng.) nu. (T3) overtime. *wopotáyimen aach angaang* our work's o.

Wopwutin nu. (loc.) a clan name.

wopwpweey See *woopw₁, -e-₂*. N. Var. *wuwapwpweey*. vo. (T6b) cut off the growing off of (a palm).

wor (3) WORA₃. [Used only impersonally with *e-₁, aa, epwe, meyi₂, ese, esapw*.] vi. be, exist. Dis. *wokkor* (ds). *aa wor* there came into existence, there is; *ese wor* or *esoor* there is not; *meyi wor* there is, there exists; *ese chchiweni (chchiweyi) wor* there is no longer; *ese pwanú (pwayi) wor* there is not again, there is none left; *ese fóókkunu (fóókkii) wor* there is truly or absolutely not. *esapw wor wún suupwa ikeey* there will be no smoking cigarettes here. With dir. suf.: *wokkoronó* continue to exist.

wora- (3) WORA₄. [In cpds. only.] unsp. observe, scrutinize. See *woráátá, woreey*.

woráátá See *wora-, -tá*. vo. (dir.) look up at. Cf. *woori*.

woreey See *wora-, -e-₂*. vo. (T6b) put a light on, shine a light on.

wores (2) WORESI. vi. wash the face.

woresi See *wores*. vo. (T2) wash (the face). *w. mosomw* w. your face.

woreyinú (1) See *woor₂, núú₂*. vi. be stained with juice from the coconut husk.

woro- (3a) WORA₅. [In cpds. only.] unsp. swallow; throat. See *woromi*.

woroor (db; 3) WORA₆. nu. (T3) stone or cement wall; stone or cement pier; stone causeway, stone embankment; dock. *worooren Chorong* the Chorong pier.

Woroorofich See *woroor, -fich*. nu. (pers.) traditional god of wall building.

woroken (Eng.) nu. organ. vi. play an organ.

woromi See *woro-, mi-*. vo. (T6a) swallow. With dir. suf.: *woromóónó*.

woromóónó See *woromi*.

woró (1) WORÓÓ. nu. (T1) name of a spell associated with swollen spots over the body. *kinin w.* rash associated with the spell. Cf. *wóró*.

woch (3) WOCHA₁. vi., adj. (be) well-preserved, long-lived, durable. *meyi w. átánaan* he is well-preserved, durable. nu. (T3) durability, longevity. *wochen átánaan!* the d. of that fellow.

-woch (2) Tn. Var. *-óch*. suf. (cc.) sort (in counting rations, kinds, varieties, species). *ewoch, ruwowoch, wúnúwoch, fowoch, nimewoch, wonowoch, fúúwoch, wanúwoch, ttiwewoch, engoon* one,...ten s.

wocha-₁ (3) WOCHA₂. N. ni. (T3) root (of a tooth). *wochan* its r. *wochen ngii* tooth's r. Syn. *apwa-*.

wocha-₂ (3) WOCHA₃. [In cpds. only.] Var. *wucha-*. unsp. eat (in reference to fish, meat and uncooked fruits and vegetables). See *wocheey₂, wochooch₁*. Cf. *a-₃*.

wocha-₃ (3) WOCHA₄. [In cpds. only.] unsp. jump an opponent (in checkers). See *wocheey₃, wochonó, wochooch₃*.

wocha-₄ (3) WOCHA₅. [In cpds. only.] unsp. tickle in the stomach. See *wocheey₄, wochooch₂*.

wocha-₅ (3) WOCHA₆. [In cpds. only.] unsp. notch, cut. See *wocheey₁, wocheni*.

wochaa-₁ (1v) See *wocha-₂, -a-₂*. [With pos. prn. only.] Var. *wuchaa-*. ni. (T1) portion (to eat) of uncooked food or cooked or uncooked meat. *wochaan* his p. *wochááy chukó* my chicken to eat.

wochaa-₂ (1v) See *wocha-₃, -a-₂*. ni. (T1) a jump (over an opponent in checkers). *wochaan* his j.

wochaamas (3) See *wocha-₂, amas*. vi. eat raw.

wochaamaseey See *wochaamas, -e-₂*. vo. (T6b) eat (something) raw.

wochaanú (1) See *wooch, énú*. Itang. nu. (loc.; T1) spirit reef.

wochang (3) See *wocha-₅, -ng*. nu. (T3) cradle for carrying a large wooden bowl. *wochangen wuunong* bowl's c.

wochááp (2) See *wocha-₂, epi-₁*. nu. (T2) dragonfly. Syn. *nifeefeechón, wusekiichén*.

wocheey₁ See *wocha-₅, -e-₂*. vo. (T6b) cut a slice off the end of the bound coconut spathe in order to keep the palm sap flowing. Dis. *wokkocheey* (ds). *wúwa w. ewe áchi* I sliced the toddy. Cf. *woseey₂, woteey*.

wocheey₂ See *wocha-₂, -e-₂*. vo. (T6b) eat (fish, meat, or uncooked fruits and vegetables). *w. kkunók* use up or waste time in visiting or other inconsequential activity that should be spent at work. Cf. *wochooch₁*.

wocheey₃ See *wocha-₃, -e-₃*. vo. (T6b) jump an opponent, take a man (in checkers). Cf. *wochooch₃*.

wocheey₄ See *wocha-₄, -e-₂*. vo. (T6b) tickle (someone) in the stomach. Cf. *wochooch₂*.

wochen nu. species of wrasse fish.

wocheni See *wocha-₅, -ni-*. vo. (T5) notch, cut notches in (e.g., the side of a canoe hull in which to set the outrigger booms).

wocheyin (2) See *wocha-₅, -ini-₅*. nu. (T2) mortise (in joinery). *wocheyinin irá* m. in a timber.

wocheyiniiy See *wocheyin, -i-₂*. vo. (T5) make a mortise in.

wochéngún (2) See *wocha-₂, ngúún*. nu. (T2) a form of sorcery used by one *itang* against another. [If one *itang* was making a speech, another present could chant a spell on his words, making him ill.]

wochooch₁ (db; 3) See *wocha-₂*. va. eat (in reference to raw fish, cooked or raw meat, uncooked fruits or vegetables). Dis. *wokkochooch* (ds). Cf. *wocheey₂*.

wochooch₂ (db; 3) See *wocha-₄*. vi. (dis.) tickle in the stomach. Cf. *wocheey₄*.

wochooch₃ (db; 3) See *wocha-₃*. vi., va. (dis.) jump men in checkers. Cf. *wocheey₃*.

wochofénú (3) See *wooch, fénú*. nu. (T3) fringing reef around an island. Syn. *wochen fénú*.

wochonó (1) See *wocha-₃, -nó*. vi. jump forwards (in checkers). Ant. *wochopáák*.

Wochonuuk (3a) See *wooch, nuuk₁*. nu. (loc.) Oroluk Island and Atoll.

wochopáák See *wocha-₃, -páák*. vi. jump backwards in checkers. Ant. *wochonó*.

wochowuuch See *wocha-₂, wuuch₁*. Itang. nu. a form of divination. [Performed by *itang* with *ipar* bananas on a mat of determine a plan of attack in war.]

wochchén vi. be brackish (of water).

wot (3) WOTA₄. vi. go aground, run on a reef (of a boat).

wota- (3) WOTA₅. unsp. arranged, in order. See *kkóót*. Cf. *wotoot, woteey*.

wotáy Var. of *wootay*.

woteengeni See *woot₂, -e-₂, ngeni*. vo. (T2) apply a husking stick to (a coconut).

woteey See *woot₂, -e-₂*. vo. (T6b) husk, remove the husk of (a coconut); clear (ground) of vegetation, weed. Syn. *óteey*. Cf. *woseey₂, wocheey₁*.

wotefich (2) See *woot₁, -fich (?)*. N. Var. *wotofich*. nu. (T2) a variety of *Colocasia* taro.

woto- (3a) WOTA₆. [In cpds. only.] unsp. side, location (in space or time).

wotoot (db; 3) See *woot₂*. va., vi. (dis.) do husking (of coconuts); do clearing (of vegetation), weeding, gardening; be cleared; weeded. nu. (T3) husking; clearing, weeding, gardening. *wotooten taka* h. coconuts.

wotofich F. of *wotefich*.

wotokaaka (1) See *woot₁, kaa-*. nu. (T1) a variety of dry-land *Colocasia* taro with red petioles.

wotonó (1) See *woto-, -nó*. nu. (loc.) (toward) the far side. *w. Wútéét, wototo Romónum* toward the far side by Wútéét, toward the near side by Romónum (said on Romónum). *w. winingách, wototo neefááf* on the far side (of the night) near dawn, on the near side near (soon after) dinner time. Ant. *wototo*.

wotopwech (3) See *woot₁, pwech*. nu. (T3) a variety of *Colocasia* taro with green petioles.

wotopwo (1) See *woot₁, pwo*. nu. (T1) a variety of *Colocasia* taro. [Its leaves were used traditionally as sails on model canoes, and hence its name.]

wotochcha (1) See *woot₁, chcha*. nu. (T1) a variety of *Colocasia* taro with red petioles.

wototo (1) See *woto-, -to*. nu. (loc.) (toward) the near side. See *wotonó* for examples.

-wow (3) WOWA. adj. (dir.) toward or in the direction of person addressed, toward you. *etiwow* go toward you; *kúkkúwow* be beside you.

wowa Wn. and Tns. contraction of *owuwa* (see *owu-*).

Wowuniyar nu. (pers.) a traditional storm god. [One of five children of the weather (*néwún rúán*), who live in the gale, sink boats in heavy seas, and blow down trees.]

woy (2) WOYI. N. Var. *way*. excl. oops! [Uttered when a person suddenly remembers or is remined of something he has forgotten or overlooked.] *woyi ko* oops, sir.

wóó-₁ (1) WÓÓ₁. ni. (prep.; T1) 1. (on) top (of); on, above, over. *wóón* on t. of him. *wóón naan cheepen* on that table. *fénúwan mé wóón saman* his land from his father. *iiy meyi pin mé wóómw* he is taboo from being above you. 2. place (of), time (of). *wóón piyepi* sandy flat area of an island below the mountain slopes; *wóón tikitik* area of rough sand that is covered at high tide. *wóón wúnúmar* season from September through December that culminates in the little breadfruit harvest (*maramen w. w.* months of this season, *meyin w. w.* breadfruit that ripens in this season).

wóó-₂ (1) WÓÓ₂. ni. (loc.; T1) surface, surface appearance, face. Dis. *wóówó* (db). *wóón, wóówóón* his s. *wóón mesey* my face.

wóósefáán (2) See *wóó-₂, sefáán*. vi. face back, be facing back.

wóók (2) WÓKU. n. (T2) cane, staff, cudgel, club, spear. *wókun* his c. *choon w.* or *niwinin w.* land acquired as spoils of war; *chóón w.* fighter, bully. *wókun kurukur* dance staff; *wókun waa* mooring stake. Cf. *wókuuk*.

wóóken (2) WÓÓKENI. (Eng.) nu. (T2) wagon. *efóch w.* one w. *waan w.* his w. *wóókenin Chuuk* Trukese w.

Wóón [Apparently derived from *wóó-₁*.] nu. (loc.) European or white man's world (including Japan). *pisekin W.* goods of European manufacture. *fin-W.* white woman; *ree-W.* white man.

Wóónirá nu. (loc.) a clan name.

wóónó See *wa-*.

wóópar (3b) See *wóó-₂, par*. vi. blush, flush; be red-faced, ruddy; be sunburned (but not peeling). Dis. *wóóparapar* (db).

wóóparapar Dis. of *wóópar*.

wóópwech (3) See *wóó-₂, pwech*. vi. be pale, white-faced. Syn. *wóóyer*.

wóóri See *wóó-₂, -ri-*. vo. (T4) face towards. With dir. suf.: *wóóraatiw* (N.) *wóóráátiw* (F.) face down on. Cf. *woori*.

wóóchááchá (1) See *wóó-₂, cháácha*. vi. be cheerful.

wóówóóyéech (db; 2: *-yéchchú-*) See *wóó-₂, ééch*. vi. be cheerful faced. Ant. *wóówóngngaw*.

wóówóngngaw (db; 3) See *wóó-₂, ngngaw*. vi. be gloomy faced. Ant. *wóówóóyéech*.

wóóyér (2) See *wóó-₂, ér₁*. vi. be pale, white-faced. Syn. *wóópwech*.

wókiipwur (3) See *wóók, pwur₁*. nu. (T3) mooring stake carried on a sailing canoe. Syn. *wókiitur, wókun waa*.

wókiitur (2) See *wóók, tur₁*. nu. (T2) mooring stake carried on a sailing canoe. Syn. *wókiipwur, wókun waa*.

wókuuk (db; 2) See *wóók*. Var. *wókuwók*. va., vi. (dis.) use as a cane, staff, cudgel, club, spear. nu. (T2) in *wókuukun esefích* (n. phr.) bow (for arrows).

wókusor (3a) See *wóók, soro-*. nu. (T3) a hold or maneuver in hand-to-hand fighting. [Against an opponent thrusting with a small knife, one seizes his knife hand with both hands, twisting the knife back and thrusting forward so he is stabbed with his own knife.]

wókuni See *wóók, -ni-*. vo. (T5) acquire a cane, staff, cudgel, club, spear. Cf. *wókuwók, wókuuk*.

wókurumw (2) See *wóók, ruumw₁*. nu. (T2) barbed spear (general term). *wókurumwun Chuuk* Trukese b. s.

wókuwók Var. of *wókuuk*.

wópw (2) WÓPWU. vi. be beat, struck, hit (with a stick or whip); be whipped. Id. *aa wópw!* or *aa wópwó!* he is talking nonsense ("he's beat"). Cf. *wech*.

wópwuni See *wópw, -ni-*. vo. (T5) beat, strike (with stick or whip); whip. Cf. *wópwuwópw*.

wópwuwópw (db; 2) See *wópw*. va., vi. (dis.) beat, strike, hit, whip. Cf. *wópwuni*.

wópwpwach (3) See *wóó-₂, pwpwach*. vi. be wrinkled (of the face), have wrinkles.

wóró (1) WÓRÓ. nu. (T1) a skin condition characterized by small bumps and experienced by some people when exposed to sea or rain (not goosepimples). *wóróón inisin* his skin bumps. Cf. *woró*. vi. have bumps on the skin.

wóchchón (4) See *wóó-₂, chón.* vi. be dark faced.

wóttam (3a) See *wóó-₂, ttam.* vi. be long-faced.

wu-₁ (2) WU₁. pref. (n.form.) male person. See *wukkó*.

wu-₂ (2) WU₂. [In this form when before words whose first vowel is *o* or *u* only.] Var. *wú-* (the common form). pref. (sub.) 1sg. sub. prn.: I. [Although a prefix, it is written as a separate word.] *wu woráátá* I look up at him. *Iyaa we wu wupwutiw me iye?* where was I born?

wu-₃ (2) WU₃. [In cpds. only.] unsp. pierce. See *wuni, wusi*.

wu-₄ (2) WU₄. [In cpds. only.] unsp. throw water on something (?). See *wuti*.

wu-₅ (2) WU₅. [In cpds. only.] Var. *wuu*. nr. (T2) fish trap. See *wunóómw, wunufeeyisin, wunupweewu*.

-wu- (2) WU₆. Var. *-u-, -ú-, -wú-*. suf. (v.form.) makes an object focussed verb of the base.

-wu (1) WUU₁. adj. (dir.) out; outside; northward. *toowu* come out. *aa péewu seni éér* it blows northward from the south. *kúkkúwuun fénú* island's outer or seaward side.

wuu- (1) WUU₃. [In cpds. only.] unsp. (u.m.) See *wuunong*.

wuu₁ (1) WUU₂. Var. *wu-₅*. nu. (T1) wicker fish trap, lobster pot. [It is made of mangrove sticks.] *eew w.* one f. t. *néwún w.* his f. t.

wuu₂ (1) WUU₅. name of the high, back, rounded vowel written *u*; name of the letter thus written.

wuufóór (3) nu. (T3) a species of parrot fish. *wuufóóren Chuuk* Trukese p. f.

wuuk₁ (3, 2) WUKA₂, WUKU₂. nu. (T3) fishnet, net (general term). *eew w.* one f. *aan w.* his f. *wuken ninnim* spider web; *wuken wiin* turtle net.

wuuk₂ (2) WUKU₃. n. (T2) fault, blame. *wukun* his f. *pwisin wukiy* my own f.

Wuumaan nu. (loc.) Uman Island. Cf. *Kuwopw*.

wuumw (2) WUMWU₃. nu. (T2) 1. earth oven, oven, furnace. *eew w.* one o. *wumwun mwemey* preparing first breadfruit from a holding a presentation to a chief; *wumwun pwoopwo* food prepared for a pregnant woman. *sooni ewe w.* kindle the o.; *féwúúw ewe w.* put rocks on the fire for the o.; *érúúw ewe w.* spread the hot rocks in the o.; *amwata* or *eeneni ewe w.* spread green grass on the hot rocks; *kkóót w.* put chunks of breadfruit in the o.; *pwénúúw* or *owufa ewe w.* spread leaves on the breadfruit chunks in the o.; *wuwaseey ewe w.* put fresh or dry grass on the leaves; *wutuut w.* throw water on the o. to make it steam; *pwénúúwénó ewe w.* cover the o. entirely with grass; *suuki ewe w.* open the o.; *pwpwo w.* pound cooked breadfruit into pudding; *ásááy ewe w.* empty the o. 2. presentation of food to a chief. Syn. *wumwusómwoon*.

wuun₁ (2) WUNU₅. Tb1. n. (T2) testicles and scrotum together. *eféw w.* one testicle. *wunun* his t. and s. *féwún w.* testicle. Syn. *suun₁*.

wuun₂ (2) WUNU₆. Tb3. nu. (T2) maggot. *emén w.* one m. *wunun nóón eey futuk* maggots in this meat. vi. have maggots. *meyi w. eey mááy* this breadfruit has m.

Wuun₃ nu. (loc.) a clan name.

Wuun₄ nu. 1. the star Aldebaran. 2. name of a month in the traditional calendar.

wuuni See *wuu₁, -ni-*. vo. (T4) catch (something) in a fish trap.

wuunong (3) See *wuu-, -nong*. nu. (T3) large and deep wooden bowl. [Used for ceremonial presentations of food.] *eew w.* one b. *sepiyan w.* his b. *wuunongen Chuuk* Trukese b.

wuunupwá (1) See *wuu₁, pwá*. nu. (T1) a type of wicker fish trap or lobster pot.

wuung (3) WUNGA. n. (T3) ridgepole (of a building). *efóch w.* one r. *wungan* its r. *wungen ewe iimw* the house's r. *pénútiwen w.* thatch that caps the r.

wuupw₁ (2) WUPWU₄. n. (T2) child, offspring, scion (of a man only). *wupwun* or *wupwun wóón* his c. *wupwun wóón iyé?* what man's child; *na semiriit wupwun wóómw* that child is yours. Cf. *naaw*.

wuupw₂ (3) WUPWA. N. n. (T3) belly, abdomen. *wupwan* his b. Syn. *nuuk, saa*.

wuupw₃ Dis. of *wupw*.

wuuch₁ (2) WUCHU₂. nu. (T2) banana (fruit and plant). *eféw w.* one b. (fruit); *efoch w.* one b. (tree or plant); *ewumw w.* one stalk of b.; *eyi* or *eyin w.* one hand of b. *wochaan w.* his b. (to eat);

fótaan w. his b. tree. *wuchun Merika* a variety of b. (syn. *peressin*).

wuuch₂ (3) WUCHCHA₁. n. (T3) of the bottom of a paddle canoe. *péén wuchchan* its longitudinal g. Syn. *fáát*.

-wuuch (3: *-wuchcha-*) WUCHCHA₂. [In cpds. only.] unsp. pain, hurt, physical discomfort. See *chewuuch, inemowuuch*.

wuut₁ (3) WUTTA. n. (T3) meeting house, boat house. *eew w.* one m. h. *wuttan* his m. h. *wutten fénú* island or district m. h. or assembly hall; *wutten mwiich* meeting house; assembly hall; *wutten waa* boat house.

wuut₂ (2) WUTU₂. n. (T2) core, interior, inside (of people, animals, fruit, things). *ewut wutun* one c. (see also *wutu-*). *wutun* its c.

wuuwu (db; 1) WUU₄. vi. bark (as a dog).

wusap (3) WUSAPA. nu. (T3) a species of reef fish.

wusek (2) WUSEKI. vi. gyrate the hips in dancing. *chóón w.* one who gyrates. *wusekin ewe feefin* the woman's gyrating.

wusekiichén See *wusek*. nu. dragonfly. Syn. *nifeefeechón, wochááp*.

wusi₁ See *wu-₃, -si-*. vo. (T5) sting, make smart. Cf. *wusuus*.

wusu-₁ (2) WUSU₁. Var. *wussu-*. ni. (T2) status, nature, way, manner, character, custom. *wusun, wussun* his s. *ifa wusumw (wussumw)?* how are you? *ifa wusun (wussun) kkeey mettóóch?* what about these things? what is the status of these things? *iyeey wusun* it is like this; *iyeen wusun* it is as follows; *ina wusun* it is like that, that's how it is, in that way. *wusun...* like, in the manner of, the status of, as for; *wusun chék...* just like, the same as; *wusun itá...* just as if. *wusun wee chék* just as it was before. Cf. *nénné*.

wusu-₂ (2) WUSU₂. [In cpds. only; presumably a back formation from *wusi*.] unsp. sting, smart.

wusuus (db; 2) See *wusu-₂*. vi. (dis.) sting, smart (as from medicine, insect bites). nu. (T2) a tree (*Excoecaria agallocha*). [Poisonous sap, whence its name; fruit used as medicine for eye trouble.] Syn. *owusuus, rowusuus, wiisuusu*.

Wusunang nu. (loc.) Ujelang Island and Atoll (Marshall Islands).

wussu- Var. of *wusu-₁*.

wuk (3a, 2) WUKA₁, WUKU₁. vi. go out of one's house for the first time in the morning; be doing the first thing of the morning. Dis. *wukkuk* (ds). With dir. suf.: *wukonong, wukonó, wukotá, wukotiw, wukoto, wukowu. iya kepwe wukonó iya?* where are you going first thing in the morning (said as an early morning greeting).

wukeey₁ See *wuk, -e-₂*. vo. (T6b) do (something) first thing or early in the morning. Syn. *owuka*. Cf. *wukkuk*.

wukeey₂ See *wuuk₁, -e-₂*. vo. (T6b) net, catch (something) in a net.

wukech (2) WUKECHI. nu. (T2) a species of large ant. *emén w.* one a. *wukechin Chuuk* Trukese a.

wukowuk₁ (db; 3) See *wuuk₁*. N. Var. *wukuuk₁*. nu. (T3) caul (in childbirth); web (of spider). *wukowuken eey monukón* this baby's c. *wukowuken ninnim* spider's w.

wukowuk₂ (db; 3) See *wuk*. N. Var. *wukuuk₂*. nu. (T3) matter in the eyes on waking in the morning. *wukowuken masan* m. in the eyes.

wukowukeyires (2) See *wukowuk₁, ráás*. nu. (T2) a variety of seaweed. *wukowukeyiresin Chuuk* Trukese s.

wukuuk₁ (db; 2) See *wuuk₁*. F. Var. *wukowuk₁*. nu. (T2) caul (in childbirth); web (of spider). *wukuukun eey monukón* this baby's c. *wukuukun ninnim* spider's w.

wukuuk₂ (db; 2) See *wuk*. F. Var. *wukowuk₂*. nu. (T2) matter in the eyes on waking in the morning. *wukuukun masan* m. in his eyes.

wukuché (1) nu. (T1) a large species of wrasse fish.

wukkó (1) See *wu-₁, kóókó*. [In reference and address.] nu. (T1) baby boy. Cf. *nikkó*.

wukkuk (ds; 2) See *wuk*. va. (dis.) do first thing in the morning. *iteyiten ráán siya w. tánnipi* every day we gardened first thing in the morning.

wumaané nu. (temp.) 19th night of the lunar month.

wumeposi (1) WUMEPOSII. Obs. (Jap. *umeboshi*) nu. (T1) pickled plum. *eféw w.* one p. *wochaan w.* his p.

wumw (2) See *wuumw*. vi. be put in an earth oven.

wumwes (2) WUMWESI. vi. be confused mentally; be crazy, insane, psychotic, out of one's mind, beside oneself. Dis. *wumwesimwes* (db) be confused, puzzled, troubled, bothered, beset. Syn. *pwuch*.

wumwesimwes Dis. of *wumwes*.

wumwowumw (db; 3) WUMWA. nu. (T3) hermit crab. *wumwowumwen Chuuk* Trukese h. c. *téén w.* h. crab's track, a design used in woodcarving.

wumwu-₁ (2) WUMWU₁. [In cpds. only.] unsp. envy. See *kkowumw, owumwuumw*.

wumwu-₂ (2) WUMWU₂. ni. (T2), suf. (cc.) 1. branching stalk (entire with its branches); stalk of bananas (with its fruit), cluster of pandanus fruit, stalk of branching coral. *ewumw, ruwowumw* or *rúwéwumw, wúnúwumw, féwumw* or *fowumw, nimewumw* or *nimowumw, wonowumw, fúúwumw, wanúwumw* or *wanuumw, ttiwewumw* or *ttiwowumw, engoon wumwun* one,...ten s. *wumwun wuuch* a s. of bananas. 2. branching vegetation. *wumwun rééré* (N.), *wumwun róóró* (F.) forest-overgrowth of leafy branches.

wumwuumw (db; 2) See *wumwu-₂*. vi. (dis.), adj. be many branched, dense, lush, thick (of vegetation or its fruit). *núú w.* coconut tree with abundant fruit.

wumwuutuut (db; 2) See *wuumw, wutuut*. nu. (T2) a kind of cooking with an earth oven (done with fermented breadfruit and involving splashing water on the oven). vi. cook in the *w.* manner.

wumwusómwoon (2) See *wuumw, sómwoon*. nu. (T2) presentation of food to a chief ("chiefly oven").

wumwukaw (3) See *wumwu-₂, awa-*. nu. (T3) a shrub (*Premna integrifolia*). [It is used in love magic, and its wood is used to make paddles.] *wumwukawen Chuuk* Trukese s. Syn. *niyóór*.

wumwuné (1) See *wuumw, nné₁*. nu. (T1) a species of reef fish. [It is prized as food.] *wumwunéén Chuuk* Trukese f.

wumwuni See *wuumw, -ni-*. vo. (T5) cook (something) in an earth oven; make earth ovens for (a chief). *raa w. sómwoon* they made e. o. for the chief.

Wumwuwa [Possibly *Wumwuwó*.] nu. (loc.) a clan name.

wun (2, 3) WUNU₁, WUNA₁. vi. be injured internally, be poisoned; be nauseated (from food).

wuna- (3) WUNA₂. [In cpds. only.] unsp. slice. See *wuneey, wunowun*.

Wunaap nu. a school of *itang* lore. [Its patron spirit is Éwúnfénú of the Wuun clan, and it is associated with Wuumaan Island.]

Wunanú nu. (loc.) Onari Island (Namonuito Atoll, known locally as *Wunaanú*).

wuneey See *wuna-, -e-₂*. vo. (T6b) slice.

wuni See *wu-₃, -ni-*. vo. (T5) pierce, put a hole in. Cf. *wunuun₁*.

wunimwoon Var. of *winimwoon*.

wuno- Var. of *wini-₁* (when followed by *wo-*).

wunooch (3) See *wuno-, wooch*. nu. (loc.; T3) (on) top of a reef. *siya nónnómw w.* we stayed on top of a r. Syn. *wóón wooch*.

wunowun (db; 3) See *wuna-*. va., vi. (dis.) slice; be sliced. *sipwe w. nippach* we shall s. squid. Cf. *wuneey*. nu. (T3) slicing. *wunowunen eey nippach* s. of this squid. *seningen w.* ear whose lobe has been cut and stretched.

wunóómw See *wu-₅*. nu. fish trap woven from grass.

wunu-₁ (2) See *wun*. ni. (T2) poison (of a substance). *wunun* its p.

wunu-₂ Var. of *wini-₁* (when followed by *wu-*).

wunu-₃ (2) See *wúnú-₁*. [In this form only in *wunuchchooch, wunuwut*.] pref. (num.) three.

wunuun₁ (db; 2) WUNU₂. [Apparnetly a back formation from *wuni*.] va., vi. (dis.) pierce; be pierced. nr. (T3) act of piercing. *wunuunun eey taka* p. of this ripe coconut.

wunuun₂ (db; 2) WUNU₃. n. (T2) appearance, what something looks like, shape, proportions (of people and things); character (of someone's actions). *wunuunun* its a. *wunuunun óómw fééfééer* the character of your actions. Syn. *nanganang, napanap₁*.

wunuun₃ (db; 2) WUNU₄. nu. (T2) a species of Lethrinid fish. *wunuunun Chuuk* Trukese f.

Wunuun₄ nu. (loc.) Ulul Island (Namonuito Atoll, known locally as *Wunowun*).

wunuunééch (2) See *wunuun₂, ééch*. vi. be well proportioned, well shaped.

wunuunungngaw (3) See *wunuun₂, ngngaw*. vi. be ill proportioned, badly shaped.

wunuung (3) See *wunu-₂, wuung*. n. (loc.; T3) top; high place, summit. *wunuungan* its t. *wunuungen chuuk* mountain top; *wunuung mékúrey* t. of my head.

Wunuungenota See *wini-₁, wuung*. [Also recorded as *Wunuunganata*.] nu. (loc.) traditional name of a ridge on Wééné (Moen) Island where government headquarters are located. [Said to derive from an *itang* twisting of *Wunuungen wootá* "high place of looking up," and to have been the traditional site of the *fanang* of Sowuwóóniiras. It is more commonly known by the Japanese name Nantakú.]

wunufeeyisin See *wu-₅, feeyisin*. nu. kind of wicker fish trap (conical with single entrance).

wunus (3, 2) WUNUSA, WUNUSU. n. (T3, T2) wholeness, entirety. *wunusan, wunusun* whole of him. *wunusen ááy káás meyinisin meyi nómw* the entire amount of all my gasoline remains (intact). *meyi wunusun eew rááń reem ne angaang* we work all day long ("it is the whole of one day for us at work"). *wunusen maram* full of the moon; *wunusen mwirinné* perfect, entirely good; *wunusen pwaapwa* absolutely or completely happy. vi., adj. (be) entire, whole; (be)full (of the moon). Dis. *wunusonus* (db) be absolutely whole, complete, perfectly intact. *rúwáánú w. ruwuuw nnewúnúngét* four and two thirds ("four entire two thirds").

wunuséech (2) See *wunus, ééch*. vi. be perfect.

wunusonus Dis. of *wunus*.

wunusungngaw (3) See *wunus, ngngaw*. vi. be completely bad.

wunupweewu (1) See *wu-₅, pwee-, -wu*. nu. (T1) large wicker fish trap (double entrance).

wunuchchooch (3) See *wunu-₃, chchooch*. num. three armfuls.

wunut (3, 2) WUNUTA, WUNUTU. nu. (T3, T2) lease rod of a loom. *efóch w.* one l. r. *wunuten* or *wunutun túúr* loom's l. r.

wunuwut (2) See *wunu-₃, wutu-*. num. 1. three cores (especially of breadfruit). 2. three chunks of cooked breadfruit.

wung (2) WUNGU. vi. be wrung out, be squeezed out by wringing (as coconut cream from grated coconut meat); be capable of having fluid content wrung out. Cf. *wúchú-₂*.

wungeni See *wuung, -ni-*. vo. (T6a) put a ridgepole on, provide with a ridgepole.

wungowung (db; 3a) See *wuung*. vi. (dis.) be high, lofty. With dir. suf.: *wungowungotá*. ni. (T3) summit, high point.

wungowungotá See *wungowung*.

wunguung (db; 2) See *wung*. va. (dis.) wring (fluid from something). n. (T2) wringing.

wungupaat (3) See *wung, paat₂*. nu. (T3) any medicinal potion made from the squeezings of bark, fruit, or other substances.

wunguti See *wung, -ti-*. vo. (T5) wring (something liquid) from something. *w. arúng* w. coconut cream (from grated coconut meat). Cf. *wunguung*.

wupw (2) WUPWU₁. vi. be fertile (of people), have increase; increase (in numbers of people). Dis. *wuupw* (ds). *aa wuupw ewe eterekes (ewe fénú)* the lineage (the island) has a high birthrate; *aa wuupw néwún átewe* that fellow has many children. Cf. *wuupw₁*.

wupweyinen (2) See *wuupw₂, -nen*. n. (T2) yaws of the throat or of the interior of the nose; sinusitis. [Believed traditionally to have been caused by chronic suppressed anger.] *wupweyinenin* his s. vi. develop yaws of the throat or nose.

wupwowupw (db; 3) See *wuupw₂*. nu. (T3) hill, mound.

wupwu-₁ (2) WUPWU₂. [In cpds. only.] unsp., suf. (cc.) breast. *ewupw, ruwowupw, wúnúwupw, féwupw, nimewupw, wonowupw, fúúwupw, wanúwupw, ttiwewupw, engoon owupwun* one,...ten breasts. Cf. *owupw*.

wupwu-₂ (2) WUPWU₃. [In cpds. only.] unsp. stabbed (with a knife).

wupwuupw (db; 2) See *wupwu*-₂. va., vi. stab (with a knife); be stabbed. *meyi feet? meyi w. reen saar* what's happening? he's stabbed by a knife.

wupwuffengen (2) See *wupwu*-₁, *ffengen*. vi. be breast-to-breast (of chickens in fighting). Cf. *wupwuri*.

wupwunuwén (2) See *wuupw*₁, *wénú*-. vi. be fatherless ("child of the bush").

wupwuri See *wupwu*-₁, *-ri*-. vo. (T5) approach (another) with breast forward (as a chicken in fighting). Cf. *wupwuffengen*.

wupwut (3) WUPWUTA. nu. (T3) 1. young coconut leaf (still light in color). *memin w.* midrib of a c. l. *wupwuten núú* coconut tree's l. 2. skirt made of young coconut leaves. [It is worn in dancing by both sexes.] *ékkénúk w.* wear a leaf skirt.

wupwutiw (3) See *wupw*, *-tiw*. vi. be born. n. (T3) birth. *wupwutiwan* his b.

wur₁ (3) WURA₁. vi. be full, filled. Dis. *wurowur* (db). With dir. suf.: *wurowu* full to overflowing; *wurowurotá* be too full, heapingly full.

wur₂ (2) WURU₁. vi. visit, take a walk or stroll; loaf, play. Dis. *wuruur* (db, the common form). Syn. *kunow*.

wuriimw (3) See *wur*₂, *iimw*. nu. (T3) paying court to women in other communities, woman stealing. [A traditional cause of war.]

wuroseni See *wur*₁, *seni*₂. vo. (T2) overflow from; be too much (big) for, be the overflow of.

wuropessúkúnó (1) See *wur*₁, *pa*-₁, *ssúk*₂, *-nó*. vi. overflow with a splash.

wuropworopwor Var. of *wúrépworopwor*.

wurowu See *wur*₁.

wurowur (db; 3) See *wur*₁. nu. (T3) fullness. With dir. suf.: *wurowurotá* over-fullness. vi. Dis. of *wur*₁.

wurowurotá See *wur*₁, *wurowur*.

wuru-₁ (2) WURU₂. [In cpds. only.] unsp. (u.m.) See *wurupap*, *wurupwin*, *wurusé*.

wuru-₂ (2) WURU₃. [In cpds. only.] unsp. separated with difficulty. See *wurufutuk*.

wuru-₃ (2) WURU₄. [In cpds. only.] unsp. inspected, examined, revealed. See *owuruur*, *wuruwo*. Cf. *wúri*₁.

wuruur₁ (db; 2) See *wur*₂. nu. (T2) visiting, excursion, amusement. vi. (dis.) go visiting. Syn. *kukkunow*.

wuruur₂ (db; 2) WURU₅. va. (dis.) gather (sugarcane only).

wurufutuk (3) See *wuru*-₂, *futuk*. vi. have flesh difficult to separate from bones (of fish); be still treasured after having been given away (of prized possessions); be grudgingly given, not eastily parted with.

wurusé (1) See *wuru*-₁, *sé* (?). nu. (T1) a tree (*Schefflera kraemeri* Harms., *Brassias actinophylla*).

wurumé (1) See *wur*₂, *méé*-₂. vi. be treated roughly (of people and animals), manhandled, jostled, pushed about.

wurumwmwot (3, 2) See *wur*₂, *-mwmwot*. vi. play about, have fun, fool around. Syn. *táy*. nu. entertainment, show, game.

wurumwmwoteey See *wurumwmwot*, *-e*-₂. vo. (T6b) tease, make sport of, make fun of. Syn. *táyiri*, *wurumwmwotiiti*.

wurumwmwotiiti See *wurumwmwot*, *-iti*. vo. (T2) tease, make sport of, make fun of. Syn. *táyiri*, *wurumwmwoteey*.

wurungngaw (3) See *wur*₂, *ngngaw*. vi. overengage in sexual incourse to the detriment of one's health.

wurupap (3) See *wuru*-₁, *paap* (?). nu. (T3) a species of bird (black and white striped, migratory). *wurupapen Chuuk* Trukese b.

wurupwin (2) See *wuru*-₁, *-pwin*. nu. (T2) a Lethrinid fish.

wuruwo (1) See *wuru*-₃, *-wo*₂. nu. (T1) origin legend, history. *wuruwoon eey fénú* history of this island. vi. argue about or discuss a legend or history.

wuruwooni See *wuruwo*, *-ni*-. vo. (T4) tell the history of.

wucha- N. var. of *wocha*-₂.

wuchaa- N. var. of *wochaa*-₁.

wuchiirek (2) See *wuuch*₁, *-rek*₂. nu. (T2) a variety of banana. [Traditionally reserved for chiefs and *itang*.]

wuchuuch (db; 2) WUCHU₁. n. (T2) foot, paw. *wuchuuchun* his f.

wuchupwech (3) See *wuuch*₁, *pwech*. nu. (T3) a variety of banana. [Traditionally reserved for chiefs and *itang*.]

wuchutopw (2) See *wuuch*₁, *topw*. nu. (T2) a variety of banana.

wuchuyaaya (1) See *wuuch*₁, *aaya*. nu. (T1) a variety of banana. [Its fiber is

used for thread in traditional loom weaving.]
wute (1) WUTEE. nu. (T1) a species of fish (8 to 10 inches long).
wuti See *wu-₄, -ti-*. vo. (T5) throw or splash water on (something, e.g. an earth oven to make it steam). Cf. *wutuut.*
wutong (Jap. *udon*) nu. noodles, noodles cooked in water or coconut milk. *eföch w.* one n. *anan w.* his n.
wutu- (2) See *wuut₂*. ni. (T2), suf. (cc.) core, interior, inside (of people, animals, fruit, things); chunk of cooked breadfruit. *ewut, ruwowut* or *rúwowut, wunuwut, fowut, nimewut, wonowut, fuuwut, wanuwut, ttiwowut, engoon wutun* one,....ten c. (in counting breadfruit cores or chunks). *wutun* its c.
wutuut (db; 2) WUTU₁. [Presumably a back formation from *wuti*.] va., vi. splash with water; be splashed upon. nu. (T2) splashing.
wutumas (3) See *wutuut, maas₃*. vi. throw or splash water on one's face.
wutteni See *wuut₁, -ni-*. vo. (T6a) acquire as a meeting house or boat house. Cf. *wuttowut.*
Wutteres See *wuut₁, ráás (?)*. [Bollig] nu. (loc.) name of the god Wonofáát's meeting house in heaven. [It is associated with war.] Cf. *resiim.*
wuttowut (db; 3) See *wuut₁*. va. (dis.) use as a meeting house or boat house. Cf. *wutteni.*
wuwa-₁ (3a) WUWA₂. [In cpds. only.] Var. *wa-*. unsp. convey, ship, carry from one place to another. See *wuweey, wuweyi, wuwoow.*
wuwa-₂ (3) WUWA₃. [In cpds. only.] unsp. tendon (?). See *wuwóór.*
wuwa (1v) WUWAA. n. (T1v) fruit, berry. *eféw w.* one f. *wuwaan* its f. *wuwáán aaw* banyan fruit; a variety of breadfruit. *wuwáán wooch* cat's eye (operculum of the turban shell, syn. *épwpwénún omos). mwmwen w.* first fruits. vi. bear fruit or berries; be fruitful, in fruit.
wuwaanong See *wuweyi.*
wuwaatá See *wuweyi.*
wuwaato See *wuweyi.*
wuwaawu See *wuweyi.*
wuwaayéech (2: *-yéchchú-*) See *wuwa, éech*. vi. bear good or plentiful fruit. nu. (T2) bearing good or plentiful fruit.
wuwas (3) WUWASA. nu. (T3) grass cover that is laid on top of food that has already been covered by leaves (*masaché*) in an earth oven. *wuwasen wuumw* ovens g. c.
wuwaseey See *wuwas, -e-₂*. vo. (T6b) lay a grass cover on (an earth oven). Syn. *wuwaseni.*
wuwaseni See *wuwas, -ni-*. vo. (T6a) lay a grass cover on (an earth oven). Syn. *wuwaseey.*
wuwangngaw (3) See *wuwa, ngngaw*. vi. bear poor or little fruit. nu. (T3) bearing poor or little fruit.
wuwap (3) WUWAPA. nu. (T3) a species of large fish. *wuwapen Chuuk* Trukese f.
wuwapw (3) WUWAPWPWA. F. Var. *kuwapw*. nu. (T3) growing tip of the palm or banana. *wuwapwpwen núú* coconut palm's g. t. Syn. *machang*. Cf. *éyirúk.*
wuwapwpweey See *wuwapw, -e-₂*. Var. *wopwpweey*. vo. (T6b) cut off the growing tip of (a palm or banana tree).
wuwaw (3) WUWAWA. nu. (T3) monarch bird of Truk. [According to legend it acquired its black markings on its head and around its beak because it ate a squid and was stained by its ink.] *wuwawen Chuuk* Trukese m. b.
Wuwáánikar nu. (loc.) a clan name.
wuwáánúúw₁ See *wuwa, -úw*. nu. a tree (*Barringtonia asiatica*). [Fruit used for fish poison and to cauterize wounds.] Syn. *kuun, sóón₁.*
Wuwáánúúw₂ nu. (loc.) a clan name.
wuwáánpóron (Pon.) nu. a Protestant pastor who has served twenty-five years and celebrated his jubilee; apostle, disciple of Jesus.
wuwáátá See *wuweyi.*
wuwáátiw See *wuweyi.*
wuweey See *wuwa-₁, -e-₂*. Var. *wuweyi*. vo. (T6b) convey, carry, transport, take, bring; drive (an automobile or motor boat). With dir. suf.: *wuweyenong, wuweeyenó, wuweeyetá, wuweeyetiw, wuweeyeto*. *epwe wuweerenó eey waa* this canoe will carry them away.
wuweeyenong See *wuweey.*
wuweeyenó See *wuweey.*

wuweeyetá See *wuweey.*
wuweeyetiw See *wuweey.*
wuweeyeto See *wuweey.*
wuweyaanong See *wuweyi.*
wuweyaatá See *wuweyi.*
wuweyaato See *wuweyi.*
wuweyaawu See *wuweyi.*
wuweyáátá See *wuweyi.*
wuweyáátiw See *wuweyi.*
wuweyi See *wuwa-$_1$, -yi-$_2$.* Var. *wuweey.* vo. (T6a) convey, carry, transport, take, bring; drive (an automobile or motor boat). Dis. *wukkuweyi* (ds). With dir. suf.: *wuweyaanong, wuweyóónó, wuweyaatá* or *wuweyáátá, wuweyáátiw, wuweyaato, wuweyaawu.* With dir. suf. and 3sg. obj. only: *wuwaanong* or *waanong, wuwóónó* or *wóónó, wuwaatá* or *wuwáátá* or *waatá* or *wáátá, wuwáátiw* or *wáátiw, wuwaato* or *waato, wuwaawow* or *waawow, wuwaawu* or *waawu. epwe wuyeyiirenó eey waa* this canoe will carry them away.
wuweyóónó See *wuweyi.*
wuwoow (db; 3a) See *wuwa-$_1$.* [Presumably from an older **wuwowu,* see *wuwowuwa-*.] Var. *wuwow.* va. (dis.) convey, carry, transport, tote. With dir. suf.: *wuwoowonong, wuwoowonó, wuwoowotá, wuwoowotiw, wuwoowoto, wuwoowowu.*
wuwoowonong See *wuwoow.*
wuwoowonó See *wuwoow.*
wuwoowotá See *wuwoow.*
wuwoowotiw See *wuwoow.*
wuwoowoto See *wuwoow.*
wuwoowowu See *wuwoow.*
wuwofóós (4) See *wuwa-$_1$, fóós.* vi. tattle, tell tales, gossip. nu. (T2) tattling, tale bearing, gossiping. *chóón w.* tale bearer, tattler.
wuwokis (2) WUWOKISI. n. (T2) verse, stanza (in the Bible, in a song). *wuwokisin eew* first v.
wuwokurukur (2) See *wuwa-$_1$, kurukur.* nu. (T2) a dance performed with orangewood staves. Syn. *tukuyá.*
wuwopwangapwang (3) See *wuwa-$_1$, pwanga-$_1$.* vi. be listless, uncooperative, making no effort.
wuwopwpwach (3) See *wuwa-$_1$, pwpwach.* vi. be lackadaisical, diffident, uninterested, enthusiastic.

wuwochchow (2) See *wuwa-$_1$, chchow.* vi. be heavy laden, loaded heavily.
wuwow Var. of *wuwoow.*
wuwóónó See *wuweyi.*
wuwóór (4) See *wuwa-$_2$, óór.* n. (T2) shin (front of leg between knee and ankle). *wowóórun* his s. *chúún w.* s. bone, fibula.
wú-$_1$ (2) WÚ$_1$. pref. (sub.) 1sg. sub. prn.: I. [Although a prefix, it is written separately except when followed by an aspect marker. Sub. prns. are used only at the beginning of narrative constructions and mark them as such.] *wúpwaapw* (indefinite future), *wúpwe* (future), *wúpwene* (uncertain future), *wúsapw* (future negative), *wúse* (negative reality), *wúte* (purposeful future negative), *wúwa* (reality).
wú-$_2$ Var. of *wi-.*
wú-$_3$ (2) WÚ$_2$. [In cpds. only.] unsp. dip out, ladle. See *wúf, wúfi.*
wú-$_4$ (2) WÚ$_3$. [In cpds. only.] unsp. attend, aware, have in mind. See *wúri$_1$, wúrú-$_1$.*
wú-$_5$ (2) WÚ$_4$. [In cpds. only.] unsp. haul, pull. See *wúr, wúri$_2$.*
wú-$_6$ (2) WÚ$_5$. [In cpds. only.] unsp. string. See *wúri$_4$, wúrúúr$_3$.*
wú-$_7$ (2) WÚ$_6$. [In cpds. only.] unsp. pound, mash with a pestle. See *wúsi, wúsúús.*
-wú- (2) WÚ$_3$. [Occurs in this form after bases ending in *éé.*] Var. *-u-, -ú-, -wu-.* suf. (v.form.) make an object focussed verb (vo.) of the base. *ngééwú* suck (*ngéénge* sucking).
wú$_1$ (3a) WÚWA$_1$. vi. be complied with, respected, observed, honored (of a tabu, law, or prohibition).
wú$_2$ (1) WÚÚ$_1$. vi. be stopped, halted (concretely, of moving things). *aa wú ewe chitoosa* the car has stopped. With dir. suf.: *wúúnó* be stopped, halted, ceased, ended (figuratively as well as concretely). *aa wúúnó aach angaang* our work has ceased.
wú$_3$ (2) WÚÚ$_2$. vi. stand erect, be upright. *aa wú ewe mwáán* the man stood. With dir. suf.: *wúútá* stand up.
wúú$_1$ [Possibly derived from *wú-$_1$* plus *wú$_1$.*] interj. I agree; yes (in confirmation of a positive statement), no (in confirmation of a negative statement).

wúú₂ (3) WÚWA₂. n. (T3) neck. wúwan his n. úkún wúwan back or nape of his n. Cf. chiyor, neewú, núkúnúú.

wúú₃ (1) WÚÚ₃. nu. (T1) name of the high, central, unrounded vowel written ú; name of the letter thus written.

wúúf (3) WÚFA. n. (T3) garment that drapes or covers the upper part of the body; dress, shirt, jacket, coat, etc. eché w. one g. wúfan his g. péwún w. sleeve (fo shirt, coat, etc.).

wúúk₁ (2) WÚKÚ₄. n. (T2), suf. (cc.) tail, rear end. ewúk, rúwéwúk, wúnúwúk, féwúk, niméwúk, wonéwúk, fúúwúk, wanúwúk, ttiwéwúk, engoon wúkún one,...ten t. wúkún its t. Cf. maach.

wúúk₂ (2) WÚKKÚ. n. (T2), suf. (cc.) nail, fingernail, toenail, claw. ewúk, rúwéwúk, wúnúwúk, féwúk, niméwúk, wonéwúk, fúúwúk, wanúwúk, ttiwéwúk, engoon wúkkún one,...ten nails or claws. wúkkún his n. wúkkún kattu cat's claw.

wúúk₃ (2) WÚKÚ₅ (?). nu. (T2) white-tailed tropic bird or bo'sun bird (*Phaethon lepturus*).

Wúúmeeyón See wú₁ (?), mee-, -ón. nu. (pers.) spirit of the late afternoon (nekkunuyón). [It makes infants sick; therefore women traditionally avoided carrying their infants outside of the house in the late afternoon.]

wúún₁ (3) WÚNA₂. n. (T3), suf. (cc.) hair (of head or body, of person or animal), fur, feather, scale (of fish). ewún, rúwéwún, wúnúwún, féwún, niméwún, wonowún, fúúwún, wanúwún, ttiwewún, engoon wúnan one,...ten h. wúnan his h. wúnen maan animal h., fur, wool, feather; wúnen siipw wool. wúnen kattu cat's paw fern (*Lycopodium cernuum*, "cat's hair").

wúún₂ (3) WÚNA₃. nu. (T3) 1. rope used to pull a tree in a desired direction when chopping it down. wúnen eey irá r. for this tree. 2. a vine (*Derris elliptica*). [It is used as a rope to haul logs and as fish poison.] Syn. wúúp. 3. aerial root of the mangrove. 4. (Itang) chief (from the metaphor wúnen fénú).

wúún₃ (2: wúnú-, wunu-) WÚNÚ₅. nu. (T2) extreme part, top. wúnún chuuk mountain top; wúnún éwú masthead; wúnún fénú cape, point (of an island); wúnún irá tree top; wúnún máchew spear point; wúnún panen irá branch end. Cf. wún₂, wúnúún₂, wúnúún₃.

wúún₄ (3) WÚNNA. n. (T3) pillow, head rest. wúnnan his p. wúnnen pachaaw the light shell remains of a marin animal that float on the water ("shark's pillow").

wúún₅ (dc; 2) See wúún₂. va. use a rope to pull a tree in a desired direction when chopping it down. Cf. wún₄.

wúúnó See wú₂.

wúúngeni See wú₂, ngeni. vo. (T2) stop for. aa w. kkeey paasiisé he stopped for these passengers.

wúúp (3) WÚPA. nu. (T3) a vine (*Derris elliptica*). [Its roots and stems are used for fish poison, and the long vine is used as rope to haul logs.] wúpen Chuuk Trukese v. Syn. wúún₂. Cf. -úw.

wúúr₁ (3) WÚRA₂. nu. (T3) langusta, Japanese spiny lobster (*Panulirus japonicus* von Siebold). wúren Chuuk Trukese l.

wúúr₂ (3) WÚRA₃. nu. (T3) supporting post. wúren iimw corner post of a house, upright timber supporting the wall plate.

wúút₁ (2) WÚTTÚ. [Presumably a back formation from wútti.] vi. be pulled out, drawn out, extracted (as a tooth, or a nail from a board). With dir. suf.: wúttúnó, wúttúwu. aa wúttúnó futuken átánaan that fellow has lost weight.

wúút₂ (3) WÚTA₂. nu. (T3) rain. wúten ikenáy today's r. chénún w. rain water (as in a cistern); chénún fáán w. raindrops (as they fall on one). aa púng w. the r. falls. Syn. ráán₁.

wúútá See wú₃.

wúúwenewen (3) See wú₃, wenewen. vi. stand up straight.

wúf (2) See wú-₃, -fi-. [Presumably a back formation from wúfi.] vi. be dipped out, scooped up, ladled out (of liquids).

wúfeni See wúúf, -ni-. vo. (T6a) acquire as an upper garment. Cf. wúféwúf.

wúféwúf (db; 3) See wúúf. va. (dis.) wear, use, borrow (an upper garment). Cf. wúfeni.

wúfi See wú-₃, -fi-. vo. (T5) dip out, scoop up, ladle out (a liquid). Cf. wúfúúf.

wúfúúf (db; 2) See *wúf.* va. (dis.) dip out, scoop up, ladle out (liquids). Cf. *wúfi.*

wúsangi (1) WÚSANGII. (Jap.) nu. (T1) rabbit. *emén w.* one r. Syn. *rapich.*

wúsen (2) WÚSENI. nu. (T2) 1. sand flea. *wúsenin Chuuk* Trukese s. f. 2. (F.) a species of scorpion fish. Syn. *íneyinó.*

wúsi See *wú-₇, -si-.* vo. (T5) pound, grind, or mash (something) with a pestle or pounder. Cf. *wúsúús.*

wúsúús (db; 2) WÚSÚ. [Presumably a back formation from *wúsi.*] va. pound or mash with a pestle. nu. (T2) 1. pounding or mashing with a pestle. *wúsúúsún kkón* p. of breadfruit pudding. 2. (F.) pestle, breadfruit pounder. *aan w., néwún w.* his p. Syn. *pwpwo₂.*

wússa- (3) WÚSSA. [In cpds. only.] unsp. height. See *wússeyisómw.*

wússeyisómw nu. house or meeting house whose crossbeam is high enough to give considerable head clearance for someone standing upright ("chief's height"). [One of the *chimwenúúren iimw.*]

wúk (2) See *wúúk₁* or *wúkú-₂.* vi. end, terminate. With dir. suf.: *wúkútiw* terminate, come to an end.

Wúkeecheni nu. (pers.) name of a Fesinimw woman who was the mother of Woonap, legendary hero of Wuumaan (Uman) Island.

wúkiiti See *wúkú-₁, -iti.* vo. (T2) be as much as, be as big as, be equal to (in amount or size).

wúkú-₁ (2) WÚKÚ₁. [In cpds. only.] unsp. measure, amount. See *éwúkú, éwúkúúk, wúkúúk₁.*

wúkú-₂ (2) WÚKÚ₂. [In cpds. only.] unsp. chopped off, lopped off. See *wúkúfi, wúkúúk₂.*

wúkúúk₁ (db; 2) See *wúkú-₁.* n. (T2) size, amount, extent, quantity, quality. *wúkúúkún* his s., its amount. *wúkúúkún chék* just so much and no more, exact amount; *wúkúúkún tekiya* height. *ifa wúkúúkún nowumw mwooni?* how much money do you have? what is the extent of your money? *ifa wúkúúkún faansowun óómw sukuun?* how long have you attended school? vi. be of a (specified) amount, measure (a specified amount). *w. ffengen* be of the same size, quantity, or quality.

wúkúúk₂ (db; 2) See *wúkú-₂.* va., vi. cut off, chop off, lop off (as with an axe); be cut, chopped, or lopped off. nu. (T2) chopping.

-wúkúúk (db; 2) WÚKÚ₃. [In cpds. only.] unsp. vibrate heavily, shake. See *pwéwúkúúk.*

wúkúúkééch (2) See *wúkúúk₁, ééch.* vi. 1. be the right size or quantity, be an appropriate size. 2. be moderate, temperate (as in drinking).

wúkúfi See *wúkú-₂, -fi-.* vo. (T5) cut off, chop off, lop off.

Wúkúniik See *wúúk₁, iik.* nu. (loc.) name of a star of constellation (Cassiopeia, "fish's tail"). *táán W., tonen W.* positions on the traditional sidereal compass used in navigation.

wúkúngeni See *wúkú-₁, ngeni.* vo. (T2) be as much as, compare favorably with, measure up to. Dis. *wúkúúk ngeni* (db).

wúkúngngaw (3) See *wúkú-₁, ngngaw.* vi. be insufficient (in amount), not enough. nu. (T3) a bad or insufficient amount, insufficiency. *wúkúngngawen aach ómónnááta* the insufficiency of our preparing it.

wúkúpar (3) See *wúúk₁, par.* nu. (T3) a bird (with green body and red tail). Syn. *nikitirúúng, niwúkúpar, túrin wén.*

wúkúpwech (2) See *wúúk₁, pwech.* N. Var. *niwúkúpwech.* nu. (T2) a species of trigger fish. *emén w.* one t. f. *wúkúpwechin* t. f. of (a given region).

wúkúché (1) See *wúúk₁, chéé.* nu. (T1) a species of wrasse fish. *wúkúchéén Chuuk* Trukese w. f.

wúkúchchen (2) See *wúúk₁, chchen₂.* nu. (T2) a species of goatfish. *wúkúchchenin Chuuk* Trukese g.

wúkútiw See *wúk.*

wúkúttumw (2) See *wúkú-₁, ttumw₃.* vi. be insufficient, not enough (of things). *meyi w. eey irá* this timber is not long enough. nu. (T2) insufficiency. *wúkúttumwun eey irá* i. of this timber.

wúkkún Dis. of *wún₁.*

wúkkúrá Dis. of *wúrá.*

wúma- (3a) WÚMA. [In cpds. only.] unsp. shape; character. See *éwúma, wúméwúm.*

wúméwúm (db; 3a) See *wúma-.* n. (T3) shape; character. *wúméwúman* his s. *meyi feet wúméwúman?* what is its s.?

wúméwúméech (db; 2) See *wúméwúm, éech*. vi., adj. (be) of pleasing shape, well-shaped; (be) lovely. *w. ngeni* (vo. phr.) be kind to, be merciful to, do good to.

wúméwúméngngaw (db; 3) See *wúméwúm, ngngaw*. vi. be of unpleasant shape, ill-shaped. *w. ngeni* (vo. phr.) be unkind to, be unmerciful to, do evil to.

wún₁ (2) WÚNÚ₁. va. drink; smoke (tobacco); take (medicine). Dis. *wúkkún* (ds). *wúwa w. sáfey* I took medicine (unspecified as to amount); *wúwa w. ewe suupwa* I smoked from the cigarette (unspecified amount); *wúse wúkkún piyé* I don't drink beer. *ewe w. nánew* that drinking yesterday. Cf. *wúnúmi*.

wún₂ (2) WÚNÚ₂. vi. be ended, terminated; lifted (of a taboo). *wúnún ewe róóng* lifting of the taboo for the dead. Cf. *wúún₃*.

wún₃ (3a) WÚNA₁. vi. stretch, be stretched (of the body). With dir. suf.: *wúnénó* rear back (as a child being carried). Syn. *aawúún*. Cf. *aawúnna, ewúnna*.

wún₄ (2) See *wúún₂*. vi. be agreed or united in the chief's name. *meyi w. eey fénú* this island is a. Cf. *wúún₅*.

Wúnaap nu. a school of *itang* associated with Wuumaan (Uman) Island.

wúnapwe (1) See *wúún₂, pwee₁*. vi. tie knots in a coconut leaf for divining purposes.

wúnaw (3) WÚNAWA. nu. (T3) breakfast. *sipwe áni w. kkón* we shall eat a b. of breadfruit pudding. vi. eat breakfast.

wúneey See *wúún₂, -e-₂*. vo. (T6b) use a rope on (a tree) to pull it in a desired direction when chopping it down. Cf. *wúún₅*.

wúnefi See *wúún₁, -fi-*. vo. (T6a) pluck (feathers, hair).

wúnenipot (3) See *wúún₂, potopot*. nu. (T3) a vine (*Derris trifoliata*). *wúnenipoten* v. of (a given region). Syn. *wúpenipot*.

wúné- (4) WÚNÉ. [In cpds. only.] unsp. whirl, twirl. See *ewúna, ewúnúún*.

wúnénó₁ (1) See *wúún₁, -nó*. vi. be rendered hairless, be plucked of feathers.

wúnénó₂ See *wún₃*.

wúnéwún Dis. of *wúún₁*.

wúningách Var. of *winingách*.

wúnoop (3) WÚNOOPA. nu. (T3) lower and flaring part of a breadfruit pounder. *wúnoopen eey wúsúús* lower part of this pounder.

wúnú-₁ (2) WÚNÚ₃. Var. *wunu-₄, ini-₁*. pref. (num.) three. See *iniik, wunuchchooch, wunuwut, wúnúchamw, wúnúchchi, wúnúchef, wúnúché, wúnúchú, wúnúchúk, wúnúféw, wúnúffaat, wúnúffit, wúnúfich, wúnúfóch, wúnúfutuk, wúnúngaf, wúnúngát, wúnúngéréw, wúnúngin, wúnúkis, wúnúkit, wúnúkkamw, wúnúkkap, wúnúkkumw, wúnúkum, wúnúkumwuch, wúnúkup, wúnúmach, wúnúmas, wúnúmataf, wúnúmech, wúnúmeech, wúnúmeet, wúnúmén, wúnúmma, wúnúmmech, wúnúmmék, wúnúmwénú, wúnúmwmwun, wúnúmwmwú, wúnúmwmwún, wúnúmwu, wúnúmwú₁, wúnúmwú₂, wúnúmwúch, wúnúnnú, wúnúpa, wúnúpachang, wúnúpan, wúnúpeche, wúnúpeek, wúnúpé, wúnúpék, wúnúpéw, wúnúpino, wúnúpinúk, wúnúpu, wúnúpwang, wúnúpwey, wúnúpwéét, wúnúpwi, wúnúpwin, wúnúpwopw, wúnúpwór, wúnúpwpwaaw, wúnúpwpwún₁, wúnúpwúkú, wúnúpwún, wúnúsap, wúnúsángá, wúnúsáwá, wúnúseeng, wúnúsen, wúnúsópw₁, wúnúsópw₂, wúnússaar, wúnússak, wúnússar, wúnússáát, wúnússát, wúnússupw, wúnútinewupw, wúnútip, wúnútit, wúnúttiit, wúnúttún, wúnútú, wúnútúkúm, wúnútún, wúnúúwéw, wúnúwo, wúnúwoch, wúnúwumw, wúnúwupw, wúnúwúk₁, wúnúwúk₂, wúnúwút, wúnúyaf, wúnúyang, wúnúyef, wúnúyem, wúnúyé, wúnúyék, wúnúyi, wúnúyin₁, wúnúyin₂, wúnúyipw, wúnúyiyey, wúnúyowut, wúnúyó, wúnúyóch*. Cf. *één₁*.

wúnú-₂ (2) WÚNÚ₄ (*ÉNÚ). [In cpds. only.] unsp. thick (of flat objects). See *maanúún*.

wúnú-₃ (2) WÚNÚ₅. [In cpds. only.] unsp. breadfruit. See *wúnúmar, wúnniinaf, wúnnúpwún*.

wúnú-₄ Var. of *wini-₁*.

wúnú-₅ (3) WÚNÚ₆. [In cpds. only.] Var. *wúnnú-₁*. unsp. lie, sleep. See *wúnni, wúnnúfátán, wúnúún₁*. Cf. *won*.

wúnú-₆ (2) WÚNÚ₇. [In cpds. only.] unsp. drawn out, extracted. See *wútti*.

wúnúún₁ (db; 2) See *wúnú*-₅. vi. (dis.) be numb, asleep (of arm or leg); be anaesthetized. nr. (T2) numbness. *wúnúúnún pecheey* n. of my leg.

wúnúún₂ (db; 3) See *wúún*₃. n. (T3) tip, physical extremity, highest point, top. *wúnúúnan* its t. *wúnúúnen chuuk* mountain top; *wúnúúnen irá* tree top; *wúnúúnen éwú* masthead. Cf. *wúnúún*₃.

wúnúún₃ (db; 2, 3) See *wúún*₃. nu. (T2, T3) projection (of land or reef into the sea, of tree branch); cape, point (of land). *wúnúúnún, wúnúúnen* p. of. *siya pwenniiy wúnúúnen Chéésinifé* we rounded the tip of Chéésinife. Cf. *wúnúún*₂.

wúnúúnowu (db; 1) See *wúnúún*₃, -*wu*. vi. project out, extend or stick far out (as a cape, point of land, tree branch). *neyi w. naan panen irá* that tree branch sticks far out. nu. (T1) long projection. *wúnúúnowuun fénú* point of land (of fringing reef).

wúnúúch (3) See *wúnú*-₄, *chche*-₁. n. (loc.; T3) skin, bark, outer part of something (as distinct from wrapping). *wúnúchchan* his s.

wúnúúwéw (2) See *wúnú*-₁, -*wúwéw*. num. three amounts of fermented breadfruit suitable for kneading.

wúnúféw (2) See *wúnú*-₁, -*féw*. num. three lumps or globular objects (e.g., stones, balls, fruit).

wúnúfich (3a) See *wúnú*-₁, *ficha*-. num. three strips of coconut, pandanus, or other palm leaf prepared for plaiting mats.

wúnúfóch (4) See *wúnú*-₁, *fóchu*-. num. three long objects (e.g., sticks, vehicles, legs, teeth, timbers, shovels).

wúnúfutuk (3) See *wúnú*-₁, *futuk*. num. three pieces of meat.

wúnúffaat (3) See *wúnú*-₁, *ffaata*-. num. three strings of fish.

wúnúffit (3) See *wúnú*-₁, *fitta*-. num. three leaf packages of small fish.

wúnúsap (3) See *wúnú*-₁, *saap*. num. three cheeks (especially of fish).

wúnúsángá (1) See *wúnú*-₁, *sángá*. num. three basketfuls of fish. Syn. *wúnúsáwá*.

wúnúsáwá (1) See *wúnú*-₁, *sáwá*. num. three basketfuls of fish. Syn. *wúnúsángá*.

wúnúseeng (3) See *wúnú*-₁, *seeng*. num. three lengths between joints.

wúnúsen (2) See *wúnú*-₁, -*sen*. num. three coils of rope. [Each coil is 30 to 100 fathoms long according to local custom.]

wúnúsópw₁ (4) See *wúnú*-₁, *sópwu*-₂. num. three segments.

wúnúsópw₂ (4) See *wúnú*-₁, *sópwu*-₃. num. three burdens of tied together breadfruit.

wúnússaar (2) See *wúnú*-₁, -*ssaar*. Var. *wúnússar*. num. three slices.

wúnússak (3) See *wúnú*-₁, *ssaka*-. num. three pieces of copra.

wúnússar N. of *wúnússaar*.

wúnússáát (2, 3) See *wúnú*-₁, -*ssáát*. Var. *wúnússát*. num. three slivers, longitudinal slices, splinters.

wúnússát N. of *wúnússáát*.

wúnússupw (2) See *wúnú*-₁, *ssupwu*-. num. three tiny drops.

wúnúkis (2) See *wúnú*-₁, *kisi*-. num. three little things or bits. Syn. *wúnúngin*.

wúnúkit (3) See *wúnú*-₁, -*kit*. num. thirty thousand.

wúnúkum (2) See *wúnú*-₁, *kumu*-. num. three mouthfuls or swallows of liquid.

wúnúkumwuch (2) See *wúnú*-₁, *kumwuch*. num. three fistfuls or handfuls (of something); three hooves, paws, feet (of animals).

wúnúkkamw (3b) See *wúnú*-₁, *kkamw*. num. three fragments or pieces (of cloth, paper).

wúnúkkap (3) See *wúnú*-₁, *kkap*. num. three cupfuls.

wúnúkkumw (2, 3) See *wúnú*-₁, *kkumw*₁. num. three portions of premasticated food.

wúnúkkú- (2) See *wúnú*-₄, *kúkkú*-. ni. (loc.; T2) immediate proximity; beside, next to, close to. *wúnúkkún* next to him.

wúnúma- (3) See *wún*₁, -*ma*-. ni. (T3) drink, smoke, thing to be drunk or smoked (by someone). *wúnúmey, wúmúmwomw, wúnúman* my, your, his d. *wúnúmen naan áát* that boy's d.

wúnúmas (3) See *maas*₃. num. three goggle lenses or other aids to vision;

three piercing or working ends (e.g., spear points).
wúnúmar (3) See *wúnú-₃, maar.* nu. (T3) 1. fermented breadfruit (in *wóón w.* season of f. b.). [The season lasts from September through December and is associated with the little breadfruit harvest in December.] *maramen wóón w.* the months of f. b. season. *meyin wóón w.* breadfruit that ripens during the f. b. season. 2. one of four traditional annual feasts. [It was made at the beginning of the *wóón wúnúmar* season and involved a presentation of fermented breadfruit to the district chief.] vi. prepare f. b. *raa w. ngeni ewe sómwoon* they prepared f. b. to present to the chief.
wúnúmach (3) See *wúnú-₁, macha-.* F. num. three fishtails (in counting fish). Cf. *wúnúwúk₁*.
wúnúmataf (3) See *wúnú-₁, matafa-.* num. three small portiions, small amounts, little bits.
wúnúmeech (2) See *wúnú-₁, -meech.* F. Var. *wúnúmech, wúnúmmech.* num. three portions of mashed breadfruit.
wúnúmeet (3) See *wúnú-₁, meet₂.* num. three strands (of hair, rope).
wúnúmech N. var. of *wúnúmeech.*
wúnúmén (2) See *wúnú-₁, maan₁.* num. three persons or creatures (of people, mammals, birds, fish, and insects; but not of lobsters, crabs, sea cucumbers, or shellfish); three knives, guns, files, scissors.
wúnúmi See *wún₁, -mi-.* vo. (T5) drink; smoke(tobacco); take (medicine); eat (honey); ingest (something) without chewing.
wúnúmma (1) See *wúnú-₁, -mma.* num. three mouthfuls of premasticated food.
wúnúmmech N. var. of *wúnúmeech.*
wúnúmmék (2) See *wúnú-₁, mékkú-.* num. three fragments.
wúnúmwénú (1) See *wúnú-₁, mwénú-.* num. three ells (lengths from elbow to fingertip).
wúnúmwu E.Wn. of *wúnúmwú₂.*
wúnúmwú₁ (1) See *wúnú-₁, mwúú-₁.* F. Var. *wúnúmwmwú.* num. three torn fragments (of rag or string).
wúnúmwú₂ (1) See *wúnú-₁, mwúú-₂.* Var. *wúnúmwu.* num. three sea cucumbers; three pieces of feces.

wúnúmwúch (2) See *wúnú-₁, -mwúch.* num. three pieces of firewood.
wúnúmwmweeráán N. of *winimwmweeráán.*
wúnúmwmweey See *wúnú-₄, mwmwa-, -e-₂.* vo. (T6b) be the first to do or use (something). *aa w. ewe kanapwus* he was the f. prisoner in the jail. *aa w. ne waawa naan waa* he was the f. to use that canoe. *iyé aa w. eey angaang?* who was the f. to do this work?
wúnúmwmwék See *wúnú-₁, mwékkú-.* N. num. one bit or morsel (of mashed food). Syn. *wúnúpwey.*
wúnúmwmwun (3) See *wúnú-₁, mwmwuna-.* Var. *wúnúmwmwún.* num. three portions of *mwatún.* Syn. *wúnútún.*
wúnúmwmwú N. of *wúnúmwú₁.*
wúnúmwmwún F. of *wúnúmwmwun.*
wúnúnnú (1) See *wúnú-₁, nnúú-.* num. three loaves of breadfruit pudding or amounts of breadfruit to be mashed into pudding loaves.
wúnúngaf (3) See *wúnú-₁, ngaaf.* num. three fathoms, three times the distance from fingertip to fingertip of outstretched arms.
wúnúngát (4) See *wúnú-₁, -ngát.* num. three general class of things (the usual term); three concave or hollow objects (Syn. *wúnúpwang*). With c. pref. and ptv. const.: *éwúnúngátin* or *éwúnúngátan* third one. With dis. c. pref.: *ékkéwúnúngát* be three at a time. With pref. *nne-₂: eew nnewúnúngátin* one third part.
wúnúngéréw (2) See *wúnú-₁, -ngéréw.* num. three thousand.
wúnúngin (2) See *wúnú-₁, ngini-.* num. three little things or bits. Syn. *wúnúkis.*
wúnúpa (1) See *wúnú-₁, -pa.* num. three fronds, garlands, stalks with leaves. [Of palm trees, banana trees, *Cyrtosperma*, and also of leis or garlands, necklaces, bead belts.] Cf. *wúnúpan.*
wúnúpan (3) See *wúnú-₁, paan₁.* num. three branches with leaves (of trees other than palms and bananas). Syn. *wúnúpachang.*
wúnúpachang (3) See *wúnú-₁, pachang₁.* num. three branches with leaves. Syn. *wúnúpan.*

wúnúpeek (2) See *wúnú-₁, peek₂*. num. three sides, pages.

wúnúpeche (1) See *wúnú-₁, peche*. num. three lower or hind limbs (of humans, birds, and animals only).

wúnúpé (1) See *wúnú-₁, péé-₁*. num. three empty containers.

wúnúpék (2) See *wúnú-₁, péék₂*. num. three chips, chopped off pieces, cigarette butts.

wúnúpéw (2) See *wúnú-₁, -péw*. num. three wings or things worn over hand or arm (e.g., gloves).

wúnúpino (1) See *wúnú-₁, pino*. num. three small packages of breadfruit pudding.

wúnúpinúk (2) See *wúnú-₁, pinúk*. num. three tied bundles, reams of paper.

wúnúpu (1) See *wúnú-₁, puu-₂*. num. three strokes in swimming (in measuring distance).

wúnúppa- (3) See *wúnú-₄, ppa-*. ni. (loc.; T3) edge (of road, stream, gully). *wúnúppan* its e. Syn. *óroppa-*.

wúnúpwang (3) See *wúnú-₁, pwaang*. num. three holes, caves, cavities, pits, tunnels, hollows. Cf. *wúnúngát*.

wúnúpwey (2) See *wúnú-₁, -pwey*. num. three pinches or morsels of breadfruit pudding.

wúnúpwéét (2) See *wúnú-₁, pwéét*. num. three noses.

wúnúpwi (1) See *wúnú-₁, pwii-₁*. num. three groups, groves, flocks, schools, herds, swarms, convoys, prides, etc.

wúnúpwin (2) See *wúnú-₁, pwiin₃*. num. three nights.

wúnúpwopw (2) See *wúnú-₁, pwoopw*. num. three tree trunks, bases, foundations, causes, sources, beginnings, origins, reasons.

wúnúpwór (4) See *wúnú-₁, pwóór*. num. three boxes or crates (of something).

wúnúpwúkú (1) See *wúnú-₁, -pwúkú*. num. three hundred.

wúnúpwún (2) See *wúnú-₁, pwúún₁*. Var. *wúnúpwpwún*. num. three pieces (broken off).

wúnúpwpwaaw (2) See *wúnú-₁, pwpwaaw*. num. three home-made cigarettes.

wúnúpwpwún₁ N. of *wúnúpwún*.

wúnúpwpwún₂ (2) See *wúnú-₃, pwpwún₁*. nu. (T2) food set aside for a menstruating woman; left-over food cooked or eaten by a menstruating woman.

wúnúchamw (3) See *wúnú-₁, -chamw*. num. three foreheads, brows, or similarly class objects (e.g., visors, stem-bases of coconut fronds); three fishheads.

wúnúchef See *wúnú-₁, -chef*. num. three tentacles (of octopus or squid); three pieces of firewood. Syn. *wúnúwút, wúnúyó*.

wúnúché (1) See *wúnú-₁, -ché*. num. three thin flat objects of any kind (e.g., sheets, leaves, planks); three songs.

wúnúchú (1) See *wúnú-₁, chúú*. num. three bone segments (of meat).

wúnúchúk (2) See *wúnú-₁, chúúk*. num. three coconut-leaf baskets (of something); three basketfuls.

wúnúchchi (1) See *wúnú-₁, -chchi*. num. three drops.

wúnútinewupw (2) See *wúnú-₁, tinewupw*. num. three yards (lengths from center of chest to outstretched fingertips).

wúnútip (3) See *wúnú-₁, tiip₂*. num. three slices, chunks, cut segments (of breadfruit and taro only).

wúnútit (2) See *wúnú-₁, -tit*. num. three strings (of breadfruit, usually ten to a string). Syn. *wúnúttiit*.

Wúnútiw nu. (loc.) Ulithi Island and Atoll (Western Caroline Islands).

wúnútú (3) See *wúnú-₁, túú*. Tbl. num. three vulvas (in counting sexual encounters).

wúnútúkúm (3) See *wúnú-₁, túkúm*. num. three packages (of something).

wúnútún (2) See *wúnú-₁, túnú-*. F. Var. *wúnúttún*. num. three portions of *mwatún* pudding. Syn. *wúnúmwmwun*.

wúnúttiit (2) See *wúnú-₁, ttiit₂*. num. three strings of ten breadfruit each. Syn. *wúnútit*.

wúnúttún N. of *wúnútún*.

wúnúwo (1) See *wúnú-₁, -wo₁*. num. three clumps (of bananas).

wúnúwoch See *wúnú-₁, -woch*. Tn. num. three sorts, kinds, rations, varieties, species. Syn. *wúnúyóch*.

wúnúwumw (2) See *wúnú-₁, wumwu-₂*. num. three branching stalks (of bananas, fruit, clusters of pandanus keys, coral).

wúnúwupw (2) See *wúnú-₁, wupwu-*. num. three breasts.

wúnúwúk₁ (2) See *wúnú-₁, wúúk₁*. num. three tails (in counting fish). Syn. *wúnúmach*.

wúnúwúk₂ (2) See *wúnú-₁, wúúk₂*. num. three fingernails, toenails, claws.

wúnúwún (3a) See *wúnú-₁, wúún₁*. num. three feathers, scales, hairs.

wúnúwút (2) See *wúnú-₁, -wút*. num. three fingers or toes; three octopus tentacles, insect legs. Cf. *wúnúchef, wúnúyó*.

wúnúyaf (3b) See *wúnú-₁, -af*. num. three pieces of intestine.

wúnúyang (3) See *wúnú-₁, -ang*. num. three finger spans; three entire limbs (of an animal).

wúnúyef (2) See *wúnú-₁, eef₁*. num. three bunches of ripe coconuts.

wúnúyem (2) See *wúnú-₁, eem*. num. three ear lobes.

wúnúyep (2) See *wúnú-₁, epi-₁*. num. three butt ends, lower ends, west ends.

wúnúyé (1) See *wúnú-₁, -é*. num. three hairs.

wúnúyék (2) See *wúnú-₁, ékkú-*. num. three nets.

wúnúyi (3) See *wúnú-₁, -i*. Rmn. num. three hands of bananas. Syn. *wúnúyin₁, wúnúyiyey*.

wúnúyin₁ (3) See *wúnú-₁, ina-₂*. N. num. three hands of bananas. Syn. *wúnúyi, wúnúyiyey*.

wúnúyin₂ (2) See *wúnú-₁, ini-₂*. num. three shoots.

wúnúyipw (3) See *wúnú-₁, -ipw*. num. three steps, footprints, soles; three items of footwear.

wúnúyiyey (3) See *wúnú-₁, iyeyiya-*. num. three hands of bananas. Syn. *wúnúyi, wúnúyin₁*.

wúnúyowut (3) See *wúnú-₁, owut*. num. three rows of thatch.

wúnúyó (1) See *wúnú-₁, óó₁*. num. three tentacles (of octopus or squid). Syn. *wúnúchef, wúnúwút*.

wúnúyóch (4) See *wúnú-₁, -óch*. num. three sorts, rations, kinds, varieties, species. Syn. *wúnúwoch*.

Wúnnan nu. a school of *itang* lore. [Its patron spirit is Paawén of the Sápenó clan, and it is associated with Fónómó District, Wútéét (Udot) Island, and Éét (Eot) Island.]

wúnneni See *wúún₄, -ni-*. vo. (T6a) acquire as a pillow. Cf. *wúnnéwún*. lean against or on. Syn. *wúnni*.

wúnnéwún (db; 3) See *wúún₄*. va. use as a pillow. Cf. *wúnneni*.

wúnni See *wúnú-₅, -ni-*. vo. (T6a) lean on. Cf. *wúnneni*.

wúnniinaf (3) See *wúnú-₃, -inaf*. F. nu. (T3) a variety of breadfruit. Syn. *meyimwotow, neepwoopwo*.

wúnnú-₁ (dc; 2) See *wúnú-₅*. [In cpds. only.] vi. lie, sleep. See *wúnnúfátán, wúnnútá*.

wúnnú-₂ (dc; 2) See *wún₁*. nr. (T2) drinking; smoking (tobacco); taking (medicine). *wúnnún piyé* beer d.

wúnnúfátán (4) See *wúnnú-₁, fátán*. vi. sleep about anywhere; spread, be epidemic (of sickness).

wúnnúpaat (dc; 3) See *wúnnú-₂, paat₂*. vi. drink or smoke incessantly.

wúnnúpwún See *wúnú-₃*. nu. a variety of breadfruit. Cf. *wúnúpwpwún*.

wúnnútá (1) See *wúnnú-₁, -tá*. vi. (with *wóón*) lay one's head upon, make a pillow of. *aa w. wóón pecheen átewe* he made a pillow of that fellow's feet.

wúnchipa (1) WÚNCHIPAA. (Jap.) nu. (T1) Japanese swamp cabbage.

wúnteng (2) WÚNTENGI. (Jap.) va., vi. drive (an automobile). nu. (T2) driving.

wúntengiiy See *wúnteng, -i-₂*. vo. (T5) drive (an automobile).

wúntookay (3) WÚNTOOKAYA. (Jap. *undookai*) nu. (T3) athletic meet.

wúng (2) WÚNGÚ. vi. be blown, sounded (of a trumpet); make a sudden loud noise (as the roar of a motor or a clap of thunder). Dis. *wúngúúng* (db) be sounding (as a trumpet), roar (as a motor), rumble (as thunder). *wúngúúngún paach* rumbling of thunder.

-wúng (3) WÚNGA. [In cpds. only.] unsp. (u.m.) See *éwúng, éwúngéwúng, neewúng*.

wúngúúng Dis. of *wúng*.

wúngúri See *wúng, -ri-*. vo. (T5) strike up (a sudden sound, as a clap of thunder). *naan irá aa w. paach* that tree has s. up thunder (on being hit by lightning).

wúp (2) See *wúúp*. vi. fish with fish poison.

wúpenipot (3) See *wúúp, potopot*. nu. (T3) a vine (*Derris trifoliata*). [It is used as hauling rope, to tie bundles, and to make fish poison.] *wúpenípoten* v. of (a given region). Syn. *wúnenípot*.

wúr (2) WÚRÚ₁. [Presumably a back formation from *wúri₂*.] vi. be hauled, pulled, hoisted. Dis. *wúrúúr* (db).

wúra- (3) WÚRA₁, KÚRA₂. [In cpds. only.] unsp. speak, converse, say. See *ékúrang₁, wúrá*.

wúraanong See *wúri₂*.

wúraato See *wúri₂*.

wúraawu See *wúri₂*.

wúraté (1) See *wúúr₂, té₁* (?). nu. (T2) kingpost (upright timber between tiebeam and ridgepole). *wúratéén iimw* house's k. Syn. *pwéét*.

wúrá (1) See *wúra-*. F. va. say, speak, opine; (with *reen*) pronounce. [Regularly used to intorduce a quotation.] *aa wúráá wo, wúpwenee nó* he said, I am going to go. *meet ena ke w.?* what did you say? *meet ke w. reen sáát?* how do you pronounce *sáát*? Syn. *ará, árá, érá*. Cf. *wúreni*.

wúráátá See *wúri₂*.

wúráátiw See *wúri₂*.

wúreni See *wúra-, -ni-*. vo. (T6a) speak to, tell (someone). Syn. *areni, áreni, éreni*. Cf. *wúrá*.

wúrépworopwor (4) See *wúúr₂, pwór*. Var. *wuropworopwor*. n. (T2) hunchback, stooped condition. *wúrépworopworun* his h. vi. be hunchbacked, stooped, bent of back.

wúrécháy Itang. nu. (T2) a chief and his *eterekes* (lineage).

wúri₁ See *wú-₄, -ri-*. N. Var. *weri*. vo. (T5) see, behold. Syn. *kúna*. Cf. *wúrúúr₁*.

wúri₂ See *wú-₅, -ri-*. vo. (T5) 1. drag, haul, tow, hoist. With dir. suf.: *wúraanong, wúraato, wúraawu, wúráátá, wúráátiw. wúróónó* drag off, haul away, elope with. Syn. *éwúrú₂*. Cf. *wúrúúr₂*. 2. strike, attack (as a sickness). *aa wúriyey sáát* the *sáát* sickness attacked me. *aa w. pwichikkaren ewe roong* the heat of the spell attacked him.

wúri₃ See *wú-₆*. vo. (T5) string together (flowers in a lei or shells in a necklace). Cf. *wúrúúr₃*.

wúróónó See *wúri₂*.

wúrú-₁ (2) WÚRÚ₂. [In cpds. only. Presumably a back formation from *wúri₁*.] unsp. aware. See *éwúrú, wúrúng, wúrúúr₁, wúrúúw*. Cf. *rú₁*.

wúrú-₂ (2) WÚRÚ₃. [In cpds. only. Presumably a back formation from *wúri₄*.] unsp. string together. See *wúrúúr₃*.

wúrúúr₁ (db; 2) See *wúrú-₁*. n. (T2) expectation, understanding, awareness. *wúrúúrún* his e. *ifa wúrúúrumw óómw kepwe niwinnó Toon?* when do you expect to return to Toon (Tol) Island? *pwata ina wúrúúrumw ngé wúwa pe ne witiwit?* What was your understanding when I died waiting? (said to someone who was late for date). *wúrúúrún...* it was expected that..., it was thought that..., it eemed that... *wúrúúrún wúpwenee pe reen átánaan ngé Piyer aa émwéchú* it seemed that I was going to be killed by that fellow, but Piyer grabbed him.

wúrúúr₂ (db; 2) See *wúr*. nu. (T2) halyard. vi. (dis.) haul on a halyard. With dir. suf.: *wúrúúrútá* haul up sail; *wúrúúrútiw* lower sail. va., vi. haul, pull, hoist, tow; be hauled, pulled, hoisted, towed. Cf. *wúri₂*.

wúrúúrúnó (db; 1) See *wúr, -nó*. vi. (dis.) 1. be hauled away; elope. 2. be postponed. nu. (T1) 1. elopement. 2. postponement.

wúrúúrúnúpwin See *wúr, pwiin₃*. nu. (pers.) traditional goddess of sexual madness. [Daughter of *Inemes*, she lives in the sky and used to manifest herself by possessing people. She could take a man as her lover by possessing a woman and demanding that he sleep with her, or she could possess a man and demand a woman. To refuse her demands led to sickness and death. When her wants were satisfied, she would return to the sky.]

wúrúúrúpwich vi. swim on one's back. Syn. *ááseneetá*.

wúrúúw See *wúrú-₁, -ú-*. vo. (T5) be aware of, think of. Id. *si w. chék ngé...* suddenly ("we are hardly aware of it when")...

wúrúng (3) See *wúrú-₁, -ng*. F. [In idiomatic usage only.] vi. be aware. Id. *sipwe w. chék aa war* we will scarcely know it before he arrives. Syn. *rú₁*.

wúrúrááán (2) See *wúrú-₁, rááán₂*. vi. tell the day of the month or night of the moon (according to traditional lunar count).

wúchú-₁ (2) WÚCHÚ₁. [In cpds. only.] Var. *wichi-*. unsp. shaken (as a cloth). See wúchúúch₁, wúchúk, wúchúki. Cf. chúngú-.

wúchú-₂ (2) WÚCHÚ₂. [In cpds. only.] unsp. pressed. See chééwúch, wúchúúch₂. Cf. wung.

wúchúúch₁ (db; 2) See wúchú-₁. Var. wichiwich₂. va., vi. shake out; be shaken (as a cloth). Cf. wúchúk, wúchúki.

wúchúúch₂ (db; 2) See wúchú-₂. nu. (T2) pressing or expressing (juices or coconut cream from a bundle of fruit or copra by pressing a bar of wood on a cradle). minen w. a press (with all its parts); néwún w. press cradle (made from a curved heavy piece of wood on which materials to be pressed are placed); wúren néwún w. supporting post of a press cradle; wáán w. press bar (made from a thin log that is pressed down on the cradle).

wúchúúw See wúchú-₂, -ú-. vo. (T5) press out, express (juice or oil) on a press. Cf. wúchchúúw.

wúchúk (2) See wúchú-₁, -ki-. [Presumably a back formation from wúchúki.] Var. wichik. vi. be shaken, shaken out (physically, as a cloth). Dis. wúchúkúchúk (db). Cf. wúchúúch₁.

wúchúki See wúchú-₁, -ki-. Var. wichiki. vo. (T5) shake out (a cloth). Cf. wúchúúch₁.

wúchchú- (2) WÚCHCHÚ. [In cpds. only.] unsp. steer a canoe by working the paddle in a manner opposite to that of normal steering.

wúchchúúw See wúchchú-, -ú-. vo. (T5) steer (a paddle canoe) by working the paddle in the opposite direction of normal paddling. Cf. wúchúúw.

wút (3) See wúút₂. vi. rain, be raining.

-wút (2) WÚTÚ₁. suf. (cc.) finger, toe (in counting). ewút, rúwéwút, wúnúwút, féwút, niméwút, wonéwút, fúúwút, wanúwút, ttiwéwút, engoon éwútún one,... ten f. or t.; fitéwút how many f. or t. Cf. éwút₂.

wúta- (3) WÚTA₁. [In cpds. only.] unsp. stroke (with the penis). See wúteey.

wúta (1) WÚTAA. n. (T1) a class of magical medicines. wútaan m. for his benefit. wútaan áppán m. to make a child crawl (when it is late in learning to do so); wútaan iik or ótoowik m. to make fish plentiful; wútaan máay or ótoomey m. to make breadfruit plentiful.

wúteey See wúta-, -e-₂. Tbl. vo. (T6b) stroke (a woman's genitals) with the penis.

wútek (2) WÚTEKI. vi., adj. good, fine, suitable, pleasing. [Traditionally the preferred word in the presence of brother and sister, father and daughter, and mother and son.] Syn. ééch, mwirinné.

wúteyiti See wút, -iti. vo. (T2) rain upon.

Wútéét nu. (loc.) Udot Island.

wútésássár (ds; 4) See wúút₂, sár₁. F. nu. (T2) ephemeral rain squall. Syn. wútésessen.

wútésessen (db; 2) See wúút₂, sen₁. N. nu. (T2) ephemeral rain squall. Syn. wútésássár.

wúténger (3) See wúút₂, nger. nu. (T3) a quick, short splash of rain that passes immediately. [A sign of someone's having died or that a woman is about to give birth.] Dis. wúténgerenger (db).

wútécha (1) See wúút₂, chcha. nu. (T1) rain of blood, bloody rain (word in a spell).

wútéchchin (2) See wúút₂, chchin. vi. be showery, alternating sun and rain. [A sign of possible heavy wind and harbinger of breadfruit.]

wúti Var. of witi.

wútiwit Var. of witiwit.

wútiwitinó Var. of witiwitinó.

wútú- (2) WÚTÚ₂. F. [In cpds. only.] unsp. fire making with the fireplow. See wútúút, wútúúw.

wútúút (db; 2) See wútú-. F. va. make fire by the fire-plow method. siya w. ááf we made fire. nu. (T2) fireplow; make fire with a fireplow. néwún w. pointed one of the two sticks in the f. (the one held in the hands).

wútúúw See wútú-, -ú-. vo. (T5) make (fire) with a fireplow.

wúttaawu See wútti.

wúttáátá See wútti.

wútti See wúnú-₆, -ti-. [Presumably from *wúnti, cf. Tonga unuhi and Samoa unusi.] vo. (T5) pull out, draw out, extract (nails, splinters, etc.). aa mwechen w. naan chuufén ngé ese chú he wanted to p. out that nail but it did not come out. With dir. suf.: wúttáátá lift up (one's leg), pull out or lift up (a post or plant from the ground); wúttaawu draw out, extract. Cf. wúút₁, wúttúút.

wúttúút (db; 2) See *wúút*₁. Var. *wúttúwút*. va., vi. pull out, draw out, extract; draw lots. *chóón w. nii* dentist, dental surgeon. Cf. *wútti*. nu. (T2) extraction, drawing out; draw (in cards); lottery, raffle; election. *wúttúútún Romónum* Romónum's lottery or election.

wúttúnó See *wúút*₁.

wúttúwu See *wúút*₁.

wúttúwút Var. of *wúttúút*.

wúwaseyirúk (2) See *wúú*₂, *sááy*, *rúk*. nu. (T2) a method of fighting around an earth oven. Cf. *wuwas*.

wúwan (3) WÚWANA. n. (T3) grey hair, white hair. *ewún w.* one g. h. *wúwanan* his g. h. vi. have grey or white hair.

wúwet N. vi. be tired, weary, lazy. Syn. *chipwang*. Cf. *wetin*.

wúwéngngaw (3) See *wú*₁, *ngngaw*. vi. be not complied with, not observed, respected, or honored (of a tabu or law).

-wúwéw (2) See *éwúwéw*. suf. (cc.) amount of fermented breadfruit suitable for kneading. *ewúwéw, rúwéwúwéw, wúnúúwéw, féwúwéw, nimewúwéw, wonéwúwéw, fúúwéw, wanúúwéw, ttiwewúwéw, engoon éwúwéwún* one,...ten a. of f. b.

wúwéyééch (2: -*yéchchú*-) See *wú*₁, *ééch*. vi. be well complied with, well observed, respected, or honored (of a taboo or law).

wúwiiti See *wú*₂, -*iti*. vo. (T2) stop until.

Y

-y₁ (2) YI₁. suf. (pos.) 1st sg. pos. prn.: my; belonging to, benefitting, or a part of me. *wáá-y* my canoe (*waa*), *awe-y* my mouth (*aaw*), *pwééti-y* my nose (*pwéét*). Cf. *-ey*.

-y₂ (3a: *-ye-*) YA. [Occurs with object focussed verbs whose bases end in *aa, áá, ee, ii, óó,* or directional suffixes, and reduces to nothing after bases ending in the single vowel *i*.] Var. *-a-₃, -w.* suf. (obj.) 3sg. obj. prn.: him, her, it; marker of object to follow that is specific (as against general) and definite as to limit or extent (as against indefinite). *ataa-y* destroy it (*ta* destroyed), *ámáá-y* kill him (*má* dead), *wochee-y* eat it raw (*wochooch* eat raw), *fichii-y* snip it (*ffich* snipped), *ómóó-y* erase it (*mó* erased), *angotoo-y* take in hand reaching hither (*angoto* reach or take hither), *angúwuu-y* take in hand reaching outside (*angowu* reach or take outside). With dir. suf.: *ataa-ye-nó* destroy it away, *angee-ye-tá* take it up.

-ya- (3) See *-a-₁*. [Used only with suf. pos. prns.] Var. *-a-₁, -wa-*. suf. (n.form.; T3) object or product of an action. [Suffixed to verb bases ending it *-á, -e, -i* to indicate the thing that is involved in the action in relation to the actor.] *-yan* o. or p. of his action. *fini-ya-* thing chosen by someone (*fini* chose), *fanee-ya-* or *fánáá-ya-* thing adzed or to be adzed by someone (*fanee-y* cut with an adze).

-ya₁ (1) AA₃. [In cpds. only.] suf. (adj.) high, elevated, lofty. *teki-ya* by high, of high rank; *e-teki-yaa-y* cause to be high, elevate.

-ya₂ (1) AA₄. [In cpds. only.] difficult, hard (to do). *féére-ya* d. to make or do.

-yey See *-ey*.

-yi-₁ (2) See *-i-₁*. [Occurs in this form after bases ending in *-e, -aa, -áá, -ee, -éé, -oo, -óó*.] Var. *-i-₁, -wi-*. suf. (rel.) links its antecedent as an attribute, member, part, property or possession of what follows; of, for. [It has a more honorific, refined, or polite connotation than *-n* or *-ni-* and is more commonly used in *itang* talk.] *niye-yi-sómw* woman of a chiefly clan (cf. *niye-ni-mwár* woman of a commoner clan).

-yi-₂ (2) YI₂. [Shifts to *-yu-* when followed by 2nd sg. obj. prn. *-k* and to *-ya-* when followed by 3rd sg. obj. prn. plus directional suffix.] Var. *-e-₂, -i-₂*. suf. (v.form.) makes an object focussed verb of the base. *wuwe-yi-yey* carry me (cf. *wuwa-*), *wuwe-yu-k* carry you (sg.), *wuwe-yi* carry it, *wuwe-ya-a-to* carry it hither, *réé-yi* grope for it (cf. *ré₁*).

www.ingramcontent.com/pod-product-compliance
Lightning Source LLC
Chambersburg PA
CBHW031540300426
44111CB00006BA/125